The Gender / Sexuality Reader

The Gender / Sexuality Reader

Culture, History, Political Economy

edited by
Roger N. Lancaster
and Micaela di Leonardo

ROUTLEDGE
New York and London

Published in 1997 by

Routledge
29 West 35th Street
New York, NY 10001

Published in Great Britain in 1997 by

Routledge
11 New Fetter Lane
London EC4P 4EE

Printed in the United States of America
Design: Jack Donner

Library of Congress Cataloging-in-Publication Data

The gender / sexuality reader : culture, history, political economy /
    edited by Roger N. Lancaster and Micaela di Leonardo
        p.   cm.
    Includes bibliographical references.
    ISBN 0–415–91004–8 (alk. paper). — ISBN 0–415–91005–6 (pbk.: alk. paper)
        1. Sex role—Cross-cultural studies.   2. Gender identity—Cross-cultural studies.
    3. Body, Human—Social aspects.   4. Feminist anthropology.   I. Lancaster, Roger N., 1959–
    II. di Leonardo, Micaela, 1949–
    GN479.65.G475   1997
    305.3—dc21   96–39187
                                                                                   CIP

Contents

MAKING MARKS AND DRAWING BOUNDARIES: CORPOREAL PRACTICES

Part Nine Re-Imagining Bodies

How to think the body now. Performativity, "post-fordist" bodies in the age of AIDS, and subversive carnal practices in an unlikely place: Three topically distinct, methodologically juxtaposed yet uncannily consonant pieces on body, identity, and selfhood

Acknowledgments

The production of this *Reader* was like the making of gender and sexuality writ small: complex, historical, multisited, contested—and deeply, innately social. We first acknowledge one another's effort, and the development of a beautiful Stakhanovite colleagueship in hard times. So many others generously gave advice and assistance that we cannot name them all here. Ken Wissoker gave us selfless advice on selections, framing, and interpretations. Phyllis Jacobson, of *New Politics*, published a spin-off piece of ours, and we thank her for her reading of our Introduction, as we also thank Lisa Freeman. Contributors themselves—we single out Susan Gal, Nancy Scheper-Hughes, Judith Stacey, and Patricia Zavella—were actively engaged in this project's conception and development. We are also terribly grateful to all those contributors who gave aid and comfort in various ways: by revising previously published material; by enduring condensations of longer pieces; by securing copyright permissions; and by proofreading typescripts.

At Columbia, a number of graduate students helped with various research tasks. Andy Bickford, Alex·Costley, Marcial Godoy, and Rhoda Kanaaneh have each lent a helpful hand to this project. Marcial, moreover, assisted with the editing of some of the longer pieces. Advanced undergraduates in "The Anthropology of Gender and Sexuality" were exceptionally sharp trouble-shooters; they helped test-drive much of this material in a very rewarding class. Roger's colleague Jean Franco was an inexhaustible resource—a font of information and inspiration.

At Northwestern, students in "Advanced Feminist Theory" and in "The Anthropology of Gender" also field-tested much of our work, to the benefit of our choices and writing. Micaela's graduate students Gina Pérez and Jacqueline Pegg provided highly competent research assistance.

At George Mason, Ligia Artiles and Orsolya Berty helped out by tracking down articles and researching library listings. Special gratitude is owed Roger's graduate assistant, Lisa Breglia, for heroic measures above and beyond the call of duty. Lisa's keen eye for proofreading, her sense of style, her command of content, and her research skills have saved us many an embarrassment. Thanks, too, to the Department of Sociology and Anthropology at George Mason, for virtually unlimited used of photocopiers, as well as for generous franking privileges—material conditions without which the paperwork demands of this project would have posed an insurmountable obstacle.

Finally, this project has seen a succession of editors and handlers at Routledge: Max Zutty, Anne Sanow, Marlie Wasserman, Eric Zinner, Bill Germano, and Linda Hollick—each of whom had a hand in shaping its development. Special thanks to Alan Wieder and Karen Deaver, who nurtured the *Reader* through its final stages of editing, grooming, and production.

—RNL, MdL

Introduction
Embodied Meanings, Carnal Practices

Micaela di Leonardo and Roger N. Lancaster

em.bod.y tr. v. 1. To invest with or as if with bodily form; make corporeal; to incarnate. 2. To represent in bodily form; personify. 3. To make part of a united whole.

—*American Heritage Dictionary*

Sometime in the 1960s, to paraphrase Virginia Woolf, Western understandings of gender and sexuality changed irreversibly.[1] To those who have simply lived gender and sexuality but never studied them, such a statement may seem like the proverbial joke about the weather: everybody talks about it, but nobody does anything about it. In reality, though, gender relations and sexuality are not like the weather: they are not given phenomena "over there," impervious to human agency. Nor are they to be understood as precultural drives anchored deeply "inside us," beyond the reach of social influences.

Even the most self-evident "givens" of sexual embodiment belong not to some ubiquitous human nature but to the shifting world of cultural meanings and social practices. Ethnographic research shows that human beings articulate extraordinarily varied notions of sexuality—of gendered, sexual bodies—and that these understandings are intricately interwoven within dense cultural fabrics.[2] Historical research shows that people have repeatedly altered both their own sexual practices and their mental constructions of erotic desire. These changes have never sprung into being *ex nihilo*, out of nothing. Metamorphoses in sexual and gender relations have always been inseparably linked to political, economic, and cultural changes.[3]

American popular culture does admit this point in some common representations—for example, in the oversimplified notion of the repressed and oppressed Victorian woman versus the politically and sexually liberated modern woman of "You've come a long way, baby" advertising fame. Actual historical shifts, however, are not only far more complex than popular cultural representations allow; popular culture itself is also an inseparable part of change in gender and sexual relations. For these reasons, we need to glance at our historical blind spot, the recent past, and the sea changes it has wrought in our apprehensions and actions.[4]

Over the past three decades in the Anglophone West, four linked political and intellectual movements—the sexual revolution, feminism, gay liberation, and civil rights/race-minority power—have altered common perceptions of proper women's and men's lives, of sexual behavior, and of the very substance of that consummate American right, the pursuit of happiness. Many individuals, as well, have become more self-conscious about the ways in which race and ethnicity have entered into cultural representations of bodies, and into ideas about sexual desire and potency.

These interconnected political and popular-cultural shifts have been both stage-setting for and symbiotic with new theory and research on gender, sexuality, and the body.

While it has frequently been confused with women's liberation, the 1960s sexual revolution in the United States both predated the second wave of feminism and in large part involved a loosening of sexual and social restrictions for heterosexual men only.[5] By the "sexual revolution," we mean shifts in popular culture and aggregate behavior toward more explicit discussions and representations of heterosexuality and less censure of heterosexual experiences outside monogamous marriage. In *The Hearts of Men* (1983), Barbara Ehrenreich documents the way in which this movement, spearheaded by men's magazines and other elements of popular culture, dethroned the former cultural ideal of the good husband and father—the breadwinner—and raised in its place the image of the playboy: a hyper(hetero)sexual, single male who proved his sophisticated masculinity equally by bedding numerous (presumably contracepting) women and by consuming the appropriate commodities. As many feminists have pointed out, this cultural shift "liberated" women only to accede to frequent and extramarital heterosexual encounters, but not necessarily to control their own sexual lives.

Although a strong current of the women's movement has always emphasized sexual and reproductive freedom, second-wave feminist concerns in fact tended to run counter to the playboy ideal.[6] (By "feminism," we indicate the critical examination of gender relations from the position of protest against women's unequal status.[7]) Where sexual revolutionaries saw seduction, feminists often saw coercion; "sexual pleasure" too frequently indexed pleasure for the male alone. (Anne Koedt, for example, published "The Myth of the Vaginal Orgasm" in *Radical Feminism* [1973], thus popularizing the feminist implications of Kinsey's much earlier research.) Prostitution shifted from a delightful service and the subject of randy humor to one means—often unpleasant and sometimes dangerous—for women to gain access to wages unavailable to them in the respectable labor market. Many feminist theorists retraced the path of some Victorian woman's movement figures—Frederick Engels, John Stuart Mill, Emma Goldman—who asserted the fundamentally prostituted, resources-for-sex nature of legal heterosexual marriage itself, in the absence of equal rights and women's independent access to a means of livelihood. Mass-marketed pornography, that commodity most notably linked to the sexual revolution, was transmogrified through the feminist gaze from proof of "sexual freedom" into a variety of forms: from childish wish-fulfillment and everyday objectification to satanic enactment of violent misogyny. As radical feminist Robin Morgan aphorized, "Pornography is the theory; rape is the practice." While feminist activists and scholars worked in many ways against the grain of the sexual revolution, at the same time they followed its contours and took advantage of its shibboleth-toppling stance to discuss sexual and bodily matters with a new, unladylike frankness.

In so doing, second-wave feminists drew especially on the work of the key between-the-waves feminist, Simone de Beauvoir. Her magisterial postwar tome, *The Second Sex* (1953), argued famously that while in reality "woman is made, not born," in dominant ideology—which both reflects and reinforces male power—she is the essential Other to the male Self. It would be difficult to overstate de Beauvoir's influence on subsequent feminist theory. Her social constructionism aided the second-wave creation of the sex/gender dichotomy. Her emphasis on the practical, even contrived nature of gendered existence continues to aid in the fight against both conservative nostalgia for "purer," more traditional sex roles as well as cultural feminist notions of a universally altrustic, sexless, and oppressed Womanhood.[8] De Beauvoir's focus on ideology facilitated the development of a feminist analysis of male bias. And her unflinching consideration of women's varying psychologies and sexual expressions (she was particularly sensitive about lesbianism) encouraged later generations of feminists to push past intellectual and political boundaries in their work on gender and sexuality.

After the Stonewall Riots of 1969, gay rights activism flourished and—like the civil rights movement and second-wave feminism—quickly became a sustained political and intellectual movement.[9] Building on earlier homophile movements, on strands of sex research that did not treat homosexuality as pathological, and on an urban gay subculture that had been expanding since the end of World War II, this movement drew personnel (lesbians had been prominent in the early second wave), tropes, and tactics from feminism. Like feminism, the gay movement has politicized the conditions of personal life and everyday culture.[10] Like feminism, it has been critical of received notions of masculinity and femininity, of "proper" ways of inhabiting this or that body. At the same time, however, the gay movement has both mediated and transformed relations between feminism and the sexual revolution, for if gay/lesbian liberation most audibly echoes themes from the earlier sexual revolution, it has translated the terms of sexual freedom and expression into an idiom that is anathema to privileged heterosexual masculinity.

With varying degrees of success and through struggles that continue today, gay and lesbian activists have publicly championed all that is positive, pleasurable, and creative in same-sex desire while opposing the obvious sources of antigay oppression: police harassment, social stigma, religious bigotry, psychiatric persecution, and sodomy laws. In the process, these concrete struggles have revealed the less obvious heteronormative premises deeply embedded in law, science, philosophy, official kinship, and vernacular culture—assumptions that necessarily stratify the allocation of legal rights and social privileges; assumptions that tend to diminish the full humanity of gay people.[11]

From the beginning, activists identified gay and lesbian "silence" and "invisibility"—tokens of this diminution—as the major obstacles in the way of effective struggle. Paradoxically, "closeting" protects the individual from the most onerous consequences of social intolerance while at the same time reinforcing and empowering that very system of intolerance. The solution? Self-disclosure—"coming out of the closet." This inaugural event and pivotal, enduring fixture in gay/lesbian politics is part precondition, part method; part message, part medium.[12] Because it sets up a particularly powerful convection that draws a private self into the public world, the discursive technology of coming out has been appropriated far beyond the arena of the gay community and has become a common motif in wider popular cultures and political struggles. In substance no less than in form of struggle, the gay/lesbian movement has played a major part in redesigning the modern social environment. Redefining same-sex intimacy as a normal expression of human sexuality has had unexpected ripple effects in larger cultural understandings: in helping the intellectual demise of conservative Freudianism; in redirecting visions of proper kinship and family relations; in toppling certain rigid assumptions about the nature of masculinity, femininity, and carnal pleasures; and in helping to normalize alternative modes of heterosexual expression.

Finally, the black civil rights movement, associated with other American race-minority struggles and with the florescence of international antiracist (building on earlier anticolonial) movements, spurred recognition of the ways in which sexuality and the very perception of human corporeality are not only "gendered" and understood in terms of "appropriate" or "normal" desires but are also intimately and intricately inscribed with race. In popular culture, this insight heightened awareness that "the personal is political," and that sexuality and power are mutually imbricated. At the academic and intellectual levels, this insight drew on and helped to further earlier work investigating the intersections of class, caste, and sexuality. Scholars and activists have traced the racist history of the American rape/lynching complex and its effects into the present; have identified and fought the unacknowledged race-ing of human bodily aesthetic evaluations; have taken up positions critical of the colonial gaze, with its unfettered access—visual and erotic—to "native" bodies; and have noted the complicated intersections of race, gender, power, and nation as they have played themselves out over centuries.[13]

This anthology, then, represents a set of the current intellectual endpoints of these late twentieth-century transformative movements. Gathered here is a selection of some of the most sophisticated work in English bearing on the intersection of these three analytically distinct yet practically intertwined domains: gender/sexuality/body. Unlike much recent writing on these topics, which largely focuses on textual analysis, we foreground here cross-cultural ethnographic and historical research by anthropologists, although our contributors also represent sociology, political science, economics, philosophy, biology, comparative literature, and—especially—history. We have specifically sought out essays in which feminism and women's studies come together with lesbian/gay studies and queer theory, as filtered through critical perspectives on race, class, and colonialism.

We consider historical political-economic interpretations to be central to this theoretical mix and use their vantage in organizing this volume. What do we mean by "political economy"? William Roseberry provides perhaps the best description. It is

> the attempt to constantly place culture in time, to see a constant interplay between experience and meaning in a context in which both experience and meaning are shaped by inequality and domination [and the] attempt to understand the emergence of particular peoples at the conjunction of local and global histories, to place local populations in the larger currents of world history. (1990: 49)

Such a practice is thus sensitive both to the varying and contested meanings particular groups parlay, and to the ways in which people live within world history—to the connections and disjunctions created by the rise and fall of states, and particularly by the spread of (not only Western) colonialism and the growth of global capitalism.

Contextualizing gender, sexuality, and human bodily experience within the historical vicissitudes of colonialism, imperialism, and class stratification allows a textured consideration of the crosscutting meanings of racial constructions in these domains. It also allows for the emergence of a robust, many sided—and politically relevant—form of social constructionism. These diverse linkages between the local and the global, present and past, familiar and "exotic," have enabled us to organize these essays into fresh thematic sections that speak to one another across time, space, and discipline—and to engage the reader in reframing old conceptions in the light of new, rigorous scholarship. Thus we *embody*, in its various meanings, a vast and sprawling interdisciplinary effort: we bring it into corporeal existence, and our organization suggests the connections that make a coherent whole of such a large number of pieces on so many topics by scholars from such disparate disciplines.

Our emphasis on political economy, like our selection of ethnographically grounded and historically specific materials, is intended as an "intervention" in the field of study represented here. Over the course of the 1980s, a substantial current of gender and sexuality studies withdrew to a narrow, disengaged, and frequently idealistic conception of social constructionism. Postmodernists habitually and synecdochically misidentified Marxism and political economy with older, reductionist, mechanistic schools of thought—"discarded grand theories"—or with less sophisticated schools in the present, such as world systems theory, and thus often simply ignored political-economic contexts in their writing.[14] Ironically, it was in the same decade that work in political economy became increasingly historically sophisticated; discarded social evolutionism and its associated teleology; abandoned earlier, mechanistic models (in which an economic "base" somehow "determines" the contents of a cultural "superstructure"); and took on culture, language, race, and gender as key analytic categories. Indeed, in anthropology, the term "culture and political economy" signaled this new, inclusive sophistication (see di Leonardo 1991a and b).

Historical political economy neither reduces sexual expression to a consequence of "material life"—as if sexual bodies were not material—nor imagines that human sexual and reproductive lives can be considered apart from the changing political economies in which those lives are embedded. Those political economies *include* dominant and contesting constructions of gender, race, sexual "perversions," and nationality—constructions that themselves carry traces of long and complicated histories of conquest, resistances, exploitation, national liberation movements, and neocolonial structures. They also include, in particular, "sexualized" states—states' ubiquitous uses of gender, sexual, and racial ideologies in order to enact their own legitimacy and control over citizens—as well as their more overt "enactments" through law and bureaucratic policy.

We hope here to bridge a chasm between the headiest aspirations and the worst failures of post–New Left scholarship on gender, sexual, and body politics. Our contributors draw on the best insights of what is today articulated under the generic name of "cultural theory" (e.g., semiotics, deconstruction, discourse theory, reflexive approaches). But they bring together the critical analysis of cultural meanings with the careful consideration of material practices. While focusing on specific events, they keep the historical horizon in clear view; even while considering intimate relations and experiences, they attend to those changes in production, consumption, technology, and law that set the stage for everyday life. In sum, this volume works to introduce postmodern subjects to political-economic approaches and thus to reassert the critical-theoretical roots of social constructionism.

This intellectual frame *a priori* prevents the theoretical and political impasses of identity politics, that modern Western tendency to assume that politics derives from the unanimous interests of certain fixed "identities"—gender, race/ethnicity, sexual preference.[15] Identity politics, very obviously, elides the operations of history and political economy, most particularly the workings of class. Not quite so obviously, it asserts the transhistorical and cross-cultural existence of only *certain* global identities. This one-sidedness denies the history and historicity, for example, of the widely varying ways sexualities have been understood and practiced, as well as the creation and transmogrification of particular racial, ethnic, or national identities over time.

Our contributors, taken as a whole, not only engage with and fill out the historical political-economic frame; they also correct both conservative and identity-politics distortions of contemporary debates involving gender, reproduction, race, and sexuality. They accept and rely on science, but demand that we see it as an historical, powerful *practice*, necessarily subject to a sociology-of-knowledge investigation. Their work is militantly antiracist, and integral to that stance is the understanding that race oppression is not only central to understanding sexuality but it is also itself various, shifting, and embedded in political economy. Moreover, they work against the retrogressive racial and gender mau-mauing that identity politics has unleashed—the notion that only xes should dare speak to x issues. Our contributors are women and men, gay and straight, multiracial and multinational, junior and senior scholars—but we have chosen them on the basis of their work, not their physiognomies or self-presentations. While considering their own embodied positionalities and their effects on fieldwork and scholarship, these scholars do not consider social status a substitute for that careful labor. Nor are they daunted by gender, racial, or sexual identity from taking full responsibility for investigating social inequalities they may not have experienced personally. Finally, this volume escapes the parochial framing of so much contemporary work on gender and sexuality in its resolutely feminist *and* gay studies, in its global and historical sweep.

We have organized this rich material into nine thematic sections under three large rubrics. Our first frame, "embodiments of history: local meanings, global economies," offers a first immersion in the placement of culture in time. Part 1, "Moving Borders: Genders, Sexualities, Histories," mixes disciplines (anthropology, historiography, literary criticism, political economy), time periods (the colonial era to the present), cultural locales, and genres in offering the reader critical takes on received wisdom of the present and recent past—whether purveyed from colonial offices, ivied halls, or television talk shows. The three pieces, read against one another, follow in de Beauvoir's footsteps to illuminate, in the concept of "degeneracy," the connections among different modes of social inequality—gender, sexuality, race, class—and their intersections over long centuries of colonialism and capitalist growth. The second section, "Modes of Reproduction: Kinship, Parenthood, States," builds on the first with theoretical overviews and case-study materials that break up our frozen, culture-bound notions of family. These essays consider how different social practices—state power, neocolonialism, nation building, technology—affect gendered parenthood around the globe and vice versa. This section, as well, lays to rest the canard that feminists and gays have "politicized" family issues. Definitions of affinity and consanguinity; the legal allotment of interpersonal rights and responsibilities; the distribution of medical resources and the disposition of various powers over bodies; the bringing into being successive generations of human beings in specific social settings: these are, and always have been, profoundly political questions, as these pieces attest.[16]

The final part of this frame, "The Social Construction of Identities: Comparative Sexualities," offers detailed historical and ethnographic accounts of shifting hetero- and homosexualities, of femininities and masculinities, and suggests some of the ways identity work has dynamically interplayed with systems of kinship, with conditions of labor, with nationalisms and their attendant representational regimes, and, not least of all, with women's and men's aspirations for a better life. Like all the essays in the larger frame, these pieces discern the making of genders, sexualities, and bodies at the conjuncture of the local and the global. They affirm that identities are at once sites of contestation *and* equivocation.

The middle frame, "making marks and drawing boundaries: corporeal practices," engages particularly with the roles of language, representation, and practice in historical and cross-cultural embodiments of gender. Part 4, "Bodies of Knowledge and the Politics of Representation," deals with specific histories of authoritative, scholarly, medical, and scientific discourses, unraveling their braided ramifications into the present. Like Donna Haraway's wide-ranging work, these essays show how such representations are affected by—and in turn affect—the politics of gender, sexuality, race, and class.[17] Each suggests how a "political economy of the body" both grounds and is conditioned by "political economy" in its usual sense.[18] Part 5, "Marks and Signs: The Social Skin," enters into classic anthropological terrain in its focus on the gendered varieties of human adornments and alterations of the body—but with a difference, as two out of three of these pieces "anthropologize" the West rather than the rest. In so doing, they erase orientalizing tropes and allow a larger perspective, animated neither by imperialist structures of feeling nor by romantic, defensive identity politics, on the bond between power and meaning in bodily alteration. The final part in this frame, "Polyvalent Pleasures: Resistances, Reinscriptions, and Dispersals," departs from the usual Derridean depiction of "the mark" as a "violent inscription" to consider marks also in their creative, affirmative, and life-sustaining capacities.[19] Depicting very different cultural and life experiences, these essays offer responsible considerations of sexual agency—of the pursuit of pleasure within constraints—by women and men living in specific times and places. Like other sections in this frame, the pieces in this section also suggest some of the ways in which systems of power, tactics of resistance, and corporeal experiences are intimately, intricately intertwined.

The last frame, "appropriations, contestations, and adaptations: toward a history of the present," focuses the volume's theoretical lens on contemporary hot-button political issues. "Sex Wars, Culture Wars" initiates the theme with sharp, timely pieces on violence against women, pornography, and the politics of "family values."[20] "Traveling Theory: Transnational and Postcolonial Interlocutions," considers bodies in motion—across and between, rather than simply within, cultures and nations. These detailed analyses of the multiple engagements of gender/ sexual constructions with state power, and their inevitable imbrication with the processes of racial stigma and valorization, reflect on contemporary state sexual politics—opening up and enriching our understanding of issues central to the evolving "new world order."

Given the volatility of that order, not to say of contemporary scholarship, it would be deceptive to conclude a volume of this sort complacently. We thus end, somewhat contentiously, with "Re-Imagining Bodies," a section that raises more questions than it answers and that reopens the fundamental questions of this field of scholarship: How are we to represent bodies, their meanings, their experiences? More specifically: How are we to understand corporeal existence, and its relation to body practices, after the deluge of deconstruction; after the succession of feminism and gay/lesbian studies by queer theory; in an era of AIDS, cyborgs, post-Fordist production, widening inequalities, and institutionalized crises? And against such a backdrop, how might we reimagine the human capacity for play, sensuousness, subversion, and creativity at the end of the twentieth century?

Bodies are ineluctably political, but embodied power is not unidimensional—nor does it find a home outside history, outside our capacity for struggle and change. Feminism, gay studies, race research, and historical political economy, working together on global materials, enable us to unfasten the intellectual straitjackets binding us as we rethink carnal knowledge, as we work to embody liberatory meanings for all humanity.

NOTES

Portions of this introduction first appeared in di Leonardo and Lancaster's longer essay, "Gender, Sexuality, Political Economy," published in the journal *New Politics* 21 (vol. 6, no. 8; Summer 1996), 29–43.

1. We have stolen the notion of this literary paraphrase from Thomas Laqueur, this volume.
2. On the variety of carnal practices, as interwoven with systems of kinship, ritual, political economy, etc., see, for example, Besnier 1994; di Leonardo 1984; Herdt 1987; Herzfeld 1985; Kelly 1976; Lancaster 1988, 1992; various contributors to Ortner and Whitehead 1981; Roscoe 1991; Turner 1995; Williams 1988.
3. See, for instance, Bérubé 1990; Bynum 1991; D'Emilio 1983; Freedman and D'Emilio 1988; Greenberg 1988; Halperin 1990; Katz 1990; Laqueur 1990; Padgug 1979; Riley 1988; various contributors to Snitow et al. 1983; Weeks 1977.
4. For a closer look at the relationships between post–1960s political and intellectual movements, see di Leonardo and Lancaster, 1996.
5. See Abelove 1992 and Laqueur 1990 on an earlier sexual revolution attendant to the rise of industrialism in England.
6. See especially 1980s and '90s' debates between antipornography and prosex feminists; for example, the contributors to Segal and McIntosh 1992 and Vance 1984; versus arguments by Dworkin 1981, 1987; and MacKinnon 1987, 1992. For useful reviews, see Hunt 1991, 1993; Kipnis 1992; Segal 1994; Valverde 1989.
7. By this definition, feminism is neither very recent nor particularly Western or white. See, for example, Jayawardena 1986. Here, however, we trace a specifically Western and recent tradition of feminist theorizing.
8. See Echols 1989 and di Leonardo 1994 on the devolution of radical into cultural feminism.
9. See Duberman 1993 for a lively history of the Stonewall Riots. For two early classics of gay theory, see Altman 1993 and Hocquenghem 1993.
10. Pioneering studies of gay and lesbian life in the United States include: Altman 1982; D'Emilio 1983; Faderman 1981, 1991; Kennedy and Davis 1993; Nestle 1992; Newton 1979, 1993; Weston 1991.
11. Arguably, this has been the densest and most provocative area of gay/lesbian theory. See Butler 1993; Rich 1993; Rubin 1975, 1984; Treichler 1988; and various contributions to Duberman et al. 1989 and Warner 1993.
12. On the productive dynamics of concealment and revelation, see Sedgwick's classic (1990).
13. See Fanon 1967; Gilman 1985; Gould 1985; Hall 1979; JanMohamed 1992; Said 1978, 1993; Stoler 1995; Szwed 1975; Truong 1993.
14. See, for example, Taussig 1987. For an engaging critique of such tendencies, see Jameson's foreword to Lyotard 1984.
15. See di Leonardo 1994, Escoffier 1985.
16. This domain is particularly richly engaged in contemporary anthropology. See Ginsburg and Rapp 1991, 1995. See also Glenn et al. 1994.
17. See Haraway 1989, 1991.
18. See Lancaster's 1995 discussion of what the term "political economy of the body" might mean.
19. See Derrida's framings (1976), especially "The Violence of the Letter," 101–40.
20. See Harvey and Gow 1994 for cross-cultural considerations of gender and violence.

REFERENCES AND FURTHER READING:

Abelove, Henry. 1992. "Some Speculations on the History of 'Sexual Intercourse' During the 'Long Eighteenth Century' in England." In *Nationalisms and Sexuality*, ed. Andrew Parker, Mary Russo, Doris Sommer, and Patricia Yaeger, 335–42. New York: Routledge.

Altman, Dennis. 1982. *The Homosexualization of America, the Americanization of the Homosexual*. New York: St. Martin's.

———. 1993 (1971). *Homosexual Oppression and Liberation*. New York: New York University Press.

Bérubé, Allan. 1990. *Coming Out Under Fire: The History of Gay Men and Women in World War Two*. New York: Free Press.

Besnier, Niko. 1994. "Polynesian Gender Liminality Through Time and Space." *Third Sexes, Third Genders*, ed. Gilbert Herdt. New York: Zone.

Butler, Judith. 1993. *Bodies That Matter: On Discursive Limits of "Sex."* New York: Routledge.

Bynum, Caroline Walker. 1991. *Fragmentation and Redemption: Essays on Gender and the Human Body in Medieval Religion*. New York: Zone.

de Beauvoir, Simone. 1953 [1949]. *The Second Sex*. New York: Knopf.

D'Emilio, John. 1983. *Sexual Politics, Sexual Communities: Making of a Homosexual Minority in the U.S.* Chicago: University of Chicago Press.

Derrida, Jacques. 1976 [1967]. *Of Grammatology*. Trans. Gayatri Chakravorty Spivak. Baltimore: Johns Hopkins University Press.

di Leonardo, Micaela. 1984. *Varieties of Ethnic Experience: Kinship, Class, and Gender Among California Italian-Americans*. Ithaca, NY: Cornell University Press.

———. 1991a. "Introduction. Gender, Culture, and Political Economy: Feminist Anthropology in Historical Perspective." In *Gender at the Crossroads of Knowledge: Feminist Anthropology in the Postmodern Era*, ed. Micaela di Leonardo, 1–51. Berkeley: University of California Press.

———. 1991b. "Habits of the Cumbered Heart: Ethnic Community and Women's Culture as Invented Traditions." In *Golden Ages, Dark Ages: Imagining the Past in Anthropology and History*, eds., William Roseberry and Jay O'Brien, 234–52. Berkeley: University of California Press.

———. 1994. "White Ethnicities, Identity Politics, and Baby Bear's Chair." *Social Text* 41: 165–91.

di Leonardo, Micaela, and Roger N. Lancaster. 1996. "Gender, Sexuality, Political Economy." *New Politics* 21 (6 [8]) (Summer): 29–43.

Duberman, Martin. 1993. *Stonewall*. New York: Dutton.

Duberman, Martin Bauml, Martha Vincinus, and George Chauncey, Jr., eds. 1989. *Hidden from History: Reclaiming the Gay and Lesbian Past*. New York: Penguin.

Dworkin, Andrea. 1981. *Pornography: Men Possessing Women*. New York: Free Press.

———. 1987. *Intercourse*. New York: Free Press.

Echols, Alice. 1989. *Daring To Be Bad: Radical Feminism in America, 1967–75*. Minneapolis: University of Minnesota Press.

Ehrenreich, Barbara. 1983. *The Hearts of Men: American Dreams and the Flight from Commitment*. New York: Anchor.

Escoffier, Jeffrey. 1985. "Sexual Revolution and The Politics of Gay Identity." *Socialist Review* 81/82: 119–54.

Faderman, Lillian. 1981. *Surpassing the Love of Men: Romantic Friendship and Love Between Women from the Renaissance to the Present*. New York: Morrow.

———. 1991. *Odd Girls and Twilight Lovers: A History of Lesbian Life in the Twentieth Century America*. New York: Columbia University Press.

Fanon, Frantz. 1967. *Black Skin, White Masks*. New York: Grove.

Freedman, Estelle B., and John D'Emilio, eds. 1988. *Intimate Matters: A History of Sexuality in America*. New York: Harper and Row.

Gilman, Sander. 1985. *Difference and Pathology: Stereotypes of Sexuality, Race, and Madness*. Ithaca, NY: Cornell University Press.

Ginsburg, Faye, and Rayna Rapp. 1991. "The Politics of Reproduction." *Annual Review of Anthropology* 20: 311–43.

———, eds. 1995. *Conceiving the New World Order: The Global Politics of Reproduction.* Berkeley: University of California Press.

Glenn, Evelyn Nakano, Grace Chang, and Linda Rennie Forcey, eds. 1994. *Mothering: Ideology, Experience, and Agency.* New York: Routledge.

Gould, Stephen Jay. 1985. "The Hottentot Venus." In *The Flamingo's Smile*, 291–301. Boston: Norton.

Greenberg, David F. 1988. *The Construction of Homosexuality.* Chicago: University of Chicago Press.

Hall, Jacquelyn Dowd. 1979. *Revolt Against Chivalry: Jessie Daniel Ames and the Women's Campaign Against Lynching.* New York: Columbia University Press.

Halperin, David. 1990. *One Hundred Years of Homosexuality and Other Essays on Greek Love.* New York: Routledge.

Haraway, Donna J. 1989. *Primate Visions: Gender, Race, and Nature in the World of Modern Science.* New York: Routledge.

———. 1991. *Simians, Cyborgs, and Women: The Reinvention of Nature.* New York: Routledge.

Harvey, David. 1990. *The Condition of Postmodernity.* Cambridge, MA: Blackwell.

Harvey, Penelope, and Peter Gow, eds. 1994. *Sex and Violence: Issues in Representation and Experience.* London: Routledge.

Herdt, Gilbert. 1987 [1981]. *Guardians of the Flutes: Idioms of Masculinity.* New York: Columbia University Press.

Herzfeld, Michael. 1985. *The Poetics of Manhood: Contest and Identity in a Cretan Mountain Village.* Princeton: Princeton University Press.

Hocquenghem, Guy. 1993 (1972). *Homosexual Desire.* Durham, NC: Duke University Press.

Hunt, Lynn, ed. 1991. *Eroticism and the Body Politic.* Baltimore: Johns Hopkins University Press.

———. 1993. *The Invention of Pornography: Obscenity and the Origins of Modernity, 1500–1800.* New York: Zone.

JanMohamed, Abdul R. 1992. "Sexuality On/Of the Racial Border: Foucault, Wright, and the Articulation of 'Racialized Sexuality.'" In *Discourse of Sexuality From Aristotle to AIDS*, ed. Domna C. Stanton, 94–116. Ann Arbor: University of Michigan Press.

Jayawardena, Kumari. 1986. *Feminism and Nationalism in the Third World.* London: Zed Press.

Katz, Johnathan. 1990. "The Invention of Heterosexuality." *Socialist Review.* 20 (1): 7–34.

Kelly, Raymond C. 1976. "Witchcraft and Sexual Relations: An Exploration of the Social and Semantic Implications of the Structure of Belief." In *Man and Woman in the New Guinea Highlands*, ed. Paula Brown and Georgeda Buchbinder, 36–53. Washington, DC: American Anthropological Association.

Kennedy, Elizabeth, and Madeline Davis. 1993. *Boots of Leather, Slippers of Gold: The History of a Lesbian Community.* New York: Routledge.

Kipnis, Laura. 1992. "(Male) Desire and (Female) Disgust: Reading Hustler." In *Cultural Studies*, ed. Lawrence Grossberg, Cary Nelson, and Paula Treichler. New York: Routledge.

Koedt, Anne. 1973. "The Myth of the Vaginal Orgasm." In *Radical Feminism*, ed. Anne Koedt, Ellen Levine, and Anita Rapone, 246–58. New York: Quadrangle/New York Times.

Lancaster, Roger N. 1988. "Subject Honor and Object Shame: The Construction of Male Homosexuality and Stigma in Nicaragua." *Ethnology* 27 (2): 111–25.

———. 1992. *Life Is Hard: Machismo, Danger, and the Intimacy of Power in Nicaragua.* Berkeley and Los Angeles: University of California Press.

———. 1995. "'That We Should All Turn Queer?' Homosexual Stigma in the Making of Manhood and the Breaking of a Revolution in Nicaragua." In *Conceiving Sexualities: Approaches to Sex Research in a Postmodern World*, ed. Richard Parker and John Gagnon, 135–56. New York: Routledge.

Laqueur, Thomas. 1990. *Making Sex: Body and Gender From the Greeks to Freud.* Cambridge: Harvard University Press.

Lyotard, Jean-Francois. 1984. *The Postmodern Condition: A Report on Knowledge.* Foreword by Fredric Jameson. Minneapolis: University of Minnesota Press.

MacKinnon, Catharine. 1987. *Feminism Unmodified: Discourses on Life and Law.* Cambridge: Harvard University Press.

———. 1992. "Does Sexuality Have a History?" In *Discourses of Sexuality: From Aristotle to AIDS,* ed., Donna Stanton, 117–36. Ann Arbor: University of Michigan Press.

Nestle, Joan, ed. 1992. *The Persistent Desire: A Femme-Butch Reader.* Boston: Alyson.

Newton, Esther. 1979. *Mother Camp: Female Impersonation in America.* Chicago: University of Chicago Press.

———. 1993. *Cherry Grove, Fire Island: Sixty Years in America's First Gay and Lesbian Town.* Boston: Beacon.

Ortner, Sherry, and Harriet Whitehead, eds. 1981. *Sexual Meanings: The Cultural Construction of Gender and Sexuality.* Cambridge: Cambridge University Press.

Padgug, Robert A. 1979. "Sexual Matters: On Conceptualizing Sexuality in History." *Radical History Review* 20: 3–33.

Rich, Adrienne. 1993 [1980, 1982]. "Compulsory Heterosexuality and Lesbian Existence." In *The Lesbian and Gay Studies Reader,* ed. Henry Abelove, Michèle Aina Barale, and David M. Halperin, 227–54. New York: Routledge.

Riley, Denise. 1988. *Am I That Name? Feminism and the Category of 'Women' in History.* Minneapolis: University of Minnesota Press.

Roscoe, Will. 1991. *The Zuni Man-Woman.* Albuquerque: University of New Mexico Press.

Roseberry, William. 1990. *Anthropologies and Histories.* New Brunswick, NJ: Rutgers University Press.

Rubin, Gayle. 1975. "The Traffic in Women: Notes on the Political Economy of Sex." in *Toward an Anthropology of Women,* ed., Rayna Reiter. New York: Monthly Review Press.

———. 1984. "Thinking Sex: Notes for a Radical Theory of the Politics of Sexuality." In *Pleasure and Danger: Exploring Female Sexuality,* ed., Carol Vance, 267–319. Boston: Routledge and Kegan Paul.

Said, Edward. 1978. *Orientalism.* New York: Pantheon.

———. 1993. *Culture and Imperialism.* New York: Knopf.

Sedgwick, Eve Kosofsky. 1990. *Epistemology of the Closet.* Berkeley: University of California Press.

Segal, Lynne. 1994. *Straight Sex: Rethinking the Politics of Pleasure.* Berkeley: University of California Press.

Segal, Lynne, and Mary McIntosh, eds. 1992. *Sex Exposed: Sexuality and the Pornography Debate.* New Brunswick, NJ: Rutgers University Press.

Snitow, Ann, Christen Stansell, and Sharon Thompson, eds. 1983. *Powers of Desire: The Politics of Sexuality.* New York: Monthly Review Press.

Stoler, Ann Laura. 1995. *Race and the Education of Desire: Foucault's* History of Sexuality *and the Colonial Order of Things.* Durham, NC: Duke University Press.

Szwed, John F. 1975. "Race and the Embodiment of Culture." *Ethnicity* 2: 19–33.

Taussig, Michael. 1987. "The Rise and Fall of Marxist Anthropology." *Social Analysis* 21: 101–13.

Treichler, Paula A. 1988. "AIDS, Homophobia, and Biomedical Discourse: An Epidemic of Signification." In *AIDS: Cultural Analysis, Cultural Activism,* ed., D. Crimp, 31–70. Cambridge: MIT.

Truong, Thanh-Dam. 1993. *Sex, Money, and Morality: Sex Tourism in Southeast Asia.* London: Zed.

Turner, Terence. 1995. "Social Body and Embodied Subject: Bodiliness, Subjectivity, and Sociality Among the Kayapo." *Cultural Anthropology* 10 (2): 143–70.

Valverde, Mariana. 1989. "Beyond Gender Dangers and Private Pleasures: Theory and Ethics in the Sex Debates." *Feminist Studies* 15 (2) (Summer): 237–54.

Vance, Carol, ed. 1984. *Pleasure and Danger: Exploring Female Sexuality.* Boston: Routledge & Kegan Paul.

Warner, Michael, ed. 1993. *Fear of a Queer Planet: Queer Politics and Social Theory.* Minneapolis: University of Minnesota Press.

Weeks, Jeffrey. 1977. *Coming Out: Homosexual Politics in Britain from the Nineteenth Century to the Present.* London: Quartet.

Weston, Kath. 1991. *Families We Choose: Lesbians, Gays, Kinship.* New York: Columbia University Press.

Williams, Walter. 1988. *The Spirit of the Flesh: Sexual Diversity in American Indian Culture.* Boston: Beacon Press.

Embodiments of History

Local Meanings, Global Economies

Part One

MOVING BORDERS
Genders, Sexualities, Histories

1 Carnal Knowledge and Imperial Power

Gender, Race, and Morality in Colonial Asia

Ann Laura Stoler

Over the last fifteen years the anthropology of women has fundamentally altered our understanding of colonial expansion and its consequences for the colonized. More recent attention to the structures of colonial authority has placed new emphasis on the quotidian assertion of European dominance in the colonies, on imperial interventions in domestic life, and thus on the cultural prescriptions by which European women and men lived (Callan and Ardener 1984; Knibiehler and Goutalier 1985, 1987; Callaway 1987; Strobel 1987). Having focused on how colonizers have viewed the indigenous Other, we are beginning to sort out how Europeans in the colonies imagined themselves and constructed communities built on asymmetries of race, class, and gender—entities significantly at odds with the European models on which they were drawn.

Feminist attempts to engage the gender politics of Dutch, French, and British imperial cultures converge on some strikingly similar observations; namely, that European women in these colonies experienced the cleavages of racial dominance and internal social distinctions very differently than men precisely because of their ambiguous positions as both subordinates in colonial hierarchies and as active agents of imperial culture in their own right (Callan and Ardener 1984; Knibiehler and Goutalier 1985; Reijs et al. 1986; Callaway 1987). Concomitantly, the majority of European women who left for the colonies in the late nineteenth and early twentieth centuries confronted profoundly rigid restrictions on their domestic, economic, and political options, more limiting than those of metropolitan Europe at the time and sharply contrasting with the opportunities open to colonial men.

In one form or another, these studies raise a basic question: In what ways were gender inequalities essential to the structure of colonial racism and imperial authority? Was the strident misogyny of imperial thinkers and colonial agents a byproduct of received metropolitan values ("they just brought it with them"), a reaction to contemporary feminist demands in Europe

Ann Laura Stoler is Professor of Anthropology, History, and Women's Studies at the University of Michigan, Ann Arbor. Her most recent publications include *Race and the Education of Desire: Foucault's* History of Sexuality *and the Colonial Order of Things* (Duke, 1995); a volume coedited with Frederick Cooper, *Tensions of Empire: Colonial Cultures in a Bourgeois World* (California, 1997), and "Racial Histories and their Regimes of Truth," forthcoming in the journal *Political Power and Social Theory* (1997). Her earlier book, *Capitalism and Confrontation in Sumatra's Plantation Belt* (Yale, 1985), won the 1991 Harry Benda Prize for its outstanding contribution to Southeast Asian Studies and was recently republished (Michigan, 1995).

("women need to be put back in their breeding place"), or a novel and pragmatic response to the conditions of conquest? Was the assertion of European supremacy in terms of patriotic manhood and racial virility an expression of imperial domination or a defining feature of it?

Focusing on French Indochina and the Dutch East Indies in the early twentieth century but drawing on other contexts, I suggest that the very categories of "colonizer" and "colonized" were secured through forms of sexual control that defined the domestic arrangements of Europeans and the cultural investments by which they identified themselves. In treating the sexual and conjugal tensions of colonial life as more than a political trope for the tensions of empire writ small, but as a part of the latter in socially profound and strategic ways, I examine how gender-specific sexual sanctions and prohibitions not only demarcated positions of power but prescribed the personal and public boundaries of race.

Colonial authority was constructed on two powerful but false premises. The first was the notion that Europeans in the colonies made up an easily identifiable and discrete biological and social entity; a "natural" community of common class interests, racial attributes, political affinities, and superior culture. The second was the related notion that the boundaries separating colonizer from colonized were thus self-evident and easily drawn (Stoler 1989). Neither premise reflected colonial realities. Tensions between bureaucrats and planters, settlers and transients, missionaries and metropolitan policy makers, *petits blancs* (lower-class whites), and monied entrepreneurs have always made Euro-colonial communities more socially fractious and politically fragile than many of their members professed (see, for example, Cooper 1980; Drooglever 1980; Ridley 1981; Comaroff and Comaroff 1986; Kennedy 1987; Prochaska, 1989). Internal divisions developed out of competing economic and political agendas—conflicts over access to indigenous resources, frictions over appropriate methods for safeguarding European privilege and power, competing criteria for reproducing a colonial elite and for restricting its membership.

The markers of European identity and the criteria for community membership were never fixed. Rather, they defined fluid, permeable, and historically disputed terrain. The colonial politics of exclusion was contingent on constructing categories. Colonial control was predicated on identifying who was "white," who was "native," and which children could become citizens rather than subjects, designating who were legitimate progeny and who were not.

What mattered was not only one's physical properties but also who counted as "European" and by what measure. Skin shade was too ambiguous; bank accounts were mercurial; religious beliefs and education were crucial but never completely sufficient. Social and legal standing derived from the cultural prism through which color was viewed, from the silences, acknowledgments, and denials of the social circumstances in which one's parents had sex. Sexual unions based on concubinage, prostitution, or church marriage derived from the hierarchies of rule; but in turn, they were negotiated relations, contested classifications, which altered individual fates and the very structure of colonial society (Matinez-Alier 1974; Ming 1983; Taylor 1983). Ultimately inclusion or exclusion required regulating the sexual, conjugal, and domestic life of *both* Europeans in the colonies and their colonized subjects.

POLITICAL MESSAGES AND SEXUAL METAPHORS

Colonial observers and participants in the imperial enterprise expressed unwavering interest in the sexual interface of the colonial encounter. Probably no subject is discussed more than sex in colonial literature and no subject more frequently invoked to foster the racist stereotypes of European society (Pujarniscle 1931: 106; Loutfi 1971: 36). With the sustained presence of Europeans in the colonies, sexual prescriptions by class, race, and gender became increasingly central to the politics of empire and subject to new forms of scrutiny by colonial states.

The salience of sexual symbols as graphic representations of colonial dominance is relatively unambiguous and well-established. Edward Said, for example, has argued that the sexual submission and possession of Oriental women by European men "fairly *stands for* the pattern of relative strength between East and West, and the discourse about the Orient that it enabled" (1978: 6, my emphasis). He describes Orientalism as a "male perception of the world," "a male power-fantasy," "an exclusively male province," in which the Orient is penetrated, silenced, and possessed (1978:207). Sexuality, then, serves as a loaded metaphor for domination, but Said's critique is not (nor does it claim to be) about those relations between women and men. Sexual images illustrate the iconography of rule, not its pragmatics. Sexual asymmetries and visions convey what is "really" going on elsewhere, at another political epicenter. They are tropes to depict other centers of power.

Sexual domination has been carefully considered as a discursive symbol, instrumental in the conveyance of other meanings, but has been less often treated as the substance of imperial policy. Was sexual dominance, then, merely a graphic substantiation of who was, so to speak, on the bottom and who was on the top? Was the medium the message, or did sexual relations always "mean" something else, stand in for other relations, evoke the sense of *other* (pecuniary, political, or some possibly more subliminal) desires? This analytic slippage between the sexual symbols of power and the politics of sex runs throughout the colonial record—as well as through contemporary commentaries on it. Some of this may be due to the polyvalent quality of sexuality; symbolically rich and socially salient at the same time. But sexual control was more than a convenient metaphor for colonial domination; it was, as I argue here, a fundamental class and racial marker implicated in a wider set of relations of power.

In the sections that follow I look at the relationship between the domestic arrangements of colonial communities and their wider political structures. Part I draws on colonization debates over a broad period (sixteenth-twentieth c.) in an effort to identify the long-term intervention of colonial authorities in issues of "racial mixing," settlement schemes, and sexual control. In examining debates over European family formation, over the relationship between subversion and sex, I look at how evaluations of concubinage, and of morality more generally, changed with new forms of racism and new gender-specific expressions of them.

Part II treats the protection and policing of European women within the changing politics of empire. It traces how accusations of sexual assault related to new demands for political rights and restricted demarcations of social space in response to them. Part III addresses what I call the "cultural hygiene" of colonialism. Taking the early twentieth century as a breakpoint, I take up the convergent metropolitan and colonial discourses on health hazards in the tropics, race-thinking, and social reform as they related to shifts in the rationalization of rule. In tracing how fears of "racial degeneracy" were grounded in class-specific sexual norms, I return to how and why racial difference was constituted and culturally coded in gendered terms.

PART I: SEX AND OTHER CATEGORIES OF COLONIAL CONTROL

Who bedded and wedded with whom in the colonies of France, England, Holland, and Iberia was never left to chance. Unions between Annamite women and French men, between Portuguese women and Dutch men, between Spanish men and Inca women produced offspring with claims to privilege, whose rights and status had to be determined and prescribed. From the early 1600s through the twentieth century the sexual sanctions and conjugal prohibitions of colonial agents were rigorously debated and carefully codified. It is in these debates over matrimony and morality that trading and plantation company officials, missionaries, investment bankers, military high commands, and agents of the colonial state confronted one another's visions of empire and the settlement patterns on which rule would rest.

In 1622, the Dutch East Indies Company (VOC) arranged for the transport of six poor but marriageable young Dutch women to Java, providing them with clothing, a dowry upon marriage, and a contract binding them to five years in the Indies (Taylor 1983: 12). Aside from this and one other short-lived experiment, immigration of European women to the East was consciously restricted for the next two hundred years. VOC shareholders argued against female emigration on several counts: the high cost of transporting married women and daughters (Blussé 1986: 161); the possibility that Dutch women (with stronger ties than men to the Netherlands?) might hinder permanent settlement by goading their burgher husbands to quickly lucrative but nefarious trade, and then repatriate to display their newfound wealth; the fear that Dutch women would enrich themselves through private trade and encroach on the company's monopoly; and the prediction that their children would be sickly and force families to repatriate, ultimately depleting the colony of permanent and loyal settlers.

The Dutch East Indies Company enforced the sanction against female migration by selecting bachelors as their European recruits and by promoting both extramarital relations and legal unions between low-ranking employees and imported slave women. Although there were Euro-Asian marriages, government regulations made concubinage a more attractive option by prohibiting European men with native wives and children from returning to Holland (Ming 1983: 69; Blussé 1986: 173). The VOC saw households based on Euro-Asian unions, by contrast, as having distinct advantages; individual employees would bear the costs of dependents; children of mixed unions were considered stronger and healthier; and Asian women made fewer (economic and emotional) demands. Finally, it was thought that men would be more likely to settle permanently by establishing families with local roots.

Concubinage served colonial interests in other ways. It permitted permanent settlement and rapid growth by a cheaper means than the importation of European women. Salaries of European recruits to the colonial armies, bureaucracies, plantation companies, and trading enterprises were kept artificially low. This was possible not only because the transport of European women and family support was thereby eliminated, as was often argued, but also because local women provided domestic services for which new European recruits would otherwise have had to pay. In the mid-nineteenth century, such arrangements were de rigueur for young civil servants intent on setting up households on their own (Ritter 1956: 21). Despite some clerical opposition by the nineteenth century concubinage was the most prevalent living arrangement for European men (van Marle 1952: 485). Nearly half of the Indies' European male population in the 1880s was unmarried and living with Asian women (Ming 1983: 70). It was only in the early twentieth century that concubinage was politically condemned.

In Asia and Africa, corporate and government decision-makers invoked the social services that local women supplied as "useful guides to the language and other mysteries of the local societies" (Malleret 1934: 216; Cohen 1971: 122). The medical and cultural know-how of local women was credited with keeping many European men alive in their initial confrontation with tropical life (Braconier 1933). Handbooks for incoming plantation employees bound for Tonkin, Sumatra, and Malaya urged men to find a bed-servant as a prerequisite to quick acclimatization (Nieuwenhuys 1959: 19; Dixon 1913: 77). In Malaysia, commercial companies encouraged the procurement of local "companions for psychological and physical well-being"; to protect European staff from the ill-health that sexual abstention, isolation, and boredom were thought to bring (Butcher 1979: 200, 202). Even in the British empire, where the colonial office formally banned concubinage in 1910, it was tacitly condoned and practiced long after (Hyam 1986b, 49; Kennedy 1987: 175). In the Indies, a simultaneous sanction against concubinage among civil servants was only selectively enforced; it had little effect on domestic arrangements outside of Java and no perceptible impact on the European households in Sumatra's newly opened plantation belt where Japanese and Japanese huishoudsters (as Asian mistresses were sometimes called) remained the rule rather than the exception (Clerkx 1961: 87–93; Stoler 1985a: 31–34; Lucas 1986: 84).

While the term concubinage commonly referred to the cohabitation outside of marriage between European men and Asian women, in fact, it glossed a wide range of arrangements that included sexual access to a non-European woman as well as demands on her labor and legal rights to the children she bore. Thus, to define it as cohabitation perhaps suggests more social privileges than most women who were involved in such relations enjoyed. Many colonized women combined sexual and domestic service within the abjectly subordinate contexts of slave or "coolie" and lived in separate quarters. On the plantations in East Sumatra, for example, where such arrangements were structured into company policies of labor control, Javanese women picked from the coolie ranks often retained their original labor contracts for the duration of their sexual and domestic service (Lucas 1986: 186).

To say that concubinage reinforced the hierarchies on which colonial societies were based is not to say that it did not make those distinctions more problematic at the same time. In such regions as North Sumatra, grossly uneven sex ratios often made for intense competition among male workers and their European supervisors for indigenous women. *Vrouwen perkara* (disputes over women) resulted in assaults on whites, new labor tensions, and dangerous incursions into the standards deemed essential for white prestige (Stoler 1985a: 33; Lucas 1986: 90–91). Metropolitan critics were particularly disdainful of these liaisons on moral grounds—all the more so when these unions *were* sustained and affectively significant relationships, thereby contradicting the racial premise of concubinage as an emotionally unfettered convenience. But perhaps most important, the tension between concubinage as a confirmation and compromise of racial hierarchy was realized in the progeny that it produced, "mixed bloods," poor "Indos," and abandoned *métis* children who straddled the divisions of ruler and ruled and threatened to blur the colonial divide. These *voorkinderen* (literally, "children from a previous marriage/union," but in this colonial context usually marking illegitimate children from a previous union with a non-European woman) were economically disadvantaged by their ambiguous social status and often grew up to join the ranks of the impoverished whites (Nieuwenhuys 1959: 21).

Concubinage was a domestic arrangement based on sexual service and gender inequalities that "worked" as long as European identity and supremacy were clear. When either was thought to be vulnerable, in jeopardy, or less than convincing, at the turn of the century and increasingly through the 1920s, colonial elites responded by clarifying the cultural criteria of privilege and the moral premises of their unity. Structured sex in the politically safe context of prostitution, and where possible in the more desirable context of marriage between "full-blooded" Europeans, replaced concubinage (Taylor 1977: 29).

Restrictions on European Women in the Colonies

Colonial governments and private business not only tolerated concubinage but actively encouraged it—principally by restricting the emigration of European women to the colonies and by refusing employment to married male European recruits. Although most accounts of colonial conquest and settlement suggest that European women chose to avoid early pioneering ventures, the choice was rarely their own (cf. Fredrickson 1981: 109). In the Indies, a government ordinance of 1872 made it impossible for any soldier below the rank of sergeant major to be married; and even above that rank, conditions were very restrictive (Ming 1983: 70). In the Indies army, marriage was a privilege of the officer corps, whereas barrack-concubinage was instituted and regulated for the rank and file. Through the 1920s and 1930s, formal and informal prohibitions set by banks, estates, and government services operating in Africa, South Asia, and Southeast Asia restricted marriage during the first three to five years of service while some simply prohibited it altogether.

Many historians assume that these bans on employee marriage and on the emigration of European women lifted when specific colonies were politically stable, medically upgraded, and economically secure. In fact marriage restrictions lasted well into the twentieth century, long after rough living and a scarcity of amenities had become conditions of the past. In India as late as 1929, British employees in the political service were still recruited at the age of twenty-six and then prohibited from marriage during their first three probationary years (Moore-Gilbert 1986: 48). On the Ivory Coast, employment contracts in the 1920s also denied marriage with European women before the third tour, which meant a minimum of five years' service, so that many men remained unmarried past the age of thirty (Tirefort 1979: 134).

European demographics in the colonies were shaped by these economic and political exigencies and thus were enormously skewed by sex. Among the laboring immigrant and native populations as well as among Europeans in the late nineteenth and early twentieth centuries, the number of men was, at the very least, double that of women, and sometimes exceeded the latter by twenty-five times. Although in the Netherlands Indies, the overall ratio of European women to men rose from 47:100 to 88:100 between 1900 and 1930, representing an absolute increase from 4,000 to 26,000 Dutch women (Taylor 1983: 128), in outlying areas such as on Sumatra's plantation belt in 1920 there were still only 61 European women per 100 men (*Koloniale Verslag* quoted in Lucas 1986: 82). On Africa's Ivory Coast, European sex ratios through 1921 were still 1:25 (Tirefort 1979: 31). In controlling the availability of European women and the sorts of sexual access allowed, colonial state and corporate authorities avoided salary increases as well as the proliferation of a lower-class European settler population. Such policies in no way muted the internal class distinctions within the European communities; they simply shaped the social geography of the colonies by fixing the conditions under which European privileges could be attained and reproduced.

Sex, Subversion, and White Prestige

The marriage prohibition revealed how deeply the conduct of private life and the sexual procliv-ities individuals expressed were tied to corporate profits and the security of the colonial state. Nowhere was the connection between sex and subversion more openly contested than in North Sumatra in the early 1900s. Irregular domestic arrangements were thought to encourage subver-sion as strongly as acceptable unions could avert it. Family stability and sexual "normalcy" were thus linked to political agitation or quiescence in very concrete ways.

Since the late nineteenth century, the major North Sumatran tobacco and rubber companies had neither accepted married applicants nor allowed them to take wives while in service (Schoevers 1913: 38; Clerkx 1961: 31–34). Company authorities argued that new employees with families in tow would be a financial burden, risking the emergence of a "European prole-tariat" and thus a major threat to white prestige (*Kroniek 1917:* 50; *Sumatra Post* 1913). Low-ranking plantation employees protested against these company marriage restrictions, an issue that mobilized their ranks behind a broad set of demands (Stoler 1989*a*: 144). Under employee pres-sure, the prohibition was relaxed to a marriage ban for the first five years of service.

Domestic arrangements thus varied as government officials and private businesses weighed the economic versus political costs of one arrangement over another, but such calculations were invari-ably meshed. Europeans in high office saw white prestige and profits inextricably linked, and atti-tudes toward concubinage reflected that concern (Brownfoot 1984: 181). Thus in Malaya through the 1920s, concubinage was tolerated precisely because "poor whites" were not. Government and plantation administrators argued that white prestige would be imperiled if European men became impoverished in attempting to maintain middle-class life styles and European wives. Colonial morality and the place of concubinage in it was relative, given the "particular anathema with which the British regarded 'poor whites'" (Butcher 1979: 26). In late nineteenth century Java, in contrast, concubinage itself was considered to be a major source of white pauperism and vigor-ously condemned at precisely the same time that a new colonial morality passively condoned ille-gal brothels (Het Pauperisme Commissie 1901; Nieuwenhuys 1959: 20–23; Hesselink 1987: 208).

What constituted morality vacillated, as did the very definition of white prestige—and what its defense should entail. A discursive obsession with white prestige was a basic feature of colonial mentality. White prestige and its protection loom as the primary cause of a long list of otherwise inexplicable colonial postures, prejudices, fears, and violences. What upheld that prestige was not a constant; concubinage was socially lauded at one time and seen as a political menace at another. White prestige was a gloss for different intensities of racist practice, gender specific and culturally coded. Although many accounts contend that white women brought an end to concubinage, its decline came with a much wider shift in colonial relations along more racially segregated lines—

in which the definitions of prestige shifted and in which Asian, Creole, and European-born women were to play new roles.

PART II: EUROPEAN WOMEN AND RACIAL BOUNDARIES

Perhaps nothing is as striking in the sociological accounts of European colonial communities as the extraordinary changes that are said to accompany the entry of white women. These adjustments shifted in one direction: toward European life styles accentuating the refinements of privilege and new etiquettes of racial difference. Housing structures in the Indies were partitioned, residential compounds in the Solomon Islands enclosed, servant relations in Hawaii formalized, dress codes in Java altered, food and social taboos in Rhodesia and the Ivory Coast codified. Taken together, these changes encouraged new kinds of consumption and new social services catering to these new demands (Boutilier 1984; Spear 1963; Woodcock 1969; Cohen 1971).

The arrival of large numbers of European women thus coincided with an embourgeoisment of colonial communities and with a significant sharpening of racial categories. European women supposedly required more metropolitan amenities than men and more spacious surroundings to allow it; they had more delicate sensibilities and therefore needed suitable quarters—discrete and enclosed. Women's psychological and physical constitutions were considered more fragile, demanding more servants for the chores they should be spared. In short, white women needed to be maintained at elevated standards of living, in insulated social spaces cushioned with the cultural artifacts of "being European." Segregationist standards were what women "deserved," and more importantly what white male prestige required that they maintain.

Racist but Moral Women, Innocent but Immoral Men

Colonial rhetoric on white women was full of contradictions. At the same time that new female immigrants were chided for not respecting the racial distance of local convention, an equal number of colonial observers accused these women of being more avid racists in their own right (Spear 1963; Nora 1961). Allegedly insecure and jealous of the sexual liaisons of European men with native women, bound to their provincial visions and cultural norms, European women, it was and is argued, constructed the major cleavages on which colonial stratification rested. Thus Percival Spear, in commenting on the social life of the English in eighteenth-century India, asserted that women "widened the racial gulf" by holding to "their insular whims and prejudices" (1963: 140). Writing about French women in Algeria two hundred years later, the French historian Pierre Nora claimed that these "parasites of the colonial relationship in which they do not participate directly, are generally more racist than men and contribute strongly to prohibiting contact between the two societies" (1961: 174). For the Indies, "it was jealousy of the dusky sirens . . . but more likely some say . . . it was . . . plain feminine scandalization at free and easy sex relations" that caused a decline in miscegenation (Kennedy 1947: 164).

Such bald examples are easy to find in colonial histories of several decades ago. Recent scholarship is more subtle but not substantially different. In the European community on the French Ivory Coast, ethnographer Alain Tirefort contends that "the presence of the white woman separated husbands from indigenous life by creating around them a zone of European intimacy" (1979: 197). Gann and Duignan state simply that it was "the cheap steamship ticket for women that put an end to racial integration in British Africa" (1978: 242; also see O'Brien 1972: 59). In such narratives, European women are positioned both as marginal players on the colonial stage and as principal actors. They are charged with dramatically reshaping the face of colonial society, imposing racial distance in African and Asian contexts where "relatively unrestrained social intermingling . . . had been prevalent in earlier years" (Cohen 1971: 122; Vere Allen 1970: 169). European women are not only the true bearers of racist beliefs but also hard-line operatives who put racism into practice, encouraging class distinctions among whites while fostering new racial antagonisms, formerly muted by sexual access.

Are we to believe that sexual intimacy with European men yielded social mobility and political rights for colonized women? Or even less likely, that because British civil servants bedded with Indian women, somehow Indian men had more "in common" with British men and enjoyed more parity? Colonized women could sometimes parlay their positions into personal profit and small rewards, but these were *individual* negotiations with no social, legal, or cumulative claims. European male sexual access to native women was not a leveling mechanism for asymmetries in race, class, or gender (Strobel 1987: 378; Degler 1986: 189).

Male colonizers positioned European women as the bearers of a redefined colonial morality. But to suggest that women fashioned this racism out of whole cloth is to miss the political chronology in which new intensities of racist practice arose. In the African and Asian contexts already mentioned, the arrival or large numbers of European wives, and particularly the fear for their protection, followed from new terms and tensions in the colonial contract. The presence and protection of European women was repeatedly invoked to clarify racial lines. It coincided with perceived threats to European prestige (Brownfoot 1984: 191), increased racial conflict (Strobel 1987: 378), covert challenges to the colonial order, outright expressions of nationalist resistance, and internal dissension among whites themselves (Stoler 1989a: 147–49).

If white women were the primary force behind the decline of concubinage, as is often claimed, they did so as participants in a much broader shift in racial politics and colonial plan (Knibiehler and Goutalier 1985: 76). This is not to suggest that European women were passive in this process, as the dominant themes in many of their novels attest (Taylor 1977: 27). Many European women did oppose concubinage—not because they were categorically jealous of, and threatened by, Asian women as often claimed (Clerkx 1961), but, more likely, because of the double standard it condoned for European women (Lucas 1986: 94–95). The voices of European women had little resonance until their objections coincided with a realignment in racial and class politics in which they were strategic to both.

Race and the Politics of Sexual Peril

The gender-specific requirements for colonial living were constructed on heavily racist evaluations, which pivoted on images of the heightened sexuality of colonized men (Tiffany and Adams 1985). In this frame, European women needed protection because men of color had "primitive" sexual urges and uncontrollable lust, aroused by the sight of white women (Strobel 1987: 379; Schmidt 1987: 411). In some colonies, that sexual threat remained an unlabeled potential; in others it was given a specific name. The "Black Peril" referred throughout Africa and much of the British Empire to the professed dangers of sexual assault on white women by black men.

In Southern Rhodesia and Kenya in the 1920s and 1930s, preoccupations with the "Black Peril" gave rise to the creation of citizens' militias, ladies' riflery clubs, and investigations as to whether African female domestic servants would not be safer to employ than men (Kirkwood 1984: 158; Schmidt 1987: 412; Kennedy 1987: 128–47; Hansen 1989). In New Guinea, alleged attempted assaults on European women by Papuan men prompted the passage of the White Women's Protection Ordinance of 1926, which provided "the death penalty for any person convicted for the crime of rape or attempted rape upon a European woman or girl" (Inglis 1975: vi). And in the Solomon Islands authorities introduced public flogging in 1934 as punishment for "criminal assaults on [white] females" (Boutilier 1984: 197).

What do these cases have in common? First, the rhetoric of sexual assault and the measures used to prevent it had virtually no correlation with actual incidences of rape of European women by men of color. Just the contrary: there was often no ex post facto evidence, nor any at the time, that rapes were committed or that rape attempts were made (Schmidt 1987; Inglis 1975; Kirkwood 1984; Kennedy 1987; Boutilier 1984). Moreover, the rape laws were race specific; sexual abuse of black women was not classified as rape and therefore was not legally actionable, nor did rapes committed by white men lead to prosecution (Mason 1958: 246–47). If these accusations of sexual threat were not prompted by the fact of rape, what did they signal and to what were they tied?

Allusions to political and sexual subversion of the colonial system went hand in hand. The term "Black Peril" referred to sexual threats, but it also connoted the fear of insurgence, of some perceived nonacquiescence to colonial control more generally (van Onselen 1982; Schmidt 1987; Inglis 1975; Strobel 1987; Kennedy 1987: 128–47). Concern over protection of white women intensified during real and perceived crises of control—provoked by threats to the internal cohesion of the European communities or by infringements on its borders. Thus colonial accounts of the Mutiny in India in 1857 are full of descriptions of the sexual mutilation of British women by Indian men despite the fact that no rapes were recorded (Metcalf 1964: 290). In New Guinea, the White Women's Protection Ordinance followed a large influx of acculturated Papuans into Port Moresby in the 1920s. Resistant to the constraints imposed on their dress, movement, and education, whites perceived them as arrogant, "cheeky," and without respect (Inglis 1975: 8, 11). In post–World War I Algeria, the political unease of *pieds noirs* (local French settlers) in the race of "a whole new series of [Muslim] demands" manifested itself in a popular culture newly infused with strong images of sexually aggressive Algerian men (Sivan 1983: 178).

Second, rape charges against colonized men were often based on perceived transgressions of social space. "Attempted rapes" turned out to be "incidents" of a Papuan man "discovered" in the vicinity of a white residence, a Fijian man who entered a European patient's room, a male servant poised at the bedroom of a European woman asleep or in half-dress (Boutilier 1984: 197; Inglis 1975: 11; Schmidt 1987: 413). With such a broad definition of danger in a culture of fear, all colonized men of color were threatening as sexual and political aggressors.

Third, accusations of sexual assault frequently followed upon heightened tensions within European communities—and renewed efforts to find consensus within them. Rape accusations in South Africa, for example, coincided with a rash of strikes between 1890 and 1914 by both African and white miners (van Onselen 1982: 51). As in Rhodesia after a strike by white railway employees in 1929, the threat of native rebellion brought together conflicting members of the European community in common cause where "solidarity found sustenance in the threat of racial destruction" (Kennedy 1987: 138).

During the late 1920s, when labor protests by Indonesia workers and European employees were most intense, Sumatra's corporate elite expanded their vigilante organizations, intelligence networks, and demands for police protection to ensure their women were safe and their workers "in hand" (Stoler 1985a).

In Sumatra's plantation belt, subsidized sponsorship of married couples replaced the recruitment of single Indonesian workers and European staff, with new incentives provided for family housing and *gezinvorming* ("family formation") in both groups. This recomposed labor force of family men in "stable households" explicitly weeded out politically "undesirable elements" and the socially malcontent. With the marriage restriction finally lifted for European staff in the 1920s, young men sought wives among Dutch-born women while on leave in Holland or through marriage brokers by mail. Higher salaries, upgraded housing, elevated bonuses, and a more mediated chain of command between colonized fieldworker and colonial staff served to clarify both national and racial affinities and to differentiate the further political interests of European from Asian workers (Stoler 1985a).

The remedies searched for alleviate sexual danger were sought in new prescriptions for securing white control; increased surveillance of native men, new laws stipulating severe corporeal punishment for the transgression of sexual and social boundaries, and the creation of areas made racially off-limits. These went with a moral rearmament of the European community and reassertions of its cultural identity. Charged with guarding cultural norms, European women were instrumental in promoting white solidarity. It was partly at their own expense, as they were to be nearly as closely policed as colonized men (Strobel 1987).

Policing European Women and Concessions to Chivalry

Although native men were the ones legally punished for alleged sexual assaults, European women were frequently blamed for provoking those desires. New arrivals from Europe were accused of being too familiar with their servants, lax in their commands, indecorous in their speech and in their dress (Vellut 1982: 100; Kennedy 1987: 141; Schmidt 1987: 413). In Papua New Guinea, "everyone" in the Australian community agreed that rape assaults were caused by a "younger generation of white women" unschooled in the proper treatment of servants (Inglis 1975: 80). In Rhodesia as in Uganda, sexual anxieties persisted in the absence of any incidents and restricted women to activities within the European enclaves (Gartrell 1984: 169). The immorality act of 1916 "made it an offense for a white woman to make an indecent suggestion to a male native" (Mason 1958: 247). As in the American South, "the etiquette of chivalry controlled white women's behavior even as [it] guarded caste lines" (Dowd Hall 1984: 64). A defense of community, morality, and white male power was achieved by increasing control over and consensus among Europeans, by reaffirming the vulnerability of white women and the sexual threat posed by native men, and by creating new sanctions to limit the liberties of both.

European colonial communities in the early twentieth century assiduously controlled the movements of European women, and, where possible, imposed on them restricted and protected roles. This is not to say that European women did not work; some openly questioned the sexist policies of their male superiors. However, by and large their tasks buttressed rather than contested the established racial order (Ralston 1977; Knibiehler and Goutalier 1985; Callaway 1987: 111; Ramuschack n.d.).

Particularly in the colonies with small European communities as opposed to those of large-scale settlement, there were few opportunities for women to be economically independent or to act politically on their own. The "revolt against chivalry"—the protest of American Southern white women to lynchings of black men for alleged rape attempts—had no counterpart among European women in Asia and Africa (Dowd Hall 1984). Firmly rejecting expansion based on the "poor white" (petit blanc) Algerian model, French officials in Indochina dissuaded *colons* with insufficient capital from entry and promptly repatriated those who tried to remain. Single women were seen as the quintessential petits blancs; with limited resources and shopkeeper aspirations, they presented the dangerous possibility that straitened circumstances would lead them to prostitution, thereby degrading European prestige at large.

Professional competence did not leave single European women immune from marginalization. Single professional women were held in contempt as were European prostitutes, with surprisingly similar objections. White prostitutes threatened prestige, while professional women needed protection; both fell outside the social space to which European colonial women were assigned—namely, as custodians of family welfare and respectability, and as dedicated and willing subordinates to, and supporters of, colonial men. The rigor with which these norms were applied becomes more comprehensible when we see why a European family life and bourgeois respectability became increasingly tied to notions of racial survival, imperial patriotism, and the political strategies of the colonial state.

PART III: WHITE DEGENERACY, MOTHERHOOD, AND THE EUGENICS OF EMPIRE

de • gen • er • ate (adj.) [L. *degeneratus,* pp. of *degenerare,* to become unlike one's race, degenerate < *degener,* not genuine, base < *de-,* from + *genus,* race, kind: see *genus*]. 1. to lose
former, normal, or higher qualities. 2. Having sunk below a former or normal condition,
character, etc.; deteriorated. 3. morally corrupt; depraved- (n.) a degenerate person, esp. one
who is morally depraved or sexually perverted- (vi.) -*at'ed, 'at'ing.* 1. to decline or become
debased morally, culturally, etc. . . . 2. Biol. to undergo degeneration; deteriorate. (*Webster's
New World Dictionary* 1972: 371)

European women were essential to the colonial enterprise and the solidification of racial boundaries in ways that repeatedly tied their supportive and subordinate posture to community cohesion and colonial security. These features of their positioning within imperial politics were powerfully reinforced at the turn of the century by a metropolitan bourgeois discourse (and an eminently anthropological one) intensely concerned with notions of "degeneracy" (Le Bras 1981: 77). Middle-class morality, manliness, and motherhood were seen as endangered by the intimately linked fears of "degeneration" and miscegenation in scientifically construed racist believers (Mosse 1978: 82). Degeneration was defined as "departures from the normal human type . . . transmitted through inheritance and lead[ing] progressively to destruction" (Morel quoted in Mosse 1978: 83). Due to environmental, physical, and moral factors, degeneracy could be averted by positive eugenic selection or, negatively, by eliminating the "unfit" and/or the environmental and cultural contagions that gave rise to them (Mosse 1978: 87; Kevles 1985: 70–84).

Eugenics entailed distinctions that were elitist, racist, and misogynist in principle and practice (Gordon 1976: 395; Davin 1978; Hammerton 1979). Its proponents advocated a pro-natalist policy toward the white middle and upper classes, a rejection of women's work roles that might compete with motherhood, and "an assumption that reproduction was not just a function but the purpose . . . of women's life" (Gordon 1974: 134). In France, England, Germany, and the United States, eugenics placed European women of "good stock" as "the fountainhead of racial strength" (Ridley 1981: 91), exalting the cult of motherhood while subjecting it to the scrutiny of this new scientific domain (Davin 1978: 12).

As part of metropolitan class politics, eugenics reverberated in the colonies in predictable as well as unexpected forms. The moral, biological, and sexual referents of the notion of degeneracy (distinct in the dictionary citation above), were invariably meshed. The "colonial branch" of eugenics embraced a theory and practice concerned with the vulnerabilities of white rule and new measures to safeguard European superiority. Designed to control the procreation of the "unfit" lower orders, eugenics targeted "the poor, the colonized, or unpopular strangers" (Hobsbawm 1987: 253). Eugenic discourse permeated how metropolitan observers viewed the "degenerate" lifestyle of colonials, and how colonial elites admonished the behavior of "degenerate" members among themselves (Koks 1931: 179–189). Whereas studies in Europe and the United States focused on the inherent propensity of the impoverished classes to criminality, in the Indies delinquency among "European" children was biologically linked to the amount of "native blood" children born of mixed marriages had inherited from their native mothers (Branconier 1918: 11). Eugenics provided a new biological idiom in which to ground the medical and moral basis for anxiety over the security of European hegemony and white prestige. It reopened debates over segregated residence and education, new standards of morality, sexual vigilance, and the rights of *certain* Europeans to rule.

Eugenic thinking was manifest not in the direct importation of metropolitan practices such as sterilization, but in a translation of the political *principles* and the social values that eugenics implied. Eugenic statements pronounced what kind of people should represent Dutch or French rule, how they should bring up their children, and with whom they should socialize. A common discourse was mapped onto different immediate exigencies of empire with variations on a gender-specific theme exalting motherhood and domesticity.

Formulae to secure European rule pushed in two directions: on the one hand, away from ambiguous racial genres and open domestic arrangements, and on the other hand, toward an upgrading, homogenization, and a clearer delineation of European standards; away from miscegenation toward white endogamy; away from concubinage toward family formation and legal marriage (Taylor 1983). As stated by the Netherlands Indies' Eugenic Society, "eugenics is nothing other than belief in the possibility of preventing degenerative symptoms in the body of our beloved *moedervolken*, or in cases where they may already be present, of counteracting them" (Rodenwaldt 1928: 1).

Like the modernization of colonialism itself, with its scientific management and educated technocrats with limited local knowledge, colonial communities of the early twentieth century were rethinking the ways in which their authority should be expressed. This rethinking took the form of asserting a distinct colonial morality, explicit in its reorientation toward the racial and class markers of "Europeanness," emphasizing transnational racial commonalities despite national differences—distilling a *homo europeaus* for whom superior health, wealth, and education were tied to racial endowments and a White Man's norm. Thus the novelist Pujarniscle, a participant-observer in France's colonial venture, wrote: "One might be surprised that my pen always returns to the word *blanc* (white) or 'European' and never to 'Français' . . . in effect colonial solidarity and the obligations that it entails allies all the peoples of the white races" (1931: 72; also see Delavignette 1946: 41).

Such sensibilities colored imperial policy in nearly all domains with fears of physical contamination giving new credence to fears of political vulnerability. Whites had to guard their ranks—in quantity and in kind—to increase their numbers and to ensure that their members blurred neither biological nor political boundaries. In the metropole the socially and physically "unfit," the poor, the indigent, and the insane, were either to be sterilized or prevented from marriage. In the colonies it was these very groups among Europeans who were either excluded from entry or institutionalized while they were there and eventually sent home (Arnold 1979; Vellut 1982: 97).

In sustaining a vision that good health, virility, and the ability to rule were inherent features of what it took to be "European," whites in the colonies had to adhere to a politics of exclusion that policed their members as well as the colonized. Measures were taken both to avoid poor white migration and to produce a colonial profile that highlighted the manliness, well-being, and productivity of European men. Within this equation, protection of manhood, national identity, and racial superiority were meshed (Loutfi 1971: 112–113; Ridley 1981: 104). Thus British colonial administrators were retired by the age of fifty-five, ensuring that

> no Oriental was ever allowed to see a Westerner as he ages and degenerated, just as no Westerner needed ever to see himself, mirrored in the eyes of the subject race, as anything but a vigorous, rational, ever-alert young Raj. (Said 1978: 42)

In the twentieth century, these "men of class" and "men of character" embodied a modernized and renovated image of rule; they were to safeguard the colonies against physical weakness, moral decay, and the inevitable degeneration that long residence in the colonies encouraged, and against the temptations that interracial domestic situations had allowed.

THE CULTURAL DYNAMICS OF DEGENERATION

> The *colon* is, in a common and etymological sense, a barbarian. He is a non-civilized person, a "new-man," . . . it is he who appears as a savage. (Dupuy 1955: 188)

The shift in imperial thinking that we can identify in the early twentieth century surely focuses on the Otherness of the colonized but also on the Otherness of colonials themselves. In metropolitan France, a profusion of medical and sociological tracts pinpointed the colonial as a distinct and degenerate social type, with specific psychological and physical features (Maunier 1932; Pujarniscle 1931). Some of that difference was attributed to the debilitating results of climate and social milieu, from staying in the colonies too long:

> The climate affects him, his surroundings affect him, and after a certain time, he has become, both physically and morally, a completely different man. (Maunier 1932: 169)

People who stayed "too long" were in grave danger of overfatigue; of individual and racial degeneration (Le Roux 1898: 222); of physical breakdown (not just illness); of cultural contamination and neglect of the conventions of supremacy, and of *disagreement* about what those conventions were (Dupuy 1955: 184–185).

Colonial medicine reflected and affirmed this slippage between physical, moral, and cultural degeneracy in numerous ways. The climatic, social, and work conditions of colonial life gave rise to a specific set of psychotic disorders affecting *l'equilibre cerebral* and predisposing Europeans in the tropics to mental breakdown (Hartenberg 1910; Abatucci 1910). Neurasthenia was the most common manifestation, a mental disorder identified as a major problem in the French empire and accounting for more than half the Dutch repatriations from the Indies to Holland (Winckel 1938: 352). In Europe and America, it was "the phantom disease . . . the classic illness of the late nineteenth century" encompassing virtually all "pscyhopatho or neurological conditions," and intimately linked to sexual deviation and to the destruction of social order itself" (Gilman 1985; 199, 202).

Whereas in Europe neurasthenia was considered to be a consequence of "modern civilization" and its high-pitched pace (Showalter 1987: 135), in the colonies its etiology took the *reverse* form. Colonial neurasthenia was allegedly caused by a *distance* from civilization and European community and by proximity to the colonized. The susceptibility of a colonial (man) was increased by an existence "outside of the social framework to which he was adapted in France, isolation in outposts, physical and moral fatigue, and modified food regimes" (Joyeux 1937: 335).

Some doctors considered the only treatment to be *le retour en Europe* (Joyeux 1937; 335; Pujarniscle 1931: 28). Others prescribed a local set of remedies, high morals, and hard work. This included sexual moderation, a "regularity and regimentation" of work, abstemious diet, physical exercise, and *European* camaraderie, buttressed by a solid (and stolid) family life with European children and a European wife (Grall 1908: 51). Guides to colonial living in the 1920s and 1930s reveal this marked shift in outlook; Dutch, French, and British doctors now denounced the unhealthy, indolent lifestyles of "old colonials," extolling the energetic and engaged activities of the new breed (and team) of colonial husband and wife (Raptchinsky 1941: 46). Considered most prone to neurasthenia, anemia, and depression, women were exhorted to actively participate in household management and childcare, and to divert themselves with botanical collections and "good works" (Chivas-Baron 1929; Favre 1938).

Children on the Colonial Divide: Degeneracy and the Dangers of Métissage

> [Young colonial men] are often driven to seek a temporary companion among the women of color; this is the path by which, as I shall presently show, contagion travels back and forth, contagion in all senses of the word. (Maunier 1932: 171)

Racial degeneracy was thought to have social causes and political consequences, both tied to the domestic arrangements of colonialism in specific ways. *Métissage* (interracial unions) generally, and concubinage in particular, represented the paramount danger to racial purity and cultural identity in all its forms. Through sexual contact with women of color European men "contracted" not only disease but debased sentiments, immoral proclivities, and extreme susceptibility to decivilized states (Dupuy 1956: 198).

By the early twentieth century, concubinage was denounced for undermining precisely those things that it was charged with fortifying decades earlier. The weight of competing discourses on local women shifted emphasis with those dangerous, passionate, and evil features of their characters overshadowing their protective role. In the new equation they became the primary bearers of ill health and sinister influences. Adaptation to local food, language, and dress, once prescribed as healthy signs of acclimatization, were now the sources of contagion and loss of (white) self. The benefits of local knowledge and sexual release gave way to the more pressing demands of respectability, the community's solidarity, and its mental health. Concubinage became the source of individual breakdown and ill-health, of racial degeneration and political unrest. Children born of these unions were seen as "the fruits of a regrettable weakness" (Mazet 1932: 8), physically marked and morally marred with "the defaults and mediocre qualities of their mothers" (Douchet 1928: 10).

Concubinage was not as economically tidy and politically neat as colonial policymakers had hoped. It was about more than sexual exploitation and unpaid domestic work; it was about children—many more than official statistics often revealed—and about who was to be acknowledged as a European and who was not. Concubine children posed a classificatory problem, impinging on political security and white prestige. The majority of such children were not recognized by their fathers, nor were they reabsorbed into local communities as authorities often claimed. The legal system favored a European upbringing, but made no demands on European men to provide it. The more socially asymmetric and perfunctory the relationship between man and woman, the more likely the children were to end up as wards of the state, subject to the scrutiny and imposed charity of the European-born community at large.

Concubine children invariably counted among the ranks of the European poor. Many Indo-Europeans, including Creole children born in the Indies of European parents, had become increasingly marginalized from strategic political and economic positions in the early twentieth century despite the fact that the new educational facilities were supposed to have provided new opportunities for them. In the 1920s and 1930s, Indies-born and educated youth were uncomfortably squeezed between an influx of new colonial recruits from Holland and the educated *inlander* (native) population with whom they were in direct competition for jobs (Mansvelt 1932: 295). The fear of concubinage was tied to the political fear that such Eurasians would demand economic access, political rights, and express their own interests through alliance with (and leadership of) organized opposition to Dutch rule.

Racial prejudice against *métis* was often, as in the Belgian Congo, "camouflaged under protestations of 'pity' for their fate, as if they were *'malheureux'* [unhappy] beings by definition" (Vellut 1982: 103). The protection of *métis* children in Indochina was an empathetic *cause célèbre* of European women at home and abroad. The French assembly on feminism, organized for the colonial exposition of 1931, devoted a major part of its proceedings to the plight of *métis* children and their native mothers, echoing the campaigns for *la recherche de paternité* by French feminists a half-century earlier (Moses 1984: 208). The assembly called for "the establishment of centers [in the colonies] where abandoned young girls or those in moral danger could be made into worthy women" (Knibiehler and Goutalier 1987: 37). European colonial women were urged to oversee the "moral protection" of *métis* youths, to develop their "natural" inclination toward French society, to turn them into "collaborators and partisans of French ideas and influences" instead of revolutionaries (Chenet 1936: 8; Knibiehler and Goutalier 1987: 35; Sambuc 1931: 261). The gender breakdown was clear: moral instruction would avert sexual promiscuity among *métisse* girls and political precocity among *métis* boys who might otherwise become militant men.

Orphanages for abandoned European and Indo-European children were a prominent feature of Dutch, French, and British colonial cultures. In the Netherlands Indies by the mid-eighteenth century, state orphanages for Europeans were established to prevent "neglect and degeneracy of the many free-roaming poor bastards and orphans of Europeans" (quoted in Braconier 1917: 293). By the nineteenth century, church, state, and private organizations had become zealous backers of orphanages, providing some education and strong doses of moral instruction. In French Indochina in the 1930s, virtually every colonial city had a home and society for the protection of abandoned *métis* youth (Sambuc 1931: 256–257; Malleret 1934: 220).

Whether these children were in fact "abandoned" by their Asian mothers is difficult to establish; the fact that *métis* children living in native homes were sometimes *sought out* by the state and private organizations and placed in these institutions suggests other interpretations (Taylor 1983). Public assistance in India, Indochina, and the Netherlands Indies was designed both to keep fair-skinned children from running barefoot in native villages and to curtail the proliferation of European pauper settlements. The need for specific kinds of religious and secular education and socialization was symptomatic of a more general fear; namely, that these children would grow into *Hollander-haters*, patricides, and anticolonial revolutionaries; that as adult women they would fall into prostitution; that as adult men with lasting ties to native women and indigenous society they would become enemies of the state, *verbasterd* (degenerate) and *décivilisé* (Angoulvant 1926: 102; Pouvourville 1926).

EUROPEAN WOMEN, RACE, AND MIDDLE-CLASS MORALITY

> A man remains a man as long as he stays under the watch of a woman of his race. (George Hardy quoted in Chivas-Baron 1920: 103)

Rationalizations of imperial rule and safeguards against racial degeneracy in European colonies merged in the emphasis on particular moral themes. Both entailed a reassertion of European conventions, middle-class respectability, more frequent ties with the metropole, and a restatement of what was culturally distinct and superior about how colonials ruled and lived. For those women who came to join their spouses or to find husbands, the prescriptions were clear. Just as new plantation employees were taught to manage the natives, women were schooled in colonial propriety and domestic management. French manuals, such as those on colonial hygiene in Indochina, outlined the duties of colonial wives in no uncertain terms. As "auxiliary forces" in the imperial effort, they were to "conserve the fitness and sometimes the life of all around them" by ensuring that "the home be happy and gay and that all take pleasure in clustering there" (Grall 1908: 66; Chailley-Bert 1897). Practical guides to life in the Belgian Congo instructed (and indeed warned) *la femme blanche* that she was to keep "order, peace, hygiene and economy" (Favre 1938: 217), "perpetuate a vigorous race," while preventing any "laxity in our administrative mores" (ibid.: 256; Travaux du Groupe d'Etudes Coloniales 1910: 10).

This "division of labor" contained obvious asymmetries. Men were considered more susceptible to moral turpitude than women, who were thus held responsible for the immoral states of men. European women were to safeguard prestige, morality, and insulate their men from the cultural and sexual contamination of contact with the colonized (Travaux . . . Coloniales 1910: 7). Racial degeneracy would be curtailed by European women charged with regenerating the physical health, the metropolitan affinities, and the imperial purpose of their men (Hardy 1929: 78).

George Mosse has characterized European racism as a "scavenger ideology," annexing nationalism and bourgeois respectability in such a way that control over sexuality was central to all three (1985: 10, 133–152). If the European middle class sought respectability "to maintain their status and self-respect against the lower-classes, and the aristocracy," in the colonies respectability was a defense against the colonized, and a way of more clearly defining themselves (ibid. 1985: 5). Good colonial living now meant hard work, no sloth, and physical exercise rather than sexual release, which had been one rationale for condoning concubinage and prostitution in an earlier period. The debilitating influences of climate could be surmounted by regular diet and meticulous personal hygiene, over which European women were to take full charge. British, French, and Dutch manuals on European household management in the tropics provided detailed instructions in domestic science, moral upbringing, and employer-servant relations. Adherence to strict conventions of cleanliness and cooking occupied an inordinate amount of women's time, while cleanliness itself served as a "prop to a Europeanness that was less than assumed" (Ridley 1981: 77). Both activities entailed a constant surveillance of native nursemaids, laundrymen, and live-in servants, while demanding a heightened domesticity for European women themselves.

Leisure, good spirit, and creature comforts became the obligation of women to provide, the racial duty of women to maintain. Sexual temptations with women of color would be curtailed by a happy, *gezellig* (cozy) family life, much as "extremist agitation" among Javanese plantation workers was to be averted by selecting married recruits and providing family housing where men would feel *senang* (happy/content) and "at home" (Stoler 1985a: 42–44). Moral laxity would be eliminated through the example of vigilant women whose status rested on their sexual restraint and dedication to their homes and their men.

IMPERIAL PRIORITIES: MOTHERHOOD VERSUS MALE MORALITY

The perceptions and practices that bound women's domesticity to national welfare and racial purity were not confined to colonial women alone. Child rearing in late nineteenth-century Britain was hailed as a national, imperial, and racial duty, as it was in France, Holland, the United States, and Germany at the same time (Davin 1978: 13; Smith-Rosenberg 1973: 351; Bock 1984: 274; Stuurman 1985). In France, where declining birth rates were of grave concern, fecundity itself had become "no longer something resting with couples" but with "the nation, the state, the race . . ." (Le Bras 1981: 90). Popular colonial authors such as Pierre Mille pushed child bearing as women's "essential contribution to the imperial mission of France" (Ridley 1981: 90). With motherhood at the center of empire building, pronatalist politics in Europe forced some improvement in colonial medical facilities, the addition of maternity wards, and increased information and control over the reproductive conditions of both European and colonized women. But the belief that the colonies were medically hazardous for white women meant that motherhood in the tropics was both a precarious and ambivalent endeavor.

Real and imagined concern over individual reproduction and racial survival contained and compromised white colonial women in a number of ways. Tropical climates were said to cause low fertility, prolonged amenorrhea, and permanent sterility (Rodenwaldt 1928: 3). Belgian doctors confirmed that "the woman who goes to live in a tropical climate is often lost for the reproduction of the race" (Knibiehler and Goutalier 1985: 92; Vellut 1982: 100). The climatic and medical conditions of colonial life were associated with high infant mortality, such that "the life of a European child was nearly condemned in advance" (Grall 1908: 65). A long list of colonial illnesses ranging from neurasthenia to anemia supposedly hit women and children hardest (Price 1939: 204).

These perceived medical perils called into question whether European-born women and thus the "white race" could actually reproduce if they remained in the tropics for an extended period of time. An international colonial medical community cross-referenced one another in citing evidence of racial sterility by the second or third generation. French observers could flatly state that unions among Creole Dutch in the Indies were sterile after two generations (Angoulvant 1926: 101).

Like the discourse on degeneracy, the fear of sterility was less about the biological survival of whites than about their political viability and cultural reproduction. These concerns were evident in the early 1900s, coming to a crescendo in the 1930s when white unemployment hit the colonies and the metropole at the same time. The depression made repatriation of impoverished Dutch and French colonial agents unrealistic, prompting speculation as to whether European working classes could be relocated in the tropics without causing further racial degeneration. Although white migration to the tropics was reconsidered, poor white settlements were rejected on economic, medical and psychological grounds. Whatever the solution, such issues hinged on the reproductive potential of European women, and thus on invasive questionnaires concerning their "acclimatization," and detailed descriptions of their conjugal histories and sexual lives.

Imperial perceptions and policies fixed European women in the colonies as "instruments of race-culture" in what proved to be personally difficult and contradictory ways. Childrearing decisions faithfully followed the sorts of racist principles that constrained the activities of women charged with childcare (Grimshaw 1983: 507). Medical experts and women's organizations recommended strict surveillance of children's activities (Mackinnon 1920: 944) and careful attention to those with whom they played. Virtually every medical and household handbook in the Dutch, French, and British colonies warned against leaving small children in the unsupervised care of local servants. In the Netherlands Indies, it was the "duty" of the *hedendaagsche blanke moeder* (the modern white mother) to take the physical and spiritual upbringing of her offspring away from the *babu* (native nursemaid) and into her own hands (Wanderken 1943: 173).

Precautions had to be taken against "sexual danger," uncleanly habits of domestics, against a "Stupid negress" who might leave a child exposed to the sun (Bauduin 1941; Bérenger-Féraud 1875: 491). Even in colonies where the climate was not considered unhealthy, European children supposedly thrived well "only up to the age of six" (Price 1939: 204) when native cultural influences were thought to come into stronger play. Thus, in late nineteenth-century Hawaii, native nursemaids commonly looked after American children until the age of five, at which point "prattlers" were confined to their mothers' supervision, prevented from learning the local language, and kept in a "walled yard adjacent to the bedrooms . . . forbidden to Hawaiians" (Grimshaw 1983: 507).

In the Netherlands Indies, where educational facilities for European children were considered excellent, it was still deemed imperative to send them back to Holland to avoid the "precocity" associated with the tropics and the "danger" of contact with *Indische* youths not from "full-blooded European elements" (Bauduin 1941: 63).

> We Dutch in the Indies live in a country which is not our own. . . . We feel instinctively that our blonde, white children belong to the blonde, white dunes, the forests, the moors, the lakes, the snow. . . . A Dutch child should grow up in Holland. There they will acquire the characteristics of their race, not only from mother's milk but also from the influence of the light, sun and water, of playmates, of life, in a word, in the sphere of the fatherland. This is not racism. (Bauduin 1941: 63–64)

Such patriotic images culturally coded racial distinctions in powerful ways. Dutch identity was represented as a common (if contested) cultural sensibility in which class convention, geography, climate, sexual proclivity, and social contact played central roles.

In many colonial communities, school-age children were packed off to Europe for education and socialization, but this was rarely an unproblematic option. Married European women were confronted with a difficult set of choices that entailed separation either from their children or husbands (Angoulvant 1926: 101). Frequent trips between colony and metropole not only separated families but also broke up marriages and homes. Such conflicting responsibilities profoundly affected the social space European women (not only wives) occupied, the tasks for which they were valorized, and the economic activities in which they could feasibly engage.

THE STRATEGIES OF RULE AND SEXUAL MORALITY

The political etymology of colonizer and colonized was gender and class specific. The exclusionary politics of colonialism demarcated not just external boundaries but also interior frontiers, specifying internal conformity and order among Europeans themselves. I have tried to show that the categories of colonizer and colonized were secured through notions of racial difference constructed in gender terms. Redefinitions of acceptable sexual behavior and morality emerged during crises of colonial control precisely because they called into question the tenuous artifices of rule *within* European communities and what marked their borders. Even from the limited cases we have reviewed, several patterns emerge. First and most obviously, colonial sexual prohibitions were racially asymmetric and gender specific. Sexual relations might be forbidden between white women and men of color but not the other way around. Second, interdictions against interracial unions were rarely a primary impulse in the strategies of rule. In India, Indochina, and South Africa in the early centuries—colonial contexts usually associated with sharp social sanctions against interracial unions—"mixing" has been systematically tolerated and even condoned.

I have focused on late colonialism in Asia, but colonial elite intervention in the sexual life of their agents and subjects was by no means confined to this place or period. In sixteenth-century Mexico, mixed marriages between Spanish men and Christianized Indian women were encouraged by the crown until mid-century, when colonists felt that "the rising numbers of their own mestizo progeny threatened the prerogatives of a narrowing elite sector" (Nash 1980: 141). In eighteenth- and early nineteenth-century Cuba, mild opposition to interracial marriage gave way to a "virtual prohibition" from 1864 to 1874 when "merchants, slave dealers and the colonial powers opposed [it] in order to preserve slavery" (Martinez-Alier 1974: 39).

Changes in sexual access and domestic arrangements have invariably accompanied major efforts to reassert the internal coherence of European communities and to redefine the boundaries of privilege distinguishing colonizer from colonized. Although the chronologies vary from one colonial context to another, we can identify some parallel shifts in the strategies of rule and in sexual morality. Concubinage fell into moral disfavor at the same time that new emphasis was placed on the standardization of European administration. While this occurred in some colonies by the early twentieth century and in others later on, the correspondence between rationalized rule, bourgeois respectability, and the custodial power of European women to protect their men seems strongest during the interwar years, when British, French, and Dutch policymakers moved from an assimilationist to a more segregationist, separatist colonial stance. The reorganization of colonial investments along corporate and multinational lines brought with it a push for a restructured and more highly productive labor force; and with it more strident nationalist and labor movements resisting those demands.

An increasing rationalization of colonial management produced radical shifts in notions of how empires should be run, how agents of empire should rule, and where, how, and with whom they should live. Critical to this restructuring was a new disdain for colonials *too* adapted to local custom, too removed from the local European community, and too encumbered with intimate native ties.

At the same time medical expertise confirmed the salubrious benefits of European camaraderie and frequent home leaves; of a *cordon sanitaire*, not only around European enclaves but also around each European man and his home. White prestige became redefined by the conventions that would safeguard the moral respectability, cultural identity, and physical well-being of its agents, with which European women were charged. Colonial politics locked European men and women into a routinized protection of their physical health and social space in ways that bound gender prescriptions to the racial cleavages between "us" and "them."

It may be, however, that we should not be searching for congruent colonial chronologies (attached to specific dates) but rather for similar shifts in the *rhythms* of rule and sexual management, for similar internal patterns within specific colonial histories themselves. For example, we know that the Great Rebellion in India in 1857 set off an entire restructuring of colonial morality in which political subversion was tied to sexual impropriety and was met with calls for middle-class respectability, domesticity, and increased segregation—all focusing on European women—nearly a half-century earlier than in colonies elsewhere. Looking to a somewhat longer *durée* than the colonial crises of the early twentieth century, we might consider British responses to the Mutiny not as an exception but as a template, thereby emphasizing the "modular" quality of colonial preceptions and policies that were built on new international standards of empire, on specific metropolitan priorities, and that were always responsible to the local challenges of those who contested European rule.

I have focused here on the multiple levels at which sexual control figured in the substance, as well as the iconography, of racial policy and imperial rule. But colonial politics was not just about sex; nor did sexual relations reduce to colonial politics. On the contrary, sex in the colonies was about sexual access and reproduction, class distinctions and racial demarcations, nationalism and European identity—in different measure and not at all at the same time. These major shifts in the positioning of women were not, as we might expect, signaled by the penetration of capitalism per se but by more subtle changes in class politics, imperial morality, and as responses to the vulnerabilities of colonial control. European culture and class politics resonated in colonial settings; class and gender discriminations were transposed into racial distinctions and reverberated in the metropole as they were fortified on colonial ground. Sexual control was both an instrumental image for the body politic, a salient part standing for the whole, and itself fundamental to how racial politics were secured and how colonial projects were carried out.

NOTE

For a longer and fully-annotated version of this essay, see Micaela di Leonardo, ed., *Gender at the Crossroads of Knowledge* (California, 1991), 51–101.

BIBLIOGRAPHY

Abatucci. 1910. Le milieu africain considéré au point de vue de ses effets sur le systéme nerveux de l'européen. *Annales d'Hygiène et de Médecine Coloniale* 13: 328–35.

Adas, M. 1989. *Machines as the measure of men.* Ithaca: Cornell University Press.

Angoulvant, Gabriel. 1926. *Les Indes Néerlandaises.* Paris: Le Monde Nouveau.

Archive d'Outre-Mer. Aix-en-Provence, France.

Arnold, David. 1979. European orphans and vagrants in India in the nineteenth century. *The Journal of Imperial and Commonwealth History* 7: 2, 104–27.

———. 1983. White colonization and labour in nineteenth-century India. *Journal of Imperial and Commonwealth History* 7: 2, 133–58.

Bajema, Carl, ed. 1976. *Eugenics then and now.* Stroudsburg, Pa.: Dowden, Hutchinson & Ross.

Baroli, March. 1967. *La vie quotidienne des Français en Algérie.* Paris: Hachette.

Bauduin, D. C. M. 1941 (1927). *Het Indische Leven.* 'S-Gravenhage: H.P. Leopolds.

Beidelman, Thomas. 1982. *Colonial evangelism.* Bloomington: Indiana University Press.

Blumberger, J. Th. P. 1939. *De Indo-Europeesche Beweging in Nederlandsch-Indie.* Haarlem: Tjeenk Willink.

Blussé, Leonard. 1986. *Strange company: Chinese settlers, mestizo women and the Dutch in VOC Batavia.* Dordrecht: Foris.

Bock, Gisela. 1984. Racism and sexism in Nazi Germany: Motherhood, compulsory sterilization, and the state. In *When biology became destiny: Women in Weimar and Nazi Germany.* New York: Monthly Review Press, pp. 271–96.

Boutilier, James. 1984. European women in the Solomon Islands, 1900–1942. In *Rethinking women's roles: Perspectives from the Pacific.* Denise O'Brien and Sharon Tiffany, eds., 173–99. Berkeley, Los Angeles, London: University of California Press.

Braconier, A. de. 1913. Het Kazerne-Concubinaat in Ned-Indie. *Vragen van den Dag* 28: 974–95.

———. 1917. Het Pauperisme onder de in Ned. Oost-Indie levende Europeanen. *Nederlandsch-Indie* (1st yr.): 291–300.

———. 1918. *Kindercriminaliteit en de verzorging van misdadig aangelegde en verwaarloosde minderjarigen in Nederlandsche-Indie.* Baarn: Hollandia-Drukkerij.

———. 1933. Het Prostitutie-vraagstuk in Nederlandsche-Indie. *Indisch Gids* 55: 2, 906–28.

Brand, J. van den. 1904. *Nogeens: De Millionen uit Deli.* Amsterdam: Hoveker & Wormser.

Brink, K. B. M. Ten. 1920. *Indische Gezondheid.* Batavia: Nillmij.

Brou, A. M. N. 1907. Le Métis Franco-Annamite. *Revue Indochinoise* (July 1907): 897–908.

Brownfoot, Janice N. 1984. Memsahibs in colonial Malaya: A study of European wives in a British colony and protectorate 1900–1940. In *The incorporated wife.* Hillary Callan and Shirley Ardener, eds. London: Croom Helm.

Butcher, John. 1979. *The British in Malaya, 1880–1941: The social history of a European community in colonial Southeast Asia.* Kuala Lumpur: Oxford University Press.

Callan, Hilary, and Shirley Ardener. 1984. *The incorporated wife.* London: Croom Helm.

Callaway, Helen. 1987. *Gender, culture and empire: European women in colonial Nigeria.* London: Macmillan.

Chailley-Bert, M. J. 1897. *L'Emigration des femmes aux colonies.* Union Coloniale Française-conference, 12 January 1897. Paris: Armand Colin.

Chenet, Ch. 1936. Le role de la femme française aux Colonies: Protection des enfants métis abandonnés. *Le Devoir des Femmes* (15 February 1936): 8.

Chivas-Baron, C. 1929. *La Femme française aux colonies.* Paris: Larose.

Clerkx, Lily. 1961. *Mensen in Deli.* Amsterdam: Sociologisch-Historisch Seminarium for Zuidoost-Azie.

Cock, J. 1980. *Maids and madams.* Johannesburg: Ravan.

Cohen, William. 1971. *Rulers of empire: The French colonial service in Africa.* Stanford, CA: Hoover Institution Press.

———. 1980. *The French encounter with Africans: White response to blacks, 1530–1880.* Bloomington: Indiana University Press.

Comaroff, John, and Jean Comaroff. 1986. Christianity and colonialism in South Africa. *American Ethnologist* 13: 1–22.

Cool, F. 1938. De Bestrijding der Werkloosheidsgevolgen in Nederlandsch-Indie gedurende 1930–1936. *De Economist* 87: 135–47, 217–43.

Cooper, Frederick. 1987. *On the African waterfront.* New Haven: Yale University Press.

Corneau, Grace. 1900. *La femme aux colonies.* Paris: Librarie Nilsson.

Courtois, E. 1900. Des Règles Hygiéniques que doit suivre l'Européen au Tonkin. *Revue Indochinoise* 83: 539–41, 564–66, 598–601.

Davin, Anna. 1978. Imperialism and motherhood. *History Workshop* 5: 9–57.

Delavignette, Robert. 1946. *Service Africain.* Paris: Gallimard.

Dixon, C. J. 1913. *De Assistent in Deli.* Amsterdam: J. H. de Bussy.

Doorn, Jacques van. 1983. *A divided society: Segmentation and mediation in late-colonial Indonesia.* Rotterdam: CASA.

———. 1985. Indie als Koloniale Maatschappy. In *De Nederlandse samenleving sinds 1815.* F. L. van Holthoon, ed. Assen: Maastricht.

Douchet. 1928. *Métis et congaies d'Indochine.* Hanoi.

Dowd Hall, Jacquelyn. 1984. "The mind that burns in each body": Women, rape, and racial violence. *Southern Exposure* 12: 6, 61–71.

Drooglever, P. J. 1980. *De Vaderlandse Club, 1929–42.* Franeker: T. Wever.

Dupuy, A. 1955. La personnalité du colon. *Revue d'Histoire Economique et Sociale* 33: 1, 77–103.

Encyclopedie van Nederland-Indie. 1919. S'Gravenhage: Nijhoff and Brill.

Engels, Dagmar. 1983. The age of consent act of 1891: Colonial ideology in Bengal. *South Asia Research* 3 (2): 107–34.

Fanon, Franz. 1967 (1952). *Black skin, white masks.* New York: Grove.

Favre, J.-L. 1938. *La vie aux colonies* Paris: Larose.

Feuilletau de Bruyn, Dr. W. K. H. 1938. Over de Economische Mogelijkheid van een Kolonisatie van Blanken op Nederlandsch Nieuw-Guinea. In *Comptes Rendus du Congrès International de Géographie, Amsterdam.* Brill: Leiden, pp. 21–29.

Fredrickson, George. 1981. *White supremacy: A comparative study in American and South African history.* New York: Oxford University Press.

Gaitskell, Deborah. 1983. Housewives, maids or mothers: Some contradictions of domesticity for Christian women in Johannesburg, 1903–39. *Journal of African History* 24: 241–56.

Gann, L. H., and Peter Duignan. 1978. *The rulers of British Africa, 1870–1914.* Stanford, CA: Stanford University Press.

Gantes, Gilles de. 1981. *La population française au Tonkin entre 1931 et 1938*. Mémoire de Maitrise, Aix-en-Provence: Université de Provence, Centre d'Aix: Institut d'Histoire des Pays d'Outre Mer.

Gartrell, Beverley. 1984. Colonial wives: Villains or victims? In *The Incorporated Wife*. Hillary Callan and Shirley Ardener, eds. 165–85. London: Croom Helm.

Gilman, Sander L. 1985. *Difference and pathology: Stereotypes of sexuality, race, and madness*. Ithaca: Cornell University Press.

Gordon, Linda. 1976. *Woman's body, woman's right: A social history of birth control in America*. New York: Grossman.

Grall, Ch. 1908. *Hygiène Coloniale appliquée: Hygiène de l'Indochine*. Paris: Ballière.

Grimshaw, P. 1983. "Christian woman, pious wife, faithful mother, devoted missionary": Conflicts in roles of American missionary women in nineteenth-century Hawaii. *Feminist Studies* 9: 3, 489–521.

Hammerton, James. 1979. *Emigrant gentlewomen: Genteel poverty and female emigration 1830–1914*. London: Croom Helm.

Hansen, Karen Tranberg. 1984. Negotiating sex and gender in urban Zambia. *Journal of Southern African Studies* 10: 2, 218–38.

_____. 1989. *Distant companions: Servants and employers in Zambia, 1900–1985*. Ithaca: Cornell University Press.

Hardy, George. 1929. *Ergaste ou la Vocation Coloniale*. Paris: Armand Colin.

Hartenberg. 1910. Les Troubles Nerveux et Mentaux chez les coloniaux. Paris.

Harwood, Dorothy. 1938. The possibility of white colonization in the tropics. In *Comptes Rendu du Congrès International de Géographie*. Leiden: Brill, pp. 131–40.

Hermans, E. H. 1925. *Gezondscheidsleer voor Nederlandsche-Indie*. Amsterdam: Meulenhoff.

Hesselink, Liesbeth. 1987. Prostitution: A necessary evil, particularly in the colonies: Views on prostitution in the Netherlands Indies. In *Indonesia Women in Focus*. E. Locher-Scholten and A. Niehof, eds., 205–24. Dordrecht: Foris.

Het Pauperisme Commissie. 1901. *Het Pauperisme onder de Europeanen*. Batavia: Landsdrukkerij.

_____. 1903. *Rapport der Pauperisme-Commissie*. Batavia: Landsdrukkerij.

Heyningen, Elizabeth Van B. 1984. The social evil in the Cape Colony 1868–1902: Prostitution and the contagious disease acts. *Journal of Southern African Studies* 10 (2): 170–97.

Hobsbawm, Eric. 1987. *The Age of Empire, 1875–1914*. London: Weidenfeld and Nicholson.

Hunt, Nancy. 1988. Le bébé en brousse: European women, African birth spacing and colonial intervention in breast feeding in the Belgian Congo. *International Journal of African Historical Studies* 21: 3.

Hyam, Ronald. 1986a. Empire and sexual opportunity. *The Journal of Imperial and Commonwealth History* 14: 2, 34–90.

_____. 1986b. Concubinage and the colonial service: The Crewe circular (1909). *The Journal of Imperial and Commonwealth History* 14: 2, 34–90.

Inglis, Amirah. 1975. *The White Women's Protection Ordinance: Sexual anxiety and politics in Papua*. London: Sussex University Press.

Jaurequiberry. 1924. *Les Blancs en Pays Chauds*. Paris: Maloine.

Jordan, Winthrop. 1968. *White over black: American attitudes toward the Negro, 1550–1812*. Chapel Hill: University of North Carolina Press.

Joyeux, Ch., and A. Sice. 1937. Affections exotiques du système nerveux. *Précis de Médicine Coloniale*. Paris: Masson.

Kantoor van Arbeid. 1935. *Werkloosheid in Nederlandsch-Indie*. Batavia: Landsdrukkerij.

Kennedy, Dane. 1987. *Islands of white: Settler society and culture in Kenya and Southern Rhodesia, 1890–1939*. Durham, NC: Duke University Press.

Kennedy, Raymond. 1947. *The ageless Indies*. New York: John Day.

Kevles, Daniel. 1985. *In the name of eugenics*. Berkeley, Los Angeles, London: University of California Press.

Kirkwood, Deborah. 1984. Settler wives in Southern Rhodesia: A case study. In *The Incorporated Wife*. H. Callan and S. Ardener, eds. London: Croom Helm.

Knibiehler, Yvonne, and Regine Goutalier. 1985. *La femme au temps des colonies*. Paris: Stock.

_____. 1987. *"Femmes et Colonisation"*: Rapport Terminal au Ministère des Relations Extérieures et de la Cooperation. Aix-en-Provence: Institut d'Histoire des Pays d'Outre-Mer.

Koks, Dr. J. Th. 1931. *De Indo*. Amsterdam: H. J. Paris.

Kroniek 1917. Oostkust van Sumatra-Instituut. Amsterdam: J. H. de Bussy.

Kroniek 1933. Oostkust van Sumatra-Instituut. Amsterdam: J. H. de Bussy.

Kuklick, Henrika. 1979. *The imperial bureaucrat: The colonial administrative service in the Gold Coast, 1920–1939*. Stanford, CA: Hoover Institution Press.

La Femme dan les Sociétés Coloniales. 1982. Table Ronde CHEE, CRHSE, IHPOM. Institut d'Histoire des Pays d'Outre-Mer, Université de Provence.

Lanessan, J.-L. 1889. *Indochine Française*. Paris: Felix Alcan.

Le Bras, Hervé. 1981. Histoire secrète de la fécondité. *Le Débat* 8: 76–100.

Le Roux. 1898. *Je Deviens Colon*. Paris.

Loutfi, Martine Astier. 1971. *Littérature et Colonialisme*. Paris: Mouton.

Lucas, Nicole. 1986. Trouwverbod, inlandse huishousdsters en Europese vrouwen: Het concubinaat in de planterswereld aan Sumatra's Oostkust 1860–1940. In *Vrouwen in de Nederlandse Kolonien*. J. Reijs, et al. Nijmeen: SUN, pp. 78–97.

Mackinnon, Murdoch. 1920. European Children in the Tropical Highlands. *Lancet* 199: 944–45.

Malleret, Louis. 1934. *L'Exotisme Indochinois dans la Littérature Française depuis 1860*. Paris: Larose.

Mannoni, Octavio. 1956. *Prospero and Caliban: The psychology of colonization*. New York: Praeger.

Mansvelt, W. 1932. De Positie der Indo-Europeanen. *Kolonial Studien* 16: 290–311.

Marks, Shula, ed. 1987. *Not either an experimental doll: The separate worlds of three South African women*. Bloomington: Indiana University Press.

Marle, A. van. 1952. De group der Europeanen in Nederlands-Indie. *Indonesie* 5(2): 77–121; 5 (3): 314–41; 5(5): 481–507.

Mason, Philip. 1958. *The birth of a dilemma*. New York: Oxford University Press.

Maunier, M. René. 1932. *Sociologie Coloniale*. Paris: Domat-Montchrestien.

Mazet, Jacques. 1932. *La Condition Juridique des Métis*. Paris: Domat-Montchrestien.

McClure, John A. 1981. *Kipling and Conrad: The colonial fiction*. Cambridge: Harvard University Press.

Mercier, Paul. 1965. The European community of Dakar. In *Africa: Social problems of change and conflict*. Pierre van den Berghe, ed., 284–304. San Francisco: Chandler.

Metcalf, Thomas, 1964. *The aftermath of revolt: India, 1857–1870*. Princeton: Princeton University Press.

Ming, Hanneke. 1983. Barracks-concubinage in the Indies, 1887–1920. *Indonesia* 35 (April): 65–93.

Moore-Gilbert, B. J. 1986. *Kipling and "orientalism."* New York: St. Martin's.

Moses, Claire Goldberg. 1984. *French feminism in the nineteenth century*. Albany: SUNY Press.

Mosse, George. 1978. *Toward the Final Solution*. New York: Fertig.

_____. 1985. *Nationalism and sexuality*. Madison: University of Wisconsin Press.

Nandy, Ashis. 1983. *The intimate enemy: Loss and recovery of self under colonialism*. Delhi: Oxford University Press.

Nash, J. 1980. Aztec women: The transition from status to class in empire and colony. In *Women and Colonization: Anthropological Perspectives*. M. Etienne and E. Leacock, eds., 134–148. New York: Praeger.

Nieuwenhuys, Roger. 1959. *Tussen Twee Vaderlanden*. Amsterdam: Van Oorschot.

Nora, Pierre. 1961. *Les Français d'Algerie*. Paris: Julliard.

O'Brien, Rita Cruise. 1972. *White society in Black Africa: The French in Senegal*. London: Faber & Faber.

Onselen, Charles van. 1982. Prostitutes and proletarians, 1886–1914. In *Studies in the social and economic history of the Witwatersrand 1886–1914*, vol. 1. New York: Longman, pp. 103–162.

Ons Nageslacht: Orgaan Van de Eugenetische vereeniging in Ned-Indie. Batavia.

Painter, N. I. 1988. "Social equality": Miscegenation, labor and power. In *The Evolution of Southern Culture*. N. Bartley, ed. Athens: University of Georgia Press.

Pourvourville, Albert de. 1926. Le Métis. In *Le Mal d'Argent*. Paris: Monde Moderne, pp. 97–114.

Price, Grenfell A. 1939. *White settlers in the Tropics*. New York: American Geographical Society.

Prochaska, David. 1989. *Making Algeria French: Colonialism in Bone, 1870–1920*. Cambridge: Cambridge University Press.

Pujarniscle, E. 1931. *Philoxène ou de la littérature coloniale*. Paris.

Ralston, Caroline. 1977. *Grass huts and warehouses: Pacific beach communities of the nineteenth century*. Canberra: ANU Press.

Ramuschack, Barbara. N.d. Cultural missionaries, maternal imperialist, feminist allies: British women activists in India, 1865–1945. In *Women Studies International* (forthcoming).

Raptchinsky, B. 1941. *Kolonisatie van blanken in de tropen*. Den Haag: Bibliotheek van Welten en Denken.

Reijis, J., E. Kloek, U. Jansz, A. de Wildt, S. van Norden, and M. de Bat. 1986. *Vrouwen in de Nederlandse Kolonien*. Nijmegen: SUN.

Ridley, Hugh. 1981. *Images of imperial rule*. New York: Croom Helm.

Rodenwaldt, Ernest. 1928. Eugenetische Problemen in Nederlandsche-Indie. In *Ons Nageslacht*. Orgaan van de Eugenetische Vereeniging in Nederland-Indie (1928): 1–8.

Ross, Ellen, and Rayna Rapp. 1980. Sex and society: A research note from social history and anthropology. *Comparative Studies in Society and History* 22: 1, 51–72.

Said, Edward W. 1978. *Orientalism*. New York: Vintage.

Sambuc. 1931. Les Métis Franco-Annamites en Indochine. *Revue du Pacifique*, 256–72.

Schneider, William. 1982. Toward the improvement of the human race. The history of eugenics in France. *Journal of Modern History* 54: 269–91.

Schoevers, T. 1913. Het leven en werken van den assistent bij de Tabakscultuur in Deli. *Jaarboek der Vereeniging "Studiebelangen."* Wageningen: Zomer, pp. 3–43.

Schmidt, Elizabeth. 1987. Ideology, economics, and the role of Shona women in Southern Rhodesia, 1850–1939. Ph.D. dissertation, University of Wisconsin.

———. N.d. "Race, sex and domestic labour: The question of African female servants in Southern Rhodesia, 1900–1939." MS.

Showalter, Elaine. 1987. *The female malady*. New York: Penguin.

Simon, Pierre-Jean. 1981. *Rapatriés d'Indochine: Un village franco-indochnois en Bourbonnais*. Paris: Harmattan.

Sivan, Emmanuel. 1983. *Interpretations of Islam, past and present*. Princeton: Darwin.

Smith-Rosenberg, C., and C. Rosenberg. 1973. The female animal: Medical and biological views of woman and her role in nineteenth-century America. *Journal of American History* 60: 2, 332–56.

Spear, Percival. 1963. *The nabobs*. London: Oxford University Press.

Spencer, J. E., and W. L. Thomas. 1948. The hill stations and summer resorts of the orient. *Geographical Review* 38: 4, 637–51.

Stepan, Nancy. 1982. *The idea of race in science: Great Britain, 1880–1960*. London: Macmillan.

Stocking, George. 1982 (1968). *Race, culture, and evolution*. Chicago: University of Chicago Press.

Stoler, Ann. 1985a. *Capitalism and confrontation in Sumatra's plantation belt, 1870–1979*. New Haven: Yale University Press.

———. 1985b. Perceptions of protest: Defining the dangerous in colonial Sumatra. *American Ethnologist* 12:4, 642–658.

———. 1989a. Rethinking colonial categories: European communities and the boundaries of rule. *Comparative Studies in Society and History* 13 (1): 134–61.

Strobel, Margaret. 1987. Gender and race in the nineteenth- and twentieth-century British empire. In *Becoming visible: Women in European history*. Boston: Houghton Mifflin.

Stuurman, Siep. 1985. *Verzuiling, Kapitalisme en Patriarchaat*. Nijmegen: SUN.

Sumatra Post. Medan, Sumatra.

Sutherland, Heather. 1982. Ethnicity and access in colonial Macassar. In *Papers of the Dutch-Indonesia historical conference*. Dutch and Indonesian Steering Committees of the Indonesian Studies Programme. Leiden: Bureau of Indonesian Studies, pp. 250–77.

Takaki, Ronald. 1977. *Iron Cages*. Berkeley, Los Angeles, London: University of California Press.

Taylor, Jean. 1977. The world of women in the colonial Dutch novel. *Kabar Seberang* 2: 26–41.

———. 1983. *The social world of Batavia*. Madison: University of Wisconsin Press.

Tirefort, A. 1979. "Le Bon Temps": La Communauté Française en Basse Cote d'Ivoire pendant l'Entre-Deux Guerres, 1920–1940. Troisième Cycle, Centre d'Etudes Africaines.

Travaux du Groupe d'Etudes Coloniales. 1910. *La Femme Blanche au Congo*. Brussels: Misch and Thron.

Treille, G. 1888. *De l'Acclimatation des Europeens dans les Pays Chauds*. Paris: Octave Doin.

Union Géographique International. 1938. *Comptes Rendus du Congres International de Géographie, Amsterdam 1938*. Leiden: Brill.

Van-Helten, Jean J., and K. Williams. 1983. "The crying need of South Africa": The emigration of single British women to the Transvaal, 1901–1910. *Journal of South African Studies* 10: 1, 11–38.

Veerde, A. G. 1931. Onderzoek naar den omvang der werkloosheid op Java (November 1930–June 1931). *Koloniale Studien* 16: 242–73, 505–33.

Vellut, Jean-Luc. 1982. Materiaux pour une image du Blanc dan la société coloniale du Congo Belge. In *Stérotypes Nationaux et Préjugés Raciaux aux XIXe et XXe Siècles*. Jean Pirotte, ed. Leuven: Editions Nauwelaerts.

Vere Allen, J. de. 1970. Malayan civil service, 1874–1941: Colonial bureaucracy/Malayan elite. *Comparative Studies in Society and History* 12: 149–78.

Wanderken, P. 1943. Zoo leven onze kinderen. In *Zoo Leven Wij in Indonesie*. Deventer: Van Hoever, pp. 172–187.

Wertheim, Willem. 1959. *Indonesian society in transition*. The Hague: Van Hoever.

White, Luise. 1990. The Comforts of Home: Prostitution in Colonial Nairobi. Chicago: University of Chicago Press.

Winckel, C.W.F. 1938. The feasibility of white settlements in the tropics: A medical point of view. In *Comptes Rendus du Congrès International de Géographie, Amsterdam*, vol. 2, sect. IIIc. Leiden: Brill, pp. 345–56.

Woodcock, George. 1969. *The British in the Far East*. New York: Atheneum.

2 Scientific Racism and the Invention of the Homosexual Body

Siobhan Somerville

One of the most important insights developed in the fields of lesbian and gay history and the history of sexuality is the notion that homosexuality and, by extension, heterosexuality are relatively recent inventions in Western culture, rather than transhistorical or "natural" categories of human beings. As Michel Foucault and other historians of sexuality have argued, sexual acts between two people of the same sex had been punishable through legal and religious sanctions well before the late nineteenth century, but these acts did not necessarily define individuals as homosexual per se.[1] Only in the late nineteenth century did a new understanding of sexuality emerge, in which sexual acts and desires became constitutive of identity. Homosexuality as the condition, and therefore identity, of particular bodies is thus a production of that historical moment.

Medical literature, broadly defined to include the writings of physicians, sexologists, and psychiatrists, has been integral to this historical argument. Although medical discourse was by no means the only—nor necessarily the most powerful—site of the emergence of new sexual identities, it does nevertheless offer rich sources for at least partially understanding the complex development of these categories in the late nineteenth and early twentieth centuries. Medical and sexological literature not only became one of the few sites of explicit engagement with questions of sexuality during this period but also held substantial definitional power within a culture that sanctioned science to discover and tell the truth about bodies.

As historians and theorists of sexuality have refined a notion of the late nineteenth-century "invention" of the homosexual, their discussions have drawn primarily upon theories and histories of gender. George Chauncey, in particular, has provided an invaluable discussion of the ways in which paradigms of sexuality shifted according to changing ideologies of gender during this period.[2] He notes a gradual change in medical models of sexual deviance, from a notion of sexual inversion, understood as a reversal of one's sex role, to a model of homosexuality, defined as deviant sexual object choice. These categories and their transformations, argues Chauncey,

Siobhan Somerville is assistant professor of English and Women's Studies at Purdue University. She has published articles in *American Literature* and *Journal of the History of Sexuality*, and is completing a book on the interdependence of discourses of race and sexuality in late nineteenth- and early-twentieth-century American culture, focusing on scientific, cinematic, and literary texts.

reflected concurrent shifts in the cultural organization of sex/gender roles and participated in prescribing acceptable behavior, especially within a context of white, middle-class, gender ideologies.

While gender insubordination offers a powerful explanatory model for the "invention" of homosexuality, ideologies of gender also, of course, shaped and were shaped by dominant constructions of race. Indeed, although it has received little acknowledgment, it is striking that the "invention" of the homosexual occurred at roughly the same time that racial questions were being reformulated, particularly in the United States. This was the moment, for instance, of *Plessy v. Ferguson*, the 1896 U.S. Supreme Court ruling that insisted that "black" and "white" races were "separate but equal." Both a product of and a stimulus to a nationwide and brutal era of racial segregation, this ruling had profound and lasting effects in legitimating an apartheid structure that remained legally sanctioned for more than half of the twentieth century. The *Plessy* case distilled in legal form many widespread contemporary fears about race and racial difference at the time. A deluge of "Jim Crow" and antimiscegenation laws, combined with unprecedented levels of racial violence, most visibly manifested in widespread lynching, reflected an aggressive attempt to classify and separate bodies as either "black" or "white."

Is it merely a historical coincidence that the classification of bodies as either "homosexual" or "heterosexual" emerged at the same time that the United States was aggressively policing the imaginary boundary between "black" and "white" bodies? Although some historians of sexuality have included brief acknowledgments of nineteenth-century discourses of racial difference, the particular relationship and potentially mutual effects of discourses of homosexuality and race remain unexplored.[3] This silence around race may be due in part to the relative lack of explicit attention to race in medical and sexological literature of the period. These writers did not self-consciously interrogate race, nor did they regularly identify by race those whose gender insubordination and/or sexual transgression brought them under the medical gaze in these accounts.[4] Yet the lack of explicit attention to race in these texts does not mean that it was irrelevant to sexologists' endeavors. Given the upheavals surrounding racial definition during this period, it is reasonable to imagine that these texts were as embedded within contemporary racial ideologies as they were within ideologies of gender.

Take, for instance, the words of Havelock Ellis, whose massive *Studies in the Psychology of Sex* was one of the most important texts of the late nineteenth-century medical and scientific discourse on sexuality in the United States and Europe. "I regard sex as the central problem of life," wrote Ellis in the general preface to the first volume. Justifying such unprecedented boldness toward the study of sex, Ellis explained:

> And now that the problem of religion has practically been settled, and that the problem of labour has at least been placed on a practical foundation, the question of sex—*with the racial questions that rest on it*—stands before the coming generations as the chief problem for solution.[5]

Despite Ellis's oddly breezy dismissal of the problems of labor and religion, which were far from settled at the time, this passage points suggestively to a link between sexual and racial anxieties. Yet what exactly did Ellis mean by "racial questions"? More significantly, what was his sense of the relationship between racial questions and the "question of sex"? Although Ellis himself left these issues unresolved, his elliptical declaration nevertheless suggested that a discourse of race—however elusively—somehow hovered around or within the study of sexuality.

In this article, I offer speculations on how late nineteenth- and early twentieth-century discourses of race and sexuality might be not merely juxtaposed but also brought together in ways that illuminate both. I suggest that the concurrent bifurcations of categories of race and sexuality were not only historically coincident but in fact structurally interdependent and perhaps mutually productive. My goal, however, is not to garner and display unequivocal evidence of the direct influence of racial categories on those who were developing scientific models of homosexuality. Nor am I interested in identifying individual writers and thinkers as racist or not. Rather, my focus here is on racial ideologies, the cultural assumptions and systems of representation about race through which individuals understood their relationships within the world.[6] My emphasis lies in understanding the relationships between the medical/scientific discourse on sexuality and the dominant scientific discourse on race during this period, that is, scientific racism.

My approach combines literary and historical methods of reading, particularly those that have been so crucial to lesbian and gay studies—the technique of reading to hear "the inexplicable presence of the thing not named,"[7] of being attuned to the queer presences and implications in texts that do not otherwise name them. Without this collective project to see, hear, and confirm queer inflections where others would deny their existence, it is arguable that gay and lesbian studies itself, and more broadly our knowledge and understanding of the historical and cultural meanings of sexuality, would be impoverished, if not impossible. In a similar way, I propose to use the techniques of queer reading, but to modulate my analysis from a focus on sexuality and gender to one alert to racial resonances as well.

My attention, then, is focused on the racial pressure points in exemplary texts from the late nineteenth-century discourse on sexuality, including those written by Ellis and other writers of the period who made explicit references to homosexuality. I suggest that the structures and methodologies that drove dominant ideologies of race also fueled the pursuit of scientific knowledge about the homosexual body: both sympathetic and hostile accounts of homosexuality were steeped in assumptions that had driven previous scientific studies of race.[8] My aim is not to replace a focus on gender and sexuality with one on race but, rather, to understand how discourses of race and gender buttressed one another, often competing, often overlapping, in shaping emerging models of homosexuality.

I suggest three broadly defined ways in which discourses of sexuality seem to have been particularly engaged—sometimes overtly, but largely implicitly—with the discourse of scientific racism. All of these models constructed both the nonwhite body and the nonheterosexual body as pathological to greater or lesser extents. Although I discuss these models in separate sections here, they often coexisted, despite their contradictions. These models are speculative and are intended as a first step toward understanding the myriad and historically specific ways in which racial and sexual discourses shaped each other at the moment in which homosexuality entered scientific discourse.

VISIBLE DIFFERENCES: SEXOLOGY AND COMPARATIVE ANATOMY

Ellis's *Sexual Inversion*, the first volume of *Studies in the Psychology of Sex* to be published, became a definitive text in late nineteenth-century investigations of homosexuality.[9] Despite the series' titular focus on the psychology of sex, *Sexual Inversion* was a hybrid text, poised in methodology between the earlier field of comparative anatomy, with its procedures of bodily measurement, and the nascent techniques of psychology, with its focus on mental development.[10] In *Sexual Inversion* Ellis hoped to provide scientific authority for the position that homosexuality should be considered not a crime but, rather, a congenital (and thus involuntary) physiological abnormality. Writing *Sexual Inversion* in the wake of England's 1885 Labouchère Amendment, which prohibited "any act of gross indecency" between men, Ellis intended in large part to defend homosexuality from "law and public opinion," which, in his view, combined "to place a heavy penal burden and a severe social stigma on the manifestations of an instinct which to those persons who possess it frequently appears natural and normal."[11] In doing so, Ellis attempted to drape himself in the cultural authority of a naturalist, eager to exert his powers of observation in an attempt to classify and codify understandings of homosexuality.[12]

Like other sexologists, Ellis assumed that the "invert" might be visually distinguishable from the "normal" body through anatomical markers, just as the differences between the sexes had traditionally been mapped upon the body. Yet the study of sexual difference was not the only methodological precedent for the study of the homosexual body. In its assumptions about somatic differences, *Sexual Inversion*, I suggest, also drew upon and participated in a history of the scientific investigation of race.

Race, in fact, became an explicit, though ambiguous, structural element in Ellis's *Sexual Inversion*. In chapter 5, titled "The Nature of Sexual Inversion," Ellis attempted to collate the evidence contained in his collection of case studies, dividing his general conclusions into various analytic categories. Significantly, "Race" was the first category he listed, under which he wrote, "All my cases, 80 in number, are British and American, 20 living in the United States and the rest being British. Ancestry, from the point of view of race, was not made a matter of special investigation" (p. 264). He then listed the ancestries of the individuals whose case studies he included, which he identified as "English . . . Scotch . . . Irish . . . German . . . French . . . Portuguese . . . [and] more or less Jewish" (p. 264). He concluded that "except in the apparently frequent presence of the German element, there is nothing remarkable in this ancestry" (p. 264). Ellis used the term "race" in this passage interchangeably with national origin, with the possible exception of Jewish identity. These national identities were perceived to be at least partially biological and certainly hereditary in Ellis's account, though subordinate to the categories "British" and "American." Although he dismissed "ancestry, from the point of view of race" as a significant category, its place as the first topic within the chapter suggested its importance to the structure of Ellis's analysis.[13]

Ellis's ambiguous use of the term "race" was not unusual among scientific and medical studies from this period, during which it might refer to groupings based variously on geography, religion, class, or color.[14] The use of the term to mean a division of people based on physical (rather than genealogical or national) differences had originated in the late eighteenth century, when Carl von Linnaeus and Johann Friedrich Blumenbach first classified human beings into distinct racial groups.[15] Blumenbach's work in turn became a model for the nineteenth-century fascination with anthropometry, the measurement of the human body. Behind these anatomical measurements lay the assumption that the body was a legible text, with various keys or languages available for reading its symbolic codes. In the logic of biological determinism, the surface and interior of the individual body rather than its social characteristics, such as language, behavior, or clothing, became the primary sites of its meaning. "Every peculiarity of the body has probably some corresponding significance in the mind, and the cause of the former are the remoter causes of the latter," wrote Edward Drinker Cope, a well-known American paleontologist, summarizing the assumptions that fueled the science of comparative anatomy.[16] Although scientists debated which particular anatomical features carried racial meanings—skin, facial angle, pelvis, skull, brain mass, genitalia—nevertheless the theory that anatomy predicted intelligence and behavior remained remarkably constant. As Nancy Stepan and Sander Gilman have noted, "The concepts within racial science were so congruent with social and political life (with power relations, that is) as to be virtually uncontested from inside the mainstream of science."[17]

Supported by the cultural authority of an ostensibly objective scientific method, these readings of the body became a powerful instrument for those seeking to justify the economic and political disenfranchisement of various racial groups within systems of slavery and colonialism. As Barbara Fields has noted, however, "Try as they would, the scientific racists of the past failed to discover any objective criterion upon which to classify people; to their chagrin, every criterion they tried varied more within so-called races than between them."[18] Although the methods of science were considered to be outside the political and economic realm, in fact, as we know, these anatomical investigations, however professedly innocent their intentions, were driven by racial ideologies already firmly in place.[19]

Ideologies of race, of course, shaped and reflected both popular and scientific understandings of gender. As Gilman has argued, "Any attempt to establish that the races were inherently different rested to no little extent on the sexual difference of the black."[20] Although popular racist mythology in the nineteenth-century United States focused on the supposed difference between the size of African American and white men's genitalia, the male body was not necessarily the primary site of medical inquiry into racial difference.[21] Instead, as a number of medical journals from this period demonstrate, comparative anatomists repeatedly located racial difference through the sexual characteristics of the female body.[22]

In exploring the influence of scientific studies of race on the emerging discourse of sexuality, it is useful to look closely at a study from the genre of comparative anatomy. In 1867, W. H. Flower and James Murie published an "Account of the Dissection of a Bushwoman," which carefully catalogued the "more perishable soft structures of the body" of a young Bushwoman.[23] They placed their study in a line of inquiry concerning the African woman's body that had begun at least a half-century earlier with French naturalist Georges Cuvier's description of the woman popularly known as the "Hottentot Venus," or Saartje Baartman, who was displayed to European audiences fascinated by her "steatopygia" (protruding buttocks).[24] Significantly, starting with Cuvier, this tradition of comparative anatomy located the boundaries of race through the sexual and reproductive anatomy of the African female body, ignoring altogether the problematic absence of male bodies from these studies.

Flower and Murie's account lingered on two specific sites of difference: the "protuberance of the buttocks, so peculiar to the Bushman race," and "the remarkable development of the labia minora," which were "sufficiently well marked to distinguish these parts from those of any ordinary varieties of the human species" (p. 208). The racial difference of the African body, implied Flower and Murie, was located in its literal excess, a specifically sexual excess that placed her body outside the boundaries of the "normal" female. To support their conclusion, Flower and Murie included corroborating "evidence" in the final part of their account. They quoted a secondhand report, "received from a scientific friend residing at the Cape of Good Hope," describing the anatomy of "two pure bred Hottentots, mother and daughter" (p. 208). This account also focused on the women's genitalia, which they referred to as "appendages" (p. 208). Although their account ostensibly foregrounded boundaries of race, their portrayal of the sexual characteristics of the Bushwoman betrayed Flower and Murie's anxieties about gender boundaries. The characteristics singled out as "peculiar" to this race—the (double) "appendages"—fluttered between genders, at one moment masculine, at the next moment exaggeratedly feminine. Flower and Murie constructed the site of *racial* difference by marking the sexual and reproductive anatomy of the African woman as "peculiar"; in their characterization, sexual ambiguity delineated the boundaries of race.

The techniques and logic of late nineteenth-century sexologists, who also routinely included physical examinations in their accounts, reproduced the methodologies employed by comparative anatomists like Flower and Murie. Many of the case histories in Krafft-Ebing's *Psychopathia Sexualis*, for instance, included a paragraph detailing any anatomical peculiarities of the body in question.[25] Krafft-Ebing could not draw any conclusions about somatic indicators of "abnormal" sexuality, but physical examinations nevertheless remained a staple of the genre. In Ellis's *Sexual Inversion*, case studies often focused more intensely on the bodies of female "inverts" than on those of their male counterparts.[26] Although the specific sites of anatomical inspection (hymen, clitoris, labia, vagina) differed in various sexological texts, the underlying theory remained constant: women's genitalia and reproductive anatomy held a valuable and presumably visual key to ranking bodies according to norms of sexuality.

Sexologists reproduced not only the methodologies of the comparative anatomy of races but also its iconography. One of the most consistent medical characterizations of the anatomy of both African American women and lesbians was the myth of an unusually large clitoris.[27] As late as 1921, medical journals contained articles declaring that "a physical examination of [female homosexuals] will in practically every instance disclose an abnormally prominent clitoris." Significantly, this author added, "This is particularly so in colored women."[28] In an earlier account of racial differences between white and African American women, one gynecologist had also focused on the size and visibility of the clitoris; in his examinations, he had perceived a distinction between the "free" clitoris of "negresses" and the "imprisonment" of the clitoris of the "Aryan American woman."[29] In constructing these oppositions, such characterizations literalized the sexual and racial ideologies of the nineteenth-century "Cult of True Womanhood," which explicitly privileged white women's sexual "purity" while implicitly suggesting African American women's sexual accessibility.[30]

The case histories in Ellis's *Sexual Inversion* differed markedly according to gender in the amount and degree of attention given to the examination of anatomical details. "As regards the sexual organs it seems possible," Ellis wrote, "so far as my observations go, to speak more definitely of inverted women than of inverted men" (p. 256). Ellis justified his greater scrutiny of women's bodies in part by invoking the ambiguity surrounding women's sexuality in general: "We are accustomed to a much greater familiarity and intimacy between women than between men, and we are less apt to suspect the existence of any abnormal passion" (p. 204). To Ellis, the seemingly imperceptible differences between "normal" and "abnormal" intimacies between women called for greater scrutiny into the subtleties of their anatomy. He included the following detailed account as potential evidence for understanding the fine line between the lesbian and the "normal" woman:

> *Sexual Organs*—(a) Internal: Uterus and ovaries appear normal. (b) External: Small clitoris, with this irregularity, that the lower folds of the labia minora, instead of uniting one with the other and forming the frenum, are extended upward along the sides of the clitoris, while the upper folds are poorly developed, furnishing the clitoris with a scant hood. The labia majora depart from normal conformation in being fuller in their posterior half than in their anterior part, so that when the subject is in the supine position they sag, as it were, presenting a slight resemblance to fleshy sacs, but in substance and structure they feel normal. (p. 136)

This extraordinary taxonomy, performed for Ellis by an unnamed "obstetric physician of high standing," echoed earlier anatomical catalogues of African women. The exacting eye (and hand) of the investigating physician highlighted every possible detail as meaningful evidence. Through the triple repetition of "normal" and the use of evaluative language like "irregularity" and "poorly developed," the physician reinforced his position of judgment. Without providing criteria for what constituted "normal" anatomy, the physician simply proclaimed irregularity based on his own powers of sight and touch. Moreover, his characterization of what he perceived as abnormal echoed the anxious account by Flower and Murie. Although the description of the clitoris in this account is a notable exception to the tendency to exaggerate its size, the account nevertheless scrutinized another site of genital excess. The "fleshy sacs" of this woman, like the "appendages" fetishized in the earlier account, invoked the anatomy of a phantom male body inhabiting the lesbian's anatomical features.

Clearly, anxieties about gender shaped both Ellis's and Flower and Murie's taxonomies of the lesbian and the African woman. Yet their preoccupation with gender cannot be understood as separate from the larger context of scientific assumptions during this period, which one historian has characterized as "the full triumph of Darwinism in American thought."[31] Gender, in fact, was crucial to Darwinist ideas. One of the basic assumptions within the Darwinian model was the belief that, as organisms evolved through a process of natural selection, they also showed greater signs of differentiation between the (two) sexes. Following this logic, various writers used sexual characteristics as indicators of evolutionary progress toward civilization. In *Man and Woman*, for instance, Ellis himself cautiously suggested that since the "beginnings of industrialism," "more marked sexual differences in physical development seem (we cannot speak definitely) to have developed than are usually to be found in savage societies."[32] In this passage, Ellis drew from theories developed by biologists like Patrick Geddes and J. Arthur Thomson, who stated in their important work *The Evolution of Sex* that "hermaphroditism is primitive; the unisexual state is a subsequent differentiation. The present cases of normal hermaphroditism imply either persistence or reversion."[33] In characterizing either lesbians' or African American women's bodies as less sexually differentiated than the norm (always posited as white heterosexual women's bodies), anatomists and sexologists drew upon notions of natural selection to dismiss these bodies as anomalous "throwbacks" within a scheme of cultural and anatomical progress.

THE MIXED BODY

The emergence of evolutionary theory in the late nineteenth century foregrounded a view of continuity between the "savage" and "civilized" races, in contrast to earlier scientific thinking about race, which had focused on debates about the origins of different racial groups. Proponents of monogeny argued that all races derived from a single origin. Those who argued for polygeny believed that different races descended from separate biological and geographical sources, a view, not coincidentally, that supported segregationist impulses.[34] With Darwin's publication of *Origin of the Species* in 1859, the debate between polygeny and monogeny was superseded by evolutionary theory, which was appropriated as a powerful scientific model for understanding race. Its controversial innovation was its emphasis on the continuity between animals and human beings. Evolutionary theory held out the possibility that the physical, mental, and moral characteristics of human beings had evolved gradually over time from apelike ancestors.[35] Although the idea of continuity depended logically on the blurring of boundaries within hierarchies, it did not necessarily invalidate the methods or assumptions of comparative anatomy. On the contrary, notions of visible differences and racial hierarchies were deployed to corroborate Darwinian theory.

The concept of continuity was harnessed to the growing attention to miscegenation, or "amalgamation," in social science writing during the first decades of the twentieth century in the United States. Edward Byron Reuter's *The Mulatto in the United States*, for instance, pursued an exhaustive quantitative and comparative study of the "mulatto" population and its achievements in relation to those of "pure" white or African ancestry. Reuter traced the presence of a distinct group of mixed-race people back to early American history: "Their physical appearance, though markedly different from that of the pure blooded race, was sufficiently marked to set them off as a peculiar people."[36] Reuter, of course, was willing to admit the viability of "mulattoes" only within a framework that emphasized the separation of races. Far from using the notion of the biracial body to refute the belief in discrete markers of racial difference, Reuter perpetuated the notion by focusing on the distinctiveness of this "peculiar people."

Miscegenation was, of course, not only a question of race but also one of sex and sexuality. Ellis recognized this intersection implicitly, if not explicitly. His sense of the "racial questions" inherent in sex was surely informed by his involvement with eugenics, the movement in Europe and the United States that, to greater or lesser degrees, advocated selective reproduction and "race hygiene."[37] In the United States, eugenics was both a political and scientific response to the growth of a population beginning to challenge the dominance of white political interests. The widespread scientific and social interest in eugenics was fueled by anxieties expressed through the popularized notion of (white) "race suicide." This phrase, invoked most notably by Theodore Roosevelt, summed up nativist fears about a perceived decline in reproduction among white Americans. The new field of eugenics worked hand in hand with growing antimiscegenation sentiment and policy, provoked not only by attempts for political representation among African Americans but also by the influx of large populations of immigrants.[38] As Mark Haller has pointed out, "Racists and [immigration] restrictionists . . . found in eugenics the scientific reassurances they needed that heredity shaped man's personality and that their assumptions rested on biological facts."[39] Ellis saw himself as an advocate for eugenics policies. On behalf of the British National Council for Public Morals, Ellis wrote several essays concerning eugenics, including

The Problem of Race Regeneration, a pamphlet advocating "voluntary" sterilization of the unfit as a policy in the best interest of "the race."[40] Further, in a letter to Francis Galton in 1907, Ellis wrote, "In the concluding volume of my Sex 'Studies' I shall do what I can to insinuate the eugenic attitude."[41]

The beginnings of sexology, then, were related to and perhaps even dependent on a pervasive climate of eugenicist and antimiscegenation sentiment and legislation. Even at the level of nomenclature, anxieties about miscegenation shaped sexologists' attempts to find an appropriate and scientific name for the newly visible object of their study. Introduced into English through the 1892 English translation of Krafft-Ebing's *Psychopathia Sexualis*, the term "homosexuality" itself stimulated a great deal of uneasiness. In the 1915 edition of *Sexual Inversion*, Ellis reported that "most investigators have been much puzzled in coming to a conclusion as to the best, most exact, and at the same time most colorless names [for same-sex desire]." Giving an account of the various names proposed, such as Ulrichs's "Uranian" and Westphal's "contrary sexual feeling," Ellis admitted that "homosexuality" was the most widely used term. Far from the ideal "color-less" term, however, "homosexuality" evoked Ellis's distaste for its mixed origins; in a regretful aside, he noted that "it has, philologically, the awkward disadvantage of being a bastard term compounded of Greek and Latin elements" (p. 2). In the first edition of *Sexual Inversion*, Ellis stated his alarm more directly: "'Homosexual' is a barbarously hybrid word."[42] A similar view was expressed by Edward Carpenter, an important socialist writer in England and an outspoken advocate of homosexual and women's emancipation at the time. Like Ellis, Carpenter winced at the connotations of illegitimacy in the word: "'homosexual,' generally used in scientific works, is of course a bastard word. 'Homogenic' has been suggested, as being from two roots, both Greek, i.e., 'homos,' same, and 'genos,' sex."[43] Carpenter's suggestion of course resonated both against and within the vocabularies of eugenics and miscegenation. Performing these etymological gyrations with almost comic literalism, Ellis and Carpenter expressed pervasive cultural anxieties about questions of racial origins and purity. Concerned above all else with legitimacy, they attempted to remove and rewrite the mixed origins of "homosexuality." Ironically, despite their suggestions for alternatives, the "bastard" term took hold among sexologists, thus yoking together, at least rhetorically, two kinds of mixed bodies—the racial "hybrid" and the invert.

Although Ellis exhibited anxieties about biracial bodies, for others who sought to naturalize and recuperate homosexuality, the evolutionary emphasis on continuity offered potentially useful analogies. Xavier Mayne, for example, one of the earliest American advocates of homosexual rights, wrote, "Between whitest of men and the blackest negro stretches out a vast line of inter-mediary races as to their colours: brown, olive, red tawny, yellow."[44] He then invoked this model of race to envision a continuous spectrum of gender and sexuality: "Nature abhors the absolute, delights in the fractional . . . Intersexes express the half-steps, the between-beings."[45] In this anal-ogy, Mayne reversed dominant cultural hierarchies that privileged purity over mixture. Drawing upon irrefutable evidence of the "natural" existence of biracial people, Mayne posited a direct analogy to a similarly mixed body, the intersex, which he positioned as a necessary presence within the natural order.

Despite Carpenter's complaint about "bastard" terminology, he, like Mayne, also occasionally appropriated the scientific language of racial mixing in order to resist the association between homosexuality and degeneration. In *The Intermediate Sex*, he attempted to theorize homosexual-ity outside of the discourse of pathology or abnormality; he too suggested a continuum of gen-ders, with "intermediate types" occupying a place between the poles of exclusively heterosexual male and female. In an appendix to *The Intermediate Sex*, Carpenter offered a series of quotations supporting his ideas, some of which drew upon racial analogies:

Anatomically and mentally we find all shades existing from the pure genus man to the pure genus woman. Thus there has been constituted what is well named by an illustrious exponent of the science

"The Third Sex" . . . As we are continually meeting in cities women who are one-quarter, or one-eighth, or so on, *male* . . . so there are in the Inner Self similar half-breeds, all adapting themselves to circumstances with perfect ease.[46]

Through notions of "shades" of gender and sexual "half-breeds," Carpenter appropriated dominant scientific models of race to construct and embody what he called the intermediate sex. These racial paradigms, along with models of gender, offered Carpenter a coherent vocabulary for understanding and expressing a new vision of sexual bodies.

SEXUAL "PERVERSION" AND RACIALIZED DESIRE

By the early twentieth century, medical models of sexuality had begun to shift in emphasis, moving away from a focus on the body and toward psychological theories of desire. It seems significant that this shift took place within a period that also saw a transformation of scientific notions about race. As historians have suggested, in the early twentieth century, scientific claims for exclusively biological models of racial difference were beginning to be undermined, although these models have persisted in popular understandings of race.[47]

In what ways were these shifts away from biologized notions of sexuality and race related in scientific literature? One area in which they overlapped and perhaps shaped one another was through models of interracial and homosexual desire. Specifically, two cultural taboos—miscegenation and homosexuality—became linked in sexological and psychological discourse through the model of "abnormal" sexual object choice.

The convergence of theories of "perverse" racial and sexual desire shaped the assumptions of psychologists like Margaret Otis, whose analysis of "A Perversion Not Commonly Noted" appeared in a medical journal in 1913. Otis noted that in all-girl institutions, including reform schools and boarding schools, she had observed widespread "love-making between the white and colored girls."[48] Otis's explicit discussion of racial difference and homosexuality was extremely rare amidst the burgeoning social science literature on sexuality in the early twentieth century.[49] Both fascinated and alarmed, Otis remarked that this perversion was "well known in reform schools and institutions for delinquent girls," but that "this particular form of the homosexual relation has perhaps not been brought to the attention of scientists" (p. 113). Performing her ostensible duty to science, Otis carefully described these rituals of interracial romance and the girls' "peculiar moral code." In particular, she noted that the girls incorporated racial difference into courtship rituals self-consciously patterned on traditional gender roles: "One white girl . . . admitted that the colored girl she loved seemed the man, and thought it was so in the case of the others" (p. 114). In Otis's account, the actions of the girls clearly threatened the keepers of the institutions, who responded to the perceived danger with efforts to racially segregate their charges (who were, of course, already segregated by gender). Otis, however, left open the motivation for segregation: Did the girls' intimacy trouble the authorities because it was homosexual or because it was interracial? Otis avoided exploring this question and offered a succinct theory instead: "The difference in color, in this case, takes the place of difference in sex" (p. 113).

Otis's account participated in the gradual shift in medical and scientific literature away from a model of inversion as a physiological difference and toward a model of homosexuality as "abnormal desire." Despite Otis's focus on desire rather than physiology, however, her characterization of the schoolgirls' "system" of romance drew upon and perpetuated stereotypes based on the earlier anatomical models. She used a simple analogy between race and gender in order to understand their desire: black was to white as masculine was to feminine.

Significantly, Otis characterized this phenomenon as a type of "the homosexual relation" and not as a particular form of interracial sexuality. Recent historical studies of the lesbian subject at the turn of the century in the United States offer a useful context for considering the implications of Otis's account. In a compelling analysis of Alice Mitchell's highly publicized

1892 murder of her lover Freda Ward, Lisa Duggan has argued that what initially pushed the women's relationship beyond what their peers accepted as normal was Mitchell's decision to pass as a man.[50] Passing, according to Duggan, was "a strategy so rare among bourgeois white women that their plan was perceived as so radically inappropriate as to be insane."[51] Duggan characterizes passing as a kind of red flag that visually marked Mitchell and Ward's relationship. Suddenly, with the prospect of Mitchell's visible transformation from "woman" to "man," the sexual nature of their relationship also came into view—abnormal and dangerous to the eyes of their surveyors.

Following Duggan's line of analysis, I suggest that racial difference performed an important visual function in Otis's account. In turn-of-the-century American culture, where Jim Crow segregation erected a structure of taboos against any kind of public (non-work-related) interracial relationship, racial difference visually marked the alliances between the schoolgirls as already suspicious. In a culture in which Ellis could remark that he was accustomed to women being on intimate terms, race became a visible marker for the sexual nature of that liaison. In effect, the institution of racial segregation and its cultural fiction of "black" and "white" produced the girls' interracial romances as "perverse."[52]

It is possible that the discourse of sexual pathology, in turn, began to inform scientific understandings of race. By 1903, a southern physician drew upon the language of sexology to legitimate a particularly racist fear: "A perversion from which most races are exempt, prompts the negro's inclinations towards the white woman, whereas other races incline toward the females of their own."[53] Using the medical language of perversion to naturalize and legitimate the dominant cultural myth of the black rapist, this account characterized interracial desire as a type of congenital abnormal sexual object choice. In the writer's terms, the desire of African American men for white women (though not the desire of white men for African American women) could be understood and pathologized by drawing upon emergent models of sexual orientation.[54]

DIVERGENCES IN RACIAL AND SEXUAL SCIENCE

The inextricability of the "invention" of homosexuality and heterosexuality from the extraordinary pressures attached to racial definition in the late nineteenth century obtained at a particular historical moment. Although sexologists' search for physical signs of sexual orientation mirrored the methods of comparative racial anatomists, the modern case study marked a significant departure from comparative anatomy by attaching a self-generated narrative to the body in question. As Jeffrey Weeks has written, Krafft-Ebing's *Psychopathia Sexualis* was a decisive moment in the "invention" of the homosexual because "it was the eruption into print of the speaking pervert, the individual marked, or marred, by his (or her) sexual impulses."[55]

The case study challenged the tendency of scientific and medical writers to position the homosexual individual as a mute body whose surface was to be interpreted by those with professional authority. Whether to grant a voice, however limited, to the homosexual body was a heavily contested methodological question among sexologists. The increasingly central position of the case study in the literature on homosexuality elicited concern from contemporary professionals, who perceived an unbridgeable conflict between autobiography and scientific objectivity. Invested in maintaining authority in medical writing, Morton Prince, for example, a psychologist who advocated searching for a "cure" to homosexuality, described in exasperation his basic distrust of the case history as a source of medical evidence, especially in the case of "perverts":

> Even in taking an ordinary medical history, we should hesitate to accept such testimony as final, and I think we should be even more cautious in our examination of autobiographies which attempt to give an analysis, founded on introspection, of the feelings, passions and tastes of degenerate individuals who attempt to explain their first beginnings in early childhood.[56]

For Prince, the "speaking pervert" was a challenge to the "truth" of medical examination and threatened to contradict the traditional source of medical evidence, the patient's mute physical body as interpreted by the physician. In Prince's view, the case history also blurred the boundaries between the legal and medical spheres:

> Very few of these autobiographies will stand analysis. Probably there is no class of people whose statements will less stand the test of a scorching cross-examination than the moral pervert. One cannot help feeling that if the pervert was thus examined by an independent observer, instead of being allowed to tell his own story without interruption, a different tale would be told, or great gaps would be found, which are now nicely bridged, or many asserted facts would be resolved into pure inferences.[57]

A "different tale" indeed. Prince's focus on "testimony" and "cross-examination" illustrated the overlapping interests and methods of the medical and the legal spheres. His tableau of litigation placed the homosexual individual within an already guilty body, one that defied the assumption that it was a readable text; its anatomical markers did not necessarily correspond to predictable sexual behaviors. The sure duplicity of this body demanded investigation by the prosecutor/physician, whose professional expertise somehow guaranteed his access to the truth.

Ellis, who sought legitimacy both for himself as a scientist and for the nascent field of sexology, also worried about the association between autobiographical accounts and fraud. In *Sexual Inversion*, he stated that "it may be proper, at this point, to say a few words as to the reliability of the statements furnished by homosexual persons. This has sometimes been called in[to] question" (p. 89). Although he also associated the homosexual voice with duplicity, Ellis differed from Prince by placing this unreliability within a larger social context. He located the causes of insincerity not in the homosexual individual but in the legal system that barred homosexuality: "We cannot be surprised at this [potential insincerity] so long as inversion is counted a crime. The most normal persons, under similar conditions, would be similarly insincere" (p. 89).

With the movement toward the case study and toward psychoanalytic models of sexuality, sexologists relied less and less upon the methodologies of comparative anatomy and implicitly acknowledged that physical characteristics were inadequate evidence for the "truth" of the body in question. Yet the assumptions of comparative anatomy did not completely disappear; although they seemed to contradict more psychological understandings of sexuality, notions of biological difference continued to shape cultural understandings of sexuality, particularly in popular representations of lesbians and gay men.

TROUBLING SCIENCE

My efforts here have focused on the various ways in which late nineteenth- and early twentieth-century scientific discourses on race became available to sexologists and physicians as a way to articulate emerging models of homosexuality. Methodologies and iconographies of comparative anatomy attempted to locate discrete physiological markers of difference through which to classify and separate types of human beings. Sexologists drew upon these techniques to try to position the "homosexual" body as anatomically distinguishable from the "normal" body. Likewise, medical discourses on sexuality appear to have been steeped in pervasive cultural anxieties toward "mixed" bodies, particularly the mulatto, whose symbolic position as a mixture of black and white bodies was literalized in scientific accounts. Sexologists and others writing about homosexuality borrowed the model of the mixed body as a way to make sense of the "invert." Finally, racial and sexual discourses converged in psychological models that understood "unnatural" desire as a marker of perversion, in these cases, interracial and same-sex sexuality became analogous.

Although scientific and medical models of both race and sexuality held enormous definitional power at the turn of the century, they were variously and complexly incorporated, revised, resisted, or ignored both by the individuals they sought to categorize and within the larger cultural imagination. My speculations are intended to raise questions and to point toward possibilities for further historical and theoretical work. How, for instance, were analogies between race and sexual orientation deployed or not within popular cultural discourses? In religious discourses? In legal discourses? What were the material effects of their convergence or divergence? How have these analogies been used to organize bodies in other historical moments and, most urgently, in our own?

In the last few years alone, for example, there has been a proliferation of "speaking perverts" in a range of cultural contexts, including political demonstrations, television, magazines, courts, newspapers, and classrooms. Despite the unprecedented opportunities for lesbian, gay, bisexual, and queer speech, however, recent scientific research into sexuality has reflected a determination to discover a biological key to the origins of homosexuality. Highly publicized new studies have purported to locate indicators of sexual orientation in discrete niches of the human body, ranging from a particular gene on the X chromosome to the hypothalamus, a structure of the brain.[58] In an updated and more technologically sophisticated form, comparative anatomy is being granted a peculiar cultural authority in the study of sexuality.

These studies, of course, have not gone uncontested, arriving as they have within a moment characterized not only by the development of social constructionist theories of sexuality but also, in the face of AIDS, by a profound and aching skepticism toward prevailing scientific methods and institutions. At the same time, some see political efficacy in these new scientific studies, arguing that gay men and lesbians might gain access to greater rights if sexual orientation could be proven an immutable biological difference. Such arguments make an analogy, whether explicit or unspoken, to earlier understandings of race as immutable difference. Reverberating through these arguments are echoes of late nineteenth- and early twentieth-century medical models of sexuality and race, whose earlier interdependence suggests a need to understand the complex relationships between constructions of race and sexuality during our own very different historical moment. How does the current effort to rebiologize sexual orientation and to invoke the vocabulary of immutable difference reflect or influence existing cultural anxieties and desires about racialized bodies? To what extent does the political deployment of these new scientific "facts" about sexuality depend upon reinscribing biologized racial categories? These questions, as I have tried to show for an earlier period, require a shift in the attention and practices of queer reading and lesbian and gay studies, one that locates questions of race as inextricable from the study of sexuality, rather than as a part of our peripheral vision.

NOTES

Many thanks to those who generously read and commented on earlier versions of this article, especially Hazel Carby, Lisa Cohen, Susan Edmunds, Heather Hendershot, Regina Kunzel, David Rodowick, Michael Rogin, and the anonymous referees for the *Journal of the History of Sexuality*.

1. See, e.g., Michel Foucault, *The History of Sexuality*, vol. 1 (New York: Vintage, 1980); George Chauncey, "From Sexual Inversion to Homosexuality: Medicine and the Changing Conceptualization of Female Deviance," *Salmagundi* 58–59 (Fall 1982–Winter 1983): 114–46; Jeffrey Weeks, *Sex, Politics, and Society: The Regulation of Sexuality since 1800* (New York: Longmans, 1981); and David Halperin, "Is There a History of Sexuality?" in *The Lesbian and Gay Studies Reader*, ed. Henry Abelove, Michèle Aina Barale, and David M. Halperin (New York: Routledge, 1993), pp. 416–31. On the invention of the classification of heterosexuality, see Jonathan Katz, "The Invention of Heterosexuality," *Socialist Review* 20 (1990): 17–34. For a related and intriguing argument that locates the earlier emergence of hierarchies of reproductive over nonreproductive sexual activity, see Henry

Abelove, "Some Speculations on the History of 'Sexual Intercourse' During the 'Long Eighteenth Century' in England," *Genders* 6 (1989): 125–30.

2. Chauncey, from "Sexual Inversion to Homosexuality."

3. Exceptions include David Halperin's brief but provocative suggestion that "all scientific inquiries into the aetiology of sexual orientation, after all, spring from a more or less implicit theory of sexual races" in "Homosexuality: A Cultural Construct," in his *One Hundred Years of Homosexuality: And Other Essays on Greek Love* (New York: Routledge, 1990), p. 50; and Abdul R. JanMohamed, "Sexuality on/of the Racial Border: Foucault, Wright, and the Articulation of 'Racialized Sexuality,'" in *Discourses of Sexuality: From Aristotle to AIDS*, ed. Domna C. Stanton (Ann Arbor, MI: University of Michigan Press, 1992), pp. 94–116.

4. For a brief discussion of the invisibility of African Americans as subjects or researchers in sexology, see Janice Irvine, *Disorders of Desire: Sex and Gender in Modern American Sexology* (Philadelphia: Temple University Press, 1990), p. 43.

5. Havelock Ellis and John Addington Symonds, *Studies in the Psychology of Sex*, vol. 1, *Sexual Inversion* (London: Wilson and Macmillan, 1897; reprint New York: Arno, 1975), x emphasis added. Ellis originally co-authored *Sexual Inversion* with John Addington Symonds. For a discussion of their collaboration and the eventual erasure of Symonds from the text, see Wayne Koestenbaum, *Double Talk: The Erotics of Male Literary Collaboration* (New York: Routledge, 1989), pp. 43–67.

6. My use of the concept of ideology draws upon Barbara Fields, "Slavery, Race, and Ideology in the United States of America," *New Left Review* 181 (1990): 95–118; Louis Althusser, "Ideology and Ideological State Apparatuses (Notes Towards an Investigation)," in his *Lenin and Philosophy and Other Essays*, trans. Ben Brewster (New York: Monthly Review Press, 1971), pp. 121–73; and Teresa de Lauretis, "The Technology of Gender," in her *Technologies of Gender: Essays on Theory, Film, and Fiction* (Bloomington, IN: Indiana University Press, 1987), pp. 1–30.

7. I borrow this phrase from Willa Cather's essay, "The Novel Démeublé," in her *Not Under Forty* (New York: Knopf, 1922), p. 50.

8. I am not implying, however, that racial anxieties caused the invention of the homosexual, nor that the invention of the homosexual caused increased racial anxieties. Both of these causal arguments seem simplistic and, further, depend upon separating the discourses of race and sexuality, whose convergence, in fact, I am eager to foreground.

9. Havelock Ellis, *Studies in the Psychology of Sex*, vol. 2, *Sexual Inversion*, 3rd ed., revised and enlarged (Philadelphia: F.A. Davis, 1915). Further references to this edition will be noted parenthetically unless otherwise stated. Although *Sexual Inversion* was published originally as vol. 1, Ellis changed its position to vol. 2 in the 2d and 3d eds., published in the United States in 1901 and 1915, respectively. In the later editions, vol. 1 became *The Evolution of Modesty*.

10. For a different interpretation of Ellis's relationship to comparative anatomy and psychiatry, see Arnold I. Davidson, "Sex and the Emergence of Sexuality," *Critical Inquiry* 14 (Autumn 1987): 16–48.

11. Ellis, *Sexual Inversion* (1900), xi. For discussions of legal battles surrounding the publication of *Sexual Inversion*, see Jeffrey Weeks, "Havelock Ellis and the Politics of Sex Reform," in Sheila Rowbotham and Jeffrey Weeks, *Socialism and the New Life: The Personal and Sexual Politics of Edward Carpenter and Havelock Ellis* (London: Pluto Press, 1977), p. 154; and Phyllis Grosskurth, *Havelock Ellis: A Biography* (New York: Knopf, 1980), pp. 191–204.

12. For further discussion of Ellis's similarity to Charles Darwin as a naturalist and their mutual interest in "natural" modesty, see Ruth Bernard Yeazell, "Nature's Courtship Plot in Darwin and Ellis," *Yale Journal of Criticism* 2 (1989): 33–53.

13. Elsewhere in *Sexual Inversion*, Ellis entertained the idea that certain races or nationalities had a "special proclivity" to homosexuality (p. 4), but he seemed to recognize the nationalistic impulse behind this argument and chided those who wielded it: "The people of every country have always been eager to associate sexual perversions with some other country than their own" (pp. 57–58).

14. Classic discussions of the term's history include Peter I. Rose, *The Subject Is Race* (New York:

Oxford University Press, 1968), pp. 30–43; and Thomas F. Gossett, *Race: The History of an Idea in America* (Dallas: Southern Methodist University Press, 1963). For a history of various forms and theories of biological determinism, see Stephen Jay Gould, *The Mismeasure of Man* (New York: Norton, 1981).

15. On Blumenbach, see John S. Haller, Jr., *Outcasts from Evolution: Scientific Attitudes of Racial Inferiority, 1859–1900* (Urbana, IL: University of Illinois Press, 1971), pp. 4–6.

16. Quoted in ibid., p. 196. On Cope, see also Gould, *The Mismeasure of Man*, pp. 115–18.

17. Nancy Leys Stepan and Sander Gilman, "Appropriating the Idioms of Science: The Rejection of Scientific Racism," in *The Bounds of Race: Perspectives on Hegemony and Resistance*, ed. Dominick LaCapra (Ithaca, NY: Cornell University Press, 1991), p. 74.

18. Fields, "Slavery, Race, and Ideology," p. 97, n.3.

19. Haller, *Outcasts from Evolution*, p. 48.

20. Sander Gilman, *Difference and Pathology: Stereotypes of Sexuality, Race, and Madness* (Ithaca, NY: Cornell University Press, 1985), p. 112.

21. According to Gilman, "When one turns to autopsies of black males from [the late nineteenth century], what is striking is the absence of any discussion of the male genitalia" (p. 89). The specific absence of male physiology as a focus of nineteenth-century scientific texts, however, should not minimize the central location of the African American male body in popular cultural notions of racial difference, especially in the spectacle of lynching, which had far-reaching effects on both African American and white attitudes toward the African American male body. One might also consider the position of the racialized male body in one of the most popular forms of nineteenth-century entertainment, the minstrel show. See Eric Lott, *Love and Theft: Blackface Minstrelsy and the American Working Class* (New York: Oxford University Press, 1993).

22. The *American Journal of Obstetrics* (*AJO*) was a frequent forum for these debates. On the position of the hymen, e.g., see C. H. Fort, "Some Corroborative Facts in Regard to the Anatomical Difference between the Negro and White Races," *AJO* 10 (1877): 258–59; H. Otis Hyatt, "Note on the Normal Anatomy of the Vulvo-Vaginal Orifice," *AJO* 10 (1877): 253–58; A. G. Smythe, "The Position of the Hymen in the Negro Race," *AJO* 10 (1877): 638–639; Edward Turnipseed, "Some Facts in Regard to the Anatomical Differences between the Negro and White Races," *AJO* 10 (1877): 32–33. On the birth canal, see Joseph Taber Johnson, "On Some of the Apparent Peculiarities of Parturition in the Negro Race, with Remarks on Race Pelves in General," *AJO* 8 (1875): 88–123. This focus on women's bodies apparently differed from earlier studies. See Londa Schiebinger, *Nature's Body: Gender in the Making of Modern Science* (Boston: Beacon, 1993), esp. pp. 143–83.

23. W. H. Flower and James Murie, "Account of the Dissection of a Bushwoman," *Journal of Anatomy and Physiology* 1 (1887): 208. Subsequent references will be noted parenthetically within the text. For brief discussions of this account, see Gilman, pp. 88–89; and Anita Levy, *Other Women: The Writing of Class, Race, and Gender, 1832–1898* (Princeton, NJ: Princeton University Press, 1991), pp. 70–72.

24. Georges Cuvier, "Extraits d'observations faites sur le cadavre d'une femme connue à Paris et à Londres sous le nom de Vénus Hottentote," *Mémoires du Musée d'histoire naturelle* 3 (1817): 259–74. On Baartman, see Schiebinger, *Nature's Body*, pp. 160–72; and Stephen Jay Gould, *The Flamingo's Smile* (New York: Norton, 1985), pp. 291–305.

25. Richard von Krafft-Ebing, *Psychopathia Sexualis*, 12th ed., trans. Franklin S. Klaf (1902; reprint, New York: Putnam, 1965).

26. This practice continued well into the twentieth century. See, e.g., Jennifer Terry, "Lesbians under the Medical Gaze: Scientists Search for Remarkable Differences," *Journal of Sex Research* 27 (August 1990): 317–39; and "Theorizing Deviant Historiography," *Differences* 3 (Summer 1991): 55–74.

27. In the first edition of *Sexual Inversion*, Ellis, who did search the lesbian body for masculine charac-

teristics, nevertheless refuted this claim about the clitoris: "There is no connection, as was once supposed, between sexual inversion in women and an enlarged clitoris" (p. 98).

28. Perry M. Lichtenstein, "The 'Fairy' and the Lady Lover," *Medical Review of Reviews* 27 (1921): 372.

29. Morris, "Is Evolution Trying To Do Away with the Clitoris?" Paper presented at the meeting of the American Association of Obstetricians and Gynecologists, St. Louis, September 21, 1892, Yale University Medical Library, New Haven, CT.

30. See Hazel Carby, *Reconstructing Womanhood: The Emergence of the Afro-American Woman Novelist* (New York: Oxford University Press, 1987), pp. 20–39; and Barbara Welter, "The Cult of True Womanhood, 1820–1860," in her *Dimity Convictions: The American Woman in the Nineteenth Century* (Columbus: University of Ohio Press, 1976), pp. 21–41.

31. George Fredrickson, *The Black Image in the White Mind: The Debate on Afro-American Character and Destiny, 1817–1914* (New York: Harper and Row, 1971), p. 246.

32. Havelock Ellis, *Man and Woman: A Study of Human Secondary Sexual Characters*, 4th ed. (1894; New York: Scribner's, 1911), p. 13. Of course, the "beginnings of industrialism" coincided with the late eighteenth century, the period during which, as Schiebinger has shown, anatomists began looking for more subtle marks of differentiation. See Londa Schiebinger, *The Mind Has No Sex? Women in the Origins of Modern Science* (Cambridge, MA: Harvard University Press, 1989), pp. 189–212.

33. Patrick Geddes and J. Arthur Thomson, *The Evolution of Sex* (London: W. Scott 1889; New York: Scribner, 1890), p. 80. Ellis no doubt read this volume closely, for he had chosen it to inaugurate a series of popular scientific books (the Contemporary Science Series) that he edited for the Walter Scott company. For more on this series, see Grosskurth, *Havelock Ellis*, pp. 114–117.

34. For a full account of the debates around monogeny and polygeny, see Gould, *The Mismeasure of Man*, pp. 30–72. Polygeny was a predominantly American theoretical development and was widely referred to as the "American school" of anthropology.

35. See Nancy Stepan, *The Idea of Race in Science: Great Britain, 1800–1960* (Hamden, CT: Archon Books, 1982), p. 53.

36. Edward Byron Reuter, *The Mulatto in the United States: Including a Study of the Role of Mixed-Blood Races throughout the World* (Boston: Gorham Press, 1918), p. 338.

37. Francis Galton (a cousin of Charles Darwin) introduced and defined the term "eugenics" in his *Inquiries into Human Faculty and Its Development* as "the cultivation of the race" and "the science of improving stock, which . . . takes cognisance of all influences that tend in however remote a degree to give to the more suitable races or strains of blood a better chance of prevailing speedily over the less suitable than they otherwise would have had" (1883; reprint, New York: AMS Press, 1973, p. 17).

38. On Roosevelt, see Thomas G. Dyer, *Theodore Roosevelt and the Idea of Race* (Baton Rouge, LA: Louisiana State University Press, 1980). See also John Higham, *Strangers in the Land: Patterns of American Nativism, 1860–1925* (New Brunswick, NJ: Rutgers University Press, 1955; reprint, 1963), pp. 146–57.

39. Mark H. Haller, *Eugenics: Hereditarian Attitudes in American Thought* (New Brunswick, NJ: Rutgers University Press, 1963), p. 144.

40. Jeffrey Weeks, *Sexuality and Its Discontents: Meanings, Myths, and Modern Sexualities* (Boston: Routledge and Kegan Paul, 1985), p. 76; Grosskurth, *Havelock Ellis*, p. 410. See also Havelock Ellis, "The Sterilization of the Unfit," *Eugenics Review* (October 1909): 203–206.

41. Quoted by Grosskurth, *Havelock Ellis*, p. 410.

42. Ellis and Symonds, *Sexual Inversion* (1897), p. 1n.

43. Edward Carpenter, "The Homogenic Attachment," in his *The Intermediate Sex: A Study of Some Transitional Types of Men and Women*, 5th ed. (London: George Allen and Unwin, 1918), p. 40n.

44. Xavier Mayne [Edward Irenaeus Prime Stevenson], *The Intersexes: A History of Similisexualism As A Problem in Social Life* ([Naples?], ca. 1908]; reprint, New York: Arno, 1975), p. 14.

45. Ibid., pp. 15, 17.

46. Quoted in Carpenter, *The Intermediate Sex*, pp. 133, 170. Carpenter gives the following citations for these quotations: Dr. James Burnet, *Medical Times and Hospital Gazette*, vol. 34, no. 1497 (London, November 10, 1906); and Charles G. Leland, *The Alternate Sex* (London: William Rider and Son, 1904), p. 57.

47. In *New People: Miscegenation and Mulattoes in the United States* (New York: Free Press, 1980), Joel Williamson suggests that a similar psychologization of race was underway by 1900 (p. 108). See also Elazar Barkan, *The Retreat of Scientific Racism: Changing Concepts of Race in Britain and the United States Between the World Wars* (New York: Cambridge University Press, 1992). On legal analogies between sodomy and miscegenation, see Andrew Koppelman, "The Miscegenation Analogy: Sodomy Law as Sex Discrimination," *Yale Law Journal* 98 (November 1988): 145–64; and Janet Halley, "The Politics of the Closet: Towards Equal Protection for Gay, Lesbian, and Bisexual Identity," *UCLA Law Review* 36 (1989): 915–76. I am grateful to Julia Friedlander for bringing this legal scholarship to my attention.

48. Margaret Otis, "A Perversion Not Commonly Noted," *Journal of Abnormal Psychology* 8 (June–July 1913): 113. Subsequent references will be noted parenthetically within the text.

49. Chauncey, in "From Sexual Inversion to Homosexuality," notes that "by the early teens the number of articles or abstracts concerning homosexuality regularly available to the American medical profession had grown enormously" (p. 115, n. 3).

50. Lisa Duggan, "The Trials of Alice Mitchell: Sensationalism, Sexology, and the Lesbian Subject in Turn-of-the-Century America," *Signs: Journal of Women in Culture and Society* 18 (Summer 1993): 791–814.

51. Ibid., p. 798.

52. In a useful discussion of recent feminist analyses of identity, Lisa Walker suggests that a similar trope of visibility is prevalent in white critics' attempts to theorize race and sexuality. See her "How to Recognize a Lesbian: The Cultural Politics of Looking Like What You Are," *Signs* (Summer 1993): 866–90.

53. W. T. English, "The Negro Problem from the Physician's Point of View," *Atlanta Journal-Record of Medicine* 5 (October 1903): 468.

54. On the other hand, antilynching campaigns could also invoke the language of sexology. Although the analogy invoked sadism, rather than homosexuality, in 1935 a psychologist characterized lynching as a kind of "Dixie sex perversion . . . much that is commonly stigmatized as cruelty is a perversion of the sex instinct." Quoted in Phyllis Klotman, "'Tearing a Hole in History': Lynching as Theme and Motif," *Black American Literature Forum* 19 (1985): 57. The original quote appeared in the *Baltimore Afro-American* (March 16, 1935).

55. Weeks, *Sexuality and Its Discontents*, p. 67.

56. Morton Prince, "Sexual Perversion or Vice? A Pathological and Therapeutic Inquiry," *Journal of Nervous and Mental Disease* 25 (April 1898): 237–56; reprinted in *Psychotherapy and Multiple Personality: Selected Essays*, ed. Nathan G. Hale (Cambridge, MA: Harvard University Press 1975), p. 91.

57. Prince, *Psychotherapy and Multiple Personality*, p. 92.

58. See Simon LeVay, *The Sexual Brain* (Cambridge, MA: MIT Press, 1993); and Dean Hamer, *The Science of Desire: The Search for the Gay Gene and the Biology of Behavior* (New York: Simon and Schuster, 1994).

3 White Lies, Black Myths

Rape, Race, and the Black "Underclass"

Micaela di Leonardo

Indifferent nature caroled and flickered, a vault of green above me. I was lying on my back at the bottom of a ravine, sometime in the early evening of a sunny July day in a suburban New Haven, Connecticut, neighborhood, and I had just become another statistic.

"All right, I'm leaving. But I'm not going far. If you make a sound, I'll come back and cut your head off." My rapist disappeared up the ravine. No reason to believe him—he was just trying to immobilize me while he escaped—and besides, I felt a desperate need for the safety of human companionship. I pulled on my running clothes and scrambled up after him. I ran out into the middle of the street and jumped in front of the first passing car. "I've been raped, please help me," I pleaded to the older white couple as the woman rolled down the passenger window. "I can't help you," she snapped, and the car sped away. I scanned the houses across the street and pelted up the steps of the only one with a car in the driveway. A black woman in her thirties in a white uniform opened the door and let me in the moment I explained myself. "Please just be quiet because my old people are asleep and I don't want them to know about this." She phoned the police, brought me a glass of water, and when she saw me standing in front of the mirror, picking leaves out of my hair and staring at my cut and bleeding face, advised me not to clean myself up before the cops came. "You know what they're like." Our eyes locked. We knew what they were like.

But I was frantic with the leftover adrenaline of the rape experience. My mind was rushing and tumbling still, reviewing the mental gymnastics I'd gone through, the strategies I'd played to keep the rapist from killing me. Now that I was safe, I wanted him caught. I persuaded my protector to leave the house with me to question a young black couple doing yard work next

Micaela di Leonardo teaches anthropology and women's studies at Northwestern University. She has written *The Varieties of Ethnic Experience* (Cornell, 1984) and *Exotics at Home: Anthropologies, Others, American Modernity* (Chicago, forthcoming); she also edited *Gender at the Crossroads of Knowledge: Feminist Anthropology in the Postmodern Era* (California, 1991). She writes frequently for *The Nation* and *The Village Voice*, and received the 1996 Anthropology in the Media Award from the American Anthropological Association. Currently a Senior Fellow at the Alice Berline Kaplan Humanities Center at Northwestern University, she is writing about race, class, and gender in New Haven, Connecticut.

door. Had they seen a man running up the street? No, they hadn't seen anything. There was a silence, and then the guy fixed me with a look: "Was he black?"

"Yeah," I said, "he was black."

I am white.

Or am I? Postmodern-era rhetoric lauds the disclosure of writers' "positionality," since—in the decidedly unpostmodern bromide—"You see from where you stand." I personally don't believe we live in the cacophonous but noncommunicating Tower of Babel universe that genuine adherence to the determinism of positionality would envision. The thrust of twentieth-century anthropology, my chosen field, is the gallant and detailed documentation of our species' capacity to stretch cognition, to empathize with others' positions and apprehensions. But I *do* believe that the "I was there" documentary style is most persuasive in the current climate. So let me persuade you that I have stood and seen from many positions in the American race/class/sex tangle. You might say I'm a hologram of American racial tension and interracial harmony, of class privilege and ressentiment, of feminist triumph and female victimization. (I'm also an academic specialist on race, class, and gender in America, past and present; nowadays, given right-wing attacks on "tenured radicals" and the unfortunately attackable work some of us have put out, that and a quarter will get you a pack of gum.) So, a report from the holographic front, starting with the image of gender/race/sexual violence.

When I scrambled up that ravine on July 16, 1987, the white couple who spurned me, the black woman who took me in and succored me, and the black man who queried my rapist's race certainly knew I was white. So did the black police, male and female, who came screeching up within minutes. But they and others—many others, for years afterward—also perceived me, iconically, as White Rape Victim of Black Man, the modern Northern embodiment of the Southern rape-lynching complex. I hated to spoil their fun, but I was something else: the former rape crisis counselor and feminist professor who had read the scholarship on rape, who knew the statistics, and who therefore ended up, with no small sense of irony, lecturing cops, coworkers, relatives, and friends alike on the tiny percentage (perhaps one in nine) of all sexual assaults that fit the heavily symbolic strange-black-on-white-woman model. Hell, I had taught classes at Yale on the topic, in those arcadian prerape days when my effervescent teaching assistants joked that I was "into violence against women." And to add to my statistical knowledge, I had been sexually attacked by a stranger and date-raped by an ex-boyfriend—both white—and had been sexually harassed on the street by literally hundreds of men, almost all of them white.

Knowledge, however, does not necessarily command emotion. Among the many violent reactions I had in the weeks following the rape—including despair, helplessness, a sense that my life was over—was a visceral, desperate fear of all strange black and brown men. Walking alone in Mount Pleasant, an inner-city Washington, DC neighborhood, I had a panic attack as it seemed that each of the dozens of Central American men streaming toward and past me on the sidewalk was about to pull a knife and stab me. (I knew, of course, that my country's foreign policy had, metaphorically, pulled a knife and stabbed them.) I flew to Northern California, my childhood home, to stay with a kindly friend in Santa Cruz and to heal among the redwoods. Walking on the campus's fennel- and bay-scented paths above the Pacific, I experienced what I decided was an uncomfortable but salutary shift: I was afraid of *all* the strange men I encountered. And in yuppie Santa Cruz, nearly all those men were white.

In the months after the rape, the Sinatra ballad "I'll Never Be the Same" ran like a tape loop through my head. I never will be the same. I am permanently more fearful, more anxious, more ready to believe that the frail threads of civility, health, and happiness will unravel; that murder and mayhem, cancer, heart attacks, car and plane crashes, are behind that thin veil, just around that sunny corner. But I know, intellectually, that the world did not change when I was knocked down that ravine. There's a nasty right-wing aphorism from the 1960s: a conservative is a liberal who's been mugged. But individual experiences shouldn't change well-thought-out opinions. I didn't need the rape to become a feminist; and, in corollary, the rape could not make me a racist. What we need as American citizens, it seems to me, is what my postrape interlocutors—many of whom were black—needed: a bracing dose of the facts. I'll never forget the poignant scene in which a friend's lover, a working-class black man I was meeting for the first time, offered me a heartfelt apology for his race. His ignorance of the facts of race and rape was far more painful to me—and to him—than were the racist assumptions of some of my white coworkers. That ignorance and those assumptions, though, are mixed indissolubly in our American stew of white racism, racial self-hatred and whistle-in-the-dark racial defense. But our collective national supper of ignorance has many more courses than race and sexual violence; our daily diet of lies and half-truths is so abundant, comes from so many sources, that it seems impossible to reform. But let me try. We are living in the midst of a terrible new gestalt, as bad as the old Southern rape complex—or worse, because now there's almost nowhere to hide. The discourse is no longer regional but national, and, unlike the last time around, it is widely believed across class, race, and former political divides. After all, William Julius Wilson, a liberal black sociologist, is the architect of "underclass" theory. But in order to address this issue, let me add another angle of diffraction to my autobiographical holographic image, to enter into the real world of gender, class, and race in America.

In the years since the rape, I've become another sort of statistic. A black colleague and I fell in love and married, and I inherited a black teenage son and a large, lively, and far-flung black family. I now "pass" in many directions, living out the real Italian American/black alliance so far beyond Spike Lee's cartoonish and misogynist vision. I've become an "honorary" black American, warmly welcomed among kin, friends, and in public places. (There are few more courteous environments in America than black working-class bars.) And I see and feel in both black and white. At one and the same time now, I fear for my purse and person around young kids, who are often black and brown—and fear for my husband's and son's safety at the hands of white mobs and police. And not without cause: each of them has been threatened by whites and harassed unjustly by police. In a final ironic twist on my own rape experience, a frantic white woman called Yale library security guards on my middle-aged professor husband when he stooped down to retrieve a book on a shelf near her.

My newly expanded understanding of white danger to black Americans, however, is not purely altruistic. In the eyes of many whites, I am now, as they say, tarred with the same brush. I, not my husband, was the victim of the sly, sexually insinuating remarks made by male and female faculty at a Southern university where we were being recruited for jobs. And the new racist right has a special place in its heart—and its plans—for me and my intermarrying sisters. William Pierce's *The Turner Diaries*—offered for sale, according to Elinor Langer in *The Nation*, by every far-right mail order business in America—is a fantasy of the violent overthrow of the U.S. government by "patriots." The entry for "August 1, 1993" describes in loving detail the Los Angeles streetscape after the Day of the Rope: miscegenating women hang "from tens of thousands of lampposts," their "grisly forms" hung with placards stating "I defiled my race." Just as I had never given out my last name when I volunteered as a rape counselor (rapists had deliberately targeted pioneering women in crisis centers), we decided, when we married, not to place announcements in newspapers. It was bad enough that my husband received hate mail at the University every time he gave an interview or published an op-ed piece.

But white Americans have been reading and hearing about the daily insults, discrimination, and dangers minority Americans face for three decades now. Unfortunately, no matter how many careful statistical studies of mortgage discrimination are published, no matter how many police beatings are videotaped, such publicity is mere sideshow to the main event in mass media and white public life since Reagan: the unremitting representation of black and brown violence, crime, laziness, and sexual profligacy. This discourse is our current national morality play, and it authorizes certain standard white scripts—scripts that are no less intensely felt at the grassroots for being written and disseminated from above. There are more or less genteel lines in our race play, dinner theater vs. soap opera versions, but they all tie directly into our new American orthodoxy, belief in an urban "underclass." This term has gained currency in both yellow journalism's accounts of inner-city "jungles" of drugs and crime and in the rarified reaches of quantitative social science. It's a grab-bag word with no fixed meaning. Writers have variously defined underclass membership in terms of residence (inner city), employment and housing status (illegal only; tenements, shelters, or the streets), reproductive status (illegitimate children, no attentive fathers), criminal status (non-white collar only), and drug use (preferably crack cocaine). Media stories abound of "wilding" youth, crack babies, shoot-outs in high schools, teenage drug dealers with gold chains, beepers, and BMWs; and the ubiquitous news standbys of whites mugged, raped, and killed by street criminals of color all conduce to our public sense of American cities as menaced by dark, savage hordes.

Writers explain the underclass according to political allegiance. Conservatives rely on the new scientific racism, proclaiming that black and brown Americans are culturally or even genetically inferior. They were "conditioned by 10,000 years of selective breeding for personal combat and the anti-work ethic of jungle freedoms," according to Marianne Mele Hall, the notorious Reagan administration appointee, and were therefore unfit for civic life. Great Society programs just "spoiled" them, encouraging a sense of entitlement that led to laziness, drug use, and crime, particularly crime against whites. Liberals focus on the deindustrialization of American cities, painting a historical picture of the simultaneous flight from inner cities of jobs for the unskilled and of middle-class minorities, leaving behind a jobless black and brown population with no role models to check irresponsible behavior. Both conservatives and liberals pat themselves on the back for their new "toughness" in admitting minorities' "moral failures" and encourage invidious comparisons with so-called model minorities. These are usually Asian Americans, but sometimes particular Hispanic populations such as Cubans (but not Puerto Ricans) and Mexicans (but only in Chicago, not California, where *they're* the underclass) will do.

Model minority rhetoric is actually a very old American movie script, produced each generation with new titles and character names. When I was an anthropologist among my own ethnic population in the 1970s, I discovered an entire scholarly literature purporting to investigate American economic mobility that was actually in the business of assigning ethnic report cards: Poles B-, Italians C+, Irish B+, Jews A-, etc. The grades differed according to the criteria used (including—surprise!—the ethnicity of the evaluator), but the key principles were constant: ethnic populations' differential economic statuses were solely due to their "culturally determined" differential behaviors. Sound familiar? The whole schmear, to stay in period, has simply been transposed from intrawhite ethnic to black versus Latino versus Asian. My people, in other words, used to be the underclass.

My family's history, in fact, helps to explain what the shift in blame-labeling really means, helps to answer the heartfelt we've-been-through-the-Depression white ethnic cry: Why can't they be like us?

Well, why can't they? What exactly are and were "we" like? Members of my father's family certainly suffered, worked hard, and were exploited on the road to social mobility. My grandparents were immigrant agricultural laborers and cannery workers in Northern California. Each of their eight children also worked in fields and canneries. The Depression transformed ordinary immigrant poverty into acute suffering. Children were pulled out of school and set to work or to mind even younger children. When they whined that they were hungry, my grandmother told them, with baleful realism, to "eat knuckles." There was an organizing drive and a strike at the cannery, and my grandfather crossed picket lines to bring home a meager salary. My teenage uncle Tony, the oldest son, unable to bear the severe work regimen imposed on him by his parents, ran away and went on the bum. Years later, my father looked up from the school playground to see his disheveled brother staring at him through the holes in the fence.

But then, like the twentieth-century god from a machine, came the war. The canneries went on overtime schedules to cope with government production demands, and there was abundant work for everyone. Even better, Hammond Aircraft in South San Francisco geared up for war construction, and my aunts Ann and Rosalie quit the cannery and took the commuter train daily from Sunnyvale. Yes, Rose (but never Rosie) was a riveter. Uncle Tony got work as a carpenter, was classified as part of essential war production, and spent the duration stateside. Uncle Sam enlisted in the Navy, and my father, trying to beat bad eyesight into the Air Force, went to Hawaii after Pearl Harbor to do construction work—the folklore was that Island physical standards were lower. He finally gave up and enlisted in the Army.

No one died, no one was even wounded. My father and uncle Sam were demobbed. Sam, married, with a son, got work as a car salesman. My father, who had desultorily attended San Jose State before the war (I've seen his transcript, which gives credence to all those tales of pool halls, reefer, and hitchhiking to San Francisco), moved back home and enrolled in a special University of Santa Clara combined A.B./law school program for returned vets. His law school class was a panoply of the Santa Clara County ethnic Catholic population—Irish, Italian, Eastern European, Spanish (but not Mexican; they were beyond the pale until the civil rights movement). He married my mother, who supported him by working as a department store buyer through the end of the program. My aunts, shut out of their high-paying wartime jobs, joined the burgeoning ranks of postwar women clericals. Lucille and Jeannie took advantage of the high quality, low-cost California junior college system to gain further business skills, and Rosalie, who had married a small businessman, took night school classes to become a bookkeeper.

Everyone married, everyone bought houses on the GI Bill, often in new developments around the Valley that one of my uncles, a contractor, helped to build. Most had children who, with the exception of Tony's parochial school phalanx, went to well-funded public schools. And, even with largely working-class careers, the Silicon Valley downturn, the national recession, four divorces, and two early widowhoods in the original sibling group, the entire family today is in relatively comfortable straits. Individuals are working toward or are on pensions. Houses are valued at up to twenty times their original prices. Two families have sold out and retired to cheaper Central Valley locations on the proceeds.

It's obvious that my kin benefited from the growing Santa Clara Valley economy from the 1940s on and from the formerly liberal California government, which took responsibility for maintaining public services and infrastructure—highways, public transportation, libraries, schools. I myself went to Berkeley as an undergraduate and graduate student, working my way through most of my graduate career and emerging debt free, thanks to then cheap rental housing and a tuition bill that today looks like the price of a loaf of bread. My father's legal career got an early boost precisely because the expansive postwar state government condemned vast tracts of farmland for roads and public buildings. Panicked immigrant farmers flocked to his office, where he adjusted them to the inevitability of losing their land, fought the state to jack up the selling price—and took a healthy cut for himself.

But we all profited in many other ways that aren't so obvious. Proposition 13, for example, was voted in just in time to roll back my relatives' property taxes—but after their children had benefited from good public schools. Now that cash-strapped California has pulled the plug on schools and whole districts have gone belly up, most of my cousins can afford to pay for private education for their children. And as California has gone, so has the nation. Buying into the housing market, relying on public transportation, getting unionized jobs with decent pension plans—it's all the same story. What was, is no longer. Those attempting to enter the mobility queue—not because they just got here but because they've been kept off until recently—just aren't facing the same circumstances. For many of them, it's as if the Depression never ended.

Well, and what if it hadn't?

If the Depression hadn't ended, if gnawing poverty, a sense that things might never get better, a feeling that they were appallingly low on the status hierarchy (the local WASP doctor forbade his daughter to date my father), had gone on year after year, a horrified social worker entering the Di Leonardo household would without doubt have certified it "underclass." After all, they were ten of them crowded into a three-bedroom house; they received government surplus food and clothing; children were both forced to work illegally and often left unsupervised. (During one afternoon my father persuaded my spunky Aunt Ann to climb into a spare tire and rolled her down a hill. Then there was the time that two of the aunts, little girls, were trying to cut a rock with a knife, and the knife slipped.) My grandfather drank home-made wine to excess and, in his frustration, beat his children. During one thrashing my father shouted, "But Pop, I didn't do anything!" "You will," was the grim reply. Nor was drug abuse confined to my grandfather. During another unsupervised lull, one of my aunts (who would not like to be named), a toddler, got into the wine cache. She was found later, drunk as a skunk, beating her round Di Leonardo skull against the wall and shouting, "My head is an egg and I can't break it."

These are the stories they tell around the dinner table, at rosaries and weddings and Christmas parties, with consummate narrative skill. I can see them: I'm in my teens and twenties, my father is still alive, and he and my uncles and aunts, one after the other, shout that no, that isn't the way it happened, you sit down and *I'll* tell it. Lovely Ann jumps up, her brown eyes sparkling with intelligence. How beautiful, how stylish, how witty they all are—and how much I love them. It is only years later that I realize how painful are the materials they have transformed rhetorically into affectionate familial humor.

But what about those current model minorities? Granted that my people (and, by extension, all working-class American white ethnics), after much suffering, got a well-deserved, government-funded leg up during and after the war—a leg that wasn't there for minorities. Granted that after years of interethnic comparisons, nobody much cares anymore whether Irish, Jews, Poles or Italians have higher median incomes, better families, or lower crime rates. Nor do scholars now glibly claim, as did Harvard historian Stephen Thernstrom in 1973, that Irish Americans "lacked any entrepreneurial tradition" or that Italian Americans lived in a subculture "that directed energies away from work." What about current groups, like Cubans and Koreans who, without extra help, seem to be such hard-working, prosperous good citizens? Isn't it true that they just have better cultures?

Well, no, it isn't true—unless "culture" means being floated upward on a tide of U.S. foreign policy dollars. Pre-Mariel Cuban migrants were the elite of that country, arriving with cash and cushy educational training; and, as Joan Didion and others have noted, were bankrolled at very high levels, as "anti-Castro activists," by the CIA. You can start a lot of small businesses from the CIA welfare rolls. Korea's "economic miracle" was stimulated by heavy American anticommunist military spending. Some of its beneficiaries, in terms both of excellent educations and pioneering grubstakes, have largely replaced American Jews in the inner-city small entrepreneur niche.

These considerations of access to cash and class background rarely occur to whites when they wave Asian, Cuban, and other groups' economic report cards in black, Puerto Rican, and Mexican faces. But equally important to our current morality play are presumptions about how American cities have declined, and about black and brown predilections to vice as the "urban underclass."

Underclass ideology, like all Big Lies, employs partial truths to propel its narrative. (The Nazis, after all, told the truth about German Jewish prominence in trade and finance. They simply failed to admit that anti-Semitic law and practice had squeezed Jews into those occupational niches.) It's certainly true that American urban areas and the United States as a whole have deindustrialized, that upwardly mobile minorities have dispersed from former ghettoes, and that unemployment, street crime, and female-headed households are more common in black and brown poor neighborhoods than elsewhere. But just exactly how did this state of affairs come to pass and what does it really mean? Here underclass writers fall back on those mainstays of the fuzzy-minded undergraduate, the use of passive verb forms and of reifications to avoid dealing with the complexities and stark politics of real human agents.

The wide array of postwar government subsidies that so coddled my relatives and other white Americans not only did not help minorities: they literally made things worse for them. The FHA deliberately fostered segregated white housing until the passage of the Fair Housing Act in 1968. Government subsidies for suburban infrastructures not only encouraged the often-remarked hemorrhage of higher-income taxpayers from cities but also drained infrastructure funding from urban areas. And then that much-heralded government infusion of cash, urban renewal, actually exchanged cheap housing for hospitals, sports arenas, and convention centers—all nice things to have, no doubt, but not if they put you out on the street. (Ninety percent of all the housing destroyed by urban renewal was never replaced, and two-thirds of those displaced were black or Hispanic.) The real estate speculation spiral of the 1970s and 1980s was the poison cherry on the arsenic cake for poor minorities' housing aspirations, pricing them out of the private housing market just as the federal government abandoned its commitment to the provision of low-cost housing. We white, middle-class Americans know what housing price inflation has meant in our lives—higher and higher shares of income siphoned off, being unable to buy a house or apartment, or becoming so ridiculously house-poor that you can't afford a meal out. Just imagine, then, what it has meant for those not only poor or working class but also minority, since it's well documented that high percentages of banks, landlords, and realtors still discriminate by race. My relatives had to endure a great deal in their youth, but never this particular combination of disastrous economic shift and overwhelming social bias.

It's the same story with jobs. Just as civil rights laws come into effect, boom, employers move good working-class jobs to the suburbs and abroad, unions lose ground and accept cutbacks and givebacks. And then schools: Jonathon Kozol points out that American schools are now more segregated—both by race and by resources—than they were in the 1960s. And of course higher education now costs much more and delivers less, in terms of position and salary, than it did thirty years ago. Even those minorities who persevere find their rewards appallingly low: black men with four years of college make, on average, the same salaries as white male high school graduates. Law firms hire very few blacks—or minorities, period. Even that bastion of political correctness, the American academy, provides little refuge. Disproving white male Ph.D.s whining about affirmative action candidates taking all their jobs, the proportion of all American professors who are black has risen only one-tenth of one percent since 1960.

All of these "statistical patterns" and "economic forces" are the results of hundreds of thousands of *intentional* decisions over time. Individuals and government agencies act both to exclude minorities and to defund public venues where they are concentrated. Against such overwhelming odds, a few years of half-hearted affirmative action has been just spitting into the wind. Black and brown comfort, convenience—lives themselves—just don't seem as valuable to whites. And they act accordingly, from the White House to the state house to the courthouse, townhouse, and tract house. But what about the argument that minorities have just brought discrimination on themselves by, in the black phrase, acting ugly? After all, aren't blacks and Hispanics simply more likely to have bad families, use drugs, commit crimes, be on welfare when they could be working?

The short, surprising answer is no. The longer answer engages our perceptions of social phenomena through class and racial lenses. Returning to my *paesani*: Progressive Era reformers, social scientists in the 1950s, even into the 1960s, perceived Italian American and other ethnic families as purely pathological. Edward Banfield dubbed the southern Italian *Weltanschauung* "amoral familism" and saw the contamination spreading in the United States. With the white ethnic movement of the 1970s, though, "ethnic families" were reworked in the public mind as warm, cozy, and close—as opposed to "disorganized" black families and "cold" WASP families with their newly absent "selfish, professional" feminist wives and mothers (never mind that white ethnic women were quite prominent among early feminists). So a great deal depends on spin, and the political power to enforce your spin on the public mind.

Our national family spin has undergone some instructive curlicues in the past two decades. In the 1970s we heard a great deal about the American family crisis: that turned out to be about rising divorce rates and women working outside the home. Although rightists still engage in some obligatory hand-wringing, American mass media have now accepted as *faits accompli*, the ubiquity of divorce and remarriage, blended families, and working mothers. Single motherhood, pioneered by entertainment figures, is also widely accepted, despite Dan Quayle—as long as the single mother is a white professional. Here we enter the two-tiered system: in other words, what's sauce for middle-class whites is not sauce for working-class and impoverished minorities. But as a public, we don't even have an accurate sense of what sauces we're judging. Most Americans, for example, believe that we are witnessing an "epidemic" of black teenage pregnancy and that women on welfare have many children, possibly to qualify for increased benefits. But black teenage birth rates have been have been going *down* for more than three decades, and the majority of women on welfare (who aren't black, anyway) have only one or two children, fewer than women *not* on welfare—not to mention that increased benefits wouldn't even keep you in diapers. It's true that black women tend to have their children at earlier ages than do whites, but University of Michigan public health professor Arline Geronimus has proven, through careful quantitative work, that having babies earlier doesn't make poor women poorer. In fact, given the accumulated physical stresses of extreme poverty, early childbearing may be better for the health of mother and child and takes advantage of grandmothers' energies before they become too rundown to help out. The point, one would hope, is to raise poor people out of poverty, not to prevent them from reproducing at all. There is overwhelming global demographic evidence, in any event, that raised standards of living, especially women's perceptions of rising social and economic opportunity, lead to later births and smaller families.

These are hard facts, but facts mean little in the face of race, class, and gender bias encouraged from the Oval Office on down. As well, we've been coached to deplore the minority female-headed family, the absent black father, and the drug-taking mother who endangers her fetus's health. But we're scapegoating minorities for being part of larger national trends. The number of *white* female-headed families is rising fast; large proportions of *white* men at all income levels (the higher the level, the higher the proportion) don't pay child support and abandon their children after divorce. And a recent study indicates that pregnant women of all races take drugs that may endanger their fetuses at the same rates, but doctors report black women to the authorities ten times more often than whites. In addition, black women are *less* likely than whites to smoke when pregnant. Even the image of the drug-taking, minority high school dropout is a lie: studies indicate that fewer black than white kids take drugs, and they have virtually the same high school graduation rates.

What really is true is that most minorities are much poorer than most whites—kept poorer by the concatenation of tens of thousands of individual white actions that maintain the condition despite often valiant efforts to escape. And it's also true that poverty encourages family discord and channels criminal tendencies toward the street. You don't get many chances to run million-dollar white-collar scams from the projects.

Finally, it's really true that many American teenagers of all races and economic statuses are disappointing human beings. But they are so for particular, societywide reasons. They've come of age in the "mean season"—an era of rightist reaction, income bifurcation, and political demobilization—and they're frustrated, angry, and often dumb with it. Every cohort matures physically at a slightly earlier age, is even less able to handle adult responsibilities, and is subject to an even greater mass advertising onslaught. Many want the expensive commodities that are deliberately targeted at them, and if their parents can't buy them, some proportion of kids will steal or rob to get them. (Mercer Sullivan documents, in a New York study, a cohort of working-class white boys who regularly mugged the most vulnerable group in their neighborhood: recent Polish immigrants stumbling out of local bars on weekends.) Antifeminist backlash has hit them hard, and too many adolescent boys of all races and classes identify successful masculinity with exploitation of and contempt for girls and women. You didn't like 2 Live Crew? Try Guns 'N' Roses, a phenomenally popular white metal band with explicitly sexist, racist, and homophobic lyrics. From an adult perspective, a significant proportion of all adolescents today are Martians. They wear funny clothes, they like terrible music, they're loud, stupid, vulgar, and disrespectful. The real question is: whose Martians are they? Journalist Ken Auletta claimed that one indication of the existence of a minority underclass was the propensity of adolescents to "walk five abreast . . . seemingly unaware that they are monopolizing the sidewalk." But Yale undergraduates used to shove me right into the gutter with great regularity. Now I'm at Northwestern, where the scrubbed-face, corn-fed students bike and rollerblade on sidewalks all over town, cannoning into the local elderly so often that there is talk of outlawing them (the kids, not the elderly) within a defensive perimeter. But no one claims that elite college students exhibit savage behavior and need (either or both) special role models or preventive detention. We just don't perceive "our" Martians the way we perceive "theirs."

It's not only a matter of perception, but of resources. Affluent white families are able to spread a class net under their deviant, self-destructive, criminally inclined, or just plain dull offspring. Fat camps, computer camps; military schools; high-class drug rehab; hospitalization for anorexia and bulimia; SAT, GRE, LSAT, and MCAT courses; lawyers who swing parole; fines and community service instead of jail time for their clients; entrance to colleges by virtue of family alumni and donations instead of accomplishments—need I go on? I have a file of newspaper wedding announcements detailing the strength of the upper-class safety net: children who clearly didn't even manage to graduate from some fifth-rate school, whose parents then ensconced them in family business sinecures or bought them horse farms or antique stores to run.

My own early inadvertent trampolining on the class net gave me a palpable sense of its resilience. It was 1965. I was fifteen, intellectual, antiwar, rebellious, cloistered by parental strictures and dull suburban residence. My friend Nina, doyenne of the local Unitarian youth group, invited me to an exciting party for local SNCC workers. Since my parents would never have allowed me to attend, we arranged a "sleepover." The party was a bust: the SNCC-ers looked down their elderly interracial activist noses at us. All the kids with cars left early, and the rest were stranded miles from our homes. One boy with a motorcycle set off to ferry one kid home, intending to come back for the rest of us in turn. The cops caught us waiting on the street, enjoyed themselves in elaborate insults of our hippie appearance, and carted us off to the Campbell police station. Terrified of my parents' reaction, I gave a false name and a friend's phone number, hoping that his mother would rescue me. But then not trusting to fate, I determined to try to rescue myself. We'd been dumped, unsupervised, in a waiting room while the cops went off to phone. I got up and tried the door. Unlocked. I flew like a bird from a cage, and began a five-hour trek home, through backyards and side streets (I found out later the entire town force was out in full cry after me), steering by hit-and-miss, asking directions once from a man lying under his car doing a night-owl repair job and once from a Chinese newsboy who lectured me on the grid layout of American streets. At dawn I triumphantly let myself into my parents' home, well prepared with a cover story. My father appeared, tousled and haggard, in the hallway. "So. You really made the festa, eh?" My friends had given me up. The cops were on the way.

Then ensued the requisite conference during which the police decided to take me to juvenile hall and charge me. Halfway there one cop turned around in the seat to say, with the consummate *Schadenfreude* I've come to associate with *Vanity Fair*, "So your parents may have a big house but you're going to juvey anyway." He was wrong. Rich kids can even get away with pissing off the cops. My father had me sprung by noon.

I am arguing for a class and race corrective to our tendency to see the minority poor and working class as profoundly different beings from our white middle-class selves, as not quite equal citizens, as people who must behave better than the rest of us just to escape censure. I am *not* saying that we should "excuse and coddle" criminals. I've lived in liberal and leftist circles for more than two decades, and never yet have I heard anyone say that robbers, rapists, and murderers shouldn't be jailed. Given an adequate weapon at the time, I would cheerfully have killed my rapist. I even become furious with litterers and have been known to slam the occasional umbrella down on the hoods of cars stopped in pedestrian crosswalks. What I have heard, and what I know to be true on the basis of scholarship—as well as common sense—is that highly stratified economic and political structures give rise to high levels of property crime. Change those structures and you can reduce that crime, just as gun control would slash the murder rate, just as genuine equality for women would reduce incidents of rape and battery—just as real oversight could have prevented the already wealthy from ripping us all off in the S&L, BCCI, HUD, and Wall Street frauds. While the corner mugger is terrifying and may physically harm us, white collar criminals are just as common, and their financial damage to the commonweal is many orders of magnitude greater. Doctors run Medicare mills; scientists fake their data; lawyers bilk old ladies; insurers transfer annuities to companies that go bankrupt, erasing thousands of people's pensions; car dealers defraud manufacturers and customers, and the literate general public is mutilating precious public library books for profit at crisis rates. So who's acting ugly?

We're so accustomed, though, to public sneering against "knee-jerk" liberals that we need to change venue to tell the story straight. Imagine yourself in Victorian London, a city of grotesque poverty and shameless wealth. Vast armies of prostitutes promenade the streets, alarming the wives and daughters of the bourgeoisie. Public drunkenness—of men and women, even of children— is common, and street crime so ubiquitous that, according to *London Labor and the London Poor* chronicler Henry Mayhew, individuals specialize in stealing and ransoming the dogs of the wealthy, in "child-stripping" (as Dickens's sinister Mrs. Brown does to Florence Dombey), in removing lead from housetops, in stealing handkerchiefs and brooches, and in throwing coal off river barges to be retrieved from the mud.

The immigrant Irish bulk large among the poor and criminal, thus seeming to legitimize theories of their racial inferiority. Prominent, progressive-seeming Victorian writers are as vilely racist toward them as are *soi-disant* liberals toward the black and brown poor today. Thackeray asked, "Have they nothing else to do—or is it that they *will* do nothing but starve, swagger and be idle in the streets?" Arthur Young wrote that Irish prefer "drinking, wrangling, quarreling, fighting, ravishing, etc." Disraeli himself wrote in *The Times* of London that "this wild, reckless, indolent, uncertain and superstitious race have no sympathy with the English character. Their fair ideal of human felicity is an alternation of clannish broils and coarse idolatry."

Sound familiar? Equally familiar is the common bourgeois analysis of the situation: the poor were "demoralized" by charity, which should be ended to force them to toil honestly, and greatly needed the renewed proximity, as behavioral models, of "residents of a better class." But with historical hindsight, we know that economic growth, rising real wages, and the Labour government's provision of subsidized housing, health care, and education swept away all these "moral failings"—until Thatcher re-created them with widespread poverty and homelessness in the 1980s. A similar story with more complicated demographics can be told about the white poor in the United States in the same eras. How then can we be so criminally callous as to mouth the cruel, self-righteous, and empirically bankrupt language of the Victorian victim-blamers?

Another clarifying mode of approach, one that makes use of living memory rather than historical research, is the analogy between race and gender bias. Now the race/gender analogy (likening women to oppressed minorities) is, as I frequently warn students, inherently limited and dangerous. If women are like blacks, then who the hell are black women? Most women live intimately with men; native-born racial minorities, now that they are rarely servants, are largely domestically segregated from whites. And so on. But like chemotherapy, the race/gender analogy may be poison but can be used therapeutically when there's a cancer on the body politic.

The year 1970 was a heady one for American feminism but not for me, child bride to a much older professor, desperately trying to ape her sophisticated elders. It's time for after-dinner conversation at a Berkeley hills dinner party. Our hosts are urbane belletrists; our fellow guests, an up-and-coming liberal historian and his nonworking wife. The historian expresses himself firmly on the subject of "women's lib": how ridiculous! Our host supports him: when we observe "those women in supermarkets"—dull creatures waddling up the aisles with screaming babies and piled carts—how can we imagine that they have intellectual potential?

Later that evening the historian's wife takes me aside to explain, with tears in her eyes, that she can't possibly go back to school or to work for some years to come. She can't trust her husband not to beat the children in her absence.

How hard can it be to see the analogy? Just as our host despised those fat housewives for not having his class and gender privilege, too many whites and upper-status minorities despise poor black and brown people for not already having been born into middle-class households. Beneath many a waddling housewife's carapace was (and is) the potential to become a doctor, a lawyer, a corporate chief—even without losing weight. Why do we so often assume that Shandra and Tyrone, Isabel and Hector from the projects haven't the same potential? Just as only some women have yet been able to benefit economically from feminist reforms, just as it's clear we're in the middle of a serious gender backlash, so for only a minority of minorities is "equality of opportunity" anything more than a sick joke.

Finally, those bombastic alpha males at the dinner party fully included the females around the table in their contempt for the housewife in the supermarket. We may not have waddled, but we were expected to quack with the rest of the ducks. No more. We know that women vary among themselves as much as they differ from men. Women are serial murderers, child torturers, thieves like Leona Helmsley—and I don't hang my head in shame. In the 1970s, one of my working-class paesans said, "Oh when I read about a criminal, I just pray that his name doesn't end in an e, o, i, or a." But in the 1990s, Italian Americans don't feel soiled by John Gotti's existence. No, that uneasy stance has been bequeathed to blacks and some Latins. When will we progress sufficiently that we don't identify far-flung, variegated minority populations as if they were tiny, homogeneous units?

There is another, more benign, but no less wrong, interpretation of racial minority lives—the contention of "cultural difference." Proponents, especially those concerned with educational issues, adjure us to understand that poor blacks in particular don't think, don't talk, don't behave the same as the rest of us and need special coaching toward assimilation. Or perhaps we need special coaching to be "sensitive." Now, I'm an anthropologist, and my guild *owns* culture; we invented the damned term. But it's become a Frankenstein monster, rampaging across the landscape of national life. Sure, poor minorities are culturally different from whites; but they're also culturally different from each other, and whites are culturally divided too. On the one hand, we're all Americans, we all watch television, we all know who Madonna is. On the other hand, we live in different regions of a large, sprawling country, and we associate with one another along lines of class, race, gender and sexual preference. Have you made a catalogue phone order recently? Chances are you talked to a white Southern woman (the companies can hire them cheaply). If you aren't Southern yourself, you probably found her a little hard to understand. But did you think, "Boy, does she need to assimilate to the rest of us"? No, you probably thought she had a cute accent, reminiscent of mint juleps. Region counts. Outerborough Jews and Italians sound more like outerborough blacks and Puerto Ricans (hey, just listen to Rosie Perez) than like white Chicagoans. White Texans sound more like black Texans than like white Iowans. Social status counts even more. You can buy your way up from "dirty Spic" to "charming Spanish gentleman." Most of all, though, what counts is whether individuals *want* to understand one another, see a benefit in putting effort into it, feel a likeness to one another. Want to, or are forced to. Some anthropologists taped an argument between two black adolescent boys in the early 1970s, just at the point of militant switchover from Negro to black. One boy kept repeating, "I'm not black, I'm reddish brown." His frustrated interlocutor finally invoked the bottom line: "Inna white man's eyes you black."

And that's it. The real key to the perception of cultural difference is politics. If populations wish to see themselves as alike because of a common experience of discrimination—or a common perception of group superiority—they will do so. No matter how much effort it takes, they will learn to move their bodies, their tongues, their brains in new ways, all the while protesting that they have always been thus. Or, of course, they can simply ignore the palpable differences among themselves and proclaim a "common culture."

But if we wish to see a population as distinct from ourselves, we will complain bitterly that we don't understand them and demand that "they" assimilate to some television ideal of middle-class whiteness. So the one cultural marker all black Americans have in common is not "black English," not signifying, not rapping, but the frustrated knowledge that whites think they're inferior.

In the early 1960s, my father told me with great emphasis of a local white attorney known for civil rights work who happened to be mugged and beaten by blacks. At the hospital, the press moved in like sharks, gleefully asking him how he felt now, after being attacked by "those people." With great, dignified contempt, the lawyer enunciated through his wired jaw, "It wasn't a feast of giggles." Nothing much nowadays is a feast of giggles, and what we all need is that attorney's ability *not* to be the "liberal who got mugged," his ability to distinguish between individual experience and larger social realities. We need not to romanticize, not to play down, not even to forgive street crime, but to speak honestly about and act strongly against the criminals who segregate and further impoverish minorities and so set the stage for street crime—in our names, and with our tax dollars.

I've offered up the multiple facets of a personal hologram, different triangulations of race, class, and gender from the 1930s to the present, from California to Connecticut and points in between. But frankly, to my mind, autobiography is really just *shtick*. You could be a white male: you could grow up in Alaska, North Dakota, or Vermont; you could have dated only whites with last names like Jones or Smith; you could be nearly albino yourself; and still grasp the nonreality of the "underclass," still send back the poisoned courses of our national race supper. All that's necessary is to overcome our collective bad faith, to admit, in detail and with the political will to change, how public policy coddles whites and squeezes minorities. Part of that admission involves giving up our two-tiered sexism, part of it mandates understanding the paradox of race as simultaneously real and socially constructed, part of it turns on how thoroughly government—whether under Democratic or Republican hegemony—shapes all of our social and economic lives.

My father used to tell a wonderful dialect joke in which the paesan faces the judge in the courtroom: "Ajudge-a, I beena here thirty year now, my children they tell me I got to getta the citizenashippa. I know George Washington-a, I lovva this country, but I can no spikka the English too good. I don know if I can passa the test." And the judge leans down from the bench and says, "Don ju worry. In thissa court, you gonna get your citizenashippa."

In a very real sense, the minority poor haven't yet gotten their citizenship. But to what court can we turn in these parlous times?

POSTSCRIPT, 1996

A whimsical greeting card from the 1970s declares "Things are getting worse," and opens to the request, "Please send chocolate." In the four years since this piece was published, things have indeed gotten worse: American incomes have become more unequal, the poor are poorer, government is doing less than ever to achieve equal rights, and "common sense," as evidenced by media clichés and politicians' statements, is more overwhelmingly reflexively racist, sexist, and mean spirited than at any time since the 1960s. Obviously bogus notions that have been repeatedly disproven—such as *The Bell Curve*'s claims of race-linked intelligence—receive vast media attention; while heartbreaking, government- and elite-caused inequities—such as widespread homelessness and unemployment—continue to be ignored or attributed to the actions of their victims. No amount of chocolate could recompense this mean season.

These appalling developments are connected to shifts in what the late Marxist literary critic Raymond Williams called "structures of feeling"—embodied ideas, intellectualized emotions that powerfully frame the ways in which we collectively apprehend human social reality. Our American structures of feeling, in the face of two decades' unremitting war against the poor, are characterized by "compassion fatigue"—a collective weariness of, a desire to avoid taking responsibility for rising human misery in our rich country and abroad. But compassion fatigue arises in particular in boomerang response to the false framing of "compassion" itself as the appropriate response to poverty and unequal opportunity. There is nothing wrong—indeed, there is a great deal right—with feeling empathy with the poor and a desire to do individual good works to ameliorate their lot. But the actions of individuals, in the long run, cannot even begin to overturn the governmental creation and enhancement of poverty. Only forcing government to change its labor, finance, housing, and social welfare policies can reverse our country's production of poverty. Moreover, compassion depends too much, in our cultural context, on the notion of "innocent" victims—on morality plays—rather than on clear thinking about historical shifts and relations among law, finance, real estate, and labor, and their effects on aggregated individuals, whether or they seem as cuddly, as innocent, as dolphins or baby seals.

This confusion of responses to individuals and to media stereotypes—the gangbanger, the minority male rapist, the pregnant crack addict, and the "good" white ethnics of the past who were never feckless or criminal and "made it with no help"—with real social analysis, a genuine consideration of the political economy of race, ethnicity, and gender in the past and present United States, was the impetus for my piece. It struck a chord in readers, and *The Village Voice* was flooded with requests to duplicate it for course and organizing use. Many individuals wrote me personal responses. The most affecting was from a progressive woman whose parents were immigrants from Eastern Europe:

I am 75 now. (yes, 75 yrs.) And, I see a society that has turned its back on understanding others. That is not their interest. All we hear is the rhetoric of anger, hate, excuses and rationale. . . .

I trained to teach deaf children (at Columbia Univ.) My first job was at Maryland School for the Blind, a residential school for blind and deaf children. But when I got there I discovered the black blind and black deaf children were housed in the back—in old, dilapidated buildings, far from the beautiful grounds, far from the white blind children—up front. I taught the black deaf children. The heat was turned off at 10 PM. . . .

As a result [of the witch-hunts of McCarthyism in the 1950s] we have people who are ignorant, misinformed, dis-connected, and victimized. They are constantly manipulated—by the media, by politicians, by so-called leaders. And, they applaud automatically to the rhetoric of "patriotism," "violence," and any other weapons.

What a waste.

Interesting and instructive as well, though, were the negative responses, particularly the white racist mail. A Louisiana man wrote that I had "studied too many books filled with distortions," and

I felt sorry for her . . . such as her prejudice towards people of the South . . . and her warped views of society when it comes to the police, welfare, and racial attitudes of America. It was obvious she has no knowledge of what goes on in the Deep South . . . especially Louisiana.

He went on to laud former Ku Klux Klan leader David Duke's "messages about crime, welfare, and high taxes," while expressing dislike for Duke the person.

An anonymous, handwritten letter extraordinarily exemplifies the frame of mind I wrote against:

I hope I can enlighten you on few things that for all your rhetoric and statistics, you seem to overlook or are unwilling to see . . .

What New York blacks especially fail to understand is that unfortunately human nature goes by one bad apple spoils the whole bunch. I personally believe that anyone who is willing to commit to education and perseverance can achieve their goals no matter what their problems or race.

Also, I think you should be ashamed for degrading your race when we have taken responsibility for the wrongs our ancestors (*not us*) committed. The entire white race is not responsible for the fear blacks have *earned* or for the few misguided white bigots who have commited racial crimes. Inspite of that or the statistics anyone quotes, we all know the truth and see everyday that the largest crimes statistics are black on black or black on white. I suggest you remember that the next time you write an article based on half-truths and personal bias . . .

A Concerned Queens Woman

Note that both texts misstate the article's arguments; ignore all the historical material, the race/gender analogy, all considerations of governmental policy (except the man's tossed-off reference to "police and welfare"), and my clear anticrime stance. They attribute my perspective, which they misrepresent as "anti-South" and "antiwhite," either to "books filled with distortions" or to a personal relationship. The "Queens Woman," in her indignation at my degrading my race, fails to notice that the piece is a paean to my dead father, who was most certainly white. Both writers exhibit a deep refusal to credit scholarly work, a kind of militant anti-intellectualism that allows individuals to imagine that political notions need not be justified with reference to the real world beyond personal anecdote. This is even more ironic, given my emphatic and repeated point that I was using the memoir form only to lend emotional force to facts and analysis that might otherwise be ignored as boring.

But this anti-intellectualism is not limited to white racists (who often, of course, appear more "genteel" and "intelligent" than these letter writers); it is also characteristic of black nationalist apprehensions of social reality. A black woman journalist wrote the *Voice* (and I excerpt according to "fair use" provisions):

I'm not an honorary black person. I'm a real one. Therefore, I have very little patience with people like di Leonardo who feel that they know what our problems are, and how to deal with them. Black people have a historical problem with white people attempting to define them and telling them what to do. . . . We already have to deal with racism. Add white paternalism to that and it's no wonder we can't get together among ourselves and work it out.

I responded:

[This woman] "read" my race and marital status, not my article, which had nothing to do with guilt, paternalism, or "telling blacks what to do." She seems unconcerned with my main theme, minority poverty and the race- and gender-biased policies that have created and maintain it. "Real black people" like Clarence Thomas, Thomas Sowell, Louis Sullivan, Glenn Loury, Shelby Steele, Stephen Carter, and Samuel Pierce have participated enthusiastically in constructing "spinning," and enforcing those policies. You can't just read out from appearance to politics. And denying whites the right to speak out against racism just lets them off the hook.

I wrote, of course, about "honorary blackness" and "passing" for rhetorical effect, not to "co-opt" black culture—an entity whose homogeneity I took pains to disprove. (And many black readers wrote to thank me for the article; I was even invited to appear on Black Entertainment Television.) But I think a larger issue is being joined here, in all three letters, one that also surfaced in friends' reports on some classroom responses to the piece. That issue is the triumph of identity politics in American public culture, of mistaken notions of the literal embodiment of truth.

Identity politics, or the appropriateness of "speaking from experience," without reference beyond the self, as a woman or man, gay or straight or bisexual, black or Latino or Asian or other minority, has become ubiquitous in American life over the past two decades. It derives from the obviously democratic impulse to credit "voices" that had theretofore not been heard in public culture, as well as from the phenomenological insight that knowledge itself is intersubjective—produced through affect-laden human interactions, apprehended differently depending on individuals' social locations and varying social situations.

But the problems with identity politics are manifold. Many critics have pointed out the ways in which it elides class differences and thus allows self-interested conservative members of particular populations to dominate the airwaves, claiming to "speak for" all blacks or all gays or all women, and so on, while ignoring those who are working class or impoverished except to adjure them to pull themselves up by their bootstraps. It is also anti-intellectual, participating in the historical amnesia of American public culture concerning earlier, strongly felt "identities"—such as union membership—for which millions fought and died. It denies the need to, even the possibility of getting beyond the self, of considering aggregate human behavior, capital flows, governmental policies and their entailments. It thus truly assumes a Tower of Babel in which groups can never communicate or act beyond their "primary identities."

And finally, identity politics is always doomed to failure both because it denies the need to organize nonmembers for particular political goals, and because of its essentialism, its falsification, oversimplification of the workings of identity even in the present. Barbara Epstein has tellingly noted that "a politics of identity encounters not only the problem of the fragility of particular categories of identity, but the fact that everyone occupies various categories at once. One may be female and white, or black but male; virtually everyone is vulnerable to some charge of privilege." Identity politics, we might say, assumes an oversimplified body, one that can be socially marked in only one way. This is not how human beings live or ever have lived.

The real key here is our willingness to think about how our socially marked bodies intersect with the rest of the material world, how they are differentially housed, fed, employed, educated: about economic functioning, government policy, institutional structures, and aggregate human social behavior. The only way to construct and test arguments about these phenomena—phenomena that channel all our personal experiences—is to learn enough about them so that we can newly see the ways in which they determine the built environments in which we operate and channel our varying opportunities and constraints, the differing trajectories of our daily lives. For this reason, and to give readers access to the sources of all my specific claims, I offer below a list of books and articles on the topics about which I wrote.

Selected Readings

On white ethnicity, underclass ideology, and actual political economy, see: Stephen Steinberg, *The Ethnic Myth: Race, Ethnicity and Class in America* (Boston: Beacon Press, 2d ed., 1981); Micaela di Leonardo, *The Varieties of Ethnic Experience: Kinship, Class and Gender Among Northern California Italian-Americans* (Ithaca, NY: Cornell University Press, 1984); Adolph L. Reed Jr., "The Underclass as Myth and Symbol: The Poverty of Discourse about Poverty," *Radical America* vol. 24 (January 1992): 21–40; Michael Katz, *In the Shadow of the Poorhouse: A Social History of Welfare in America* (New York: Basic Books, 1986), and *The "Underclass" Debate: Views From History* (Princeton: Princeton University Press, 1993); Frank Levy, *Dollars and Dreams: The Changing American Income Distribution* (New York: Norton, 1988); Frances Piven and Richard Cloward, *The New Class War: Reagan's Attack on the Welfare State and Its Consequences* (New York: Pantheon, 1982); Fred Block et al., eds., *The Mean Season: The Attack on the Welfare State* (New York: Pantheon, 1987); Holly Sklar, *Chaos or Community? Seeking Solutions, Not Scapegoats, for Bad Economics* (Boston: South End Press, 1995).

For careful treatments of crime, drugs, race, and youth, see: Mercer Sullivan, *"Getting Paid:" Youth Crime and Work in the Inner City* (Ithaca, NY: Cornell University Press, 1989); Elliot Currie, *Reckoning: Drugs, the Cities, and the American Future* (New York: Hill and Wang, 1993); United States General Accounting Office, "Teenage Drug Use: Uncertain Linkages with Either Pregnancy or School Dropout" (Washington, DC: U.S. Government Printing Office, 1991).

On the urban renewal debacle, past and present segregated housing, segregated and unequal education today, and the political economy of American cities, see: Martin Anderson, *The Federal Bulldozer* (Cambridge: MIT Press, 1962); Dennis Judd, *Politics of American Cities* (New York: Scott, Foresman, 1988); Thomas Lee Philpott, *The Slum and the Ghetto: Neighborhood Deterioration and Middle-Class Reform, Chicago, 1880–1930* (New York: Oxford University Press, 1978); Arnold Hirsch, *Making the Second Ghetto: Race and Housing in Chicago, 1940–1960* (Cambridge: Cambridge University Press, 1983); Susan and Norman Fainstein, eds., *Restructuring the City: The Political Economy of Urban Development* (New York: Longman, 1983); Douglas S. Massey and Nancy Denton, *American Apartheid: Segregation and the Making of the Underclass* (Cambridge: Harvard University Press, 1992); Michael Quint, "Racial Gap Found on Mortgages: Loan-Denial Rate Said to Be Double for Minorities," *New York Times*, October 22, 1993; Jonathon Kozol, *Savage Inequalities: Children in America's Schools* (New York: Crown, 1991); John R. Logan and Harvey Molotch, *Urban Fortunes: The Political Economy of Place* (Berkeley: University of California Press, 1978).

On women, race, reproduction and welfare, see: Arline Geronimus and Sanders Korenman, "The Socioeconomic Consequences of Teen Childbearing Reconsidered," *Quarterly Journal of Economics* (Vol. 107, November 1992); Arline Geronimus, "Maternal Youth or Family Background? Preliminary Findings on the Health Disadvantages of Infants with Teenage Mothers," Research Report no.91–204, Population Studies Center, University of Michigan, 1991; Linda Gordon, ed., *Women, the State, and Welfare* (Madison: University of Wisconsin Press, 1990); Virginia Morris, "Docs Let Pregnant Whites Off the Drug Hook," *New Haven Register*, April 26, 1990; Molly McNulty, "Pregnancy Police: The Health Policy and Legal Implications of Punishing Pregnant Women for Harm to Their Fetuses," *Review of Law and Social Change*, vol. 16, no. 2 (1987–88); Rickie Solinger, *Wake Up Little Susie: Single Pregnancy and Race before Roe vs. Wade* (New York: Routledge, 1992); Jill Quadagno, *The Color of Welfare: How Racism Undermined the War on Poverty* (New York: Oxford University Press, 1992).

On false notions of "traditional" American families, and accurate narratives of American family history, see: Steven Mintz and Susan Kellogg, *Domestic Revolutions: A Social History of American Family Life* (New York: Free Press, 1988); Stephanie Coontz, *The Way We Never Were: American Families and the Nostalgia Trap* (New York: Basic Books, 1992); Barrie Thorne and Marilyn Yalom, *Rethinking the Family: Some Feminist Questions*, rev. ed., (Boston: Northeastern University Press, 1992).

On race, class, and sexual violence against women, see: Diana Russell, *The Politics of Rape: The Victim's Perspective* (New York: Stein and Day, 1975), and *Sexual Exploitation: Rape, Child Sexual Abuse, and Workplace Harassment* (Beverly Hills: Sage, 1984); Micaela di Leonardo, "The Political Economy of Street Harassment," *Aegis* (Summer 1981); Brett Williams, "Babies and Banks: The 'Reproductive Underclass' and the Raced, Gendered Masking of Debt," in Steven Gregory and Roger Sanjek, eds., *Race* (New Brunswick, NJ: Rutgers University Press, 1994). On the new racist Right, see Elinor Langer, "The American Neo-Nazi Movement Today," *The Nation*, July 16/23, 1990.

For accounts of Victorian parallels to the present and British racism against the Irish, see: my preface to the reissue of Jack London's 1903 *People of the Abyss* (New York: Lawrence Hill, 1995); L. P. Curtis, *Anglo-Saxon and Celt* (New York: New York University Press, 1968).

Finally, for insightful commentary on identity politics, multiculturalism and the New Right, see: Pat Aufderheide, ed., *Beyond PC: Toward a Politics of Understanding* (St. Paul, MN: Greywolf Press, 1992) (Barbara Epstein's article is in this book); Micaela di Leonardo, "White Ethnicities, Identity Politics, and Baby Bear's Chair," *Social Text*, no. 41 (1994); Ellen Messer-Davidow, "Manufacturing the Attack on Liberalized Higher Education, *Social Text*, no. 36 (1993); William Roseberry, "Multiculturalism and the Challenge of Anthropology," *Social Research*, vol. 59, no. 4 (1992).

Part Two

MODES
OF REPRODUCTION
Kinship, Parenthood,
States

4   Is There a Family?

New Anthropological Views

Jane Collier, Michelle Z. Rosaldo, Sylvia Yanagisako

This essay poses a rhetorical question in order to argue that most of our talk about families is clouded by unexplored notions of what families "really" are like. It is probably the case, universally, that people expect to have special connections with their genealogically closest relations. But a knowledge of genealogy does not in itself promote understanding of what these special ties are about. The real importance of The Family in contemporary social life and belief has blinded us to its dynamics. Confusing ideal with reality, we fail to appreciate the deep significance of what are, cross-culturally, various ideologies of intimate relationship, and at the same time we fail to reckon with the complex human bonds and experiences all too comfortably sheltered by a faith in the "natural" source of a "nurture" we think is found in the home.

This essay is divided into three parts. The first examines what social scientists mean by The Family. It focuses on the work of Bronislaw Malinowski, the anthropologist who first convinced social scientists that The Family was a universal human institution. The second part also has social scientists as its focus, but it examines works by the nineteenth-century thinkers Malinowski refuted, for if—as we shall argue—Malinowski was wrong in viewing The Family as a universal human institution, it becomes important to explore the work of theorists who did not make Malinowski's mistakes. The final section then draws on the correct insights of nineteenth-century theorists to sketch some implications of viewing The Family not as a concrete institution designed to fulfill universal human needs, but as an ideological construct associated with the modern state.

Jane F. Collier is Professor of Anthropology at Stanford University. Much of her work focuses on the relationship of gender inequality to other forms of social inequality. She has written about gender asymmetry in so-called classless societies and is currently completing a book on family change in a Spanish village.

Michelle Zimbalist Rosaldo was Associate Professor of Anthropology at Stanford University. Before her untimely death in 1981, she co-edited *Woman, Culture, and Society* with Louise Lamphere (Stanford, 1974) and authored *Knowledge and Passion: Ilongot Notions of Self and Social Life* (Cambridge, 1980).

Sylvia Yanagisako is Professor of Anthropology at Stanford University. She is the author of *Transforming the Past: Kinship and Tradition among Japanese Americans* (Stanford, 1985), as well as numerous articles on kinship and gender. She is coeditor with Jane Collier of the collection *Gender and Kinship: Essays Toward a Unified Analysis* (Stanford, 1987) and with Carol Delaney of the collection *Naturalizing Power: Essays in Feminist Cultural Analysis* (Routledge, 1994). She is currently writing a book on family firms in the silk industry of northern Italy.

MALINOWSKI'S CONCEPT OF THE FAMILY

In 1913 Bronislaw Malinowski published a book called *The Family Among the Australian Aborigines*[1] in which he laid to rest earlier debates about whether all human societies had families. During the nineteenth century, proponents of social evolution argued that primitives were sexually promiscuous and therefore incapable of having families because children would not recognize their fathers.[2] Malinowski refuted this notion by showing that Australian aborigines, who were widely believed to practice "primitive promiscuity," not only had rules regulating who might have intercourse with whom during sexual orgies but also differentiated between legal marriages and casual unions. Malinowski thus "proved" that Australian aborigines had marriage, and so proved that aboriginal children had fathers, because each child's mother had but a single, recognized husband.

Malinowski's book did not simply add data to one side of an ongoing debate. It ended the debate altogether, for by distinguishing coitus from conjugal relationships, Malinowski separated questions of sexual behavior from questions of the family's universal existence. Evidence of sexual promiscuity was henceforth irrelevant for deciding whether families existed. Moreover, Malinowski argued that the conjugal relationship, and therefore The Family, had to be universal because it fulfilled a universal human need. As he wrote in a posthumously published book:

> The human infant needs parental protection for a much longer period than does the young of even the highest anthropoid apes. Hence, no culture could endure in which the act of reproduction, that is, mating, pregnancy, and childbirth, was not linked up with the fact of legally-founded parenthood, that is, a relationship in which the father and mother have to look after the children for a long period, and, in turn, derive certain benefits from the care and trouble taken.[3]

In proving the existence of families among Australian aborigines, Malinowski described three features of families that he believed flowed from The Family's universal function of nurturing children. First, he argued that families had to have clear boundaries, for if families were to perform the vital function of nurturing young children, insiders had to be distinguishable from outsiders so that everyone could know which adults were responsible for the care of which children. Malinowski thus argued that families formed bounded social units, and to prove that Australian families formed such units, he demonstrated that aboriginal parents and children recognized one another. Each aboriginal woman had a single husband, even if some husbands had more than one wife and even if husbands occasionally allowed wives to sleep with other men during tribal ceremonies. Malinowski thus proved that each aboriginal child had a recognized mother and father, even if both parents occasionally engaged in sexual relations with outsiders.

Second, Malinowski argued that families had to have a place where family members could be together and where the daily tasks associated with child rearing could be performed. He demonstrated, for example, that aboriginal parents and their immature children shared a single fire—a home and hearth where children were fed and nurtured—even though, among nomadic aborigines, the fire might be kindled in a different location each night.

Finally, Malinowski argued that family members felt affection for one another—that parents who invested long years in caring for children were rewarded by their own and their children's affections for one another. Malinowski felt that long and intimate association among family members fostered close emotional ties, particularly between parents and children, but also between spouses. Aboriginal parents and their children, for example, could be expected to feel the same emotions for one another as did English parents and children, and as proof of this point, Malinowski recounted touching stories of the efforts made by aboriginal parents to recover children lost during conflicts with other aborigines or with white settlers and efforts made by stolen aboriginal children to find their lost parents.

Malinowski's book on Australian aborigines thus gave social scientists a concept of The Family that consisted of a universal function, the nurturance of young children, mapped onto (1) a bounded set of people who recognized one another and who were distinguishable from other like groups; (2) a definite physical space, a hearth and home; and (3) a particular set of emotions, family love. This concept of The Family as an institution for nurturing young children has been enduring, probably because nurturing children is thought to be the primary function of families in modern industrial societies. The flaw in Malinowski's argument is the flaw common to all functionalist arguments: Because a social institution is observed to perform a necessary function does not mean either that the function would not be performed if the institution did not exist or that the function is responsible for the existence of the institution.

Later anthropologists have challenged Malinowski's idea that families always include fathers, but, ironically, they have kept all the other aspects of his definition. For example, later anthropologists have argued that the basic social unit is not the nuclear family including father but the unit composed of a mother and her children: "Whether or not a mate becomes attached to the mother on some more or less permanent basis is a variable matter."[4] In removing father from the family, however, later anthropologists have nevertheless retained Malinowski's concept of The Family as a functional unit, and so have retained all the features Malinowski took such pains to demonstrate. In the writings of modern anthropologists, the mother-child unit is described as performing the universally necessary function of nurturing young children. A mother and her children form a bounded group, distinguishable from other units of mothers and their children. A mother and her children share a place, a home and hearth. And, finally, a mother and her children share deep emotional bonds based on their prolonged and intimate contact.

Modern anthropologists may have removed father from The Family, but they did not modify the basic social science concept of The Family in which the function of child rearing is mapped onto a bounded set of people who share a place and who "love" one another. Yet it is exactly this concept of The Family that we, as feminist anthropologists, have found so difficult to apply. Although the biological facts of reproduction, when combined with a sufficiently elastic definition of marriage, make it possible for us, as social scientists, to find both mother-child units and Malinowski's conjugal-pairs-plus-children units in every human society, it is not all clear that such Families necessarily exhibit the associated features Malinowski "proved" and modern anthropologists echo.

An outside observer, for example, may be able to delimit family boundaries in any and all societies by identifying the children of one woman and that woman's associated mate, but natives may not be interested in making such distinctions. In other words, natives may not be concerned to distinguish family members from outsiders, as Malinowski imagined natives should be when he argued that units of parents and children have to have clear boundaries in order for child-rearing responsibilities to be assigned efficiently. Many languages, for example, have no word to identify the unit of parents and children that English speakers call a "family." Among the Zinacantecos of southern Mexico, the basic social unit is identified as a "house," which may include from one to twenty people.[5] Zinacantecos have no difficulty talking about an individual's parents, children, or spouse; but Zinacantecos do not have a single word that identifies the unit of parents and children in such a way as to cut it off from other like units. In Zinacanteco society, the boundary between "houses" is linguistically marked, while the boundary between "family" units is not.

Just as some languages lack words for identifying units of parents and children, so some "families" lack places. Immature children in every society have to be fed and cared for, but parents and children do not necessarily eat and sleep together as a family in one place. Among the Mundurucu of tropical South America, for example, the men of a village traditionally lived in a men's house together with all the village boys over the age of thirteen; women lived with other women and young children in two or three houses grouped around the men's house.[6] In Mundurucu society, men and women ate and slept apart. Men ate in the men's house, sharing food the women had cooked and delivered to them; women ate with other women and children in their own houses. Married couples also slept apart, meeting only for sexual intercourse.

Finally, people around the world do not necessarily expect family members to "love" one another. People may expect husbands, wives, parents, and children to have strong feelings about one another, but they do not necessarily expect prolonged and intimate contact to breed the loving sentiments Malinowski imagined as universally rewarding parents for the care they invested in children. The mother-daughter relationship, for example, is not always pictured as warm and loving. In modern Zambia, girls are not expected to discuss personal problems with, or seek advice from, their mothers. Rather, Zambian girls are expected to seek out some older female relative to serve as confidante.[7] Similarly, among the Cheyenne Indians who lived on the American Great Plains during the last century, a mother was expected to have strained relations with her daughters.[8] Mothers are described as continually admonishing their daughters, leading the latter to seek affection from their fathers' sisters.

Of course, anthropologists have recognized that people everywhere do not share our deep faith in the loving, self-sacrificing mother, but in matters of family and motherhood, anthropologists, like all social scientists, have relied more on faith than evidence in constructing theoretical accounts. Because we *believe* mothers to be loving, anthropologists have proposed, for example, that a general explanation of the fact that men marry mother's brothers' daughters more frequently than they marry father's sisters' daughters is that men naturally seek affection (i.e., wives) where they have found affection in the past (i.e., from mothers and their kin).[9]

LOOKING BACKWARD

The Malinowskian view of The Family as a universal institution—which maps the "function" of "nurturance" onto a collectivity of specific persons (presumably "nuclear" relations) associated with specific spaces ("the home") and specific affective bonds ("love")—corresponds, as we have seen, to that assumed by most contemporary writers on the subject. But a consideration of available ethnographic evidence suggests that the received view is a good deal more problematic than a naive observer might think. If Families in Malinowski's sense are *not* universal, then we must begin to ask about the biases that, in the past, have led us to misconstrue the ethnographic record. The issues here are too complex for thorough explication in this essay, but if we are to better understand the nature of "the family" in the present, it seems worthwhile to explore the question, first, of why so many social thinkers continue to believe in Capital-Letter Families as universal institutions, and second, whether anthropological tradition offers any alternatives to a "necessary and natural" view of what our families are. Only then will we be in a position to suggest "new anthropological perspectives" on the family today.

Our positive critique begins by moving backward. In the next few pages, we suggest that tentative answers to both questions posed above lie in the nineteenth-century intellectual trends that thinkers like Malinowski were at pains to reject. During the second half of the nineteenth century, a number of social and intellectual developments—among them, the evolutionary researches of Charles Darwin, the rise of "urban problems" in fast-growing cities; and the accumulation of data on non-Western peoples by missionaries and agents of the colonial states—contributed to what most of us would now recognize as the beginnings of modern social science. Alternately excited and perplexed by changes in a rapidly industrializing world, thinkers as diverse as socialist Frederick Engels[10] and bourgeois apologist Herbert Spencer[11]—to say nothing of a host of mythographers, historians of religion, and even feminists—attempted to identify the distinctive problems and potentials of their contemporary society by constructing *evolutionary* accounts of "how it all began." At base, a sense of "progress" gave direction to their thought, whether, like Spencer, they believed "man" had advanced from the love of violence to a more civilized love of peace or, like Engels, that humanity had moved from primitive promiscuity and incest toward monogamy and "individual sex love." Proud of their position in the modern world, some of these writers claimed that rules of force had been transcended by new rules of law,[12] while others thought that feminine "mysticism" in the past had been supplanted by a higher male "morality."[13]

At the same time, and whatever else they thought of capitalist social life (some of them criticized, but none wholly abhorred it), these writers also shared a sense of moral emptiness and a fear of instability and loss. Experience argued forcefully to them that moral order in their time did not rest on the unshakable hierarchy—from God to King to Father in the home—enjoyed by Europeans in the past.[14] Thus, whereas Malinowski's functionalism led him to stress the underlying continuities in all human social forms, his nineteenth-century predecessors were concerned to understand the facts and forces that set their experiential world apart. They were interested in comparative and, more narrowly, evolutionary accounts because their lives were torn between celebration and fear of change. For them, the family was important not because it had at all times been the same but because it was at once the moral precondition for, the triumph of, and the victim of developing capitalist society. Without the family and female spheres, thinkers like Ruskin feared we would fall victim to a market that destroys real human bonds.[15] Then again, while men like Engels could decry the impact of the market on familial life and love, he joined with more conservative counterparts to insist that our contemporary familial forms benefited from the individualist morality of modern life and reached to moral and romantic heights unknown before.

Given this purpose and the limited data with which they had to work, it is hardly surprising that the vast majority of what these nineteenth-century writers said is easily dismissed today. They argued that in simpler days such things as incest were the norm; they thought that women ruled in "matriarchal" and peace-loving states or, alternatively, that brute force determined the primitive right and wrong. None of these visions of a more natural, more feminine, more sexy, or more violent primitive world squares with contemporary evidence about what, in technological and organizational terms, might be reckoned relatively "primitive" or "simple" social forms. We would suggest, however, that whatever their mistakes, these nineteenth-century thinkers *can* help us rethink the family today, at least in part because we are (unfortunately) their heirs, in the area of prejudice, and partly because their concern to characterize difference and change gave rise to insights much more promising than their functionalist critics may have thought.

To begin, although nineteenth-century evolutionary theorists did not believe The Family to be universal, the roots of modern assumptions can be seen in their belief that women are, and have at all times been, defined by nurturant, connective, and reproductive roles that *do not change* through time. Most nineteenth-century thinkers imaged social development as a process of differentiation from a relatively confused (and thus incestuous) and indiscriminate female-oriented state to one in which men fight, destroy their "natural" social bonds, and then forge public and political ties to create a human "order." For some, it seemed reasonable to assume that women dominated, as matriarchs, in the undifferentiated early state, but even these theorists believed that women everywhere were "mothers" first, defined by "nurturant" concerns and thus excluded from the business competition, cooperation, social ordering, and social change propelled and dominated by their male counterparts. And so, while nineteenth-century writers differed in their evaluations of such things as "women's status," they all believed that female reproductive roles made women different from and complementary to men and guaranteed both the relative passivity of women in human history and the relative continuity of "feminine" domains and functions in human societies. Social change consisted in the acts of men, who left their mothers behind in shrinking homes. And women's nurturant sphere was recognized as a complementary and necessary corrective to the more competitive pursuits of men, not because these thinkers recognized women as political actors who influence the world, but because they feared the unchecked and morally questionable growth of a male-dominated capitalist market.

For nineteenth-century evolutionists, women were associated, in short, with an unchanging biological role and a romanticized community of the past, while men were imaged as the agents of all social process. And though contemporary thinkers have been ready to dismiss manifold aspects of their now-dated school of thought, on this point we remain, perhaps unwittingly, their heirs. Victorian assumptions about gender and the relationship between competitive male markets and peace-loving female homes were not abandoned in later functionalist schools of thought at least in part because pervasive sexist biases make it easy to forget that women, like men, are important actors in *all* social worlds. Even more, the functionalists, themselves concerned to understand all human social forms in terms of biological "needs," turned out to strengthen earlier beliefs associating action, change, and interest with the deeds of men because they thought of kinship in terms of biologically given ties, of "families" as units geared to reproductive needs, and finally, of women as mere "reproducers" whose contribution to society was essentially defined by the requirements of their homes.

If most modern social scientists have inherited Victorian biases that tend ultimately to support a view uniting women and The Family to an apparently unchanging set of biologically given needs, we have at the same time failed to reckon with the one small area in which Victorian evolutionists were right. They understood, as we do not today, that families—like religions, economies, governments, or courts of law—are *not* unchanging but the product of various social forms, that the relationships of spouses and parents to their young are apt to be different things in different social orders. More particularly, although nineteenth-century writers had primitive society all wrong, they were correct in insisting that *family* in the modern sense—a unit bounded, biologically as well as legally defined, associated with property, self-sufficiency, with affect and a space "inside" the home—is something that emerges not in Stone Age caves but in complex state-governed social forms. Tribal peoples may speak readily of lineages, households, and clans, but—as we have seen—they rarely have a word denoting Family as a particular and limited group of kin; they rarely worry about differences between legitimate and illegitimate heirs or find themselves concerned (as we so often are today) that what children and/or parents do reflects on their family's public image and self-esteem. Political influence in tribal groups in fact consists in adding children to one's home and, far from distinguishing Smith from Jones, encouraging one's neighbors to join one's household as if kin. By contrast, modern bounded Families try to keep their neighbors out. Clearly their character, ideology, and functions are not given for all times. Instead, to borrow the Victorian phrase, The Family is a "moral" unit, a way of organizing and thinking about human relationships in a world in which the domestic is perceived to be in opposition to a politics shaped outside the home, and individuals find themselves dependent on a set of relatively noncontingent ties in order to survive the dictates of an impersonal market and external political order.

In short, what the Victorians recognized and we have tended to forget is, first, that human social life has varied in its "moral"—we might say its "cultural" or "ideological"—forms, and so it takes more than making babies to make Families. And having seen The Family as something more than a response to omnipresent, biologically given needs, they realized too that Families do not everywhere exist; rather, The Family (thought to be universal by most social scientists today) is a moral and ideological unit that appears, not universally, but in particular social orders. The Family as we know it is not a "natural" group created by a state that recognizes Families as units that hold property, provide care and welfare, and attend particularly to the young—a sphere conceptualized as a realm of love and intimacy *in opposition* to the more "impersonal" norms that dominate modern economies and politics. One can, in nonstate social forms, find groups of genealogically related people who interact daily and share material resources, but the contents of their daily ties, the ways they think about their bonds and their conception of the relationship between immediate "familial" links and other kinds of sociality, are apt to be different from the ideas and feelings we think rightfully belong to families we know. Stated otherwise, because our notions of The Family are rooted in a contrast between "public" and "private" spheres, we will not find that Families like ours exist in a society where public and political life is radically different from our own.

Victorian thinkers rightly understood the link between the bounded modern Family and the modern state, although they thought the two related by a necessary teleology of moral progress.

Our point resembles theirs not in the *explanations* we would seek but in our feeling that if we, today, are interested in change, we must begin to probe and understand change in the families of the past. Here the Victorians, not the functionalists, are our rightful guides because the former recognized that *all* human social ties have "cultural" or "moral" shapes, and more specifically, that the particular "morality" of contemporary familial forms is rooted in a set of processes that link our intimate experiences and bonds to public politics.

TOWARD A RETHINKING

Our perspective on families therefore compels us to listen carefully to what the natives in other societies say about their relationships with genealogically close kin. The same is true of the natives in our own society. Our understanding of families in contemporary American society can be only as rich as our understanding of what The Family represents symbolically to Americans. A complete cultural analysis of The Family as an American ideological construct, of course, is beyond the scope of this essay. But we can indicate some of the directions such an analysis would take and how it would deepen our knowledge of American families.

One of the central notions in the modern American construct of The Family is that of nurturance. When antifeminists attack the Equal Rights Amendment, for example, much of their rhetoric plays on the anticipated loss of the nurturant, intimate bonds we associate with The Family. Likewise, when pro life forces decry abortion, they cast it as the ultimate denial of nurturance. In a sense, these arguments are variations of a functionalist view that weds families to specific functions. The logic of the argument is that because people need nurturance, and people get nurtured in The Family, then people need The Family. Yet if we adopt the perspective that The Family is an ideological unit rather than merely a functional unit, we are encouraged to subject this syllogism to closer scrutiny. We can ask, first, What do people mean by nurturance? Obviously, they mean more than mere nourishment—that is, the provision of food, clothing, and shelter required for biological survival. What is evoked by the word nurturance is a certain kind of relationship: a relationship that entails affection and love, that is based on cooperation as opposed to competition, that is enduring rather than temporary, that is noncontingent rather than contingent upon performance, and that is governed by feeling and morality instead of law and contract.

The reason we have stated these attributes of The Family in terms of oppositions is because in a symbolic system the meanings of concepts are often best illuminated by explicating their opposites. Hence, to understand our American construct of The Family, we first have to map the larger system of constructs of which it is only a part. When we undertake such an analysis of The Family in our society, we discover that what gives shape to much of our conception of The Family is its symbolic opposition to work and business—in other words, to the market relations of capitalism. For it is in the market, where we sell our labor and negotiate contract relations of business, that we associate with competitive, temporary, contingent relations that must be buttressed by law and legal sanctions.

The symbolic opposition between The Family and market relations renders our strong attachment to The Family understandable, but it also discloses the particularity of our construct of The Family. We can hardly be speaking of a universal notion of The Family shared by people everywhere and for all time because people everywhere and for all time have not participated in market relations out of which they have constructed a contrastive notion of the family.

The realization that our idea of The Family is part of a set of symbolic oppositions through which we interpret our experience in a particular society compels us to ask to what extent this set of oppositions reflects real relations between people and to what extent is also shapes them. We do not adhere to a model of culture in which ideology is isolated from people's experience. On the other hand, neither do we construe the connection between people's constructs and people's experience to be a simple one of epiphenomenal reflection. Rather, we are interested in understanding how people come to summarize their experience in folk constructs that gloss over the diversity, complexity, and contradictions in their relationships. If, for example, we consider the second premise of the aforementioned syllogism—the idea that people get "nurtured" in families—we can ask how people reconcile this premise with the fact that relationships in families are not always this simple or altruistic. We need not resort to the evidence offered by social historians (e.g., Philippe Aries[16] and Lawrence Stone[17]) of the harsh treatment and neglect of children and spouses in the history of the Western family, for we need only read our local newspaper to learn of similar abuses among contemporary families. And we can point to other studies, such as Young and Willmott's *Family and Kinship in East London*,[18] that reveal how people often find more intimacy and emotional support in relationships with individuals and groups outside The Family than they do in their relationships with family members.

The point is not that our ancestors or our contemporaries have been uniformly mean and nonnurturant to family members but that we have all been both nice and mean, both generous and ungenerous, to them. In like manner, our actions toward family members are not always motivated by selfless altruism but are also motivated by instrumental self-interest. What is significant is that, despite the fact that our complex relationships are the result of complex motivations, we ideologize relations within The Family as nurturant while casting relationships outside The Family—particularly in the sphere of work and business—as just the opposite.

We must be wary of oversimplifying matters by explaining away those disparities between our notion of the nurturant Family and our real actions toward family members as the predictable failing of imperfect beings. For there is more here than mere disjunction of the ideal and the real. The American construct of The Family, after all, is complex enough to comprise some key contradictions. The Family is seen as representing not only the antithesis of the market relations of capitalism; it is also sacralized in our minds as the last stronghold against The State, as the symbolic refuge from the intrusions of a public domain that constantly threatens our sense of privacy and self-determination. Consequently, we can hardly be surprised to find that the punishments imposed on people who commit physical violence are lighter when their victims are their own family members.[19] Indeed, the American sense of the privacy of the things that go on inside families is so strong that a smaller percentage of homicides involving family members are prosecuted than those involving strangers.[20] We are faced with the irony that in our society the place where nurturance and noncontingent affection are supposed to be located is simultaneously the place where violence is most tolerated.

There are other dilemmas about The Family that an examination of its ideological nature can help us better understand. For example, the hypothesis that in England and the United States marriages among lower-income ("working-class") groups are characterized by a greater degree of "conjugal role segregation" than are marriages among middle-income groups has generated considerable confusion. Since Bott observed that working-class couples in her study of London families exhibited more "segregated" conjugal roles than "middle-class" couples, who tended toward more "joint" conjugal roles,[21] researchers have come forth with a range of diverse and confusing findings. On the one hand, some researchers have found that working-class couples indeed report more segregated conjugal role-relationships—in other words, clearly differentiated male and female tasks, as well as interests and activities—than do middle-class couples.[22] Other researchers, however, have raised critical methodological questions about how one goes about defining a joint activity and hence measuring the degree of "jointness" in a conjugal relationship.[23] Platt's finding that couples who reported "jointness" in one activity were not particularly likely to report "jointness" in another activity is significant because it demonstrates that "jointness" is not a general characteristic of a relationship that manifests itself uniformly over a range of domains. Couples carry out some activities and tasks together or do them separately but equally; they also have other activities in which they do not both participate. The measurement of the "jointness" of conjugal relationships becomes even more problematic when we recognize that what one individual or couple may label a "joint activity" another individual or couple may consider a "separate activity." In Bott's study, for example, some couples felt that all activities carried out by husband and wife in each other's presence were

> similar in kind regardless of whether the activities were complementary (e.g. sexual intercourse, though no one talked about this directly in the home interview), independent (e.g. husband repairing book while the wife read or knitted), or shared (e.g. washing up together, entertaining friends, going to the pictures together). It was not even necessary that husband and wife should actually be together. As long as they were both at home it was felt that their activities partook of some special, shared, family quality.[24]

In other words, the distinction Bott drew among "joint," "differentiated," and "autonomic" (independent) relationships summarized the way people thought and felt about their activities rather than what they were observed to actually do. Again, it is not simply that there is a disjunction between what people say they do and what they in fact do. The more cogent point is that the meaning people attach to action, whether they view it as coordinated and therefore shared or in some other way, is an integral component of that action and cannot be divorced from it in our analysis. When we compare the conjugal relationships of middle-income and low-income people, or any of the family relationships among different class, age, ethnic, and regional sectors of American society, we must recognize that our comparisons rest on differences and similarities in ideological and moral meanings as well as on differences and similarities in action.

Finally, the awareness that The Family is not a concrete "thing" that fulfills concrete "needs" but an ideological construct with moral implications can lead to a more refined analysis of historical change in the American or Western family than has devolved upon us from our functionalist ancestors. The functionalist view of industrialization, urbanization, and family change depicts The Family as responding to alterations in economic and social conditions in rather mechanistic ways. As production gets removed from the family's domain, there is less need for strict rules and clear authority structures in the family to accomplish productive work. At the same time, individuals who now must work for wages in impersonal settings need a haven where they can obtain emotional support and gratification. Hence, The Family becomes more concerned with "expressive" functions, and what emerges is the modern "companionate family." In short, in the functionalist narrative, The Family and its constituent members "adapt" to fulfill functional requirements created for it by the industrialization of production. Once we begin to view The Family as an ideological unit and pay due respect to it as a moral statement, however, we can begin to unravel the more complex, dialectical process through which family relationships and The Family as a construct were mutually transformed. We can examine, for one, the ways in which people and state institutions acted, rather than merely reacted, to assign certain functions to groupings of kin by making them legally responsible for these functions. We can investigate the manner in which the increasing limitations placed on agents of the community and the state with regard to negotiating the relationships between family members enhanced the independence of The Family. We can begin to understand the consequences of social reforms and wage policies for the age and sex inequalities in families. And we can elucidate the interplay between these social changes and the cultural transformations that assigned new meanings and modified old ones to make The Family what we think it to be today.

Ultimately, this sort of rethinking will lead to a questioning of the somewhat contradictory modern views that families are things we need (the more "impersonal" the public world, the more we need them) and at the same time that loving families are disappearing. In a variety of ways, individuals today *do* look to families for a "love" that money cannot buy and find; our contemporary world makes "love" more fragile than most of us hope and "nurturance" more self-interested than we believe.[25] But what we fail to recognize is that familial nurturance and the social forces that turn our ideal families into mere fleeting dreams are *equally* creations of the world we know *today*. Rather than think of the ideal family as a world we lost (or, like the Victorians, as a world just recently achieved), it is important for us to recognize that while families symbolize deep and salient modern themes, contemporary families are unlikely to fulfill our equally modern nurturant needs.

We probably have no cause to fear (or hope) that The Family will dissolve. What we can begin to ask is what we *want* our families to do. Then, distinguishing our hopes from what we have, we can begin to analyze the social forces that enhance or undermine the realization of the kinds of human bonds we need.

NOTES

1. Bronislaw Malinowski, *The Family Among the Australian Aborigines* (London: University of London Press, 1913).

2. Lewis Henry Morgan, *Ancient Society* (New York: Holt, 1877).

3. Bronislaw Malinowski, *A Scientific Theory of Culture* (Chapel Hill: University of North Carolina Press, 1944), p. 99.

4. Robin Fox, *Kinship and Marriage* (London: Penguin, 1967), p. 39.

5. Evon Z. Vogt, *Zinacantan: A Maya Community in the Highlands of Chiapas* (Cambridge, Mass.: Harvard University Press, 1969).

6. Yolanda and Robert Murphy, *Women of the Forest* (New York: Columbia University Press, 1974).

7. Ilsa Schuster, *New Women of Lusaka* (Palo Alto, CA: Mayfield, 1979).

8. E. Adamson Hoebel, *The Cheyennes: Indians of the Great Plains* (New York: Holt, Rinehart and Winston, 1978).

9. George C. Homans and David M. Schneider, *Marriage, Authority, and Final Causes* (Glencoe, Ill.: Free Press, 1955).

10. Frederick Engels, *The Origin of the Family, Private Property and the State*, in *Karl Marx and Frederick Engels: Selected Works*, vol. 2 (Moscow: Foreign Language Publishing House, 1955).

11. Herbert Spencer, *The Principles of Sociology*, vol. 1, *Domestic Institutions* (New York: Appleton, 1973).

12. John Stuart Mill, *The Subjection of Women* (London: Longmans, Green, Reader and Dyer, 1869).

13. J. J. Bachofen, *Das Mutterrecht* (Stuttgart, 1861).

14. Elizabeth Fee, "The Sexual Politics of Victorian Social Anthropology," in *Clio's Banner Raised*, ed. M. Hartman and L. Banner (New York: Harper & Row, 1974).

15. John Ruskin, "Of Queen's Gardens," in *Sesame and Lilies* (London: J. M. Dent, 1907).

16. Philippe Aries, *Centuries of Childhood*, trans. Robert Baldick (New York: Vintage, 1962).

17. Lawrence Stone, *The Family, Sex, and Marriage in England 1500–1800* (London: Weidenfeld and Nicholson, 1977).

18. Michael Young and Peter Willmott, *Family and Kinship in East London* (London: Routledge and Kegan Paul, 1957).

19. Henry P. Lundsgaarde, *Murder in Space City: A Cultural Analysis of Houston Homicide Patterns* (New York: Oxford University Press, 1977).

20. Ibid.

21. Elizabeth Bott, *Family and Social Network: Roles, Norms, and External Relationships in Ordinary Urban Families* (London: Tavistock, 1957).

22. Herbert J. Gans, *The Urban Villagers* (New York: Free Press, 1962); C. Rosser and C. Harris, *The Family and Social Change* (London: Routledge and Kegan Paul, 1965).

23. John Platt, "Some Problems in Measuring the Jointness of Conjugal Role-Relationships," *Sociology* 3 (1969): 287–97; Christopher Turner, "Conjugal Roles and Social Networks: A Re-examination

of an Hypothesis," *Human Relations* 20 (1967): 121–30; and Morris Zelditch Jr., "Family, Marriage and Kinship," in *A Handbook of Modern Sociology*, ed. R. E. L. Faris (Chicago: Rand McNally, 1964), pp. 680–707.

24. Bott, *Family and Social Network*, p. 240.

25. Rayna Rapp, "Family and Class in Contemporary America: Notes Toward an Understanding of Ideology," *Science and Society* 42 (Fall 1978): 278–300.

5 Lifeboat Ethics

Mother Love and Child Death in Northeast Brazil

Nancy Scheper-Hughes

I have seen death without weeping
The destiny of the Northeast is death
Cattle they kill
To the people they do something worse
      —Anonymous Brazilian singer (1965)

"Why do the church bells ring so often?" I asked Nailza de Arruda soon after I moved into a corner of her tiny mud-walled hut near the top of the shantytown called the Alto do Cruzeiro (Crucifix Hill). I was then a Peace Corps volunteer and a community development/health worker. It was the dry and blazing hot summer of 1965, the months following the military coup in Brazil, and save for the rusty, clanging bells of N.S. das Dores Church, an eerie quiet had settled over the market town that I call Bom Jesus da Mata. Beneath the quiet, however, there was chaos and panic. "It's nothing," replied Nailza, "just another little angel gone to heaven."

Nailza had sent more than her share of little angels to heaven, and sometimes at night I could hear her engaged in a muffled but passionate discourse with one of them, two-year-old Joana. Joana's photograph, taken as she lay propped up in her tiny cardboard coffin, her eyes open, hung on a wall next to one of Nailza and Ze Antonio taken on the day they eloped.

Nailza could barely remember the other infants and babies who came and went in close succession. Most had died unnamed and were hastily baptized in their coffins. Few lived more than a month or two. Only Joana, properly baptized in a church at the close of her first year and placed under the protection of a powerful saint, Joan of Arc, had been expected to live. And Nailza had dangerously allowed herself to love the little girl.

In addressing the dead child, Nailza's voice would range from tearful imploring to angry recrimination: "Why did you leave me? Was your patron saint so greedy that she could not allow me one child on this earth?" Ze Antonio advised me to ignore Nailza's odd behavior, which he understood as a kind of madness that, like the birth and death of children, came and went. Indeed, the premature birth of a stillborn son some months later "cured" Nailza of her "inappropriate" grief, and the day came when she removed Joana's photo and carefully packed it away.

Nancy Scheper-Hughes is Professor and Chair in the Department of Anthropology at the University of California, Berkeley, where she directs the doctoral training program in Medical Anthropology. Her books include *Saints, Scholars, and Schizophrenics: Mental Illness in Rural Ireland* (California, 1979) and *Death Without Weeping: The Violence of Everyday Life in Brazil* (California, 1992), which won the Bryce Wood Award (Latin American Studies Association), the Harry Chapin Media Award (World Hunger Year), the Pietre Prize (Centro Internazionale di Etnostoria, Italy), and the Wellcome Prize (Royal Anthropological Institute). Her current research and writing is about the transition to democracy in South Africa, where she was Chair of Social Anthropology at the University of Cape Town in 1993–94.

More than fifteen years elapsed before I returned to the Alto do Cruzeiro, and it was anthropology that provided the vehicle of my return. Since 1982 I have returned several times in order to pursue a problem that first attracted my attention in the 1960s. My involvement with the people of the Alto do Cruzeiro now spans a quarter of a century and three generations of parenting in a community where mothers and daughters are often simultaneously pregnant.

The Alto do Cruzeiro is one of three shantytowns surrounding the large market town of Bom Jesus in the sugar plantation zone of Pernambuco in Northeast Brazil, one of the many zones of neglect that have emerged in the shadow of the now tarnished economic miracle of Brazil. For the women and children of the Alto do Cruzeiro, the only miracle is that some of them have managed to stay alive at all.

The Northeast is a region of vast proportions (approximately twice the size of Texas) and of equally vast social and developmental problems. The nine states that make up the region are the poorest in the country and are representative of the Third World within a dynamic and rapidly industrializing nation. Despite waves of migrations from the interior to the teeming shantytowns of coastal cities, the majority still live in rural areas on farms and ranches, sugar plantations, and mills.

Life expectancy in the Northeast is only forty years, largely because of the appallingly high rate of infant and child mortality. Approximately one million children in Brazil under the age of five die each year. The children of the Northeast, especially those born in shantytowns on the periphery of urban life, are at a very high risk of death. In these areas, children are born without the traditional protection of breast-feeding, subsistence gardens, stable marriages, and multiple adult caretakers that exists in the interior. In the hillside shantytowns that spring up around cities or, in this case, interior market towns, marriages are brittle, single parenting is the norm, and women are frequently forced into the shadow economy of domestic work in the homes of the rich or into unprotected and oftentimes "scab" wage labor on the surrounding sugar plantations, where they clear land for planting and weed for a pittance, sometimes less than a dollar a day. The women of the Alto may not bring their babies with them into the homes of the wealthy, where the often-sick infants are considered sources of contamination, and they cannot carry the little ones to the riverbanks where they wash clothes because the river is heavily infested with schistosomes and other deadly parasites. Nor can they carry their young children to the plantations, which are often several miles away. At wages of a dollar a day, the women of the Alto cannot hire baby sitters. Older children who are not in school will sometimes serve as somewhat indifferent caretakers. But any child not in school is also expected to find wage work. In most cases, babies are simply left at home alone, the door securely fastened. And so many also die alone and unattended.

Bom Jesus da Mata, centrally located in the plantation zone of Pernambuco, is within commuting distance of several sugar plantations and mills. Consequently, Bom Jesus has been a magnet for rural workers forced off their small subsistence plots by large landowners wanting to use every available piece of land for sugar cultivation. Initially, the rural migrants to Bom Jesus were squatters who were given tacit approval by the mayor to put up temporary straw huts on each of the three hills overlooking the town. The Alto do Cruzeiro is the oldest, the largest, and the poorest of the shantytowns. Over the past three decades many of the original migrants have become permanent residents, and the primitive and temporary straw huts have been replaced by small homes (usually of two rooms) made of wattle and daub, sometimes covered with plaster. The more affluent residents use bricks and tiles. In most Alto homes, dangerous kerosene lamps have been replaced by light bulbs. The once tattered rural garb, often fashioned from used sugar sacking, has likewise been replaced by store-bought clothes, often castoffs from a wealthy *patrão* (boss). The trappings are modern, but the hunger, sickness, and death that they conceal are traditional, deeply rooted in a history of feudalism, exploitation, and institutionalized dependency.

My research agenda never wavered. The questions I addressed first crystallized during a veritable "die-off" of Alto babies during a severe drought in 1965. The food and water shortages and the political and economic chaos occasioned by the military coup were reflected in the hand-written entries of births and deaths in the dusty, yellowed pages of the ledger books kept at the public registry office in Bom Jesus. More than 350 babies died in the Alto during 1965 alone—this from a shantytown population of little more than 5,000. But that wasn't what surprised me. There were reasons enough for the deaths in the miserable conditions of shantytown life. What puzzled me was the seeming indifference of Alto women to the deaths of their infants, and their willingness to attribute to their own tiny offspring an aversion to life that made their death seem wholly natural, indeed all but anticipated.

Although I found that it was possible, and hardly difficult, to rescue infants and toddlers from death by diarrhea and dehydration with a simple sugar, salt, and water solution (even bottled Coca-Cola worked fine), it was more difficult to enlist a mother herself in the rescue of a chid she perceived as ill-fated for life or better off dead, or to convince her to take back into her threat-ened and besieged home a baby she had already come to think of as an angel rather than as a son or daughter.

I learned that the high expectancy of death, and the ability to face child death with stoicism and equanimity, produced patterns of nurturing that differentiated between those infants thought of as thrivers and survivors and those thought of as born already "wanting to die." The survivors were nurtured, while stigmatized, doomed infants were left to die, as mothers say, *a mingua*, "of neglect." Mothers stepped back and allowed nature to take its course. This pattern, which I call mortal selective neglect, is called passive infanticide by anthropologist Marvin Harris. The Alto situation, although culturally specific in the form that it takes, is not unique to Third World shan-tytown communities and may have its correlates in our own impoverished urban communities in some cases of "failure to thrive" infants.

I use as an example the story of Zezinho, the thirteen-month-old toddler of one of my neigh-bors, Lourdes. I became involved with Zezinho when I was called in to help Lourdes in the delivery of another child, this one a fair and robust little tyke with a lusty cry. I noted that while Lourdes showed great interest in the newborn, she totally ignored Zezinho who, wasted and severely malnourished, was curled up in a fetal position on a piece of urine- and feces-soaked cardboard placed under his mother's hammock. Eyes open and vacant, mouth slack, the little boy seemed doomed.

When I carried Zezinho up to the community day-care center at the top of the hill, the Alto women who took turns caring for one another's children (in order to free themselves for part-time work in the cane fields or washing clothes) laughed at my efforts to save Ze, agreeing with Lourdes that here was a baby without a ghost of a chance. Leave him alone, they cautioned. It makes no sense to fight with death. But I did do battle with Ze, and after several weeks of force-feeding (malnourished babies lose their interest in food), Ze began to succumb to my ministra-tions. He acquired some flesh across his taut chest bones, learned to sit up, and even tried to smile. When he seemed well enough, I returned him to Lourdes in her miserable scrap-material lean-to, but not without guilt about what I had done. I wondered whether returning Ze was at all fair to Lourdes and to his little brother. But I was busy and washed my hands of the matter. And Lourdes did seem more interested in Ze now that he was looking more human.

When I returned in 1982, there was Lourdes among the women who formed my sample of Alto mothers—still struggling to put together some semblance of life for a new grown Ze and her five other surviving children. Much was made of my reunion with Ze in 1982, and everyone enjoyed retelling the story of Ze's rescue and of how his mother had given him up for dead. Ze would laugh the loudest when told how I had had to force-feed him like a fiesta turkey. There was no hint of guilt on the part of Lourdes and no resentment on the part of Ze. In fact, when questioned in private as to who was the best friend he ever had in life, Ze took a long drag on his cigarette and answered without at trace of irony, "Why my mother, of course." "But of course," I replied.

Part of learning how to mother in the Alto do Cruzeiro is learning when to let go of a child who shows that it "wants" to die or that it has no "knack" or no "taste" for life. Another part is learning when it is safe to let oneself love a child. Frequent child death remains a powerful shaper of maternal thinking and practice. In the absence of firm expectation that a child will survive, mother love as we conceptualize it (whether in popular terms or in the psychobiological notion of maternal bonding) is attenuated and delayed with consequences for infant survival. In an environment already precarious to young life, the emotional detachment of mothers toward some of their babies contributes even further to the spiral of high mortality—high fertility in a kind of macabre lock-step dance to death.

The average woman of the Alto experiences 9.5 pregnancies, 3.5 child deaths, and 1.5 still-births. Seventy percent of all child deaths in the Alto occur in the first six months of life, and 82 percent by the end of the first year. Of all deaths in the community each year, about 45 percent are of children under the age of five.

Women of the Alto distinguish between child deaths understood as natural (caused by diarrhea and communicable diseases) and those resulting from sorcery, the evil eye, or other magical or supernatural afflictions. They also recognize a large category of infant deaths seen as fated and inevitable. These hopeless cases are classified by mothers under the folk terminology "child sickness" or "child attack." Women say that there are at least fourteen different types of hopeless child sickness, but most can be subsumed under two categories—chronic and acute. The chronic cases refer to infants who are born small and wasted. They are deathly pale, mothers say, as well as weak and passive. They demonstrate no vital force, no liveliness. They do not suck vigorously; they hardly cry. Such babies can be this way at birth or they can be born sound but soon show no resistance, no "fight" against the common crises of infancy: diarrhea, respiratory infections, tropical fevers.

The acute cases are those doomed infants who die suddenly and violently. They are taken by stealth overnight, often following convulsions that bring on head banging, shaking, grimacing, and shrieking. Women say it is horrible to look at such a baby. If the infant begins to foam at the mouth or gnash its teeth or go rigid with its eyes turned back inside its head, there is absolutely no hope. The infant is "put aside"—left alone—often on the floor in a back room, and allowed to die. These symptoms (which accompany high fevers, dehydration, third-stage malnutrition, and encephalitis) are equated by Alto women with madness, epilepsy, and worst of all, rabies, which is greatly feared and highly stigmatized.

Most of the infants presented to me as suffering from chronic child sickness were tiny, wasted famine victims, while those labeled as victims of acute child attack seemed to be infants suffering from the deliriums of high fever or the convulsions that can accompany electrolyte imbalance in dehydrated babies.

Local midwives and traditional healers, praying women, as they are called, advise Alto women on when to allow a baby to die. On midwife explained: "If I can see that a baby was born unfortuitously, I tell the mother that she need not wash the infant or give it a cleansing tea. I tell her just to dust the infant with baby powder and wait for it to die." Allowing nature to take its course is not seen as sinful by these often very devout Catholic women. Rather, it is understood as cooperating with God's plan.

Often I have been asked how consciously women of the Alto behave in this regard. I would have to say that consciousness is always shifting between allowed and disallowed levels of awareness. For example, I was awakened early one morning in 1987 by two neighborhood children who had been sent to fetch me to a hastily organized wake for a two-month-old infant whose mother I had unsuccessfully urged to breast-feed. The infant was being sustained on sugar water, which the mother referred to as *soro* (serum), using a medical term for the infant's starvation regime in light of his chronic diarrhea. I had cautioned the mother that an infant could not live on *soro* forever.

The two girls urged me to console the young mother by telling her that it was "too bad" that her infant was so weak that Jesus had to take him. They were coaching me in proper Alto etiquette. I agreed, of course, but asked, "And what do *you* think?" Xoxa, the eleven-year-old, looked down at her dusty flip-flops and blurted out, "Oh, Dona Nanci, that baby never got enough to eat, but you must never say that!" And so the death of hungry babies remains one of the best kept secrets of life in Bom Jesus da Mata.

Most victims are waked quickly and with a minimum of ceremony. No tears are shed, and the neighborhood children form a tiny procession, carrying the baby to the town graveyard where it will join a multitude of others. Although a few fresh flowers may be scattered over the tiny grave, no stone or wooden cross will mark the place, and the same spot will be reused within a few months' time. The mother will never visit the grave, which soon becomes an anonymous one.

What, then, can be said of these women? What emotions, what sentiments motivate them? How are they able to do what, in fact, must be done? What does mother love mean in this inhospitable context? Are grief, mourning, and melancholia present, although deeply repressed? If so, where shall we look for them? And if not, how are we to understand the moral visions and moral sensibilities that guide their actions?

I have been criticized more than once for presenting an unflattering portrait of poor Brazilian women, women who are, after all, themselves the victims of severe social and institutional neglect. I have described these women as allowing some of their children to die, as if this were an unnatural and inhuman act rather than, as I would assert, the way any one of us might act, reasonably and rationally, under similarly desperate conditions. Perhaps I have not emphasized enough the real pathogens in this environment of high risk: poverty, deprivation, sexism, chronic hunger, and economic exploitation. If mother love is, as many psychologists and some feminists believe, a seemingly natural and universal maternal script, what does it mean to women for whom scarcity, loss, sickness, and deprivation have made that love frantic and robbed them of their grief, seeming to turn their hearts to stone?

Throughout much of human history—as in a great deal of the impoverished Third World today—women have had to give birth and to nurture children under ecological conditions and social arrangements hostile to child survival, as well as to their own well-being. Under circumstances of high childhood mortality, patterns of selective neglect and passive infanticide may be seen as active survival strategies.

They also seem to be fairly common practices historically and across cultures. In societies characterized by high childhood mortality and by a correspondingly high (replacement) fertility, cultural practices of infant and child care tend to be organized primarily around survival goals. But what this means is a pragmatic recognition that not all of one's children can be expected to live. The nervousness about child survival in areas of northeast Brazil, northern India, or Bangladesh, where a 30 percent or 40 percent mortality rate in the first years of life is common, can lead to forms of delayed attachment and a casual or benign neglect that serves to weed out the worst bets so as to enhance the life chances of healthier siblings, including those yet to be born. Practices similar to those that I am describing have been recorded for parts of Africa, India, and Central America.

Life in the Alto do Cruzeiro resembles nothing so much as a battlefield or an emergency room in an overcrowded inner city public hospital. Consequently, morality is guided by a kind of "lifeboat ethics," the morality of triage. The seemingly studied indifference toward the suffering of some of their infants, conveyed in such sayings as "little critters have no feelings," is understandable in light of these women's obligation to carry on with their reproductive and nurturing lives.

In their slowness to anthropomorphize and personalize their infants, everything is mobilized so as to prevent maternal overattachment and, therefore, grief at death. The bereaved mother is told not to cry, that her tears will dampen the wings of her little angel so that she cannot fly up to her heavenly home. Grief at the death of an angel is not only inappropriate, it is also a symptom of madness and of a profound lack of faith.

Infant death becomes routine in an environment in which death is anticipated and bets are hedged. While the routinization of death in the context of shantytown life is not hard to understand, and quite possible to empathize with, its routinization in the formal institutions of public life in Bom Jesus is not as easy to accept uncritically. Here the social production of indifference takes on a different, even a malevolent cast.

In a society where triplicates of every form are required for the most banal events (registering a car, for example), the registration of infant and child death is informal, incomplete, and rapid. It requires no documentation, takes less than five minutes, and demands no witnesses other than office clerks. No questions are asked concerning the circumstances of the death, and the cause of death is left blank, unquestioned and unexamined. A neighbor, grandmother, older sibling, or common-law husband may register the death. Since most infants die at home, there is no question of a medical record.

From the registry office, the parent proceeds to the town hall, where the mayor will give him or her a voucher for a free baby coffin. The full-time municipal coffinmaker cannot tell you exactly how many baby coffins are dispatched each week. It varies, he says, with the seasons. There are more needed during the drought months and during the big festivals of Carnaval and Christmas and São Joao's Day because people are too busy, he supposes, to take their babies to the clinic. Record keeping is sloppy.

Similarly, there is a failure on the part of city-employed doctors working at two free clinics to recognize the malnutrition of babies who are weighed, measured, and immunized without comment and as if they were not, in fact, anemic, stunted, fussy, and irritated starvation babies. At best, the mothers are told to pick up free vitamins or health "tonic" at the municipal chambers. At worst, clinic personnel will give tranquilizers and sleeping pills to quiet the hungry cries of "sick-to-death" Alto babies.

The church, too, contributes to the routinization of, and indifference toward, child death. Traditionally, the local Catholic church taught patience and resignation to domestic tragedies that were said to reveal the imponderable workings of God's will. If an infant died suddenly, it was because a particular saint had claimed the child. The infant would be an angel in the service of his or her heavenly patron. It would be wrong, a sign of a lack of faith, to weep for a child with such good fortune. The infant funeral was, in the past, an event celebrated with joy. Today, however, under the new regime of "liberation theology," the bells of N.S. das Dores parish church no longer peal for the death of Alto babies, and no priest accompanies the procession of angels to the cemetery where their bodies are disposed of casually and without ceremony. Children bury children in Bom Jesus da Mata. In this most Catholic of communities, the coffin is handed to the disabled and irritable municipal gravedigger, who often chides the children for one reason or another. It may be that the coffin is larger than expected and the gravedigger can find no appropriate space. The children do not wait for the gravedigger to complete his task. No prayers are recited and no sign of the cross made as the tiny coffin goes into its shallow grave.

When I asked the local priest, Padre Marcos, about the lack of church ceremony surrounding infant and childhood death today in Bom Jesus, he replied: "In the old days, child death was richly celebrated. But those were the baroque customs of a conservative church that wallowed in death and misery. The new church is a church of hope and joy. We no longer celebrate the death of child angels. We try to tell mothers that Jesus doesn't want all the dead babies they send him." Similarly, the new church has changed its baptismal customs, now often refusing to baptize dying babies brought to the back door of a church or rectory. The mothers are scolded by the church attendants and told to go home and take care of their sick babies. Baptism, they are told, is for the living; it is not to be confused with the sacrament of extreme unction, which is the anointing of the dying. And so it appears to the women of the Alto that even the church has turned away from them, denying the traditional comfort of folk Catholicism.

The contemporary Catholic church is caught in the clutches of a double bind. The new theology of liberation imagines a kingdom of God on Earth based on justice and equality, a world without hunger, sickness, or childhood mortality. At the same time, the church has not changed its official position on sexuality and reproduction, including its sanctions against birth control, abortion, and sterilization. The padre of Bom Jesus da Mata recognizes this contradiction intuitively, although he shies away from discussions on the topic, saying he prefers to leave questions of family planning to the discretion and the "good consciences" of his impoverished parishioners. But this, of course, sidesteps the extent to which those good consciences have been shaped by traditional church teachings in Bom Jesus, especially by his recent predecessors. Hence, we can begin to see that the seeming indifference of Alto mothers toward the death of some of their infants is but a pale reflection of the official indifference of church and state to the plight of poor women and children.

Nonetheless, the women of Bom Jesus are survivors. One woman, Biu, told me her life history, returning again and again to the themes of child death, her first husband's suicide, abandonment by her father and later by her second husband, and all the other losses and disappointments she had suffered in her long forty-five years. She concluded with great force, reflecting on the days of Carnaval '88 that were fast approaching:

> No, Dona Nanci, I won't cry, and I won't waste my life thinking about it from morning to night. . . . Can I argue with God for the state that I'm in? No! And so I'll dance and I'll jump and I'll play Carnaval! And yes, I'll laugh and people will wonder at a *pobre* like me who can have such a good time.

And no one did blame Biu for dancing in the streets during the four days at carnaval—not even on Ash Wednesday, the day following Carnaval '88 when we all assembled hurriedly to assist in the burial of Mercea, Biu's beloved *casula*, her last-born daughter who had died at home of pneumonia during the festivities. The rest of the family barely had time to change out of their costumes. Severino, the child's uncle and godfather, sprinkled holy water over the little angel while he prayed: "Mercea, I don't know whether you were called, taken, or thrown out of this world. But look down at us from your heavenly home with tenderness, with pity, and with mercy." So be it.

6 Population

Delusion and Reality[1]

Amartya Sen

1.

Few issues today are as divisive as what is called the "world population problem." With the approach this autumn of the International Conference on Population Development in Cairo, organized by the United Nations, these divisions among experts are receiving enormous attention and generating considerable heat. There is a danger that in the confrontation between apocalyptic pessimism, on the one hand, and a dismissive smugness, on the other, a genuine understanding of the nature of the population problem may be lost.

Visions of impending doom have been increasingly aired in recent years, often presenting the population problem as a "bomb" that has been planted and is about to "go off." These catastrophic images have encouraged a tendency to search for emergency solutions which treat the people involved not as reasonable beings, allies facing a common problem, but as impulsive and uncontrolled sources of great social harm, in need of strong discipline.

Such views have received serious attention in public discussions, not just in sensational headlines in the popular press, but also in seriously argued and widely read books. One of the most influential examples was Paul Ehrlich's *The Population Bomb*, the first three sections of which were headed "Too Many People," "Too Little Food," and "A Dying Planet."[2] A more recent example of a chilling diagnosis of imminent calamity is Garrett Hardin's *Living within Limits*.[3] The arguments on which these pessimistic visions are based deserve serious scrutiny.

If the propensity to foresee impending disaster from overpopulation is strong in some circles, so is the tendency, in others, to dismiss all worries about population size. Just as alarmism builds on the recognition of a real problem and then magnifies it, complacency may also start off from a

Amartya Sen is Lamont University Professor and Professor of Economics and Philosophy at Harvard University. He studied in Calcutta and Cambridge, and has taught at Cambridge and in Calcutta, Delhi, and London. Prior to Harvard, he was Drummond Professor of Political Economy at Oxford. His publications include *Collective Choice and Social Welfare* (1970), *Poverty and Famine* (1980), *Choice, Welfare, and Measurement* (1982), *On Ethics and Economics* (1987), and *Inequality Reexamined* (1992). He is a former President of the Econometric Society, the International Economic Association, the Indian Economic Association, and the American Economic Association.

reasonable belief about the history of population problems and fail to see how they may have changed by now. It is often pointed out, for example, that the world has coped well enough with fast increases in population in the past, even though alarmists had expected otherwise. Malthus anticipated terrible disasters resulting from population growth and a consequent imbalance in "the proportion between the natural increase of population and food."[4] At a time when there were fewer than a billion people, he was quite convinced that "the period when the number of men surpass their means of subsistence has long since arrived." However, since Malthus first published his famous *Essay on Population* in 1798, the world population has grown nearly six times larger, while food output and consumption per person are considerably higher now, and there has been an unprecedented increase both in life expectancies and in general living standards.[5]

The fact that Malthus was mistaken in his diagnosis as well as his prognosis two hundred years ago does not, however, indicate that contemporary fears about population growth must be similarly erroneous. The increase in the world population has vastly accelerated over the last century. It took the world population millions of years to reach the first billion, then 123 years to get to the second, 33 years to the third, 14 years to the fourth, 13 years to the fifth billion, with a sixth billion to come, according to one UN projection, in another 11 years.[6] During the last decade, between 1980 and 1990, the number of people on earth grew by about 923 million, an increase nearly the size of the total world population in Malthus's time. Whatever may be the proper response to alarmism about the future, complacency based on past success is no response at all.

IMMIGRATION AND POPULATION

One current worry concerns the regional distribution of the increase in world population, about 90 percent of which is taking place in the developing countries. The percentage rate of population growth is fastest in Africa—3.1 percent per year over the last decade. But most of the large increases in population occur in regions other than Africa. The largest absolute increases in numbers are taking place in Asia, which is where most of the world's poorer people live, even though the rate of increase in population has been slowing significantly there. Of the worldwide increase of 923 million people in the 1980s, well over half occurred in Asia—517 million in fact (including 146 million in China and 166 million in India).

Beyond concerns about the well-being of these poor countries themselves, a more self-regarding worry causes panic in the richer countries of the world and has much to do with the current anxiety in the West about the "world population problem." This is founded on the belief that destitution caused by fast population growth in the third world is responsible for the severe pressure to emigrate to the developed countries of Europe and North America. In this view, people impoverished by overpopulation in the "South" flee to the "North." Some have claimed to find empirical support for this thesis in the fact that pressure to emigrate from the South has accelerated in recent decades, along with a rapid increase in the population there.

There are two distinct questions here: first, how great a threat of intolerable immigration pressure does the North face from the South; and second, is that pressure closely related to population growth in the South, rather than to other social and economic factors? There are reasons to doubt that population growth is the major force behind migratory pressures, and I shall concentrate here on that question. But I should note in passing that immigration is now severely controlled in Europe and North America, and insofar as Europe is concerned, most of the current immigrants from the third world are not "primary" immigrants but dependent relatives—mainly spouses and young children—of those who had come and settled earlier. The United States remains relatively more open to fresh immigration, but the requirements of "labor certification" as a necessary part of the immigration procedure tend to guarantee that the new entrants are relatively better educated and more skilled. There are, however, sizable flows of illegal immigrants, especially to the United States and to a lesser extent to southern Europe, though the numbers are hard to estimate.

What causes the current pressures to emigrate? The "job-worthy" people who get through the immigration process are hardly to be seen as impoverished and destitute migrants created by the sheer pressure of population. Even the illegal immigrants who manage to evade the rigors of border control are typically not starving wretches but those who can make use of work prospects in the North.

The explanation for the increased migratory pressure over the decades owes more to the dynamism of international capitalism than to just the growing size of the population of the third world countries. The immigrants have allies in potential employers, and this applies as much to illegal farm laborers in California as to the legally authorized "guest workers" in automobile factories in Germany. The economic incentive to emigrate to the North from the poorer Southern economies may well depend on differences in real income. But this gap is very large anyway, and even if it is presumed that population growth in the South is increasing the disparity with the North—a thesis I shall presently consider—it seems unlikely that this incentive would significantly change if the Northern income level were, say, twenty times that of the Southern as opposed to twenty-five times.

The growing demand for immigration to the North from the South is related to the "shrinking" of the world (through revolutions in communication and transport), reduction in economic obstacles to labor movements (despite the increase in political barriers), and the growing reach and absorptive power of international capitalism (even as domestic politics in the North has turned more inward looking and nationalistic). To try to explain the increase in immigration pressure by the growth rate of total population in the third world is to close one's eyes to the deep changes that have occurred—and are occurring—in the world in which we live, and the rapid internationalization of its cultures and economies that accompanies these changes.

FEARS OF BEING ENGULFED

A closely related issue concerns what is perceived as a growing "imbalance" in the division of the world population, with a rapidly rising share belonging to the third world. That fear translates into worries of various kinds in the North, especially the sense of being overrun by the South. Many Northerners fear being engulfed by people from Asia and Africa, whose share of the world population increased from 63.7 percent in 1950 to 71.2 percent by 1990, and is expected, according to the estimates of the United Nations, to rise to 78.5 percent by 2050 AD.

It is easy to understand the fears of relatively well-off people at the thought of being surrounded by a fast growing and increasingly impoverished Southern population. As I shall argue, the thesis of growing impoverishment does not stand up to much scrutiny; but it is important to address first the psychologically tense issue of racial balance in the world (even though racial composition as a consideration has only as much importance as we choose to give it). Here it is worth recollecting that the third world is right now going through the same kind of demographic shift—a rapid expansion of population for a temporary but long stretch—that Europe and North America experienced during their industrial revolution. In 1650 the share of Asia and Africa in the world population is estimated to have been 78.4 percent, and it stayed around there even in 1750.[7] With the industrial revolution, the share of Asia and Africa diminished because of the rapid rise of population in Europe and North America: for example, during the nineteenth century, while the inhabitants of Asia and Africa grew by about 4 percent per decade or less, the population of "the area of European settlement" grew by around 10 percent every decade.

Even now the combined share of Asia and Africa (71.2 percent) is considerably *below* what its share was in 1650 or 1750. If the United Nations' prediction that this share will rise to 78.5 percent by 2050 comes true, then the Asians and the Africans would return to being proportionately almost exactly as numerous as they were before the European industrial revolution. There is, of course, nothing sacrosanct about the distribution of population in the past; but the sense of a growing "imbalance" in the world, based only on recent trends, ignores history and implicitly presumes that the expansion of Europeans earlier on was natural, whereas the same process happening now to other populations unnaturally disturbs the "balance."

COLLABORATION VERSUS OVERRIDE

Other worries involving the relation of population growth to food supplies, income levels, and the environment reflect more serious matters.[8] Before I take up those questions, a brief comment on the distinction between two rival approaches to dealing with the population problem may be useful. One involves voluntary choice and a collaborative solution, and the other overrides voluntarism through legal or economic coercion.

Alarmist views of impending crises tend to produce a willingness to consider forceful measures for coercing people to have fewer children in the third world. Imposing birth control on unwilling people is no longer rejected as readily as it was until quite recently, and some activists have pointed to the ambiguities that exist in determining what is or is not "coercion."[9] Those who are willing to consider—or at least not fully reject—programs that would use some measure of force to reduce population growth often point to the success of China's "one child policy" in cutting down the national birth rate. Force can also take an indirect form, as when economic opportunities are changed so radically by government regulations that people are left with very little choice except to behave in ways the government would approve. In China's case, the government may refuse to offer housing to families with too many children—thus penalizing the children as well as the dissenting adults.

In India the policy of compulsory birth control that was initiated during the "emergency period" declared by Mrs. Gandhi in the 1970s was decisively rejected by the voters in the general election in which it—along with civil rights—was a major issue. Even so, some public health clinics in the Northern states (such as Uttar Pradesh) insist, in practice, on sterilization before providing normal medical attention to women and men beyond a certain age. The pressures to move in that direction seem to be strong, and they are reinforced by the rhetoric of "the population bomb."

I shall call this general approach the "override" view, since the family's personal decisions are overridden by some agency outside the family—typically by the government of the country in question (whether or not it has been pressed to do so by "outside" agencies, such as international organizations and pressure groups). In fact, overriding is not limited to an explicit use of legal coercion or economic compulsion, since people's own choices can also be effectively overridden by simply not offering them the opportunities for jobs or welfare that they can expect to get from a responsible government. Override can take many different forms and can be of varying intensity (with the Chinese "one child policy" being something of an extreme case of a more general approach).

A central issue here is the increasingly vocal demand by some activists concerned with population growth that the highest "priority" should be given in third world countries to family planning over other public commitments. This demand goes much beyond supporting family planning as a part of development. In fact, proposals for shifting international aid away from development in general to family planning in particular have lately been increasingly frequent. Such policies fit into the general approach of "override" as well, since they try to rely on manipulating people's choices through offering them only some opportunities (the means of family planning) while denying others, no matter what they would have themselves preferred. Insofar as they would have the effect of reducing health care and educational services, such shifts in public commitments will not only add to the misery of human lives, they may also have, I shall argue, exactly the opposite effect on family planning than the one intended, since education and health care have a significant part of the *voluntary* reduction of the birth rate.

The "override" approach contrasts with another, the "collaborative" approach, that relies not on legal or economic restrictions but on rational decisions of women and men, based on expanded choices and enhanced security, and encouraged by open dialogue and extensive public discussions. The difference between the two approaches does not lie in government's activism in the first case as opposed to passivity in the second. Even if solutions are sought through the decisions and actions of people themselves, the chance to take reasoned decisions with more knowledge and a greater sense of personal security can be increased by public policies, for example, though expanding educational facilities, health care, and economic well-being, along with providing better access to family planning. The central political and ethical issue, concerning the "override" approach do not lie in its insistence on the need for public policy but in the ways it significantly reduces the choices open to parents.

THE MALTHUS-CONDORCET DEBATE

Thomas Robert Malthus forcefully argued for a version of the "override" view. In fact, it was precisely this preference that distinguished Malthus from Condorcet, the eighteenth-century French mathematician and social scientist from whom Malthus had actually derived the analysis of how population could outgrow the means of living. The debate between Condorcet and Malthus in some ways marks the origin of the distinction between the "collaborative" and the "override" approaches, which still compete for attention.[10]

In his *Essay on Population*, published in 1798, Malthus quoted—extensively and with approval—Condorcet's discussion, in 1795, of the possibility of overpopulation. However, true to the Enlightenment tradition, Condorcet was confident that this problem would be solved by reasoned human action: through increases in productivity, through better conservation and prevention of waste, and through education (especially female education) which would contribute to reducing the birth rate.[11] Voluntary family planning would be encouraged, in Condorcet's analysis, by increased understanding that if people "have a duty toward those who are not yet born, that duty is not to give them existence but to give them happiness." They would see the value of limiting family size "rather than foolishly . . . encumber[ing] the world with useless and wretched beings."[12]

> Even though Malthus borrowed from Condorcet his diagnosis of the possibility of overpopulation, he refused to accept Condorcet's solution. Indeed, Malthus's essay on population was partly a criticism of Condorcet's "Enlightenment reasoning" and even the full title of Malthus's famous essay specifically mentioned Condorcet. Malthus argued that there is no reason whatever to suppose that anything beside the difficulty of procuring in adequate plenty the necessaries of life should either *indispose* this greater number of persons to marry early, or *disable* them from rearing in health the largest families.[13]

Malthus thus opposed public relief of poverty: he saw the "poor laws" in particular as contributing greatly to population growth.[14]

Malthus was not sure that any public policy would work, and whether "overriding" would in fact be possible: "The perpetual tendency in the race of man to increase beyond the means of subsistence is one of the great general laws of animated nature which we can have no reason to expect will change."[15] But insofar as any solution would be possible, it could not come from voluntary decisions of the people involved, or from acting from a position of strength and economic security. It must come from overriding their preferences through the compulsions of economic necessity, since their poverty was the only thing that could "indispose the greater number of persons to marry early, or disable them from rearing in health the largest families."

DEVELOPMENT AND INCREASED CHOICE

The distinction between the "collaborative" approach and the "override" approach thus tends to correspond closely to the contrast between, on the one hand, treating economic and social development as the way to solve the population problem and, on the other, expecting little from development and using, instead, legal and economic pressures to reduce birth rates. Among recent writers, those such as Gerard Piel[16] who have persuasively emphasized our ability to solve problems through reasoned decisions and actions have tended—like Condorcet—to find the solution of the population problem in economic and social development. They advocate a broadly collaborative approach, in which governments and citizens would together produce economic and social conditions favoring slower population growth. In contrast, those who have been thoroughly skeptical of reasoned human action to limit population growth have tended to go in the direction of "override" in one form or another, rather than concentrate on development and voluntarism.

Has development, in fact, done much to reduce population growth? There can be little doubt that economic and social development, in general, has been associated with major reductions in birth rates and the emergence of smaller families as the norm. This is a pattern that was, of course, clearly observed in Europe and North America as they underwent industrialization, but that experience has been repeated in many other parts of the world.

In particular, conditions of economic security and affluence, wider availability of contraceptive methods, expansion of education (particularly female education), and lower mortality rates have had—and are currently having—quite substantial effects in reducing birth rates in different parts of the world.[17] The rate of world population growth is certainly declining, and even over the last two decades its percentage growth rate has fallen from 2.2 percent per year between 1970 and 1980 to 1.7 percent between 1980 and 1992. This rate is expected to go steadily down until the size of the world's population becomes nearly stationary.[18]

There are important regional differences in demographic behavior; for example, the population growth rate in India peaked at 2.2 percent a year (in the 1970s) and has since started to diminish, whereas most Latin American countries peaked at much higher rates before coming down sharply, while many countries in Africa currently have growth rates between 3 and 4 percent, with an average for sub-Saharan Africa of 3.1 percent. Similarly, the different factors have varied in their respective influence from region to region. But there can be little dispute that economic and social development tends to reduce fertility rates. The regions of the third world that lag most in achieving economic and social development, such as many countries in Africa, are, in general, also the ones that have failed to reduce birth rates significantly. Malthus's fear that economic and social development could only encourage people to have more children has certainly proved to be radically wrong, and so have all the painful policy implications drawn from it.

This raises the following question: in view of the clear connection between development and lower fertility, why isn't the dispute over how to deal with population growth fully resolved already? Why don't we reinterpret the population problem simply as a problem of underdevelopment and seek a solution by encouraging economic and social development (even if we reject the oversimple slogan "development is the most reliable contraceptive")?

In the long run, this may indeed be exactly the right approach. The problem is more complex, however, because a "contraceptive" that is "reliable" in the long run may not act fast enough to meet the present threat. Even though development may dependably work to stabilize population if it is given enough time, there may not be, it is argued, time enough to give. The death rate often falls very fast with more widely available health care, better sanitation, and improved nutrition, while the birth rate may fall rather slowly. Much growth of population may meanwhile occur.

This is exactly the point at which apocalyptic prophecies add force to the "override" view. One claim, then, that needs examination is that the world is facing an imminent crisis, one so urgent that development is just too slow a process to deal with it. We must try right now, the argument goes, to cut down population growth by drastic and forceful means if necessary. The second claim that also needs scrutiny is the actual feasibility of adequately reducing population growth through these drastic means, without fostering social and economic development.

2.

POPULATION AND INCOME

It is sometimes argued that signs of an imminent crisis can be found in the growing impoverishment of the South, with falling income per capita accompanying high population growth. In general, there is little evidence for this. As a matter of fact, the average population of "low-income" countries (as defined by the World Bank) has been not only enjoying a rising gross national product (GNP) per head but also a growth rate of GNP per capita (3.9 percent per year for 1980–1992) that is much faster than those for the "high-income" countries (2.4 percent) and for the "middle-income" ones (0 percent).[19]

The growth of per capita GNP of the population of low-income countries would have been even higher had it not been for the negative growth rates of many countries in sub-Saharan Africa, one region in which a number of countries have been experiencing economic decline. But the main culprit causing this state of affairs is the terrible failure of economic production in sub-Saharan Africa (connected particularly with political disruption, including wars and military rule), rather than population growth, which is only a subsidiary factor. Sub-Saharan Africa does have high population growth, but its economic stagnation has contributed much more to the fall in its per-capita income.

With its average population growth rate of 3.1 percent per year, had sub-Saharan Africa suddenly matched China's low population growth of 1.4 percent (the lowest among the low-income countries), it would have gained roughly 1.7 percent in per capita GNP growth. The real income per person would still have fallen, even with that minimal population growth, for many countries in the region. The growth of GNP per capita is *minus* 1.9 percent for Ethiopia, *minus* 1.8 percent for Togo, *minus* 3.6 percent for Mozambique, *minus* 4.3 percent for Niger, *minus* 4.7 percent Ivory Coast, not to mention Somalia, Sudan, and Angola, where the political disruption has been so serious that no reliable GNP estimates even exist. A lower population growth rate could have reduced the magnitude of the fall in per capita GNP, but the main roots of Africa's economic decline lie elsewhere. The complex political factors underlying the troubles of Africa include, among other things, the subversion of democracy and the rise of combative military rulers, often encouraged by the cold war (with Africa providing "client states"—from Somalia and Ethiopia to Angola and Zaire—for the superpowers, particularly from the 1960s onward). The explanation of sub-Saharan Africa's problems has to be sought in these political troubles, which affect economic stability, agricultural and industrial incentives, public health arrangements, and social services—even family planning and population policy.[20]

There is indeed a very powerful case for reducing the rate of growth of population in Africa, but this problem cannot be dissociated from the rest of the continent's woes. Sub-Saharan Africa lags behind other developing regions in economic security, in health care, in life expectancy, in basic education, and in political and economic stability. It should be no great surprise that it lags behind in family planning as well. To dissociate the task of population control from the politics and economics of Africa would be a great mistake and would seriously mislead public policy.

POPULATION AND FOOD

Malthus's exact thesis cannot, however, be disputed by quoting statistics of income per capita, for he was concerned specifically with food supply per capita, and he had concentrated on "the proportion between the natural increase of population and food." Many modern commentators, including Paul Ehrlich and Garrett Hardin, have said much about this, too. When Ehrlich says, in his *Population Bomb*, "too little food," he does not mean "too little income," but specifically a growing shortage of food.

Is population beginning to outrun food production? Even though such an impression is often given in public discussions, there is, in fact, no serious evidence that this is happening. While there are some year-to-year fluctuations in the growth of food output (typically inducing, whenever things slacken a bit, some excited remarks by those who anticipate an impending doom), the worldwide trend of food output per person has been firmly upward. Not only over the two centuries since Malthus's time, but also during recent decades, the rise in food output has been significantly and consistently outpacing the expansion of world population.[21]

But the total food supply in the world as a whole is not the only issue. What about the regional distribution of food? If it were to turn out that the rising ratio of food to population is mainly caused by increased production in richer counties (for example, if it appeared that U.S. wheat output was feeding the third world, in which much of the population expansion is taking place), then the neo-Malthusian fears about "too many people" and "too little food" may have some plausibility. Is this what is happening?

In fact, with one substantial exception, exactly the opposite is true. The largest increases in the production of food—not just in the aggregate but also per person—are actually taking place in the third world, particularly in the region that is having the largest absolute increases in the world population, that is, in Asia. The many millions of people who are added to the populations of India and China may be constantly cited by the terrorized—and terrorizing—advocates of the apocalyptic view, but it is precisely in these countries that the most rapid rates of growth in food output per capita are to be observed. For example, between the three-year averages of 1979–1981 and 1991–1993, food production per head in the world moved up by 3 percent, while it went up by only 2 percent in Europe and went down by nearly 5 percent in North America. In contrast, per capita food production jumped up by 22 percent in Asia generally, including 23 percent in India and 39 percent in China.[22] (See Table 1.)

During the same period, however, food production per capita went down by 6 percent in Africa, and even the absolute size of food output fell in some countries (such as Malawi and Somalia). Of course, many countries in the world—from Syria, Italy, and Sweden to Botswana in Africa—have had declining food production per head without experiencing hunger or starvation since their economies have prospered and grown; when the means are available, food can be easily bought in the international market if it is necessary to do so. For many countries in sub-Saharan Africa, the problem arises from the fact that the decline in food production is an integral part of the story of overall economic decline, which I have discussed earlier.

Table 1   Indices of Food Production Per Capita

	1979–1981 Base Period	1991–1993
World	100	103
Europe	100	102
North America	100	95
Africa	100	94
Asia	100	122
including		
India	100	123
China	100	139

Source: FAO Quarterly Bulletin of Statistics.

Difficulties of food production in sub-Saharan Africa, like other problems of the national economy, are not only linked to wars, dictatorships, and political chaos. In addition, there is some evidence that climatic shifts have had unfavorable effects on parts of that continent. While some of the climatic problems may be caused partly by increases in human settlement and environmental neglect, that neglect is not unrelated to the political and economic chaos that has characterized sub-Saharan Africa during the last few decades. The food problem of Africa must be seen as one part of a wider political and economic problem of the region.[23]

THE PRICE OF FOOD

To return to "the balance between food and population," the rising food production per capita in the world as a whole, and in the third world in general, contradicts some of the pessimism that characterized the gloomy predictions of the past. Prophecies of imminent disaster during the last few decades have not proved any more accurate than Malthus's prognostication nearly two hundred years ago. As for new prophecies of doom, they cannot, of course, be contradicted until the future arrives. There was no way of refuting the theses of W. Paddock and P. Paddock's popular book *Famine—1975!*, published in 1968, which predicted a terrible cataclysm for the world as a whole by 1975 (writing off India, in particular, as a basket case), until 1975 actually arrived. The new prophets have learned not to attach specific dates to the crises they foresee, and past failures do not seem to have reduced the popular appetite for this creative genre.

However, after noting the rather dismal forecasting record of doomsayers, we must also accept the general methodological point that present trends in output do not necessarily tell us much about the prospects of further expansion in the future. It could, for example, be argued that maintaining growth in food production may require proportionately increasing investments of capital, drawing them away from other kinds of production. This would tend to make food progressively more expensive if there are "diminishing returns" in shifting resources from other fields into food production. And, ultimately, further expansion of food production may become so expensive that it would be hard to maintain the trend of increasing food production without reducing other outputs drastically.

But is food production really getting more and more expensive? There is, in fact, no evidence for that conclusion either. In fact, quite the contrary. Not only is food generally much cheaper to buy today, in constant dollars, than it was in Malthus's time, but it also has become cheaper during recent decades. As a matter of fact, there have been increasing complaints among food exporters, especially in the third world, that food prices have fallen in relation to other commodities. For example, in 1992, a United Nations report recorded a 38 percent fall in the relative prices of "basic foods" over the last decade.[24] This is entirely in line with the trend, during the last three decades, toward declining relative prices of particular food items, in relation to the prices of manufactured goods. The World Bank's adjusted estimates of the prices of particular food crops, between 1953–1955 and 1983–1985, show similarly steep declines for such staples as rice (42 percent), wheat (57 percent), sorghum (39 percent), and maize (37 percent).[25]

Not only is food getting less expensive, but we also have to bear in mind that the current increase in food production (substantial and well ahead of population growth, as it is) is itself being kept in check by the difficulties in selling food profitably, as the relative prices of food have fallen. Those neo-Malthusians who concede that food production is now growing faster than population often point out that it is growing "only a little faster than population," and they are inclined to interpret this as evidence that we are reaching the limits of what we can produce to keep pace with population growth.

But that is surely the wrong conclusion to draw in view of the falling relative prices of food and the current difficulties in selling food, since it ignores the effects of economic incentives that govern production. When we take into account the persistent cheapening of food prices, we have good grounds to suggest that food output is being held back by a lack of effective demand in the market. The imaginary crisis in food production, contradicted as it is by the upward trends of total and regional food output per head, is thus further debunked by an analysis of the economic incentives to produce more food.

DEPRIVED LIVES AND SLUMS

I have examined the alleged "food problem" associated with population growth in some detail because it has received so much attention both in the traditional Malthusian literature and in the recent writings of neo-Malthusians. In concentrating on his claim that growing populations would not have enough food, Malthus differed from Condorcet's broader presentation of the population question. Condorcet's own emphasis was on the possibility of "a continual diminution of happiness" as a result of population growth, a diminution that could occur in many different ways—not just through the deprivation of food, but through a decline in living conditions generally. This more extensive worry can remain, even when Malthus's analysis of the food supply is rejected.

Indeed, average income and food production per head can go on increasing even as the wretchedly deprived living conditions of particular sections of the population get worse, as they have in many parts of the third world. The living conditions of backward regions and deprived classes can decline even when a country's economic growth is very rapid on the average. Brazil during the 1960s and 1970s provided an extreme example of this. The sense that there are just "too many people" around often arises from seeing the desperate lives of people in the large and rapidly growing urban slums—*bidonvilles*—in poor countries, sobering reminders that we should not take too much comfort from aggregate statistics of economic progress.

But in an essay addressed mainly to the population problem, what we have to ask is not whether things are just fine in the third world (they obviously are not), but whether population growth is the root cause of the deprivations that people suffer. The question is whether the particular instances of deep poverty we observe derive mainly from population growth rather than from other factors that lead to unshared prosperity and persistent and possibly growing inequality. The tendency to see in population growth an explanation for every calamity that afflicts poor people is now fairly well established in some circles, and the message that gets transmitted constantly is the opposite of the old picture postcard: "Wish you weren't here."

To see in population growth the main reason for the growth of overcrowded and very poor slums in large cities, for example, is not empirically convincing. It does not help to explain why the slums of Calcutta and Bombay have grown worse at a faster rate than those of Karachi and Islamabad (India's population growth rate is 2.1 percent per year, Pakistan's 3.1), or why Jakarta has deteriorated faster than Ankara or Istanbul (Indonesian population growth is 1.8 percent, Turkey's 2.3), or why the slums of Mexico City have become worse more rapidly than those of San José (Mexico's population growth rate is 2.0, Costa Rica's 2.8), or why Harlem can seem more and more deprived when compared with the poorer districts of Singapore (U.S. population growth rate is 1.0, Singapore's is 1.8). Many causal factors affect the degree of deprivation in particular parts of a country—rural as well as urban—and to try to see them all as resulting from over-population is the negation of social analysis.

This is not to deny that population growth may well have an effect on deprivation, but only to insist that any investigation of the effects of population growth must be part of the analysis of economic and political processes, including the effects of other variables. It is the isolationist view of population growth that should be rejected.

THREATS TO THE ENVIRONMENT

In his concern about "a continual diminution of happiness" from population growth, Condorcet was a pioneer in considering the possibility that natural raw materials might be used up, thereby making living conditions worse. In his characteristically rationalist solution, which relied partly on voluntary and reasoned measures to reduce the birth rate, Condorcet also envisaged the development of less improvident technology: "The manufacture of articles will be achieved with less wastage in raw materials and will make better use of them."[26]

The effects of a growing population on the environment could be a good deal more serious than the food problems that have received so much attention in the literature inspired by Malthus. If the environment is damaged by population pressures, this obviously affects the kind of life we lead, and the possibilities of a "diminution in happiness" can be quite considerable. In dealing with this problem, we have to distinguish once again between the long and the short run. The short-run picture tends to be dominated by the fact that the per capita consumption of food, fuel, and other goods by people in third world countries is often relatively low; consequently the impact of population growth in these countries is not, in relative terms, so damaging to the global environment. But the problems of the local environment can, of course, be serious in many developing economies. They vary from the "neighborhood pollution" created by unregulated industries to the pressure of denser populations on rural resources such as fields and woods.[27] (The Indian authorities had to close down several factories in and around Agra, since the façade of the Taj Mahal was turning pale as a result of chemical pollution from local factories.) But it remains true that one additional American typically has a larger negative impact on the ozone layer, global warmth, and other elements of the earth's environment than dozens of Indians and Zimbabweans put together. Those who argue for the immediate need for forceful population control in the third world to preserve the global environment must first recognize this elementary fact.

This does not imply, as is sometimes suggested, that as far as the global environment is concerned, population growth in the third world is nothing to worry about. The long-run impact on the global environment of population growth in the developing countries can be expected to be large. As the Indians and Zimbabweans develop economically, they too will consume a great deal more, and they will pose, in the future, a threat to the earth's environment similar to that of people in the rich countries today. The long-run threat of population to the environment is a real one.

3.

WOMEN'S DEPRIVATION AND POWER

Since reducing the birth rate can be slow, this and other long-run problems should be addressed right now. Solutions will no doubt have to be found in the two directions to which, as it happens, Condorcet pointed: (1) developing new technology and new behavior patterns that would waste little and pollute less, and (2) fostering social and economic changes that would gradually bring down the growth rate of population.

On reducing birth rates, Condorcet's own solution not only included enhancing economic opportunity and security, but also stressed the importance of education, particularly female education. A better-educated population could have a more informed discussion of the kind of life we have reason to value; in particular it would reject the drudgery of a life of continuous child bearing and rearing that is routinely forced on many third world women. That drudgery, in some ways, is the most immediately adverse consequence of high fertility rates.

Central to reducing birth rates, then, is a close connection between women's well-being and their power to make their own decisions and bring about changes in the fertility pattern. Women in many third world countries are deprived by high birth frequency of the freedom to do other things in life, not to mention the medical dangers of repeated pregnancy and high maternal mortality, which are both characteristic of many developing countries. It is thus not surprising that reductions in birth rates have been typically associated with improvement of women's status and their ability to make their voices heard—often the result of expanded opportunities for schooling and political activity.[28]

There is nothing particularly exotic about declines in the birth rate occurring through a process of voluntary rational assessment, of which Condorcet spoke. It is what people do when they have some basic education, know about family planning methods and have access to them, do not readily accept a life of persistent drudgery, and are not deeply anxious about their economic security. It is also what they do when they are not forced by high infant and child mortality rates to be so worried that no child will survive to support them in their old age that they try to have many children. In country after country the birth rate has come down with more female education, the reduction of mortality rates, the expansion of economic means and security, and greater public discussion of ways of living.

DEVELOPMENT VERSUS COERCION

There is little doubt that this process of social and economic change will over time cut down the birth rate. Indeed, the growth rate of world population is already firmly declining—it came down from 2.2 percent in the 1970s to 1.7 percent between 1980 and 1992. Had imminent cataclysm been threatening, we might have had good reason to reject such gradual progress and consider more drastic means of population control, as some have advocated. But that apocalyptic view is empirically baseless. There is no imminent emergency that calls for a breathless response. What is called for is systematic support for people's own decisions to reduce family size through expanding education and health care, and through economic and social development.

It is often asked where the money needed for expanding education, health care, etc., would be found. Education, health services, and many other means of improving the quality of life are typically highly labor-intensive and are thus relatively inexpensive in poor countries (because of low wages).[29] While poor countries have less money to spend, they also need less money to provide these services. For this reason many poor countries have indeed been able to expand educational and health services widely without waiting to become prosperous through the process of economic growth. Sri Lanka, Costa Rica, Indonesia, and Thailand are good examples, and there are many others. While the impact of these social services on the quality and length of life have been much studied, they are also major means of reducing the birth rate.

By contrast with such open and voluntary developments, coercive methods, such as the "one child policy" in some regions, have been tried in China, particularly since the reforms of 1979. Many commentators have pointed out that by 1992 the Chinese birth rate has fallen to 19 per 1,000, compared with 29 per 1,000 in India, and 27 per 1,000 for the average of poor countries other than China and India. China's total fertility rate (reflecting the number of children born per woman) is now at "the replacement level" of 2.0, compared with India's 3.6 and the weighted average of 4.9 for low-income countries other than China and India.[30] Hasn't China shown the way to "solve" the population problem in other developing countries as well?

4.

CHINA'S POPULATION POLICIES

The difficulties with this "solution" are of several kinds. First, if freedom is valued at all, the lack of freedom associated with this approach must be seen to be a social loss in itself. The importance of reproductive freedom has been persuasively emphasized by women's groups throughout the world.[31]

The loss of freedom is often dismissed on the grounds that because of cultural differences, authoritarian policies that would not be tolerated in the West are acceptable to Asians. While we often hear references to "despotic" Oriental traditions, such arguments are no more convincing than a claim that compulsion in the West is justified by the traditions of the Spanish Inquisition or of the Nazi concentration camps. Frequent references are also made to the emphasis on discipline in the "Confucian tradition"; but that is not the only tradition in the "East," nor is it easy to assess the implications of that tradition for modern Asia (even if we were able to show that discipline is more important for Confucius than it is for, say, Plato or Saint Augustine).

Only a democratic expression of opinion could reveal whether citizens would find a compulsory system acceptable. While such a test has not occurred in China, one did in fact take place in India during "the emergency period" in the 1970s, when Indira Gandhi's government imposed compulsory birth control and suspended various legal freedoms. In the general elections that followed, the politicians favoring the policy of coercion were overwhelmingly defeated. Furthermore, family planning experts in India have observed how the briefly applied programs of compulsory sterilization tended to discredit voluntary birth control programs generally, since people became deeply suspicious of the entire movement to control fertility.

Second, apart from the fundamental issue of whether people are willing to accept compulsory birth control, its specific consequences must also be considered. Insofar as coercion is effective, it works by making people do things they would not freely do. The social consequences of such compulsion, including the ways in which an unwilling population tends to react when it is coerced, can be appalling. For example, the demands of a "one-child family" can lead to the neglect—or worse—of a second child, thereby increasing the infant mortality rate. Moreover, in a country with a strong preference for male children—a preference shared by China and many other countries in Asia and North Africa—a policy of allowing only one child per family can easily lead to the fatal neglect of a female child. There is much evidence that this is fairly widespread in China, with very adverse effects on infant mortality rates. There are reports that female children have been severely neglected as well as suggestions that female infanticide occurs with considerable frequency. Such consequences are hard to tolerate morally, and perhaps politically also, in the long run.

Third, what is also not clear is exactly how much additional reduction in the birth rate has been achieved through these coercive methods. Many of China's longstanding social and economic programs have been valuable in reducing fertility, including those that have expanded education for women as well as men, made health care more generally available, provided more job opportunities for women, and stimulated rapid economic growth. These factors would themselves have reduced the birth rates, and it is not clear how much "extra lowering" of fertility rates has been achieved in China through compulsion.

For example, we can determine whether many of the countries that match (or outmatch) China in life expectancy, female literacy rates, and female participation in the labor force actually have a higher fertility rate than China. Of all the countries in the world for which data are given in the *World Development Report 1994*, there are only three such countries: Jamaica (2.7), Thailand (2.2), and Sweden (2.1)—and the fertility rates of two of these are close to China's (2.0). Thus the additional contribution of coercion to reducing fertility in China is by no means clear, since compulsion was superimposed on a society that was already reducing its birth rate and in which education and jobs outside the home were available to large numbers of women. In some regions of China the compulsory programs needed little enforcement, whereas in other—more backward—regions, it had to be applied with much severity, with terrible consequences in infant mortality and discrimination against female children. While China may get too much credit for its authoritarian measures, it gets far too little credit for the other, more collaborative and participatory, policies it has followed, which have themselves helped to cut down the birth rate.

CHINA AND INDIA

A useful contrast can be drawn between China and India, the two most populous countries in the world. If we look only at the national averages, it is easy to see that China with its low fertility rate of 2.0 has achieved much more than India has with its average fertility rate of 3.6. To what extent this contrast can be attributed to the effectiveness of the coercive policies used in China is not clear, since we would expect the fertility rate to be much lower in China in view of its higher percentage of female literacy (almost twice as high), higher life expectancy (almost ten years more), larger female involvement (by three quarters) in the labor force, and so on. But India is a country of great diversity, whose different states have very unequal achievements in literacy, health care, and economic and social development. Most states in India are far behind the Chinese provinces in educational achievement (with the exception of Tibet, which has the lowest literacy rate of any Chinese or Indian state), and the same applies to other factors that affect fertility. However, the state of Kerala in Southern India provides an interesting comparison with China, since it too has high levels of basic education, health care, and so on. Kerala is a state within a country, but with its 29 million people, it is larger than most countries in the world (including Canada). Kerala's birth rate of 18 per 1,000 is actually lower than China's 19 per 1,000, and its fertility rate is 1.8 for 1991, compared with China's 2.0 for 1992. These low rates have been achieved without any state coercion.[32]

The roots of Kerala's success are to be found in the kinds of social progress Condorcet hoped for, including among others, a high female literacy rate (86 percent, which is substantially higher than China's 68 percent). The rural literacy rate is in fact higher in Kerala—for women as well as men—than in every single province in China. Male and female life expectancies at birth in China are respectively 67 and 71 years; the provisional 1991 figures for men and women in Kerala are 71 and 74 years. Women have been active in Kerala's economic and political life for a long time. A high proportion do skilled and semi-skilled work and a large number have taken part in educational movements.[33] It is perhaps of symbolic importance that the first public pronouncement of the need for widespread elementary education in any part of India was made in 1817 by Rani Gouri Parvathi Bai, the young queen of the princely state of Travancore, which makes up a substantial part of modern Kerala. For a long time public discussions in Kerala have centered on women's rights and the undesirability of couples marrying when very young.

This political process has been voluntarily and collaborative, rather than coercive, and the adverse reactions that have been observed in China, such as infant mortality, have not occurred in Kerala. Kerala's low fertility rate has been achieved along with an infant mortality rate of 16.5 per 1,000 live births (17 for boys and 16 for girls), compared with China's 31 (28 for boys and 33 for girls). And as a result of greater gender equality in Kerala, women have not suffered from higher mortality rates than men in Kerala, as they have in the rest of India and in China. Even the ratio of females to males in the total population in Kerala (above 1.03) is quite close to that of the current ratios in Europe and America (reflecting the usual pattern of lower female mortality whenever women and men receive similar care). By contrast, the average female to male ratio in China is 0.94 and in India as a whole 0.93.[34] Anyone drawn to the Chinese experience of compulsory birth control must take note of these facts.

The temptation to use the "override" approach arises at least partly from impatience with the allegedly slow process of fertility reduction through collaborative, rather than coercive, attempts. Yet Kerala's birth rate has fallen from 44 per 1,000 in the 1940s to 18 by 1991—not a sluggish decline. Nor is Kerala unique in this respect. Other societies, such as those of Sri Lanka, South Korea, and Thailand, which have relied on expanding education and reducing mortality rates—instead of on coercion—have also achieved sharp declines in fertility and birth rates.

It is also interesting to compare the time required for reducing fertility in China with that in the two states in India, Kerala and Tamil Nadu, which have done most to encourage voluntary and collaborative reduction in birth rates (even though Tamil Nadu is well behind Kerala in each respect).[35] Table 2 shows the fertility rates both in 1979, when the one-child policy and related programs were introduced in China, and in 1991. Despite China's one-child policy and other

Table 2 Fertility Rates in China, Kerala, and Tamil Nadu

	1979	1991
China	2.8	2.0
Kerala	3.0	1.8
Tamil Nadu	3.5	2.2

Sources: For China, Xizhe Peng, *Demographic Transition in China* (Oxford University Press, 1991), Li Chengrui, *A Study of China's Population* (Beijing: Foreign Language Press, 1992), and *World Development Report 1994.* For India, *Sample Registration System 1979–80* (New Delhi: Ministry of Home Affairs, 1982) and *Sample Registration System: Fertility and Mortality Indicators 1991* (New Delhi: Ministry of Home Affairs, 1993).

coercive measures, its fertility rate seems to have fallen much less sharply than those of Kerala and Tamil Nadu. The "override" view is very hard to defend on the basis of the Chinese experience, the only systematic and sustained attempt to impose such a policy that has so far been made.

FAMILY PLANNING

Even those who do not advocate legal or economic coercion sometimes suggest a variant of the "override" approach—the view, which has been getting increasing support, that the highest priority should be given simply to family planning, even if this means diverting resources from education and health care as well as other activities associated with development. We often hear claims that enormous declines in birth rates have been accomplished through making family planning services available, without waiting for improvements in education and health care.

The experience of Bangladesh is sometimes cited as an example of such success. Indeed, even though the female literacy rate in Bangladesh is only around 22 percent and life expectancy at birth no higher than 55 years, fertility rates have been substantially reduced there through the greater availability of family planning services, including counseling.[36] We have to examine carefully what lessons can, in fact, be drawn from this evidence.

First, it is certainly significant that Bangladesh has been able to cut its fertility rate from 7.0 to 4.5 during the short period between 1975 and 1990, an achievement that discredits the view that people will not voluntarily embrace family planning in the poorest countries. But we have to ask further whether family planning efforts may themselves be sufficient to make fertility come down to really low levels without providing for female education and the other features of a fuller collaborative approach. The fertility rate of 4.5 in Bangladesh is still quite high—considerably higher than even India's average rate of 3.6. To begin stabilizing the population, the fertility rates would have to come down closer to the "replacement level" of 2.0, as has happened in Kerala and Tamil Nadu, and in many other places outside the Indian subcontinent. Female education and the other social developments connected with lowering the birth rate would still be much needed.

Contrasts between the records of Indian states offer some substantial lessons here. While Kerala, and to a smaller extent Tamil Nadu, have surged ahead in achieving radically reduced fertility rates, other states in India in the so-called Northern heartland (such as Uttar Pradesh, Bihar, Madhya Pradesh, and Rajasthan), have very low levels of education, especially female education, and of general health care (often combined with pressure on the poor to accept birth control measures, including sterilization, as a qualifying condition for medical attention and other public services). These states all have high fertility rates—above 4.0. The regional contrasts within India strongly argue for the collaborative approach, including active and educated participation of women.

The threat of an impending population crisis tempts many international observers to suggest that priority be given to family planning arrangements in the third world countries over other commitments such as education and health care, a redirection of public efforts that is often recommended by policymakers and at international conferences. Not only will this shift have negative effects on people's well-being and reduce their freedoms, it can also be self-defeating if the goal is to stabilize population.

The appeal of such slogans as "family planning first" rests partly on misconceptions about what is needed to reduce fertility rates, but also on mistaken beliefs about the excessive costs of social development, including education and health care. As has been discussed, both these activities are highly labor intensive, and thus relatively inexpensive even in very poor economies. In fact, Kerala, India's star performer in expanding education and reducing both death rates and birth rates, is among the poorer Indian states. Its domestically produced income is quite low— lower indeed in per capita terms than even the Indian average—even if this is somewhat deceptive, for the greatest expansion of Kerala's earnings derives from citizens who work outside the state. Kerala's ability to finance adequately both educational expansion and health coverage depends on both activities being labor-intensive; they can be made available even in a low-income economy when there is the political will to use them. Despite its economic sluggishness, an issue that Kerala will undoubtedly have to address before long (perhaps by reducing bureaucratic controls over agriculture and industry, which have stagnated), its level of social development has been remarkable, and that has turned out to be crucial in reducing fertility rates. Kerala's fertility rate of 1.8 not only compares well with China's 2.0, but also with the U.S.'s and Sweden's 2.1, Canada's 1.9, and Britain's and France's 1.8.

The population problem is serious, certainly, but neither because of "the proportion between the natural increase of population and food" nor because of some impending apocalypse. There are reasons for worry about the long-term effects of population growth on the environment; and there are strong reasons for concern about the adverse effects of high birth rates on the quality of life, especially for women. With greater opportunities for education (especially female education), reduction of mortality rates (especially of children), improvement in economic security (especially in old age), and greater participation of women in employment and in political action, fast reductions in birth rates can be expected to result through the decisions and actions of those whose lives depend on them.

This is happening right now in many parts of the world, and the result has been a considerable slowing down of world population growth. The best way of dealing with the population problem is to help to spread these processes elsewhere. In contrast, the emergency mentality based on false beliefs in imminent cataclysms leads to breathless responses that are deeply counterproductive, preventing the development of rational and sustainable family planning. Coercive policies of forced birth control involve terrible social sacrifices, and there is little evidence that they are more effective in reducing birth rates than serious programs of collaborative action.[37]

NOTES

1. This paper draws on my lecture arranged by the "Eminent Citizens Committee for Cairo '94" at the United Nations in New York on April 18, 1994, and also on research supported by the National Science Foundation. This essay is reprinted from the *New York Review of Books*, September 22, 1994.

2. Paul Ehrlich, *The Population Bomb* (Ballantine, 1968). More recently Paul Ehrlich and Anne H. Ehrlich have written *The Population Explosion* (Simon and Schuster, 1990).

3. Garrett Hardin, *Living within Limits* (Oxford University Press, 1993).

4. Thomas Robert Malthus, *Essay on the Principle of Population As It Affects the Future Improvement of Society with Remarks on the Speculation of Mr. Godwin, M. Condorcet, and Other Writers* (London: J. Johnson, 1798), chapter 8; in the Penguin classics edition, *An Essay on the Principle of Population* (1982), p. 123.

5. See Simon Kuznets, *Modern Economic Growth* (Yale University Press, 1966).

6. Note by the Secretary-General of the United Nations to the Preparatory Committee for the International Conference on Population and Development, Third Session, A/Conf.171/PC/5, February 18, 1994, p. 30.

7. Philip Morris Hauser's estimates are presented in the National Academy of Sciences publication *Rapid Population Growth: Consequences and Policy Implications*, vol. 1 (Johns Hopkins University Press, 1971). See also Simon Kuznets, *Modern Economic Growth*, chapter 2.

8. For an important collection of papers on these and related issues see Sir Francis Graham-Smith, F.R.S., editor, *Population—The Complex Reality: A Report of the Population Summit of the World's Scientific Academies*, issued by the Royal Society and published in the U.S. by North American Press, Golden, Colorado. See also D. Gale Johnson and Ronald D. Lee, editors, *Population Growth and Economic Development, Issues and Evidence* (University of Wisconsin Press, 1987).

9. Hardin, *Living within Limits*, p. 274.

10. Paul Kennedy, who has discussed important problems in the distinctly "social" aspects of population growth, has pointed out that this debate "has, in one form or another, been with us since then," and "it is even more pertinent today than when Malthus composed his *Essay*," in *Preparing for the Twenty-first Century* (Random House, 1993), pp. 5–6.

11. On the importance of "enlightenment" traditions in Condorcet's thinking, see Emma Rothschild, "Condorcet and the Conflict of Values," *The Historical Journal*, Vol. 39, no. 3 (September 1996).

12. Marie Jean Antoine Nicholas de Caritat Marquis de Condorcet's *Esquisse d'un Tableau Historique des Progrès de l'Esprit Humain, Xe Epoque* (1795). English translation by June Barraclough, *Sketch for a Historical Picture of the Progress of the Human Mind*, with an introduction by Stuart Hampshire (Weidenfeld and Nicolson, 1955), pp. 187–92.

13. T. R. Malthus, *A Summary View of the Principle of Population* (London: John Murray, 1830); in the Penguin classics edition (1982), p. 243; italics added.

14. On practical policies, including criticism of poverty relief and charitable hospitals, advocated for Britain by Malthus and his followers, see William St. Clair, *The Godwins and the Shelleys: A Biography of a Family* (Norton, 1989).

15. Malthus, *Essay on the Principle of Population*, Chapter 17; in the Penguin classics edition, *An Essay on the Principle of Population*, pp. 198–199. Malthus showed some signs of weakening in this belief as he grew older.

16. Gerard Piel, *Only One World: Our Own to Make and to Keep* (Freeman, 1992).

17. For discussions of these empirical connections, see R. A. Easterlin, editor, *Population and Economic Change in Developing Countries* (University of Chicago Press, 1980); T. P. Schultz, *Economics of Population* (Addison-Wesley, 1981); J. C. Caldwell, *Theory of Fertility Decline* (Academic Press, 1982); E. King and M. A. Hill, editors, *Women's Education in Developing Countries* (Johns Hopkins University Press, 1992); Nancy Birdsall, "Economic Approaches to Population Growth" in *The Handbook of Development Economics*, edited by H. B. Chenery and T. N. Srinivasan (Amsterdam: North Holland, 1988); Robert Cassen, et al., *Population and Development: Old Debates, New Conclusions* (New Brunswick: Overseas Development Council / Transaction Publishers, 1994).

18. World Bank, *World Development Report 1994* (Oxford University Press, 1994), Table 25, pp. 210–11.

19. World Bank, *World Development Report 1994*, Table 2.

20. These issues are discussed in my joint book with Jean Drèze, *Hunger and Public Action* (Oxford University Press, 1989), and the three volumes edited by us, *The Political Economy of Hunger* (Oxford University Press, 1990), and also in my paper "Economic Regress: Concepts and Features," *Proceedings of the World Bank Annual Conference on Development Economics 1993* (World Bank, 1994).

21. This is confirmed by, among other statistics, the food production figures regularly presented by the United Nations Food and Agricultural Organization (see the *FAO Quarterly Bulletin of Statistics*, and also the *FAO Monthly Bulletins*).

22. For a more detailed picture and references to data sources, see my "Population and Reasoned Agency: Food, Fertility and Economic Development," in *Population, Economic Development, and the*

Environment, edited by Kerstin Lindahl-Kiessling and Hans Landberg (Oxford University Press, 1994); see also the other contributions in this volume. The data presented here have been slightly updated from later publications of the FAO.

23. On this see my *Poverty and Famines* (Oxford University Press, 1981).

24. See UNCTAD VIII, Analytical Report by the UNCTAD Secretariat to the Conference (United Nations, 1992), table V-S, p. 235. The period covered is between 1979–1981 to 1988–1990. These figures and related ones are discussed in greater detail in my paper "Population and Reasoned Agency," cited earlier.

25. World Bank, *Price Prospects for Major Primary Commodities,* vol. 2 (World Bank, March 1993). Annex tables 6, 12, and 18.

26. Condorcet, *Esquisse d'un Tableau Historique des Progrès de l'Esprit Humain;* in 1968 reprint, p. 187.

27. The importance of "local" environmental issues is stressed and particularly explored by Partha Dasgupta in *An Inquiry into Well-Being and Destitution* (Oxford University Press, 1993).

28. In the monograph by Jean Drèze and myself called *India: Economic Development and Social Opportunities* (New Delhi: Oxford University Press, 1995), we discuss the importance of women's political agency in rectifying some of the more serious lapses in Indian economic and social performance—not just pertaining to the deprivation of women themselves.

29. See Jean Drèze and Amartya Sen, *Hunger and Public Action* (Oxford University Press, 1989), which also investigates the remarkable success of some poor countries in providing widespread educational and health services.

30. World Bank, *World Development Report 1994,* p. 212; and *Sample Registration System: Fertility and Mortality Indicators 1991* (New Delhi: Ministry of Home Affairs, 1993).

31. See the discussions, and the literature cited, in Gita Sen, Aerienne German, and Lincoln Chen, editors, *Population Policies Reconsidered: Health, Empowerment, and Rights* (Harvard Center for Population and Development Studies/International Women's Health Coalition, 1994).

32. On the actual processes involved, see T. N. Krishnan, "Demographic Transition in Kerala: Facts and Factors," in *Economic and Political Weekly,* vol. 11 (1976), and P. N. Mari Bhat and S. I. Rajan, "Demographic Transition in Kerala Revisited," in *Economic and Political Weekly,* vol. 25 (1990).

33. See, for example, Robin Jeffrey, "Culture and Governments: How Women Made Kerala Literate," in *Pacific Affairs,* Vol. 60 (1987).

34. On this see my "More Than 100 Million Women Are Missing," *New York Review of Books,* December 20, 1990; Ansley J. Coale, "Excess Female Mortality and the Balance of the Sexes: An Estimate of the Number of 'Missing Females'," *Population and Development Review,* no. 17 (1991); Amartya Sen, "Missing Women," *British Medical Journal,* no. 304 (March 1992); Stephan Klasen, "'Missing Women' Reconsidered," *World Development,* vol. 22, no. 7 (July 1996).

35. Tamil Nadu has benefited from an active and efficient voluntary program of family planning, but these efforts have been helped by favorable social conditions as well, such as a high literacy rate (the second highest among the sixteen major states), a high rate of female participation in work outside the home (the third highest), a relatively low infant mortality rate (the third lowest), and a traditionally higher age of marriage. See also T. V. Antony, "The Family Planning Programme—Lessons from Tamil Nadu's Experience," *Indian Journal of Social Science,* vol. 5 (1992).

36. World Bank and Population Reference Bureau, *Success in a Challenging Environment: Fertility Decline in Bangladesh* (World Bank, 1993).

7 State Fatherhood

The Politics of Nationalism, Sexuality, and Race in Singapore

Geraldine Heng and Janadas Devan

Postcolonial governments are inclined, with some predictability, to generate narratives of national crisis, driven perhaps—the generous explanation—to reenact periodically the state's traumatic if also liberating separation from colonial authority, a moment characteristically founding the nation itself *qua* nation. Typically, however, such narratives of crisis serve more than one category of reassurance: by repeatedly focusing anxiety on the fragility of the new nation, its ostensible vulnerability to every kind of exigency, the state's originating agency is periodically reinvoked and ratified, its access to wide-ranging instruments of power in the service of national protection continually consolidated. It is a post-Foucauldian truism that they who successfully define and superintend a crisis, furnishing its lexicon and discursive parameters, successfully confirm themselves the owners of power, the administration of crisis operating to revitalize ownership of the instruments of power even as it vindicates the necessity of their use.

If a postcolonial government remains continually in office for decades beyond its early responsibility for the nation's emergence, as is the case in the Republic of Singapore, the habit of generating narratives of crisis at intervals becomes an entrenched, dependable practice. While the metaphors deployed, causes identified, and culpabilities named in the detection of crisis necessarily undergo migration, accusation by the government of Singapore—whose composite representation is overwhelmingly male, Chinese, and socioeconomically and educationally privileged—has been increasingly directed in recent years to such segments of society as do not give

Geraldine Heng teaches medieval literature and women's studies at the Department of English, University of Texas at Austin. Her book-in-progress, *Empire of Magic: Medieval Romance and the Politics of Cultural Fantasy*, considers the nexus of romance, medieval empire-formation and colonization, the politics of gender and sexuality, and issues of language and emergent nationalisms. Her most recent article on Singapore, "'A Great Way to Fly': Nationalism, the State, and the Varieties of Third-World Feminism," appears in Feminist Genealogies, Colonial Legacies, Democratic Futures, eds. M. Jaqui Alexander and Chandra Talpade Mohanty (Routledge, 1996).

Janadas Devan is a Singaporean writer presently based in Austin, Texas. He was educated at the University of Singapore and Cornell University. He writes for newspapers and journals in Southeast Asia and the United States, and is currently working on a book on Singapore, *Model Nation: An Anatomy of the Rational State*.

back an image of the state's founding fathers to themselves. Precise adequacy on the part of the citizenry to an ideal standard of nationalism then becomes referenced, metonymically, to the successful if fantasmatic reproduction of an ideal image of its fathers. Crisis is unerringly discovered—threats to the survival and continuity of the nation, failures in nationalism—when a distortion in the replication or scale of a composition deemed ideal is fearfully imagined.

NATIONALISM AND SEXUALITY: IDEOLOGIES OF REPRODUCTION

That an obsession with ideal replication in the register of the imaginary can lend itself to somatic literalization—transformed through acts of state power into a large-scale social project of *biological* reproduction—is the disturbing subtext of one of the most tenacious and formidable of state narratives constructed in Singapore's recent history, with consequences yet proliferating at the time of this article. Hinging precisely on a wishful fantasy of exact self-replication, this narrative of crisis posits, as the essential condition of national survival, the regeneration of the country's population (its heterogeneous national body) in such ratios of race and class as would faithfully mirror the population's original composition at the nation's founding moment, retrospectively apotheosized. In an aggressive exposition of paternal distress in August 1983 that ranges authoritatively over such subjects as genetic inheritance and culture, definitions of intelligence, social and economic justice and responsibility, and gender theory, the nation's father of founding fathers, Prime Minister Lee Kuan Yew, leveled an extraordinary charge against the nation's *mothers*, incipient and actual—accusing them of imperiling the country's future by willfully distorting patterns of biological reproduction. The disclosure of a reproductive crisis took place, suitably, on the anniversary of the state's birth, during the Prime Minister's annual National Day Rally speech, as part of the celebrations commemorating the country's emergence as a national entity.[1]

The crisis, as formulated by him, received this inflection: highly-educated women in Singapore, defined as those with a university degree, were not producing babies in sufficient numbers to secure their self-replacement in the population, either because of a failure to marry, or, having married, a failure to bear more than 1.65 children per married couple, he declared. On the other hand, poorly educated women, defined as those who do not complete the equivalent of an elementary school education (women of "no education" or "no qualifications," as they came to be called), were reproducing too freely, generating 3.5 children each; women with only an elementary education, producing 2.7 children, were also outstripping the "graduate mothers," as the Prime Minister called them.

This was a problem, Lee reasoned, because graduate mothers produced genetically-superior offspring, the ability to complete a university education attesting to superior mental faculties, which would be naturally transmitted to offspring through genetic inheritance. Eighty percent of a child's intelligence, Lee explained, citing certain studies in genetics and sociobiology, was predetermined by nature, while nurture accounted for the remaining 20 percent. Within a few generations, the quality of Singapore's population would measurably decline, with a tiny minority of intelligent persons being increasingly swamped by a seething, proliferating mass of the unintelligent, untalented, and genetically inferior; industry would suffer, technology deteriorate, leadership disappear, and Singapore lose its competitive edge in the world. Since his was a tiny country of no natural resources and few advantages other than the talents of its people, if measures were not immediately taken to counteract the downhill slide caused by "lopsided" female reproductive sexuality, a catastrophe of major proportions was imminent a scant few generations down the line.[2]

It would seem that men did not figure prominently in the Prime Minister's dystopian vision, because his statistics revealed to him that Singapore women as a rule selected mates of equal or superior academic standing; graduate mothers alone, therefore, could be relied on to guarantee the genetic purity of the tribe. Closer examination of his tables consequently revealed that class and race, however, were the major, suppressed categories of his anxiety, since the women of recalcitrant fertility were by and large Chinese, upper- and middle-class professionals, while those of inordinate reproductive urges and no university degrees comprised, by a stunning coincidence, working-class women of Malay and Indian ethnic origin—members, that is, of Singapore's minority racial groups. The Chinese majority, then 76 percent, was shrinking at the terrifying rate of 7 percent in each generation, even as Malays, a mere 15 percent, were wildly proliferating by 4 percent per generation, and Indians, then 6 percent of the population, by 1 percent. The threat of impending collapse in the social and economic order, for which an unruly, destabilizing, and irresponsible feminine sexuality was held to account, was covertly located at the intersecting registers of race and class. Chaos, in this prophecy of national disaster, was visualized as the random interplay of excess and deficiency among female bodies, which, left unregulated, would produce disabling, ungovernable, and unsafe equations of class and race.[3]

If Lee's articulation of genetic inheritance, culture, education, intelligence, and reproductive sexuality seems inordinately mechanical, his faith in the assumed infallibility (and univocity) of statistics oddly uncritical, and his commitment to the logic of racial and class regulation relentless, it is because he subscribes, without apology, to a projective model of society as an economic and social machine. His stated preference, on the controversial issue of intelligence, for genetic catalogues and theories of determination over such arguments as would consider the interplay of social, psychic, historical, cultural, environmental, *and* genetic forces operating on the human subject (the reductive impatience leading him to extract, from a small-scale study on identical twins by Thomas Bouchard of the University of Minnesota, easy, simplistic axioms and catch-phrases on universal essences of human nature, expressed in tidy percentages) merely evinces a concomitant desire for the human organism to function, also, like a machine. The language of eugenics is precisely for Lee a language of efficient automation—a syntax and grammar congenially identical to his own, and to that routinely employed by his ministers and cohorts in public discourse—the appeal of eugenics residing, for him, in its very promise, however fugitive it might seem to others, of state-of-the-art biological replication: a superior technology to guarantee the efficient manufacture of superior-quality babies (the machine of eugenics confirming the body machine).[4]

The investment in mechanical models of human reproduction, social formations, and the body, exposes, of course, the desire for an absolute mastery, the desire that mastery be absolutely possible. Functional machines in everyday life—machines as they are recognized by Lee, and used in Singapore society—are predictable and orderly, blessedly convenient: malfunctioning ones can be adjusted, faulty components replaced, and the whole made to work again with a minimum of fuss. Most pointedly, a machine presupposes—indeed, requires—an operator, since a machine commonly exists in the first place in order to be operated: relieving all suspicion that full supervisory control may be impossible (exorcising, that is, the specter of desire, instability, and an unconscious from human formations), the trope of the machine comfortingly suggests that what eludes, limits, or obstructs absolute knowability, management, and control can be routinely evacuated.

The indictment of women, then—working class and professional, Malay, Indian, and Chinese—inscribes a tacit recognition that feminine reproductive sexuality refuses, and in refusing, undermines the fantasy of the body-machine, a conveniently operable somatic device: thus also undoing, by extension, that other fantasied economy, society as an equally operable contraption. Indeed, the disapproval, simultaneously, of an overly productive and a non(re)productive feminine sexuality registers a suspicion of that sexuality as noneconomic, driven by pleasure: sexuality for its own sake, unproductive of babies, or babies for their own sake, unproductive of social and economic efficiency.[5] That women of minority races should stand accused of a runaway irresponsibility, moreover, neatly conjoins two constituencies of society believed to be most guilty of pursuing the noneconomy of pleasure (pleasure as, indeed, noneconomic): the female, and the "soft" Indian/Malay citizen, whose earthly sexuality, putative garrulousness, laziness, emotional indulgence, or other distressing irrationality conform to reprobate stereotypes of ethnicity and gender that have, in recent years, prominently found their way into public discourse.

In the months that followed his sketch of a future, feminine-instigated apocalypse, contro-versy of a sort arose around the issue, whose political volatility was at once and slyly undercut, however, by its characterization in the national press and electronic media (which are in Singa-pore either directly state owned, state dominated, or subject to severely restrictive licensing laws) as a "Great Marriage Debate." Its reduction to merely a "debate," and over merely an old, respectable, and comfortably familiar institution, marriage, strategically moved the issue away from any explicit recognition of or engagement with its deeply political, and politically extreme, content. The English-language newspapers would have it, moreover, that the vast majority of their readers were concerned merely to help the Prime Minister accomplish his goal of increased numbers of graduate babies; and since access to popular opinion through media uninflected by state control was, and still remains, unavailable, the character of public response could only be gauged from what was selected for publication in newspaper letters' columns, or broadcast on state-run radio and television programming.[6]

Even as public discussion began, however (a discussion mercilessly regulated by speeches and pronouncements from government cohorts of every description, all tirelessly repeating and expa-tiating at length on the Prime Minister's arguments in a concerted drive to overwhelm public opinion), the government moved with characteristic pre-emptive speed to launch a comprehen-sive system of incentives and threats, together with major changes of social policy, to bend the population in the diction of the Prime Minster's will. Cash awards of S$10,000 were offered to working-class women, under careful conditions of educational and low-income eligibility, to restrict their childbearing to two children, after which they would "volunteer" themselves for tubal ligation. The scheme was piously tricked out in the language of philanthropic concern and state munificence—one fawning newspaper headline even proclaiming it the "Govt's $10,000 Helping Hand for the Low Income Families" [sic]. At the same time as the formal statement from the Prime Minister's Office grandly and unctuously trumpeted its benevolence, maternity charges in public (that is, government-run) hospital wards most frequently used by working-class mothers were increased for those who had already given birth to their state-preferred quota of two children.[7]

To entice graduate women to have more children, on the other hand, generous tax breaks, medical insurance privileges, and admission for their children to the best schools in the country were promised, *inter alia*—prompting legal scholars and others to object that such discriminatory, class-inflected practices were manifestly and blatantly unconstitutional.[8] Changes in school admis-sions policy to further privilege the privileged were nonetheless implemented, the government countering criticism with a massive disinformation effort that shamelessly sought to persuade the disadvantaged that their children, too, would profit from the new hierarchies ("Non-graduates Will also Benefit," one newspaper headline soothingly cajoled the public; another announced, with unremitting cruelty, "More Good News for Non-graduate Mums: All Primary Schools are of Fairly Equal Standard").[9] Other transformations in social policy followed—altered entrance criteria to the country's only existing university to favor men over women applicants, since the Prime Minister's statistics had suggested to him that male more than female university graduates tended to marry and have children;[10] a revised family-planning program that now urged *all who could afford it* to have at least three children (where its former policy encouraged the two-child family as the ideal norm for all, equally); and, more recently, the suggestion that certain restric-tions may be placed on legalized abortion, freely available in Singapore since 1974[11]—but with their relationship to the priorities advertised in the so-called Great Marriage Debate officially denied, minimized, or simply passing unreported and undiscussed. Among its own employees, the government decided to require members of the Civil Service in the higher echelons—Division One officers, who no doubt qualify as intelligent—to submit detailed personal information on themselves and their families, including their "marital status, the educational qualifications of their spouses, and the number of children" they had; and at last one civil servant was summarily selected ("assigned") to undergo an experiment in the use of commercial matchmaking services abroad.[12]

Cabinet ministers began to exhort graduate women to marry and bear children *as a patriotic duty*. Obediently taking their cue from the government, two (nonfeminist) women's organizations accordingly proposed, in a disturbing collusion with state patriarchy, that women be *required* to bear children as a form of National Service—the equivalent, in feminine, biological terms, of the two-and-a-half year military service compulsorily performed by men for the maintenance of national defense.[13] A sexualized, separate species of nationalism, in other words, was being adopted for women: as patriotic duty for men grew out of the barrel of a gun (phallic nationalism, the wielding of a surrogate technology of the body in national defense), so would it grow, for women, out of the recesses of the womb (uterine nationalism, the body *as* a technology of defense wielded by the nation). Men bearing arms, and women bearing children; maternal and/as military duty: the still-recent history of Nazi Germany grimly but not uniquely reminds us that certain narratives of nationalism and dispositions of state power specifically require the exercise of control over the body, the track of power on bodies being visited differently according to gender. The demand that women serve the nation biologically, with their bodies—that they take on themselves, and submit themselves to, the public reproduction of nationalism in the most private medium possible, forcefully reveals the anxious relationship, in the fantasies obsessing state patriarchy, between reproducing power and the power to reproduce: the efficacy of the one being expressly contingent on the containment and subsumption of the other.[14]

As the Prime Minister himself spoke with ominous nostalgia of the traditional means by which women had been variously coerced into bearing children in most Asian cultures of the past, the dependence of paternal power—its assurance of regenerative survival—on the successful conscription and discipline of female reproductive sexuality within hierarchical structures dominated by patriarchs, explicitly surfaced. Lee spoke feelingly of the past, when families could enforce the marriage of their daughters by arranging marriages of convenience without their daughters' consent.[15] He expressed regret at his government's socialist policies in the heady days of early postcolonial independence, when women's suffrage and universal education relinquished to women some control over their biological destinies.[16] He speculated thoughtfully on the possibility of reintroducing polygamy (by which he meant *polygyny* rather than polyandry), outlawed in Singapore since the Women's Charter of 1961, and voiced frank, generous admiration of virile Chinese patriarchs of the past, whose retinues of wives, mistresses, and illegitimate children unquestionably testified, under principles of social Darwinism, to their own, and thus their children's genetic superiority.[17]

Men, it would seem, figured prominently in Lee's dystopian vision after all. Behind the ostensible crisis of maternity and reproduction—too much or too little, never exactly enough—was a crisis of *paternity* and reproduction. A few women suggested, with irony, that if increased numbers of superior children were exclusively the issue, then women ought to be encouraged, nay, urged to have children outside the institution of marriage, with all stigmatization of single mothers and illegitimate offspring removed. Many women, they challenged, did not wish to marry, but wished nonetheless to have children; should not the government in their urgent desire recommend moves toward women-headed families?[18] Recognizing the threat to patriarchal authority vested in the traditional Asian family—after which its own hierarchies and values were after all patterned—the government conspicuously failed to generate enthusiasm for this alternative. A future in which women might conceive and raise children with the support of society, but without the check of a paternal signifier, could not be thought, even in the name of putative national survival. Addressing as it did the hidden stake in Lee's narrative of crisis, whose undisclosed object of concern was precisely the stable replication of the paternal signifier and its powers, this vision of women-led families struck at the core of state fatherhood itself, the institutional basis on which governmental patriarchy was posited.[19]

The narrative behind Lee's narrative could then be read: a fantasy of self-regenerating father-hood and patriarchal power, unmitigated, resurgent, and in endless (self-) propagation, inexhaustibly reproducing its own image through the pliant, tractable conduit of female anatomy—incidental, obedient, and sexually suborned female bodily matter. His sentimental indulgence in the saving visions of a reactionary past, selectively idealized, stages that past as the exclusive theater of omnipotent fathers: state fathers, whose creative powers incorporate and subsume the maternal function, as attested by their autonomous birthing of a nation. The subsequent show of protective solicitude over the national offspring then aggressively, if fantasmatically, replays the cherished moment of paternal delivery: by arresting change and difference in the national body, and wishfully transfixing the population in its original composition at birth, a living testimony to the founding moment is made perpetually available, a constantly present reminder; and the fearful threat of material transmogrification—growth, alteration, difference, the transformations wrought by an undisclosed, never-certain future (imagined, conveniently, as issuing from mothers, that displaced, but ever-looming, ever-returning source of threat and competition)—is simultaneously warded off and disengaged.

Out of that obsession with a pastness ideologically configured had come, then, the script of a dangerous agenda of racial and class manipulation: the very agenda explicitly renounced by the publicly subscribed goals—democracy, equality, and social justice, regardless of race, gender, creed, or class—on which Lee's government had so prided itself, for which it had won the country freedom from Britain, and by which its public mandate to govern today is still declaratively based. It is as a defense against his fear of the future—a future which finds its representation and threat, for him, in a race-marked, class-inflected, ungovernable female body (so commonly figured as the receptacle of the future that it is the perennial locus of social accusation and experiment)—that Lee's Great Marriage Debate was invented. The past—that ground in which the powers of reproduction and the reproduction of power had seemed miraculously to converge in a self-legitimating moment of plenitude echoing through time—served, in this case, as in the case of so many other nations and nationalisms, as the imaginary treasure-house of a superannuated political fantasy.

NATIONALISM AND RACE: REPRODUCTIONS OF IDEOLOGY

Concurrent with the rhetoric of crisis identifying what might be called the threat from within the nation that inaugurates the Great Marriage Debate, there has also been over recent years the discovery of a threat from without, a *cultural* crisis of an equally disturbing magnitude. Represented as the intensified danger of contamination by the West, this particular crisis has required the formulation of related themes in defense of the social body—the retrieval of a superior, "core" Chinese culture in the name of a fantasmatic "Confucianism"; the promotion of Mandarin, the preferred dialect of the ruling class of imperial China, as the master language of Chineseness; and the concoction of a "national ideology," grounded in a selective refiguration of Confucianism, to promote the interests of the state.

All three themes take shape as urgent national priorities to combat this other, external threat to the survival, prosperity, and identity of the nation: "Western" values, variously depicted as individualism, relativism, and hedonism at worst, or as an unstable pluralism and a needlessly liberal democracy at best.[20] The decadent individualism of the West, cabinet ministers declare, has caused the economic decline of the United States relative to Japan, South Korea, Taiwan, and Singapore, the so-called four Asian tigers; concomitantly, these East Asian economies are said to owe their prosperity to their Confucian-based cultures, their "communitarian value system," industry, thrift, and social cohesiveness being attributed to a changeless Confucian *essence* that has been preserved intact through the ages, an essence that not only survives transmission without alteration, but that also has made possible rapid industrial development. Taught in Singapore schools since 1982, Confucianism has been offered as an option to Chinese secondary students, who are encouraged to study it in place of a religion in "moral education" classes. Preceding this initiative by a few years is the "Speak Mandarin" campaign for the preservation of Chineseness: if all Chinese Singaporeans spoke Mandarin, this argument goes, they could communicate without the use of English across dialect boundaries; Chinese values would be disseminated without the dilution and distraction that multiple dialects threaten, and the auditory unity of a common tongue would assuage the dangers of the West.[21]

Like the script of the "Great Marriage Debate," racial and sexual categories are conjoined in the attribution of value and accusation in the detection of crisis. Prime Minister Lee has often reiterated his conviction that the industrial prominence of East Asian societies over the relatively less developed economies of the Indian subcontinent and Malay archipelago is rooted in the "hard" values of the former over the "soft" cultures of the latter, unapologetically proffering, in simultaneous praise and contempt, figures of phallocentric toughness and gynocentric laxity that are scarcely disguised. Indians, moreover, Lee confidently proclaims, are "naturally contentious"; like women, they are loquacious and theatrical, too indulgent and irresponsible ("soft") to be capable of the social discipline of "hard" Confucian cultures that renders East Asian societies increasingly potent as political powers to challenge the West. Lest one miss the point, Lee has mused aloud if Singapore could have achieved its economic and social strides if the population had been composed of an Indian racial majority and a Chinese minority, instead of the other way around. State politics instituted to manipulate female reproductive sexuality in preferred ratios of race and class leave no doubt as to what his government believes the answer to be.[22]

Because almost all Singaporeans under the age of forty speak English today with varying degrees of fluency—93 percent of primary-school-age children are in schools where it is the language of instruction—they are deemed uniquely vulnerable to infection by the West, unlike Japanese, Koreans, and Taiwanese. Encouraged by British colonial policy for over a century, the dominance of English was institutionalized after decolonization by Lee's own government, which established it as the preferred language of education and business and as the *de facto* language of government: a privileged medium of access to Western science and technology that augmented the nation's attractions to multinational capital. In the 1950s and '60s, when the Malayan Communist Party was influential among the Chinese-educated in Singapore and Malaya, the policy of both the British colonial administration and the postcolonial governments that succeeded it involved the diminution in social and political status of Chinese education: "left-wing activist," "Communist," and "Chinese-educated" were virtually synonymous, interchangeable terms ("the English-educated," as Lee put it then, "do not riot"). The association of English with progress and economic enfranchisement resulted, by the mid-1970s, in a considerable reduction in the number of Chinese schools and the closure of the only Chinese-language university in Singapore.

Ironically, thirty years after independence, the very political authority that had institutionalized the language now expresses "doubt about the wisdom of teaching Singaporeans English." "If one went back to Korea, Taiwan, or Hong Kong 100 years from now," Lee speculated in a wistful fantasy of paternal control, "their descendants would be recognizable because what they took in from the West was what their leaders decided to translate into their books, newspapers and t.v. programmes." In Singapore, on the other hand, "we have given everybody a translator in his pocket and all doors are open." In this nightmare vision—the unresisted seduction of a vulnerable, "soft," social body feminized by language ("all doors are open")—Lee saw "a wholesale revision of values, attitudes of good and bad, or role-models and so on."[23] English, once the conduit of rapid economic development that consolidated the power and legitimacy of the new state and its founding fathers, is now a dangerous passage facilitating an invasion of difference that would rupture the continuity of cultural identity and alter the course of ideal generational propagation.

These changing fantasmatic definitions of threats to the state, requiring sporadic redeployment of valid and invalid identities, languages, and cultures in narratives of history and national survival, reveal, then, the essentialist counters of race and culture as amenable to arbitrary representations, inflected by interests of state power. Differences *within* cultures and races—and the conflation of these two terms is a necessary gesture in the essentialist discourse of nationalism—are converted into differences *between* cultures and races, into differences that strategically serve to distinguish valid, enabling, or potent cultural identities from those other identities represented as seductive and disabling, subverting the firmness of national purpose. Narratives of history and survival thus deployed in the production of differences support specific formations of power; the past itself becomes a category produced by present causes to legitimate the exigent directives of the state, and is punctually offered as a reusable counter to vindicate genealogies of state dispensation. Each construction of an essential identity requires a reconfiguring of the past: the equation of "Confucian Chineseness" with the interests of the state demands not only the discounting of Singapore history in the 1950s and 1960s, but also a radical retroping of the enabling conditions of economic development and modern nationhood. No longer is an absorption of Western values, liberal democracy, technological organization, and habits of objectivity deemed *sine qua non* the legitimizing prerequisites of a modern state. That Singapore, like Japan, Korea, and Taiwan, has "arrived" as a developed economy is to be traced instead to the presence in these societies of "core" Confucian virtues—to the efflorescence, as it were, of what has always been there, fully present, denying the perceived absence or lack that instigated the movement toward the West in the immediate postcolonial period. Locating the ideological source of the modern East Asian state in an unchanging Confucian essence allows, moreover, the idealized recuperation of the entire history of Chinese culture as a seamless narrative of continuity and cohesion, suffering neither a fall (as into communism) nor a lack—allows, that is, an ideological fantasy of transgenerational replication, where a signifying essence gendered in a particular modality of authority reproduces itself across history and national boundaries in unobstructed transcendent resurgence. The history of Singapore is then a single moment in the history of Chinese racial culture, written into an integrated script of transnational ideological revitalization.

The mystifications exercised in this figuration of (trans)national ideology should not, however, be read as implying irrationality. The very discovery of Confucianism is articulated by the need to manage, not to resist, an increasingly successful industrial nation. Confucianism accordingly is promoted in Singapore as constitutive of the rational organization of society and has itself been submitted to stringent inquiry that it might be systematically delivered as an object of knowledge, a rational and authoritative epistemology. Confucian scholars are hired from abroad (from metropolitan centers such as Harvard and Princeton, among others) to staff an Institute of East Asian Philosophy at the National University of Singapore: they help to formulate the syllabi and design the texts for school courses, sift Confucian tenets consciously for useful emphases and prescriptions, and systematize the propagation of the subject. Bizarre as this programmatic exercise might seem to Western eyes, it merely repeats, in effect, the modalities of producing and using knowledge long assumed in the West by the social sciences, including the discourse Edward Said calls Orientalism. Based on expertise and scholarly systematization, the knowledge produced is then delivered as a rational, objective, disinterested, and coherent (philosophical) system, conferring legitimacy on the state which establishes the promise of a truly rational organization of society, even as it enables the state to police the boundaries of permissible discourse through the continued regulation of knowledge. Thus mantled in objectivity and knowledge, the state assumes what Foucault calls its "pastoral" function, subjecting its citizens to a "set of very specific patterns" that totalizes the operation of an apparently benign, implicitly paternal power.[24] In Singapore, the paradigms of economic or corporate management and their protocols of rationality serve at once as the model and chief beneficiary of the state's pastoral power, submitting citizens to a structure of values that best subtends, with minimal fuss and resistance, the efficient working of state corporatism and multinational capital.[25] The location of this structure of values in Confucianism, moreover, and the figuration of Confucianism itself as racial and (trans)national identity, continuous with other East Asian societies and with an organically fecund past, stages the modern state and nationalism as merely the theater where a primordial paternal signifier can gather to itself new instruments of potency, without the irritation of difference to trouble its timeless sway. The description of history as the movement and repetition of the same discovers an aggressive and ruthless absorption of contemporary forms of power: few nations can boast the degree of thoroughness to which the founders of Singapore have carried the paternal logic of the modern state.

The policies of the Singapore government cannot therefore be dismissed as an instance of a peculiarly irrational but unique oriental despotism, for their exercise of power is enabled, in large measure, by the reinscription of *Western* modes of discourse in an Asian context. Represented as an invasive threat to Singapore society from without, Western modalities are in fact already operating as instruments of power for the local production of subjects *within* the nation. The strategic deployment of selective material from contemporary metropolitan disciplines such as genetics and sociobiology (in the fabricated exigency dubbed the "Great Marriage Debate") is one explicit instance of state collusion with Western institutions of power/knowledge. Indeed, the domestication of an economy of power operative and operable as rationality—knowledge as a technique, a circuit, of power—is crucially necessary to the constitution of a "native" center of authority. Though the ultimate horizon of complicity between authoritative knowledges in the metropolitan West and formations of power in the postcolonial state is beyond the scope of this article, a few of the productive effects of this complicity can be briefly described.

The institution of what can be called, for suggestive convenience, an "internalized orientalism" makes available to *postcolonial* authority the knowledge-power that *colonial* authority wielded over the local population, and permits, in Singapore, an overwhelmingly Western-educated political elite to dictate the qualities that would constitute Chineseness. Internalized orientalism allows the definition of an idealized Chineseness fully consonant with the requirements of a modern market economy, and supplies the mechanism of justification by which qualities deemed undesirable (and projected as forms of racial and sexual accusation) may be contained or excised. Thus simultaneously concerned with replication and containment, internalized orientalism supervises the erasure of the rich cultural resources of dialects spoken over countless generations, and arbitrarily names Mandarin the single repository of core Chinese virtues so as to facilitate cultural dissemination and bring within the possibility of governance a Chineseness that might otherwise have remained, like female reproductive habits, too resistantly diverse and prolific.

Ignoring the materiality of Chinese history, internalized orientalism writes its own narratives of history and nationalism, in service to the state. In the effort to establish congruence between the individual's place in a "natural institution like the family" and the individual's loyalty to an "omnipresent government" (see note 20), the Singapore brand of Confucianism suppresses the fact that loyalty to family and clan functioned frequently in Chinese history to subtract from loyalty to the state.[26] State fatherhood specifically requires, of course, the intimate articulation of the traditional family with the modern state, and the ostensible homology of the one to the other, claimed by Singapore Confucianism, facilitates and guarantees the transfer of the paternal signifier *from* the family *to* the state, the metaphor of state as family then rendering "natural" an "omnipresent government."[27]

For all the anti-Western rhetoric that characterizes this detection of crisis, then, internalized orientalism in fact supplies state fatherhood with an efficient mechanism for the processing of Western culture—an apparatus of definition, selection, and control that manipulates the rationalizing power of Western modes of knowledge and organization for the efficient management of local capitalism, even as it sets aside as waste what is deemed seductively decadent and dangerous: in short, it presents the ideal regulative machine to the modern Asian state. Whether it provisions the state with a schematic Confucianist system of knowledge or selected statistics from genetics and sociobiology, internalized orientalism serves a paternal master: a gendered formation of power absorbed in fantasmatic repetition, and seeking a reliable machinery of efficient self-regeneration. Recent discoveries of national crisis—in female reproductive sexuality and the social insufficiency that must be rectified by Confucianism, Mandarin, and a national ideology— mark significant breaches, or failures of repetition. The narratives of identity, sexuality, history, culture, and nationalism officially issued with their discovery merely reinstate the proper mechanisms of correction.

In the reproductions of ideology contained in these narratives, then, a dream of a timeless paternal essence merges, splendid, transcendent, immortal.[28] Masking its power in myriad forms, but somehow always managing to reveal itself, this paternal signifier moves across history, and national boundaries, harboring within itself a Chinese soul wielding a Western calculus of choice (so the fantasy goes). Triumphantly resurfacing through many ages, countries, and cultures, always appropriating to itself new, and ever-puissant forms of contemporary power, it finds that it is checked nonetheless in its primordial play, in one location on the globe, by a troublesome figure of difference. Invariably, that figure is feminine. Whether represented by actual women (as in the Great Marriage Debate) or "other" races and cultures whose identifying characteristics are implicitly feminized—whether, that is, it is a sexual, or a social, body that haunts and threatens— the figure of threat, auguring economic and social disintegration, dismantling the foundations of culture, undermining, indeed, the very possibility of a recognizable future, is always, and unerringly, feminine. The Great Marriage Debate, and the great cultural crises in Singapore—the threats from within and without—merely reposition an age-old reminder, repeated in the scripts of many nations, many nationalisms:

Women, and all signs of the feminine, are by definition always and already antinational.

NOTES

1. The trope of father and daughter is so commonly invoked in Singapore to express the relationship between the governing political party that won Singapore independence from Britain (the People's Action Party, or PAP), and the nation itself, as to be fully naturalized, passing unremarked. Singapore is never imagined, by its government or citizens, as a "mother" or "mother country" (identifications reserved exclusively for the ancestral countries of origin of Singapore's various racial groups—India, China, etc.) but rather as a female child, or at best, an adolescent girl or "young lady." A letter to a national newspaper, entitled "Dear PAPa . . . ," and signed by "Singapore, A Young Lady," in the persona of a respectful growing daughter petitioning for greater freedom from her stern father, captures the tenor of the relationship perfectly (*The Straits Times* [Singapore], January 5, 1985). (An answering letter, fictitiously from "PAPa," subsequently appeared in the same newspaper.) The psychic economy of the nation prominently circulates between these two gendered positions, tropes of the mother appearing only as counters of facilitation in and reinforcement of the father-daughter dyad.

2. "If we continue to reproduce ourselves in this lopsided way, we will be unable to maintain our present standards. Levels of competence will decline. Our economy will falter, the administration will suffer and the society will decline. For how can we avoid lowering performance when for every two graduates (with some exaggeration to make the point), in 25 years' time there will be one graduate, and for every two uneducated workers, there will be three?" ("Talent for the Future: Prepared Text of the Prime Minister, Mr. Lee Kuan Yew's Speech at the National Day Rally Last Night," *The Straits Times* (Singapore), August 15, 1983.

3. Lest anyone assume that Lee's articulation of race, class, and gender in the detection of reproductive crisis is unique to Singapore, attention might be drawn to the increasing number of articles in popular U.S. magazines that describe similar discoveries in alarmist, prophetic tones like his—see, e.g., "A Confederacy of Dunces: Are the Best and the Brightest Making Too Few Babies?" in *Newsweek* (May 22, 1989); and R. J. Herrnstein, "IQ and Falling Birthrates," in the *Atlantic Monthly* (May 1989), the latter glossed by the cover headline: "In this Issue: Why are Smart Women Having Fewer Children?" Lee, in the latter article, is admiringly played up as a stalwart example of farsighted and courageous leadership that dares to take measures to rectify envisaged future disaster. Significantly,

he is cast in this favorable light with Arthur Balfour, the prime minister of Britain who moaned in 1905 that "everything done towards opening careers to the lower classes did something towards the degeneration of the race." The eugenic nightmare of a representative of British high imperialism is echoed thus across the century—the cadences of alarm, fear, and threat remaining unchanged—by the postcolonial prime minister of (a formerly British) Singapore. Nor is Lee's reductive faith in the genetic transmission of intelligence a subscription exclusive now to retrograde third world autocrats. Even as a redoubtable Jay Gould stirred himself to counter Lee's misuse of scientific arguments ("Singapore's Patrimony [and Matrimony]: The Illogic of Eugenics Knows Neither the Boundaries of Time nor Geography," *Natural History*, May 1984), U.S. genetic determinists Thomas Bouchard, John Karlsson, and the seemingly indefatigable William Shockley lent themselves to eager support of Lee's vision: "The Singapore program," says Shockley, "is discriminate in a very constructive way. Discrimination is a valuable attribute. Discrimination means the ability to select a better wine from a poorer wine. The word has become degraded. And social engineering? As soon as you've got welfare programs, where you prevent improvident people from having their children starve to death, you are engaged in a form of social engineering. Of genetic engineering even. We have these things going on now, but we're not looking at what effects they have, and that's where the humanitarianism is irresponsible" (see "The Great Debate Over Genes," *Asiaweek*, March 2, 1984).

4. Lee has, on occasion, referred to the people of Singapore as "digits," their inherited attributes as "hardware" to be "programmed" with "software" (ideology, education, culture, etc.). A cohort of his recently suggested, in public, that people "interface" more with one another to increase human communication and understanding. Typically, Lee's National Day Rally speeches (the August 1983 one is no exception) begin with a report of the nation's economic progress for the year in a detailed statistical format, the machinery of statistics representing, for him, and for his government, the power of a penultimate, absolute, and unarguable force. That his statistics in this particular instance are not immovable, however, is suggested by curious vagrancies in the figures subsequently cited, with confident authority, by various government individuals in his support (the "1.6" children born to graduate parents sometimes mutating, for instance, into "1.3" or "1.7" children).

5. Thomas Laqueur's contention that feminine pleasure (and in particular the female orgasm) was historically read as essential to the economy of female reproductive sexuality suggests that its functional removal from that economy has specifically marked it as superfluous, irrelevant ("Orgasm, Generation, and the Politics of Reproductive Biology," in Catherine Gallagher and Thomas Laqueur, eds., *The Making of the Modern Body: Sexuality and Society in the Nineteenth Century* [Berkeley: University of California Press, 1987], pp. 1–41). The pleasurable and the economic are not only read as separate in Singapore today, but inimical (the trope of the machine allowing no role for pleasure, which by its very concession of uselessness, nonnecessity, and excess disables the fantasies of order and regularity on which a local notion of the economic must depend): indeed, pleasure is tacitly suspected of subverting what would otherwise have been an economic reproductive sexuality, distorting this instead into its opposite, a self-indulgent noneconomy.

6. The *Straits Times*, publishing 31 of the 101 letters it received immediately following the Prime Minister's speech, defended its decision not to publish the remaining 71 letters thus: "Sifting through the pile, one can detect some misunderstanding of Prime Minister Lee Kuan Yew's message. Most of the correspondents did not address their thoughts to the main issue: The better-educated segment of the population should be encouraged to have more children (than what they are having now) to bring about a more balanced reproduction rate. Instead, they interpreted the speech as one more setback for the less intelligent in our society" (A. S. Yeong, "What the Others Said: An Analysis of Unpublished Letters on the PM's National Day Rally Speech," *The Straits Times* [Singapore], August 29, 1983). Among the letters published—no doubt because it was thought acute and useful—was an argument to do away with the right of every adult citizen to an equal vote in national elections: "If, at any stage, there is a threat to progress due to increasing numbers of incompetent people, government may even think of introducing a weightage factor for every vote

that comes from a 'qualified' person so that power and administration are kept in the hands of truly competent persons. In a democratic set-up, the principle of 'one person one vote' is fast becoming a menace to society" (G. Rangarajan, "Maintain a Competent Majority," letter to *The Straits Times* [Singapore], August 19, 1983).

7. The statement from the Prime Minister's Office declares, in officialese borrowed from sociology: "Unless we break this low education large family cycle, we will have a small but significant minority of our people permanently trapped in a poverty subculture, whilst the rest of the population will move even further up the economic and social ladder" (Margaret Thomas, "Govt's $10,000 Helping Hand for the Low Income Families," *The Sunday Monitor* [Singapore], June 3, 1984). The aim of this money incentive, according to the report, "is to encourage poorly-educated and low-income Singaporeans . . . to stop at two so that their children will have a better chance in life." The writer of this article, driven to notice the coincidence of class and race in the encouragement of this particular group of citizens, nonetheless finds in it an opportunity to play up the dewy-eyed innocence and ingenuous charity of the proposal: "Though it is not spelt out in the statement, a significant proportion of the people caught in the poverty trap are Malays. . . . The relatively disadvantaged position of the Malay community is a matter of concern to both leaders of the community and the Government."

8. The relevant clause in the Constitution, article 16(1)(a), reads: "There shall be no discrimination against any citizens of Singapore on the grounds of religion, race, descent or place of birth . . . in the administration of any educational institution maintained by a public authority and, in particular, the admission of pupils or students or the payment of fees." Of six unnamed "legal experts" consulted by one newspaper, four agreed that the privileging of certain children over others in the proposed new admissions policy was in direct contravention of this clause (see Siva Arasu, "Unconstitutional? What Legal Experts Say," *The Sunday Times* [Singapore], March 4, 1984). Protests against the scheme were lodged by one government Member of Parliament (Tan Ban Huat, "A Violation of Constitution, Says Dr. Toh," *The Straits Times* [Singapore], February 13, 1984); the lone opposition-party Member then in Parliament (see "House Throws Out Motion by Jeya on Entry Scheme," *The Straits Times* [Singapore], March 14, 1984); the National University of Singapore Students' Union, in a petition carrying 3,000 signatures (Hedwig Alfred, "NUS Students' Union Wants to Meet Dr. Tay," *The Straits Times* [Singapore], March 14, 1984); and "500 undergraduates, or nearly 40 percent" of the student population of the Nanyang Technological Institute ("NTI Students Pen Protests Against Priority Plan: A Class System Would Arise, They Say," *The Sunday Times* [Singapore], February 19, 1984).

9. The Minister of State for Education at the time, Dr. Tay Eng Soon, repeatedly characterized the country's top schools (a description earned on the basis of examination results and the traditional reputation of the institutions) as schools that were merely "popular" as a consequence of public misconception (see "Equal Standard, Equal Chances" and Hedwig Alfred, "More Good News for Non-Grad Mums: All Primary Schools Are of Fairly Equal Standard—Dr. Tay," *The Sunday Times* [Singapore], March 4, 1984). In the midst of public anxiety, resentment, and anger over the proposed changes, the Minister admitted, in an interview with *The Straits Times*, that for all the fuss and trouble, only 200 children were eligible for the new privileges that year (June Tan, "Non-Graduates Will Also Benefit," *The Straits Times* [Singapore], January 24, 1984). Despite Tay's firm assurance in January 1984 that the new policy would be a permanent one, public opinion nevertheless triumphed, and the demise of the scheme was announced in March 1985: "Education Minister Dr. Tony Tan has decided that Singapore can do without the controversial priority scheme which favoured the children of graduate mothers but made a whole lot of people angry" (see "Graduate Mum Scheme to Go," *The Straits Times* [Singapore], March 26, 1985).

10. In August 1983, Lee pronounced the larger number of male to female university graduates a source of satisfaction (Bob Ng, "PM: Watch This Trend: Talent Problem Will Worsen When Women Graduates Are No Longer in the Minority," *The Straits Times* [Singapore], August 22, 1983). By

October, a change in university admissions policy was announced: "This more-girls-fewer-boys trend was worrying, [the Vice-Chancellor] said, on general principles. Asked if the new policy had anything to do with the Great Marriage Debate—that many women graduates are staying unmarried because a lot of male graduates are marrying less educated women—he said it was unfair to say so. But if [the National University of Singapore] continued to take in more girls than boys, 'the problem of unmarried women graduates will be aggravated'" (June Tan and Abdullah Tarmugi, "NUS Relaxes Rule on Second Language: To Redress Imbalance between Male and Female Undergrads," *The Sunday Times* [Singapore], October 30, 1983).

11. "Whatever the changes, the two-child family will remain the norm, except that now well-educated parents who have the means to bring up children in a good home are encouraged to have more than two" (June Tan, "New Family Planning Slogan: Message Will Tell Different Things to Different People," *The Straits Times* [Singapore], January 31, 1984). A year later, in 1985, restrictions on abortion began to be publicly discussed (Irene Hoe, "When MPs Shake Their Heads Over Unwed Mums," *The Straits Times* [Singapore], March 17, 1985).

12. The information to be furnished compulsorily was formidably exhaustive: "They must state whether the spouse has a pass degree or is an honors graduate, and if so, which class, the year it was obtained and the name of the college or university. Those with spouses having a pass degree or lower qualifications have to furnish details of the examinations they sat for, the subjects taken, the grades achieved, the name of the school and the year they got their certificates" (see "Officials Asked to Disclose Spouses' Education," *The Straits Times* [Singapore], September 9, 1983; and Teresa Ooi, "Singapore Diplomat is Asked to Try Out Match-Making Service," *The Straits Times* [Singapore], September 18, 1983).

13. Tsang So-Yin, "The National Service for Women," *The Straits Times* (Singapore), August 17, 1983. Sunday columnist Irene Hoe tartly responded: "If childbirth is indeed national service, the women in the S[ingapore] C[ouncil of] W[omen's] O[rganizations] should be the first to volunteer—before they seek to draft other women" ("The National Service for Women: If Childbirth Is That, These Women Leaders Should Set an Example," *The Sunday Times* [Singapore], August 21, 1983). For the homology between military service and maternal service in cultural representation, see Nancy Huston, "The Matrix of War: Mothers and Heroes," in Susan Rubin Suleiman, ed., *The Female Body in Western Culture* (Cambridge, MA: Harvard University Press, 1986), pp. 119–36.

14. Alice Jardine finds "a climate of sustained . . . paranoia" to exist whenever "the *regulation* of the mother's body . . . [serves] as ground for a monolithic, nationalistic ideology" ("Opaque Texts and Transparent Contexts: The Political Difference of Julia Kristeva," in Nancy K. Miller, ed., *Poetics of Gender* [New York: Columbia University Press, 1986], p. 108). Laurie Langbauer suggests that "the mother's confinement during delivery" in the nineteenth century represents an attempted immobilization of a certain fear of feminine regenerative uncontrollability—the physical transfixing of the woman being itself an admission of her "controlling power" of reproduction ("Women in White, Men in Feminism," *Yale Journal of Criticism*, 2, 2 [1989], p. 223).

15. "In the old days, matchmakers settled these affairs. . . . I remember, as a young boy, hearing my grandmother talk, and she got my aunt married off. She was already 20 plus . . . and there was a widow with no children. Well educated, highly suitable. The result is a family of five, all of whom made it to university. My cousins. . . . We are caught betwixt and between, from an old world in which these matters are thoroughly considered and carefully investigated and properly arranged, to this new world of hit and miss" ("Talent for the Future").

16. "When we adopted these policies they were manifestly right, enlightened and the way forward to the future. With the advantage of blinding hindsight, educating everybody, yes, absolutely right. Equal employment opportunities, yes, but we shouldn't get our women into jobs where they cannot, at the same time, be mothers. . . . You just can't be doing a full-time, heavy job like that of a doctor or engineer and run a home and bring up children . . . we must think deep and long on the profound changes we have unwittingly set off" ("Talent for the Future").

17. "Mr. Lee told an audience of university students that polygamy allowed the mentally and physically vibrant to reproduce. He said that in the old society, successful men had more than one wife. Citing the example of former Japanese Prime Minister Kakuei Tanaka as a man who had a wife and a mistress and children by both, he said the more Tanakas there were in Japan, the more dynamic its society would be" (Kong Sook Chin, "Woman MP Questions Notion of Polygamy," *The Sunday Times* [Singapore], December 28, 1986).

18. In a forum conducted by *The Sunday Times*, two women, who went by the pseudonymous names of "Veronica" and "Mrs. Chan," produced the following dialogue: "Mrs. Chan: 'No woman would support polygamy.' Veronica: 'But there are women like me who would love to have children even though we're unmarried.' Mrs. Chan: 'Yes, a lot of women would like that. Our laws should not penalize such women. Those who are professional and financially self-supporting are quite capable of bringing up their children alone. We should encourage single motherhood, allow such interested women to have artificial insemination.' Veronica: 'It needn't be by artificial means.' (Laughter)" (Tan Lian Choo, "Marriage and the Single Girl: The Sunday Times Roundtable," *The Sunday Times* [Singapore], July 20, 1986).

19. Single motherhood appears to make patriarchy of the first world as much as the third world variety equally queasy. In a *Newsweek* article (October 31, 1988) on what seems to be a highly successful program of state-supported single motherhood in Sweden (the title of which—"What Price Motherhood? An Out-of-Wedlock Baby Boom in Sweden"—strategically projects an affect of doubt and skeptical disapproval), Neil Gilbert, "who heads the Family Welfare Research Group at the University of California at Berkeley," is quoted as saying piously: "If people aren't willing to make commitments . . . you wonder what kind of society you will have down the line."

20. Professor Tu Wei Ming of Harvard University, the government's most prominent Confucian "expert," has offered the view that "democratic institutions . . . are institutions that, if not diametrically opposed to, are at least in basic conflict with *natural* organizations such as family. . . . Some very deep-rooted Confucian-humanistic values are values that need to be fundamentally transformed to be totally compatible with democratic institutions." The newspapers that published the text of Professor Tu's talk glossed it thus: "Democratic institutions are opposed to basic Confucianist ideas like the primacy of the family, an *omnipresent* government, and a preference for a community of trust rather than an adversarial relationship" (emphasis ours). See "When Confucianism Grapples with Democracy," *The Sunday Times* [Singapore], November 27, 1988).

21. Singaporeans are commanded by the most prominent slogan in the campaign to "Speak More Mandarin, Less Dialects" [sic], as if Mandarin itself were not a dialect. Mandarin is now referred to as the "mother tongue" of all Chinese, though virtually all Chinese in Singapore, left to themselves, would likely identify their "mother tongues" as Teochew, Hokkien, Cantonese, Hainanese, Shanghainese, Hakka, or some other regional dialect spontaneously used in their family. Their official "mother tongue," by contrast, has to be acquired through formal education, a large percentage of Chinese schoolchildren proving so inept at it as to require extensive extracurricular private tuition. The government has gone to great lengths, nonetheless, to promote Mandarin, including dubbing Cantonese feature films and soap operas from Hong Kong into Mandarin for Singapore television, and instituting a campaign to discourage taxi drivers—notoriously resistant to government regulation—from speaking in dialect. By the government's own estimate, the measures have been successful; 87 percent of Chinese Singaporeans, they claim, can now speak Mandarin.

22. Recently, in defending a government policy to import up to 100,000 Chinese from Hong Kong to redress declining birth rates among Chinese Singaporeans, Lee repeated the scenario of crisis he sketched in inaugurating the Great Marriage Debate in marginally more delicate terms: "Let us just maintain the status quo. And we have to maintain it or there will be a shift in the economy, both the economic performance and the political backdrop which makes that economic performance possible" (see "Hongkongers' Entry Won't Upset Racial Mix," *The Straits Times Weekly Overseas Edition*, August 26, 1989).

23. See N. Balakrishnan, "Pledge of Allegiance: Core Values Touted as an Antidote to Westernisation," *Far Eastern Economic Review* (Hong Kong), February 9, 1989.

24. Michel Foucault, "Afterword: The Subject and Power," in Hubert L. Dreyfus and Paul Rabinow, *Michel Foucault: Beyond Structuralism and Hermeneutics* (Chicago: University of Chicago Press, 1983), pp. 213–14.

25. Significantly, the notion that East Asian industrial powers owe their prosperity to a Confucian essence circulates prominently also in the West, repeated so often in U.S. print and electronic media as to be naturalized as fact. The image of a ruthlessly efficient Confucianist Orient, with a highly commendable "communitarian value system"—celebrated in the West chiefly, one suspects, for the purpose of promoting a particular reorganization within Western industrial societies—is shared by the Orient itself to promote a similar agenda: the efficient management of capitalism.

26. For instance, in *The Gates of Heavenly Peace: The Chinese and Their Revolution, 1895–1980* (New York: Viking, 1981), Jonathan Spence quotes a writer who blamed "Chinese faith in the family for having destroyed all possibilities of true patriotism" (340), and cites Lu Xun's contempt for Confucian scholars, the fictionist asserting in a story that these Confucianists had survived through the centuries because they "had never laid down their lives to preserve a government" (122).

27. Recently, speaking on the problem of escalating emigration from Singapore, First Deputy Prime Minister Goh Chok Tong introduced a plaintive inflection of the trope of state as family: "No country is perfect just as no family is perfect. But we do not leave our family because we find it imperfect or our parents difficult" ("The Emigration Problem," *The Straits Times* [Singapore], October 6, 1989).

28. Personal immortality is sometimes claimed by the representatives of paternal essentialism as well. An issue of *Newsweek* (November 19, 1990) quoted Prime Minister Lee as saying, in concern over the future of Singapore: "Even from my sickbed, even if you are going to lower me in my grave and I feel that something is going wrong, I'll get up."

8 Gender in the Post-Socialist Transition

The Abortion Debate in Hungary

Susan Gal

INTRODUCTION[1]

The fall of communism in Eastern Europe has had profoundly gendered effects. Women's experiences of the economic and political changes have been different from those of men; the implications for women's lives are often more damaging. Equally important, in all the countries of Eastern Europe, questions of procreation and reproduction became, for a time, the focus of intense public debate and legislative action. In Hungary, as in many countries of the region, the lenient regulations of the late communist era that assured easy access to abortion were challenged after 1989, at the highest parliamentary levels.

It is important to ask why questions of abortion gained such attention, especially since, in contrast to other social problems of the post-socialist period such as inflation, ethnic tension, rising unemployment, and loss of state-supported social services, abortion regulations were not a source of popular discontent.[2] I argue that the insistent debates about abortion reveal the ways in which politics has been (re)constituted in Eastern Europe. Reproduction, as an issue, allowed "morality" and "nature" to be invoked to justify the power of groups and factions newly vying for control of the political process.

This suggests that, in order to understand the direction of social change in Eastern Europe since the end of communism, it is not enough to examine the aspects of social life that mainstream social science has identified as crucial: privatization, marketization, democratization, the growth of civil society, and new forms of the state. We must also consider the discourses and practices of gender. These affect not only interpersonal matters, but also the political economy of large-scale social transformations.[3] For example, the practices of procreation and reproduction have far-reaching effects on such matters as the population's size and age composition, as well as various parameters of the labor force. Yet my aim here is not to analyze such practices in themselves, but rather to explicate the public *discourse* about reproduction that accompanied the end of communism.

Susan Gal is Professor of Anthropology at the University of Chicago. She writes about the language of politics and politics of language, especially as these intersect with gender categories and everyday practices. She is currently co-organizer (with Gail Kligman) in a comparative analysis of gender discourses, women's strategies, and economic change across post-socialist Eastern Europe.

A focus on discourse is important for two reasons. First, in discussing Eastern Europe there is a tendency to assume that American and Western European observers already understand the terms in which people frame their concerns. The words themselves appear familiar because, like "human rights," or "free press," "abortion" is an active term in American public debates, about which Eastern Europeans are well informed. They need to be, because they must often orient to the transnational legal institutions of the European Community, the global financial and moral linkages of the IMF and the Catholic Church. Moreover, Eastern European political arguments have also been borrowed into American and Western European debates.

Yet, despite some deceptive parallels, "abortion" in Hungary is embedded in a different field of meanings than its cognates elsewhere in the world. If we view the debate about abortion in Hungary as part of a politics of reproduction, potentially comparable to similar processes in other parts of the globe, then it is important to specify exactly how it was differently encoded, differently linked to other political questions. For example, we should be able to differentiate it from American debates about abortion in the late nineteenth century that were part of arguments for racial supremacy and medical hegemony (Mohr 1978, Petchesky 1984); from Western European conceptions about reproduction as part of the welfare state's responsibility toward women and children (Glendon 1987); or from arguments about abortion that pitted women's privacy, pleasure, and autonomy against society's moral revitalization in twentieth-century America (Luker 1984, Ginsberg 1989). Thus, it is not that politicization of reproduction is peculiar to any region, or to the present transformations in Eastern Europe, but rather that the nature of that politicization reveals much about the polity in which it occurs.

Second, a focus on discourse and the debates around abortion allows us to turn this link between politics and reproduction around, and ask not how politics influences ideas about reproduction, but rather how the issue of reproduction constitutes one of the means by which claims for political power are made, and through which they are widely understood as natural and legitimate. Thus, in the present case, the abortion debate turns out not only to be very much about abortion, but also an argument in absentia with communism and a scramble for newly available forms of symbolic capital. Indeed, it is a contest for control of the emerging principles of political rule. It allows us to see the many ironies evident in the attempt to make a new social order against a previous one whose elements are nevertheless the only building materials at hand.

Because it makes politics, the abortion debate was an integral part of the restratification of Hungarian society in the wake of communism. In contrast to the arena of privatization, which allowed the reproduction of old elites based on existing expertise, social networks, social positions, and the consequent access to information and capital, the abortion debate was linked most closely to the political sphere where new elites were forming at the same time as they constructed the cultural grounds to produce, justify, and legitimate their own mobility.[4]

After a brief sketch of reproductive politics in socialist Hungary, I discuss two strands of argument in the two years of controversy leading up to the 1992 parliamentary vote. The first strand came from the populist writers and their allies, including Christian professionals, as well as the centrist and conservative political parties who were part of Hungary's first, post-1989, coalition government (1990–1994). The second was produced by writers, academics, and journalists aligned with the parties who claimed the label "liberal," and who constituted the parliamentary opposition during those years. In discussing these debates, I draw on approaches to textuality that have been emerging in contemporary linguistic anthropology (e.g., Briggs and Bauman 1992, Gal 1991), briefly indicating some of the defining characteristics of public pronouncements within each position, and how such texts engage each other.

NOTES ON THE POLITICS OF REPRODUCTION UNDER SOCIALISM

Disputes about abortion and the related issues of childcare, welfare, and motherhood emerged repeatedly in Hungarian politics during the state socialist period. Although discussed under the rubric of "socialist planning," "population," or "health," they were often linked to industrial and foreign policy as well. These political precedents, and the institutional and personal memories produced through these policies, formed the material out of which new traditions could be built, and constrained what was seen as possible and desirable in the 1990–92 debate.

Official abortion regulations following the Second World War required the consent of two physicians whose professional judgments about the health risks to the mother formed the basis of the decision. These regulations had emerged through a process of medical professionalization and heated political debate during the 1930s.[5] But with the consolidation of Communist rule in 1949, abortion ceased to be a matter of medical judgment and became instead the object of centrally determined social planning. Policies concerning it were important enough to be personally made and signed by a whole series of Communist Party first secretaries. I focus here not so much on the details of these regulations but on how they were justified. Three quite separate phases of abortion regulation can be discerned, roughly corresponding to the waxing and waning of more general reformist strategies within the Party.

The first, between 1949 and 1954, was an extremely restrictive ban that criminalized abortion, putting in place a strident anti-abortion information campaign and a series of reporting practices that in effect put the adult population under surveillance. Not coincidentally, this followed closely the Soviet policy of the period. The 1953 abortion regulation refused the possibility of abortion even on medical grounds. The emphasis in official announcements was on the military and production needs of Hungary and the responsibility of every person to subordinate personal choice to the overriding interests of the socialist state. The death of Stalin and internal changes in Hungarian leadership ended this restrictive period, so that during the more general liberalizations following 1956, abortion was allowed to adult women on demand. This change was understood by the public as the retreat of the state from private life. It was widely regarded as an officially unacknowledged but important victory of the 1956 revolution. By the 1960s, an independent trend toward lower fertility along with the rise in number of abortions produced its effect: the Hungarian population, like many in Western Europe, was not replacing itself.

In response to this demographic decline, and also as part of the general political retrenchment following the reforms of 1968, a new and restrictive abortion policy was put into place in 1973–74. The regulations were publicly justified as a protection of women's health against the ravages of abortion, but no such negative effects were ever empirically demonstrated. More broadly, a media campaign reasserted the rationale of national over individual interests and attacked the "unhealthy" spirit of individualism (leading to birth control) as unacceptable in a socialist society. The 1973 policy was in force, though administered increasingly more leniently, until the late 1980s when abortion became available more-or-less on demand.

There was no popular outcry against this policy after the fall of the communist government in 1989. Rather, a small group calling itself "Defenders of the Fetus" appealed to the Supreme Court of Hungary, arguing, in the new climate of rights and rule of law, that something as important as abortion policy should at least be in the form of a law, ratified by Parliament, rather than simply a paternalistic regulation, ordered by the Central Committee. The Court ruled that because the right to life was safeguarded by the Hungarian constitution, a decision had to be made by Parliament about the circumstances under which this could be abrogated; it mandated that the legislative body make the decision by the end of 1992.

The law finally passed by Parliament was a compromise measure, judged "liberal" by much of the Hungarian and even the international press. But on close scrutiny, it shows several restrictive aspects as well. Its requirements of familial consent, waiting period, repeated visits to clinics, and raised prices put anti-abortion pressure on poor women, rural women, and women whose families disapprove of the decision. The arguments by which such a policy was made and understood, in the context of previous abortion regulation, are the center of interest here.

POPULIST WRITERS AND CHRISTIAN PROFESSIONALS

Opposition to abortion was an integral part of the cultural understandings that organized the political opposition to communism in the 1980s in Hungary. Among the populist writers who constituted one strand of this opposition, references to abortion appeared regularly. On September 27, 1987, about 150 writers, scholars, technical workers, and others took part in a semilegal meeting held outside of Budapest that was later sanctified as the first successful large-scale public action of the many politically diverse social groups and networks that constituted the growing opposition to the government. Many of the participants have since become prominent in Hungarian government and political life. The dominant themes of the meeting were economic and civil reform. Yet, the complaints of the populists were pointedly not economic. The meeting was opened by one such writer who said: Hungarians had "become crippled in our moral attitudes, in our beliefs . . . and thus unable to be born in proper circumstances and in sufficient numbers" (Lezsák 1991: 6). To understand the conspicuous place of reproduction in this jeremiad, we must see how this writer has positioned himself with respect to earlier debates.

A distinctive feature of discussions about abortion in Hungary for over a century has been the assumption that it is a problem of declining population. And this evokes, among educated people, echoes of another worry: the imminent death of the nation. This fear was enunciated by populist writers in the 1930s who turned to investigations of the countryside in an effort to redefine national identity. Such redefinitions were made necessary by the massive and traumatic losses of land and hence population that were suffered by Hungary when the Treaty of Trianon redistributed Hungarian territories among the victors of the First World War. In several rural regions, the writers (re)discovered a tradition of population control that had been in existence since the abolition of serfdom. Well-to-do Hungarian peasants restricted reproduction to a single child, usually in order to keep the patrimony undivided and viable. This was usually accomplished through social pressure exerted by elder generations, especially women (Vásáry 1989).

For the populists this was an emotionally wrenching sociopolitical phenomenon, as threatening to the nation as the diminution of population brought about by the Treaty of Trianon. They invoked Herder's eighteenth-century prophecy that Hungarians would soon be lost among the more numerous Germans and Slavs, and tied this prediction directly to reproductive practices and the dangers of "rural matriarchy." Populist writers argued that Hungarian peasants were deliberately, selfishly, and wrong-headedly destroying themselves. Unless the populists could save them, the nation would simply die out and be forgotten by the world.[6]

The populists of 1987 evoked memories of this older debate by using similar rhetorical figures. They talked of abortion as "national catastrophe" and a "biological Trianon." They likened the "four million Hungarians" (not fetuses or babies, but Hungarians) lost through abortion to the Hungarian losses in sixteenth-century patriotic battles against the Turks. And, like the writers of the 1930s, they linked these losses to a lack of national consciousness and a lack of appropriate morality. Another speech, delivered at the same meeting in 1987, reveals some of the other ways in which opposition to abortion was constructed as part of nationalist feeling, and how a continuity with the earlier discourse—indeed, the recontextualization of that earlier discourse into the current circumstances—was accomplished:

This is a nation that has seen harder times [even than now]. . . . We are probably the first in the world not only in suicide and mortality, not only in failure to be born . . . but also in production of emigrants. It started with the staggering losses [of Trianon], it continued after 1920 with further expulsions through which many valuable brains ended up in the service of foreigners. The high point was the departure of Béla Bartók; then came the forced emigration of 1945–48 during which a great variety of spiritual forces left the homeland in masses. This was topped only by the exodus of 1956. And in our own days there is the flood out of Transylvania. . . . So, there is a basis for our fear of death. (Csurka 1991: 24).

Note how this passage creates an apparently coherent historical fate for the nation by linking selected events in chronological order. Through a formal parallelism we are invited to understand that suicides are the same kind of social phenomenon as abortion [the failure to be born], which is in turn equivalent to territorial diminution, as well as to waves of emigration, no matter how distinct their motivation: Béla Bartók left Hungary expressly to escape impending fascism, while the 1945–1948 emigration was made up, in part, of fascists.

Furthermore, the passage is a fine example of textual invention of tradition. Its form suggests that communism is an enemy of the nation because the form implicitly equates communism, which is understood by listeners as responsible for the current rate of suicide, abortion, the emigration of 1956 and emigration from Transylvania, with those foreign enemies of Hungary who were responsible for the losses of Trianon, and 1945–1948. And indeed, with every liberalization of abortion after 1956, communist ideologues worried not only about the response of the Soviet Union and about the effect on population, but also that lenience towards abortion would incite "anti-Communist feeling" among a new generation of potentially influential populist intellectuals. They feared the party would be seen as indifferent to population decline and hence as "against the nation." Being against abortion was equated with being against the death of the nation, which became, by 1987, an important element in opposition to "alien" Communist rule.

When populist writers equated the high rate of abortion with the immorality of state socialism, their rhetoric dovetailed precisely with the religiously based arguments of conservative, Christian doctors and lawyers.[7] But these professionals emphasized not responsibilities toward the nation but the need for morality in life choices about family and money. Along with other critics in Hungary, they noted that communism socialized many functions of the bourgeois family and devalued motherhood in a misguided attempt to equalize and even homogenize the sexes. By seeking the centralization of all power, state socialism destroyed social solidarities outside the family and thus promoted an atomization of social life. This, they argued, produced a "selfish" obsession with financial success and a concomitant neglect of ethics, care, and concern for other people.

A sordid interest in money, and a "cynical materialism," were linked in such discussions to the high rate of abortion: Those who would choose not to give birth because of financial insecurity or lack of an apartment in which to raise children were labeled materialistic and unethical for putting creature comforts above responsibilities to higher ethical values, such as life, the good of humanity, or even the Hungarian nation. Just as the communist rhetoric of the 1950s and 1970s asked people (and especially women) to unselfishly produce children for the sake of industrial development in a socialist collectivity, so the populists and conservative professionals asked for renunciation of selfishness, but this time in the interests of humanity, morality, and nation.

In addition, members of the legal and medical professions charged state socialism with a disregard for expertise, specifically their own expertise in medicine, law, or medical ethics. Like the charge of immorality, the neglect of professional expertise in favor of party loyalty is a longstanding criticism of the socialist state. The doctors argued against abortion not only for the sake of the fetus but also for the sake of their own assessment of mothers' health. Regardless of what women want, they said, doctors know best. Lawyers, in keeping with their expertise, demanded the restitution of rights denied in previous regulations. The appeal to rights was also a familiar feature of anticommunist discourse. But who exactly is being deprived of rights here? Anti-abortion lawyers argued that in the abortion decision there are four interested parties: the fetus, the mother, the father, and society. Of these, the communist regulations required only the mother's voice. It is the exclusion of the fetus, the father and society that must be rectified. Lawyers were pleased to speak for all three.

In these writings women were figured as willfully ignorant: sad dupes of the communist system. Because of supposedly generous maternity leaves and favorable divorce and custody laws, women were also seen as the corrupted beneficiaries of the communist state. In much of this material an implicit equation was drawn between women allied with the former communist state, as against men who were linked to a new, law-governed, state and society.

It is striking that the abortion debate helped to form and brought into a single anti-abortion camp a number of emerging groups, as well as different strands of anticommunist argument. What linked these groups and arguments is that the anti-abortion stances were clearly tied to enhancing the groups' professional interests and presence in the social space between state and family that was legalized and expanded in the wake of socialism. Their arguments buttressed their own claims to morality and expertise, and hence for the indispensability and rightness of their leadership at the higher echelons of society. By discussing the naturalized and moralized issues of reproduction, they were proposing far more than any particular policy. They were implicitly proposing principles for judging leaders in a historical moment when the basis for such judgment was very much a matter of contention.

LIBERALS AND THE CONSTRUCTION OF POLITICS

Let us turn now to writings about abortion from newspapers published by writers aligned with the liberal parties, those who were the parliamentary opposition in the years of the abortion debate. In contrast to the dramatic, even grandiose, rhetoric of the populists and the professionals warning against abortion, we find in the *Beszélő* and the *Magyar Narancs* articles filled with puns, bitter parody, or savagely funny put-downs. One article on the abortion question was titled: "Kis jogi pornográfia," literally "A little pornography about the law." This plays on the earlier title of a remarkable and much admired avant-garde novel *Kis magyar pornográfia* (A short survey of Hungarian pornography), which was itself a parody of all those titles published by the Communist presses (A short survey of art/history/literature) that pretended to educate the new socialist man with canned versions of arts and letters in Hungarian. I have selected an example of this kind of article, to provide the flavor:

> Those who argue against abortion on the grounds of church or legal principles, are not able to see past the fact of egg fertilization. They don't realize that fact is preceded by another, one which is the greatest in a person's life, the most intimate, without exaggeration the most sacred: making love. In the course of legal arguments, this sacred act is turned into a sacrilege. The bed is first the object of searchlights, then it is tossed into the street. . . . [W]hat many people object to in pornography is that it takes exactly the most inner moments and tries to put these in front of the public, thereby destroying their intimacy. A law about abortion would do just that. . . . This is no longer a woman's problem. . . . The question is not whether one should ban or allow abortion, but rather whether or not one can, or should at all, regulate such a phenomenon by legal means. (Ráduly 1992: 5).

The tongue-in-cheek quality of this article is evident in the use of theological terms to discuss sex and pornography, the high moral tone combined with the outrageous suggestion that laws about abortion are a kind of pornography (the latter a growing phenomenon, by the way, on sale on the streets of Budapest, and one that the churches and nationalists are firmly against). By agreeing with the religious and legal minded that sex is sacred, this young man is able to parody those with grand moral claims.

But the frame of the playful argument is nevertheless serious: It introduces the notion of privacy on which all the arguments of liberal writers rest. However, for these writers, "the private" is not equivalent to the Western European bourgeois category of privacy, familiar since the nineteenth century. On the contrary, we must look for this writer's meaning by taking his style seriously. Through his ironic handling of otherwise serious issues, he is establishing an intertextual link to a Hungarian tradition that stands specifically opposed to that of the populist writers. The precedents these stylistic traits evoke are the left-liberal, modernist, often Jewish, cosmopolitan intellectuals of fin-de-siècle Hungary, and more recently, the anticommunist dissident intellectuals of the 1970s and 1980s. In short, he aligns himself with the self-styled "liberals," the producers of samizdat literature. These are the former theorists of "antipolitics," that strategy for surviving communism that was described by György Konrád (1984) for Hungary and Václav Havel (1988) for Czechoslovakia.

It was exactly such writers who argued in the 1980s that the private sphere, including the second economy and those few social spaces not occupied by the socialist state, were the places where dissident male intellectuals could enact antipolitics, behaving as if they lived outside the socialist state. As a substitute for an unattainable democratic politics, they envisioned the creation of a private civil society. This oxymoronic ideal entailed the celebration of the private as no longer a woman's preserve but rather a means of political action for men. Yet, theorists also looked back nostalgically to an idealized, prewar bourgeois family, arguing that under socialism women should be, but alas were not, a haven against the heartless state.[8] Although this image was not salient in writing about women and reproduction within the liberal parties during the abortion debate, neither was support for a notion of women's rights, although liberal writers were conspicuously obsessed with rights in general. Instead, as we have seen, the availability of abortion was defended on quite different grounds.

These grounds become clearer in another article (Mink 1991: 22–25), which though serious, nevertheless used the same playful allusion in its title (*Kis magyar abortusztörténet*, or A short history of Hungarian abortion), thereby making the same intertextual link to an artistic avant-garde and to political dissidence. The article is a chronological discussion of previous historical experiments restricting abortion in Europe. In establishing precedents, the author lists Stalin's Soviet Union, Hitler's Germany, Rákosi's Hungary of the 1950s, and Ceauşescu's Romania. Not coincidentally, these regimes are moments of horror in the historical imagination of most Hungarians, quite apart from their abortion policies. By making the proposed restriction of 1992 the endpoint of this sequence, the author implicitly censures such restriction, noting in passing that this restriction, like the predecessors he lists, relies, in part, on fear of increase among minority populations, especially the Hungarian Gypsies.

This too is an invention of tradition, an argument built with the same strategies of decontextualization and recontextualization as those used by the populist in my earlier example. What is most striking about the liberal article, however, is that in the end the author rejects his own form of argument and thus fundamentally refuses to agree with the populist even at the level of discursive strategies. After lining up his historical examples, he says:

> None of this, of course, touches the moral judgment of the issue. . . . The decision about that is not a historical question, but one about moral philosophy, and so it is not part of our subject matter in this article. (Mink 1991: 25)

The decision about abortion is thus a private, ethical issue, and not a question for political debate at all.

Although the liberal newspapers and politicians offered a much more lenient proposal for legalized abortion than the populist writers and the governing coalition, we see that in both cases the arguments involved considerably more than abortion alone. For the liberal writers, abortion had just as little to do with women and their rights as for the populists, and just as much to do with morality. Where they differed decisively was in their stance on the relation of morality to the state, and the implicit images of the state itself.

The arguments of the liberal parties suggested a minimal state, one that would neither construct nor assume a unity of purpose in the populace; one that would make a sharp divide between the sphere of the state and the sphere of private decision. The private, for them, would include property in the unbridled workings of the capitalist market, but included as well reproductive moral judgments deemed to be the concern only of the citizen-individuals, undistinguished by gender or ethnicity, that such a state would ideally construct as subjects.

In contrast, the populists presupposed a state built on moral consensus, one that would represent a national and ethnic unity, in which there would be little public debate because a political authority would decide what is best for the entire community. To be qualified to create and run such a state, one would have to have just the qualities the conservative professionals and populist writers claimed to be their own: Leaders would have to be ethnically one with the nation (Hungarian, and not Jew or Gypsy). And they would have to be especially sensitive on moral issues. For them, this is precisely what made the abortion issue so suitable for public debate. The moral sensitivity of conservatives could be materially demonstrated exactly by their concern about the primal, naturalized issues of life and death in reproduction and abortion. As one might expect from their position, the liberal parties were not particularly interested in arguing about abortion as a public policy matter.[9] But for the governing parties, who were largely impotent in vital questions of economic reorganization, regulating abortion provided a palpable way of putting into practice their image of the paternal state, while also allowing them to appear to provide the leadership in morality that everyone had agreed was missing from everyday life.

SOME OF THE WOMEN

But the abortion debate was not only about forms of state power. It was also about abortion and therefore about women's bodies. To what extent, then, is the kind of state-society relation implicitly proposed by populists and liberals likely to engage women's political energies? The women who will have to live with the new law did not participate very much in the battles for discursive hegemony described above. Rather, they constituted a marginal voice, quieted by charges of selfishness and by their own critiques of the double and triple day that communism demanded of women. In Poland the threat of restricted abortion is partly what energized women's movements. This has happened only on a very small scale in Hungary. Several tiny groups were formed. One of these, made up of professionals and entrepreneurial women, organized a forum to discuss abortion. Vociferously disagreeing with anti-abortion arguments, they emphasized, in their own version of anticommunist argument, that once again decisions were to be made about and for them, but without their participation.

More privately, my discussions with Hungarian women in urban as well as rural settings revealed a sense of bafflement and irritation about these debates. At Christmastime 1992, I received a letter from an acquaintance, a woman of forty with a recently earned college diploma, who lives in a village where I have done fieldwork since 1987. She wrote in alarm about the beating of Gypsies in the streets of Budapest, about the anti-Semitic statements of members of the government, and then she asked: "And meanwhile, what are they doing in Parliament? Eighty-year-old men, those idiots, amuse themselves by screaming against abortion when unemployment is enormous and the potential parents themselves have nothing to eat." This letter highlights a broad phenomenon, by taking abortion for granted. As some of the anti-abortion writings themselves either stated or assumed, many Hungarian women have a sense of entitlement concerning abortion, and this seems to be substantiated by recent polls (Pongrácz and Molnár 1991). More than seventy percent of the population agreed that abortion should be available even for "social reasons."

Women described to me the possible loss of abortion as a lack of "civility" in the country, a return to the "eastern" backwardness and barbarity of the Stalinist years.[10] They saw abortion as a major, often the only, form of contraception. Even the most pious Catholic women, active for years in the village church, expressed a conviction that abortion must remain legal. One of these, in her late forties, paused significantly when I put the question to her, and answered, "They couldn't possibly take that away." Urban women often responded with anger to my question: In the face of the high cost of housing in Budapest, "who is going to give me the space to put another child at the kitchen table?" Echoing the words of my acquaintances, a woman interviewed anonymously in a weekly newspaper said, "As long as society can't assure me the money to raise my child, they shouldn't have anything to do with this question" (1990: 80). Clearly some women are creating a discourse about abortion—one involving visions of a good society: civility, economic responsibility—that is not congruent with any of the others I have discussed.

Yet there is another aspect to the larger issue of women, work, reproduction, and family. Even more than in the village where I have conducted fieldwork, educated women in Budapest expressed great frustration in trying to balance wage-work responsibilities and the demands of housework and motherhood. While socialism met some of its (unasked) promises to women in Hungary by engineering their massive entrance into the labor force, it did not provide adequate childcare nor a rearrangement of gender roles to ease housework. The resultant difficulties of managing both kinds of work have been laid at the feet of state socialism by many women. It is the system they blamed for not allowing them the choice of being full-time mothers.

Furthermore, when abortion decisions were left to women, this was seen by many not as a chance for autonomy, but as the state allowing men to abandon women and children. More subtly, many women in their thirties and forties expressed a sense of guilt about their supposed lack of skills in child rearing and housekeeping. They expressed a feeling of inadequacy because of their lack of training (caused by their own labor force participation and their mothers' wage work) in the "civilized womanly arts" of decoration, dress, and nurturance. Thus, ironically, a critique of state socialism for these women included the demand for higher wages for men to support wives and children. If this set of conceptions includes a further valorization of "motherhood," as many populists and Christian organizations argue it should, this may yet provide grounds for women to oppose abortion and acquiesce in a new organization of their subordination within the broader arena of Hungarian politics.

CONCLUSION

In Hungary, as elsewhere in the world, the abortion debate made politics. But abortion had specific meanings in Hungary at this historical juncture. For instance, cultural conceptualizations about abortion were not linked to sexuality and women's right to privacy, as in the current American debate, but rather to ideas about nationhood, the unnaturalness and immorality of communism, and the defense of civility. By looking carefully at speeches and writings produced within the Hungarian abortion debate, I have tried to specify some of the textual strategies through which opposing views were constructed.

Most striking, however, is the way in which all positions in the Hungarian debate were arguments, in absentia, with a state socialism that no longer existed. An image of a godless, immoral, overly ideological communism was everyone's foil. The debate itself was thus an attempt to construct a new politics against, and out of, the materials provided by the old. Yet, despite the participants' explicit goal to make a novel and more "open" political life, the abortion debate produced unintended, ironic continuities with the old. While touted for its new tolerance of many parties, ideas, and stances, it also made some political positions invisible or impossible.

The continuities are inseparable from the anticommunism itself. In arguing for the indispensability of their expertise, conservative professionals and politicians stressed the importance of knowledge, in contrast to communism's supposedly exclusive reliance on those who showed party loyalty. Yet, the arguments of the conservatives doubtless sounded familiar to those who had lived under the infantilizing tutelage of a "vanguard" Communist Party. For, like their communist predecessors, each of these experts, as well as the conservative politicians, implied that ordinary people should not make decisions for themselves; the experts and leaders knew better what should be best for everyone. Similarly familiar were the calls by populists and conservative politicians for women's unselfishness. Though the cause was now the "nation" rather than the needs of "socialist society," sacrifices to be made in the name of a larger collectivity were hardly new to Hungarians.

Despite the emergence of genuine diversity in political debate, some political positions disappeared from view. The defense of women's rights and autonomy was incompatible with anti-communism, at this historical moment, despite the general concern with civil and human rights. For liberals, claims for special women's rights would have been antithetical to the moral purity of a creed that ideally made no distinctions of identity among "citizen-individuals." But it was impossible for conservatives as well, because women's rights were discursively linked to state socialism and to women's supposed advantages under that system. The paternalistic communist state, by socializing some household tasks, and by supporting women and children directly, rather than through the men of a household, allowed a level of autonomy for women that is unusual in other political systems. Yet, women themselves often experienced this support as inadequate and oppressive, and were not vocal in its defense.

Debates about abortion were not invented, of course, by post-socialist critics. State socialist planners had also been deeply involved in a politics of reproduction, attempting to shape procreative practices through legal and discursive means in the service of various and changing political goals: communist militarism and industrialization, emulation of Soviet models, or reformist attempts to rescue the failing political-economic system. What is distinctive about the post-socialist debate is that the reverse relation was more salient: Arguments about abortion and the proper forms of reproduction were not the means to reach already defined political goals. They were presented rather to justify and naturalize broad political visions and thereby gain moral ballast for their proponents. Discussed in the guise of the abortion debate were wide-ranging political questions: What should be the form of the state? What is a legitimate subject of political debate? By which criteria—ethnicity, morality, expertise—should leaders be chosen?

Rather than the shaping of reproductive practices for political ends, we see the shaping of politics through a coded discussion of reproductive practices. The social process of reproduction gains its power to moralize politics because it is already constituted, in the tradition discussed here, as a natural, primal phenomenon involving life and death. Thus, in the newly constituted field of Hungarian politics, the abortion debate allowed groups and alliances to create themselves through such debates. They made claims about their own political value, while simultaneously constructing the means by which such value was to be measured.

NOTES

1. My thanks to Judith Gerson, Katherine Verdery, and József Böröcz for their generous comments. All translations are my own.

2. For reports on the situation of women in East Europe since 1989, and questions of reproduction particularly, see the special section of *Signs* (1991), the special issue of *German Politics and Society* (1991–92), and *Feminist Review* (Winter 1991). Only in Romania, where abortion was banned, were regulations popularly opposed, see Kligman (1993).

3. The general link between politics and gender has been made most forcefully by Scott (1988); on politics of reproduction see Ginsberg and Rapp (1991).

4. For a discussion of the importance of discursive factors in the transition from socialism, see Verderey (1991); Stark (1992) and Böröcz (in press) provide overviews of economic transformation, and Róna-Tas (1991) notes the greater mobility among political elites. My discussion of the self-legitimation of political elites relies on Bourdieu's (1991) notion of "symbolic power."

5. An excellent source of information about Hungarian abortion policy from the 1930s to the present is Sándor (1992).

6. An important collection of the 1930s' debates about abortion, population, and the one-child system can be found in the journal *Nyugat* (1933).

7. My analysis of the positions of conservative and professional groups draws on my reading of the daily and weekly press from 1990 to the end of 1991. Further specific citations can be found in Gal (1994).

8. Joanna Goven (1993) has shrewdly analyzed this link between gender and dissent in Hungary.
9. This is not to say that liberals did not write copiously about the abortion issue. Indeed, one former dissident, philosopher, and liberal political leader published an important philosophical discussion of the issue (Kis 1992).
10. Civility is a central notion in Hungarian discourse about national identity, and part of the social geography that often locates Hungary not quite in "Europe" but somewhere between "East" and "West." For a discussion of this discourse, see Gal 1991.

REFERENCES

Anonymous. 1990. Interview in *168 Ora*, p. 8.

Böröcz, József. (In press). Simulating the great transformation: Property change under prolonged informality in Hungary. *Archives européenes de Sociologie*.

Bourdieu, Pierre. 1991. *Language and symbolic power*. Cambridge: Cambridge University Press.

Briggs, Charles, and Bauman, Richard. 1992. Genre, intertextuality and social power. *J. of Linguistic Anthropology* 2:2: 131–72.

Csurka, István. 1991. Untitled comments. *In* S. Agócs (ed.), *Lakitelek 1987*, p. 24. Budapest: Püski.

Elfogy a magyarság? (Will the Hungarians come to an end?) *Nyugat* (special issue), 1933.

Feminist Review. Special issue on East European women. Winter 1991.

Gal, Susan. 1994. Gender in the post-socialist transition: The abortion debate in Hungary. *East European Politics and Societies*, 8:2: 256–86.

———. 1991. Bartók's funeral: Representations of Europe in Hungarian political rhetoric. *American Ethnologist* 18: 440–58.

German Politics and Society. 1991–92. Special issue on women and gender.

Ginsberg, Faye. 1989. *Contested Lives*. Berkeley: University of California Press.

——— and Rayna Rapp. 1991. The politics of reproduction. *Annual Review of Anthropology*. 20: 311–44.

Glendon, Mary. 1987. *Abortion and divorce in Western law: American failures, European challenges*. Cambridge: Harvard University Press.

Goven, Joanna. 1993. Gender politics in Hungary: Autonomy and antifeminism. *In* N. Funk and M. Mueller (eds.). *Gender politics and post-communism: Reflections from Eastern Europe and the former Soviet Union*. New York: Routledge.

Havel, Václav. 1988. Antipolitical politics. *In* J. Keane (ed.). *Civil society and the state*. London: Verso.

Kis, János. 1992. *Az abortuszról* (About abortion). Budapest: Cserepfalvi.

Kligman, Gail. 1993. The politics of reproduction in Ceauşescu's Romania: A case study in political culture. *East European Politics and Societies* 6:3: 364–418.

Konrád, György. 1984. *Antipolitics*. San Diego: Harcourt, Brace.

Lezsák, Sándor. 1991. Köszöntöm vedégeinket, barátainkat (Greetings to our guests and friends). *In* S. Agócsa (ed.), *Lakitelek 1987*, p. 6. Budapest: Puski.

Luker, Kristin. 1984. *Abortion and the politics of motherhood*. Berkeley: University of California Press.

Mink, András. 1991. Kis magyar abortusztörténet (A short history of Hungarian abortion). *Beszélö*, Nov. 30, pp. 22–25.

Mohr, James. 1978. *Abortion in America: The origins and evolution of national policy*. New York: Oxford University Press.

Petchesky, Rosalind. 1984. *Abortion and woman's choice*. Boston: Northeastern University Press.

Pongrácz, Marietta, and Edit Molnár. 1991. Az abortuszkérdés Magyarországon (The abortion question in Hungary). *Statisztikai Szemle* 69:7: 509–31.

Ráduly, János S. 1992. Kis jogi pornográfia (A little pornography about the law). *Magyar Narancs*, March 18, p. 5.

Róna-Tas, Ákos. 1991. The selected and the elected: The making of the new Parliamentary elite in Hungary. *East European Politics and Societies* 5:3: 357–94.

Sándor, Judit (ed.). 1992. *Abortusz és . . .* (Abortion and . . .) Budapest: Literatura Medica.

Scott, Joan. 1988. *Gender and the politics of history*. New York: Columbia University Press.

Signs. 1991. Special section on Eastern Europe.

Stark, David. 1992. Path dependence and privatization strategies in East Central Europe. *East European Politics and Societies* 6:1: 17–54.

Vásáry, Ildikó. 1989. The sin of Transdanubia: The one child system in rural Hungary. *Continuity and Change* 4:3: 429–68.

Verdery, Katherine. 1991. Theorizing socialism: A prologue to the "transition." *American Ethnologist*, 18: 419–39.

9   Fetal Images

The Power of Visual Culture in the Politics of Reproduction

Rosalind Pollack Petchesky

> [Ultimately] the world of "being" can function to the exclusion of the mother. No need for mother—provided that there is something of the maternal: and it is the father then who acts as—is—the mother. Either the woman is passive; or she doesn't exist. What is left is unthinkable, unthought of. She does not enter into the oppositions, she is not coupled with the father (who is coupled with the son).
>
> —Hélène Cixous, *Sorties*

In the mid-1980s, with the United States Congress still deadlocked over the abortion issue and the Supreme Court having twice reaffirmed "a woman's right to choose,"[1] the political attack on abortion rights moved further into the terrain of mass culture and imagery. Not that the "prolife movement" has abandoned conventional political arenas; rather, its defeats there have hardened its commitment to a more long-term ideological struggle over the symbolic meanings of fetuses, dead or alive.

Antiabortionists in the United States and elsewhere have long applied the principle that a picture of a dead fetus is worth a thousand words. Chaste silhouettes of the fetal form, or voyeuristic-necrophilic photographs of its remains, litter the background of any abortion talk. These still images float like spirits through the courtrooms, where lawyers argue that fetuses can claim tort liability; through the hospitals and clinics, where physicians welcome them as "patients"; and in front of all the abortion centers, legislative committees, bus terminals, and other places that "right-to-lifers" haunt. The strategy of antiabortionists to make fetal personhood a self-fulfilling prophecy by making the fetus a *public presence* addresses a visually oriented culture. Meanwhile, finding positive images and symbols of abortion hard to imagine, feminists and other prochoice advocates have all too readily ceded the visual terrain.

Beginning with the 1984 presidential campaign, the neoconservative Reagan administration and the Christian Right accelerated their use of television and video imagery to capture political discourse—and power.[2] Along with a new series of "Ron and Nancy" commercials, the Reverend Pat Robertson's "700 Club" (a kind of right-wing talk show), and a resurgence of Good versus Evil kiddie cartoons, American television and video viewers were bombarded with the newest "prolife" propaganda piece, *The Silent Scream*. *The Silent Scream* marked a dramatic shift in

Rosalind Pollack Petchesky is Professor of Political Science and Women's Studies at Hunter College of the City University of New York and founder and international coordinator of the International Reproductive Rights Research Action Group (IRRRAG). Her book, *Abortion and Woman's Choice: The State, Sexuality and Reproductive Freedom* (Northeastern University, 1990), won the Joan Kelly Prize of the American Historical Association, and her many articles on reproductive and sexual politics have been translated into several languages. Petchesky is the general editor of IRRRAG's forthcoming book, *Negotiating Reproductive Rights: Women's Perspective Cross-Culturally* (Zed Press, 1997). In 1995 she was the recipient of a MacArthur Fellows Award.

the contest over abortion imagery. With formidable cunning, it translated the still and now-stale images of fetus as "baby" into real-time video, thus (1) giving those images an immediate inter-face with the electronic media; (2) transforming antiabortion rhetoric from a mainly religious/ mystical to a medical/technological mode; and (3) bringing the fetal image "to life." On major network television the fetus rose to instant stardom, as *The Silent Scream* and its impresario, Dr. Bernard Nathanson, were aired at least five different times in one month, and one well-known reporter, holding up a fetus in a jar before ten million viewers, announced: "This thing being aborted, this potential person, sure looks like a baby!"

My interest in this essay is to explore the overlapping boundaries between media spectacle and clinical experience when pregnancy becomes a moving picture. In what follows, I attempt to understand the cultural meanings and impact of images like those in *The Silent Scream*. Then I examine the effect of routine ultrasound imaging of the fetus not only on the larger cultural cli-mate of reproductive politics but also on the experience and consciousness of pregnant women. Finally, I shall consider some implications of "fetal images" for feminist theory and practice.

DECODING *THE SILENT SCREAM*

Before dissecting its ideological message, I should perhaps describe *The Silent Scream*. The film's actual genesis seems to have been an article in the *New England Journal of Medicine* by a noted bioethicist and a physician, claiming that early fetal ultrasound tests resulted in "maternal bond-ing" and possibly "fewer abortions." According to the authors, both affiliated with the National Institutes of Health, upon viewing an ultrasound image of the fetus, "parents [that is, pregnant women] probably will experience a shock of recognition that the fetus belongs to them" and will more likely resolve "ambivalent" pregnancies "in favor of the fetus." Such "parental recognition of the fetal form," they wrote, "is a fundamental element in the later parent-child bond."[3] Although based on two isolated cases, without controls or scientific experimentation, these asser-tions stimulated the imagination of Dr. Bernard Nathanson and the National Right-to-Life Committee. The resulting video production was intended to reinforce the visual "bonding" theory at the level of the clinic by bringing the live fetal image into everyone's living room. Dis-tributed not only to television networks but also to schools, churches, state and federal legislators, and anyone (including the opposition) who wants to rent it for fifteen dollars, the video cassette provides a mass commodity form for the "prolife" message.

The Silent Scream purports to show a medical event, a real-time ultrasound imaging of a twelve-week-old fetus being aborted. What we see in fact is an image of an image of an image; or, rather, we see three concentric frames: our television or VCR screen, which in turns frames the video screen of the filming studio, which in turns frames a shadowy, black-and-white, pulsat-ing blob: the (alleged) fetus. Throughout, our response to this set of images is directed by the figure of Dr. Nathanson—sober, bespectacled, leaning professorially against the desk—who func-tions as both medical expert and narrator to the drama. (Nathanson is in "real life" a practicing obstetrician-gynecologist, ex-abortionist, and well-known antiabortion crusader.) In fact, as the film unfolds, we quickly realize that there are *two* texts being presented here simultaneously—a medical text, largely visual, and a moral text, largely verbal and auditory. Our medical narrator appears on the screen and announces that what we are about to see comes to us courtesy of the "dazzling" new "science of fetology," which "exploded in the medical community" and now enables us to witness an abortion—"from the victim's vantage point." At the same time we hear strains of organ music in the background, ominous, the kind we associate with impending doom. As Nathanson guides his pointer along the video screen, "explaining" the otherwise inscrutable movements of the image, the disjunction between the two texts becomes increasingly jarring. We *see* a recognizable apparatus of advanced medical technology, displaying a filmic image of vibrat-ing light and shaded areas, interspersed with occasional scenes of an abortion clinic operating table (the only view of the pregnant woman we get). This action is moderated by someone who "looks like" the paternal-medical authority figure of the proverbial aspirin commercial. He occasionally interrupts the filmed events to show us clinical models of embryos and fetuses at various stages of development. Meanwhile, however, what we *hear* is more like a medieval morality play, spoken in standard antiabortion rhetoric. The form on the screen, we are told, is "the living unborn child," "another human being indistinguishable from any of us." The suction cannula is "moving violently" toward "the child"; it is the "lethal weapon" that will "dismember, crush, destroy," "tear the child apart," until only "shards" are left. The fetus "does sense aggression in its sanctuary," attempts to "escape" (indicating more rapid movements on the screen), and finally "rears back its head" in "a silent scream"—all to a feverish pitch of musical accompaniment. In case we question the nearly total absence of a pregnant woman or of clinic personnel in this scenario, Nathanson also "informs" us that the woman who had this abortion was a "feminist," who, like the young doctor who performed it, has vowed "never again"; that women who get abortions are themselves exploited "victims" and "castrated"; that many abortion clinics are "run by the mobs." It is the verbal rhetoric, not of science, but of *Miami Vice.*

Now, all of this raises important questions about what one means by evidence, or "medical information," because the ultrasound image is presented as a document testifying that the fetus is "alive," is "human like you or me," and "senses pain." *The Silent Scream* has been sharply confronted on this level by panels of opposing medical experts, *New York Times* editorials, and a Planned Parenthood film. These show, for example, that at twelve weeks the fetus has no cerebral cortex to receive pain impulses; that no "scream" is possible without air in the lungs; that fetal movements at this stage are reflexive and without purpose; that the image of rapid frantic movement was undoubtedly caused by speeding up the film (camera tricks); that the size of the image we see on the screen, along with the model that is continually displayed in front of the screen, is nearly twice the size of a normal twelve-week fetus, and so forth.[4] Yet this literal kind of rebuttal is not very useful in helping us to understand the ideological power the film has despite its visual distortions and verbal fraud.

When we locate *The Silent Scream* where it belongs, in the realm of cultural representation rather than of medical evidence, we see that it embeds ultrasound imaging of pregnancy in a moving picture show. Its appearance as a medical document both obscures and reinforces a coded set of messages that work as political signs and moral injunctions. (As we shall see, because of the cultural and political context in which they occur, this may be true of ultrasound images of pregnancy in general.) The purpose of the film is obviously didactic: to induce individual women to abstain from having abortions and to persuade officials and judges to force them to do so. The medical authority figure—paternalistic and technocratic at the same time—delivers these messages less by his words than by the power of his image and his persona.

As with any visual image, *The Silent Scream* relies on our predisposition to "see" what it wants us to "see" because of a range of influences that come out of the particular culture and history in which we live. The aura of medical authority, the allure of technology, the cumulative impact of a decade of fetal images—on billboards, in shopping center malls, in science-fiction blockbusters like *2001: A Space Odyssey*—all rescue the film from utter absurdity; they make it credible. "The fetal form" itself has, within the larger culture, acquired a symbolic import that condenses within it a series of losses—from sexual innocence to compliant women to American imperial might. It is not the image of a baby at all but of a tiny man, a homunculus.

The most disturbing thing about how people receive *The Silent Scream*, and indeed all the dominant fetal imagery, is their apparent acceptance of the image itself as an accurate representation of a real fetus. The curled-up profile, with its enlarged head and finlike arms, suspended in its balloon of amniotic fluid, is by now so familiar that not even most feminists question its authenticity (as opposed to its relevance). I went back to trace the earliest appearance of these photos in popular literature and found it in the June 1962 issue of *Look* (along with *Life*, the major mass-circulating "picture magazine" of the period). It was a story publicizing a new book, *The First Nine Months of*

Life, and it featured the now-standard sequel of pictures at one day, one week, seven weeks, and so forth.[5] In every picture the fetus is solitary, dangling in the air (or its sac) with nothing to connect it to any life-support system but "a clearly defined umbilical cord." In every caption it is called "the baby" (even at forty-four days) and is referred to as "he"—until the birth, that is, when "he" turns out to be a girl. Nowhere is there any reference to the pregnant woman, except in a single photograph at the end showing the newborn baby lying next to the mother, both of them gazing off the page, allegedly at "the father." From their beginning, such photographs have represented the fetus as primary and autonomous, the woman as absent or peripheral.

Fetal imagery epitomizes the distortion inherent in all photographic images: their tendency to slice up reality into tiny bits wrenched out of real space and time. The origins of photography can be traced to late nineteenth-century Europe's cult of science, itself a byproduct of industrial capitalism. Its rise is inextricably linked with positivism, that flawed epistemology that sees "reality" as discrete bits of empirical data divorced from historical process or social relationships.[6] Similarly, fetal imagery replicates the essential paradox of photographs whether moving or still, their "constitutive deception" as noted by postmodernist critics: the *appearance* of objectivity, of capturing "literal reality." As Roland Barthes puts it, the "photographic message" appears to be "a message without a code." According to Barthes, the appearance of the photographic image as "a mechanical analogue of reality," without art or artifice, obscures the fact that the image is heavily constructed, or "coded"; it is grounded in a context of historical and cultural meanings.[7]

Yet the power of the visual apparatus's claim to be "an unreasoning machine" that produces "an unerring record" (the French word for "lens" is *l'objectif*) remains deeply embedded in Western culture.[8] This power derives from the peculiar capacity of photographic images to assume two distinct meanings, often simultaneously: an empirical (informational) and a mythical (or magical) meaning. Historically, photographic imagery has served not only the uses of scientific rationality, as in medical diagnostics and record keeping, and the tools of bureaucratic rationality, in the political record keeping and police surveillance of the state.[9] Photographic imagery has also, especially with the "democratization" of the hand-held camera and the advent of the family album, become a magical source of fetishes that can resurrect the dead or preserve lost love. And it has constituted the escape fantasy of the movies. This older, symbolic, and ritualistic (also religious?) function lies concealed within the more obvious rationalistic one.

The double text of *The Silent Scream*, noted earlier, recapitulates this historical paradox of photographic images; their simultaneous power as purveyors of fantasy and illusion yet also of "objectivist 'truth.'"[10] When Nathanson claims to be presenting an abortion from the "vantage point of the [fetus]," the image's appearance of seamless movement through real time—*and* the technologic allure of the video box, connoting at once "advanced medicine" and "the news"—render his claim "true to life." Yet he also purveys a myth, for the fetus—if it had any vantage point—could not possibly experience itself as if dangling in space, without a woman's uterus and body and bloodstream to support it.

In fact, every image of a fetus we are shown, including *The Silent Scream*, is viewed from the standpoint neither of the fetus nor of the pregnant woman but of the camera. The fetus as we know it is a fetish. Barbara Katz Rothman observes that "the fetus in utero has become a metaphor for 'man' in space, floating free, attached only by the umbilical cord to the spaceship. But where is the mother in that metaphor? She has become empty space."[11] Inside the futurizing spacesuit, however, lies a much older image. For the autonomous, free-floating fetus merely extends to gestation the Hobbesian view of born human beings as disconnected, solitary individuals. It is this abstract individualism, effacing the pregnant woman and the fetus's dependence on her, that gives the fetal image its symbolic transparency, so that we can read in it our selves, our lost babies, our mythic secure past.

Although such receptions of fetal images may help to recruit antiabortion activists, among both women and men, denial of the womb has more deadly consequences. Zoe Sofia relates the film *2001: A Space Odyssey* to "the New Right's cult of fetal personhood," arguing that "every technology is a reproductive technology . . . in science fiction culture particularly, technologies are perceived as modes of reproduction in themselves, according to perverse myths of fertility in which man replicates himself without the aid of woman." The "Star Child" of *2001* is not a living organic being but "a biomechanism, . . . a cyborg capable of living unaided in space." This "child" poses as the symbol of fertility and life but in fact is the creature of the same technologies that bring cosmic extermination, which it alone survives. Sofia sees the same irony in "the right-wing movement to protect fetal life" while it plans for nuclear war. Like the fetal baby in *2001*, "the pro-life fetus may be a 'special effect' of a cultural dreamwork which displaces attention from the tools of extermination and onto the fetal signifier of extinction itself." To the extent that it diverts us from the real threat of nuclear holocaust and comes to represent the lone survivor, the fetal image signifies not life but death.[12]

If the fetus-as-spaceman has become inscribed in science fiction and popular fantasy, it is likely to affect the appearance of fetal images even in clinical contexts. The vantage point of the male onlooker may perhaps change how women see their own fetuses on, and through, ultrasound imaging screens. *The Silent Scream* bridges these two areas of cultural construction, video fantasy-land and clinical biotechnics, enlisting medical imagery in the service of mythic-patriarchal messages. But neither arena, nor the film itself, meets a totally receptive field. Pregnant women respond to these images out of a variety of concrete situations and in a variety of complex ways.

OBSTETRICAL IMAGING AND MASCULINE/VISUAL CULTURE

We have seen the dominant view of the fetus that appears in still and moving pictures across the mass-cultural landscape. It is one where the fetus is not only "already a baby," but more—a "baby man," an autonomous, atomized minispace hero. This image has not supplanted the one of the fetus as a tiny, helpless, suffering creature but rather merged with it (in a way that uncomfortably reminds one of another famous immortal baby). We should not be surprised, then, to find the social relations of obstetrics—the site where ultrasound imaging of fetuses goes on daily—infiltrated by such widely diffused images.

Along with the external political and cultural pressures, traditional patterns endemic to the male-dominated practice of obstetrics help determine the current clinical view of the fetus as "patient," separate and autonomous from the pregnant woman. These patterns direct the practical applications of new reproductive technologies more toward enlarging clinicians' control over reproductive processes than toward improving health (women's or infants'). Despite their benefits for individual women, amniocentesis, in vitro fertilization, electronic fetal monitoring, routine cesarean deliveries, ultrasound, and a range of heroic "fetal therapies" (both in utero and ex utero) also have the effect of carving out more and more space/time for obstetrical "management" of pregnancy. Meanwhile, they have not been shown to lower infant and perinatal mortality/morbidity, and they divert social resources from epidemiological research into the causes of fetal damage.[13] But the presumption of fetal "autonomy" ("patienthood" if not "personhood") is not an inevitable requirement of the technologies. Rather, the technologies take on the meanings and uses they do because of the cultural climate of fetal images and the politics of hostility toward pregnant women and abortion. As a result, the pregnant woman is increasingly put in the position of adversary to her own pregnancy/fetus, either by having presented a "hostile environment" to its development or by actively refusing some medically proposed intervention (such as a cesarean section or treatment for a fetal "defect").[14]

Similarly, the claim by antiabortion polemicists that the fetus is becoming "viable" at an earlier and earlier point seems to reinforce the notion that its treatment is a matter between a fetus and its doctor. In reality, most authorities agree that twenty-four weeks is the youngest a fetus is likely to survive outside the womb in the foreseeable future; meanwhile, over 90 percent of pregnant women who get abortions do so in the first trimester, fewer than 1 percent do so past the twentieth week.[15] Despite these facts, the *images* of younger and younger, and tinier and tinier, fetuses being "saved," the point of viability being "pushed back" *indefinitely*, and untold aborted fetuses being "born alive" have captured recent abortion discourse in the courts, the headlines, and television drama.[16] Such images blur the boundary between fetus and baby; they reinforce the idea that the fetus's identity as separate and autonomous from the mother (the "living, separate child") exists from the start. Obstetrical technologies of visualization and electronic/surgical intervention thus disrupt the very definition, as traditionally understood, of "inside" and "outside" a woman's body, of pregnancy as an "interior" experience. As Donna Haraway remarks, pregnancy becomes integrated into a "high-tech view of the body as a biotic component or cybernetic communications system"; thus, "who controls the interpretation of bodily boundaries in medical hermeneutics [becomes] a major feminist issue."[17] Interpreting boundaries, however, is a way to contest them, not to record their fixity in the natural world. Treating a fetus as if it were outside a woman's body, because it can be viewed, is a political act.

This background is necessary to an analysis that locates ultrasound imaging of fetuses within its historical and cultural context. Originating in sonar detectors for submarine warfare, ultrasound was not introduced into obstetrical practice until the early 1960s—some years after its accepted use in other medical diagnostic fields.[18] The timing is significant, for it corresponds to the end of the baby boom and the rapid drop in fertility that would propel obstetrician-gynecologists into new areas of discovery and fortune, a new "patient population" to look at and treat. "Looking" was mainly the point, because, as in many medical technologies (and technologies of visualization), physicians seem to have applied the technique before knowing precisely what they were looking for. In this technique, a transducer sends sound waves through the amniotic fluid so they bounce off fetal structures and are reflected back, either as a still image (scan) or, more frequently, a real-time moving image "similar to that of a motion picture," as the American College of Obstetricians and Gynecologists (ACOG) puts it.[19]

Although it was enthusiastically hailed among physicians for its advantages over the dangers of X-ray, ultrasound imaging in pregnancy is currently steeped in controversy. A 1984 report by a joint National Institutes of Health/Food and Drug Administration panel found "no clear benefit from routine use," specifically, "no improvement in pregnancy outcome" (either for the fetus/infant or the woman), and no conclusive evidence either of its safety or harm. The panel recommended against "routine use," including "to view . . . or obtain a picture of the fetus" or "for educational or commercial demonstrations without medical benefit to the patient" ("the patient" here, presumably, being the pregnant woman). Yet it approved of its use to "estimate gestational age," thus qualifying its reservations with a major loophole. At least one-third of all pregnant women in the United States are now exposed to ultrasound imaging, and that would seem to be a growing figure. Anecdotal evidence suggests that many if not most pregnancies will soon include ultrasound scans and presentation of a sonogram photo "for the baby album."[20]

How can we understand the routinization of fetal imaging in obstetrics even though the profession's governing bodies admit the medical benefits are dubious? The reason ultrasound imaging in obstetrics has expanded so much are no doubt related to the reasons, economic and patriarchal, for the growth in electronic fetal monitoring, cesarean sections, and other reproductive technologies. Practitioners and critics alike commonly trace the obstetrical technology boom to physicians' fear of malpractice suits. But the impulses behind ultrasound also arise from the codes of visual imagery and the construction of fetal images as "cultural objects" with historical meanings.

From the standpoint of clinicians, at least three levels of meaning attach to ultrasound images of fetuses. These correspond to (1) a level of "evidence" or "report," which may or may not motivate diagnosis and/or therapeutic intervention; (2) a level of surveillance and potential social control; and (3) a level of fantasy or myth. (Not surprisingly, these connotations echo the textual structure of *The Silent Scream*.) In the first place, there is simply the impulse to view, to get a picture of the fetus's anatomical structures in motion, and here obstetrical ultrasound reflects the impact of new imaging technologies in all areas of medicine. One is struck by the lists of "indications" for ultrasound imaging found in the *ACOG Technical Bulletin* and the *American Journal of Obstetrics and Gynecology* indexes. Although the "indications" include a few recognizable "abnormal" conditions that might require a "non-routine" intervention (such as "evaluation of ectopic pregnancy" or "diagnosis of abnormal fetal position"), for the most part they consist of technical measurements, like a list of machine parts—"crown rump length," "gestational sac diameter," fetal sex organs, fetal weight—as well as estimation of gestational age. As one neonatologist told me, "We can do an entire anatomical workup!"[21]

Of course, none of this viewing and measuring and recording of bits of anatomical data gives the slightest clue as to what *value* should be placed on this or any other fetus, whether it has a moral claim to heroic therapy or life at all, and who should decide.[22] But the point is that the fetus, through visualization, is being treated as a patient already, is being given an ordinary checkup. Inferences about its "personhood" (or "babyhood"), in the context of the dominant ways of seeing fetuses, seem verified by sonographic "evidence" that it kicks, spits, excretes, grows.

Evidentiary uses of photographic images are usually enlisted in the service of some kind of action—to monitor, control, and possibly intervene. In the case of obstetrical medicine, ultrasound techniques, in conjunction with electronic fetal monitoring, have been used increasingly to diagnose fetal distress and abnormal presentation leading to a prediction of prolonged labor or breech birth. These findings then become evidence indicating earlier delivery by cesarean section, evoking the correlation some researchers have observed between increased use of electronic fetal monitoring and ultrasound and the threefold rise in the cesarean section rate in the last fifteen years.[23]

Complaints by feminist health advocates about unnecessary caesareans and excessive monitoring of pregnancy are undoubtedly justified. Even the profession's own guidelines suggest that the monitoring techniques may lead to misdiagnoses or may themselves be the cause of the "stresses" they "discover."[24] One might well question a tendency in obstetrics to "discover" disorders where they previously did not exist, because visualizing techniques compel "discovery," or to apply techniques to wider and wider groups of cases.[25] On the whole, however, diagnostic uses of ultrasound in obstetrics have benefited women more than they've done harm, making it possible to define the due date more accurately, to detect anomalies, and to anticipate complications in delivery. My question is not about this level of medical applications but rather about the cultural assumptions underlying them. How do these assumptions both reflect and reinforce the larger culture of fetal images sketched above? Why has the impulse to "see inside" come to dominate ways of knowing about pregnancy and fetuses, and what are the consequences for women's consciousness and reproductive power relations?

The "prevalence of the gaze," or the privileging of the visual, as the primary means to knowledge in Western scientific and philosophical traditions has been the subject of a feminist inquiry by Evelyn Fox Keller and Christine R. Grontkowski. In their analysis, stretching from Plato to Bacon and Descartes, this emphasis on the visual has had a paradoxical function. For sight, in contrast to the other senses, has as its peculiar property the capacity for detachment, for objectifying the thing visualized by creating distance between knower and known. (In modern optics, the eye becomes a passive recorder, a camera obscura.) In this way, the elevation of the visual in a hierarchy of senses actually has the effect of debasing sensory experience, and relatedness, as modes of knowing: "Vision connects us to truth as it distances us from the corporeal."[26]

Some feminist cultural theorists in France, Britain, and the United States have argued that visualization and objectification as privileged ways of knowing are specifically masculine (man the viewer, woman the spectacle).[27] Without falling into such essentialism, we may suppose that the language, perceptions, and uses of visual information may be different for women, as pregnant subjects, than they are for men (or women) as physicians, researchers, or reporters. And this difference will reflect the historical control by men over science, medicine, and obstetrics in Western society and over the historical definitions of masculinity in Western culture. The deep gender bias of science (including medicine), of its very ways of seeing problems, resonates, Keller argues, in its "common rhetoric." Mainly "adversarial" and "aggressive" in its stance toward what it studies, "science can come to sound like a battlefield."[28] Similarly, presentations of scientific and medical "conquests" in the mass media commonly appropriate this terrain into Cold War culture and macho style. Consider this piece of text from *Life*'s 1965 picture story on ultrasound in pregnancy, "A Sonar 'Look' at an Unborn Baby":

> The astonishing medical machine resting on this pregnant woman's abdomen in a Philadelphia hospital is "looking" at her unborn child in precisely the same way a Navy surface ship homes in on enemy submarines. Using the sonar principle, it is bombarding her with a beam of ultra-high-frequency sound waves that are inaudible to the human ear. Back come the echoes, bouncing off the baby's head, to show up as a visual image on a viewing screen. (p. 45)

The militarization of obstetrical images is not unique to ultrasonography (most technologies in a militarized society either begin or end in the military); nor is it unique to its focus on reproduction (similar language constructs the "war on cancer"). Might it then correspond to the very culture of medicine and science, its emphasis on visualization as a form of surveillance and "attack"? For some obstetrician-gynecologist practitioners, such visualization is patently voyeuristic; it generates erotic pleasure in the nonreciprocated, illicit "look." Interviewed in *Newsweek* after *The Silent Scream* was released, Nathanson boasted: "With the aid of technology, we stripped away the walls of the abdomen and uterus and looked into the womb."[29] And here is Dr. Michael Harrison writing in a respected medical journal about "fetal management" through ultrasound:

> The fetus could not be taken seriously as long as he [*sic*] remained a medical recluse in an opaque womb; and it was not until the last half of this century that *the prying eye of the ultrasonogram* . . . rendered the once opaque womb transparent, *stripping the veil of mystery from the dark inner sanctum* and *letting the light of scientific observation fall on the shy and secretive fetus*. . . . The sonographic voyeur, *spying on the unwary fetus*, finds him or her a surprisingly active little creature, and not at all the passive parasite we had imagined.[30]

Whether voyeurism is a "masculinist" form of looking, the "siting" of the womb as a space to be conquered can only be had by one who stands outside it looking in. The view of the fetus as a "shy," mysterious "little creature," recalling a wildlife photographer tracking down a gazelle, indeed exemplifies the "predatory nature of a photographic consciousness."[31] It is hard to imagine a pregnant woman thinking about her fetus this way, whether she longs for a baby or wishes for an abortion.

What we have here, from the clinician's standpoint, is a kind of *panoptics of the womb*, whose aim is "to establish normative behavior for the fetus at various gestational stages" and to maximize medical control over pregnancy.[32] Feminist critics emphasize the degrading impact fetal-imaging techniques have on the pregnant woman. She now becomes the "maternal environment," the "site" of the fetus, a passive spectator in her own pregnancy.[33] Sonographic detailing of fetal anatomy completely displaces the markers of "traditional" pregnancy, when "feeling the baby move was a 'definitive' diagnosis." Now the woman's *felt* evidence about the pregnancy is discredited in favor of the more "objective" data on the video screen. We find her "on the table with the ultrasound scanner to her belly, and on the other side of the technician or doctor, the fetus on the screen. The doctor . . . turns *away* from the mother to examine her baby. Even the heartbeat is heard over a speaker removed from the mother's body. The technology which makes the baby/fetus more 'visible' renders the woman invisible."[34]

Earlier I noted that ultrasound imaging of fetuses is constituted through three levels of meaning—not only the level of evidence (diagnosis) and the level of surveillance (intervention), but also that of fantasy or myth. "Evidence" shades into fantasy when the fetus is visualized, albeit through electronic media, as though removed from the pregnant woman's body, as though suspended in space. This is a form of fetishization, and it occurs repeatedly in clinical settings whenever ultrasound images construct the fetus through "indications" that sever its functions and parts from their organic connection to the pregnant woman. Fetishization, in turn, shades into surveillance when physicians, "right-to-life" propagandists, legislatures, or courts impose ultrasound imaging on pregnant women in order "to encourage 'bonding.'" In some states, the use of compulsory ultrasound imaging as a weapon of intimidation against women seeking abortions has already begun.[35] Indeed, the very idea of "bonding" based on a photographic image implies a fetish: the investment of erotic feelings in a fantasy.[36] When an obstetrician presents the patient with a sonographic picture of the fetus "for the baby album," it may be a manifestation of the desire to reproduce not only babies but also motherhood.

But feminist critiques of "the war against the womb" often suffer from certain tendencies toward reductionism. First, they confuse masculine rhetoric and fantasies with actual power relations, thereby submerging women's own responses to reproductive situations in the dominant (and victimizing) masculine text. Second, if they do consider women's responses, those responses are compressed into Everywoman's Reproductive Consciousness, undifferentiated by particular historical and social circumstances; biology itself becomes a universal rather than an individual, particular set of conditions. To correct this myopia, I shall return to the study of fetal images through a different lens, that of pregnant women as viewers.

PICTURING THE BABY—WOMEN'S RESPONSES

The scenario of the voyeuristic ultrasound instrument/technician, with the pregnant woman displaced to one side passively staring at her objectified fetus, has a certain phenomenological truth. At the same time, anecdotal evidence gives us another, quite different scenario when it comes to the subjective understanding of pregnant women themselves. Far from feeling victimized or pacified, they frequently express a sense of elation and direct participation in the imaging process, claiming it "makes the baby more real," "more our baby"; that visualizing the fetus creates a feeling of intimacy and belonging, as well as a reassuring sense of predictability and control.[37] (I am speaking here of women whose pregnancies are wanted, of course, not those seeking abortions.) Some women even talk about themselves as having "bonded" with the fetus through viewing its image on the screen.[38] Like amniocentesis, in vitro fertilization, voluntary sterilization, and other "male-dominated" reproductive technologies, ultrasound imaging in pregnancy seems to evoke in many women a sense of greater control and self-empowerment than they would have if left to "traditional" methods or "nature." How are we to understand this contradiction between the feminist decoding of male "cultural dreamworks" and (some) women's actual experience of reproductive techniques and images?

Current feminist writings about reproductive technology are not very helpful in answering this kind of question. Works such as Gena Corea's *The Mother Machine* and most articles in the anthology, *Test-Tube Women*, portray women as the perennial victims of an omnivorous male plot to take over their reproductive capacities. The specific forms taken by male strategies of reproductive control, while admittedly varying across times and cultures, are reduced to a pervasive, transhistorical "need." Meanwhile, women's own resistance to this control, often successful, as well as their complicity in it, are ignored; women, in this view, have no role as agents of their reproductive destinies.

But historical and sociological research shows that women are not just passive victims of reproductive technologies and the physicians who wield them. Because of their shared reproductive situation and needs, women throughout the nineteenth and twentieth centuries have often *generated* demands for technologies such as birth control, childbirth anesthesia, or infertility treatments, or they have welcomed them as benefits (which is not to say the technologies offered always met the needs).[39] We have to understand the market for oral contraceptives, sterilization, in vitro fertilization, amniocentesis, and high-tech pregnancy monitoring as a more complex phenomenon than either the victimization or the male-womb-envy thesis allows.

At the same time, theories of a "feminist standpoint" or "reproductive consciousness" that would restore pregnant women to active historical agency and unify their responses to reproductive images and techniques are complicated by two sets of circumstances.[40] First, we do not simply imbibe our reproductive experience raw. The dominant images and codes that mediate the material conditions of pregnancy, abortion, and so forth, determine what, exactly, women "know" about these events in their lives, their *meaning* as lived experience. Thus, women may see in fetal images what they are told they ought to see. Second, and in dialectical tension with the first, women's relationships to reproductive technologies and images differ depending on social differences such as class, race, and sexual orientation, and biological ones such as age, physical disability, and personal fertility history. Their "reproductive consciousness" is constituted out of these complex elements and cannot easily be generalized or, unfortunately, vested with a privileged insight.

How different women see fetal images depends on the context of the looking and the relationship of the viewer to the image and what it signifies. Recent semiotic theory emphasizes "the centrality of the moment of reception in the construction of meanings." The meanings of a visual image or text are created through an "interaction" process between the viewer and the text, taking their focus from the situation of the viewer.[41] John Berger identifies a major contextual frame defining the relationship between viewer and image in distinguishing between what he calls "photographs which belong to private experience" and thus connect to our lives in some intimate way, and "public photographs," which excise bits of information "from all lived experience."[42] Now, this is a simplistic distinction because "private" photographic images become imbued with "public" resonances all the time; we "see" lovers' photos and family albums through the scrim of television ads. Still, I want to borrow Berger's distinction because it helps indicate important differences between the meanings of fetal images when they are viewed as "the fetus" and when they are viewed as "my baby."

When legions of right-wing women in the antiabortion movement brandish pictures of gory dead or dreamlike space-floating fetuses outside clinics or in demonstrations, they are participating in a visual pageant that directly degrades women—and thus themselves. Wafting these fetus pictures as icons, literal fetishes, they both propagate and celebrate the image of the fetus as autonomous space-hero and the pregnant woman as "empty space." Their visual statements are straightforward representations of the antifeminist ideas they (and their male cohorts) support. Such right-wing women promote the public, political character of the fetal image as a symbol that condenses a complicated set of conservative values—about sex, motherhood, teenage girls, fatherhood, the family. In this instance, perhaps it makes sense to say they participate variously in a "phallic" way of looking and thus become the "complacent facilitators for the working out of man's fantasies."[43]

It is not only antiabortionists who respond to fetal images, however. The "public" presentation of the fetus has become ubiquitous; its disembodied form, now propped up by medical authority and technological rationality, permeates mass culture. We are all, on some level, susceptible to its coded meanings. Victor Burgin points out that it does no good to protest the "falseness" of such images as against "reality," because "reality"—that is, how we experience the world, both "public" and "private"—"is itself constituted through the agency of representations."[44] This suggests that women's ways of seeing ultrasound images of fetuses, even their own, may be affected by the cumulative array of "public" representations, from *Life* magazine to *The Silent Scream*. And it possibly means that some of them will be intimidated from getting abortions—although as yet we have little empirical information to verify this. When young women seeking abortions are coerced or manipulated into seeing pictures of fetuses, their own or others, it is the "public fetus" as moral abstraction they are being made to view.

But the reception and meanings of fetal images also derive from the particular circumstances of the woman as viewer, and these circumstances may not fit neatly within a model of women as victims of reproductive technologies. Above all, the meanings of fetal images will differ depending on whether a woman wishes to be pregnant or not. With regard to wanted pregnancies, women with very diverse political values may respond positively to images that present their fetus as if detached, their own body as if absent from the scene. The reasons are a complex weave of socioeconomic position, gender psychology, and biology. At one end of the spectrum, the "pro-life" women Kristin Luker interviewed strongly identified "the fetus" with their own recent or frequent pregnancies; it became "my little guy." Their circumstances as "devout, traditional women who valued motherhood highly" were those of married women with children, mostly unemployed outside the home, and remarkably isolated from any social or community activities. That "little guy" was indeed their primary source of gratification and self-esteem. Moreover— and this fact links them with many women whose abortion politics and life styles lie at the opposite end of the spectrum—a disproportionate number of them seem to have undergone a history of pregnancy or child loss.[45]

If we look at the women who comprise the market for high-tech obstetrics, they are primarily those who can afford these expensive procedures and who have access to the private medical offices where they are offered. Socially and demographically, they are not only apt to be among the professional, educated, "late-childbearing" cohort who face greater risks because of age (although the average age of amniocentesis and ultrasound recipients seems to be moving rapidly down). More importantly, whatever their age or risk category, they are likely to be products of a middle-class culture that values planning, control, and predictability in the interests of a "quality" baby.[46] These values preexist technologies of visualization and "baby engineering" and create a predisposition toward their acceptance. The fear of "nonquality"—that is, disability—and the pressure on parents, particularly mothers, to produce fetuses that score high on their "stress test" (like infants who score high on their Apgar test and children who score high on their SATs) is a cultural as well as a class phenomenon. Indeed, the "perfect baby" syndrome that creates a welcoming climate for ultrasound imaging may also be oppressive for women, insofar as they are still the ones who bear primary responsibility—and guilt—for how the baby turns out.[47] Despite this, "listening to women's voices" leads to the unmistakable conclusion that, as with birth control generally, many women prefer predictability and will do what they can to have it.

Women's responses to fetal picture taking may have another side as well, rooted in their traditional role in the production of family photographs. If photographs accommodate "aesthetic consumerism," becoming instruments of appropriation and possession, this is nowhere truer than within family life—particularly middle-class family life.[48] Family albums originated to chronicle the continuity of Victorian bourgeois kin networks. The advent of home movies in the 1940s and 1950s paralleled the move to the suburbs and backyard barbecues.[49] Similarly, the presentation of a sonogram photo to the dying grandfather, even before his grandchild's birth,[50] is a 1980s way of affirming patriarchal lineage. In other words, far from the intrusion of an alien, and alienating, technology, it may be that ultrasonography is becoming enmeshed in a familiar language of "private" images.

Significantly, in each of these cases it is the woman, the mother, who acts as custodian of the image—keeping up the album, taking the movies, presenting the sonogram. The specific relationship of women to photographic images, especially those of children, may help to explain the attraction of pregnant women to ultrasound images of their own fetus (as opposed to "public" ones). Rather than being surprised that some women experience bonding with their fetus after viewing its image on a screen (or in a sonographic "photo"), perhaps we should understand this as a culturally embedded component of desire. If it is a form of objectifying the fetus (and the pregnant woman herself as detached from the fetus), perhaps such objectification and detachment are necessary for her to feel erotic pleasure in it.[51] If with the ultrasound image she first recognizes the fetus as "real," as "out there," this means that she first experiences it as an object she can possess.

Keller proposes that feminists reevaluate the concept of objectivity. In so doing they may discover that the process of objectification they have identified as masculinist takes different forms, some that detach the viewer from the viewed and some that make possible both erotic and intellectual attachment.[52] To suggest that the timing of maternal-fetus or maternal-infant attachment is a biological given (for example, at "quickening" or at birth), or that "feeling" is somehow more "natural" than "seeing," contradicts women's changing historical experience.[53] On the other hand, to acknowledge that bonding is a historically and culturally shaped process is not to deny its reality. That women develop powerful feelings of attachment to their ("private") fetuses, especially the ones they want, complicates the politics of fetal images.

Consider a recent case in a New York court that denied a woman damages when her twenty-week fetus was stillborn, following an apparently botched amniocentesis. The majority held that, because the woman did not "witness" the death or injury directly, and was not in the immediate "zone of danger" herself, she could not recover damages for any emotional pain or loss she suffered as a result of the fetus's death. As one dissenting judge argued, the court "rendered the woman a bystander to medical procedures performed upon her own body," denying her any rights based on the emotional and "biological bond" she had with the fetus.[54] In so doing, the majority implicitly sanctioned the image of fetal autonomy and maternal oblivion.

As a feminist used to resisting women's reduction to biology, I find it awkward to defend their biological connection to the fetus. But the patent absurdity and cruelty of this decision underscore the need for feminist analyses of reproduction to address biology. A true biological perspective does not lead us to determinism but rather to infinite *variation*, which is to say that it is historical.[55] Particular lives are lived in particular bodies—not only women's bodies but, just as relevantly, aging, ill, disabled, or infertile ones. The material circumstances that differentiate women's responses to obstetrical ultrasound and other technologies include their own biological history, which may be experienced as one of limits and defeats. In fact, the most significant divider between pregnant women who welcome the information from ultrasound and other monitoring techniques and those who resent the machines or wish to postpone "knowing" may be personal fertility history. A recent study of women's psychological responses to the use of electronic fetal monitors during labor "found that those women who had previously experienced the loss of a baby tended to react positively to the monitor, feeling it to be a reassuring presence, a substitute for the physician and an aid to communication. Those women who had not previously suffered difficult or traumatic births . . . tended to regard the monitor with hostility, as a distraction, a competitor."[56]

Infertility, pregnancy losses, and women's feelings of desperation about childlessness have many sources, including cultural pressures, environmental hazards, and medical misdiagnosis or neglect.[57] Whatever the sources, however, a history of repeated miscarriages, infertility, ectopic pregnancy, or loss of a child is likely to dispose a pregnant woman favorably to techniques that allow her to visualize the pregnancy and *possibly* to gain some control over its outcome.[58] Pregnancy as biosocial experience acts on women's bodies in different ways, with the result that the relation of their bodies, and consciousness, to reproductive technologies may also differ.

Attachment of pregnant women to their fetuses at earlier stages in pregnancy becomes an issue, not because it is cemented through "sight" rather than "feel," but when and if it is used to

obstruct or harass an abortion decision.[59] In fact, there is no reason any woman's abortion decision should be tortured in this way, because there is no medical rationale for requiring her to view
an image of her fetus. Responsible abortion clinics are doing ultrasound imaging in selected
cases—*only* to determine fetal size or placement, where the date of the woman's last menstrual
period is unknown, the pregnancy is beyond the first trimester, or there is a history of problems,
or to diagnose an ectopic pregnancy. But in such cases the woman herself does not see the image,
because the monitor is placed outside her range of vision and clinic protocols refrain from showing her the picture unless she specifically requests it.[60] In the current historical context, to consciously limit the uses of fetal images in abortion clinics is to take a political stance, to resist the
message of *The Silent Scream*. This reminds us that the politics of reproductive technologies are
constructed contextually, out of who uses them, how, and for what purposes.

The view that "reproductive engineering "is imposed on "women as a class," rather than being
sought by them as a means toward greater choice,[61] obscures the particular reality not only of
women with fertility problems and losses but also of other groups. For lesbians who utilize sperm
banks and artificial insemination to achieve biological pregnancy without heterosexual sex, such
technologies are a critical tool of reproductive freedom. Are lesbians to be told that wanting their
"own biological children" generated through their own bodies is somehow wrong for them but
not for fertile heterosexual couples?[62] The majority of poor and working-class women in the
United States and Britain still have no access to amniocentesis, in vitro fertilization, and the rest,
although they (particularly women of color) have the highest rates of infertility and fetal impair-
ment. It would be wrong to ignore their lack of access to these techniques on the grounds that
worrying about how babies turn out, or wanting to have "your own," is only a middle-class (or
eugenic) prejudice.

In Europe, Australia, and North America, feminists are currently engaged in heated debate
over whether new reproductive technologies present a threat or an opportunity for women. Do
they simply reinforce the age-old pressures on women to bear children and to bear them to certain specifications, or do they give women more control? What sort of control do we require in
order to have reproductive freedom, and are there/should there be any limits on our control?[63]
What is the meaning of reproductive technologies that tailor-make infants, in a context where
child care remains the private responsibility of women and many women are growing increasingly
poor? Individual women, especially middle-class women, are choosing to utilize high-tech
obstetrics, and their choices may not always be ones we like. It may be that chorionic villus sampling, the new first-trimester prenatal diagnostic technique, will increase the use of selective abortion for sex. Moreover, the bias against disability that underlies the quest for the "perfect child"
seems undeniable. Newer methods of prenatal diagnosis may mean that more and more abortions
become "selective," so that more women decide "to abort the particular fetus [they] are carrying
in hopes of coming up with a 'better' one next time."[64] Are these choices moral? Do we have a
right to judge them? Can we even say they are "free"?

On the other hand, techniques for imaging fetuses and pregnancies may, depending on their
cultural contexts and uses, offer means for empowering women, both individually and collectively. We need to examine these possibilities and to recognize that, at the present stage in history,
feminists have no common standpoint about how women ought to use this power.

CONCLUSION

Images by themselves lack "objective" meanings; meanings come from the interlocking fields of
context, communication, application, and reception. If we removed from the ultrasound image of
The Silent Scream its title, its text, its sound narrative, Dr. Nathanson, the media and distribution
networks, and the whole antiabortion political climate, what would remain? But, of course, the
question is absurd because no image dangles in a cultural void, just as no fetus floats in a space
capsule. The problem clearly becomes, then, how do we change the contexts, media, and con-

sciousness through which fetal images are defined? Here are some proposals, both modest and utopian.

First, we have to restore women to a central place in the pregnancy scene. To do this, we must create new images that recontextualize the fetus, that place it back into the uterus, and the uterus back into the woman's body, and her body back into its social space. Contexts do not neatly condense into symbols; they must be told through stories that give them mass and dimension.

Second, we need to separate the power relations within which reproductive technologies, including ultrasound imaging, are applied from the technologies themselves. If women were truly empowered in the clinic setting, as practitioners and patients, would we discard the technologies? Or would we use them differently, integrating them into a more holistic clinical dialogue between women's felt knowledge and the technical information "discovered" in the test tube or on the screen? Before attacking reproductive technologies, we need to demand that all women have access to the knowledge and resources to judge their uses and to use them wisely, in keeping with their own particular needs.

Finally, we should pursue the discourse now begun toward developing a feminist ethic of reproductive freedom that complements feminist politics. What ought we to choose if we become genuinely free to choose? Are some choices unacceptable on moral grounds, and does this mean under any circumstances, or only under some? Can feminism reconstruct a joyful sense of childbearing and maternity without capitulating to ideologies that reduce women to a maternal essence? Can we talk about morality in reproductive decision making without invoking the specter of maternal duty? On some level, the struggle to demystify fetal images is fraught with danger, because it involves *re-embodying* the fetus, thus representing women as (wanting-to-be or not-wanting-to-be) pregnant persons. One way out of this danger is to image the pregnant woman, not as an abstraction, but within her total framework of relationships, economic and health needs, and desires. Once we have pictured the social conditions of her freedom, however, we have not dissolved the contradictions in how she might use it.

NOTES

This article was originally published in *Feminist Studies*, Vol. 13, No. 2 (Summer 1987) and, in a somewhat shortened version, in *Reproductive Technologies*, ed. Michelle Stanworth (London and Minneapolis: Polity Press/University of Minnesota, 1987).

1. *City of Akron v. Akron Center for Reproductive Health*, 426 U.S. 416 [1983]; and *Thornburgh v. American College of Obstetricians and Gynecologists*, 54 LW 4618, 10 June 1986. From a prochoice perspective, the significance of these decisions is mixed. Although the court's majority opinion has become, if anything, more liberal and more feminist in its protection of women's "individual dignity and autonomy," this majority has grown steadily narrower. Whereas in 1973 it was seven to two, in 1983 it shrank to six to three and then in 1986 to a bare five to four, while the growing minority becomes ever more conservative and antifeminist. [Note: This article was originally written prior to the Supreme Court's 1992 decision in *Planned Parenthood of Southeastern Pennsylvania v. Casey*. In five separate opinions denoting significant splits within the court, five of the justices concurred in upholding *Roe's* main finding that a woman's right to choose abortion "before viability" is a matter of basic liberty under the Fourteenth Amendment. Yet a majority of the court also held that all the restrictions on abortion imposed by the Pennsylvania statute, with the one exception of spousal consent, did not impose "undue burden" on this constitutionally protected liberty.)

2. See Paul D. Erickson, *Reagan Speaks: The Making of an American Myth* (New York: New York University Press, 1985); and Joanmarie Kalter, "TV News and Religion," *TV Guide* 9 and 16 (November 1985, for analyses of these trends.

3. John C. Fletcher and Mark I. Evans, "Maternal Bonding in Early Fetal Ultrasound Examinations," *New England Journal of Medicine* 308 (1983): 392–93.

4. Planned Parenthood Federation of America, *The Facts Speak Louder: Planned Parenthood's Critique of*

"The Silent Scream" (New York: Planned Parenthood Federation of America, n.d.). A new film, *Silent Scream II*, appeared too late to be reviewed in this article.

5. These earliest photographic representations of fetal life, made by the Swedish photographer Lennart Nilsson, were reproduced in "Babies before Birth," *Look* 26 (June 5, 1962): 19–23; "A Sonar Look at an Unborn Baby," *Life* 58 (January 165, 1965): 45–46; and Geraldine L. Flanagan, *The First Nine Months of Life* (New York: Simon & Schuster, 1962).

6. For a history of photography, see Alan Trachtenberg, ed. *Classic Essays on Photography* (New Haven: Leete's Island Books, 1980); and Susan Sontag, *On Photography* (New York: Delta, 1973), esp. 22–23.

7. Roland Barthes, "The Photographic Message," in *A Barthes Reader,* ed. Susan Sontag (New York: Hill & Wang, 1982), 194–210. Compare Hubert Danish: "The photographic image does not belong to the natural world. It is a product of human labor, a cultural object whose being . . . cannot be dissociated precisely from its historical meaning and from the necessarily datable project in which it originates." See his "Notes for a Phenomenology of the Photographic Image," in *Classic Essays on Photography*, 287–90.

8. Lady Elizabeth Eastlake, "Photography," in *Classic Essays on Photography*, 39–68, 65–66; John Berger, *About Looking* (New York: Pantheon, 1980), 48–50; and Andre Bazin, "The Ontology of the Photographic Image," in *Classic Essays on Photography*, 237–40, 241.

9. Allan Sekula, "On the Invention of Photographic Meaning," in Victor Burgin, ed., *Thinking Photography* (London: Macmillan, 1982), 84–109; and Sontag, *On Photography*, 5, 21.

10. Stuart Ewen and Elizabeth Ewen, *Channels of Desire: Mass Images and the Shaping of American Consciousness* (New York: McGraw-Hill, 1982), 33.

11. Barbara Katz Rothman, *The Tentative Pregnancy: Prenatal Diagnosis and the Future of Motherhood* (New York: Viking, 1986), 114.

12. Zoe Sofia, "Exterminating Fetuses: Abortion, Disarmament, and the Sexo-Semiotics of Extraterrestrialism," *Diacritics* 14 (1984): 47–59.

13. Rachel B. Gold, "Ultrasound Imaging During Pregnancy," *Family Planning Perspectives* 16 (1984): 240–43, 240–41; Albert D. Haverkamp and Miriam Orleans, "An Assessment of Electronic Fetal Monitoring," *Women and Health* 7(1982): 126–34, 128; and Ruth Hubbard, "Personal Courage Is Not Enough: Some Hazards of Childbearing in the 1980s," in *Test-Tube Women: What Future for Motherhood?* ed. Rita Arditti, Renate Duelli Klein, and Shelley Minden (Boston: Routledge & Kegan Paul, 1984), 331–55, 341.

14. Janet Gallagher, "The Fetus and the Law—Whose Life Is It, Anyway?" *Ms.* (Sept. 1984); John Fletcher, "The Fetus as Patient: Ethical Issues," *Journal of the American Medical Association* 246 (1981): 772–73; and Hubbard, "Personal Courage Is Not Enough," 350.

15. David A. Grimes, "Second-Trimester Abortions in the United States," *Family Planning Pespectives* 16 (1984): 260–65; and Stanley K. Henshaw et al., "A Portrait of American Women Who Obtain Abortions," *Family Planning Pespectives* 17 (1985): 90–96.

16. In her dissenting opinion in the *Akron* case, Supreme Court Justice Sandra Day O'Connor argued that *Roe v. Wade* was "on a collision course with itself" because technology was pushing the point of viability indefinitely backward. In *Roe* the court had defined "viability" as the point at which the fetus is "potentially able to live outside the mother's womb, albeit with artificial aid." After that point, it said, the state could restrict abortion except when bringing the fetus to term would jeopardize the woman's life or health. Compare Nancy K. Rhoden, "Late Abortion and Technological Advances in Fetal Viability: Some Legal Considerations," *Family Planning Perspectives* 17 (1985): 160–61. Meanwhile, a popular weekly television program, *Hill Street Blues*, in March 1985 aired a dramatization of abortion clinic harassment in which a pregnant woman seeking an abortion miscarries and gives birth to an extremely premature fetus-baby, which soon dies. Numerous newspaper accounts of "heroic" efforts to save premature newborns have made front-page headlines.

17. Donna Haraway, "A Manifesto for Cyborgs: Science, Technology, and Socialist Feminism in the 1980s," *Socialist Review* 80 (1985): 65–107.

18. Gold, 240; and David Graham, "Ultrasound in Clinical Obstetrics," *Women and Health* 7 (1982): 39–55.

19. American College of Obstetricians and Gynecologists, "Diagnostic Ultrasound in Obstetrics and Gynecology," *Women and Health* 7 (1982): 55–58 (reprinted from ACOG, *Technical Bulletin*, no. 63 [October 1981]).

20. Madeleine H. Shearer, "Revelations: A Summary and Analysis of the NIH Consensus Development Conference on Ultrasound Imaging in Pregnancy," *Birth* 11 (1984): 23–36, 25–36, 30; Gold, 240–41.

21. Dr. Alan Fleishman, personal communication (May 1985).

22. For a discussion of these issues, see Rosalind P. Petchesky, *Abortion and Woman's Choice: The State, Sexuality and Reproductive Freedom* (Boston: Northeastern University, 1990, revised), chap. 9.

23. Kathy H. Sheehan, "Abnormal Labor: Caesareans in the U.S.," *The Network News* (National Women's Health Network) 10 (July/August 1985): 1, 3; and Haverkamp and Orleans, 127.

24. ACOG, "Diagnostic Ultrasound in Obstetrics and Gynecology," 58.

25. Stephen B. Thacker and H. David Banta, "Benefits and Risks of Episiotomy," in *Women and Health* 7 (1982): 173–80.

26. Evelyn Fox Keller and Christine R. Grontkowski, "The Mind's Eye," in *Discovering Realty: Feminist Perspectives on Epistemology, Metaphysics, Methodology, and Philosophy of Science*, ed. Sandra Harding and Merrill B. Hintikka (Dordrecht: D. Reidel, 1983), 107–24.

27. Luce Iragaray, "Ce Sexe qui n'en est pas un," in *New French Feminisms: An Anthology*, ed. Elaine Marks and Isabelle de Courtivron (New York: Schocken, 1981), 99–106, 101; Annette Kuhn, *Women's Pictures: Feminism and Cinema* (London: Routledge & Kegan Paul, 1982), 601–65, 113; Laura Mulvey, "Visual Pleasure and Narrative Cinema," *Screen* 16 (1979): 6–18; and E. Ann Kaplan, "Is the Gaze Male?" in *Powers of Desire: The Politics of Sexuality*, ed. Ann Snitow, Christine Stansell, and Sharon Thompson (New York: Monthly Review Press, 1983), 309–27, 324.

28. Evelyn Fox Keller, *Reflections on Gender and Science* (New Haven: Yale University, 1985), 123–24.

29. Melinda Beck et al., "America's Abortion Dilemma," *Newsweek* 105 (14 Jan. 1985): 20–29, 21 (italics added).

30. This passage is quoted in Hubbard, 348, and taken from Michael R. Harrison et al., "Management of the Fetus with a Correctable Congenital Defect," *Journal of the American Medical Association* 246 (1981): 774 (italics added).

31. Haraway, 89; Sontag, *On Photography*, 13–14.

32. This quotation comes from the Chief of Maternal and Fetal Medicine at a Boston hospital, as cited in Hubbard, 349. Compare it with Graham, 49–50.

33. For examples, see Hubbard, 350; and Rothman, 113–15.

34. Rothman, 113.

35. Gold, 242.

36. Kaplan, 324. Compare Jessica Benjamin, "Master and Slave: The Fantasy of Erotic Domination," in *Powers of Desire*, 280–99, 295. This article was originally published as "The Bonds of Love: Rational Violence and Erotic Domination," *Feminist Studies* 6 (Spring 1980): 144–74.

37. Hubbard, 335; Rothman, 202, 212–13, as well as my own private conversations with recent mothers.

38. Rothman, 113–14.

39. Linda Gordon, *Woman's Body, Woman's Right: A Social History of Birth Control in America* (New York: Grossman, 1976): Angus McLaren, *Birth Control in Nineteenth-Century England* (London: Croom Helm, 1978); Jane Lewis, *The Politics of Motherhood: Child and Maternal Welfare in England, 1900–1939* (London: Croom Helm, 1980), chap. 4; Rosalind P. Petchesky, "Reproductive Freedom: Beyond a Woman's Right to Choose," in *Women: Sex, and Sexuality*, ed. Catharine R. Stimpson and

Ethel Spector Person (Chicago: University of Chicago Press), 1981, 92–116 (originally in *Signs* 5 [Summer 1980]); and Petchesky, *Abortion and Woman's Choice*, chaps. 1 and 5.

40. Mary O'Brien, *The Politics of Reproduction* (Boston: Routledge and Kegan Paul, 1983), chap. 1; and Nancy Hartsock, *Money, Sex, and Power* (New York: Longman, 1983), chap. 10.

41. Kuhn, 43–44.

42. Berger, 51.

43. Irigaray, 100.

44. Burgin, 9.

45. Kristin Luker, *Abortion and the Politics of Motherhood* (Berkeley: University of California, 1984), 138–39, 150–51.

46. Michelle Fine and Adrienne Asch, "Who Owns the Womb?" *Women's Review of Books* 2 (May 1985): 8–10; Hubbard, 336.

47. Hubbard, 344.

48. Sontag, *On Photography*, 8.

49. Patty Zimmerman, "Amateurs, the Avant-Garde, and Ideologies of Art," *Journal of Film and Video*, Summer/Fall 1986, 63–85.

50. Rothman, 125.

51. Lorna Weir and Leo Casey, "Subverting Power in Sexuality," *Socialist Review* 14 (1984): 139–57.

52. Keller, *Reflections on Gender and Science*, 70–73, 98–100, 117–20.

53. Compare this to Rothman, 41–42.

54. David Margolick, "Damages Rejected in Death of Fetus," *New York Times*, 16 June 1985, 26.

55. See Denise Riley, *War in the Nursery: Theories of the Child and Mother* (London: Virago, 1983), 17 and chaps. 1–2, generally, for an illuminating critique of feminist and Marxist ideas about biological determinism and their tendency to reintroduce dualism.

56. Brian Bates and Allison N. Turner, "Imagery and Symbolism in the Birth Practices of Traditional Cultures," *Birth* 12 (185): 33–38.

57. Rebecca Albury, "Who Owns the Embryo?" in *Test-Tube Women*, 54–67, 57–58.

58. Rayna Rapp has advised me, based on her field research, that another response of women who have suffered difficult pregnancy histories to such diagnostic techniques may be denial—simply not wanting to know. This too, however, may be seen as a tactic to gain control over information, by censoring bad news.

59. Coercive, invasive uses of fetal images, masked as "informed consent," have been a prime strategy of antiabortion forces for some years. They have been opposed by prochoice litigators in the courts, resulting in the Supreme Court's repudiation on three different occasions of specious "informed consent" regulations as an unconstitutional form of harassment and denial of women's rights. See *Akron*, 1983; *Thornburgh*, 1986.

60. I obtained this information from interviews with Maria Tapia-Birch, administrator in the Maternal and Child Services Division of the New York City Department of Health; and with Jeanine Michaels, social worker, and Lisa Milstein, nurse-practitioner, at the Eastern Women's Health Clinic in New York, who kindly shared their clinical experience with me. Subsequent to this writing, the court upheld such a biased counseling, or "informed consent," provision in the Pennsylvania statute that was declared constitutional in *Planned Parenthood v. Casey* (1992). See n. 1, above.

61. Corea, 313.

62. Compare Fine and Asch.

63. Samuel Gorovitz, "Introduction: The Ethical Issues," *Women and Health* 7 (1982): 1–8, 1.

64. Hubbard, 334.

Part Three

THE SOCIAL CONSTRUCTION
OF IDENTITIES

Comparative Sexualities

10   Sex and Society

A Research Note from Social History and Anthropology

Ellen Ross and Rayna Rapp

"The personal is political" was a central insight of the wave of feminism that gathered momentum in the 1960s. Within that phrase is condensed the understanding that the seemingly most intimate details of private existence are actually structured by larger social relations. Attention to the personal politics of intimate life soon focused on sexuality, and many canons of sexual meaning were challenged. The discovery of erotic art and symbols as male centered, the redefinition of lesbian sexuality as positive and life-affirming, and the dismantling of the two orgasm theory as a transparently male perception of the female body were among the products of this critique. Such reinterpretations suggest that social definitions of sex may change rapidly and in the process transform the very experience of sex itself.[1]

Sexuality's biological base is always experienced culturally, through a translation. The bare biological facts of sexuality do not speak for themselves; they must be expressed socially. Sex feels individual, or at least private, but those feelings always incorporate the rules, definitions, symbols, and meanings of the worlds in which they are constructed. "The mind can be said to be our most erogenous zone," as one commentator has phrased it,[2] and breakthroughs in sexual counseling have revealed that sexual dysfunction is best cured by teaching people to fantasize, a social response rather than a biological repair.[3] Conversely, without a social context to define them as legitimate, the sexual experiences of generations of American women were confused and distorted; properly brought-up Victorian women were taught that they need never be "bothered" by sexual passions, while their more "liberated" daughters learned that orgasms were their anatomical destiny.[4]

Ellen Ross received her Ph.D. in History from the University of Chicago, and is Professor of History and Women's Studies at Ramapo College in New Jersey. A specialist in modern British history, her current work is on middle-class women "travelers" among London's poor in the nineteenth and twentieth centuries. Her book *Love and Toil: Motherhood in Outcast London 1870–1918* was published by Oxford University Press in 1993.

Rayna Rapp teaches in the Department of Anthropology, New School for Social Research, where she chairs the Master's Program in Gender Studies and Feminist Theory. She is editor of *Toward an Anthropology of Women* and the co-editor of *Promissory Notes: Women in the Transition to Socialism; Articulating Hidden Histories,* and *Conceiving the New World Order: The Global Politics of Reproduction.* Her book, *Moral Pioneers: Fetuses, Families, and Amniocentesis,* forthcoming from Routledge, analyzes the social impact and cultural meaning of prenatal diagnosis in the United States.

If the biological facts do not speak for themselves, neither do the social ones. While it has become a standard tenet of sociology and social psychology that all human behavior, including sexual behavior, is shaped by social contexts, those contexts remain cloudy. The classics of the social science of sex divide either into mere catalogues of sexual variation (replete with initiation rites, puberty ceremonies, coital positions, *ad infinitum* among exotic peoples)[5] or vague assertions that sexual behavior is taught and learned in social groups.[6] As recent innovative essays by Michel Foucault and Jeffrey Weeks point out, scholars are just beginning to investigate the plasticity of sexuality in Western European history and its embeddedness in other social arenas.[7]

But *how* society specifically shapes sexuality still remains abstract. How are we to weight and evaluate the claims of the different domains of society on the prescription and behavior surrounding sex? How, for example, do family contexts, religious ideologies, community norms, and political policies interact in the formation of sexual experience? Here we intend to bring the theories and methods of anthropology and social history to bear on the problem of structuring social contexts.

We realize that the most popular perspective on the social shaping of sexuality focuses on individuals in family contexts, almost to the detriment of larger social connections. This is most powerfully exemplified by psychoanalytic theory, which attempts to bridge the seeming gap between the social and biological worlds by describing human personality as a product of the experiences of love, hate, power, and conflict in families. Such experiences are presumed to leave important residues in the unconscious. Adult sexuality is thus a central aspect of personality, which takes form in earliest childhood. Experiences of dependency, merging, and separating, initially focused on the mothering figure, resonate deeply throughout adult sexual life.

Recent feminist revisions of psychoanalytic theory have focused on the social construction of motherhood under conditions of male dominance. They reveal the centrality of female parenting in the psychic structuring of gender identity. Scholars such as Gayle Rubin, Nancy Chorodow, Dorothy Dinnerstein, Juliet Mitchell, and Jane Flax have demonstrated how complex and deeply "unnatural" the social process of creating gendered and heterosexual beings is.[8] Such theories underline the tenacity with which sexuality is intertwined with unconscious relations of dominance not easily or automatically affected by social reform.

A focus on the psychoanalytic, however, holds the social world at bay, awarding it only minimal importance in the shaping of consciousness and sexuality. The examples cited below suggest that the social contexts in which sexual experience occurs are continually changing. While a truly social and historical theory of sexuality requires an explicit link between society and enduring psychic structure, such links are as yet far from clear.

The solution to the problem of connecting the individual unconscious and the wider society is not to read directly, as psychohistorians do, from a supposed universal psychosexual conflict between parents and children to general, society wide antagonisms. Christopher Lasch, for example, posits a direct connection between the alleged decrease of paternal authority within families and the crisis of contemporary American capitalism.[9] In the hands of such scholars, the study of society becomes a mere meditation on psychosexual development and social history becomes superfluous.

The analysis of psychosexual development is a complement to the study of society, not its ahistorical replacement. Sexuality both generates wider social relations and is refracted through the prism of society. As such, sexual feelings and activities express all the contradictions of power relations—of gender, class, and race. We can never assume, for example, that the sexual experiences of black slave women and white plantation women—though sometimes involving the same class of men—were the same. To examine these sexual experiences we do not intend to focus on "disembodied" sex acts. Rather, we will sketch out the series of contexts that condition, constrain, and socially define these acts.

Attempting to describe the link between society and individual sexuality, we initially saw these contexts spiraling outward from the individual toward the larger world. Social relations that appear peripheral to individual sexual practices (labor migration, for example) may in fact influence them profoundly through intervening social forms (e.g., by limiting available sexual partners and influencing the age of marriage). Gayle Rubin suggests that intermeshed gears provide a better image; in the ratio of the gears would be found the narrower and broader determinants of sexual experience.[10] But we cannot measure such ratios, and this metaphor is too mechanical to describe relationships in constant flux. More satisfactory is Clifford Geertz's image of an onion, which he used in describing the permeation of culture in the human experience.[11] In sexuality as in culture, as we peel off each layer (economies, politics, families, etc.), we may think that we are approaching the kernel, but we eventually discover that the whole is the only "essence" there is. Sexuality cannot be abstracted from its surrounding social layers.

Whatever metaphor best represents the social embeddedness of sexuality, it must be able to contain at least the following contexts: (1) kinship and family systems, (2) sexual regulations and definitions of communities, and (3) national and world systems. We do not claim that any one of these contexts is causal, or that our list is complete. But we will claim that each and all of them simultaneously set up the external limits on sexual experience and give shape to individual and group behavior. As social contexts, they both mirror and are lived through the salient power divisions in any society: class, caste, race, gender, and heterosexual dominance. Such divisions are internalized at the most intimate level of sexual fantasies and feelings and become part of human personality itself. We will discuss each of the spiraling contexts to illustrate our conviction that sexuality is shaped by complex, changing social relations and thus has a history. Like all histories, it is capable of further transformation through the struggles of "sexual politics."

FAMILY FORMS AND KINSHIP SYSTEMS

It is an axiom of cultural anthropology that family forms, embedded in kinship systems, vary cross-culturally and often over time within a single culture. Kinship systems encompass such basic relations as marriage patterns, the tracing of descent, and inheritance not only of specific offices or possessions but also of more abstract rights and obligations. All these aspects of kinship systems have a potential impact on sexuality: kin terminologies, inheritance practices, and marriage patterns are significant in sexual socialization.

Kinship terminologies, for example, may carry crucial information on degrees of incest, acceptable marriage partners, and even the "gray area" within which some kinsfolk may be available for sexual relations but not for marriage. The fourteen kin categories named in Dravidian terminologies (found in parts of South Asia, Australia, and the Pacific) orient children not only to naming their parents, or siblings, but to knowing their potential mothers- and fathers-in-law and their potential spouses as well.[12] In such kinship systems, major messages mapping permissible and outlawed sexual partners are transmitted in language itself. While most Western languages designate many fewer kin classifications than this, the power to name—and thus legitimate or abolish—a sexual relation within the family may occur locally and informally. In the villages of southeastern France, for example, many young brides are referred to as "little mother" from the day they enter the new husband's family. Such a kin term conveys not only the centrality of producing future heirs for the stem family, but the desexualization of the conjugal dyad as well.[13]

In delineating permissible or necessary marriage partners, kinship systems usually specify sexual objects as well. Among the Banaro of northern New Guinea, for instance: "When a woman is married, she is initiated into intercourse by the sib-friend [a member of the same sib or clan, a kin group organized by common descent] of her groom's father. After bearing a child by this man, she begins to have intercourse with her husband. She also has an institutionalized partnership with the sib-friend of her husband. A man's partners include his wife, the wife of his sib-friend, and the wife of his sib-friend's son."[14] In such a system, as Rubin points out, there are multiple triangulated heterosexual bonds set up in both the sib-friend and marriage systems. The point is not only that people are socially constructed as "heterosexual," but as specifically sib-friend and cross-cousin sexual as well. (A cross-cousin is a kinsperson who is the child of the opposite-sexed sibling of the parent of the person to whom he/she is related. For example, my mother's brother's children are my cross-cousins—cross-sex of the connecting parental genera-tions—while my mother's sister's children are my parallel cousins.) Sexual socialization is no less specific to each culture than is socialization to ritual, dress, or cuisine.

Permissible objects of sexual passion may be redefined as official definitions of family bound-aries change. In an extremely thoughtful comparison of Catholic and Protestant family strategies and affective relations in early modern France, Natalie Davis points out that "back in the thir-teenth century, people remembered the days when one could not marry within the seventh degree, that is, any of the descendants of one's great-great-great-great-great grandparents. Then, at the Lateran Council of 1215, it became and remained within the fourth degree: one was for-bidden to marry any one of the descendant of one's sixteen great-great grandparents."[15] The contraction of the field in which incestuous unions were defined affected what were natural or permissible sexual experiences among kinsfolk, godparents, and their offspring. Medieval and Renaissance theologians debated the relative merits of directing passion inside and outside of nuclear families: the sixteenth-century Jesuit Edmond Auger reasoned that "'our carnal desires' are by nature strongest towards those closest to us and would be boundless if we married them."[16] Such theological speculation parallels modern anthropology's romance with the relation between incest prohibitions and the creation of marriage alliances.[17]

Incest prohibitions are not the only boundaries to sex and marriage that family systems set up. As many demographic and family historians remind us, European marriage patterns from at least as far back as the seventeenth century through the nineteenth century were based on a late age of marriage and a high proportion of persons who remained permanently celibate, that is, unmar-ried.[18] Such people might be domestic servants, prostitutes, or members of religious orders or armies, but often their celibacy was generated by the inheritance system into which they were born. Examining family practices among the late seventeenth- and eighteenth-century squirearchy of England, a group that favored impartibility (the practice of inheritance by a single person, by custom often the eldest male child, which ensures that estates remain undivided), Lawrence Stone found a celibacy rate of about 25 percent among daughters and younger sons, a rate more than twice as high as that of the sixteenth century. These low rates of nuptiality he attributes to primogeniture.[19] It is not only the sexual experiences of the young that are struc-tured by inheritance systems, but also those of adults, especially widows. For though the English countryside in many regions had a substantial "female presence" of inheriting daughters or widows, their remarriage was always problematic for the children of the first marriage.[20] In the Cambrian parish of Kikby Lonsdale, a widow lost her "freebench"—her common law right to a portion of her husband's estate during her lifetime—if she either remarried or had sexual inter-course.[21] In such an example, the property and sexual relations of widows become fused.

The sexual life of celibates was probably quite different from that of the married population. As eighteenth-century observers noted, "The unmarried Ladies and Gentlemen . . . of moderate fortunes . . . are unable to support the Expense of Family . . . they therefore acquiesce in Celibacy; Each Sex compensating itself, as it can, by other Diversions."[22] Such diversions might include "a variety of alternatives [which] are and probably were available, notably, lonely or mutual masturbation, oral or anal sex, homosexuality, bestiality, adultery with married women whose offspring are attributed to their husbands, and resort to prostitutes."[23] While this list was compiled by Stone in discussing alternatives to heterosexual premarital intercourse, it would equally apply to permanent celibates. As Jack Goody points out, even when more than one son married, the opportunities for love and romance might vary with inheritance practice. In tradi-tional France, a common cultural perception was that first sons married as their families dictated, while second sons married "for love."[24]

While we have discussed inheritance as if it were generated out of family relations, it is important to note that inheritance patterns actually integrate family members (and their sexuality) into national and even international movements in law and in class formation. As E. P. Thompson notes, the "grid of inheritance" in any locality reflects the efforts of geographically wider social classes to secure the property, offices, and training of their offspring in a world that is continuously changing.[25] Inheritance laws legislated by a central state implicate family formation and sexual patterns at the local level. What appear as local patterns organized around kinship are often products of much wider social relations.

COMMUNITIES AS LOCI OF SOCIAL RELATIONS

Families and kin groups cannot organize sexuality for themselves; the partners and patterns they require are usually rooted in wider communities, where lively traditions of sexual prescription—courting behavior, ritual prohibitions, and sexual socialization—are played out. The varied use of charivari rituals illustrates how local sexual norms are intricately intertwined with other values. These were rituals that occurred in France and England dating from the seventeenth century or earlier, in which neighbors serenaded offenders of moral values—especially values in the sexual/domestic realm—with "rough music" (banging, whistling, etc.), sometimes parading an effigy of the offender. Charivaris were directed not only against henpecked husbands, adulterers, notorious seducers, and homosexuals, but also against merchants who cheated customers, talebearers, habitual drunks, strikebreakers, those who worked during festival times, and magistrates issuing unpopular decisions.[26] The "Rebecca Riots" in southern Wales in the 1840s used the charivari form in both the "public" and "private" domains: against newly built toll roads and farm dispossessions, but also against the Bastardy Clauses of the 1834 Poor Law.[27]

But the community practices surrounding sexuality represent more than local traditions, for communities are also termini of worldwide economic, social, political, and cultural systems. They simultaneously exhibit patterns that are regionally rooted and also reflect the larger world. The introduction of rural industry into some English and Welsh farming communities in the early modern period, for example, changed courtship and marriage to reflect the new value that children's, and especially daughters', labor represented to the family economy as a whole. Earlier patterns in which parents arranged children's marriages through precontracts or spousals gave way in many areas to more clandestine courtship arranged by the young people themselves. Night-courting—peer-group-supervised heterosexual pairing, common in nineteenth-century northern Europe—was one such method. The use of intermediaries in bargaining between parents and children suggests the tensions involved in young peoples' marital decisions. Bridal pregnancy may have been a trump card in children's hands as they asserted autonomy from the family economy via their own sexuality.[28]

Many of the aspects of community sociability—peer groups, the transmission of sexual knowledge, ritual boundaries to permissible or impermissible sexual relations, the involvement of Church regulations on sex that we discuss in this section—reflect both the autonomy of community groups and the presence of a larger social world. Peer groups exhibit this ambiguity especially clearly, for while at the village level it may appear that the young men, for example, have complete control over the regulation of courtship, the ages at which the young may marry or the degree to which bastards may be supported are established by social forces, or laws, originating outside of local communities.

Peer groups are found in many cultures and they serve a variety of functions. Perhaps most importantly, they organize intergenerational relationships outside the family itself. Links between generations are especially significant in systems that depend on family economies, where relations of production cannot be separated from those of kinship, marriage, and reproduction. In such systems, peer regulation of sex and marriage is crucial to the politics and economics of both family and community life. Peer groups are often age based, but because they encompass cultural experience beyond simple shared chronology, they are not reducible to demographic age-cohorts. In the French language, generational age and marriage status are conflated: *vieille fille/vieux garçon* translates as spinster/bachelor, but its literal meaning is aged girl/aged boy. In traditional Irish villages, unmarried men are boys, no matter what their chronological age.[29]

Given a marriage pattern in town and country in which there is a long period between the age of sexual maturity and the age of marriage, highly ritualized management of celibacy and courtship was common in early modern Europe. In describing the history of youth groups in eighteenth-century England and Germany, John Gillis notes:

> Horizontal bonding of young single persons was a feature not only of the schools and universities, but also of many of the professions, the army, the bureaucracy, and the clergy as well. The clergy was the only one in which celibacy was an essential aspect of the brotherhood; but as a requirement of apprenticeship and as a kind of extended rite of passage, it was a feature of all trades and professions. In the crafts, journeymen's associations upheld the ideal of continence and the delay of marriage, relying on an elaborate imagery and ritual of "brotherhood" to solidify the social and moral bonds within their group . . . [for example] perhaps a primary function of the *Wanderjahr* was to take young men out of the marriage market during those years when such a step would have had disastrous results for the entire community, and thus prolong the state of semidependence until a place for them opened up in the normal course of the generational cycle.[30]

As the massive process of proletarianization and urbanization broke down the productive and reproductive patterns of traditional Europe, "traditions of youth were redrawn along class lines."[31] Working-class youth, by the later nineteenth century, were more economically and sexually autonomous at younger ages than were middle-class youngsters. Their peer groups were often labeled "promiscuous" and "delinquent" by middle-class observers, whose own children were sequestered in single-sex schools, universities, social clubs, and fraternal orders. "Adolescence" was increasingly used to describe the period of prolonged professional training to which middle-class offspring were subjected, during which time they were considered to be asexual.[32]

For Western Europe, evidence of ritualized structuring of courting dates back a considerable time. In French peasant villages from medieval almost through modern times, groups of unmarried men, the "abbeyes" Natalie Davis describes, restricted the pool of marriageable young people and maintained village endogamy—marriage within a specified social group in a community—by fighting or fining strangers who came to court local girls.[33] Adolescent peer groups in traditional European villages might even more directly supervise sexual activity. Recently, historians have drawn attention to "night-courting" in northern France, the Vendée, Alsace, Germany, Switzerland, and Scandinavia.[34] In night-courting as practiced in many parts of Scandinavia, young unmarried men gathered at a central place on Saturday nights and set off on a round of visits to the houses of the village's unmarried women, hoping to leave one of their number with each woman. Couples spent the rest of the night in the women's beds, and courted according to detailed rules that outlined what clothing needed to be left on, what body parts might touch, and so on. At the end of the night, the group of men reformed, and public mockery was the fate of couples found violating these rules.[35] "Accidents are rare," according to a 1795 report on the practice in Neuchâtel.[36] Church spokesmen, especially in Catholic regions, attacked these practices as immoral from as early as the seventeenth century. But they survived in some places to the end of the nineteenth century, only to be deplored as primitive and immoral by middle-class lay observers. Yet the loss of such peer regulation, either through its actual suppression or through the breakup of communities, seems to be one of the cluster of forces that led to increased illegitimacy rates.[37]

Sexuality is a notorious source of tension between adolescent peer groups and adults. The teenage girls studied by Molly Dougherty in a rural black town in the Southern United States play their peers against their adult kinswomen as they enter into heterosexual relationships. Attitudes toward sexual experimentation and courting are relaxed and positive among peers; adult women may castigate the teenagers for early pregnancy, but they also supervise the transition to the elevated status motherhood provides for the young girls. Teenage sex and its consequences are negotiated between the peer and parenting generations, allowing young women to test bonds in both directions as they court.[38]

Peer groups formed in adolescence may have an impact on the affective and sexual lives of their members throughout adulthood. Among the best-studied adult peers are the all-female networks that nineteenth-century middle-class American women formed. Girlhood friendships, often begun at boarding schools, deepened as the women began to share a common domestic fate and religious culture in which they were defined as the more sensitive and spiritual of the sexes. These homoerotic friendships were nurtured in the informal but enduring bonds between women whose context is erased if sexuality is investigated only within the heterosexual marital dyad.[39]

Communities are the loci not only of the regulation of sexual partners and practices, but also of the transmission of sexual knowledge as well. Indeed, before the proliferation of "how-to" books, communities were the only source of knowledge about sex and reproduction. Formulas for contraceptive substances and abortifacients, and access to midwives or abortionists, were in the hands of village women in traditional Europe, as were concepts of when it was acceptable to use them.[40] Urban females' networks also were sources of information, and pre–World War I British evidence suggests that abortion was more common in urban areas at least in part because such information networks could operate there.[41] In Sheffield in the 1890s, for instance, lead contamination of the water supply suggested to some women that a lead powder commonly used around the house might also bring on miscarriages. From there the word spread to Leicester, Nottingham, Birmingham, and other towns, all by word of mouth.[42]

Loss of contact through migration could mean the absence of vital knowledge about sexuality and procreation. The early twentieth-century letters collected by the Women's Cooperative Guild on maternity in Britain eloquently speak of such losses. Many women knew close to nothing about sex or reproduction, even at their first pregnancy.[43] The especially high rates of illegitimacy and infanticide among French and English nineteenth-century servants suggest not only their isolation from country or town working-class communities but also their ignorance about contraception, abortifacients, and abortionists.[44]

Some contemporary non-Western cultures have well-organized procedures for the transmission of sexual knowledge. Verrier Elwin investigated child and adolescent dormitories among the Muria of Bastar, a central Indian tribe, where children from the age of six or seven spend increasing amounts of time living with their peers. Young members are taught by slightly older ones, and a range of sexual skills is transmitted, including techniques of massage, foreplay, and mutual satisfaction. Young girls are taught to think of their bodies as "ripening fruit"; they are taught, too, that "when the clitoris sees the penis coming, she smiles." Intense dyads are broken up by enforcement of shifting partners; it is only among the older adolescents that "serious" courting leading to marriage is permitted.[45]

The amount of autonomy from wider institutions that community practices express varies widely. Charivaris, night-courting, and gossip enforcing sexual norms seem to genuinely express at least a part of community opinion. Priests and parsons, while important members of the community and influenced by its values, are also representatives of powerful national or international organizations. Their presence has of course tremendous power to shape sexual attitudes and experiences, but that molding has not always represented official theological positions. Although canon law, judicial procedure, and confessional practice all condemned "sins against nature," by medieval times contraception was viewed as more heinous when practiced inside of marriage than when used in illicit sex. In the hierarchy of sins, an adulterous union that was sterile was less sinful in the clergy's eyes than one that produced offspring. In examining community confessional records, Jean-Louis Flandrin suggests that the "Malthusian revolution" spread, in sixteenth- and seventeenth-century village France, via illicit relationships. But by the latter half of the eighteenth century, husbands and wives had created a cultural innovation: they had moved contraception out of the adulterous affair and into the marriage bed. Thus the Church's teachings distinguishing levels of sin prepared the way for marital experimentation.[46] Flandrin also thinks that the eighteenth-century clergy's increasing emphasis on duty and obligation to offspring encouraged family limitation as well. It made responsibilities to the already born more salient, allowing parents to consider contraception "for the sake of" their children.[47] Thus, official Church discourse on sexual practices was transformed as it was appropriated at the community level.

SEX AND "WORLD SYSTEMS"

Large-scale social institutions and forces may appear distant and abstract, but they actually influence the intimate experiences people have, defining the circumstances under which shifting sexual mores are played out. The Roman Catholic Church, for example, is organized to operate simultaneously at the international, national, local, and intimate levels. Other institutions may exhibit a sexual regulatory aspect, as national laws frequently do. The discussion that follows focuses first on the power of such large-scale institutions to shape sexuality. It then suggests an examination of less formalized, but perhaps more pervasive forces—economic or demographic change, shifting town/country relations—that affect sexual transformations.

All of the world's major religions serve as arbiters of moral systems, an important aspect of which is usually sexuality, as amply demonstrated in the history of Roman Catholicism. Even before the Protestant Reformation, Catholic doctrine had begun to tighten the connections between sexuality, marriage, and procreation. It increasingly campaigned against all nonmarital and nonprocreative forms of sexuality. The Church's definition of marriage, for example, became more rigorous, sharply differentiating the married from the unmarried and making the difference between licit and illicit sex more important. Medieval practice came close to assuming that couples who had intercourse were indeed married, for at that point the promise to marry carried more weight than any public ceremony that might take place, and it was widely believed that cohabitation was what made marriage official. Gradually, witnesses to the marriage were required; then a priest's presence, to administer a sacrament previously offered by the couple themselves; and finally the betrothal promise lost its binding character.[48]

The same rigidifying of Church definitions occurred on the subject of concubinage, the open acknowledgment of illicit sexual relations and paternity, with support for mother and child. The Counter-Reformation campaign against clerical concubinage was accompanied by an effective one against lay concubinage as well. By the mid-seventeenth century, it was successful and the practice was rare in France; only kings and the greatest lords openly acknowledged their bastards. The campaign against concubinage may account for the steady decline in illegitimacy figures in seventeenth-century France and in England. But it meant particular victimization for unmarried mothers, now stigmatized and far more likely to flee their communities. The abolition of concubinage also spelled disaster for the children, as bastards in disproportionate numbers ended up as foundlings and almost certainly faced early death.[49]

Legal systems provide a material background against which sexual relations are played out, whether they affect sexuality directly (e.g., legitimacy clauses, the outlawing of abortion, and sex codes defining prostitution) or at a distance (e.g., welfare and the responsibilities of fathers). Laws defining paternity, for example, are important in setting up the context in which sexuality occurs. Their effect does not necessarily result from forcing fathers to support their illegitimate children. Few women in England, either before or after the 1834 Bastardy Clause undermined putative fathers' legal obligations, seem to have applied for child support, and we know too well how few divorced fathers in contemporary America pay child support consistently over the years. Rather, as such laws become known, they help to establish an atmosphere that changes the sexual balance of power. The commissioners investigating the causes of the "Rebecca Riots" in 1844 were convinced that this is what had happened in southern Wales. Traditional marriage and courtship patterns in England had condoned premarital pregnancies, and eighteenth-century legislation made it relatively easy for mothers of bastards to collect regular support payments. The Bastardy Clauses to the 1834 Poor Law Amendment Act assigned financial responsibility solely to the mothers (or their parishes).[50] Now, courting men seemed to feel a new license to avoid marriage. "It is a bad time for the girls, Sir," a woman reported to a Haverfordwest Poor Law Guardian who testified before the Commission. "The boys have their own way."[51] The Bastardy Clauses were probably among the factors that influenced a shift in popular sexual culture: an earlier tradition of lively female sexual assertiveness as traced in folk ballads and tales gave way to a more prudish, cautious image of womanhood by the 1860s. Such a transformation appears quite rational in light of the shifting legal environment.[52] What Flandrin calls the "legal disarming of women vis-à-vis their seducers" took place earlier and more thoroughly in France. In the seventeenth century it was legally possible for a seducer, unless he married the woman, to be charged with rape if the woman was under twenty-five. As the penalty for rape was death, many seducers charged in court no doubt preferred marriage. The Civil Code of 1804, however, forbade searching for putative fathers and made unmarried women solely responsible for their children.[53]

Throughout Europe and in America, the mid- to late-nineteenth century witnessed a hardening of legal definitions of sexual outcasts, as sexual behavior came under increasing state and cultural surveillance. It is from this period that many of the sex and vice codes still prevalent in Western societies can be dated. In England, a series of Contagious Diseases Acts passed from 1864 on to control venereal disease in the army and navy by registering prostitutes had the effect of stigmatizing the women and isolating them from the working-class neighborhoods in which they lived and worked. Although a campaign to repeal the acts was ultimately successful, its social purity orientation led to still further sexually restrictive legislation. The Criminal Law Amendment Act, an omnibus crime bill passed in 1885, raised the age of consent for girls from thirteen to sixteen in response to a movement to "save" working-class girls from the perceived evils of "white slavery" and aristocratic male lust. The newly increased powers of the police were turned not on the wealthy buyers of sex, but on its poorer sellers. Lodging-house keepers were commonly prosecuted as brothel keepers, and prostitutes were often uprooted and cast out from their neighborhoods. Forced to find new lodging in areas of cities more specialized in vice, they became increasingly dependent on male pimps once community support, or at least toleration, of their occupation was shattered by legal prosecution.[54]

In the Labouchere Amendment to the same 1885 act, all forms of sexual activity between men (with consent, in private as well as in public) were subject to prosecution. This represents a dramatic extension of the definition of male homosexuality (and its condemnation) beyond the "abominations of buggery" clauses promulgated under Henry VIII and remaining in force in the centuries that followed.[55] The Labourchere Amendment was followed in 1898 by the Vagrancy Act, which turned police attention to homosexual solicitation. Antihomosexual legislation was passed in an atmosphere of a purity campaign that viewed homosexuality as a vice of the rich visited on the poor. But the effects of the legislation were turned against working-class homosexuals, who were most likely to be tried, while wealthier men were often able to buy their way out of public notice and prosecution. As Jeffrey Weeks points out, the sex codes and their effects must be viewed in relation to evolving notions of respectability in both working-class and lower-middle-class culture. One aspect of that respectability was sexual; another was the growing belief in the purity and innocence of childhood. Both converged in support for the sex codes, which raised the age of consent and identified and outlawed a range of male homosexual activities.[56] It is within this cultural milieu that sexually specialized neighborhoods, cultures, and commodities were probably given impetus to evolve.[57]

Less obvious to the eye than Church policies or legal systems, but still more central in structuring sexual experience, are social and economic forces that, for example, determine the availability of resources for marriage, or the possibility of finding in expanding urban areas a setting for homosexual contacts. To analyze for Western society this widest level of determinants of sexuality would be tantamount to writing the first volume of a sexual *Capital*. Here we want merely to suggest that the intimate experience of sexuality is intertwined with the most global of social forces. The complex of transformations that accompanied the development of industrial capitalism in Western Europe—including increased wage-labor dependency and massive urban migration—generated statistical clues to changing sexual patterns.

The availability of wage labor in general made it possible for larger proportions of people to marry (especially by the nineteenth century) and for marriage to take place at earlier ages as couples could support themselves without waiting for sizable dowries or inheritances. For the eighteenth- and early nineteenth-century Leicestershire village of Shepshed, for example, knitters working for wages in domestic industry had different demographic patterns from those of artisans or the farming population. The knitters' wage dependency allowed them earlier marriage and encouraged more children, who were also employable.[58] In nineteenth-century industrial cities, too, waged workers tended to marry at greater rates than did the populations of towns with large artisanal or commercial sectors.[59]

Migration from country to city left profound, though complex, demographic traces, creating new situations in which migrants experienced courtship, sex, marriage, and childbearing. Different kinds of towns—commercial, industrial, or mining, as Louise Tilly and Joan Scott have shown—provided migrants with different demographic and economic situations. In textile cities like Preston or Mulhouse, where the demand for both female and child labor was high, women outnumbered men and marriages were late. Where the labor force was chiefly male and jobs for women few, as in mining and metalworking centers like Carmaux and Anzin, women were scarce and marriage ages tended to be lower.[60]

While urban life seemed to promote illegitimacy in France, massive proletarianization in the English countryside is linked to higher rates of illegitimacy there.[61] Rising rates of illegitimacy may appear to be a new development, but recent work suggests that behind the figures lie traditional courtship and sexual patterns, reproduced under new and difficult circumstances. Young women, away from their families and communities to work as servants or in manufacturing jobs, courted and had sexual relations with traditional expectations that marriage would take place should a pregnancy result. But in the new situations of commercial and industrial towns, employment for many men was too unstable to permit marriage, and community pressure on them to support their bastards was weak.[62] Under new conditions of urbanization, old sexual patterns led to new social consequences.

From as early as the twelfth century, towns had provided foci for the formation of male homosexual subcultures. There is evidence of distinct homosexual communities in Italian towns in the fourteenth century, French from the fifteenth, and British by the seventeenth. In the relative anonymity of eighteenth-century London, a network of cafes, bars, meeting places, and brothels thrived, serving a wide clientele that represented most of the city's major occupations.[63] As the labeling of homosexuals as deviants became sharper toward the end of the nineteenth century, this subculture tightened, subdivided, and generated a political arm, which was predominantly upper and upper-middle class.[64] The lesser visibility of lesbian subgroups in history probably reflects not only the lower level of legal persecution to which they were apparently subjected, but, more importantly, that lesbians (like heterosexual women) have had far less independence than men and fewer resources on which to base their subcultures.[65]

Behind the dramatic economic and demographic changes of the era of industrialization in Europe lie cultural and ideological changes far harder to penetrate. The transformation of social relations of labor provides a general context for shifting symbolic relations, including the symbolism of sex and gender.

Domestic service, for example, was the most common waged occupation for women in England and France well into the twentieth century. It carried with it a specific demographic pattern, conditions of labor, and conditions of culture as well. Stringent codes of class and gender marked the relation between master and servant as one of personal dominance and subordination. Female servants lived as dependents, tied to their masters' households. One aspect of their subordination was expressed in exaggerated codes of meekness and cleanliness. Another was asexuality, transgression of which could lead to serious consequences, such as being "'placed' in institutional substitutes for homes: Homes for Orphans, Charity Homes, Homes for Fallen Women."[66] "No followers" rules imposed secrecy on courting and sexual behavior.

In an analysis of illegitimacy among London domestics in the nineteenth century, John Gillis traces the subtle and contradictory circumstances that led some upper servants to unwed pregnancy and abandonment of children. "Better" servants and their suitors, usually skilled or semi-skilled workers, shared their masters' sense of respectability. They aimed to acquire some economic security as a basis for marriage. The men were quite geographically mobile, unlike the women, who were tied to bourgeois households. A too-early pregnancy might lead men to abandon women who lacked the savings and employment skills on which to found a new household.[67]

The strange romance of two Victorians illustrates the complicated intersection between erotic experience and wider social forces, such as the institutionalized patterns of dominance and subordination that prevailed between servant-keeping bourgeois families and their female servants.[68] Hannah Cullwick was a twenty-one-year-old kitchen servant when she met twenty-five-year-old Arthur J. Munby in London in 1854. Munby was in London studying to become a barrister, but his real passion was the working woman—pit brow women, crossings-sweepers, milk carriers, farm laborers, and lower servants all fascinated him.

By the time they met, both Hannah and Arthur had already focused their sexual and romantic fantasies not only on the opposite sex but also on the opposite class. Munby's passion for working women was paralleled by Hannah's decision that any sweetheart she was to have "shall be someone much above me; and I will be his slave."[69]

Class polarities structured their relationship. Munby's sensual appreciation of Hannah Cullwick focused on her large size (which he exaggerated), sturdiness, large red hands and arms, and the frequently dirty face and arms her work produced. Munby loved to watch Cullwick scrubbing her master's front steps, and he found it natural that she should wash his feet and polish his boots. Hannah in turn cherished her servitude and passed up many chances for high-paying and comfortable upper servants' jobs because she could not give up her "lowliness."

A troubled secret marriage took place in 1872. It was followed by a few years of domestic life, Hannah posing as her husband's servant and both partners enjoying the game while Munby continued his regular round of bachelor activities. Marriage exacerbated their class differences. Their erotic life remained frustrating: rare kissing, cuddling, and Munby's sitting on his wife's large lap seem to have comprised the more directly "sexual" parts of their relationship.

As Lenore Davidoff suggests in her sensitive study of this relationship, the contradictions in Munby's emotional life may well be traced to the common upper-middle-class practice of hiring country women as the nearly full-time caretakers of children. His erotic biography comes into classic Freudian focus when we learn that another woman named Hannah served as a nurse in the Munby household throughout his childhood.[70] Hannah Cullwick's fixation on gentlemen and her association between romantic love and servitude are less classically oedipal: their analysis opens up the connection between patriarchy and class oppression.

CONCLUSION

We have argued that understanding sexuality requires critical attention to the idea that sex is a lived and changing relationship and not an "essence" whose content is fixed. Sex cannot be studied as a series of "acts"; nor should the sexual component in all social relations be ignored.

It is no accident, however, that contemporary culture tempts us to reify sex as a thing-in-itself. The modern perception of sex is an ideological reflection of real changes that have occurred in the contexts of daily life within which sexuality is embedded. The separation, with industrial capitalism, of family life from work, of consumption from production, of leisure from labor, of personal life from political life, has completely reorganized the context in which we experience sexuality. These polarities are grossly distorted and miscast as antinomies in modern ideological formulations, but their seeming separation creates an ideological space called "personal life," one defining characteristic of which is sexual identity.[71] Modern consciousness permits, as earlier systems of thought did not, the positing of "sex" for perhaps the first time as having an "independent" existence. While we have discussed family and kinship systems, communities, and large-scale institutional and informal forces as though they were separate contexts for shaping sexuality, they are, of course, interdependent. The power of each in relation to all others to provide the meaning and control of sexuality shifts with historical time. Recently, for example, a common American complaint is that families are losing control over their children's sexual education and behavior, challenged by public schools, the mass media, and state policies (which grant sex education and abortions to teenagers, even without parental consent). The power of families and communities to determine sexual experience has indeed sharply diminished in the past two centuries, allegedly allowing for individual sexual "liberation."

Although the movement toward self-conscious sexuality has been hailed by modernists as liberatory, it is important to remember that sexuality in contemporary times is not simply released or free-floating. It continues to be socially structured, but we would argue that the dominant power to define and regulate sexuality has been shifting toward the group of what we have labeled large-scale social and economic forces, the most salient of which is perhaps the state. States now organize many of the reproductive relations that were once embedded in smaller-scale contexts. Sexuality thus enters the "social contract," connecting the individual citizen and the state. In the process, an ideological space is created that allows us to "see" sex as a defining characteristic of the individual person, "released" from the traditional restraints of family and community. The rise of the two great ethnosciences of sexual and personal liberation—sexology and psychoanalysis—have accompanied this transformation, attempting to explain and justify it.[72]

But the ideology of sexual freedom and the right to individual self-expression have come increasingly into conflict with both state hegemony and the residual powers of more traditional contexts such as family and community control. Today, abortion, sterilization abuse, sex education, homosexual rights, and welfare and family policies are explosive political issues in the United States and much of Western Europe. For as states claim a greater and greater interest in the structuring of sexuality, sexual struggles increasingly become part of public, consciously defined politics. All the salient power divisions in any society—class, race, gender, and heterosexual dominance—structure the consciousness, demands, and resources different groups bring to these, as to any other, political issues. Politicians attentive to the sexualization of policy and the politicization of sexuality now know what scholars ignore at their peril: such issues have never been simply "private" or "personal," but are eminently part of the public domain.

NOTES

This paper was originally written for an innovative conference, "Writing the History of Sexuality and Power," New York University, March 1978. Many friends read and criticized earlier drafts of this paper. We especially want to thank Shirley Lindenbaum, Harriet Rosenberg, Gayle Rubin, Sara Ruddick, Judith Walkowitz, and Eric Wolf.

1. The definition of what constitutes sexuality is currently under debate. Some analysts stress the biological basis of the experience, focusing on organic and neurological response; others, more committed to a psychoanalytic perspective, stress the role of fantasy—originating in childhood—in eliciting these responses. As the recent work of Michel Foucault suggests, however, both positions

presuppose that "sex" as a category of human experience can be isolated and is uniform throughout history (*The History of Sexuality*, vol. 1: *An Introduction*, tr. Robert Hurley [New York: Pantheon, 1978]).

2. John Gagnon and Bruce Henderson, "The Social Psychology of Sexual Development," in *Family in Transition*, ed. Arlene S. Skolnick and Jerome H. Skolnick, 2d ed. (Boston and Toronto: Little, Brown, 1977), pp. 116–22, 118.

3. The classic works are William H. Masters and Virginia E. Johnson, *Human Sexual Response* (Boston: Little, Brown, 1966); and idem., *Human Sexual Inadequacy* (Boston: Little, Brown, 1970).

4. A summary of this transformation is found in Michael Gordon, "From an Unfortunate Necessity to a Cult of Mutual Orgasm: Sex in American Marital Education Literature, 1830–1940," in *Studies in the Sociology of Sex*, ed. James Henslin (New York: Appleton Century Crofts, 1960).

5. For example, Havelock Ellis, *Studies in the Psychology of Sex*, 2 vols. (New York: Random House, 1937–1942); Fernando Henriques, *Love in Action: The Sociology of Sex* (New York: Dutton, 1960).

6. James M. Henslin, "The Sociological Point of View," in *Studies in the Sociology of Sex*, pp. 1–6; Gagnon and Henderson, "The Social Psychology of Sexual Development"; Clellan S. Ford and Frank A. Beach, *Patterns of Sexual Behavior* (New York: Harper and Row, 1972), chap. 13.

7. Foucault, *History of Sexuality*; Jeffrey Weeks, "Movements of Affirmation: Sexual Meaning and Homosexual Identities," *Radical History Review* 2 (Spring/Summer 1979): 164–80; Robert Padgog, "Sexual Matters: On Conceptualizing Sexuality in History," ibid., pp. 3–24.

8. Nancy Chodorow, *The Reproduction of Mothering* (Berkeley and Los Angeles: University of California Press, 1978); Dorothy Dinnerstein, *The Mermaid and the Minotaur: Sexual Arrangements and Human Malaise* (New York: Harper and Row, 1976); Jane Flax, "The Conflict between Nurturance and Autonomy in Mother-Daughter Relationships and Within Feminism," *Feminist Studies* 4, no. 2 (June 1978): 171–89; Juliet Mitchell, *Psychoanalysis and Feminism* (New York: Pantheon, 1974); Gayle Rubin, "The Traffic in Women: Notes on the 'Political Economy' of Sex," in *Toward an Anthropology of Women*, ed. Rayna R. Reiter (New York: Monthly Review Press, 1975).

9. Christopher Lasch, *Haven in a Heartless World* (New York: Basic Books, 1977).

10. Personal communication, June 1979.

11. Clifford Geertz, "The Impact of the Concept of Culture on the Concept of Man," in *New Views of the Nature of Man*, ed. J. Platt (Chicago: University of Chicago Press, 1966), pp. 93–118; reprinted in Clifford Geertz, *The Interpretation of Cultures* (New York: Basic Books, 1973).

12. Roger M. Keesing, *Kin Groups and Social Structure* (New York: Holt, Rinehart and Winston, 1975), chap. 7.

13. Rayna Rapp, unpublished field notes, Provence (France), 1969, 1970, 1971–1972.

14. Richard Thurnwald, "Banaro Society," *Memoirs of the American Anthropological Association* 3, no. 4 (1916): 251–391; summarized and cited in Rubin, "The Traffic in Women," p. 166.

15. Natalie Zemon Davis, "Ghosts, Kin and Progeny: Some Features of Family Life in Early Modern France," *Daedalus* 106, no. 2 (Spring 1977): 87–114, 101. See also Jean-Louis Flandrin, *Families in Former Times: Kinship, Household and Sexuality*, tr. Richard Southern (Cambridge: Cambridge University Press, 1979), pp. 19–23.

16. Davis, "Ghosts," pp. 102–103.

17. Classic essays on incest prohibitions are found in Nelson Graburn, ed., *Readings in Kinship and Social Structure* (New York: Harper and Row, 1971), chap. 14; Robin Fox, *Kinship and Marriage* (Harmondsworth, England: Penguin Books, 1967), chap. 2. Lévi-Strauss's most famous work, *Elementary Structures of Kinship*, tr. James H. Bell, John R. von Sturmer, and Rodney Needham (Boston: Beacon Press, 1969), is founded on this question.

18. Louise Tilly and Joan Scott, *Women, Work and Family* (New York: Holt, Rinehart and Winston, 1978), p. 26; Lutz K. Berkner, "Recent Research on the History of the Family in Western Europe," *Journal of Marriage and the Family* 35 (August 1973): 395–405; Lawrence Stone, *The Family, Sex and Marriage in England, 1500–1800* (New York: Harper and Row, 1977), chap. 2.

19. Stone, *Family, Sex and Marriage*, pp. 44, 46–48.

20. E. P. Thompson, "The Grid of Inheritance: A Comment," in *Family and Inheritance*, ed. Jack Goody, Joan Thirsk, and E. P. Thompson (Cambridge: Cambridge University Press, 1976), p. 349.

21. Alan Macfarlane, *The Origins of English Individualism* (Oxford: Basil Blackwell, 1978), p. 82.

22. Corbyn Morris, "Observations on the Past Growth and Present State of the City of London" (1751), cited in J. Hajnal, "European Marriage Patterns in Perspective," in *Population in History*, ed. D. V. Glass and D. E. C. Eversley (Chicago: Aldine, 1965), pp. 101–43.

23. Stone, *Family, Sex and Marriage*, pp. 615–16.

24. Jack Goody, *Production and Reproduction: A Comparative Study of the Domestic Domain* (Cambridge: Cambridge University Press), p. 63.

25. Thompson, "Grid of Inheritance," p. 360.

26. E. P. Thompson, "'Rough Music': Le charivari anglais," *Annales E.S.C.* 27 (March–April 1972): 285–312, 293, 305.

27. U. R. Q. Henriques, "Bastardy and the New Poor Law," *Past and Present* 37 (July 1967): 103–29, 118.

28. Interesting speculations on generational power relations in handicraft families appear in Hans Medick, "The Proto-Industrial Family Economy," *Social History* 1, no. 3 (October 1976): 291–315; and John Gillis, "Resort to Common-Law Marriage in England and Wales, 1700–1850," unpublished manuscript.

29. Rayna Rapp, unpublished field notes; Conrad Arensberg and Solon T. Kimball, *Family and Community in Ireland*, 2d ed. (Cambridge: Harvard University Press, 1968), p. 55.

30. John R. Gillis, *Youth and History: Tradition and Change in European Age Relations, 1770–Present* (New York and London: Academic Press, 1974), pp. 22–23.

31. Ibid., p. 38.

32. Ibid., chaps. 2, 3, and 4.

33. Natalie Zemon Davis, "The Reasons of Misrule," in *Society and Culture in Early Modern France* (Stanford, Calif.: Stanford University Press, 1975), pp. 97–123, 104–105; Flandrin, *Families in Former Times*, pp. 34–35.

34. Pierre Caspard, "Conceptions pré-nuptiales et développement du capitalisme dans la Principauté de Neuchâtel (1678–1820)," *Annales E.S.C.* 29, no. 4 (July–August 1974): 989–1008, 993–96; Edward Shorter, *The Making of the Modern Family* (New York: Basic Books, 1975), pp. 102–105; Michael Drake, *Population and Society in Norway, 1735–1865* (Cambridge: Cambridge University Press, 1969), pp. 138–45.

35. Shorter, *Making of the Modern Family*, pp. 102–103. The sources on which his account is based are listed in notes 53–59, p. 298.

36. Caspard, "Conceptions pré-nuptiales," p. 995.

37. Jean-Louis Flandrin, "Repression and Change in the Sexual Life of Young People in Medieval and Early Modern Times," *Journal of Family History* 2, no. 3 (September 1977): 196–210, 200–203, 205.

38. Molly Dougherty, *Becoming a Woman in Rural Black Culture* (New York: Holt, Rinehart and Winston, 1978), part 3, pp. 71–107.

39. Carol Smith-Rosenberg, "The Female World of Love and Ritual: Relations Between Women in Nineteenth-Century America," *Signs* 1, no. 2 (Autumn 1975): 1–29. See also Nancy Cott, *The Bonds of Womanhood* (New Haven: Yale University Press, 1977).

40. Jacques Gélis, "Sages-femmes et accoucheurs: l'obstétrique populaire au XVII et XVIII sièles," *Annales E.S.C.* 32 (September–October 1977): 927–57; Mireille Laget, "La naissance aux siècles classiques. Pratique des accouchements et attitudes collectives en France XVII et XVIII siècles," ibid., pp. 958–92.

41. Patricia Knight, "Women and Abortion in Victorian and Edwardian England." *History Workshop* 4 (Autumn 1977): 57–69, 58–59.

42. Angus McLaren, *Birth Control in Nineteenth-Century England* (London: Croom Helm, 1978), p. 242; Knight, "Women and Abortion," p. 60.

43. See Margaret L. Davies, ed., *Maternity, Letters from Working Women*, reprint ed. (New York and London. W. W. Norton, 1978), p. 56.

44. John R. Gillis, "Servants, Sexual Relations, and the Risks of Illegitimacy in London 1801–1900," *Feminist Studies* 5, no. 1 (Spring 1979): 142–73; Theresa M. McBride, *The Domestic Revolution* (New York: Holmes and Meier, 1976), chap. 6.

45. Verrier Elwin, *Kingdom of the Young* (Oxford: Oxford University Press, 1947).

46. Jean-Louis Flandrin, "Contraception, Marriage and Sexual Relations in the Christian West," in *Biology of Man in History*, ed. Robert Forster and Orest Ranum, tr. Elborg Forster and Patricia M. Ranum (Baltimore and London: Johns Hopkins University Press, 1975), pp. 23–47.

47. Flandrin, *Families in Former Times*, pp. 211–12.

48. Sir Frederick Pollock and Ferderick William Maitland, *The History of English Law Before the Time of Edward I*, 2 vols., 2d ed. reissue (Cambridge: Cambridge University Press, 1968): 2, chap. 6; Willystine Goodsell, *A History of Marriage and the Family*, rev. ed. (New York: Macmillan, 1934); O. R. McGregor, *Divorce in England, A Centenary Study* (London: Heinemann, 1957).

49. Flandrin, *Families in Former Times*, pp. 180–84.

50. Henriques, "Bastardy and the New Poor Law," pp. 118–19.

51. Quoted in ibid., p. 119.

52. Gillis, "Servants, Sexual Relations and the Risks of Illegitimacy."

53. Flandrin, "Repression and Change," p. 204.

54. Judith R. Walkowitz and Daniel J. Walkowitz, "'We Are Not Beasts of the Field'": Prostitution and the Poor in Plymouth and Southampton Under the Contagious Diseases Acts," *Feminist Studies* 1, nos. 3–4 (Winter-Spring 1973); Judith Walkowitz, "The Making of an Outcast Group," in *A Widening Sphere*, ed. Martha Vicinus (Bloomington: Indiana University Press, 1977); pp. 72–93, 85–87; and Judith Walkowitz, *Prostitution and Victorian Society: Women, Class and the State* (Cambridge: Cambridge University Press, 1980).

55. Guido Ruggiero, "Sexual Criminality in the Early Renaissance: Venice 1338–1358," *Journal of Social History* 8 (Summer 1975): 17–37; Randolph Trumbach, "London's Sodomites: Homosexual Behavior and Western Culture in the Eighteenth Century," *Journal of Social History* 11 (Fall 1977): 1–33; Jeffrey Weeks, *Coming Out: Homosexual Politics in Britain from the Nineteenth Century to the Present* (London and New York: Quartet Books, 1977), pp. 1–44; Louis Crompton, review of *Coming Out* by Weeks: *Socialism and the New Life* by Jeffrey Weeks and Sheila Rowbotham; and *Homosexuality and Literature* by Jeffrey Meyers, in *Victorian Studies* 22, no. 2 (Winter 1979): 211–13.

56. Weeks, *Coming Out*, pp. 19–20.

57. This view is implicit in Weeks's *Coming Out*.

58. David Levine, *Family Formation in an Age of Nascent Capitalism* (New York: Academic Press, 1977).

59. Tilly and Scott, *Women, Work and Family*, pp. 93–96. See also Lynn H. Lees, *Exiles of Erin: Irish Migration in Victorian London* (Manchester: Manchester University Press, 1979) for a discussion of changes in ages of marriage of rural Irish who migrated to London at the time of the famine; and Louise A. Tilly, "The Family Wage Economy of a French Textile City: Roubaix, 1872–1906," *Journal of Family History* 4, no. 4 (Winter 1979): 381–94.

60. Tilly and Scott, *Women, Work and Family*, p. 96.

61. Edward Shorter, "Illegitimacy, Sexual Revolution and Social Change in Modern Europe," *Journal of Interdisciplinary History* 1 (Autumn 1971): 231–72.

62. Shorter's "Female Emancipation, Birth Control and Fertility in European History" (*American Historical Review* 78, no. 3 [June 1973]: 605–40) opened a debate on the sources of Europe's high birth and illegitimacy rates in the era of early industrialization. On illegitimacy, the weight of scholarship supports the view that the urban migration of young women made them especially vulnerable to illegitimate pregnancies. See Louis A. Tilly, Joan W. Scott, and Miriam Cohen, "Women's Work and European Fertility Patterns," *Journal of Interdisciplinary History* 6, no. 3 (Winter 1976): 447–76; and Cissie Fairchilds, "Female Sexual Attitudes and The Rise of Illegitimacy: A Case Study," *Journal of Interdisciplinary History* 8, no. 4 (Spring 1978): 627–67.

63. Trumbach, "London's Sodomites"; Weeks, *Coming Out*, pp. 35–42; Mary Mackintosh, "The Homosexual Role," in *Family in Transition*, ed. Arlene S. Skolnick and Jerome H. Skolnick (Boston: Little, Brown, 1971), pp. 231–42, 236–38.

64. Weeks, *Coming Out*, part 4.

65. Ibid., p. 89.

66. Leonore Davidoff, "Mastered for Life: Servant and Wife in Victorian and Edwardian England," *Journal of Social History* 8 (Summer 1974): 404–28, 413–14.

67. Gillis, "Servants, Sexual Relations, and the Risks of Illegitimacy," p. 167.

68. The discussion that follows is based on Derek Hudson, *Munby, Man of Two Worlds: The Life and Diaries of Arthur J. Munby, 1828–1910* (Boston: Gambit, Inc.); and on Leonore Davidoff's interpretive study, "Class and Gender in Victorian England: The Diaries of Arthur J. Munby and Hannah Cullwick," *Feminist Studies* 5, no. 1 (Spring 1979): 87–142.

69. Hudson, *Munby*, p. 69.

70. Davidoff, "Class and Gender," pp. 87–100.

71. Although they have very different theoretical perspectives; both Eli Zaretsky and Christopher Lasch believe that sexual identity takes shape in "personal" space, Eli Zaretsky, "Capitalism, the Family, and Personal Life, Part 1," *Socialist Revolution* 3, nos. 1–2 (January–April 1973): 69–126; and Christopher Lasch, "The Family as a Haven in a Heartless World," *Salmagundi* 34 (Fall 1976): 42–55; and idem, "The Waning of Private Life," *Salmagundi* 36 (Winter 1977): 3–15.

72. The labeling of sexology and psychoanalysis as "ethnoscience," suggesting a folk system of understanding that is quite logical, but based on "wrong" assumptions linked to turn-of-the-century social perceptions, is Gayle Rubin's. Seeing the context in which these models of personal relationships developed as a part of changes in wider social power arrangements is the contribution of Foucault and of Donzelot. See Michel Foucault, *The History of Sexuality*, and Jacques Donzelot, *The Policing of Families*, tr. Robert Hurley (New York: Pantheon Books, 1979).

11 Capitalism and Gay Identity

John D'Emilio

For gay men and lesbians, the 1970s were years of significant achievement. Gay liberation and women's liberation changed the sexual landscape of the nation. Hundreds of thousands of gay women and men came out and openly affirmed same-sex eroticism. We won repeal of sodomy laws in half the states, a partial lifting of the exclusion of lesbians and gay men from federal employment, civil rights protection in a few dozen cities, the inclusion of gay rights in the platform of the Democratic Party, and the elimination of homosexuality from the psychiatric profession's list of mental illnesses. The gay male subculture expanded and became increasingly visible in large cities, and lesbian feminists pioneered in building alternative institutions and an alternative culture that attempted to embody a liberatory vision of the future.

In the 1980s, however, with the resurgence of an active right wing, gay men and lesbians face the future warily. Our victories appear tenuous and fragile; the relative freedom of the past few years seems too recent to be permanent. In some parts of the lesbian and gay male community, a feeling of doom is growing: analogies with McCarthy's America, when "sexual perverts" were a special target of the Right, and with Nazi Germany, where gays were shipped to concentration camps, surface with increasing frequency. Everywhere there is the sense that new strategies are in order if we want to preserve our gains and move ahead.

I believe that a new, more accurate theory of gay history must be part of this political enterprise. When the gay liberation movement began at the end of the 1960s, gay men and lesbians had no history that we could use to fashion our goals and strategy. In the ensuing years, in building a movement without knowledge of our history, we instead invented a mythology. This mythical history drew on personal experience, which we read backward in time. For instance, most lesbians and gay men in the 1960s first discovered their homosexual desires in isolation, unaware of others and without resources for naming and understanding what they felt. From this experi-

John D'Emilio is Director of the Policy Institute of the National Gay and Lesbian Task Force. His books include *Sexual Politics, Sexual Communities: the Making of a Homosexual Minority in the United States, 1940–1970* (Chicago, 1983); *Making Trouble: Essays on Gay History, Politics, and the University* (Routledge, 1992); and, with Estelle Freedman, *Intimate Matters: A History of Sexuality in America* (Harper and Row, 1988). He is currently writing a biography of Bayard Rustin.

ence, we constructed a myth of silence, invisibility, and isolation as the essential characteristics of gay life in the past as well as the present. Moreover, because we faced so many oppressive laws, public policies, and cultural beliefs, we projected this onto an image of the abysmal past until gay liberation, lesbians, and gay men were always the victims of systematic, undifferentiated, terrible oppression.

These myths have limited our political perspective. They have contributed, for instance, to an overreliance on a strategy of coming out—if every gay man and lesbian in America came out, gay oppression would end—and have allowed us to ignore the institutionalized ways in which homophobia and heterosexism are reproduced. They have encouraged, at times, an incapacitating despair, especially at moments like the present: How can we unravel a gay oppression so pervasive and unchanging?

There is another historical myth that enjoys nearly universal acceptance in the gay movement, the myth of the "eternal homosexual." The argument runs something like this: gay men and lesbians always were and always will be. We are everywhere; not just now, but throughout history, in all societies and all periods. This myth served a positive political function in the first years of gay liberation. In the early 1970s, when we battled an ideology that either denied our existence or defined us as psychopathic individuals or freaks of nature, it was empowering to assert that "we are everywhere." But in recent years it has confined us as surely as the most homophobic medical theories, and locked our movement in place.

Here I wish to challenge this myth. I want to argue that gay men and lesbians have *not* always existed. Instead, they are a product of history, and have come into existence in a specific era. Their emergence is associated with the relations of capitalism; it has been the historical development of capitalism—more specifically, its free labor system—that has allowed large numbers of men and women in the late twentieth century to call themslves gay, to see themselves as part of a community of similar men and women, and to organize politically on the basis of that identity.[1] Finally, I want to suggest some political lessons we can draw from this view of history.

What, then, are the relationships between the free labor system of capitalism and homosexuality? First, let me review some features of capitalism. Under capitalism, workers are "free" laborers in two ways. We have the freedom to look for a job. We own our ability to work and have the freedom to sell our labor power for wages to anyone willing to buy it. We are also freed from the ownership of anything except our labor power. Most of us do not own the land or the tools that produce what we need, but rather have to work for a living in order to survive. So, if we are free to sell our labor power in the positive sense, we are also freed, in the negative sense, from any other alternative. This dialectic—the constant interplay between exploitation and some measure of autonomy—informs all of the history of those who have lived under capitalism.

As capital—money used to make more money—expands, so does this system of free labor. Capital expands in several ways. Usually it expands in the same place, transforming small firms into larger ones, but it also expands by taking over new areas of production: the weaving of cloth, for instance, or the baking of bread. Finally, capital expands geographically. In the United States, capitalism initially took root in the Northeast, at a time when slavery was the dominant system in the South and when noncapitalist Native American societies occupied the western half of the continent. During the nineteenth century, capital spread from the Atlantic to the Pacific, and in the twentieth, U.S. capital has penetrated almost every part of the world.

The expansion of capital and the spread of wage labor have effected a profound transformation in the structure and functions of the nuclear family, the ideology of family life, and the meaning of heterosexual relations. It is these changes in the family that are most directly linked to the appearance of a collective gay life.

The white colonists in seventeenth-century New England established villages structured around a household economy, composed of family units that were basically self-sufficient, independent, and patriarchal. Men, women, and children farmed land owned by the male head of household. Although there was a division of labor between men and women, the family was truly an interdependent unit of production: the survival of each member depended on the cooperation of all. The home was a workplace where women processed raw farm produces into food for daily consumption; where they made clothing, soap, and candles; and where husbands, wives, and children worked together to produce the goods they consumed.

By the nineteenth century, this system of household production was in decline. In the Northeast, as merchant capitalists invested the money accumulated through trade in the production of goods, wage labor became more common. Men and women were drawn out of the largely self-sufficient household economy of the colonial era into a capitalist system of free labor. For women in the nineteenth century, working for wages rarely lasted beyond marriage; for men, it became a permanent condition.

The family was thus no longer an independent unit of production. But although no longer independent, the family was still interdependent. Because capitalism had not expanded very far, because it had not yet taken over—or socialized—the production of consumer goods, women still performed necessary productive labor in the home. Many families no longer produced grain, but wives still baked into bread the flour they bought with their husband's wages; or, when they purchased yarn or cloth, they still made clothing for their families. By the mid-1800s, capitalism had destroyed the economic self-sufficiency of many families, but not the mutual dependence of the members.

This transition away from the household family-based economy to a fully developed capitalist free labor economy occurred very slowly, over almost two centuries. As late as 1920, 50 percent of the U.S. population lived in communities of fewer than 2,500 people. The vast majority of blacks in the early twentieth century lived outside the free labor economy, in a system of sharecropping and tenancy that rested on the family. Not only did independent farming as a way of life still exist for millions of Americans, but even in towns and small cities women continued to grow and process food, make clothing, and engage in other kinds of domestic production.

But for those people who felt the brunt of these changes, the family took on new significance as an affective unit, an institution that produced not goods but emotional satisfaction and happiness. By the 1920s among the white middle class, the ideology surrounding the family described it as the means through which men and women formed satisfying, mutually enhancing relationships and created an environment that nurtured children. The family became the setting for a "personal life," sharply distinguished and disconnected from the public world of work and production.[2]

The meaning of heterosexual relations also changed. In colonial New England the birth rate averaged over seven children per woman of childbearing age. Men and women needed the labor of children. Producing offspring was as necessary for survival as producing grain. Sex was harnessed to procreation. The Puritans did not celebrate *hetero*sexuality but rather marriage; they condemned *all* sexual expression outside the marriage bond and did not differentiate sharply between sodomy and heterosexual fornication.

By the 1970s, however, the birth rate had dropped to under two. With the exception of the post–World War II baby boom, the decline has been continuous for two centuries, paralleling the spread of capitalist relations of production. It occurred even when access to contraceptive devices and abortion was systematically curtailed. The decline has included every segment of the population—urban and rural families, blacks and whites, ethnics and WASPs, the middle class and the working class.

As wage labor spread and production became socialized, then, it became possible to release sexuality from the "imperative" to procreate. Ideologically, heterosexual expression came to be a means of establishing intimacy, promoting happiness, and experiencing pleasure. In divesting the household of its economic independence and fostering the separation of sexuality from procreation, capitalism has created conditions that allow some men and women to organize a personal life around their erotic/emotional attraction to their own sex. It has made possible the formation of urban communities of lesbians and gay men and, more recently, of a politics based on a sexual identity.

Evidence from colonial New England court records and church sermons indicates that male and female homosexual behavior existed in the seventeenth century. Homosexual *behavior*, however, is different from homosexual *identity*. There was, quite simply, no "social space" in the colonial system of production that allowed men and women to be gay. Survival was structured around participation in a nuclear family. There were certain homosexual acts—sodomy among men, "lewdness" among women—in which individuals engaged, but family was so pervasive that colonial society lacked even the category of homosexual or lesbian to describe a person. It is quite possible that some men and women experienced a stronger attraction to their own sex than to the opposite sex—in fact, some colonial court cases refer to men who persisted in their "unnatural" attractions—but one could not fashion out of that preference a way of life. Colonial Massachusetts even had laws prohibiting unmarried adults from living outside family units.[3]

By the second half of the nineteenth century, this situation was noticeably changing as the capitalist system of free labor took hold. Only when *individuals* began to make their living through wage labor, instead of as parts of an interdependent family unit, was it possible for homosexual desire to coalesce into a personal identity—an identity based on the ability to remain outside the heterosexual family and to construct a personal life based on attraction to one's own sex. By the end of the century, a class of men and women existed who recognized their erotic interest in their own sex, saw it as a trait that set them apart from the majority, and sought others like themselves. These early gay lives came from a wide social spectrum: civil servants and business executives, department store clerks and college professors, factory operatives, ministers, lawyers, cooks, domestics, hoboes, and the idle rich: men and women, black and white, immigrant and native born.

In this period, gay men and lesbians began to invent ways of meeting each other and sustaining a group life. Already, in the early twentieth century, large cities contained male homosexual bars. Gay men staked out cruising areas, such as Riverside Drive in New York City and Lafayette Park in Washington. In St. Louis and the nation's capitol, annual drag balls brought together large numbers of black gay men. Public bathhouses and YMCAs became gathering spots for male homosexuals. Lesbians formed literary societies and private social clubs. Some working-class women "passed" as men to obtain better-paying jobs and lived with other women—lesbian couples who appeared to the world as husband and wife. Among the faculties of women's colleges, in the settlement houses, and in the professional associations and clubs that women formed, one could find lifelong intimate relationships supported by a web of lesbian friends. By the 1920s and 1930s, large cities such as New York and Chicago contained lesbian bars. These patterns of living could evolve because capitalism allowed individuals to survive beyond the confines of the family.[4]

Simultaneously, ideological definitions of homosexual behavior changed. Doctors developed theories about homosexual*ity*, describing it as a condition, something that was inherent in a person, a part of his or her "nature." These theories did not represent scientific breakthroughs, elucidations of previously undiscovered areas of knowledge; rather, they were an ideological response to a new way of organizing one's personal life. The popularization of the medical model, in turn, affected the consciousness of the women and men who experienced homosexual desire so that they came to define themselves through their erotic life.[5]

These new forms of gay identity and patterns of group life also reflected the differentiation of people according to gender, race, and class that is so pervasive in capitalist societies. Among whites, for instance, gay men have traditionally been more visible than lesbians. This partly stems from the division between the public male sphere and the private female sphere. Streets, parks, and bars, especially at night, were "male space." Yet the greater visibility of white gay men also reflected their larger numbers. The Kinsey studies of the 1940s and 1950s found significantly more men than women with predominantly homosexual histories, a situation caused, I would argue, by the fact that capitalism had drawn far more men than women into the labor force, and at higher wages. Men could more easily construct a personal life independent of attachments to the opposite sex, whereas women were more likely to remain economically dependent on men. Kinsey also found a strong positive correlation between years of schooling and lesbian activity. College-educated white women, far more able than their working-class sisters to support themselves, could survive more easily without intimate relationships with men.[6]

Among working-class immigrants in the early twentieth century, closely knit kin networks and an ethic of family solidarity placed constraints on individual autonomy that made gayness a difficult option to pursue. In contrast, for reasons not altogether clear, urban black communities appeared relatively tolerant of homosexuality. The popularity in the 1920s and 1930s of songs with lesbian and gay male themes—"B.D. Woman," "Prove It on Me," "Sissy Man," "Fairey Blues"—suggests an openness about homosexual expression at odds with the mores of whites. Among men in the rural West in the 1940s, Kinsey found extensive incidence of homosexual behavior, but, in contrast with the men in large cities, little consciousness of gay identity. Thus, even as capitalism exerted a homogenizing influence by gradually transforming more individuals into wage laborers and separating them from traditional communities, different groups of people were also affected in different ways.[7]

The decisions of particular men and women to act on their erotic/emotional preference for the same sex, along with the new consciousness that this preference made them different, led to the formation of an urban subculture of gay men and lesbians. Yet at least through the 1930s this subculture remained rudimentary, unstable, and difficult to find. How, then, did the complex, well-developed gay community emerge that existed by the time the gay liberation movement exploded? The answer is to be found during World War II, a time when the cumulative changes of several decades coalesced into a qualitatively new shape.

The war severely disrupted traditional patterns of gender relations and sexuality, and temporarily created a new erotic situation conducive to homosexual expression. It plucked millions of young men and women, whose sexual identities were just forming, out of their homes, out of towns and small cities, out of the heterosexual environment of the family, and dropped them into sex-segregated situations—as GIs, as WACs and WAVEs, in same-sex rooming houses for women workers who relocated to seek employment. The war freed millions of men and women from the settings where heterosexuality was normally imposed. For men and women already gay, it provided an opportunity to meet people like themselves. Others could become gay because of the temporary freedom to explore sexuality that the war provided.[8]

Lisa Ben, for instance, came out during the war. She left the small California town where she was raised, came to Los Angeles to find work, and lived in a women's boarding house. There she met for the first time lesbians who took her to gay bars and introduced her to other gay women. Donald Vining was a young man with lots of homosexual desire and few gay experiences. He moved to New York City during the war and worked at a large YMCA. His diary reveals numerous erotic adventures with soldiers, sailors, marines, and civilians at the Y where he worked, as well as at the men's residence club where he lived, and in parks, bars, and movie theaters. Many GIs stayed in port cities like New York, at YMCAs like the one where Vining worked. In his oral histories of gay men in San Francisco, focusing on the 1940s, Allan Bérubé has found that the war years were critical in the formation of a gay male *community* in the city. Places as different as San Jose, Denver, and Kansas City had their first gay bars in the 1940s. Even severe repression could have positive side effects. Pat Bond, a lesbian from Davenport, Iowa, joined the WACs during the 1940s. Caught in a purge of hundreds of lesbians from the WACs in the Pacific, she did not return to Iowa. She stayed in San Francisco and became part of a community of lesbians. How many other women and men had comparable experiences? How many other cities saw a rapid growth of lesbian and gay male communities?[9]

The gay men and women of the 1940s were pioneers. Their decisions to act on their desires formed the underpinnings of an urban subculture of gay men and lesbians. Throughout the 1950s and 1960s, the gay subculture grew and stabilized so that people coming out then could more easily find other gay women and men than in the past. Newspapers and magazines published articles describing gay male life. Literally hundreds of novels with lesbian themes were published.[10] Psychoanalysts complained about the new ease with which their gay male patients found sexual partners. And the gay subculture was found not just in the largest cities. Lesbian and gay male bars existed in places like Worcester, Massachusetts, and Buffalo, New York; in Columbia, South Carolina, and Des Moines, Iowa. Gay life in the 1950s and 1960s became a nationwide phenomenon. By the time of the Stonewall Riots in New York City in 1969—the event that ignited the gay liberation movement—our situation was hardly one of silence, invisibility, and isolation. A massive, grass-roots liberation movement could form almost overnight precisely because communities of lesbians and gay men existed.

Although gay community was a precondition for a mass movement, the oppression of lesbians and gay men was the force that propelled the movement into existence. As the subculture expanded and grew more visible in the post–World War II era, oppression by the state intensified, becoming more systematic and inclusive. The Right scapegoated "sexual perverts" during the McCarthy era. Eisenhower imposed a total ban on the employment of gay women and men by the federal government and government contractors. Purges of lesbians and homosexuals from the military rose sharply. The FBI instituted widespread surveillance of gay meeting places and of lesbian and gay organizations, such as the Daughters of Bilitis and the Mattahine Society. The post office placed tracers on the correspondence of gay men and passed evidence of homosexual activity on to employers. Urban vice squads invaded private homes, made sweeps of lesbian and gay male bars, entrapped gay men in public places, and fomented local witch hunts. The danger involved in being gay rose even as the possibilities of being gay were enhanced. Gay liberation was a response to this contradiction.

Although lesbians and gay men won significant victories in the 1970s and opened up some safe social space in which to exist, we can hardly claim to have dealt a fatal blow to heterosexism and homophobia. One could even argue that the enforcement of gay oppression has merely changed locales, shifting somewhat from the state to the arena of extralegal violence in the form of increasingly open physical attacks on lesbians and gay men. And, as our movements have grown, they have generated a backlash that threatens to wipe out our gains. Significantly, this New Right opposition has taken shape as a "pro family" movement. How is it that capitalism, whose structure made possible the emergence of a gay identity and the creation of urban gay communities, appears unable to accept gay men and lesbians in its midst? Why do heterosexism and homophobia appear so resistant to assault?

The answers, I think, can be found in the contradictory relationship of capitalism to the family. On the one hand, as I argued earlier, capitalism has gradually undermined the material basis of the nuclear family by taking away the economic functions that cemented the ties between family members. As more adults have been drawn into the free labor system, and as capital has expanded its sphere until it produces as commodities most goods and services we need for our survival, the forces that propelled men and women into families and kept them there have weakened. On the other hand, the ideology of capitalist society has enshrined the family as the source of love, affection, and emotional security, the place where our need for stable, intimate human relationships is satisfied.

This elevation of the nuclear family to pre-eminence in the sphere of personal life is not accidental. Every society needs structures for reproduction and childbearing, but the possibilities are not limited to the nuclear family. Yet the privatized family fits well with capitalist relations of production. Capitalism has socialized production while maintaining that the products of socialized labor belong to the owners of private property. In many ways, child rearing has also been progressively socialized over the last two centuries, with schools, the media, peer groups, and employers taking over functions that once belonged to parents. Nevertheless, capitalist society maintains that reproduction and child rearing are private tasks, that children "belong" to parents, who exercise the rights of ownership. Ideologically, capitalism drives people into heterosexual families: each generation comes of age having internalized a heterosexist model of intimacy and personal relationships. Materially, capitalism weakens the bonds that once kept families together so that their members experience a growing instability in the place they have come to expect happiness and emotional security. Thus, while capitalism has knocked the material foundation away from family life, lesbians, gay men, and heterosexual feminists have become the scapegoats for the social instability of the system.

This analysis, if persuasive, has implications for us today. It can affect our perception of our identity, our formulation of political goals, and our decisions about strategy.

I have argued that lesbian and gay identity and communities are historically created, the result of a process of capitalist development that has spanned many generations. A corollary of this argument is that we are *not* a fixed social minority composed for all time of a certain percentage of the population. *There are more of us* than one hundred years ago, more of us than forty years ago. And there may very well be more gay men and lesbians in the future. Claims made by gays and nongays that sexual orientation is fixed at an early age, that large numbers of visible gay men and lesbians in society, the media, and the schools will have no influence on the sexual identities of the young, are wrong. Capitalism has created the material conditions for homosexual desire to express itself as a central component of some individuals' lives; now, our political movements are changing consciousness, creating the ideological conditions that make it easier for people to make that choice.

To be sure, this argument confirms the worst fears and most rabid rhetoric of our political opponents. But our response must be to challenge the underlying belief that homosexual relations are bad, a poor second choice. We must not slip into the opportunistic defense that society need not worry about tolerating us, since only homosexuals become homosexuals. At best, a minority group analysis and a civil rights strategy pertain to those of us who already are gay. It leaves today's youth—tomorrow's lesbians and gay men—to internalize heterosexist models that it can take a lifetime to expunge.

I have also argued that capitalism has led to the separation of sexuality from procreation. Human sexual desire need no longer be harnessed to reproductive imperatives, to procreation; its expression has increasingly entered the realm of choice. Lesbians and homosexuals most clearly embody the potential of this split, since our gay relationships stand entirely outside a procreative framework. The acceptance of our erotic choices ultimately depends on the degree to which society is willing to affirm sexual expression as a form of play, positive and life-enhancing. Our movement may have begun as the struggle of a "minority," but what we should now be trying to "liberate" is an aspect of the personal lives of all people—sexual expression.[11]

Finally, I have suggested that the relationship between capitalism and the family is fundamentally contradictory. On the one hand, capitalism continually weakens the material foundation of family life, making it possible for individuals to live outside the family, and for a lesbian and gay male identity to develop. On the other hand, it needs to push men and women into families, at least long enough to reproduce the next generation of workers. The elevation of the family to ideological pre-eminence guarantees that capitalist society will reproduce not just children but also heterosexism and homophobia. In the most profound sense, capitalism is the problem.[12]

How do we avoid remaining the scapegoats, the political victims of the social instability that capitalism generates? How can we take this contradictory relationship and use it to move toward liberation?

Gay men and lesbians exist on social terrain beyond the boundaries of the heterosexual nuclear family. Our communities have formed in that social space. Our survival and liberation depend on our ability to defend and expand that terrain, not just for ourselves but for everyone. That means, in part, support for issues that broaden the opportunities for living outside traditional heterosexual family units: issues like the availability of abortion and the ratification of the Equal Rights Amendment, affirmative action for people of color and for women, publicly funded day care and other essential social services, decent welfare payments, full employment, the rights of young people—in other words, programs and issues that provide a material basis for personal autonomy.

The rights of young people are especially critical. The acceptance of children as dependents, as belonging to parents, is so deeply ingrained that we can scarcely imagine what it would mean to treat them as autonomous human beings, particularly in the realm of sexual expression and choice. Yet until that happens, gay liberation will remain out of our reach.

But personal autonomy is only half the story. The instability of families and the sense of impermanence and insecurity that people are now experiencing in their personal relationships are real social problems that need to be addressed. We need political solutions for these difficulties of personal life. These solutions should not come in the form of a radical version of the profamily position, of some left-wing proposals to strengthen the family. Socialists do not generally respond to the exploitation and economic inequality of industrial capitalism by calling for a return to the family farm and handicraft production. We recognize that the vastly increased productivity that capitalism has made possible by socializing production is one of its progressive features. Similarly, we should not be trying to turn back the clock to some mythic age of the happy family.

We do need, however, structures and programs that will help to dissolve the boundaries that isolate the family, particularly those that privatize child rearing. We need community- or worker-controlled day care, housing where privacy and community coexist, neighborhood institutions—from medical clinics to performance centers—that enlarge the social unit where each of us has a secure place. As we create structures beyond the nuclear family that provide a sense of belonging, the family will wane in significance. Less and less will it seem to make or break our emotional security.

In this respect, gay men and lesbians are well situated to play a special role. Already excluded from families as most of us are, we have had to create, for our survival, networks of support that do not depend on the bonds of blood or the license of the state, but that are freely chosen and nurtured. The building of an "affectional community" must be as much a part of our political movement as are campaigns for civil rights. In this way we may prefigure the shape of personal relationships in a society grounded in equality and justice rather than exploitation and oppression, a society where autonomy and security do not preclude each other but coexist.

NOTES

This essay is a revised version of a lecture given before several audiences in 1979 and 1980. I am grateful to the following groups for giving me a forum in which to talk and get feedback: the Baltimore Gay Alliance, the San Francisco Lesbian and Gay History Project, the organizers of Gay Awareness Week 1980 at San Jose State University and the University of California at Irvine, and the coordinators of the Student Affairs Lectures at the University of California at Irvine.

Lisa Duggan, Estelle Freedman, Jonathan Katz, Carole Vance, Paula Webster, Bert Hansen, Ann Snitow, Christine Stansell, and Sharon Thompson provided helpful criticisms of an earlier draft. I especially want to thank Allan Bérubé and Jonathan Katz for generously sharing with me their own research, and Amber Hollibaugh for many exciting hours of nonstop conversation about Marxism and sexuality.

1. I do not mean to suggest that no one has ever proposed that gay identity is a product of historical change. See, for instance, Mary McIntosh, "The Homosexual Role," *Social Problems* 16 (1968): 182–92; Jeffrey Weeks, *Coming Out: Homosexual Politics in Britain* (New York: Quartet Books,

1977). It is also implied in Michel Foucault, *The History of Sexuality*, vol. 1: *An Introduction*, tr. Robert Hurley (New York: Pantheon, 1978). However, this does represent a minority viewpoint, and the works cited above have not specified how it is that capitalism as a system of production has allowed for the emergence of a gay male and lesbian identity. As an example of the "eternal homosexual" thesis, see John Boswell, *Christianity, Social Tolerance, and Homosexuality* (Chicago: University of Chicago Press, 1980), where "gay people" remains an unchanging social category through fifteen centuries of Mediterranean and Western European history.

2. See Eli Zaretsky, *Capitalism, the Family, and Personal Life* (New York: Harper and Row, 1976); and Paula Fass, *The Damned and the Beautiful: American Youth in the 1920s* (New York: Oxford University Press, 1977).

3. Robert F. Oaks, "'Things Fearful to Name': Sodomy and Buggery in Seventeenth-Century New England," *Journal of Social History* 12 (1978): 268–81; J. R. Roberts, "The Case of Sarah Norman and Mary Hammond," *Sinister Wisdom* 24 (1980): 57–62; and Jonathan Katz, *Gay American History* (New York: Crowell, 1976), pp. 16–24, 568–71.

4. For the period from 1870 to 1940 see the documents in Katz, *Gay American History*, and idem., *Gay/Lesbian Almanac* (New York: Crowell, 1983). Other sources include Allan Bérubé, "Lesbians and Gay Men in Early San Francisco: Notes Toward a Social History of Lesbians and Gay Men in America," unpublished paper, 1979; Vern Bullough and Bonnie Bullough, "Lesbianism in the 1920s and 1930s: A Newfound Study" *Signs* 2 (Summer 1977): 895–904.

5. On the medical model see Weeks, *Coming Out*, pp. 23–32. The impact of the medical model on the consciousness of men and women can be seen in Louis Hyde, ed., *Rat and the Devil: The Journal Letters of F. O. Matthiessen and Russell Cheney* (Hamden, Conn.: Archon, 1978), p. 47; and in the story of Lucille Hart in Katz, *Gay American History*, pp. 258–79. Radclyffe Hall's classic novel about lesbianism, *The Well of Loneliness*, published in 1928, was perhaps one of the most important vehicles for the popularization of the medical model.

6. See Alfred Kinsey et al., *Sexual Behavior in the Human Male* (Philadelphia: W. B. Saunders, 1948), and *Sexual Behavior in the Human Female* (Philadelphia: W. B. Saunders, 1953).

7. On black music, see "AC/DC Blues: Gay Jazz Reissues," Stash Records, ST-106(1977); and Chris Albertson, *Bessie* (New York: Stein and Day, 1974). On the persistence of kin networks in white ethnic communities see Judith Smith, "Our Own Kind: Family and Community Networks in Providence," in *A Heritage of Her Own*, ed. Nancy F. Cott and Elizabeth H. Pleck (New York: Simon and Schuster, 1979), pp. 393–411; on differences between rural and urban male homoeroticism see Kinsey et al., *Sexual Behavior in the Human Male*, pp. 455–57, 630–31.

8. The argument and the information in this and the following paragraphs come from my book *Sexual Politics, Sexual Communities: The Making of a Homosexual Minority in the United States, 1940–1970* (Chicago: University of Chicago Press, 1983). I have also developed it with reference to San Francisco in "Gay Politics, Gay Community: San Francisco's Experience," *Socialist Review* 55 (January-February 1981): 77–104.

9. Donald Vining, *A Gay Diary, 1933–1946* (New York: Pepys Press, 1979); "Pat Bond," in Nancy Adair and Casey Adair, *Word Is Out* (New York: New Glide Publications, 1978), pp. 55–65; and Allan Bérubé, "Marching to a Different Drummer: Coming Out During World War II," a slide/talk presented at the annual meeting of the American Historical Association, December 1981, Los Angeles. A shorter version of Bérubé's presentation can be found in *The Advocate*, October 15, 1981, pp. 20–24.

10. On lesbian novels see *The Ladder*, March 1958, p. 18; February 1960, pp. 14–15; April 1961, pp. 12–13; February 1962, pp. 6–11; January 1963, pp. 6–13; February 196, pp. 12–19; February 1965 pp. 19–23; March 1966, pp. 22–26; and April 1967, pp. 8–13. *The Ladder* was the magazine published by the Daughters of Bilitis.

11. This especially needs to be emphasized today. The 1980 annual conference of the National Organization for Women, for instance, passed a lesbian rights resolution that defined the issue as one of

"discrimination based on affectional/sexual preference/orientation," and explicitly disassociated the issue from other questions of sexuality such as pornography, sadomasochism, public sex, and pederasty.

12. I do not meant to suggest that homophobia is "caused" by capitalism or is to be found only in capitalist societies. Severe sanctions against homoeroticism can be found in European feudal society and in contemporary socialist countries. But my focus in this essay has been the emergence of a gay identity under capitalism, and the mechanisms specific to capitalism that made this possible and that reproduce homophobia as well.

12 Transformations of Homosexuality-Based Classifications[1]

David F. Greenberg

SEXUAL CATEGORIES

The world is endlessly varied, infinitely complex. To facilitate communication and collective action, humans map their perceptions of the world's plenitude cognitively into categories that simplify complexity. They ignore some features of the terrain, highlight others, and sometimes represent features that don't exist.

Categories that are too gross to capture important meaningful variations are sometimes criticized for being "stereotypes"; they fail to recognize distinctions that ought to be taken into account. When used to make decisions that affect the life chances of those categorized, categories become instrumentalities of power. But reliance on simplified categories is unavoidable. Human language and social life would be impossible without it.

Some category systems may offer practical advantages over others: if one is classifying some plants as "foods" and others as "not foods," there will be survival value in placing toxic plants in the second category rather than in the first. But the choice of criteria of relevance are not given in the world being categorized. In classifying whales as mammals rather than fish, taxonomists take certain criteria (bearing young alive, being warm-blooded, having lungs) rather than others (living in an aquatic habitat, lacking arms and legs) as determinate. A different choice could have been made.[2]

As a rule, collective categories do not wholly structure individual perceptions and action. In every society, individual biographies are to some extent unique. Distinctive experiences and life goals enable individuals to interpret collective categories idiosyncratically, devise their own, and challenge others'.

In complex societies, conceptual systems and categories are likely to vary in systematic ways with social location. Exposure to others' classification systems often makes one's own less than totally hegemonic. Lack of opportunity, and the need to coordinate one's actions with those of

The author of numerous books and articles spanning several fields of study, **David F. Greenberg** has been a theoretical high energy physicist, a civil rights and prisoners' rights activist, and a draft resister. Now Professor of Sociology at New York University, he does research and teaches courses on crime, law, deviance, and statistics, and studies ancient languages. He is a member of Democratic Socialists of America.

others who may not share one's own classification scheme, can prevent people from acting on the basis of their own ideational system. Incentives and disincentives associated with lines of action can shift individuals' preference schedules, leading to the choice of one course of conduct instead of another. Nevertheless, a mapping of collective categories often helps explain individual perceptions and behaviors.

Where these collective categories are absent, individuals can be at a loss how to classify themselves. The mid-eighteenth-century Englishwoman, Charlotte Charke, who sometimes wore men's clothes and courted women, but lived outside of any subculture that could have given meaning to these practices, referred to herself not as a butch lesbian but as "a NONPAREIL OF THE AGE," one of the "Wonders of Ages past, and those to come," and an "Oddity," as if she were unique."[3]

Recent comparative and historical investigation has made clear that the categories and assumptions of cognitive schemes for thinking and speaking about sex vary with time and place. Tomas Almaguer, for example, observes that "the Mexican-Latin American sexual system" has no concept analogous to the North American-European "gay man."[4] When the Moslem Hanbalite jurisconsult Ibn al-Gauzi (d. circa 1200 A.D.) wrote, "He who claims that he experiences no desire [when looking at beautiful male youths] is a liar, and if we could believe him, he would be an animal, not a human being,"[5] he was clearly working with a different set of assumptions about the wellsprings of erotic attraction than was Jeremy Bentham, who wrote, "Should a man of his free choice prefer a male to a female I see not what reason there would be for applying the word natural to the one rather than the other."[6] The Comte de Berssac in the Marquis de Sade's novel, *Justine*, offered still another construction: "We deviates, you see, are biologically different from other men: like them we also enjoy an Altar of Sodom lined with the same sensitive membranes which adorn your Altar of Venus."[7] And though Sade invokes anatomy here, he does so in a way that is quite different from the biological researchers who recently claimed to have found a gene that governs sexual orientation.

These conceptual differences force us to problematize the relationship between act and identity. It is no longer possible to speak casually of ancient Greeks or medieval Christian monks who experienced passionate longings for other men as "gay,"[8] taking for granted that men living hundreds of years ago thought of themselves as contemporary gay men do. Gayness and homosexuality were largely absent from their mental universe.

KINSHIP-STRUCTURED SOCIETIES

Behavior that present-day Western observers identify as homosexual occurs quite widely in small-scale bands and tribes. Where such relationships among males are institutionalized, they commonly take one of two possible forms. In the *pederastic*, semen of an older male is placed in or on the body of a youth. In some New Guinea and Latin American Indian groups, the practice is universal and mandatory. Neither partner is considered a distinct type of person.

In the *transgenderal* type, one of the parties abandons an original gender identity. Usually the gender abandoned is male, but sometimes it is female. The gender-changer may be regarded as a member of the opposite sex, or as an occupant of a "third" gender role. Often they take a sexual partner of the same anatomical sex, but this is not invariably so. It is gender behavior and identity, not sexual expression, that is critical in this classification scheme; our highlighting this phenomenon as "transgenderal homosexuality" reveals the priorities of a modern Western classification scheme not shared by the peoples among whom this phenomenon is found.

When the gender-changer's sex partners are of the same sex, their gender identities are invariably conventional. Where relationships of this sort are institutionalized, the conventionally gendered partner is given no special name or identity, but the gender-changer is considered a distinct type of person.

CLASSICAL ANTIQUITY

The pederastic form of same-sex relationships was a prominent feature of ancient Greek and Roman civilization. In these civilizations, male erotic interest in persons of the same sex was generally assumed to be universally present and psychologically normal, but not exclusive.

Plutarch's *Dialogue on Love* illustrates this thinking about homoeroticism. One of the interlocutors in the dialogue maintains:

> The noble lover of beauty engages in love wherever he sees excellence and splendid natural endowment without regard for any difference in physiological details. He will be fairly and equally disposed toward both sexes, instead of supposing that males and females are as different in the matter of love as they are in their clothes.

Nor was there any compulsion to restrict oneself to one sex. In Lucian's short story, "The Ship or the Wishes" (second century A.D.), Timolaus wishes he owned a ring that will

> make the pretty boys and women and whole peoples fall in love with me—no one will fail to love me and think me desirable: I shall be on every tongue. Most women will hang themselves in despair, boys will be mad for me and think themselves blessed if I but glance at one of them, and pine away for grief if I but ignore them.[9]

These excerpts from poems in *The Greek Anthology*—[10]

> The love of women touches not my heart, but brands have heaped unquenchable coals of fire on me. (XII.17, Anonymous)

> Persistent Love, thou ever whirlest at me no desire for women, but the lightning of burning longing for males (XII.87, Anonymous)

—demonstrate that some Greeks did have exclusive sexual interests, at least at the time they wrote. The poets may have mentioned it because it was so atypical.

An adult in ancient Greece and Rome standardly took a prepubescent youth for a partner, an adolescent whose body hair had not yet begun to grow. In Greece, relations with a citizen youth were ideally supposed to have a pedagogical function. The older lover was supposed to teach his beloved how to be a virtuous citizen. At the same time, the older lover was supposed to marry and have children, though some may not have done so. Sexual relations might also be had with members of other subordinate categories, such as slaves.

Sexual roles in these relationships were prescribed. The boy was expected to show affection to his older lover, but not to respond sexually. Thus Xenophon remarks, "The boy does not share in the man's pleasure in intercourse, as a woman does; cold sober, he looks upon the other drunk with sexual desire."[11] As in our own times, the norm was not always followed. Greek vase paintings show some youths taking the initiative or responding to an older man's sexual overtures.

An adult male was not supposed to take the receptive role. According to Plutarch, "Those who enjoy playing the passive role we treat as the lowest of the low, and we have not the slightest degree of respect for them." The passive role was the role played by a woman, a youth, or slave; it was shameful for an adult man—though not for a youth or slave. A youth's subordination to an older man was "natural" and temporary; and a slave was by definition subordinate to his master. Of course, some adults did take the passive role. Efforts were made to explain their anomalous preference for the receptive role.

This qualified acceptance of male homosexual expression began to weaken in late antiquity, when Stoic philosophers argued that the ideal life was one of sexual abstinence, because sex distracted one from philosophical contemplation. But philosophers considered this an ideal mainly for themselves; they never expected the entire population to live up to it. Some Stoics accepted sexual relations between persons of the same sex and those of opposite sex on the same basis, as long as they were kept within moderation. Others thought that sex should be restricted to an opposite-sex spouse, and only for reproduction. This, however, was merely an opinion. The philosophers had neither the intention nor the means of imposing their views on others.

Sex in Early Christianity

Christianity synthesized Hellenistic doctrines of Stoic sexual self-restraint with an older Jewish sexual morality in which sexual activity between two males was—for reasons that are still debated—a capital offense. The prohibition was directed against a particular type of *behavior*, and did not single out a particular *type of person*.

Ambiguities of wording make it difficult to be certain, but Saint Paul may have extended the Jewish prohibition of male-male sex to relations between females in his Letter to the Romans. Males who engage in sexual relations with other males, he added, were deserving of death.

This expression of Christian charity must be placed in the context of early Christian thinking about women and heterosexual sex. The Pauline Epistles allowed married couples to engage in sexual activity, but only because it was better to marry than to burn; sex had no positive value of its own. Subsequent generations of Christians took this antipathy to sex even further. In the second and third centuries A.D., virginity came to constitute the core of personal virtue. Some bishops held that only virgins could be saved, and would not baptize someone who had ever had sexual intercourse. Saint Augustine, whose checkered sexual career before he became a Christian would have precluded his own salvation under the more stringent standard, formulated the criteria that made sexual activity acceptable to the Church: it had to be within a marital relationship and of the sort that could potentially be procreative. These criteria left no basis for a sexual relationship between same-sex partners.

After Christianity became the official religion of the Roman Empire, it was in a position to impose Christian standards of sexual virtue on the Roman population. By the early sixth century, this influence is seen in the provision of the Justinian code for putting men to death for sexual activity with other males.

Sodomy in Medieval Christendom

The invading Germans were not as restrictive about homoeroticism as Christianity was; some had institutionalized pederastic initiation rituals. Yet some shared the Greco-Roman contempt for male effeminacy, and may have punished men who played a receptive sexual role in relation to other men.

As the Roman Catholic Church tried to shape moral standards in the British Isles and in Western Europe, it tried to discipline sinners, especially those who violated its sexual norms. These efforts were not entirely successful. There may have been a fair amount of homoeroticism between monks within the medieval monasteries, nuns in nunneries, and between knights and their squires. According to Orderic, a monk who chronicled English and Norman politics in the late eleventh and early twelfth centuries, the young Norman noblemen were worthy of being burned because they "shamelessly abandoned themselves to the foulest Sodomitical practices."[12]

Though Christian teaching forbade all same-sex sexual relations, repressing them was a low priority. In 1102, Anselm, then bishop of Canterbury, urged that those who had such relations not be punished too harshly because "this sin has hitherto been so public that hardly anyone is embarrassed by it, and many have therefore fallen into it because they were unaware of its seriousness." The churchman Jacques de Vitry, writing of Paris in 1230, noted that the "abominable vice sodomy so filled the city that it was held a sign of honor if a man kept one or more concubines."[13]

Repression against male-male sexual activity grew in thirteenth-century Europe, probably as an unanticipated consequence of the Gregorian reforms. To prevent priests from giving Church property to their sons, and to position the priesthood as morally superior to the laity, Church reformers tried to put an end to priestly marriages and concubinage. In closing off heterosexual outlets, the Church intensified the homoerotic atmosphere of the monastery. Yet same-sex relations posed just as great a threat to the moral standing of the priesthood as opposite-sex relations did. Church reformers tried to eliminate both. Ultimately they extended their repressive stance toward same-sex relations among the laity as well. Sodomy became criminal under national legislation promulgated by the centralizing monarchs, as well as in the municipal statutes of individual cities.

Medieval explanations for sodomy were entirely voluntaristic, notwithstanding the existence of other perspectives (astrology, Galenic medicine) that explained behavior more deterministically. William of Bologna, a thirteenth-century surgeon, probably writing under the influence of Arab medical treatises, was a rare exception: he explained sexual relations between women as due to a growth emanating from the mouth of the womb and appearing outside the vagina as a pseudo-penis.

It is noteworthy that in medieval law and in Christian teachings, sodomy could include opposite-sex as well as same-sex contacts, and contacts with nonhuman animals. Some married couples were burned at the stake after being convicted of sodomy for engaging in anal intercourse. Peter Cantor, a professor of theology at the University of Paris in the late twelfth century, classified coitus interruptus as sodomy; and a sixteenth-century Dutch writer, Joost van Damhouder, counted intercourse with Turks, Saracens, and Jews as sodomitical on the grounds that to a Christian, infidels were equivalent to "dogs and animals."

Though sexual relations between females were not prohibited in the Jewish Bible, Christian writers classified them as sinful based on their interpretation of an ambiguous passage in the first chapter of Paul's Letter to the Romans. On the other hand, they did not always consider them sodomitical because women did not penetrate one another. Yet some theologians, including Aquinas, did consider sexual relations between women to be sodomy. In France, Spain, Switzerland, Germany, and Italy, medieval and early modern secular law made sexual relations between females a capital offense, but when Henry VIII made "buggery"—the equivalent of sodomy—capital in 1533, relations between females were not mentioned.[14] In the rare prosecutions of women for sex with one another, it was almost always for the use of "material instruments," which could penetrate. It is clear that "sodomy" could take on multiple meanings (as it can now) and cannot simply be equated with the modern term "homosexuality." Homosexuality encompasses both men and women, but sodomy often did not. Equally, homosexuality excludes sex with animals and with opposite-sex partners.

URBANIZATION AND SOCIAL CHANGE

Several developments provided the impetus for change from this premodern pattern of same-sex relationships. One was the rise of large cities. Urbanization makes it possible to enter into sexual relationships discreetly, without the knowledge of family, neighbors, and employers. This protection is critical when disclosure can lead to ostracism, loss of job, and legal penalties. Cities also facilitate the establishment of networks and institutions centered on homoeroticism by bringing together people with specialized tastes, creating the critical mass needed to make specialized institutions viable.

The larger medieval towns already had populations large enough to make male prostitution economically viable. Richard of Devizes, an English monk writing at the end of the twelfth century, noted the existence of male prostitution in London. By the fifteenth and sixteenth centuries, male homosexual[15] networks could be found in Paris, Rouen, and Cologne; and street theater performances during the annual Carnival celebration sometimes had homoerotic themes. Nothing so elaborate is documented for England, but there, too, "male love" was a recognized phenomenon mentioned in literary sources.[16]

The existence of social networks involving male-male eroticism has been particularly well documented for Renaissance Italy. Between 1432 and 1502, approximately 25 percent of the male population of Florence—by modern standards a remarkably high percentage—was arrested on sodomy charges.[17] In 1488, Venice sealed off the porch of Santa Maria Mater Domini to stop it from being used as a gathering spot by local sodomites. According to Saint Bernardino of Siena, Florence and others, Tuscan cities of the early fifteenth century had such a reputation for sodomy that Genoa would not hire Tuscan schoolmasters. Some said that boys were more likely than girls to be sexually assaulted on the streets. To stop female streetwalkers from dressing as boys to attract customers, the Florentine city fathers banned female-to-male transvestism, and tried to recruit female prostitutes from other cities. The seventeenth-century Scottish traveler William Lithgow found boy prostitution to be common and widely accepted even in the smaller towns of Italy.

With time, social networks grew into elaborate subcultures. The Brazilian historian Luiz Mott has written about seventeenth-century Lisbon:

> There were inns openly patronized by sodomites, balls where transvestites danced and played instruments, much street prostitution, and men who served as go-betweens for male sexual encounters. . . . All classes participated, with clergy heavily represented.

Seville also had a visible subculture based on male-male eroticism.

These urban subcultures were able to develop and grow even in the presence of extremely harsh laws because the most severe penalties were rarely imposed. Between 1348 and 1461, death penalties were imposed in about ten sodomy cases tried in Florence. These were typically cases in which the partner was an extremely young child, where a rape took place, or where there were other collateral offenses like robbery or burglary that might have been capital in their own right.

The sculptor Cellini, convicted twice of consensual sodomy, was handled more typically. The first time he was fined; the second time he was placed under house arrest. Notwithstanding these convictions for activities that the Church designated as sinful, he received commissions for his sculptures from the Church, and was buried with full honors when he died.

Many relationships between males were not exclusive. The Renaissance Italian painter Caravaggio lived for years with one of his male models, but later had an affair with a woman. The model married and fathered a son. John Donne satirized a man who lusted for "a plumpe muddy whore, or prostitute boy." Ben Jonson's comedy *Epicoene* refers to a well-to-do man who has "a mistress abroad and his ingle (a youthful male lover) at home."

On the other hand, some of the relationships were thought to be exclusive. In a novella of Sabadino, a man informs his priest that he has never sinned with a woman because "women disgust me to the point that when I just look at them I only want to vomit." When he wanted a diversion, he said, he turned only to boys. Sir Anthony Welcome, a courtier of James I, referred to Anthony Ashley, clerk of the privy council, as someone "who never loved any but boys," and "naturally loved men." Yet, as far as we can tell from surviving records, this seems to have been unusual. In fact, Ashley married twice, and fathered a daughter. That homoerotic interest was usually not exclusive of heteroerotic interest undoubtedly discouraged the creation of distinct identities and interests based on homoeroticism.

FEMALE-FEMALE RELATIONSHIPS IN EARLY MODERN EUROPE

Women's lives were more constrained than men's in early modern Europe, limiting their opportunities for establishing intimate relationships with women (or with men!). Yet there were possibilities. Starting in the seventeenth century some women left their natal villages in Holland and Germany, disguised themselves as men, and practiced men's occupations. Some married women and lived with them, often until the cross-dressing woman died or was discovered to be anatomically female. The couples were isolated from one another, but some cases were widely publicized and may have served as examples to other women. When caught, it was usually just the cross-dressing partner who was punished, suggesting that the infraction was primarily of a gender norm, not of a sexual norm.

Once women were admitted into occupations in which they could be self-supporting without changing their gender identity (or had some way of being economically independent), they could more easily take women lovers. By the late eighteenth century there were French cafés patronized by *tribades*[18] who worked as actresses, as well as by women of the court.

England saw a parallel development. In 1773, the Frenchman Bachaumont wrote in a letter that the opera star Mlle. Heinel was settling in England: "Her tastes for women will find there attractive satisfaction, for though Paris furnishes many tribades it is said that London is herein superior." Travel diaries written toward the end of the century mention clubs or tribades in London and Bath. The tribade was by this time a recognized social type.

THE SECULARIZATION OF CULTURE

The partial secularization of European cultural life made it possible to think about sexual relations in ways that were not predetermined by church teachings. Louvois, war minister under Louis XIV, commented in 1666 that sexual relations between males might not be so bad: lovers of men would be less reluctant to go to war than married men with wives. Salon wits observed that the problem of underpopulation in early civilizations had long been overcome, making it safe to abandon biblical pronatalism. Men of the Middle Ages would not have voiced such cynical and skeptical opinions so freely.

Exploration brought knowledge of non-Western cultures that, unlike Islam, were located far enough away as to pose no military threat. The eighteenth-century French *philosophe* Diderot used the example of the Tahitians, whose naked women welcomed French sailors with open arms and legs, to argue that Western sexual morality is unnecessarily repressive and unhealthy.

Deterministic modes of explanation began to appear. They were already present in Renaissance physics and astronomy, where they were introduced to account for the behavior of inanimate matter. However, once an explanatory framework is introduced, its application is easily extended. Thus, Marsilio Ficino, the fifteenth-century Italian Platonist, reviving Hellenistic ideas about sex, observed that some men "naturally love males," while others do not, this disposition being dictated by astrological configurations at birth. Angelo Firenzuola contended in his *Dialogue on the Beauty of Women* (early sixteenth century), that "Jupiter makes some women lovers of women, others lovers of men." Here we find not only a deterministic explanation of anomalous sexual patterns, but the notion of mutually exclusive object choices.

Yet the influence of these deterministic explanations was limited. For the most part, sexual contacts with persons of the same sex continued to be understood voluntaristically. Thus the sixteenth-century Puritan John Rainolds (1549–1607) wrote that sexual attraction to another man was something to which "men's natural corruption and viciousness is prone." If that is so, what distinguishes those who act on their attraction from those who do not is their choice to do so; the attraction itself is not distinctive to a particular type of person.

By the eighteenth century, the successes of Newtonian physics and of engineering science won wider acceptance for notions of mechanical causality and its applicability to human beings. Diderot argued that "the abominable tastes" (of males, for males) come from "the abnormal nervous systems in young men and from the decaying of the brains of old men. From the lure of beauty in Athens, the scarcity of women in Rome, the fear of the pox in Paris." The existence of berdaches[19] among the American Indians, he thought, was due to the hot climate, the status of women, and the morphology of Indian penises.

When a discourse denigrating a particular group circulates in a society, members of the devalued group often find a way to appropriate that discourse for its own purposes. Men who were sexually attracted to men did so by drawing on deterministic world views to argue that they had not chosen their attraction; it reflected an inclination over which they had no control. When one of the characters in the anonymously written play, *L'ombre de Deschauffours*, maintains, "In nature everyone has his own inclination," another replies that this inclination is formed at birth.[20]

This etiological determinism was embraced in the second half of the nineteenth century by Karl Heinrich Ulrichs, a civil servant in Hanover, who in 1864 began publishing pamphlets calling for the normalization of sexual relations between same-sex partners. In the next generation such figures as Magnus Hirschfeld in Germany, and Havelock Ellis in England, took up the cause—and the deterministic reasoning.

Legal reforms reflected the secularization of intellectual life that had been developing in civil society. The Napoleonic Code, which decriminalized voluntary sexual conduct between adults, reflected the weakening of religious influences and the rise of *laissez-faire* economics. Once one accepts the position that contractual freedom provides a superior method for organizing social life, the logic is easily extended from business transactions to sexual transactions. Individuals were to be free to decide for themselves what their sex lives were to be as long as they didn't impose themselves on unwilling partners or on minors.

THE RETURN OF MALE EFFEMINACY

Among the men who participated in the social networks forming in early modern England and Europe, one finds a phenomenon present in some band and tribal societies as well as in classical antiquity but that seems to have largely disappeared for a thousand years: male effeminacy joined with homoeroticism. Medieval and Renaissance sodomites did not generally cross-dress, or adopt women's mannerisms.[21]

The re-emergence of male effeminacy is best documented in England at the beginning of the eighteenth century, where effeminate men were sufficiently well-known to be given a special name, "mollies." They gathered in taverns, where they cross-dressed and mimicked women.

As none of the mollies left accounts of themselves, we are completely ignorant as to what being a molly meant to them. Was it a playful toying with gender conventions—something like an early version of camp? Was it a way to make themselves more acceptable as partners to men who were accustomed to female partners? Or did it entail a more serious self-identification as "essentially female"?

We don't know. The answer may not have been the same for all mollies. However, contemporaries worried about the phenomenon, just as men of classical antiquity did. Thus the anonymous *Satan's Harvest Home*, published in England in 1749, argued that boys were coming to be raised at home rather than being apprenticed. Pampered at home by their mothers, and kept from the rough-and-tumble play of boys, they were growing up effete, never having had the chance to acquire the manly traits that would enable them to dominate, and thus satisfy, women. Such men, "unable to pleasure the women, chuse rather than to run into unnatural vices with one another, than to attempt what they are but too sensible they cannot perform."

Much of what we would call homosexuality was unconnected with the molly subculture. Participants may never have connected their own activities with the monstrous sodomy they read or even wrote about. Thus, Meredith Davy, a Somerset laborer accused of having sexual relations over a period of years with his apprentice who shared his bed, seemed bewildered when charged with sodomy. King James I wrote with nostalgia to Buckingham about "that night in bed together at Farnham," yet wrote in a letter to his son that sodomy was so foul a sin that no king could ever forgive it.

The stereotype linking gender anomaly with homoeroticism was sufficiently well established by the early nineteenth century that writers of fiction could draw on it freely. Thus in Balzac's *Splendeurs et misères des courtesans* (1843), when the director of a Paris jail takes a British visitor on a tour of his establishment, he points disgustedly to one building as the one "where the queens hang out." When the visitor asks what they are, he is told, "They are the third sex, my Lord." In an 1835 novel by Theophile Gautier, one character is described having "the body and soul of a woman, the spirit and strength of a man." She proclaims herself "a third sex which has not yet got a name." Ulrichs was probably influenced by this popular idea when he attributed same-sex eroticism to an anomaly of fetal development in which a male soul became incorporated in a female body, or vice versa.

Social networks based on homoerotic interest formed in U.S. cities after the Civil War, and some of them featured male cross-dressers. A physician wrote in 1871 of "restaurants frequented by men in women's attire, yielding themselves to indescribable lewdness." A quarter of a century later, Colin Scott described the social world of these cross-dressers as including

> coffee-clatches, where the members dress themselves with aprons, etc, and knit, gossip and cro-
> chet. . . . The avocations which inverts follow are frequently feminine in their nature. They are fond
> of the actor's life and particularly that of the comedian requiring the dressing in female attire, and the
> singing in imitation of a female voice, in which they often excel.

That earlier waves of immigrants from Europe, where networks of cross-dressers had been func-
tioning for some time, did not bring this phenomenon to the United States suggests that such networks can only flourish when cities are large enough to sustain them. Before the Civil War, American cities were not large enough for a cultural transplant to take root.

Some historians have suggested that the notion of homosexuals being effeminate, or of lesbians being masculine, was an invention of European physicians of the late nineteenth century.[22] The historical evidence clearly refutes this contention. Gender transformation was not invented by doctors in the late nineteenth century; for men it developed indigenously within the sodomitical subcultures that formed in early modern European and nineteenth-century American cities.

MEDICAL JURISDICTION OVER SAME-SEX RELATIONS

Some medical doctors of the late nineteenth century became interested in same-sex sexual rela-
tions from Ulrichs' pamphlets or from other campaigners for the normalization of same-sex sexual activity; others learned of it from their patients, or as court psychiatrists asked to render expert opinions about men being prosecuted on sodomy charges. The psychiatrists appropriated from the early homophile literature the notion that same-sex eroticism designated a distinct type of individual, but saw that individual as exhibiting a medical pathology.

The German physician Karl Westphal adopted this new perspective in 1869, when he published the case history of a patient with "contrary sexual feelings," who, when young

> was particularly fond of boys' games, and liked to dress as a boy. Since her eighth year had a liking for
> young girls—not all, but certain ones. Made love to them, kissed them, embraced them, at times suc-
> ceeded in touching their genitals. From the eighteenth to her twenty-third year had frequent oppor-
> tunity to gratify her desire.

At 35, she "still had a great desire to be a man."

Soon everything was being forced into the mold of gender. Dr. Blumer (1883), a physician at the New York State Lunatic Asylum, described one of his patients as having "contrary sexual feeling" even though the patient found the thought of sex with another man loathsome. The diagnosis was made on the basis of his long eyelashes, womanlike voice and intonation, and occasional lisp, his talent in writing fiction, and his excellence at playing the piano and composing music.

A new term, "invert," appeared in the literature to designate those who had "contrary sexual feelings." The term applied to both men and women, and connoted gender reversal as much as anomalous sexual desire or behavior. Around the same time, the term "homosexual" was introduced by the translator Károly Mária Kertbeny, and eventually displaced the cumbersome "contrary sexual feeling" and "inversion." In the context of a culture that considered departures from gender prescriptions to be signs of psychopathy, these terms were clearly stigmatizing.[23] Some right-wing German homosexual men opposed the medicalization of homosexuality, rejected male effeminacy, and tried to link male homoeroticism with hyper-masculinity.

Nevertheless, the stereotype provided a protective cover for those who did not fit the stereotype. The eminent Vienna psychiatrist Richard von Krafft-Ebing, called in as a forensic psychiatrist to examine a defendant in a sodomy trial, concluded that he could not possibly have been guilty of passive homosexuality. "He possessed neither the peculiarities of the male prostitute nor the clinical marks of effemination; and he had not the anthropological and clinical stigmata of the female-man. He was, in fact, the very opposite of this."

The stereotype of the invert as effeminate was so dominant that nineteenth-century observers never commented on an important transformation in homoerotic expression then taking place: the shift from an age-differentiated pattern to one in which the partners were adults who were not differentiated into active and passive partners. This shift can be attributed to the egalitarian political culture of modern democracies and to the sharpening of social distinctions between youths and adults.

Although the effeminate male and masculine female were among those who sought and had sexual relations with others of their sexes, many of the latter were entirely conventional in their gender presentation. This fact came to light from time to time. For example, many of the men arrested in the "Vere Street Scandal" in 1810, when a London tavern was raided, had blue-collar occupations. Working in these occupations was considered the epitome of masculinity. Yet the stereotype of the male invert as effeminate persisted.

It did so because gender was so salient an issue to professionals in the late nineteenth century. Women were clamoring for admission to higher education and for the right to vote. They sought the abolition of prostitution and denounced the salons, thus challenging two institutions that catered to male privilege. Embattled and threatened men responded by claiming that differences between the sexes were large, innate, and ineradicable. Any attempt to abolish them by educating women or admitting them into the professions would violate the natural laws of the human body and ruin women's health.

As the capitalist economies of Europe and North America matured, middle-class employment increasingly entailed white-collar work that was not physically demanding and thus did not confer masculinity. Imperial expansion into Asia and Africa by military means seemed to require a macho masculinity that the domestic economy could not be counted on to produce. President Theodore Roosevelt worried: "The greatest danger that a long period of profound peace offers to a nation is that of creating effeminate tendencies in young men."

In these circumstances, masculine women and effeminate men were perceived as threats to the absolute division of humanity into two distinct, complementary subspecies. Their threat to the boundaries that defined a radical dichotomy of tender was viewed with anxiety, alarm, and hostility.

The identification of homoerotic interests with breaches of gender standards not only expressed anxieties of the late nineteenth and early twentieth centuries; it held the additional advantage for psychiatrists and medical researchers that it could be integrated within a larger cognitive framework that had been developing during the nineteenth century. Developmental embryology had demonstrated that the human fetus is initially not differentiated anatomically into male and female; it rather has rudimentary structures capable of developing into both male and female sex organs. As the embryo develops, one set of structures disappears, so that at birth the typical human appears as either male or female. Where this fails to happen, a hermaphrodite is born. The concept of psychic hermaphroditism, referring to someone whose "soul" is not completely male or female, was but a short conceptual step.

Well-publicized successes of medicine in dealing with previously intractable illnesses encouraged physicians to expand their jurisdiction over many forms of behavior by reconceiving them as manifestations of a medical pathology. Thus, toward the end of eighteenth century, physicians began to argue that habitual heavy drinking stemmed from a disease of the will that created an irresistible craving for alcohol. In the nineteenth century this explanation became widely accepted.

The same claim for professional jurisdiction was being made in relation to homosexuality. Writing in an American medical journal in 1884, a Dr. George Shrady said of men and women with "abnormal instincts" that "conditions once considered criminal are really pathological, and come within the province of the physician . . . the profession can be entrusted to sift the degrading and vicious from what is truly morbid." This medicalization was by no means benign. Hereditary degeneracy posed a threat not merely because of what living degenerates might do, but because they risked the future of the species. Physicians proposed to cope with this threat by sterilizing degenerates or imprisoning them for life.

Even the religious were influenced by the new perspective. A physician writing in *Revue de l'hypnotisme* observed in 1909, "Today we see a curious phenomenon: the Catholic Church and Protestant Church rank themselves, in relation to homosexuality, on the side of medicine; they declare that sexual inversion is an anomaly of nature, a sickness, and that the paragraphs [of the criminal code] against the inverts are unjustified."

The campaigns for homosexual rights in Germany, and the psychiatric and sexological literature, spread the idea that one could have a distinctive sexuality and that this sexuality could motivate behavior. Among the many explanations that were proposed to account for the Jack-the-Ripper murders and mutilations of prostitutes in London toward the end of the nineteenth century was the suggestion that they reflected some type of sexual psychopathology. It was one of the first occasions in which homicide was explained *sexually*.[24]

Freud broke with the medical analysis of homoeroticism only to a degree. He was familiar with embryo research and drew on it when he suggested that homosexuality could be a developmental disorder in which the disorder occurred after birth rather than before. By proposing that heterosexuality was an outcome of the resolution of the Oedipal complex, Freud implicitly asserted that heterosexuality is not foreordained but instead needs as much explanation as homosexuality. In some of his writings he distinguished gender identity from object choice, making possible the recognition of conventionally masculine lovers of men and conventionally feminine lovers of women, as homosexuals. He may have been influenced by that tendency in the German homophile that repudiated male effeminacy.

The idea of the unconscious—one of Freud's central concepts—implies the possible existence of latent homosexuality. In psychoanalytic thought, all people have a hidden core identity whose essence is sexual. However, that identity does not dichotomize neatly into the categories of homosexual and heterosexual. Rather, homosexuality is part of everyone's sexual history, if only in fantasy, or sublimated in same-sex friendship. This claim potentially depathologizes homosexuality. At times Freud specifically denied that homosexuality was an illness. Yet he was also not able to accept fully that it was just as normal a form of sexual expression as heterosexuality.

Even when Freud was not directly addressing homosexuality, his writings developed ideas that were important for the conceptualization of homosexuality. In arguing that masturbation and premarital sex could be healthy, and in endowing women with sexual desire, Freud was publicly breaking the boundaries of what was considered acceptable in polite, middle-class Victorian society. In some medical writings of the nineteenth century, normal healthy women were not supposed to want sex or to enjoy it. Uncorrupted, they would never take the initiative. Though some medical specialists argued otherwise, literature claiming sexual anesthesia for women circulated very widely. At a time when middle-class women were beginning to pursue careers, this slight liberation was an accommodation to new possibilities available to women.

At times the belief that women did not want sexual contact immunized them from prosecution. In 1819, an English judge in a libel suit in 1819 in which two schoolmistresses were accused of a lesbian relationship said, "No such case was ever known in Scotland, or in Britain. . . . I do believe that the crime here alleged has no existence." Another judge remarked, "According to the known habits of women in this country, there is no indecency in one woman going to bed with another." From the late eighteenth to the early twentieth centuries, middle-class and professional women were able to live together unobtrusively in "Boston marriages," relatively free from harassment or persecution because the stereotype of women as asexual meant that they could not possibly be lovers.[25]

Overall, the sexualization of women was probably a positive one for them, but progress had its price. The publicity Freud's writings gave to the possibility of lesbianism brought romantic relationships under greater suspicion. At the same time, they helped make possible the establishment of "lesbian" as an identity independent of a woman's gender identity or role in the relationship.

CONTEMPORARY CONTROVERSY

Once the idea that homosexuality is a condition that underlies behavior gains currency, and it is thought that the condition can be caused by some prior condition or event, the door is open for all kinds of fads and fancies to be invoked and studied as possible explanations for it. Psychoanalysis has offered only one set of possibilities. Other proposals have come from endocrinology, genetics, and neuro-anatomy.

Until recently, this research was carried out largely by medical specialists who rarely questioned the common view that homosexuality was pathological. Drawing on their professional training, they attempted to identify its causes in the body or in the mind in the hope of finding a workable "treatment" that would turn homosexuals into heterosexuals.

In recent years, the medical/psychiatric establishment has substantially abandoned the belief that a homosexual orientation in itself is necessarily pathological and has largely stopped looking for a "cure." Nevertheless, the search for a cause persists, and the search has largely been organized around the commonsense scheme in which people are "homosexual" or "heterosexual," even though the scheme itself has been criticized as time-bound and oversimplified. The attention this body of research receives is due mainly to its politicization by spokespersons for the gay movement, who hope that if a biological cause of homosexuality can be identified, the case for gay rights will be strengthened. At the same time, skeptics have questioned the assumptions that underlie the research, and argue that the case for gay rights does not rest on the etiology of sexual orientation.

In the decades following the Second World War, and especially in the last quarter-century, the gay political movement in the United States and Western Europe has relied heavily on "identity politics," defining its constituency as those who share a common sexual orientation, understood by most activists to be biologically determined, though the lesbian-feminist movement has at times found another rhetoric appealing. It attributes heterosexuality to male compulsion, and contends that any woman has the potential to choose lesbianism—and should do so, to establish solidarity with other women instead of "sleeping with the enemy."

In recent years new configurations of sexual categories have appeared. Bisexuals, often marginalized and sometimes scorned by both gays and straights, have claimed a distinct identity. A more radical conceptual reconfiguration has emerged under the aegis of "queer" politics. The category "queer" includes men and women, and extends to transvestites and pre- and postoperative transsexuals. It argues that the rigid distinctions between these categories used in diagnosis and treatment are not necessarily meaningful. Some anatomically male "transgenderists" take estrogen, yet, as they do not seek sex reassignment surgery, do not meet the traditional psychiatric criteria for classification as "transsexual."[26] Are they transvestites? Transsexuals? Or what? Rigid, dichotomous category schemes have difficulty coming to terms with such individuals.

Queer theory emphasizes the performativity of gender, and views sexual identities as products of social disciplinary practices. Insofar as behavior is theatrical, it need not be attributed to any underlying trait or "essence" of the actor. Seen in this way, masculinity, femininity, queerness, straightness are not so much what one is, but what one does.[27]

The inability of repression to banish queerness from human life implies that it is present not just in a discrete population of "gays" but also in the lives and culture of "straights," even though they are not always aware of it. In like manner, the straight is present in the queer. Queer theory aims to undermine the binaries of sex and gender.[28]

Strategically, queer activism has implied a repudiation of assimilationist politics. The category queer was launched as a tactic for building a politics based on the common status of being excluded, marginalized, or outlawed, rather than on a common *identity* (as a homosexual, a transsexual, or whatever).

As a political thrust, this effort has had very limited success. Arguably, it relied overly on linguistic magic to achieve unity, without giving enough attention to programmatic concerns. Notwithstanding the goal of wide inclusion, some older gays still regard "queer" as an insult, and do not identify themselves in this way. Some have argued that the queer refusal to assimilate is possible only for a privileged white, male elite, and thus excludes those who "are fighting just to eat and live."[29]

Queer theorists have also been concerned with the problems posed by the fact that people possess multiple identities; they are not merely gay or straight, but are also white, Asian, black, Latino, male, female. Queer theorists remind us that when we use a broad, abstract category like "gay," it is easy to forget the diversity the category encompasses.

Heterogeneity of categories is inherent in all classification systems, but becomes especially troubling when particular kinds of diversity are obscured. Feminists have argued that the abstract human in philosophical discourse often turns out to be implicitly male, so that differences of sex and gender are never even noticed, much less theorized. In like manner, queer theorists contend that the abstract gay in academic and political writings often turns out to be implicitly white, male, and middle-class, concealing the distinct experiences and subjectivities of all others. Recognition of the ways multiple identities intersect and inflect one another has become a central theme in queer studies, where it is seen as having a political significance connected with emancipatory projects of such marginalized groups as blacks and Latinos.

These controversies remind us that categorical schemes differ not only between cultures; but that they also vary within the cultures of complex societies, and can be the site of political contest.

NOTES

I am grateful to Roger Lancaster for helpful comments on an earlier draft.

1. Where documentation is not provided here, the reader should refer to David F. Greenberg, *The Construction of Homosexuality* (Chicago: University of Chicago Press, 1988).

2. John Law and Peter Lodge, *Science for Social Scientists* (New York: Macmillan, 1984).

3. Quoted in Lisa Moore, "'She Was Too Fond of Her Mistaken Bargain': The Scandalous Relations of Gender and Sexuality in Feminist Theory," *Diacritics* (1991): 89–101.

4. Tomas Almaguer, "Chicano Men: A Cartography of Homosexual Identity and Behavior," *differences* 3 (1991).

5. Quoted in James A. Bellamy, "Sex and Society in Islamic Popular Literature," pp. 23–42, in A. L. Sayyi-Marsot (ed.), *Society and the Sexes in Medieval Islam* (Malibu: Udena, 1979).

6. Louis Crompton, "Jeremy Bentham's Essay on 'Paederasty' Part 2," *Journal of Homosexuality* 4 (1978): 99.

7. Quoted in Antony Copley's *Sexual Moralities in France, 1780–1980* (New York: Routledge, 1989).

8. John Boswell uses this language in *Christianity, Social Tolerance, and Homosexuality: Gay People in Western Europe from the Beginning of the Christian Era to the Fourteenth Century* (Chicago: University of Chicago Press, 1980).

9. Robert A. Padgug, "Sexual Matters: On Conceptualizing Sexuality in History," *Radical History Review* 20 (1979): 3–33.

10. *The Greek Anthology*, tr. W. R. Paton. (New York: G. P. Putnam's Sons, 1926).

11. *Banquet* 8.21.

12. Ordericus Vitalis, *Ecclesiastical History of England and Normandy* VIII.10 (see also VIII.4). Corroboration can be found in Henry of Huntington, *Chronicle* (London: Henry G. Bohn, 1853), pp. 248–49; William of Malmesbury, *Chronicle of the Kings of England* (IV.1).

13. Quoted in Arlo Karlen, *Sexuality and Homosexuality: A New View* (New York: W. W. Norton, 1971).

14. Louis Crompton, "The Myth of Lesbian Impunity: Capital Laws from 1270–1791," *Journal of Homosexuality* 6 (1980/81): 11–26.

15. Here I use a contemporary term; we don't know whether participants in these networks would have thought of themselves in ways that resemble the self-identity of modern homosexuals.

16. Bruce R. Smith, *Homosexual Desire in Shakespeare's England: A Cultural Poetics* (Chicago: University of Chicago Press, 1991); Joseph Cady, "'Masculine Love,' Renaissance Writing, and the 'New Invention' of Homosexuality," *Journal of Homosexuality* 23 (1990): 9–40.

17. Ninety-seven percent of the passives were age twenty or under. It is unlikely that all who engaged in sodomy were arrested. The proportion who participated may have been substantially larger. Michael J. Rocke, "Il Controllo dell'Omosessualità a Firenze nel XV Secolo: Gli *Ufficiali di Notte*," *Quaderni Storici* N.S. 66 (1987): 701–23.

18. Randolph Trumbach, "London's Sapphists: From Three Sexes to Four Genders in the Making of Modern Culture," pp. 111–36, in Gilbert Herdt (ed.), *Third Sex/Third Gender: Beyond Sexual Dimorphism in Culture and History* (New York: Zone Books, 1994).

19. The berdache was a "third gender role" found in many American Indian groups. The role was occupied by anatomically normal males; they often engaged in sexual relations with conventionally gendered men.

20. The play dates from 1739. Deschauffours had been broken on the wheel for sodomy some years earlier.

21. There were occasional exceptions. William of Malmesbury's *Chronicle* IV.1 refers to effeminate pathics who wore pointed shoes and walked with a mincing gait. Antonio Beccadelli's *Hermaphroditus*, published in 1425 A.D., refers to the "effeminate Lentulo" who couldn't even call his bottom his own because he owed it to half the world (I.14). However, these men were not considered effeminate because they engaged in sexual activity with other men but because of the role they played with them. Their male partners were not thought to be effeminate. That was also true of the male partners of the cross-dressing male prostitute (who also had numerous female sexual partners) arrested in London in 1394 A.D. (Favid Lorenzo Boyd and Ruth Mazo Karras, "The Interrogation of a Male Transvestite Prostitute in Fourteenth-Century London," *GLQ* 1 (1995): 459-65. Because the receptive partner in the Italian Renaissance (and probably in earlier times as well) was usually a youth, few adult males would have been labeled "effeminate" because of the role they played. Male effeminacy was known in early modern England, and was personified in the fop. But fops were thought to be excessively attracted to women, not to men.

22. Michel Foucault, *The History of Sexuality*, vol. 1: *An Introduction* (New York: Vintage, 1980).

23. Harry Oosterhuis, "Homosexual Emancipation in Germany Before 1933: Two Traditions," *Journal of Homosexuality* 22 (1991): 1–28.

24. Deborah Cameron and Elizabeth Frazer, *The Lust to Kill: A Feminist Investigation of Sexual Murder* (New York: New York University Press, 1987).

25. "Romantic friendships" between men were likewise not viewed with suspicion in the nineteenth

century even when they entailed strong emotional bonds (E. Anthony Rotundo, "Romantic Friendship," *Journal of the History of Sexuality* 23 [1989]:1–25). No one, for example, accused Abraham Lincoln of being a sodomite, even though he developed a strong attachment to the man whose bed he shared for four years while he was practicing law in Springfield, Ill. Charley Shiveley, "Big Buck and Big Lick: Abe Lincoln and Walt Whitman," pp. 125–37 in Winston Leyland (ed.), *Gay Roots: Twenty Years of Gay Sunshine* (San Francisco: Gay Sunshine Press, 1991).

26. Anne Bolin, "Transcending and Transgendering: Male-to-Female Transsexuals, Dichotomy and Diversity," pp. 447–85 in Gilbert Herdt (ed.), *Third Sex, Third Gender: Beyond Sexual Dimorphism in Culture and History*. (New York: Zone).

27. Kath Weston, "Do Clothes Make the Woman? Gender Performance Theory and Lesbian Eroticism," *Genders* 17: 1–21.

28. Alexander Doty, *Making Things Perfectly Queer* (Minneapolis: University of Minnesota Press, 1993).

29. Miguel Gutierrez, quoted in Steve Cosson, "Queer," *OUT/LOOK* 11 (1991): 16.

13   Seed of the Nation

Men's Sex and Potency in Mexico

Matthew C. Gutmann

PAPA'S SONS

Alfredo Pérez's wandering father, like many men of the older generations according to Alfredo, was absent for most of his son's life. Before his father died, however, Alfredo Pérez found him and, as he recounts,

> I took my wife and children to see him. He asked me to forgive him. I told him, "Don't worry about it, Papa. I'm no one to judge you, only God." A week later he died. When he died, well, we went to the burial and to the vigil. A lot of people began looking at me. I saw my sisters, and they said to me, "Look, we want to introduce you to Papa's son." So a man said to me, "Glad to meet you, my name is Alfredo Pérez." And then another, "How do you do? My name is Alfredo Pérez." I met five Alfredos, all with the same last name, all my half-brothers—Alfredo Pérez, Alfredo Pérez, Alfredo Pérez, each one.

Alfredo sees himself as similar to his father in certain respects—he talks about his own wild years with alcohol and affairs—but those days are now long past. Today, he says, his family is what counts.

"I've been married for thirty-two years, and we've had our ups and downs. I fight with her, we say things to each other. But she respects me, and I her. Even though we fight and we stop talking for a day or two, afterwards we're happy. And that's the way we will go through life, God willing. But the fine thing is to have some children who respect and admire you. I see now how they respect and admire and love me, and it's a *semilla* [seed] that I planted and taught to grow straight and tall."

As with his father before him, one's self-identification as a man is connected for Alfredo with insemination, financial maintenance, and moral authority, all of which are in turn largely predicated on men's relationships with women. At the same time, unlike his father, long-term mar-

Matthew Gutmann received his Ph.D. in Anthropology from Berkeley in 1995 and is now Assistant Professor at Brown University. He is the author of *The Meanings of Macho: Being a Man in Mexico City* (California, 1996) and has published papers on gender, critical theory, and Mexico. Parts of this essay are excerpted with permission from the author's book, *The Meanings of Macho*.

riage has become a symbol to Alfredo of his having consistently fulfilled his masculine responsibilities to provide financially for his wife and children.

Alfredo Pérez and his namesake brothers are from the *colonias populares* of Mexico City, where between 1992 and 1994 I carried out ethnographic fieldwork on the changing meanings and practices of being a working-class man in the Mexican capitol.[1] In contrast to those scholars who feel they have discovered a "typical" Mexican, Latin American, or Spanish-speaking masculinity, in my research I have instead been repeatedly confronted with the diversity of male identities. Similarly, the stereotyped image of a generalized Mexican male sexuality—polygamous, potent, and prolific—that together with poorly defined notions of ubiquitous Mexican machismo has long enjoyed currency in the social sciences and more popularly, seems today all the more inappropriate.[2] Rather than seeking to define the parameters of a homogenous Mexican male identity, therefore, in trying to understand gender and sexuality in Mexico we must examine the influence of generational differences and other factors like class, ethnic group, and region, and explore how these impinge on the realities of what it means to be a man, *ser hombre*, in contemporary Mexico.

Sexual identities, roles, and relations do not remain frozen in place, either for individuals or for groups. There is continuous contention and confusion over what constitute sexualities among women and men: they mean different things to different people at different times. And sometimes different things to the same person at the same time. In Mexico City today, men and women express greater self-consciousness about sexuality, not in the sense that they talk more about sex, but that their manner of talking about sex is different. Two key factors have contributed to these transformations in Mexico: first, the greater accessibility and widespread use of modern methods of birth control in the past twenty years throughout the country; and second, in a less obvious but still significant fashion, the open challenge of homosexuality as a major form of sexual life and expression in Mexico City and some other urban centers.[3]

Birth control and homosexuality have been central to changing notions of modern male sexuality in Mexico. Nor is it coincidental that the authoritative portrayals (see below) of twentieth-century Mexican national identity—arguments for an essential *mexicanidad*, or Mexicanness—highlight Mexican masculinity, and especially male potency in the form of the infamous Mexican Macho. It follows that if Mexican male sexuality, especially in the guise of man-as-progenitor, has long been romantically linked to cultural nationalist versions of *mexicanidad*, then changes in male sexuality will necessarily be involved in defining transformations in the modern Mexican nation.

The study of men in Mexico is not new, of course, as male ethnographers have been interviewing and examining men there for decades. However, what has generally not been done by anthropologists in Mexico or elsewhere until quite recently is to study men *as men* (see Godelier 1986: 76). Nor is the case of Latin America unique.[4] Indeed, even when men are studied as engendered and engendering beings, there is still a tendency to isolate them from women as if male and female gender identities and practices were easily segregated. This last problem is in turn compounded by the curious efforts by some, though not all, anthropologists presently writing about masculinity and manhood to avoid engaging seriously with feminist theory.

We will do better if we understand gender as referring to the ways in which differences and similarities related to physical sexuality of both women and men are understood, contested, organized, and practiced by societies. Which should not imply that what it means *physically* to be a man or a woman can be taken for granted; it must be explained. Understanding the body and sexuality requires an examination of cultural and historical factors and not simply an inspection of genitalia.[5]

COLONIA SANTO DOMINGO

In the case of Mexico, beginning in the 1940s, national identity came to be associated with certain sexually charged kinds of masculinity, in particular the sexually potent (macho) man: one who is physically vital, prolific, and powerful. In much of the nationalist rhetoric of the era since then, to be examined below, women became the silenced partners of Mexican male patriots. Nonetheless, especially beginning in the late 1960s in Mexico, political and social challenges to dominant gender relations and mores—in the forms of feminism and movements for gay and lesbian rights—provided an opening for questioning and defying social standards regarding issues like female marital fidelity and homosexuality. These developments combined with others like greater access to birth control led to a profound decoupling of sex from procreation in Mexico. And in this way as well, some of the bulwark of cultural nationalist versions of Mexican (male) sexuality has been undermined.

I came to know Alfredo Pérez in Colonia Santo Domingo, a *colonia popular* on the southside of Mexico City, where he and his family arrived in the mid-1970s. This was a few years after the 1971 invasion by thousands of "parachutist" families into the area of volcanic lava flows and caves known as the Pedregales. Among the residents of this self-built neighborhood of Santo Domingo, who now number over 100,000, women as well as men have been active as community organizers and leaders, first to build roads, and then to bring in electricity, schools, and other social necessities. Because of a conjuncture of special circumstances present as well in other communities in Mexico and Latin America in the last twenty years, popular social moments marked by varying degrees of independence from state control have played a prominent role in the cultural politics of Colonia Santo Domingo since the invasion.

In part because grass-roots feminist struggles (see Stephen 1997), such as those occurring in many of Mexico City's *colonias populares*, have generally had an oppositional character with respect to the Mexican state and ruling PRI party, and in part because Mexican national symbolism has come to be closely identified with macho potency, in the 1970s and 1980s women's gender and sexual identities developed in ways far less tied to notions of national culture in Mexico. Indeed, women in Colonia Santo Domingo and elsewhere in Mexico City have often sought to confront their men by explicitly opposing Mexican national gender categories. As a consequence men have been rebuked on two interconnected fronts, nationalism and masculinity, and thus for many what it means to be a man (or a woman) is less evident today in Mexico City than ever before.

In this essay I briefly examine three topics held by many to exemplify Mexican masculinity: the *casa chica*, where male sexuality has achieved international renown through the seeming institutionalization of men's adultery; contemporary sex between men, which is indicative of transformations in what it means to have sex and what it means to be Mexican; and finally, defining statements of *mexicanidad* regarding Mexican male sexuality and national character. Each of these topics may be analyzed as a distinctly "male" province; yet each may also be seen as an illustration of male-female relations in Mexico City's *colonias populares*.

LA CASA CHICA

In Oscar Lewis's (1961) affectionate portrait of Mexican working-class family life, *The Children of Sánchez*, he discusses many sexual practices in the capitol in the 1950s. Overly confident in the resilience of cultural practices, I was sure when I began fieldwork in 1992 that one of these, *la casa chica* (the small house), was still an entrenched institution. After all, Jesús Sánchez, whose children are the subject of Lewis's book, usually seemed to have a mistress or second wife, depending upon how you defined the relationship, whom he maintained in *la casa chica* (or *segundo frente* [second front]). *La casa chica* is usually thought of as the arrangement whereby a Mexican man keeps a woman other than his wife in a residence separate from his main (*casa grande*) household, and is discussed as a modern form of urban polygamy common in all social strata in Mexico, and by no means the prerogative of only wealthy men.[6]

Information on *la casa chica* was initially easy to come by. One man in a Christian Base Community in Colonia Ajusco (that borders Santo Domingo) spoke to me disparagingly of a brother of his who maintained *three* different households simultaneously, and did this on a factory worker's wages. A few weeks later, Luciano was welding a pipe in our apartment. Neighbors had already told me Luciano had a *casa chica*, so I was especially looking forward to talking with him. I asked Luciano about his family, and he told me that he and his wife were *separados* (separated). They had not lived together for years, he said. When I asked where he was living then, he replied, "Not far from here." But though he no longer shared a home with his "wife"—Luciano fumbled over what to call her—because the house and the land were in his name, getting divorced was out of the question; in a divorce he would risk losing all the property.

On another occasion I mentioned to a friend, Margarita, that I was surprised I had not encountered the famous *casa chica* in Santo Domingo. Margarita paused a moment and then said to me carefully, "¿Sabes qué? Carmela es la casa chica [You know what? Carmela is *la casa chica*]." Carmela, a woman in her late thirties whom I had previously met, had lived for twelve years with the man she always referred to as her husband. But, it turned out, this man was legally married to (though separated from) another woman with whom he had four children, the youngest then thirteen. Carmela's "husband" had legally adopted her son from an earlier relationship, and she and this man later had a daughter.

After a few months of fieldwork, I was getting quite wary of what *la casa chica* meant to different people, and how everyone referred to the "husbands" and "wives" of those involved in *las casas chicas*. By the time Rafael told me in December that his brother was living in their home with his *casa chica*, I had also grown a little weary of the term.

"Is he married to another woman?" I asked Rafael.

"Yes, he's been married for years," came the reply. "Of course, they haven't been together since he's been with this new woman, but he's still married to the first one."

Then a neighbor happened to mention a remarkable but more "classical" *casa chica* arrangement a couple of blocks from where we lived in Santo Domingo.

"You know the tire repair place on the corner? Well, a guy used to live over it with two sisters. He lived with them both!"

"In the same house?" I asked suspiciously.

"No."

"But each sister knew about the other one?"

"They knew about it and each tried to outdo the other, trying to get him to realize that she was better. He lived with the two sisters, two days with one, two with the other."

"What were they thinking?"

"Their mother was the really stupid one. She used to say that he was her *doble yerno* [double-son-in-law]. If the mother thought this, what could you expect from the daughters?"

Yet how the phrase *la casa chica* is used in daily conversation is often quite removed from such classical patterns. Rafael, who works in maintenance at the National University (UNAM) that borders Santo Domingo, once told me that 60 percent of his fellow employees at UNAM have *casas chicas*. I looked astonished. "Yes, I am talking about women as well as men." It soon became apparent that Rafael was talking about people having extramarital affairs; for him *casa chica* was a catchy analogue.

So too, while Margarita refers to Carmela as "*la casa chica*," and although by Carmela's own account the man she lives with cheated on her early in their relationship, this man has been faithful to Carmela for seven years and he is her "husband." As for Luciano's arrangement, a few weeks after fixing our pipes, and after we had gotten to know each other better, he told me that for several years he had lived with a woman other than his "first wife." He and the "second wife" now have two children together. In responding to questions about "your spouse" in a formal survey I conducted, Luciano always answered with regard to this second woman.

Most of the *casas chicas* that I know of in Mexico City that conform to a pattern of urban polygamy—where a man shuttles between two (or more) households and the "wives" are often ignorant of each other—are maintained by well-paid workers or men from the middle and upper classes. Other than the factory worker with three "wives," generally the only workers who can afford this kind of set-up are truckers or migrants to the United States, or men who have higher-paying jobs in the electrical, telephone, or petroleum industries.

So what, then, *is* the meaning of *la casa chica* and what shape does it take in the lives of people in Colonia Santo Domingo? At least in some instances, rather than referring to urban polygamy, *la casa chica* is used to describe second (or later) marriages. In other words, it frequently refers to serial monogamy, and if adultery occasionally occurs, it does so within *this* context. The approach many people take to *la casa chica* is in part a product of Catholic doctrine and antidivorce sanctions. Mexican working-class men as well as women have learned to manipulate the cultural rituals and social laws of machismo, not unlike the sixteenth-century rural French, who were, as Natalie Davis (1983:46) writes, a people with "centuries of peasant experience in manipulating popular rituals and the Catholic law on marriage."

This is especially true for the poor, who cannot as easily arrange and afford church annulments of their marriages. Men are culturally expected to financially maintain their (first) "wives" forever, just as these women expect to be supported—not that this situation always obtains. That is, for many men and women *la casa chica* is the best resolution to a situation in which legal divorce is out of the question. It is the way serial monogamy is practiced by many people in a society in which one often must be "married" to one's first spouse for life. The fact that few women and men necessarily intend in this manner to subvert Catholic rules regarding marriage-for-life does not take away from the creative (and subversive) quality of their actions.

In addition to prohibitions against divorce emanating from the Catholic Church, there are other factors that impinge on the situation. After divorce, first wives can more easily prevent fathers from seeing their children. And men such as Luciano can also lose property rights if their de facto divorces become de jure, and if they marry other women and end up living elsewhere.

The traditional *casa chica* arrangement, in which one man lives simultaneously with more than one woman and "family," may or may not persist in the upper echelons of Mexican society. But it is not common in Colonia Santo Domingo, at least not in this sense of urban polygamy.[7] My argument is instead threefold: first, that the expression *la casa chica* is used in a variety of ways in *colonias populares*, many of which ways have little to do with adultery as this latter term is defined by men and women involved in these unions; second, that these multiple meanings of *la casa chica* are illustrations of a cultural practice that has emerged in the context of Catholic laws on marriage; and third, that this cultural practice should be seen as part of a manipulative popular response to the church's ban on divorce.

Popular approaches to the *casa chica* in Santo Domingo are thus exemplary of Gramsci's (1929–35: 333) notion of contradictory consciousness, as the unpredictable exigencies of the living enter into lively contest with the oppressive traditions and bromides of dead generations. And, therefore, as Herzfeld (1987: 84) makes clear in another context, in instances such as the daily references and practices relating to the *casa chica* we should, rather than merely bearing witness to an "enforced passivity" induced from on high, especially and instead see "the quality of active social invention" in defiance of official discourse and control.

SEX BETWEEN MEN

If many Mexican male identities used to be wrapped up in adultery and siring many children, especially male children, today these are less central concerns. Such issues are still important to varying degrees to some men, but in Mexico City many younger men (and women) have begun thinking more reflexively about their bodies than their fathers and mothers ever did, and today there is a growing sense that sexuality is as much a possibility as it is an ultimatum, that there are multiple sexualities—not just two—and that sexuality can and does change.

As mentioned earlier, two key elements have contributed to these transformations. The first of these is the greater accessibility and widespread use of modern methods of birth control in the past twenty years in Mexico.[8] Following tremendous population growth as a result of a rise in average life expectancy from 25 years in 1900 to 66 years in 1980, birth rates have been cut in half in the last two decades in Mexico (Zavala de Cosío 1992: 16). Such demographic transitions are undoubtedly related to changes in the meanings and practices of maternity, paternity, gender, and sexual identities overall in Mexican society, for if women and couples are having fewer children, presumably this is a result of either increased use of birth control or decreased sexual relations between women and men. Either way, changing cultural attitudes and behavior are deeply involved in the statistics. The changes involving women that are made apparent in the lower birth rates imply re-evaluations and changes among men as well. For if womanhood is no longer so closely tied to motherhood, for example, then manhood too may be at least partially recast, though this does not necessarily manifest itself in immediate shifts regarding parenting practices by women or men.

Adult men have rarely died from childbirth in Mexico or anywhere else, but the separation of sex from pregnancy, childbirth, and child rearing has had a profound impact on them as well as on women, and altered more than just fertility rates. Sexuality increasingly has the ability to culturally transform personal and family life. And sexuality, potentially at least, is likewise more than ever before able to be itself transformed, including sexuality in relation to romantic love. Sexuality in this context is less tied to biological imperatives and more associated with desire, that is, subjective and transitory.[9]

In Santo Domingo and other *colonias populares* in Mexico City, sex is today less taken for granted than in earlier generations, and people talk not only of distinctions between the sexualities of men and women but to a greater extent now of differences among men and among women. Sex has a social history today and not just a biological evolution. For instance, friends in Santo Domingo occasionally mention *las casas de las locas* (the houses of the crazy-queens), where gay cross-dressers and transvestites are said to live. But reference is usually made to these houses in the past, and no one ever seems able to say where such a house might be today. Nonetheless, despite the fact that political movements for homosexual and lesbian human rights are less visible in Mexico today than they were in the late 1970s, the organized struggles of lesbians and gays and their supporters in Mexico have had real, if often collateral, importance for residents of Santo Domingo.[10]

Gaining even a rough picture of the sexual practices of men is complicated enough, not least of all for lack of common definitions: What *is* a heterosexual act? What *is* homosexuality? There is the possibility that men denied to me, or even to themselves, certain episodes of their youth. Carlos Monsiváis says that, at least in the past, sex between males sixteen to twenty-five years old used to be "a habit of youth" in the *colonias populares* of Mexico City (interview by author, 20 February 1993). Still, regardless of the sex practiced or dreamed about by men in Santo Domingo, many have undoubtedly been greatly influenced through what they have seen, heard, and in some cases done outside (or inside) the *colonia*.

It is hardly coincidental that the Zona Rosa, the part of Mexico City best known as a converging area for homosexuals, is also a major tourist district and the site of Metro Insurgentes, the busiest stop on the city's subway line. Millions of people pass through the Zona Rosa each day on their way to and from work and shopping. In addition, the Zona Rosa is a favorite spot among more adventurous teenagers from Colonia Santo Domingo, a place they go to hang out on Friday and Saturday nights. In sites such as the Zona Rosa, people in Mexico City have great access and exposure to people of different cultural orientations, including people of different sexual preferences. Such cross-cultural and cross-sexual intermingling is one feature of life in Mexico City that makes the capital stand out from most other parts of the country.[11]

The Alameda Park is where many young women who work in wealthy homes during the week as *muchachas* go on Sunday, their day off, hoping young men will buy them sodas or *paletas* (popsicles). The Alameda, next to Bellas Artes, another tourist attraction, is also where young *prostitutos* (male prostitutes), usually adolescent Indian men, cruise the pathways looking for business. Many of the *prostitutos'* clients are foreigners, and nearly all are men from the middle and upper strata—some of the people who frequent this part of the Centro Histórico of Mexico City.

Younger men in Santo Domingo who are particularly prone to using sexual innuendo are also more inclined to make insulting and/or defensive comments about homosexuality. However, even the contemporary homophobic language used by young men in the community reveals cultural creativity in response to the new provocation of multiple sexualities in Mexico City. While riding together on the way to matches, the young men on the River Plate *futbol* team, who come from Santo Domingo or the neighboring pueblo of Los Reyes, usually slap and pinch each other a lot. Amid all this grabbing and touching, two or three of the fifteen young men regularly and loudly jeer the others. Often, employing a kind of generic slur, they accuse one or another of their teammates of being a *maricón*, a queer. Instead of merely responding in kind, the accused often retorts with the more sophisticated insult, "Yeah, well you're a *bisexual!*"

Such rejoinders show no more expansive understanding than the frequent opinion voiced by older men in Santo Domingo that there are more *maricas* (faggots) and machos among the rich, as if to imply that (what they see as) sexual deviance—and sexual *access*—is greater within the elites. But comments about *bisexuales* do announce a growing lexicon that points to new understandings on some level that people *have* sexualities, that these sexualities are part of what makes someone who she or he is, and that alternative sexualities are viable, at least for some.

Among youth in Santo Domingo, the tensions of contradictory consciousness and practices with respect to sexuality are often evident. In addition to the most vocal members of the River Plate futbol team who give voice to homophobia, there are also youth in the *colonias populares* for whom homosexuals and bisexuals are not so much seen as a group apart as they are accepted as one group among many within the culturally accepted boundaries of sexuality. Among some working class youth, sexual experimentation among youth of the same sex is considered positive and a rite of passage.[12] This makes it all the more impossible and erroneous to neatly categorize youth, as individuals or groups, as even heterosexual, homosexual, or bisexual. After all, it is precisely from such labels that these youth are attempting to escape—even as they articulate and manipulate such markers.

Sexualities in Colonia Santo Domingo are thus thoroughly implicated in constructions of gender identities, yet they also operate to a real degree on their own trajectories.[13] That is, sexuality is considered by many in the *colonia* as a discrete category that is never simply subsumed by considerations of masculinity and/or femininity, and indeed plays as much of a role in the constitution of gender categories as gender plays in forming ways of thinking about and acting on transformations of sexuality.

SEXING THE MEXICAN NATION

The consolidation of the Mexican nation, ideologically and materially, was fostered early on not only in the gun battles on the wild frontier, not only in the voting rituals of presidential politics, but also in the imagining and inventing of *mexicanidad* in the national cinema, whose Golden Age began in the late 1930s. Although there were female leads in the movies of the period, on the silver screen it was the manly actors who most came to embody the restless and explosive potential of the emerging Mexican nation. And of all the male movie stars of this era, one stood out as "a macho among machos." Ever the handsome and pistol-packing *charro* (singing cowboy) with his melodious and eminently male tenor, Jorge Negrete came to epitomize the swaggering Mexican nation, singing,

> I am a Mexican, and this wild land is mine.
> On the word of a macho, there's no land lovelier and
>   wilder of its kind.
> I am a Mexican, and of this I am proud.

> I was born scorning life and death,
> And though I have bragged, I have never been cowed.[14]

In the rural cantinas, the manly temples of the golden age of Mexican cinema, the macho mood was forged. Mexico appeared on screen as a single entity, however internally incongruent, while within the nation the figures of Mexican Man and Mexican Woman loomed large—the former

> untamed, generous, cruel, womanizing, romantic, obscene, at one with family and friends, subjugated and restless . . . [the latter] obedient, seductive, resigned, obliging, devoted to her own and slave to her husband, to her lover, to her children, and to her essential failure. (Monsiváis 1992: 18)

The distinctions between being a macho and being a man were coming into clearer focus in the Mexican cinema of the 1940s:

> To be macho is now part of the scenery. To be macho is an attitude. There are gestures, movements. It is the belief that genital potency holds the key to the universe, all that. It goes from the notion of danger to the notion of bragging; that's the difference between macho and man [*hombre*]. As the song says, "If you've got to kill me tomorrow, why don't you get it over with now?"—that is being very manly [*ser muy hombre*]. "I have four wives"—that is being very macho [*ser muy macho*]. (Carlos Monsiváis, interview by author, 20 February 1993)

Then, at the end of the 1940s, Mexican machismo underwent a most refined dissection by Octavio Paz in *El laberinto de la soledad* (1950). Despite Paz's wish to speak only to a small group "made up of those who are conscious of themselves, for one reason or another, as Mexicans" (Paz 1961: 11), this work more than any other has come to represent the authoritative view of essential Mexican attributes like machismo, loneliness, and mother worship. Therefore when Paz writes, "The Mexican is always remote, from the world and from other people. And also from himself" (p. 29), he should not be taken literally but literarily. It is a beautifully written book, and part of the reason for its elegance may be that Paz was creating qualities of *mexicanidad* as much as he was reflecting on them. As he put it in his "Return to the Labyrinth of Solitude," "the book is part of the attempt of literally marginal countries to regain consciousness: to become subjects again" (Paz 1985: 330).

Paz (1961: 35) writes with regard to men and women in Mexico, "In a world made in man's image, woman is only a reflection of masculine will and desire." In Mexico, "woman is always vulnerable. Her social situation—as the repository of honor, in the Spanish sense—and the misfortune of her 'open' anatomy expose her to all kinds of dangers" (p. 38). Biology as destiny? But there is nothing inherently passive, or private, about vaginas in Mexico or anywhere else. Continuing with Paz, just as "the essential attribute of the *macho*"—or what the macho seeks to display, anyway—is power, so too with "the Mexican people." Thus *mexicanidad*, Paz tells us, is concentrated in the macho forms of "caciques, feudal lords, hacienda owners, politicians, generals, captains of industry" (p. 82).

Many Mexican men are curious about what it means to be a Mexican, and what it means to be a man. One is not born knowing these things; nor are they truly discovered. They are learned and relearned. For some, this involves a quest for one's patrimony. "Pedro Páramo is my father too," declares one of Mexico's bastard sons (Rulfo 1959: 3). Even if he is an infamous brute, a father is a father. For the Mexican macho and for the nation, it is better to have a father than to be fatherless.

In Paz and much of the literature of cultural nationalism in Mexico in recent decades, "the problem of national identity was thus presented primarily as a problem of *male* identity, and it was male authors who debated its defects and psychoanalyzed the nation" (Franco 1989: 131). In Mexico, nationalist identity and practices have long enjoyed an intimate history with masculinity. At least in the formal pronouncements about *mexicanidad*, however, it is only by implication that women have shared the same history. Building the sense and the material reality of the Mexican nation has required virtues like potency (in the sense of powerfulness, sexual and otherwise), a quality that in the Mexican national canon has generally been made a (male) gendered trait.

The correlation between manliness and potency has never been without its contradictions for ordinary people in Mexico, and authoritative statements about "being *mexicano*" have rather exclusively referred to politically and sexually potent *men*. But not only the elites speak to these issues, as seen in pragmatic and romantic nationalist statements from below (see Mallon 1995). For, nationalist discourse aside, in the daily lives of millions of women and men in rural and urban Mexico, powerful wives are not simply considered mere extensions of their husbands.

SEXUAL CONTRADICTIONS

The multiple expressions of male sexual identities in Mexico today contradict all stereotyped notions of a uniform Spanish-speaking masculinity that crosses class, ethnic group, region, sexuality, and age. As di Leonardo (1991: 30f.) shows in her discussion of the "embedded nature of gender," not only is it a mistake to study men or women in isolation, but also the category of gender itself must be examined in its interconnectedness with other major social divisions. There is not a Mexican cultural system of generally agreed-upon gender meanings and experience. Not only is there tremendous diversity with regard to gender in *colonias populares* in Mexico City, but also gender identities in Colonia Santo Domingo, as elsewhere, are products and manifestations of cultures in motion; they do not emanate from some primordial essence whose resilience bears testament to perpetual forms of inequality.

Given this analysis, it is all the more important to critique the segregated approach still prevalent in women's and men's studies. As we have seen in the case of the *casa chica* in Mexico City, such an approach is wholly unsatisfactory because it would conceal the meanings created by women and men *together*, and their joint practices aimed at circumventing pre-existing religious and civil statutes regarding marriage, divorce, and sexual fidelity. The reticence of some anthropologists who study men and masculinity to participate more openly in feminist debates often seems related to a particular methodology that *excludes* women as irrelevant to questions about male identities and activities.

Yet only by studying men *and* women, and by rejecting the false simplicity of a structuralist binary opposition man-woman, will it be possible to grasp that consciousness about and participation in sexual relations between men in Mexico's *colonias populares*, for instance, does not simply entail greater acceptance of a "third" sex and a "third" gender. What is needed instead is a thorough rejection of fixed and immutable categories of gender and sexuality, both for groups and for individuals in Mexico.

We can similarly either accept that there are multiple and shifting meanings and practices of male sexuality in Mexico, or we can essentialize what were already reified generalizations about Mexican men in the first place. Like any identity, male sexual identities in Mexico City do not reveal anything intrinsic about men there. The contradictory consciousness of many men in Colonia Santo Domingo about their own sexual identities, their sense of and experience with sex, is part of the reigning chaos of their lives at least as much as the imagined national coherence imposed from without.

Further, to paraphrase Mosse's (1985: 67) remark about modern Europe, nationalism in Mexico has had a special affinity for male society, and it has thereby helped to legitimize the dominance of men over women. As odd as women's exclusion from nationalist history may seem, it is all the more bizarre in the case of the history of sexuality. Nonetheless, in this century it was only following the emergence of grass-roots feminism and movements for gay and lesbian rights in Mexico that cliched truths about sexuality came to be broadly questioned, in the process erod-ing many stolid presumptions about Mexican and Mexican male potency.

Sex in Mexico is changing in important if uncalculated ways, as throughout this Catholic land divorce restrictions remain in place, though they are routinely and creatively dodged by some through *la casa chica*. Homophobia is a code of boyish insults, while sexual experimentation by young men with young men and young women with young women is increasingly seen as legit-imate. The sexual contradictions of a generation have effectively transformed very little and quite a lot.

NOTES

1. My thanks to Stanley Brandes, Teresita de Barbieri, Micaela di Leonardo, Mary Goldsmith, Michael Herzfeld, Louise Lamphere, Roger Lancaster, Margarita Melville, Carlos Monsiváis, Eduardo Nivón, and Nancy Scheper-Hughes for their comments on earlier drafts and/or many of the ideas that have developed into this essay. Fieldwork was conducted 1992–93, with grants from Fulbright-Hays DDRA, Wenner-Gren, National Science Foundation, Institute for Intercultural Studies, UC MEXUS, and the Center for Latin American Studies and Department of Anthropology at UC Berkeley; and 1993–95, under a grant from the National Institute of Mental Health. My gratitude as well to the Centro de Estudios Sociológicos and the Programa Interdisciplinario de Estudios de la Mujer, both at El Colegio de México, and to the Departamento de Antropología, Universidad Autónoma Metropolitana-Iztapalapa, for providing institutional support during fieldwork in Mex-ico City. Final revisions on this chapter were made while I was a Visiting Fellow at the Center for U.S.-Mexican Studies in San Diego.

2. This stereotype has been developed and/or critiqued in the following: Paz (1961); Ramos (1962); Mendoza (1963); Paredes (1971); Stevens (1973); Monsiváis (1981); de Barbieri (1990); Gilmore (1990); Lancaster (1992); Ramírez (1993); Limón (1994); Gutmann (1996).

3. I draw here on Giddens's (1992) insights regarding sexuality, love, and eroticism in modern societies. The term "homosexuality" is used guardedly in this paper to refer to sex between men and between women. In Mexico City, however, unlike the United States, people usually mean by homosexual only the man who is penetrated by another (not necessarily "homosexual") man in anal intercourse. For more on these terms and activities, and certain similarities with regard to sex between men in different parts of Latin America and among Chicanos, see Lancaster (1992) and Al-maguer (1990).

4. Recent anthropological works that either focus or contain significant sections on masculinity include: Brandes (1980); Herdt (1981); Gregor (1985); Herzfeld (1985); Godelier (1986); Gilmore (1990); Parker (1991); Fachel Leal (1992); Lancaster (1992); Welzer-Lang and Filiod (1992); Limón (1994); and Gutmann (1996).

5. For her discussion of "social constructionism," including with regard to gender, see di Leonardo (1991); see also Scott (1988: 2) on defining gender and sexuality.

6. For a recent mention of the practice, though not the name, of the *casa chica*, see Bossen (1988: 272) on middle-class households in Guatemala City. For Mexico, see also Diaz (1970: 60) and Fromm and Maccoby (1970: 149).

7. At the same time, none of my analysis regarding serial monogamy minimizes the traumatic financial and emotional impact of men who do desert their wives and children, regardless of whether these men take up with other women. Given my interests in fathers and fathering, I was in contact with more men who lived with their families, even if they were not necessarily active in parenting, than I was with those who had abandoned their wives and children. Single mothers were nonetheless common enough in the colonia.

8. In this paper I do not analyze the significant differences and inequalities between women and men regarding the utilization of birth control devices in the working class in Mexico City. For a discus-sion of this matter, see Gutmann (1996) chapter 5.

9. On "desire," see Lancaster's (1992: 270) emphasis on materialist contextualization and analysis.

10. The gay and lesbian rights movement in the United States may also have indirectly played a political role in Mexico. Although there have been comparative studies of homosexuality among Mexicans in Mexico and among Mexicans in the United States (see, for example, Magaña and Carrier [1991]), as far as I know there has been no research on the influence of the gay rights movement in the United States on Mexico, and of the movement in Mexico on the United States, via Mexican immigrants to the United States. For a treatment that at least raises relevant questions regarding the mutual influence of neighboring gay and Latino communities in San Francisco, see Castells (1983: 99–172).

11. Such public intermingling across sexual and other cultural boundaries is also evident in Ciudad Juárez and Tijuana, both on the Mexico-U.S. border.

12. This final observation is confirmed in recent research by Florinda Riquer (personal communication).

13. Which is one reason why anthropologists who study masculinity would do well to note Herdt's (1990: 434) assessment: "Generally . . . reductionism continues in studies of males, where there appears to be a compelling match between the cultural expectations ascribed to males, and the biological fact of their maleness."

14. *Yo soy mexicano, mi tierra es bravía.*
    Palabra de macho, que no hay otra tierra más linda
    *   y más brava que la tierra mía.*
    Yo soy mexicano, y orgullo lo tengo.
    Nací despreciando la vida y la muerte,
    Y si he hecho bravatas, también las sostengo.
    From the song "Yo soy mexicano."

BIBLIOGRAPHY

Almaguer, Tomás. 1991. "Chicano Men: A Cartography of Homosexual Identity and Behavior." *differences* 3(2): 75–100.

Bossen, Laurel. 1988. "Wives and Servants: Women in Middle-Class Households, Guatemala City." In *Urban Life: Readings in Urban Anthropology*, 2nd ed. George Gmelch and Walter P. Zenner, eds. Pp. 265–75. Prospect Heights: Waveland.

Brandes, Stanley H. 1980. *Metaphors of Masculinity: Sex and Status in Andalusian Folklore*. Philadelphia: University of Pennsylvania Press.

Castells, Manuel. 1983. *The City and the Grassroots: A Cross-Cultural Theory of Urban Social Movements*. Berkeley: University of California Press.

Davis, Natalie. 1983. *The Return of Martin Guerre*. Cambridge: Harvard University Press.

de Barbieri, Teresita. 1990. "Sobre géneros, prácticas y valores: Notas acerca de posibles erosiones del machismo en México." In *Normas y prácticas: Morales y cívicas en la vida cotidiana*. Juan Manuel Ramírez Sáiz, ed. Pp. 83–105. Mexico City: Porrúa / Universidad Nacional Autónoma de México.

Diaz, May N. 1970. *Tonalá: Conservatism, Responsibility, and Authority in a Mexican Town*. Berkeley: University of California Press.

di Leonardo, Micaela. 1991. "Gender, Culture, and Political Economy: Feminist Anthropology in Historical Perspective." In *Gender at the Crossroads of Knowledge: Feminist Anthropology in the Postmodern Era*. Micaela di Leonardo, ed. Pp. 1–48. Berkeley: University of California Press.

Fachel Leal, Ondina, ed. 1992. *Cultura e identidade masculina*. Cadernos de Antropologia, no. 7. Porto Alegre, Brazil: Universidade Federal do Rio Grande do Sul.

Franco, Jean. 1989. *Plotting Women: Gender and Representation in Mexico*. New York: Columbia University Press.

Fromm, Erich, and Michael Maccoby. 1970. *Social Character in a Mexican Village: A Sociopsychoanalytic Study*. Englewood Cliffs, NJ: Prentice-Hall.

Giddens, Anthony. 1992. *The Transformation of Intimacy: Sexuality, Love and Eroticism in Modern Societies*.

Stanford, CA: Stanford University Press.

Gilmore, David. 1990. *Manhood in the Making: Cultural Concepts of Masculinity.* New Haven: Yale University Press.

Godelier, Maurice. 1986. *The Making of Great Men: Male Domination and Power among the New Guinea Baruya.* Cambridge: Cambridge University Press.

Gramsci, Antonio. 1929–35 (1971). *Selections from the Prison Notebooks.* New York: International.

Gregor, Thomas. 1985. *Anxious Pleasures: The Sexual Lives of an Amazonian People.* Chicago: University of Chicago Press.

Gutmann, Matthew C. 1996. *The Meanings of Macho: Being a Man in Mexico City.* Berkeley: University of California Press.

Herdt, Gilbert. 1981. *Guardians of the Flutes: Idioms of Masculinity.* New York: McGraw-Hill.

———. 1990. "Mistaken Gender: 5-Alpha Reductase Hermaphroditism and Biological Reductionism in Sexual Identity Reconsidered." *American Anthropologist* 90(2): 433–46.

Herzfeld, Michael. 1985. *The Poetics of Manhood: Contest and Identity in a Cretan Mountain Village.* Princeton: Princeton University Press.

———. 1987. *Anthropology Through the Looking-Glass: Critical Ethnography in the Margins of Europe.* Cambridge: Cambridge University Press.

Lancaster, Roger N. 1992. *Life Is Hard: Machismo, Danger, and the Intimacy of Power in Nicaragua.* Berkeley: University of California Press.

Lewis, Oscar. 1961. *The Children of Sánchez: Autobiography of a Mexican Family.* New York: Vintage.

Limón, José. 1994. *Dancing with the Devil: Society and Cultural Poetics in Mexican-American South Texas.* Madison: University of Wisconsin Press.

Magaña, J. R., and J. M. Carrier. 1991. "Mexican and Mexican American Male Sexual Behavior and Spread of AIDS in California." *Journal of Sex Research* 28(3): 425–41.

Mallon, Florencia. 1995. *Peasant and Nation: The Making of Postcolonial Mexico and Peru.* Berkeley: University of California Press.

Mendoza, Vicente T. 1963. "El machismo en México." *Cuadernos del Instituto Nacional de Investigaciones Folklóricas* (Buenos Aires) 3:75–86.

Monsiváis, Carlos. 1981. *Escenas de pudor y liviandad.* Mexico City: Grijalbo.

———. 1992. "Las mitologías del cine mexicano." *Intermedios* 2: 12–23.

Mosse, George L. 1985. *Nationalism and Sexuality: Middle-Class Morality and Sexual Norms in Europe.* Madison: University of Wisconsin Press.

Paredes, Américo. 1971. "The United States, Mexico, and Machismo." Marcy Steen, trans. *Journal of the Folklore Institute* 8(1): 17–37.

Parker, Richard. 1991. *Bodies, Pleasures, and Passions: Sexual Culture in Contemporary Brazil.* Boston: Beacon.

Paz, Octavio. 1950. *El laberinto de la soledad.* Mexico City: Fondo de Cultura Económica.

———. 1961. *The Labyrinth of Solitude: Life and Thought in Mexico.* Lysander Kemp, trans. New York: Grove.

———. 1985. "Return to the Labyrinth of Solitude." In *The Labyrinth of Solitude and Other Writings.* Yara Milos, trans. Pp. 327–53. New York: Grove.

Ramírez, Rafael L. 1993. *Dime capitán: Reflexiones sobre la masculinidad.* Río Piedras, Puerto Rico: Ediciones Huracán.

Ramos, Samuel. 1962. *Profile of Man and Culture in Mexico.* Peter G. Earle, trans. Austin: University of Texas Press.

Rulfo, Juan. 1959. *Pedro Páramo.* Lysander Kemp, trans. New York: Grove.

Scott, Joan W. 1988. *Gender and the Politics of History.* New York: Columbia University Press.

Stephen, Lynn. 1997. *Women and Social Movements in Latin America: Power from Below.* Austin: University of Texas Press. In press.

Stevens, Evelyn. 1973. "*Marianismo:* The Other Face of *Machismo* in Latin America." In *Male and Female in Latin America*. Ann Pescatello, ed. Pp. 89–101. Pittsburgh: University of Pittsburgh Press.

Welzer-Lang, Daniel, and Marie-France Pichevin, eds. 1992. *Des Hommes et du Masculin*. Centre de Recherches et d'Etudes Anthropologiques. Lyons: Presses Universitaires.

Zavala de Cosío, María Eugenia. 1992 *Cambio de fecundidad en México y políticas de población*. Jorge Ferreiro, trans. Mexico City: El Colegio de México.

Making Marks
and Drawing Boundaries

Corporeal Practices

Part Four

BODIES OF KNOWLEDGE
AND THE POLITICS
OF REPRESENTATION

14 Secrets of God, Nature, and Life

Evelyn Fox Keller

INTRODUCTION

One virtually infallible way to apprehend the thickness (or "viscosity") of language and culture is to take a key image employed by a culture in transition and attempt to track its shifting meanings, referents, and evocative force. This indeed was the task that Raymond Williams set himself in compiling his now famous *Keywords* (1983). Almost inevitably, one quickly finds (as Williams himself found) that an entire critical vocabulary is called forth, all of its terms shifting in concert. And as the individual meanings of these words shift and reorient themselves, their collective meaning, the world view the vocabulary (or "lexicon") represents, is transformed. Tracking such a collection of keywords can thus yield a temporal and cognitive map of a cultural transformation in process.

Take, for instance, the image of "secrets" as it was evoked in sixteenth- and seventeenth-century English discourses of nature, attending in particular to how that image changed over the course of the scientific evolution—how it changed in its usage, in its denotative or connotative force; in its referentiality and its consequentiality. Of these changes, one aspect alone might be said to provide an almost perfect marker of the origins of modern science. I am thinking, of course, of the rhetorical shift in the locus of essential secrets from God to Nature. Over time, the metaphorical import of this shift was momentous; above all, it came to signal a granting of permission to enquiring minds—permission that was a psychologically necessary precursor for the coming Enlightenment. Indeed, Kant's own answer to the question "What is Enlightenment?" was simply this: "*sapere aude*"—to dare to know.

Arcana Dei signaled forbidden knowledge, the hidden affairs or workings of God, "the secret[s] which god hath set Ayein a man mai nought be let" (OED: 357)—"hyd to alle men," or at best revealed to only a chosen few. To be allowed to share in God's secrets meant to be enclosed by the same protective veil. The knowledge acquired by those privileged few who *had* gained such

Evelyn Fox Keller received her Ph.D. in theoretical physics at Harvard University, worked for a number of years at the interface of physics and biology, and is now Professor of History and Philosophy of Science in the Program in Science, Technology, and Society at MIT. Her books include *A Feeling for the Organism: The Life and Work of Barbara McClintock*; *Reflections on Gender and Science*; and, most recently, *Refiguring Life: Metaphors of Twentieth Century Biology* (Columbia, 1995). Her current research is on the history of developmental biology.

access remained similarly (and properly) shrouded in secrecy. Once known, secrets did not become open knowledge in our sense of the term; rather, knowledge itself remained secret. Indeed, knowledge and secrets were at times almost interchangeable terms (see, for example, Eamon 1984).

But between the sixteenth and early eighteenth centuries, the term "secrets" entered a new register of meanings, graphically corresponding to the crucial shift in reference from *Dei* to *naturae*—a shift that deprived them of their privileged and protected status. At one end of this new range of meanings, "secrets" came to be understood as an enticement to discreet courtship (as Francis Bacon wrote, "Enough if, on our approaching her with due respect, she condescends to show herself" [quoted in Lloyd 1984: 15]); and the other end, as a provocation demanding penetration, violation, "putting nature on the rack" and "storming her stronghold and castles" (also Bacon [cf. Keller 1985: 123]). To the new seekers of truth, the act of knowing became one of disclosure rather than enclosure. If the idea of *Arcana Dei* invited privileged entrance into a veiled inner sanctum, the expression "secrets of nature" came to be heard as an invitation to dissolving, or to ripping open, the veil of secrecy.

However, in order for the passage of sects from God to Nature to have such import for the pursuit (and with it, for the definition) of knowledge, many other terms had to shift in concert. Perhaps especially, the terms God and Nature had themselves to undergo subtle transformation as they came to mark a different—simultaneously more distant and more authoritarian—relation between God and the natural world. Once alive and intelligent, participating in (even having) soul, by the beginning of the eighteenth century, Nature had given way to nature: devoid of both intelligence and life. As Carlo Ginzburg has written, "The secrets of Nature are no longer secrets; the intellectual boldness of scientists will put Nature's gifts at our feet" (1976: 41). He might have said as well that Nature, relieved of God's presence, had itself become transformed— newly available to inquiry precisely because it was newly defined as an object.

But still, between availability and compulsion is quite a long way, and in order to understand why the move from God to Nature lent to "secret" the sense not merely of accessibility but, in addition, of demanding penetration, something else is needed. In particular, it is necessary to add the terms "woman" and "life" to the shifting lexicon,[1] paying special note, as we do, to the rhetorical import of the role of gender in that discursive transformation.

WOMEN, LIFE, AND NATURE

Recent literature in feminist theory has called for a critical examination by historians and sociologists of science of the significance of the gender markings that have pervaded virtually all of the discourse of modern science, and that were especially prominent in early writings. In particular, a series of arguments have been put forth for the central role played by the metaphoric equation, first, between woman and nature, and collaterally, between man and mind, in the social construction of modern science, especially in the articulation of new criteria for certain knowledge and in the demarcation of scientific from other forms of knowledge (see, especially, Merchant 1981; Keller 1985; Hardin 1986). From this perspective, it would be tempting indeed to think of the passage of secrets from God to Nature in the sixteenth and seventeenth centuries as a simple retagging from male to female—as it were, a sex-change operation on the term "secrets." But such a view is itself a consequence of the reconfiguration that this passage signaled—a reconfiguration in which the meanings of male and female (as well as of God and Nature) were themselves both participants and products. In other words, along with the change of meaning for the terms God and Nature went a simultaneous change of meaning for the terms man and woman. The very construction, "secrets of nature," called forth a metaphoric convergence between women, life, and nature that bound these terms together in a new way and, in so doing, contributed to changes in all their meanings. What was new was not the metonymic use of women to stand for life, or even, by extension, as representation of nature; rather, the newness lay in the naming of the conjunction between women, life and nature as the locus (or refuge) of *secrets that did not belong to God*. It is in this move—in the wedge between Nature and God that was rhetorically inserted by such a shift in reference—that the language of secrets acquired its most radically new implication: not respect for the status of things as they are and must be, but first, permission, then, a challenge, and finally, a moral imperative for change.

Of course, it might be argued, since the affiliation between Woman, Nature, and Life had been established long before the period we are discussing, that it had always served to guarantee a latent antithesis between God and Nature, even before those terms had themselves become officially separate. Indeed, as Gillian Beer has observed, one effect of personifying nature as female is to promote just this separation, to distinguish nature from God (Beer, in Jordanova 1986: 233). But in fact, before naming nature as female could work to properly effect such a distinction, any residual trace of a divine image had itself to be more fully erased from the term "woman." The latent antithesis between God and Nature, or for that matter, between God and female, does not become fully manifest until a wedge has been inserted between both parts of the dyadic construct, woman/nature, and the divine. God cannot stand in antithetical relation to either nature or to woman until He is first made to stand apart; antithesis can only work to drive deeper a wedge that is already in place. However, once in place, the tension between male and female then can (and inescapably does) come to work on behalf of a process that ends in radical schism—finally, not only between God and Nature, God and woman, but also between male and female.

It is just this complex process of interlocking separations growing into demarcations that, I am suggesting, is marked, and facilitated, by the naming (or renaming) of "secrets" as belong to "Nature" rather than to "God." That renaming *could* come to signal the loss of His protection precisely because of the pre-existing tension between the terms. Yet it is only *with* such a renaming that the language of secrets could now be heard as an invitation to exposure, as a call to arms. The net effect of the demarcations that emerged from the new configurations—demarcations between God and Nature, between God and woman, and between woman and man—was to transform the implication of Nature's obscure interiority for enquiring men from an intimation of exclusion to a certainty; banishing forever any possibility of participation; making of that interiority a secret that, once no longer forbidden, must be exposed precisely because it cannot be shared.

It might be said that the cultural function of secrets is always to articulate a boundary—an interior not visible to outsiders, the demarcation of a separate domain, a sphere of autonomous power. Belonging to God, that sphere was inviolable. And as long as the power associated with women, nature, and life was seen as belonging to, or at least blessed by, God, it too was inviolable. The critical move in the transformation of these relations came in the disassociation of these powers from God, and accordingly, in the dissolution of the sanctions an earlier association had guaranteed. Unless severely checked, the power that had been and continued to be associated with women, nature, and life, once disassociated from God, automatically took on an autonomy that seemed both psychologically and conceptually intolerable. No longer a part of, it took on the guise of a challenge to the powers of God and man. A key development in this transformation— indeed, in the very disassociation of nature from God—was, of course, the change in conception of God contributed by Reformation theology, a change that radically emphasized the absoluteness of His sovereignty.

GOD AND NATURE

The connections between Reformation theology in seventeenth-century England and the scientific revolution, and the particular notion of "positive sanctions," first argued by Robert Merton in 1938, have, in the intervening fifty years, become familiar territory to historians of science. Gary Deason (1986) reminds us of one such link that is surely pertinent here. Though more than one hundred fifty years separated the architects of the scientific revolution from the beginnings of

Protestantism, many of their arguments bear a striking resemblance to those of Luther and Calvin before them. For Calvin, as for Luther, to assure God's "radical sovereignty" it was necessary to retrieve the world of animate and inanimate objects from the Aristotelians and Thomists, relieving these objects of their intrinsic activity and recasting as His "instruments." To godly men, "These are . . . nothing but instruments to which God continually imparts as much effectiveness as he wills, and according to his own purpose bends and turns them to either one action or another" (Calvin, quoted in Deason 1986: 176–77). In almost identical language, Robert Boyle argued against the Aristotelian view of a personified nature on the grounds that it "seems to detract from the honour of the great author and governor of the world" (Boyle 1744, 4: 361). To grant activity to nature is to detract from "the profound reverence we owe the divine majesty, since it seems to make the Creator differ too little by far from a created (not to mention an imaginary) Being" (Boyle 1744, 4: 366; in Deason 1986: 180). Moses, Boyle reminds us,

> has not a word of nature: and whereas philosophers presume, that she, by her plastic power and skill, forms plants and animals out of the universal matter, the divine historian ascribes the formation of them to God's immediate *fiat* . (1744, 4: 368)

In much the same spirit, Newton may have been even more deeply committed to the belief that homage to God required that matter be seen as brute, passive, in a word, pure inertia—capable only of resistance to force, and not of generating (or causing) it. That even gravity, the force that by his own account derives from "the quantity of solid matter which [articles] contain,"

> should be innate, inherent and essential to Matter . . . is to me so great an Absurdity, that I believe no Man who has in philosophical Matters a competent Faculty of thinking, can ever fall into it. (in Deason 1986: 183)

For Newton, all motion and all life derived from without, from "active Principles" associated not with material nature, but with God.

> And if it were not for these Principles, the Bodies of the Earth, Planets, Comets, Sun, and all things in them would grow cold and freeze, and become inactive Masses; and all Putrefaction Generation, Vegetation and Life would cease, and the Planets and Comets would not remain in their Orbs. (in Deason 1986: 184)

As Deason writes, "the radical sovereignty of God required the animation of nature to come from God alone and not from matter" (183).

Deason's point is well taken. But still missing from his analysis is the work done on and by the marks of gender in the language of God and nature. There are not two terms in the transformation to which Boyle and Newton contribute so importantly, but in fact three, each of which is itself at least dual. Rather than a simple renegotiation between God and nature, seventeenth-century rhetoric aimed at a renegotiation of the relation between sets of cultural entities that could at the time still be treated as relatively coherent dyads: God and father; nature and mother; man and brother. (The last dyad, man and brother, is generally tacit in these texts, appearing only obliquely, if at all.) To see the actual workings of this rhetoric, it is necessary to reread the same texts for the marks of gender. I choose one essay in particular, Boyle's *A Free Inquiry into the Vulgarly Received Notion of Nature*, to illustrate how only a slightly more attentive reading permits us to see much of the complexity of the linguistic and cultural reorientation that Boyle, here as elsewhere, actively sought to effect. Boyle himself was of course only one actor among many in this transformation, and the rhetorical structures of his writing were effective precisely to the extent that they spoke to the readers of his time. My primary purpose in singling out this particular essay, however, is as much to exemplify a method of reading as it is to make an example of a particular method of writing.

REREADING BOYLE

Boyle announces both his intention and his strategy in the title itself: one notion of nature, already devalued by the label "vulgar," is to be replaced by another, the result of "free inquiry." The term "free" is used by Boyle throughout his text interchangeably with "bold." His title thus announces the author as one who (anticipating Kant) "dares to know." The object of Boyle's inquiry is clear enough—it is "right ideas" of "nature herself." But before Boyle even identifies the "wrong" or "vulgar" ideas of nature from which he dissents (we learn only along the way that it is the picture of nature as active, potent, and intelligent), he sets out to examine the constraints that bond some men to "vulgar" notions—that is, those commonly (but mistakenly) held scruples that require a special freedom and daring to overcome.

Two such scruples are named in the very first section of his discourse. First is the compunction of filial obligation, raised only to be cast in immediate a priori doubt:

> It may seem an ingrateful and unfilial thing to dispute against nature, that is taken by mankind for the common parent of us all. But though it be an undutiful thing, to express a want of respect for an acknowledged parent, yet I know not, why it may not be allowable to question one, that a man looks upon but as a pretended one, . . . *whether she be so or no;* and until it appear to me, that she is so, I think it my duty to pay my gratitude, not to I know not what, but to that deity, whose wisdom and goodness . . . designed to make me a man. . . . (Boyle 1744, 4: 361) (my italics)

This first scruple, re-presented as a question, is immediately followed by two counterscruples of Boyle's own:

> I might add, that it not being half so evident to me, that what is called nature is my parent, as that all men are my brothers, by being the offspring of God . . . I may justly prefer the doing of them a service, by disabusing them, to the paying of her a ceremonial respect.

But even "setting allegories aside,"

> I have sometimes seriously doubted, whether the vulgar notion of nature has not been both injurious to the glory of God, and a great impediment to the soiled and useful discovery of his works. (Boyle 1744, 4: 361)

Thus Boyle begins his opening argument for transferring veneration from nature to God with a tacit reversal, invoking not paternal but maternal uncertainty, inserting doubt where there had heretofore been none. As in Boyle's other writings, skepticism is employed here as a "rhetorical tool"—invoked to "challenge the authority of a particular discursive tradition" (Golinski 1987: 59).[2] Doubt is, after all, the very stuff of "free inquiry"—so long, that is, as it is not debarred by faith. Assurance that *this* question at least is not so debarred is given promptly: "I know not," he writes, "why it may not be allowable to question . . . whether she be so or no." In other words, Boyle's first task is to create the space for a question, and this he accomplishes by invoking the authority of "free inquiry." But from where does that authority derive? From the very first moment of his text. The authority of "free inquiry" is rooted in the tacit opposition between "free" and "vulgar" that Boyle has inserted in his opening title.

Having thus authorized himself—and his readers—to replace what had commonly been taken to be a certainty by a question, the field is now open for new (or newly invoked) kinds of certification. For this, Boyle looks with one eye to the evidence of his own senses and, with the other, to biblical authority. Though philosophers may presume of nature "that she, by her plastic power and skill, forms plants and animals out of the universal matter," Boyle reminds us that the Bible tells us differently:

> God said, let the earth ring forth the living creature after its kind.... And God (without any mention of nature) made the beast of the earth after his kind. (Boyle 1744, 4: 368)

The particular difference Boyle wishes to note is underscored by both the subject of and the actual verb designating creation, and by the gender of the originary parent or model of living beings: From "she," with "her" plastic powers, the biblical quotation shifts, first, to "it," the earth, still retaining sufficient active power to enable it to "bring forth," and finally, to "Him," who "made" the beast of the earth (as it were) after "his" kind.

At the very least, the reader feels obliged to conclude that it is not "half so evident" that nature is not a true parent after all, and accordingly, that the scruple of filial respect does not apply. Instead, a counterscruple—wedding scientific doubt with religious certainty—ought prevail. Together, the logical doubt that will be revealed by a free inquiry, and the theological certainty that is by definition not open to question, combine to argue for a reorientation of affiliation. Fraternal duty (propelled by free inquiry) and paternal gratitude (guaranteed by faith) are made one: True veneration belongs only to Him who "makes me a man," who, "setting allegories aside," binds all men in a brotherhood dedicated to "the solid and useful discovery of his works."

The second scruple that Boyle attributes to common belief is closely related to the first: It follows from the view of nature as an agent, or "viceregent" of God, and hence as sacrosanct. The identification of this second scruple, a "scruple of conscience," is in fact preceded by just the sort of rhetorical polarization Deason describes:

> I think it more consonant to the respect we owe to divine providence, to conceive . . . God [as] a most free, as well as almost wise agent. . . . This, I say, I think to be a notion more respectful to divine providence, than to imagine, as we commonly do, that God has appointed an intelligent and powerful Being, called nature, to be as his viceregent, continually watchful for the good of the universe in general . . . . I am the more tender of admitting such a lieutenant to divine providence, as nature is fancied to be, because I shall hereafter give you some instances, in which it seems, that, if there were such a thing, she must be said to act too blindly and impotently, to discharge well the part she is to be trusted with. (Boyle 1744, 4: 362–63)

Nature is demoted from her position as viceregent, first, in the name of "the respect we owe to divine providence," and second, in the name of a promised (empirical) demonstration. Having thus disparaged the role of nature, any lingering "scruple of conscience" concerning the "removal of [her] boundaries" is automatically undetermined:

> To this I add, that the veneration, wherewith men are imbued for what they call nature, has been a discouraging impediment to the empire of man over the inferior creatures of God: for many have not only looked upon it, as an impossible thing to compass, but as something of impious to attempt, the removing of those boundaries, which nature seems to have put and settled among her productions: and whilst they look upon her as such a venerable thing, some make a kind of scruple of conscience to endeavor so to emulate any of her works, as to excel them. (Boyle 1744, 4: 363)

The offense committed in making "a Goddess" of nature, "as if it were a kind of Antichrist, that usurped a great share in the government of the world" (Boyle 1744, 4: 364), is an offense simultaneously against God and against man. Precisely because the two are kin, like father and son, to delimit the "empire of man" is tacitly to delimit the empire of God; it is for the glory of God that men must seek to "emulate" and "excel" the works of nature. Man himself is of course exempted—neither to be counted among those works that had been commonly through of as hers (but must now be recognized as God's), nor in fact as a part of nature. He stands beyond her boundaries. Not only is nature not a true parent after all—merely, as Boyle describes her later in the same text, "a great . . . pregnant automaton" (1744, 4: 373); but perhaps more to the point, her domain, though it encompasses all animal kind, does not include the sons of God:

> I shall here consider the world [that is, the "corporeal works of God"] but as the great system of things corporeal, as it once really was towards the close of the sixth day of the creation, when God had finished all his material works, but had not yet created man. (Boyle 1744, 4: 364)

Arriving only on the seventh day, man stands apart, and above—his proximity to God measured by his distance from nature, and proven by his ability to examine "the nature of the spring, that gets all [the parts of "the great automaton"] amoving" (Boyle 1744, 4: 358)—in short, by his capacity to "emulate" and "excel" the workings of her parts. The knowledge thus acquired provides not only (at least some) proof of men's proximity to God, but, as well, to each other. Its function is to cement the brotherhood of man under the fatherhood of God. So conceived, knowledge must be "freely and generously communicated" (Boyle 1655)—not secreted for either personal glory or personal gain.[3]

On the place of woman in this new cosmology, Boyle is virtually silent.[4] But though unspoken, she is doubly figured, and doubly dispossessed: once, explicitly, as the mother who is not, and again, implicitly, as the unnamed wife of the man who is. Truly a spokesman of his time, Boyle leaves her to oscillate ambiguously between deconstructed nature and reconstructed man. And indeed, there she will remain for almost the entire history of modern science, dislocated without a clearly viable relocation in view.

THE PROBLEM OF LIFE

At least part of the reason for the enduring uncertainty in the status of "woman," oscillating between nature and man, can be identified quite readily: It lies in the problem of life, a problem that can be described simultaneously in terms of the science of life and in terms of the language of life—but perhaps especially, as a problem evident in the life of the language of science.

There is indeed a sense in which the workings of language can be said to have a life of their own, yet more complex than the above (already rather convoluted) reading suggests. Especially, it might be said that the metaphor of "secrets of nature" has had a life of its own, with its own built-in mortality. Notice, for example, how, with the reorientation between God and Nature just described, the conjunction between Woman, Nature, and life that was itself so useful a rhetorical resource in the secularization of nature, is set on a course that ultimately works toward its own dissolution: Once Nature's secrets are penetrated, nature no longer holds that which had marked it with the personalizing "N," that is, as alive; "Nature" can no longer serve as a trope (or prosopopeia) for the world of living creatures. If the metaphoric passage of "secrets" marked a wedge between Nature and God that in turn licensed an all-out crusade on Nature's secrets, the very success of that crusade guaranteed the emergence of a new kind of wedge, now between nature and life. It is this new wedge that leads Richard Westfall (1972) to write in hindsight of the revolution that "banished life from the universe," and that, even before much had happened, had led Henry More to complain to Descartes of "the sharp and cruel blade [with] which in one blow, so to speak, [you] dared to despoil of life and sense practically the whole race of animals, metamorphosing them into marble statues and machines" (Easlea 1983: 23). The life of Man was of course not so despoiled; for Boyle, as for Descartes, man is set apart by his "rational soul" (1744,

4: 364), arriving on the scene only on the seventh day of creation. Indeed, in certain respects, the deanimation of nature seemed merely to enhance man's own sense of animation, an animation now, however, marked more by difference from than by kinship with the rest of the natural world.

Were it the case that the same wedge that had "banished life from the universe" had placed Woman squarely on the side of Man, equally (or similarly) severed from nature, the history of science might have looked quite different. As it was, however, the metaphoric structure of the entire discourse precluded such a turn. That structure propelled the tropic course of scientific language in a rather different direction, a direction that, for the short run at least, left the identification of women with nature ambiguously intact. On the one hand it was precisely the survival of the metaphoric link between woman and nature that facilitated the reflection of nature's deanimation, desanctification, and mechanization in the social domain; that is, that facilitated the parallel and contemporaneous taming (or "passification") of the image of Woman that has been noted by social historians.[5] On the other hand, it was precisely the survival of women's still mysterious relation to the production of life—especially, of the life that mattered most (that is, our own)—that sustained the identification of women with nature, and that simultaneously provided the irreducible ground of resistance to the final mechanization of nature. As long as the generation of life—human life/all life—remained beyond our grasp, both women and nature would retain some of their/its sense of residual potency.[6] Machines might be powerful, but they are not omnipotent; to imagine them capable of generation, as Descartes did, was to go beyond the bounds of credulity. Fontanelle (d. 1657) put it quite simply in his early retort to Descartes:

> Do you say that Beasts are Machines just as Watches are? Put a Dog Machine and a Bitch machine side by side, and eventually a third little Machine will be the result, whereas two Watches will lie side by side all their lives without ever producing a third Watch. (from Jacob 1973: 63)

In other words, as long as mechanism failed to provide a plausible solution to the mysteries of genesis and generation, a trace of divine blessing survived; one pocket of secrecy remained sacrosanct.

For a brief while, a radically different solution to the problem of generation enjoyed some popularity. In this solution, generation was attributed not to mechanical forces, but to divine creation. If, harking back to St. Augustine, living beings came into existence with the creation of the universe, the direct result of divine intervention, and nature (and woman) merely the vessel in which they grow, then the mysteries of genesis and generation are not properly nature's secrets, but God's.[7] In short time, however, this solution too came to be regarded by most scientific thinkers as lacking in credibility; it could accommodate neither the evidence of ordinary senses nor that of scientific investigations. By the beginning of the eighteenth century, it would have to be admitted that here, in the twin problems of genesis and generation, where the domains of women, life, nature, and God could not be clearly demarcated, a limit to man's "dare to know" stood firm.

CONCLUSION

For all the rhetorical persuasiveness and scientific acumen of Bacon, Descartes, Boyle, and Newton; long after Henry Oldenburg's invitation to suitors with "boldness and importunity," who could "penetrate into Nature's antechamber to her inner closet" (from Easlea 1983: 26); long after Halley had sung his praises of Newton's prowess in "penetrating . . . into the abstrusest secrets of Nature"; long even after Alexander Pope's dictum that, after Newton, "All was *Light*"; the most vital of nature's laws lay, still, "hid in Night." A full two centuries would follow in which the most "penetrating genius" of human culture would reveal many of the "most mysterious recesses of nature," and yet, even so, it would still have to be granted that the secrets of greatest importance to men remained as they'd begun, as Davenant had written in 1630, "lock'd" in Nature's "cabinet" (OED: 357). In the early nineteenth century, Sir Humphrey Davy complained that "the skirt only of the veil which conceals these mysterious and sublime processes has been lifted up" (quoted in Easlea 1983: 28). Across the channel, using almost identical language, Francois Magendie wrote: "Nature has not up to the present permitted man to raise the veil which hides from him the understanding of vital phenomena" (quoted in Mendelsohn 1965: 216). The same basic observation would be heard, again and again, in England, in France, and in Germany, until well into the second half of the nineteenth century.

As long as the problems of genesis and generation would remain recalcitrant, the ambiguity that continued to animate the metaphoric relation between women, nature, and life would also endure. Indeed, it could be said that it is these mysteries that constitute the very source of the ambiguity. In turn, however, that same ambiguity functioned as a force impinging on the status of "woman" in the larger cultural field, a force that was simultaneously generative and constraining. Above all, it permitted, and even required, an understanding of "woman" that could mediate, at one and the same time, between man and nature, and between animate and inanimate. One might say that it is just this ambiguity that is captured by the enduring trope "secrets of nature"— indeed, that maintains its entire metaphoric structure.

But there is also a dynamic at work within this language that is itself quintessentially dialectical. The survival of the ambiguous relation between women, life, and nature rests on the endurance of an inaccessible domain—on a domain of difference that maintains the life of the metaphor, "secrets of nature." At the same time, however, the tropic structure of this metaphor itself constitutes a relentless pressure aimed at its dissolution. Once resolved, once the secrets of genesis and generation are completely revealed, once nature has become truly lifeless, so too, in that moment, the metaphor of "secrets of nature" will also have died. And because the life of language is always *in* culture, it should come as no surprise that many of the social norms that had served all along to nourish and animate it will also have died.[8]

Perhaps the only surprise is how very long this process would take to work itself out. We might marvel at the longevity of the language that has continued to animate the scientific project even as both that project, and that language, worked to deanimate the source that provided them with their vital energies.

In retrospect, we might say that those who had "dared to know" had lacked the means to know; that Davy's (or Magendie's) remarks reflected the inadequacy of the instruments (both conceptual and technological) available to seventeenth- and eighteenth-century mechanists for fully penetrating N/nature's ultimate secret, that the force of nature's resistance was too great. But in actuality, these remarks also reflected a human (or cultural) resistance that worked alongside natural resistance to keep this boldest of all crusades beyond the reach of Newton's gaze.

In the late eighteenth and early nineteenth centuries, this human resistance manifested itself in the demarcation of a separate domain of nature or living beings, and with it, a separate domain of science. And for a while at least, the demarcation of "life," and the parallel demarcation of "biology," served to provide living beings with something of a refuge from the incursions of seventeenth- and eighteenth-century mechanism. Eventually, of course, mechanism did prevail. But before this final conquest, indeed, before the "Secret of life" could even be named as a fitting quest for natural science, life itself would first have to be relieved of the residual sense of sublimity that had, despite all the efforts to the mechanical philosophers, continued to attach to the nature of animal and plant forms. Secrets would have to make a final passage, from nature to life—a passage that both marked an facilitated the transformation of twentieth-century science and culture, much as the earlier passage, from God to nature, had marked and facilitated the transformations of that period; a passage that was necessary if the ordinary people that scientists are were to condone the rhetoric and the technology required for the dissolution of this last stronghold. When that happened, a new religion would be resurrected: a God neither of "man" nor "woman," but of atoms and molecules. For the one religious reference that Francis Crick is willing to embrace, he quotes Salvador Dalí:

> And now the announcement of Watson and Crick about DNA. This is for me the real proof of the existence of God. (Crick 1966: 1)

NOTES

I am indebted to the National Endowment for the Humanities for supporting the work for this essay during my stay at the Institute for Advanced Study in 1987–88.

1. It is T. S. Kuhn who has introduced the term "lexicon" into the history and philosophy of science to denote a "structured vocabulary" of scientific terms (see, for example, Kuhn 1989). My own use of the term, although indebted to Kuhn, is conspicuously looser: Because my "structured vocabulary" influences terms denoting social as well as scientific categories, it will be considerably more difficult to delimit than Kuhn's.

2. Golinski's very interesting analysis of Boyle's use of skepticism as a rhetorical strategy focuses especially on its use in the *Skeptical Chymist* to "challenge the authority of the prevalent ode of chemical discourse, and to initiate a restructured discourse" (Golinski 1987: 61).

3. See Golinski (1987: 66) for some interesting remarks about the boundaries of class implicit in Boyle's arguments against "the retention of 'secrets and receipts' for commercial gain."

4. Elizabeth Potter makes an interesting argument showing that the absence of women in Boyle's discourse and cosmology is neither neutral nor idle, but rather that it actively works to frame man as *the* scientific presence (see Potter 1989).

5. The significance of this transformation for shifting social norms of gender (that is, for actual men and women) is not an explicit subject of this paper, but it is an obviously related question of fundamental importance. A brief discussion, as well as some references to the literature on this subject, can be found in Keller (1985) (cf. especially chapter 3).

6. As well, it might be added, as sexual agency. Consider, for example, that it was only toward the end of the eighteenth century that "medical science and those who relied upon it cease[d] to regard the female orgasm as relevant to generation" (Laqueur 1986: 1).

7. Although, to my knowledge, Boyle himself was not an explicit advocate of such preformationist (or pre-existence) theories, and even seems to have vacillated both on the question of preexistence and on the adequacy of purely mechanical accounts of generation (see, for example, Pyle 1987), I think it can be argued that his argument in "A Free Inquiry . . ." did help to set the stage for the preformationist arguments that followed. (For further discussion of seventeenth-century preformationism, see Bowler, 1971; Roger 1971; Gasking 1967.)

8. The change in the language of science of the second half of the twentieth century, and the parallel changes in the social norms that we witness around us, are of course a subject of their own. Some of the interactions between scientific language, technology, and social norms characteristic of our own time will be elaborated in a later essay; here I wish only to call attention to the existence of such interactions.

15 Orgasm, Generation, and the Politics of Reproductive Biology

Thomas Laqueur

Sometime in the late eighteenth century human sexual nature changed, to paraphrase Virginia Woolf. This essay gives an account of the radical eighteenth-century reconstitution of female, and more generally human, sexuality in relation to the equally radical Enlightenment political reconstitution of "Man"—the universalistic claim, stated with starkest clarity by Condorcet, that the "rights of men result simply from the fact that they are sentient beings, capable of acquiring moral ideas and of reasoning concerning these ideas. [And that] women, having these same qualities, must necessarily possess equal rights."[1]

Condorcet moves immediately to biology and specifically to reproductive biology to justify his position. Exposure to pregnancy, he says is no more relevant to women's political rights than is male susceptibility to gout. But of course the facts or supposed facts of female physiology were central to Condorcet, to Mill, to feminists as well as antifeminists, to liberalism in its various forms and also to its enemies. The body generally, but especially the female body in its reproductive capacity and in distinction from that of the male, came to occupy a critical place in a whole range of political discourses. It is this connection between politics and a new disposition of male and female that concerns me here.[2]

Near the end of the century of Enlightenment, medical science and those who relied upon it ceased to regard the female orgasm as relevant to generation. Conception, it was held, could take place secretly, with no tell-tale shivers or signs of arousal. We no longer linked the loci of pleasure with the mysterious infusing of life into matter. Routine accounts, like that in a popular Renaissance midwifery text of the clitoris as that organ "which makes women lustful and take delight in copulation," without which they "would have no desire, nor delight, nor would they ever conceive," came to be regarded as controversial if not manifestly stupid.[3] Sexual orgasm moved to the periphery of human physiology. Previously a deeply embedded sign of the generative process,

Thomas Laqueur is Professor of History at the University of California, Berkeley. He is the author, most recently, of *Making Sex: Body and Gender from the Greeks to Freud* (Harvard, 1990), a book which expands on the themes raised in the present essay. He is currently completing a book on the meanings of death in the eighteenth and nineteenth centuries, and is engaged in two new projects: a study of names, lists, and memory from the American Civil War to the present; and a study of autoeroticism and economies of desire, 1712–1995.

orgasm became simply a feeling, albeit an enormously charged one, whose existence was a matter for empirical inquiry or armchair philosophizing.

The new conceptualization of the female orgasm, however, was but one formulation of a more radical eighteenth-century reinterpretation of the female body in relation to that of the male. For several thousand years it had been a commonplace that women have the same genitals as men, except that, as Nemesius, bishop of Emesa in the sixth century, put it: "Theirs are inside the body and not outside it." Galen, who in the second century A.D. developed the most powerful and resilient model of the homologous nature of male and female reproductive organs, could already cite the anatomist Herophilus (third century B.C.) in support of his claim that a woman has testes with accompanying seminal ducts very much like the man's, one on each side of the uterus, the only difference being that the male's are contained in the scrotum and the female's are not.[4]

For two millennia the organ that by the early nineteenth century had become virtually a synecdoche for woman had no name of its own. Galen refers to it by the same word he uses for the male testes, *orchis*, permitting context to make clear with which sex he is concerned. As late as 1819, the *London Medical Dictionary* is still somewhat muddled in its nomenclature: "Ovaria: formerly called female testicles; but now supposed to be the receptacles of ova or the female seed." Indeed, doggerel verse of the nineteenth century still sings of these hoary homologies after they have disappeared from learned texts:

> . . . though they of different sexes be,
> Yet on the whole they are the same as we,
> For those that have the strictest searchers been,
> Find women are but men turned outside in.

By 1800 this view, like that linking orgasm to conception, had come under devastating attack. Writers of all sorts were determined to base what they insisted were fundamental differences between male and female sexuality, and thus between man and woman, on discoverable biological distinctions. In 1803, for example, Jacques Moreau de la Sarthe, one of the founders of "moral anthropology," argued passionately against the nonsense written by Aristotle, Galen, and their modern followers on the subject of women in relation to men.[5] Not only are the sexes different, they also are different in every conceivable respect of body and soul, in every physical and moral aspect. To the physician or the naturalist, the relation of woman to man is "a series of oppositions and contrasts." Thus the old model, in which men and women were arrayed according to their degree of metaphysical perfection, their vital heat, along an axis whose telos was male, gave way by the late eighteenth century to a new model of difference, of biological divergence. An anatomy and physiology of incommensurability replaced a metaphysics of hierarchy in the representation of women in relation to men.[6]

But neither the demotion of female orgasm nor the biology of incommensurability of which it was a part follow simply from scientific advances. True, by the 1840s it had become clear that, at least in dogs, ovulation could occur without coition and thus presumably without orgasm. And it was immediately postulated that the human female, like the canine bitch, was a "spontaneous ovulator," producing an egg during the periodic heat that in women was known as the menses. But the available evidence for this half-truth was at best slight and highly ambiguous. Ovulation, as one of the pioneer twentieth-century investigators in reproductive biology put it, "is silent and occult: neither self-observation by women nor medical study through all the centuries prior to our own era taught mankind to recognize it." Indeed, until the 1930s standard medical advice books recommended that to *avoid* conception women should have intercourse during the middle of their menstrual cycles—i.e., during days twelve through sixteen, now known as the period of *maximum* fertility. Until the 1930s even the outlines of our modern understanding of the hormonal control of ovulation were unknown. Thus, while scientific advances might in principle have caused a change in the understanding of the female orgasm, in fact, the reevaluation of pleasure occurred a century and a half before reproductive physiology came to its support.[7]

The shift in the interpretation of the male and female bodies, however, cannot have been due, even in principle, primarily to scientific progress. In the first place, the "oppositions and contrasts" between the female and the male have been self-evident since the beginning of time: the one gives birth and the other does not, to state the obvious. Set against such momentous truths, the discovery, for example, that the ovarian artery is not, as Galen would have it, the homologue of the vas deferens is of relatively minor significance. Thus, the fact that at one time male and female bodies were regarded as hierarchically, that is vertically, ordered and that at another time they came to be regarded as horizontally ordered, as opposites, as incommensurable, must depend on something other than one or even a set of real or supposed "discoveries."

In addition, nineteenth-century advances in developmental anatomy (germ-layer theory) pointed to the common origins of both sexes in a morphologically androgenous embryo and thus not to their intrinsic difference. Indeed, the Galenic homologies were by the 1850s reproduced at the embryological level: the penis and the clitoris, the labia and the scrotum, the ovary and the testes shared common origins in fetal life. Finally, and most tellingly, no one was very interested in looking at the anatomical and concrete physiological differences between the sexes until such differences became politically important. It was not, for example, until 1797 that anyone bothered to reproduce a detailed female skeleton in an anatomy book so as to illustrate its difference from the male. Up to this time there had been one basic structure for the human body, of the male.[8]

Instead of being the consequence of increased scientific knowledge, new ways of interpreting the body were rather, I suggest, new ways of representing and indeed of constituting social realities. As Mary Douglas wrote, "The human body is always treated as an image of society and . . . there can be no natural way of considering the body that does not involve at the same time a social dimension." Serious talk about sexuality is inevitably about society. Ancient accounts of reproductive biology, still persuasive in the early eighteenth century, linked the experiential qualities of sexual delight to the social and indeed the cosmic order. Biology and human sexual experience mirrored the metaphysical reality on which, it was thought, the social order too rested. The new biology, with its search for fundamental differences between the sexes and its tortured questioning of the very existence of women's sexual pleasure, emerged at precisely the time when the foundations of the old social order were irremediably shaken, when the basis for a new order of sex and gender became a critical issue of political theory and practice.[9]

THE ANATOMY AND PHYSIOLOGY OF HIERARCHY

The existence of female sexual pleasure, indeed the necessity of pleasure for the successful reproduction of humankind, was an unquestioned commonplace well before the elaboration of ancient doctrines in the writings of Galen, Soranus, and the Hippocratic school. Poor Tiresias was blinded by Juno for agreeing with Jove that women enjoyed sex *more* than men. The gods, we are told in the *Timaeus*, "contrived the love of sexual intercourse by constructing an animate creature of one kind in us men, and another in women"; only when the desire and love of the two sexes unite them are these creatures calmed. Galen's learned texts, *On the Seed* and the sections on the reproductive organs in *On the Usefulness of the Parts of the Body*, are intended not to query but rather to explain the obvious: "why a very great pleasure is coupled with the exercise of the generative parts and a raging desire precedes their use."[10]

Heat is of critical importance in the Galenic account. It is, to begin with, the sign of perfection, of one's place in the hierarchical "great chain of being." Humans are the most perfect of animals, and men are more perfect than women by reason of their "excess of heat." Men and women are, in this model, not different in kind but in the configuration of their organs; the male is a hotter version of the female, or to use the teleologically more appropriate order, the female is the cooler, less perfect version of the male.[11]

Understanding the machinery of sex thus becomes essentially an exercise in topology: "Turn outward the woman's, turn inward, so to speak, and fold double the man's, and you will find the same in both in every respect." Galen invites his readers to practice mentally the admittedly difficult inversions.

> Think first please, of the man's [external genitalia] turned in and extending inward between the rectum and the bladder. If this should happen, the scrotum would necessarily take the place of the uterus with the testes lying outside, next to it on either side.

The penis in this exercise becomes the cervix and vagina; the prepuce becomes the female pudenda and so forth, continuing on through the various ducts and blood vessels. Or, he suggests, try it backwards:

> Think too, please, of the converse, the uterus turned outward and projecting. Would not the testes [ovaries] then necessarily be inside it? Would it not contain them like a scrotum? Would not the neck [the cervix], hitherto concealed inside the perineum but now pendant, be made into the male member?[12]

If the female is a replica of the male, with the same organs inside rather than outside the body, why then, one might ask, are women not men? Because they have insufficient heat to extrude the organs of reproduction and, as always for Galen, because form befits function. Nature in her wisdom has made females cooler, allowing their organs to remain inside and providing there a safe, guarded place for conception and gestation. Moreover, if women were as hot as men, semen planted in the womb would shrivel and die like seed cast upon the desert; of course, the extra nutriment needed by the fetus would likewise burn off. The fact remains that women, whatever their special adaptations, are but variations of the male form, the same but lower on the scale of being and perfection.[13]

In this model, sexual excitement and the "very great pleasure" of climax in both men and women are understood as signs of a heat sufficient to concoct and comingle the seed, the animate matter, and create new life. Friction heats the body as it would two objects rubbing together. The chafing of the penis, or even its imagined chafing in nocturnal emission, warms the male organ and, through its connections to veins and nerves, every other part of the body. As warmth and pleasure build up and diffuse, the increasingly violent movement of the whole man causes the finest part of the blood to be concocted into semen, a kind of foam that finally bursts forth powerfully and uncontrollably like an epileptic seizure, to use the analogy Galen borrowed from Democritus.[14]

In women, the rubbing of the vagina and the neck of the womb performs the same function though, some writers would argue, with a somewhat different rhythm of delight. The author of the Hippocratic treatise *The Seed* maintains, for example, that heat in women builds up more gradually, resulting in a pleasure at once more sustained and less intense than the male's. Though her orgasm occurs whether she emits before or after the man, it is most intense if it occurs at the moment the sperm and its heat touches the womb. Then, like a flame flaring when wine is sprinkled on it, the woman's heat blazes most brilliantly. The nuances of the orgasm thus represent the inner workings of the body as well as the cosmic order of perfection.

Like a great steam generator, the whole body warms up to produce the seed; the sensations of intercourse and the orgasm itself indicate that everything is working as it should. But in this model sexual pleasure is not specifically genital, despite the fact that intercourse is viewed as the relieving of a localized itch and the organs of copulation as sources, through friction, of heat.

Orgasm's warmth, though more vehement and exciting, is in kind no different from other warmth and can be produced in some measure by food, wine, or the power of imagination.

Ancient medicine bequeathed to the Renaissance a physiology of flux and corporeal openness, one in which blood, mother's milk, and semen were fungible fluids, products of the body's power to concoct its nutriment. Thus, not only could women turn into men, as writers from Pliny to Montaigne testified (see below), but bodily fluids could turn easily into one another. This is not only explained why pregnant women, who, it was held, transformed food into nourishment for the fetus, and new mothers, who transformed the catamenial elements into milk, did not menstruate; it also accounted for the observation that obese women, who transformed the normal plethora into fat, and dancers, who used up the plethora in exercise, did not menstruate either and were thus generally infertile. Menstrual blood and menstrual bleeding were, moreover, regarded as no different than blood and bleeding generally. Thus Hippocrates views nosebleed and the onset of menstruation as equivalent signs of the resolution of fevers. A woman vomiting blood will stop if she starts to menstruate, and it is a good sign if epistaxis occurs in a woman whose courses have stopped. Similarly, bleeding in men and in women is regarded a physiologically equivalent. If melancholy appears "after the suppression of the catamenial discharge in women," argues Araeteus the Cappadocian, "or the hemorrhoidal flux in men, we must stimulate the parts to throw off their accustomed evacuation."[15]

Indeed, the menses, until one hundred years before its phantasmagoric nineteenth-century interpretations by Michelet and others, was still regarded, as it had been by Hippocrates, as but one form of bleeding by which women rid themselves of excess materials. Albrecht von Haller, the great eighteenth-century physiologist, argues that in puberty the plethora "in the male, vents itself frequently through the nose . . . but in the female the *same* plethora finds a more easy vent downward." Herman Boerhaave, the major medical teacher of the generation before Haller, cites a number of cases of men who bled regularly through the hemorrhoidal arteries, the nose, or the fingers or who, if not bled prophylactically, developed the clinical signs, the tenseness of the body, of amenorrhea. Even the enlightened Frederick the Great had himself bled before battle to relieve tension and facilitate calm command.[16]

The fungibility of fluids thus represented in a different register the anatomical homologies described earlier. The higher concoction of male semen with respect to that of the female and the fact that males generally rid themselves of nutritional excesses without frequent bleeding bore witness both to the essential homology between the economies of nutrition, blood, and semen in men and women, and to the superior heat and greater perfection of the male. Sexual heat was but an instance of the heat of life itself, an orgasm in both sexes the sign of warmth sufficient to transform one kind of bodily fluid into its reproductively potent forms and to assure a receptive place for the product of their union. In this context, it is not difficult to see why Galen's clinical judgments on the relationship between pleasure and fertility, or between the absence of pleasure and barrenness, should have become commonplace in both learned and popular Renaissance medical literature.

Thus, to ensure "generation in the time of copulation," the right amount of heat, made manifest by normal sexual pleasure and in the end by orgasm, must be produced. Talk and teasing, several books suggest, were the first resort. Women should be prepared with lascivious words, writes John Sadler, having pointed out earlier the importance of mutual orgasm; sometimes the problem is neither the womb nor other impediments in either spouse,

> except only in the manner of the act as when in the emission of the seed, the man is quicke and the woman too slow, whereby there is not a concourse of both seeds at the same instant as the rules of conception require.

He further recommends wanton behavior, "all kinde of dalliance" and "allurement to venery."

Then, if the man still found his mate "to be slow, and more cold, he must cherish, embrace, and tickle her." He must

> handle her secret parts and dugs, that she may take fire and be enflamed in venery, for so at length the wombe will strive and waxe fervent with desire of casting forth its own seed, and receiving the man's seed to be mixed together therein.

The womb, as another writer notes almost a century later, "by Injoyment Naturally receives Seed for Generation . . . as Heat [attracts] Straws or Feathers." Be careful, warn Ambroise Pare and others, not to leave a woman too soon after her orgasm, "lest aire strike the open womb" and cool the seeds so recently sown.[17] If all this fails, the Renaissance pharmacopoeia was full of useful drugs that worked either directly or by sympathetic magic. Pare recommends "fomenting her secret parts with a decoction of hot herbes made with muscadine, or boiled in other good wine," and rubbing civet or muske into the vagina. Submerge the privates in a warm sitz bath of junipers and chamomile, advises another authority. The heart of a male quail around the neck of a man and the heart of a female around the neck of a woman were said to enhance love, presumably because of the lecherous character of birds generally and perhaps of quails in particular; a concoction of ale hoof and pease straw was also indicated.[18]

In the Renaissance, as in late antiquity, an unbreakable bond between orgasm and fulfillment of the command to be fruitful and multiply linked personal experience to a greater social and cosmic order. On the one hand, concupiscence and the irresistible attractions of sexual rapture stood as marks in the flesh of mankind's fall from grace, of the essential weakness of the will. But on the other hand, pleasure was construed as precisely what compelled men and women to reproduce themselves, despite what prudence or individual interest might dictate. The import of the Timaeus's account of creation was that in both men and women brazenly *self-willed* genitals assured the propagation of the species through their love of intercourse even if reason might urge abstinence. This notion is elaborated with an especial poignancy for women in the popular Renaissance literature. Only "ardent appetite and lust" prevented the "bitter decay in short time of mankind"; only the fact that a mercifully short memory and an insatiable desire made women forget the dangerous agonies of childbirth allowed the human race to continue. If the bearing of children was God's offer of consolation for the loss of eternal life, the lethean pleasures of sex were a counterweight to its pain. The biological "invisible hand" of delight made them cooperate in assuring the immortality of the species and the continuity of society.[19]

Male and female bodies in these Renaissance accounts were, as is perhaps obvious, still very much like those of Galen. Consider the influential engravings in Andreas Vesalius's epoch-marking *De humani corporis fabrica* and his more popular *Tabulae sex*, all of which reinforce the hoary model through striking new representations. When Vesalius is self-consciously trying to emphasize the homologies between male and female organs of generation (figs. 1 and 2) and, even more telling, when he is not (fig. 3), he is firmly in the camp of the "ancients," however much he might rail against the authority of Galen in other contexts. But the anatomical accuracy of Galen is not what is at issue here. The female reproductive system can be, and indeed on occasion was still in the late nineteenth century, "accurately" rendered in the manner of Vesalius long after the old homologies had lost their credibility (figs. 4 and 5). But after the late seventeenth century and the collapse of the hierarchical model there was, in general, no longer any reason to draw the vagina and external pudenda in the same frame with the uterus and the ovaries. Bodies did not change, but the meanings of the relationship between their parts did.[20]

Seventeenth-century audiences still gave credence to a whole collection of tales, going back at least to Pliny, that illustrate the structural similarities and thus the mutability of male and female bodies. Sir Thomas Browne, in his *Enquiries into Vulgar and Common Errors* (1646), devotes an entire chapter to the question of whether "every hare is both male and female." He concludes

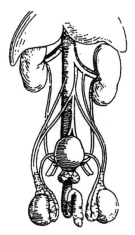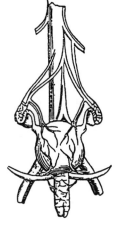

Figs. 1 and 2. Andreas Vesalius, male and female reproductive organs, *Tabulae Sex.* From *The Anatomical Drawings of Andreas Vesalius*, ed. Charles D. O'Malley and J.B. de C.M. Saunders (New York, 1982).

that "as for the mutation of sexes, or transition of one into another, we cannot deny it in Hares, it being observable in Man." Ambroise Pare, the great sixteenth-century surgeon, recounts the case of one Germain Garnier, christened Marie, who was serving in the retinue of the king. Germain was a well-built young man with a thick, red beard who until he was fifteen had lived and dressed as a girl, showing "no mark of masculinity." But then, in the heat of puberty,

> as he was in the fields and was rather robustly chasing his swine, which were going into a wheat field, [and] finding a ditch, he wanted to cross over it, and having leaped, at that very moment the genitalia and the male rod came to be developed in him, having ruptured the ligaments by which they had been held enclosed.

Marie, soon to be renamed, hastened home to his/her mother, who consulted physicians and surgeons, all of whom assured her that her daughter had become her son. She took him to the bishop, who called an assembly that decided that indeed a transformation had taken place. "The shepard received a man's name: instead of Marie . . . he was called Germain, and men's clothing was given him." (Some persisted in calling him Germain-Marie as a reminder that he had once been a girl.) Montaigne tells the same story, "attested to by the most eminent officials of the town." There is still, he reports, in the area "a song commonly in the girls' mouths, in which they warn one another not to stretch their legs too wide for fear of becoming males, like Marie Germaine."[21]

How were transformations like Marie's possible? The learned Caspar Bauhin explains how "women have changed into men," namely, "The heat having been rendered more vigorous, thrusts the testes outward." Such transformations, however, seem to work only up the "great chain of being."

> We therefore never find in any true story that any man ever became a woman, because Nature tends always toward what is most perfect and not, on the contrary, to perform in such a way that what is perfect should become imperfect.[22]

Fig. 3. Vesalius, uterus, vagina, and external pudenda from a young woman, *De humani corporis.* This illustration was not made to illustrate homologies with the male organ. From *Anatomical Drawings of Vesalius.*

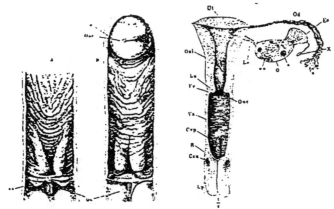

Figs. 4 and 5. Frontal cross section of female genitals (*left*); front wall of the vagina (*right*); from Jakob Henle, *Handbuch der systematischen Anatomie des Menschen*, vol. 2 (Braunschweig, 1866). These illustrations show that the geometric relations depicted in fig. 3 are not intrinsically implausible.

Moreover, the Galenic structure survived the discovery of a new, and one would think totally incompatible, homology: that of the clitoris to the penis. Jane Sharp, whose 1671 midwifery guide was last reprinted in 1728, could happily argue at one point in her work that the vagina, "which is the passage for the yard, resembleth it turned inward," while arguing two pages later and with no apparent embarrassment, that the clitoris is the female penis. "It will stand and fall as the yard doth and makes women lustful and take delight in copulation," thus helping to assure the conditions necessary for conception. The labia thus fit nicely into both systems of analogies. They give women great pleasure in copulation and, as the ancients said, defend the matrix from outward violence, but they are also, as John Pechy puts it, "that wrinkled membranous production, which clothes the Clitoris like a foreskin." This left open the question of whether the vagina or the clitoris were to be thought of as the female penis, though both could be regarded as erectile organs. One midwifery manual notes that "the action of the clitoris is like that of the yard, which is erection" and, on the very same page, that "the action of the neck of the womb [the vagina and cervix] is the same with that of the yard; that is to say, erection." Thus, until the very end of the seventeenth century there seemed no difficulty in holding that women had an organ homologous, through topological inversion, to the penis inside their bodies, the vagina, and another one morphologically homologous to the penis, outside, the clitoris.[23]

Perhaps the continued power of the systemic, genitally unfocused account of sex inherited by Renaissance writers from antiquity—the view of the sexually excited body as a great boiler, heating up to blow off steam—explains why mutually incompatible interpretations of male and female genitals caused so little consternation. Seventeenth-century writers seem to have welcomed the idea that male and female pleasure was located in essentially the same kind of organ. They remained undisturbed by the clitoris's supposed dual function—licit pleasure in heterosexual intercourse and illicit pleasure in "tribadism." They elaborate the penis/clitoris homology with great precision: the outward end of the clitoris, one physician writes, is like the glans of the penis, and like it "the seat of the greatest pleasure in copulation in women." According to another, the tip of the clitoris is, therefore, also called the "amoris dulcedo."

The ancient account of bodies and sexual pleasures was not ultimately dependent for its support simply on facts or supposed facts about the body, even though it was articulated in the concrete language of anatomy and physiology. Were it otherwise, the system of homologies would have fallen well before its time from the sheer weight of readily apparent difficulties. The recognition of the clitoris is a case in point. The word *clitoris* makes its first known English appearance in 1615 when Helkiah Crooke argues that it *differs* from the yard: "[It] is a small body, not continued at all with the bladder, but placed in the height of the lap. The clitoris hath no passage for the emission of seed; but the virile member is long and hath a passage for seed." Yet, one can easily set beside this quite correct list of facts equally unexceptional observations supporting the contrary view. The clitoris, for example, is called the *tentigo* in Thomas Vicary's enormously popular *The Anatomie of the Body of Man* (1586), a term borrowed from the eleventh-century Arab medical writer Albucasis meaning in Latin "a tenseness or lust; an erection." It *is*, of course, erectile and erotogenous, and thus a "counterfeit yard," if one chooses to emphasize these features.[24]

The homological view survived not only the potential challenge posed by the anatomist Colombo's discovery of the clitoris, but other expressions of skepticism as well. Crooke, in the text cited above, attacks the Galenic homologies in general, pointing out that the scrotum of a man is thin-skinned while the base of the womb, its homologue, is "a very thicke and tight membrane." Again, this is scarcely a telling point when compared with the self-evident fact that the womb carries a baby while the penis does not. Moreover, the topological inversions suggested by Galen are, and were known to be, manifestly implausible if taken literally. Recall the mind-bending metaphor of the womb as a penis inside itself, like the eyes of a mole, or perfectly formed but hidden within, like the eyes of other animals *in utero*.

The fact that criticisms of the Galenic model not only are self-evident but also were sprinkled throughout the literature is a reminder that the cultural construction of the female in relation to the male, while expressed in terms of the body's concrete realities, was more deeply grounded in assumptions about the nature of politics and society. It was the abandonment of these assumptions in the Enlightenment that made the hierarchically ordered system of homologies hopelessly inappropriate. The new biology, with its search for fundamental differences between the sexes and between their desires, emerged at precisely the time when the foundations of the old social order were irremediably shaken. Indeed, as Havelock Ellis discovered, "It seems to have been reserved for the nineteenth century to state that women are apt to be congenitally incapable of experiencing complete sexual satisfaction and are peculiarly liable to sexual anaesthesia." But what happens to the old biology, to its complex of metaphors and relations? In some respects nothing happened to it; or, in any case, nothing happened very fast.[25]

POLITICS AND THE BIOLOGY OF SEXUAL DIFFERENCE

When in the 1740s the young Princess Maria Theresa was worried because she did not immediately become pregnant after her marriage to the future Hapsburg emperor, she asked her physician what she ought to do. He is said to have replied:

> Ceterum censeo vulvam Sanctissimae Majestatis ante coitum esse titillandum [Moreover I think the vulva of Her Most Holy Majesty is to be titillated before intercourse].

The advice seems to have worked as she bore more than a dozen children. Similarly, Albrecht von Haller, one of the giants of eighteenth-century biological science, still postulated an erection of both the external and the internal female reproductive organs during intercourse and regarded woman's orgasm as a sign that the ovum has been ejaculated from the ovary. Although he is well aware of the existence of the sperm and the egg and of their respective origins in the testes and ovaries, and has no interest in the Galenic homologies, the sexually aroused female in his account bears a remarkable resemblance to the male under similar circumstances.

> When a woman, invited either by moral love, or a lustful desire of pleasure, admits the embraces of the male, it excites a convulsive constriction and attrition of the very sensible and tender parts; which lie within the contiguity of the external opening of the vagina, after the same manner as we observed before of the male.

The clitoris grows erect, the nymphae swell, venous blood flow is constricted, and the whole external genitalia becomes turgid as the system works "to raise the pleasure to the highest pitch." A small quantity of lubricating mucous is expelled in this process, but

> the same action which, by increasing the heights of pleasure, causes a greater conflux of blood to the whole genital system of the female, occasions a much more important alteration in the interior parts.

The uterus becomes turgid with in flowing blood; likewise the fallopian tubes become erect "so as to apply the ruffle or fingered opening of the tube to the ovary." Then, at the moment of mutual orgasm, the "hot male semen" acting on this already excited system causes the extremity of the tube to reach still further until, "surrounding and compressing the ovarium in fervent congress, [it] presses out and swallows a mature ovum." The extrusion of the egg, Haller points out finally to his learned readers, who would probably have read this torrid account in the original Latin,

> is not performed without great pleasure to the mother, nor without an exquisite unrelatable sensation of the internal parts of the tube, threatening a swoon or fainting fit to the future mother.[26]

The problem with which this essay began thus remains. Neither advances in reproductive biology nor anatomical discoveries seem sufficient to explain the dramatic revaluation of the female orgasm that occurred in the late eighteenth century and the even more dramatic reinterpretation of the female body in relation to that of the male. Rather, a new model of incommensurability triumphed over the old hierarchical model in the wake of new political agendas. Writers from the eighteenth century onward sought in the facts of biology a justification for cultural and political differences between the sexes that were crucial to the articulation of both feminist and antifeminist arguments. Political theorists beginning with Hobbes had argued that there is no basis in nature for any specific sort of authority—of a king over his people, of slaveholder over slave, nor, it followed, of man over woman. There seemed no reason why the universalistic claims made for human liberty and equality during the Enlightenment should exclude half of humanity. And, of course, revolution, the argument made in blood that mankind in all its social and cultural relations could be remade, engendered both a new feminism and a new fear of women. But feminism itself, and indeed the more general claims made by and for women to public life—to write, to vote, to legislate, to influence, to reform—was also predicated on difference.

Thus, women's bodies in their corporeal, scientifically accessible concreteness, in the very nature of their bones, nerves, and, most important, reproductive organs, came to bear an enormous new weight of cultural meaning in the Enlightenment. Arguments about the very existence of female sexual passion, about women's special capacity to control what desires they did have, and about their moral nature generally were all part of a new enterprise seeking to discover the anatomical and physiological characteristics that distinguished men from women. As the natural body itself became the gold standard of social discourse, the bodies of women became the battleground for redefining the most ancient, the most intimate, the most fundamental of human relations: that of woman to man.

It is relatively easy to make this case in the context of explicit resistance to the political, economic, or social claims of women. Prominent male leaders in the French Revolution, for example, strenuously opposed increased female participation in public life on the grounds that women's physical nature, radically distinguished from that of men and represented most powerfully in the organs of reproduction, made them unfit for public life and better suited to the private sphere. Susanna Barrows maintains that fears born of the Paris Commune and of the new political possibilities opened up by the Third Republic generated an extraordinarily elaborate physical anthropology of sexual difference to justify resistance to change. In the British context, the rise of the women's suffrage movement in the 1870s elicited a similar response. Tocqueville argues that in the

United States democracy had destroyed the old basis for patriarchal authority and that consequently it was necessary to trace anew and with great precision "two clearly distinct lines of action for the two sexes." In short, wherever boundaries were threatened arguments, for fundamental sexual differences were shoved into the breach.[27]

But reinterpretations of the body were more than simply ways of reestablishing hierarchy in an age when its metaphysical foundations were being rapidly effaced. Liberalism postulates a body that, if not sexless, is nevertheless undifferentiated in its desires, interest, or capacity to reason. In striking contrast to the old teleology of the body as male, liberal theory begins with a neuter body, sexed but without gender, and of no consequence to cultural discourse. The body is regarded simply as the bearer of the rational subject, which itself constitutes the person. The problem for this theory, then, is how to derive the real world of male dominion of women, of sexual passion and jealousy, of the sexual division of labor and cultural practices generally from an original state of genderless bodies. The dilemma, at least for theorists interested in the subordination of women, is resolved by grounding the social and cultural differentiation of the sexes in a biology of incommensurability that liberal theory itself helped bring into being. A novel construal of nature comes to serve as the foundation of otherwise indefensible social practices.

For women, of course, the problem is even more pressing. The neuter language of liberalism leaves them, as Jean Elshtain recently argues, without their own voice. But more generally the claim of equality of rights based on an essential identity of the male and female, body and spirit, robs women both of the reality of their social experience and of the ground on which to take political and cultural stands. If women are indeed simply a version of men, as the old model would have had it, then what justifies women writing, or acting in public, or making any other claims for themselves as women? Thus feminism, too—or at least historical versions of feminisms—depends upon and generates a biology of incommensurability in place of the teleologically male interpretation of bodies on the basis of which a feminist stance is impossible.[28]

Rousseau's essentially antifeminist account is perhaps the most theoretically elaborated of the liberal theories of bodies and pleasures, but it is only one of a great many examples of how deeply a new biology is implicated in cultural reconstruction. In the state of nature, as he imagined it in the first part of *A Discourse on Inequality*, there is no social intercourse between the sexes, no division of labor in the rearing of young, and, in a strict sense, no desire. There is, of course, brute physical attraction between sexes, but it is devoid of what he calls "moral love," which "shapes this desire and fixes it exclusively on one particular object, or at least gives the desire for this chosen object a greater degree of energy." In this world of innocence there is no jealousy or rivalry, no marriage, no taste for this or that woman; to men in the state of nature "every woman is good." Rousseau is remarkably concrete in specifying the reproductive physiology of women that must, in his view, underlie this condition. Hobbes, he argues, erred in using the struggle of male animals for access to females as evidence for the natural combativeness of the primitive human state. True, he concedes, there is bitter competition among beasts for the opportunity to mate, but this is because for much of the year females refuse the male advance.

But women, he points out, have no such periods of abstinence and are thus not in short supply:

> No-one had ever observed, even among savages, females having like those of other species fixed periods of heat and exclusion. Moreover, among several of such animals, the whole species goes in heat at the same time, so that there comes a terrible moment of universal passion, a moment that does not occur in the human species, where love is never seasonal.

Reproductive physiology and the nature of the menstrual cycle bear an enormous weight here; the state of nature is in large measure conceptualized as dependent on the supposed biological differences between women and beasts.[29]

But what happened to this primitive state of desire? Rousseau gives an account of the geographical spread of the human race, of the rise of the division of labor, of how in developing a dominion over animals man "asserted the priority of his species, and so prepared himself from afar to claim priority for himself as an individual." But the individuation of desire, the creation of what he calls the moral part of love ("an artificial sentiment"), and the birth of imagination ("which causes such havoc amongst us") are construed as the creation of women and, specifically, as the product of female modesty. The *Discourse* presents this modesty as volitional and instrumental: "[It is] cultivated by women with such skill and care in order to establish their empire over men, and so make dominant the sex that ought to obey." But in *Emile* modesty is naturalized: "While abandoning women to unlimited desires, He [the Supreme Being] joins modesty to these desires in order to constrain them." And somewhat later in a note Rousseau adds: "The timidity of women is another instinct of nature against the double risk they run during their pregnancy." Indeed, throughout *Emile* he argues that natural differences between the sexes are represented and amplified in the form of moral differences that society erases only at its peril.[30]

Book 5 begins with the famous account of sexual difference and sameness. "In everything not connected with sex, woman is man. . . . In everything connected with sex, woman and man are in every respect related but in every respect different." But, of course, a great deal about women *is* connected with sex: "The male is male only at certain moments. The female is female her whole life. . . . Everything constantly recalls her sex to her." "Everything," it turns out, is everything about reproductive biology: bearing young, suckling, nurturing, and so on. Indeed the chapter becomes a catalogue of physical and consequently moral differences between the sexes; the former, as Rousseau says, "lead us unawares to the latter." Thus, "a perfect woman and a perfect man ought not to resemble each other in mind any more than in looks." From the differences in each sex's contribution to their union, it follows that "one ought to be active and strong, the other passive and weak." The problem with Plato, Rousseau argues, is that he excludes "families from his regime and no longer knowing what to do with women, he found himself *forced to make them men.*" It is precisely this sameness of "the exercises" Plato gives men and women, this "civil promiscuity which throughout confounded the two sexes in the same employments and the same labors and which cannot fail to engender the most intolerable abuses," to which Rousseau objects. But what are these objectional abuses?

> I speak of that subversion of the sweetest sentiments of nature, sacrificed to an artificial sentiment which can only be maintained by them—as though there were no need for a natural base on which to form conventional ties; as though the love of one's nearest were not the principle of the love one owes the state; as though it were not by means of the small fatherland which is the family that the heart attaches itself to the large one; as though it were not the good son, the good husband, and the good father [all males of course] who make the good citizen.

Finally, returning to the ostensible subject of the book, Rousseau concludes that "once it is demonstrated that man and woman are not and ought not to be constituted in the same way in either their character or temperament, it follows that they ought not to have the same education."[31]

For Rousseau a great deal depends, it turns out, on the natural modesty of women and on their role, distinct from the male's in reproducing the species. Indeed, all of civilization seems to have arisen in consequence of the secular fall from innocence when the first woman made herself temporarily unavailable to the first man. But Rousseau is simply pushing harder on a set of connections that are commonplace in the Enlightenment—although by no means always so antifeminist in their interpretation.

Most prominently among the figures of the Scottish Enlightenment, John Millar argues for the crucial role of women and their virtues in the progress of civilization. Far from being lesser men, they are treated in his *Origin of the Distinctions of Ranks* as both a moral barometer and as an active agent in the improvement of society. Millar's case begins with the claim that sexual relations, being most susceptible "to the peculiar circumstances in which they are placed and most liable to be influenced by the power of habit and education," are the most reliable guide to the character of a society. In barbarous societies, for example, women accompanied men to war and were scarcely different from them; in peaceful societies that had progressed in the arts, a woman's "rank and station" were dictated by her special talents for rearing and maintaining children and by her "peculiar delicacy and sensibility," whether these derived from her "original constitution" or her role in life. Thus, civilization in Millar's account leads to an increasing differentiation of male and female social roles; this greater differentiation of roles—and specifically what he takes to be improvements in the lot of women—are signs of moral progress. But women themselves in more civilized societies are also the engines of further advance. "In such a state, the pleasures which nature has grafted upon love between the sexes, become the source of an elegant correspondence, and are likely to have a general influence upon the commerce of society." In this, the highest state—he is thinking of French salon society and of the *femme savant*—

> [women are] led to cultivate those talents which are adapted to the intercourse of the world, and to distinguish themselves by polite accomplishments that tend to heighten their personal attractions, and to excite those peculiar sentiments and passions of which they are the natural objects.

Thus, desire among civilized men, and indeed modern civilization, is inextricably bound up in Millar's moral history with feminine accomplishment.[32]

It is hardly surprising in the context of Enlightenment thought that the moral and physical differentiation of women from men is also critical to the political discourse of women writers—from Anna Wheeler and early socialists at one end of the political spectrum through the radical liberalism of Mary Wollstonecraft to the domestic ideology of Hannah More and Sarah Ellis. For Wheeler and others, as Barbara Taylor argues, the denial or devaluation of female passion is to some degree part of a more general devaluation of passion. Reason, they dare to hope, would be triumphant over the flesh.

But the nature of female passion and of the female body is unresolved in Wheeler's work. Her book, *An Appeal of One-Half the Human Race, Women, Against the Pretensions of the Other Half, Men, To Retain Them in Political and Thence in Civil and Domestic Slavery*, jointly written with William Thompson, is a sustained attack on James Mill's argument that the interests of women and children are subsumed—i.e., are virtually represented by—the interests of husbands and fathers. This "moral miracle," as they call it, would be credible were Mill right in holding that women are protected against abuse because men "will act in a kind way toward women in order to procure from her those gratifications, the zest of which depends on the kindly inclinations of one party yielding them." Since women are themselves free from sexual desire, they are in an excellent bargaining position vis-à-vis men, who are decidedly not liberated from their bodies. Nonsense, say Wheeler and Thompson. If women are, "like the Greek Asphasia," cold and sexless, the argument might have force. But not only is woman, like man, sexed and desirous but, in the current state of affairs, "Woman is more the slave of man for gratification of her desires than man is to woman." The double standard allows men to seek gratification outside of marriage but forbids it to women.[33]

Both Wheeler and Thompson's analysis of the sorry shape of the male world and their need to claim some political ground for women lead them dramatically to change their emphasis and make almost the opposite case as well. In a chapter entitled "Moral Aptitude for Legislation More Probable in Women than Men," woman is represented not as equally passionate as man but as more moral, more empathetic, and generally better able to act in accord with the common interest and not merely out of self-interest. Whether women had these traits in some hypothetical state of nature or acquired them through a kind of moral Lamarckianism is unclear, but in the modern world they demonstrate a greater susceptibility to pain and pleasure, a more powerful desire to promote the happiness of others, and a more developed "moral aptitude" than men. These, Wheeler and Thompson argue, are the most important qualities in a legislator. It is, moreover, precisely women's inferior strength and her inability to oppress others through superior force as men are wont to do that will ensure that they rule fairly and justly. Moreover, women as mothers and as the weaker sex need a world at peace far more than men, and they would thus be constitutionally more likely to legislate ways to obtain it. Wheeler and Thompson's arguments are more poignantly put than this summary suggests, but they contribute to a construction of woman not very different from that of the domestic ideologists.

As a radical liberal, Mary Wollstonecraft is caught in much the same dilemma. On the one hand, liberal theory pushes her to declare that the neutral, rational subject has in essence no sex. On the other hand, she was in her own life only too aware of the power, indeed the destructive violence, of sexual passion. Moreover she seems to have held, with Rousseau, that civilization increases desire and that "people of sense and reflection are most apt to have violent and constant passions and to be preyed on by them." Finally, as Zillah Eisenstein argues, for Wollstonecraft to subscribe to the notion of the subject as genderless would be to deny what to her were manifestly present, the particular qualities of women's experiences.[34]

Her solution was to take for women the moral high ground. Blessed with a unique susceptibility "of the attached affections," women's special role in the world is to civilize men and raise up children to virtue. In the *Female Reader*, Wollstonecraft lays on a heavy dose of religion, which she says will be "the solace and support" of her readers when they find themselves, as they often will, "amidst the scenes of silent unobserved distress." "If you wish to be loved by your relations and friends," she counsels without detectable irony, "prove that you can love them by governing your temper." Good humor, cheerful gaiety, and the like are not to be learned in a day. Indeed, as Barbara Taylor argues, Wollstonecraft shares with early socialist feminists a commitment to "passionlessness," whether out of some sense of its political possibilities, an acute awareness of passion's dangers, or a belief in the special undesiring qualities of the female body.[35]

In any case, Wollstonecraft's arguments for the differences between the sexes begin to sound very much like Sarah Ellis's, however profound the political chasm that divided the two women. In *Wives of England*, one of the canonical works of domestic ideology, Ellis argues that from the wife and mother, "as head of a family and mistress of a household, branch off in every direction trains of thought, and tones of feeling, operating upon those more immediately around her, but by no means ceasing there . . . extending outwards in the same manner, to the end of all things." This influence is born of the heightened moral sensibilities with which the female organism seems blessed. Though women are to have no role in the world of mundane politics, they are to confront issues

> such as extinction of slavery, the abolition of war in general, cruelty to animals, the punishment of death, temperance, and many more, on which, neither to know, nor to feel, is almost equally disgraceful.

In short, women's politics must be the politics of morality.[36]

All of this is not intended as an argument that writers from Hobbes, through Rousseau and on to Ellis, were all engaged in precisely the same theoretical or political undertaking. Rather, I have sought to display the wide range of apparently unrelated political agendas in which a new differentiation of the sexes occupied a critical place. Desire was given a history, and the female body distinguished from the male's, as the seismic transformations of European society between the seventeenth and the nineteenth centuries put unbearable pressure on old views of the body and its pleasures. A biology of hierarchy grounded in a metaphysically prior "great chain of being" gave way to a biology of incommensurability in which the relationship of men to women, like that of apples to oranges, was not given as one of equality or inequality but rather as a *difference* whose meaning required interpretation and struggle.

REPRODUCTIVE BIOLOGY AND THE CULTURAL RECONSTRUCTION OF WOMEN

I want now to turn from political and moral theory to the sciences of reproductive biology, to the seemingly unpromising domain of ovarian and uterine histology and the clinical observation of menstruation and fertility. Aldous Huxley's remark that "the science of life can confirm the intuitions of the artist, can deepen his insights and extend the range of his vision" could as well be said of those who produced what he takes to be a prior and culturally pure knowledge. The dry and seemingly objective findings of the laboratory and the clinic become, within the disciplines practiced there, the stuff of art, of new representations of the female as a creature profoundly different from the male. And this "art," clothes in the prestige of natural science, becomes in turn the specie, the hard currency of social discourse.[37]

But I do not want to give the impression that reproductive biology or clinical gynecology are simply exercises in ideology. I will therefore begin by describing a critically important discovery of the early nineteenth century: that some mammals—nineteenth-century researchers believed all mammals—ovulate spontaneously during regularly recurring periods of heat, independently of intercourse, conception, pleasure, or any other subjective phenomena. Until the early 1840s, the question of when and under what conditions ovulation took place was as obscure as it had been in 1672 when de Graaf argued that what he called the female testicle actually produced eggs.

In humans, the evidence for spontaneous ovulation was, in the early nineteenth century, highly ambiguous. Numerous anecdotal clinical reports, based on increasingly available autopsy material, claimed that cicatrices—scars remaining after a wound, sore, or ulcer has healed—can be demonstrated on ovaries of virgins and that these are left there by the release of an ovum and, more to the point, by the release of numerous ova corresponding to the number of menstrual cycles that the woman had had. But what, if anything, did this prove? Very little. Johann Friederich Blumenbach, professor of medicine at Göttingen and one of the most distinguished physicians of Europe, for example, had been among the first to notice by the late eighteenth century that ovarian follicles burst without the presence of semen or even "without any commerce with the male." But he concluded from these cases only that, on occasion, "venereal ardour alone . . . could produce, among the other great changes in the sexual organs, the enlargement of the vesicles" and even their rupture. Johannes Muller, professor of physiology at Berlin, a leading proponent of biological reductionism, concludes that scars on the ovaries of virgins mark anomalous ovulations. Thus, while the exact forces causing the egg to be thrust into the fallopian tube remained unknown, the evidence until the 1840s was by no means sufficient to establish the normal occurrence of ovulation independent of coition, venereal arousal, or even conception.[38]

The critical experiment establishing spontaneous ovulation in dogs and by extension other mammals was elegantly simple. In the novelistic style that characterizes so much early nineteenth-century scientific reporting, Theodor L. W. Bischoff tells his reader that on 18 and 19 December 1843 he noted that a large bitch in his possession had begun to go into heat. On the nineteenth he allowed her contact with a male dog, but she refused its attentions. He kept her securely imprisoned for two more days and then brought on the male dog again; this time, she was interested but the animals were separated before coition could take place. At ten o'clock, two days later, i.e., on the morning of the 23rd, he cut out her left ovary and fallopian tubes and carefully closed the wound. The Graafian follicles in the excised ovary were swollen but had not yet burst. Five days later, he killed the dog and found in the remaining ovary four developing corpus lutei filled with serum; careful opening of the tubes revealed four eggs. He concludes:

I do not think it is possible to demonstrate with any more thoroughness the whole process of the ripening and expulsion of the eggs during heat, independently of coition, than through this dual observation on one and the same animal.

And of course if ovulation occurs independently of coition, it must also occur independently of fecundation.

Granted that dogs and pigs go into heat and during this period ovulate whether they mate or not, what evidence was there that women's bodies behave in a similar manner? No one prior to the early twentieth century had claimed to have seen a human egg outside the ovary. Bischoff admitted that, in the absence of such a discovery, there was no direct proof for the extension of his theory to women, but he was sure that an egg would be found soon enough. In fact, an unfertilized egg was not reported until 1930, and then in the context of an argument against the nineteenth-century view relating heat to menstruation. Thus, the crucial experimental link—the discovery of the egg—between menstruation on the one hand and the morphology of the ovary on the other was lacking in humans. The role of the ovaries in the reproductive cycle of mammals was imperfectly understood until the publication of a series of papers beginning in 1900, while the hormonal control of ovulation by the ovary and the pituitary remained unknown until the 1930s.[39]

But despite the paucity of evidence in humans, the discovery of spontaneous ovulation in dogs and other mammals was of enormous importance in the history of representing women's bodies. Beginning in the middle of the nineteenth century, the ovaries came to be regarded as largely autonomous control centers of reproduction in the female animal, and in humans they were thought to be the essence of femininity itself. "Propter solum ovarium mulier est id quod est," as the French physician Achilles Chereau puts it; it is only because of the ovary that woman is what she is. Moreover, menstruation in women came to be interpreted as the precise equivalent of the heat in animals, marking the only period during which women are normally fertile. Widely cited as Pouchet's eighth law, the view as that "the menstrual flow in women corresponds to the phenomena of excitement which manifests itself during the rut [*l'époque des amours*] in a variety of creatures and especially in mammals." The American physician Augustus Gardner drew out the implications of the menstruation/rut analogy less delicately: "The bitch in heat has the genitals tumefied and reddened, and a bloody discharge. The human female has nearly the same." "The menstrual period in women," announces the *Lancet* in 1843, "bears a strict physiological resemblance" to the heat of "brutes."[40]

With these interpretations of spontaneous ovulation, the old physiology of pleasure and the old anatomy of sexual homologies were definitively dead. The ovary, whose distinction from the male testes had only been recognized a century earlier, became the driving force of the whole female economy, with menstruation the outward sign of its awesome power. As the distinguished British gynecologist Mathews Duncan put it, in an image too rich to be fully teased apart here: "Menstruation is like the red flag outside an auction sale; it shows that something is going on inside." And that something, as will become clear, was not a pretty sight; the social characteristics of women seemed writ in blood and gore. The silent workings of a tiny organ wighing in on the average seven grams in humans, some two to four centimeters long, and the swelling and subsequent rupture of the follicles within it, came to represent synecdochically what it was to be a woman.[41]

But why would anyone believe that menstruation was in women what heat was in dogs? The answer lies outside the bounds of science in a wide range of cultural demands on the enterprise of interpretation. Consider, for example, the answer Bischoff himself offers: the equivalence of menstruation and heat is simply common sense. If one accepts spontaneous ovulation during periods of heat in mammals generally, it "suggests itself." In any case, there is much indirect evidence for the equation of heat and menstruation, in addition to the authority of the "most insightful physicians and naturalists" from the earliest times on.

In fact the analogy was far from evident, and most of those from antiquity to Bischoff's day who gave their views on the subject repudiated it. Haller's *Physiology* is quite explicit on the point that, while there are "some animals, who, at the time of their venal copulation, distil blood from their genitals," menstruation is peculiar "to the fair sex [of] the human species." Moreover, in contrast to bleeding in animals, menstruation for Haller is quite independent of the periodicity of sexual desire. Intercourse neither increases nor decreases the menstrual flux; women deny a heightened "desire of venery" during their periods and report rather being "affected by pain and languor." Finally, sexual pleasure is localized "in the entrance of the pudendum" and not in the uterus, from which the menses flow. Blumenbach, among the most widely reprinted and translated text of the next generation, joins Pliny in arguing that only women menstruate, though cautioning his readers that the investigation of the "periodical nature of this hemorrhage is so difficult that we can obtain nothing beyond probability" and should thus be careful not to offer mere conjecture as fact.[42]

What scant facts there were seemed more anthropological than biological, and these came under severe attack. In a masterful review of the literature up to 1843, Robert Remak, professor of neurology at Posen, argues that even if one grants that, as do healthy women, all or some mammals have regularly recurring periods of bleedings and that the bleeding in animals originates in the uterus and not from the turgescent external genitalia—neither concession being warranted by the evidence—there remains "one further circumstance on which to ground the most radical difference between menstruation and the periodical flow of blood from the genitals of animals":

> In female animals the bleeding accompanies heat [*brunst*], the period of the most heightened sexual drive, the only time the female will allow the male access, and the only time she will conceive. Quite to the contrary, in women the menstrual period is scarcely at all connected to increased sexual desire nor is fecundity limited to its duration; indeed a kind of instinct keeps men away from women during the menses—some savage people like certain African and American tribes isolate menstruating women in special quarters—and experience shows that there is no time during the inter-menstrual period when women can not conceive. It follows therefore that the animal heat is totally missing in women. . . . Indeed the absence of menstruation in animals is one of the features that distinguish man from the beasts.

Johannes Muller, in his 1843 textbook, comes to similar conclusions. He modestly points out that neither the purposes nor the causes of the periodical return of the menses are known. Quite probably, however, it exists to "*prevent* in the human female the periodical return of sexual excitation [*brunst*]" that occurs in animals. Common sense, in short, does not explain why nineteenth-century investigators would want to view the reproductive cycle of women as precisely equivalent to that of other animals.[43]

Professional politics and the imperatives of a particular philosophy of science offer perhaps part of an answer. As Jean Borie points out, Pouchet's is "une gynaecologie militante"; the same can be said of that of many of his colleagues, especially his French ones. Their mission was to free women's bodies from the stigma of clerical prejudice and centuries of popular superstition and, in the process, to substitute the physician for the priest as the moral preceptor of society. Sexuality would shift from the realms of religion to those of science triumphant. At the heart of the matter lay the faith that reproduction, like nature's other mysteries, was in essence susceptible to rational analysis. Thus, in the absence of specific evidence of human ovulation, "logic" for Pouchet would dictate that women functioned no differently from the bitch, sow, or female rabbit, who in turn followed the same fundamental laws as mollusks, insects, fishes, or reptiles. He explicitly calls his readers' attention to the pristinely scientific, experimentally grounded, character of his work and its avoidance of metaphysical, social, and religious concerns. Thus, there were considerable professional and philosophical attractions to the position that menstruation was like heat and that a sovereign organ, the ovary, ruled over the reproductive processes that made women what they were.[44]

But this radical naturalization, this reduction of women to the organ that differentiates them from men, was not in itself a claim for their association with nature as against culture and civilization. The argument for the equation of heat and menstruation could be just as easily used to prove women's moral elevation as to prove the opposite. Indeed the very fact that women, on account of their recurrent cycles of rut, were more bound to their bodies than were men was evidence on some accounts for their superior capacity to transcend the brutish state. Arguing against those who held that the lack of animal-like lust or behavioral disturbances in women belied the new theory of spontaneous ovulation, one noted authority draws attention to "the influence exercised by moral culture on the feelings and passions of humanity." Observe "the marvelous power exercised by civilization on the mind of her who, from her social position, is rendered the charm of man's existence." Is it a wonder that the creature who can subjugate her own feelings, simulate good cheer when her heart is rent in agony, and in general give herself up to the good of the community can exercise control "the more energetically, at a time [menstruation] when she is taught that a stray thought of desire would be impurity, and its fruition pollution." But then, as if to back off from this model of woman as being simultaneously a periodically excited time bomb of sexuality and a model for the power of civilization to keep it from exploding, G. F. Girdwood concludes that "to aid her in her duty, nature has wisely provided her with the sexual appetite slightly developed."[45]

The interpretive indigestion of this passage, its sheer turning in on itself, bears witness to the extraordinary cultural burden that the physical nature of women—the menstrual cycle and the functions of the ovaries—came to bear in the nineteenth century. Whatever one thought about women and their rightful place in the world could, it seemed, be mapped onto their bodies, which in turn came to be interpreted anew in the light of these cultural demands. The construal of the menstrual cycle dominant from the 1840s to the early twentieth century rather neatly integrates a particular set of discoveries into a biology of incommensurability. Menstruation, with its attendant aberrations, became a uniquely and distinguishingly female process. Moreover, the analogy now assumed between heat and menstruation allowed evidence hithertofore used against the equivalence of the reproductive cycles of women and brutes to be reinterpreted to mean the opposite. Behavior hidden in women, just as ovulation is hidden, could be made manifest by associating it with the more transparent behavior of animals.

Thus, for example, the author of one of the most massive compilations of moral physiology in the nineteenth century could argue that the quite mad behavior of dogs and cats during heat, their flying to satisfy the "instinct which dominates all else," leaping around an apartment and lunging at windows, repeated "so to speak indefinitely" if the venereal urge were not satisfied, is but a more manifest version of what the human female too experiences. Since both women and brutes are thought to be subject to the same "orgasme de l'ovulation," and since the bursting of the ovarian follicle was marked by the same deluge of nervous excitement and bleeding in both, whatever discomfort adolescent girls might feel at the onset of menstruation and whatever irritability or tension a woman might experience during her menses could be magnified through the metaphors of this account and reinterpreted as but the tip of a physiological volcano. Menstruation, in short, was a minimally disguised heat. Women would behave like brutes were it not for the thin veneer of civilization. Language, moreover, adjusted to the new science. The whole cultural baggage of *brunst, rut, heat*—words hithertofore applied only to animals—and the neologism *estrous*, derived from the Latin *oestrum*, "gadfly," meaning a kind of frenzy and introduced to describe a process common to all mammals, was subtly or not so subtly laden on the bodies of women.[46]

Menstrual bleeding thus becomes the sign of a periodically swelling and ultimately exploding ovarian follicle whose behavioral manifestation is an "estrous," "brunst," or "rut." But what one saw on the outside was only part of the story; the histology of the uterine mucosa and of the ovary revealed much more. Described in seemingly neutral scientific language, the cells of the endometrium or corpus luteum became re-presentations, redescriptions of the social theory of sexual incommensurability. Walter Heape, the militant antisuffragist and reader in zoology at Cambridge University, for example, is absolutely clear on what he thinks of the female in relation to the male body. Though some of the differences between men and women are "infinitely subtle, hidden" and others "glaring and forceful," the truth of the matter, he argues, is that

> the reproductive system is not only structurally but functionally fundamentally different in the Male and the Female; and since all other organs and systems of organs are affected by this system, it is certain that the Male and Female are essentially different throughout.

They are, he continues, "complementary, in no sense the same, in no sense equal to one another; the accurate adjustment of society depends on proper observation of this fact." A major set of these facts were evident, for Heape and many others, in the uterus. It should be noted, however, that the basic histology of menstruation—let alone its causes—was not established until the classic 1908 paper of L. Adler and F. Hitschmann. Previous descriptions, as these two young Viennese gynecologists noted, were demonstrably inadequate. The point here is less that so little was known about menstruation than that it was described in a way that created, through an extraordinary leap of the synecdochic imagination, a cellular correlative to the socially distinguishing characteristics of women. Histology mirrored with uncanny clarity what it meant to be female.[47]

Today, the uterus is described as passing through two stages, rather colorlessly designated "secretory" and "proliferative," during each menstrual cycle. In the nineteenth and early twentieth centuries it was said to proceed through a series of at least four and as many as eight stages. Its "normal" stage was construed as "quiescence," followed by "constructive" and "destructive" stages and a stage of "repair." Menstruation, as one might surmise, was defined as occurring at the destructive stage, when the uterus gave up its lining. As Heape puts it, in an account redolent of war reportage, the uterus during the formation of the menstrual clot is subject to "a severe, devastating, periodic action." The entire epithelium is torn away at each period,

> leaving behind a ragged wreck of tissue, torn glands, ruptured vessels, jagged edges of stroma, and masses of blood corpuscles, which it would seem hardly possible to heal satisfactorily without the aid of surgical treatment.

Mercifully, this is followed by the recuperative stage and a return to normalcy. Little wonder that Havelock Ellis, steeped in this rhetoric, would conclude that women live on something of a biological roller coaster. They are, "as it were, periodically wounded in the most sensitive spot in their organism and subjected to a monthly loss of blood." The cells of the uterus are in constant, dramatic flux and subject to soul-wrenching trauma. Ellis concludes, after ten pages of still more data on the physiological and psychological periodicity in women, that the establishment

> of these facts of morbid psychology, are very significant; they emphasize the fact that even in the healthiest woman a worm however harmless and unperceived, gnaws periodically at the roots of life.[48]

A gnawing worm is by no means the only metaphor of pain and disease employed to interpret uterine or ovarian histology. The bursting of the follicle is likened by Rudolph Virchow, the father of modern pathology, to teething, "accompanied with the liveliest disturbance of nutrition and nerve force." For the historian Michelet, woman is a creature "wounded each month," who suffers almost constantly from the trauma of ovulation, which in turn is at the center, as Thérèse Moreau has shown, of a physiological and psychological phantasmagoria dominating her life. Less imaginatively, a French encyclopedia likens follicular rupture to "what happens at the rupture of an acute abscess." The German physiologist E. F. W. Pfluger likens menstruation to surgical debridement, the creation of a clean surface in a wound or, alternatively, to the notch used in grafting a branch onto a tree, to the "innoculationschnitt." Imperatives of culture or the unconscious, not positive science, informed the interpretations of the female body more or less explicitly in these accounts.[49]

While all of the evidence presented so far is by men and produced in a more or less antifeminist context, image making, the construction of the body through science, occurs in feminist writers as well. Mary Putnam Jacobi's *The Question of Rest for Women During Menstruation* (1886), for example, is a sustained counterattack against the view that "the peculiar changes supposed to take place in the Graafian vesicles at each period . . . involve a peculiar expenditure of nervous force, which was so much dead loss to the individual life of the woman." Women were therefore unfit for higher education, a variety of jobs, and other activities that demand large expenditures of the mental and physical energy that was thought to be in such short supply. Since the "nervous force" was commonly associated in higher animals and in women with sexual arousal, Jacobi's task becomes one of severing the sexual from the reproductive life of women, of breaking the ties between the two postulated in the ovarian theory of Bischoff, Pouchet, Adam Raciborski, and others.[50]

Much of her book is taken up with a compilation of the real or supposed empirical failings of this view. But though many of her criticisms are well taken, she neither offers a more compelling new theory of the physiology of ovulation nor gives a clearer picture of cellular changes in the uterine mucosa during the menstrual cycle than do those she is arguing against.[51]

Jacobi does, however, offer a new metaphor: "All the processes concerned in menstruation converge, not toward the sexual sphere, but the *nutritive*, or one department of it—the reproductive." The acceleration of blood flow to the uterus "in obedience to a *nutritive* demand" is precisely analogous to the "afflux of blood to the muscular layer of the stomach and intestines after a meal." Jacobi, like her opponents, tended to reduce woman's nature to woman's reproductive biology. But for her, the essence of female sexual difference lay not in periodically recurring nervous excitement nor in episodes of engorgement, rupture, and release of tension but rather in the quiet processes of nutrition. Far from being periodical, ovulation in Jacobi's account is essentially random: "The successive growth of the Graafian vesicles strictly resembles the successive growth of buds on a bough." Buds, slowly opening into delicate cherry or apple blossoms and, if fertilized, into fruit, are a far cry from the wrenching and sexually intense swellings of the ovary imagined by the opposing theory.[52]

Indeed, Jacobi's woman is in many respects the inverse of that of Pouchet, Raciborski, or Bischoff. For these men, the theory of spontaneous ovulation demanded a woman shackled to her body, woman as nature, as physical being, even if the tamed quality of her modern European avatar spoke eloquently of the power of civilization. For Jacobi, on the other hand, spontaneous ovulation implied just the opposite. Biology provides the basis for a radical split between woman's mind and body, between sexuality and reproduction. The female body carries on its reproductive functions with no mental involvement; conversely, the mind can remain placidly above the body, free from its constraints. Jacobi's first effort at a metaphorical construction of this position uses fish whose ova are extruded without "sexual congress, and in a manner analogous to the process of defecation and micturition." In higher animals, sexual congress is necessary for conception, but ovulation remains spontaneous and independent of excitement. From this, it follows, according to Jacobi, that *"the superior contribution of the nutritive element of reproduction made by the female is balanced by an inferior dependence upon the animal or sexual element: in other words, she is sexually inferior."*[53]

Of course, Jacobi cannot deny that in lower animals female sexual instinct is tied exclusively to reproduction and that a ruptured follicle or follicles are invariably found during the rut. She nevertheless maintains that there is no proof of anything but a coincidental relationship between the state of the ovaries and the congested state of the external and internal genitalia that seems to signal sexual readiness. But in women, she adamantly maintains, "the sexual instinct and reproductive capacity remain distinct; there is no longer any necessary association between sexual impulse, menstruation, and the dehiscence of ova." Indeed, her entire research program is devoted to showing that the menstrual cycle may be read as the ebb and flow of female nutritive rather than sexual activity, that its metabolic contours are precisely analogous to those of nutrition and growth. And this brings one back to the metaphor of the ovary as fruit blossom. The woman buds as surely and as incessantly as the "plant, continually generating not only the reproductive cell, but the nutritive material without which this would be useless." But how, given that women generally eat less than men, do they obtain a nutritive surplus? Because "it is the possibility of making this reserve which constitutes the *essential peculiarity* of the female sex."[54]

The point here is not to belittle Jacobi's scientific work but rather to emphasize the power of cultural imperatives, of metaphor, in the production and interpretation of the rather limited body of data available to reproductive biology during the late nineteenth century. At issue is not whether Jacobi was right in pointing out the lack of coincidence between ovulation and menstruation in women and wrong in concluding that there is therefore no systematic connection between the two. Rather, both she and her opponents emphasized some findings and rejected others on largely extrascientific considerations. In the absence of an accepted research paradigm, their criteria were largely ideological—seeing woman either as civilized animal or as mind presiding over a passive, nutritive body.

But perhaps even the accumulation of fact, even the coherent and powerful modern paradigm of reproductive physiology in contemporary medical texts, offers but slight restraint on the poetics of sexual difference. Indeed, the subject itself seems to inflame the imagination. Thus, when W. F. Ganong's 1977 *Review of Medical Physiology*, a standard reference work for physicians and medical students, allows itself one moment of fancy, it is on the subject of women and the menstrual cycle. Amid a review of reproductive hormones, of the process of ovulation and menstruation described in the cold language of science, one is quite unexpectedly hit by a rhetorical bombshell, the only lyrical moment linking the reductionism of modern biological science to the experiences of humanity in 599 pages of compact, emotionally subdued prose:

Thus, to quote an old saying, "Menstruation is the uterus crying for lack of a baby."

Cultural concerns have free license here, however embedded they may be in the language of science. As in nineteenth-century texts, synechdochic leaps of the imagination seem to view woman as the uterus, which in turn is endowed, through the by-now familiar turn of the pathetic fallacy, with feelings, with the capacity to cry. The body remains an arena for the construction of gender even though modern research paradigms do, of course, isolate the experimental and interpretive work of reproductive biology from extrascientific pressures far more than was possible in the essentially preparadigmatic research of the nineteenth century.[55]

Scientific advances, I have argued, did not destroy the hierarchical model that construed the female body as a lesser, turned-inward version of the male, nor did it banish female orgasm to the physiological periphery. Rather, the political, economic, and cultural transformations of the eighteenth century created the context in which the articulation of radical differences between the sexes became culturally imperative. In a world in which science was increasingly viewed as providing insight into the fundamental truths of creation, in which nature as manifested in the unassailable reality of bones and organs was taken to be the only foundation of the moral order, a biology of incommensurability became the means by which such differences could be authoritatively represented. New claims and counterclaims regarding the public and private roles of women were thus contested through questions about the nature of their bodies as distinguished from those of men. In these new discursive wars, feminists as well as antifeminists sacrificed the idea of women as inherently passionate; sexual pleasure as a sign in the flesh of reproductive capacity fell victim to political exigencies.

NOTES

For a complete and fully-annotated version of this essay, see the author's piece in C. Gallagher, and T. Laqueur ed., *The Making of the Modern Body* (California, 1987), 1–41.

1. Condorcet, "On the Admission of Women to the Rights of Citizenship" (1791), in *Selected Writings*, ed. Keith Michael Baker (Indianapolis, 1976), 98.
2. Ibid., 98.
3. Wisdom of Solomon 7.2 and Philo *Legum allegoriae* 2.7, cited in Peter Brown, "Sexuality and Society in the Fifth Century A.D.: Augustine and Julian of Eclanum," in *Tria corda: Scritti in onore di Arnaldo Momigliano*, ed. E. Gabba (Como, 1983), 56; Mrs. Jane Sharp, *The Midwives Book* (1671), 43–44.
4. Nemesius of Emesa, *On the Nature of Man* (Philadelphia, 1955), 369; Galen *De semine* 2.1, in *Opera omnia*, ed. C. G. Kuhn, 20 vols. (1821–33), 4:596.
5. Bartholomew Parr, ed., *The London Medical Dictionary*, vol. 2 (Philadelphia, 1819), 88–89; *Aristotle's Masterpiece* (1803; reprint ed., New York, 1974), 3.
6. Jacques Moreau de la Sarthe, *Histoire naturelle de la femme*, vol. 1 (Paris, 1803), 15, which sounds the theme of the entire volume.
7. George W. Corner, "The Events of the Primate Ovarian Cycle," *British Medical Journal*, no. 4781 (23 August 1952): 403. On older views of the fertile period of the menstrual cycle see, for example, the Roman Catholic authority Carl Capellmann, *Fakultativ Sterilität ohne Verletzung der Sittengesetze* (Aachen, 1882), who taught that days fourteen to twenty-five are "safe," while fertility rises just before the menses and continues until day fourteen. Marie Stopes, in her immensely popular manuals *Married Love* (10th ed., London, 1922), 191, and *Contraception* (London, 1924), 85, advised that maximum fertility occurs just after cessation of the menses. For the popularity of these views well into the 1930s see Carl G. Hartman, *Time of Ovulation in Women* (Baltimore, 1936), 149 and passim.
8. For an early and clearly presented table of embryological homologies, see Rudolf Wagner, ed., *Handwörterbuch der Physiologie*, vol. 4 (Braunschweig, 1853), s.v. "Zeugung," 763. Regarding skeletons, see Londa Scheibinger, "Skeletons in the Closet: The First Illustrations of the Female Skeleton in Eighteenth-Century Anatomy," in *The Making of the Modern Body*, ed. by Catherine Gallagher and Thomas Laqueur (California, 1987) 42–82. 1759 is an alternative date for the first representation of the female skeleton; see ibid.
9. Mary Douglas, *Natural Symbols* (New York, 1982), 70.
10. Plato *Timaeus* 91A-C, Loeb Classical Library, ed. R. G. Bury (Cambridge, Mass., 1929), 248–50; Galen, *On the Usefulness of the Parts of the Body*, ed. and trans. Margaret May, 2 vols. (Ithaca, N.Y., 1968), 2: 640.
11. Ibid., 1: 382 and n. 78; 2: 628, 630.
12. Ibid., 2: 628–29.
13. Ibid., 2: 630–31 and, more generally, 636–38.
14. Ibid., 2: 640–43. The allusion to Democritus is probably the following: "Coition is a slight attack of apoplexy: man gushes forth from man, and is separated by being torn apart with a kind of blow"; 68B.22, in *Die Fragmente der Vorsokratiker*, ed. Diels-Kranz (Berlin, 1956). Galen is clearly in sympathy here with the Hippocratic treatise *The Seed*, in *Hippocratic Writings*, ed. G.E.R. Lloyd (London, 1978), 317–21. Aristotle argues that the emission of semen in men is due "to the penis being heated by its movement"; in addition, "maturation" or a final concoction of the semen takes place through the heating of copulation. See Aristotle *Generation of Animals* 717b24 and 717a5, in *The Complete Works of Aristotle*, ed. Jonathan Barnes, 2 vols. (Princeton, N.J., 1984).
15. This is all quite commonplace in classical medicine. See, for examples, Aristotle *Generation of Animals* 727a3–15, 776a15–33 on milk and *History of Animals* 581b30–583b2 on semen and menstrual

blood as plethora and on menstrual blood finding its way to the breasts and becoming milk; Aetius of amida, *Tetrabiblion*, trans. James V. Ricci (Philadelphia, 1950); Hippocrates *Aphorisms* 32 and 33 and *Epidemics* 1.16, in *The Medical Works of Hippocrates*, ed. and trans. John Chadwick and W. N. Mann (Oxford, 1950). Renaissance texts, both popular and learned, repeated much of this lore; see, for example, Patricia Crawford, "Attitudes to Menstruation in Seventeenth-Century England," *Past and Present*, no. 91 (1981): 48–73.

16. The earliest version of the hemorrhoidal bleeding/menstruation equivalency I have encountered is in Aristotle, *Generation of Animals* 27a10, where he notes that women in whom the menstrual discharge is normal are not troubled with hemorrhoidal bleeding or nosebleeds. See J. B. [John Bulwer], *Anthropometamorphosis: Man Transformed of the Artificial Changeling* (1653), 390; and Albrecht von Haller, *Physiology: Being a Course of Lectures*, vol. 2 (1754), paragraph 816, p. 293, my emphasis. For further clinical notes on the connection between menstrual and other bleeding see John Locke, *Physician and Philosopher . . . with an Edition of the Medical Notes*, Wellcombe History of Medicine Library, n.s., vol. 2 (London, 1963), 106, 200.

17. John Sadler, *The Sicke Woman's Private Looking Glass* (1636), 118 and 110–18 more generally; Pierre Dionis, *A General Treatise of Midwifery* (1727, from a late seventeenth-century French text), 57 (on the importance of the imagination); Ambroise Pare, "Of the Generation of Man," in *The Works of the Famous Cirurg . . .* , trans. Thomas Johnson (1634), book 24, pp. 889–90; Robert Barrett, *A Companion for Midwives* (1699), 62.

18. Pare, "Of the Generation of Man," 889; Trotulla, *Diseases of Women*, 16; William Sermon, *The Ladies Companion or the English Midwife* (1671), 13; Sadler, *Looking Glass*, 118ff.

19. Euchar Roesslin, *The Byrth of Mankynde* (1545), fol. 28. This text, or thinly disguised versions of it, was widely reprinted in large numbers of vernacular and Latin editions; the trope of a succession of children as a merciful God's comfort for the sting of death was often attributed to St. John Chrysostom, presumably to Homily XVIII on Gen. 4.1, "And Adam Knew Eve as His Wife."

20. J. B. de C. M. Saunders and Charles D. O'Malley, *The Anatomical Drawings of Andreas Vesalius* (New York, 1982), points out that figs. 2 and 3 were drawn to illustrate the Galenic homologies while the penislike vagina in fig. 4 is simply an artifact of having to remove the organs in a great hurry. A useful table of the homologies Vesalius sought to illustrate are given in L. R. Lind, ed., *The Epitome of Andreas Vesalius* (New York, 1949), 87. These representations became the standards for more than a century in both popular and learned tracts; see for example Alexander Read, *A Description of the Body of Man* (1634), 128, for an English version; and Fritz Weindler, *Geschichte der gynäkologische-anatomischen Abbildung* (Dresden, 1908).

21. Sir Thomas Browne, *Pseudodoxia Epidemica or Enquiries into Very Many Received Tenents and Commonly Presumed Truths*, vol. 2 of *The Works of Sir Thomas Browne*, ed. Geoffrey Keynes (London, 1928), book 3, chap. 17, pp. 212–13, 216; Browne denies the vulgar belief in the annual alteration of sex in hares; Ambroise Pare, *On Monsters and Marvels*, ed. and trans. Janis L. Pallister (Chicago, 1982), 32; *Montaigne's Travel Journal* (San Francisco, 1983), 6.

22. Caspar Bauhin, *Theatrum Anatomicum* (Basel, 1605), as cited in William Harvey, *Lectures on the Whole Anatomy* (1616), ed. and trans. C. D. O'Malley, F. N. L. Poynter, and K. F. Russell (Berkeley, 1961), 132 and 467n.

23. On the discovery of the clitoris see Renaldo Colombo, *De re anatomica* (1572), book 2, chap. 16, pp. 447–48; Sharp, *Midwives Book*, 44–45; John Pechey, *Complete Midwives Practice* (London, 1698), 49.

24. Helkiah Crooke, *A Description of the Body of Man* (1615), 250; Thomas Vicary's work is also known as *The Englishman's Treasure* (1585), 53.

25. Havelock Ellis, *Studies in the Psychology of Sex*, vol. 3 (Philadelphia, 1923), 194; the phenomenon Ellis observes is, I suggest, of eighteenth-century origins.

26. Cited in V. C. Medvei, *A History of Endocrinology* (Boston, 1982), 357; Haller, *Physiology*, paragraphs 823–26, pp. 301–3. Haller, at the time he wrote these passages, was an ovist; that is, he believed that

the egg contained the new life and that the sperm merely activated its development. But the same sorts of accounts were also written by spermaticists.

27. See for examples Jane Abray, "Feminism in the French Revolution," *American Historical Review* 80, no. 1 (February 1975): 43–62; Susanna Barrows, *Distorting Mirrors* (New Haven, 1981), chap. 2; Susan Sleeth Mosedale, "Science Corrupted: Victorian Biologists Consider 'The Woman Question,'" *Journal of the History of Biology* 11, no. 1 (Spring 1978): 1–55; Elizabeth Fee, "Nineteenth-Century Craniology: The Study of the Female Skull," *Bulletin of the History of Medicine* 53, no. 3 (Fall 1979): 915–33; Lorna Duffin, "Prisoners of Progress: Women and Evolution," in Sara Delamont and Lorna Duffin, eds., *Woman: Her Cultural and Physical World* (New York, 1978), 56–91. For two contemporary English articulations of these themes see Grant Allen, "Plain Words on the Woman Question," *Fortnightly Review*, n.s., 46 (October 1889): 274; and W. L. Distant, "On the Mental Differences Between the Sexes," *Journal of the Royal Anthropological Institute* 4 (1875): 78–87. Alexis de Tocqueville, *Democracy in America*, ed. Phillips Bradley, vol. 2 (New York, 1945), 223.

28. Jean Elshtain, *Public Man, Private Woman* (Princeton, N.J., 1981), chap. 3.

29. Jean-Jacques Rousseau, *A Discourse on Inequality*, trans. Maurice Cranston (Harmondsworth, 1984), 104.

30. Ibid., 102–3, 110; *Emile; or, On Education*, trans. Allan Bloom (New York, 1979), book 5, pp. 359 and 362n.

31. Ibid., 357–58, 362–63; my emphasis.

32. John Millar, *Origin of the Distinctions of Ranks* (Basel, 1793), 14, 32, 86, 95–96.

33. Anna Wheeler and William Thompson, *An Appeal of One-Half the Human Race, Women, Against the Pretensions of the Other Half, Men, to Retain Them in Political and Thence in Civil and Domestic Slavery* (London, 1825), 60–61, emphasis in text.

34. Zillah Eisenstein, *The Radical Future of Liberal Feminism* (New York, 1981), chap. 5, pp. 89–112; Mary Wollstonecraft, *Thoughts on the Education of Daughters . . .* (1787), 82.

35. Mary Wollstonecraft, *Female Reader* (1789), vii; Taylor, *Eve*, 47–48. I take the term "passionlessness" and an understanding of its political meaning in the early nineteenth century from Nancy Cott's pioneering article "Passionlessness: An Interpretation of Victorian Sexual Ideology, 1790–1850," *Signs* 4, no. 21 (1978): 219–36.

36. Sarah Ellis, *The Wives of England* (London, n.d.), 345, and *The Daughters of England, Their Position in Society, Character & Responsibilities* (London, 1842), 85. Mitzi Myers, "Reform or Ruin: A Revolution in Female Manners," *Studies in the Eighteenth Century* 11 (1982): 199–217, makes a persuasive case for considering writers as politically as the domestic ideologists and Mary Wollstonecraft as engaged in the same moral enterprise.

37. Aldous Huxley, *Literature and Science* (New York, 1963), 67; quoted in Peter Morton, *The Vital Science: Biology and the Literary Imagination, 1860–1900* (London, 1984), 212.

38. For references to some of the English and French clinical reports see William Baly, *Recent Advances in the Physiology of Motion, the Senses, Generation, and Development* (London, 1848), 46n.; Johann Friedrich Blumenbach, *The Elements of Physiology*, trans. John Elliotson (1828), 483–84; Johannes Muller, *Handbuch der Physiologie des Menschen*, vol. 2 (Coblenz, 1840), 644–56 and 643–49 generally on the release of the ovum.

39. Bischoff, *Beweis*, 43; Q. U. Newell et al., "The Time of Ovulation in the Menstrual Cycle as Checked by Recovery of the Ova from the Fallopian Tubes," *American Journal of Obstetrics and Gynecology* 19 (February 1930): 180–85; on the discovery of the reproductive hormones see A. S. Parkes, "The Rise of Reproductive Endocrinology, 1926–1940," *Journal of Endocrinology* 34 (1966): xx–xxii; Medvei, *History*, 396–411; and George W. Corner, "Our Knowledge of the Menstrual Cycle, 1910–1950," *The Lancet* 240, no. 6661 (28 April 1951); 919–23.

40. Achilles Chereau, *Memoires pour servir a l'étude des maladies des ovaires* (Paris, 1844), 91; Pouchet, *Théorie positive*, 227; Augustus Gardner, *The Causes and Curative Treatment of Sterility, with a Prelimi-*

nary Statement of the Physiology of Generation (New York, 1856), 17; *Lancet*, 28 January 1843, 644.

41. Duncan is cited as the epigraph of chapter 3, "The Changes That Take Place in the Non-Pregnant Uterus During the Oestrous Cycle," in F. H. A. Marshall, *The Physiology of Reproduction* (New York, 1910), 75.

42. Bischoff, *Beweis*, 40 and 40–48 generally on this point; Haller, *Physiology*, paragraph 812, p. 290 (p. 419 of the 1803 English edition); Blumenbach, *Elements*, 461–62; the oft-repeated allusion to Pliny is from his *Natural History* 7.15.63.

43. Robert Remak, "Über Menstruation und Brunst," *Neue Zeitschrift für Geburtskunde* 3 (1843): 175–233, esp. 176; Muller, *Handbuch*, 640.

44. Jean Borie, "Une Gynecologie passionée," in Jean-Paul Aron, ed., *Misérable et glorieuse: La Femme du XIX siècle* (Paris, 1980), 164ff.; Angus McLaren, "Doctor in the House: Medicine and Private Morality in France, 1800–1850," *Feminist Studies* 2, no. 3 (1974–75): 39–54; Pouchet, *Théorie positive*, introduction, 12–26 (on the use of "logic" in the absence of hard evidence see his discussion of the first law, esp. 15), 444–46 (summary of his programmatic statement).

45. G. F. Girdwood, "On the Theory of Menstruation," *Lancet*, 7 (October 1844); 315–16.

46. Adam Raciborski, *Traité de la menstruation* (Paris, 1868), 46–47 and 43–47 generally; his *De la puberté et de l'âge critique chez la femme* (Paris, 1844) was often cited, along with Bischoff, as having established the existence of spontaneous ovulation in humans; *orgasme* was primarily a medical term in the nineteenth century meaning an increase of vital energy to a part often associated with turgescence (see *Littre*, s.v. "orgasme"); the first use I have found of the term *"estrous"* to refer to the reproductive cycle of humans as well as other mammals is in Walter Heape, "The 'Sexual Season' of Mammals and the Relation of the 'Proestrum' to Menstruation," *Quarterly Journal of the Microscopical Society*, 2nd ser., 44, no. 1 (November 1900): 1–70 and esp. 29–40.

47. Walter Heape, *Sex Antagonism* (London, 1913), 23; F. Hitschmann and L. Adler, "Der Bau der Uterusschleimhaut des geschlechtsreifen Weibes mit besonderer Berucksichtigung der Menstruation," *Monatsschrift für Geburtshulfe und Gynäkologie* 27, no. 1 (1908): 1–82, esp. 1–8, 48–59.

48. Walter Heape's account of the stages of menstruation is in his "The Menstruation of *Semnopithecus entellus*," *Philosophical Transactions of the Royal Society of London*, ser. B, 184, part 1 (1894): 411–66 plus plates, esp. 421–40; the quotation is from Marshall's summary *Physiology*, 92; Havelock Ellis, *Man and Woman: A Study of Human Secondary Sexual Characteristics* (London, 1904), 284, 293.

49. Rudolph Virchow, *Der puerperale Zustand: Das Weib und die Zelle* (1848), 751, as cited in Mary Jacobi, *The Question of Rest for Women During Menstruation* (New York, 1886), 110. According to Michelet (*L'Amour*, 393), the ovary was of course not the only source of woman's fundamental sickness: "Ce siècle sera nommé celui des maladies de la matrice," he argues, having identified the fourteenth century as that of the plague and the sixteenth as that of syphilis (iv). See Thérèse Moreau, *Le Sang de l'histoire* (1982); A. Charpentier, *Cyclopedia of Obstetrics and Gynecology*, trans. Egbert H. Grandin (New York, 1887), part 2, p. 84; for Pfluger see Hans H. Simmer, "Pfluger's Nerve Reflex Theory of Menstruation: The Product of Analogy, Teleology and Neurophysiology," *Clio Medica* 12, no. 1 (1977): 57–90, esp. 59.

50. Jacobi, *Question of Rest*, 1–25, 81, and 223–32 passim.

51. Ibid., section 3, pp. 64–115, is devoted to laying out and criticizing the so-called ovarian theory of menstruation.

52. Ibid., 98–100.

53. Ibid., 83, 165; emphasis is in the text.

54. Ibid., 99, 167–68.

55. W. F. Ganong, *Review of Medical Physiology*, 8th ed. (Los Altos, Calif., 1977), 332 and 330–44 passim.

16   How to Build a Man

Anne Fausto-Sterling

How does one become a man? Although poets, novelists, and playwrights long past answered with discussions of morality and honor, these days scholars deliberate the same question using a metaphor—that of social construction. In the current intellectual fashion, men are made, not born. We construct masculinity through social discourse, that array of happenings that covers everything from music videos, poetry, and rap lyrics to sports, beer commercials, and psychotherapy. But underlying all of this clever carpentry is the sneaking suspicion that one must start with a blueprint—or, to stretch the metaphor yet a bit more, that buildings must have foundations. Within the soul of even the most die-hard constructionist lurks a doubt. It is called the body.

In contrast, biological and medical scientists feel quite certain about their world. For them, the body tells the truth. (Never mind that postmodern scholarship has questioned the very meaning of the word "truth.") My task in this essay is to consider the truths that biologists extract from bodies, human and otherwise, to examine scientific accounts—some might even say constructions—of masculinity. To do this, I will treat the scientific/medical literature as yet another set of texts open to scholarly analysis and interpretation.

What are little boys made of? While the nursery rhyme suggests "snips and snails, and puppy-dogs tails," during the past seventy years, medical scientists have built a rather more concrete and certainly less fanciful account. Perhaps the single most influential voice during this period has been that of psychologist John Money. Since at least the 1920s, embryologists have understood that during fetal development a single embryonic primordium—the indifferent fetal gonad—can give rise to either an ovary or a testis. In a similar fashion, both male and female external genitalia arise from a single set of structures. Only the internal sex organs—uteri, fallopian tubes, prostates, sperm transport ducts—arise during embryonic development from separate sets of

---

Anne Fausto-Sterling received her Ph.D. in Developmental Genetics and has spent thirty years working as a laboratory biologist. She has produced additional scholarship in the field of gender and science and is interested in the social nature of scientific knowledge. Her first book, *Myths of Gender: Biological Theories about Women and Men* (Basic) appeared in a second edition in 1992. She is currently writing a book with the tentative title: *Body Building: How Biologists Construct Sexuality*. She is Professor of Medical Science and Women's Studies at Brown University.

structures. In the 1950s, Money extended these embryological understandings into the realm of psychological development. As he saw it, all humans start on the same road, but the path rapidly begins to fork. Potential males take a series of turns in one direction, potential females in another. In real time, the road begins at fertilization and ends during late adolescence. If all goes as it should, then there are two, and only two, possible destinations—male and female.

But, of course, all does not always go as it should. Money identified the various forks in the road by studying individuals who took one or more wrong turns. From them, he derived a map of the normal. This is, in fact, one of the very interesting things about biological investigators. They use the infrequent to illuminate the common. The former they call abnormal, the latter normal. Often, as is the case for Money and others in the medical world, the abnormal requires management. In the examples I will discuss, management means conversion to the normal. Thus, we have a profound irony. Biologists and physicians use natural biological variation to define normality. Armed with this description, they set out to eliminate the natural variation that gave them their definitions in the first place.[1]

How does all this apply to the construction of masculinity? Money lists ten road signs directing a person along the path to male or female. In most cases these indicators are clear, but, as in any large city these days, graffiti sometimes makes them hard to read and the traveler ends up taking a wrong turn. The first sign is *chromosomal sex,* the presence of an X or a Y chromosome. The second is *gonadal sex*: when there is no graffiti, the Y or the X instructs the fetal gonad to develop into a testis or an ovary. *Fetal hormonal sex* marks the third fork: the embryonic testis must make hormones that influence events to come—particularly the fourth *(internal morphologic sex)*, fifth *(external morphologic sex),* and sixth *(brain sex)* branches in the road. All of these, but especially the external morphologic sex at birth, illuminate the road sign for step number seven, *sex of assignment and rearing.* Finally, to become either a true male or a true female in John Money's world, one must produce the right hormones at puberty *(pubertal hormonal sex),* acquire and express a consistent *gender identity and role*, and, to complete the picture, be able to reproduce in the appropriate fashion *(procreative sex).*[2]

Many medical texts reproduce this neat little scheme, and suggest that it is a literal account of the scientific truth, but they neglect to point out how, at each step, scientists have woven into the fabric their own deeply social understandings of what it means to be male or female. Let me illustrate this for several of the branches in the road. Why is it that usually XX babies grow up to be female while XYs become male? Geneticists say that it is because of a specific Y chromosome gene, often abbreviated SDY (for "Sex-Determining Gene" on the Y). Biologists also refer to the SDY as the Master Sex-Determining Gene and say that in its *presence* a male is formed. Females, on the other hand, are said to be the default sex. In the *absence* of the master gene, they just naturally happen. The story of the SDY begins an account of maleness that continues throughout development. A male embryo must activate this master gene and seize its developmental pathway from the underlying female ground plan.

When the SDY gene starts working, it turns the indifferent gonad into a functional testis. One of the first things the testis does is to induce hormone synthesis. It is these molecules that take control of subsequent developmental steps. The first hormone to hit the decks (MIS, or Mullerian Inhibiting Substance) suppresses the development of the internal female organs, which lie in wait ready to unveil their feminine presence. The next, fetal testosterone, manfully pushes other embryonic primordia to develop both the internal and external trappings of physical masculinity. Again, medical texts offer the presence/absence hypothesis. Maleness requires the presence of special hormones; in their absence, femaleness just happens.[3]

Up to this point, two themes emerge. First, masculinity is an active presence that forces itself onto a feminine foundation. Money sometimes calls this "The Adam Principle—adding something to make a male." Second, the male is in constant danger. At any point male development can be derailed; a failure to activate SDY, and the gonad becomes an ovary; a failure to make MIS, and the fetus can end up with fallopian tubes and a uterus superimposed on an otherwise male body; a failure to make fetal testosterone, and, despite the presence of a testis, the embryo develops the external trappings of a baby girl. One fascinating contradiction in the scientific literature illustrates my point. Most texts write that femaleness results from the absence of male hormones, yet at the same time scientists worry about how male fetuses protect themselves from being femininized by the sea of maternal (female) hormones in which they grow.[4] This fear suggests, of course, that female hormones play an active role, after all; but most scientists do not pick up on that bit of logic. Instead, they hunt for special proteins the male embryo makes in order to protect itself from maternally induced feminization. (It seems that mother is to blame even before birth.)

Consider now the birth of a boy-child. He is perfect: Y chromosomes, testes descended into their sweet little scrotal sacs, a beautifully formed penis. He is perfect—except that the penis is very tiny. What happens next? Some medical texts refer to a situation such a this as a social emergency, others see it as a surgical one. The parents want to tell everyone about the birth of their baby boy; the physicians fear he cannot continue developing along the road to masculinity. They decide that creating a female is best. Females are imperfect by nature, and if this child cannot be a perfect or near-perfect male, then being an imperfect female is the best choice. What do the criteria physicians use to make such choices tell us about the construction of masculinity?

Medical managers use the following rule of thumb:

Genetic females should always be raised as females, preserving reproductive potential, regardless of how severely the patients are virilized. In the genetic male, however, the gender of assignment is based on the infant's anatomy, predominantly the size of the phallus.[5]

Only a few reports on penile size at birth exist in the scientific literature, and it seems that birth size in and of itself is not a particularly good indicator of size and function at puberty. The average phallus at birth measures 3.5 cm (1 to 1.5 inches) long. A baby boy born with a penis measuring only 0.9 inches raises some eyebrows, but medical practitioners do not permit one born with a penis less than 0.6 inches long to remain as a male.[6] Despite the fact that the intact organ promises to provide orgasmic pleasure to the future adult, it is surgically removed (along with the testes) and replaced by a much smaller clitoris which may or may not retain orgasmic function. When surgeons turn "Sammy" into "Samantha," they also build her a vagina. Her primary sexual activity is to be the recipient of a penis during heterosexual intercourse. As one surgeon recently commented, "It's easier to poke a hole than build a pole."

All this surgical activity goes on to ensure a congruous and certain sex of assignment and sex of rearing. During childhood, the medical literature insists, boys must have a phallus large enough to permit them to pee standing up, thus allowing them to "feel normal" when they play in little boys' peeing contests. In adulthood, the penis must become large enough for vaginal penetration during sexual intercourse. By and large, physicians use the standard of reproductive potential for making females and phallus sizes for making males, although Suzanne J. Kessler reports one case of a physician choosing to reassign as male a potentially reproductive genetic female infant rather than remove a well-formed penis.[7]

At birth, then, masculinity becomes a social phenomenon. For proper masculine socialization to occur, the little boy must have a sufficiently large penis. There must be no doubt in the boy's mind, in the minds of his parents and other adult relatives, or in the minds of his male peers about the legitimacy of his male identification. In childhood, all that is required is that he be able to pee in a standing position. In adulthood, he must engage in vaginal heterosexual intercourse. The discourse of sexual pleasure, even for males, is totally absent from this medical literature. In fact, male infants who receive extensive penile surgery often end up with badly scarred and thus physically insensitive members. While no surgeon finds this outcome desirable, in assigning sex to an intersexual infant, sexual pleasure clearly takes a backseat to ensuring heterosexual conventions. Penetration in the absence of pleasure takes precedence over pleasure in the absence of penetration.

In the world of John Money and other managers of intersexuality, men are made, not born. Proper socialization becomes more important than genetics. Hence, Money and his followers have a simple solution to accidents as terrible as penile amputation following infant circumcision: raise the boy as a girl. If both the parents and the child remain confident of his newfound female identity, all will be well. But what counts as good mental health for boys and girls? Here, Money and his coworkers focus primarily on female development, which becomes the mirror from which we can reflect the truth about males. Money has published extensively on XX infants born with masculinized genitalia. Usually such children are raised as girls, receiving surgery and hormonal treatments to feminize their genitalia and to ensure feminine puberty. He notes that frequently such children have a harder time than usual achieving clarity about their femininity. Some signs of trouble are these: in the toddler years, engaging in rough-and-tumble play, and hitting more than other little girls do; in the adolescent years, thinking more about having a career and fantasizing less about marriage than other little girls do; and, as an adolescent and young adult, having lesbian relationships.

The homologue to these developmental variations can be found in Richard Green's description of the "Sissy Boy Syndrome." Green studied little boys who developed "feminine" interests—playing with dolls, wanting to dress in girls' clothing, not engaging in rough-and-tumble play. These boys, he argued, are at high risk for becoming homosexuals. Money's and Green's ideas work together to present a picture of normality. And, surprise, surprise, there is no room in the scheme for a normal homosexual. Money makes a remarkable claim. Genetics and even hormones count less in making a man or a woman than does socialization. In sustaining that claim, his strongest evidence, his trump card, is that the child born a male but raised a female becomes a heterosexual female. In their accounts of the power of socialization, Money and his coworkers defined heterosexual in terms of the sex of rearing. Thus, a child raised as a female (even if biologically male) who prefers male lovers is psychologically heterosexual, although genetically she is not.

Again, we can parse out the construction of masculinity. To begin with, normally developing little boys must be active and willing to push one another around; maleness and aggression go together. Eventually, little boys become socialized into appropriate adult behavior, which includes heterosexual fantasy and activity. Adolescent boys do not dream of marriage, but of careers and a professional future. A healthy adolescent girl, in contrast, must fantasize about falling in love, marrying, and raising children. Only a masculinized girl dreams of a professional future. Of course, we know already that for men the true mark of heterosexuality involves vaginal penetration with the penis. Other activities, even if they are with a woman, do not really count.

This might be the end of the story, except for one thing. Accounts of normal development drawn from the study of intersexuals contain internal inconsistencies. How *does* Money explain the higher percentage than normal of lesbianism, or the more frequent aggressive behavior among masculinized children raised as girls? One could imagine elaborating on the socialization theme: parents aware of the uncertain sex of their children subconsciously socialize them in some intermediary fashion. Shockingly for a psychologist, however, Money denies the possibility of subconsciously driven behavior. Instead, he and the many others who interpret the development of intersexual children resort to hormonal explanations. If an XX girl, born with a penis, surgically "corrected" shortly after birth, and raised as a girl, subsequently becomes a lesbian, Money and others do not look to faulty socialization. Instead, they explain this failure to become heterosexual by appealing to hormones present in the fetal environment. Excess fetal testosterone caused the masculinization of the genitalia; similarly, fetal testosterone must have altered the developing brain, readying it to view females as appropriate sexual objects. Here, then, we have the last bit of the picture painted by biologists. By implication, normal males become sexually attracted to females because testosterone affects their brain during embryonic development. Socialization reinforces this inclination.

Biologists, then, write texts about human development. These documents, which take the form of research papers, textbooks, review articles, and popular books, grow from interpretations of scientific data. Often written in neutral, abstract language, the texts have the ring of authority. Because they represent scientific findings, one might imagine that they contain no preconceptions, no culturally instigated belief systems. But this turns out not to be the case. Although based in evidence, scientific writing can be seen as a particular kind of cultural interpretation—the enculturated scientist interprets nature. In the process, he or she also uses that interpretation to reinforce old or build new sets of social beliefs. Thus, scientific work contributes to the construction of masculinity, and masculine constructs are among the building blocks for particular kinds of scientific knowledge. One of the jobs of the science critic is to illuminate this interaction. Once this is done, it becomes possible to discuss change.

NOTES

1. In the 1950s Dr. John Money argued that gender was merely a matter of body image and upbringing. One of his most dramatic cases, offered over and over again in defense of his viewpoints, was a pair of twin boys. One suffered a circumcision accident at the age of eight months and lost his penis. Money decided to raise this child as a girl, advised that "she" be castrated, given reconstructive genital surgery, and at puberty be given female hormones. Money claimed that this child easily assumed a female identity and grew into a woman who accepted her gender identity. Recently, however, Dr. Milton Diamond and Keith Sigmundson (Archives of Pediatric and Adolescent Medicine, March 1997) found and interviewed Money's patient, now in his thirties. In fact he never accepted his female identity, and as a teenager demanded to learn his whole medical history and decided to continue life as a male, even though he did not have a functional penis. This case report made the front pages of the New York Times and a debate now rages about how to interpret this new information.

2. For a popular account of this picture, see John Money and Patricia Tucker, Sexual Signatures: On Being a Man or a Woman (Boston: Little, Brown, 175).

3. The data do not actually match the presence/absence model, but this does not seem to bother most people. For a discussion of this point, see Anne Fausto-Sterling, "Life in the XY Corral," Women's Studies International Forum 12 (1989): 319–31; Anne Fausto-Sterling, "Society Writes Biology/Biology Constructs Gender," Daedalus 116 (1987): 61–76; and Anne Fausto-Sterling, Myths of Gender: Biological Theories about Women and Men (New York: Basic Books, 1992).

4. I use the phrase "male hormone" and "female hormone" as shorthand. There are, in fact, no such categories. Males and females have the same hormones, albeit in different quantities and sometimes with different tissue distributions.

5. Patricia Donahoe, David M. Powell, and Mary M. Lee, "Clinical Management of Intersex Abnormalities," Current Problems in Surgery 8 (1991): 527.

6. Robert H. Danish, Peter A. Lee, Thomas Mazur, James A. Amrhein, and Claude J. Migeon, "Micropenis II: Hypogonadotropic Hypogonadism," Johns Hopkins Medical Journal 146 (1980): 177–84.

7. Suzanne J. Kessler, "The Medical Construction of Gender: Case Management of Intersexed Infants," Signs 16 (1990).

17 Baboons with Briefcases vs. Langurs with Lipstick

Feminism and Functionalism in Primate Studies

Susan Sperling

Studies of monkeys and apes have never been just about monkeys and apes. With the rise of evolutionary thought in nineteenth-century Europe, our views of the nonhuman primates became firmly tied to our understanding of our own development over evolutionary time. In the Western imagination, primates have become important to the iconography of human gender, as primate studies have become central to academic and popular discourses about gendered animal and human bodies.

Two theories of ultimate causality have dominated primatological models for the origins of monkey, ape, and human gendered behavior: structural-functionalism and sociobiology. The structural-functionalist model, British social anthropology's key contribution to twentieth-century social science, explains the structural pattern of social institutions in terms of how they function as integrated systems to fulfill individual and societal human needs. Anthropologists in the period following World War II translated this theory to their observations of nonhuman primates; they viewed savanna baboon behaviors as adaptations that "functioned" both to promote individual survival and to maintain stable troop life. As we shall see, this perspective structured much theory about the evolution of human gendered behaviors as extrapolated from studies of baboons and other monkeys and apes. Male dominance was viewed as functioning to organize and control the troop in much the same way as political leadership functions in human cultures. There are many problems with this simple analogy.

In the mid-1970s, sociobiology replaced structural-functionalism as the pre-eminent explanatory model. According to the sociobiologists, behaviors always evolve to maximize the reproductive fitness of individuals (the relative percentage of genes passed on to future generations). Although differing in some significant ways, both models explain the existence of gender-dimorphic behaviors as functioning to increase evolutionary fitness and as controlled in unspecified

Susan Sperling studied physical anthropology at Berkeley where she has developed research on popular and academic discourses about the relationships of human beings to primates and to other animals. She is currently writing about recent ethnographic research on attitudes towards animals in a variety of contexts, including their use as food and in scientific research. She lives in the San Francisco Bay Area where she teaches in the Medical Anthropology Program at UCSF and at Chabot College.

ways by genes. Both kinds of functionalist arguments for the origin of sexually dimorphic behaviors among humans explain these behaviors as adaptations to past selective pressures in primate or hominid phylogeny. In the past, many of these reconstructions have been overtly sexist; some more recent functionalist hypotheses have attempted to redress former androcentric biases. But these new narratives, although more palatable for some feminists, rest on poor empirical foundations. We do not fully understand the biological, social, and ecological roots of nonhuman primate aggression or dominance. "Fully alternative accounts" of the development of gendered behaviors in primates can, and must, be developed. Feminist sociobiology does not represent progress for feminist evolutionary science because it suggests a biological essentialism at the heart of human behavior. In following its path, we abandon those research strategies that might lead us to insights about gendered aspects of human aggression, among other things. But in order to understand feminist sociobiology and its deficiencies, we need a better sense of the unfolding story of primate studies and structural-functionalist and sociobiological models.

For a quarter century, functionalist reductionism in primatology has seemed almost immune to sophisticated arguments about evolutionary epistemology in other disciplines; primatologists who have addressed this problem have sometimes found themselves tarred with the brush of "anti-Darwinism" and "antievolutionism." Stephen Jay Gould (1986) has written of the frustrations involved in critiquing adaptationism: "A former student of mine recently completed a study proving that color patterns of certain clam shells did not have the adaptive significance usually claimed. A leading journal rejected her paper with the comment: 'Why would you want to publish such nonresults?'"[1] As Gould points out, the study of gender differences suffers from the same bias, a problem in what is privileged as publishable. Measured gender differences are reported and attract attention from the press. What we do not know is how often such differences are not found and the result not published.

Other things shape behavior besides genes and shape it in important ways for the organisms in question. As biologist Susan Oyama (1985) points out, an ant larva may become a worker or a queen, depending on nutrition, temperature, and other variables, just as a male rodent may exhibit nurturant behaviors when exposed to certain stimuli. Control does not flow only from the gene outward. To understand the vastly more complex developmental sequences involved in the acquisition of gendered primate behavior, we must study it developmentally rather than attempting to reduce discourse to arguments about ultimate genetic fitness. There is much more to understanding the development of behavior than retrospectively hypothesizing its adaptive function. Considering the presently confounding array of data on gender-role dimorphism in different primate species, it seems that three things are likely to provide both better questions and answers about behavioral dimorphism: emphasis on both context and development of behavior, a rejection of essentialism and gender dualism, and a focus on the interaction been organisms and their environments of development. This mandates not the complete abandonment of functionalist models but their integration with other levels of causality.

An obsession with gender-role dimorphism (sexually differing behaviors) as an adaptive mechanism has impeded our understanding of the origins and maintenance of such sexually distinct behaviors in primates—behaviors that, after all, vary greatly both within and across species. Functionalist interpretations of primate behavior view sexually dimorphic traits as end points of natural selection and attempt to explain the selective pressures that might have brought these traits into being, while failing to explain their mechanisms of development and great variety of expressions. These approaches propose a kind of Panglossian philosophy that all behavior is adaptive, although there is much accumulating evidence that this is by no means the case.

The uses of nonhuman primate behavior for understanding human evolution raise important epistemological questions about how we know things in evolutionary science; feminist scholars and others in the evolutionary sciences are beginning to address these questions. Researchers must begin to examine the multiply contingent pathways along which biological systems develop and the complex ways in which extraorganismic factors interact with organisms at every stage of development. Emphasis on contingency in the development of biological and behavioral systems leads inevitably away from the biological essentialism (the belief that gendered behaviors are genetically determined) so pervasive in functionalist evolutionary models in primatology. I want to argue for a deconstruction of all functionalist models, including sociobiological ones, of sex-linked primate behaviors. I think we can hope for more accurate, fuller, more coherent approaches to the study of primate gender differences (some of which may help us to understand aspects of human behavior) than those proposed by functionalists of the last two decades. Unfortunately, epistemological critiques of functionalism are rarely raised outside the scholarly enclaves in which evolutionary biologists meet. Such discourse almost never reaches social scientists, among whom the debate has been disastrously constructed as one between reductionists in the biological and evolutionary sciences—who contend that genetic mechanisms selected over phylogenetic history control important human behaviors—and feminists and other cultural constructionists who deny that biology has any important role in human experience. In both scholarly and popular discussions, writers disseminate the currently privileged functionalist model in journals, at conferences, and in the popular press. Although a number of primatologists have argued for years against the obsession with ultimate causality that has come to dominate the field, their ideas have not been widely conveyed outside the discipline.

STRUCTURAL-FUNCTIONALIST MODELS OF PRIMATE GENDERED BEHAVIOR

When I first began my tenure as a graduate student in physical anthropology at the University of California, Berkeley, in the 1970s, modern primate studies had emerged from a period in which a relatively small number of researchers collected natural histories of a variety of primate species in the field and had entered an era of widespread structural-functionalist model building. The first period, the natural history stage of primate studies, occurred roughly between 1950 and 1965. In the second stage (from the mid-1960s to the late 1970s), data from a variety of field studies, particularly those of savanna baboons and the chimpanzees of the Gombe Reserve in Tanzania, were incorporated into structural-functionalist models for human evolution centered on the sexual division of labor, the origins of the family, and the origins of human gendered behavior. The third phase came in the late 1970s with the hegemony of sociobiology as the functionalist model par excellence for understanding behavioral evolution.

The first wave of postwar anthropological primatology included a number of long-term studies that laid the foundations of the discipline. Most of these studies were descriptive natural histories with few explicit links made to human evolution. During the second stage of primatology, which began in the mid-1960s, structural-functionalist analysis became central to the problem-oriented studies that replaced the earlier emphasis on natural history. Primatology was then, as it is today, a heterogeneous field that included research on proximate causal factors affecting social behavior and on the complex interaction between social structure, behavior, and ecology (socio-ecology). But it is the structural-functionalist grand theory builders, those who have focused exclusively on ultimate causality, who have been the progenitors of the most influential and popular visions of primate behavior. In the functionalist models of the 1960s and 1970s, all aspects of behavior within a primate troop were explained as adaptive mechanisms. Thus, the roles of females and males in different species were interpreted as selected during the phylogenetic history of the species because they "functioned" to promote survival.

Lynda Marie Fedigan (1982) has reviewed many of the evolutionary reconstructions by primatologists of this period. She points out that the "baboonization" of early human life in such models rested on a savanna ecological analogy: since protohominids evolved on the African savanna, presumably they would have shared certain selective pressures with modern baboon troops, particularly for predator protection by large males. Washburn, DeVore (1961), and other early baboon researchers had viewed male dominance as functioning to organize troop members hierarchically and to control overt aggression. Fedigan argues that the other primary model for protohominid evolution, that of the chimpanzees studied by Goodall at the Gombe Reserve in Tanzania, was far preferable. Here the analogy rested on a phylogenetic relationship between chimp and human, which is immensely closer. This model emphasized the mother-offspring bond, sharing within the matrifocal family, the immigration of young females to new groups, birth spacing, and temporary sex bonding. It is to this chimpanzee behavioral model that the first wave of feminist authors, in particular the constructors of the "woman the gatherer" model, would turn for primatological evidence of the social centrality of females in early hominid evolution.

Fedigan points out that the "baboonization" of protohominids became so common that by the early to mid-1970s not a single introductory text in human evolution omitted reference to it. As Rowell (1974) and other critics of this model stressed, many of the generalizations and assumptions about the functions of male dominance made by early baboon researchers like Washburn and DeVore were unsubstantiated by data from other research sites. Rowell's studies of troop movement among forest baboons, for instance, indicated that the direction of daily foraging routes was determined by a core of mature females rather than by the dominant males. As feminist scholars such as Sandra Harding (1986) and Donna Haraway (1989) note, women primatologists often have had a different vision of group structure and behavior because they attended to female actors in a way that male primatologists did not. This focus on female behavior in baboons and in a variety of other species became fuel for the critical deconstructions of the baboon model during the 1970s. In addition, a number of studies questioned the assumption that male dominance conferred a reproductive advantage on particular males, thus contributing to selection for male aggression.

Despite such criticisms, the insertion of primatological data into structural-functionalist models for the evolution of gendered human behavior continued. The practice was borrowed by scholars outside of primatology, and soon found its way into popular writings. A statement by psychologists Carol McGuiness and Karl Pribram (Goldman 1978) illustrates this phenomenon: "In all primate societies the dominant males control territorial boundaries and maintain order among lesser males by containing and preventing their aggression, the females tending the young and forming alliances with other females. Human primates follow this same pattern so remarkably that it is not difficult to argue for biological bases for the type of social order that channels aggression to guard the territory which in turn maintains an equable environment for the young."[2]

McGuinness's and Pribam's interpretation appeared in *Psychology Today*, one of many popular journals publishing articles on human nature and its biological roots. Although the template here is the savanna baboon troop as described by Washburn and DeVore—and contested early in this period by Rowell and others who call into question all of the fundamental assumptions of the savanna model—"all primate species" collapsed the diversity and specificity of data on primates into a single category, "primate societies." Here, and in a plethora of popular books and articles published during this period, monkeys and apes were used explicitly as exemplars of earlier stages of human evolution. The ubiquitous primate ancestral group now occupied a position like that of "tribal societies" in the evolutionary schemas of nineteenth-century anthropologists. The diffusion of cultural relativism into all branches of modern social science had made it embarrassing and untenable to fit tribal groups into this early evolutionary slot. If "primitives" were to be considered our equals with complex and meaningful cultures, they could not also represent the protohuman past. In this new way of thinking, monkeys and apes became the early ancestral group from which human institutions could be seen to have evolved.

This replacement of human "primitives" by nonhuman primates also relates to global political events of the postwar period. Following WWII, a number of key academics publicly rejected eugenics and the biology of race as legitimate areas of concern within evolutionary science, thereby setting the agenda for decades of antiracist physical anthropology. Colonial liberation and the West's subsequent Cold War courtship of developing nations helped to make politically untenable the positioning of human tribal societies as human evolutionary precursors. The Third World and its peoples could no longer occupy the place assigned them by early Western evolutionists' origin accounts; now baboons and chimpanzees would replace them. But while the Victorians had downgraded tribal peoples to primitive exemplars of the Western past, postwar evolutionists *upgraded* nonhuman primates to fill the newly vacant slot on the putative evolutionary ladder.

One consequence of this key insertion of the nonhuman primate in the Western symbolic niche for "primitive progenitor" was an implied obliteration of the border between human and nonhuman. The passage by McGuiness and Pribram is a mass of terminological ambiguities. What is meant by terms such as "the division of labor" when referring to nonhuman primates? Does this term mean the same thing when applied to human groups? Monkeys and apes do not have a division of labor along gender lines as do human cultures; each animal performs subsistence tasks in approximately the same way as the others, consuming on the spot what is individually foraged. Human divisions of labor by sex are complex historical and socioeconomic phenomena embroidered with symbolic meanings unavailable to animals. But when DeVore and Hall (1965) wrote that "the baboon troop is organized around the dominance hierarchy of adult males," they meant it both literally and figuratively. They perceived dominant males as "culturally" binding together a loose, potentially chaotic aggregate of females, subadult males, and young. In the same work, they offered a spatial schematization of primate societies, a series of concentric circles with the most dominant animals in the center. DeVore and Hall visualized male dominance as the cement of primate social organization. This paralleled British social anthropology's view of the politics of small scale societies as all-male endeavors. As Sylvia Yanagisako (1979) has shown, crucial social anthropological texts often presented thick descriptions of male networks and their power relations and thin descriptions of female networks, which were assumed to represent a kind of eternal set of female relational networks devoid of either power or meaning.

Social anthropologist and popularizer Robin Fox is typical of the many writers who sought evolutionary legitimations of male dominance among humans in primate field studies. In *Biosocial Anthropology* (1975a), Fox was quite explicit about his use of nonhuman primates as replacements for human "primitives":

> We know a great deal about primates which can tell us what is behaviorally available to our order in general and, therefore, what must have been available by way of a behavioral repertoire to our ancestors . . . "early man" then, in this sense, was less like modern man gone wild than like a primate tamed. *And even if we cannot deduce accurately the kinship systems of early man [sic] from those of the most primitive humans, we can do something better, we can distill the essence of kinship systems on the basis of comparative knowledge and find the elements of such systems that are logically, and hence in all probability chronologically, the "elementary forms of kinship."*[3]

The differences between Fox's assumptions and those of the Victorian evolutionists are negligible. Fox traced the evolution of human kinship through the primates, borrowing, as he admits, "somewhat recklessly from the jargon of social anthropology, descent and alliance."[4] According to his analysis, these two elements are present in nonhuman primate social systems but are combined only in human groups. He divides primate social systems into two types, single-male and multimale groups, of which all have in common "a threefold division of the larger group into: a) adult males; b) females and young; c) peripheral males. We can look at any primate social system, including our own, in terms of the 'accommodations' made between these three blocks."[5] The phylogenetic histories of different primates are thus collapsed into several categories with a certain internal consistency but little relationship to actual data. Once Fox raises the question of the relationship of complex human behaviors to nonhuman primate behavioral variation, his evidence becomes a confusing array of randomly chosen bits and pieces of behavior from species with varying phylogenetic proximity to one another and to humans. An important consequence of this approach is that it obscures many of the culturally unique aspects of human kinship, among them the widespread existence of putative kin among human cultures, that make it fundamentally different from social relations among nonhumans.

Examples of this missing link approach to the use of nonhuman primate behavior abound in the literature of this period, often focusing on gendered behavior and its presumed "functions." Many popularizations of this approach have had a wide audience. In one such account, the sexologist and gerontologist Alex Comfort (1966) explained the presumed continual receptivity of human females:

> At some point in primate evolution, the female became receptive all year round and even throughout pregnancy. This apparently trifling change in behavior was probably the trigger, or one of the triggers, which set off the evolution of man [sic]. Between baboons and higher apes we find the effects of this change. Baboons behave very like other pack-living animals. Higher apes, with sexual activity continuing all the year round, and unrelated to heat, develop a heterosexual social life which is not confined to the coital encounter.[6]

Comfort's order of ascent is baboon, ape, and human, and the characteristic "continual sexual receptivity" is traced along this ladder in much the same way that the Victorians associated "primitive promiscuity" with savages, group marriage with barbarians, and monogamy with civilized humans.

As we move up and down the phylogenetic scale, monkeys and apes are anthropomorphized, and behaviors of diverse species are used as simple analogues of human characteristics. Much of the second-wave scholarly and popular evolutionary writing that uses nonhuman primate models reproduces this logical failing. Selected examples of group structure, kinship, and dominance behavior in nonhuman primates are viewed as precursors of human social structure and behavior. The influence of these models on popular perceptions of the relationship of humans to animals and of the meanings of gender divisions has been profound.

Nonhuman primates became the missing link in the evolutionary models of the late 1960s and 1970s. But nonhuman primates are as unwieldy a link as were the "primitives" of the early evolutionists. All living species of organisms have undergone separate histories combining both evolutionary and chance events. There is immense variation in behavior among primate species, and cross-phylum generalizations are hard to make. For instance, sexual behavior among monkeys and apes exhibits a wide variety of patterns that defy neat phylogenetic analysis. Monkeys display a variety of mating patterns, but the most telling data in this regard are from the apes. There are significant differences between the sexual behavior of chimpanzees, gorillas, and orangutans that in no way relate to their phylogenetic closeness to humans. For instance, hormonal and behavioral states appear closely correlated in gorilla reproductive behavior, somewhat less so in chimps, and least of all in orangutans. But chimpanzees are much more closely related to humans than are orangutans. This finding contradicts the linear evolutionist's view that the closer a species' phylogenetic relationship to humans, the less its sexual behavior is hormonally controlled and the greater the resemblance to human reproductive behavior.

SOCIOBIOLOGY AND THE EVOLUTION OF GENDERED BEHAVIOR IN PRIMATES

The 1975 publication of *Sociobiology: The New Synthesis* by Harvard entomologist Edward O. Wilson was a signal event for students of animal behavior in numerous disciplines. Wilson makes two major assertions in *Sociobiology*: that all important social behaviors are genetically controlled, and that natural selection of the genome is caused by a set of specific adaptive mechanisms (kin selection) that produce behaviors maximizing an organisms's ability to contribute the greatest number of genes to the next generation. Wilson took the concept of kin selection and applied it to all animal and human behavior from the social insects to humans, suggesting that the social sciences and biological sciences be subsumed by sociobiology. It is not surprising that many scientists viewed the idea of their disciplines' cannibalistic incorporation into the body of sociobiology as an unsavory prospect. Some objected on political grounds to its explicit reductionism and potential for racist and sexist interpretations. The Boston-based collective Science for the People (1976) issued a critical attack on sociobiology, calling it another form of biological determinism like nineteenth-century eugenics and Social Darwinism. At the same time, sociobiology began to establish a foothold in American and European departments of anthropology, zoology, and psychology. As structural-functionalism had earlier, sociobiology became the grand theory conveyed to social scientists interested in human evolution and widely popularized through newspaper and magazine articles and popular books. By the mid-1980s, a number of important empirical critiques appeared, deconstructing the logic of sociobiological arguments. But these have yet to be widely circulated outside classes and seminars in evolutionary theory.

Early sociobiological views of the evolution of human gendered behaviors incorporated primatological data and viewed males and females as having differential reproductive strategies. Because of the presumably greater "investment" of female primates in infant rearing, female behaviors were viewed as selected because they advanced a female's chances of gaining male protection during vulnerable periods for herself and her offspring (offspring are seen as fleshy packets of shared genes). Females frequently were pictured as conservative, coy, and passive. By contrast, it behooved males to inseminate as many females as possible, thus forwarding their attempted genetic monopoly of the future. Wilson wrote: "It pays males to be aggressive, hasty, fickle and undiscriminating. In theory it is more profitable for females to be coy, to hold back until they can identify the male with the best genes. Human beings obey this biological principle faithfully."[7] DeVore and other sociobiologists have maintained that the sexual and romantic interest of middle-aged men in younger women and their presumed lack of interest in their female age cohorts stem from selective pressures on male primates to inseminate as many fertile females as possible.

Wilson (1978) applied sociobiological arguments to the meaning of the middle-class nuclear family in American culture:

> The building block of nearly all human societies is the nuclear family. The populace of an American industrial city, no less than a band of hunter-gatherers in the Australian desert, is organized around this unit. In both cases the family moves between regional communities, maintaining complex ties with primary kin by means of visits (or telephone calls and letters) and the exchange of gifts. During the day the women and children remain in the residential area while the men forage for game or its symbolic equivalent in the form of money. The males cooperate in bands or deal with neighboring groups.[8]

It is no coincidence that sociobiology and the second wave of Western feminism were simultaneous occurrences. Early sociobiologists clearly envisioned their new model as "disproving" feminism. The sociobiologist Pierre Van den Berghe wrote: "Neither the National Organization for Women nor the Equal Rights Amendment will change the biological bedrock of asymmetrical parental investment."[9] Phillip Kitcher (1985) has commented on the sexism of many sociobiological arguments:

> Sometimes the expression is tinged with regretful sympathy for ideals of social justice (Wilson), at other times with a zeal to *epater les feministes* (Van den Berghe). [I]t is far from clear that sociobiologists appreciate the political implications of the views they promulgate. These implications become

clear when a *New York Times* series on equal rights for women concludes with a serious discussion of the limits that biology might set to women's aspirations, and when the new right in Britain and France announces its enthusiasm for the project of human sociobiology.[10]

More recently, a feminist discourse in sociobiology has shifted attention to the presumed gender-specific reproductive strategies of female primates. By stressing female variance, feminist sociobiologists assert that selection acts on females as well as males to encode genetic programs for enhanced fitness. The primatologist Sarah Hrdy (1986), an important contributor to this literature, has lauded the emphasis in sociobiology on variance in reproductive success for contributing a bracing dose of feminism to primatology. Thus, these researchers see female mate choice and female elicitation of male support and protection in rearing young as integral to the competitive strategies of females vis-à-vis other females.[11] They describe "prolonged female receptivity" in some nonhuman primates and human females as an evolved mechanism to manipulate male behavior. Variation in mothering styles and skills, and the degree of selfishness of caretakers, are said to reflect variance in reproductive interests that are sometimes at odds with those of offspring. They also describe (as kin-selection strategies) competition between females whenever fertility and the rearing of young are limited by access to resources and the competition of dominant females on behalf of their offspring by eliminating competitors or forestalling reproduction in the mothers of potential competitors. The new female primate is dressed for success and lives in a troop that resembles the modern corporation: now everyone gets to eat power lunches on the savanna.

This new view of females among academic sociobiologists is mirrored in popular journalism about primate infanticide and infant abuse, and interfemale aggression and competition. Here, human females are portrayed as bearers of behavioral homologues from their nonhuman primate ancestors and early hominid past predisposing them toward certain modes of interindividual competition, rather than as the passive and nurturant weaklings of some former functionalist models. In these newer accounts, female competition has taken center stage. It is tempting to blame journalists and science writers for these lurid images and their extension to human females, but that would be a mistake: the academic sociobiological model is clearly meant to apply across the primate order to humans. DeVore (Anderson 1986) for example, interprets soap operas to reflect his vision of female reproductive strategies:

> Soap operas have a huge following among college students, and the female-female competition is blatant. The women on these shows use every single feminine wile. On the internationally popular soap *Dynasty*, for example, a divorcee sees her ex-husband's new wife riding a horse nearby. She knows the woman to be newly pregnant, so she shoots off a gun, which spooks the horse, which throws the young wife, and makes her miscarry. The divorcee's own children are living with their father and this woman; the divorcee doesn't want this new young thing to bring rival heirs into the world to compete with her children.
>
> Whole industries turning out everything from lipstick to perfume to designer jeans are based on the existence of female competition. The business of courting and mating is after all, a negotiation process, in which each member of the pair is negotiating with those of the opposite sex to get the best deal possible, and to beat out the competition from one's own sex. . . . I get women in my class saying I'm stereotyping women, and I say sure, I'm stereotyping the ones who make lipstick a multibillion dollar industry. It's quite a few women. Basically, I appeal to students to look inside themselves: what are life's little dilemmas? When your roommate brings home a guy to whom you're extremely attracted, does it set up any sort of conflict in your mind?[11]

Many sociobiologists disclaim the reductionism of their popular interpreters; Wilson (1978) and Hrdy (1981) have both published statements about the importance of human cultural transmission and the possibility of change in human social relations caused by cultural factors. This is disingenuous; it has now become fashionable for both biological and environmental reductionists to claim interactionism as the only reasonable view and then to revert immediately to the reductionist theories that belie their assertions. In fact, academic sociobiologists draw the same conclusions as their journalistic interpreters.

WHAT WE KNOW ABOUT GENDERED PRIMATE BEHAVIOR

Modern biological and behavioral studies have exposed the fallacy of basic arguments essential to reductionist theories of ultimate causality. Scientists now criticize many former assertions about reliably differentiating behavioral dimorphisms across primate phyla as based on incomplete data. The more we know about nonhuman primate behavior, the more examples of intraspecific and interspecific variety emerge. Several common functionalist assertions about gender differences now appear to be unsubstantiated. For instance, male monkeys and apes of a variety of different species have been described as more aggressive than conspecific females. Barbara B. Smuts (1987), however, finds no consistent gender difference in frequencies of aggression in numerous primate species. She focuses on the contextual factors influencing agonistic behaviors in both males and females, including how males and females influence each other, rather than positing inherent, genetically controlled behavioral dimorphisms.

Another recently challenged functionalist theory about nonhuman primates is that social dominance is highly correlated with reproductive success and that dominance behaviors have been selected over the phylogenetic histories of species. Irwin S. Bernstein (1968, 1987), in reviewing data from numerous primate studies, suggests that there is little association between dominance rank and reproductive success. Fedigan summarizes the whole era of reports on male copulations, mating success, consortship, and male dominance and concludes that none of the measures provides a convincing picture of dominant males monopolizing estrous females. High levels of male aggression and wounding during the breeding season may have more to do with male mobility, "xenophobia," and rank instability among males during the breeding season than with fighting over females.

Aggression, reproduction access, and dominance are emerging as more complex, variable, and context dependent and, as well, subject to generalizations easily applied cross-phyla. And not all primate species show a pattern of male protection from predators for females and young (their own or those of other males); indeed, many do not. Robert S. O. Harding and Dana K. Olson (1986) report that the vivid displays of male patas (a type of African monkey), long assumed to distract predators from females and young, who remained frozen in the grass, now appear to be associated with intermale competition during the breeding season. To complicate the picture further, these large African cercopithecines were thought to live in exclusively single-male groups. In fact, it is now clear that patas females mate with a variety of males.

How can we generalize with any certainty about gendered behavior in nonhuman primates? We know that female primates conceive, gestate, and lactate, and that in most species it is the female primarily who nurtures the young (although nonhuman primate "nurturance" should not be confused with the cultural traditions with which this word is associated in human groups). Males inseminate females. There is little or no sexual division in subsistence labor among nonhuman primates, one fact among many other that makes them strikingly different from human beings. All nonhuman primates forage for themselves, and there is little sharing of food, with a few exceptions, such as the occasional opportunistic hunting by some male chimps and baboons. In many, but not all, species of monkeys and apes, males are larger than females, more muscular, and have larger canines. Size dimorphism seems to be important in a number of species in giving priority of access to environmental incentives (such as desired grooming partners or preferred foods), but larger males by no means always dominate smaller females. Aggressive and affiliative behaviors of male and female primates vary depending on the species, social context, and individual. In fact, we are confronted with an enormous range of variations in intraspecific and interspecific behavior that defies neat classificatory schemas. Yet, rather than study the ontogeny of behaviors across the life span of individual animals, a daunting task but one likely to yield some important clues about the development and maintenance of behaviors, many primatologists have generally continued to posit tidy ex post facto explanations about function.

TOWARD AN EPIGENETIC PERSPECTIVE ON GENDERED PRIMATE BEHAVIOR

A recent and more refined discourse in evolutionary studies has suggested that important influences on the development of organisms cannot be explained by reductionist-adaptationist models. Bernstein (1987) has noted the concentration on function rather than mechanism in the literature and points out that while functional consequences may influence genetic change in a population's future, they do not always reflect evolutionary history. The concept that evolution always produces ideal solutions ignores many other factors that may have had varying degrees of importance in a species' history: random processes, phylogenetic inertia, environmental change, and the random nature of mutation. The zoologist Hans Kummer (1971) noted, "Discussions of adaptiveness sometimes leave us with the impression that every trait observed in a species must by definition be ideally adaptive, whereas all we can say with certainty is that it must be tolerable, since it did not lead to extinction."[12]

Whether they propose masculinist or feminist arguments, both structural-functionalism and sociobiology commit the fallacy of affirming the consequent. In 1951, the ethologist Niko Tinbergen (Bernstein 1987) posed a set of questions for understanding the reason for the existence of a biological structure: (1) What were the immediate preceding events leading to changes producing the structure or behavior? (2) What are the consequences of the structure (its functions)? (3) What processes from conception to the present have influenced the attributes of the structure? and (4) What were the evolutionary selective pressures that influenced the genetic contributions to the structure? It is important to note that the second and fourth questions are separate: function is a future consequence; it is not the same as evolutionary history, because environments are not constant. The first and third questions deal with proximal and developmental factors that bring about behaviors, levels of analysis often completely ignored by functionalists but likely to yield the most interesting developmental data on gendered behavior. Tinbergen's classic construction throws into relief the error of trying to answer all questions at the level of function alone, as so many of the grand theory builders in modern primatology have done, without explicating proximal cause and mechanism.

Although linear functionalist agendas have prevailed in reconstructions of the evolution of human gendered behavior, views of what female and male monkeys and apes are doing, and why they are doing it, have changed considerably. Primates are icons for us. They seem to live at the boundary of nature and culture, and, as Haraway (1978a, 1987b, 1989) has brilliantly elucidated, the ways they appear in current Western symbolism reflect the political and socioeconomic discourses of the historical periods during which primate studies have developed as a discipline. But postmodern feminist deconstructions of primatology have tended to avoid the issue of good science versus bad science.

On the other hand, Sandra Harding (1986) suggests that the elimination of masculine bias in science requires "a fundamental transformation of concepts, methods and interpretations; an examination of the very logic of scientific inquiry."[13] I propose that the movement away from linear functionalist models in primatology toward a more robust epigenetic vision of evolutionary biology fits squarely within Harding's proposed course of action. The resistance to this change is strong: the linear reductionism of the past is clean and orderly, whereas for many, the ambiguity of the kind of approach I am suggesting is often unbearably messy. Such an approach is also time-consuming; primates are long-lived species, and the research strategies necessary for a full explication of gendered behavior require life history studies, a difficult prospect within the current structure of academic science (in which most primatological data are acquired for doctoral dissertations during one or two field seasons).

Can there be an evolutionary biology that does more than retell functionalist stories in a less sexist format? An approach that looks at genetic and extragenetic factors in the origin, diversity, and persistence of gender dimorphic behavior is more useful, although more complicated and problematic, than reductionist-functionalist models. Life history studies of primates, which view development from the perspective of both proximate and ultimate causality, are necessary to our future understanding of all aspects of behavior, including gendered behaviors.

Feminists in the social sciences have often turned away from a consideration of evolutionary biology because of their awareness of the dangers of its frequently reductionist paradigms. But a more robust and sophisticated primate ethology may have something to offer by elucidating developmental mechanisms that apply across primate species and by defining the important differences between human and nonhuman primates. Human gendered behavior involves uniquely human cultural, cognitive, and linguistic characteristics that appear to be recent developments in hominid evolution and that are not shared by other primates. Biological anthropologists can contribute to an understanding of human gendered behavior only by attending first to its historical, economic, and cultural causes. Without a sophisticated grasp of human social behavior, they have little to offer the social sciences by way of theorizing about biological "roots" of complex human behaviors. Recent discourse in the social and biological sciences points out problems with normative studies that assume that behaviors are fixed dimorphisms to be measured in adulthood. Recent critiques in evolutionary theory challenge reductionist-adaptationist models that collapse variation into theories of male and female reproductive strategies. Primatologists must attend to these arguments as well as acknowledge that the human world has never existed before and that its conditions are constantly changing. This fact sets important limitations on what we can know about human evolution from studies of monkeys and apes.

Ultimately, langurs in lipstick are not an improvement over baboons with briefcases: we must return them all to their natural environments. This mandates changes in research styles involving description and coherent explanation of what actually happens during life-cycle development. With more sophisticated methodologies and more robust theoretical models, primatology may yet have something valuable to offer those of us interested in gendered human behavior.

NOTES

I want to acknowledge Abraham Sperling for pointing out the importance of critical deconstruction early in my development. Some of the ideas in this paper are the result of a long, ongoing dialogue with Micaela di Leonardo about anthropology, feminism, and the relationship between social theory and evolutionary science. I gratefully acknowledge her help in the articulation of these topics as presented here. Donna Haraway's perspectives on modern primate studies have played an important role in my approach to various functionalist agendas in primatology.

1. Gould, Stephen J. 1986. Cardboard Darwinism. *New York Review of Books* (September 25): 50–51.
2. Quoted in Goldman, David. 1978. Special Abilities of the Sexes: Do They Begin in the Brain? *Psychology Today* 12, No. 6 (November): 56.
3. Fox, Robin. 1975. *Biosocial Anthropology*. New York: Wiley: 11.
4. Ibid. 11.
5. Ibid. 13.
6. Comfort, Alex. 1966. *The Nature of Human Nature*. New York: Harper and Row: 13.
7. Wilson, Edward O. 1978. *On Human Nature*. Cambridge: Harvard University Press: 552.
8. Ibid. 553.
9. Quoted in Kitcher, Phillip. 1985. *Vaulting Ambition: Sociobiology and the Quest for Human Nature*. Cambridge: MIT Press.
10. Ibid. 6.

11. Quoted in Anderson, Duncan M. 1986. The Delicate Sex: How Females Threaten, Starve, and Abuse One Another. *Science 86*, No. 3: 43–48.

12. Quoted in Bernstein, Irwin S. 1987. The Evolution of Nonhuman Primate Behavior. *Genetica* 73: 101.

13. Harding, Sandra. 1986. *The Science Question in Feminism*. Ithaca: Cornell University Press: 108.

BIBLIOGRAPHY

Altmann, Jeanne. 1974. Observational Study of Behavior: Sampling Methods. *Behaviour* 49: 227–67.

———. 1980. *Baboon Mothers and Infants*. Cambridge, Mass: Harvard University Press.

Altmann, Stuart A., ed. 1962. A Field Study of the Sociobiology of Rhesus Monkeys, *Macaca mulatta*. *Annals of the New York Academy of Sciences* 102 (2): 338–435.

Altmann, Stuart A., and Jeanne Altmann. 1970. *Baboon Ecology: African Field Research*. Chicago: University of Chicago Press.

Anderson, Duncan M. 1986. The Delicate Sex: How Females Threaten, Starve, and Abuse One Another. *Science*, 86 (April): 43–48.

Ardrey, Robert. 1961. *African Genesis*. London: Collins.

———. 1966. *The Territorial Imperative*. New York: Atheneum.

———. 1970. *The Social Contract*. New York: Atheneum.

———. 1976. *The Hunting Hypothesis*. New York: Atheneum.

Bateson, Patrick. 1981. Ontogeny of Behaviour. *British Medical Bulletin* vol. 37, (2): 159–64.

Birke, Linda. 1986. Women, Feminism and Biology: The Feminist Challenge. New York: Metheun.

Bernstein, Irwin S. 1968. Primate Status Hierarchies. *American Zoologist* 8: 741(abstract).

———. 1987. The Evolution of Nonhuman Primate Social Behavior. *Genetica* 73: 99–116.

Blier, Ruth, ed. 1984. *Science and Gender: A Critique of Biology and its Theories on Women*. New York: Pergamon.

———, ed. 1986. *Feminist Approaches to Science*. New York: Pergamon.

Bogess, Jane. 1979. Troop Male Membership Changes and Infant Killing in Langurs (*Presbytis entellus*). *Folia Primalogica* 32: 65–107.

Bourne, Geoffrey. 1971. *The Ape People*. New York: Signet.

Buettner-Janusch, John, ed. 1962. The Relative of Man: Modern Studies of the Relation of Evolution of Nonhuman Primates to Human Evolution. *Annals of the New York Academy of science* 102 (2): 181–514.

Burton, Frances D. 1977. Ethology and the Development of Sex and Gender Identity in Nonhuman Primates. *Acta Biotheoretica* 26: 1–18.

Bygott, J. D. 1979. Agonistic Behavior, Dominance, and Social Structure in Wild Chimpanzees of the Gombe National Park. In Hamburg and McCown (1979), 405–28.

Campbell, Bernard, ed. 1972. *Sexual Selection and the Descent of Man, 1871–1971*. Chicago: Aldine.

Carpenter, Clarence R. 1964. *Naturalistic Behavior of Nonhuman Primates*. University Park: Pennsylvania State University Press.

Cheney, Dorothy L. 1977. Social Development of Immature Male and Female Baboons. Ph.D Thesis. University of Cambridge.

Cheney, Dorothy L., Robert M. Seyfarth, and Barbara Smuts. 1986. Social Relationships and Social Cognition in Nonhuman Primates. *Science* 234 (12 December 1986): 161–66.

Chevalier-Skolnikoff, Suzanne. 1971a. The Ontogeny of Communication in *Macaca speciosa*. Ph.D thesis. University of California, Berkeley.

———. 1971b. The Female Sexual Response in Stumptail Monkeys (*Macaca speciosa*), and its Broad Implications for Female Mammalian Sexuality. Paper presented at the American Anthropological Association Meeting, New York City.

Clutton-Brock, Timothy H. 1983. Behavioural Ecology and the Female. *Nature* 306:716.

Crook, John Hurrell and Stephen Garltan. 1966. On the Evolution of Primate Societies. *Nature* 210: 1200–03.

Collias, Nicholas E., and Charles H. Southwick. 1952. A Field Study of Population Density and Social Organization in Howling Monkeys. *Proceedings of the American Philosophical Society* 96: 143–56.

Comfort, A. 1966. *The Nature of Human Nature.* New York: Harper and Row.

Dahlberg, Francis, ed. 1981. *Woman the Gatherer.* New Haven: Yale University Press.

Daly, Martin, and Margo Wilson. 1978. *Sex, Evolution, and Behavior.* North Scituate, Mass.: Duxbury Press.

Dawkins, R. 1976. *The Selfish Gene.* London: Oxford University Press.

DeVore, Irven. 1962. The Social Behavior and Organization of Baboon Troops. Ph.D Thesis, University of Chicago.

———, ed. 1965a. *Primate Behavior: Field Studies of Monkeys and Apes.* New York: Holt, Rinehart and Winston.

———. 1965b. Male Dominance and Mating Behavior in Baboons. In F. A. Beach, ed. *Sex and Behavior,* New York: Krieger, pp. 266–89.

DeVore, Irven and K.R.L. Hall. 1965. Baboon Social Behavior. In *Primate Behavior: Field Studies of Monkeys and Apes.* New York: Holt, Rinehart, and Winston.

de Waal, F. 1982. *Chimpanzee Politics: Power and Sex Among Apes.* New York: Harper and Row.

Dolhinow, Phyllis, ed. 1972. *Primate Patterns.* New York: Holt, Rinehart and Winston.

———. and Naomi Bishop. 1972. The Development of Motorskills an Social Relationships among Primates through Play. In Dolhinow 1972, pp. 312–37.

Eimerl, Sarel and Irven De Vore. 1965. *The Primates.* Life Nature Library. New York: Time, Inc.

Fausto-Sterling, Anne. 1985. *Myths of Gender: Biological Theories about Women and Men.* New York: Basic Books.

Fedigan, Linda Marie. 1982. *Primate Paradigms: Sex Roles and Social Bonds.* Montreal: Eden Press.

———. 1983. Dominance and Reproductive Success in Primates. *Yearbook of Physical Anthropology* 26: 91–129.

———. 1986. The Changing Role of Women in Models of Human Evolution. *Annual Review of Anthropology* 15: 25–66.

Fedigan, Linda Marie and Laurence Fedigan. N.D. Gender and the Study of Primates. American Anthropological Association: Project on Gender Curriculum. In manuscript.

Fisher, Helen. 1982. *The Sex Contract: The Evolution of Human Behavior.* New York: Morrow.

Fossey, Dian. 1970. Making Friends with Mountain Gorillas.*National Geographic Magazine* 137: 48–68.

———. 1983. *Gorillas in the Mist.* Boston: Houghton-Mifflin.

Fox, Robin. 1968. The Evolution of Human Sexual Behavior. *New York Times Magazine,* March 24, pp. 32ff.

———. 1975a. Primate Kin and Human Kinship. In *Biosocial Anthropology.* New York: Wiley.

———, ed. 1975b. *Biosocial Anthropology.* New York: John Wiley and Sons.

Jamieson, Ian G. 1986. The Functional Approach to Behavior: Is It Useful? *American Naturalist.* 127: 195–208.

Galdikas, Birute. 1980. Living with Orangutans. *National Geographic Magazine* 157 (6): 880–53.

Gartlan, John S. 1964. Dominance in East African Monkeys. *Proceedings of the East African Academy* 2: 75–79.

Gilmore, Hugh. 1981. From Radcliffe-Brown to Sociobiology: Some Aspects of the Rise of Primatology within Physical Anthropology. *Journal of Physical Anthropology* 56 (4): 387–92.

Goldman, D. 1978. Special Abilities of the Sexes: Do They Begin in the Brain? *Psychology Today* 12 (6): 48ff.

Goodall, Jane. 1963. My Life Among the Wild chimpanzees. *National Geographic Magazine* 124 (2): 272–308.

———. 1971. *In The Shadow of Man.* Boston: Houghton-Mifflin.

———. 1986. *The Chimpanzees of Gombe: Patterns of Behavior.* Cambridge, Mass.: Harvard University Press.

Gould, Stephen Jay. 1986. Cardboard Darwinism. *New York Review of Books* (September 25): 47–54.

Gould, Stephen Jay. and E. Vrba. 1982. Exaptation—A Missing Term in the Science of Form. *Paleobiology* 8: 4–15.

Hall, K. R. L., and Irven DeVore. 1965. Baboon Social Behavior. In DeVore (1965): 53–110.

Hamburg, David A. 1963. Emotions in the Perspective of Human Evolution. In Knapp, ed. *Expressions of Emotions in Man*. New York: International Universities Press, pp. 300–17.

Hamburg, David A. and Elizabeth McCown, eds. 1979. *The Great Apes*. Menlo Park, Calif: Benjamin/Cummings.

Hamilton, W. D. 1963. The Evolution of Altruistic Behavior. *American Naturalist* 97: 354–56.

———. 1964. The Genetical Evolution of Social Behavior, I and II. *Journal of Theoretical Biology* 7: 1–52.

Haraway, Donna J. 1978a. Animal Sociology and a Natural Economy of the Body Politic, Part I. A Political Physiology of Dominance. *Signs* 4: 21–36.

———. 1978b. Animal Sociology and a Natural Economy of the Body Politic, Part II: The Past is the Contested Zone: Human Nature and Theories of Production and Reproduction in Primate Behavior Studies. *Signs* 4: 37–60.

———. The Biological Enterprise: Sex, Mind, and Profit from Human Engineering to Sociobiology. *Radical History Review*, 20: 206–37.

———. 1983. The Contest for Primate Nature: Daughters of Man the Hunter in the Field, 1960–80. In Mark Kann, ed. *The Future of American Democracy: Views from the Left*. Philadelphia: Temple University Press, pp. 175–207.

———. 1986. Primatology is Politics by Other Means: Women's Place is in the Jungle. In Blier (1986), 77–118.

———. 1988. Situated Knowledges: The Science Question in Feminism as a Site of Discourse on the Privilege of Partial Perspective. *Feminist Studies* 14(3): 575–600.

———. 1989. *Primate Visions: Gender, Race, and Nature in the World of Modern Science*. New York: Routledge.

Harding, Robert S. O., and Dana K. Olson. 1986. Patterns of Mating Among Male Patas Monkeys in Kenya. *American Journal of Primatology* 11: 343–58.

Harding, S. 1986. *The Science Question in Feminism*. Ithaca: Cornell University Press.

Hausfater, Glenn. 1975. Dominance and Reproduction in Baboons: A Quantitative Analysis. *Contributions to Primatology*, 7. Basel: Karger.

Hausfater, Glenn and Sarah Blaffer Hrdy, eds. 1984. *Infanticide: Comparative and Evolutionary Perspective*. New York: Aldine.

Hinde, Robert, ed. 1983. *Primate Social Relationships: An Integrated Approach*. Sunderland, Mass.: Sinauer.

Hodos, W. 1970. Evolutionary Interpretation of Neural and Behavioral Studies of Living Vertebrates. *The Neurosciences* 2.

Hrdy, Sarah Blaffer. 1977. *Langurs of Abu*. Cambridge, Mass: Harvard University Press.

———. 1981. *The Woman That Never Evolved*. Cambridge, Mass.: Harvard University Press.

———. 1986. Empathy, Polyandry, and the Myth of the Coy Female. In Blier (1986), 119–46.

Hubbard, Ruth. 1982. Have only Men Evolved? In Hubbard, Henifin, and Fried (1982), 17–46.

Jay, P., ed. 1968. *Primates: Studies in Adaptation and Variability*. New York: Holt, Rinehart and Winston.

Jolly, A. 1966. *Lemur Behavior*. Chicago: Chicago University Press.

Jones, Clara B. 1981. The Evolution and Socioecology of Dominance in Primate Groups: Theoretical Formulation, Classification, and Assessment. *Primates* 22: 70–83.

Jordanova, Ludmila J. 1980. Natural facts: A Historical Perspective on Science and Sexuality. In MacCormack and Strathern (1980), 42–69.

Kaye, Howard L. 1986. *The Social Meaning of Modern Biology: From Social Darwinism to Sociobiology*. New Haven: Yale University Press.

Keller, Evelyn Fox. 1983. *A Feeling for the Organism*. New York: Freeman.

———. 1985. *Reflections on Gender and Science*. New Haven: Yale University Press.

———. 1987. Reproduction and the Central Project of Evolutionary Theory. *Biology and Philosophy* 2: 73–86.

Kevles, B. 1976. *Watching the Wild Apes*. New York: Dutton.

Kinzey, Warren G., ed. 1987. *The Evolution of Human Behavior: Primate Models*. Albany: SUNY Press.

Kitcher, P. 1985. *Vaulting Ambition: Sociobiology and the Quest for Human Nature*, Cambridge, Mass.: MIT Press.

Kummer, Hans. 1971. *Primate Societies: Group Techniques of Ecological Adaptation*. Chicago: Aldine.

Lancaster, Jane B. 1973. In Praise of the Achieving Female Monkey. *Psychology Today* 7(4): 30–36, 99.

Leavitt, R. 1975. *Peaceable Primates and Gentle People*. New York: Harper and Row.

Lee, R., and I. DeVore, eds. 1968. *Man the Hunter*. Chicago: Aldine.

Leibowitz, L. 1978. *Females, Males, Families: A Biosocial Approach*. Belmont, Calif: Duxbury.

Lewontin, R.C., Steven Rose, and Leon J. Kamin. 1984. *Not in Our Genes: Biology, Ideology and Human Nature*. New York: Pantheon.

Lovejoy, O. 1981. The origin of man. *Science* 211 (4,480): 341–50.

MacCormack, C. and Marilyn Strathern, eds., 1980. *Nature, Culture, Gender*. Cambridge: Cambridge University Press.

Martin, M., and B. Voorhies. 1975. *Female of the Species*. New York: Columbia University Press.

Maynard-Smith, J. 1964. Group Selection and Kin Selection. *Nature* 201: 1145–47.

Morris, Desmond. 1967. *The Naked Ape*. New York: McGraw-Hill.

————, ed. 1978. *Primate Ethology*. London: Weidenfeld and Nicolson.

Nadler, R. 1981. Laboratory Research on Sexual Behavior of the Great Apes. In *Reproductive Biology of the Great Apes*, ed. C. E. Graham. New York: Academic Press.

Napier, John R., and N. A. Barnicot, eds. 1963. *The Primates: Symposium of the London Zoological Society*, no. 10.

————, and P. H. Napier. 1967. *A Handbook of Living Primates*. New York: Academic Press.

Nishida, T. 1972. Preliminary Information on the Pygmy Chimpanzees (*Pan panicus*) of the Congo Basin. *Primates* 13: 415–25.

Oyama, S. 1985. *The Ontogeny of Information: Development Systems and Evolution*. Cambridge: Cambridge University Press.

Patterson, Francine. 1978. Conversations with a Gorilla. *National Geographic* 154: 438–65.

Poirier, Frank, ed. 1972. *Primate Socialization*. New York: Random House.

Radcliffe-Brown, A. R. 1952. *Structure and Function in Primitive Society*. New York: Free Press.

Reite, Martin, and Nancy Caine, eds. 1983. *Child Abuse: The Nonhuman Primate Data*. New York: Alan Liss.

Rieter, Rayna Rapp, ed. 1975. *Toward an Anthropology of Women*. New York: Monthly Review Press.

Reynold, P. 1981. *On the Evolution of Human Behavior: The Argument from Animals to Man*. Berkeley: University of California Press.

Richard, Alison F. 1981. Changing Assumptions in Primate Ecology. *American Anthropology* 83: 517–33.

————. 1985. *Primates in Nature*. New York: Freeman.

Rosaldo, Michelle Z., and Louise Lamphere, eds. 1974. *Woman, Culture, and Society*. Palo Alto: Stanford University Press.

Rowell, T. 1966. Forest Living Baboons in Uganda. *Journal of Zoology* 149: 344–64.

————. 1972. *The Social Behaviour of Monkeys*. Middlesex, England: Penguin Books.

————. 1974. The concept of dominance *Behavioral Biology* 11: 131–54.

Sade, Donald S. 1965. Some Aspects of Parent-Offspring and Sibling Relations in a Group of Rhesus Monkeys, with a Discussion of Grooming. *American Journal of Physical Anthropology* 23 (1): 1–17.

————. 1967. Determinants of Dominance in a group of free-ranging rhesus monkeys. In S.A. Altmann (1967) 99–114.

Small, Meredith, ed. 1984. *Female Primates: Studies by Women Primatologists*. New York: Alan Liss.

Smuts, B. B. 1984. *Sex and Friendship in Baboons*. Chicago: Aldine.

Smuts, B. B., Dorothy L. Cheney, Robert M. Seyfarth, Richard W. Wrangham, and Thomas T. Struhsaker, eds. 1987. *Primate Societies*. Chicago: University of Chicago Press.

Sociobiological Study Group of Science for the People. 1976. Sociobiology—Another Biological Determinism. *Biosciences* 26 (3): 182–86.

Southwick, C., ed. 1963. Primate Social Behavior. Princeton: Van Nostrand.

Sperling, S. 1988. *Animal Liberators: Research and Morality.* Berkeley: University of California Press.

Strum, S. 1982. Agonistic Dominance in Male Baboons: An Alternate View. *International Journal of Primatology* 3: 175–202.

Strusaker, T. 1971. Social Behaviour of Mother and Infant Vervet Monkeys (*Cercopithecus aethiops*) *Animal Behaviour* 19: 233–50.

Sussman, R. L., ed. 1979. *Primate Ecology: Problem Oriented Field Studies.* New York: Wiley.

Symons, D. 1979. *The Evolution of Human Sexuality.* New York: Oxford University Press.

Tanner, N. 1981. *On Becoming Human.* Cambridge: Cambridge University Press.

Tanner, N. and Adrienne Zihlman. 1976. Women in Evolution, part I: Innovation and Selection in Human Origins. *Signs* 1: 585–608.

Tiger, Lionel, and R. Fox. 1971. *The Imperial Animal.* New York: Holt, Rinehart and Winston.

Trivers, R. 1972. Parental Investment and Sexual Selection. In Campbell (1972), 136–79.

Washburn, S. L. 1961. *The Social Life of Early Man.* Viking Fund Publication in Anthropology, no. 31. New York: Wenner-Gren Foundation for Anthropological Research. Chicago: Aldine.

Washburn, S. L., and Irven De Vore. 1961. Social Behavior of Baboons and Early Man. In Washburn (1961), 91–105.

Washburn, S. L., and Phyllis J., eds. 1972. *Perspective in Human Evolution*, vol. 2. New York: Holt, Rinehart and Winston.

Williams, George C. 1966. *Adaptation and Natural Selection.* Princeton: Princeton University Press.

Wilson, Edward O. 1975. *Sociobiology: The New Synthesis.* Cambridge: Harvard University Press.

———. 1978. *On Human Nature.* Cambridge: Harvard University Press.

Wynne-Edwards, V. C. 1962. *Animal Dispersion in Relation to Social Behaviour.* New York: Hafner.

Yanagisako, Sylvia. 1979. Family and Household: The Analysis of Domestic Groups. *Annual Reviw of Anthropology* 8: 161–205.

Zihlman, A. 1978. Women and Evolution, Part 2. Subsistence and Social Organization among Early Hominids. *Signs* 4: 4–20.

———. 1985. Gathering Stories for Hunting Human Nature. *Feminist Studies* 11: 364–77.

18   The Violence of Rhetoric
On Representation and Gender

Teresa de Lauretis

> Older women are more skeptical in their heart of hearts than any man; they believe in the superficiality of existence as in its essence, and all virtue and profundity is to them merely a way to cover up this "truth," a very welcome veil over a *pudendum*—in other words, a matter of decency and shame, and nothing more!
>
> —Friedrich Nietzsche, *The Gay Science*

> Even the healthiest woman runs a zigzag course between sexual and individual life, stunting herself now as a person, now as a woman.
>
> —Lou Andreas-Salomé, *Zur Psychologie der Frau*

Woman's skepticism, Nietzsche suggests, comes from her disregard for truth. Truth does not concern her. Therefore, paradoxically, woman becomes the symbol of Truth, of that which constantly eludes man and must be won, which lures and resists, mocks and seduces, and will not be captured. This skepticism, this truth of nontruth, is the "affirmative woman" Nietzsche loved and was, Derrida suggests. It is the philosophical position Nietzsche himself occupies and speaks from—a position that Derrida locates in the terms of a rhetoric, "between the 'enigma of this solution' and the 'solution of this enigma'" (Derrida 1976b: 51).[1] The place from where he speaks, the locus of his enunciation, is a constantly shifting place within discourse (philosophy), a rhetorical function and construct; and a construct that—call it *différance*, displacement, negativity, internal exclusion, or marginality—has become perhaps the foremost rhetorical trope of recent philosophical speculation. However, in speaking from that place, from the position of woman, Nietzsche need not "stunt" himself "now as a person, now as a woman," as his contemporary and sometime friend Lou Andreas-Salomé admittedly did.[2] The difference between them, if I may put it bluntly, is not *différance* but gender.

If Nietzsche and Derrida can occupy and speak from the position of woman, it is because that position is vacant and, what is more, cannot be claimed by women. To anticipate a point that will be elaborated later on, I simply want to suggest that while the question of woman for the male philosophers is a question of style (of discourse, language, writing—of philosophy), for Salomé, as in most present-day feminist thinking, it is a question of gender—of the social construction of

Teresa de Lauretis is Professor of the History of Consciousness at the University of California, Santa Cruz. She is the author of numerous essays and books on semiotics, psychoanalysis, film, literature, and feminist theory, including *Alice Doesn't: Feminism, Semiotics, Cinema* (Indiana, 1984) and *Technologies of Gender: Essays on Theory, Film, and Fiction* (Indiana, 1987). Her most recent book in English is *The Practice of Love: Lesbian Sexuality and Perverse Desire* (Indiana, 1994).

"woman" and "man," and of the semiotic production of subjectivity. And whereas both style and gender have much to do with rhetoric, the latter (as I use the term and will attempt to articulate it) has also much to do with history, practices, and the imbrication of meaning with experience; in other words, with the mutually constitutive effects in semiosis of what Peirce called the "outer world" of social reality and the "inner world" of subjectivity.

With this in mind, let me then step into the role of Nietzsche's older woman and cast my considerations on the semiotic production of gender between the rhetoric of violence and the violence of rhetoric.

The very notion of a "rhetoric of violence" presupposes that some order of language, some kind of discursive representation is at work not only in the concept "violence" but in the social practices of violence as well. The (semiotic) relation of the social to the discursive is thus posed from the start. But once that relation is instated, once a connection is assumed between violence and rhetoric, the two terms begin to slide and, soon enough, the connection will appear to be reversible. From the Foucauldian notion of a rhetoric of violence, an order of language that speaks violence—names certain behaviors and events as violent, but not others, and constructs objects and subjects of violence, and hence violence as a social fact—it is easy to slide into the reverse notion of a language that, itself, produces violence. But if violence is in language, before if not regardless of its concrete occurrences in the world, then there is also a violence of rhetoric, or what Derrida has called "the violence of the letter" (1976a: 101–140).

I will contend that both views of the relation between rhetoric and violence contain and indeed depend upon the same representation of sexual difference, whether they assume the "fact" of gender or, like Derrida, deny it; and further, that the representation of violence is inseparable from the notion of gender, even when the latter is explicitly "deconstructed" or, more exactly, indicted as "ideology." I contend, in short, that violence is en-gendered in representation.

VIOLENCE EN-GENDERED

In reviewing the current scholarship on family violence, Wini Breines and Linda Gordon begin by saying, "Only a few decades ago, the term 'family violence' would have had no meaning: child abuse, wife beating, and incest would have been understood but not recognized as serious social problems" (Breines and Gordon 1983: 490). In particular, while child abuse had been "discovered" as far back as the 1870s, but later lost visibility, social science research on wife beating (more often called "spouse abuse" or "marital violence") is altogether recent; and incest, though long labeled a crime, was thought to be rare and, in any event, not related to (family) violence. In other words, the concept of a form of violence institutionally inherent—if not quite institutionalized—in the family, did not exist as long as the expression "family violence" did not.

Breines and Gordon, a sociologist and a historian, are keenly aware of the semiotic, discursive dimension of the social. Thus, they go on to argue, if the great majority of scholarly studies still come short of a coherent understanding of family violence as a social problem, the reason is that, with the exception of feminist writers, clinicians, and a few male empirical researchers, the work in this area fails to analyze the terms of its own inquiry, especially terms such as family, power, and gender. For, Breines and Gordon maintain, violence between intimates must be seen in the wider context of social power relations; and gender is absolutely central to the family. In fact, we may add, it is as necessary to the constitution of the family as it is itself, in turn, forcefully constructed and inevitably reproduced by the family. Moreover, they continue, institutions like the medical and other "helping professions" (e.g., the police and the judiciary) are complicit, or at least congruent, with "the social construction of battering." For example, a study (Stark et al. 1979) of how the emergency room of a city hospital treated women for injuries or symptoms while completely ignoring the causes, if the injuries resulted from battering, shows how the institution of medicine "coerce[s] women who are appealing for help back into the situations and relationships that batter them. It shows a system taking women who were hit, and turning them into battered women" (Breines and Gordon 1983: 519).

The similarity of this critical position with that of Michel Foucault, himself a social historian, is striking, though no reference is made to his works (among them, *Discipline and Punish* and *The History of Sexuality* would be quite germane). But what the similarity makes apparent and even more striking is the difference of the two positions; that difference being, again, gender—not only the notion of gender, which is pivotal to the argument of Breines and Gordon, and largely irrelevant to Foucault's, but also, I will dare say, the gender of the authors. For it is feminism, the historical practice of the women's movement and the discourses that have emerged from it—like the collective speaking, confrontation, and reconceptualization of the female's experience of sexuality—that inform the epistemological perspective of Breines and Gordon. They refute the idea that all violence is of similar origin, whether that origin be located in the individual (deviance) or in an abstract, transhistorical notion of society ("a sick society"). And they counter the dominant representation of violence as a "breakdown in social order" by proposing instead that violence is the sign of "a power struggle for the *maintenance* of a certain kind of social order" (1983: 511). But which kind of social order is in question, to be maintained or to be dismantled, is just what is at stake in the discourse on family violence. It is also where Breines and Gordon differ from Foucault.

As they see it, both the intrafamily and the gender-neutral methodological perspectives on incest, for instance, which are often found combined, are motivated by the desire to explain away a reality too uncomfortable or threatening to nonfeminists. (In spite of the agreement among statistical studies that, in cases of incest as well as child sexual abuse, 92 percent of the victims are females and 97 percent of the assailants are males, "predictably enough, until very recently the clinical literature ignored this feature of incest, implying that, for example, mother-son incest was as prevalent as father-daughter incest" [Breines and Gordon 1983: 523].) Such studies not only obscure the actual history of violence against women but, by disregarding the feminist critique of patriarchy, they effectively discourage analysis of family violence from a context of both societal and *male* supremacy. Following up on the insights provided by Breines and Gordon, one can see that this is undoubtedly the rhetorical function of gender-neutral expressions such as "spouse abuse" or "marital violence," which at once imply that both spouses may equally engage in battering the other, and subtly hint at the writer's or speaker's nonpartisan stance of scientific and moral neutrality. In other words, even as those studies purport to remain innocent of the ideology or of the rhetoric of violence, they cannot avoid and indeed purposefully engage in the violence of rhetoric.

Foucault, on his part, is well aware of the paradox. The social, as he envisions it, is a field of forces, a crisscrossing of practices and discourses involving relations of power. With regard to the latter, individuals, groups, or classes assume variable positions, exercising at once power and resistance in an interplay of nonegalitarian but mobile, changeable relations; for the very existence of power relations "depends on a multiplicity of points of resistance . . . present everywhere in the power network" (Foucault 1980: 94). Both power and resistance, then, operate concurrently in "the strategic field" that constitutes the social, and both traverse or spread across—rather than inhere in or belong to—institutions, social stratifications, and individual unities. However, it is power, not resistance nor negativity, that is the positive condition of knowledge. Far from being an agency of repression, power is a productive force that weaves through the social body as a network of discourses and generates simultaneously forms of knowledge and forms of subjectivity or what we call social subjects. Here, one would think, the rhetoric of power and the power of rhetoric are one and the same thing. Indeed, he writes,

> this history of sexuality, or rather this series of studies concerning the historical relationships of power and the discourse on sex is, I realize, a circular project in the sense that it involves two endeavors that refer back to one another. We shall try to rid ourselves of a juridical and negative representation of power, and cease to conceive of it in terms of law, prohibition, liberty, and sovereignty. But how then do we analyze what has occurred in recent history with regard to this thing—seemingly one of the

most forbidden areas of our lives and bodies—that is sex? How, if not by way of prohibition and blockage, does power gain access to it? (1980: 90)

His answer posits the notion of a "technology" of sex, a set of "techniques for maximizing life" (1980: 123) developed and deployed by the bourgeoisie since the end of the eighteenth century in order to ensure its class survival and continued hegemony. Those techniques involved the elaboration of discourses (classification, measurements, evaluation, etc.) about four privileged "figures" or objects of knowledge: the sexualization of children and the female body, the control of procreation, and the psychiatrization of anomalous sexual behavior as perversion. These discourses—which were implemented through pedagogy, medicine, demography, and economics, were anchored or supported by the institutions of the state, and became especially focused on the family—served to disseminate and to "implant" those figures and modes of knowledge into each individual, family, and institution. This technology "made sex not only a secular concern but a concern of the state as well; to be more exact, sex became a matter that required the social body as a whole, and virtually all of its individuals, to place themselves under surveillance" (1980: 116).

Sexuality, then, is not a property of bodies or something originally existent in human beings, but the product of that technology. What we call sexuality, Foucault states, is "the set of effects produced in bodies, behaviors, and social relations" by the deployment of "a complex political technology" (1980: 127), which is to say, by the deployment of sexuality. The analysis is in fact circular, however attractive or fitting. Sexuality is produced discursively (institutionally) by power, and power is produced institutionally (discursively) by the deployment of sexuality. Such a representation, like Foucault's view of the social, leaves no event or phenomenon out of the reach of *its* discursive power; nothing escapes from the discourse of power, nothing exceeds the totalizing power of discourse. His conclusion, therefore, is at best paradoxical. "We must not think that by saying yes to sex, one says no to power. . . . The rallying point for the counterattack against the deployment of sexuality ought not to be sex-desire, but bodies and pleasures" (1980: 157)—as if bodies and pleasures existed apart from the discursive order, from language or representation. But then they would exist in a space which his theory precisely locates outside the social.

I have suggested elsewhere that there may be a discrepancy between Foucault's theory and his radical politics (his interventions in issues of capital punishment, prison revolts, psychiatric clinics, judiciary scandals, etc.), a discrepancy that can be accounted for by a contradiction perhaps inescapable at this time in history: the twin and opposite pull exerted on any progressive or radical thinker by the positivity of political action, on one front, and the negativity of critical theory, on the other. The contradiction is most evident, for me, in the efforts to elaborate a feminist theory of culture, history, representation, or subjectivity. Since feminism begins at home, so to speak, as a collective reflection on practice, on experience, on the personal as political, and on the politics of subjectivity, a feminist theory only exists as such insofar as it refers and constantly comes back to these issues. The contradictory pressure toward affirmative political action (the "counterattack") and toward the theoretical negation of patriarchal culture and social relations is glaring, unavoidable, and probably even constitutive of the specificity of feminist thought. In Foucault, the effect of that discrepancy (if my hypothesis is correct) has prompted charges of "paradoxical conservatism."[3]

For example, his political stance on the issue of rape, in the context of the reform of criminal law in France, has been criticized by French feminists as more subtly pernicious than the traditional, "naturalist" ideology. Arguing for decriminalization (and the desexualization) of rape, in a volume published in 1977 by the Change collective with the title *La folie encerclée*, Foucault proposed that rape should be treated as an act of violence like any other, an act of aggression rather than a sexual act. A similar position was also held by some American feminists (e.g., Brownmiller 1975), though with the opposite intent with regard to its juridical implications, and has been acutely criticized within American feminism: "Taking rape from the realm of 'the sexual,' placing it in the realm of 'the violent,' allows one to be against it without raising any questions about the extent to which the institution of heterosexuality has defined force as a normal part of [(hetero)sexual relations]" (MacKinnon 1979: 219). In the terms of Foucault's theoretical analysis, his proposal may be understood as an effort to counter the technology of sex by breaking the bond between sexuality and crime; an effort to enfranchise sexual behaviors from legal punishment, and so to render the sexual sphere free from intervention by the state. Such a form of "local resistance" on behalf of the men imprisoned on, or subject to, charges of rape, however, would paradoxically but practically work to increase and further to legitimate the *sexual* oppression of women. As Monique Plaza puts it, it is a matter of "our costs and their benefits." For what is rape if not a sexual practice, she asks, an act of *sexual* violence? While it may not be exclusively practiced on women, "rape is sexual essentially because it rests on the very social difference between the sexes. . . . It is *social sexing* which is latent in rape. If men rape women, it is precisely because they are women in a social sense"; and when a male is raped, he too is raped "as a woman" (Plaza 1980: 31).

This allows us to unravel the contradiction at the heart of Foucault's modest proposal, a contradiction that his analysis of sexuality does not serve to resolve: to speak against sexual penalization and repression, in our society, is to uphold the sexual oppression of women, or better, to uphold the practices and institutions that produce "woman" in terms of the sexual, and then oppression in terms of gender. (Which of course is not to say that oppression is not also produced in other terms.) To release "bodies and pleasures" from the legal control of the state, and from the relations of power exercised through the technology of sex, is to affirm and perpetuate the present social relations that give men rights over women's bodies. To decriminalize rape is, as Plaza states—making full use of the rhetoric of violence in her political confrontation with Foucault— to "defend the rights of the rapists . . . from the position of potential rapist that you are 'subjected' to by your status as a man" (1980: 33). Here Plaza sharply identifies the problem in Foucault's own "enunciative modality" (defined in Foucault 1972); that is to say, the place or sociosexual position from which he speaks, that of the male or male-sexed subject. For sexuality, not only in the general and traditional discourse but in Foucault's as well, is not construed as gendered (as having a male form and a female form), but simply as male. Even when it is located, as it very often is, *in* the woman's body, sexuality is an attribute or property of the male. It is in this sense, in light of that "enunciative modality" common to all the accepted discourses in Western culture (but not only there), that Adrienne Rich's notion of "compulsory heterosexuality" acquires its profoundest resonance and productivity. And in this sense her argument is not at the margins of feminism, as she seems to fear, but quite central to it (Rich 1980).

The historical fact of gender, the fact that it exists in social reality, that it has concrete existence in cultural forms and actual weight in social relations, makes gender a political issue that cannot be evaded or wished away, much as one would want to, be one male or female. For even as we agree that sexuality is socially constructed and overdetermined, we cannot deny the particular specification of gender that is the issue of that process; nor can we deny that precisely such a process finally positions women and men in an antagonistic and asymmetrical relation. The interests of men and women or, in the case in question, of rapists and their victims, are exactly opposed in the practices of social reality, and cannot be reconciled rhetorically. This is the blind spot in Foucault's radical politics and antihumanist theory, both of which must and do appeal to feminists as valuable contributions to the critique of ideology (see for example Martin [1982], and Doane et al. [1984]). Therefore, illuminating as his work is to our understanding of the mechanics of power in social relations, its critical value is limited by his unconcern for what, after him, we might call "the technology of gender"—the techniques and discursive strategies by which gender is constructed and hence, I argue, violence is engendered.

But there may be another chestnut in the fire, another point at issue. To say that (A) the concept of "family violence" did not exist before the expression came into being, as I said earlier, is not the same as saying that (B) family violence did not exist before "family violence" became part of the discourse of social science. The enormously complex relation binding expression, content, and referent (or sign, meaning, and object) is what makes (A) and (B) not the same. It seems to me that of the there—the concept, the expression, and the violence—only the first two belongs to Foucault's discursive order. The third is somewhere else, like "bodies and pleasures," outside the social. Now, for those of us whose bodies and whose pleasures are out there where the violence is (in that we have no language, enunciative position, or power apparati to speak them), the risk of saying yes to sex-desire and power is relatively small, and amounts to a choice between the devil and the deep blue sea. If we then want to bring our bodes and our pleasures closer, where we might see what they are like; better still, where we might represent them from another perspective, construct them with another standard of measurement, or understand them within other terms of analysis; in short, if we want to attempt to know them, we have to leave Foucault and turn, for the time being, to Peirce.

For Peirce, the object has more weight, as it were. The real, the physical world and empirical reality are of greater consequence to the human activity of semiosis, as outlined by Charles Sanders Peirce, than they are to the symbolic activity of signification, as defined in Saussure's theory of language and re-elaborated in contemporary French thought. Saussure's insistence on the arbitrary or unmotivated nature of the linguistic sign caused semiology to extend the categorical distinction between language (*langue*, the language system) and reality to all forms and processes of representation, and thus to posit an essential discontinuity between the orders of the symbolic and the real. Thereafter, not only would the consideration of the referent be no longer pertinent—or even possible—to the account of signification process; but the different status of the signifier and the signified would be questioned. The signified would be seen as either inaccessible, separated from the signifier by the "bar" of repression (Lacan 1966: 497), or equally engaged in the "play of differences" that make up the system of signifiers and the domain of signification (Derrida 1976a: 7). The work of the sign, in brief, would have no reference and no purchase on the real. For Peirce, on the other hand, the "outer world" enters into semiosis at both ends of the signifying process: firstly through the object, more specifically the "dynamic object," and secondly through the final interpretant. This complicates the picture in which a signifier would immediately correspond to a signified (Saussure) or merely refer to another signifier (Lacan, Derrida). Take the famous definition:

> A sign, or representamen, is something which stands to somebody for something in some respect or capacity. It addresses somebody, that is, it creates in the mind of that person an equivalent sign, or perhaps a more developed sign. That sign which it creates I call the *interpretant* of the first sign. The sign stands for something, its *object*. It stands for that object, not in all respects, but in reference to a sort of idea, which I have sometimes called the *ground* of the representation. (Peirce 2.228)

As Umberto Eco observes in "Peirce and the semiotic foundations of openness" (Eco 1979: 175–99), the notions of meaning, ground, and interpretant all pertain in some degree to the area of the signified, while interpretant and ground also pertain in some degree to the area of the referent (object). Moreover Peirce distinguishes between the dynamic object and the immediate object, and it is the notion of ground that sustains the distinction. The dynamic object is external to the sign: it is that which "by some means contrives to determine the sign to its representation" (4.536). The immediate object, instead, is internal; it is an "Idea" or a "mental representation," "the object as the sign itself represents it" (4.536).

From the analysis of the notion of "ground" (a sort of context of the sign, which makes pertinent certain attributes or aspects of the object and thus is already a component of meaning), Eco argues that not only does the sign in Peirce appear as a textual matrix; the object, too, "is not necessarily a thing or a state of the world but a rule, a law, a prescription: it appears as the operational description of a set of possible experiences" (Eco 1979: 181).

> Signs have a direct connection with Dynamic Objects only insofar as objects determine the formation of a sign; on the other hand, signs only "know" Immediate Objects, that is, meanings. There is a difference between the *object of which a sign is a sign* and the *object of a sign*: the former is the Dynamic Object, a state of the outer world; the latter is a semiotic construction. (Eco 1979: 193)

But the immediate object's relation to the representamen is established by the interpretant, which is itself another sign, "perhaps a more developed sign." Thus, in the process of unlimited semiosis, the nexus object-sign-meaning is a series of ongoing mediations between "outer world" and "inner" or mental representations. The key term, the principle that supports the series of mediations, is of course the interpretant.

As Peirce sees it, "the problem of what the 'meaning' of an intellectual concept is can only be solved by the study of the interpretants, or proper significate effects, of signs" (5.475). He then describes three general classes:

1.   "The first proper significate effect of a sign is a *feeling* produced by it." This is the *emotional* interpretant. Although its "foundation of truth" may be slight at times, often this remains the only effect produced by a sign such as, for example, the performance of a piece of music.

2.   When a further significate effect is produced, however, it is "through the mediation of the emotional interpretant"; and this second type of meaning effect he calls the *energetic* interpretant, for it involves an "effort," which may be a muscular exertion but is more usually a mental effort, "an exertion upon the Inner World."

3.   The third and final type of meaning effect that may be produced by the sign, through the mediation of the former two, is "a *habit-change*": "a modification of a person's tendencies toward action, resulting from previous experiences or from previous exertions." This is the "ultimate" interpretant of the sign, the effect of meaning on which the process of semiosis, in the instance considered, comes to rest. "The real and living logical conclusion *is* that habit," Peirce states, and designates the third type of significate effect, the *logical* interpretant. But immediately he adds a qualification, distinguishing this logical interpretant from the concept or "intellectual" sign:

> The concept which is a logical interpretant is only imperfectly so. It somewhat partakes of the nature of a verbal definition, and is as inferior to the habit, and much in the same way, as a verbal definition is inferior to the real definition. The deliberately formed, self-analyzing habit—self-analyzing because formed by the aid of analysis of the exercises that nourished it—is the living definition, the veritable and final logical interpretant. (5.491)

The final interpretant, then, is not "logical" in the sense in which a syllogism is logical, or because it is the result of an "intellectual" operation like deductive reasoning. It is logical in that it is "self-analyzing," or, we might say, in that it makes sense of the emotion and muscular/mental effort which preceded it by providing a conceptual representation of that effort. Such a representation is implicit in the notion of habit as a "tendency toward action" and in the solidarity of habit and belief (5.538).

Peirce's formulation of the ultimate interpretant maps another path or a way back from semiosis to reality. For Eco, it provides the "missing link" between signification and concrete action. The final interpretant, he states, is not a Platonic essence or a transcendental law of signification but a result, as well as a rule: "To have understood the sign as a rule through the series of its interpretants means to have acquired the habit to act according to the prescription given by the sign. . . . The action is the place in which the *haecceitas* ends the game of semiosis" (Eco 1979:

194–95). But we should go further in our reading of Peirce, and so enter into a territory where Eco fears to tread, the terrain of subjectivity.

When Peirce speaks of habit as the result of a process involving emotion, muscular and mental exertion, and some kind of conceptual representation (the "final logical interpretant"), he is thinking of individual persons as the subject of such a process. If the modification of consciousness, the habit or habit-change, is indeed the meaning effect, the "real and living" conclusion of each single process of semiosis, then where "the game of semiosis" ends, time and time again, is not exactly "concrete action," as Eco sees it, but a person's (subjective) disposition, a readiness (to action), a set of expectations. For the chain of meanings comes to a halt, however temporarily, by anchoring itself to somebody, to some body, an individual subject.[4] Thus, as we use signs or produce interpretants, their significate effects must pass through each of us, each body and each consciousness, before they may produce an effect or an action upon the world. Finally, then, the individual's habit as a semiotic production is both the result and the condition of the social production of meaning.

Clearly, this reading of Peirce points toward a possible elaboration of semiotics as a theory of culture that hinges on a historical, materialist, *and* gendered subject—a project that cannot be pursued here. What I wish to stress, for the sake of the present discussion, is the sense of a certain weight of the object in semiosis, an overdetermination wrought into the work of the sign by the real, or what we take as reality, even if it is itself already an interpretant; and hence the sense that experience (habit), however misrecognized or misconstrued, is indissociable from meaning; and therefore that practices—events and behaviors occurring in social formations—weigh in the constitution of subjectivity as much as does language. In that sense, too, violence is not simply "in" language or "in" representation, but is also thereby en-gendered.

VIOLENCE AND REPRESENTATION

When one first surveys the representations of violence in general terms, there seem to be two kinds of violence with respect to its object: male and female. I do not mean by this that the "victims" of such kinds of violence are men and women, but rather that the object on which or to which the violence is done is what establishes the meaning of the represented act; and that object is perceived or apprehended as either feminine or masculine. An obvious example of the first instance is "nature," as in the expression "the rape of nature," which at once defines nature as feminine and rape as violence done to a feminine other (whether its physical object be a woman, a man, or an inanimate object). Speculating on the particular rhetoric of violence that permeates the discourse in which scientists describe their encounter with the unknown, Evelyn Fox Keller finds a recurrent thematics of conquest, domination, and aggression reflecting a "basic adversarial relation to the object of study."

> Problems, for many scientists are things to be "attacked," "licked" or "conquered." If more subtle means fail, then one resorts to "brute force," to the "hammer and tongs" approach. In the effort to "master" nature, to "storm her strongholds and castles," science can come to sound like a battlefield. Sometimes, such imagery becomes quite extreme, exceeding even the conventional imagery of war. Note, for example, the language in which one scientist describes his pursuit: "I liked to follow the workings of another mind through these minute, teasing investigations to see a relentless observer get hold of Nature and squeeze her until the sweat broke out all over her and her sphincters loosened. (Keller 1983: 20)

The "genderization of science," as Keller calls the association of scientific thought with masculinity and of the scientific domain with femininity, is a pervasive metaphor in the discourse of science, from Bacon's prescription of "a chaste and lawful marriage between Mind and Nature" to Bohr's chosen emblem, the yin-yang symbol, for his coat of arms (Keller 1978: 413, 432). It is a compelling representation, whose effects for the ideology and the practice of science, as well as for the subjectivity of individual scientists, are all the more forceful since the representation is treated as a myth; that is to say, while the genderization of science is admitted and encouraged in the realm of common knowledge, it is simultaneously denied entry or currency in the realm of formal knowledge (Keller 1978: 410). This is the case not only in the hard sciences, so-called, but also more often than not in the "softer" disciplines and even, ironically enough, in the study of myth.

The other kind of violence is that which in *Violence and the Sacred* René Girard has aptly called "violent reciprocity," the acting out of "rivalry" between brothers or between father and son, and which is socially held in check by the institution of kinship, ritual, and other forms of mimetic violence (war and sport come immediately to mind). The distinctive trait here is the "reciprocity" and thus, by implication, the equality of the two terms of the violent exchange, the "subject" and the "object" engaged in the rivalry; and consequently the masculinity attributed, in this particular case, to the object. For the subject of the violence is always, by definition, masculine; "man" is by definition the subject of culture and of any social act.[5]

In the mythical text, for example, according to Lotman's theory of plot typology, there are only two characters, the hero and the obstacle or boundary. The first is the mythical subject, who moves through the plot-space establishing differences and norms. The second is but a function of that space, a marker of boundary, and therefore inanimate even when anthropomorphized.

> Characters can be divided into those who are mobile, who enjoy freedom with regard to plot-space, who can change their place in the structure of the artistic world and cross the frontier, the basic topological feature of this space, and those who are immobile, who represent, in fact, a function of this space. Looked at typologically, the initial situation is that a certain plot-space is divided by a *single* boundary into an internal and an external sphere, and a *single* character has the opportunity to cross that boundary. . . . Inasmuch as closed space can be interpreted as "a cave," "the grave," "a house," "woman" (and, correspondingly, be allotted the features of darkness, warmth, dampness), entry into it is interpreted on various levels as "death," "conception," "return home" and so on; moreover all these acts are thought of as mutually identical. (Lotman 1979: 167–68)

In the mythical text, then, the hero must be male regardless of the gender of the character, because the obstacle, whatever its personification (sphinx or dragon, sorceress or villain), is morphologically female—and indeed, simply the womb, the earth, the space of his movement. As he crosses the boundary and "penetrates" the other space, the mythical subject is constructed as human being and as male; he is the active principle of culture, the establisher of distinction, the creator of differences. Female is what is not susceptible to transformation, to life or death; she (it) is an element of plot-space, a topos, a resistance, matrix and matter.

Narrative cinema, too, performs a similar inscription of gender in its visual figuration of the masculine and the feminine positions. The woman, fixed in the position of icon, spectacle or image to be looked at, bears the mobile look of both the spectator and the male character(s). It is the latter who commands at once the action and the landscape, and who occupies the position of subject of vision, which he relays to the spectator. As Laura Mulvey shows in her analysis of the complex relations of narrative and visual pleasure, "sadism demands a story" (1975: 14). Thus, if Oedipus has become a paradigm of human life and error, narrative temporality and dramatic structure, one may be entitled to wonder whether that is purely due to the artistry of Sophocles or the widespread influence of Freud's theory of human psychic development in our culture; or whether it might not also be due to the fact that, like the best of stories and better than most, the story of Oedipus weaves the inscription of violence (and family violence, at that) into the representation of gender.

I will now turn to two celebrated critical texts that exemplify two discursive strategies deployed in the construction of gender and two distinctive rhetorical configurations of violence. The first is Lévi-Strauss's reading, in "The effectiveness of symbols" (Lévi-Strauss 1967), of a Cuna incantation performed to facilitate difficult childbirth; a reading that prompts him to make a daring parallel between shamanistic practices and psychoanalysis, and allows him to elaborate his crucial notion of the unconscious as symbolic function. The shaman's cure consists, he states, "in making explicit a situation originally existing on the emotional level and in rendering acceptable to the mind pains which the body refuses to tolerate" by provoking an experience "through symbols, that is, through meaningful equivalents of things meant which belong to another order of reality" (1967: 192, 196). Whereas the arbitrary pains are alien and unacceptable to the woman, the supernatural monsters evoked by the shaman in his symbolic narrative are part of a coherent system on which the native conception of the universe is founded. By calling upon the myth, the shaman reintegrates the pains within a conceptual and meaningful whole, and "provides the sick [sic] woman with a *language*, by means of which unexpressed, and otherwise inexpressible, psychic states can be immediately expressed" (1967: 193). Both the shaman's cure and psychoanalytic therapy, argues Lévi-Strauss, albeit with an inversion of all the elements, are done by means of a manipulation carried out through symbols that constitute a meaningful code, a language.

Let us consider now the structure of the myth in question and the performative value of the shaman's narrative. For, after all, the incantation is a ritual, though based on myth. It has, that is, a practical purpose: it seeks to effect a physical, somatic transformation in its addressee. The main actors are the shaman, performing the incantation, and the woman in labor whose body is to undergo the transformation, to become actively engaged in expelling the full-grown fetus and bringing forth the child. In the myth that subtends the incantation, one would think, the hero must be a woman or at least a female spirit, goddess, or totemic ancestor. But it is not so. Not only is the hero a male, personified by the shaman, as are his helpers, also symbolized with decidedly phallic attributes; and not only is the incantation intended to effect the childbearing woman's identification with the male hero in his struggle with the villain (a *female* deity who has taken possession of the woman's body and soul). But more importantly, the incantation aims at detaching the woman's identification or perception of self from her own body. It seeks to sever her identification with a body that she must come to perceive precisely as a space, the territory in which the battle is waged. The hero's victory then results in his recapturing the woman's soul, and his descent through the landscape of her body symbolizes the (now) unimpeded descent of the fetus along the birth canal.

The effectiveness of symbols, the work of the symbolic function in the unconscious, would thus effect a splitting of the female subject's identification into the two mythical positions of hero (the human subject) and boundary (spatially fixed object or personified obstacle—her body). The doubt that the apprehension of one's body or oneself as obstacle, landscape or battlefield may not "provide the . . . woman with a language" does not cross the text. But whether or not this construct would "make sense" to the Cuna woman for whose benefit the ritual is presumably performed, Lévi-Strauss's interpretation must be acceptable in principle to Lotman, Girard, and any others who look on the history of the human race from the anthropological perspective and within an epistemology wherein "biological" sexual difference is the ground (in Peirce's term) of gender. In that perspective, woman remains outside of history. She is Mother and Nature, matrix and matter, "an equivalent more universal than money," as Lea Melandri accurately phrased it (1977: 27). The discourse of the sciences of man constructs the object as female and the female as object. This, I suggest, is its rhetoric of violence, even when the discourse presents itself as humanistic, benevolent or well-intentioned.

Indeed, Derrida criticizes Lévi-Strauss's paternalistic attitude toward his objects of study (the Nambikwara) as well as the naiveté by which he regards them as an "innocent" people because they have no written language. In such a community, described in the autobiographical *Tristes Tropiques*, violence would be introduced by Western civilization, and actually erupts as the anthropologist (Lévi-Strauss himself, who recounts the event) teaches a group of children how to write. The "revenge" of one little girl, struck by another during the "Writing Lesson," consists in revealing to the anthropologist the "secret" of the other girl's proper name, which the Nambik-wara are not allowed to use. What is ingenuous, for Derrida, is Lévi-Strauss's ostensible belief that writing is merely the phonetic notation of speech, and that violence is an effect of written language (civilization) rather than of language as such; for "all societies capable of producing, that is to say of obliterating, their proper names, and of bringing classificatory difference into play, practice writing in general" (Derrida 1976a: 109).

> To name, to give names that it will on occasion be forbidden to pronounce, such is the originary violence of language which consists in inscribing within a difference, in classifying, in suspending the vocative absolute. To think the unique *within* the system, to inscribe it there, such is the gesture of the arche-writing: arche-violence, loss of the proper, of absolute proximity, of self-presence. . . . Out of this arche-violence, forbidden and therefore confirmed by a second violence that is reparatory, protective, instituting the "moral," prescribing the concealment of writing and the effacement and obliteration of the so-called proper name which was already dividing the proper, a third violence can *possibly* emerge or not (an empirical possibility) within what is commonly called evil, war, indiscretion, rape; which consists of revealing by effraction the so-called proper name, the originary violence which has severed the proper from its property and its self-sameness [*propriété*]. (1976a: 112)

Empirical or common violence (and we cannot help remaking the text's own classifactory play in the listing of signifiers—evil, war, indiscretion, rape) is "more complex" than the other two levels to which it refers, namely, arche-violence and law. Unfortunately for us, however, Derrida is not concerned to analyze it or to suggest why, how, or when it may possibly emerge. He only implies that the emergence of empirical violence, the fact of violence in society, is no accident, though Lévi-Strauss would need to see it as an accident in order to maintain his belief in the natural innocence and goodness of the primitive culture. From Rousseau and the eighteenth century, Derrida concludes, Lévi-Strauss has inherited an archaeology that "is also a teleology and an eschatology": "The dream of a full and immediate presence closing history [suppresses] contradiction and difference" (1976a: 115).

The rhetorical construct of a "violence of the letter," the originary violence that preempts presence, identity, and property or propriety, is perhaps more accessible in another of Derrida's own works, *Spurs*, where he performs a reading of Nietzsche and, with him, addresses just what he claimed that Lévi-Strauss suppressed—contradiction and difference. This could be my second textual *exemplum*, whereby to illustrate what I earlier called the violence of rhetoric. It would support my contention that, while Derrida's discourse denies the fact of gender, its "becoming woman" depends on the same construct of sexual difference precisely if naively and traditionally articulated by Lévi-Strauss (1969).

Were I to do so, however, I would earn Derrida's contempt for "those women feminists so derided by Nietzsche," I would put myself in the position of one "who aspires to be like a man," who "seeks to castrate" and "wants a castrated woman" (Derrida 1976b: 53). I shall not do so, therefore. Decency and shame prevent me, though nothing more. I shall instead approach Derrida's text obliquely—a gesture the philosopher may not find displeasing—by way of another's reading, or a quadruple displacement, if you will.

"The discourse of man," writes Gayatri Spivak, "is in the metaphor of woman" (1983: 169). The problem with phallocentrism "is not merely one of psycho-socio-sexual behavior [as, we recall, Foucault would have it] but of the production and consolidation of reference and meaning" (1983: 169). Derrida's critique of phallocentrism—deconstruction—takes the woman as "model" for the deconstructive discourse. It takes the woman as model because, as Spivak reads (Derrida reading) Nietzsche. the woman can fake an orgasm, while the man cannot:

Women impersonate themselves as having an orgasm even at the time of orgasm. Within the historical understanding of women as incapable of orgasm, Nietzsche is arguing that impersonating is woman's only sexual pleasure. (Spivak 1983: 170)

Thus, in what appears to me as a case of inscribing gender with a vengeance, Derrida searches for
the name of the mother in *Glas*; elsewhere he uses the "name of woman" to question the "we-
men" of the philosophers (Spivak 1983: 173); and *Dissemination* takes the hymen as figure for the
text, the undecidability of meaning, the "law of the textual operation—of reading, writing, philosophizing" (1983: 175).

Deconstruction thus effects "a feminization of the practice of philosophy," Spivak observes
(with a phrase that reminds me immediately of Keller's "genderization of science"), adding that
she does not regard it as "just another example of the masculine use of woman as instrument of
self-assertion" (1983: 173). For if man can never "fully disown his status as subject," and if desire
must still "be expressed as man's desire," yet the deconstructor's enterprise—seeking his own displacement "by taking the woman as object or figure"—is an "unusual and courageous" one.
Regretfully, one must infer, Spivak is led to admit that the question of woman, asked in the way
Nietzsche and Derrida ask it, "is *their* question, not *ours*" (1983: 184). Then she suggests, "with
respect," that such a feminization of philosophy as serves the male deconstructor "might find its
most adequate legend in male homosexuality defined as criminality, and that it cannot speak for
the woman" (1983: 177). One can only conclude that, insofar as the "deconstructor" is a woman,
the value of that critical practice ("the patriarchy's own self-critique") is at best ambiguous. We
can produce, as Spivak recommends, "useful and scrupulous fake readings in the place of the passively active fake orgasm" (1983: 186), but we will not have come any closer to understanding,
representing, or reconstructing our bodies and our pleasures otherwise.

For the female subject, finally, gender marks the limit of deconstruction, the rocky bed (so to
speak) of the "abyss of meaning." Which is not to say that woman, femininity, or femaleness are
any more or any less outside discourse than anything else is. This is precisely the insistent emphasis of feminist criticism: gender must be accounted for. It must be understood not as a "biological" difference that lies before or beyond signification, nor as a culturally constructed object of
masculine desire, but as semiotic difference—a different production of reference and meaning
such as, not Derrida and not Foucault, but possibly Peirce's notion of semiosis may allow us to
begin to chart. Clearly, the time of "replacing feminist criticism" (Kamuf 1982) has not come.

NOTES

1. In Barbara Harlow's translation of *Spurs*, the quotations from Nietzsche incorporated in Derrida's
   text are given in the words of the English translation by Thomas Common (*Joyful Wisdom* [New
   York: Frederick Ungar, 1960]). I have preferred to use Walter Kaufmann's translation in *The Gay
   Science* (1974), both below and, somewhat modified, in my epigraph above, which is from paragraph
   64. In the passage cited by Derrida from *Die fröhliche Wissenschaft* (§ 71, "On female chastity"),
   Nietzsche is speaking of the contradiction that upper-class women, reared in total ignorance of sexuality, must encounter at the moment of marriage. From their supposed ignorance of sex, Nietzsche
   mockingly laments, women are "hurled, as by a gruesome lightning bolt, into reality and knowledge,
   by marriage—precisely by the man they love and esteem most! To catch love and shame in a contradiction and to be forced to experience at the same time delight, surrender, duty, pity, terror, and
   who knows what else, in the face of the unexpected neighborliness of god and beast! . . . Even the
   compassionate curiosity of the wisest student of humanity is inadequate for guessing how this or that
   woman manages to accommodate herself to *this solution of the riddle*, and to *the riddle of a solution*, and
   what dreadful, far-reaching suspicions must stir in her poor, unhinged soul—and how the ultimate
   philosophy and skepsis of woman casts anchor at this point!" I have italicized the phrases that
   Derrida takes out of context and recasts in the frame of his interpretation of Nietzsche. As will be

discussed later, Derrida reads in Nietzsche a progressive valorization of woman as a self-affirming power, "a dissimulatress, an artist, a dionysiac"; and this is the "affirmative woman" that Derrida takes as his model for "writing," for the critical operation of questioning, doubting, or "deconstructing" all truths.

2. For an interesting discussion of Salomé's writing, figure, and historiographical "legend" from the perspective of present-day feminism, see Martin. The quotation from Salomé's *Zur Psychologie der Frau*, which appears at the beginning of this essay, is cited in Martin (1982: 29).

3. "Paradoxical conservatism," I have argued, "is a very appropriate phrase for a major theoretician of social history who writes of power and resistance, bodies and pleasures and sexuality as if the ideological structures and effects of patriarchy had nothing to do with history, as if they had no discursive status or political implications. The rape and sexual extortion performed on little girls by young and adult males is a 'bit of theater,' a petty 'everyday occurrence in the life of village sexuality,' purely 'inconsequential bucolic pleasures' [Foucault 1980: 31–32]. What really matters to the historian is the power of institutions, the mechanisms by which these bits of theater become, he claims, pleasurable for the individuals involved—the men *and* the women, former little girls—who thus become complicit with those institutional apparati" (de Lauretis 1984: 94). This passage, which I take the liberty of reprinting here, occurs in the context of my analysis of a film, Nicolas Roeg's *Bad Timing: A Sensual Obsession* (1980), in light of some of Foucault's ideas. The film is an interesting study of "marital violence," and an excellent visual-narrative text for a discussion of violence, representation, and gender.

4. My reading of Peirce's definition of the sign, and thus of the relationship of sign and subject, bears a comparison with Lacan's ostensibly antithetical formula ("a signifier represents a subject for another signifier"). I must again refer interested readers to chapter 6 of my book (1984), "Semiotics and Experience," where a fuller discussion of Eco is also to be found.

5. Studies in language usage demonstrate that, if the term "man" includes women (while the obverse is not true, for the term "woman" is always gendered, i.e., sexually connoted), it is only to the extent that, in the given context, women are (to be) perceived as nongendered "human beings," and thus as man (see Spender 1980). For example, Lévi-Strauss's theory of kinship (1969) is based on the thesis that women are both like men and unlike men: they are human beings (like men), but their special function in culture and society is to be exchanged and circulated among men (unlike men). Because of their "value" as means of sexual gratification and reproduction, women are the means—objects and signs—of social communication (among human beings). Nevertheless, as he is unwilling to exclude women from humanity or "mankind," he compromises by saying that women are also human beings, although in the symbolic order of culture they do not speak, desire, or produce meaning *for themselves*, as men do, by means of the exchange of women. One can only conclude that, in so far as women are human beings, they are (like) men.

REFERENCES

Andreas-Salomé, Lou (1978). *Zur Psychologie der Frau*, ed. by Gisela Brinker-Gabler. Frankfurt: Fischer Taschenbuch Verlag.

Breines, Wini, and Gordon, Linda (1983). The New Scholarship on Family Violence. *Signs: A Journal of Women in Culture and Society* 8(3), 490–531.

Brownmiller, Susan (1975). *Against Our Will: Men, Women and Rape.* New York: Simon and Schuster.

Change (1977). *La folie encerclée.* Paris: Seghers/Laffont.

de Lauretis, Teresa (1984). *Alice Doesn't: Feminism, Semiotics, Cinema.* Bloomington: Indiana University Press.

Derrida, Jacques (1976a). *Of Grammatology*, trans. by Gayatri Chakravorty Spivak. Baltimore and London: Johns Hopkins University Press.

———— (1976b). *Éperons. Les styles de Nietzsche.* Venice: Corbo e Fiore. [This is a four-language edition; the English translation is by Barbara Harlow.]

Doane, Mary Ann, Mellencamp, Patricia, and Williams, Linda (eds.) (1984). *Re-Vision: Essays in Feminist Film Criticism*. Los Angeles: American Film Institute.

Eco, Umberto (1979). *The Role of the Reader: Explorations in the Semiotics of Texts*. Bloomington and London: Indiana University Press.

Foucault, Michel (1972). *The Archaeology of Knowledge*, trans. by A. M. Sheridan Smith. London: Irvington.

———. (1980). *The History of Sexuality, Vol. I: An Introduction*, trans. by Robert Hurley. New York: Vintage Books.

Girard, René (1977). *Violence and the Sacred*, trans. by Patrick Gregory. Baltimore and London: Johns Hopkins University Press.

Kamuf, Peggy (1982). Replacing Feminist Criticism. *Diacritics* 12, 42–47.

Keller, Evelyn Fox (1978). Gender and Science. *Psychoanalysis and Contemporary Thought* (September), 409–433.

———. (1983). Feminism as an Analytic Tool for the Study of Science. *Academe* (September-October), 15–21.

Lacan, Jacques (1966). *Écrits*. Paris: Éditions du Seuil.

Lévi-Strauss, Claude (1961). *Tristes Tropiques*, trans. by John Russell. New York: Criterion.

———. (1967). *Structural Anthropology*, trans. by Claire Jacobson and Brooke Grundfest Schoept. Garden City: Anchor Books.

———. (1969). *The Elementary Structures of Kinship*, trans. by James Harle Bell, John Richard von Sturmer, and Rodney Needham. Boston: Beacon Press.

Lotman, Jurij (1979). The Origin of Plot in the Light of Typology, trans. by Julian Graffy. *Poetics Today* 1(1–2), 161–84.

MacKinnon, Catharine (1979). *Sexual Harassment of Working Women: A Case of Sex Discrimination*. New Haven, Conn.: Yale University Press.

Martin, Biddy (1982). Feminism, Criticism, and Foucault. *New German Critique* 27, 3–30.

———. (1991). *Woman and Modernity: The (Life)styles of Lou Andreas-Salomé*. Ithaca, N.Y.: Cornell University Press.

Melandri, Lea (1977). *L'infamia originaria*. Milan: Edizioni L'Erba Voglio.

Mulvey, Laura (1975). Visual Pleasure and Narrative Cinema. *Screen* 16(3), 6–18.

Nietzsche, Friedrich (1974). *The Gay Science*, trans. by Walter Kaufmann. New York: Vintage Books.

Peirce, Charles Sanders (1931–1958). *Collected Papers*, Charles Hartshorne and Paul Weiss (eds.). Cambridge, Mass: Harvard University Press.

Plaza, Monique (1980). Our costs and their benefits, trans. by Wendy Harrison. *m/f* 4, 28–39. [Originally in *Questions féministes*, no. 3 (May 1978).]

Rich, Adrienne (1980). Compulsory Heterosexuality and Lesbian Existence. In *Signs: A Journal of Women in Culture and Society* 5(4), 631–60.

Spender, Dale (1980). *Man Made Language*. London: Routledge and Kegan Paul.

Spivak, Gayatri Chakravorty (1983). Displacement and the Discourse of Woman. In *Displacement: Derrida and After*, ed. by Mark Krupnick, 169–95. Bloomington: Indiana University Press.

Stark, Evan, Flitcraft, Anne, and Frazier, William (1979). Medicine and Patriarchal Violence: The Social Construction of a "Private" Event. *International Journal of Health Services* 9(3), 461–93.

19 From Nation to Family

Containing African AIDS

Cindy Patton

Current AIDS-control efforts have invented a heterosexual "African AIDS" that promotes a new kind of colonial domination by reconstructing Africa as an uncharted, supranational mass. Whatever the overt concerns of the international health workers for containing AIDS in (within?) the continent, their construal of "Africa" as the margin of economic/cultural "development" and as the "heart" of the AIDS epidemic helps to stabilize a Euro-America adrift in a postmodern condition of lost metanarratives and occluded origins. As a totalizing grand history of nations has given way to a transcendent account of chance intersections of germs and bodies, the map of the postcolonial world has now been redrawn as a graph of epidemiologic strike rates. Because international AIDS policy has discouraged or overlooked serious attempts to prevent HIV transmission through health education, community organizing, and improved bloodbanking, this new Africa-with-no-borders functions as a giant agar plate, etched by the "natural history" of the AIDS epidemic.[1]

The very labeling of "African AIDS" as a heterosexual disease quiets the Western fear that heterosexual men will need to alter their own sexual practices and identity. If the proximate (homosexual) AIDS allows such men to ignore their local complicity in "dangerous" practices that lead to the infection of ("their") women, then a distant "African AIDS," by correlating heterosexual danger with Otherness/thereness, performs the final expiative act for a Western heterosexual masculinity that refuses all containment. Erased in this process are the colonially inscribed borders of sub-Saharan countries, while new borders are drawn between the "African family" and a "modernizing society" populated by "single people" who have been dying at an appalling rate throughout the epidemic. The nation, once the colonial administrative unit *par excellence*, has

Cindy Patton was intensively involved in gay and AIDS activism throughout the 1980s. In addition to her work with the AIDS Action Committee in Boston, she served as a consultant to the World Health Organization's Global Program on AIDS and, in the early 1980s, worked as an ethnographer on a Center for Disease Control study of HIV counseling in methadone clinics. She now teaches lesbian and gay studies in the Graduate Institute for Liberal Arts at Emory University in Atlanta. Her works include *Sex and Germs: the Politics of AIDS* (1985), *Making It: A Woman's Guide to Sex in the Age of AIDS* (with Janis Kelly) (1987), *Inventing AIDS* (1990), *Last Served? Gendering the HIV Pandemic* (1994), *Fatal Advice* (1996), and a forthcoming volume, *Who I Am: Making American Political Identities* (with Harry Denny).

been replaced in the minds of healthworkers with (an image of) the bourgeois family, thereby constituting what had never truly existed before in Africa as the only defense against modernization and its "diseases." In what follows, I explore some of the implications of this movement from nation to family as the preferred prophylaxis in the catastrophe of "African AIDS."

MAPPING "AFRICAN AIDS"

Accompanying a *New York Times* article "AIDS in Africa: A Killer Rages On" (whose headline continues "AIDS Is Spreading Rapidly and Ominously Throughout Africa") is a nearly full-page chart, "AIDS in Africa: An Atlas of Spreading Tragedy."[2] These headlines displace responsibility for the epidemic—who exactly is this killer? what is the tragedy?—and elide the disease's biological mechanics in exploiting its symbolic resonances. The article's spatialization of AIDS in its accompanying map of the continent simultaneously locates countries and underscores the irrelevance of their borders: in *this* Africa, disease transcends nation. Replacing what had been colonialism's heart of darkness is the calculated horror of a new interior density, represented on the map by dark-to-light shadings corresponding to HIV attack rates. The "AIDS belt" supposed to exist in central Africa is depicted here not only as the "heart" of the regional epidemic but as the imagined origin of the entire global pandemic. Yet the "evidence" employed by the map reveals the duplicities of Western discourse about AIDS in Africa: seroprevalence rates for the continent are concocted from sensationalist media accounts of specific locations and from the records of epidemiologists working from strictly limited samples (often as few as 100 people) of pregnant women, prostitutes, and clients with sexually transmitted diseases. When not enough AIDS is found, it needs to be imagined, as the key to the *Times'* map suggests:

> The shadings on this map indicate the percentage of sexually active adults believed to be infected with the AIDS virus in major urban areas. Rural rates tend to be much lower. The numbers are based on the latest available data, which may understate current rates. Blank spots do not necessarily mean an absence of AIDS.

Despite its disclaimers about "missing data," there are in fact no "blank spots" on the map; the *Times* fills in the *entire* surface, lumping together countries with "infection rates less than 5 percent" with those for which "data [is] not available." Although we are told that high attack rates (of HIV, which is consistently conflated here with AIDS) are characteristic only of urban areas, whole countries are shaded to indicate "At least 5 percent to 10 percent," "At least 10 percent to 20 percent," and "At least 20 percent." The curious use of the nonexclusive "at least" for the increasingly darker/denser shadings suggests that errors in data will always underestimate "AIDS" for a country. But the note on "sources" at the bottom of the map gives us a clearer indication of the accuracy of the epidemiologic data from which the map is derived:

> Surveys of subgroups are useful but must be interpreted with caution. Urban infection rates cannot be extrapolated to rural areas. Rates among prostitutes, soldiers, hospital patients, and patients at clinics for sexually transmitted diseases tend to be far higher than in the population at large. Blood donor figures may overstate prevalence if donors are recruited among high-risk groups or understate it if efforts are made to avoid high-risk donors. Often, surveys of pregnant women visiting prenatal clinics are considered the best indicator of infection among the adult population.

In this brief summary of data offered for the twenty-four countries that appear to have data (this leaves as "blank spots" another twenty-nine, which include some of the continent's largest),[3] the *Times* acknowledges that seroprevalence studies vary from nation to nation, but all of these studies have been used indiscriminately to present the worst case scenario within any given country. While HIV is certainly an important African health concern, seroprevalence rates are rising *everywhere* and not just in African locales. The *Times*, however, suggests no reason for singling out Africa as exceptional and offers no comparative data on rates in Euro-America or other global regions (Asia, the Pacific Rim, Eastern Europe, Central and South America, and the Caribbean are the real "blank spots" on the *Times*'s map). The article's one comparison to the U.S. serves to inscribe "their AIDS" as heterosexual in comparison with "our AIDS":

> In contrast with the pattern in the United States, AIDS in Africa is spreading mainly through het-erosexual intercourse, propelled by long-neglected epidemics of venereal disease that facilitates viral transmission. . . . In the United States, gay men and residents of a few inner-city pockets face com-parable devastation, but over all, fewer than 1 percent of adults are believed to be infected with the AIDS virus.

"Inner-city pockets" is of course a reference to poor people of color, the internal blank spot of the U.S. If the horror of the American crisis is the confrontation (of white heterosexuals) with both homosexuality and the feared black underclass, the tragedy in Africa seems rather more unthinkable: "Strange new issues are in the air. Where the disease spread earliest and large num-bers have already died, as in Uganda, frightened young men and women are starting to realize that even marriage may be risky."

If AIDS has been thought to sail or jet[4] between the Euro-American countries, it is repre-sented by the *Times* as traveling by truck throughout Africa. An insert showing trucks on a dusty road and entitled "Dangerous Traffic" tells us that:

> The highways of East and Central Africa, such as this one west of Kampala, Uganda, have been major conduits for AIDS. A study of Kenya of 317 truck drivers of varied nationalities found that three-fourths frequently visited prostitutes but that only 30 percent ever used condoms. One in four was infected with HIV. In 1986, 35 percent of drivers studied in Kampala were infected. Most prostitutes and barmaids along trucking routes are infected.

While the direction of infection is obscured here (truck drivers to prostitutes or prostitutes to truck drivers?), the conflation of truckers with their penises and of roads with vaginas is abun-dantly clear. If truck drivers "unloading" their "dangerous cargo" is a more compelling trope than the usual evocation of urban prostitutes spewing germs to hapless clients, this is because the spread of AIDS in Africa is itself hardly unrelated to the spread of "modernization."

INVENTING AFRICAN AIDS

By 1986, Western media and scientists worldwide had created the linguistic distinction between "AIDS" and "African AIDS" that makes the *Times*'s map readable. These designations are informal names for the more technical World Health Organization terms, Pattern One and Pattern Two. Pattern One describes epidemiologic scenarios where "homosexual behavior" and "drug injec-tion" are considered the primary means of HIV transmission. Because Pattern One (or, as the unmarked category, simply "AIDS") is coded racially as "white," African American communities— where homosexuality is presumed to be absent—are now said to exhibit features of Pattern Two ("African AIDS"). Pattern Two indicates places where transmission is held to be "almost exclusively heterosexual."[5] Synonymous with "African AIDS," Pattern Two is a linguistic construction con-fusing an epidemiologic description (however unuseful) with an emerging "history" of the epi-demic. The Caribbean has "African AIDS" but Latin America has "AIDS," an unprecedented if barely conscious recognition of indigenous homosexualities. A third category, Pattern Three, rec-ognizes the emergence of "heterosexual" AIDS outside Euro-America and Africa in places where HIV arrived "late" and largely through postcolonial sex tourism and international bloodbanking.

The "history" of the epidemic reflected in these categories inverts the crucial epidemiologic issues. Rather than asking how HIV moved from the Pattern One countries (where AIDS was diagnosed first by epidemiologists' accounts) to the Pattern Two countries, the scientifically endorsed history of AIDS shows HIV originating in Africa and then moving to North America.[6] The scientific distinction between AIDS/gay/white/Euro-American and African AIDS/heterosexual/black/African/U.S.-inner-city neatly fails to inquire how HIV traveled from the bodies of U.S. homosexual men into the bodies of "Africans" a continent and ocean away, or how "African AIDS" then returned to diasporal African communities in the U.S. The blank spot within the Euro-American mind makes it far easier to imagine an alternative causal chain running from monkeys to Africans to queers than to recall the simple fact that the West exports huge quantities of unscreened blood to its Third World client states (much less acknowledge that black and white Americans have sex—gay as well as straight—and share needles with each other).

This difference between Patterns One and Two thus helps white, Euro-American heterosexuals evade the idea that they might themselves be vulnerable since African (and African American) heterosexuality is so evidently different than Euro-American. Euro-American heterosexuality is "not at risk" as long as local AIDS is identified as homosexual and heterosexual AIDS remains distant. The projected difference of African heterosexuality and the asserted absence of African homosexuality[7] continue to drive not only the forms of epidemiologic research (for example, researchers have been more interested in finding bizarre and distinctive "African" sexual practices[8] than in documenting transfusion-related cases) but also the forms of educational intervention whose focus in Africa is almost exclusively on promoting monogamy or, in more "sensitive" campaigns, "stable polygamy."

My earlier work on "African AIDS" investigated how Western scientific representations of the national and sexual cultures of postcolonial Africa direct the international AIDS research agenda. Reading conference documents and media reports on "AIDS in Africa," I marked the links between apparently innocuous or obviously fantastic assumptions made about Africa(ns) within Western discourse and the conduct and direction of Western science. In particular, I showed how the persistent Western description of Africa as a "catastrophe" and as "heterosexual" justified as altruistic the genocidal Western practices and policies toward their client-state "Others."

Because "African AIDS" is simultaneously "different" and "similar," conflicts in Western AIDS discourse, ethics, and medical research can be rationalized by drawing upon research undertaken throughout the continent. For example, while data from African clinics convinces Westerners that heterosexual transmission is possible (because all intercourse is the same), this same data is also read as suggesting that widespread transmission among heterosexuals is not likely enough to require the universal adoption of the condom (because Africans engage in other exotic sexual practices and polygamy).[9] Diagnosis of AIDS in Africa is said to be unreliable because medical facilities are alleged to be poor; this licenses demographers to multiply known cases by exorbitant factors in order to obtain a "true" (i.e., catastrophic) picture of AIDS in "Africa." But "African" diagnosis becomes a problem (and for epidemiologists rather than clinicians) only because the definition of AIDS is derived from the U.S. experience of largely well-cared-for, middle-class men who become inexplicably weak and unable to fight common illness. The fall from "previous health" is not a feasible diagnostic distinction in countries (or among U.S. women or those living in the inner city, for that matter) where people have received little health care or where infectious diseases and nutritional deficiencies make it difficult to distinguish between clinical AIDS and malaria, anaemia, tuberculosis, etc.

An important note on the terms I've employed here: in Western discourse, Africa, a continent of roughly eleven and a half million square miles and fifty-three countries, is treated as a homogenous sociopolitical block. Yet this supposedly "unknown" continent—unknown, that is, to its pale neighbors to the north—is in fact far more culturally, linguistically, religiously, and socially diverse than North America and Europe. Collapsing the many cultures residing on the continent into "Africa" is an act of political and cultural violence. In order to complicate "Africa" as a Western construction, I employ the equivalent constructions "North American" and "Euro-

American" to indicate the collection of relatively homogeneous northern administrative states as we appear to our southern neighbors. The resultant vagueness Euro-Americans will experience in this strategy should be read back from the "Other" point of view: "North Americans" in particular should consider their own discomfort at having their cultural space discursively reduced in this way.

But this is not the only critical reduction occurring in Western discourse about Africa: as a term, "Africa" can mean both the land mass and its people precisely because the people of Africa have been considered to be coextensive with the continent, a conflation I evoke through the shorthand "Africa(ns)." This conflation has been eloquently described by Frantz Fanon: what is done to the "African body," especially woman's body, is a metaphor for what is to be done to the continent, and vice versa.[10]

IMPLODING BORDERS

The flattening out of the racial, ethnic, and cultural diversity of non-European-descended Africans into a singular autochthonous people performed an important function during the era of colonialism. Carving up the land was not sufficient; a narrative reconstruction of Africa's "uncivilized" prehistory was necessary to justify the colonial presence. The colonial taxonomist's "racial" distributions—"Semites," "hamites," "negroes," "nilotes," "half-hamites," "bantus," "Khoisans," not to mention "Italians" and peoples of the Asian subcontinent ("Indian," another site of colonialist reduction through arbitrary racial taxonomic schemes)—mapped an Africa prior to colonial border construction in order to deny the social orders and political/cultural groups of *people* ("Zulus," "Sabaeans," "Berbers," "Ibos," etc.) who lived, intermarried, fought battles, and traded culture and religion with one another before the incursion of Europeans. These are peoples whose racial and sexual histories seemed always to defy the new administrative borders, but the Europeans still insisted that "natives" must be placed somewhere—spatialized—and organized properly through sexual and genealogical successions—temporalized.

Such a displacement of the political and social onto the sexual and racial has returned today, with similarly self-justifactory motives, as the narrative logic underwriting Western accounts of AIDS among the peoples of Africa. Again, spatial demarcation and temporal sequence organize historical narrative. In obvious ways ("AIDS began in Africa"), insidious ways ("AIDS 'jumped species' from green monkeys to 'African' humans"), and subtle ways (persistent descriptions of truck drivers, miners, "prostitutes," and soldiers traversing the continent), the Euro-American story of "African AIDS" concerns not only racial difference but also territory transected and borders gone out of control. But rather than continuing to adduce African "backwardness" as an excuse for colonial plunder, AIDS epidemiology offers "African sexuality" as a rationale for unethical experimentation and unwillingness to pursue education and community organizing projects that could decrease transmission of HIV. No longer content to carve up a massified Africa into "proper" nations, AIDS media reportage offers a view of African sexuality—alternately described as traditional (polygamy) or condemned as modern (rural-urban social breakdown resulting in "prostitution")—which now requires rapid reorganization into bourgeois families.

This is the side of "African AIDS" I wish to take up here: "containment" through the promotion of racist and heterophobic conceptions of "safe sex." Reading the *Times*'s map alongside the new pamphlet series "Strategies for Hope," collaboratively produced by British international relief organizations and two African national AIDS committees,[11] I want to show how "self-help" manuals for use in Anglophone communities in Africa recall previous border constructions in seeking to promote as "safe sex" a bourgeois "African family" that has never in fact existed.

STRATEGIES FOR HOPE

With an international recession underway, the only capital-intensive educational projects possible in poor countries are collaborative ones with (largely) European international relief organizations. The set of concepts underlying "African AIDS" have become so naturalized today that such projects must rewrite local experience to conform to the internationally adopted narrative. The Euro-American fascination with a "different" African sexuality can routinely be glimpsed in epidemiologic studies and newspaper accounts (witness this sidebar to the *Times* article discussed previously):

> Studies in the United States show that transmission of the AIDS virus during vaginal intercourse is usually quite difficult, especially from female to male. But research in Africa has revealed conditions that multiply the danger. . . . One is the rampant extent of sexually transmitted diseases . . . above all, chancroid, which causes festering ulcers. . . . A second major factor . . is the lack of male circumcision in much of Africa. . . . Researchers are just now turning attention to little-known sexual practices that might also raise transmission odds. . . . In parts of Central Africa . . . women engage in a practice known as "dry sex." In variations of the practice, designed to increase friction during intercourse, women use herbs, chemical powders, stones, or cloth in the vagina to reduce lubrication and cause swelling. . . . Promiscuity helps drive the epidemic. While data do not exist for comparing sexual behavior on different continents, surveys do show that extramarital sex is commonplace in Africa.

The Western imaginary runs wild in these few lines: the easy slide between the gaping vagina and the gaping hole that, on the map, is the "heart" of African AIDS; the undisguised preoccupation with the shape and size of African penises; the assertion of a relative promiscuity, which even the author admits has no data to support it; the conflation of "extramarital" and "promiscuous"—all of these together form a shorthand litany of the "difference" of African sexuality. Such accounts, however, are not limited to the Western media but can be discovered in educational materials designed specifically for "African" use. The following is taken from the "Strategies for Hope" pamphlet series:

> HIV infection in Africa is spread primarily by *heterosexual intercourse*. It affects sexually active men and women in equal numbers, rather than subgroups of the population such as male homosexuals or intravenous drug users. (Homosexuality and intravenous drug use are rare in Africa.) High-risk sexual behavior therefore consists of sexual intercourse with more than one partner. (Pamphlet 1, 3)

The claim in the colonial voice-over to this ostensibly "local" pamphlet that "African" homosexuality is rare is extraordinarily duplicitous. Indeed, same-sex affective and domestic relations were not at all unusual in many precolonial cultures. When colonial and especially British administrators arrived, they were distressed by these relationships, which often played key roles in the distribution of goods and the maintenance of lineages. Colonial law grouped these disparate practices together under one name, "homosexuality," which it pronounced uncivilized and banned by law. Thus contemporary denials by African leaders of the category "homosexuality" are as often a refusal of the European notion of static homosexual identity as they are a denial of same-sex affective and domestic relations. Neocolonialists now can denigrate homosexuality as a Western import and thereby gain increased control over indigenous economic and social relations by tightening control over the remaining cross-sex relations.[12]

In the context of the reigning transnational distinctions between "AIDS" and "African AIDS," (bad) individuals are routinely figured against (good) families, a strategy that both denies the existence of Euro-American gay people's social networks and excommunicates them from their blood relatives. The language employed in the pamphlets—"HIV infection in Africa is primarily a *family disease*, rather than a disease affecting mainly single people" (Pamphlet 1, 3; emphasis in original)—begins to reveal what is at stake. The homophobic Section 28 in Britain (similar to the Helms Amendment in the U.S.) was not content to refuse government funding to projects that "promote homosexuality" but also derided "pretend families." The unit to be sanctioned and protected is thus the statistical minority, the bourgeois family—white, heterosexual, mother and father, small number of children. The logo for the 1987 International AIDS Conference in Stockholm proposed a similarly compacted description of the AIDS epidemic: here was a stylized (and nude) mother and father, each holding a hand of the small child who stood between them. To the Western mind, AIDS is most importantly a threat to the family, and a double one—not simply the threat of an entire family being infected, but also the threat of growing numbers of single people challenging the supremacy of the family unit.

Besides "African AIDS," the only other media image of a "family with AIDS" that has received wide attention focuses on the hemophiliac, the less celebrated Other whose "feminine" bleeding shores up heterosexual masculinity. The October 1988 *Scientific American*, a special issue entitled "What Science Knows About AIDS," presents a full-page picture of a white, North American family (the Burkes, who were outspoken advocates for the rights of people with HIV). We are told that the father is a hemophiliac who "infected" his wife before he knew he was himself infected, and she in turn gave birth to an infected son. Even as the Burkes' membership in a community of blood-product users is completely elided in the magazine's account, this apparently isolated family encodes the story of the tragic innocence of those who lack knowledge, pitted against those who do or should have had it (gay men and drug users are said to infect "knowingly" or recklessly). Though the article's passive constructions describing how wife and son "became infected" minimize the heterosexual component of the "Burkes' AIDS," the fact of the matter is that, throughout this account, Mr. Burke's hemophilia has itself been sufficient to undercut his masculine identity. We have a glimpse here of the power of heterosexual culture's own heterophobia: the horror of this North American "family with AIDS" is that the unit was actually engaging in the identity-bestowing activities of a small, well-disciplined family.

The African family's purported problem is its similar inability to construct itself properly as a small, well-disciplined unit. Oddly enough, the families (that is, everyone defined as "not an individual") in the "Strategies for Hope" pamphlets are comprised of multiple adults, not just "polygamous" units but "sisters" who "often visited the nearby rural bar, where they sold chicken . . . and sexual favors" (Pamphlet 1, 19). Like homosexuality, the Euro-American category of "the prostitute"—an individual with a professional identity as a sex worker—is seen as distinct from those who engage in the traditional practice of "selling favors." Located outside the confines of the family proper, "prostitutes" are singled out by the media to bolster support for "family values" and by epidemiologists to mark the historical progress of HIV through a country or city. Such "prostitutes" are said to have "Western" AIDS since they are constructed as "single people"; they are not as recuperable into families as are the women who seem to mimic traditional female roles by selling chicken and sexual favors. In the "Strategies for Hope" series, the various extramarital and nonmarital sexual relations that have resulted in "family AIDS" (as represented in the thirteen "true story" inserts in the pamphlets) are considered, in contrast, to form part of "family life." The issue, it becomes clear, is not sex per se but the failure to organize it within the disciplined borders of the bourgeois family.

The pamphlets invoke a nostalgia for a less urban Africa in which "traditional family values" once prevailed—and this despite the reality that polygamy and age-specific sexual experimentation were the dominant organizational strategies in the many different cultural strands of this "tradition." In a gesture remarkably like Thatcher's privatization and Reagan's New Altruism, the pamphlets posit the family as the idealized site for support, care, and education: "Even in urban communities the family retains much of its cohesive power, although weakened to some extent by the spread of 'modern' attitudes and values" (Pamphlet 3, 3). Instead of noticing how this conception of the family-as-primary-political-unit disempowers both women and the community, this odd *recto-verso* history of the rise of the bourgeois family in Africa secures as "traditional" the mother-father-child unit by conflating the image of the single urban person ("prostitute" and perhaps migrant workers and truck drivers) with the image of "the modern." But what, after all, could be more modern than the bourgeois family?

Legible throughout the pamphlets is the heterophobic dread of the condom. The litany that "Africans won't use condoms," which formed a crucial part of Western rationalizations for pursuing vaccine trials,[13] is repeated under the guise of "cultural sensitivity" in this Christian missionary/British neocolonial collaboration:

> *Sexual attitudes and habits* are different form those of industrialized countries. Resistance to the idea of using condoms is widespread, especially among men. Many years of intensive health education and attitude-forming would be required to achieve sustained attitudinal and behavioral change in this area.
>
> Condoms do have a significant—but limited—role in AIDS control in Africa, but promoting the use of condoms is a diversion from the central issue of *sexual behavior.* The practice of having multiple sexual partners is the main causal factor in the transmission of HIV in Africa. Promoting the use of condoms does not address this issue. It advocates a technical solution to a problem which can be addressed only through fundamental changes in social attitudes, values, and behavior. (Pamphlet 3, 21)[14]

Such distinctions are of course completely ludicrous—Euro-American heterosexual men seem no less resistant to condom use than African men; condom use and sexual behavior are scarcely two separable matters; the spatial dispersions invoked in the image of HIV-infected truck drivers and wandering prostitutes are only slightly more imaginative than the idea of mobile yuppies with bicoastal life styles transporting HIV around the U.S. or, as Pattern Three implicitly suggests, around the world. The crucial point here is that bourgeois family units in Africa—understood, from the outset, to be free of infection—must not rely upon condom use to prevent infection, for how otherwise could they succeed in reproducing themselves? Conversely, since those outside the family must be prevented from reproducing, it is they alone who must be urged to use condoms. The already infected persons, especially women, in their haphazard, defamilialized units are thus to be "eliminated" in a kind of final prophylactic solution. Advocated only for "people already infected with HIV or those who engage in recognizably high-risk sexual behavior" (such as sex with "prostitutes"), condoms "reduce but *do not eliminate the risk of transmission*" (Pamphlet 3, 21). "Elimination" of transmission slides easily into elimination of persons: what is implicit here is a brave new world of monogamous or faithful polygamous relationships[15] that will rise from the ashes of the "modernization" that, in its destruction of "traditional values," becomes a "cause" of AIDS.

If any doubts remain about the nature of the pamphlet series, its descriptions of AIDS counseling make it clear that the "cure" for AIDS in Africa lies in the proliferation of bourgeois families. "Communication" is repeatedly proscribed for counselors and families. Although noting that other social support networks continue to exist (though always fractured by "modernization"), the pamphlets urge one-on-one, paraprofessional counseling to replace functioning social relations involving grandmothers, cousins, or jokesters who teach about sexuality. In the abstract, such programs seem desirable in a crisis setting, but their longer-term effect is to destroy existing social relations while promoting disciplining interventions from the local clinic.

The TASO project of Uganda (Pamphlet 2) follows precisely from this model of the reconstructed bourgeois family and describes how the transition "back" to the family and the "elimination" of the already infected will be managed. I do not want to undercut the important work of TASO, modeled on the grass-roots "self-help" (though largely gay male) people-living-with-AIDS movement in the West.[16] Instead, I want to underline what is presented here as "appropriate" AIDS work. While this organization has been enormously helpful, it is crucial to realize that the conception of "self-help" as employed in its project is as culture bound as the idea of the bourgeois family. *Self*-help arises only in the context of already existing (or already denied) *state*-mediated services, hence the emphasis on "self-" rather than on community mobilization. Not surprisingly, most of the TASO clients whose stories appear in this pamphlet are men who are themselves both counselors and clients of the five-year-old organization. These stories suggest in effect that the organization has become a kind of surrogate family; indeed, a client named Gilbert has moved to a house near the TASO office, where he now works part-time, so that he "can see a lot more of his children. . . . As a father I feel much closer to my children" (Pamphlet 2, 24). These transitional family units, "victims" of the modernization that permitted the disease of Western single people to invade the African family, are presented as evidence for the "safeness" of bourgeois families to come. Though never specifically addressed in the pamphlet, the paradigmatic act that defines the bourgeois family—regulated heterosexual intercourse—is itself to be protected from the condom. In one sweep, the pamphlet's refusal to promote universal condom use paves the way for the virtual genocide of anyone outside the chastity-before-marriage-monogamous-couple and enables Euro-American epidemiologists to name the "difference" constitutive of "African AIDS." *If only they'd had proper families.*[17]

African social patterns once were deemed unnatural or hypernatural (uncivilized) by the West, but African sex is still considered profoundly natural, too close to the body and its supposedly prediscursive desires to be able to accommodate the inhibiting condom. Having failed to demonstrate anatomical, behavioral, or even sociomedical differences between Euro-American and African sex acts, international AIDS workers now conclude that intercourse itself must ultimately be declared safe, and that the "risk" be situated in its practice outside the legitimate borders of the bourgeois family. Those who cannot be contained within this family will be simply left to die, but such an outcome will be rapid because "African AIDS" seems inexplicably to move faster than "AIDS" (largely because the Western drug companies cannot make any money there). "Africa" is thus once more experiencing border constructions that mask state-sponsored genocide as indigenous social and cultural formation are elided in the interests of a brave new world of disease-free—and controllable—bourgeois family units.

NOTES

This essay differs in its focus from the version given at the Nationalisms and Sexualities Conference, a version which has already appeared at several stages and in different forms: "Inventing African AIDS," *City Limits* [London], 363 (September 1988); "Inventing African AIDS," *New Formations*, 10 (Spring 1990); and "Inventing African AIDS," in my *Inventing AIDS* (New York: Routledge, 1990). I am indebted to Erica Carter who spent a good deal of time preparing the latter two manuscripts, and to Andrew Parker who helped with this new version. I am grateful as well to Eve Kosofsky Sedgwick for hosting a symposium on this topic at Duke University in September 1989.

For related analyses see especially Paula A. Treichler, "AIDS and HIV Infection in the Third World: A First World Chronicle," in Barbara Kruger and Phil Mariani, eds., *Remaking History* (Seattle: Bay Press, 1989); Treichler, "AIDS, Africa, and Cultural Theory," *Transition*, 51 (1991); and Simon Watney, "Missionary Positions," *Critical Quarterly*, 30, 1 (Autumn 1989).

1. "Natural history" is the term employed within epidemiology to describe the development of a disease, epidemic, or pandemic if left to run its course. The desire to learn the natural history of HIV/AIDS has resulted in debates, for example, about whether the few remaining long-time infected by asymptomatic men in a San Francisco "natural history" cohort should now "be allowed" to take prophylactic AZT or pentamidine, two of the most widely accepted life-prolonging drugs. Researchers in Africa have expressed a similar wish to allow existing conditions to continue to "see what happens." In one study of the effectiveness of contraceptive sponges for interrupting HIV transmission, researchers gave half of the targeted women (who were sex workers) placebos—in essence a wad of cotton. Despite early data suggesting that both groups in the study

were becoming infected at a rapid rate, the experiment continued for three years until "statistically sound samplings" were obtained. Tragically, the same research data showed that sex workers in an adjoining district had been able to get many of their male clients to use condoms, thereby decreasing not only HIV transmission in these women but other sexually transmitted diseases overall. For more on such experiments, see my *Inventing AIDS*.

2. *New York Times*, September 16, 1990, pp. 1, 14. The map and accompanying article, "What Makes the 2 Sexes So Vulnerable to Epidemic," appear on p. 15.

3. Specific information is given for: "Most Severely Affected"—Malawi, Rwanda, Uganda, Zambia; "Urban Rate 10 percent to 20 percent—Burundi, Ivory Coast, Tanzania, Zimbabwe, Central African Republic, Congo, Guinea Bissau, Kenya, and Zaire (Rwanda has the same percentages but is placed in the "Most Severely Affected" category apparently because of a single study showing a 30 percent rate of seroprevalence in a cohort of pregnant women in the capital city); and "Ominous Signs"—Angola, Burkina Faso, Mali, Ethiopia, Ghana, Namibia, Nigeria, Senegal, Sierra Leone, South Africa, and Sudan.

4. I am alluding here to the highly publicized accounts that suggest (based on fantasy) that either Tall Ships sailors who toured the world in 1976 or "Patient Zero," a steward on Air Canada in the early 1980s, brought AIDS to the U.S. See Randy Shilts, *And the Band Played On* (New York: St. Martin's Press, 1987).

5. This assumption of heterosexuality seems to be based only on the simple statistical fact that the male to female ratio in Africa as a whole is about 1:1. Scientists have been slow to recognize, however, that the number of women who receive transfusions (and thus the transfusion-related HIV infection) has been grossly underestimated. Since it is standard medical practice throughout much of Africa to give whole blood transfusions for malarial, nutritional, or maternal anemia, scientists have consistently conflated pregnancy with transfusions as "risk" factors. See Alan Fleming, "Prevention of Transmission of HIV by Blood Transfusion in Developing Countries," Global Impact of AIDS Conference (London, March 8–10, 1988).

6. A scientist of the stature of Luc Montaigne has persistently maintained, despite contrary epidemiologic data, that "AIDS" started in "Africa." His claim is based on the genetic similarity of a simian immunodeficiency virus found in monkeys. This insistence is an updating of racist evolutionary theory, only in place of the old missing link between apes and homo sapiens, the new missing link connects monkeys with North Americans. By a clever sleight of hand, the AIDS-came-from-Africa theory first situates the virus as more or less dormant in Africa and then transports it to Europe and/or America, where it rapidly disseminates. At the same time, so this theory runs, a variant of the virus suddenly proliferates in Africa (urbanization is cited as an explanation—but this process was already well underway before the onset of the epidemic).

7. I remain perplexed by Westerners' insistence that there is no homosexuality in Africa—after all, it would have been much simpler to lay AIDS at the door of a single "perversion." Yet Western homosexual panic works overtime in AIDS discourse: homosexuality is more controllable if it can be retained as a category of Western bourgeois culture. To acknowledge other homosexualities would implicitly challenge Western notions that homosexuality is a symptom of cultural decadence, even if "primitive" homosexualities can be written off on that basis. But such panic also enables the denial of miscegenation through the denial of cross-race homosexual congress. This is nowhere clearer than in South African AIDS discourse, where both "white (homosexual)" AIDS and "black (heterosexual)" AIDS are said to exist. Well into the 1980s, South African commentators would wryly note that apartheid may have "saved" South African blacks from AIDS. Studies of male relations in the mines, conducted as gay history, were appropriated as "proof" of the effectiveness of sexual apartheid (perhaps the least violent but most fundamental aspect of racial separation): black miners, it was argued, did not acquire AIDS while in the male-only dormitories since they had "intercourse" only with their female partners.

8. The persistent effort to establish an African heterosexual "difference" began with allegations that

Africans favored anal intercourse because it is, as many media reports called it, "a primitive form of birth control." This assumed that HIV transmission was paradigmatically sodomitic; the handful of Army cases in which men alleged that they had been infected by prostitutes also rested on this idea since, as one researcher told me, "their wives wouldn't do it (permit anal intercourse)." Sadly, for the Western sexual imagination, epidemiologists failed to find higher rates of anal intercourse, or any other exotic practice, to explain differences between "African" and "Euro-American" heterosexual practice. But researchers and journalists are still searching, as can be seen in a passage from the *Times* on "dry sex" that I discuss below. Who knows what lurks in the Euro-American male imaginary here—"African" penises smaller than fantasized? "African" vaginas even larger than feared?

9. See, for example, Robert E. Gould, "Reassuring News About AIDS: A Doctor Tells Why *You* May Not Be at Risk," *Cosmopolitan* (January 1988), p. 147: "The data I gathered concerning heterosexual intercourse in Africa show marked differences from the way it is usually practiced in the United States."

10. See especially Frantz Fanon, "Unveiling Algeria," in *A Dying Colonialism* (New York: Monthly Review press, 1965). I am also indebted here to Kirstin McDougall, whose unpublished manuscript on maternal metaphors in AIDS discourse confirms that such slippage occurs not only in Western but also in Anglophone African media.

11. The three "Strategies for Hope" pamphlets, published jointly by ACTIONAID in London, the African Medical and Research Foundation in Nairobi, and World in Need in Colchester (U.K.), are now distributed widely by the World Health Organization Global Program on AIDS. The series includes two pamphlets about Zambia and one about Uganda; these have been reviewed, respectively, by the National AIDS Surveillance Committee of Zambia and the National AIDS Control Programme of Uganda. Pamphlet One is entitled *From Fear to Hope: AIDS Care and Prevention at Chikankata Hospital, Zambia*, authored by U.K.-based Glen Williams, who is also the series editor. Pamphlet Two, by U.K.-based Janie Hampton, is called *Living Positively with AIDS: The AIDS Support Organisation (TASO), Uganda*. The third pamphlet is *AIDS Management: An Integrated Approach*, by Williams and Capt. (Dr.) Ian D. Campbell, Chief Medical Officer of the Salvation Army Hospital in Chikankata, Zambia.

12. For more general information on the inscription of sexual cultures as subaltern, see especially T. Dunbar Moody, "Migrancy and Male Sexuality in South African Gold Mines," *Journal of South African Studies*, 14, 2 (January 1988), pp. 228–56; Lourdes Arguelles and B. Ruby Rich, "Homosexuality, Homophobia, and Revolution: Notes Toward an Understanding of the Cuban Lesbian and Gay Male Experience," in Martin Duberman, Martha Vicinus, and George Chauncey Jr., eds., *Hidden from History* (New York: New American Library, 1989); Pat Caplan, ed., *The Cultural Construction of Sexuality* (New York: Tavistock, 1987); "Homecoming," *Black/Out*, 2, 1 (Fall 1986); and Alfred Machela, "The Work of the Rand Gay Organization," Conference on Homosexual Identity Before, During, and After HIV (Stockholm, June 1988).

13. For the longer argument on Western medical ethics and proposed vaccine trials, see my *Inventing AIDS*.

14. To their credit, in Pamphlet 3, the authors emphasize that condoms are not currently being supplied to African countries in sufficient supply to meet potential demand (21). However, this can hardly be used as an excuse not to promote condom usage at all, since it is probably easier and quicker to increase condom supplies than it is to promote "monogamy." Indeed, the ease with which the lack-of-supply argument becomes an excuse for not promoting condoms is rooted in the widespread notion that "in Africa, AIDS is a disease of poverty."

15. See Pamphlet 1, which invokes "traditional values and norms of sexual behavior, which have been lost in the recent wave of 'modernization,'" and which defines "stable polygamy" as a form of "safe sex" (20).

16. It is critical to recognize how limiting are the terms of the international health regime; many local

strategies remain "unreadable" because they defy the standardizations favored by the World Health Organization.

17. I am indebted here to the brief sections on the construction of the "Algerian" family in Malek Al-loula, *The Colonial Harem*, trans. Myrna Godzich and Wlad Godzich (Minneapolis: University of Minnesota Press, 1986). A similar pattern occurs in the media reportage about AIDS in Africa, where the existing "African" family is often implicitly denigrated for having, besides a surfeit of children, either too many parents or too few (usually the father has died or has run off).

20 The Color of Sex

Postwar Photographic Histories of Race and Gender in *National Geographic Magazine*

Catherine A. Lutz and Jane L. Collins

Race is, as Henry Gates has said, "a trope of ultimate, irreducible difference between cultures, linguistic groups, or adherents of specific belief systems that—more often than not—also have fundamentally opposed economic interests" (1985: 5). It is a trope that is particularly dangerous because it "pretends to be an objective term of classification." Gates points to the profoundly social nature of racial classification. Social groups engaged in struggle define racial boundaries in the contexts of that struggle; powerful groups then invoke biology in a post-hoc justification of the boundaries they have drawn. Those in power elaborate observable physical differences—no matter how subtle—into explanations, affirmations, and justifications for inequality and oppression. Once this work is done, and the boundaries are intact, racist theory produces full-blown descriptions of culture and personality that juxtapose powerful ego and degraded/dangerous alter, "lending the sanction of God, biology or the natural order to presumably unbiased descriptions of cultural tendencies and differences" (Gates 1985: 5).

As Gates and others have so eloquently pointed out, racial difference—and its supposed cultural concomitants—is thus not the *source* of the many contemporary conflicts where it is said to be at issue. It is never a simple matter of two groups in contact finding themselves so physically and culturally different that they just cannot get along. Rather, racial and cultural difference become coded ways of talking about other differences that matter—differences in power and in interests.[1] For this reason—however absolute and intransigent they may seem—racial/racist theories must retain flexibility and are frequently ambiguous. As Omi and Winant (1986: x) have said, race is an inherently unstable "complex of social meanings, constantly being transformed by

Jane Collins is Professor of Sociology and Women's Studies at the University of Wisconsin, Madison. She is author of *Unseasonal Migrations: The Effects of Rural Labor Scarcity in Peru* (Princeton, 1988), and coauthor (with Martha Gimenez) of *Work Without Wages: Comparative Studies of Domestic Labor and Self-Employment* (SUNY, 1990).

Catherine Lutz is Professor of Anthropology at the University of North Carolina, Chapel Hill. She has researched ethnopsychology on a Micronesian atoll (*Unnatural Emotions*, 1988), the gendered social contexts of American psychology and anthropology ("The Gender of Theory," 1995), and militarization in American history and contemporary social life (*Making Soldiers in the Public Schools*, with Lesley Bartlett, 1995). Lutz and Collins are co-authors of *Reading National Geographic* (Chicago, 1993).

political struggle." To work to uncover the social arrangements that give rise to and reproduce racism is to place its analysis in realms of human agency and to emphasize the specificity of its historical forms.

TRANQUIL RACIAL SPACES

National Geographic magazine is the product of a society deeply permeated with racism as a social practice and with racial understandings as ways of viewing the world. It sells itself to a reading public that—while they do not consider themselves racist—turn easily to race as an explanation for culture and for social outcome. The Geographic headquarters itself has had few black employees up to the present, despite the predominantly African American citizenry of Washington, D.C. It is not surprising, therefore, that while race is rarely addressed directly in the magazine, white American racial categories powerfully structure the images contained in its pages.

One of the most powerful (and distinctive) tenets of racism in the United States is the idea that "blackness" is an all-or-nothing phenomenon. Racial law through the period of the Civil War, and after, held that any "black" ancestry was sufficient to define one as black. As recently as 1983, this type of reasoning was upheld by the State Supreme Court of Louisiana, when it refused to allow a woman descended from an eighteenth-century white planter and a black slave to change the classification on her birth certificate from "colored" to "white" (Omi and Winant 1986: 57). The laws in question, and the cultural preconceptions upon which they were based, insistently denied the reality of interracial sexual relations or of the sexual exploitation that so frequently accompanied the master/slave relation. They insisted on pure and unequivocal categories with which to reason about difference. Such airtight categories were viewed as necessary to guard the privileges of "whites" as absolute, and to justify the denial of equality to "blacks" as an impossibility.

Nevertheless, when Euramericans turned their eyes outside the borders of their own country, other forms of reasoning prevailed. Evolutionist thought dominated attempts to understand the human diversity of the non-European world. Such thinking needed a continuum, and one that was grounded in nature. Skin color is obviously highly variable, only with some difficulty made to accommodate the simple binary classification "black"/"white" in the United States. A continuum of skin color was thus a perfect biological substratum on which to graft stories of human progress or cultural evolution.

Late nineteenth-century fairs and expositions frequently organized the world cultures they presented along an evolutionary scale. These almost always corresponded to a racial continuum, as Rydell (1984) has noted, from the "savagery" of the dark-skinned Dahomeyans, to the Javanese "Brownies," to the "nearly-white" Chinese and Japanese. As evolutionary trajectories were reproduced over the course of the twentieth century, in anthropological theory and in white popular consciousness, they almost always were connected to a scale of skin color, which was then construed, in many cases, as an independent form of verifying their correctness.

As we examined *National Geographic* photographs, we hypothesized that it was this more differentiated scale—rather than the simple binary opposition called into play for analyzing American culture—that would inform the ways *National Geographic* would portray, and readers would interpret, images of the third world. Distinctions in popular stereotypes of the peoples of Northern and sub-Saharan Africa, or of Melanesia and Polynesia, indicated that Euramericans drew conclusions about others based on the *degree* of darkness of skin color. As we analyzed constructions of race in *National Geographic* photographs, we thus coded them in a way that would allow us to determine whether "bronze" peoples were portrayed different from those who would be more commonly seen as "black"; to see, in other words, if simply binary constrictions informed the images, or if more complex evolutionary schema structured their messages.[2]

The period for which we analyzed photographs—1950–86—encompassed times of great turmoil in racially defined relationships in the United States. The late 1950s and early sixties saw struggles to overturn racial codes that were more intense than any since the Civil War era. Participants in the civil rights movement sought to obtain basic civil liberties for African Americans; they used the egalitarian verbiage of federal law to challenge the restrictive laws and practices of states and municipalities. Such changes did not simply require a change in the legal codes and their implementation, however; they also demanded, as Omi and Winant have argued, "a paradigm shift in established systems of racial meanings and identities" (1986: 90).

Nonviolent tactics such as freedom rides, marches, attempts to desegregate key southern school districts and universities, and sit-ins at segregated lunchrooms characterized the period up until the passage of the 1964 Civil Rights Act and the voting rights legislation of 1965. By the mid-sixties, however, many who had worked and hoped for these changes were disillusioned. Changes in legislation had profound symbolic value, and materially benefitted a small number of middle-class African Americans. But they did not alter the economic circumstances of the vast majority of blacks living in poverty, and they did not adequately challenge the tremendous and continuing burden of institutional racism. This led to an increasing radicalization of key branches of the civil rights movement and to angry rioting in places like Watts and Newark (Harding 1981; Carson 1981).

The civil rights movement contested white privilege and its counterpart, the institutionalized oppression of black Americans. It also contested the very meaning of race in American culture. As white Americans were deprived of one of the master tropes explaining their privileged position in the world, race became an uncomfortable topic for them. This discomfort was reflected in the pages of *National Geographic*. Clearly the magazine did not cover the turmoil in U.S. cities during the period. At the same time, it sought to ease anxieties in its portrayal of the third world. As late as the early 1950s, the Euramerican reading public could comfortably view Asian and African peoples attending white explorers and photographers—carrying them across rivers, pulling them in rickshaws, carrying their packs and bags. By the late sixties, however, these images were too disturbing, the possibility of rebellion and anger was too present. White travelers simply disappeared from the pictures, removing the possibility of conflictual relationships.

With this action, third world spaces were cleared for fantasy. Black and bronze peoples of Africa, Asia, and Latin America were shown going about their daily lives—happy, poor but dignified, and attuned to basic human values. The photographs themselves were not all that different from those of previous decades; however, in the racially charged context of the fifties and sixties, their meaning had changed. The implicit contrast with Watts and Newark, or even with Selma and Montgomery, operated behind the scenes. The third world was constituted as safe, comfortable space, where race was not an issue and where white people did not have to re-evaluate the sources of their privilege.

Apparently, though, in the minds of *National Geographic* editors, too much of even a reassuring fantasy could be disturbing. Until 1961, the numbers of white, black, or bronze people occurring in any given issue of *National Geographic* was variable. In 1952, for example, only about 15 percent of people depicted in articles on the Third World were dark-skinned; in 1958, the figure was about 46 percent. Beginning in 1961, however, a remarkably stable pattern began to appear. For the next twenty-five years the percentage of dark-skinned people in any issue held very constant at about 28 percent. People who could be categorized as bronze formed a fairly regular 60 percent of the total, with the remaining 12 percent constituted by light or white-skinned third world peoples. The intense stability of this pattern, and particularly the almost invariant proportion of dark-skinned people represented, suggests that editorial attention may have been focused on the issue.

This is admittedly indirect evidence. We did not find anyone at *National Geographic* who was willing to say that skin color per se was a consideration in putting together issues (although conversations in planning meetings suggest that it may well be). We do know, however, that *National Geographic*'s marketing department gathered significant amounts of data on the popularity of different kinds of articles and that Africa was by far the least popular world region. By marketing definitions, African peoples constituted a difficult topic; to the extent that market concerns drive content, one would thus expect some sort of regulation of their coverage.

In photographs where dark-skinned peoples were portrayed, there were interesting regularities—contributing to an overall image of contentment, industriousness, and simplicity. The activity level of individuals portrayed in the photographs, for example, clearly sorted out on an evolutionary scale marked by skin color. Individuals coded as black were most likely to be depicted in high levels of activity—engaged in strenuous work or athletics. People coded white were most likely to be engaged in low-level activity—seated or reclining, perhaps manipulating something with their hands, but rarely exerting themselves. Those coded bronze were most likely to be found engaged in activities that fell somewhere between the two extremes, such as walking or herding animals. In keeping with this pattern, people of color (both black and bronze) were most likely to be portrayed at work in the photographs we examined, while people with white skin were most likely to be found at rest.

Portraying people at work is in keeping with an editorial policy that demands a focus on the positive as construed in the United States, that is, the work ethic. It is possible to imagine that editors sought to counter images of the laziness of non-white peoples (in the Euramerican imagination) by deliberately presenting an alternative view. At the same time, in the contradictory manner that is characteristic of colonial / neocolonial mentality (see Bhabha 1983)—it is also possible that deeply ingrained notions of racial hierarchy made it seem more "natural" for dark-skinned peoples to be at work and engaged in strenuous activity. White ambivalence around the black male seems often to center around issues of strength: while vigor is good for the worker to have, it also has the threatening connotations of potential rebelliousness, and so some hobbling often follows the rendition of strength.

Few topics have occupied as much space in colonial discourse as the relationship of blacks to labor. As Euramericans sought to build wealth on the backs of colonized peoples and slaves, they sought to continually refine methods of maximizing the labor they were able to extract. Colonial administrators and plantation bosses continually reported on the successes and failures of innovations in the process. The double mentality reflected in the reports was plain—while people of color were inherently suited to labor, they never wanted to work hard enough in the fields of their white masters. The image of a tremendous capacity to work, coupled with an unwillingness to do so, gave rise to contradictory stereotypes. The heritage of these stereotypes and the labor relations that gave rise to them can be traced in the strenuously employed black bodies portrayed in the pages of *National Geographic*.

In equally regular ways, black and bronze peoples were more likely to be portrayed as poor and technologically backward. Individuals coded as white were more likely to be wealthy and less likely to be poor than other categories. Still, only 21 percent of black and 16 percent of bronze people were photographed in contexts of poverty. Fully 70 percent of the former and 72 percent of the latter were shown without any markers of wealth or poverty, and some of each group were portrayed as wealthy. There is clearly a tension at work in the photographs. The greater poverty of darker-skinned individuals may, in part, be empirically determined; it is also in keeping with popular Euramerican stereotypes of the degraded status of dark-skinned peoples. On the other hand, *National Geographic*'s policy of focusing on the positive and avoiding advocacy precludes too heavy an emphasis on impoverishment. Dark-skinned peoples have a somewhat greater tendency to be poor—one might construe the statistical weight of the photographs as saying—but, in general, they live well.

Individuals coded white were most likely to be depicted with machines of one kind or another; black and bronze individuals were most likely to be shown with simple tools of local manufacture. Not surprisingly, people of color were more often depicted as engaged in ritual. This variable also sorted out along an evolutionary/skin color continuum: the darker the skin color, the more likely to engage in ritual practices. In classic evolutionist terms, superstition (represented by ritual) and science (represented by technology) were counterposed. Similarly, the darker the skin color of an individual, the less likely he or she was to be depicted in Western-style clothing. The darker the skin of the people portrayed, the less they were associated with things European, and the more exotic they were rendered.

Given these trends, it was somewhat surprising to find that dark-skinned peoples were not photographed in natural settings (that is, in landscapes or greenery) more often than their lighter-skinned counterparts. They were, however, more likely to appear in settings where surroundings were not clearly discernible. Such portrayals tend to aestheticize the materials upon which they focus. In this case, they force attention to the lines, shapes and colors of the bodies themselves, rather than providing information about the context in which the bodies appear. Because such photos were relatively numerous, dark-skinned people consequently appeared in *social* surroundings less frequently.

People coded black or bronze were more likely to be photographed in large groups than those coded white. They were less likely to be portrayed alone or in small intimate groups. People of color were therefore less often the subject of individualized photographic accounts, attentive to "biographic" features and life circumstances. They were more often portrayed as part of a mass, perhaps thereby suggesting to readers that they had relatively undifferentiated feelings, hopes, or needs. Individuals coded as black and bronze were far more likely to be photographed gazing into the camera than individuals coded white—a stance that, while complex and sometimes ambiguous—frequently suggests availability and compliance.

Despite some Euramerican stereotypes, dark skin was not associated with evidence of aggression in the pages of *National Geographic* through most of the period we have examined. Aggression is generally taboo as a topic for *National Geographic* photographs, except in the highly specific case of depicting U.S. military power. Additionally, however, to retain its status as a place where white U.S. readers go to assuage their fears about race and cultural difference, *National Geographic* must studiously avoid photographs that might suggest a potential threat from colonized and formerly colonized peoples. To depict anger, violence, or the presence of weapons is to evoke the fear that they might be turned to retaliation. They serve as an uncomfortable reminder of a world given to struggles for independence, revolutions, and rebellions.

In the marketplaces of images, *National Geographic* relies on two intertwined strategies. It relies on recognition—on offering readers what they already know and believe, in new and appealing ways. Its reputation and sales also turn on the classic humanism with which it portrays the world. In its depictions of "nonwhite" peoples, the humanist mission—to portray all humans as basically the same "under the skin"[3]—comes into conflict with Western "commonsense knowledge" about the hierarchy of races.

The organization of photographs into stories about cultural evolution (couched in more "modern" terms of progress and development) provides the partial resolution of this contradiction. These stories tell the Euramerican public that their race prejudice is not so wrong; that at one point people of color *were* poor, dirty, technologically backward, and superstitious—and some still are. But this is not due to intrinsic or insuperable characteristics. With guidance and support from the West, they can in fact overcome these problems, acquire the characteristics of civilized peoples and take their place alongside them in the world. In the context of this story, the fact that bronze peoples are portrayed as slightly less poor, more technologically adept, serves as proof that progress is possible—and fatalistically links progress to skin color.

At the same time, the "happy-speak" policies of *National Geographic* have meant that for people of color—as for others—the overall picture is one of tranquility and well-being. We are seldom confronted with historical facts of racial or class violence, with hunger as it unequally affects black and white children, or with social movements that question established racial hierarchies. One photographer expressed this poignantly, pointing to a photograph of an African family in a 1988 issue on population. "The story is about hunger," he said, "but look at these people. It's a roman-tic picture."

This is not to say that no one at the National Geographic Society is attentive to these issues. Dedicated photographers and editors worked hard in the 1970s to produce and push into print two deeply disturbing accounts of apartheid. And while this attempt engendered a repressive movement within the Society's Board of Trustees, an article critical of South African black home-lands appeared in February 1986.

The same strategies, however, pursued in different epochs, can have different meanings and consequences. The humanist side of *National Geographic* in the 1950s and 1960s denied social problems; it also provided images of people of color living their lives in relatively dignified ways. It gave short shrift to poverty and disharmony, but it permitted a certain amount of identification across racial boundaries. In a period when racial boundaries were highly visible and when African Americans were struggling for equal rights under the law, these images could be read, at least in part, as subtle arguments for social change.

The 1970s have been characterized as a period of "racial quiescence," when social movements waned and conflicts receded (Omi and Winant 1986: 2). Racial oppression did not cease, but it was not as openly contested. In turn, the 1980s saw a backlash in undisguised attempts to dis-mantle legislation protecting civil rights and nondiscriminatory practices. These moves did not require—and, in fact, assiduously avoided, an explicitly racial discourse. Busing, originally imple-mented to desegregate schools, was overturned under banners of "community control" and "parental involvement." Rejections of racially balanced textbooks were couched in terms of bat-tles against "secular humanism" and "political correctness." And in the 1988 presidential cam-paign, movements of people of color were recast as "special interests" (Oni and Winant 1986: 125).

In such a context, classic humanism takes on pernicious overtones. The denial of race as a *social* issue, in a society with a profoundly racist history and where institutional racism still exists, fore-closes dialogue on the issues. *National Geographic* has not intentionally contributed to this fore-closure; it goes on producing pictures in much the same way it has for years. And yet the message that we are all alike under the skin takes on new meaning in a social context that denies that dis-crimination exists or that race has been used to consolidate the privilege of some and oppress others. The racism of the 1980s was not confrontational and defiant; it simply turned its back on the issues. The tranquil racial spaces of *National Geographic* can only contribute to this willed ignorance.

THE WOMEN OF THE WORLD

National Geographic photographs of the women of the world tell a story about the women of the United States over the post–World War II period. It is to issues of gender in white American readers' lives, such as debates over women's sexuality or whether women doing paid labor can mother their children adequately, that the pictures refer as much as to the lives of third world women. Seen in this way, the *National Geographic's* women can be placed alongside the other women of American popular culture: the First Lady, the woman draped over an advertisement's red sports car, the Barbie doll, the woman to whom the Hallmark Mother's Day card is addressed. Rather than treating the photos as simply images of women, we can set them in the context of a more complex cultural history of the period, with the sometimes radical changes it brought to the lives of the women who are the readers (or known to the male readers) of the magazine.

The photographs of *National Geographic* are indispensible to understanding issues of gender because the magazine is one of the very few popular venues trafficking in large numbers of images of black women. While the photographs tell a story about cultural ideals of femininity, the nar-rative threads of gender and race are tightly bound up with each other. In the world at large, race and gender are clearly not separate systems, and as Trinh (1989), Moore (1988), Sacks (1989), and others have reminded us.

For the overwhelmingly white readers of the *Geographic*, the dark-skinned women of distant regions serve as touchstones, giving lessons both positive and negative about what women are and should be (compare Botting 1988). Here, as elsewhere, the magazine plays with possibilities of the other as a flexible reflection—even a sort of funhouse mirror—for the self. The women of the world are portrayed in sometimes striking parallel to popular images of American womanhood of the various periods of the magazine's production—for instance, as mothers and beautiful objects. At certain times, with certain races of women, however, the *Geographic's* other women provide a contrast to stereotypes of white American women—they are presented as hard-working bread-winners in their communities.

As with American women in popular culture, Third World women are portrayed less frequently than men: one-quarter of the pictures we looked at focus primarily on women.[4] The situation has traditionally not been that different in the anthropological literature covering the non-Western world, and it may be amplified in both genres where the focus is on cultural difference or exoticism. Given the association between women and the natural world, men and things cultural (Ortner 1974), a magazine that aspires to describe the distinctive achievements of civilizations might be expected to highlight the world of men. But like the "people of nature" in the Fourth World, women have been treated as all the more precious for their nonutilitarian, nonrationalistic qualities. Photographs of women become one of the primary devices by which the magazine depicts "universal human values," and these include the values of family love and the appreciation of female beauty itself.[5] We turn to these two issues now, noting that each of them has had a consistent cultural content through the postwar period, during historical changes that give the images different emphases and form through the decades.

The motherhood of man. There is no more romantic set of photographs in the *Geographic* than those depicting the mothers of the world with their children. There is the exuberant picture showing the delight of a Kurd mother holding her infant. Filling much space, as an unusually high percentage of the magazine's mother-child pictures do, the photograph covers two pages despite the relative lack of information in it. Its classical composition and crisp, uncluttered message are similar to those in many such photos. They often suggest the Western tradition of madonna painting, and evoke the Mother's Day message: this relationship between mother and child, they say, is a timeless and sacred one, essentially and intensely loving regardless of social and historical context—the foundation of human social life rather than cultural difference. The family of man, these pictures might suggest, is first of all a mother-child unit, rather than a brotherhood of solidarity between adults.[6]

For the magazine staff and readers of the 1950s, there must have been even more power in these images than we see in them today. The impact of the photos would have come from the intense cultural and social pressures on middle-class women to see their most valued role as that of mother (Margolis 1984). The unusually strong pressure of this period is often explained as motivated by desires to place returning World War II veterans (and men in general) in those jobs available and by anxieties about the recent war horror and the future potential for a nuclear conflagration, which made the family seem a safe haven (May 1988). As a new cult of domesticity emerged, women were told—through both science and popular culture—that biology, morality, and the psychological health of the next generation required their commitment to full-time mothering. This ideological pressure persisted through the 1950s despite the rapid rise in female employment through the decade.

The idealization of the mother-child bond is seen in everything from the warm TV relationships of June Clever with Wally and the Beaver to the cover of a *Life* magazine issue of 1956 devoted to "The American Woman" showing a glowing portrait of a mother and daughter lovingly absorbed in each other; all of this is ultimately and dramatically reflected in the period's rapidly expanding birth rate. This idealization had its counterpoint in fear of the power women were given in the domestic domain. In both science and popular culture, the mother was criticized for being smothering, controlling, oversexualized, and, a bit later, overly permissive (Ehrenreich and English 1978, 1988).

The *National Geographic*'s treatment of children can be seen as an extension of these ideologies of motherhood and the family. As the "woman question" came to be asked more angrily in the late 1950s, there was a gradual erosion of faith in the innocence of the mother-infant bond and even in the intrinsic value of children (Ehrenreich and English 1978), centered on fears of juvenile delinquency and the later 1960's identification of a "generation gap." The *National Geographic*, however, continued to print significant numbers of photographs of children, perhaps responding to their increasingly sophisticated marketing information which indicated that photographs of children and cute animals were among their most popular pictures.

In the *National Geographic*'s pictures of mother and child, it often appears that the nonwhite mother is backgrounded, with her gaze and the gaze of the reader focused on the infant. The infant may in fact be an even more important site for dealing with white racial anxieties, by virtue of constituting an acceptable black love object. A good number of pictures in the postwar period have the form of these two: one a Micronesian and the other an Iraqi infant, from 1974 and 1976 respectively, each peacefully asleep in a cradle with the mother visible behind. The peacefulness constitutes the antithesis of the potentially threatening differences of interest, dress, or ritual between the photographed adult and the reader.

Women and their breasts. The "nude" woman sits, stands or lounges at the salient center of *National Geographic* photography of the non-Western world. Until the phenomenal growth of mass circulation pornography in the 1960s, the magazine was known as the only mass culture venue where Americans could see women's breasts. Part of the folklore of Euramerican men, stories about secret perusals of the magazine emerged time after time in our conversations with *National Geographic* readers. People vary in how they portray the personal or cultural meaning of this nakedness, some noting it was an aid to masturbation, others claiming it failed to have the erotic quality they expected. When white men tell these stories about covertly viewing black women's bodies, they are clearly not recounting a story about a simple encounter with the facts of human anatomy or customs; they are (perhaps unsuspectingly) confessing a highly charged— but socially approved—experience in this dangerous territory of projected, forbidden desire and guilt. Such stories also exist (in a more charged, ironic mode) in the popular culture of African Americans—for example, in Richard Pryor's characterization of *National Geographic* as the black man's *Playboy*.

The racial distribution of female nudity in the magazine conforms, in pernicious ways, to Euramerican myths about black women's sexuality. Lack of modesty in dress places black women closer to nature. Given the pervasive tendency to interpret skin color as a marker of evolutionary progress, it is assumed that white women have acquired modesty along with other characteristics of civilization. Black women remain backward on this scale, not conscious of the embarrassment they should feel at their nakedness (Gilman 1985: 114–15, 193). Their very ease unclothed stigmatizes them.

In addition, black women have been portrayed in Western art and science as both exuberant and excessive in their sexuality. While their excess intrigues, it is also read as pathological and dangerous. In the texts produced within white culture, Haraway writes, "Colored women densely code sex, animal, dark, dangerous, fecund, pathological" (1989:154). Thus for the French surrealists of the 1930s, the exotic, unencumbered sexuality of non-Western peoples—and African women in particular—represented an implicit criticism of the repression and constraint of European sexuality. The Africanism of the 1930s, like an earlier Orientalism, evidenced both a longing for—and fear of—the characteristics attributed to non-Western peoples (Clifford

1988: 61). The sexuality of black women that so entertained French artists and musicians in cafes and cabarets, however, had fueled earlier popular and scientific preoccupation with the Hottentot Venus and other pathologized renditions of black women's bodies and desires (Gilman 1985).

The *Geographic*'s distinctive brand of cultural relativism, however, meant that this aspect of black sexuality would be less written in by the institution than read in by readers, particularly in comparison with other visual venues such as Hollywood movies. One can see the distinctive *Geographic* style in comparison with *Life* photography of non-Western women. A stronger cultural viewpoint on race is at work in a 1956 *Life* article on "other women," which ran next to an article on American women of various regions of the country. The two articles read as a kind of beauty pageant, with all the photographs emphasizing the sitter's appearance, sexuality, and passivity. Ultimately, the magazine's editors judged American women the better-looking set (many captions also noted the "natural," "healthy," wholesome—non-perverted?—quality of the American women), but the adjectives they used to caption the non-Western women describe their sense of the more passive and sexually explicit stance of the other women. So they are variously praised for their "fragility," "great softness," "grace," "languorous" qualities, and eagerness "to please"; "the sensuous quality often seen in women of the tropics" was found in one Malayan woman. The hypersexual but passive woman here replicates the one found by many Westerners in their imaginary African travels throughout the last century (Hammond and Jablow 1977). In the *Life* article, all of the non-Western women except the one Chinese "working girl" (and many of the American women), touch themselves, their clothes, or fans in the usual pose for characterizing female self-involvement (Goffman 1979).

If *National Geographic* trades in the sexuality of black women, it is less comfortable with that of black men. Men coded black were far more likely than those coded white to appear bare-chested in the pages of the magazine—often in poses that drew attention to musculature and strength. The *National Geographic* has apparently tried to include pictures of "handsome, young men" (Abramson 1987: 143). The magazine has been extremely skittish, however, about portraying male genitals. A respect for the facts has not inhibited the careful erasure of all evidence of male penises from photographs. In cultures where men do not customarily wear pants, the magazine has relied on careful extensions of loin clothes, the drawing in of shorts, or simply air-brushing away body parts to avoid offending the white reading public. The fear of—and desire to erase—black male sexuality has a long tradition in Euramerican culture. It reached its fullest and most heinous development in the paranoid fantasies of organizations such as the Ku Klux Klan and in the castrations and lynchings of southern black men for real or imputed advances toward white women (Carby 1985: 307–308). Haraway (1989) and Torgovnick (1990) offer vivid examples and analyses of the evidence of miscegenation and black abduction anxieties in American popular culture materials, such as the Tarzan stories and movies. Masquerading as taste or propriety, however, the underlying anxiety also finds its place in the pages of *National Geographic*.

Like the nude and its role in Western high art painting (Hess and Nochlin 1972; Betterton 1987; Nead 1990), nudity in *Geographic* photographs has had a potential sexual, even pornographic, interpretation. Such interpretations would obviously threaten the magazine's legitimacy and sales, achieved through its self-definition as a serious, relatively high-brow, family magazine. Pornography represents just the opposite values: "disposability, trash," the deviant, the unrespectable, the low class (Nead 1990: 325). Like fine art, science attempts to frame the nude female body as devoid of pornographic attributes. While art aestheticizes it, science dissects, fragments, and otherwise desexualizes it. The *National Geographic* nude has at times done both of these contradictory things.

Two important stylistic changes can be identified in photos of women's bodies in the magazine, one related to changes in commercial photography of women and the other to the growing tolerance of "aesthetic" pictures in the *Geographic* of the eighties. Beginning in the late fifties, certain changes in the way women were photographed in commercials began to be reflected in

National Geographic images. In early advertisements of the period, women are shown directly involved in the use of a product, as when a woman with a fur stole is shown being helped into her 1955 Chrysler by the doorman of an obviously upscale building. By contrast, a 1966 Chevrolet ad depicts a woman lying on the roof of the car putting on lipstick, with a small inset photo that shows her sitting on the roof being photographed by a man. The ads of the 1950s show women as domestic royalty; the later ads place them in more straightforwardly sexual roles and postures.

In *National Geographic* documentary images as well, we find a shift, coming some years after that in commercial photography; the naked woman moves from being just an ethnographic fact ("this is the way they dress as they go about their lives") to presentation as in part an aesthetic and sexual object. After 1970, naked women are less often shown framed with men, less often mothering, more often dancing or lounging.[7] The erotic connotations of the horizontal woman (known and drawn on by advertisers [Goffman 1979]), and of the woman absorbed in dance, combine with more romantic, aesthetic styles to create photos which follow the inflation of sexualized images of women in the culture at large (Wolf 1991).

A second explanation for changes in the rendering of the nude woman is found in the increasing tolerance of a more aesthetic rendering of all subjects in the *Geographic*. Aesthetic style, however, has special implications and nuances when the photos are of women. What arises after the fifties in the *Geographic* is not just a more self-consciously aesthetic style, but also a style whose uses elsewhere in the culture were centered on photography of women, as in fashion and other commercial work.

The cultural debate (however minor in scale and impact) over whether the nudity in the *Geographic* was or is appropriate follows shifting and conflicting definitions of acceptable portrayals of women's bodies (Nead 1990). At issue is not simply whether women's bodies are displayed, but what the cultural context of those images is (Myers 1987; Vance 1990); that context includes the sexualization of the breasts, the objectification of women, the racist understanding of black femininity, and the shame that inheres in American culture to sexuality itself.[8] Nonetheless, the still heavily white male photographic and editorial staff at the *Geographic* appears relatively unaffected by feminist critiques of the use of women's bodies or the critique of colonial-looking relations (Gaines 1988) that prompt both the frequent inclusion and a particular distorted reading by subscribers of the nude black woman's body.

The kitchen debates in Africa: Woman's place in the march of progress. In a subtly nuanced analysis of the genre of 1980s Hollywood success movies, Traube (1989) details the influence of the Reagan years and a particular moment of labor demography and consumer capitalism in the construction of the films' plots and styles. These films describe, among other things, the gender-specific dangers and possibilities of the world of managerial work for the middle-class youth who view these movies on their way to corporate work lives. Specifically, they include "warning of the feminizing effects of deference on men and, conversely, the masculinizing effects of ambition on women" (1989: 291). The *National Geographic*'s women do not provide as easy an identificatory anchor for the magazine's readers as do these movie's characters, but their image, too, has responded to changes in the politics and rate of American women's labor force participation. They have also played a role in articulating longstanding cultural notions about the role of women in socioeconomic development overseas.

Against the indolent native of colonialist discourse, the *Geographic*'s industrious native toils in response to an editorial policy which calls for a sympathetic other. Women's work is portrayed, however, as less intellectually demanding and more toilsome than that of men. Take the Melanesian man and woman set up on opposite pages (April 1969: 574–75). A male archer on the left is labeled, "man, the hunter" and, on the right, a photo of a woman with child in netbag carrying a large load of firewood, "woman, the laborer." The woman smiles under her burden, perhaps thereby evoking images long in circulation in Western culture: these are images which romanticize the hard-working black woman, often ignoring the difference between her enduring and enjoying (much less opposing) oppression (hooks 1981: 6). In this latter cultural discourse, the black woman could endure what no lady could and therefore revealed her more natural, even animal nature (81–82). For many readers of the *Geographic*, it may be an easy step from the celebration of the strong, working woman to her dehumanization as someone with less than human abilities to withstand those burdens.[9]

Cultural ambivalence toward women working outside the home has been profound during the postwar period, when women's waged employment grew from 25 percent in 1940 to 40 percent in 1960. More of this is accounted for by African American women, half of whom were employed in 1950, with their waged work continuing at high rates in the following decades. The ideological formulation of the meaning of women's work has changed. Working women in the fifties were defined as helpmates to their husbands. Only much later did women's work come to be seen by some as a means to goals of independence and self-realization (Chafe 1983), although even here, as Traube (1989) points out, messages were widely available that women's success in work was threatening to men. This ambivalence occasionally shows up in the *Geographic* when the laboring woman is presented as a drudge or when her femininity, *despite her working*, is emphasized. An example of the latter is found in a photograph of a Burmese woman shown planting small green shoots in a garden row (June 1974: 286). Retouching has been done both to her line of plants and to the flowers which encircle her hair. The sharpening and coloring of these two items lets the picture much more clearly tell a narrative about her femininity and her productivity and about how those two things are not mutually exclusive.

More often, however, the labor of women as well as other aspects of their lives are presented by the *Geographic* as central to the march of progress in their respective countries. Women are constructed as the vanguard of progress in part through the feminizing of the developing nation state itself (Kabbani 1986; cf. Shaffer 1988). How does this work? In the first instance, those foreign states are contrasted, in some Western imaginations, with a deeply masculine American national identity (Krasniewitz 1990; Jeffords 1989), a gendering achieved through the equation of the West (*in* the West, of course) with strength, civilization, rationality, and freedom, its other with vulnerability, primitivity, superstition, and the binds of tradition. Once this equation has been made, articles can be titled as in the following instance where progress is masculinized and the traditional nation feminized: "Beneath the surge of progress, old Mexico's charm and beauty life undisturbed" (October 1961).

Fanon (1965: 39) pointed out in his analysis of French colonial attitudes and strategies concerning the veil in Algeria that the colonialists' goal, here as elsewhere in the world, was "converting the woman, winning her over to the foreign values, wrenching her free from her status" as a means of "shaking up the [native] man" and gaining control of him. With this and other motives, those outsiders who would "develop" the Third World have often seen the advancement of non-Western women as the first goal to be achieved, with their men's progress thought to follow rather than precede it. In the nineteenth century, evolutionary theory claimed that the move upward from savagery to barbarism to civilization was indexed by the treatment of women, in particular by their liberation "from the burdens of overwork, sexual abuse, and male violence" (Tiffany and Adams 1985: 8). It "saw women in non-Western societies as oppressed and servile creatures, beasts of burden, chattels who could be bought and sold, eventually to be liberated by 'civilization' or 'progress,' thus attaining the enviable position of women in Western society" (Etienne and Leacock 1980: 1), who were then expected to be happy with their place.[10] The *Geographic* has told a much more upbeat version of this story, mainly by presenting other women's labors positively.

The continuation of these ways of thinking into the present can be seen in how states defined as "progressive" have been rendered by both Western media like the *National Geographic* and the non-Western state bureaucrats concerned. Graham-Brown (1988) and Schick (1990) describe how photographic and other proof of the progress or modernity of states like Turkey and pre-revolutionary Iran has often been found primarily in the lives of their women, and particularly in their unveiling.[11] Indeed, as Schick points out, "a photograph of an unveiled woman was not much different from one of a tractor, an industrial complex, or a new railroad; it merely symbolized yet another one of men's achievements" (1990: 369).

Take the example from the *Geographic's* January 1985 article on Baghdad. Several photographs show veiled women walking through the city's streets. One shot shows women in a narrow alley. The dark tones of the photograph are a function of the lack of sunlight reaching down into the alley, but they also reproduce the message of the caption. Playing with the associations between veil and past that are evoked for most readers, it says, "In the shadows of antiquity, women in long black abayas walk in one of the older sections of the city." A few pages earlier, we learn about the high-rise building boom in the city and the changing roles of women in a two-page layout that shows a female electrical engineer in a hard hat and jeans organizing a building project with a male colleague. The caption introduces her by name and goes on: "Iraqi women, among the most progressive in the Arab world, constitutes 25 percent of the country's work force and are guaranteed equality under Baath Party doctrine." On the opposite page, the modern buildings they have erected are captioned, "New York on the Tigris." The equation of the end point (Manhattan) with the unveiled woman is neatly laid out.

The celebration of simultaneous women's liberation and national progress is not the whole story, of course. The magazine also communicates—in a more muted way through the fifties and into the sixties—a sense of the value of the "natural," Gemeinshaft-based life of the people without progress. Progress can be construed as a socially corrosive process as it was in the late nineteenth century, when non-Western women were seen as superior to their Western counterparts because too much education had weakened the latter (Ehrenreich and English 1978: 114), sapping vitality from their reproductive organs. The illiterate woman of the non-Western world still lives with this cultural inheritance, standing for the woman "unruined" by progress.

An example of the contradictory place of progress is found in two photographs that draw attention to housewives. In the first, an Inuit woman wearing a fur trimmed parka stands in front of a washing machine: "Unfamiliar luxury" the caption says, "a washing machine draws a housewife to the new 'Tuk' laundromat, which also offers hot showers" (July 1968). This picture is explicitly structured around the contrast between the premodern and the modern, with the evaluative balance falling to the luxurious present. It might have still resonated for readers with the image from 1959 of Nixon and Khrushchev arguing over the benefits of capitalism next to a freshly minted washing machine and dryer at the American National Exhibition in Moscow. In those debates, Nixon could argue that the progress of American society under capitalism is found in its ability to provide labor-saving devices to women. "I think that this attitude toward women is universal. What we want is to make easier the life of our housewives," he said. In the gender stories told during the cold war, family life and commodities provided what security was to be found in the post-Hiroshima, post-Holocaust world (May 1988). The non-Western woman, too, could be deployed as proof of capitalism's value, of the universal desire for these goods, and of the role of women in the evolution of society.

From January 1971, however, an article titled "Housewife at the End of the World" documents the adventures of an Ohio woman settling in Tierra del Fuego, and congratulates her on adapting to local norms of self-sufficiency and simplicity. The last photo's caption articulates the theme of the whole article: "Life in this remote land spurs inventiveness. . . . My special interests keep me so busy I have little time to miss the conveniences I once knew." The North American woman chooses to forgo the benefits of progress in search of an authentically simple place, as her "younger sister" climbs the ladder in the other direction.

In stories of progress and/or decline, Western and non-Western women have often been played off of one another in this way, each used to critique the other in line with different purposes and in the end leaving each feeling inadequate. The masculine writer/image maker/consumer thereby asserts his own strength, both through his right to evaluate and through his completeness in contrast to women. Although non-Western men cannot be said to fare well in these cultural schemes, they are used less frequently and in other ways (Honour 1989) to either critique or shore up white men's masculinity.

In sum, the women of the non-Western world represent a population aspiring to the full femininity achieved in Western cultures, and, in a more secondary way, they are a repository for the lost femininity of "liberated" Western women. Both an ideal and thus a critique of modern femininity, they are also a measure to tell the Western family how far it has advanced. They are shown working hard and as key to their countries' progress toward some version of the Western consumer family norm. The sometimes contradictory message these pictures can send to middle class women is consistent with cultural ideologies in the United States that both condemn and affirm the woman who would be both mother and wage laborer. We can see the women of the *National Geographic* playing a role within a social field where the Cold War was being waged and where social changes in kinship structures and gender politics were precipitated by the entrance of white women into the paid labor force in larger and larger numbers.

NOTES

1. This is not to deny that there are complex correspondences between culture and racial categories as socially deployed. Once race has been used to marginalize and isolate social groups, shared experiences of oppression, coping and resistance may give rise to shared cultural premises. The "culture" or "cultures" that result, however, are at least partly a consequence of the deployment of racial categories and not evidence of the validity of the categories themselves.

2. The authors and an anthropology graduate student coded the photographs. Intercoder agreement occurred for 86 percent of all decisions. We resolved disagreements through discussion between coders. The photographic features coded included world location, gender, age, activity type, surroundings, dress style, wealth or poverty indicators, nudity, presence of technology, vantage, and camera gaze. A complete description of these features may be found in Lutz and Collins (1993: 285).

3. In part because of its focus on everyday life, *National Geographic* does not trade in the standardized images of black people that have been common in western art—some of which have been characterized by Honour (1989) as "heroes and martyrs," "the benighted," "the defiant," and "the pacified."

4. This proportion is based on those photos in which adults of identifiable gender are shown (N=510). Another 11 percent show women and men together in roughly equal numbers, leaving 65 percent of the photos depicting mainly men.

5. The popularity of this notion in American culture, which *National Geographic* relies on as much as feeds, is also one wellspring for American feminism's focus on universal sisterhood, that is, its insistence, particularly in the 1970s, that Western and non-Western women will easily see each other as similar or sharing similar experiences.

6. Edward Steichen's *Family of Man* exhibition, first displayed in the United States in 1955, also included a substantial section devoted to mothers and infants, nicknamed "Tits and Tots" by the staff of photographers who organized it (Meltzer 1978). This exhibit was immensely popular when it toured, and the catalogue became a bestselling book.

7. This is based on the twenty photos in our sample of 592, where women are shown without shirts on; half of that number occurred from 1950 to 1969 and the other half from 1970 to 1986 (one would, of course, expect there to be somewhat fewer such photos as urbanization and change in dress styles spread across the globe). Some of the same phenomena noted here have been found in advertising in American family magazines (that is, a decrease in images of married women shown in child care and an increase in those showing them at recreation), although in the latter ads the trends begin earlier, in the later 1940s (Brown 1981).

8. The *Geographic*'s breasts should be seen against the broader background of the social changes in the industrial West around sexuality. Foucault (1978) has noted that those changes have been mistakenly associated with a "liberation" of sexuality. In fact, he suggests, with the emergence of the modern state and its regulatory needs has come an obsession with "talking" about and managing sex— through science, state policy, clinical medicine, and now photography.

9. That step may have been taken by white feminism as well, hooks points out: "When the women's movement was at its peak and white women were rejecting the role of breeder, burden bearer, and sex object, black women were celebrated for their unique devotion to the task of mothering; for their 'innate' ability to bear tremendous burdens; and for their ever-increasing availability as sex object. We appeared to have been unanimously elected to take up where white women were leaving off" (1981: 6). See Hammond and Jablow 1977 for an analysis of the particular strength of the notion of non-white women as beasts of burden in the case of African women; see also Collins (1991).

10. Western feminism in the 1970s may have simply transformed rather than fundamentally challenged the terms of this argument as well when it argued that the women of the world were oppressed by men and to be liberated by feminism as defined in the West (see Amos and Parmar 1984).

11. Although feminist anthropology has analyzed and critiqued these kinds of assumptions, it has nonetheless often continued a basic evolutionary discourse in the assumption that Ong has identified: "Although a common past may be claimed by feminists, Third World women are often represented as mired in it, ever arriving at modernity when Western feminists are already adrift in postmodernism" (1988: 87).

REFERENCES

Abramson, Howard S. 1987. National Geographic: Behind America's Lens on the World. New York: Crown.

Amos, V., and Prathiba Parmar. 1984. Challenging Imperial Feminism. Feminist Review 17: 3–20.

Betterton, Rosemary, ed. 1987. Looking On: Images of Femininity in the Visual Arts and Media. London: Pandora.

Bhabha, Homi K. 1983. The Other Question—Homi K. Bhabha Reconsiders the Stereotype and Colonial Discourse. Screen 24(6): 18–36.

Botting, Wendy. 1988. Posing for Power/Posing for Pleasure: Photographies and the Social Construction of Femininity. Binghamton, NY: University Art Gallery.

Brown, Bruce W. 1981. Images of Family Life in Magazine Advertising: 1920–1978. New York: Praeger.

Canaan, Joyce, 1984. Building Muscles and Getting Curves: Gender Differences in Representations of the Body and Sexuality among American Teenagers. Paper presented at the Annual Meeting of the American Anthropological Association, Denver.

Carby, Hazel. 1985. "On the Threshold of Woman's Era": Lynching, Empire and Sexuality in Black Feminist Theory. In Race, Writing and Difference, ed. H. Gates, pp. 301–16. Chicago: University of Chicago Press.

Carson, Claybourne. 1981. In Struggle: SNCC and the Black Awakening of the 1960s. Cambridge: Harvard University Press.

Chafe, William. 1983. Social Change and the American Woman, 1940–70. In A History of Our Time: Readings on Postwar America, ed. William Chafe and Harvard Sitkoff, pp. 147–65. New York: Oxford University Press.

Clifford, James. 1988. The Predicament of Culture: Twentieth-Century Ethnography, Literature and Art. Cambridge: Mass.: Harvard University Press.

Collins, Patricia Hill. 1991. Black Feminist Thought. Boston: Unwin Hyman.

Ehrenreich, Barbara and Deirdre English. 1978. For Her Own Good: 150 Years of the Experts' Advice to Women. Garden City, NY: Anchor Press/Doubleday.

Etienne, Mona, and Eleanor Leacock. 1980. Women and Colonization: Anthropological Perspectives. New York: Praeger.

Fanon, Frantz. 1965. A Dying Colonialism. New York: Grove Press.

Foucault, Michel. 1978. The History of Sexuality. Vol. 1, trans. R. Hurley. New York: Random House.

Gaines, Jane. 1988. White Privilege and Looking Relations: Race and Gender in Feminist Film Theory. Screen 29 (4): 12–27.

Gates, Henry Louis, Jr. 1985. Writing "Race" and the Difference it Makes. In "Race," Writing, and Difference, ed. H. L. Gates, pp. 1–20. Chicago: University of Chicago Press.

Gilman, Sander. 1985. Difference and Pathology: Stereotypes of Sexuality, Race, and Madness. Ithaca: Cornell University Press.

Goffman, Erving. 1979. Gender Advertisements. New York: Harper and Row.

Graham-Brown, Sarah. 1988. Images of Women: The Portrayal of Women in Photography of the Middle East, 1860–1950. London: Quartet Books.

Hammond, Dorothy and Alta Jablow. 1977. The Myth of Africa. New York: Library of Social Science.

Haraway, Donna. 1989. Primate Visions: Gender, Race, and Nature in the World of Modern Science. New York: Routledge.

Harding, Vincent. 1981. There is a River: The Black Struggle for Freedom in America. New York: Harcourt Brace Jovanovich.

Hess, Thomas B., and Linda Nochlin. 1972. Women as Sex Object: Studies in Erotic Art, 1730–1970. New York: Newsweek Books.

Honour, Hugh. 1989. The Image of the Black in Western Art. Vol. 4, From the American Revolution to World War I. New York: Morrow.

hooks, bell. 1981. Ain't I a Women? Black Women and Feminism. Boston: South End.

Jeffords, Susan. 1989. The Remasculinization of America: Gender and the Vietnam War. Bloomington: Indiana University Press.

Kabbani, Rana. 1986. Europe's Myths of the Orient. Bloomington: Indiana University Press.

Krasniewicz, Louise. 1990. Desecrating the Patriotic Body: Flag Burning, Art Censorship, and the Powers of "Protoypical Americans." Paper presented at the Annual Meeting of the American Anthropological Association, New Orleans.

Lutz, Catherine A. and Jane L. Collins. 1993. Reading National Geographic. Chicago: University of Chicao Press.

Margolis, Maxine. 1984. Mothers and Such. Berkeley and Los Angeles: University of California Press.

May, Elaine Tyler. 1988. Homeward Bound: American Families in the Cold War Era. New York: Basic Books.

Meltzer, Milton. 1978. Dorothea Lange: A Photographer's Life. New York: Farrar Straus Giroux.

Moore, Henrietta. 1988. Feminism and Anthropology. Cambridge: Cambridge University Press.

Myers, Kathy. 1987. Towards a Feminist Erotica. In Looking On, ed. R. Betterton, Pp. 189–202. London: Pandora.

Nead, Lynda. 1990. The Female Nude: Pornography, Art, and Sexuality. Signs 15: 323–35.

Omi, Michael, and Howard Winant. 1986. Racial Formation in the United States: From the 1960s to the 1980s. New York: Routledge.

Ong, Aihwa. 1988. Colonialization and Modernity: Feminist Re-presentation of Women in Non-Western Societies. Inscriptions 3/4: 79–93.

Ortner, Sherry. 1974. Is Female to Male as Nature is to Culture? In Woman, Culture and Society, ed. M. Rosaldo and L. Lamphere, Pp. 67–88. Stanford: Stanford University Press.

Rydell, Robert. 1984. All the World's a Fair: Visions of Empire at American International Expositions, 1876–1916. Chicago: University of Chicago Press.

Sacks, Karen. 1989. Toward a Unified Theory of Class, Race and Gender. American Ethnologist 16: 534–50.

Schaffer, Kay. 1988. Women and the Bush: Forces of Desire in the Australian Cultural Tradition. Cambridge: Cambridge University Press.

Schick, Irvin Cemil. 1990. Representing Middle Eastern Women: Feminism and Colonial Discourse. Feminist Studies 16(2): 345–80.

Tiffany, Sharon, and Kathleen Adams. 1985. The Wild Woman: An Inquiry into the Anthropology of an Idea. Cambridge, Mass.: Schenkman.

Torgovnick, Marianna. 1990. Gone Primitive: Savage Intellects, Modern Lives. Chicago: University of Chicago Press.

Traube, Elizabeth G. 1989. Secrets of Success in Postmodern Society. Cultural Anthropology 4: 273–300.

Trinh Minh-Ha. 1989. Woman, Native, Other: Writing Postcoloniality and Feminism. Bloomington: Indiana University Press.

Vance, Carol. 1990. The Pleasures of Looking: The Attorney General's Commission on Pornography versus Visual Images. In The Critical Image, ed. Carol Squires, pp. 38–58. Seattle: Bay Press.

Wallace, Michele. 1990. Invisibility Blues: From Pop to Theory. London: Verso.

Wolf, Naomi. 1991. The Beauty Myth: How Images of Beauty are Used Against Women. New York: Morrow.

Young, Iris Marion. 1990. Breasted Experience. In Throwing Like a Girl and Other Essays in Feminist Philosophy and Social Theory, ed. I. M. Young. Bloomington: Indiana University Press.

Part Five

MARKS AND SIGNS

The Social Skin

21 Womb as Oasis

The Symbolic Context of Pharaonic Circumcision in Rural Northern Sudan

Janice Boddy

Since 1976 I have conducted ethnographic research in a small Sudanese village (Hofriyat, a pseudonym) located on the Nile some 200 km downstream of the capital city, Khartoum. Before I went to the area I was aware that Hofriyati females underwent genital surgery in childhood, and I had read several descriptions of that operation (e.g., Barclay 1964; Widstrand 1964). Nothing, however, had adequately prepared me for what I was to witness, least of all the voluminous popular exposés proclaiming the custom meaningless. As time passed in the village and understanding deepened I came to regard this form of female circumcision in a very different light. In this chapter I discuss my growing appreciation of its significance, for it is only in understanding the practice, its meaningfulness to those who undergo it—indeed, the extent to which its meanings inform women's sense of self and are embedded in the commonplace details of everyday life—that those who are committed to its eradication (e.g. Assaad 1980; el-Saadawi 1980; Hosken 1979; Morgan and Steinem 1980; W.H.O. 1979; Toubia 1995; Dareer 1982) might approach the problem with the sensitivity it demands.

VILLAGERS AND THE VILLAGE

The people of Hofriyat are Muslim. They are organized into several overtly patrilineal descent groups, only a few of which are corporate in any real sense. Furthermore, villagers are relatively endogamous: people marry within the patrilineage when possible and practical, otherwise they marry close kin of varying degrees and prefer as spouses people who live nearby. Along with most of the population of Northern Sudan, Hofriyati speak a dialect of Arabic that contains numerous remnants of earlier vernaculars, principally Nubian and Bejawi (Gasim 1965).

The geographical area in which the village lies straddles two ecological zones; it is a region wherein true desert gradually begins to give way to semidesert acadia scrub, with an average annual rainfall in the vicinity of 5 cm. Rainfall, however, is unpredictable. Some years the area receives far less than 5 cm, other years (about one in five) it receives considerably more, as

Janice Boddy is Associate Professor of Anthropology at the University of Toronto. She is author of *Wombs and Alien Spirits: Women, Men and the Zar Cult in Northern Sudan* (Wisconsin, 1989). She has written articles on culture, spirit possession, feminism, Sudanese women, and colonial history; she is co-author (with Virginia Lee Barnes) of *Aman: the Story of a Somali Girl* (Pantheon, 1994; translated into fourteen languages).

much as 15 cm. Thus, the region is marginal with respect to cultivation undertaken at any distance from the river. More than rain, it is irrigation and the annual inundation of the Nile on which farming in the area depends. Arable land is a limited commodity, confined to a narrow strip bordering the Nile, and is insufficient to support the entire population of the village. Therefore, younger men regularly leave in order to seek work in the country's larger towns and cities, while their families, typically older men, children, and womenfolk, remain behind in the village.

IN THE FIELD: 12 JUNE 1976

It is the height of the desert summer, a season of intense heat and daily sandstorms. It is also the season of purification (ayām al-ṭahūr). Schools are closed, boys and girls are home for vacation; gradually their fathers are returning to the village, on vacation from the working year spent in Khartoum, Kassala, or Port Sudan. Now is the time, I am told, when circumcisions will be performed. Boys and girls have time to recover from their respective operations without losing time at their studies, and fathers have time to host the necessary festivities and religious ceremonies and to bask in the achievement of becoming the fathers of men.

For male children, the pomp and ceremony of circumcision is rivaled only by that of their weddings. It is a major social step toward full adulthood. For little girls, the unpleasant prospect of circumcision is not balanced by the achievement of womanly social status. A girl remains a girl until she is married. Her circumcision is celebrated by the briefest and most subdued of ceremonial feasts: morning tea. There are no religious festivities associated with the event, as there are for boys. The operation, however, renders her marriageable; undergoing it is a necessary condition of becoming a woman, of being enabled to use her one great gift, fertility.

It is the twelfth of June, a day that promises to be as hot and as demanding as any yet experienced. I am to witness the circumcisions of two little girls. Zaineb calls for me at sunup; it seems we are late. We run to a ḥōsh (courtyard) in the interior of the village. When we arrive, we find that Miriam, the local midwife, has already circumcised one sister and is getting ready to operate on the second. A crowd of women, many of them grandmothers (ḥabōbat), has gathered outside the room, not a man in sight. A dozen hands push me forward. "You've got to see this up close," says Zaineb, "it's important." I dare not confess my reluctance. The girl is lying on an angareeb (native bed), her body supported by several adult kinswomen. Two of these hold her legs apart. Then she is administered a local anesthetic by injection. In the silence of the next few moments Miriam takes a pair of what look to me like children's paper scissors and quickly cuts away the girl's clitoris and labia minora. She tells me this is the lahma djewa (the inside flesh). I am surprised that there is so little blood. Then she takes a surgical needle from her midwife's kit, threads it with suture, and sews together the labia majora, leaving a small opening at the vulva. After a liberal application of antiseptic, it is all over.

The young girl seems to be experiencing more shock than pain, and I wonder if the anesthetic has finally taken effect. The women briefly trill their joyous ululation (zaghārūda) and we adjourn to the courtyard for tea. While we wait, the sisters receive the ritual ornaments (jirtig) that will protect them from harm as they recuperate.

A NOTE ON TERMINOLOGY

The operation described above is a modified version of "Pharaonic circumcision," a term widely employed both in the literature and by Sudanese themselves (ṭahāra far'owniyya). As villagers explain it, the custom is quite ancient, dating from the time of the Pharaonic Egyptians, though this point is questioned by historians, archaeologists, and medical experts alike (Barclay 1964: 238; Huelsman 1976: 123). Another phrase used in reference to this procedure, "infibulation," is perhaps technically more accurate, since the vaginal orifice is partially occluded by skin that is clasped or fastened together. Throughout the present paper I use the terms "Pharaonic circumcision," "female circumcision," and "infibulation" synonymously, while acknowledging, of course that other forms of female circumcision exist.

THE OPERATION PRIOR TO 1969

Seeing an infibulation, even in this modernized, "sterile" form, was something I had been dreading. Yet my virtual lack of emotional reaction then, and a few days later when I was permitted to photograph another of these events, horrified me more than the circumcisions themselves. It was all so matter-of-fact. However, the relative indifference with which my village friends treated the phenomenon only temporarily diffused its effect. For one night after the last of the operations had taken place, when I was as alone as one can be in the field, I suddenly felt the impact of what had taken place. I became determined to find out why this severe form of circumcision is practiced; why, in the face of orthodox Islamic disapproval and the contravening legislation of at least two modern Sudanese regimes, it persists.[1]

Granted, there have been improvements in the midwife's techniques. The operation today is less radical, somewhat more sterile, and, owing to the use of *benidj* (anesthetic), less painful that it was for local women circumcised before 1969. I remember sitting transfixed in alarm as my informants graphically recounted their own experiences. Before Miriam received government training in midwifery, female circumcisions used to be performed by *dāyat al-ḥabil* ("midwives of the rope").[2] A circular palm mat with its center removed was so placed that it fit over a freshly dug hole in the ground.[3] The girl was made to sit on the mat at the edge of the hole. Her adult female relatives held her arms and legs while the midwife, using no anesthetic and having no apparent concern for sterile procedure, scraped away all of the external genitalia, including the labīa majora, using a straight razor. Then she pulled together the skin that remained on either side of the wound and fastened it with two thorns inserted at right angles. These last were held in place by thread or bits of cloth wound around their ends. (Fresh acacia thorns produce numbness when they pierce the skin and may have helped to relieve the pain.) A straw or a reed was also inserted, posteriorly, so that when the wound healed there would be a small opening in the scar tissue to allow for elimination of urine and menstrual blood. The girl's legs were then bound together and she was made to lie on an *angareeb* for a month or more to promote healing. According to my informants, whatever the length of her recovery, it had to be less than forty days in order to distinguish it from time spent in confinement after childbirth. When the wound was thought to have healed sufficiently, the thorns were removed and the girl unbound.

To date, historical and functional explanations of this practice have been highly speculative. Many, though not all, are based principally on the testimony of male informants and so risk being labeled one-sided or chauvinistic.[4] I do not attempt to redress such shortcomings in this essay, nor to present a sexually balanced view, for most of my informants are women. Nor is it my purpose to account for the custom's remote historic origins, for even if they could be located, it is questionable whether they would contribute substantially to our understanding of its present significance. Here I wish merely to provide an interpretation of the context of Pharaonic circumcision as it is now practiced in one village in Sudan.

With little exception, arguments offered thus far are intellectually unsatisfying when taken in and of themselves, yet together they form a complex rationale that may operate (consciously or unconsciously) to sustain and justify the practice. Various authors, for example, have suggested that Pharaonic circumcision was designed to ensure chastity and to protect young women from rape (Barclay 1964; Trimingham 1965). Others (Hansell and Soderberg reported in el-Safi 1970; Dr. R. T. Ravenholt reported in Morgan and Steinem 1980) consider it to be a primitive form of birth control. And it has been argued that infibulation is thought to make women more attractive sexually, that the vaginal orifice is made smaller in order to increase the male's sexual pleasure (Barclay 1964; Trimingham 1965). According to Barclay (1964: 239), it is a common belief among male Arab Sudanese that local women are "oversexed," a condition that circumcision is intended to control. Last, and least convincing, there are those who maintain that infibulation originated among desert nomads as a hygienic practice designed to prevent vaginal infection where sanitary conditions, owing to a scarcity of water, were less than ideal (Cederblad 1968).[5]

To take up the last point first, even if it could be proven that the custom had originated in the attempt to control vaginal disorders, the sanitation argument does not explain why the custom should persist under improved conditions. It does not explain why riverine sedentaries perform Pharaonic circumcisions when there is an abundance of water at their disposal and when it is customary, if not mandatory, to bathe at least once a day. Moreover, there is no evidence to suggest that the practice does not do the opposite of its proposed intent, for urinary tract infections and problems with both micturition and menstruation are common complaints among village women.

The notion that female circumcision of any kind, whether Sunna (*khafd*, or "reduction" of the clitoris), clitoral excision, or Pharaonic, increases male enjoyment in intercourse is widespread both in Sudan and in Egypt (Assaad 1980:13; Ammar 1954: 120). With regard to the case at hand, there are several points to be considered. First the tremendous success of regional brothels, staffed by purportedly uncircumcised Ethiopian women and Southern Sudanese, must at least weaken this view (but does not obviate it entirely), especially since these establishments are patronized by married men (having direct or occasional access to women) and unmarried men alike. The growing male acceptance of recent innovations in the circumcision technique also undermines the pleasure argument. In the village where I lived there is a relatively large group of women who were circumcised before 1969 and who have never been wed.[6] Most of these women are over the age of 20, an age considered late for marriage. Yet, many younger sisters and cousins of these women, circumcised after that date in the less radical manner, are presently married. Since it is customary for elder daughters and their female parallel cousins to be married before younger sisters and parallel cousins, men are now marrying[7]—and what is more, saying that they prefer to marry—women who have been less severely mutilated. My female informants suggested the reasons for their preference to be religion *(dīn)* and an expected improvement in sexual relations over the experiences of their longer-married kinsmen.

Indeed, men who consider themselves religious often advocate adopting the Sunna (orthodox) form of female circumcision wherein only the prepuce of the clitoris is excised. I was informed by friends in Khartoum that many Western-educated Sudanese are now having their daughters "pseudocircumcised." In the latter operation, the girl is first given a Sunna circumcision and then loosely infibulated. Apparently the infibulation is reversible and is performed only so that the girl might save face before her traditionally circumcised cohorts at boarding school.[8]

By far, the majority of those who insist that Pharaonic circumcisions continue to be performed are not men but adult women, and notable among these are the *ḥabōbat* (grandmothers).[9] Any account of the practice falls short of the mark if it fails to consider why this should be so. One of the arguments mentioned earlier does suggest that circumcision is relatively advantageous to women as a form of birth control. Indeed, while this may be a latent function of the custom, as Hayes (1975) suggests, there is no evidence from my own fieldwork to support the view that limiting the number of one's children is its actual purpose. Most women in the village who have been stably married for 10 or 15 years became pregnant at least six or seven times during that period. Of these, women who tend to miscarry or to bear stillborn infants have been pregnant most often (see Boddy 1989).

By contrast, I was frequently consulted on the subject of contraception. Women nurse their babies for as long as two years, yet there is a relatively short postpartum taboo on sexual activity (two to three months). It is believed that if a woman becomes pregnant too soon after the birth of her last child, the child she is nursing will sicken and die. These circumstances, coupled with the relative fecundity of village women, probably account for the fact that several of them approached me for information about birth control pills and injections, saying that they wished to space their children further apart.

VIRGINITY, FERTILITY, AND SEXUAL COMPLEMENTARITY

Of all the explanations for Pharaonic circumcision, those referring to the preservation of chastity and the curbing of sexual desire seem most persuasive, given that in Sudan, as elsewhere in the Muslim world, a family's dignity and honor are vested in the conduct of its womenfolk (Barclay 1964; Hayes 1975; Trimingham 1965; for Egypt, see Ammar 1954; Assaad 1980; el-Saadawi 1977). As significant as this point appears to be, however, it may represent a confusion of causes with effects.

What infibulation *does*, though this is not necessarily its original purpose—nor even, perhaps, what it is intended to do in Hofriyat today—is ensure that a girl is a virgin when she marries for the first time. It does control her sexuality and makes it less likely that she will engage in extra-marital affairs. A young girl both dreads and eagerly awaits her wedding day: she welcomes the elevation in status while fearing what it implies, namely, having to endure sexual relations with her husband. Hofriyati women told me that it may take as long as two years of continuous effort before penetration can occur. For a man it is a point of honor to have a child born within a year of his marriage, and often the midwife is summoned in secret, under cover of darkness, to assist the young couple by surgically enlarging the bride's genital orifice, a service for which she charges an exorbitant fee.[10]

Because they find it so painful, most of the women I talked to said that they avoid sex as often as possible, encouraging their husbands to sleep with them only when they wish to become pregnant. Sexual relations do not necessarily become easier for the couple over time. When a woman gives birth, the midwife must be present not only to cut through the scar tissue and release the child but also to reinfibulate her once the baby is born.

Reinfibulation guarantees that after each delivery a woman's body is restored, at least superficially, to its condition prior to marriage. During her 40-day confinement period, she is re-presented to her husband as a bride and given gifts of clothing and jewelry similar to those she received at her wedding, though these are diminished in scale. Moreover, a divorced or widowed woman may undergo reinfibulation in anticipation of remarriage, thus renewing, like the recently delivered mother, her "virginal" status. According to Hayes (1975: 622), the notion of virginity assumes special significance in Northern Sudan. As she succinctly remarks with regard to Pharaonic circumcision, "in Sudan, virgins are made, not born."

> The concept of virginity in Sudan is an anomaly to the Western world. Virginity, from our point of view, is a physical condition which is absolutely (and irrevocably) changed by a specific behavior. Virginity in Sudan can be thought of as a social category, in the sense that the physiological manifestation can be socially controlled (Hayes 1975: 622).

While I am in basic agreement with this statement, I feel it requires qualification. I submit that, for Sudanese women, the social category "virgin" has somewhat less to do with sexual abstinence than it has to do with fertility. Although infibulation acts to control female sexuality, this is not its avowed purpose.[11] My friends stated that it is performed on young girls in order to make them clean (*nazeef*), smooth (*na'īm*), and pure (*ṭāhir*) (this last intended result furnishes the colloquial term for circumcision in general: *ṭāhūr* [signifying cleansing or purifying]). Women say a girl who has not been purified through circumcision may not marry, and thus may not bear children and attain a position of respect in her old age. Circumcision prepares her body for womanhood, whereas marriage provides her with the opportunity to advance her position through giving birth, especially to sons.

Explanations for infibulation found in the literature apparently confuse the sexuality of women with their ability to bear children where these aspects of womanhood ought to be distinguished (the promiscuity argument). Conversely, perhaps they tend overly to dissociate the sexuality of males from their ability to impregnate women (the pleasure argument). Male fertility is closely associated with concepts of virility, as the following incident will illustrate. Once I overheard a man talking about his beautiful *bit 'amm* (FBD) whom he wished he had married. Although this woman and her present husband had been married for over a year, she had not yet conceived. Said the man, "By God, if I had married her, she would have had twins by now!"[12]

As I demonstrate in subsequent pages, infibulation neither increases, nor for that matter limits, male sexual pleasure (this is irrelevant here) so much as it ensures or socializes female fertility. By removing their external genitalia, women are not so much preventing their own sexual pleasure (though obviously this is an effect) as enhancing their femininity. Circumcision as a symbolic act brings sharply into focus the fertility potential of women by dramatically de-emphasizing their inherent sexuality. By insisting on circumcision for their daughters, women assert their social indispensibility, an importance that is not as the sexual partners of their husbands,[13] nor, in this highly segregated, male-authoritative society, as their servants, sexual or otherwise, but as the mothers of men. The ultimate social goal of a woman is to become, with her husband, the cofounder of a lineage section. As a respected *haboba* she is "listened to," she may be sent on the *hadj* (pilgrimage to Mecca) by her husband or her sons, and her name is remembered in village genealogies for several generations.

In this society women do not achieve social recognition by behaving or becoming like men, but by becoming less like men physically, sexually, and socially (see Assaad 1980: 6). Male as well as female circumcision rites stress this complementarity. Through their own operation, performed at roughly the same age as when girls are circumcised (between five and ten years), boys become less like women: while the female reproductive organs are covered, that of the male is uncovered, or, as one Sudanese author states, "unveiled" (el-Safi 1970: 65). Circumcision, then, accomplishes the social definition of a child's sex (see Ammar 1954: 121ff; Assaad 1980: 4ff; Kennedy 1970) by removing physical characteristics deemed appropriate to his or her opposite: the clitoris and other external genitalia, in the case of females; the prepuce of the penis, in the case of males. This last is emphasized by a custom now lapsed in Hofriyat wherein one of the newly circumcised boys' grandmothers would wear his foreskin as a ring on the day of his operation.[14]

After circumcision, young boys are no longer permitted to sleep with their mothers and sisters, but must accompany their older brothers in the men's quarters. Similarly, a young girl is increasingly restricted to association with womenfolk and is expected to assume greater domestic responsibility once she has been circumcised. Indeed, the most notable feature of village life is this polarization of the sexes, most marked between men and women of childbearing age. To the outsider it almost appears as though there are two virtually separate, coexisting societies that only occasionally overlap. Men and women generally do not eat together, they occupy separate quarters in the family compound, and they associate with those of their own sex in segregated areas at ceremonies and religious events. Further, while men have ultimate authority over women, this is often far less actual than supposed. In everyday affairs, women are more strictly governed by the *habōbat* than by their male kin, and when it comes to a matter of direct control by her husband, the Hofriyati woman is expert in the art of passive resistance.

The nature of male authority is itself instructive. A woman is legally regarded as being under the control and care of her father and, after his death, of her brothers for as long as they live. When she marries she also becomes accountable to her husband, but her immediate male kin retain moral responsibility for her welfare. Theoretically, a measure of both economic and moral responsibility passes to her adult sons should she become widowed or divorced. What these men share is the right to allocate, and in the case of her husband, to use, the woman's reproductive potential.

Through marriage, a man acquires access to his wife's fertility, and she, the means to activate it. Children are the capital on which male and female careers are built but at the same time kept separate, since marriages themselves are fragile and, for men, may be polygamous. It is only through marriage that men and women might inaugurate their respective, yet mutually dependent, social careers.

INTERPRETATION

Given the polarization and heightened complementarity of the sexes as outlined above, what is it specifically about Pharaonic circumcision that, as I claim, enhances a woman's socially defined femininity, her potential fertility? If, as I suggest, the minimization of a woman's sexual enjoyment and the covering of her reproductive organs is a symbolic act, what then is the nature of this symbolism, its meaning and its context?

The question is best approached by first returning to informants' statements regarding the purposes of this custom and taking these statements to be accurate. When questioned, both men and women responded, with an opacity that indicates transparent truth, that girls are circumcised because "it is our custom" (*'ādatna*) and "it is necessary" (*ḍurūri, lazim*). As mentioned earlier, however, my closer female friends volunteered somewhat more exegetically than the custom was intended to make women pure (*ṭāhir*), clean (*nazeef*), and smooth (*na'īm*). As I began to learn the various uses and associations of these qualities, gradually piecing together what I was observing and what I was being told, it became increasingly obvious that there was a certain fit between this practice and others. A wide range of activities, concepts, and what villagers call their customs (*'ādat)* appear to be guided by a group of interrelated idioms and metaphors, sometimes explicitly formulated, but more often not. These idioms are, as I perceive them, components of an informal logic of everyday life (Geertz 1973: 10ff). In Hofriyat, they are processes and qualities relative to things and events. They underlie both ritualized and nonritualized behavior, providing a number of overlapping contexts that inform social discourse.

To describe the symbolic context of female circumcision in Hofriyat, one must trace further applications of the qualities that define it: purity, cleanliness, and smoothness. An interpretation of these qualities leads to further associations, until one is faced with a complex network of relations in which certain basic idioms predominate. Such an interpretive analysis is much like weaving and tying an elaborate macrame, some threads must be left dangling in places, only to be caught up again at a later point and reworked into the whole. With this caution to the reader, I proceed.

PURITY, BIRDS, AND FERTILITY

The only situation other than male and female circumcision and female ritual purity in which I consistently heard people use the descriptive *ṭāhir* (pure) was in reference to certain types of birds. Among domestic birds, pigeons are considered *ṭāhir* while chickens are considered *waskhan* (dirty). The former are *ṭāhir*, Hofriyati say, because they splash around in water when it is set out for them, and they reside above the ground in large tins that people suspend from the rafters of their verandas. Their meat, referred to as *lahma nazeefa* (clean flesh), is a delicacy and pigeon broth is a local panacea.[15] Chickens, by contrast, are regarded as filthy creatures that scratch in the dust, eat their own excrement, and generally make a mess of people's courtyards. Their meat is almost never eaten, as it, too, is considered dirty. Yet chickens are kept by villagers because they produce eggs, which are considered "clean food" (*akil nazeef*), food that "brings blood" (*byjeeb dum*).

Young unmarried girls who dance at wedding parties are often referred to as *hamāmāt masheen fi sūq* (pigeons going to market).[16] The girls consider themselves on display for prospective husbands, as it is usually at such affairs that arrangements for subsequent marriages are initiated. The dance performed by women at these parties is a slow and rhythmic forward step with arms extended. It is referred to as *ragees bi rugaba* (a dance from the neck), as it consists primarily of moving the head forward and backward in the controlled manner, as my informants describe it, of a little bird or pigeon walking along the ground.

Wild water birds, like those found along the Nile, are considered clean though, for the majority of villagers, inedible. Until very recently, people had the cheeks of their younger daughters marked with a small scar in the shape of a rounded "T." This is referred to by village women as *derab al-ṭayr* (bird tracks, like those left by water birds walking along the beach). It is considered a mark of beauty, a feature that greatly adds to a woman's desirability.

One can thus outline a rather strong metaphoric connection between young circumcised girls (and, for that matter, older women) and birds associated with water. Both are *naẓeef*; both domesticated water-linked birds and girls are *ṭāhir*. Girls are sometimes referred to as birds and in some circumstances they are said to act like birds. Inversely, birds of this particular category behave like humans since they "bathe."

While I was in the village, I rented a *ḥōsh* from one of the local women. Gathering dust in the ceiling corners of the main room were four ostrich eggshells, each of which was decorated differently from the rest. As I began visiting other households in the area, it became apparent that my room was typical in this respect. Questions as to the significance of these objects met with suppressed laughter form my female companions. They explained that these are *manāẓir*, visions or views, things to look at. The idiom of "seeing" is strongly developed in Hofriyat. Someone is thought to absorb qualities of what is seen, correspondingly one might effect changes in something or someone by emitting visual influences (this is the *'āyn ḥārra* [evil or "hot" eye]). Now, although the actual designs of these objects may be significant in themselves, they are highly variable and, according to my informants, subject only to the creative impulse of the painter; they may be painted by men or women. When prodded further as to their significance, my friends said that ostrich eggshells and similarly shaped gourds (now more commonly used) are so placed because the woman who sleeps in that room wishes to become pregnant. These objects are, however, permanent fixtures in the majority of homes; they are not put up and taken down at woman's whim. They are not, in others words, signals in some sexual semaphore designed to dampen or to rally a husband's consummate attention. Rather, they are fertility objects. One informant said, "We look at them because we want sons" (*āwlad*, which also means "children" in a general sense).

As fertility symbols or images these objects figure in a number of contexts. First, a man's testes are euphemistically referred to as his "eggs," of which the massive ostrich egg is considered an exaggerated specimen. Furthermore, though villagers themselves make no such explicit connection, it is noteworthy that the object is something associated with birds. Of course, only the shell of an ostrich egg is used for decoration; the egg itself is removed by making a small puncture in the shell and draining off the contents. Ostrich eggshells and their latter-day counterparts, gourds of similar size and form, are prized for their shape, their smooth rounded surfaces, and their creamy white color.

The quality "whiteness" usually is associated with concepts of cleanliness and purity. White foods are generally classed as "clean" and are thought to "bring blood," to increase the amount of blood in the body.[17] In Hofriyat these are eggs, goat's milk, goat's milk cheese, cow's milk, fish, rice, sugar, and white flour. Of these, only goat's milk and sugar may be considered staples; all are, to some extent, scarce or limited and expensive. There is another group of foods considered to be clean. These are also expensive and are usually purchased only on special occasions or for guests. Some of the most common are tinned fish, tinned jam, oranges, bananas, guavas, and grapefruit. These foods are generally associated with Europeans, Egyptians, and Lebanese, that is, with people having light—or as villagers say, "white"—skin. They are thought of as being especially clean because they are all, so to speak, "contained" or enclosed and protected from dirt and dryness.

Hofriyati are very conscious of skin color. White skin is clean, beautiful, and a mark of potential holiness. I, being Caucasian, was repeatedly told that my chances of getting into heaven, should I choose to become Muslim, were far greater than those of the average Sudani. This is because the Prophet Mohammed was white and all white-skinned peoples are in the favored position of belonging to his tribe (*gabeela*). Ranked in order of desirability, the skin color of villagers ranges from "light," or *asfar* (yellow), to *ahmar* (red, somewhat darker than *asfar*), to *akhḍar* (green, darker still), to *azrag* (blue) or "dark." The term *aswad* (black) is usually reserved to Southern Sudanese and "Africans," people who in earlier times were enslaved.

One context in which the concepts of whiteness as desirable skin coloring, cleanliness, purity, and smoothness figure prominently is that of women's cosmetics. Immediately before her wedding, a young girl goes through an elaborate regimen of physical preparation for the first time in her life. To begin with, all of her body hair must be removed, excepting that on her head. This is done using a combination of sugar, lime juice, and water, boiled until a thick, sticky concentrate remains. When it cools, the toffeelike substance is spread over the skin and, like depilatory wax, quickly pulled away, taking the hair with it. I am told that women cannot use razors for this purpose as do men, who shave their pubic hair. Women must experience "heat" and "pain" (*ḥārr*) when they depilate, whereas men use a "cold" (*bārid*) method of hair removal. It should be noted that infibulation, too, is referred to as *ḥarr*, that heat and pain generally are associated with acts of feminine purification.

After her skin has been cleared of hair, the prospective bride takes a smoke bath (*dukhāna*). If such does not already exist, a small hole is dug in the kitchen floor or other appropriate spot indoors. It is then filled with fragrant woods and lighted. The girl removes her clothing, wraps herself in a special blanket (*shamla*) made of goat or camel hair, and sits over the hole, taking care to envelop the rising smoke. She may sit this way for as long as two hours or more, adding wood from time to time and gossiping with her friends. The bath is considered a success if, when she emerges, the top layer of her skin can be sloughed off, exposing a lighter and smoother surface beneath. To remove this dead layers she massages herself with a concoction of smoked dough made from millet flour and powdered aromatic woods, known as *dilka*. When all traces of *dilka* have been rubbed away, she oils herself and applies perfume. Then her hands and feet are stained with henna, the purpose of which is both to cool and to ornament the extremities.

These preparations, which may take several days to complete, are intended to make her skin soft, smooth, clean, fragrant, and desirably lighter in color. (In fact, some women go to the extent of powdering themselves with packaged vanilla custard in order to improve the cast of their skin.) After such treatment, performed for the first time when she becomes a bride, and henceforth whenever she wants to attract the sexual attentions of her husband, a woman's body shares several qualities with the ostrich egg fertility object: both are smooth, both are clean and "white," and both are pure. What is more, the shape of the ostrich egg, with its tiny orifice, corresponds to the idealized shape of the circumcised woman's womb. So, too, the cleanliness, whiteness, and enclosedness of valued edibles evoke images of the bride and of fecundity.

A distinctive feature of objects herein described as "enclosing" is their ability to retain moisture. Similarly, a bride's cosmetic routine is supposed to prevent her from perspiring. Human sweating and the smell of sweat are considered gauche at all times, but at a wedding they are especially despicable. What is more, the association between moisture retention and "pure" and "purified" women is photo-negatively expressed by the term for prostitute, *sharmūṭa* (literally, "that which is shredded or in tatters"). But in local parlance *sharmūṭ* (masculine form) is meat that has been cut into strips and hung to dry. There is thus an implicit association between prostitutes and dried meat or flesh.

All of the above relations, which should become more firmly established as we progress, combine to signify that on the day of her wedding a young girl finally reaches a peak of potential and appropriate fertility, defined in terms of the qualities "whiteness," "smoothness," "cleanliness," "purity," "enclosedness," and "imperviousness."

THE ALTERNATIVE FERTILITY OBJECT:
DIVISION OF LABOR, FLUIDS, REPRODUCTION, AND ENCLOSEDNESS

We now turn to the web of symbolic relations that spin out from the alternative fertility object, the egg-shaped gourd (*gar'a*). Such gourds may be used in place of ostrich eggs only after they have been preserved by drying in the sun. One knows that a *gar'a* is ready to be decorated and hung in a room if, when it is shaken, its seeds can be heard to rattle inside. The vocabulary of cultivation and of farming in general provides a figurative lexicon for most things having to do with human reproduction and, to a certain extent, with village social structure. The progeny of a man or a woman is referred to as his or her *djena* (fruit) or *zuriy'a* (crop, that which is sown). A man's immediate descendants, the lineage section of which he is head, is also his *zuriy'a*.

As such, the fact that the appropriately shaped gourd contains seeds in an enclosed space is exceedingly significant. To begin with, native theories of conception have it that the fetus is formed from the union of a man's semen, spoken of as his seed, with his wife's blood. Sexual intercourse causes the woman's blood to thicken or coagulate, and she ceases menstruation until after the baby's birth. While pregnant, a woman nourishes her husband's future "crop" within her.

These ideas also relate to those concerning parents' respective contributions to the body of their child. Women told me that although young people learn differently in school these days, a child receives its bones from its father and its flesh and blood from its mother. While an adequate description of village social structure is beyond the scope of this chapter, certain of its characteristics are relevant to the symbolic interpretation given here. Just as the skeleton structures the body, so do endogamous patrilineal descent groups structure the village. But endogamy, though preferred, is not always possible in practice. What is more, adherence to endogamy is not a great concern of people entering into second or subsequent marriages. The upshot of all this is that sisters frequently marry into lineages unrelated or only distantly related to each other. And, no matter what their respective descent affiliations, the children of such women are considered close relatives. Women thus serve to link together the various named descent groups in the village. People who belong to different patrilineages, yet acknowledge relationship, say that *"bayn nehna lahma wa dum"* ("between us there is flesh and blood"). If it is through men that the social order receives its structure, its rigidity (its bones), then it is through women that it receives its fluidity and its integration (its blood and its flesh).

There are several other contexts in which fluids and moisture figure prominently as markers of femininity. The most important of these, for our present purpose, has to do with division of labor by sex. While cultivation is thought primarily to be men's work, fetching water from the wells for household consumption is traditionally considered women's work. Thus it is through their individual labors, farming and getting water, that men and women provide the household with materials for its staple food, *kisra*. Kisra is made by first mixing *dura* flour with an almost equal amount of water. Then the batter is spread thinly over a seasoned griddle and the waferlike product is removed when dry.

Now *kisra* batter is mixed by hand in a special type of container called a *gūlla*. This is a squat, rounded pottery jar, about the size of an average pumpkin, having an opening at the top slightly larger than a woman's fist. It differs from water jars (singular: *zīr*) in that the latter are far larger, capable of holding forty liters of water or more. Zirs are longer than they are round and made of a porous clay that permits sweating, hence cooling of the water they contain. Gūllas, on the other hand, must be nonporous, they must not allow anything inside of them to seep out. This feature likens them to other objects herein described as moisture retentive: foods that are contained and the cosmetically prepared body of the infibulated bride, all of which evoke the further positive qualities of cleanliness, purity, femininity, and fecundity.

Significantly, besides serving as a container in which flour and water are mixed for *kisra*, the *gūlla* has another function, relative to childbirth. If a woman miscarries when she is only a few months pregnant, the expelled matter is treated like menstrual blood and put down the latrine.

However, should she require the services of a midwife to open her up, a different method of disposal is called for. The fetus is first wrapped in a cloth, as for a corpse; then it is placed in a *gūlla* and buried somewhere within the confines of the *ḥōsh* (the house enclosure). The symbolism of this act is made more explicit when one considers what is done in the case of a stillbirth. If a baby is born but fails to breathe, its body is wrapped in a cloth and buried without ceremony just against the outer wall of the *ḥōsh*. But, should an infant expire having taken even one breath, then normal funeral procedure must be followed and the child buried in the graveyard on the outskirts of the village.

Both the *gūlla* and the *ḥōsh* appear in this context as symbols for the womb. In the case of the *gūlla*, it is an object of daily life in which the fruits of men's and women's labors are mixed. The mixture when baked produces *kisra*, the staple food, that which sustains life. It is important to note that only women mix and bake *kisra*.

Similarly, in the womb are mixed a man's seed and a woman's blood: substance and fluid, like grain and water. This mixture when formed reproduces life, and hence also sustains it. Again, only women, through their fertility, perform this reproductive task. There is, symbolically, no more fitting receptacle for an aborted "mixture" of male and female contributions than the *gūlla*, the impervious container of unbaked "life."

There is a certain level of exegesis involved in this interpretation. One of my informants thinks that the *gūlla* might be used for this purpose because in this shape it resembles the *bayt al-wilāda* (the womb; literally, the house of childbirth) and in its size it corresponds to the belly of a pregnant woman. The "house" metaphor is significant and we will return to it in the conclusion to this chapter.

Earlier I stated that the *ḥōsh*, the walled enclosure of a household area, also symbolizes the womb. More accurately, it symbolizes an initial stage in the process of becoming human. The miscarried fetus has not, strictly speaking, been born; it does not emerge with a wholly developed human body. Its progress is halted in the womb and so it must be disposed of within the *ḥōsh*. The stillborn child emerges fully developed, but does not breathe; its progress is halted or fixed at the point of birth. As it has emerged from the womb, so it is buried against the outer wall of the compound. The child who breathes but then dies is indeed fully human, for breath is the essence of life. A child who has breathed is placed with other humans who have lived, who have passed from the *ḥōsh* and the village to the grave. Significantly, women, who are associated with birth and with the *ḥōsh* in this and several other contexts, are not permitted to be present at the burial.[18] Such is the responsibility of men. Women may visit the graveyard, but only after the funeral has ended. The symbolism of village spatial organization in customs having to do with unsuccessful pregnancy thus not only expresses the physical relationship between mother (womb) and child but also describes the unsuccessful emergence of an individual into society. The child who dies at birth skips over the social phase of being, going directly from the *ḥōsh* to the grave.

FURTHER ASSOCIATIONS OF THE ḤŌSH: ENCLOSURE AND CLEANLINESS, PURITY AND SOCIALITY

Generally speaking, all enclosed areas in the village are considered clean and protected places. *Ḥōsh* yards are swept daily, as are the floors of its rooms and verandas within. Clean spaces, spaces that are inside, are social areas. They are areas of relative safety, where one is least likely to become possessed by malevolent spirits (*djinn aswad* [black *djinn*]), hence to be driven mad. *Djinn* frequent open spaces such as the desert, ruins, and rubbish heaps. The insides of *ḥayshan* (pl.) are considered relatively safer than village paths, which in turn are relatively safer than the surrounding countryside.

Yet social spaces are not always bounded by high walls. While these are desirable, some homes in the village do not have walled-in courtyards surrounding them. Instead, the open area immediately adjacent to such a structure is marked off by a ring of stones or by a thorn fence (*zarība*).

However humble its boundaries, though, such an enclosure is regularly swept smooth to maintain the distinction between it and unmarked space.

The village, too, is bounded—to the west by farmlands and the river, to the north and south by other villages, and to the east by the desert, *al-khālla* (the emptiness). The graveyard is located on the westernmost fringe of the desert, between the village and "emptiness." Thus, as one moves eastward from the river to the desert, there is a shift from conditions of relative fecundity and abundance to those of relative sterility, with humans poised between the two.

This in-between place, social space, is organized concentrically. At the hub is the *ḥōsh*, the extended family and the place where life begins. Surrounding the *ḥōsh* in the village are neighbors and kinsmen, considered one and the same by local people: they are called *nās gareeb* (those who are close or near) or *gareebna* (our relatives). In nearby villages are distant relations and affinal kin. Beyond this, one soon arrives at the periphery of the known social world.

It is appropriate to mention here that social space is also relatively bounded in an ideological sense. People marry *gareeb* (near). They ought to marry within patrilineage, preferably a FBS or FBD, but given demographic limitations they try to marry as "close" as possible (that is, other kin in a declining order of preference). Thus, it is not surprising that the best or most prestigious marriage is also the closest: between bilateral parallel cousins whose parents are parallel cousins. While it is stated by informants and in the literature that patrilateral cousins are preferred spouses, my evidence indicates that matrilateral parallel cousins and cross-cousins are also considered exceedingly close. If for some reason one must marry a more distant relative, he or she ought yet to observe the preference for territorial endogamy: neighbors are "close" by definition. Moreover, all villagers acknowledge a plethora of consanguineal and affinal ties to all other villagers. Social space as expressed through kinship and marriage thus replicates the social organization of physical space: both are based on the principle of relative enclosure within a circumscribed space.

ENCLOSURE OF PHYSICAL SPACE: THE HUMAN BODY

The above considerations lead us back to some earlier relinquished threads in the argument. Significant with respect to the concept of relative enclosure are several associations in another domain, that of the human body. With respect to established notions of aesthetic propriety, a human face, male or female, is considered beautiful if it is characterized by a small mouth and by narrow nostrils. What is more, body orifices are places where potentially dangerous *djinn* might abide. Burial customs dictate that all such orifices, including spaces between fingers and toes, be washed, perfumed, and stuffed with cotton before the corpse is wrapped and taken to the cemetery. This is to ensure the expulsion of any lingering *djinn* and to prevent the soul of the deceased from reinhabiting its mortal remains. Thus, while orifices of the human body are necessary for sustaining life, they are dangerous, not aesthetically pleasing if large, and not to be left open after death.

The idiom of closure is further dramatized by certain features of folk medicine as practiced in the village. Remedies are often based on the assumption that pain and swelling are caused by things coming apart or opening. One common cure for a headache, or "open head" (*rās maftūḥ*), is first to wrap a band of cloth around the head, then to tighten this band by twisting it with a key or a piece of wood. Alternatively, the head may be closed by the application of hot irons to four equidistant points on the skull, starting from mid-forehead. Pulled tendons and ligaments are also treated by "fire" (*nār*): hot irons are placed at either end of the affected area so that what has come apart may be fused together again by heat. The associations of heat, of fusing together, of closing, and of the aesthetic preference for small body orifices once again call to mind the practice of infibulation.

Through the course of this analysis, the idiom of relative enclosure has emerged predominant. The *ḥōsh*, the womb, and many more objects and actions of daily life; beliefs about the human body, reproduction, imperviousness, and the fertility potential of brides; the organization of space and social relations; all that I have outlined above appear over and over again in contexts that play upon this theme. These contexts culminate in further symbolic associations of the *ḥōsh*, the infibulated (enclosed) womb, and sexual differentiation.

As noted earlier, the sexes are spatially as well as socially segregated. They occupy opposite sides of the dancing ground at ceremonies and are housed and fed in different households during communal feasts. The *ḥōsh*, too, is spatially divided into men's and women's quarters, having separate entrances for each. The "front" door (no specified orientation) is known as the men's entrance and is used by official guests and strangers. The men's room (*diwān*) is generally located in the front part of the courtyard near this door. The back door is known as the women's entrance and is for the use of women, close male kin, and neighbors. Women's quarters are situated at the rear of the compound, as is the kitchen. If the *ḥōsh* is considered a politico-economic unit, internal or domestic affairs are the province of women, while external affairs, such as marketing, are handled by men. Although women are not, strictly speaking, secluded, there is a general feeling that they ought to remain within the the *ḥōsh* unless officially visiting kin.[19] Thus, there exists a fairly strong association of women with internal affairs, enclosedness, and the rear or interior of the *ḥōsh*, and of men with external affairs, nonenclosedness, and the front of the *ḥōsh*. These complementary relations provide further images with which Hofriyati think about social reproduction, a subject to which we now return.

The men's entrance to the *ḥōsh* is known as *al-khashm al-bayt* (the mouth/opening/orifice of the house). This term also refers to a group of kin. Properly speaking, a *khashm al-bayt* consists of several related lineages: it is subtribe. But in Hofriyat, as elsewhere in the Sudan (Barclay 1964: 91), this term is used only to refer to people who live in or originate from a common *ḥōsh* (compound) or *bayt* (house), hence, to a lineage section.

Extension of anatomical terms to nonanatomical subjects, such as I have described above, is common in Sudanese colloquial Arabic. For example, the supports of an *angareeb* are its "legs" (singular: *kur'a*). Doors and orifices through which things and people pass are "mouths" or "nostrils" (singular: *khashm*), and the insides of houses and other enclosed areas are "bellies" or "stomachs" (singular: *batin*).

From a converse perspective, however, nonanatomical terms are often applied to parts of the anatomy. Most important for our discussion, the word "house" is explicitly associated with the womb, for the womb is referred to as the "house of childbirth" (*bayt al-wilāda*) and the vaginal opening is its *khashm* (its door or mouth). Thus an implicit association exists between the *khashmal-bayt*, meaning the men's door of the courtyard—and, metaphorically, one man's immediate descendants—and the *khashm* of the *bayt el-wilāda*, a woman's genital orifice.[20] The men's door literally opens into an enclosed area occupied by a man's sons and daughters, his *zuriy'a*. The *khasm al-bayt al-wilada*, the door of the womb, also opens into an enclosed area that is more completely enclosed and purified by a woman's circumcision and infibulation. Just as the *ḥōsh* protects a man's descendants, so the enclosed womb protects a woman's fertility—her potential and, ultimately, that of her husband. Like the *ḥōsh* poised between the river and the desert, the womb of an infibulated woman is an oasis, the locus of appropriate human fertility.

Pharaonic circumcision, a practice which because of its apparent brutality is viewed with horror in the West, is for the women of Hofriyat an assertive symbolic act. Through it they emphasize what they hold to be the essence of femininity, morally appropriate fertility, the potential to reproduce the lineage or to found a lineage section. In that infibulation purifies, smooths, and makes clean the outer surface of the womb, the enclosure or *ḥōsh* of the house of childbirth, it socializes or, better, culturalizes a woman's fertility. Through occlusion of the vaginal orifice, her womb, both literally and figuratively, becomes a social space: enclosed, impervious, virtually impenetrable. Her social virginity, defined by qualities of enclosedness, purity, and all the rest, must periodically be reestablished at those points in her life (after childbirth and before remarriage) when her fertility once again is rendered potent.

The practice of Pharaonic circumcision, though discouraged by orthodox Islam and also by the state, is thus deeply embedded in Hofriyati culture. It is a salient expression of interiority, enclosure, an idiom that informs much of village daily life. Yet to understand infibulation in Hofriyat it is not enough to discover its logic; we must also consider how its meanings are actualized and recreated by individuals. We need, I suggest, to contemplate the implications of pharaonic circumcision for a female child's developing self-perception. Through the operation and other procedures involving heat or pain—that purify female bodies, cleanse them and make them smooth—appropriate dispositions are being inculcated in young girls, dispositions which, following Bourdieu, are inscribed in their bodies not only physically but also cognitively, and emotionally, in the form of inclinations, "schemes of perception and thought" (1977: 15). On its *own,* however, the trauma of circumcision is insufficient to shape the feminine self, to propel it in prescribed directions. Such experiences must also be meaningful to those who undergo and reproduce them. In Hofriyat, as we have seen, meaning is carefully built up through metaphors and associations immanent in the practical acts and objects of everyday life. The simple routines of fetching water or baking bread, which girls begin to perform following their circumcisions— or even, perhaps, of peeling an orange or opening a tin of fish—all reverberate with tacit messages. They are practical metaphors, the means by which a woman's subjective reality is not merely expressed but realized and maintained. A girl's circumcision orients her toward a self-image constrained by her culture's values. And as she matures she is invited to relive that experience at various points in her life: vicariously, through participating in others' operations; actually after each delivery; and metaphorically, with any procedure involving heat or pain or fluids or the qualities detailed above. The very walls of her house, its lay-out, its rooms and doors, speak to her of her self. Both in ritual and in many small moments throughout her working day informative values are implicitly restated and her dispositions reinforced. It is the coherence and interwovenness of concepts constructing womanhood in Hofriyat that render them so powerful, so compelling, so politically effective.

Those who work to eradicate female circumcision must, I assert, cultivate an awareness of the custom's local significances and of how much they are asking people to relinquish as well as gain. The stakes are high and it is hardly surprising that efforts to date have met with little success. It is, however, ironic that a practice that—at least in Hofriyat—emphasizes female fertility at a cultural level can be so destructive of it physiologically and so damaging to women's health overall. That paradox has analogies elsewhere, in a world considered "civilized," seemingly far removed from the "barbarous East." Here too, in the west from where I speak, feminine selfhood is often attained at the expense of female well-being. In parallels like these, perhaps there lies the germ of an enlightened approach to the problem.

NOTES

An early version of this paper was presented to the Anthropology Colloquium, University of Toronto, and subsequently at McMaster University, the University of Waterloo, and the University of Western Ontario. I wish to thank the members of these audiences for their comments and encouragement. I am especially grateful to Nadia Abu Zahara, Ken Burridge, Michael Lambek, and Judith Shapiro for their many helpful suggestions and criticisms of that draft. Responsibility for the final version is, of course, my own. Funding for research in Sudan was provided by a Social Sciences and Humanities Research Council of Canada Doctoral Fellowship. Professor P. L. Shinnie of the University of Calgary greatly facilitated my fieldwork in its initial stages. I am most indebted, however, to the women of Hofriyat, whose friendship, patience, grace, and wit made research among them a pleasure.

1. The Anglo-Egyptian Condominium government outlawed it in 1946, as did the May (1969) Revolution government headed by President Nimieri.
2. This refers to a method of child delivery no longer practiced in Hofriyat, where a woman about to give birth would support herself by grasping onto ropes suspended from the main ceiling beam of a room.

3. This apparatus is also basic to smoke-bathing (later discussed) and to rope-delivery (see note 2).

4. Hayes (1975) is the notable exception here. In Egypt, el-Saadawi (1977) and Assaad (1980) have investigated female genital operations using female informants.

5. All of these explanations are common currency in the Western community in Khartoum and among educated Sudanese, who are frequently hard pressed to account for the practice.

6. This group consists of 31 of 121 resident adult females between the ages of 16 and 55 in 1977, or 25.6 percent, taking age 12 as the last possible year for the operation to be performed. This is considered rather late, the average age at circumcision being somewhere between 5 and 10.

7. The objection that this merely reflects a breakdown in traditional marriage patterns consequent upon increasing modernization does not hold. Patrilateral parallel-cousin marriages and marriages between other classes of close kin occur as frequently today as they did before 1969.

8. Often, however, girls whose fathers wish to preserve them from the more severe operation are "kidnapped" by their grandmothers and Pharaonically circumcised nonetheless. For recent modifications of the operation, see Gruenbaum 1991.

9. It has been suggested to me that the habōbat are so adamantly in favor of Pharaonic circumcision because they need to justify having experienced the mutilation themselves. While I have no doubt that this is one reason for the persistence of the custom, I think it insufficient as a complete explanation of it. The cultural context, described within, is supportive of the operation. Infibulation is considered a positive change in a woman's body; it is not something negative, as the term "mutilation" implies.

10. Lest it be thought that the habōbat as a group have a vested economic interest in seeing the custom maintained, it should be mentioned that midwives are few and in the past inherited the profession from their mothers or maternal aunts.

11. It is certainly possible (even probable) that men do not share this view of female circumcision and its intended purpose. As Barclay (1964) and Trimingham (1965) suggest, their conception might well lean more toward the maintenance of chastity and sexual honor than toward infibulation as a means of enhancing fertility, which I argue is the feminine view. The two, chastity and "quality" fertility, are quite simply different sides of the same coin, for the only offspring considered socially and morally viable are those born of lawful marriages, most appropriately contracted between close kin. See Boddy (1989) for further discussion of these points.

12. Ammar (1954), however, does show that circumcision has to do with fertility. He states: "The belief is that on his or her circumcision or wedding, a person could be deprived of fertility and potency, and hence great care must be taken to avoid the evil eye, and to avoid those who are sterile and desire fertility" (1954: 122).

13. Women rarely object, and often prefer, that their husbands frequent brothels, so long as they do not spend too much money in such establishments.

14. Apropos of this complementarity, Ammar (1954: 121) notes that in Silwa, Upper Egypt (where clitoral excision is practiced): "In the colloquial language of the village, circumcision of the boy is sometimes referred to as 'cutting his pigeon' while in the case of a girl it is described as 'cutting her cockscomb'." The association of "pigeon" with the "feminine" foreskin is striking in its similarity to metaphors expressive of femininity in Hofriyat, discussed below. Further, in Silwa, circumcision and fertility are ritually associated with bread, Nile water, and eggs (Ammar 1954: 117ff), all of which are prominent symbols having like significances in Hofriyat.

15. So pure are pigeons (hamāmāt) considered to be that the persons of limited means might substitute a pair of these birds for the obligatory sacrificial ram at the 'Id al-Adha (the Islamic Great Fest) or, for that matter, whenever animal sacrifice is called for.

16. All phrases are reported as given. No effort has been made to "correct" grammar, to make it consistent with rules of classical or modern literary Arabic. The reader ought to be aware, however, that most intensive contact was with women in Hofriyat. I was frequently struck by differences between their speech and that of adult men.

17. Much of what follows appears to be based upon an ancient humoral approach to disease. Body fluids figure prominently in the assessment of relative health; likewise, heat and cold are significant qualities of various symptoms, treatments, and preventatives.

18. Males, on the other hand, are not permitted to witness childbirth.

19. Even so, a woman, when outside her *ḥōsh*, is still "enclosed" for then she must wear her *tōb*, a garment consisting of at least 9 m of cloth wound around the body and covering the head.

20. I must add that I do not recall hearing people refer to the woman's entrance to the *ḥōsh* as a *khashm*. It was always simply referred to as *al-warā'* (the back) or as *al-bāb al-warā'* (the back door).

REFERENCES

Ammar, Hamed. 1954. Growing Up in an Egyptian Village. London: Routledge and Kegan Paul.

Assaad, Marie Bassili. 1980. Female Circumcision in Egypt: Social Implications, Current Research, and Prospects for Change. Studies in Family Planning 11(1): 3–16.

Barclay, Harold. 1964. Buuri al Lamaab: A Suburban Village in the Sudan. Ithaca: Cornell University Press.

Boddy, Janice. 1989. Wombs and Alien Spirits: Women, Men and the Zar Cult in Nothern Sudan. Madison, WI: University of Wisconsin Press.

Bourdieu, Pierre. 1977. Outline of a Theory of Practice. Cambridge: Cambridge University Press.

Cederblad, M. 1968. A Child Psychiatric Study of Sudanese Arab Children. Copenhagen: Munksgaard.

Dareer, Asma El. 1982. Woman Why Do You Weep? Circumcision and Its Consequences. London: Zed.

Gasim, Awn al-Sharif. 1965. Some Aspects of Sudanese Colloquial Arabic. Sudan Notes and Records 46: 40–49.

Geertz, Clifford. 1973. The Interpretation of Cultures. New York: Basic Books.

Gruenbaum, Ellen. 1991. The Islamic Movement, Development, and Health Education: Recent Changes in the Health of Rural Women in Central Sudan. Social Science and Medicine 33(6): 637–45.

Hayes, Rose Oldfield. 1975. Female Genital Mutilation, Fertility Control, Women's Roles, and the Patrilineage in Modern Sudan: A Functional Analysis. American Ethnologist 2: 617–633.

Hosken, Franzeska P. 1979. The Hosken Report: Genital/Sexual Mutilation of Females. Lexington, MA: WIN News.

Huelsman, Ben R. 1976. An Anthropological View of Clitoral and Other Female Genital Mutilations. In The Clitoris. T. P. Lowery and T. S. Lowery, eds. pp. 111–61. St. Louis: Warren H. Green.

Kennedy, John G. 1970. Circumcision and Excision in Egyptian Nubia. Man 5: 175–191.

Morgan, Robin, and Gloria Steinem. 1980. Genital Mutilation: 30 Million Women are Victims. Ms. March: 65–67, 98, 100.

Saadawi, Nowal el-. 1977. Woman and Psychological Conflict. Cairo: el-Mu'assasa el- 'Arabiya lil- dirassat wa'l-nashr.

_____. 1980. The Question No One Would Answer. Ms. March: 68–69.

Safi, Ahmed el-. 1970. Native Medicine in the Sudan: Sources, Conception, and Methods. Khartoum: Khartoum University Press.

Toubia, Nahid. 1995. Female Genital Mutilation: A Call for Global Action. New York: Rainbow/Women Ink, (second edition).

Trimingham, J. Spencer. 1965. Islam in the Sudan. London: Oxford University Press.

Widstrand, Carl Gosta. 1964. Female Infibulation. Varia I, Occasional Papers of Studia Ethnographica Upsaliensia 20:95–124.

W.H.O. (World Health Organization). 1979. Pratiques Traditionelles Affectant la Santé des Femmes et des Enfants. Rapport d'un Séminaire Tenu à Khartoum du 10 au 15 Février 1979. Alexandria: Eastern Mediterranean Office.

22 Victorian Clitoridectomy

Isaac Baker Brown
and His Harmless Operative Procedure

Elizabeth A. Sheehan

Recent publicity concerning the World Health Organization's investigation of the practice of clitoridectomy and infibulation in Muslim countries has appropriately focused attention on the implications of these procedures for women's health and socioeconomic status. At the same time, greater international awareness of female genital mutilation has allowed westerners, including some social scientists, to view such practices as being rooted in ideologies totally foreign to the West. Criticism too deeply imbued with a sense of ethical and scientific superiority deflects attention from the cultural contexts in which female genital mutilation takes place while also denying western medicine's use of similar procedures. In an effort to overcome this tendency and to examine the persistent connection between belief system and medical practice, this article discusses the use of clitoridectomy in Victorian England and its consequences for a gynecological surgeon named Isaac Baker Brown.

THE VICTORIAN CONTEXT

For many educated Victorians, the nineteenth century heralded a new age governed by science and reason. It appeared to middle-class men such as Isaac Baker Brown that at no other time in modern history was the distinction between savagery and civilization so evident to the intelligent mind. The actions of British gentlemen were viewed as being determined by logic and Christian morality, while those of Africa and India were seen as being determined by dangerous ignorance and myth. James Brain writes that "the apparently bizarre and often bloody features" of such peoples "served to instill a sense of comforting superiority in the breasts of scholars in the technologically developed countries" (1977: 191).

Ironically, during the same period when British anthropology was beginning to catalog the strange behavior of the British Empire's colonized peoples, British gynecological medicine of the mid-nineteenth century was engaging in practices equally strange, certainly at least as "unscien-

Elizabeth A. Sheehan teaches anthropology at American University in Washington, D.C. Her research interests center on ideology, gender, and institutionalized forms of power. She has published articles on the role of university intellectuals in Irish public life and about gender in Irish literature. She is currently working on a book about representations of women in Catholic sainthood.

tific," and clearly ritual in nature. The current reevaluation of Victorian social attitudes, found particularly in areas of research such as women's history and the professionalization of medicine, provides a new perspective through which to view the role of the "women's specialist" in a society changing rapidly in the face of scientific development, political awareness, and social unrest. In many instances, professional medical attitudes of the period synthesize wider cultural attitudes of Victorian England. In this context, the brief but dramatic practice of clitoridectomy by British doctors gains significance beyond that of the sensational oddity.

Isaac Baker Brown was an eminent obstetrical surgeon in the London of the 1850s. His practice was devoted to the diseases of women, and even today textbooks still refer to his development of procedures that helped lay the foundations of modern gynecological surgery. Yet his contributions to gynecology were inextricably linked to the Victorian medical theory of biological determinism, and, viewed from a contemporary feminist perspective, Brown's lifework appears to be a classic example of upright intentions combined with medical misogyny. He advocated the use of chloroform to relieve the pain of parturition, but by doing so he ultimately encouraged the development of an obstetrical imperative that removed control over childbirth from women and placed it in the hands of doctors. More questionably, Brown's acceptance of the mid-nineteenth-century "Psychology of the Ovary" theory, whereby all medical and emotional problems of women were considered to be based on some internal malfunction of the ovaries, rationalized his frequent practice of ovariotomy as a cure for female emotional disorders. Yet while there is no defense of his use of clitoridectomy or of the manner in which he performed this operation, an examination of the material concerning the scandal of clitoridectomy in Victorian England ultimately reflects more on the behavior of the British medical profession in its scapegoating of Brown than on Brown himself.

BROWN'S PRACTICE OF CLITORIDECTOMY

Born in 1812, Isaac Baker Brown grew up in a medical family and, at an early age, qualified as a surgeon. His success as an "accoucheur," an obstetrician, led to his further interest in the medical problems of women. In 1848 he was elected a Fellow of the Royal College of Surgeons, and in 1854 published *On Surgical Diseases of Women*, a work which quickly became a standard text and established Brown's reputation as a foremost obstetrician. He helped found St. Mary's Hospital and, in 1858, opened and became chief administrator of his own hospital, the London Surgical Home for Women. Brown's Home enjoyed the patronage of several members of the Royal Family (including one of Queen Victoria's daughters) who occupied themselves with the support of charitable causes. The Home was visited frequently by prestigious members of the British and European medical establishment, who wished to observe Brown's avant garde surgical procedures. Brown's repeated success with ovariotomy, including the one he performed on his own sister, lent respectability to its practice in England. He helped popularize the operation for vesico-vaginal fistula, pioneered by the American gynecologist J. Marion Sims. Brown's professional standing at this time is indicated by the following passage taken from a review of the second edition of *On Surgical Diseases of Women*, published in the *British Medical Journal* of 2 November 1861:

> Mr. Brown has been for some time known as a surgeon who has devoted considerable attention to the improvement of the various operations necessary for the removal or amelioration of certain afflictions of the female sexual organs, and it must be admitted that this branch of surgery is under obligations to him for the improvements he has suggested and brought into practice. (*British Medical Journal* 1861: 467)

In 1865 Brown was elected president of the Medical Society of London. He was in demand as a surgeon, a lecturer, a writer, and an authority on the nervous diseases of women. From his prosperous private practice near Hyde Park, Isaac Baker Brown at age fifty-four seemed to have secured a permanent and hallowed niche in the annals of nineteenth-century medicine. It was at this time that Brown decided to publish the results of an experimental form of surgery he had been developing since 1858. In March 1866 the book *On The Curability of Certain Forms of Insanity, Epilepsy, Catalepsy, and Hysteria in Females* was published. In it Brown proposed that all of the feminine weaknesses referred to in the title could be cured by excision of the clitoris. "All unprejudiced men must adopt, more or less, the practice which I have carried out," he wrote in his book.

Brown's observation that many of the epileptic patients in his Home masturbated led to his conclusion that such a practice was related to the etiology of the disease. In *Curability*, Brown avowed that "peripheral excitement of the pudic nerve" gave rise to a disease that could be divided into eight distinct stages, beginning with hysteria, developing into epilepsy, and culminating in either idiocy or death. Brown specified the danger signs in females susceptible to this process of degeneration: "The patient becomes restless and excited, or melancholy and retiring, listless, and indifferent to the social influences of domestic life." She loses her appetite, suffers headaches and back pain, and "disturbances or irregularities in the uterine functions. Often a great disposition for novelties is exhibited, the patient desiring to escape from home, fond of becoming a nurse in hospitals, soeur de charité, or other pursuits of the like nature, according to station and opportunities. . . . To these symptoms in the single female will be added, in the married, distaste for marital intercourse" (*British Medical Journal* 1866a: 38).

Confident of the success of his procedure, Brown's tone in the book was casual and chatty, as evidenced by excerpts published in the *Journal's* review of 28 April 1866: under chloroform, "the clitoris is freely excised by scissors or knife—I always prefer scissors." The patient's improvement was usually immediate, but "it cannot be too often repeated, this improvement can only be made permanent in many cases by careful watching and moral training on the part of both parents and friends" (*British Medical Journal* 1866a: 438). However, another doctor's account of Brown's operation depicted a procedure of almost unbelievable cruelty:

> Two instruments were used: the pair of hooked forceps which Mr. Brown always uses in clitoridectomy, and a cautery iron such as he uses in dividing the pedicle in ovariotomy. . . . The clitoris was seized by the forceps in the usual manner. The thin edge of the red-hot iron was then passed around its base until the organ was severed from its attachment, being partly cut or sawn, and partly torn away. After the clitoris was removed, the nymphae on each side were severed in a similar way by a sawing motion of the hot iron. After the clitoris and nymphae were got rid of, the operation was brought to a close by taking the back of the iron and sawing the surfaces of the labia and the other parts of the vulva which had escaped the cautery, and the instrument was rubbed down backwards and forwards till the parts were more effectually destroyed than when Mr. Brown uses the scissors to effect the same result. (*British Medical Journal* 1867: 407–8)

The immediate reaction to Brown's book is difficult to determine. The *British Medical Journal's* review was surprisingly scathing, considering Brown's position in the profession and the respect accorded to previous accounts of his work in the pages of the *Journal*. The review disputed Brown's claims for his operation, questioned the extremity of the procedure, and observed that the moral training and careful watching Brown recommended following the operation might in themselves cure the disorder. The review conceded that the practice of clitoridectomy might be of some value in certain forms of nervous disease. Brown's basic contention that masturbation caused specific illnesses was not disputed: as the *Journal* review declared, "It has long been an established fact, that onanism practiced to the extent supposed by Mr. Brown will occasion all the various disorders named by him." The review astutely observed, however, that whatever improvement in the patient's condition that occurred following the operation might be attributable more to the shock of the operation to the nervous system than to the efficacy of the procedure itself as a cure for epilepsy (*British Medical Journal* 1866a: 439–40).

Yet the topic of clitoridectomy was not a completely new one for the editors of the *Journal*. Brown himself had been publishing reports of his earlier experiences with the procedure since March 1858 within the *Journal*'s pages, and even within the *Journal*'s review of *Curability* a footnote noted that a Viennese surgeon had been quoted in the *Journal* as saying, "I don't hesitate in cases of habitual onanism, especially in widows and particular in cases where the vice has produced psychical disturbances, to recommend the operation" (*British Medical Journal* 1866a: 439). On 16 June 1866 the *Journal* reported a case of a clitoridectomy (performed by a surgeon other than Brown) that proved of no value, the symptoms having returned within a month of the operation (*British Medical Journal* 1866b: 637). However, the same issue carried in its correspondence column a letter from a physician who questioned the importance of the clitoris at all to the female enjoyment of sex, maintaining that its removal was of little consequence and calling clitoridectomy a "harmless operative procedure" (F.R.S. 1866: 654).

THE CONTROVERSY OVER CLITORIDECTOMY

The nature of the dispute over clitoridectomy reflects the contradiction expressed in nineteenth-century literature on female genitals. In 1818 the clitoris was not even mentioned in a textbook description of female reproductive anatomy; by 1866 it was being viewed as the source of several severe but unconnected disorders. An 1856 medical dictionary offers an unusual translation of the Greek root of the word *clitoris*—"a servant who invites guests"—and describes its structure as being similar to that of the penis, without mentioning an analogous sexual role (Duglison 1856: 214).

It would appear that the medical profession wanted it both ways: the clitoris was so unimportant to a normal woman as not to be missed if removed, yet lurking in its tissue was the greatest threat to female welfare ever known. If any other operation had been shown to have been of such negligible value, it would have been abandoned. Clitoridectomy was practiced in Victorian England in spite of its failure to effect cures for the disorders it was intended to relieve.

The lack of distinction between the physical and mental aspects of women's health was further confused by the conventional Victorian image of female sexuality. Any malaise or symptom that could not be accounted for by a clearly physical cause was attributed to an emotional one, brought about by a tendency toward promiscuity, nymphomania, or masturbation. The number of clitoridectomies performed in England during the period when Brown was practicing is impossible to determine. The fact that the operation is described in literature published well after the 1860s lends support to the idea that only Brown's particularly well-publicized application of the procedure was discouraged, while clitoridectomy in and of itself remained an acceptable medical technique. Additionally, widespread belief in the dangers of masturbation to the female sensibility was never disputed in the discussion concerning Brown's use of the operation.

Rigid Victorian attitudes toward sex, which reinforced the strength of the middle-class patriarchal family and attempted to impose order on the tumultuous social conflict of nineteenth-century England, developed into a form of pseudo-science to which both medical doctors and early social scientists adhered. Some doctors claimed that promiscuous women could be known by the size and shape of their genitals, particularly the clitoris. Masturbation led to madness, some said even to death. The tremendous freedom with which such beliefs were applied to patients' lives and the basis they formed for operating procedures are incredible when one realizes that throughout most of the nineteenth century even the basic process of menstruation remained largely misunderstood.

The false separation of early western medicine from ancient health and ritual practice obscures the point at which clitoridectomy moved into a realm of the Hippocratic tradition. The first reference to the operation in European medicine extends back at least to the sixth century A.D., when a man named Aetius recommended the use of the operation in the case of an enlarged or tumorous clitoris (McKay 1901: 197). The use of the procedure for similar reasons is routinely noted in most medical texts of the late eighteenth and early nineteenth centuries, and from the descriptions given, these seem to have been performed as a way of relieving discomfort and dispelling fluids collected in a diseased clitoris.

What Isaac Baker Brown can be credited with is publicizing the theory that nervous disorders could be cured by such a procedure. It was not until the mid-nineteenth century that a causal connection between various vaguely defined nervous diseases and masturbation of the clitoris was made. Accounts from this period do not clarify often whether the patient was suffering from an actual physical irregularity of the clitoris or whether masturbation and hysterical symptoms indicated a potential for a more serious disorder best eliminated by removal of the clitoris. The rationale for performing the operation varied from patient to patient. Brown and his followers offered clitoridectomy as a cure for physical, mental, and moral disturbances, despite the fact that a more scientific segment of the medical profession had begun to realize that not all disorders of the female genitals were based on immoral or otherwise irregular conduct. Parent-Duchatelet's 1857 study of Parisian prostitutes had disclosed that the clitoris "was found to be of normal size in females of the most unbridled passions" (Churchill 1857:61). Yet an edition of the *Church Times* of 1866, quoted in the *British Medical Journal*, circulated the following message to British clergymen:

> We desire to call attention of the clergy especially to a little book, which will enable them to suggest a remedy for some of the most distressing cases of illness which they frequently discover among their parishioners. Epileptic afflictions have long been considered usually incurable. Mr. Baker Brown, F.R.C.S., the eminent surgeon, has discovered and applied with great success . . . a surgical remedy for certain forms of epilepsy and kindred diseases. . . . The clergy will be doing a service, especially to their poorer parishioners, by bringing [the operation] under the notice of medical men. (*British Medical Journal* 1866a: 456)

An important element of the debate over clitoridectomy was the personal antagonism Brown incurred from his colleagues, although this antagonism does not appear to be evident prior to the publication of *Curability*. The development of gynecology as a legitimate branch of medicine had been a slow process. Male medical practitioners of the nineteenth century had struggled with great difficulty to gain precedence over the methods of midwives and the fears of women patients. With the expansion of surgical treatment for female genital disorders not directly related to reproduction, gynecology began to distinguish itself from obstetrics. The delicate nature of the gynecologist's work required the maintenance of the highest standards of impersonal professionalism. This attitude was aptly expressed by a member of the profession who spoke at the Obstetrical Society's investigation of Brown's practices:

> I assume we meet here as gentlemen constituting a public body, who have emerged from the difficulties and clouds under which we lay during previous centuries, having achieved a position satisfying the public that their health in our hands, as men of honour and gentlemen, is safe. (*British Medical Journal* 1857: 407)

Medical journals of the period reflect a private-men's-club attitude toward the entire medical profession, an exclusivity and class consciousness that encouraged the perception of the physician as a member of an elite group. The columns of the *Journal* included editorials on the state of public morality as well as social notes on the activities of the nobility. The fear of traducing the medical profession's honor by the injudicious spread of information concerning intimate health problems led to an attempt to withhold such information from the public. The *Journal's* final criticism of Brown's book in its review had been a request that "a serious medical work on the subject of Female Masturbation should bear on its outward *facies* none of those characters which belong to the class of works which lie upon drawing-room tables" (*British Medical Journal* 1866a: 440). Information on matters such as gynecological operations could appeal only to prurient public interest and was especially harmful to female morals. "It is a dirty subject," the editors of the *Journal* said of clitoridectomy, and one requiring "absolute purity of speech, thought, and expression" (*British Medical Journal* 1866c: 665). Such "purity of speech" apparently extended to an explanation of the operation to the patient herself. In the Obstetrical Society's inquiry into the practice of clitoridectomy, it became evident from testimony that many women who had had the procedure performed had been told merely that they were going to have a "slight operation on the external parts" (*British Medical Journal* 1867: 397).

The medical profession's attack on Brown appears to have been prompted in part by his desire to gain public recognition for his "cure" for epilepsy and hysteria. By seeking to publicize his theories about clitoridectomy, Brown brought to light in exquisite detail practices that up till then had been employed quietly by others as well as Brown, and for similar purposes. Brown had been reporting his use of the procedure for hysteria and related problems in the *British Medical Journal* since the 1850s. Several discussions of the topic appeared in issues of the *Journal* preceding the controversy aroused by Brown and his book. Even after *Curability's* publication early in 1866, but prior to the call for an investigation of Brown's techniques, many other doctors not only admitted having performed the operation but also declared it to be of value in many cases. At a meeting of the Obstetrical Society reported in the 15 December 1866 issue of the *Journal*, Sir John Fife, Sir James Simpson, Dr. Beatty, and Dr. Savage were reported by other obstetricians as having performed the operation or recommended it to their female patients. Dr. West, author of a well-known text on women's diseases, disparaged Brown's work and wrote that "public attempts to excite the attention of non-medical persons, and especially of women, to the subject of self-abuse in the female sex are likely to injure society, and to bring discredit on the medical profession" (West 1866: 677). It may be that it was the publicity that West most despised, as Brown claimed that West himself had attempted to cure a woman with "hysterical symptoms of an epileptoid nature, which he attributed to masturbation," by application of caustics to the clitoris, and that the failure of this treatment had caused West to recommend clitoridectomy to the patient (Brown 1866: 676).

The call for the censuring of Brown paralleled the medical profession's belated decision to abandon publicly the advocacy of clitoridectomy. Brown's attempts to save himself from personal ruin led to the transgression of his naming in print other British gentlemen who had been past supporters of his operation. The requests for Brown's removal from the Obstetrical Society accelerated as continued public discussion of the issue of clitoridectomy began to expose the faulty theoretical structure of Victorian medical practice concerning women. The sometimes glaringly hypothetical nature of such practice was evident in remarks such as one made by a Dr. Routh, another obstetrician, in reference to clitoridectomy: "Suppose it failed?" he said. "Was it necessarily the wrong step to have taken?" (*British Medical Journal* 1866c: 673). While condemning Brown's operation, few doctors disputed his contention that female emotional disorder was based on genital dysfunction. Brown's particular methods were slurred at the same time that accepted medical theory of the period supported the widespread practice of ovariotomy as a cure for hysteria.

Brown's private virtue as well as his professional ethical code were assailed violently as the debate over clitoridectomy intensified. He spent the months following the *Journal's* review of *Curability* defending himself against the attacks of his former colleagues, who denied all past association with him aside from professional courtesy. London's great doctors withdrew from him and addressed virulent letters concerning Brown's character to the *Journal*, whose editors saw fit to include anonymous contributions in its pages as well. A Harley Street physician, Dr. Greenhalgh, wrote of "the censures of an indignant profession. . . . My contention also is that women have unwittingly been made the victims of operations of the nature of which they were wholly ignorant" (Greenhalgh 1867: 42). Yet Brown wrote that "Dr. Greenhalgh was once my friend; and as such, always received the most courteous attention at my hands in his *numerous* visits to the London Surgical Home" (Brown 1867: 19).

In the 5 January 1867 issue of the *Journal*, Brown himself called for the appointment of a committee to investigate the results of clitoridectomy, and offered to refrain from performing the operation without consultation from another doctor until the committee could prepare a report. "If the investigation should prove that my views have a false foundation, and that the operation is useless, I will give it up altogether. On the other hand, if the evidence be in my favor, as I believe it will be, I shall continue to practice it in proper cases" (Brown 1867: 19).

On 25 February 1867, the Council of the Obstetrical Society met and decided that the notoriety and debate surrounding Brown's practice of clitoridectomy justified a recommendation for Brown's expulsion from the Society. On 3 April, the Society met to hear testimony concerning Brown's surgical procedures and professional conduct. The fifteen-page transcript of this "trial," which appears in the 6 April issue of the *Journal*, is a fascinating document, extremely readable as a synthesis of Victorian attitudes concerning women, health, and sex.

Members of the Society from all over England were present. The meeting room overflowed with excited and outspoken men calling for Brown's expulsion, who cheered and applauded as Brown was denounced by a series of highly outraged doctors and surgeons, while the defendant was denied the opportunity to reply until the latter part of the evening. Mr. Haden, a surgeon, described Brown's methods as obscene quackery and speculated on the scenario that might have taken place on the occasion of many clitoridectomies. He pictured a husband or father bringing the woman to the doctor's office, assured that a simple, unspecified surgical procedure would provide a cure for her epilepsy or other disorder:

> The patient is taken up and put under chloroform, and her clitoris is cut out before she has recovered from the anesthetic. Down comes the promoter of the scheme to the expectant victim below; invites him to write a cheque for 100 or 200 guineas.

If the man objected, he might be informed that:

> "Your daughter," or "your wife," as the case may be, "has undergone a disgraceful mutilation, because she has been given to disgraceful practices; if you can afford to tell your friends this, and to tell the man who is to marry her that she has had her clitoris cut out, and that for all disgraceful purposes, well and good; but if you cannot afford to tell them this, I think you had better pay the money and say no more about it." (*British Medical Journal* 1867: 397)

Except in his brief and blunt description of the operation itself, Haden characterized the man involved, husband or father, as the victim, and viewed the repercussions of the operation as bearing directly on another man, the future husband. Haden also saw the iniquity of the situation largely in financial terms. The man who must pay for the operation was threatened with exposure unless he could "afford" to risk other men knowing what had been done to his wife or daughter. A definite implication of blackmail, an affront to all gentlemen, was made by Haden in his colorful description of Brown's supposed scheme, and by doing so Haden further slandered Brown in the eyes of these "men of honour."

Brown denied vehemently that he had ever demanded any fees from patients in his Home or performed the operation without explaining to the patient some approximation of what he intended to do. Another surgeon in the room pointed out that few operations of any kind were explained to the patient, lest he or she refuse to undergo them. One by one, the members of the Society rose and expressed their shock at the behavior of this mountebank who threatened the good name of their brotherhood, the strength of which lay in its increasing support from the Victorian middle class. "Obstetricians, beyond other men, are not only the guardians of life, but, by force of circumstance, often also the guardians of female honor and purity" (*British Medical Journal* 1867: 388).

When finally given a chance to speak, Brown accurately pinpointed the crux of the entire debate:

> Mr. Brown: The whole of this hinges upon the neglect of the Council in investigating the subject of clitoridectomy as scientific men. Instead of examining the subject, which I challenged them to do again and again, they have neglected it, and tried to get rid of it by expelling me. . . . I maintain my late colleagues in this room have all performed this operation. . . . I have come to the conclusion that the operation of clitoridectomy was a justifiable operation—not my operation, recollect, gentlemen, but an operation, as Dr. Haden has showed, that has been practiced from the time of Hippocrates, and has been mentioned by all writers since that period again and again.

Later on in the proceedings Brown stated:

> If the operation is so bad, and so unfounded in practice, then ignore it and come to a proper determination upon it. If you, as a Society, say it is a subject which cannot be treated, it is not an operation that can be performed, then come down and say so, and if I perform it afterwards, expel me.

> The President of the Society: It is the manner in which you perform it. It is the manner in which you perform the operation, not the operation itself.

> Mr. Brown: Who is to decide it? Will you tell us what your ethical laws are? Will you tell me that my practise has been different from that of any other man in this room who now performs clitoridectomy? . . . I say, if you condemn the operation of clitoridectomy, and call it quackery, be honest men and have it investigated scientifically. (*British Medical Journal* 1867: 402)

Needless to say, Brown's line of self-defense did little to win him support. The Obstetrical Society's vote was taken: 194 for removal, 38 against removal, 5 nonvoters. "So severe a punishment as this has not fallen upon any man holding a respectable position in our profession in the memory of any of us," said the editors of the *British Medical Journal* on 6 April 1867 (*British Medical Journal* 1867: 388).

A few days later, Brown resigned from his fellowship in the Medical Society of London, of which he had once been president. The Society's acceptance of this resignation provoked another controversy when several members resigned from it themselves, in protest against Brown's having been allowed to withdraw from that prestigious body with some degree of self-respect. In addition, Brown resigned from the board of the hospital he had himself founded, the London Surgical Home for Women, obliged, he said, by the state of his health.

For five years Brown virtually disappeared from public notice. A book of his written prior to the clitoridectomy controversy was published in 1867, *On Safe Delivery from the Pains of Labour*, advocating "painless parturition with full mental consciousness." The book's influence was almost entirely negated by the onus of its author's sensational expulsion. Brown's work was mentioned no more in the *Journal*, nor was clitoridectomy, although medical textbooks continued to refer to the operation. A series of strokes progressively made Brown an invalid until, in April 1872, the Baker Brown Charitable Fund was announced in the *British Medical Journal* to help the outcast who was "suffering from severe illness (paralysis) and great pecuniary distress" (*British Medical Journal* 1872: 377). The *Journal* listed weekly the donors and their donations, including many from former patients. A total of £440 10s. 6d. was raised, a considerable figure for that time. But even in its well-publicized charity, the British medical profession succeeded in disparaging Brown. A letter describing the administration of the money, published in the 23 January 1873 issue of the *Journal* and written by the treasurer of the fund, Forbes Winslow, details the allotment of three guineas a week to Brown to maintain himself. "He is still paralyzed, and requires the constant assistance of a nurse, being unable to stand alone, dress, or feed himself. In fact, he is nearly as helpless as a new-born child" (Winslow 1873: 106). With some alarm, Winslow noted that improved medical treatment had increased the likelihood of Brown outliving his fund; thus, his remittance was cut back to two guineas a week.

Dr. Winslow's fears were groundless. On 1 February 1873, less than a week after the publication of his letter in the *Journal*, Isaac Baker Brown was attacked with vomiting and headache. He became unconscious and died on 3 February, at age sixty-one. The *Journal*'s gracious obituary, published on 8 February, reserved the sad story of Brown's fall from grace to the end of its tribute. "The important services of the early workers in this branch (gynecology) have hardly met with sufficient acknowledgement, and this has especially occurred in the case of the subject of our present notice" (*British Medical Journal* 1873: 159).

An interesting postscript to Brown's story was added in 1889 by Lawson Tait, one of the most prominent of nineteenth-century British gynecologists, in his book *Diseases of Women and Abdominal Surgery*. Summarizing the scandal surrounding Brown's operation, Tait claimed that Brown suffered from "extensive cerebral softening" (during the same period that Brown wrote two books and ran a small hospital), but also added an illuminating passage stating that the uproar concerning Brown might not have occurred "had he not been pursued by a rival as relentless as he was cruel and persevering . . . a large part of the evidence against him being furnished from the commonplace book of his rival, who seems to have dogged his steps for years" (Tait 1889: 63). Tait did not, of course, indicate who this individual might have been, but further wrote that the humiliation of Brown had "one disastrous result . . . the operation of clitoridectomy was absolutely discarded, and I have never heard a surgeon say he had performed it since 1867. Yet I am certain in many cases it would be useful." Apparently, Tait's medical theories cannot have been too different from those of Brown, as there is little else but promiscuity or masturbation implied when Tait wrote, in the same volume, that "reasons altogether too disgusting for publication" caused him to perform a clitoridectomy on a woman in 1886, thus saving her from "suicide or the asylum" (Tait 1889: 63).

The British medical establishment succeeded in its main desire: to get rid of Isaac Baker Brown. Evidently it did little to discredit the medical reasoning behind clitoridectomy, particularly in America, where it was recommended in the textbooks of several well-known gynecologists. In his 1859 study, *Woman: Her Diseases and Remedies*, Charles Meigs had proposed the practice of the operation, citing the case of a nine-year-old nymphomaniac (Meigs 1859: 151), but as late as 1897, Thomas Allbutt's *A System of Gynecology* stated that in cases of nervous disorder thought to be caused by an enlarged clitoris, "it may be necessary to amputate the clitoris, or to excise the nymphae. In a case of my own great benefit followed the excision of the labia minora in a highly neurotic girl, who was thus restored from a state of chronic invalidism to one of health and usefulness" (Allbutt 1897: 97). The last clitoridectomy known to have been performed in this country to correct emotional disorder was done in the 1940s on a five-year-old girl (Ehrenreich and English 1973: 34).

As wrong as he was in advocating this "harmless operative procedure," the scientific investigation that Brown had called for to justify his methods might have helped dispel some of the myths concerning female anatomy and psychology that flourished in the secrecy of the medical profession and in the social mores of the times. Yet, as we have seen in our own era, it is often too difficult and too threatening to recognize one's vested interest in preserving behavior that reifies our own world view. We may say we know where myth ends and science begins, but for each of us it will be at a different point. The British medical profession did not wish to examine the theoretical structure that fulfilled its desire to mold public conscience and private behavior. The pillorying of Isaac Baker Brown succeeded in avoiding the obvious issues, and the fiat of the medical profession's outright control over women's bodies continued well into this century.

REFERENCES

Allbutt, Thomas and W. S. Playfair, eds. 1897. *A System of Gynecology*. New York: Macmillan Company.

Brain, James L. 1977. Sex, Incest, and Death: Initiation Rites Reconsidered. *Current Anthropology* 18:191–98.

British Medical Journal

> 1861. Review of *On Surgical Diseases of Women*, by Isaac Baker Brown, 2 November: 467.

> 1866a. Review of *On the Curability of Certain Forms of Insanity, Epilepsy, Catalepsy, and Hysteria in Females*, by Isaac Baker Brown. 28 April: 438–40.

>> Report of *Church Times* article on clitoridectomy. 28 April: 438–40.

> 1866b. Report of Operation of Clitoridectomy. 16 June: 637.

> 1866c. Report of Meeting of the Obstetrical Society. 15 December: 672–75.

> 1867. Report of Obstetrical Society Meeting to Investigate Isaac Baker Brown's Practice of Clitoridectomy. 6 April: 395–410.

>> Editorial on Obstetrical Society Meeting to Investigate Isaac Baker Brown's Practice of Clitoridectomy. 6 April: 387–88.

> 1872. Announcement of Opening of Baker Brown Charitable Fund. 6 April: 377.

> 1873. Obituary for Isaac Baker Brown. 8 February: 158.

Brown, Isaac Baker. 1866. Correspondence. *British Medical Journal*. 15 December: 676.

> 1867. Correspondence. *British Medical Journal*. 12 January: 19.

Churchill, F. 1857. *On the Diseases of Women*. 4th ed. Dublin: Fannin and Company.

Duglison, Robley. 1856. *Medical Lexicon: A Dictionary of Medical Science*. 3d ed. Philadelphia: Blanchard and Leas.

Ehrenreich, Barbara, and Deirdre English. 1973. *Complaints and Disorders: The Sexual Politics of Sickness*. Old Westbury, N.Y.: Feminist Press.

F.R.S. 1866. Correspondence. *British Medical Journal*. 16 June: 654.

Greenhalgh, William. 1867. Correspondence. *British Medical Journal*. 12 January: 42.

McKay, W.V.S. 1901. *History of Ancient Gynecology*. London: Bailliere, Tindall, and Cox.

Meigs, Charles D. 1859. *Woman: Her Diseases and Remedies*. Philadelphia: Blanchard and Leas.

Tait, Lawson. 1889. *Diseases of Women and Abdominal Surgery*. Philadelphia: Blanchard and Leas.

West, Dr. 1866. Correspondence. *British Medical Journal*. 15 December: 677.

Winslow, Forbes. 1873. Report on Allocation of Money from Isaac Baker Brown Fund. *British Medical Journal*. 25 January: 106.

23   "Material Girl"

The Effacements of Postmodern Culture

Susan Bordo

PLASTICITY AS POSTMODERN PARADIGM

In a culture in which organ transplants, life-extension machinery, microsurgery, and artificial organs have entered everyday medicine, we seem on the verge of practical realization of the seventeenth-century imagination of body as machine. But if we have technically and technologically realized that conception, it can also be argued that metaphysically we have deconstructed it. In the early modern era, machine imagery helped to articulate a totally determined human body whose basic functionings the human being was helpless to alter. The then-dominant metaphors for this body—clocks, watches, collections of springs—imagined a system that is set, wound up, whether by nature or by God the watchmaker, ticking away in predictable, orderly manner, regulated by laws over which the human being has no control. Understanding the system, we can help it to perform efficiently, and we can intervene when it malfunctions. But we cannot radically alter its configuration.

Pursuing this modern, determinist fantasy to its limits, fed by the currents of consumer capitalism, modern ideologies of the self, and their crystallization in the dominance of U.S. mass culture, Western science and technology have now arrived, paradoxically but predictably (for it was an element, though submerged and illicit, in the mechanist conception all along), at a new, postmodern imagination of human freedom from bodily determination. Gradually and surely, a technology that was first aimed at the replacement of malfunctioning parts has generated an industry and an ideology fueled by fantasies of rearranging, transforming, and correcting, an ideology of limitless improvement and change, defying the historicity, the mortality, and, indeed, the very materiality of the body. In place of that materiality, we now have what I will call cultural plastic. In place of God the watchmaker, we now have ourselves, the master sculptors of that plastic.

Susan Bordo is Professor of Philosophy and holds the Singletary Chair of Humanities at the University of Kentucky. She is author of *The Flight to Objectivity: Essays on Cartesianism and Culture* (SUNY, 1987) and *Unbearable Weight: Feminism, Western Culture, and the Body* (California, 1993), which was named one of the New York Times Notable Books for 1993. A collection of recent essays, *Twilight Zones: The Hidden Life of Cultural Images from Plato to O.J.*, is forthcoming (California, 1997), and she is currently working on *My Father's Body and Other Unexplored Regions of Sex, Masculinity, and the Male Body* (under contract with Farrar, Straus, and Giroux).

This disdain for material limits and the concomitant intoxication with freedom, change, and self-determination are enacted not only on the level of the contemporary technology of the body but also in a wide range of contexts, including much of contemporary discourse on the body, both popular and academic. In this essay, looking at a variety of these discursive contexts, I attempt to describe key elements of this paradigm of plasticity and expose some of its effacements—the material and social realities it denies or renders invisible.

PLASTIC BODIES

"Create a masterpiece, sculpt your body into a work of art," urges *Fit* magazine. "You visualize what you want to look like, and then you create that form." "The challenge presents itself: to rearrange things."[1] The precision technology of body-sculpting, once the secret of the Arnold Schwarzeneggers and Rachel McLishes of the professional body-building world, has now become available to anyone who can afford the price of membership in a gym (Figure 1). "I now look at bodies," says John Travolta, after training for the movie *Staying Alive*, "almost like pieces of clay that can be molded."[2] On the medical front, plastic surgery, whose repeated and purely cosmetic employment has been legitimated by Michael Jackson, Cher, and others, has become a fabulously expanded industry, extending its domain from nose jobs, face lifts, tummy tucks, and breast augmentations to collagen-plumped lips and liposuction-shaped ankles, calves, and buttocks (Figure 2). In 1989, 681,000 procedures were done, up 80 percent over 1981; over half of these were performed on patients between the ages of eighteen and thirty-five.[3] The trendy *Details* magazine describes "surgical stretching, tucking and sucking" as "another fabulous [fashion] accessory" and invites readers to share their cosmetic-surgery experiences in their monthly

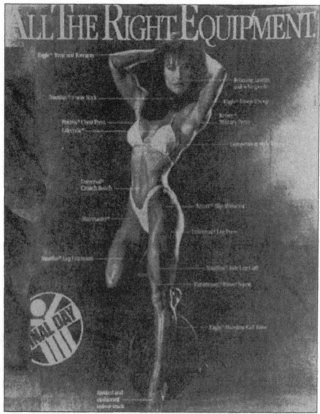

FIGURE 1

FIGURE 2

column "Knife-styles of the Rich and Famous." In that column, the transportation of fat from one part of the body to another is described as breezily as changing hats might be:

> Dr. Brown is an artist. He doesn't just pull and tuck and forget about you. . . . He did liposuction on my neck, did the nose job and tightened up my forehead to give it a better line. Then he took some fat from the side of my waist and injected it into my hands. It goes in as a lump and, then he smooths it out with his hands to where it looks good. I'll tell you something, the nose and neck made a big change, but nothing in comparison to how fabulous my hands look. The fat just smoothed out all the lines, the veins don't stick up anymore, the skin actually looks soft and great. [But] you have to be careful not to bang your hands.[4]

Popular culture does not apply any brakes to these fantasies of rearrangement and self-transformation. Rather, we are constantly told that we can "choose" our own bodies (Figures 3 and 4). "The proper diet, the right amount of exercise and you can have, pretty much, any body you desire," claims Evian. Of course, the rhetoric of choice and self-determination and the breezy analogies comparing cosmetic surgery to fashion accessorizing are deeply mystifying. They efface not only the inequalities of privilege, money, and time that prohibit most people from indulging in these practices, but also the desperation that characterizes the lives of those who do. "I will do anything, *anything*, to make myself look and feel better," says Tina Lizardi (whose "Knife-styles"

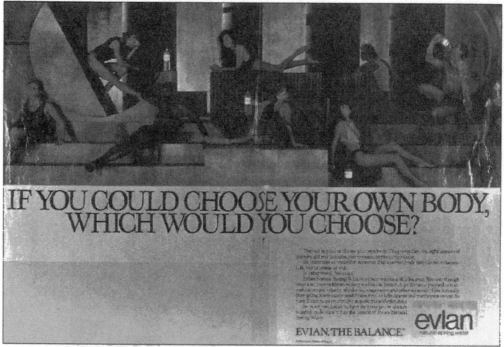

FIGURE 3

FIGURE 4

experience I quoted from above). Medical science has now designated a new category of "poly-surgical addicts" (or, in more casual references, "scalpel slaves") who return for operation after operation, in perpetual quest of the elusive yet ruthlessly normalizing goal, the "perfect" body.[5] The dark underside of the practices of body transformation and rearrangement reveals botched and sometimes fatal operations, exercise addictions, eating disorders. And of course, despite the claims of the Evian ad, one cannot have *any* body that one wants—for not every body will *do*. The very advertisements whose copy speaks of choice and self-determination visually legislate the effacement of individual and cultural difference and circumscribe our choices (Figure 5).

That we are surrounded by homogenizing and normalizing images—images whose content is far from arbitrary, but is instead suffused with the dominance of gendered, racial, class, and other cultural iconography—seems so obvious as to be almost embarrassing to be arguing here. Yet contemporary understandings of the behaviors I have been describing not only construct the situation very differently but also do so in terms that preempt precisely such a critique of cultural imagery. Moreover they reproduce, on the level of discourse and interpretation, the same conditions that postmodern bodies enact on the level of cultural practice: a construction of life as plastic possibility and weightless choice, undetermined by history, social location, or even individual biography. A 1988 *Donahue* show offers my first illustration.

FIGURE 5

The show's focus was a series of television commercials for DuraSoft colored contact lenses. In these commercials as they were originally aired, a woman was shown in a dreamlike, romantic fantasy—for example, parachuting slowly and gracefully from the heavens. The male voiceover then described the woman in soft, lush terms: "If I believed in angels, I'd say that's what she was—an angel, dropped from the sky like an answer to a prayer, with eyes as brown as bark." [Significant pause] "No . . . I *don't think so.*" [At this point, the tape would be rewound to return us to:] "With eyes as violet as the colors of a child's imagination." The commercial concludes: "DuraSoft colored contact lenses. Get brown eyes a second look" (see Figure 6).

The question posed by Phil Donahue: Is this ad racist? Donahue clearly thought there was controversy to be stirred up here, for he stocked his audience full of women of color and white women to discuss the implications of the ad. But Donahue was apparently living in a different decade from most of his audience, who repeatedly declared that there was nothing "wrong" with the ad, and everything "wrong" with any inclinations to "make it a political question." Here are some comments taken from the transcript of the show:

FIGURE 6

"Why does it have to be a political question? I mean, people perm their hair. It's just because they like the way it looks. It's not something sociological. Maybe black women like the way they look with green contacts. It's to be more attractive. It's not something that makes them—I mean, why do punk rockers have purple hair? Because they feel it makes them feel better." [white woman]

"What's the fuss? When I put on my blue lenses, it makes me feel good. It makes me feel sexy, different, the other woman, so to speak, which is like fun." [black woman]

"I perm my hair, you're wearing make-up, what's the difference?" [white woman]

"I want to be versatile . . . having different looks, being able to change from one look to the other." [black female model]

"We all do the same thing, when we're feeling good we wear new makeup, hairstyles, we buy new clothes. So now it's contact lenses. What difference does it make?" [white woman]

"It goes both ways . . . Bo Derek puts her hair in cornstalks, or corn . . . or whatever that thing is called. White women try to get tan." [white woman]

"She's not trying to be white, she's trying to be different." [about a black woman with blue contact lenses]

"It's fashion, women are never happy with themselves."

"I put them in as toys, just for fun, change. Nothing too serious, and I really enjoy them." [black woman][6]

Some points to note here: first, putting on makeup, styling hair, and so forth are conceived of only as free *play*, fun, a matter of creative expression. This they surely are. But they are also experienced by many women as necessary before they will show themselves to the world, even on a quick trip to the corner mailbox. The one comment that hints at women's (by now depressingly well documented) dissatisfaction with their appearance trivializes that dissatisfaction and puts it beyond the pale of cultural critique: "It's fashion." What she means is, "It's *only* fashion," whose whimsical and politically neutral vicissitudes supply endless amusement for women's eternally superficial values. ("Women are never happy with themselves.") If we are never happy with ourselves, it is implied, that is due to our female nature, not to be taken too seriously or made into a political question. Second, the content of fashion, the specific ideals that women are drawn to embody (ideals that vary historically, racially, and along class and other lines) are seen as arbitrary, without meaning; interpretation is neither required nor even appropriate. Rather, all motivation and value come from the interest and allure—the "sexiness"—of change and difference itself. Blue contact lenses for a black woman, it is admitted, make her "other" ("the other woman"). But that "other" is not a racial or cultural "other"; she is sexy because of the piquancy, the novelty, the erotics of putting on a different self. *Any* different self would do, it is implied.

Closely connected to this is the construction of *all* cosmetic changes as the same: perms for the white women, cornrows on Bo Derek, tanning, makeup, changing hairstyles, blue contacts for black women—all are seen as having equal political valence (which is to say, *no* political valance) and the same cultural meaning (which is to say, *no* cultural meaning) in the heterogeneous yet undifferentiated context of the things "all" women do "to be more attractive." The one woman in the audience who offered a different construction of this behavior, who insisted that the styles we aspire to do not simply reflect the free play of fashion or female nature—who went so far, indeed, as to claim that we "are brainwashed to think blond hair and blue eyes is the most beautiful of all," was regarded with hostile silence. Then, a few moments later, someone challenged: "Is there anything *wrong* with blue eyes and blond hair?" The audience enthusiastically applauded this defender of democratic values.

This "conversation"—a paradigmatically postmodern conversation, as I will argue shortly—effaces the same general elements as the rhetoric of body transformation discussed earlier. First, it effaces the inequalities of social position and the historical origins that, for example, render Bo Derek's cornrows and black women's hair-straightening utterly noncommensurate. On the one hand, we have Bo Derek's privilege, not only as so unimpeachably white as to permit an exotic touch of "otherness" with no danger of racial contamination, but her trend-setting position as a famous movie star. Contrasting to this, and mediating a black woman's "choice" to straighten her hair, is a cultural history of racist body-discriminations such as the nineteenth-century comb-test, which allowed admission to churches and clubs only to those blacks who could pass through their hair without snagging a fine-tooth comb hanging outside the door. (A variety of comparable tests—the pine-slab test, the brown bag test—determined whether one's skin was adequately light to pass muster.)[7]

Second, and following from these historical practices, there is a disciplinary reality that is effaced in the construction of all self-transformation as equally arbitrary, all variants of the same trivial game, without differing cultural valance. I use the term *disciplinary* here in the Foucauldian sense, as pointing to practices that do not merely transform but *normalize* the subject. That is, to repeat a point made earlier, not every body will do. A 1989 poll of *Essence* magazine readers revealed that 68 percent of those who responded wear their hair straightened chemically or by hot comb.[8] "Just for fun"? For the kick of being "different"? When we look at the pursuit of beauty as a normalizing discipline, it becomes clear that not all body transformations are the same. The general tyranny of fashion—perpetual, elusive, and instructing the female body in a pedagogy of personal inadequacy and lack—is a powerful discipline for the normalization of *all* women in this culture. But even as we are all normalized to the requirements of appropriate feminine insecurity

FIGURE 7

and preoccupation with appearance, more specific requirements emerge in different cultural and historical contexts, and for different groups. When Bo Derek put her hair in cornrows, she was engaging in normalizing feminine practice. But when Oprah Winfrey admitted on her show that all her life she has desperately longed to have "hair that swings from side to side" when she shakes her head (Figure 7), she revealed the power of racial as well as gender normalization, normalization not only to "femininity" but also to the Caucasian standards of beauty that still dominate on television, in movies, in popular magazines. (When I was a child, I felt the same way about my thick, then curly, "Jewish" hair as Oprah did about hers.) Neither Oprah nor the *Essence* readers nor the many Jewish women (myself included) who ironed their hair in the 1960s have creatively or playfully invented themselves here.

DuraSoft knows this, even if Donahue's audience does not. Since the campaign first began, the company has replaced the original, upfront magazine advertisement with a more euphemistic variant, from which the word *brown* has been tastefully effaced. (In case it has become too subtle for the average reader, the model now is black—although it should be noted that DuraSoft's failure to appreciate brown eyes also renders the eyes of most of the world not worth "a second look" [Figure 8].) In the television commercial, a comparable "brownwash" was effected; here "eyes as brown as . . ." was retained, but the derogatory nouns—"brown as boots," "brown as bark"—were eliminated. The announcer simply was left speechless: "eyes as brown as . . . brown as . . .," and then, presumably having been unable to come up with an enticing simile, shifted to "violet." As in the expurgated magazine ad, the television commercial ended: "Get *your* eyes a second look."

When I showed my students these ads, many of them were as dismissive as the *Donahue* audience, convinced that I was once again turning innocent images and practices into political issues. I persisted: if racial standards of beauty are not at work here, then why no brown contacts for blue-eyed people? A month later, two of my students triumphantly produced a Dura-Soft ad for brown contacts (Figure 9), appearing in *Essence* magazine, and with an advertising campaign directed solely at *already* brown-eyed consumers, offering the promise *not* of "getting blue eyes a second look" by becoming excitingly darker, but of "subtly enhancing" dark eyes, by making them *lighter* brown. The creators of the DuraSoft campaign clearly know that not all differences are the same in our culture, and they continue, albeit in ever more mystified form, to exploit and perpetuate that fact.[9]

PLASTIC DISCOURSE

The *Donahue* DuraSoft show (indeed, any talk show) provides a perfect example of what we might call a postmodern conversation. All sense of history and all ability (or inclination) to sustain cultural criticism, to make the distinctions and discriminations that would permit such criticism, have disappeared. Rather, in this conversation, "anything goes"—and any positioned social critique (for example, the woman who, speaking clearly for consciousness of racial oppression, insisted that the attraction of blond hair and blue eyes has a cultural meaning significantly different from that of purple hair) is immediately destabilized. Instead of distinctions, endless *differences* reign—an undifferentiated pastiche of differences, a grab bag in which no items are assigned any more importance or centrality than any others. Television is, of course, the great teacher here, our modeler of plastic pluralism: if one *Donahue* show features a feminist talking about battered wives, the next show will feature mistreated husbands. Women who love too much, the sex habits of priests, disturbed children of psychiatrists, daughters who have no manners, male strippers, relatives who haven't spoken in ten years all have their day alongside incest, rape, and U.S. foreign policy. All are given equal weight by the great leveler—the frame of the television screen.

This spectacle of difference defeats the ability to sustain coherent political critique. Everything is the same in its unvalanced difference. ("I perm my hair, you're wearing makeup, what's the difference?") Particulars reign, and generality—which collects, organizes, and prioritizes, sus-

FIGURE 8

pending attention to particularity in the interests of connection, emphasis, and criticism—is suspect. So, whenever some critically charged degeneralization was suggested on Donahue's Dura-Soft show, someone else would invariably offer a counterexample—I have blue eyes, and I'm a black woman; Bo Derek wears cornrows—to fragment the critique. What is remarkable is that people accept these examples as *refutations* of social critique. They almost invariably back down, utterly confused as to how to maintain their critical generalization in the face of the destabilizing example. Sometimes they qualify, claiming they meant some people, not all. But of course, they meant neither all nor some. They meant *most*—that is, they were trying to make a claim about social or cultural *patterns*—and that is a stance that is increasingly difficult to sustain in a postmodern context, where we are surrounded by endlessly displaced images and are given no orienting context in which to make discriminations.

Those who insist on an orienting context (and who therefore do not permit particulars to rein in all their absolute "difference") are seen as "totalizing," that is, as constructing a falsely coher-

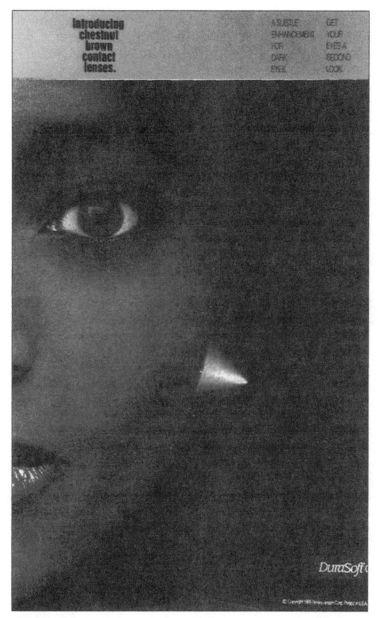

FIGURE 9

ent and morally coercive universe that marginalizes and effaces the experiences and values of others. ("Is there anything *wrong* with blue eyes and blond hair?") As someone who is frequently interviewed by local television and newspaper reporters, I have often found my feminist arguments framed in this way, as they were in an article on breast-augmentation surgery. After several pages of "expert" recommendations from plastic surgeons, my cautions about the politics of female body transformation (none of them critical of individuals contemplating plastic surgery, all of them of a cultural nature) were briefly quoted by the reporter, who then went on to end the piece with a comment on *my* critique—from the director of communications for the American Society of Plastic and Reconstructive Surgery:

Those not considering plastic surgery shouldn't be too critical of those who do. It's the hardest thing for people to understand. What's important is if it's a problem to that person. We're all different, but we all want to look better. We're just different in what extent we'll go to. But none of us can say we don't want to look the best we can.[10]

With this tolerant, egalitarian stroke, the media liaison of the most powerful plastic surgery lobby in the country presents herself as the protector of "difference" against the homogenizing and stifling regime of the feminist dictator.

Academics do not usually like to think of themselves as embodying the values and preoccupations of popular culture on the plane of high theory or intellectual discourse. We prefer to see ourselves as the demystifyers of popular discourse, bringers-to-consciousness-and-clarity rather than unconscious reproducers of culture. Despite what we would *like* to believe of ourselves, however, we are always within the society that we criticize, and never so strikingly as at the present post-modern moment. All the elements of what I have here called postmodern conversation—intoxication with individual choice and creative *jouissance*, delight with the piquancy of particularity and mistrust of pattern and seeing coherence, celebration of "difference" along with an absence of critical perspective differentiating and weighing "differences," suspicion of the totalitarian nature of generalization along with a rush to protect difference from its homogenizing abuses—have become recognizable and familiar in much of contemporary intellectual discourse. Within this theoretically self-conscious universe, moreover, these elements are not merely embodied (as in the *Donahue* show's DuraSoft conversation) but explicitly thematized and *celebrated*, as inaugurating new constructions of the self, no longer caught in the mythology of the unified subject, embracing of multiplicity, challenged the dreary and moralizing generalizations about gender, race, and so forth that have so preoccupied liberal and left humanism.

For this celebratory, academic postmodernism, it has become highly unfashionable—and "totalizing"—to talk about the grip of culture on the body. Such a perspective, it is argued, casts active and creative subjects as passive dupes of ideology; it gives too much to dominant ideology, imagining it as seamless and univocal, overlooking both the gaps that are continually allowing for the eruption of "difference" and the polysemous, unstable, upon nature of all cultural texts. To talk about the grip of culture on the body (as, for example, in "old" feminist discourse about the objectification and sexualization of the female body) is to fail to acknowledge, as one theorist put it, "the cultural work by which nomadic, fragmented, active subjects confound dominant discourse."[11]

So, for example, contemporary culture critic John Fiske is harshly critical of what he describes as the view of television as a "dominating monster" with "homogenizing power" over the perceptions of viewers. Such a view, he argues, imagines the audience as "powerless and undiscriminating" and overlooks the fact that:

Pleasure results from a particular relationship between meanings and power. . . . There is no pleasure in being a "cultural dope." . . . Pleasure results from the production of meanings of the world and of self that are felt to serve the interests of the reader rather than those of the dominant. The subordinate may be disempowered, but they are not powerless. There is a power in resisting power, there is a power in maintaining one's social identity in opposition to that proposed by the dominant ideology, there is a power in asserting one's own subcultural values against the dominant ones. There is, in short, a power in being different.[12]

Fiske then goes on to produce numerous examples of how *Dallas, Hart to Hart*, and so forth have been read (or so he argues) by various subcultures to make their own "socially pertinent" and empowering meanings out of "the semiotic resources provided by television."

Note, in Fiske's insistent, repetitive invocation of the category of power, a characteristically postmodern flattening of the terrain of power relations, a lack of differentiation between, for example, the power involved in creative *reading* in the isolation of one's own home and the power held by those who control the material production of television shows, or the power involved in public protest and action against the conditions of that production and the power of the dominant meanings—for instance, racist and sexist images and messages—therein produced. For Fiske, of course, there *are* no such dominant meanings, that is, no element whose ability to grip the imagination of the viewer is greater than the viewer's ability to "just say no" through resistant reading of the text. That ethnic and subcultural meaning *may* be wrested from *Dallas* and *Hart to Hart* becomes for Fiske proof that dominating images and messages are only in the minds of those totalitarian critics who would condescendingly "rescue" the disempowered from those forces that are in fact the very medium of their creative freedom and resistance ("the semiotic resources of television").

Fiske's conception of power—a terrain without hills and valleys, where all forces have become "resources"—reflects a very common postmodern misappropriation of Foucault. Fiske conceives of power as in the *possession* of individuals or groups, something they "have"—a conception Foucault takes great pains to criticize—rather than (as in Foucault's reconstruction) a dynamic of noncentralized forces, its dominant historical forms attaining their hegemony, not from magisterial design or decree, but through multiple "processes, of different origin and scattered location," regulating and normalizing the most intimate and minute elements of the construction of time, space, desire, embodiment.[13] This conception of power does *not* entail that there are no dominant positions, social structures, or ideologies emerging from the play of forces; the fact that power is not held by any *one* does not mean that it is equally held by *all*. It is in fact not "held" at all; rather, people and groups are positioned differentially within it. This model is particularly useful for the analysis of male dominance and female subordination, so much of which is reproduced "voluntarily," through our self-normalization to everyday habits of masculinity and femininity. Within such a model, one can acknowledge that women may indeed contribute to the perpetuation of female subordination (for example, by embracing, taking pleasure in, and even feeling empowered by the cultural objectification and sexualization of the female body) without this entailing that they have power in the production and reproduction of sexist culture.

Foucault does insist on the *instability* of modern power relations—that is, he emphasizes that resistance is perpetual and unpredictable, and hegemony precarious. This notion is transformed by Fiske (perhaps under the influence of a more deconstructionist brand of postmodernism) into a notion of resistance as *jouissance*, a creative and pleasurable eruption of cultural "difference" through the "seams" of the text. What this celebration of creative reading as resistance effaces is the arduous and frequently frustrated historical struggle that is required for the subordinated to articulate and assert the value of their "difference" in the face of dominant meanings—meanings that often offer a pedagogy directed at reinforcement of feelings of inferiority, marginality, ugliness. During the early fifties, when *Brown v. the Board of Education* was wending its way through the courts, as a demonstration of the destructive psychological effects of segregation black children were asked to look at two baby dolls, identical in all respects except color. The children were asked a series of questions: Which is the nice doll? Which is the bad doll? Which doll would you like to play with? The majority of black children, Kenneth Clark reports, attributed the positive characteristics to the white doll, the negative characteristics to the black. When Clark asked one final question, "Which doll is like you?" they looked at him, he says, "as though he were the devil himself" for putting them in that predicament, for forcing them to face the inexorable and hideous logical implications of their situation. Northern children often ran out of the room; southern children tended to answer the question in shamed embarrassment. Clark recalls one little boy who laughed, "Who am I like? That doll! It's a nigger and I'm a nigger!"[14]

Failing to acknowledge the psychological and cultural potency of normalizing imagery can be just as effective in effacing people's experiences of racial oppression as lack of attentiveness to cultural and ethnic differences—a fact postmodern critics sometimes seem to forget. This is not to deny what Fiske calls "the power of being different"; it is, rather, to insist that it is won through ongoing political *struggle* rather than through an act of creative interpretation. Here, once again, although many postmodern academics may claim Foucault as their guiding light, they differ from him in significant and revealing ways. For Foucault, the metaphorical terrain of resistance is explicitly that of the "battle"; the "points of confrontation" may be "innumerable" and "instable," but they involve a serious, often deadly struggle of embodied (that is, historically situated and shaped) forces.[15] Barbara Kruger exemplifies this conception of resistance in a poster that represents the contemporary contest over reproductive control through the metaphor of the body as battleground (Figure 10). Some progressive developers of children's toys have self-consciously entered into struggle with racial and other forms of normalization. The Kenya Doll (Figure 11) comes in three different skin tones ("so your girl is bound to feel pretty and proud") and attempts

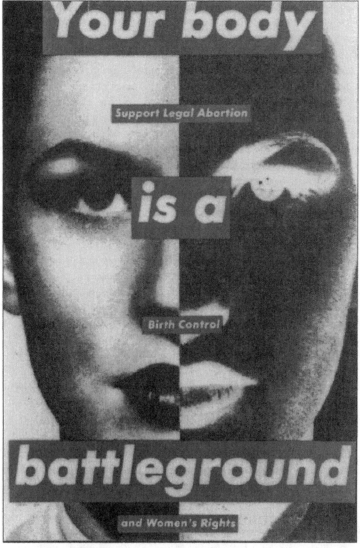

FIGURE 10

to create a future in which hair-straightening *will* be merely one decorative option among others. Such products, to my mind, are potentially effective "sites of resistance" precisely because they recognize that the body is a battleground whose self-determination has to be fought for.

The metaphor of the body as battleground, rather than postmodern playground, captures, as well, the *practical* difficulties involved in the political struggle to empower "difference." *Essence* magazine has consciously and strenuously tried to promote diverse images of black strength, beauty, and self-acceptance. Beauty features celebrate the glory of black skin and lush lips; other departments feature interviews with accomplished black women writers, activists, teachers, many of whom display styles of body and dress that challenge the hegemony of white Anglo-Saxon standards. The magazine's advertisers, however, continually play upon and perpetuate consumers' feelings of inadequacy and insecurity over the racial characteristics of their bodies. They insist that, in order to be beautiful, hair must be straightened and eyes lightened; they almost always employ models with fair skin, Anglo-Saxon features, and "hair that moves," insuring association of their products with fantasies of becoming what the white culture most prizes and rewards.

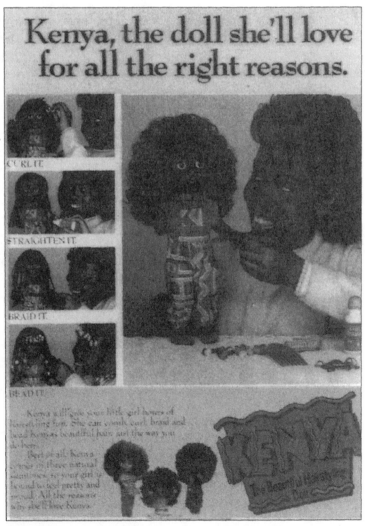

FIGURE 11

This ongoing battle over the black woman's body and the power of its "differences" ("differences" that actual black women embody to widely varying degrees, of course) is made manifest in the twentieth-anniversary issue, where a feature celebrating "The Beauty of Black" faced an advertisment visually legislating virtually the opposite (and offering, significantly, "escape") (Figures 12 and 13). This invitation to cognitive dissonance reveals what *Essence* must grapple with, in every issue, as it tries to keep its message of African American self-acceptance clear and dominant, while submitting to economic necessities on which its survival depends. Let me make it clear here that such self-acceptance, not the reverse tyranny that constructs light-skinned and Anglo-featured African Americans as "not black enough," is the message *Essence* is trying to convey, against a culture that *denies* "the Beauty of Black" at every turn. This terrain, clearly, is not a playground but a minefield that constantly threatens to deconstruct "difference" *literally* and not merely literarily.

FIGURE 12

"Material Girl": Madonna as Postmodern Heroine

John Fiske's conception of "difference," in the section quoted above, at least imagines resistance as challenging specifiable historical forms of dominance. Women, he argues, connect with subversive "feminine" values leaking through the patriarchal plot of soap operas; blacks laugh to themselves at the glossy, materialist-cowboy culture of *Dallas*. Such examples suggest a resistance directed against *particular* historical forms of power and subjectivity. For some postmodern theorists, however, resistance is imagined as the refusal to embody *any* positioned subjectivity at all; what is celebrated is continual creative escape from location, containment, and definition. So, as Susan Rubin Suleiman advises, we must move beyond the valorization of historically suppressed values (for example, those values that have been culturally constructed as belonging to an inferior, female domain and generally expunged from Western science, philosophy, and religion) and toward "endless complication" and a "dizzying accumulation of narratives."[16] She appreciatively

FIGURE 13

(and perhaps misleadingly) invokes Derrida's metaphor of "incalculable choreographies"[17] to capture the dancing, elusive, continually changing subjectivity that she envisions, a subjectivity without gender, without history, without location. From this perspective, the truly resistant female body is not the body that wages war on feminine sexualization and objectification, but the body that, as Cathy Schwichtenberg has put it, "uses simulation strategically in ways that challenge the stable notion of gender as the edifice of sexual difference . . . [in] an erotic politics in which the female body can be refashioned in the flux of identities that speak in plural styles."[18] For this erotic politics, the new postmodern heroine is Madonna.

This celebration of Madonna as postmodern heroine does not mark the first time Madonna has been portrayed as a subversive culture-figure. Until the early 1990s, however, Madonna's resistance has been interpreted along "body as battleground" lines, as deriving from her refusal to allow herself to be constructed as a passive object of patriarchal desire. John Fiske, for example, argues that this was a large part of Madonna's original appeal to her "wanna-bes"—those hordes of middle-class preteeners who mimicked Madonna's moves and costumes. For the "wanna-bes," Madonna demonstrated the possibility of a female heterosexuality that was independent of patriarchal control, a sexuality that defied rather than rejected the male gaze, teasing it with her own gaze, deliberately trashy and vulgar, challenging anyone to call her a whore, and ultimately not giving a damn how she might be judged. Madonna's rebellious sexuality, in this reading, offered itself not as coming into being through the look of the "other," but as self-defining and in love with, happy with itself—an attitude that is rather difficult for women to achieve in this culture and that helps to explain, as Fiske argues, her enormous appeal for pre-teen girls.[19] "I like the way she handles herself, sort of like take it or leave it; she's sexy but she doesn't need men . . . she's kind of there all by herself," says one. "She gives us ideas. It's really women's lib, not being afraid of what guys think," says another.[20]

Madonna herself, significantly and unlike most sex symbols, has never advertised herself as disdainful of feminism nor constructed feminists as man-haters. Rather, in a 1985 *Time* interview, she suggests that her lack of inhibition in "being herself" and her "luxuriant" expression of "strong" sexuality constitute her brand of feminist celebration.[21] Some feminist theorists would agree. Molly Hite, for example, argues that "asserting female desire in a culture in which female sexuality is viewed as so inextricably conjoined with passivity" is "transgressive":

> Implied in this strategy is the old paradox of the speaking statue, the created thing that magically begins to create, for when a woman writes—self-consciously from her muted position as a woman and not as an honorary man—about female desire, female sexuality, female sensuous experience generally, her performance has the effect of giving voice to pure corporeality, of turning a product of the dominant meaning-system into a producer of meanings. A woman, conventionally identified with her body, writes about that identification, and as a consequence, femininity—silent and inert by definition—erupts into patriarchy as an impossible discourse.[22]

Not all feminists would agree with this, of course. For the sake of the contrast I want to draw here, however, let us grant it, and note, as well, that an argument similar to Fiske's can be made concerning Madonna's refusal to be obedient to dominant and normalizing standards of female *beauty*. I am now talking, of course, about Madonna in her more fleshy days. In those days, Madonna saw herself as willfully out of step with the times. "Back in the fifties," she says in the *Time* interview, "women weren't ashamed of their bodies." (The fact that she is dead wrong is not relevant here.) Identifying herself with her construction of that time and what she calls its lack of "suppression" of femininity, she looks down her nose at the "androgynous" clothes of our own time and speaks warmly of her own stomach, "not really fat" but "round and the skin is smooth and I like it." Contrasting herself to anorectics, whom she sees as self-denying and self-hating, completely in the thrall of externally imposed standards of worthiness, Madonna (as she saw herself) stood for self-definition through the assertion of her own (traditionally "female" and now anachronistic) body-type (Figure 14).

Of course, this is no longer Madonna's body type. Shortly after her 1987 marriage to Sean Penn, she began a strenuous reducing and exercise program, now runs several miles a day, lifts weights, and has developed, in obedience to dominant contemporary norms, a tight, slender, muscular body (Figure 15). Why did she decide to shape up? "I didn't have a flat stomach anymore," she has said. "I had become well-rounded." Please note the sharp about-face here, from pride to embarrassment. My goal here, however, is not to suggest that Madonna's formerly voluptuous body was a nonalienated, freely expressive body, a "natural" body. While the slender body is the current cultural ideal, the voluptuous female body is a cultural form, too (as are all bodies), and was a coercive ideal in the fifties. My point is that in terms of Madonna's own former lexicon of meanings—in which feminine voluptuousness and the choice to be round in a culture of

FIGURE 14

the lean were clearly connected to spontaneity, self-definition, and defiance of the cultural gaze—the terms set by that gaze have now triumphed. Madonna has been normalized; more precisely, she has self-normalized. Her "wanna-bes" are following suit. Studies suggest that as many as 80 percent of nine-year-old suburban girls (the majority of whom are far from overweight) are making rigorous dieting and exercise the organizing discipline of their lives.[23] They do not require Madonna's example, of course, to believe that they must be thin to be acceptable. But Madonna clearly no longer provides a model of resistance or "difference" for them.

None of this "materiality"—that is, the obsessive body-praxis that regulates and disciplines Madonna's life and the lives of the young (and not so young) women who emulate her—makes its way into the representation of Madonna as postmodern heroine. In the terms of this representation (in both its popular and scholarly instantiations), Madonna is "in control of her image, not trapped by it"; the proof lies in her ironic and chameleon-like approach to the construction of her identity, her ability to "slip in and out of character at will," to defy definition, to keep them guessing.[24] In this coding of things, as in the fantasies of the polysurgical addict (and, as I argue in *Unbearable Weight*, the eating-disordered woman), *control* and *power*, words that are invoked over

FIGURE 14

and over in discussions of Madonna, have become equivalent to *self-creating*. Madonna's new body has no material history; it conceals its continual struggle to maintain itself, it does not reveal its pain. (Significantly, Madonna's "self-exposé," the documentary *Truth or Dare*, does not include any scenes of Madonna's daily workouts.) It is merely another creative transformation of an ever-elusive subjectivity. "More Dazzling and Determined Not to Stop Changing" as *Cosmopolitan* describes Madonna: " . . . whether in looks or career, this multitalented dazzler will never be trapped in any mold!"[25] The plasticity of Madonna's subjectivity is emphasized again and again in the popular press, particularly by Madonna herself. It is how she tells the story of her "power" in the industry: "In pop music, generally, people have one image. You get pigeonholed. I'm lucky enough to be able to change and still be accepted . . . play a part, change characters, looks, attitudes."[26]

Madonna claims that her creative work, too, is meant to escape definition. "Everything I do is meant to have several meanings, to be ambiguous," she says, She resists, however (in true post-modern fashion), the attribution of serious artistic intent; rather (as she told *Cosmo*), she favors irony and ambiguity, "to entertain myself" and (as she told *Vanity Fair*) out of "rebelliousness and a desire to fuck with people."[27] It is the postmodern nature of her music and videos that has most entranced academic critics, whose accolades reproduce in highly theoretical language the notions emphasized in the popular press. Susan McClary writes:

> Madonna's art itself repeatedly deconstructs the traditional notion of the unified subject with finite ego boundaries. Her pieces explore . . . various ways of constituting identities that refuse stability, that remain fluid, that resist definition. This tendency in her work has become increasingly pronounced; for instance, in her recent controversial video "Express Yourself" . . . she slips in and out of every subject position offered within the video's narrative context . . . refusing more than ever to deliver the security of a clear, unambiguous message or an "authentic" self.[28]

Later in the same piece, McClary describes "Open Your Heart to Me," which features Madonna as a porn star in a peep show, as creating "an image of open-ended *jouissance*—an erotic energy that continually escapes containment."[29] Now, many feminist viewers may find this particular video quite disturbing, for a number of reasons. First, unlike many of Madonna's older videos, "Open Your Heart to Me" does not visually emphasize Madonna's subjectivity or desire—as "Lucky Star," for example, did through frequent shots of Madonna's face and eyes, flirting with and controlling the reactions of the viewer. Rather, "Open Your Heart to Me" places the viewer in the position of the voyeur by presenting Madonna's body as object, now perfectly taut and tightly managed, for display. To be sure, we do not identify with the slimy men, drooling over Madonna's performance, who are depicted in the video; but, as E. Ann Kaplan has pointed out, the way men view women *in* the filmic world is only one species of objectifying gaze. There is also the viewer's gaze, which may be encouraged by the director to be either more or less objectifying.[30] In "Open Your Heart to Me," as in virtually all rock videos, the female body is offered to the viewer purely as a spectacle, an object of sight, a visual commodity to be consumed. Madonna's weight loss and dazzling shaping-up job make the spectacle of her body all the more compelling; we are riveted to her body, fascinated by it. Many men and women may experience the primary reality of the video as the elicitation of desire *for* that perfect body; women, however, may also be gripped by the desire (very likely impossible to achieve) to *become* that perfect body.

These elements can be effaced, of course, by a deliberate abstraction of the video from the cultural context in which it is historically embedded—the continuing containment, sexualization, and objectification of the female body—and in which the viewer is implicated as well and instead treating the video as a purely formal text. Taken as such, "Open Your Heart to Me" presents itself as what E. Ann Kaplan calls a "postmodern video": it refuses to "take a clear position vis-à-vis its images" and similarly refuses a "clear position for the spectator within the filmic world . . . leaving him/her decentered, confused."[31] McClary's reading of "Open Your Heart to Me" emphasizes precisely these postmodern elements, insisting on the ambiguous and unstable nature of the relationships depicted in the narrative of the video, and the frequent elements of parody and play. "The usual power relationship between the voyeuristic male gaze and object" is "destabilized," she claims, by the portrayal of the male patrons of the porno house as leering and pathetic. At the same time, the portrayal of Madonna as porno queen-object is deconstructed, McClary argues, by the end of the video, which has Madonna changing her clothes to those of a little boy and tripping off playfully, leaving the manager of the house sputtering behind her. McClary reads this as "escape to androgyny," which "refuses essentialist gender categories and turns sexual identity into a kind of play." As for the gaze of the viewer, she admits that it is "risky" to "invoke the image of porn queen in order to perform its deconstruction," but concludes that the deconstruction is successful: "In this video, Madonna confronts the most pernicious of her stereotypes and attempts to channel it into a very different realm: a realm where the feminine object need not be the object of the patriarchal gaze, where its energy can motivate play and nonsexual pleasure."[32]

I would argue, however, that despite the video's evasions of clear or fixed meaning there *is* a dominant position in this video: it is that of the objectifying gaze. One is not *really* decentered and confused by this video, despite the "ambiguities" it formally contains. Indeed, the video's postmodern conceits, I would suggest, facilitate rather than deconstruct the presentation of Madonna's body as an object on display. For in the absence of a coherent critical position telling us how to read the images, the individual images themselves become preeminent, hypnotic, fixating. Indeed, I would say that ultimately this video is entirely about Madonna's body, the narrative context virtually irrelevant, an excuse to showcase the physical achievements of the star, a video centerfold. On this level, any parodic or destabilizing element appears as cynically, mechanically tacked on, in bad faith, a way of claiming trendy status for what is really just cheesecake—or perhaps, soft-core pornography.

Indeed, it may be worse than that. If the playful "tag" ending of "Open Your Heart to Me" is successful in deconstructing the notion that the objectification, the sexualization of women's bodies is a serious business, then Madonna's *jouissance* may be "fucking with" her youthful viewer's perceptions in a dangerous way. Judging from the proliferation of rock and rap lyrics celebrating rape, abuse, and humiliation of women, the message—not Madonna's responsibility alone, of course, but hers among others, surely—is getting through. The artists who perform these misogynist songs also claim to be speaking playfully, tongue-in-cheek, and to be daring and resistant to transgressors of cultural structures that contain and define. Ice T, whose rap lyrics gleefully describe the gang rape of a woman—with a flashlight, to "make her tits light up"—claims that he is only "telling it like it is" among black street youth (he compares himself to Richard Wright), and he scoffs at feminist humorlessness, implying, as well, that it is racist and repressive for white feminists to try to deny him his indigenous "style." The fact that Richard Wright embedded his depiction of Bigger Thomas within a critique of the racist culture that shaped him, and that *Native Son* is meant to be a *tragedy*, was not, apparently, noticed in Ice T's postmodern reading of the book, whose critical point of view he utterly ignores. Nor does he seem concerned about what appears to be a growing fad—not only among street gangs, but in fraternity houses as well—for gang rape, often with an unconscious woman, and surrounded by male spectators. (Some of the terms popularly used to describe these rapes include "beaching"—the woman being likened to a "beached whale"—and "spectoring," to emphasize how integral a role the onlookers play.)

My argument here is a plea, not for censorship, but for recognition of the social contexts and consequences of images from popular culture, consequences that are frequently effaced in postmodern and other celebrations of "resistant" elements in these images. To turn back to Madonna and the liberating postmodern subjectivity that McClary and others claim she is offering: the notion that one can play a porno house by night and regain one's androgynous innocence by day does not seem to me to be a refusal of essentialist categories about gender, but rather a new inscription of mind/body dualism. What the body does is immaterial, so long as the imagination is free. This abstract, unsituated, disembodied freedom, I have argued in this essay, glorifies itself only through the effacement of the material praxis of people's lives, the normalizing power of cultural images, and the continuing social realities of dominance and subordination.

NOTES

1. Quoted in Trix Rosen, *Strong and Sexy* (New York: Putnam, 1983), pp. 72, 61.
2. "Travolta: 'You Really Can Make Yourself Over,'" *Syracuse Herald-American*, Jan. 13, 1985.
3. "Popular Plastic Surgery," *Cosmopolitan* (May 1990): 96.
4. Tina Lizardi and Martha Frankel, "Hand Job," *Details* (Feb. 1990): 38.
5. Jennet Conant, Jeanne Gordon, and Jennifer Donovan, "Scalpel Slaves Just Can't Quit," *Newsweek* (Jan. 11, 1988): 58–59.
6. *Donahue* transcript 05257, n.d., Multimedia Entertainment, Cincinnati, Ohio.
7. Dahleen Glanton, "Racism Within a Race," *Syracuse Herald-American*, Sept. 19, 1989.
8. *Essence* reader opinion poll (June 1989): 71.
9. Since this essay first appeared, DuraSoft has altered its campaign once more, renaming the lenses "Complements" and emphasizing how "natural" and subtle they are. "No one will know you're wearing them," they assure. One ad for "Complements" features identical black twins, one with brown eyes and one wearing blue lenses, as if to show that DuraSoft finds nothing "wrong" with brown eyes. The issue, rather, is self-determination: "Choosing your very own eye color is now the most natural thing in the world."
10. Linda Bien, "Building a Better Bust," *Syracuse Herald-American*, March 4, 1990.
11. This was said by Janice Radway in an oral presentation of her work, Duke University, Spring, 1989.
12. John Fiske, *Television Culture* (New York: Methuen, 1987), p. 19.
13. Michel Foucault, *Discipline and Punish* (New York: Vintage, 1979), p. 138.
14. Related in Bill Moyers, "A Walk Through the Twentieth Century: The Second American Revolution," PBS Boston.
15. Foucault, *Discipline and Punish*, pp. 26–27.
16. Susan Rubin Suleiman, "(Re)Writing the Body: The Politics and Poetics of Female Eroticism," in Susan Rubin Suleiman, ed., *The Female Body in Western Culture* (Cambridge: Harvard University Press, 1986), p. 24.
17. Jacques Derrida and Christie V. McDonald, "Choreographies," *Diacritics* 12, no. 2 (1982): 76.
18. Cathy Schwichtenberg, "Postmodern Feminism and Madonna: Toward an Erotic Politics of the Female Body," paper presented at the University of Utah Humanities Center, National Conference on Rewriting the (Post)Modern: (Post)Colonialism/Feminism/Late Capitalism, March 30–31, 1990.
19. John Fiske, "British Cultural Studies and Television," in Robert C. Allen, ed., *Channels of Discourse* (Chapel Hill: University of North Carolina Press, 1987), pp. 254–90.
20. Quoted in John Skow, "Madonna Rocks the Land," *Time* (May 27, 1985): 77.
21. Skow, "Madonna Rocks the Land," p. 81.
22. Molly Hite, "Writing—and Reading—the Body: Female Sexuality and Recent Feminist Fiction," in *Feminist Studies* 14, no. 1 (Spring 1988): 121–22.
23. "Fat or Not, 4th Grade Girls Diet Lest They Be Teased or Unloved," *Wall Street Journal*, Feb. 11, 1986.
24. Catherine Texier, "Have Women Surrendered in MTV's Battle of the Sexes?" *New York Times*, April 22, 1990, p. 31.
25. *Cosmopolitan* (July 1987): cover.
26. David Ansen, "Magnificent Maverick," *Cosmopolitan* (May 1990): 311.
27. Ansen, "Magnificent Maverick," p. 311; Kevin Sessums, "White Heat," *Vanity Fair* (April 1990): 208.

28. Susan McClary, "Living to Tell: Madonna's Resurrection of the Fleshy," *Genders*, no. 7 (Spring 1990): 2.

29. McClary, "Living to Tell," p. 12.

30. E. Ann Kaplan, "Is the Gaze Male?" in Ann Snitow, Christine Stansell, and Sharon Thompson, eds., *Powers of Desire: The Politics of Sexuality* (New York: Monthly Review Press, 1983), pp. 309–27.

31. E. Ann Kaplan, *Rocking Around the Clock: Music Television, Postmodernism and Consumer Culture* (New York: Methuen, 1987), p. 63.

32. McClary, "Living to Tell," p. 13.

Part Six

POLYVALENT PLEASURES
Resistances, Reinscriptions,
and Dispersals

24   The Carnivalization of the World

Richard Parker

Sin, the saying goes, does not exist beneath the equator. It is an idea that has been traced as far back as the writings of the austere Dutch historian Gaspar von Barlaeus, in his seventeenth-century chronicle *Rerum per Octennium in Brasilien* (Barlaeus 1980). First published in 1660, Barlaeus's work; would become a classic document of the Dutch occupation of northeast Brazil (see Freyre 1956, Boxer 1957).

> All wickedness was amusement and play, making known among the worst the epiphany: "—On the other side of the equinoctial line there is no sinning"—, as if morality did not pertain to all places and peoples, but only to the northerners, and as if the line that divides the world separated as well virtue from vice. (Barlaeus 1980, 49)

Barlaeus's chronicle seems to have marked Brazil out as somehow unique and problematic: hardly, in this instance, a tropical Eden, but rather a land of sin and wickedness, whose inhabitants seemed to believe that the universal laws of morality and virtue did not apply to them. With his northern severity, Barlaeus, of course, could only scoff at such a misguided notion before going on to outline the renewed sense of order that Dutch rule had gradually been able to enforce upon the chaotic existence of the tropics. Surely he could not have imagined the impact that his own words would later have in shaping a very different understanding of the world.

In the early 1970s, at the height of the military dictatorship that lasted from 1964 until the return to civilian rule in 1984, the poet and novelist Ledo Ivo published his prize-winning political allegory *Ninho de Cobras* (Snakes' nest), set in the provincial port city of Maceió, in the northeastern state of Alagoas, during World War II (see Ivo 1981). Exploring the underside of

---

Richard G. Parker is Professor of Medical Anthropology and Human Sexuality and Chair of the Department of Health Policy and Institutions in the Institute of Social Medicine at the State University of Rio de Janeiro, as well as Secretary General of the Brazilian Interdisciplinary AIDS Association (ABIA) and a director of the Commission on Citizenship and Reproduction (CCR) in Brazil. He has carried out long-term research in Brazil for more than fifteen years, focusing on gender, sexuality, HIV/AIDS and public policy. Recent English-language publications include *Sexuality, Politics, and AIDS in Brazil* (with Herbert Daniel, Falmer, 1993), and *Conceiving Sexuality: Approaches to Sex Research in a Postmodern World* (edited with John H. Gagnon, Routledge, 1995).

social and political life in Maceió, Ivo focused on the often conflicting perceptions of reality that result as much from political as from psychological repression. The almost mythical power of the past in the present reappears throughout his text. It is most evident, however, in a chapter entitled *A Festa* (the Portuguese term for both "party" and "festival"), following the description of a night-long party held by members of the local elite at Dina's, one of Maceió's leading houses of prostitution, when Ivo echoes the words of Barlaeus for his own purposes:

> "Beyond the Equator sin does not exist," Barlaeus had noted when writing the chronicle of the Dutch period. Then that landscape had been part of New Holland and through the rows of crooked streets and warehouses bursting with sugar passed the worst scum of the earth. Besides the Portuguese, there were Dutch, French, Scots, Englishmen, Jews, and Germans who, sought after or hunted by the Inquisition and other tribunals which foreshadowed the eve of the stake or the gallows, had arrived there with their dreams and vices. . . . "Beyond the Equator, sin does not exist," they alleged in word or in thought; and they killed Indians and Blacks and their own white companions. They sacked plantations, robbed warehouses and ravaged women, depositing in them, in their burning or Negro cunts, the seeds of the green or blue eyes of those red-haired and white-featured Northeasterners of today. This permissive code has crossed the centuries. And today, in Maceió's turbulent brothels, when somebody shouts "everybody naked," or wild orgies splash creek or ocean waters awakened by man's lasciviousness, a hidden tradition surfaces once again. It is a tradition of creatures faithful to the life of the flesh and the senses and suffocated by the Church and the State. . . . It is as if the Alagoans momentarily remembered those remote times when everything was permitted. (Ivo 1981, 113–15)

In the face of centuries of social development and repression, the vision of a past in which, as Ivo puts it, "everything was permitted" continues to interrupt the flow of social action. What Ivo describes as a "hidden tradition" surfaces to give meaning to contemporary life.

Here, in the present, however, what is most striking about this "hidden tradition" is the degree to which it has been re-created in positive, rather than negative, terms. A vision of evil and wickedness has given way to a kind of playful celebration of the most fundamental possibilities of life. This quality has been captured by Chico Buarque de Hollanda in *Não Existe Pecado ao Sul do Equador* ("Sin Doesn't Exist to the South of the Equator"), his reinvention of Barlaeus, and one of the most successful songs of the past two decades of Brazilian popular music:

> Sin doesn't exist
> on the side beneath the equator.
> Let us commit a sin
> spread open, sweaty, all steamy.
> Let me be your depraved doormat,
> your devilish bouquet, stream of love.
> When it's a lesson of disorder,
> look out, get out from under, I'm the professor.
> Leave sadness aside,
> Come to eat, dine on me,
> *sarapatel, caruru, tucupi tacacá,*
> See if you can use me, abuse me, soil me,
> Because your mixed-blooded woman can't wait.
> Leave sadness aside,
> Come to eat, dine on me,
> *sarapatel, caruru, tucupi tacacá,*
> See if you can exhaust me, put me on your table,
> Because your Dutchwoman can't wait.

Playing on the double entendre of the human body as a world unto itself, and the waist as an equatorial line dividing north from south, *Não Existe Pecado ao Sul do Equador* takes Ledo Ivo's text one step further, suggesting that if sin exists, it is only in the mind. True to the transgressive logic of erotic ideology, beneath the waist is a world of pleasures and passions, of tastes and flavors, that would be unimaginable in Barlaeus's northern reality.

Once again, then, what emerges from these various texts, fragmentary as they are, is a vision of a world divided, split into two sharply opposed modes of being or forms of experience. The seriousness and severity of daily life, which is made possible only through the repression of desires and the prohibition of pleasures, is contrasted with a rebellious world of sensuality and satisfaction in which the pleasures of the body can escape the restrictions imposed by an oppressive social order. It is a vision of a world free from sin and given over to the sensuality of the body, and it is most fully realized today in the experience of *carnaval*, the annual pre-Lenten festival that has existed in the West since the early days of Christianity but that has taken its most elaborate form in contemporary Brazilian culture.

Like the myths of origin that tell of the formation of a uniquely sexual people in an exotic land, the carnivalesque tradition has taken on new meaning, beneath the equator, as somehow definitive of the peculiar character of Brazilian reality (see Da Matta 1978). For Brazilians and foreigners alike, the *carnaval* has become almost synonymous with Brazil itself. Yet even if it were nothing else, *carnaval* would still be the clearest example in contemporary Brazilian life of those peculiar moments when a hidden tradition comes out of hiding and an entire society discovers and reinvents itself—when, for a few brief days, myths of origin take shape in cultural performance, the past invades the present, and the sensuality of the body defies sin. It is a time when everything is permitted, when anything is possible.

CELEBRATING THE FLESH

The carnivalesque tradition has, of course, already been described and analyzed extensively by any number of writers (see, for example, Bakhtin 1968; Baroja 1979; Burke 1978; Gaignebet and Florentin 1974; Ladurie 1979). It has been interpreted, through its essential opposition to the world of daily life, as a kind of ritual of reversal or rebellion in which social life is turned on its head and time played back to front (Davis 1975, Leach 1961, Turner 1969). It has been seen as a world of laughter, of madness and play, in which the established order of daily life dissolves in the face of an almost utopian anarchy, in which all hierarchical structures are overturned and the fundamental equality of all human beings is proclaimed. Above all else, it has been understood as a celebration of the flesh in which the repressions and prohibitions of normal life cease to exist and every form of pleasure is suddenly possible (Bakhtin 1968). Indeed, even the name of the festival itself has been interpreted as meaning "a farewell to flesh" (from the Latin *carnis* or "flesh" and *vale* or "farewell")—a kind of final triumph of sensuality before Lent (Leach 1972).

The sensuality of the carnivalesque tradition is nowhere more evident than in Brazilian *carnaval*, which is arguably the most elaborate, widespread recreation of the logic of the festival anywhere in the contemporary world. No less than the traditional carnival of medieval Europe, the modern Brazilian *carnaval* embodies a single, overriding ethic: the conviction that in spite of all the evidence to the contrary, there still exists a time and place where complete freedom is possible. If the carnivalesque tradition has taken root in Brazil, however, it has hardly remained stagnant. On the contrary, it has clearly continued to change and grow in response to the specific circumstances of Brazilian life, merging with the "hidden tradition" of the Brazilian past that is essential to the understandings that Brazilians have built up of themselves as a people. In other words, the *carnaval* itself has been "Brazilianized" and has itself become a kind of metaphor with its own highly complicated set of meanings.

Once again, some sense of what all of this means on the ground, of how it is experienced and understood by the people who participate in it, can best be approached through the language that they use to make sense of it. The world of *carnaval* is a world of diverse pleasures. As Nancy Scheper-Hughes has noted, one of the key metaphors structuring the Brazilian perception of reality is the notion of normal daily life (as opposed to the world created by the *carnaval*) as a kind of *luta*, "struggle" (Scheper-Hughes 1988). This *luta* takes many forms and is played out on a number of different levels, but it clearly characterizes the nature of day-to-day existence, filled, as it is, with *trabalho* (work) and *sofrimento* (suffering):

> The meaning of this is that life, survival, is an eternal war. The struggle for our daily bread . . . The struggle for a miserable salary . . . The struggle because of a lack of hope . . . In itself, everything in order to arrive at the end is simply a total struggle to the death. (Antônio)

This linear (and ultimately tragic) trajectory of one's life is interrupted each year by the cyclical rhythm of the seasons, by the time outside of time, during *carnaval*, when the work and suffering of daily life give way to a world of *risos* (laughter). Here, in this world of laughter, the normal conditions of human existence, marked as they are by an almost overwhelming *tristeza* (sadness), are transformed in the *felicidade* (happiness) and *alegria* (joy or elation) of the festival:

> It's like in that song from the film Black Orpheus: *Tristeza nao tem fim, felicidade sim* (Sadness has no end, but happiness ends). Leaving sadness, the struggle of day-to-day life, forgotten inside an imaginary drawer, the people allow themselves to be carried away by the reality of fantasy (*uma fantasia real*) in the three days of *carnaval*. They are three days of merrymaking, sweat, and beer, but everything comes to an end on Shrove Tuesday. (João)

In these fleeting moments of happiness, the daily struggle of life is reinvented, transformed into *brincadeira* (play, fun, amusement, joking, etc.). No longer the deadly serious battle for existence, the playful struggles of the *carnaval* take on an altogether different form in the chaotic battles of the traditional *entrudo* (a ritualized street fighting in which the participants pelt one another with filth, garbage, mud, excrement, or urine); the somewhat tamer jests and jokes of *foliões* (literally, "merrymakers" or "revellers," but derived from the French terms for madness and madmen); the *brincando* (playing) with water pistols, clubs, or similar weapons in the street; or even the playful *campeonatos* (championships) of the great *escolas de samba* (samba schools) that are a focus today for the *carnaval* of Rio de Janeiro.

The use of the verb *brincar* (to play) is instructive, for it is especially here, in this notion, that the sexual meanings in the symbolic structure of the festival are most evident. *Brincando* (playing) can take shape on any number of different levels. On the one hand, it refers to the apparently innocent play of children, the *brinquedos* (toys) and *brincadeiras* (fun and games) that everyone remembers from their childhood:

> In the life of a child, the word *brincar* is perhaps one of the most frequently used, not to mention "to eat" and "to drink." This word is heard all the time in the life of the child, not only from the child himself, but from everyone around him. (Rose)

At the same time, however, there is less innocent play of early adolescence and even adulthood—the *brincadeiras sexuais* (sexual play) that has such an important place in the formation of the erotic universe:

> The *brincadeiras sexuais* in the life of a child around the age of puberty pass from the material toys (*brinquedos*) to the playthings (*brinquedos*) of the sexual organs. . . . The doll and the toy car are left aside, or almost totally forgotten, in order to give room for the so-called *brincadeiras* of discovery of the body in transition to adulthood. (Rose)

It is this notion of play as not only pleasurable, but also profoundly sexual in nature, that shapes the fully adult use of *brincar* as a synonym for both sexual intercourse itself and erotic play more generally:

> The verb *brincar* is also used. "I want to play (*brincar*) with you" or "I want to play (*brincar*) in your cunt (or your ass, or your mouth)." "Let's play a good game (*brincadeira*). "I have a toy (*brinquedo*) here that you will like." "Can I put my toy (*brinquedo*) in your garage?" (João)

Linking the play of children to that of adults, then, and true to the totalizing and transgressive logic of erotic ideology, the use of *brincar* breaks down the kinds of hierarchical categories and distinctions that normally order daily life. It builds up another, very different, understanding of human experience, in which enjoyment and pleasure become the focus of attention, the most important reason for being.

It is hardly surprising, then, that *brincar* should be used as well as the verb for "doing *carnaval*":

> *Brincar* is used also for the *carnaval*. You say that you are going "to play" (*brincar*) the *carnaval*. "Let's play (*brincar*) the *carnaval*." This verb was chosen because of giving adults the liberty to let everything out during these three days of merrymaking and paganism for the Christians. To play (*brincar*) the *carnaval* is to dance, to drink, to fuck, to get high, to kill, and to die. They are days to let out your emotions like a child—but the adult, when he plays (*brinca*) the *carnaval*, these are perhaps the only days of the year that he can really be himself and not some jester from everyday life. (João)

The past that is recreated in the carnivalesque present is at once social and individual: the hidden tradition of an unruly and sensual historical past and the repressed freedom of childhood. For young and old alike, the oversized *chupeta* (pacifier) is among the most common *brinquedos* used during the *carnaval*, and since its original recording in 1937, *Mamae Eu Quero* ("Mommy I Want"), with all of its possible meanings, has continued as perhaps the most popular of all *carnaval* songs:

> Mommy I want,
> Mommy I want,
> Mommy I want to suckle.
> Give me the pacifier,
> Give me the pacifier,
> Give me the pacifier,
> So that the baby won't cry.

Recreating a world outside of time, a world where wishes and desires can always be satisfied, this emphasis on sucking and suckling breaks down the lines that separate children from adults and the divisions that separate one individual body from another.

This emphasis on union, on the fundamentally erotic merging of the body with other bodies, is especially evident in the experience of the carnivalesque crowd—the *massa* (mass) of revelers playing *carnaval* (see Bakhtin 1968).

> During the *carnaval* you stop being the master of your own body. The mass becomes master . . . (Alexandre)

Losing control, losing mastery, over one's body and merging with the bodies of others, the individual finds himself integrated into the masses, or perhaps more accurately, the *povo* (people). The *povo* in turn is offered a new and different awareness of its sensuality, its material unity and community. For a few brief moments, hierarchy and patronage collapse, and the masses rule the streets.

Within this unruly crowd, bodies not only rub up against one another and, at least in symbolic terms, merge into one: they can be exchanged and transformed. The *carnaval* proposes that fantasy should become reality, and *fantasia*, the very term used to describe the mental images of psychic fantasy, is also used for the costumes of *carnaval*. Through *fantasias* and masks, individual reality is transformed and the fantastic reality of *carnaval* is created. The diversity and complexity of the *carnaval* costumes defies description, ranging from clownlike fools and Chaplinesque tramps to grotesque monsters, anthropomorphic animals, skeletons, and ghostlike representations of death. While many of these fantastic disguises might just as likely be found today in the carnivals of Europe or the Caribbean, and obviously draw on a carnivalesque tradition that subsumes the Brazilian *carnaval*, it is not surprising that just as many have taken a particularly Brazilian turn. The characters of a number of imaginary figures, such as Zé Pereira, from carnivals of the past, are recreated and become popular motifs in the present. *Pretos-Velhos* (Old Blacks, who are among the principal *guias*, or "guides," in ecstatic trance religions such as *Umbanda*), and any number of other figures from the world of the Afro-Brazilian religious cults, are common in the world of *carnaval*. And while indigenous peoples have been driven further and further into decay and extinction, costumed *grupos de indios* (groups of Indians) have become a special focus in carnival celebrations throughout Brazil.

Marginalized and oppressed in contemporary life, in the world of *carnaval* these figures come to the center of attention. They call up a violent Brazilian past, yet they integrate it into a form derived originally from Europe. Indeed, in properly cannibalistic fashion, they almost devour that form: they ingest it, digest it, and spit it out again in what is somehow a distinctly Brazilian shape. They create a present that is clearly part of a broader carnivalesque tradition, while at the same time uniquely Brazilian—the quintessential expression of the Brazilian spirit.

The playful manipulation of sexual images dominates this world of masks and costumes. Joking clowns adopt enormous, clublike phalluses that can be used to beat upon the bodies of other merrymakers. Grotesque, diabolical, or monstrous figures combine the body parts of male and female in order to create ambiguous *andróginos* (androgynes). Men transform themselves into women, and women (though somewhat less commonly) into men. Indeed, no symbolic form dominates the symbolism of the festival as completely as transvestism.

The transvestism of the festival is anything but a single, structural phenomenon. On the contrary, it is multiple and varied. There are the comic *blocos de sujos* (groups of filthy ones), for example, whose gender-crossing is relatively balanced between male and female, and whose tone is largely comic or absurd:

> In the 1950s, 1960s, and even the 1970s, it was common for children to cross-dress and go out asking for coins. . . . The girls would put on, and put on even today, large asses, and with their faces hidden they can play (*brincar*) and say improper things to people or flirt with the guys that they are after. They liberate themselves a little more than normal. The boys put on large false breasts and let people play with their boobs and with asses made out of pillows. This transvestism starts very early. Parents help to make the costumes, and sometimes the whole family goes out together cross-dressed, or in large groups called *blocos de sujos*—which may or may not use masks, but with heavy makeup and extravagant feminine clothes. (João)

While the *blocos de sujos* often seem to focus on the mundane and ordinary—maids, housewives, and the like—in building up their comic transformations, there are also far more stylized and serious performances. Young adolescent males from the lower sectors dress as high-class whores and call themselves *piranhas*. Homosexually identified males from the more modern middle sectors choose low-cut gowns exposing their masculine chests, make use of an exaggerated makeup, and sprinkle glitter in their beards or mustaches in a carnivalesque version of what has been described in English as "gender-fuck" (Read 1980, 17–18). And most ubiquitous, the *travestis* (transvestites) who usually work the shadowy streets of almost all major Brazilian cities during daily life become absolute centers of attention with their elaborate gowns and stylized performances. What at first glance appears to be a unified symbolic inversion takes shape, upon closer inspection, then, as a set of transformations as diverse as the sexual universe more generally. Celebrating the confusion and ambiguity, but building up subjective meanings as varied as their subjects, these multiple transvestisms push and pull at the seams of any system of meanings that would seek to separate the world into two distinct, opposed, and hierarchically related categories, in order to organize the better part of collective life around this separation.

As the emphasis on transvestism obviously suggests, the sexual universe that the *carnaval* opens up is altogether different from the world of daily life. The festival creates a special time and space, opposed to this everyday life, when the silent, and sometimes perverse, pleasures that occur "within four walls" escape their boundaries and create a fully public world in which, like the private world of erotic ideology, anything is possible. The two seem to reinforce one another, each providing a kind of model for the other, and even in the cyclical passage of time, they are intimately tied together:

> The sexual rhythm of the year gets faster during the summer, principally with the arrival of *carnaval*. With the heat of the summer, people have more energy for everything. . . . Everyone tries to find the sun, and the beaches become super-full with sweaty and golden bodies. Clothes become a key for the exhibitionism and display of the body, of the gifts of nature. Everything is very semi-nude, especially in cities where there are beaches. The nights are exhilarating, and there is no place where there aren't people. They are hot nights, propitious for love, sex, freedom of the body. In the summer, nothing is a sin (*nada é pecado*), principally with the arrival of *carnaval* mixing with the summer and tropicalism of this country. Everything comes to a climax in the *carnaval*. . . . This is the key that closes the psychological summer of the Brazilians. After the *carnaval*, the sun is still there for a few months, but the interior heat and the hope don't generate so much excitement as in the summer that comes before *carnaval*. (Antônio)

Linking notions about the sensuality of *sol* (sun), *suar* (sweat), *praia* (beach), and *verão* (summer) to the practice of *sacanagem* (transgressive sexual interaction), then, the *carnaval* embodies a "tropical" vision of the world. Like the carnivals of the northern hemisphere, this *carnaval*, too, offers a vision of the future: a utopian vision of the possibilities of life in a tropical paradise, somewhere south of the equator, where the struggles, suffering, and sadness of normal human existence have been destroyed by pleasure and passion. In the *carnaval*, everything is permitted, as it would be in the best of all possible worlds. The polymorphous pleasures of erotic ideology become the norm, rather than the transgression of the established order, and the fullest possibilities of sexual life take concrete form in the play of human bodies:

> During the *carnaval* everything is permitted in terms of sex or drugs. The *carnaval* balls are, in certain places, a true orgy. Everything is permitted. You understand? There is no censorship, and the unrestrained exhibitionism and the desire to expose oneself are very common in the carnivalesque atmosphere. During this period, sex is present everywhere, and bodies, souls, and semen are left at their will, giving to everyone the freedom to do what they really desire. It is a good period for prostitution and the buyers of pleasure. Everything is sold, everything is bought, everything is given, everything is received with a lewd and inviting smile on the face. Beaches, corners, bars, bathrooms, parks, buses, trains, and other places are stages for sensuality and sex. The streets become completely given over to the beat of *samba* and the frenzy of sweaty bodies having sex. (João)

Impersonal sex between strangers who may never see one another again, sex in groups, sex in the streets or on the beach, sex in public, in full view rather than hidden within four walls—all become part and parcel of the play of *carnaval*. Sexual transactions that cross the lines of class, age, and race, lesbian and homosexual interactions, exhibitionism, and any number of other marginal pleasures become possible in a world where repression and oppression cease to exist. Playing, pressing up against other bodies (and ultimately losing one's own) in the crowd, entering the bodies of unknown partners, their faces hidden behind masks or beneath makeup—anything is possible in a world where sin ceases to exist. Freeing the imagination from the seemingly interminable struggles that are inevitably one's lot in life, it offers a better world, a world of pleasure and satisfaction, of joy and happiness. Even if these few moments of pleasure and joy must always come to an end on the morning of *Quarta-Feira de Cinzas* (Ash Wednesday), they nonetheless hold out the possibility of something better than the endless sadness of daily life. They offer *esperança* (hope), and they root it in pleasures and passions of the people as a whole.

IN THE WHEEL OF SAMBA

Carnaval in Rio de Janeiro, Recife, or Salvador is not just a somewhat more contemporary version of the traditional carnivals of Venice, Madrid, or Lisbon. It has not merely responded to, but has in fact fully integrated, a distinctly Brazilian reality into its symbolic structure. Through a kind of cannibalism that modernists of the 1920s and 1930s could not help but admire, the contemporary Brazilian *carnaval* seems to have fed upon a traditional European form in order to invest it with a particularly Brazilian content. Just as sexuality has been seen as the concrete mechanism of the racial mixture that is understood as fundamental to the formation of the Brazilian people, the *carnaval*, with its symbolism of sexuality, and its own mixture of European, Amerindian, and African cultural traits, has increasingly been offered up as the most authentic expression of the underlying ethos of Brazilian life.

That the *carnaval* should have provided fertile ground for the elaboration of both indigenous and African cultural traditions is hardly surprising. Because the festival creates a space outside of the normal social order, outside of the structures necessary for *civilização* (civilization), it takes shape as something somehow *primitivo* (primitive) and *selvagem* (savage). It is understood as a time when the most "primitive" and "savage" urges of the individual unconscious rise up and play themselves out on an elaborate stage. To many early observers, there was really little difference between the pagan excesses of *carnaval* and the excessive ceremonies of the pagans. The grotesque anthropophagous ceremonies of the native Brazilians and the orgiastic dances of the African slaves seemed to flow into and merge with the obscene celebration of the flesh during *carnaval*, and it is not unexpected that the symbolism of these "savage" performances should have been incorporated into the festival (Sebe 1986).

The symbolism of anthropophagy is especially well suited to the semantic structure of the *carnaval*. The transgression of a food taboo can easily be linked to the transgression of sexual taboos in a symbolic construct focused on devouring the flesh of another human body in order to incorporate it within one's own. As a symbol of incorporation, then, anthropophagy can be invested with layers of meaning ranging from cannibalism itself, to the act of sexual intercourse, to the mixture of races and cultures that is taken as definitive of Brazilian reality. In the persons of the *blocos de índios*, the use of masks and costumes harking back to the totemism of the native Brazilian tribes, and the altogether unruly and chaotic incorporation of "savage" imagery (ranging from the use of colored feathers and headdresses to bows and arrows), the symbolism of the *carnaval* not only overturns the order of daily life, but offers an interpretation of Brazilian reality as less modern and civilized than savage and primitive (see Sebe 1986, 48–53).

As important as this configuration focused on indigenous culture has obviously been, however, the distinctly Brazilian character of *carnaval* has been most clearly asserted in the music and dance derived from the African cultures of a slave-holding society. The *batucadas* (the rhythmic beating of percussion instruments) and *sambas* (both a style of dance and a specific type of music) that dominate the contemporary *carnaval* are interpreted in terms of their African roots, and their perceived sensuality is linked to the milieu from which they emerged. African music and dance have been seen, in turn, as closely associated secular expressions of African culture that were originally derived from the context of religious ritual, but that took on new meaning, at least in part, because of the encouragement of the slaveowners themselves, who viewed them in erotic terms and saw them as useful in increasing the size of their herds:

> The *samba* dance was introduced in Brazil by the Africans. In the slave quarters, and in their rituals, the dance began to take on great force. It was seen, even by the masters, as an erotic dance—a kind of aphrodisiac. You understand? The slaves spent their days at forced labor on the plantations. At night, they got together in circles, and with the palms of their hands and a few primitive drums began to sing and dance *samba*. The ritualization of the *mulata* woman's walk and the agile grace of the feet of the *mulato* man began to spread in Brazilian culture. From the most remote and marginalized places, it was gradually introduced into the general culture, and now it is not known as just a part of black culture, but is generalized and known worldwide. (Sérgio)

Following the freed slaves from the rural plantations to the cities, and up into the hills and *favelas* of Rio de Janeiro and Salvador, *rodas de samba* (wheels or circles of *samba*) sung and danced to the beating rhythms of the *batucada* situated themselves at the margins of Brazilian society—in the shantytowns where even the police were unwilling to venture, in the Afro-Brazilian religious cults with their perceived emphasis on witchcraft and sorcery, in the bohemian bars associated with crime and prostitution. Yet like the *sambistas* (*samba* composers or dancers) who invented them, they come down from the hills each year for *carnaval*, when the most marginal elements of Brazilian society come to the center of the social universe and create a world of fantasy and happiness.

Like the symbolism of anthropophagy, the symbolic associations of the *samba* are particularly well fitted to the world of *carnaval*. Recreating the festival in Brazilian terms, *samba* simultaneously reproduces the erotic focus of carnivalesque symbolism. In its rhythms and movements, as much as in its lyrics, it reinvents the body, freeing it (as on the plantations) from the discipline of work and opening it up to the experience of pleasure:

> The first thing that is important for the *samba*, in order for you to really dance the *samba*, is that you have to let your body go free. You have to be light, to have free movements. The second thing is to make it charming. And to get across the grace of the *samba*, you have to smile, to let out energy with your face. It's the happiness (*felicidade*) of *carnaval*. The third thing is to place the *samba* principally in the arms, in the belly, in this part here. . . . The *samba* is divided between the head, the torso, and the limbs. With the head, it's the movement that announces the *samba*. With the smile, with singing, with the music . . . You understand? With the torso, you give lascivious movements, sexual movements. With the feet, you give the rhythm and the movement of the *samba*. If you have a good foot, if you know how to move with your feet, your body will go along in the swaying movement also. . . . The rhythm, the movement that comes from the feet, fills the whole body with the shake-shake (*mexe-mexe*) of the *samba*. The belly, the ass, the thighs, the belly-button. . . . These are the most important parts of the body for the lasciviousness of the *samba*. . . . The movements are well defined with the movements of sex. (João)

Rising up from the feet and filling the entire body with life, the movement of the *samba* opens out, like the outstretched arms that are among the most characteristic gestures of the *carnaval*, to *abraçar* (embrace) the world. Reproducing the strangely controlled madness that has always been associated with the *carnaval*, but giving it a specifically Brazilian cast, *samba* frees the body from the daily constraints imposed upon it, defying sadness and suffering within the space of the festival. Like the symbolism of *carnaval* more generally, it celebrates the flesh. It focuses on the sensuality of the body. It offers a vision of the world given over to the pleasure and passion, joy and ecstasy.

The role of *samba* in the *carnaval* also plays into the wider system of inversions that bring the most marginalized sectors of Brazilian society to the center of the festive world. Just as *samba* descends from the *favelas*, so too do the *sambistas*—the poorest (and darkest) segments of urban society, whose struggles and suffering in an oppressive economic and social system cannot be stated strongly enough, become the focus of the *carnaval:*

> In the *carnaval*, the poorest *sambista* goes out to play (*brincar*) costumed (*fantasiado*) as a king of France or Portugal. In daily life he has no importance within the society. But on the avenue, he's the professor. (Sérgio)

If the poor and the powerless can become kings and queens, however, this carnivalesque inversion is hardly the only way in which the *sambista* comes down from the hills in order to take center stage during the festival. The symbolism of *carnaval* works as much through intensification as through inversion, and it is perhaps in the figures of the *malandro* (translated, at best, as a "rogue" or a "scoundrel") and the *mulata* (a dark-skinned, mulatto woman) that the marginalized reality of the *favela* is most clearly enacted in carnivalesque performance.

Treated normally as a "bad element," a dangerous good-for-nothing who is likely to be a criminal, a racketeer, or a thief, in the carnivalization of the world the *malandro* becomes a kind of culture hero—a trickster, really, known for his ability to circumvent the rules and regulations of the established order:

> The *malandro* always likes to "put something over on" or "rob" other people. He's a man who is looking for freedom—freedom of expression and financial freedom . . . Society labels him as an assailant or a thief. It treats being a *malandro* as if it were like being a bum, an easy and dangerous life. . . . (Jorge)

If it is the mark of the *malandro* that he is able to find a way around the structures of authority, it is no less clear that he lives not for hard work or struggle, but for pleasure and sensuality:

> The *malandro* is a poet, an artist of life. Most times, he doesn't like to work. He waits for everything to fall from the sky. He lives for pleasure, for *sacanagem, carnaval*, all these things. (José)

Like the *malandro*, the *mulata* is given a key role in the symbolic universe of the *carnaval*. Defined, ever since the days of slavery (as the writings of Gilberto Freyre made so evident), as an erotic ideal in Brazilian culture, the *mulata* is perceived as the perfect embodiment of the heat and sensuality of the tropics (see Sant'Anna 1984).

> The *mulata* is the black goddess of Brazilian culture. She is a symbol of sexuality and fertility, and is known as one of the most beautiful women in the world. She possesses movements and gestures that no other kind of woman possesses. Like the way she walks, talks, smiles, makes love. . . . Her voluptuous way of moving her body is imitated by many, but only the *mulata* has such grace in moving her behind. (João)

Yet if the *mulata* appears as an ideal of female attraction, it is an ideal that exists within the paradoxes of Brazilian life, within the double standard of a patriarchal tradition developed in a slaveholding society. Perhaps best captured in a proverb cited by Freyre, the *mulata* has been held up as a sexual, rather than social ideal: *Branca para casar, mulata para foder, negra para trabalhar* (White woman for marrying, *mulata* woman for fucking, black woman for working) (Freyre 1956). In the most sensual of celebrations, however, the *mulata*, perhaps even more forcefully than the *malandro*, comes to the center of attention:

> The *mulata* is known as a sexual symbol of the *carnaval*. It's the *mulata* who knows how to stir things up, who knows how to *samba* and play. She is the symbol of the attractive woman, the Brazilian woman. (Wilson)

In the elaborate theater of the *carnaval*, the *mulata* thus emerges as the most concrete symbol of a much broader ethos. Embodying an entire ideology, she becomes a representation of Brazil itself—of the Brazilian people, formed from the mixture of three races and cultures, somehow marginal and distant (beneath the equator) from the world's great centers of wealth and power, yet possessing a seductive charm that sets them apart from any other people anywhere on the face of the earth.

If much of the sexual symbolism of *carnaval* seems to undercut the certainty of established classifications, relativizing and destroying them through grotesque combinations or elaborate transvestisms, then in a strange way this world of *samba* that has been integrated into the structure of Brazilian *carnaval* seems to display them in an intensified or exaggerated form. *Samba* itself, at least in its most popular manifestations, is created within a fundamentally male space: the popular bars where the predominantly male composers spend their free time, and where women who wish to avoid being labeled as *putas* or *piranhas* are unlikely to venture. Even the language, the poetry, of *samba* is a kind of male discourse, which often focuses on the suffering and injustice imposed, it is claimed, upon men by women.

Even here, however, as everywhere in the world of *carnaval*, things are not always all that they seem to be—or, perhaps more accurately, things are often *more* than they seem to be. If the symbolism of the *samba* displays the hierarchy of gender in particularly stark form, it simultaneously calls into question the neatly ordered structures of bourgeois sexual morality. It offers up a sexuality that is at once primitive, savage, and tropical. Situating itself within a structure of fantasies that is perhaps as old as the first European contact with the non-European world, it plays on a whole set of white images about black sexuality and sensuality. Transforming these images into a vision of a uniquely Brazilian sexuality—a vision built up in the rhythms and movements of *samba*, the trickery and cunning of *malandragem*, and the voluptuous pleasures of the *mulata*—this configuration identifies itself as somehow more "authentic" or "true" to the tropical nature of Brazilian reality, and certainly as more "alive," than the pale conformity of the bourgeois order could ever be. If it reproduces in exaggerated form certain oppressive structures from the world of normal daily life, it simultaneously uses these structures to overthrow others in the kind of constant, playful, sarcastic movement characteristic of a world that has been *carnavalizado* (carnivalized). From the point of view of the elite, it is here that both its fascination and danger lie.

THE GREATEST SHOW ON EARTH

For as long as there has been a historical record of the festival, it has been marked by discord and debate. At the same time that the transgressive values of the *carnaval* have been loudly proclaimed in the streets, they have been constantly criticized by the voices of restraint and order. Like the myths of origin that tell of a licentious past, an atmosphere of "sexual intoxication" resulting in the mixture of distinct races, and ultimately, the formation of the Brazilian people, the sometimes violent and always sensual performances of the *carnaval* have been met with a profound ambivalence (see Turner 1983). It has been the object of extensive criticism as well as outright repression. Over the course of more than a century, there has been an ongoing effort (particularly in Rio de Janeiro, where the festival has been most visible to the wider world) to domesticate the most savage expressions of the carnivalesque tradition, to find a way of organizing its disorder. Ironically, this process has contributed to the attention that has been focused on the festival, to its gradual development as a symbol for an even larger reality.

From the early colonial period on, the celebration of *carnaval* in Brazil was marked by a sharp dichotomy that has continued on up to the present: a distinction between the *carnaval da rua* (*carnaval* in the street) and the *carnaval do salão* (*carnaval* in the large hall or ballroom). This opposition between *rua* and *salão*, in turn, has been translated into any number of other oppositions between the popular classes and the elite, between the influences of African or Amerindian cultures and the predominance of European patterns, and so on. The *carnaval da rua*, perhaps most frequently described as the *entrudo*, was characterized by its unruly and rebellious nature, its violence and dirtiness, as the *foliõs* pushed, shoved, and pelted one another with water, mud, urine, and other unidentified substances. It was the *carnaval* of the poor, which meant that its participants were overwhelmingly black—the so-called savage, primitive, African elements in Brazilian society. The *carnaval do salão*, by contrast, was a celebration of the white elite, regulated by invitations or paid admission. Held most often in large theaters, the elaborate *bailes* (balls) were modeled on Portuguese and Italian celebrations and characterized by their elaborate costumes and disguises (see Da Matta 1978; Eneida 1958; Sebe 1986).

By the middle of the nineteenth century, the celebration of the *entrudo* had become the object of considerable concern on the part of the elite, and by 1853, an edict had been issued banning the *entrudo* as a carnivalesque game. While a succession of similar mandates issued over the course of the next fifty years would never completely succeed in doing away with the *entrudo*, the battle lines had clearly been drawn, and an attempt to civilize the *carnaval* had begun. Gradually, this process took shape through the formation of somewhat more organized groups, derived from different classes and communities that came together to celebrate the festival. Beginning in the 1850s, for example, members of the rising middle classes came together to form what were known as *Grandes Sociedades* (Great Societies) which paraded through the streets of the city in elaborate costumes, marching to the music of brass bands and pulling floats that often focused on political issues of the day, as well as organizing balls for the participation of their members. The poorer sectors, in turn, adapted this notion to the more scattered reality of the traditional *entrudo*, joining in somewhat less ordered groups known as *cordões* (cordons), *ranchos* (literally, "strolling persons"), and *blocos* (blocks). Composed largely of members of the working class or the petit-bourgeoisie, the *cordões* and the *ranchos*, like the Great Societies, paraded in costume throughout the city, marching to the music of bands and choruses. The *blocos* were made up of the poorest segments of the population, and had little formal structure aside from the spontaneous grouping of the festival, when participants would dress up in old clothes and comic hats in order to parade about as Zé Pereiras or comic clowns (Eneida 1958; Sebe 1986).

Given the significant presence of poor blacks and mulattos, it was principally in the *blocos* that the influence of *samba* was first felt during the 1920s and 1930s. The earliest samba schools arose out of a number of the larger, better organized *blocos* during the twenties and were closely linked to specific neighborhoods, principally *favelas*, that existed on the margins of Brazilian society. As highly visible organizations of poor blacks—and, hence, in the eyes of the elite, of *malandros, vagabundos* (vagrants or vagabonds), and *marginais* (marginals)—the same schools were subject, especially during this early period, to more than a small amount of harassment on the part of the police, and were themselves extremely concerned with projecting an image that would be respected and accepted by the elite sectors of the society. Their marginal position within society as a whole led to an ongoing struggle over just how they would be incorporated not only within the festival, but within the world of normal daily life.

The position of the samba schools changed radically, however, in the 1930s, with the rise of populist politics and the emergence of Getulio Vargas as president of Brazil. In seeking to recruit support among the lower sectors—and thus to incorporate them into the existing political structure—populist politicians began to turn significant attention to the schools and to offer public funding for their activities. By 1934, the *União Geral de Escolas de Samba* (General Union of Samba Schools) had been formed and had begun, with the blessing of the government of Rio de Janeiro, to sponsor a *carnaval* parade of up to thirty different schools. City authorities, newspapers, and the police had all become involved in planning and organizing the *desfile* (parade or review), and an increasingly elaborate set of rules and regulations had been invented in order to organize a competition between the schools. The most notable requirement was the stipulation that the *enredos* (plots) of the *sambas* presented by the schools were to be based upon "national motifs"—on the events or personalities of Brazilian history. At the same point that elite writers such as Gilberto Freyre were turning to history in order to create myths of origin, the participants in *carnaval* were being pushed to turn to history in order to create ritual, in order to present a reading of the Brazilian past to the Brazilians in the present. The elaborate performances of the samba schools would become a way of representing the past—again, not necessarily in terms of any kind of empirical, historical understanding, but along the lines of a particular ideology, a cultural construction.

By the 1950s and 1960s, the samba schools had achieved a remarkable degree of legitimacy within the wider society. The *sambistas* had come down from the hills to perform at the very heart of the *carnaval* in Rio de Janeiro—and like the *carnaval* in Rio more generally, had been held up to Brazil as a whole as a kind of model for the performance of the festival. Indeed, even the membership of the schools had been transformed. While they continued to be based in predominantly poor black neighborhoods, they had been subject to what has been described as an "invasion" on the part of the predominantly white middle and upper classes:

> From the 1960s on, the samba schools became fashionable for every type of social class. They weren't just made up of only blacks and poor people anymore, but of everyone who was attracted by the *batuques* of *agogos* (a percussion instrument consisting of two different sized bells that are hit with a stick), *tambores chocalhos* (rattling gourd percussion instruments), and every type of instrument that awakens in the hearts and minds of the Brazilian the contagious rhythm of the carnivalesque plots. (José)

This invasion of the schools by the middle and upper classes has been interpreted in different ways. It has been seen as a sign of the incorporation of the marginal *sambista* into the structure of the global society, as evidence of the hegemonic appropriation of a popular form of black expression by the white elite, and as a product of the inclusion and *communitas* of the *carnaval* itself. Whatever else it may be, however (and it is all of these things), it is vivid evidence of the extent to which the world of *samba* has come to the center of the carnivalesque world while the festival itself has become a massive spectacle—what by 1965 could be described, without exaggeration, as *o maior espetáculo popular do mundo* (the largest popular spectacle in the world) or *o maior show da terra* (the greatest show on earth) (see Sebe 1986, 72–73).

As befits the greatest show on earth, the parade of the samba schools has moved to the central avenues of downtown Rio—indeed, since the early 1980s, a whole avenue has been set aside for it, and a huge concrete structure known popularly as the *Sambódromo* (Sambadrome) has been constructed as a permanent replacement for the temporary bleachers of the past. The competition between the schools has been divided into three levels: *Grupo I*, the *superdesfile* (superparade) of the largest schools, parading with anywhere from 2,000 to 3,500 members, *Grupo II*, of slightly smaller, intermediate schools; and *Grupo II*, made up of the smallest schools.

Placing thousands of performers on the avenue, each school arranges its component parts in slightly different ways, depending upon the demands of its particular theme. Yet even this variation takes place within an overall structure that has itself become an accepted tradition throughout Brazil. The parade of the samba schools has not only become central to the shape of the festival in Rio but has also become largely synonymous with Brazilian *carnaval* more generally—a quintessential expression of everything that the *carnaval* involves and, certainly, among the most widely popular parts of the festival. Ordered and controlled by the state, it has also replaced the frightening chaos of carnivalesque play with what is, in its own way, a highly disciplined alternative. However, it has hardly succeeded in silencing the all-encompassing sensuality that is so fundamental to the whole meaning of the festival. It would be more accurate to suggest that the parade, as well as the samba schools more generally, has managed to incorporate the whole carnivalesque system of meanings into its own structure at the same time that it has incorporated itself into the wider structure of the *carnaval*.

Focusing on the world of *samba*, with all of its connotations of savagery, poverty, and marginality, yet recreating this world as a fantastic spectacle of color and movement, the parade creates a kind of utopian illusion:

> The parade of the samba schools is called the greatest show on earth. The beauty of the colors of the costumes, accompanied by the steps of the *samba* as well as the plot, gives an incredible beauty. The sequins, precious and semi-precious stones, satins, silks, and purpurins fluttering in plumes. . . . It is a parade of great happiness and incredible energy. It is one of the marvels of the world. (Oscar)

This world is as far from the abject poverty of the *favelas* as is imaginable. And without ever losing sight of the often oppressive, exploitative bureaucratization and commercialization of the festival, it is still a world in which the experience of oppression and exploitation is swept away in a sense of freedom—a world in which the masses are healthy and energetic, well fed and well informed.

Linking the passion of the carnivalesque present to the dream of liberty in the future, this utopian vision incorporates, as well, the whole sexual symbolism of the *carnaval*. The sexual imagery of the festival is most vividly displayed in the world of plumes and papier-mâché. As in less organized forms of carnivalesque play—in fact, all the more forcefully because of its highly organized nature—the schools focus on sexuality and sensuality as intimately linked to the deepest meaning of the festival:

> The parade has become a type of stage for sensuality, with its floats and its different sections in their tropical, sensual frenzy. . . . The bodies are for the most part semi-nude, showing the energy of hot, happy, virile bodies. . . . The couples of *passistas* or *sambistas* intertwine with their legs and with movements of their buttocks in a totally sensual form. The in and out movements of their legs, bellies, sexes, and buttocks give the connotation of an eternal sexual climax. (José)

The symbolism of *carnaval* has responded most clearly (even if in a particularly stylized way) to the changing shape of the Brazilian sexual universe through the parade of the schools. Over the course of the past decade, for example, the increasingly open expression of female sexuality has been pushed, each year, to an extreme in the performances of the schools:

> Nowadays, there are enormous floats with dozens of beautiful women partially or, many times, totally naked. Wearing only plumes on their heads to cover up from what the most extreme might say, they would otherwise be totally nude. Strong, young, muscular men, with small loincloths, are placed on these floats also. The demonstration of their sexual attributes, as much of the man as of the woman, has been one of the great attractions of the parade of the samba schools. (Francisco)

As well as women, the most marginalized groups of transvestites and homosexuals have come more to the center of carnivalesque performance in the samba schools, and they can customarily be found not only in the *alas* but also among the most important *destaques* ("eminences," specific individuals who stand out from the crowd because of their elaborate costumes) in even the most traditional schools:

> Transvestism and homosexuality have been important parts of the samba schools. There are special floats for male homosexual *destaques* with their luxurious and extremely feminine costumes. They dress up as Gal Costa or Maria Bethania, or other famous figures from pop music or television. The number of gay groups in the parade has increased every year. They develop all sorts of different types, from the most sophisticated to the most grotesque. They stuff their costumes with large asses, hips, breasts, and bellies. Fruits and vegetables are used often as well. . . . Squash, pears, oranges, watermelons, cucumbers, or the traditional manioc root as a phallic symbol . . . the manioc root is used a lot for the joke of the carnivalesque prick. The carrot and the banana also. You're going to see this a lot with the *destaques* on the floats during *carnaval*. (João)

Sexual meanings have been fundamental to the highly ordered pageantry of the schools. Indeed, in the drama and spectacle of the parade, as much as in other forms of carnivalesque play, sexual imagery has not only responded to changes taking place in the everyday world but has also pushed the structures and meanings of daily life beyond their limits, incorporating even the most marginal elements of the Brazilian sexual universe into the heart of the carnivalized world.

The impact of this presentation of the sexual universe has been magnified by the attention the schools have received. Broadcast live to every region of the nation, the parade characterizes the festival for the widest possible public. Marketed, both at home and abroad, as the greatest show on earth, the parade has become synonymous with the *carnaval* as a whole. Undercutting the sobriety of daily life in a world of motion, music, and color, this remarkable pageant is the greatest illusion of all. Yet in the reality of fantasy that it creates, it pushes up against the repressive limits that structure the world of convention. It plays with them and stretches them. Like every form of carnivalesque play, it offers an alternative vision of life as it might be rather than as it is. As much as the more haphazard chaos that it was originally designed to replace, the organized chaos of the parade shapes and defines the nature of sexual life in contemporary Brazil. Ironically, in so doing, it has shaped and defined the nature of Brazil itself.

CARNAVAL AS METAPHOR

The vision of *carnaval* is quite clearly utopian—a model of the world as it might be rather than as it is. It is also, of course, an illusion, and no matter how fully they throw themselves into its peculiar reality, its participants never completely lose sight of its fleeting quality:

> Everyone knows that *carnaval* is an illusion created to forget about day-to-day life in such difficult times. There are songs that refer to the *carnaval* as "smoke," "wind," "light," or "heat." There is a song that says "for everything comes to an end on Ash Wednesday." Another highlights love: "Love that takes place in the *carnaval* disappears in smoke." They are three days of fun and madness, until Wednesday, when everything begins again. (Maria)

Yet if the ephemeral, imaginary character of the *carnaval* is not lost on the men and women who live it each year, neither is its power to transform experience, and even, perhaps, to change the world around it:

> In spite of being an illusion, the *carnaval* still possesses great psychological power for the Brazilian. They say that liberty went to live in some other place. . . . So *carnaval* tries to search for liberty. It is a utopia that in reality is real and not just a dream. Within this surrealism of the *carnaval*, it is possible to imagine a better world, a world that is really made up of true fantasies and freedom. (Antonio)

Within the space of the festival, it becomes possible not only to transgress the restrictions of daily life, but to push the limits, to reinvent the possibilities, of that wider social and cultural universe. Built, perhaps, on shifting sand, but rebuilt each year again, this often contradictory capacity for transformation, for the continued search for freedom and happiness, lies at the heart of the whole carnivalesque fantasy. It is central to the meaning of the *carnaval* within Brazilian culture.

Because of its internal contradictions, one can read this symbolic configuration in any number of different ways. For example, it is impossible to ignore the extent to which the symbolic structures of the festival exaggerate the most oppressive structures of the real world—male fantasies and desires continue to define a particular vision of female sexuality, and, for that matter, bourgeois morality continues to organize the expression of what is perceived to be a more "savage" or "primitive" sensuality:

> There are various interpretations—from sexism to the sin of the flesh. Because everything is permitted in these days, there are controversial ideas about what is called "morality" and "proper conduct." There are certain intellectuals, or false-intellectuals, that talk about the "opium of the people." Others deplore the worship of high luxury or of carnality. But, in reality, these people are a pretentious minority. For the majority of Brazilians, playing (*brincar*) the *carnaval* is an authentic expression of the people (*povo*). Playing the *carnaval* is to feel free. It is to feel extremely Brazilian. (Jorge)

Thus it is also impossible to ignore the degree to which carnivalesque imagery destroys conventional assumptions, offering women as well as men, the *povo* as well as the bourgeoisie, the opportunity to manipulate the webs of meaning and the systems of power in which they find themselves enmeshed, to create a sense of themselves as a whole, an identity as a people. What is most striking about the *carnaval* is its ability to encode and articulate so many different, often contradictory, meanings and thus to open itself up to so many divergent interpretations.

Because of this ability to incorporate contradictory interpretations within a single whole, the *carnaval* has offered a fundamentally popular counterpart to the myths of origin of elite writers such as Paulo Prado and Gilberto Freyre, with their emphasis on the formation of the Brazilian people through the process of racial mixture. With all of its chaos and confusion, its contradictions and its juxtapositions, its exaggerated sexuality and its transgressive laughter, the *carnaval* stands as an ironic answer to the search for a sense of identity that has troubled Brazilian thinking for more than a century. As much as the stories that Brazilians have told themselves about their own formation as a people, it has offered its own reading of Brazilian reality—a reading focused, like the myths of origin, on the sensual nature of Brazilian life, on the chaotic mixture of races and cultures that has given rise to a new world in the tropics. While the elite myths of origin have focused on the past as a way of giving meaning to the present, however, the more popular performances of the *carnaval* have themselves cannibalized this past not simply as a way of reinventing the present, but as a means of inventing a future. The symbolic system that they create is ultimately less closed than open, and the identity that they suggest, less singular than plural—like the *carnaval* itself, diverse and multiple, based not so much on the fusion of opposites as on the juxtaposition of differences.

In its invention of another (more fundamentally popular) reading of Brazilian reality as still in the process of becoming, the *carnaval* has emerged as far more than a secular ritual marking out the cycle of the year. It has become a metaphor for Brazil itself—or at the very least, for those qualities that are taken as most essentially Brazilian, as the truest expression of Brazilianness. No less than the myths of origin, it has become a story that Brazilians tell themselves about themselves (about their past, certainly, but also about their future). It is a story that they use as yet another frame of reference that allows them to manipulate, rearrange, and even reinvent the contours of their own sexual universe. It suggests, to Brazilians and outsiders alike, that here beneath the equator life might best be understood and appreciated as a work in progress, that reality is complex and multiple, and that nothing is ever quite what it appears to be. Even what appears the most absolute can always be transformed, it would seem, in a world where sin ceases to exist and anything is possible.

NOTE

For a complete and fully-annotated version of this essay, see chapter six of the author's Bodies, Pleasures, and Passions: Sexual Culture in Contemporary Brazil (Boston: Beacon, 1991), 136–164. Copyright and permissions are held by the author.

BIBLIOGRAPHY

Bakhtin, Mikhail. 1968. *Rabelais and His World*. Cambridge, Mass.: MIT Press.

Barlaeus, Gaspar. 1980. *História dos Feitos Recentemente Praticados durante Oito Anos no Brasil*. Recife: Fundação de Cultura Cidade do Recife.

Baroja, Julio Caro. 1979. *El Carnaval: Analisis Historico-Cultural*. Madrid: Taurus Ediciones.

Boxer, C. R. 1957. *The Dutch in Brazil, 1624–1654*. Oxford: Clarendon Press.

Burke, Peter. 1978. *Popular Culture in Early Modern Europe*. New York: Harper and Row.

Da Matta, Roberto. 1978. *Carnavais, Malandros, e Heróis: Para uma Sociologia do Dilema Brasileiro*. Rio de Janeiro: Zahar Editores.

Davis, Natalie Zemon. 1975. *Society and Culture in Early Modern France*. Stanford, CA: Stanford University Press.

Eneida. 1958. *História do Carnaval Caroica*. Rio de Janeiro: Editora Civilização Brasileira.

Freyre, Gilberto. 1956. *The Masters and the Slaves: A Study in the Development of Brazilian Civilization*. New York: Alfred A. Knopf.

Gaignebet, Claude, and Marie-Claude Florentin. 1974. *Le Carnaval: Essais de Mythologie Populaire*. Paris: Payot.

Ivo, Lêdo. 1981. *Snakes' Nest*. New York: New Directions Books.

Ladurie, Emmanuel Le Roy. 1979. *Carnival in Romans*. New York: Braziller.

Leach, Edmund. 1961. *Rethinking Anthropology*. London: Athlone.

Leach, Maria, ed. 1972. *Funk and Wagnall's Standard Dictionary of Folklore, Mythology, and Legend*. New York: Funk and Wagnall's.

Read, Kenneth E. 1980. *Other Voices: The Style of a Male Homosexual Tavern*. Novato, CA: Chandler and Sharp.

Scheper-Hughes, Nancy. 1988. "The Madness of Hunger: Sickness, Delirium, and Human Needs." *Culture, Medicine, and Psychiatry* 12(4): 1–30.

Sebe, José Carlos. 1986. *Carnaval, Carnavais*. São Paulo: Editora Ática.

Turner, Victor. 1969. *The Ritual Process: Structure and Anti-Structure*. Chicago: University of Chicago Press.

———. 1983. "Carnaval in Rio: Dionysian Drama in an Industrializing Society." In *The Celebration of Society: Perspectives on Contemporary Cultural Performance*, ed. Frank E. Manning, 103–24. Bowling Green, OH: Bowling Green University Popular Press.

25   Sisters and Queers

The Decentering of Lesbian Feminism

Arlene Stein

Recently, a forty-four-year-old mother of two boys told me that "in the old days," the 1970s, she could go to a particular place—a cafe or women's center, for example—to find the lesbian community in her medium-sized town. But by the late 1980s, when she broke up with a long-time lover, she went out searching again for that community and couldn't find it. Another woman I knew expressed fears about the number of lesbian friends she had lost to heterosexual conversions, having become convinced that more and more women were forsaking their lesbianism in exchange for what she saw as the greater public respectability afforded by living with men.

Lesbian feminism emerged out of the most radical sectors of the women's movement in the early 1970s. Young women who "came out through feminism," as the saying went, attempted to broaden the definition of lesbianism, to transform it from a medical condition or, at best, a sexual "preference" into a collective identity that transcended rampant individualism and its excesses as well as compulsory gender and sex roles. It was a movement that spawned the most vibrant and visible lesbian culture that had ever existed in this country.

But by the mid-1980s, the vision of a Lesbian Nation that would stand apart from the dominant culture as a sort of haven in a heartless (male/heterosexual) world, began to appear ever more distant. In contrast to the previous decade, lesbian culture and community began to seem placeless. This complaint was common, particularly among women who came of age in the 1970s, when becoming a lesbian meant coming into a community committed to some shared values. Philosopher Janice Raymond sounded the call of alarm in a women's studies journal in 1989:

Arlene Stein teaches sociology at the University of Oregon. Her recent research analyzes shifts in lesbian identity, consciousness, and culture from the 1970s to the present. The anthology *Sisters, Sexperts, Queers: Beyond the Lesbian Nation* (Plume 1993) was a Lambda Literary Award nominee. The essay included in this volume is adapted from the author's book, *Sex and Sensibility: Stories of a Lesbian Generation* (California, 1997).

Alison Bechdel has been studiously chronicling the vagaries of Lesbian Nation since 1983. Her comic strip runs in over fifty queer and alternative papers from Frisco to Halifax, and she has six *Dykes to Watch Out For* collections in print, all published by Firebrand Books. She lives in Vermont.

We used to talk a lot about lesbianism as a political movement—back in the old days when lesbian-ism and feminism went together, and one heard the phrase lesbian feminism. Today we hear more about lesbian sadomasochism, lesbians having babies and everything lesbians need to know about sex.[1]

As she and others explained it, the 1980s and 1990s brought a retrenchment from the radical visions of the previous decade. A triumphant conservatism had shattered previously cohesive les-bian communities.

While many of these assertions are unquestionably true, the death-of-community scenario could not explain the apparent paradox that by 1990, in many urban centers, lesbian influence was in some respects nowhere *and* everywhere. In 1991, the *San Francisco Examiner* reported on the closing of the last lesbian bar in that city. How strange, the columnist noted, that "more les-bians than ever live in San Francisco but that the last lesbian bar was set to close." Bemoaning the loss of a "home base" for lesbians, the former owner of the bar said: "It's a victim of the lesbian community becoming more diverse. There is an absence of a lesbian community in the presence of a million lesbians."[2]

Reflecting this more decentered sense of community, today's lesbian "movement," if one can call it that, consists of a series of projects, often wildly disparate in approach, many of which incorporate radical and progressive elements. If the corner bar was once the only place in town, by 1990 in cities across the country there were lesbian parenting groups, support groups for women with cancer and other life-threatening diseases, new and often graphic sexual literature for lesbians, organizations for lesbian "career women" and lesbians of color, and mixed organi-zations where out lesbians played visible roles. What is new, I suggest, is the lack of any funda-mental hegemonic logic or center to these projects.[3]

The once clear connection between lesbianism and feminism, in which the former was assumed to grow naturally out of the latter, is not all that clear today. Gone is the ideal of a cul-turally and ideologically unified Lesbian Nation. A series of challenges, largely from within les-bian communities themselves, have shaken many of the ordering principles of lesbian feminism. In the following, I want to explain this process of decentering. What does it mean? Why did it occur? And what might it tell us about the trajectory of identity-based movements?[4]

IDENTITIES AND MOVEMENTS

All movements engage identities, but in recent years "identity" has become a key term, signify-ing the sense in which the goal of movements is not only to mobilize identities toward some

other end, but also to act upon collective identities themselves. In the 1960s and 1970s, in response to the widespread perception of postwar social conformity, "new" social moments politicized many people's concerns with autonomy and subjective identity, arguing for notions of political activity that challenged previously clear-cut distinctions between private and public, personal and political.

Lesbian feminism, and the women's liberation movement in general, drew heavily upon the images and symbols of Black Power and shared its commitment to authenticity, redefining and affirming the self, and achieving individuality via group identification. But when we think of social movements, typically we assume that the formation of such collective identities is relatively unproblematic, that they simply reflect "essential" differences among persons that exist prior to mobilization. We refer, for example, to a supposedly unified subject such as the "women's" moment, search for signs of collectivization and unity, and downplay evidence of discontinuities and ruptures.

Instead of assuming that collective identities simply reflect differences among persons that exist prior to mobilization, we need, I think, to look closely at the process by which movements remake identities. For it is through the process of mobilization that a sense of "group-ness" is constructed, and through which individual identities are reshaped.[5] Accordingly, I want to re-read the history of lesbian feminism as a series of identity reconstructions that are partial and strategic.

A social movement organized around sexuality may seem a peculiar site for such an examination, since sexual desires and behaviors tend to be viewed as presocial and unchanging. Over the past two decades, however, a host of scholars have argued against such assumptions, claiming, for example, that homosexuality is socially constructed, "situational, influenced and given meaning and character by its location in time and social space."[6]

Lesbian feminists took this constructionist critique very seriously. Indeed, they literally tried to remake lesbian life in this country by bringing together disaffected members of the homophile, gay liberation, and feminist movements, as well as unaffiliated women, to form autonomous lesbian organizations that would be part of the larger struggle for social and sexual freedom. Yet in the end, I will argue, the movement failed to see the constructed, indeed fragile, nature of its own collective self-concepts.

SMASHING THE CATEGORIES

To my suggestion that lesbianism is becoming decentered, one could reply that the lesbian-feminist movement, consisting of hundreds of semi-autonomous, small-scale efforts nationwide, was never centered. However, while it was never unified, it did have a hegemonic project. It was, first,

an effort to reconstruct the category "lesbian," to wrest it from the definitions of the medical experts and broaden its meaning. It was, second, an attempt to forge a stable collective identity around that category and to develop institutions that would nurture that identity. And third, it sought to use those institutions as a base for the contestation of the dominant sex/gender system.

The medical model of homosexuality, dominant for most of the twentieth century, situated sexual object choice outside of society, declaring it fixed at birth or in early childhood, and deemed it an intractable property of the individual. The "old gay" prefeminist world, a series of semisecret sub-

cultures located primarily in urban areas, formed in relation to the hegemonic belief that heterosexuality was natural and homosexuality an aberration. But for 1970s "new lesbians," the prefeminist world and the conviction that lesbians were failed women was no longer tenable or tolerable.
In place of the belief in a lesbian essence or fixed minority identity signified by an inversion of
gender, long synonymous with the image of lesbianism in the popular imagination, they substi-
tuted the universal possibility of "woman-identified" behavior.[7] As a popular saying went, "feminism is the theory, lesbianism is the practice."

In critic Eve Sedgwick's words, we see the "re-visioning, in female terms, of same-sex desire"

> as being at the very definitional center of each gender, rather than occupying a cross-gender or limi-
> nal position between them. Thus women who loved women were seen as more female . . . than those
> whose desire crossed boundaries of gender. The axis of sexuality, in this view, was not only highly
> coextensive with the axis of gender but expressive of its most heightened essence.[8]

Through its encounter with feminism, lesbianism straddled what Sedgwick has called "minori-
tizing" and "universalizing" strategies, between fixing lesbians as a stable minority group and
seeking to liberate the "lesbian" in every woman. Feminism provided the ideological glue that
wedded these two sometimes contradictory impulses.

The movement could not have emerged without the second-wave feminist insight that gender
roles are socially constructed, or without the gay liberationist application of that insight to sexuality. If the "exchange of women"—compulsory heterosexuality—was the bedrock of the
sex/gender system, as Gayle Rubin and others argued, then women who made lives with other
women were subverting the dominant order.[9] Jill Johnston and others declared that a "conspiracy
of silence" insured that for most women "identity was presumed to be heterosexual unless proven
otherwise. . . . There was no lesbian identity. There was lesbian activity." Expressing the feelings
of many middle-class women of her generation, Johnston wrote in 1973:

> For most of us the chasm between social validation and private needs was so wide and deep that the
> society overwhelmed us for any number of significant individual reasons. . . . We were all
> heterosexually identified and that's the way we thought of ourselves, even of course when doing
> otherwise.[10]

If homophobia on the part of heterosexual feminists and in society at large deterred many
women from claiming a lesbian identity, collapsing the distinction between identification and

desire minimized stigma and broadened the definition of lesbianism, transforming it into "female bonding," a more inclusive category, with which a larger number of middle-class women could identify. Indeed, there was historical precedent for this vision in the "passionate friendships" common among women of the eighteenth and nineteenth centuries.[11]

Lesbianism represented a sense of connectedness based on mutuality and similarity rather than difference. Ultimately, it was more than simply a matter of sex, poet Judy Grahn declared: "Men who are obsessed with sex are convinced that lesbians are obsessed with sex. Actually, like other women, lesbians are obsessed with love and fidelity."[12] The new, broadened definition of lesbianism resonated with many women who had long experienced their sexuality in relational rather than simply erotic terms, and who considered sexuality a relatively nonsalient aspect of identity and an insufficient basis upon which to organize a mass movement.

Centering lesbianism upon female relationality and identification, these "new lesbians" challenged medicalized conceptions that focused upon gender-inversion and masculinized sexual desire. They blurred the boundary between gay and straight women and transformed lesbianism into a normative identity that over time came to have as much—and sometimes more—to do with life-style preferences (such as choice of dress or leisure pursuits) and ideological proclivities (anticonsumerist, countercultural identifications) as with sexual desires or practices.

This shift in meaning enabled many women who had never considered the possibility of claiming a lesbian lifestyle to leave their husbands and boyfriends—some for political reasons, others in expression of deeply rooted desires, many for both. It allowed many of those who lived primarily closeted lives to come out and declare their lesbianism openly. Never before had so much social space opened up so quickly to middle-class women who dared to defy deeply held social norms about their proper sexual place. As a result, the group of women who called themselves lesbians became increasingly heterogeneous, at least in terms of sexuality.

REMAKING THE SELF

Historically, there have always been women who have had sexual/romantic relationships with other women but have not assumed the label "lesbian." There have also been women whose actual sexual desires and behaviors don't fit the common social definition of lesbian—women, for example, who identify as lesbian but who are bisexual in orientation and/or practice. There are many possible configurations of the relationship between desire, practice, and identity—many more such configurations than there are social categories to describe them.

Yet popular understandings of lesbianism assume a clear-cut relationship between sexual orientation/behavior and sexual identity. Lesbians are assumed to be women who are attracted

exclusively to other women and who claim an identity on the basis of that attraction. But for many women the relation between sexual orientation, sexual identity, and sexual practice is far from stable or uncomplicated.

Moreover, as I have suggested, such definitions change over time. Particularly before the advent of the lesbian-feminist movement, these definitions were situated primarily within the framework of medical expertise, which fixed lesbianism as a "condition" and made it synonymous with cross-gender, or mannish, attributes. It meant that a woman who took on a lesbian identity needed to overcome extreme social disapproval and formulate a favorable sense of herself, which included a "deviant" sexuality.[13] Those who took on this identity during the pre-Stonewall era were more apt to be women who had never developed stable identities as heterosexuals.

Often these women either had never had significant sexual and emotional relationships with men, or they had related to men only in an effort to hide or deny their lesbianism. One such women described her coming out in the following terms:

> I fell in love with a woman when I was about fifteen or sixteen. I don't know whether I used the term lesbian then; I knew that I loved women, and that was where I was and where I wanted to be. I didn't fall in love with men.[14]

In sociologist Barbara Ponse's terminology, she would be considered a "primary" lesbian—someone who identified homosexual feelings in herself before she understood their social significance, who did so at a relatively early age, and who experienced homosexuality less as a choice than as a compulsion. If the "old gay" world was comprised largely of women for whom lesbianism was "primary," lesbian feminists claimed that the pool of potential lesbians was much larger. Young lesbians in the early 1970s universalized the critique of compulsory heterosexuality and emphasized the possibility of coming out or "electing" lesbianism, proclaiming that it was the "feminist solution." Not only was the institution of heterosexuality constructed, activists argued, but so too were heterosexual desires. Because they were constructed, they reasoned, such desires could just as easily be reconstructed.

This fifty-two-year-old woman had been married for twenty-two years. Interviewed in the early-1970s, she described her coming out as follows:

> I began . . . to become involved with women's consciousness-raising groups, and I began to hear . . . of the idea of women being turned on to each other. It was the first time I heard about it in terms of people that I knew. . . . I was receptive but had no previous, immediate history. Like there was a part of me that had been thinking about it, and thinking, "Gee, that sounds like intellectually that's a good idea."[15]

The movement thus brought into the fold many "elective" lesbians like this woman, for whom relationships with men were often significant; some were married, some had long-term relationships with men with whom they felt they were in love and to whom they were sexually attracted. Nevertheless, they "discovered" women as sexual and emotional partners at some point, and came to identify as lesbians. Writing of this period several years later, a long-time activist recalled:

Those of us who were active in 1971 and 72 witnessed the tremendous influx of formerly heterosexual women into the Lesbian Movement. They came by the thousands. Lesbians of this background now compose the very backbone of the Lesbian Movement. . . . We put the world of men on notice that we were out to give their wives and lovers a CHOICE. We got a bad reputation as "chauvinistic." Lesbian feminism was called an "expansionist philosophy"— meaning that we were out to politically seduce (read: awaken) all women. In the

years that followed, it seems ironic to this old-gay-never-married dyke, that some of the most ardent, anti-straight women . . . were 1971's HOUSEWIVES![16]

The distinction Ponse and others have drawn between "primary" and "elective" lesbians— who differ as to their accounts of the origins of their lesbianism, the meaning of lesbian activity and lesbian feelings, and their age of entry into the lesbian community—thus suggests very different paths through which women have arrived at lesbian identity. Drawing upon object-relations psychoanalytic theory, Beverly Burch argues that the "early" or primary lesbian incorporates a greater "differentness" within her sense of self than the "later-developing" or elective lesbian.

"Primary" lesbians generally have to struggle to establish a positive sense of themselves as lesbians during adolescence, when other issues of social identity are being negotiated. Women who come out later in life, on the other hand, may have already negotiated other issues of social identity before they assume a "deviant" sexual identity. They may have established a sense of self as relatively "normal," at least in terms of their sexuality. Taking on a lesbian identity at this stage, says Burch, means coping with somewhat different issues. "It may involve a sense of loss in terms of acceptability and social ease, but losing something one has had is an experience quite different from never having had it."[17]

Moreover, as I have suggested, historical evidence shows these sexual choices to be shaped by class position. Women who joined lesbian subcultures before Stonewall were more likely to be of working-class origin, due at last in part to the fact that they tended to be less concerned with losing social status. Women encourage to "elect" lesbianism through exposure to feminism, by contrast, were more likely to come from the middle classes. With time, these and other preexisting, largely unspoken, differences in identity would pose thorny problems for the process of collectivization. Smashing the categories, it turned out, was a much simpler task than remaking the self.

BORDER SKIRMISHES

Twelve hundred women attended the first West Coast Lesbian-Feminist Conference, held in Los Angeles in June 1973. The goal of the conference was to unify lesbian feminists under a common program, but almost immediately the gathering was wracked by internal disagreements over the definition of lesbianism and, by extension, debates over who would be admitted. A male-to-female transsexual guitarist was shouted down by the crowd and prevented from performing. A prominent feminist writer and theorist was criticized for living with a man. Shortly after the conference, one woman's comment was telling: "If there was any point of unity it was that almost all lesbians are conscious of and hopeful for the development and existence of a lesbian-feminist culture/movement."[18] But a unified culture and movement implied a consensus on the meaning of lesbianism that did not exist.

During the early 1970s, such debates about who was a lesbian became commonplace throughout the country—at conferences, at women's music festivals, and within local communities. Border skirmishes around transsexualism, lesbians with boy children, bisexuality, and other issues deeply divided many lesbian events and communities. Symptomatic of the difficulty of defining the category "lesbian," they marked a growing preoccupation with fixing boundaries, making membership more exclusive, and hardening the notion of lesbian "difference."

The movement had earlier tried to broaden the base of lesbianism by loosening the boundaries around the group. But smashing some categories entailed creating others; identity politics requires defining an identity around which to mobilize. Boundary-setting became a preoccupation of the movement once it was faced with the challenge of insuring commitment and guarding against disaffection from the ranks, particularly in view of the pre-existing differences among women that I earlier identified.

If early lesbian feminism emphasized the fluidity of identity categories and the importance of self-description, with time the definition narrowed: Lesbians were biological women who do not sleep with men and who embrace the lesbian label. If they shared certain values in common, fore-most among them was their willingness to make lives apart from men. The growing symbolic importance of the notion of a "women's community" in the mid- to late 1970s signified the importance of boundary definition.[19] It centered the movement upon a rejection of men and patriarchal society. It claimed that gender is the primary basis of lesbian identity (and that all other divisions are male imposed), and argued that power was something imposed from without, by men. If power and hierarchy issues surfaced, members of the "women's community" saw this as the residue of patriarchy and male-identification, something that would fade away with time. If women within the community developed heterosexual desires, lesbians in the mid- to late 1970s tended to see this as a sign that patriarchy had been insufficiently purged.

While the language of the movement was radically constructionist, at least in terms of sexuali-ty in practice it privileged the "primary" lesbian for whom desire, exclusively lesbian, was con-gruent with identity. Studying the lesbian community in a medium-sized southern city in the 1970s, Barbara Ponse described the "biographic norm" of lesbian communities as the "gay tra-jectory," popularly known as "coming out." Lesbians assumed that this process was unidirectional. In the highly politicized milieu of lesbian communities, one did not come out and then "go back in" without suffering the consequences of such a move. Ponse concluded that the fluidity and changeability of both identity and activity at the level of the individual "may elude classification within the frameworks of the paradigms of the lesbian world, which, like the dominant culture, assume a heterosexual-homosexual dichotomy."[20]

The movement also privileged white, middle-class women, for whom lesbianism represented both a sexual choice and an oppositional identity. But for many women of color, as well as white working-class women, the choices were never so clear and unambivalent. Women of color, in particular, often felt that they were forced to pick and choose among identities. Audre Lorde wrote in 1979: "As a Black lesbian feminist comfortable with the many different ingredients of my identity . . . I find I am constantly being encouraged to pluck out some one aspect of myself and present this as the meaningful whole, eclipsing or deny-ing the other parts of self."[21] Many resisted pressures to make lesbianism their "dominant" or "master" identity.

What is problematic, I believe, was not so much that boundary-making took place—for it does in all identity-based movements—but that the discourse of the movement, rooted in notions of authenticity and inclusion, ran so com-pletely counter to it. Lesbian feminism positioned itself as the expression of the aspirations of *all* women. Like other identity-based movements, it promised the realization of individual as well as collective identity, and saw the two as intimately linked. At its best, it provided women with the strength and support to proclaim their desires for one another. It allowed many to withdraw from difficult and often abusive situations and opened up social space never before possible in this country. But at its worst, it hardened

LOIS! WHATEVER HAPPENED TO FEMINISM? WHERE HAS OUR POLITICAL ANALYSIS GONE?! AND WHY ARE ALL THESE WOMEN TRASHING EVERYTHING I STAND FOR?!

the boundaries around lesbian communities; subsumed differences of race, class, and even sexual orientation; and set up rather rigid standards for living one's life.

DILEMMAS OF IDENTITY

All identity-based movements have a tendency to fall into what Alberto Melucci has termed "integralism," the yearning for a totalizing identity, for a "master key which unlocks every door of reality." Integralism, says Melucci, rejects a pluralist and "disenchanted" attitude to life and encourages people to "turn their backs on complexity" and become incapable of recognizing difference.[22] Indeed, the contemporary sociological and historical literature on lesbian-feminist communities of the 1970s is rife with such observations.[23] Sociologist Susan Krieger looked at "the dilemmas of identity" posed by a women's community in the Midwest in the mid-1970s. She found that individuals frequently experienced a loss of self, in which they felt either overwhelmed or abandoned by the community. While noting that "all social groups confront their members with this kind of conflict," Krieger admitted that "in some groups"—namely those in which "the desire for personal affirmation from the group is great, and the complementary desire for assertion of individuality is also strong"—this experience is felt more intensely than in other groups and seems to occur more frequently.[24] Lesbian communities were often characterized by likeness, intimacy, and shared ideological orientation; they were comprised of women who were highly stigmatized. Krieger surmised that all these things contributed to the seeming difficulties their members had with maintaining their individuality amid pressures to merge and to become one with the community. Often this dynamic caused individuals to become more preoccupied with bolstering their own identities than with achieving political goals and led to internal struggles over who really belonged in the community.

While Krieger focused on gender as the primary locus of "likeness" within lesbian-feminist communities, one could also add race, class, and personal style to the mix. In many parts of the country, despite their efforts to free themselves from imposed social roles, subcultures often created new ones, prescribing sexual styles, political ideologies, and even standards of personal appearance that relatively few could successfully meet. This had the effect of excluding many women, particularly working-class women of all races, but also women who for any number of reasons may not have felt at home in the movement's countercultural milieu.

Particularly after the mid–1970s, many lesbian-feminist communities, scattered throughout the nation, became increasingly private enclaves. If earlier the movement tried to "smash the categories," substituting for the narrow, overly sexualized definitions of lesbianism a broad normative definition that welcomed all women into the fold, over time these definitions themselves nar-

rowed and became increasingly prescriptive. It is ironic, perhaps, that the very qualities that were once seen as a boon to the lesbian-feminist movement were coming to be viewed as seeds of its demise. Communities of intimacy, it turned out, were also communities of exclusion.

Individuals troubled by the inability of lesbian feminism to resolve the tension between identity and difference were faced with two basic options: They could reject identity as a basis for politics and strike out on their own, asserting their individual autonomy and personal difference. Or they could reshape identity politics and form new attachments that acknowledged "multiple" allegiances and the partial nature of lesbian identity. Indeed, as I will argue, both trends characterize the current phase of lesbian identity politics.

In the early 1980s, a series of structural and ideological shifts conspired to decenter the lesbian-feminist model of identity. First, the predominantly white and middle-class women who comprised the base of the movement aged, underwent various life-cycle changes, and settled into careers and families of various stripes—often even heterosexual ones. Second, a growing revolt emerged from within: Women of color, working-class women, and sexual minorities, three separate but overlapping groups, asserted their claims on lesbian identity politics. The next section focuses on these shifts, particularly on how sexual difference posed a challenge to lesbian-feminist constructions of identity.

SEX, RACE, AND THE DECLINE OF THE MALE THREAT?

From the mid-1970s to the early 1980s, the most visible political campaigns undertaken by the feminist movement were against pornography and sexual violence against women. For many women, straight and gay, pornography symbolized male sexuality and power and the fear that stalked women through the ordinary routines of daily life, representing all that was anathema to the vision of a female sexuality that emphasized rationality and reciprocity rather than power and coercion.

But new voices emerged, charging that the radical feminist vision glossed over real, persistent differences among women, and that it idealized women's sexuality and their relationships with one another. These women argued that all the attention upon sexual danger had minimized the possibility of women's pleasure. Highly polarized battles raged in the pages of feminist publications, as "sex radicals" branded their anti porn, anti-s/m opponents as "good girls," and came to a head in the unlikely setting of a conference at Barnard College in 1982, when anti-s/m activists picketed a speak-out on "politically incorrect sex."[25]

These political clashes, which have come to be called the "sex debates" or "porn wars," rarely addressed the subject of lesbianism explicitly. But insofar as these debates called into question the normative basis of the lesbian-feminist model of identity, lesbianism was the salient subtext. Lesbian "sex radicals" charged that somewhere in the midst of defining sexuality as male, and lesbianism as a blow against the patriarchy, desire seemed to drop out of the picture. As the editor of *On Our Backs* magazine, a popularizer of the emergent "pro-sex" lesbian sensibility, brashly claimed:

The traditional notion of femininity as gentle and nurturing creates the stereotype that lesbianism is just a hand-holding society. "Lesbians don't have sex," the story goes. Or if they do, it is this really tiresome affair—five minutes of cunnilingus on each side, with a little timer nearby, and lots of talking about your feelings and career.[26]

As "prosex" lesbians saw it, in all the talk about "woman-identification," the specificity of lesbian existence as a *sexual* identity seemed to get lost. In response, some tried to reengage with the tradition of pre-Stonewall lesbianism, which they saw as unencumbered by feminist ideological prescriptions and rooted in working-class bar culture and butch-femme roles.[27] A burgeoning sexual literature reasserted the centrality of desire and sexuality in lesbian identity and culture. Rather than making the distinction between male and male sexualities the primary political cleavage (as radical feminists had done), it acknowledged the sexual diversity implicit within the lesbian category and often invoked, symbolically at least, the sexual license of an earlier moment in gay male culture.

For many women, the onset of the AIDS crisis, which occurred nearly simultaneously, made coalition-building with gay men an even more immediate task. Centering post-Stonewall lesbian identity upon the shared rejection of men and patriarchy, lesbians had earlier disengaged from a gay liberation movement that was largely blind to their needs. But the tide of homophobia unleashed by the AIDS crisis affected lesbians as well as gay men and served at times to sharpen the differences between lesbians and heterosexual women. As the withered body of the person with AIDS replaced the once-pervasive image of the all-powerful male oppressor, the sense of male threat that underlay lesbian-feminist politics diminished further.

Lesbians in many urban centers joined the ranks of such predominantly gay male organizations as ACT UP and Queer Nation, which engaged in public actions across the nation to increase lesbian/gay visibility and puncture the "heterosexual assumption." Others attempted to construct sexualized subcultures that took their cue from an earlier era of gay male sexual experimentation. There were more co-ed gay bars, social events, and institutions. The new identifications between lesbians and gay men extended to personal style as well: clothing, music, and other forms of consumption.

By the late 1980s, even if relatively few women were directly touched by these developments, their effects could be felt in many lesbian communities. The break was largely, though not entirely, generational. An emergent lesbian politics acknowledged the relative autonomy of gender and sexuality, sexism and heterosexism.[28] It suggested that lesbians shared with gay men a sense of "queerness," a non-normative sexuality that transcends the binary distinction homosexual/heterosexual to include all who feel disenfranchised by dominant sexual norms—lesbians and gay men, as well as bisexuals and transsexuals.[29]

As a partial replacement for "lesbian and gay," the term "queer" attempted to separate questions of sexuality from those of gender.[30] But in terms of practice, this separation was incomplete. The new coexistence of gay men and women was often uneasy: ACT UP and Queer Nation chapters in many cities were marred by gender (and racial) conflicts. The new "co-sexual" queer culture could not compensate for real, persistent structural differences in style, ideology, and access to resources among men and women. This recurring problem suggested that while the new queer politics represented the assertion of a sexual difference that could not be assimilated into feminism, neither could gender be completely subsumed under sexuality. Despite their apparent commonalities, lesbians and gay men were often divided along much the same lines as heterosexual women and men.[31]

A less noisy but no less significant challenge to lesbian feminism came through the assertion of racial and ethnic identifications. At conferences and national meetings, women of color argued for the importance of acknowledging the divisions of race and class, which had long been subsumed in the interest of building a unified culture and movement. A series of influential anthologies challenged the feminist belief in the primacy of the sex/gender system, and led to the development of autonomous black, Asian, and Latina lesbian-feminist organizations.[32]

If lesbian feminism often presented itself as a totalizing identity that would subsume differences of race, class, and ethnicity and pose a united front against patriarchal society, these challenges pointed toward an understanding of lesbianism as situated in a web of multiple oppressions and identities. Lesbians of color and lesbian sex radicals questioned the belief that lesbian life could ever stand completely outside of or apart from the structures of the patriarchal culture. They problematized the once uncontested relationship between lesbianism and feminism. And they shifted lesbian politics away from its almost exclusive focus upon the "male threat," toward a more diffuse notion of power and resistance, acknowledging that lesbians necessarily operate in a society marked by inequalities of class and race, as well as of gender and sexuality.

SEVENTIES QUESTIONS FOR NINETIES WOMEN

Some might interpret the scenario I have painted, of the increasing spatial and ideological fragmentation of lesbian communities and the currently contested nature of the relationship between feminism and lesbianism, as indicative of a "post-feminist" era. Certainly, the series of cultural shifts I have described break with an earlier moment of lesbian-feminist politics. They result in large part from the difficulties lesbians have faced in mobilizing around a sense of group difference, even as these cultural shifts are made possible by the construction of that very sense of difference.

I have argued that the lesbian-feminist movement found itself torn between two projects: between fixing lesbians as a stable minority group, and seeking to liberate the "lesbian" in every woman. As I suggested earlier, feminism provided the ideological glue that wedded these two sometimes contradictory impulses. It redefined lesbianism in more expansive, universal terms, constructing a lesbian culture founded upon resistance to gender and sexual norms. While it opened up the possibility of lesbian identification to greater numbers of women than ever before, it could achieve unity only ultimately through exclusion, through a gender separatism that hardened the boundaries around it.

Younger women today are trying to carve out lesbian identities at a moment when many of the apparent certainties of the past have eroded—the meaning of lesbianism, the relationship between lesbianism and feminism, and the political potential of identity politics. They recognize that while marginalized groups construct symbolic fictions of their experience as a means of self-validation, and that compulsory heterosexuality necessitates the construction of a lesbian/gay identity, identities are always simultaneously enabling *and* constraining. As one twenty-three-year-old New Yorker recently told me:

> What I am is in many ways contradictory. I don't belong in the straight world, though I'm a white girl. . . . But I don't really belong in the feminist world because I read lesbian porn and refuse to go by a party line. On the other hand, I think I'm a feminist. It's a set of contradictions.[33]

Even as they integrate feminism into their daily lives, she and others reject the view that lesbianism is *the* feminist act, that any sexual identity is more authentic or unmediated than any other. In this sense, they are in fact "postfeminist," if that term is descriptive of the consciousness of women and men who, while holding their distance from feminist identities or politics, have been profoundly influenced by them. They simultaneously locate themselves inside and outside the dominant culture, and feel a loyalty to a multiplicity of different projects, some of them feminist-oriented, others more queer-identified, many of them incorporating elements of both critiques. And they see themselves, and their lesbianism, as located in a complex world marked by racial, class, and sexual divisions.

Indeed, this indeterminacy is deeply troubling to many women, particularly those who once held out the hope of constructing a lesbian-feminist movement that was culturally and ideologically unified. But I want to suggest that today's more "decentered" movement may present new democratic potential. Many women who felt excluded by an earlier model of identity now feel that they can finally participate in politics on their own terms. As clashes over feminist issues such as abortion, sexual harassment, and pay equity heat up over the coming years, as they are likely to do, lesbians will be on the front lines, as they have always been—only this time they will be out as lesbians. Others will continue to participate in movements that are not necessarily feminist at all, but with greater visibility than ever before.

This suggests that any unified conception of lesbian identity is reductive and ahistorical; collective identity is a production, a process. Stuart Hall's comments on ethnic resistance are relevant here.[34] In any politicization of marginal groups, he says, there are two phases. The first comprises a rediscovery of roots and implies a preoccupation with identity. Only when this "local" identity is in place can a consideration of more global questions and connections begin. For many lesbians in this country, the first phase of this movement has already occurred. We may now be seeing the arrival of the second.

NOTES

For their comments on earlier drafts of this article, I am grateful to Elizabeth Armstrong, Deborah Gerson, Sabine Hark, Liz Kotz, Nancy Solomon, Pat Stevens, Carla Trujillo, and the *SR* Bay Area collective, especially Steve Epstein. Thanks also to audiences at the Conference on Cultural Politics and Social Movements, UC Santa Cruz, and the Fifth Annual Lesbian and Gay Studies Conference, Rutgers University.

"No Dykes," is reprinted with permission from: Alison Bechdel, *Dykes to Watch Out For: The Sequel* (Ithaca, NY: Firebrand Books, 1992), strip #82, pp. 16–17.

1. Janice Raymond, "Putting the Politics Back into Lesbianism," *Women's Studies International Forum*, vol. 12, no. 2 (1989).

2. *San Francisco Examiner*, November 12, 1991, p. 3.

3. Howard Winant makes a similar argument about the politics of race in "Postmodern Racial Politics: Difference and Inequality," in *Socialist Review*, vol. 20, no. 1 (January–March 1990).

4. These ideas are based on archival research and interviews conducted primarily in the San Francisco Bay Area. Parts of the analysis may not hold true for other parts of the country, particularly nonurban areas, where the pace of change may be slower.

5. Pierre Bourdieu, "What Makes a Social Class? On the Theoretical and Practical Existence of Groups," *Berkeley Journal of Sociology*, vol. 32, (1987), p. 13. Also see Scott Lash, *Sociology of Postmodernism* (New York: Routledge, 1990); Sandra Harding's discussion of epistemologies as "justificatory strategies," in "Feminism, Science and the Anti-Enlightenment Critiques," *Feminism/Postmodernism*, ed. Linda Nicholson (New York: Routledge, 1990), p. 87.

6. Jonathan Katz, *Gay American History* (New York: Harper and Row, 1976), p. 7. See also Jeffrey Weeks, "The Development of Sexual Theory and Sexual Politics," *Human Sexual Relations*, Mike Brake (New York: Pantheon, 1982).

7. Radicalesbians, "The Woman-Identified Woman," reprinted in *For Lesbians Only*, Sarah Hoagland and Julia Penelope, eds. (London: Onlywoman Press, 1988); Adrienne Rich, "Compulsory Heterosexuality and Lesbian Existence," *Signs* (Summer 1980).

8. Eve Sedgwick, *Epistemology of the Closet* (Berkeley: University of California Press, 1990), p. 36.

9. Gayle Rubin, "The Traffic in Women," in *Toward an Anthropology of Women*, ed. Rayna Reiter (New York: Monthly Review, 1975).

10. Jill Johnston, *Lesbian Nation: The Feminist Solution* (New York: Simon & Schuster, 1973), p. 58.

11. See Caroll Smith-Rosenberg, *Disorderly Conduct* (New York: Knopf, 1985); "The Female World of Love and Ritual," in *Heritage of Her Own*, ed. Nancy F. Cott and Elizabeth Pleck (New York: Simon and Schuster, 1979).

12. Judy Grahn, "Lesbians as Bogeywoman," in *Women: A Journal of Liberation*, vol. 1, no. 4 (Summer 1970), p. 36.

13. Vivienne C. Cass, "Homosexual Identity Formation: A Theoretical Model," in *Journal of Homosexuality*, vol. 4, no. 3 (1979).

14. Barbara Ponse, *Identities in the Lesbian World: The Social Construction of Self* (Westport: Greenwood, 1978), p. 160.

15. Ibid., p. 162.

16. *Lesbian Tide* (May-June 1978), p. 19.

17. Beverly Burch, "Unconscious Bonding in Lesbian Relationships: The Road Not Taken," unpublished dissertation, Institute for Clinical Social Work, Berkeley, CA, 1989, p. 91.

18. Jeanne Cordova, *Lesbian Tide* (May-June 1973).

19. Alice Echols, *Daring to be Bad: Radical Feminism in America 1967–75* (Minneapolis: University of Minnesota Press, 1989); Bonnie Zimmerman, *The Safe Sea of Women: Lesbian Fiction 1969–1989* (Boston: Beacon Press, 1990).

20. Ponse, *Identities in the Lesbian World*, p. 139.

21. Audre Lorde, "Age, Race, Class and Sex: Women Redefining Difference," in *Sister Outsider* (Trumansburg: Crossing Press, 1984).

22. Alberto Melucci, *Nomads of the Present: Social Movements and Individual Needs in Contemporary Society* (London: Century Hutchinson, 1989), p. 209.

23. Iris Young, "The Ideal of Community and the Politics of Difference," in *Feminism/Postmodernism*, ed. Linda Nicholson (New York: Routledge, 1990); Shane Phelan, *Identity Politics: Lesbian Feminism and the Limits of Community* (Philadelphia: Temple University Press, 1989); Cheryl Cole, "Ethnographic Sub/versions," unpublished dissertation, University of Iowa, 1991.

24. Susan Krieger, *The Mirror Dane: Identity in a Woman's Community* (Philadelphia: Temple University Press, 193), p. xv.

25. Carole Vance, ed., *Pleasure and Danger: Exploring Women's Sexuality* (Boston: Routledge, 1984); B. Ruby Rich, "Feminism and Sexuality in the 1980s," *Feminist Studies*, vol. 12, no. 3 (Fall 1986).

26. From an interview with Susie Bright, October 1989.

27. Joan Nestle, "Butch-Fem Relationships," *Heresies* 12 (Summer 1981).

28. Julia Creet, "Lesbian Sex/Gay Sex: What's the Difference?" *OUT/LOOK: National Lesbian and Gay Quarterly*, no. 11 (Winter 1991); Gayle Rubin, "Thinking Sex: Notes for a Radical Theory of the Politics of Sexuality," in Vance, *Pleasure and Danger*.

29. The autonomous bisexual movement suggested a politics along similar lines, but tended to privilege self-identified bisexuals. See, for example, *Bi Any Other Name: Bisexual People Speak Out*, Loraine Hutchins and Lani Kaahumanu, eds. (Boston: Alyson, 1990).

30. Michael Warner, "Fear of a Queer Planet," *Social Text* 29 (1991); Allan Bérubé and Jeffrey Escoffier, "Queer/Nation," *OUT/LOOK: National Lesbian and Gay Quarterly*, no. 11 (Winter 1991).

31. Dan Levy, "Queer Nation in S.F. Suspends Activities," *San Francisco Chronicle*, December 27, 1991; Michele DeRanleau, "How the Conscience of an Epidemic Unraveled," *San Francisco Examiner*, October 1, 1990.

32. These included *This Bridge Called My Back: Writings by Radical Women of Color*, Cherríe Moraga and Gloria Anzaldúa (Watertown, MA: Persephone, 1981); *All the Women are White, All the Blacks are Men, But Some of Us Are Brave*, Gloria Hull, Patricia Bell Scott, and Barbara Smith, eds. (New York: Feminist Press, 1982); *Home Girls: A Black Feminist Anthology* Barbara Smith, ed. (New York: Kitchen Table / Women of Color Press, 1983).

33. From an interview with the author in 1989.

34. Stuart Hall, "Cultural Identity and Cinematic Representation," *Framework*, n. 36, 1989.

26 "Playing with Fire"
The Gendered Construction
of Chicana/Mexicana Sexuality

Patricia Zavella

Mexican sexual/gender discourse grafts a particular twist onto the Catholic Mediterranean "honor and shame" cultural configuration.[1] Rooted in dislocations generated by a history of Spanish conquest, colonization of indigenous peoples, and a war of independence, sexuality, gender, and nationalism are deeply intertwined in Mexican society.[2] According to this Mexican cultural "master narrative," women should submit to sexual repression embedded in Catholic-based discourse, institutions, and everyday practices in part because of the mythologized actions of one of their sex. The "national allegory," classically articulated by Octavio Paz, posits the betrayal of her people by Malinche, Cortés' translator and concubine, as instituting a cultural configuration in which the act of sexual intercourse (*chingar*) is seen as conquest, violation, and devaluation of women by men who are shamed for being mestizos—sons of Spanish fathers and socially denigrated Indian mothers.[3] The Virgin of Guadalupe (the "brown virgin") symbolizes proper servility and modesty for Mexican women, as well as the subversive spiritual power of the indigenous who conformed to Catholicism in form if not in faith. Male dominance and the double standard are integral in the cultural polemics of macho/chingon and virgin/whore. Feminist scholars have contested this misogynist interpretative framework on its own allegorical terms, arguing that doña Marina or Malintzin (as she was originally named) can be seen as having acted strategically in the horrific circumstances of Spanish conquest.[4]

The research on Chicana/*Mexicano*[5] sexuality in contemporary times confirms the continuing importance of Catholic repression and the double standard.[6] This research, however, often ignores the regional variations in this cultural configuration in Mexico, and it is unclear how Mexicans reared in the United States construe its meaning.[7] Moreover, Mexican residents in the U.S.—like others—do not simply follow church doctrines when it comes to decisions about contraception, abortion, or submitting to sexual violence.[8] Beyond the Church, cultural constructions in Mexico and the United States are influenced by other forces—popular culture, state

Patricia Zavella is Professor of Community Studies at the University of California, Santa Cruz. An anthropologist whose work is situated within feminist and Chicana/o studies, her scholarly interests include: feminist theory, regional political economies, the relationship between women's wages and domestic labor, family and kinship, and the social and cultural changes brought about by transnational migration of Mexicanas/os.

policies regarding the body, or increased incidents of sexually transmitted diseases. Many Chicano gay men and lesbians openly contest this interpretive framework and transgress these gendered scripts, struggling to dismantle Mexican heterosexism and homophobia by creating discourse and social spaces (what Emma Pérez calls *lengua y sitio*) for acknowledging homoerotic sexuality.[9] Lesbian theorists also claim *La Virgen de Guadalupe* as their icon, reconfiguring her as symbol of indigenous liberation and women's empowerment.

How do individuals in general construct their sense of sexual pleasure or identity in conformity and/or resistance to cultural discourse? How is power coded into sexual behavior and relationships? And how do heterosexuals and lesbians differ from one another in defining a sense of sexual subjectivity? This piece contributes to an understanding of Chicana/*Mexicana* sexuality through the use of ethnographic interviews to engage critically these questions.[10]

Using interviews to understand sexuality is problematic, as knowledge about sexuality is often "nondiscursive," that is, knowledge that is assumed rather than made explicit.[11] The people I interviewed in the course of a larger, multiraced study of poverty in Santa Cruz County, struggled to convey their ambivalent feelings or to describe experiences that they had previously repressed. I heard a common refrain: "We just *knew*. There were certain things you did not talk about, and sex was one of them" or, more pointedly, "Talking about sex meant I was a bad person. So I didn't talk about it." The interviews themselves, then, were transgressions of the silencing in which women had been trained.

The problematics of discussing sex with an interviewer are compounded by memory lapses, where the experience of childhood is, in some ways, irretrievable.[12] Some of the people I interviewed sometimes had difficulty recalling what they were taught and by whom; this in itself was telling. In these instances, I culled from their recollections of childhood experiences and admonitions to understand their enculturation regarding gender and sexuality. For others, memories were what Penelope Lively calls "brilliant frozen moments," because of their significance; yet they too were "distorted by the wisdom of maturity"[13] and influenced by the social context of the interview setting. These narratives are thus representations, "situated knowledge" at multiple levels, and should be read critically.[14] They are also, though, our only means—absent autobiography—to gain access to the self-construction of sexuality among the poor.

My purpose is to explicate the political economy of gender and sexuality among impoverished and working-class Chicanas and Mexicanas, to show how social meaning regarding sexual practices is culturally constructed. This analysis begins with two women's narratives of sexual practices and meaning, individual narratives that take place in an arena of plural, competing, and often conflicting social narratives about sexual practices and meanings. Roger Lancaster suggests that each of these spheres is "traversed by various degrees of autonomy, control, freedom and determinism, rebellion and conformity, power and love."[15] To understand the meaning of sexual practices or identity, I will examine these women's "cultural poetics" of sexual desire.

The metaphors "playing" and "fire" recurred in the cultural poetics of sexual desire among all my Chicana and Mexicana interviewees, metaphors rendered banal in popular culture.[16] Heterosexuals and lesbians indicated that in seeking sexual desire they were "playing"—flirting, teasing, or testing potential lovers. Fire contained dual meanings, signifying both the repressive forces of culturally sanctioned silence regarding Eros in Mexican society; and simultaneously, in seeking the "powers of desire,"[17] women imagined sexual pleasure as fire—"hot," "passionate," "boiling," "explosive"—and difficult to stop. They envisioned seeking out potential sexual partners as a "game" played within the limits imposed by cultural authority of church doctrines, family practices, and the sanctions of conventional society. While women did not always "win" the game, and indeed sometimes "got burned," playing was pleasurable, often because the game was taboo in some sense. Seeking a mate, then, often pushed societal parameters and made these women feel a sense of power and the ability to pursue that which they desired. During interviews, women recalled even failed loves occasionally with tears of pain, but more often with smiles and joy.

Two women speak below—a heterosexual Chicana, Mirella Hernández (a pseudonym), and a *lesbiana* Mexicana—María Pérez.[18] In presenting these particular narratives, I do not mean to impose binary oppositions—cultural vs. essential self, heterosexual and homosexual, feelings and logic. Rather, following Jean Franco, I here write women into the plot of sexuality, showing their historical agency in contesting traditional expectations. I argue that these women's cultural poetics of sexuality entailed struggling with the contradictions of repressive discourses and social practices that were often violent towards women and their own desires. I chose these women among my many informants because their narratives particularly represent, as Franco has described certain literary texts, "incandescent moments when different configurations of gender and knowledge are briefly illuminated."[19]

MIRELLA HERNÁNDEZ

Her mother immigrated from a rural Mexican village with virtually no education; her father was from New Mexico and had a high school education. Born in California and twenty-one years old, Mirella identified herself ethnically as "Mexican."

Mirella had vivid memories of experiences related to sex and family. "I've always been curious about sex," she said. She told me about an incident that occurred when she was about eight. She and a neighbor boy were in a swimming pool and they began playing by exposing their bodies. Her brother discovered them and "blackmailed me." When the brother did tattle to their mother, Mirella was forced to go apologize to the boy's parents about the incident. She recalled with embarrassment: "That was the worst." Mirella also recalled that sex itself—or anything even alluding to sex—was not to be discussed openly:

> I remember this really clearly. This lady came over when my mom was pregnant, and she told me "when your Mom buys the baby" and I thought, "You're so stupid, I know where they come from." My Mom gave me the eye, like, "don't you dare say a word," you know. Later I asked her, "Why can't I tell them where they come from?" And she just told me, "Out of respect."

Clearly, respect—for herself or for elders—meant that discussion of anything related to sex was to be avoided.

Mirella's mother was a battered woman whose alcoholic spouse would beat and rape her, sometimes in front of the children. "When I was old enough my Mom told me about it [the rape]. And sometimes we would run into their room when it was happening and catch him and I saw." Witnessing the abuse and rape was a traumatic experience for Mirella: "I felt really sick. I remember looking at my mom the next day and thinking, you know, how dirty a person could feel. I hated my father when that happened. I didn't want him to touch me. I just couldn't stand him, and even my Mom, I wouldn't let my Mom touch me; I wanted her to but I didn't want her to." Mirella's mother would occasionally call the police to stop the battering, but then would not press charges. Mirella managed to keep any knowledge about the violence at home from her friends and teachers: "I kept it a secret from everybody. I wanted everybody to think that my family was just fine." When other children talked about their families, Mirella became a master at deception: "I wouldn't say anything and pretended like everything was okay."

As Mirella became an adolescent and began to receive more explicit knowledge about her body, adults gave her mixed messages. When she began menstruating, her mother and aunts offered congratulations for her new status as a woman, which she found to be embarrassing but pleasing. Mirella also experienced a new reticence towards men:

> I knew that I could have kids now, so that was really scary. Yet it was also exciting because I thought, "I could be a mom," you know? Then after that I hated men [she laughed nervously]. I mean, I didn't want them to get too close to me, for a period of about half a year. I don't know if it was

because of my Dad, or it was just me; it was a weird feeling I got. My Mom would always say, "All men are alike, *que son cabrones*" (they're bastards). So I thought maybe they really are.

Mirella was also encouraged more to be "ladylike," foregoing her usual attire of pants for dresses, curling her hair and being allowed to wear makeup. Her father warned her about impregnation in clinical terms: "My Dad told me it took two people, you have to be in love, you know. He also said usually when you marry. And 'intercourse' was the word, it wasn't sex, it was intercourse. He explained that certain times of the month you could get pregnant, or you couldn't, which was really confusing for me." Her mother was more direct: "She'd tell me not to throw myself at boys: 'Have respect,' and 'I was never with anybody until I got married.' I always told myself, because of my mother's values, that I would not have sex until I was married." The strategy of saving her virginity for marriage and eventual motherhood would provide her with the expectation of economic stability, for the assumption was that a young man would support her in exchange for her unsullied reputation.

Mirella never received any sense that having a homosexual relationship was a possibility: "Well I heard the word 'fag,' but I didn't know what it meant. I just laughed along with everybody else." Thus she was encouraged to be feminine and celebrate her apparent fecundity, but only to a limited degree. Becoming a woman meant the possible threat of pregnancy, distasteful intimacy with men, the importance of self-respect, and the prospect of economic support.

At age fifteen, Mirella's family celebrated her *quinceañera*, a religious coming-of-age debut that indicates a young woman's availability for courtship and marriage:

> At first I didn't want one because I didn't know what it meant and I thought it was just to have a big bash. When I started going to catechism, I knew the real meaning of a *quinceañera* and why my Mom wanted me to have one. It represents purity, your virginity, which was neat, of course. But I thought I was one of the only virgins at 15 [she laughed]. I had so much fun!

Over three hundred people attended, including relatives who came up from Southern California. She worked part time to save enough to purchase all the food and the dresses for the attendants. Her mother ordered food from a caterer, at discount, since her brother worked there. Mirella's parents had separated just prior to the *quinceañera*. "It was a real turning point for us, as a family, to be able to do this on our own." This celebration of virginity and family, then, was meaningful at several levels.

Although Mirella had permission to date, her mother applied different standards of behavior to her and her brother, who was free to come and go as he pleased. Mirella always had to report where she was going, with whom, and to obey a strict curfew. She also had to leave a phone number if she changed her plans. Perhaps because she was parenting by herself (supporting her family on her wages as a cook), Mirella's mother seemed particularly vigilant: "My Mom would tell me to have fun, but be careful, you know, '*cuídate*.' I know what that means now."

Mirella's mother let her know she would be able to tell if a woman has lost her virginity:

> My Mom says she can tell under the eyes, I guess you get bags under your eyes. And she can tell when someone's pregnant, even if they're not showing just by their face, if they look drained or pale. It's weird: Our neighbor came over once and Mom asked her. And she'd be, "No, I'm not planning on having any kids," and then she turned out pregnant. I think that my Mom was trying to scare me to think, "Well if I have sex, she is going to know right off."[20]

Her mother advised Mirella to date a lot of different men so she would not end up "tied down" as she had been: "She loves the guys that I've gone out with, but she never wanted me to have a serious relationship with anybody and she doesn't know about what I've done with them. She was always open to birth control and I can talk to her about sex if I wanted to." Again, the message was mixed, with the apparent openness about discussing sex with her mother tempered by the caution: "She said, 'don't have sex until you get married, then you don't have to worry about birth control.'"

Clearly Mirella was expected to remain a virgin until marriage. She was trained and closely watched—primarily by her mother, but with strong reinforcement from Catholic catechism and with support from her brother and father—to guard her body from male abuse and to repress her own sexual desires. She came of age in northern California during the late 1980s, however, a time when Madonna was the popular cultural icon and the seductive Kenny G. was her favorite musician. Mirella received very different messages from the dominant culture and her friends than she received at home and at church. As Olaiz finds, "Among friends, women allow themselves to explore different forms of sexual expression, like dress, make-up, the way they talk, the music they listen to and how they dance to it, and how these different forms convey that a woman is attractive and available for romantic relationships."[21]

Mirella started dating her first boyfriend at sixteen, after years of flirting and "playing hard to get." Michael was four years older, white—of Portuguese ethnicity in a community that was predominantly Mexican—and from an upper middle class family. Mirella found him attractive because, "I think it was his body, which is odd because I always had the image of going out with someone who was tall and built, with green eyes and black hair [implying a Mexican]. Where he was short, with a nice body, and his eyes, his eyes talked. They were sending out these messages, like he always got what he wanted type of thing. And I wasn't the girl who gave what you wanted, which I think was a big challenge for him and it was a challenge for me." With her long, black hair and "olive" skin, Mirella's beauty was classically Mexican. Michael's mother did not approve of the relationship, was blatantly rude towards Mirella whenever she called or visited, and would not deliver messages that she had called. Mirella's brother did not approve either:

> He always told me Michael was bad news, 'cause he did drugs in high school and he was a rebel. He would always tell me that "this guy just wants one thing, to get you in the sack." I knew if I went out with him I couldn't talk to my brother about it. At first it was hush-hush; only Mom knew. When I finally told him, he said, "Well you gotta do what you have to do," and "Be careful." But that's not what I saw, because it took a long time for me to even sleep with this guy. Michael was very respectful. He was my first real love, even though then I really didn't know what love was.

Mirella, then, was playing with fire, drawn to this man but wanting to preserve her reputation as a "good girl." His membership in the local powerful white community added to the sense of taboo and enhanced the challenge. Proving her brother wrong was an added enticement. Mirella was asserting her own independence within the confines of her family's control. As has been found with other Chicanas/Mexicanas, the fact that she was in love with the man provided a rationale in which a young woman was considered respectable despite the loss of her virginity.[22]

The relationship with Michael only lasted about nine months before Mirella discovered that he had dated another young woman and was seen kissing her at a local movie theater.

> When I found out he had cheated on me, it broke my heart. And I didn't give him any chances either. It was over. I said "fuck you, that's it." It grossed me out to think that I was sleeping with him and he went out with someone else and I remember hating him. I said to myself, "Why am I so stupid, I should have listened to my Mom, I shouldn't have had sex until I get married." I was so afraid that if anyone found out, they're going to think that I'm a tramp or something. Especially if my Mom found out, she would kill me. I was the worst person.

Since neither her mother nor brother found out she had lost her virginity, her reputation remained unscathed.

It was another year and a half before Mirella felt she could trust a man enough to go out with him. During this period she reflected upon how she would conduct herself in relationships and made a profound change from her previous thinking: "I thought maybe I shouldn't fall in love, you know. It's okay just to date someone and sleep with them, that type of thing." Mirella was beginning to reconfigure her own sense of pleasure despite the confines of her life.

Her next relationship was with another white boy, Jim, a Slovenian—an ethnic group whose members owned much land in the area—but he was of working class background. Even though he was very handsome, and had an "even better body" than Michael, Mirella was attracted to his personality rather than by the challenge of dating a wealthy man: "I wasn't looking for a boyfriend, I was just bummed and not wanting to do anything. But he was really sweet and fun. I thought 'okay, not all guys are the same.'" Still, Mirella would not have sex with Jim for quite some time. Then an opportunity for privacy presented itself:

> My grandmother went away for vacation and I was taking care of her house [she laughed]. But it was really weird because my grandma's fairly religious, and everywhere you turn there's a crucifix or *santos*. I remember being in her room and there's this cross looking at me, and I thought, "Oh my God, how evil I am." But then things happened, and I could care less about what was up on the walls.

Their relationship lasted three years and the couple discussed getting married. Jim had drinking problems, however, and Mirella asserted her independence from him: "I'm not going to put up with that, not after what my mom went through. She says, 'you give him one chance and they expect more from you.' And I was giving too much and not receiving enough back." Despite "still being in love with him," Mirella ended the relationship. Meanwhile she had enrolled in a community college, working towards a nursing degree, and took a part-time job as a lab technician, moving towards economic self-sufficiency.

At the time of the interview, Mirella had just started dating another young man, a Chicano university student who was a friend of her brother's. This was the first "Hispanic" she had ever dated, and she found that their same ethnic background "really makes a difference" and was a powerful attraction of a different type:

> Now that I've dated Ray, I realize that they can understand your culture. With Ray, I don't have to teach him anything, and he knows what I'm saying when I talk to my mom in Spanish. And he's got this little saying, he calls me *"mija"* (my little daughter), which I think is the cutest thing. It gives me the neatest feeling. And I could see my mom's face light up, the first time I took him to a *quinceañera*. Ray can dance and everything. I'm happy when I go out with him.

Mirella was attracted to Ray because of his good looks, but this time she appreciated something more: "He's so smart, and that's a turn on for me. He's going to school and he's got goals and he's going for it. And that's what I'm doing too. I can talk to him about school and he understands." Even though they did not have a commitment to one another, the couple spent time together almost every night, and she had met his family. She was the first Chicana that Ray had dated also, and his mother was delighted.

The couple delayed initiating sex. Mirella was taking the pill to regulate her menstrual periods, and made it clear to him that nevertheless she was not "easy": "I explained it wasn't because I was sleeping around or anything. He said, 'that's fine.'" An educated man himself, Ray was not judgmental about Mirella's sexual past. The couple was making plans to solidify their relationship:

We were talking the other night. I haven't told Ray "I love you" straight out and he hasn't told me either. But I think I'm getting there. He asked me, "Are you falling in love?" And I told him how I felt about him and he told me. He says that he can see himself marrying me.

Mirella's ideal relationship would "work 50–50," where each was committed to the relationship, and they spent as much time on their relationship as on their careers.

I asked her directly, "What gives you sexual pleasure, or what would you desire in a sexual relationship," Mirella got flustered, stammered a bit, and then responded: "I don't think I'm turned on by just the thought of having sex. I do have to care for the person. I don't think if I wanted it, I just could have it. Because I have wanted to have sex but that hasn't happened. I don't know. If something could work out between us." Later she clarified, "I just think its a turn on to think that he's got so much going for him. He can make a life out of what he's doing, and I know that I definitely can too." In talking about meeting the rest of Ray's family, and developing their relationship, Mirella admitted, "I'm excited. I'm really excited."

A maturing young woman, Mirella Hernández now realizes that sexual relationships are not inherently dangerous and that all men are not stupid, abusive, or mistrustful. She has incorporated some of the teachings of her mother and the Catholic Church as guides for her behavior so that she would not be considered "easy"; this is one source of her self respect. But she also resisted her family's preoccupation with virginity and her mother's model of a traditional role within marriage. Now closer to economic stability herself, Mirella prefers a relationship with a man working towards a career, and she claims the right to her own sexual pleasure outside of marriage.

MARÍA PÉREZ

In contrast to Mirella, thirty-five year old María Pérez had more experiences and more reflections about them. María was reared in a small town in the state of Puebla. The daughter of mestizo campesinos, María attended all-girls schools in Mexico on scholarships and completed some college classes. Highly intelligent and precocious—as a child she won prizes during school competitions for her literary performances and superior essays—her "biggest dream" was to receive her doctorate at The Sorbonne, in Paris. While she was raised Catholic, she no longer attends church regularly, and considers herself to be "very eclectic religiously," combining a sardonic devotion to La Virgen de Guadalupe, Buddhism, and the Goddess. Formerly a bilingual community educator at a social service agency, at the time of the interview María was unemployed and the couple was experiencing dire financial difficulties, with the threat of losing their home. Initially she interrogated me about my motives, theoretical perspective, and methodological approach, and even took note of my publications. I apparently passed her test, for María was delighted to be interviewed and gave me over ten hours of her time. This moved her lover to observe, "Sure she's writing a book, but it's not just about *you*."

Like Mirella, María received traditional gender socialization as a child:

I was taught that it is very important to have a family, and sacrifice for your family. You should get married because the husband will take care of you; he has to be the provider. You need to learn how to cook, sew, clean up the house and do all the chores, and especially make good food because that will give happiness to your husband. You've got to have children because that's your role in life, as a woman, is to have children. If you don't have children, nothing in life that you may do will be meaningful.

Her family assumed that heterosexuality would be the norm.

María received clear messages that sex was sinful and sexual pleasure was to be avoided. She recalled that as a five-year-old child, she and a male cousin of the same age engaged in exploration of their bodies: "Oh, you have a penis and I don't. What do you use that for?" When her caretaker found them, she reported the incident to María's mother, who became very angry and slapped María, saying "I don't want you doing this." There was some discussion about whether her cousin had raped her, and if so her mother threatened to kill him. María was forbidden to play with her cousin again. Regarding sexual self exploration, María recalled,

> One time my mother found me exploring myself, and she was pretty pissed off. She brought me by the hand and she slapped me and she says "those things you don't do, you can get infected." Later I learned about masturbation, the concept, but it was like, "don't do it," right? Don't give yourself pleasure, that's a sin, you're being in temptation, and then God will punish you. The Ten Commandants were kind of mandatory.

María recalled that during childhood games of playing house, she usually took the male role:

> There were no boys in the school, so I became the male figure in our games. So I had a girlfriend instead of a boyfriend. Not only one, but I had two or three. We used to play movies, and because my name is María Luisa, I became Luis. I chose this: "I want to be the head general; I want to be Batman instead of Bat Girl." I remember that we played to kiss each other, but it wasn't on the mouth, it was more pretend, or we held hands. But it was the characters in the movies that we used to express those feelings.

Despite having few male companions to learn from, María was drawn to the male gender and sexual script. Through Mexican romantic cinematic images, she already had a view of men as having more than one lover, and through play was able to assert authority and power by assuming male roles.

When María became adolescent, she gained the rudimentary knowledge about conception and male-female sexual differences in a sixth grade course at school. Her mother had been reared in a convent, yet unlike many women, was relatively open to discussing menstruation and sex: "I learned that you should be a virgin when you get married, and then you should be sexually available for your husband." Other than warning her to preserve her virginity, however, María's kin offered no information about sexual relationships.

At twelve, María realized that females could have relationships with other females through the discovery of two girls at school who were in love: "Everyone said '¡jotas!' (dykes) with a horrible contempt, and I was scared." Age twelve was also when María fell in love for the first time with a young woman, a fellow classmate. But she was afraid of her desires:

> I didn't want to accept that she was it. I passed through a denial stage, you know, "How can I be in love with a girl?" Later, at secondary school I would see popular guys in the group of girls, and I would say "I wish I could *be* that boy." I pretended, "He's very handsome, and I would be honored to be his girlfriend," but I was lying all the time. I thought, "I can't let them say dyke to me. I have too much to lose, all of my prestige." So I covered up [my sexuality].

Even though María was afraid of others finding out, she persevered in a context where there were implicit mixed messages. Girls were not allowed to spend time alone together, although it was acceptable for them to sleep in the same bed in the large dormitory room. María and her friend would casually sleep together without arousing suspicion about their interest in one another: "We began to play sexually, but no more than kissing, and we never ever talked about this."

María then began a period where she perceived herself as "the most popular boy," when she had "a heap of admiring girls." She began a process of sexual exploration and play (*juego sexual*), only with women and usually with more than one. In a classic Mexican sense, María was solidifying her sense of herself as male and predator.

She then met a younger woman and the relationship became serious: "She was so young, and she had such beauty. Her body was just beginning to become defined, and it was the first time that I paid attention to the body of a woman." They were open with each other about the sexual nature of their relationship and, since they had no money, would court by writing love notes or bringing each other gifts of flowers or leaves. María composed love poems to win over her lover. Their relationship was cast in a heterosexist mold, in the sense that María played the male and her lover the female when they made a commitment. María would tell her lover "you cannot go out with other boys," and her lover responded,

> "All this time you have been with so and so and no more, you can't go out with other girls." And I would say, "well, I didn't seek them out" [she laughed sheepishly]. I was copying *los patrones machistas* (the male bosses) because I didn't have anyone else to copy. It was not easy for a girl to play the role of a boy. The role of a woman is defined. But I was a girl who desired to be a boy, and with no one to learn from. Also there was much about boys that I did not like. I didn't know much in this interior struggle. Anyway, at that time I was *muy macha, muy marimacha* (very male, very butch).

Talking about her behavior over two decades later, María was embarrassed about her past mimicry of what to her were the negative male qualities of jealousy, infidelity, and possessiveness towards her girlfriend. Reflecting upon her behavior, she said "I was a *macho* Mexican *cabrón*." María's experience parallels that of Cherríe Moraga, who noted: "In the effort to avoid embodying *la chingada*, I became the *chingón*. In the effort not to feel fucked, I became the fucker, even with women."[23]

Because they were openly lovers among themselves, the two women felt an even stronger sense that they must remain secretive about their relationship in public. They could sleep in the same bed in the large dormitory, but their sexual exploration became stifled:

> No one knew so we were careful that only we would know what was going on. And this is very important: it became an *adventure*. It had to be in a manner that was so quiet—we couldn't make any noise or movements to be able to do this. It was like the night clouds, like a smooth breeze that barely moved. We couldn't do anything else because if everyone knew, there would be a scandal. We began exploring our lips, exploring what does it feel like to be kissed, the power of a kiss. She was playing with fire.

This relationship ended when the young woman entered another school. Her lover next pursued a sexual relationship with a young man, so her "playing with fire" was temporary. María, however, was drawn to the "power of a kiss" with women.

At fifteen, María became involved with another Mexicana, Josefina, who eventually became "the love of my life," her *compañera* or wife.[24] In the initial stages of their relationship, María used the subterfuge of innuendo to communicate with her love object. "I'd say, 'Well you must love your boyfriend a lot since you won't leave him.' What I was saying is 'I want you to leave your boyfriend.' We could not really clarify what was happening." Once they did get involved, María recalled that Josefina "had the most beautiful eyes and beautiful hair. She was all woman, in the sense that she was *the* woman, *la madre abnegada, la mujer sufrida* (the self-denying mother, the suffering woman) and all that. It was very appropriate for me to get in that relationship because I was the macho prototype, a macho man in the tradition of values." As the prototypical female, Josefina was protective and nurtured María:

> She believes that no one would love me like her. She's right. She was mother, even in the sense of nurturing me. I became a baby sometimes in her arms. Sometimes when she embraced me, she made me feel like I had regained something, completed something that I missed when I was a child. I

became mature with her. And I taught her how to be independent, how to be less preoccupied and focus on the qualification, to get an A. You had to fight for it.

María's vision of gender roles for women, then, was "defined" and restricting, complementing those for men which were assertive and strong.

The lovers suffered through an initial period of denial, then admitted their feelings for one another.

> It was really a Romeo and Juliet thing; it was very passionate, very intense and we were running from it, like it can't be. I had my first real sexual relationship with her. She was the woman who taught me how to kiss. Not like before. With Josefina, it was the giving part and the exchanging part of the kiss, where you lose yourself in the pleasure of kissing somebody.

The lovers would be together for nine years, and experienced the full panoply of romantic feelings:

> We did it all. We had passion, we had confrontations, we had growing, we had turbulence, we had the caring. It was a struggle against everything. We were claiming our right to be in love. We couldn't avoid touching each other in front of everybody. It was like water boiling over, you know, when you're boiling water and it gets out of control? It was not possible for us to deny we loved each other. We would hold hands and walk in front of everybody, we said, "We don't care, fuck you, our love is meant to be and we are gonna defend it no matter what."

The school officials suspected the girls were lovers and sent them to a psychologist, who was sympathetic: "She would smile. She knew exactly what was happening, and she wanted us to be careful. She didn't want us to sleep together. But that was our daily sanctuary, even though it was in the middle of a large building." The other girls began protecting them with "*la ley del hielo*," an unwritten code of honor in which no one would "break the ice" and tell the authorities. María and Josefina knew they were in love, but did not understand exactly what was happening to them. María began to investigate through books and found a term for her desires—lesbianism.

During this period María and Josefina dated several boys, "to play the role that I had a boyfriend. But the boyfriends were only a mask to cover up that there was more between Josefina and I. It was just because I was general secretary, and so forth, so I needed to do that. I had to be normal." The boyfriends did not interest María—"not even a kiss. They asked me why, and I said 'no, I take care of my honor,' something like that. And they believed in that and I manipulated that." Although María knew she preferred intimate relationships with women, she used the subterfuge of virgin honor to mask her blossoming homosexuality.

The lovers' relationship was made public inadvertently. María's mother discovered they were lovers by opening a letter from Josefina. María's father beat her and her mother was upset, raised a big scandal and eventually went to the police, but then dropped any charges. The discovery only pushed the two lovers together: "We would say, 'If the world doesn't want us we will leave this world—I will die for you and you will die for me.' We wanted to do it [commit suicide] if it became necessary." María moved out and the breach with her mother has never fully healed. María, then, was pushed out of the closet, suffering the humiliation of Mexican homophobia.

Josefina's parents were more accepting, although they did not fully approve. Eventually María became like an adopted daughter in Josefina's parents' home. Ironically, María's "father-in-law" provided her with a role model for how to be an honorable man. It would be some time, however, before María fully learned the lesson.

Despite Josefina's parents' good will, María and Josefina were not open about their lesbianism:

It was a big *secreto a voz* (unspoken secret). That is a big concept in the Latino family in Mexico, whenever some sin is going on, we have a social psychology happening here protecting the victim and the victimizer. And it has come here [to the U.S.] somehow. They say, "Don't say anything about your aunt, poor thing, she has a big problem." And it's like [groans] now I'm guilty too. You break the guilty feeling in pieces and distribute it among the whole family, but over a long period of time. Whenever someone gets pissed with somebody, they will yell it and say, "Enough is enough, I'm going to tell the secret!"

María and Josefina's relationship was a huge *secreto a voz:* "Everyone pretended that we were great friends."

María and Josefina's relationship was premised on three vows they made to one another: One was that during sex they would not engage in vaginal penetration, so they would preserve their virginity:[25] "Sex was a lot of mutual masturbation and other things, but no penetration." They waited two years before agreeing to vaginal penetration. María explained the significance of giving up one's virginity: "The social oppression to marry as a virgin, all of that, was so strong that it really was a sacrifice to lose one's virginity. It was protection for each other, until we got to the point where we could walk out on the street and say 'fuck your mother, I'm not a virgin and so what!'" Like Mirella, María was told that one could tell if a woman lost her virginity—the backs of her knees would change. A related promise was that their relationship took priority: "If we wanted to give it [virginity] to anyone, it would be among ourselves first, or it wouldn't happen." The third agreement was that "if we found a man who became the love of our life, we would end our relationship." In some ways this was a quixotic promise for, as María noted, "That was very crazy, very far from happening after nine years." Implicit in their agreement was that having a sexual relationship with a man was acceptable, because it would not seriously threaten their relationship, and that for either of them to have a relationship with another woman was considered an infidelity since it would betray their more important love as women.

María did have sexual relations with other women, and even though she described herself as "promiscuous," she made it clear that "I'm not the type of person to make out on the first date. I needed something more from the person." In one of these relationships, her lover pressured her for sex with penetration. Like the macha that she was, María cleverly asked the lover to wait: "I told her, 'I'm not ready, let me think about it.' I directed the thing with Jóse emotionally so that we got to the point of where we complied with my promise to have that experience with her and not another woman. In the end it happened and it was a good experience, very satisfying." Later María had vaginal penetration with the other woman but she had honored her and Josefina's commitment.

María was successful with other women because of the clarity of the boundaries she established with them: "I couldn't promise those women the heavens and the stars. I would say, 'I have this relationship with another woman but I can play with you sexually.'" She found sexual pleasure in her identification with the sexual prowess of men:

I was very fortunate because I've had the experience of receiving that gift [a woman's virginity] not from one woman, from many, like six, seven. A true man, whoever, if he heard this, would envy me enormously. He would say, "How did you do that, that you had all these virgins and you didn't have to marry any of them?" And I did not have to violate them either. I guess I was charming, I don't know [smiles winningly].

María still viewed herself as male—in control, guiding the relationship with Josefina, playing the field with many lovers at the same time, and gaining the ultimate male conquest, a woman's virginity. Her vision of men was that they had more power and freedom than women, and would stop at nothing to satisfy their pleasures. María sought the entitlements of Mexican masculinity even as she constructed a lesbian identity that was in opposition to patriarchal authority.

After nine years, the relationship between María and Josefina soured. The primary reason was that Josefina, the "self-denying mother," wanted children, and María could not sire children. Her voice broke as she explained the crisis:

> The last three years, our relationship was very very bad. We would make love at night and fight during the day. It was more painful to make love because we knew that we couldn't have children, that was clear. But we wanted a consummation of our relationship. When we made love, she usually ended up crying. And I was so guilty, like, "I can't!" I felt so impotent, without reason. I was not at fault for that.

Desperate, María investigated having a sex change operation and becoming a "transsexual," even though it would have been very painful. Of course she still would have been "impotent." At a cost of "a million pesos," she could not afford it.

For reasons that are not entirely clear, María decided to be faithful but Josefina had her own affair with a man, became pregnant, and fell in love with him. María was jealous and initially had doubts that Josefina was actually pregnant, fearing it was some sort of ruse. Josefina then got an abortion, and that created an irreparable rift in their relationship.

> The abortion is what hurt me, more than her being in love with somebody else. I didn't understand, why did she do that? She said, "I knew that you were jealous, and feeling sad." But it was more sad at that point in our relationship to not have it. I said, "Let's have it, it will be our child. It's good that you are pregnant. Yes, I am jealous but when you have the child, those jealousies will be gone. But let me work on it, let me process this." No. That was a very strong breach.

María's own Catholicism and desire for a child that consummated their love made Josefina's rationale for the abortion unfathomable: "When I asked her why, she said 'because I love you and I don't want you to be resentful of this. I'm gonna have it when you and I are better.' The guilt, the pressure of the guilt was too large. I couldn't believe that it happened." Unable to control Josefina on something so important, María reacted with her idea of a male response. Anticipating the *dénouement* of their relationship, María resumed her macha ways: "And then I started being unfaithful again, with two more women at the same time. I started being promiscuous." Ironically, Josefina "came out of the closet" several years after their relationship ended.

María had a number of different lovers after that, from each one learning something new. Despite promises of fidelity, she was often unfaithful. She kept track, with great respect, of the number of women who gave her the gift of their virginity. She even had a sexual relationship with a man, just as an experiment. Given his inattention to her sexual pleasure, María found straight sex boring.

In 1978, María moved to Mexico City, where she became involved in a network of other *lesbianas*. But without public safe spaces such as the lesbian bars in the United States[26] and a nascent gay and lesbian rights movement centered in Guadalajara (a day's bus ride away),[27] coming out as a lesbian was not particularly appealing to her: "We didn't say 'we're *lesbianas*,' but we would just be together. Whenever people would say something about it, we would just look at them like, 'You better shut up.'" Looking for adventure and still grieving the loss of her relationship with Josefina, María moved to the United States in 1986, about the time that Mirella was coming of age.

Here María experienced a new awareness of racism and found more openness regarding sexuality.[28] Economically her life took a tailspin; despite her middle-class credentials, she could not find a job and worked as a farm worker for about a year until she found work as a bilingual staff person in a social service agency. Her social life was a different story: She met a number of lesbians and bisexual women who were out of the closet. Indeed, a national magazine dubbed Santa Cruz as the new "lesbian utopia" (displacing Amherst, Massachusetts) and there are regular features in the local press indicating the presence of many lesbians. In this context, María began dating Latinas and white women, and with their encouragement she underwent a profound transformation. With the active support of one lover, María came out of the closet herself and began accepting herself as female: "She's very beautiful and she made me realize that if women were with me, it wasn't because I appeared to be a man or I was pretending to be a man. No, it was because I was a *woman*. So I confronted that. Now I say, 'Yeah I'm a woman and I love women.'" This reconciliation with herself even had a dramatic effect on her body. "Before, I was less femme, I didn't have large breasts. I looked like a boy." She gained weight and became more curvaceous, and changed from androgynous-looking to having a more female body type: "Because of the comfort of being accepted, I have learned to cope. And my body changed after I accepted that I was a woman. I think it was psychosomatic." With her self-described more feminine body, María now wears pants, oxford shirts, and short hair; from a distance she appears gender-neutral. María also experienced a new sense of the importance of masturbation in her life, incorporating self-pleasure as an explicit political stance, in part to counter any possible threat of AIDS, but also as part of her self-conscious attempt to redefine herself.

María is currently living with her lover (who during her interview chose the pseudonym Frida) in an open lesbian relationship. She is proud that their relationship is based on fidelity and honesty. María characterized Frida as "more femme" than herself, because of Frida's appreciation of a feminine self-presentation of her body through dress and hair styles. The couple experienced economic difficulties, as the defunding of social services in California often meant that one or both of them was temporarily unemployed. Their financial vicissitudes provided the base of the couple's desire for flexible gender expectations: "In the beginning I was the provider for a few months, and then I became the housewife. And I'm the mom sometimes, because she's younger than me, and I'm the teacher most of the time. She's a very good student." María described their love: "I'm very lucky to be with Frida. When I am in love with a woman, I'm very passionate. I'm a Scorpio so it's extreme: It's like a big explosion—*boom*."

María's coming-out story, however, is not just a process of self-actualization as she struggles with contradictions in a heterosexist society. Frida occasionally bullies María by throwing furniture or hitting walls with her fists during arguments, although according to both women Frida does not actually hit María. Despite her happiness with Frida, because of these outbursts, María considers herself a battered woman. Ironically, even as María has accepted her own womanhood, she views herself as not in control and relatively powerless to stop the violence—as *la mujer abnegada,* a suffering woman. The couple has sought help with a social service agency that provides lesbian-sensitive services for battered women so María does not see herself as a victim but as a survivor. She laments that those services are not offered in Spanish, the language of their intimacy. María hopes to establish an organization of *lesbianas Mexicanas* that could provide culturally sensitive, bilingual services for lesbians experiencing domestic violence of all types. María seeks a new kind of power—collective mutual aid with other women.

CONCLUSION

Despite being of different generations, nationalities, and sexual orientations, these two women articulated strikingly similar cultural poetics regarding gender and sexuality. They were both expected to conform to traditional Catholic expectations that women forgo sexual exploration or pleasure, guard their virginity and reputations for marriage and children, and denigrate homosexuality. This powerful cultural message created a virtual cult of virginity—not unlike that in other cultures—that was being undermined by the end of the twentieth century. Both women learned that their own bodies would alter to reveal their deviation from "purity" and a loss of status, confirming findings in other research on the importance of virginity for Mexican women.

When these women did "give up" their virginity, they heard their lovers use the language of play, referring to them as little daughters. Both heard echoes of honor and respect for their conformity to these ideals of proper womanhood, or experienced shame, anguish, and scandal for the transgressions—confirming notions Gutiérrez found much earlier in Mexican society. This cultural message contained a deep pragmatism, promising life-long economic support by a man in exchange for playing the part. Despite having more education than most Latinas, they learned few culturally sanctioned messages that confirmed their yearning and faced contending ideas about sexuality in the United States, particularly in popular culture.

These women, however, are not the subjugated, essentialized category of woman in the Mexican allegory of virgin/whore. As historical actors, they both regarded Catholic ideology as a template to be contested. Their own volition and support of other women shaped how they came to know their bodies, whom they found attractive, and the pleasure they found in sexual relationships with others. Each struggled to create a discourse about the power of love in this culturally mediated world where the female gender was subject to male dominance.

Mirella's "plot" involved coming to desire a man of her own racial background, despite the deep emotional scarring of male violence and Catholic-inspired control over her body, and having been "singed" through her social transgressions with white men. Despite the cadences of "valley girl" speech with inferences of nonchalance, her dreams carry serious economic consequences. The potential stable life together with Ray, with their combined income as a professional couple, would provide definite prospects of economic and social mobility much beyond what she could provide for herself. Mirella links the vision of a companionate ideal family—one sanctioned by institutionalized heterosexuality—with sexual pleasure.

María also recoiled from the crucible of patriarchy and Catholicism even as she was drawn to the entitlements of masculinity. She, too, was "scorched," this time because of her desire for women and for flaunting the conventions of virginity and femininity. Her choice of lesbianism means that she would not have the economic support afforded to women who marry well. María's position in marginally funded social services brings the challenge of building on her human capital and becoming economically stable with a partner in the same situation.

These women's narratives illustrate structures of gender, of sexuality, and of racialized bodies in Mexican culture that profoundly affect decisions that appear to be individualistic. While the boundaries proscribed for women seem rigid and limiting, they were certainly malleable enough for these women to create space for themselves. In following her desires, each woman subverted male dominance and reconstructed power, claiming an autonomous life and subjectivity. Each maneuvered through the fires of control to embrace the body enflamed.

NOTES

Thanks to Tomás Almaguer, Gloria Cuádraz, Micaela di Leonardo, Barbara García, Ramón Gutiérrez, Mirella Hernández, Aída Hurtado, Francisca Angulo Olaiz, María Pérez, Carter Wilson, and the graduate students in my Latino Ethnographies graduate seminar at the University of Michigan for their helpful comments on various versions of this paper.

1. David D. Gilmore, ed. *Honor and Shame and the Unity of the Mediterranean* No. 22 (Washington: American Anthropological Association, 1987); J. Peristiany, ed. *Honour and Shame: The Values of Mediterranean Society* (Chicago: University of Chicago Press, 1965); Julian Pitt-Rivers, "Honor," *International Encyclopedia of the Social Sciences* (New York, 1968), pp. 131–51.

2. Jean Franco, *Plotting Women: Gender and Representation in Mexico* (New York: Columbia University Press, 1989). This cultural configuration is specific to Mexican society; Roger Lancaster asserts that "'sexual purity' in the sense of virginity is not and never has been an important element of the Nicaraguan ideal of proper womanhood." See Roger N. Lancaster, *Life is Hard: Machismo, Danger, and The Intimacy of Power in Nicaragua* (Berkeley: University of California Press, 1992), p. 310.

3. There is a long intertextual tradition of reflection on the Mexican national character ("*lo*

mexicano"). Two key texts are: Octavio Paz, *The Labyrinth of Solitude, Life and Thought in Mexico* (New York: Grove Press, 1961) and Samuel Ramos, *Profile of Man and Culture in Mexico* (Austin: University of Texas Press, 1962). Anthropologist Claudio Lomnitz-Adler calls instead for the study of regional and intimate ideologies. See Claudio Lomnitz-Adler, *Exits from the Labyrinth: Culture and Ideology in the Mexican National Space* (Berkeley: University of California Press, 1992).

4. Adelaida R. del Castillo, "Malintzin Tenepal: A Preliminary Look into a New Perspective," in *Essays on La Mujer*, eds. Rosaura Sánchez and Rosa Martínez Cruz (UCLA: Chicano Studies Center Publications, 1977); Norma Alarcón, Chicana Feminist Literature: A Re-Vision Through Malintzin/or Malintzin: Putting flesh Back on the Object," in *This Bridge Called My Back, Writings by Radical Women of Color*, eds. Cherríe Moraga and Gloria Anzaldúa (Watertown, MA: Persephone Press, 1981); Cherríe Moraga, *Loving in the War Years: lo que nunca pasó por sus labios* (Boston: South End Press, 1983). Ramón Gutiérrez argues that in Spanish colonial society there were prescribed gender-specific rules of proper social comportment, where honor was a male attribute while shame was intrinsic to females because of their "natural weakness" and association with nature. Men were encouraged to be sexually active even through coercion or deception. "Decent" women, unless given in Church-sanctified matrimony, were shamed and dishonored through illicit sexual behavior. Thus women were to be "militantly protected" by family members and the church, their honor-virtue "fiercely contested and rather scandalously lost," and the seduction of a virgin of high status subject to legal sanctions during the eighteenth century. Low status women—who had lost institutional ties to men and/or were members of inferior racial categories—were considered sport for the prowess of men. Thus conflicts over maintaining honor—how norms and values were imposed or contested—or the repercussions of lost honor and inevitable shame, illuminate the social construction of sexuality in colonial Mexican society. See Ramón A. Gutiérrez, *When Jesus Came the Corn Mothers Went Away: Marriage, Sexuality and Power in New Mexico, 1500–1846* (Stanford: Stanford University Press, 1991).

5. The terms Chicana/o or Mexicana/o, designed to get away from the use of the generic "he" in the word Chicano or Mexicano, are cumbersome. I use Chicana/Mexicano to designate people of Mexican origin in the United States of both sexes.

6. Olivia M. Espín, "Cultural and Historical Influences on Sexuality in Hispanic/Latin Women: Implications for Psychotherapy," in *Pleasure and Danger: Exploring Female Sexuality*, Carol Vance, ed. (Boston: Routledge and Kegan Paul, 1984), pp. 149–64; Emma Guerrero Pavich, "A Chicana Perspective on Mexican Culture and Sexuality," *Journal of Social Work and Human Sexuality* 3 (Spring, 1986), pp. 47–65; Ana María Alonso and María Teresa Koreck, "Silences: 'Hispanics,' AIDS, and Sexual Practices," *Differences A Journal of Feminist Cultural Studies* 1 (1989), pp. 101–24; Amado M. Padilla and Traci L. Baird, "Mexican-American Adolescent Sexuality and Sexual Knowledge: An Exploratory Study," *Hispanic Journal of Behavioral Sciences* 13 (1, 1991), pp. 95–104.

7. Alonso and Korek, "Silences: 'Hispanics,' AIDS, and Sexual Practices." Also see James M. Taggart, Gender Segregation and Cultural Constructions of Sexuality in Two Hispanic Societies. *American Ethnologist* 19 (1, 1992), pp. 75–96; Carter Wilson, *Hidden in the Blood: AIDS in Yucatan.* (New York: Columbia University Press 1995).

8. David Alvirez, "The Effects of Formal Church Affiliation and Religiosity on the Fertility Patterns of Mexican American Catholics," *Demography* 10 (1973), pp. 19–36. Hispanic teenagers are just as likely to have an abortion as black and white teenagers. See Katherine F. Darabi, Joy Dryfoos and Dana Schwartz, "Hispanic Adolescent Fertility," *Hispanic Journal of Behavioral Sciences* 8 no. 2 (1986), pp. 157–71. For a discussion of women's escape from sexual violence, see Lourdes Argüelles and Anne Rivero, "Violence, Migration, and Compassionate Practice: Conversations with Some Women We Think We Know," *Urban Anthropology*, special issue on Latino Ethnography 22 no. 3–4 (1993), pp. 259–76.

9. Literally "tongue and place": Pérez is calling for a discourse and social space "that rejects colonial ideology and the by-products of colonialism and capitalist patriarchy—sexism, racism,

homophobia." See Emma Pérez, "Sexuality and Discourse: Notes From a Chicana Survivor," in Carla Trujillo, ed., *Chicana Lesbians: The Girls Our Mothers Warned Us About* (Berkeley: Third Woman Press, 1991), pp. 159–84. See also Cherríe Moraga, *Loving in the War Years;* Gloria Anzaldúa, *Borderlands/La Frontera: The New Mestiza* (San Francisco: spinsters/aunt lute, 1987); Juanita Ramos, ed. *Compañera: Latina Lesbians (an Anthology* (New York: Latina Lesbian History Project, 1987); Norma Alarcón, Ana Castillo and Cherríe Moraga, "The Sexuality of Latinas." Special Issue of *Third Woman* 4 (1989); Tomás Almaguer, "Chicano Men: A Cartography of Homosexual Identity and Behavior," *Differences: A Journal of Feminist Cultural Studies* 3 no. 2 (1991), pp. 75–100; Trujillo, ed. *Chicana Lesbians*; Emma Pérez, "Speaking From the Margin: Uninvited Discourse on Sexuality and Power," in *Building with Our Hands: New Directions in Chicana Studies*, Adela de la Torre and Beatriz M. Pesquera (Berkeley: University of California Press, 1993), pp. 57–74.

10. I am currently doing historical and ethnographic research on the construction of family and household among the poor in Santa Cruz County, California, thus far interviewing mainly women—Mexicanas, Chicanas and whites, heterosexual and queer. I query how people were socialized regarding sex, family and marriage; inquiring about early experiences with sexual experimentation; messages they received about their bodies, experiences regarding starting to menstruate (for women); sexual histories; notions of sexual pleasure; and current experiences and values regarding family and sex.

11. For a discussion of nondiscursive knowledge, see Michael Burawoy, et al., eds., *Ethnography Unbound: Power and Resistance in the Modern Metropolis* (Berkeley: University of California Press, 1991), p. 5. Roger M. Keesing argues that women's "muteness" or the richness of their narratives "must always be historically and contextually situated, and bracketed with doubt." See "Kwaio Women Speak: The Micropolitics of Autobiography in a Solomon Island Society," *American Anthropologist*, vol. 87 (March 1985), pp. 27–39, p. 27.

12. In autobiographical written narratives, writers often struggle with the blurring of "memory" and "reality." See Penelope Lively, *Oleander, Jacaranda: A Childhood Perceived* (New York: Harper Collins, 1994); and Judith Ortiz Cofer, *Silent Dancing: A Partial Remembrance of a Puerto Rican Childhood* (Houston: Arte Publico Press, 1990).

13. Lively, *Oleander, Jacaranda*, vii.

14. Donna Haraway, *Primate Visions: Gender, Race, and Nature in the World of Modern Science* (New York: Routledge, 1989).

15. Lancaster, *Life is Hard*, p. 318.

16. Although this trope emerged with white women as well, that analysis is beyond the scope of this paper.

17. Ann Snitow, Christine Stansell and Sharon Thompson, eds. *Powers of Desire: The Politics of Sexuality* (New York: Monthly Review Press, 1983).

18. María went over my narrative about her, making corrections regarding dates and names, and clarifying her views. She preferred that I use her real name, and viewed this disclosure as part of her process of coming out as a lesbian: "I know its a tremendous risk but this is reality, this is not fiction. They cannot deny me."

19. Franco, *Plotting Women*, p. xxiii.

20. Other Chicanas and Mexicanas reported changes that occur in women's bodies after losing their virginity, including that women's hips get wider, that they walk differently, or that their faces become more "knowing."

21. Francisca Angulo Olaiz, "Struggling to Have a Say: How Latino Adolescents Construct Themselves as Sexual Adults and What this Means for HIV Prevention Programs," Masters' thesis, Anthropology Department, University of California, Los Angeles, 1995, p. 54.

22. Based on participant observation in a southern California high school and in-depth interviews with Chicana/Latino high school students (women and men), Francisca Angulo Olaiz finds that virginity

is socially constructed. Women especially do not denigrate a woman who lost her virginity if she was in love with the man and expected permanence in the relationship. See Olaiz, "Struggling to Have a Say," chapter 3.

23. Cherríe Moraga, *Loving in the War Years*, p. 125.

24. While *compañera* literally means companion or sexual partner, María explicitly characterized Josefina as her "wife."

25. Alonso and Koreck argue that it is acceptable for a heterosexual couple to have anal intercourse prior to marriage for it does not negate a woman's vaginal virginity and is a form of birth control. See Alonso and Koreck, "Silences: 'Hispanics,' AIDS, and Sexual Practices."

26. Elizabeth Kennedy Lapovsky and Madeline D. Davis, *Boots of Leather, Slippers of Gold: The History of a Lesbian Community* (New York: Routledge, 1993).

27. Ian Lumsden, *Homosexuality: Society and the State in Mexico* (México, D.F.: Solediciones Colectivo Sol, 1991).

28. Immigrant lesbian women from various countries report experiencing shock from the differences between their home countries and the United States. See Olivia M. Espín, "Crossing Borders and Boundaries: The Life Narratives of Immigrant Lesbians," *Division* 44 (1995), pp. 18–27.

Appropriations, Contestations, and Adaptations

Toward a History of the Present

Part Seven

SEX WARS,
CULTURE WARS

27 Violence, Sexuality, and Women's Lives

Lori L. Heise

My feminist project over the last six years has been to interject the reality of violence against women into the dominant discourse on AIDS, women's health, and international family planning. My overall aim has been twofold: to improve public health policy by making it more reflective of the reality of women's lives, and to marshal some of the resources and technical know-how of the international health community to assist women's organizations fighting gender violence in the developing world.[1]

To date, the failure of the global health community to recognize gender-based abuse has put both important public health objectives and individual women at risk. By ignoring the pervasiveness of violence within relationships, for example, the current global AIDS strategy (which is based heavily on condom promotion) dooms itself to failure. The research shows that many women are afraid to even broach the subject of condom use for fear of male reprisal (Elias and Heise 1993; Rao Gupta 1993). As Anke Ehrhardt, co-director of the HIV Center for Clinical and Behavioral Studies, observes, "We have not only ignored the fact that women do not control condom use, but we have rushed head long into prevention efforts aimed at getting women to insist on condom use without taking into account that they may risk severe repercussions, such as violence and other serious threats to their economic and social support" (Ehrhardt 1991).

This is but one example of the potential costs of failing to explore the intersection of violence, sexuality, gender, and public health. In this chapter, I lay out what is known about violence and sexuality, especially with respect to its implications for women's sexual and reproductive lives. More importantly, I discuss several risks I see present in the feminist project of introducing ideas about violence and sexuality into the professional world of public health. Focusing the "biomedical gaze" on violence risks reinforcing negative images of woman as "victim," an impression that can undermine women's interests. (For example, when faced with women's initial difficulty in "negotiating" condom use, some AIDS experts recommended shifting the entire focus of

Lori L. Heise is Codirector of the Health and Development Policy Project (HDPP), a not-for-profit research and advocacy organization dedicated to integrating gender concerns and social justice perspectives into international health policy and practice. A long-time advocate for women's health internationally, Ms. Heise has worked extensively in the areas of gender-based violence, women and HIV issues, and sexual education. She can be reached by e-mail at lheise@igc.apc.org.

condom promotion and training to men, instead of exploring ways to strengthen women's ability to protect themselves.) Increased attention to the pervasiveness of violence, especially sexual violence, also risks fueling popular notions of sexuality as biologically driven and of male sexualities as "inherently predatory"—both notions experiencing a resurgence in popular culture. As I will show, however, the cross-cultural record does not support a vision of male sexuality as inherently aggressive. To the extent that male sexual behavior is aggressive in certain cultures, it is because sexuality expresses power relations based on gender.

A MULTIPLICITY OF DISCOURSES

Sexuality and gender have become the subjects of sociological and biomedical inquiry only within the last century or so. Within this short history, several distinct discourses have laid claim to the domain of human sexual experience. The first, "sexology," emerged as a discipline in the late nineteenth century. Typified by Havelock Ellis, Alfred Kinsey, and Masters and Johnson, sexology has been most concerned with sexual function, dysfunction, and the physiology of the sexual response. To its credit, sexology views women as agents of their own sexual lives, and takes as a given women's right to sexual pleasure (see Table 1).

Many feminists have criticized sexology, however, for neglecting the "dangerous" side of sex for women: abuse, unwanted pregnancy, STDs, humiliation, rape. As feminist Leonore Tiefer points out, "Sexology's nomenclature of sexual disorders does not describe what makes women unhappy about sex in the real world, but narrows and limits the vision of sexual problems to failures of genital performance" (Tiefer 1992). According to Tiefer, sexology looks at sexuality from the position of male privilege, where the sexual narrative has to do with erotics: intercourse, arousal, pleasure, erection, orgasm. "All well and good," she notes, "But hardly the stuff at the center of many women's sexual experience" (Tiefer 1992: 4).

Feminists also fault sexology for failing to confront and work against gender-based power differentials. Significantly, none of the breakthrough studies that first documented the pervasiveness of nonconsensual sex, illegal abortion, and STDs in women came from mainstream sex research. Sexology has resisted challenging male power over female sexuality—in the form of coercive sex, male-defined religious doctrine, or lack of contraceptive research—because it fears "politicizing" what it sees as a basically neutral, "scientific" subject. According to feminists, however, sexologists—like all professionals—can either *support* institutional norms which ignore women's reality, or they can *subvert* those norms. As Tiefer maintains: "Any attempt to be neutral, to be 'objective' is to support the status quo" (Tiefer 1992: 5).

A second more recent discourse on sexuality emerges from the "population control" and international health establishment. International health's interest in sex focuses almost exclusively on behaviors that have implications for demographics and/or for disease. A review of over 2,100 articles from five of the top family planning and health journals, for example, reveals that between 1980 and 1992, sexuality and male-female power dynamics are mentioned only within three narrow contexts: how women's attitudes about sexuality influence contraceptive use and effectiveness (forty-one articles); how adolescent sexual activity and contraceptive use are related to teen pregnancy (twenty-four articles); and how "high risk" sexual behaviors are related to the spread of sexually transmitted diseases, including AIDS (eleven articles) (Dixon-Mueller 1992). The preoccupation in public health has been with sexual danger and with counting disembodied acts (e.g., the number of instances of unprotected penetrative intercourse in the last month) not with meaning, context, or pleasure. In this discourse, women are frequently seen as means to an end—as "targets" for demographic initiatives or as reproductive vessels—rather than as individuals with independent needs and a right to sexual self-determination and pleasure (Dixon-Mueller 1993).

A third prominent discourse, which I shall call "antipornography feminism," is best represented by women such as Andrea Dworkin, Catharine MacKinnon, Kathleen Barry, and Evelina Giobbe. These women have dominated one side of what has come to be known in feminist cir-

Table 1   Sex Research Paradigms

Sexology	Population Control/ Public Health	Anti-Pornography Feminism	Integrated Feminist Approach
Acknowledges PLEASURE but Focuses on Genital Performance	Focuses on DANGER (STDs; unwanted pregnancy; "high risk sex")	Focuses on DANGER (Rape, child sexual abuse; pornography)	Acknowledges DANGER but Claims Women's Right to Sexual PLEASURE
Ignores Gender Power Imbalances	Attempts to Override Imbalances through Technology	Fights Against Gender-based Power Inequities	Fights Against Gender-based Power Inequities
Focuses on Behavior and Physiology	Focus on Behavior and Technology	Focuses on Context and Meaning (although tends toward negative)	Focuses on Context and Meaning but recognizes pragmatic realities
Women Seen as Agents	Women Seen as a Means to an End (e.g. to achieve demographic targets)	Women seen as Victims (or potential victims)	Women Seen as Agents Operating within Restricted Options
Adherents See themselves as Scientists	Adherents See Themselves as Practitioners	Adherents See Themselves as Activists	Adherents See Themselves as Activists and Practitioners
Risks Trivializing Women's Reality by Ignoring "Danger" Part of Sex for Women	Ignores Gender-based Power Relations to the Detriment of Program Success	Fuels Essentialist Notions of Male Sexuality as Inherently "Predatory"; Reinforces Image of Women as Victims	Seeks Strategies that Empower Women and Promote Long-Term Social Change while Meeting Women's Immediate Needs

cles as the "sex wars"—basically an internal debate over the "appropriate" boundaries (from a feminist perspective) of human sexual behavior. At issue are such themes as pornography, sado-masochism, prostitution, and how society should respond to these phenomena (Valverde 1987; Cole 1989). The antipornography feminists argue for intervention and insist that women will never achieve equality as long as their sexuality is commercialized, and as long as domination and economic exploitation are conflated with sexual pleasure. The "sex radical critique, on the other hand, sees long term danger in any effort to censor sexual behavior between consenting adults, arguing that such efforts can too easily be used against sexual minorities and women" (Vance 1984).

While my work shares a common motivation with the anti-pornography feminists, there are strains in their thought that I find troubling. I commend this paradigm for its focus on gender-based power inequities and for its activist stance, but it tends to be profoundly pessimistic, and easily degenerates into portraying women solely as victims. In their zeal to highlight the dangers of sex, antipornography feminists have also tended to overlook sex's pleasures. In a radically "sex-negative" culture, overcompensation—even in the face of a culture largely indifferent to women's victimization—carries certain dangers. It also contributes to the poplar "demonization" of men and of male sexuality. It is the importation of these pitfalls that I fear in my effort to introduce the reality of violence into the family planning and international health field. To the uninitiated, the very pervasiveness of violence can be so overwhelming as to justify dismissing the situation as impossible to change.

Understandably, such concerns have been used to question efforts to integrate violence into the public health mainstream. Rather than tolerate naivete and gender-blindness in the health and development field, however, I think antiviolence activism must seek to transform public health discourse and research, encouraging a greater emphasis on social context, meaning, power differentials, and gender. It is with this vision that I offer a new paradigm for sex research and practice within public health, combining the strength of the three other models. Table 1 includes a brief summary of the existing sex paradigms as well as a suggested model for a new approach. This new option—which I call the "integrated feminist approach"—is most closely approximated today by the women's health movement as reflected in the demands put forward by women's groups at the International Conference on Population and Development (ICPD) in Cairo.

While this chart admittedly oversimplifies three complex and pluralistic fields of inquiry, it nonetheless allows a quick (and I hope useful) comparison of some of the existing stakeholders in women's sexuality. It also summarizes the integrated approach to sexuality that I strive for in my own work. The following section explores what we currently know about violence and coercion as it relates to women's sexual and reproductive health. In the last section of this chapter, I offer an interpretation of these data and explore my concerns about the anti-pornography discourse in greater detail.

THE IMPACT OF VIOLENCE ON WOMEN'S SEXUAL AND REPRODUCTIVE LIVES

Regrettably, we know very little in social science about how violence or fear of violence operates in women's lives. Only recently have researchers begun to document the pervasiveness of gender-based abuse, and virtually no attempt has been made to investigate how violence affects women's sexuality. There are important questions in need of exploration: What is the role of coercion in sexual initiation? How do force and fear affect women's experience of sexual pleasure? How does violence affect women's reproductive health? The following section summaries the information available on each of these questions. Of necessity, much of the analysis remains speculative.

The Prevalence of Violence Against Women

The most endemic form of violence against women is wife abuse, or more accurately, abuse of women by intimate male partners. Table 2 summarizes twenty studies from a wide variety of countries that document that *one-quarter to over half* of women in many countries of the world report having been physically abused by a present or former partner. Although some of these studies are based on convenience samples, the majority are based on probability samples with a large number of respondents (e.g., Mexico, United States, Colombia, Kenya).[2]

Statistics around the world also suggest that rape is a common reality in the lives of women and girls. Six population-based surveys from the United States, for example, suggest that between one in five and one in seven U.S. women will be the victims of a completed rape in her lifetime (Kilpatrick, Edmund and Seymor 1992).[3] Moreoever, there are well-designed studies of rape among college-aged women from New Zealand (Gavey 1991), Canada (Dekeseredy and Kelly 1992), the United States (Koss, Gidycz, and Wisniewski 1987), and the United Kingdom (Beattie 1992) that reveal remarkably similar rates of completed rape across countries, when using similar survey instruments (based on Koss and Oros 1982).[4] A study among adult women (many of them college students) in Seoul, Korea, yielded slightly lower rates of completed rape, but an equally high rate of attempts (Shim 1992) (see Table 3).

Not surprisingly, given the extremely sensitive nature of the subject, reliable data on child sexual abuse are even more scarce. Nonetheless, the few studies that do exist—along with ample indirect evidence—suggest that sexual abuse of children and adolescents is a widespread phenomenon. In the United States, for example, population-based studies indicate that twenty-seven to 62 percent of women recall at least one incident of sexual abuse before the age of eighteen (Peters, Wyatt, and Finkelhor 1986).[5] An anonymous, islandwide, probability survey of Barbados revealed that one woman in three and one to two men per one hundred reported behavior constituting childhood or adolescent sexual abuse (Handwerker 1991). And in Canada, a government commission estimated that one in four female children and one in ten male children are sexually assaulted prior to the age of seventeen years (Canadian Government 1984).

Elsewhere, indirect evidence suggests cause for concern. Two studies from Nigeria, for example, document that a large percentage of female patients at STD clinics are young children. A 1988 study in Zaria, Nigeria found that sixteen percent of female patients seeking treatment for STDs were children under the age of five and another six percent were children between the ages of six and fifteen (Kisekka and Otesanya 1988). An older study in Ibadan found that twenty-two percent of female patients attending one STD clinic were under the age of ten (Sogbetun et al. 1977). Likewise, a study conducted in the Maternity Hospital of Lima, Peru revealed that ninety percent of the young mothers aged twelve to sixteen had been raped by their father, stepfather or another close relative.[6]

A final indication of the prevalence of sexual abuse comes from the observations of children themselves. In 1991, when the Nicaraguan NGO, CISAS held a national conference for the children involved in their "Child to Child" program (a project that trains youngsters ages eight to fifteen to be better child care providers for their siblings), participants identified "sexual abuse" as the number one health priority facing young people in their country.

EXPERIENCE OF SEXUAL PLEASURE

When coercion enters the sexual arena, it invariably affects women's experience of sex. While we know something about the impact of rape or sexual abuse on women's sexual functioning, little is known about how subtle or overt coercion within consensual unions affects women's sexual lives. Research indicates that from 50 to 60 percent of women who are raped experience severe sexual problems, including fear of sex, problems with arousal, and decreased sexual functioning (Burnam 1988; Becker et al. 1982). But what of forced sex within relationships or of the role of coercion in women's sexual initiation? Both are topics deserving much greater exploration.

Little information is available, for example, on the degree to which young women feel coerced into their first sexual experience. In one study, 40 percent of girls ages eleven to fifteen in Jamaica reported the reason for their first intercourse as "forced" (Allen 1982). A qualitative study of sexual initiation among adolescent girls in the United States—aptly entitled "Putting a Big Thing into a Little Hole"—indicates that many girls recall their first intercourse negatively (Thompson 1990).[7] Many girls mention pain, fear, disappointment, and a sense of not being in control of the situation. While most do not frame their experience as "coercive," few in this group were prepared for or actively wanted the sex to happen. As author Sharon Thompson observes: "Often they did not agree to sex. They gave in, they gave up, they gave out" (Thompson 1990:358).

Also at issue is how young girls experience first intercourse when forced into arranged marriages at a very young age. While the rate of child marriage is declining, a significant portion of girls are still married off before the age of fifteen, often to unknown men many years their senior (see Table 4). Evidence from a qualitative study of sexual initiation among child brides in Iran confirms that early intercourse, even when culturally supported, can be very traumatic for young girls. Anthropologist Mary Hegland interviewed exiled Iranian women living in the United States about sexual initiation in Iran (Hegland n.d.). Many gave graphic details of forced defloration of young girls, most of whom were totally ignorant of sex (often a young girl was held down by relatives while the man forced himself on her). While the women said the term "rape" would never be applied to this experience in Iran, they freely used terms like "rape" and "torture" to describe the experience after being exposed to this language in the United States. This new language merely gave voice to feelings they already had.

Given the prevalence of violence in women's lives, there is a remarkable lack of information on how it affects women's sexuality. Only one study, published recently in the *Journal of Family Violence*,

Table 2   Prevalence of Wife Abuse, Selected Countries

COUNTRY	SAMPLE SIZE	SAMPLE TYPE	FINDINGS	COMMENTS
Barbados (Handwerker 1991)	264 women and 243 men aged 20–45	Island-wide national probability sample	30% of women battered as adults	Women and men report 50% of their mothers beaten
Antigua (Handwerker 1993)	97 women aged 20–45	Random subset of national probability sample	30% of women battered as adults	Women and men report 50% of mothers beaten
Kenya (Raikes 1990)	733 women from Kissi District	District-wide cluster sample	42% "beaten regularly"	Taken from contraceptive prevalence survey
Papua New Guinea (Toft 1987)	*Rural* 736 men; 715 women; *Urban Low Income,* 368 men; 298 women; *Urban Elite* 178 men; 99 women	Rural survey in 19 villages in all regions and provinces Urban survey with oversample of elites	67% rural women beaten; 56% urban low income women beaten; 62% urban elite women beaten	Almost perfect agreement between % of women who claim to have been beaten and % of men who admit to abuse
Sri Lanka (Sonali 1990)	200 mixed ethnic, low-income women from Colombo	Convenience sample from low-income neighborhood	60% have been beaten	51% said husbands used weapons
India (Mahajan 1990)	109 men and 109 women from village in Jullundur District, Punjab	50% sample of all scheduled (lower) caste households and 50% of nonscheduled (higher) caste houses	75% of lower caste men admit to beating their wives; 22% of higher caste men admit to beatings	75% of scheduled caste wives report being beaten "frequently"
Malaysia (WAO 1993)	713 women and 508 males over 15 years old	National random probability sample of Peninsular Malaysia	39% of women have been "physically beaten by a partner in the last year"	Note: This is an annual figure; 15% of adults consider wife beating acceptable (22% of Malays)
Colombia (PROFAMILIA 1992)	3,272 urban women 2,118 rural woman	National probability sample	20% physically abused; 33% psychologically abused; 10% raped by husband	Part of Colombia's Demographic and Health survey
Costa Rica (Chacon et al. 1990)	1,388 women	Convenience sample of women attending child welfare clinic	50% report being physically abused	Sponsored by UNICEF/PAHO
Costa Rica (1990)	1,312 women aged 15–49 years	Random probability sample of urban women	51% report being beaten up to several times per year; 35% report being hit regularly	

Table 2 (Continued) Prevalence of Wife Abuse, Selected Countries

COUNTRY	SAMPLE SIZE	SAMPLE TYPE	FINDINGS	COMMENTS
Mexico (Jalisco) (Ramirez and Vazquez 1993)	1,163 rural women; 427 urban women in the state of Jalisco	Random household survey of women on DIF register	56.7% of urban women and 44.2% of rural women experienced some form of "interpersonal violence"	
Mexico (Valdez Santiago and Shrader Cox 1990)	342 women from Nezahualcoyotl	Random probability sample of women from city adjacent to Mexico City	33% had lived in a "violent relationship"	
Ecuador (CEPLAES 1992)	200 low-income women	Convenience sample of Quito barrio	60% had been "beaten" by a partner	Of those beaten, 37% were assaulted with a frequency between once a month and every day
Chile (Larrain 1993)	1,000 women in Santiago ages 22 to 55 years involved in a relationship of 2 years or more	Stratified random probability sample with a maximum sampling error of 3%	60% abused by a male intimate; 26.2% physically abused (more severe than pushes, slaps, or having an object thrown at you)	70% of those abused are abused more than once a year
Norway (Schei and Bakketeig 1989)	150 women aged 20 to 49 years in Trondheim	Random sample selected from census data	25% had been physically or sexually abused by a male partner	Definition does not include less severe forms of violence like pushing, slapping, or shoving
New Zealand (Mullen et al. 1988)	2,000 women sent questionnaire; stratified random sample of 349 women selected for interview	Random probability sample selected from electoral rolls of five contiguous parliamentary constituencies	20.1% report being "hit and physically abused" by a male partner; 58% of these women (>10% of sample) were battered more than 3 times	
United States (Straus and Gelles 1986)	2,143 married or co-habitating couples	National random probability sample	28% report at least one episode of physical violence	
United States (Grant, Preda & Martin 1991)	6,000 women state-wide from Texas	Statewide random probability sample	39% have been abused by male partner after age 18; 31% have been physically abused	>12% have been sexually abused by male partner after age 18
United States (Teske and Parker 1983)	3,000 rural women in Texas	Random probability sample of communities with 50,000 people or less	40.2% have been abused after age 18; 31% have been physically abused	22% abused within the last 12 months

Table 3   Prevalence of Rape Among College-Aged Women

COUNTRY	AUTHORS	SAMPLE	DEFINITION OF RAPE[a]	COMPLETED RAPE	COMPLETED & ATTEMPTS
Canada	DeKeseredy and Kelly 1993	National probability sample of 1,835 women at 95 colleges and universities	Anal, oral, or vaginal intercourse by force or threat of force SES #9,10	8.1% (by dating partners since high school)	23.3% (rape or sexual assault by anyone ever)
New Zealand	Gavey 1991	347 women psychology students	Anal, vaginal intercourse by force or threat; or because a man gave alcohol or drugs SES #8,9,10	14.1%	25.3%
United Kingdom	Beattie 1992	1,574 women at six universities	Vaginal intercourse by force or because a man gave alcohol or drugs SES #8,9	11.3%	19.3%
United States	Koss et al. 1987	3,187 women at 32 colleges and universities	SES #8,9,10	15.4%	27.5%
United States	Moore, Nord and Peterson 1989	Nationally representative sample of 18 to 22 years old	Forced to have sex against your will, or were raped?	12.7% of whites; 8% of blacks (before age 21)	
Seoul Korea	Shim 1992	2,270 adult women (quota sample)	SES #9,10	7.7%	21.8%

a) Estimates of rape and attempted rape are based on the legal definition of rape in the country concerned and are derived from different combinations of the following questions taken from the Sexual Experiences Survey (Koss and Oros, 1984):

4) Has a man attempted sexual intercourse (getting on top of you, attempting to insert his penis) when you didn't want to by threatening or using some degree of physical force (twisting your arm, holding you down, etc.) but intercourse did not occur?

8) Have you had sexual intercourse when you didn't want to because a man gave you alcohol or drugs?

9) Have you had sexual intercourse when you didn't want to because a man threatened or used some degree of physical force (twisting your arm, holding you down, etc.) to make you?

10) Have you engaged in sex acts (anal or oral intercourse or penetration by objects other than a penis) when you didn't want to because a man threatened or used some degree of physical force (twisting your arm, holding you down, etc.) to make you?

explicitly looks at the effects of violence on women's experience of sex (Apt and Hurlbert 1993). Compared to nonabused women in distressed marriages, women living in violent relationships had significantly lower (i.e., more negative) responses on nine scales designed to measure sexual satisfaction, intimacy, arousal, and attitudes toward sex. Nonetheless, they had significantly more intercourse.

This high rate of intercourse is not surprising given the frequency of coerced sex within physically abusive relationships. Whereas 14 percent of all U.S. wives report being physically forced to have sex against their will, the prevalence of coercive intercourse among battered women is at least 40 percent (Campbell and Alford 1989). In Bolivia and Puerto Rico, 58 percent of battered wives report being sexually assaulted by their partner, and in Colombia, the reported rate is 46

Table 4   Percentage of Women Aged 20 to 24 Today
Who Were Married Before the Age of Fifteen, Selected Countries

COUNTRY	PERCENT	YEAR OF REPORT
Uganda	17.8	1989/90
Nigeria	26.7	1990
Mali	26.7	1987
Cameroon	21.3	1991
Liberia	16.6	1986
Guatemala	12.6	1987
Dominican Republic	9.0	1991
Mexico	6.2	1987
Trinidad/Tobago	6.0	1987
Egypt*	15.0	1988
Indonesia	10.0	1991
Pakistan	11.4	1990/91

* Before the age of 16
SOURCE: Selected Demographic and Health Surveys.

percent (Isis International 1988; PROFAMILIA 1992). Given the percentage of women around the world who live with physically abusive partners, it is likely that sexual coercion within consensual unions is quite common.

There is also a remarkable gap in our knowledge about the meaning and experience of sex among women who live in non-violent relationships. Even here, the experience of sex for women is often humiliating and degrading—one they tolerate rather than enjoy. Commenting on how their husbands treated them sexually, the Iranian women interviewed above used such phrases as "I'm not a toilet," "I'm not just a hole," "It's like swallowing nasty medicine" (Hegland n.d.). In focus group discussions with Mexican women about men, sex, and marriage, many women likewise expressed deep resentment about how men treated them in sexual relationships (Folch-Lyon, Macorra, and Schearer 1981). Women in particular mentioned:

- physical abuse by husbands to coerce the wife's sexual compliance;
- widespread male infidelity;
- men's authoritarian attitude toward their wives;
- threats of abandonment if wives failed to meet their husband's sexual demands or his demand for more children; and
- an abiding sense of depersonalization, humiliation, and physical dissatisfaction during sex.

Perhaps more than anything, the Spanish phrase women commonly use for sex captures their sentiment: *"el me usa"* (he uses me). Such comments raise the question of the nature of "consent" within the patriarchal institution of marriage. Would women consent to such treatment if they had the economic resources to survive independently and the social permission to seek sexual gratification elsewhere?

Ability to Control Fertility

The family planning literature documents that, for many women, fear of male reprisal greatly limits their ability to use contraception (Dixon-Mueller 1992). Men in many cultures react negatively to birth control because they think it signals a woman's intentions to be unfaithful. (Their logic is that protection against pregnancy allows a woman to be promiscuous.) Where children are a sign of male virility, a woman's attempt to use birth control may also be interpreted as an affront to her partner's masculinity. While male approval is not always the deciding factor, studies from countries as diverse as Mexico, South Africa, and Bangladesh have found that partner approval is the single greatest predictor of women's contraceptive use.[8] When partners disapprove, women either forgo contraception or they resort to family planning methods they can use without their partner's knowledge.

The unspoken reality behind this subterfuge is that women can be beaten or otherwise abused if they do not comply with men's sexual and childbearing demands. In a recent interview, Hope Mwesigye of FIDA-Uganda, a nonprofit legal aid organization for women in Kampala, recounted the story of a young married mother who was running from a husband who regularly beat her. Despite earning a decent wage, the woman's husband refused to maintain her and their two children. To avoid bringing more children into the world whom she could not feed, the woman began using birth control without her husband's consent. The beatings began when she failed to bring forth more children; they became more brutal when he learned of her contraceptive use (Banwell 1990).

In other countries, legal provisions requiring spousal permission before dispensing birth control can actually put women at increased risk of violence. According to Pamela Onyango of Family Planning International Assistance, women in Kenya have been known to forge their partner's signature rather than open themselves to violence or abandonment by requesting permission to use family planning services (Banwell 1990). Nor are Kenyan women alone in their fear of such consequences. Researchers conducting focus groups on sexuality in Mexico and Peru found that women held similar concerns—fear of violence, desertion, or accusations of infidelity—if they brought up birth control (Folch-Lyon, Macorra, and Schearer 1981; Fort 1989). Not surprisingly, when family planning clinics in Ethiopia removed their requirement for spousal consent, clinic use rose 26 percent in just a few months (Cook and Maine 1987).

Not all women who fear violence in this context are necessarily at risk of actual abuse. In fact, some recent studies suggest that many men may be more open to family planning than most women suspect (Gallen 1986). Communication in marriage can be so limited, however, that spouses often do not know their partner's views on family planning. Women thus assume that their husband's attitude will mirror the cultural norm, which frequently says that men want large families and distrust women who use birth control. The discrepancy between women's perceptions and reality also speaks to the ability of violence to induce fear by example.

Risk of Acquiring STDs

Not surprisingly, male violence also impedes women's ability to protect themselves from HIV and other STDs. Violence can increase a woman's risk either through nonconsensual sex or by limiting her willingness and/or ability to enforce condom use. In many cultures, suggesting condom use is even more threatening than raising other forms of birth control, because condoms are widely associated with promiscuity, prostitution, and disease. By bringing up condom use, women either insinuate their own infidelity or implicitly challenge a male partner's right to conduct outside relationships. Either way, a request for condoms may trigger a violent response (Elias and Heise 1993; Worth 1991).

Indeed, an AIDS prevention strategy based solely on "negotiating" condom use assumes an equity of power between men and women that simply does not exist in many relationships. Even within consensual unions, women often lack control over the dynamics of their sexual lives. A study of home-based industrial workers in Mexico, for example, found that wives' bargaining power in marriage was lowest with regard to decisions about if and when to have sexual intercourse (Beneria and Roldan 1987). Studies of natural family planning in the Philippines, Peru, and Sri Lanka (Liskin 1981) and sexual attitudes among women in Guatemala (DataPro and

Asociación Guatemalteco para la Prevención y Control de SIDA 1991) also mention forced sex in marriage, especially when the men arrive home drunk.

Childhood sexual abuse also appears to generate responses that put individuals at increased risk of STDs, including AIDS. Several studies, for example, link a history of sexual abuse with a high risk of entering prostitution (Finkelhor 1987; James and Meyerding 1977). Researchers from Brown University found that men and women who had been raped or forced to have sex in either childhood or adolescence were four times more likely than nonabused individuals to have worked in prostitution (Zierler 1991). They were also twice as likely to have multiple partners in any single year and to engage in casual sex with partners they did not know. Women survivors of childhood sexual assault were twice as likely to be heavy consumers of alcohol and nearly three times more likely to become pregnant before the age of eighteen. These behaviors did not translate directly into higher rates of HIV among women, but men who experienced childhood sexual abuse were twice as likely to be HIV positive as men who did not.

Impacts of sexual abuse on sexual risk-taking have also been documented in a developing country—on the island of Barbados. Based on a probability survey of 407 women, anthropologist Penn Handwerker has shown that sexual abuse is the single most important determinant of high risk sexual activity during adolescence for both Barbadian men and women (Handwerker 1991). After controlling for a widerange of socioeconomic and home-environment variables (e.g., absent father), sexual abuse remains strongly linked to both the number of partners adolescents have and to their age at first intercourse. Further analysis shows that direct effects of childhood sexual abuse on partner change remain significant into the respondent's mid-thirties. For men, physical, emotional and/or sexual abuse in childhood is also highly correlated with lack of condom use in adulthood, after controlling for many other variables.[9]

Pregnancy Complications and Birth Outcomes

While pregnancy should be a time when the health and well-being of women is especially protected, surveys suggest that pregnant women are prime targets for abuse. Results from a large, prospective study of battery during pregnancy among low income women in the United States, for example, indicate that one out of *every six* pregnant women was assaulted during her present pregnancy (McFarlane 1992). The study, sponsored by the Centers for Disease Control, followed a stratified cohort of 691 white, African American, and Hispanic women for three years in Houston and Baltimore. Sixty percent of the abused women in this study reported two or more episodes of violence, and they were three times as likely as non-abused women to begin prenatal care in the third trimester. Other studies indicate that women battered during pregnancy run twice the risk of miscarriage and four times the risk of having a low birth weight baby compared with women who are not beaten (Stark et al. 1981; Bullock and McFarlane 1989). Birth weight is a powerful predictor of a child's survival prospects in the first year of life.

Battering during pregnancy is likely to have an even grater impact on Third World mothers who are already malnourished and overworked. A survey of 342 randomly sampled women in Mexico City revealed that twenty percent of those battered reported blows to the stomach during pregnancy (Valdez Santiago and Shrader Cox 1992). In another study of eighty battered women who sought judicial intervention against their partner in San Jose, Costa Rica, 49 percent report being beaten during pregnancy. Of these, 7.5 percent reported miscarriages due to the abuse (Ugalde 1988).

A prospective study of 161 women living in Santiago, Chile, likewise revealed that those women living in areas of high social and political violence had a significantly increased risk of pregnancy complications compared to women living in lower violence neighborhoods. After adjusting for potential confounders (income, education, marital status, underweight, cigarette smoking, dissatisfaction with neighborhood, life events, alienation, uncertainty, and depression), researchers found that high levels of sociopolitical violence were associated with an approximately fivefold increase in risk of pregnancy complications (such as pre-eclampsia, premature labor, threat of miscarriage, gestational hypertension, etc.) (Zapata et al. 1992). If the stress and trauma of living in a violent neighborhood can induce complications, it is reasonable to assume that living in the private hell of an abusive relationship could as well.

Some Thoughts on the Implications of These Findings

After reading the above review, it is hard not to share the profound pessimism about men and about male sexuality that runs throughout much of the antipornography literature. It is important to consider, however, the appropriate message to be taken from these data. Unfortunately, the conclusion some have drawn is that women are essentially powerless and that men must be aggressive by nature. Generally there is indignation at male abuse, but it is often accompanied by a sense that the problem runs too deep to be addressed. Whether justified by biological arguments (evolution has endowed men with an aggressive sexual nature) or sociocultural determinism (patriarchy is everywhere and not easily changed), these beliefs can rationalize inaction.

Ironically, the very research and ideas that can be used to justify inaction often come from individuals who probably would not support the use of their data in this way. I, for example, oppose the view that male sexuality is inherently aggressive or that women are essentially victims. Most of my antiviolence colleagues would likely agree, although few have made a point of arguing against the interpretation of their work in this way. Given the appeal of "essentialist" notions of sex and gender in popular culture (and the political implications of such arguments), it is my belief, however, that anyone who promotes new ideas in mainstream discourse has a responsibility not only for what they meant to say but, for how their words can be construed and used. It is out of this sense of responsibility that I offer the following interpretation of the data on sexuality and violence that I present above.

First, despite the powerful ability of violence to exact obedience and exert control, women are not totally powerless. In fact, women have proven incredibly capable of exerting agency even within the most constrained social conditions. Extremely poor women in India, for example, have been known to exert control over their sexual lives by declaring extended religious fasts, a socially sanctioned activity (imbued with taboos against sexual relations) that even violent men are reluctant to violate (Savara, personal communication). Likewise, research has shown that far from being passive, battered women often adopt complex coping and management strategies that serve to lessen the impact of the violence on themselves and their children (Browne 1987; Bowker 1983; Okun 1986). Even some prostitutes interpret their decision to turn tricks as an empowered choice—a way to make money for sexual services extracted from other women through marriage (Delacoste and Alexander 1987). This is not to say that women do not deserve broader choices than these examples imply. Such acts do represent, however, a creativity and resourcefulness in the face of powerful social forces that is important to acknowledge and affirm at all times. Failure to recognize the possibility of agency within patriarchal structures fuels fatalism and can undermine women's sense of self, with disempowering results.

In her speech "Does Sexuality Have a History?" for example, feminist attorney Catharine MacKinnon advances a very deterministic and fatalistic picture of women and sexuality. Taking issue with the prevailing view of academic historians that sexuality is basically constructed and highly plastic, MacKinnon (1991) writes:

> I would hypothesize that while ideologies about sex and sexuality may ebb and flow . . . the actual practices of sex may look relatively flat. . . . Underneath all of these hills and valleys, these ebbs and flows, there is this bedrock, this tide that has not changed much, namely male supremacy and the subordination of women. . . . For this feminists have been called ahistorical. Oh, dear. We have disrespected the profundity and fascination of all the different ways in which men fuck us in order to emphasize that however they do it, they do it. And they do it to us. (MacKinnon 1991: 6)

In a later edition of the *Michigan Quarterly*, the same journal which reprinted the original speech, author Suzanne Rhodenbaugh (1991) accuses McKinnon of committing a "new violence" by denying women the agency to define their own sexuality. In her reply essay, "MacKinnon, May I Speak?" Rhodenbaugh writes:

> MacKinnon, with probably good intention to empower women, seems to me in her essay another voice reducing us, one saying we are creatures mainly acted upon. This feels greatly over-simplified, and finally untrue. It feels further, like new injustice. For if my "history of sexuality" includes such facts as my having been raped, having been beaten by a husband, having gone through a pregnancy against my will, and all else that has happened to my body, and the sexual attention that I did not seek but was subjected to . . . then presumably as a sexual creature I'm little more than victim, and am predominantly passive. (Rhodenbaugh 1991: 442)

MacKinnon likewise implies that male sexual behavior is hegemonically abusive (however they do it, they do it. And they do it to us"). But Rhodenbaugh refuses to cede her agency, saying: "I'm just one individual woman, but I'm not of a mind to exchange the name 'invisible' for the name 'victim.' Neither name will hold me" (Rhodenbaugh 1991: 422).

Indeed, Rhodenbaugh's comments capture the essence of the dilemma faced by anti-violence activists: in exposing the reality of violence, we risk gaining visibility at the price of promoting the image of woman as victim and the notion of sex as all danger and no pleasure. One way to avoid this pitfall is always to counterbalance the pessimism engendered by the tenacity of patriarchy with examples of women's creative attempts at resistance within existing constraints. Another is constantly to imbue the antiviolence discourse with reminders of why feminists fight sexual violence in the first place. As author Naomi Wolf points out, "Feminists agitate against rape not just because it is a form of violence—but because it is a form of violence that uniquely steals from the survivor her sexual spontaneity and delight. . . . The right to say no must exist for the right to say yes to have any meaning" (Wolf 1992). Regrettably, this recognition is all too often lost in feminist discussions of sexual violence.

A second pitfall of antiviolence work is the danger of fueling popular notions of sexual essentialism by drawing attention to the pervasiveness of gender violence. Essentialist explanations for social phenomenon are generally dangerous because they provide a powerful justification for the status quo. If what exists is biologically based, then it is "natural" and by extension, "good" (or at least not open to change). Essentialist interpretations have a long history, beginning with scientists such as Freud and Konrad Lorenz who saw aggression and sexuality as "drives" or "instincts" that needed periodic release or they would "discharge" in destructive ways. This "hydraulic" image of sexuality is one that still holds much popular appeal. Indeed, the notion that men "need" frequent sex with many partners is a myth used in many cultures (including my own) to justify and condone sexual behavior by men that can be exploitative and hurtful to women.

While most psychologists now reject the drive theory, it still captures the imagination of many in the general public. The meteoric rise of author/academic Camille Paglia attests to the enduring appeal that such essentialist notions command. Although Paglia, a latter-day Freudian, would likely object to being characterized as a biological determinist, her writings and public statements smack of determinism and her analysis of sexual violence draws exclusively from biology, psychology, and ethics rather than from an analysis of power or gender role socialization. In *Sex, Art and American Culture*, for example, Paglia writes:

> Aggression and eroticism are deeply intertwined. Hunt, pursuit, and capture are biologically programmed into male sexuality. . . . I see in the simple, swaggering masculinity of the jock and in the noisy posturing of the heavy-metal guitarist certain fundamental, unchangeable truths about sex. . . . We must remedy social injustice wherever we can. But there are some things we cannot change.

There are sexual differences based in biology. Academic feminism is lost in a fog of social constructionism. (Paglia 1992: 50–53)

A careful reading of Paglia's text reveals that she does believe that the male "tendency toward brutishness" can be overridden through socialization (in some cases, at least), but it is easy to see how her purposefully provocative statements about male sexuality could be construed to support popular notions that "boys will be boys." Given the potential of such rationalizations to promote behavior harmful to women, Paglia has a responsibility not only for her beliefs but also for how her words are likely to be heard. Once she steps out of academia and onto the TV talk-show cir-cuit, Paglia has an increased duty to guard against the misuse of her ideas by paying careful atten-tion to language and by countering likely misinterpretations of her ideas.

Likewise, feminists who uncover the pervasiveness of violence should not leave the impression that aggression is an immutable part of male sexuality. With understandable frustration, some in the health and development field have reacted to the violence data with the question: What is it about male sexuality that makes men that way? I think, however, that this is the wrong question. Rather we should be asking: What is it about the construction of masculinity in different cultures that promotes aggressive sexual behavior by men? And, what is it about the construction of fem-ininity and the structure of economic and social power relations in societies that permits this behavior to continue?

The reason that it is wrong to frame the question in terms of "maleness" (which is normally interpreted to have biological roots) is because the cross-cultural record does not support the view that male violence against women is universal. Three separate cross-cultural studies confirm that there are at least a handful of societies where rape and/or wife abuse does not exist (or did not exist in the recent past). In her study of 156 tribal societies, for example, feminist anthropol-ogist Peggy Reeves Sanday classified 47 percent of the cultures she studied as essentially "rape free" (i.e., rape was totally absent or extremely rare) (Sanday 1981). Even if one cedes that some of the societies designated "rape free" probably represent inadequacies in the ethnographic record rather than truly nonviolent societies, the number of examples cited (and the descriptions of life in these societies) suggests that there are (or have been) at least some cultures not plagued by gender-based abuse.

Likewise, two other studies of wife abuse cross-culturally (Levinson 1989; Counts, Brown and Campbell 1992) unearth additional examples of cultures where gender-based violence is absent or exceedingly rare. In his ethnographic review of ninety peasant and small scale societies, Levinson (1989) identified sixteen that could be described as "essentially free or untroubled by family vio-lence." Among the Central Thai, for example, domestic violence was extremely rare according to detailed ethnographies collected in the 1960s. Central Thai families were remarkable for the absence of any meaningful division of labor by sex: men were as likely as women to carry out household duties including child care, and women as likely as men to plow or manage the family business. Divorce was common, people preferring to separate rather than live with discord. Com-munity norms disdained aggression; other nonviolent means of conflict resolution were plentiful and preferred (Phillips 1966).

The existence of such cultures—even if few in number—stands as proof that violence against women is not an inevitable outgrowth of male biology, male sexuality, or male hormones. It is "male conditioning," not the "condition of being male," that appears to be the problem. Although what it means to be "male" varies among different cultures and within different seg-ments of the same culture, the importance of the masculine mystique appears to be a common element in many, but not all, societies. In his book *Manhood in the Making: Cultural Concepts of Masculinity*, anthropologist David Gilmore notes that across many cultures "there is a constantly recurring notion that real manhood is different from simple anatomical maleness, that it is not a neutral condition that comes about spontaneously through biological maturation but rather is a precarious or artificial state that boys must win against powerful odds" (Gilmore 1991: 11). Gilmore observes that this notion exists among both peasants and sophisticated urban peoples, and among both warrior peoples and those who have never killed in anger. He argues further that "manhood" represents an "achieved status" different from parallel notions of womanhood. "As a social icon," he writes, "femininity . . . usually involves questions of body ornament or sexual allure, or other essentially cosmetic behaviors that enhance, rather than create, an inherent quality of character. An authentic femininity rarely involves tests or proofs of action." (Gilmore 1991: 11).

Although I would disagree with Gilmore's last statement (in many cultures a woman must bear a child before she is considered fully human, much less a mature, adult woman), his observations about the elusive quality of manhood are nonetheless important for our analysis of sexually aggressive behavior in men. It is my belief, shared by other theorists (such as Lancaster 1992; Stoltenberg 1989; and Olsson 1984) that it is partly men's insecurity about their masculinity that promotes abusive behavior toward women. The fear that accompanies this insecurity derives in part from a gendered system that assigns power and status to that which is male and denigrates or subordinates that which is female. Men in many cultures wage daily battle to prove to themselves and others that they qualify for inclusion in the esteemed category "male." To be "not male," is to be reduced to the status of woman or, worse, to be "queer" (see below).

Since gender is socially constructed, it must be actualized through action and sensation—by doing things that repeatedly affirm that one is really male or really female while avoiding things that leave room for doubt. As social theorist John Stoltenberg observes:

> Most people born with a penis between their legs grow up aspiring to feel and act unambiguously male, longing to belong to the sex that is male and daring not to belong to the sex that is not, and feeling this urgency for a visceral and constant verification of their male sexual [read: gender] identity—for a fleshy connection to manhood—as the driving force of their life. The drive does not originate in the anatomy. The sensations derive from the idea. The ideas give the feelings social meaning; the idea determines which sensations shall be sought. (Stoltenberg 1989: 31)

Many societies have evolved elaborate rituals and rites of passage to help induct young men into manhood. Some involve brutal hazings and tests of courage while others require endurance, aptitude, and skill. They all share the underlying premise that real men are made, not born. This feeds into men's gender insecurity.

One way to feel unambiguously male in many cultures is to dominate women, to behave aggressively, and to take risks. A "real man" in the Balkans, for example, is one who drinks heavily, fights bravely, and shows "indomitable virility" by fathering many children (Denich 1974: 250). In eastern Morocco, "true men" are distinguished based on their physical prowess and heroic acts of both feuding and sexual potency (Marcus 1987: 50). On the South Pacific island of Truk, fighting, drinking, defying the sea, and sexually conquering women are the true measures of manhood (Caughey 1970; Marshall 1979; Gilmore 1990).

Significantly, sexual conquest and potency appear as repeated themes in many cultural definitions of manhood, placing women at increased risk of coercive sex. This is as true in the United States as it is elsewhere. Recently, nine teenage boys from an upper-working-class suburb of Long Beach were arrested for allegedly molesting and raping a number of girls, some as young as ten. The boys, members of a group called the Spur Posse, acknowledge having sex with scores of underage girls as part of a sexual competition. In tabulating their sexual exploits, the boys make reference to the uniform number of the sports stars who are their heros—"I'm 44 now—Reggie Jackson." "I'm 50—David Robinson." Tellingly, some of the boys' fathers appear boastful of their sons' conquests. In a recent *New York Times* article, one father praised his son as "all man" and insisted that the girls his son had had sex with were "giving it away" (Gross 1993).

The salience of sex to some versions of masculine identity is likewise recognized in a Swedish government report on prostitution, published in 1981:

> The male confirms and proves his maleness, his virility, through his sexuality. It becomes the core, the very essence around which he consciously and unconsciously forms his idea about himself as a man. The female sexual identity has not been formed in relationship to sexuality, but in the need to be chosen by a man. . . . By being chosen the woman receives the necessary proof of her value as a woman—both in her own eyes and in others. (Olsson 1984: 73)

Indeed, some theorists go so far as to assert that notions of masculinity help construct the experience of sex itself. Speaking from an Anglo-American perspective, John Stoltenberg argues that "so much of most men's sexuality is tied up with gender-actualizing—with feeling like a real man—that they can scarcely recall an erotic sensation that had no gender-specific cultural meaning. As most men age, they learn to cancel out and deny erotic sensations that are not specifically linked to what they think a real man is supposed to feel" (Stoltenberg 1989: 33).

To the extent that masculine ideals are associated with violence, virility, and power, it is easy to see how male sexual behavior might emerge as predatory and aggressive. Indeed, the more I work on violence against women, the more I become convinced that the real way forward is to redefine what it means to be male. When masculinity is associated with aggression and sexual conquest, domineering sexual behavior and violence become not only a means of structuring power relations between men and women but also a way of establishing power relations among men. As Roger Lancaster observes in his ethnographic study of gender relations in Nicaragua, within many gendered systems sexual exploits are part of a system of posturing among men where women are merely the mediums of competition (see Lancaster 1992; see also Lancaster 1995).

Since men have a collective interest in the perpetuation of gender hierarchies, individual male behavior is closely monitored by the male community (and sometimes by mothers acting on behalf of their sons). When the behavior of men or boys does not live up to the masculine ideal, they are frequently rebuked by invoking another gendered symbol: the male homosexual, however culturally defined. "Real men" are almost always defined in opposition to the queer, the *hueco*, the *cochón*, the sissy. Homosexual stigma is invoked to enforce the masculine ideal; it becomes part of the glue that holds male dominance together.

As Lancaster points out in his Nicaraguan example, homosexual stigma helps structure and perpetuate male sexual and gender norms. Lancaster maintains that by adolescence, boys are in open competition for the status of manhood. "The signs of masculinity," he argues, "are actively struggled for, and can only be won by wresting them *away from* other boys around them" (Lancaster 1992, 1995).

Fortunately, the ethnographic record provides us with examples to prove that the world need not be constructed this way. After exhaustively reviewing existing information on masculinity cross-culturally, Gilmore notes that while "ideas and anxieties about masculinity as a special-status category of achievement are widespread in societies around the world, being expressed to varying degrees . . . they do not seem to be absolutely universal" (Gilmore 1990). He cites several exceptions: cultures where manhood is of minimal interest to men and where there is little or no social pressure to act "manly."

Among Gilmore's examples are the Semai people of Malaysia and inhabitants of Tahiti. In Tahiti, for example, there are no strict gender roles, no concept of male honor to defend, and no social expectation to "get even." Men share a cultural value of "timidity" that forbids retaliation, and even when provoked, men rarely become violent. According to Gilmore, the concept of "manliness" as separate from femininity is simply foreign to them (Gilmore 1990). An extensive ethnographic record reveals that a similar description would be appropriate for the Semai of Malaysia as well (Dentan 1979).

What is intriguing about these two examples is that they conform well to the picture of other societies known to have low or nonexistent levels of violence against women. Indeed, both Peggy Sanday's cross-cultural study of rape and the anthology, *Sanctions and Sanctuary*, a cross-cultural look at wife beating, found that one of the strongest predictors/correlates of societies with high violence against women was the presence of a masculine ideal that emphasized dominance, toughness, or male honor (Counts, Brown, and Campbell 1992).[10] While these types of studies cannot prove causality, they do begin to suggest which factors appear especially predictive of high rates of violence against women versus those that predict low rates of gender violence. Table 5 presents a simplified account of the major findings of the Levinson, Sanday, and *Sanctions and Sanctuary* studies.

Interestingly, the findings strongly support the feminist contention that hierarchical gender relations—perpetuated through gender socialization and the socioeconomic inequalities of society—are integrally related to violence against women. Male decision making in the home and economic inequality between men and women are strongly correlated with high rates of violence against women, while women having power outside of the home (either political, economic, or magical) seems to offer some protection against abuse. Another particularly strong factor seems to be the social acceptance of violence as a way to resolve conflict: where interpersonal violence is tolerated in the society at large, women are at higher risk. Given that much behavior is learned by children through modeling, this finding is hardly surprising.

This generic picture conforms well to actual ethnographic descriptions of societies with little or no violence against women. Sanday uses the Mbuti Pygmie, a forest dwelling people, to illustrate her point. Violence between the sexes, or between anybody, is virtually absent among the Mbuti Pygmie when they are in their forest environment. There is little division of labor by sex. A man is not ashamed to pick mushrooms and nuts if he finds them, or to wash and clean a baby. Decision making is by common consent; men and women have equal say because hunting and gathering are both important to the economy (Turnbull 1965). This description sounds remarkably similar to that offered for the Central Thai, the Semai of Malaysia, and the Tahitians, described earlier.

The factors that emerge as predictive of low violence are also enlightening. In addition to female power, the presence of all-female coalitions or work groups appears to be significant. Whether this operates by increasing women's economic power or through female solidarity and consciousness-raising, remains unclear. Especially significant appears to be the presence of strong

Table 5   Corrrelates of Gender Violence Based on Cross-Cultural Studies

PREDICTIVE OF HIGH VIOLENCE	PREDICTIVE OF LOW VIOLENCE
1. Violent interpersonal conflict resolution (1) (3)	1. Female power outside of the home (1) (2) (3)
2. Economic inequality between men and women (3)	2. Active community interference in violence (2) (3)
3. Masculine ideal of male dominance/ toughness/honor (1) (2)	3. Presence of exclusively female groups (work or solidarity) (2) (3)
4. Male economic and decision-making authority in the family (2)	4. Sanctuary (shelters/friends/family) (3)

(1) = Sanday 1981.

(2) = Counts, Brown, Campbell 1992.

(3) = Levinson 1989.

sanctions against violence and access to sanctuary (hence the name of the anthology, *Sanctions and Sanctuary*). Sanctions can take the form of swift legal response, or they can involve informal community sanctions, like public humiliation. Likewise, "sanctuary" can be formal shelters or merely the cultural understanding that neighbors and/or family members will take in a woman whose partner is threatening her. Violence appears especially common in cultures where women leave their natal village to get married; not only are family members not present to intervene in disputes, but it is also more difficult for the woman to seek refuge when relatives are distant (Counts, Brown, and Campbell 1992). In fact, active community or family interference in violent events emerged as an important predictor of low violence in both of the wife-beating studies.

CONCLUSION

These cross-cultural accounts suggest that the possibility of a world without violence against women is not a hopeless fantasy. Societies have existed, and may still exist, that are essentially free of gender-based abuse. But social movements must have both vision and a sense of responsibility to those who must live within today's reality. The overwhelming presence of violence in many women's lives demands that we work on two fronts: to challenge the gender-based inequities and beliefs that perpetuate male violence and to provide services and support to those attempting to survive, despite the social forces allied against them. A range of professions—public health, family planning, sexuality research—have important roles to play. They can marshal their resources to help untangle the complex web of social forces that encourage violent behavior; they can design programs to empower women and enlighten men; and they can identify and refer women to helpful services. Given the health and social consequences of abuse, this is not their prerogative but also their obligation.

NOTES

1. As it stands, most international development funders see violence as outside of their area of responsibility. International funding tends to be very sectoral, with aid streams targeted specifically to education, agriculture, population control, or health. Since antiviolence initiatives, such as crisis centers, law reform efforts, and public education do not fall easily within any of these categories, they frequently cannot get outside funding or support. The Health and Development project helps articulate the links between violence and women's health with an eye toward recruiting more health dollars for violence-related programming.

2. Although individually valid, these studies are not directly comparable because each uses a different set of questions to probe for abuse. The vast majority of studies ask the respondents whether they have been "abused," "beaten," or "involved in a violent relationship." A subset (e.g., the studies from Barbados and United States) makes this determination based on a list of "acts" that a woman may or may not have been subjected to during her lifetime (e.g., hitting with fist, biting, hit with an object, etc.). Clinical and research experience suggests that allowing women to self-define abuse, if anything, underestimates the level of physical and psychological violence in intimate relationships. In many cultures, women are socialized to accept physical and emotional chastisement as part of a husband's marital prerogative, thereby limiting the range of behaviors women consider "abusive." Moreover, women are sometimes reluctant to report abuse out of shame or fear of incriminating other family members. Both factors suggest that the prevalence rates in Table 2 are likely to underestimate actual levels of abuse.

3. All of the studies use legally grounded definitions of rape; thus, forms of penetration other than penile-vaginal are included and women were not instructed to exclude rape by husbands. Questions were typically framed to define explicitly the behaviors that should be included in the definition. For example: "Has a man made you have sex by using force or threatening to harm you? When we use the word 'sex' we mean a man putting his penis in your vagina even if he didn't ejaculate)." This is followed by: "If he did not try to put his penis in your vagina, has a man made you do other

sexual things like oral sex, anal sex, or put fingers or objects inside you by using force or threatening to harm you?"

4. The estimates in Table 3 are based on existing legal definitions of rape in the United States which recognize penetration of any orifice by physical force or threat of force, or because a woman is incapacitated due to drugs or alcohol.

5. In evaluating the sources of variability in prevalence of sexual abuse, Peters, Wyatt, and Finkelhor 1986 suggest that differences in definitions and the various methods used in these studies probably account for most of the variations reported.

6. This figure is quoted in "Rape: Can I Have This Child?" a photonovela produced by Movimiento Manuela Ramos, Lima, Peru, as part of their campaign to decriminalize abortion in cases of rape.

7. Another significant subset reported positive initiations. While recalling some lack of pleasure due to inexperience, these girls actively agreed to intercourse and considered it part of an ongoing process of sexual discovery that began earlier in life with sex play, petting, and masturbation.

8. By no means is male approval always the greatest determinant of contraceptive use. For examples of cases where it is, see Gallen (1986) and Kincaid (1992).

9. Variables controlled for include: years in legal or common law union during previous five years; raised in lower-class home; education of mother; education of father; raised in stable nuclear family; raised solely by mother; raised with a stepfather; degree of affection mother's partner showed her; degree of physical and emotional abuse to mother; degree of affection mother showed son; degree of affection mother's partner showed son; degree to which mother's partner physically and emotionally abused son; man's educational status; man's occupational status.

10. There are examples of peaceful societies that do have a notion of "achieved manhood," but generally this manhood is not linked to dominance, male honor, or aggression but to skill, often in the realm of hunting. In these societies—such as the Mbuti Pygmies and the !Kung Bushmen—hunting is not an "outlet for aggression," but is seen as "a contribution to society of both indispensable economic and spiritual value . . . truly a kind of indirect nourishing or nurturing" (Gilmore 1990: 116).

REFERENCES

Allen, S. M. (1982) "Adolescent pregnancy among 11–15 year old girls in the parish of Manchester." Dissertation for diploma in Community Health. Kingston: University of the West Indies. As cited in C. P. MacCormack and A. Draper (1987). "Social and cognitive aspects of female sexuality in Jamaica." In *The Cultural Construction of Sexuality.* Ed. P. Caplan. London: Tavistock Publications.

Apt, Carol, and Hurlbert, David (1993). "The Sexuality of Women in Physically Abusive Marriages: A Comparative Study." *Journal of Family Violence* 8 (1): 57–69.

Banwell, Suzanna Stout (1990). *Law, Status of Women and Family Planning in Sub-Saharan Africa: A Suggestion for Action.* Nairobi: The Pathfinder Fund.

Beattie, Valerie. (1992). "Analysis of the Results of a Survey on Sexual Violence in the U.K." Unpublished manuscript; available from author.

Becker, J. V.; Skinner, L. J.; Abel, G. G.; and Treacy, E. C. (1982) "Incidence and types of sexual dysfunctions in rape and incest victims." *Journal of Sex and Marital Therapy* 8: 65–74.

Beneria, L. and Roldan, M. (1987). *The Crossroads of Class and Gender.* Chicago: University of Chicago Press. As cited in R. Dixon-Mueller, "Sexuality, Gender, and Reproductive Health." Draft paper prepared for International Women's Health Coalition, New York.

Bowker, L. H. (1983) *Beating Wife Beating.* Lexington, MA: Lexington Books.

Browne, A. (1987) *When Battered Women Kill.* New York: The Free Press.

Browne, A. and Williams, K. (1992) "Resource Availability for Women at Risk and Partner Homicide." *Law and Society Review.*

Bullock, Linda F., and McFarlane, Judith. (1989) "The Birth/Weight Battering Connection." *American Journal of Nursing,* pp. 1,153–55.

Burnam, M. Audrey. (1988) "Sexual Assault and Mental Disorders in a Community Population." *Journal of Consulting and Clinical Psychology* 56 (6): 843–50.

Canadian Government. (1984) *Sexual Offenses Against Children.* Vol. 1. Ottawa: Canadian Publishing Centre.

Caughey, John L. (1970). "Cultural Values in Micronesian Society." Unpublished Ph.D. dissertation, University of Pennsylvania.

(CEPLAES) Barragan Alvarado, Lourdes; Ayala Marin, Alexandra; and Gloria Camacho Zambrano. (1992) "Proyecto Educativo Sobre Violencia de Genero en la Relacion Domestica de Pareja." Quito, Ecuador: Centro de Planificacion y Estudios Sociales.

Chacon, K. et al. (1990). "Caracteristicas de La Mujer Agredida Atendida en el Patronato Nacional de la Infancia (PANI)." Cited in Gioconda Batres and Cecilia Claramunt. *La Violencia Contra La Mujer En La Familia Costarricense: Un Problema de Salud Publica.* San Jose, Costa Rica: ILANUD.

Cole, Susan (1989). *Pornography and the Sex Crisis.* Toronto, Canada. Amanita Enterprises.

Cook, Rebecca, and Deborah, Maine (1987). "Spousal Veto Over Family Planning Services." *American Journal of Public Health* 77 (3): 339–44.

Counts, Dorothy; Brown, Judith; and Campbell, Jacquelyn (1992). *Sanctions and Sanctuary: Cultural Perspectives on the Beating of Wives.* Boulder: Westview Press.

Coy, Frederico (1990). Study cited in Delia Castillo et. al. "Violencia Hacia La Mujer en Guatemala." Report prepared for the First Central American Seminar on Violence Against Women as a Public Health Problem, Managua, Nicaragua, March 11–13, 1992.

DataPro SA and Associatión Guatemalteca para la Prevención y Control del SIDA (1991). *Guatemala City Women: Empowering a Vulnerable Group for HIV Prevention.* Guatemala City: DataPro.

DeKeseredy, Walter, and Kelly, Katherine (1993). Private communication. Preliminary data from "First National Study on Dating Violence in Canada." Family Violence Prevention Division, Department of Health and Welfare, Ottawa, Canada.

Delacoste, F. and Alexander, Priscilla (1987). *Sex Work: Writings by Women in the Sex Industry.* Pittsburgh: Cleis Press.

Denich, Bette (1974). "Sex and Power in the Balkans." In *Women, Culture, and Society.* Eds. Michelle Rosaldo and Louise Lamphere. Palo Alto: Stanford University Press.

Dentan, Robert (1979). *The Semai: A Nonviolent People of Malaya.* New York: Holt, Rinehart and Winston.

Dixon-Mueller, Ruth (1992). "Sexuality, Gender, and Reproductive Health." Draft working paper prepared for International Women's Health Coalition, New York.

——— (1993). *Population Policy and Women's Rights: Transforming Reproductive Choice.* Westport, CT: Praeger.

Ehhrardt, Anke (1991). Speech before the first National Conference on Women and HIV Infection, sponsored by the National Institutes of Health and Centers for Disease Control, Washington, DC.

Elias, Christopher, and Heise, Lori (1993). "The Development of Microbicides: A New Method of HIV Prevention for Women." Programs Division Working Paper No. 6. New York: The Population Council.

Finklehor, D. (1987) "The Sexual Abuse of Children: Current Research Reviewed." *Psychiatric Annals*, 17: 233–41.

Folch-Lyon, Evelyn; Macorra, Luis, and Schearer, S. Bruce (1981). "Focus Group and Survey Research on Family Planning in Mexico." *Studies in Family Planning* 12 (12): 409–32.

Fort, A. L. (1989). "Investigation of the Social Context of Fertility and Family Planning: A Qualitative Study in Peru." *International Family Planning Perspectives* 15 (3): 88–94.

Gallen, M. A. (1986). "Men—New Focus for Family Planning Programs." *Population Reports* Series J, No. 33.

Gavey, Nicola. (1991) "Sexual Victimization Prevalence Among New Zealand University Students." *Journal of Consulting and Clinical Psychology* 59: 464–66.

Gilmore, David. (1990). *Manhood in the Making: Cultural Concepts of Masculinity.* New Haven: Yale University Press.

Grant, Robert; Preda, Michael; and Martin, J. David (1989). "Domestic Violence in Texas: A Study of Statewide and Rural Spouse Abuse." Wichita Falls, TX: Bureau of Business and Government Research, Midwestern State University.

Gross, Jane (1993). "Where 'Boys Will Be Boys,'and Adults Are Befuddled." *New York Times*. March 29.

Handwerker, Penn (1991). "Gender Power Difference May be STD Risk Factors for the Next Generation." Paper presented at the 90th Annual Meeting of the American Anthropological Association, Chicago, Illinois.

—— (1993). "Power, Gender Violence, and High Risk Sexual Behavior: AIDS/STD Risk Factors Need to be Defined More Broadly." Private communication, Department of Anthropology, Humboldt State University, Arcata, California, February 10.

Isis International. (1988) "Campana sobre la violencia en contra de la mujer." Boletin 16–17, Red de Salud de las Mujeres Latinoamericanas y del Caribe. Santiago, Chile: Isis International.

James, J. and Meyerding, J. (1977). "Early Sexual Experience and Prostitution." *American Journal of Psychiatry* 134: 1,381–85.

Kilpatrick, D.G.; Edmunds, C.N.; and Seymour, A.K. (1992). *Rape in America: A Report to the Nation*. Arlington, VA: The National Victim Center.

Kincaid, D. Lawrence, et al. (1991). "Family Planning and the Empowerment of Women in Bangladesh." Paper presented at the Nineteenth Annual Meeting of the American Public Health Association, Atlanta, GA, November 13, 1991.

Kisekka, Mere, and Otesanya, B. (1988). "Sexually Transmitted Disease as a Gender Issue: Examples from Nigeria and Uganda." Paper given at the AFARD/AAWORD Third General Assembly on The African Crisis and the Women's Vision of the Way Out. Dakar, August.

Koss, M. P.; Gidycz, C. A. and Wisniewski, N. (1987) "The Scope of Rape: Incidence and Prevalence of Sexual Aggression and Victimization in a National Sample of Higher Education Students." *Journal of Consulting and Clinical Psychology*. 55: 162–70.

Koss, M. P., and Oros, C. J. (1982). "Sexual Experiences Survey: A Research Instrument Investigating Sexual Aggression and Victimization." *Journal of Consulting and Clinical Psychology* 50: 455–57.

Lancaster, Roger (1992). *Life is Hard: Machismo, Danger, and the Intimacy of Power in Nicaragua*. Berkeley: University of California Press.

—— (1995). "That We Should All Turn Queer? Homosexual Stigma in the Making of Manhood and the Breaking of a Revolution in Nicaragua." In *Conceiving Sexuality: Approaches to Sex Research in a Postmodern World*. Eds. Richard Parker and John Gagnon, pp. 135–56. New York: Routledge.

Larrain, Soledad (1993). "Estudio de Frecuencia de la Violencia Intrafamiliar y la Condicion de la Mujer en Chile." Santiago, Chile: Pan American Health Organization.

Levinson, David (1989). *Violence in Cross-Cultural Perspective*. Newbury Park: Sage.

Liskin, L. S. (1981). "Periodic Abstinence: How Well Do New Approaches Work?" *Population Reports*. Baltimore, MD: Johns Hopkins School of Hygiene and Public Health.

MacKinnon, Catharine (1991). "Does Sexuality Have a History?" *Michigan Quarterly Review* 30 (1): 1–11.

Mahajan, A. (1990). "Instigators of Wife Battering." In *Violence Against Women*. Ed. Sushma Sood, pp. 1–10. Jaipur, India: Arihant Publishers.

Marcus, Michael. (1987). "Horsemen are the Fence of the Land: Honor and History among the Ghiyata of Eastern Morocco." In *Honor and Shame and the Unity of the Mediterranean*. Special Pub. no. 22. Ed. David Gilmore. Washington DC: American Anthropological Association,

Marshall, Mac. (1979). *Weekend Warriors*. Palo Alto, CA: Mayfield.

McFarlane, Judith, et al. (1992) "Assessing for Abuse During Pregnancy: Severity and Frequency of Injuries and Associated Entry Into Prenatal Care." *Journal of the American Medical Society* 267 (23): 3,176–78.

Mullen, et al. (1988). "Impact on Sexual and Physical Abuse on Women's Mental Health." *Lancet* 1: 841.

Okun, L. E. (1986). *Woman Abuse: Facts Replacing Myths*. Albany: State University of New York Press.

Olsson, Hanna. (1981). "The Woman, The Love, and the Power." In *International Feminism: Networking*

Against Female Sexual Slavery. Ed. Kathleen Barry, Charlotte Bunch and Shirley Castley. New York: International Tribune Center.

Paglia, Camille (1992). *Sex, Art and American Culture.* New York: Vintage Books.

Peters, S. D.; Wyatt, G. E; and Finkelhor, D. "Prevalence." (1986). In *A Source Book on Child Sexual Abuse.* Ed. D. Finkelhor. Beverly Hills: Sage, pp. 15–59.

Phillips, H. P. (1966). *Thai Peasant Personality: The Patterning of Interpersonal Behavior in the Village of Bang Chan.* Berkeley: University of California.

PROFAMILIA (1990). *Encuestra de Prevalencia, Demografia y Salud.* (DHS) Bogota: Colombia.

——— (1992). "Estudio Sobre La Violencia Contra La Mujer en la Familia Basado en La Encuesta Real-izada a las Mujeres Maltratadas Que Acudieron At Servicio Juridico de ProFamilia Entre El 15 de Marzo de 1989 y El 30 de Marzo de 1990." In *La Violencia y Los Derechos Humanos de la Mujer.* Bo-gota: PROFAMILIA.

Raikes, Alanagh. (1990) *Pregnancy, Birthing and Family Planning in Kenya: Changing Patterns of Behavior: A Health Utilization Study in Kissi District.* Copenhagen: Centre for Development Research.

Raj-Hashim, Rita (1993). Private communication. "Summary of Survey Research Malaysia (SRM) Study on Women and Girlfriend Battery." Asian-Pacific Resource and Research Centre for Women, Kuala Lumpur, Malaysia.

Ramirez Rodriguez, Juan Carlos, and Uribe Vazquez, Griselda (1993). "Mujer y violencia: un hecho co-tidiano." *Salud Publica de Mexico.* Cuernavaca: Instituto Nacional de Salud Publica.

Rao Gupta, Geeta (1993). "Women and HIV: Lessons from a Multicountry Research Project." Paper pre-sented at the Working Group on Sexual Behavior Research Conference: International Perspectives in Sex Research. Rio de Janeiro, 22–25 April.

Rhodenbaugh, Suzanne (1991). "Catharine MacKinnon: May I Speak?" *Michigan Quarterly Review* 30 (3): 415–22.

"Rompiendo el Silencio" (1992). *La Boletina* Managua, Nicaragua: Puntos de Encuentro. Oct/Nov No.9.

Sanday, Peggy Reeves (1981). "The Socio-cultural Context of Rape: A Cross Cultural Study." *Journal of Social Issues* 37 (4): 5–27.

Savara, Mira (1993). Observation made at the Working Group on Sexual Behavior Research Conference: International Perspectives in Sex Research. Rio de Janeiro, 22–25 April.

Schei, B., and Bakketeig L. S. (1989) "Gynecological Impact of Sexual and Physical Abuse by Spouse: A Study of a Random Sample of Norwegian Women." *British Journal of Obstetrics and Gynecology* 96: 1,379–83.

Shim, Young-Hee. (1992) "Sexual Violence against Women in Korea: A Victimization Survey of Seoul Women." Paper presented at the conference on International Perspectives: Crime, Justice and Pub-lic Order. St. Petersburg, Russia, June 21–27.

Sogbetun, A. O.; Alausa, K. O.; and A. O. Osoba. (1977) "Sexually Transmitted Disease in Ibadan, Nige-ria." *British Journal of Venereal Disease* 53: 158.

Sonali, Deraniyagala. (1990) "An Investigation into the Incidence and Causes of Domestic Violence in Sri Lanka." Women in Need (WIN), Colombo, Sri Lanka.

Stark, E.; Flitcraft, A.; Zuckerman, B.; Grey, A.; Robinson, J.; and W. Frazier. (1981) *Wife Abuse in the Medical Setting: An Introduction for Health Personnel.* Monograph #7. Washington, DC: Office of Do-mestic Violence.

Stoltenberg, John (1989). *Refusing to Be a Man: Essays on Sex and Justice.* Portland, OR: Breiten Bush Books

Straus, M. A, and Gelles, R. J. (1986). "Societal Change and Change in Family Violence from 1975 to 1985 as Revealed by Two National Surveys." *Journal of Marriage and the Family* 48: 465–79.

Teske, Raymond Jr., and Parker, Mary (1983). "Spouse Abuse in Texas: A Study of Women's Attitudes and Experiences." Austin, TX: Department of Human Resources.

Thompson, Sharon (1990). "Putting a Big Thing into a Little Hole: Teenage Girls Accounts of Sexual Ini-tiation." *Journal of Sex Research* 27(3): 341–61.

Tiefer, Leonore. (1992) "Feminism Matters in Sexology." In *Sex Matters*. Ed. W. Bezemer et al. Elsevier Science Publishers.

Toft, S. (ed.) (1986). *Domestic Violence in Papua New Guinea*. Law Reform Commission Occasional Paper No. 19, Port Morseby, Papua New Guinea.

Ugalde, Juan Gerardo. (1988) "Sindrome de la Mujer Agredida." In *Mujer*, no. 5. San Jose, Costa Rica: Cefemina.

Valdez Santiago, Rosaria and Shrader Cox, Elizabeth. (1992) "La violencia hacia la mujer Mexicana como problema de salud publica: La incidencia de la violencia domestica en una microregion de Ciudad Nexahualcoyotl." Mexico City: CECOVID.

Valverde, Mariana. (1987). *Sex, Power, and Pleasure*. Philadelphia: New Society Publishers.

Vance, Carol. (ed.) (1984). *Pleasure and Danger:Exploring Women's Sexuality*. Boston: Routledge and Kegan Paul.

Wolf, Naomi. (1992). "Feminist Fatale." *New Republic*, March 16.

Worth, Dooley. (1991) "Sexual Violence Against Women and Substance Abuse." Working draft, presented to the Domestic Violence Task Force, New York, January.

Wyatt, Gail. (1988). "The Relationship Between Child Sexual Abuse and Adolescent Sexual Functioning in Afro-American and White American Women." *Annals of the New York Academy of Sciences* 528: 111–22.

Zapata, Cecelia, et al. (1992). "The Influence of Social and Political Violence on the Risk of Pregnancy Complications." *American Journal of Public Health* 82 (5): 685–90.

Zierler, Sally, et al. (1991). "Adult Survivors of Childhood Sexual Abuse and Subsequent Risk of HIV Infection." *American Journal of Public Health*, 81 (5): 572–75.

28 Rape and the Inner Lives of Black Women in the Middle West

Preliminary Thoughts on the Culture of Dissemblance

Darlene Clark Hine

One of the most remarked upon but least analyzed themes in Black women's history deals with Black women's sexual vulnerability and powerlessness as victims of rape and domestic violence. Author Hazel Carby put it baldly when she declared, "The institutionalized rape of black women has never been as powerful a symbol of black oppression as the spectacle of lynching. Rape has always involved patriarchal notions of women being, at best, not entirely unwilling accomplices, if not outwardly inviting a sexual attack. The links between black women and illicit sexuality consolidated during the antebellum years had powerful ideological consequences for the next hundred and fifty years."[1] I suggest that rape and the threat of rape influenced the development of a culture of dissemblance among Black women. By dissemblance I mean the behavior and attitudes of Black women that created the appearance of openness and disclosure but actually shielded the truth of their inner lives and selves from their oppressors.

To be sure, themes of rape and sexual vulnerability have received considerable attention in the recent literary outpourings of Black women novelists. Of the last six novels I have read and reread, for example, five contained a rape scene or a graphic description of domestic violence.[2] Moreover, this is not a recent phenomenon in Black women's writing.

Virtually every known nineteenth-century female slave narrative contains a reference to, at some juncture, the ever-present threat and reality of rape. Two works come immediately to mind: Harriet Jacobs's *Incidents in the Life of a Slave Girl* (1861) and Elizabeth Keckley's *Behind the Scenes, or Thirty Years a Slave, and Four Years in the White House* (1868). Yet there is another thread running throughout these slave narratives—one that concerns these captive women's efforts to resist the misappropriation and to maintain the integrity of their own sexuality.[3] The combined influence of rape (or the threat of rape), domestic violence, and economic oppression is key to understanding the hidden motivations informing major social protest and migratory movements in Afro-American history.

Second only to Black women's concern for sexual preservation is the pervasive theme of the

---

Darlene Clark Hine is John A. Hannah Professor of American History at Michigan State University, and is the author of many books and articles. Her scholarly and research interests include twentieth-century American history, black women's history, the Civil Rights Movement, African Americans in the learned professions, the history of black theology, and the history of blacks in science.

frustration attendant to finding suitable employment. Oral histories and autobiographical accounts of twentieth-century migrating Black women are replete with themes about work. Scholars of Black urban history and Black labor history agree that Black women faced greater economic discrimination and had fewer employment opportunities than did Black men. Black women's work was the most undesirable and least remunerative of all work available to migrants.

As late as 1930, a little over three thousand Black women, or 15 percent, of the Black female labor force in Chicago were unskilled and semiskilled factory operatives. Thus, over 80 percent of all employed Black women continued to work as personal servants and domestics. Historian Alan H. Spear pointed out that "negro women were particularly limited in their search for desirable positions. Clerical work was practically closed to them and only a few could qualify as school teachers. Negro domestics often received less than white women for the same work and they could rarely rise to the position of head servant in large households."[4]

Given that many Black women migrants were doomed to work in the same kinds of domestic service jobs they held in the South, one wonders why they bothered to move in the first place. There were some significant differences that help explain this phenomenon. A maid earning seven dollars a week in Cleveland perceived herself to be, and probably was, much better off than a counterpart receiving two dollars and fifty cents a week in Mobile, Alabama. A factory worker, even one whose work was dirty and low status, could and did imagine herself better off than domestic servants who endured the unrelenting scrutiny, interference, and complaints of household mistresses and the untoward advances of male family members.

I believe that in order to understand this historical migratory trend we need to understand the noneconomic motives propelling Black female migration. I believe that many Black women quit the South out of a desire to achieve personal autonomy and to escape both from sexual exploitation from inside and outside of their families and from the rape and threat of rape by white as well as Black males. To focus on the sexual and the personal impetus for Black women's migration in the first several decades of the twentieth century neither dismisses nor diminishes the significance of economic motives. Rather, as historian Lawrence Levine cautioned, "As indisputably important as the economic motive was, it is possible to overstress it so that the black migration is converted into an inexorable force and Negroes are seen once again not as actors capable of affecting at least some part of their destinies, but primarily as beings who are acted upon—southern leaves blown North by the winds of destitution."[5] It is reasonable to assume that some Black women were indeed "southern leaves blown North" and that there were many others who were self-propelled actresses seeking respect, control over their own sexuality, and access to well-paying jobs.

My own research on the history of Black women in the Middle West had led me to questions about how, when, and under what circumstances the majority of them settled in the region. These questions have led to others concerning the process of Black women's migration across time, from the flights of runaway slaves in the antebellum period to the great migrations of the first half of the twentieth century. The most common, and certainly the most compelling, motive for running, fleeing, migrating was a desire to retain or claim some control over ownership of their own sexual beings and the children they bore. In the antebellum period, hundreds of slave women risked their lives and those of their loved ones to run away to the ostensibly free states of the Northwest Territory, in quest of an elusive sexual freedom for themselves and freedom from slavery for their children.

Two things became immediately apparent as I proceeded with researching the history and reading the autobiographies of late nineteenth- and early twentieth-century migrating, or fleeing, Black women. First, that these women were sexual hostages and domestic violence victims in the South (or in other regions of the country) did not reduce their determination to acquire power to protect themselves and to become agents of social change once they settled in midwestern communities. Second, the fundamental tension between Black women and the rest of the society—referring specifically to white men, white women, and, to a lesser extent, Black men—

involved a multifaceted struggle to determine who would control their productive and reproductive capacities and their sexuality. At stake for Black women caught up in this ever-evolving, constantly shifting, but relentless war was the acquisition of personal autonomy and economic liberation. Their quest for autonomy, dignity, and access to opportunity to earn an adequate living was (and still is) complicated and frustrated by the antagonisms of race, class, and gender conflict and by differences in regional economies. At heart, though, the relationship between Black women and the larger society has always been, and continues to be, adversarial.

Because of the interplay of racial animosity, class tensions, gender role differentiation, and regional economic variations, Black women, as a rule, developed and adhered to a cult of secrecy, a cult of dissemblance, to protect the sanctity of inner aspects of their lives. The dynamics of dissemblance involved creating the appearance of disclosure or openness about themselves and their feelings, while actually remaining an enigma. Only with secrecy, thus achieving a self-imposed invisibility, could ordinary Black women accrue the psychic space and harness the resources needed to hold their own in the often one-sided and mismatched resistance struggle.

The inclination of the larger society to ignore those considered "marginal" actually enabled subordinate Black women to craft the veil of secrecy and to perfect the art of dissemblance. Yet it could also be argued that their secrecy or "invisibility" contributed to the development of an atmosphere inimical to realizing equal opportunity or a place of respect in the larger society. There would be no room on the pedestal for the southern Black lady. Nor could she join her white sisters in the prison of "true womanhood." In other words, stereotypes, negative images, and debilitating assumptions filled the space left empty due to inadequate and erroneous information about the true contributions, capabilities, and identities of Black women.

This line of analysis is not without problems. To suggest that Black women deliberately developed a culture of dissemblance implies that they endeavored to create, and were not simply reacting to widespread misrepresentations and negative images of themselves in white minds. Clearly, Black women did not possess the power to eradicate negative social and sexual images of their womanhood. Rather, what I propose is that in the face of the pervasive stereotypes and negative estimations of the sexuality of Black women, it was imperative that they collectively create alternative self-images and shield from scrutiny these private, empowering definitions of self. A secret, undisclosed persona allowed the individual Black woman to function, to work effectively as a domestic in white households, to bear and rear children, to endure the frustration-born violence of frequently under- or unemployed mates, to support churches, to found institutions, and to engage in social service activities, all while living within a clearly hostile white, patriarchal, middle-class America.

The problem this penchant for secrecy presents to the historian is readily apparent. Deborah Gray White has commented about the difficulty of finding primary source material for personal aspects of Black female life: "Black women have also been reluctant to donate their papers to manuscript repositories. That is in part a manifestation of the black woman's perennial concern with image, a justifiable concern born of centuries of vilification. Black women's reluctance to donate personal papers also stems from the adversarial nature of the relationship that countless black women have had with many public institutions, and the resultant suspicion of anyone seeking private information."[6]

White's allusion to "resultant suspicion" speaks implicitly to one important reason why so much of the inner life of Black women remains hidden. Indeed, the concepts of "secret" and "dissemblance," as I employ them, hint at these issues that Black women believed better left unknown, unwritten, unspoken except in whispered tones. Their alarm, their fear, or their Victorian sense of modesty implies that those who broke the silence provided grist for detractors' mills and, even more ominously, tore the protective cloaks from their inner selves. Undoubtedly, these fears and suspicions contribute to the absence of sophisticated historical discussion of the impact of rape (or threat of rape) and incidences of domestic violence on the shape of Black women's experiences.

However, the self-imposed secrecy and the culture of dissemblance, coupled with the larger society's unwillingness to discard tired and worn stereotypes, has also led to ironic incidences of misplaced emphases. Until quite recently for example, when historians talked of rape in the slavery experience they often bemoaned the damage this act did to the Black male's sense of esteem and respect. He was powerless to protect his woman from white rapists. Few scholars probed the effect that rape, the threat of rape, and domestic violence had on the psychic development of the female victims. In the late nineteenth and early twentieth centuries, as Carby has indicated, lynching, not rape, became the most powerful and compelling symbol of Black oppression. Lynching, it came to be understood, was one of the major noneconomic reasons why southern Black men migrated North.

The culture of dissemblance assumed its most institutionalized form in the founding, in 1896, of the National Association of Colored Women's Clubs (NACW). This association of Black women quickly became the largest and most enduring protest organization in the history of Afro-Americans. Its size alone should have warranted the same degree of scholarly attention paid to Marcus Garvey's Universal Negro Improvement Association. Not surprisingly, the primary objects of NACW attack were the derogatory images and negative stereotypes of Black women's sexuality. By 1914 it had a membership of fifty thousand, far surpassing the membership of every other protest organization of the time, including the National Association for the Advancement of Colored People and the National Urban League. In 1945, in Detroit, for example, the Detroit Association of Colored Women's Clubs, federated in 1921, boasted seventy-three member clubs with nearly three thousand individual members.[7]

Mary Church Terrell, the first president of the NACW, declared in her initial presidential address that there were objectives of the Black women's struggle that could be accomplished only by the "mothers, wives, daughters, and sisters of this race." She proclaimed, "We wish to set in motion influences that shall stop the ravages made by practices that sap our strength, and preclude the possibility of advancement." She boldly announced, "We proclaim to the world that the women of our race have become partners in the great firm of progress and reform. . . . We refer to the fact that this is an association of colored women, because our peculiar status in this country . . . seems to demand that we stand by ourselves."[8]

At the core of essentially every activity of NACW's individual members was a concern with creating positive images of Black women's sexuality. To counter negative stereotypes many Black women felt compelled to downplay, even deny, sexual expression. The twin obsessions with naming and combatting sexual exploitation tinted and shaped Black women's support even of the woman's suffrage movement. Nannie H. Burroughs, famed religious leader and founder of the National Training School for women and Girls at Washington, D.C., cajoled her sisters to fight for the ballot. She asserted that with the ballot Black women could ensure the passage of legislation to win legal protection against rapists. Calling the ballot a "weapon of moral defense" she exploded, "When she [a Black woman] appears in court in defense of her virtue, she is looked upon with amused contempt. She needs the ballot to reckon with men who place no value upon her virtue."[9]

Likewise, a determination to save young unskilled and unemployed Black women from having to bargain sex in exchange for food and shelter motivated some NACW members to establish boarding houses and domestic service training centers, such as the Phillis Wheatley Homes and Burrough's National Training School. This obsession with providing Black women with protection from sexual exploitation and with dignified work inspired other club members in local communities around the country to support or to found hospitals and nursing training schools.

At least one plausible consequence of this heightened mobilization of Black women was a decline in Black urban birth rates. As Black women became more economically self-sufficient, better educated, and more involved in self-improvement efforts, including participation in the flourishing Black women's club movement in midwestern communities, they had greater access to birth control information. As the institutional infrastructure of Black women's clubs, sororities, church-based women's groups, and charity organizations sunk roots into Black communities, it encouraged its members to embrace those values, behaviors, and attitudes traditionally associated with the middle classes. To urban Black middle-class aspirants, the social stigma of having many children did, perhaps, inhibit reproduction. To be sure, over time the gradually evolving male-female demographic imbalance meant that increasingly significant numbers of Black women, especially those employed in the professions, in urban midwestern communities would never marry. The point stressed here, however, is that not having children was, perhaps for the very first time, a choice enjoyed by large numbers of Black women.

There were additional burdens placed upon and awards granted to the small cadre of single, educated, professional Black women who chose not to marry or to bear children. The more educated they were, the greater the sense of being responsible, somehow, for the advance of the race and for the elevation of Black womanhood. They held these expectations of themselves and found a sense of racial obligation reinforced by the demands of the Black community and its institutions. In return for their sacrifice of sexual expression, the community gave them respect and recognition. Moreoever, this freedom and autonomy represented a socially sanctioned, meaningful alternative to the uncertainties of marriage and the demands of child rearing. The increased employment opportunities, whether real or imagined, and the culture of dissemblance enabled many migrating Black women to become financially independent and simultaneously to fashion socially useful and autonomous lives, while reclaiming control over their own sexuality and reproductive capacities.

This is not to say that Black women, once settled into midwestern communities, never engaged in sex for pay or occasional prostitution. Sara Brooks, a Black domestic servant from Alabama who migrated to Cleveland, Ohio, in the 1930s, ill-disguised her contempt for women who bartered their bodies. She declared, while commenting on her own struggle to pay the mortgage on her house, "Some women woulda had a man to live in the house and had an outside boyfriend, too, in order to get the house paid for and the bills." She scornfully added, "They meet a man and if he promises em four or five dollars to go to bed, they's grab it. That's called sellin' your own body, and I wasn't raised like that."[10] What escapes Brooks, in this moralizing moment, is that her poor and powerless Black female neighbors were extracting value from the only thing the society now allowed them to sell. As long as they occupied an enforced subordinate position within American society, this "sellin' your own body" as Brooks put it, was, I submit, Rape.

In sum, at some fundamental level all Black women historians are engaged in the process of historical reclamation. But it is not enough simply to reclaim those hidden and obscure facts and names of Black foremothers. Merely to reclaim and to narrate past deeds and contributions risks rendering a skewed history focused primarily on the articulate, relatively well-positioned members of the aspiring Black middle class. In synchrony with the reclaiming and narrating must be the development of an array of analytical frameworks that allow us to understand why Black women behave in certain ways and how they acquired agency.

The migration of hundreds of thousands of Black women out of the South between 1915 and 1945, and the formation of thousands of Black women's clubs and the NACW are actions that enabled them to put into place, to situate, a protest infrastructure and to create a self-conscious Black women's culture of resistance. Most significant, the NACW fostered the development of an image of Black women as being super moral women. In particular, the institutionalization of women's clubs embodied the shaping and honing of the culture of dissemblance. This culture, grounded as it was on the twin prongs of protest and resistance, enabled the creation of positive alternative images of their sexual selves and facilitated Black women's mental and physical survival in a hostile world.

NOTES

I benefited greatly from conversations with D. Barry Gaspar and Deborah Gray White. I am grateful to Tiffany Patterson and to Elsa Barkley Brown for their comments. An earlier version of this talk was presented as the endnote address at the First Southern Conference on Women's History, Converse College, Spartanburg, South Carolina, June 10–11, 1988.

1. Hazel V. Carby, *Reconstructing Womanhood: The Emergence of the Afro-American Woman Novelists* (New York: Oxford University Press, 1987), 39.

2. See Terry McMillan, *Mama* (Boston: Houghton Mifflin, 1987); Grace Edwards-Yarwood, *In the Shadow of the Peacock* (New York: McGraw-Hill, 1988); Alice Walker, *The Color Purple* (New York: Harcourt Brace Jovanovich, 1982); Toni Morrison, *The Bluest Eye* (New York: Washington Square Press, 1972); Gloria Naylor, *The Women of Brewster Place* (New York: Penguin, 1983).

3. Harriet A. Jacobs, *Incidents in the Life of a Slave Girl Written by Herself*, ed. Jean Fagan Yellin (Cambridge, Mass.: Harvard University Press, 1987). Elizabeth Keckley, *Behind the Scenes, or Thirty Years a Slave, and Four Years in the White House*, introduction by James Olney (New York: Oxford University Press, 1988). See also Rennie Simpson, "The Afro-American Female: The Historical Construction of Sexual Identity," in *The Powers of Desire: The Politics of Sexuality*, ed. Ann Snitow, Sharon Thompson, and Christine Stansell (New York: Monthly Review Press, 1983), 229–35.

4. Alan H. Spear, *Black Chicago: The Making of a Negro Ghetto, 1890–1920* (Chicago: University of Chicago Press, 1967), 34.

5. Lawrence W. Levin, *Black Culture and Black Consciousness: Afro-American Folk Thought from Slavery to Freedom* (New York: Oxford University Press, 1977), 274.

6. Deborah Gray White, "Mining the Forgotten: Manuscript Sources for Black Women's History," *Journal of American History* 74 (June 1987): 237–42, esp. 237–38.

7. Robin S. Peebles, "Detroit's Black Women's Clubs," *Michigan History* 70 (January/February 1986): 48.

8. Darlene Clark Hine, "Lifting the Veil, Shattering the Silence; Black Women's History in Slavery and Freedom," in *The State of Afro-American History: Past, Present, and Future*, ed. Darlene Clark Hine (Baton Rouge: Louisiana State University Press, 1986), 223–49, esp. 236–37.

9. Roslyn Terborg-Penn, "Woman Suffrage: 'First Because We Are Women and Second Because We Are Colored Women,'" *Truth: Newsletter of the Association of Black Women Historians* (April 1985); 9; Evelyn Brooks Barnett, "Nannie Burroughs and the Education of Black Women," in *The Afro-American Woman*, ed. Roslyn Terborg-Penn and Sharon Harley (Port Washington, N.Y.: Kennikat, 1978), 97–108.

10. Thordis Simonsen, ed., *You May Plow Here: The Narrative of Sara Brooks* (New York: Simon & Schuster, 1987), 219.

29 Negotiating Sex and Gender in the Attorney General's Commission on Pornography

Carole S. Vance

Larry Madigan began his testimony in the Miami federal courthouse. Dark-haired, slight, and dressed in his best suit, he fingered his testimony nervously before he was recognized by the chair. The podium and microphone at which he stood were placed at the front of the auditorium, so when the thirty-eighty-year-old looked up from his typed statement, he saw only the members of the Attorney General's Commission on Pornography. They sat on the raised dais, surrounded by staff aides, federal marshals, the court stenographer, and flags of Florida and the United States. Behind him sat the audience, respectfully arrayed on dark and immovable wood benches that matched the wood paneling which enveloped the room.

"At age 12," he began earnestly, "I was a typical, normal, healthy boy and my life was filled with normal activities and hobbies." But "all the trouble began a few months later," when he found a deck of "hard-core" pornographic playing cards, depicting penetration, fellatio, and cunnilingus. "These porno cards highly aroused me and gave me a desire I never had before," he said. Soon after finding these cards, his behavior changed: he began masturbating, attempted to catch glimpses of partially dressed neighbor women, and surreptitiously tried to steal *Playboy* magazines from the local newsstand. His chronicle went on for several minutes.

"By the age of 16, after a steady diet of *Playboy, Penthouse, Scandinavian Children,* perverted paperback books, and sexology magazines, I had to see a doctor for neuralgia of the prostate." His addiction worsened in his twenties, when he began watching pornographic videos. He went on to "promiscuous sex" with "two different women," but eventually found Christ. He concluded, "I strongly believe that all that has happened to me can be traced back to the finding of those porno cards. If it weren't for my faith in God and the forgiveness in Jesus Christ, I would now possibly be a pervert, an alcoholic, or dead. I am a victim of pornography."[1]

Carole S. Vance, an anthropologist, writes about sexuality, gender, and public policy. She teaches at the Columbia University School of Public Health in New York City. Dr. Vance organized the Barnard College sexuality conference (1982), edited *Pleasure and Danger: Exploring Female Sexuality* (Pandora, 2nd edition, 1991), and authored many articles about sexuality and gender. She has worked in many activist groups and was a founding member of FACT (Feminist Anti-Censorship Taskforce) and the American Anthropological Association's Committee on the Status of Women. Dr. Vance has also been the Doris Stevens Professor of Women's Studies at Princeton University and most recently a Visiting Fellow at the Humanities Research Centre, The Australian National University.

The audience sat in attentive silence. No one laughed. Only a few cynical reporters sitting next to me quietly elbowed each other and rolled their eyes, although their stories in the next day's papers would contain respectful accounts of Mr. Madigan's remarks and those of his therapist, Dr. Simon Miranda, who testified as an expert witness that many of his patients were being treated for mental problems brought on by pornography.

The Attorney General's Commission on Pornography, a federal investigatory commission appointed in May 1985 by then–Attorney General Edwin Meese III, orchestrated an imaginative attack on pornography and obscenity. The chief targets of its campaign appeared to be sexually explicit images. These were dangerous, according to the logic of the commission, because they might encourage sexual desires or acts. The commission's public hearings in six U.S. cities during 1985 and 1986, lengthy executive sessions, and an almost 2,000-page report[2] constitute an extended rumination on pornography and the power of visual imagery. Its ninety-two recommendations for strict legislation and law enforcement, backed by a substantial federal, state, and local apparatus already in place, pose a serious threat to free expression. Read at another level, however, the commission's agenda on pornography stands as a proxy for a more comprehensive program about gender and sexuality, both actively contested domains where diverse constituencies struggle over definitions, law, policy, and cultural meanings.

To enter a Meese Commission hearing was to enter a public theater of sexuality and gender, where cultural symbols—many dating from the late nineteenth century—were manipulated with uncanny intuition: the specter of uncontrolled lust, social disintegration, male desire, and female sexual vulnerability shadowed the hearings. The commission's goal was to implement a traditional conservative agenda on sexually explicit images and texts: vigorous enforcement of existing obscenity laws coupled with the passage of draconian new legislation.[3] To that end, the commission, dominated by a conservative majority, effectively controlled the witness list, evidence, and fact-finding procedures in obvious ways that were widely criticized for their bias.[4] But the true genius of the Meese Commission lay in its ability to appropriate terms and rhetoric, to deploy visual images and create a compelling interpretive frame, and to intensify a climate of sexual shame that made dissent from the commission's viewpoint almost impossible. The power of the commission's symbolic politics is shown by the response of both spectators and journalists to Larry Madigan's testimony, as well as by the inability of dissenting commission witnesses who opposed further restriction to unpack and thus counter the panel's subterranean linguistic and visual ploys.

Convened during Ronald Reagan's second term, the commission paid a political debt to conservatives and fundamentalists who had been clamoring for action on social issues, particularly pornography, throughout his terms of office. Pornographic images were symbols of what moral conservatives wanted to control: sex for pleasure, sex outside the regulated boundaries of marriage and procreation. Sexually explicit images are dangerous, conservatives believe, because they have the power to spark fantasy, incite lust, and provoke action. What more effective way to stop sexual immorality and excess, they reasoned, than to curtail sexual desire and pleasure at its source—in the imagination. However, the widespread liberalization in sexual behavior and attitudes in the last century, coupled with the increased availability of sexually explicit material since the 1970s, made the conservative mission a difficult, though not impossible, task.[5] The commission utilized all available tools, both symbolic and procedural.

PROCEDURES AND BIAS

Appointed to find "new ways to control the problem of pornography," the panel was chaired by Henry Hudson, a vigorous antivice prosecutor from Arlington, Virginia, who had been commended by President Reagan for closing down every adult bookstore in his district. Hudson was assisted by his staff of vice cops and attorneys and by executive director Alan Sears, who had a reputation in the U.S. Attorney's Office in Kentucky as a tough opponent of obscenity.[6] Prior to convening, seven of the eleven commissioners had taken public stands opposing pornography and supporting obscenity law as a means to control it. These seven included a fundamentalist broadcaster, several public officials, a priest, and a law professor who had argued that sexually explicit expression was undeserving of First Amendment protection because it was less like speech and more like dildos.[7] The smaller number of moderates sometimes tempered the staff's conservative zeal, but their efforts were modest and not always effective.

The conservative bias continued for fourteen months, throughout the panel's more than 300 hours of public hearings in six U.S. cities and lengthy executive sessions, which I observed.[8] The list of witnesses was tightly controlled: 77 percent supported greater control, if not elimination, of sexually explicit material. Heavily represented were law-enforcement officers and members of vice squads (68 of 208 witnesses), politicians, and spokespersons for conservative anti-pornography groups like Citizens for Decency through Law and the National Federation for Decency. Great efforts were made to find "victims of pornography" to testify,[9] but those reporting positive experiences were largely absent. Witnesses were treated unevenly, depending on whether the point of view they expressed facilitated the commission's ends. There were several glaring procedural irregularities, including the panel's attempt to withhold drafts and working documents from the public and its effort to name major corporations such as Time, Inc., Southland, CBS, Coca-Cola, and K-Mart as "distributors of pornography" in the final report, repeating unsubstantiated allegations made by the Reverend Donald Wildmon, executive director of the National Federation for Decency. These irregularities led to several lawsuits against the commission.

The barest notions of fair play were routinely ignored in gathering evidence. Any negative statement about pornographic images, no matter how outlandish, was accepted as true. Anecdotal testimony that pornography was responsible for divorce, extramarital sex, child abuse, homosexuality, and excessive masturbation was entered as "evidence" and appears as supporting documentation in the final report's footnotes.

GENDER NEGOTIATIONS

The commission's unswerving support for aggressive obscenity law enforcement bore the indelible stamp of the right-wing constituency that brought the panel into existence. Its influence was also evident in the belief of many commissioners and witnesses that pornography leads to immorality, lust, and sin. But the commission's staff and the Justice Department correctly perceived that an unabashedly conservative position would not be persuasive outside the right wing. For the commission's agenda to succeed, the attack on sexually explicit material had to be modernized by couching it in more contemporary arguments, arguments drawn chiefly from anti-pornography feminism and social science. So the preeminent harm that pornography was said to cause was not sin and immorality, but violence and the degradation of women.

To the extent that the worldviews and underlying ideologies of anti-pornography feminism and social science are deeply different from those of fundamentalism, the commission's experiment at merging or overlaying these discourses was far from simple. In general, the commission fared much better in its attempt to incorporate the language and testimony of anti-pornography feminists than that of social scientists. The cooptation of anti-pornography feminism was both implausible and brilliantly executed.

Implausible, because the panel's chair, Henry Hudson, and its executive director, Alan Sears, along with the other conservative members, were no feminists. Hudson usually addressed the four female commissioners as "ladies." He transmuted the term used by feminist anti-pornography groups, "the degradation of women," into the "degradation of femininity," which conjured up visions of Victorian womanhood dragged from the pedestal into a muddy gutter. Beyond language, conservative panelists consistently opposed proposals that feminists universally support— for sex education or school-based programs to inform children about sexual abuse, for example. Conservative members objected to sex-abuse programs for children, contending that such instruction prompted children to make hysterical and unwarranted accusations against male relatives. In addition, panelists rejected the recommendations of feminist prostitutes' rights groups like COYOTE and the U.S. Prostitutes Collective,[10] preferring increased arrests and punishment of women (though not their male customers) to decriminalization and better regulation of abusive working conditions. More comically, conservative panelists tried to push through a "vibrator bill," a model statute that would ban as obscene "any device designed or marketed as useful primarily for the stimulation of human genital organs." The three moderate female commission members became incredulous and upset when they realized that such a law would ban vibrators.

During the course of the public hearings, conservative and fundamentalist witnesses made clear that they regarded the feminist movement as a major cause of the family breakdown and social disruption which they had observed during the past twenty years. Feminists advocated divorce, abortion, access to birth control, day care, single motherhood, sexual permissiveness, lesbian and gay rights, working mothers—all undesirable developments that diminished the importance of family and marriage. Conservatives and fundamentalists were clear in their allegiance to a traditional moral agenda: sex belonged in marriage and nowhere else. Pornography was damaging because it promoted and advertised lust, sex "with no consequences," and "irresponsible" sex.

Anti-pornography feminists, in their writing and activism dating from approximately 1977, saw the damage of pornography in different terms, though other feminists (and I include myself in this group) objected to their analysis for uncritically incorporating many conservative elements of late nineteenth-century sexual culture.[11] Nevertheless, the anti-pornography feminist critique made several points that differed sharply from those made by conservatives. It argued that most, if not all, pornography was sexist (rather than immoral). It socialized men to be dominating and women to be victimized. Moreover, pornographic imagery led to actual sexual violence against women, and it constituted a particularly effective form of anti-woman propaganda. At various times, antipornography feminists have proposed different remedial strategies ranging from educational programs and consciousness-raising to restriction and censorship of sexually explicit material through so-called civil rights anti-pornography legislation, first drafted in 1983. But a consistent theme throughout anti-pornography feminism, as in most feminism, was intense opposition to and fervent critique of gender inequality, male domination, and patriarchal institutions, including the family, marriage, and heterosexuality.

The conflict between basic premises of conservative and anti-pornography feminist analyses is obvious. Nevertheless, the commission cleverly used anti-pornography feminist terms and concepts as well as witnesses to their own advantage in selective ways, helped not infrequently by anti-pornography leaders and groups themselves. Anti-pornography feminist witnesses eagerly testified before the commission and cast their personal experiences of incest, childhood sexual abuse, rape, and sexual coercion in terms of the "harms" and "degradation" caused by pornography. Anti-pornography feminist witnesses, of course, did not voice complaints about divorce, masturbation, or homosexuality, which ideologically give feminists no cause for protest, but they failed to comment on the great divide that separated their complaints from those of fundamentalists, a divide dwarfed only by the even larger distance between their respective political programs. Indeed, some prominent anti-pornography feminists were willing to understate, and most avoided mentioning, in their testimony their support for those cranky feminist demands so offensive to conservative ears: abortion, birth control, and lesbian and gay rights. Only one feminist anti-pornography group, Feminists Against Pornography from Washington, D.C., refused to tailor its testimony to please conservative members and attacked the Reagan administration for its savage cutbacks on programs and services for women.[12] Their testimony was soon cut off on the grounds of inadequate time, though other anti-pornography groups and spokespersons—including Andrea Dworkin, Catharine MacKinnon, and Women Against Pornography (New York)—would be permitted to testify at great length.

In the context of the hearing, the notion that pornography "degrades" women proved to be a particularly helpful unifying term, floating in and out of fundamentalist as well as anti-pornography feminist testimony. By the second public hearing, "degrading" had become a true crossover term—used by moral majoritarians, vice cops, and aggressive prosecutors, as well as anti-pornography feminists. Speakers didn't notice, or chose not to, that the term "degradation" had very different meanings in each community. For anti-pornography feminists, pornography degrades women when it depicts or glorifies sexist sex: images that put men's pleasure first or suggest that women's lot in life is to serve men. For fundamentalists, "degrading" was freely applied to all images of sexual behavior that might be considered immoral, since in the conservative worldview immorality degrades the individual and society. "Degrading" was freely applied to visual images that portrayed homosexuality, masturbation, and even consensual heterosexual sex. Even images of morally approved marital sexuality were judged "degrading," since public viewing of what should be a private experience degraded the couple and the sanctity of marriage. These terms provided by anti-pornography feminists—"degrading," "violence against women," and "offensive to women" (though conservatives couldn't resist adding the phrase "and children")—were eagerly adopted by the panel and proved particularly useful in giving it and its findings the gloss of modernity and some semblance of concern with human rights.

Although the commission happily assimilated the rhetoric of anti-pornography feminists, it decisively rejected their remedies. Conservative men pronounced the testimony of Andrea Dworkin "eloquent" and "moving" and insisted on including her statement in the final report, special treatment given to no other witness. But antipornography feminists had argued against obscenity laws, saying they reflected a moralistic and antisexual tradition that could only harm women. Instead, they favored ordinances, such as those developed for Minneapolis and Indianapolis by Dworkin and MacKinnon,[13] that would outlaw pornography as a violation of women's civil rights. The commission never seriously entertained the idea that obscenity laws should be repealed; given its conservative constituency and agenda, it couldn't have.

The commission's report summarily rejected Minneapolis-style ordinances. These had been "properly held unconstitutional" by a recent Supreme Court decision, the panel agreed, because they infringed on speech protected under the First Amendment. But the panel cleverly, if disingenuously, argued that traditional obscenity law could be used against violent and degrading material in a manner "largely consistent with what this ordinance attempts to do," ignoring anti-pornography feminists' vociferous rejection of obscenity laws. The panel recommended that obscenity laws be further strengthened by adding civil damages to the existing criminal penalties. This constitutes a major defeat for anti-pornography feminists. But unlike social scientists, who protested loudly over the commission's misuse of their testimony, the anti-pornography feminists did not acknowledge the panel's distortion. Instead, they commended the panel for recognizing the harm of pornography and continued to denounce obscenity law,[14] without coming to grips with the panel's commitment to that approach.

Even more startling were MacKinnon's and Dworkin's statements to the press that the commission "has recommended to Congress the civil rights legislation women have sought,"[15] and this comment by Dorchen Leidholdt, founder of Women Against Pornography: "I am not embarrassed at being in agreement with Ed Meese."[16] Over the course of the hearings, it seems that each group strategized how best to use the other. However, the vast power and resources of the federal government, backed by a strong fundamentalist movement, made it almost inevitable that the Meese Commission would benefit far more in this exchange than anti-pornography feminists.

The commission attempted another major appropriation of feminist issues by recasting the problem of violence against women. Since the backlash against feminism began in the mid-1970s, conservative groups most decisively rejected feminist critiques of violence in the family, particularly assertions about the prevalence of marital rape, incest, and child sexual abuse. Such sexual violence was rare, they countered, and exaggerated by feminists only because they were "man-haters" and "lesbians" who wanted to destroy the family. Accordingly, conservatives consistently opposed public funding for social services directed at these problems: rape hotlines, shelters for abused wives, programs to identify and counsel child victims of incest. Such programs would destroy the integrity of the family, particularly the authority of the father, conservatives believed.

The commission hearings document inequality, patriarchy, and women's powerlessness a startling reversal in the conservative discourse on sexual violence. Conservative witnesses now claimed that there is an epidemic of sexual violence directed at women and children, even in the family. Unlike the feminist analysis, which points to inequality, patriarchy, and women's powerlessness as root causes, the conservative analysis singles out pornography and its attendant sexual liberalization as the responsible agents. Men are, in a sense, victims as well, since once their lust is aroused, they are increasingly unable to refrain from sexual aggression. It is clear that the conservative about-face seeks to respond to a rising tide of concern among even right-wing women about the issues of violence and abuse, while at the same time seeking to contain it by providing an alternative narrative: the appropriate solution lies in controlling pornography, not challenging male domination; pornography victimizes men, not just women. In that regard, it is striking that the victim witnesses provided by anti-pornography feminist groups were all female, whereas those provided by conservatives included many men.

Ironically, the conservative analysis ultimately blames feminism for violence against women. To the extent that feminists supported a more permissive sexual climate, including freer sexual expression, and undermined marriage as the only appropriate place for sex and procreation, they promoted an atmosphere favorable to violence against women. The commission's symbolic and rhetorical transformations were skillful. The panel not only appropriated anti-pornography feminist language to modernize a conservative agenda and make it more palatable to the mainstream public, but it also used issues of male violence successfully raised by feminists to argue that the only reliable protection for women was to be found in returning to the family and patriarchal protection.

THE PLEASURES OF LOOKING

The commission's campaign against sexually explicit images was filled with paradoxes. Professing belief in the most naive and literalist theories of representation, the commissioners nevertheless shrewdly used visual images during the hearings to establish "truth" and manipulate the feelings of the audience. Arguing that pornography had a singular and universal meaning that was evident to any viewer, the commission staff worked hard to exclude any perspective but its own. Insisting that sexually explicit images had great authority, the commissioners framed pornography so that it had more power in the hearing than it could ever have in the real world. Denying that subjectivity and context matter in the interpretation of any image, they created a well-crafted context that denied there was a context.

The foremost goal of the commission was to establish "the truth" about pornography—that is, to characterize and describe the sexually explicit material that was said to be in need of regulation. Pornographic images were shown during all public hearings, as witnesses and staff members alike illustrated their remarks with explicit, fleshy, often full-color images of sex. The reluctance to view this material that one might have anticipated on the part of fundamentalists and conservatives was nowhere to be seen. The commission capitalized on the realistic representational form of still photos and movie and video clips, stating that the purpose of viewing these images was to inform the public and themselves about "what pornography was really like." Viewing was carefully orchestrated, and a great deal of staff time went toward organizing the logistics and technologies of viewing. Far from being a casual or minor enterprise, the selection and showing of sexually explicit images constituted one of the commission's major interventions.

The structure of viewing was an inversion of the typical context for viewing pornography. Normally private, this was public, with slides presented in federal courthouse chambers before hundreds of spectators in the light of day. The viewing of pornography, usually an individualistic and libidinally anarchic practice, was here organized by the state—the Department of Justice, to be exact. The ordinary purpose in viewing, sexual pleasure and masturbation, was ostensibly absent, replaced instead by dutiful scrutiny and the pleasures of condemnation.

These pleasures were intense. The atmosphere throughout the hearings was one of excited repression: witnesses alternated between chronicling the negative effects of pornography and making sensationalized presentations of "it." Taking a lead from feminist anti-pornography groups, everyone had a slide show: the FBI, the U.S. Customs Service, the U.S. Postal Service, and sundry vice squads. At every "lights out," spectators would rush to one side of the room to see the screen, which was angled toward the commissioners. Were the hearing room a ship, we would have capsized many times.

Alan Sears, the executive director, told the commissioners with a grin that he hoped to include some "good stuff" in their final report, and its two volumes and 1,960 pages faithfully reflect the censors' fascination with the thing they love to hate. The report lists in alphabetical order the titles of material found in sixteen adult bookstores in six cities: 2,370 films, 725 books, and 2,325 magazines, beginning with *A Cock Between Friends* and ending with *69 Lesbians Munching*. A detailed plot summary is given for the book, *The Tying Up of Rebecca*, along with descriptions of sex aids advertised in the books, their costs, and how to order them.

The commission viewed a disproportionate amount of atypical material, which even moderate commissioners criticized as "extremely violent and degrading."[17] To make themselves sound contemporary and secular, conservatives needed to establish that pornography was violent rather than immoral and, contradicting social science evidence, that this violence was increasing.[18] It was important for the panel to insist that the images presented were "typical" and "average" pornography, but typical pornography—glossy, mainstream porn magazines directed at heterosexual men—does not feature much violence, as the commission's own research (soon quickly suppressed) confirmed.[19] The slide shows, however, did not present many carefully airbrushed photos of perfect females or the largely heterosexual gyrations (typically depicting intercourse and oral sex) found even in the most hard-core adult bookstores. The commission concentrated on atypical material, produced for private use or for small, special-interest segments of the market or confiscated in the course of prosecutions. The slides featured behavior that the staff believed to be especially shocking: homosexuality, excrement, urination, child pornography, bestiality (with over twenty different types of animals, including chickens and elephants), and especially sadomasochism (SM).

The commission relied on the realism of photography to amplify the notion that the body of material shown was accurate and therefore, they implied, representative. The staff also skillfully mixed atypical and marginal material with pictorials from *Playboy* and *Penthouse*, rarely making a distinction between types of publications or types of markets. The desired fiction was that all pornography was the same. Many have commented on the way all photographic images are read as fact or truth, because the images are realistic. This general phenomenon is true for pornographic images as well, but it is intensified when the viewer is confronted by images of sexually explicit acts which he or she has little experience viewing (or doing) in real life. Shock, discomfort, fascination, repulsion, and arousal all operate to make the image have an enormous impact and seem undeniably real.

The action depicted was understood as realistic, not fantastic or staged for the purposes of producing an erotic picture. Thus, images that played with themes of surrender or domination were read as actually coerced. A nude woman holding a machine gun was clearly dangerous, a panelist noted, because the gun could go off (an interpretation not, perhaps, inaccurate for the psychoanalytically inclined reader). Images of obviously adult men and women dressed in exaggerated fashions of high-school students were called child pornography.

Sadomasochistic pornography had an especially strategic use in establishing that sexually explicit imagery was "violent." The intervention was effective, since few (even liberal critics) have been willing to examine the construction of SM in the panel's argument. Commissioners saw a great deal of SM pornography and found it deeply upsetting, as did the audience. Photographs included images of women tied up, gagged, or being "disciplined." Viewers were unfamiliar with the conventions of SM sexual behavior and had no access to the codes participants use to read these images. The panel provided the frame: SM was nonconsensual sex that inflicted force and violence on unwilling victims. Virtually any claim could be made against SM pornography and, by extension, SM behavior, which remains a highly stigmatized and relatively invisible sexuality. As was the case with homosexuality until recently, invisibility reinforces stigma, and stigma reinforces invisibility in a circular manner.

The redundant viewing and narration of SM images reinforced several points useful to the commission—pornography depicted violence against women and promoted male domination. An active editorial hand was at work, however, to remove reverse images of female domination and male submission; these images never appeared, though they constitute a significant portion of SM imagery. Amusingly, SM pornography elicited hearty condemnation of "male dominance," the only sphere in which conservative men were moved to critique it throughout the course of the hearing.

The commission called no witnesses to discuss the nature of SM, either professional experts or typical participants.[20] Given the atmosphere, it was not surprising that no one defended it. Indeed, producers of more soft-core pornography joined in the condemnation, perhaps hoping to direct the commission's ire to groups and acts more stigmatized than themselves.[21] The commission ignored a small but increasing body of literature that documents important features of SM sexual behavior, namely consent and safety. Typically, the conventions we use to decipher ordinary images are suspended when it comes to SM images. When we see science fiction movies, for example, we do not leave the theater believing that the special effects were real or that the performers were injured making the films. But the commissioners assumed that images of domination and submission were both real and coerced.

In addition, such literalist interpretations were evident in the repeated assertions that all types of sexual images had a direct effect on behavior. The idea that sexual images could be used and remain on a fantasy level was foreign to the commission, as was the possibility that individuals might use fantasy to engage with dangerous or frightening feelings without wanting to experience them in real life. This lack of recognition is consistent with fundamentalist distrust and puzzlement about the imagination and the symbolic realm, which seem to have no autonomous existence; for fundamentalists, imagination and behavior are closely linked. If good thoughts lead to good behavior, a sure way to eliminate bad behavior is to police bad thoughts.

The voice-over for the visual segments was singular and uniform, which served to obliterate the actual diversity of people's response to pornography. But sexually explicit material is a contested ground precisely *because* subjectivity matters. An image that is erotic to one individual is revolting to a second and ridiculous to a third. The object of contestation *is* meaning. Age, gender, race, class, sexual preference, erotic experience, and personal history all form the grid through which sexual images are received and interpreted. The commission worked hard to eliminate diversity from its hearings and to substitute instead its own authoritative, often uncontested, frequently male, monologue.

It is startling to realize how many of the Meese Commission's techniques were pioneered by anti-pornography feminists between 1977 and 1984. Claiming that pornography was sexist and promoted violence against women, anti-pornography feminists had an authoritative voice-over, too, though for theorists Andrea Dworkin and Catharine MacKinnon and groups like Women Against Pornography, the monologic voice was, of course, female. Although anti-pornography feminists disagreed with fundamentalist moral assumptions and contested rather than approved, male authority, they carved out new territory with slide shows depicting allegedly horrific sexual images, a technique the commission heartily adopted. Anti-pornography feminists relied on victim testimony and preferred anecdotes to data. They, too, shared a literalist interpretive frame and used SM images to prove that pornography was violent.

The Meese Commission was skilled in its ability to use photographic images to establish the so-called truth and to provide an almost invisible interpretive frame that compelled agreement with its agenda. The commission's true gift, however, lay in its ability to create an emotional atmosphere in the hearings that facilitated acceptance of the commission's world-view. Its strategic use of images was a crucial component of this emotional management. Because the power of this emotional climate fades in the published text, it is not obvious to most readers of the commission's report. Yet it was and is a force to be reckoned with, both in the commission and, more broadly, in all public debates about sexuality, especially those that involve the right wing.

RITUALS OF SEXUAL SHAME

An important aspect of the commission's work was the ritual airing and affirmation of sexual shame in a public setting. The panel relentlessly created an atmosphere of unacknowledged sexual arousal and fear. The large amount of pornography shown, ostensibly to educate and repel, was nevertheless arousing. The range and diversity of images provided something for virtually everyone, and the concentration on taboo, kinky, and harder-to-obtain material added to the charge. Part of the audience's discomfort may have come from the unfamiliarity of seeing sexually explicit images in public, not private, settings, and in the company of others not there for the express purpose of sexual arousal. But a larger part must have come from the problem of experiencing sexual arousal in an atmosphere where it is condemned. The commission's lesson was a complex one, but it taught the importance of managing and hiding sexual arousal and pleasure in public, while it reinforced secrecy, hypocrisy, and shame. Unacknowledged sexual feelings, though, did not disappear but developed into a whirlwind of mute, repressed emotion that the Meese Commission channeled toward its own purpose.

Sexual shaming was also embedded in the interrogatory practices of the chair. Witnesses appearing before the commission were treated in a highly uneven manner. Commissioners accepted virtually any claim made by anti-pornography witnesses as true, while those who opposed restriction of sexually explicit speech were often met with rudeness and hostility. The panelists asked social scientist Edward Donnerstein if pornographers had tried to influence his research findings or threatened his life. They asked actress Colleen Dewhurst, testifying for Actor's Equity about the dangers of censorship in the theater, if persons convicted of obscenity belonged to the union, and if the union was influenced by organized crime. They questioned her at length about the group's position on child pornography.

Sexual shame was also ritualized in how witnesses spoke about their personal experiences with images. "Victims of pornography" told in lurid detail of their use of pornography and eventual decline into masturbation, sexual addiction, and incest. Some testified anonymously, shadowy apparitions behind translucent screens. Their first-person accounts, sometimes written by the commission's staff,[22] featured a great elaboration of the sexual damage caused by visual images. To counter these accounts there was nothing but silence: descriptions of visual and sexual pleasure were absent. The commission's chair even noted the lack and was fond of asking journalists if they had ever come across individuals with positive experiences with pornography. The investigatory staff had tried to identify such people to testify, he said, but had been unable to find any. Hudson importuned reporters to please send such individuals his way. A female commissioner helpfully suggested that she knew of acquaintances, "normal married couples living in suburban New Jersey," who occasionally looked at magazines or rented X-rated videos with no apparent ill effects. But she doubted they would be willing to testify about their sexual pleasure in a federal courthouse, with their remarks transcribed by the court stenographer and their photos probably published in the next day's paper as "porn-users."

Though few witnesses chose to expose themselves to the commission's intimidation through visual images, the tactics used are illustrated in the differential treatment of two female witnesses, former *Playboy* Playmate Micki Garcia and former *Penthouse* Pet of the Year Dottie Meyer. Garcia accused Playboy Enterprises and Hugh Hefner of encouraging drug use, murder, and rape (as well as abortion, bisexuality, and cosmetic surgery) in the Playboy mansion. Her life was endangered by her testimony, she claimed. Despite the serious nature of some of these charges and the lack of any supporting evidence, her testimony was received without question.[23] Meyer, on the other hand, testified that her association with *Penthouse* had been professionally and personally benefi-cial. At the conclusion of her testimony, the lights dramatically dimmed and large blow-ups of several *Penthouse* pictorials were flashed on the screen; with rapid-fire questions the chair demanded that she explain sexual images he found particularly objectionable. Another male com-missioner, prepared by the staff with copies of Meyer's nine-year-old centerfold, began to pepper her with hectoring questions about her sexual life: Was it true she was preoccupied with sex? Liked sex in cars and alleyways? Had a collection of vibrators? Liked rough-and-tumble sex?[24] The female commissioners were silent. His sexist cross-examination was reminiscent of that directed at a rape victim, discredited and made vulnerable by any admission or image of her own sexuality. Suddenly, Dottie Meyer was on trial, publicly humiliated because she dared to present herself as unrepentantly sexual, not a victimized woman.

The ferocious attack on Dottie Meyer—and by extension on any displays of women's sexual pleasure in the public sphere—is emblematic of the agenda of conservatives and fundamentalists on women's sexuality. Although they presented their program under the guise of feminist lan-guage and concerns, their abiding goal was to reestablish control by restricting women—and their desires—within ever-shrinking boundaries of the private and the domestic. The falsity of the panel's seemingly feminist rhetoric was highlighted by the moment when a lone woman speaking of her own sexual pleasure was seen as a greater threat than all male "victims" of pornography who had assaulted and abused women. The conspicuous absence of any discourse that addressed women's definitions of their own sexual pleasures, that enlarged rather than constricted the domain of their public speech or action, unmasked this agenda. Unmasked, too, was the com-mission's primary aim: not to increase the safe space for women, but to narrow what can be seen, spoken about, imagined, and—they hope—done. The invisibility and subordination of female sexual pleasure in the commission's hearings is a that which conservatives and fundamentalists would like to extend to the entire culture. Feminist language, disembodied from feminist princi-ples and programs, was used to advance the idea that men, women, and society could be pro-tected only through the suppression of female desire. In the face of false patriarchal protections embedded in shame and silence, feminists need to assert their entitlement to public speech, vari-ety, safety, and bodily and visual pleasures.

NOTES

I am grateful to Frances Doughty, Lisa Duggan, Ann Snitow and Sharon Thompson for reading early drafts and for helpful comments, criticism, and encouragement. Thanks also to Faye Ginsburg and Anna Tsing for thoughtful suggestions and patience.

Thanks to the Rockefeller Foundation for a Humanist-in-Residence Fellowship (1987–88) at the Cen-ter for Research on Women, Douglass College, Rutgers, the State University, New Brunswick, New Jer-sey, which supported my research and writing.

Parts of this analysis have appeared in "The Meese Commission on the Road," The *Nation*, 243, 3 (2–9 August 1986), pp. 65, 76–82; and "The Pleasures of Looking: The Attorney General's Commission on Pornography versus Visual Images," in Carol Squiers, ed., *The Critical Image: Essays on Contemporary Pho-tography* (Seattle: Bay Press, 1990), pp. 38–58. Earlier versions of this paper were presented at the annual meeting of the Society for Photographic Education, Rochester, New York, 17 March 1989; at the panel *Gender Rituals and the Sexual Self*, American Anthropological Association, 21 November 1987; and at the panel *Contested Domains of Reproduction, Sexuality, Family and Gender in America*, American Ethnological Society, Wrightsville Beach, North Carolina, 24 April 1986. Thanks to panelists and members of the audience for helpful comments.

NOTES

This essay first appeared in Faye Ginsburg and Anna L. Tsing, eds., *Uncertain Terms: Negotiating Gender in American Culture* (Beacon, 1990), 118–34. It is reprinted here with the kind permission of Carole S. Vance, who holds copyright and permissions.

1. Attorney General's Commission on Pornography, Miami transcript, public hearing, November 21, 1985.

2. Attorney General's Commission on Pornography, *Final Report*, 2 vols. (Washington, D.C.: U.S. Government Printing Office, 1986).

3. See *Final Report*, pp. 433–58, for a complete list of the panel's recommendations. These include mandating high fines and long jail sentences for obscenity convictions, appointing a federal task force to coordinate prosecutions nationwide, developing a computer data bank to collect information on individuals suspected of producing pornography, and using punitive RICO legislation (the Racketeer Influenced and Corrupt Organizations Act, originally developed to fight organized crime) to confiscate the personal property of anyone convicted of the "conspiracy" of producing pornography. For sexually explicit material outside the range of legal prosecution, the commission recommended that citizen activist groups target and remove material in their communities which they find "dangerous or offensive or immoral."

4. For a detailed critique of procedural irregularities, see Barry Lynn, *Polluting the Censorship Debate: A Summary and Critique of the Attorney General's Commission on Pornography* (Washington, D.C.: American Civil Liberties Union, 1986).

5. For changes in sexual patterns in the last century, see (for England) Jeffrey Weeks, *Sex, Politics and Society: The Regulation of Sexuality Since 1800* (New York: Longman, 1981); and (for America) John D'Emilio and Estelle B. Freedman, *Intimate Matters* (New York: Harper and Row, 1988). For a history of pornography, see Walter Kendrick, *The Secret Museum* (New York: Viking, 1987).

6. Sears went on to become the executive director of Citizens for Decency Through Law, a major conservative anti-pornography group. (The group has since changed its name to the Children's Legal Foundation.)

7. Attorney Frederick Schauer argued that sexually explicit expression that was arousing was less like speech and more like "rubber, plastic, or leather sex aids." See "Speech and 'Speech'—Obscenity and 'Obscenity': An Exercise in the Interpretation of Constitutional Language," *Georgetown Law Journal* 67 (1979), 899–923, especially pp. 922–23.

8. My analysis is based on direct observation of the commission's public hearings and executive sessions, supplemented by interviews with participants. All the commission's executive sessions were open to the public, following the provision of sunshine laws governing federal advisory commissions. Commissioners were specifically prohibited from discussing commission business or engaging in any informal deliberations outside of public view.

   Public hearings were organized around preselected topics in six cities: Washington, D.C. (general), Chicago (law enforcement), Houston (social science), Los Angeles (production and distribution), Miami (child pornography), and New York (organized crime). Each public hearing typically lasted two full days. Commission executive sessions were held in each city in conjunction with the public hearings, usually for two extra days. Additional work sessions occurred in Washington, D.C., and Scottsdale, Arizona.

9. Victims of pornography, as described in the *Final Report*, included "Sharon, formerly married to a medical professional who is an avid consumer of pornography," "Bill, convicted of the sexual molestation of two adolescent females," "Dan, former Consumer of Pornography (sic)," "Evelyn,

Mother and homemaker, Wisconsin, formerly married to an avid consumer of pornography," and "Mary Steinman, sexual abuse victim."

10. Los Angeles transcript, public hearing, October 17, 1985.

11. Major works of anti-pornography feminism include Andrea Dworkin, *Pornography: Men Possessing Women* (New York: G. P. Putnam, 1979); Susan Griffin *Pornography and Silence: Culture's Revenge Against Nature* (New York: Harper and Row, 1981); Laura Lederer, ed., *Take Back the Night* (New YorK: William Morrow, 1980); Catharine A. MacKinnon, "Pornography, Civil Rights, and Speech," *Harvard Civil Rights-Civil Liberties Law Review*, vol. 20, 1–70.

　　Opinion within feminism about pornography was, in fact, quite diverse, and it soon became apparent that the antipornography view was not hegemonic. For other views, see Carole S. Vance, ed., *Pleasure and Danger: Exploring Female Sexuality* (New York: Routledge & Kegan Paul, 1984); Varda Burstyn, ed., *Women Against Censorship,* (Vancouver: Douglas & McIntyre, 1985); and Kate Ellis et al., eds., *Caught Looking: Feminism, Pornography, and Censorship* (New York: Caught Looking, Inc., 1986).

12. Washington, D.C., transcript, public hearing, June 20, 1985.

13. For the version passed in Indianapolis, see Indianapolis, Ind., code section 16–3 (q) (1984); and Andrea Dworkin, "Against the Male Flood: Censorship, Pornography, and Equality," *Harvard Women's Law Journal* 9 (1985), 1–19. For a critique, see Lisa Duggan, Nan Hunter, and Carole S. Vance, "False Promises: Feminist Antipornography Legislation in the U.S.," in *Women Against Censorship*, ed. Varda Burstyn (Toronto: Douglas & McIntyre, 1985), 130–51.

14. Women Against Pornography press conference, July 9, 1986, New York.

15. Statement of Catharine A. MacKinnon and Andrea Dworkin, July 9, 1986, New York, distributed at a press conference organized by Women Against Pornography following the release of the Meese Commission's *Final Report*.

16. David Firestone, "Battle Joined by Reluctant Allies," *Newsday*, July 10, 1986, p. 5.

17. Statement of commissioners Judith Becker and Ellen Levine, *Final Report*, p. 199. In addition, they wrote: "We do not even know whether or not what the Commission viewed during the course of the year reflected the nature of most of the pornographic and obscene material in the market; nor do we know if the materials shown us mirror the taste of the majority of consumers of pornography."

18. Recent empirical evidence does not support the often-repeated assertion that violence in pornography is increasing. In their review of the literature, social scientists Edward Donnerstein, Daniel Linz, and Steven Penrod conclude, "At least for now, we cannot legitimately conclude that pornography has become more violent since the time of the 1970 obscenity and pornography commission" (in *The Question of Pornography: Research Findings and Policy Implications* [New York: Free Press, 1987], 91).

19. The only original research conducted by the commission examined images found in the April 1986 issues of best-selling men's magazines (*Cheri, Chic, Club, Gallery, Genesis, High Society, Hustler, Oui, Penthouse, Playboy, Swank*). The study found that "images of force, violence, or weapons" constituted less than 1 percent of all images (0.6 percent), hardly substantiating the commission's claim that violent imagery in pornography was common. Although the results of this study are reported in the draft, they were excised from the final report.

20. For recent works on SM, see Michael A. Rosen, *Sexual Magic: The S/M Photographs* (San Francisco: Shaynew Press, 1986); Geoff Mains, *Urban Aboriginals* (San Francisco: Gay Sunshine Press, 1984); Samois, ed., *Coming to Power*, 2d ed. (Boston: Alyson Press, 1982); Gini Graham Scott, *Dominant Women, Submissive Men* (New York: Praeger, 1983); Thomas Weinberg and G. P. Levi Kamel, *S and M: Studies in Sadomasochism* (Buffalo: Prometheus Books, 1983); Gerald and Caroline Greene, *S-M: The Last Taboo* (New York: Grove Press, 1974).

21. The proclivity of mildly stigmatized groups to join in the scapegoating of more stigmatized groups

is explained by Gayle Rubin in her discussion of sexual hierarchy (Gayle Rubin, "Thinking Sex: Notes for a Radical Theory of the Politics of Sexuality" in *Pleasure and Danger: Exploring Female Sexuality*, ed. Carole S. Vance [Boston: Routledge & Kegan Paul, 1984], 267–319.)

22. Statement of Alan Sears, executive director (Washington, D.C. transcript, June 18, 1985).

23. Los Angeles transcript, public hearing, October 17, 1985.

24. New York City transcript, public hearing, January 22, 1986.

30   The Neo-Family-Values Campaign

Judith Stacey

In November of 1992 there was impeccable cause to imagine that the family wars in the United States were about to abate. The extent and irreversibility of family change, assisted by Murphy Brown, the Republican Convention fiasco and the Year of the Woman, seemed to have vanquished the family-values brigades. Who would have predicted that even the liberal media would scramble to rehabilitate Dan Quayle's image before Bill and Hillary had survived their blistering first 100 days?

Yet that is exactly what happened. DAN QUAYLE WAS RIGHT, blared the April 1993 cover of the *Atlantic Monthly*, a magazine popular with the very cultural elite whom the former vice-president had blamed for the decline of Western civilized family life. Far from withering, a revisionist campaign for family values flourished under Democratic skies. While Clinton's job stimulus package suffered a silent demise, pro-family values stories mushroomed in magazines, newspapers, on radio and TV talk shows, and in scholarly journals. The *Atlantic* cover story by Barbara Dafoe Whitehead[1] ignited "the single strongest public response to any issue ever published by the *Atlantic* since at least 1981,"[2] and was recycled from sea to rocky sea. A *New York Times* op-ed, "The Controversial Truth: Two-Parent Families are Better," by Rutgers University sociologist David Popenoe, also enjoyed acclaim, with retreads and derivatives appearing from the *Chronicle of Higher Education* to the Santa Rosa, California *Press Democrat*.[3] In the winter of 1992–1993 issue of *American Scholar*, Senator Daniel Patrick Moynihan, a founding father of post-World War II family crisis discourse, added to his hefty inventory of family values jeremiads. James Q. Wilson, the Collins Professor of Management and Public Policy at UCLA, earlier proponent of racial theories of criminality, weighed in with a featured family-values essay in *Commentary*.[4] From "This Week with David Brinkley" to the "MacNeil-Lehrer News Hour," television followed suit, featuring guests like Popenoe, who chanted kaddish over an idealized family past.

Judith Stacey, the Streisand Professor of Contemporary Gender Studies and Professor of Sociology at the University of Southern California, has written and lectured extensively on the politics of family change. Her recent book, *In the Name of the Family: Rethinking Family Values in the Postmodern Age* (Beacon, 1996), challenges the research and politics behind contemporary campaigns for family values. She is also the author of *Brave New Families: Stories of Domestic Upheaval in Late Twentieth Century America* (Basic, 1990) and *Patriarchy and Socialist Revolution in China* (California, 1983).

Because the rhetoric of family-values discourse seems so familiar, most progressives have failed to recognize, or to respond appropriately to, what is dangerously novel here. I would have committed a similar error, had my book, *Brave New Families*, not become a target for the new, family security guards.[5] Quoting from it, Popenoe portrayed me as an antifamily extremist, and numerous spin-offs reprinted the lines while deriding my support for family diversity.[6] This unsolicited notoriety fueled my efforts to understand how and why a revival of the family-values campaign coincided with the very changing of the political guard that I had expected would spell its decline.

PSEUDO-SCHOLARLY CULTURAL COMBAT

Old-fashioned family-values warriors, like Jerry Falwell, Dan Quayle, and Pat Buchanan, are right-wing Republicans and/or fundamentalist Christians, overtly antifeminist, antihomosexual, and politically reactionary. Their profamily campaign suffered its nadir during the 1992 electoral season—from Quayle's infamous Murphy Brown speech through the ill-advised family-values orgy of the Republican Convention to defeat at the polls. This campaign continues to exert powerful influence over the Republican Party. In contrast, the revisionist campaign has an explicitly centrist politics, rhetoric, and ideology. A product of academicians rather than clerics, it grounds its claims in secular social science instead of religious authority, and eschews antifeminism for a postfeminist family ethic.

While the right wing may prove the prime beneficiary of current family-values discourse, it is not its primary producer. Rather, an interlocking network of scholarly and policy institutions, think thanks, and commissions began mobilizing during the late 1980s to forge a national consensus on family values that rapidly shaped the family ideology and politics of the Clinton administration and his New Democratic party. Central to this effort are the Institute for American Values, codirected by David Blankenhorn and Barbara Dafoe Whitehead (author of the *Atlantic* article), and its sponsored research offshoot, the Council on Families in America, cochaired by David Popenoe and Jean Bethke Elshtain. The former, which Popenoe describes as a "nonpartisan public policy organization," sponsors the latter, whose seventeen members depict themselves as "a volunteer, nonpartisan program of scholarly research and interdisciplinary deliberation on the state of families in America. We come from across the human sciences and across the political spectrum."[7]

"This is an attempt to bring people together who could convince the liberal intelligentsia that the family was in trouble and that this was a big problem," Popenoe explained to me in an interview. "Most of us are neoliberal—you know, New Democrats, affiliated with the Progressive Policy Institute. We try to keep to the middle of the road."[8] The political network and the funding sources of these center-laners merge with those of the communitarians—a movement once characterized by its founder, sociologist Amitai Etzioni, as "struggling for the soul of the Clinton Administration."[9] They are linked as well with those of the Democratic Leadership Council's Progressive Policy Institute. Political scientist William Galston, who was Clinton's chief domestic policy adviser until he resigned in June of 1995, is a communitarian as well as a member of the Council on Families. Blankenhorn, Popenoe and Elshtain are all communitarians, as is Henry Cisneros. Al Gore spoke at a 1991 communitarian teach-in.

Galston coauthored a family policy position paper for the Progressive Policy Institute,[10] which echoed themes from a conference cosponsored by the Institute for American Values at Stanford University in 1990. The conference volume, *Rebuilding the Nest*, edited by Blankenhorn, Elshtain, and Steven Bayme, helped guide the deliberations of the National Commission on Children, which issued the 1991 Rockefeller Report, *Beyond Rhetoric: A New American Agenda for Children and Families*.[11] Governor Bill Clinton of Arkansas was a member of that commission.

According to Popenoe these groups share the same benefactors, like the Randall, Smith Richardson, Scaife, and Mott foundations, and the Brookings and American Enterprise institutes; more of them are conservative than liberal as Popenoe acknowledged.[12] With such support, revisionists are self-consciously waging a cultural crusade to restore the privileged status of life-long, heterosexual marriage. Declaring that "the principal source of family decline over the past three decades has been cultural," Whitehead urged the Institute for American Values readership to join a cultural mobilization to restore nuclear family supremacy.[13] Wilson's *Commentary* essay went further, calling "this raging cultural war" over family values "far more consequential than any of the other cleavages that divide us."[14] *Newsweek* columnist Joe Klein applauded revisionist proposals for "a massive antipregnancy [sic] and proselytizing campaign similar to the antismoking and -drug crusades of recent years. 'Those *worked*,' says presidential adviser William Galston. 'They really changed behavior patterns, and this might, too.'"[15]

If the effects of this campaign on sexual and conjugal behavior in the private sphere remain to be seen, it quickly achieved an astonishing, and disturbing, impact on the public behavior and policy priorities of the Clinton administration. It took scarcely a year to convert Clinton from representing himself as a proud icon of a strong single mom's glory into a repentant Quayle acolyte. "Hurray for Bill Clinton. What a difference a year makes," Quayle gloated in December 1993, right after *Newsweek* had published the president's revised family credo: "Remember the Dan Quayle speech? There were a lot of very good things in that speech," Clinton acknowledged. "Would we be a better-off society if babies were born to married couples? You bet we would."[16] The rhetorical means through which Clinton's family-values makeover occurred merit close scrutiny.

FEIGNING ICONOCLASTIC COURAGE

In one of the more effective rhetorical ploys of the revisionist campaign, these mainstream social scientists, policy lobbyists, and prominent political office holders and advisers have been able to ride the coat tails of the antipolitical correctness crusade by positioning themselves as dissident challengers of a formidable, intolerant, ideological establishment. Popenoe, for example, is associate dean of Social and Behavioral Sciences at Rutgers University, as well as codirector of the Council on Families in America. Wilson occupies an endowed professorship of management of public policy at UCLA, and Elshtain, an endowed professorship of theology at the University of Chicago. Etzioni was the 1994–1995 President of the American Sociological Association. And Senator Moynihan, well . . .

Yet, Wilson characterized those scholars who reject a nostalgic view of 1950s families as "policy elites."[17] During a radio debate over the superiority of the two-parent family, Popenoe portrayed me and other feminist sociologists as part of the "liberal social science establishment."[18] Whitehead laments, "It is nearly impossible to discuss changes in family structure without provoking angry protest,"[19] citing as evidence enraged responses in the mid-1960s to Moynihan's *The Negro Family: The Case for National Action*, which had labeled the rising percentages of Black single-mother families a "tangle of pathology." She attributes to ideological pressures some of the caution exercised by researchers who do not support the claim that single-parent families are deficient. "Some are fearful that they will be attacked by feminist colleagues," Whitehead claims, "or, more generally, that their comments will be regarded as an effort to turn back the clock to the 1950s—a goal that has almost no constituency in the academy."[20]

Wilson predicted that were the president to exercise leadership in condemning unwed childbearing, he would elicit "dismayed groans from sitcom producers and ideological accusations from sociology professors [like yours truly], but at least the people would know that he is on their side."[21] Exploiting popular resentment against PC cultural elites builds upon the tradition of disingenuous populism honed by former Republican vice-presidents Spiro Agnew and Dan Quayle. At the same time, it pays tribute to the considerable, albeit precarious, influence over gender and family discourse that feminism has achieved during the past quarter-century. Inside the academy, many centrists probably do feel threatened and displaced by feminist scholars. They are fighting back.

CONSTRUCTING SOCIAL SCIENTIFIC STIGMA

While the right-wing family-values campaign appeals to religious and traditional patriarchal authority for its family vision, centrists are engaged in an active process of transmuting into a newly established, social scientific "truth" one of the most widely held prejudices about family life in North America—the belief in the superiority of families composed of married, heterosexual couples, and their biological children. Revisionists argue that the presence or absence of two married, biological parents in the household is the central determinant of a child's welfare, and thereby of our society's welfare. They identify fatherless families as the malignant root of escalating violence and social decay, claiming such families generate the lineage of unemployed, undomesticated, familyless fathers, as John Gillis aptly puts it,[22] who threaten middle-class tranquility.

Through the sheer force of categorical assertion, repetition, and cross-citation of each other's publications, these social scientists seem to have convinced most of the media, the literate public, and Clinton himself that a fault-free bedrock of social science research validates the particular family values that they and most Americans claim to favor, but fail to practice. "In three decades of work as a social scientist," asserted Popenoe in his *New York Times* op-ed, "I know of few other bodies of data in which the weight of evidence is so decisively on one side of the issue: on the whole for children, two-parent families are preferable to single-parent and stepfamilies."[23] In the *Atlantic* story three months later, Whitehead quoted these very lines as authority for a similar assertion: "The social arrangement that has proved most successful in ensuring the physical survival and promoting the social development of the child is the family unit of the biological mother and father."[24] Whitehead also relied on Moynihan's essay "Defining Deviancy Down," which blamed "broken families" for almost all of our current social crises. Moynihan, in turn, had quoted an earlier essay by Whitehead in support of a similar argument.[25] Moynihan, Whitehead, and Popenoe all cited the National Commission on Children's Rockefeller Report, and the Report returned the favor with frequent citations of essays by Popenoe and his associates in the Institute for American Values and the Council for Families in America.[26]

Then, when in April 1993 Popenoe defined the ideal family in the *Chronicle of Higher Education*, he paraphrased views that he and Blankenhorn both had expressed in *Rebuilding the Nest* and which Whitehead and the Rockefeller Report had endorsed: "What are the characteristics of an *ideal* family environment for childrearing? The Council believes they are an enduring family with two biological parents that regularly engages in activities together; has many of its own routines, traditions, and stories; and provides a great deal of contact between adults and children."[27] With minor editorial revisions, the Council on Families in America reprinted this definition as one of eight propositions on family life.[28]

It is not often that the social construction or more precisely here, the political construction of knowledge is quite so visible or incestuous as in the reciprocal citation practices of these cultural crusaders. Through such means, they seem to have convinced President Clinton and most of the public that "it is a confirmed empirical generalization," as Popenoe maintains, that nontraditional families, "are not as successful as conventional two-parent families."[29] Yet, the current status of social scientific knowledge on the success of diverse family structures is far more complex, and the views of family scholars far more heterogeneous, than revisionists pretend. Social scientists continue actively to debate whether family form or processes determine diverse family outcomes and whether our family or socioeconomic crisis has generated its counterpart.[30] For example, in a judicious, comprehensive review essay on the cumulative research on changing parent-child relations, prominent family sociologist David Demo concluded that "the consequences of maternal employment, divorce, and single-parent family structure have been greatly exaggerated, and that researchers need to investigate processes more directly influencing children, notably economic hardship and high levels of marital and family conflict."[31] In fact, according to Demo, "the accumulated evidence is sufficiently consistent to wonder whether we, as researchers, are asking the most important questions, or whether we, like the families we are trying to study, are more strongly influenced by traditional notions of family formality."[32]

The revisionist social scientists suppress these debates by employing social-scientific sleights of hand. For example, they rest their claims on misleading comparison groups and on studies, like Judith Wallerstein's widely cited research on divorcing parents, that do not use any comparison groups at all.[33] While it is true that, on average, children whose parents divorce fare slightly worse than those whose parents remain married, this reveals little about the impact of divorce on children. To address that question, one must compare children of divorce not with all children of married parents, but with those whose unhappily married parents do not divorce. In fact, research indicates that high-conflict marriages harm children more than do low-conflict divorces. "There is abundant evidence," David Demo concludes, "that levels of family conflict are more important than type of family structure for understanding children's adjustment, self-esteem, and other measures of psychological well-being."[34] Unhappily married parents must ask themselves not whether divorcing or staying married is worse for children in general, but which would be worse for their particular children in their particular unhappy marriage.

Centrists use additional statistical tricks to exaggerate advantages some children from two-parent families enjoy over their single-parented peers. For example, they pretend that correlation proves causality and ignores mediating variables, or they treat small and relative differences as though they were gross and absolute. In fact, most children from both kinds of families turn out reasonably all right, and when other parental resources—like income, education, self-esteem, and a supportive, social environment—are roughly similar, signs of two-parent privilege largely disappear. Most research indicates that a stable, intimate relationship with one responsible, nurturant adult is a child's surest route to becoming the same kind of adult. In short, the research scale tips handily toward those who stress the quality of family relationships over their form.[35]

Once dissenting scholarly views on the pathology of single-parent families had been muffled or marginalized, only a rhetorical baby step was needed to move from the social to the moral inferiority of such families. Ergo, the remarkably respectful public response that American Enterprise Institute scholar Charles Murray received in November 1993 to his overtly punitive quest to restigmatize unwed childbearing via Dickensian welfare politics. "My proposition is that illegitimacy is the single most important social problem of our time—more important than crime, drugs, poverty, illiteracy, welfare, or homelessness because it drives everything else," Murray declared in defense of his proposal "to end all economic support for single mothers." Forcing single mothers off of welfare would slash nonmarital childbearing, Murray reasoned, because, "the pressure on relatives and communities to pay for the folly of their children will make an illegitimate birth the socially horrific act it used to be, and getting a girl pregnant something boys do at the risk of facing a shotgun."[36] Instead of receiving timely visits from the ghosts of Christmases past, present, and future, Murray was soon the featured guest on *This Week with David Brinkley*. Even in liberal San Francisco, an op-ed by a supporter of Murray's proposals from the right-wing Hoover Institute upstaged the more charitable Christmas week commentaries aired on the local affiliate of National Public Radio.[37]

By then, revisionists had deftly paved the yellow brick road to Murray's media coronation. "Bringing a child into the world outside of marriage," Blankenhorn had asserted three years earlier, "is almost always personally and socially harmful."[38] In December of 1992, Moynihan congratulated himself on having predicted the epidemic of single-parent families and its calamitous social consequences nearly thirty years earlier. "There is one unmistakable lesson in American history," he had written in 1965; "a community that allows a large number of young men to grow up in broken families, dominated by women . . . asks for and gets chaos."[39]

Thus, by the time the 1993 holiday season began, the ideological mortar had dried firmly enough to encourage *Newsweek* columnist Joe Klein's view that "the issue is so elemental, the question so basic, the answer so obvious," that one should not have to ask a president, as the magazine just had done, whether it is "immoral for people to have children out of wedlock?" Klein applauded when President Clinton, himself possessed of dubious parentage and out-of-wedlock, half-siblings who seem to surface intermittently, answered "much as Dan Quayle, to whom he gave considerable credit, might have: 'I believe this country would be a lot better off if children were born to married couples.'" After all, Klein lamented:

> It's a measure of our social fragility and moral perversity that the president's statement will be controversial in certain circles even though there's now a mountain of data showing illegitimacy to be the smoking gun in a sickening array of pathologies—crime, drug abuse, physical and mental illness, welfare dependency. Bill Clinton's morality will, no doubt, be seen as hopelessly retro—or worse, as cynical politics—in Hollywood, where he was off raising money over the weekend and where out-of-wedlock births are quite the fashion.[40]

Indeed, by then, the revisionist cultural onslaught had been so effective that even Donna Shalala, the token feminist progressive in Clinton's cabinet, felt politically compelled to recite its moralist mantra: "I don't like to put this in moral terms, but I do believe that having children out of wedlock is just wrong." A dyed-in-the-wool, but curious, White House liberal confided, off the record, to *Newsweek*, "I'd like to see the Murray solution tried somewhere—just to see, y'know, what might happen."[41] In June 1994, *before* the right-wing Republican mid-term electoral rout, Clinton sent a welfare "reform" proposal to Congress with caps on childbearing and benefits that promised to satisfy such curiosity. Then, in the 1996 electoral season, he signed the Republican version of welfare repeal.

THE NEW POSTFEMINIST FAMILISM

Despite inflated claims to iconoclasm, revisionists promote family values that seem, at first glance, tediously familiar. Sounding like card-carrying conservatives in academic drag, they blame family breakdown for everything from child poverty, declining educational standards, substance abuse, homicide rates, AIDS, infertility, and teen pregnancy to narcissism and the Los Angeles riots. They attribute family breakdown, in turn, to a generalized decline in family values, which, in its turn, they often associate with feminism, the sexual revolution, gay liberation, excessively generous welfare policies and escalating demands for social rights.

While orthodox and revisionist family preachers share obvious affinities, centrists take wiser note of present demographic and cultural terrain than do their right-wing counterparts. Because they claim to decry rampant individualism, they tend to acknowledge greater public and corporate responsibility for family decline and redress than is palatable to family-values hardliners. Many used to claim to support the Progressive Policy Institute's call for a guaranteed working wage that would lift families with full-time workers out of poverty. Most also claim to favor family-friendly workplace reforms like flextime, family leaves, and flexible career paths.[42] Disappointingly, however, they devote much less of their political energies to these more progressive goals than to the cultural campaign that has done much to undermine such reforms.

Perhaps the most significant distinction between the traditional and neo-family values campaigns is in gender ideology. Departing from the explicit antifeminism and homophobia of a Jesse Helms or Pat Buchanan, family centrists accommodate their family values to postindustrial society and postfeminist culture.[43] They temper their palpable nostalgia for Ozzie and Harriet with rhetorical gestures toward gender equality. "The council does not bemoan the loss of 'the traditional nuclear family,' with its strict social roles, distinguishing between male breadwinners and female homemakers," Popenoe maintains. "Recognizing" instead "the importance of female equality and the changing conditions of modern society, we do not see the previous model of lifelong, separate gender roles within marriage as either desirable or possible on a society-wide scale. But we do believe strongly that the model of the two-parent family, based on a lasting, monogamous marriage, is both possible and desirable."[44] Blankenhorn too once espoused post-feminist ideology: "Strengthening family life in the 1990s cannot and should not mean the repeal of the past 30 years of new opportunities for women in the workplace and in public life. Just as today's cultural ethos of individualism affects men just as much as women, so must a revived ethos of family life affect the behavior and priorities of both sexes."[45]

Revisionists place great emphasis on reviving paternal commitment. Wilson lauds efforts by the National Center for Neighborhood Enterprise "that try to encourage men to take responsibility for their children."[46] Blankenhorn has turned combatting fatherlessness into his overarching mission. Joining forces with Don Eberly, a former aide to Jack Kemp, he formed a national organization of fathers to "restore to fatherhood a sense of pride, duty, and reward."[47] Combining a massive promotional tour for his 1995 book, *Fatherless America*, with a campaign for The National Fatherhood Initiative, Blankenhorn has been actively crusading against "excesses of feminism" like the belief that "men will not become new fathers unless they do half the diaper changes or bottle feedings." Instead, his campaign promotes a neo-traditional model of fatherhood, in which "the old father, with some updating in the nurturing department, will do just fine."[48]

Such postfeminist ideology appeals to many conservative feminists and to many liberals. It builds upon a body of thought I once labeled new conservative feminism, to which family centrists Elshtain and Sylvia Hewlett made formative contributions.[49] One of the defining features of this ideology is its weak stomach for sexual politics. Centrists offer tepid support, at best, for abortion rights, often supporting restrictions like spousal and parental notification, partly with the claim that these could hold men more paternally accountable.[50]

Rather than confront the internal contradictions, unjust power relations, and global economic reorganization that underlie the decline of life-long marriage, revisionists promote what Whitehead terms a New Familism, in which postfeminist women willingly, admirably, and self-consciously *choose* to place familial needs above the demands of "a life defined by traditional male models of career and success." "In the period of the New Familism," Whitehead exults, "both parents give up something in their work lives in order to foster their family lives. The woman makes the larger concession, but it is one she actively elects and clearly sees as temporary."[51] Popenoe explicitly proposes what he calls "revising the cultural script" for modern marriages by making such "temporary" asymmetrical gender concessions a normative feature in his model of the "modified traditional nuclear family."[52]

AND OTHER EUPHEMISMS FOR INJUSTICE

1. The "Stability" of Gender Inequality

One need hardly be a paranoid feminist to penetrate the shallow veneer of revisionist commitments to gender equality. Defending a lengthy lament by Popenoe about American family decline, family sociologist Norval Glenn, for example, conceded that there is "a rational basis for concern that attempts to 'put the family back together' may tend to erase recent feminist gains." Likewise, Wilson acknowledged that "what is at stake, of course, is the role of women."[53]

Of course. Few feminists were confused when Quayle lashed out at Murphy Brown. Perhaps a few more will be misled by the higher-toned, centrist retreat of his views. Yet, despite lip-service to gender equality, the revisionist campaign does not redress marital inequalities or question that women bear disproportionate responsibility for their children and families. That Wilson and Glenn recognize the gender stakes in this rhetorical contest underscores how much more communitarian talk of family values impugns the individualism of women than that of men. Postfeminist family ideology appropriates some feminist critiques of conventionally masculine work priorities while appealing to those conventionally feminine maternalist values of women that some feminist scholars like Carol Gilligan and Deborah Tannen have made popular. This ideology also exploits women's weariness with the incompatibility of postindustrial work and family demands, as well as their anxiety over the asymmetrical terms of the heterosexual courtship and marriage market and of women's vulnerability to divorce-induced poverty.

Centrists often blame excessive divorce rates as well as unwed motherhood on a general rise of selfishness—gender unspecified. To curb such indulgence, they advocate measures to restrict access to divorce, such as mandatory waiting periods and counseling and the reinstatement of fault criteria in divorce laws. Typically, they present their proposals for these restrictive measures under a child-centered mantle that taps women's all-too-ready reservoirs of guilt about failing to serve the best interests of their children.

The backlash against no-fault divorce is gaining popularity among politicians. Republican Governor Terry Brandstad of Iowa denounced no-fault divorce in his 1996 State of the State Message. In February 1996, Michigan became the first state to consider a bill to revoke no-fault divorce in cases where one spouse opposes the divorce, and several other states are considering following Michigan's lead. Arguing that people "must begin to see the connection between divorce and other problems, especially poverty and juvenile delinquency," Jessie Dalman, the Republican sponsor of the Michigan bill, augmented the child-protection rationale with a direct appeal to women's fear of impoverishment.[54] Likewise, Dan Jarvis, director of the Michigan Family Forum policy group that has campaigned vigorously for this bill, portrayed it as protecting women: "Let's say a homemaker has a husband who cheats on her. Under the proposed law, she would have the upper hand. She can say: 'All right, you want your divorce? You can have it. But it's going to cost you.'"[55]

Many women—especially homemakers—and their children indeed have been impoverished by the unfair effects of current no-fault divorce property settlements, as feminist scholars and lawyers have documented.[56] The current unjust economic consequences of no-fault divorce laws constitute a serious problem in need of serious legislative and judicial reforms. It is a postfeminist sleight of hand, however, to pretend that repeal of no-fault divorce is the only or best possible remedy, or that it will promote greater gender equality in marriage. The rhetoric against no-fault erroneously implies that men seek a disproportionate number of contemporary divorces and that women have greater interests than men in sustaining their marriages. Unfortunately, the reverse is closer to the truth. Women seek a disproportionate number of contemporary divorces, despite the unjust consequences they risk in doing so, often because they find the injustices and difficulties of their marriages even harder to bear.[57]

Whether revisionist efforts to affix a tepid norm of gender equality to family-values rhetoric are well intentioned or disingenuous, their marriage seems ill-fated. Principles of egalitarianism and stability frequently collide, and, as in too many traditional marriages, the former are sacrificed to the latter. Revisionists, unlike both orthodox family-values advocates and feminists, rarely confront a disturbing contradiction at the heart of the Western ideal of a fully volitional marriage system: historically, stable marriage systems have rested upon coercion, overt or veiled, and on inequality. Proposals to restrict access to divorce implicitly recognize this unpleasant contradiction, one that poses a thorny dilemma for a democracy. If, as many feminists fear, a stable marriage system depends upon systemic forms of inequality, it will take much more than moralistic jeremiads bemoaning family decline, or even mandatory waiting and counseling prerequisites to divorce, to prop up contemporary marital stability.

This bleaker, feminist analysis of contemporary marital fragility, rather than the "family optimism" that revisionists attribute to social scientists who do not share their views,[58] explains some of the political passions at stake in our dispute. Without coercion, as Wilson concedes, divorce and single motherhood rates will remain high. Indeed, I agree with Popenoe that women's capacity to survive outside marriage, however meagerly, explains why both rates rose so sharply in recent decades. Marriage became increasingly fragile as it became less economically obligatory, particularly for women. These developments expose the inequality and coercion that always lay at the vortex of the supposedly voluntary, "companionate marriage" of the traditional nuclear family.

I do not dispute Glenn's judgment that "male-female equality in a society in which the quality of life is mediocre for everyone is hardly anyone's idea of utopia."[59] However, perhaps because I am less willing to sacrifice women's precarious gains on the chimerical altar of social stability, I am more motivated to find alternative social responses to our misdiagnosed familial ills.

2. The "Biology" of Heterosexism

Homophobia also plays a closeted role in the centrist campaign, one that could prove more insidious than right-wing gay-bashing. Wilson includes popular discomfort with same-sex marriage in his sympathetic inventory of the family values of "reasonable people."[60] Popenoe makes one foray at a definition of the family broad enough to encompass "homosexual couples, and all other family types in which dependents are involved," only to retreat instantly to the linguistic mantra favoring "two biological parents" that pervades revisionist rhetoric.[61] Moynihan's conviction that children need to grow up in families that provide them with a "stable relationship to male authority" is echoed by Whitehead's undocumented claim that research demonstrates "the importance of both a mother and a father in fostering the emotional well-being of children."[62] Blankenhorn, once again, goes even further by explicitly condemning lesbian childbearing. Indeed, his book formally proposes restricting access to donor sperm and alternative insemination services exclusively to married couples with fertility problems. "In a good society," Blankenhorn maintains, "people do not traffic commercially in the production of radically fatherless children."[63]

Elshtain unapologetically concedes that when she and her colleagues affirm a heterosexual family model, "we are privileging relations of a particular kind in which certain social goods are at stake."[64] Doing so panders to popular heterosexist prejudice. Despite consistent research findings that lesbians and gays parent at least as successfully as heterosexuals,[65] the Council on Families in America refuses to advocate equal marriage, adoption, or childbearing rights for the former. Rather, it remains faithful to Etzioni's credo: "There are some issues, such as abortion and gay rights, that we know communitarians cannot agree on, so we have completely avoided them."[66]

Such evasion abets the social agenda and political strategy of organized reactionaries. Homophobia has become the wedge issue of the new right family warriors. When Republicans sought to scuttle passage of the Family Leave Act in January 1993, the newly inaugurated Clinton's own first family-values offering, they did so by attempting to saddle it with a rider to prevent lifting the ban on gays in the military. Likewise, Falwell seized upon Clinton's nomination of a lesbian to an undersecretary post as an opportunity to flood the coffers of his Liberty Alliance. Urging readers to send donations of twenty-five dollars with a "Stop the Lesbian Nomination Reply Form," Falwell warned that, "President Clinton's nomination of Roberta Achtenberg, a lesbian, to the Department of Housing and Urban Development is a threat to the American family. . . . Achtenberg has dedicated her life to winning the 'rights' of lesbians to adopt little babies. Please help me stop her nomination."[67] The Traditional Values Coalition, based in Anaheim, claims to have sold 45,000 copies of the videotape, "Gay Rights, Special Rights," that they designed expressly to mobilize antigay sentiment among African-Americans.[68]

Ironically, the identification of Republicanism with such intolerance, with the notion, as Representative Constance Morella of Maryland put it, that "if you don't talk a certain way, raise your kids a certain way, love a certain way and pray a certain way, you are most certainly not welcome here," alarms many Republican Party moderates. However, a forum they convened in May of 1993 to reorient the Party foundered on just this faultline, with conservatives supporting Buchanan's view that "traditional values is the last trump card the Republican Party possesses."[69]

Centrist ideology colluded with a homophobic, right-wing agenda at a dangerous moment, help-ing to pave the way for the lop-sided victory of the antigay Defense of Marriage Act, which Clinton signed into law in September 1996.

3. Making a "Career" of Class Bias

Less obvious than the gender and sexual stakes of family-values rhetoric, perhaps, are ways it also serves as a sanitized decoy for less reputable prejudices of class and race. Having studied working-class families struggling to sustain body, soul, and kin ties in the economically depressed Silicon Valley during the mid-1980s, I cannot help but wonder what sort of family culture revisionists like Whitehead, Popenoe, and other communitarians inhabit. Perhaps, their moralistic images of selfish, hedonistic adults who place their own emotional and sexual pleasures and career ambitions above the needs of their vulnerable children derive from observations of some occupants who reside in a professional-corporate social cocoon.

Such caricatures bear little resemblance to twenty-something Carole, a laid-off electronics assembler and Fotomat envelope stuffer, a wife and mother of four, who left and returned to her abusive husband before she died of cancer. Nor do they apply to Lanny, another twenty-some-thing, laid-off drafter, who divorced the substance-abusing father of her young daughter after discovering he had "snorted away" the down payment she had laboriously accumulated to pur-chase a house. They do not fit Jan, a forty-year-old lesbian social-service worker, who continues to contribute time, resources, and love to the son of a former lover. They do not adequately depict the hard choices or the family realities that confront any of the women I studied, or, I would venture, those of the vast majority of citizens. The idiom of careers that family-values enthusiasts employ suggests ignorance of how few adults in this postindustrial age enjoy the luxury of joining a new familism by choosing to place their children's needs above the demands of their jobs.

4. Willie Horton in Whiteface

Wherever class bias flourishes in the United States race can seldom be far behind, for, in our soci-ety, these two axes of injustice are always hopelessly entangled. Quayle's attack on Murphy Brown was an ill-fated attempt to play the Willie Horton card in whiteface. Without resorting to overtly racist rhetoric, the image conjured up frightening hordes of African-American welfare "queens" rearing infant fodder for sex, drugs, and videotaped uprisings, such as had just erupted in Los Angeles. As anthropologist Elizabeth Traube points out, "shadow traces of African-American family practices are inscribed in postfeminist visions of the family," and *Murphy Brown* directly exploits symbolic effects of this ancestry with its opening theme Motown soundtrack.[70] Lurking in Murphy's shadows were descendants of the pathological "black matriarchs" Moynihan had permanently etched into the collective consciousness nearly three decades ago.[71]

In case anyone in fin-de-siècle U.S.A. remained ignorant of the racial coding of family-values discourse, Charles Murray used a megaphone to teach them a crash course. His *Wall Street Journal* op-ed, reprinted by the *Philadelphia Inquirer* under the title "The Emerging White Underclass and How to Save It," warned whites that their family patterns now resemble that malignant "tangle of pathology" that Moynihan diagnosed in 1965 among African Americans. Displaying greater hon-esty than most revisionists, Murray concluded by speaking the unspeakable: "The brutal truth is that American society as a whole could survive when illegitimacy became epidemic within a comparatively small ethnic minority. It cannot survive the same epidemic among whites."[72]

Racial anxiety runs as subtext to the entire history of family-crisis discourse in the United States, which long predates Moynihan's incendiary 1965 report. It reaches back a century to xenophobic fears that in the face of high fertility among eastern and southern European migrants, native white women, whose birth rates were declining were threatening their tribe with "race suicide." It reaches back much further into the history of colonial settler fears of the diverse sexual and kinship practices of indigenous cultures, as well as to rationales that esteemed, white scholars offered for African American slavery—that it helped civilize the heathen by teaching family values to a species that lacked these.

If marriage was a form of racial privilege under slavery, it is rapidly becoming so again today. Sociologist William Wilson has constructed a chauvinistic, but still stunning, "marriageable Black male index" that graphs the increasing scarcity of Black men who are neither unemployed nor incarcerated. Wilson's index indirectly demonstrates that male breadwinning and marriage are becoming interactive badges of race and class status.[73] Indeed, the greatest contrast in family patterns and resources in the U.S. today is between two steady-earner and single-mother households, and these divide notably along racial lines. Perhaps this is why presidential voting patterns in 1992 displayed a family gap more pronounced than the gender gap. Married voters heavily favored Bush, while the unmarried shored up Clinton's precarious margin of victory.[74] A campaign that sets couple- and single-parent families at odds has political consequences. Centrist Democrats have begun to erode the advantage Republicans enjoy among the largely white, middle-class, heterosexual, two-parent family set.

THE EMERGING CONSERVATIVE CULTURAL "CONSENSUS"

In the long run, however, such a strategy is unlikely to succeed. As leaders of the right-wing Christian profamily movement recognized, with delight, family-values ardor more readily promotes their reactionary agenda. Gary Bauer, president of the right-wing Family Research Council and editor of the fundamentalist *Focus on the Family Citizen*, gloats that there are encouraging "signs that a pro-family consensus, which has been forming for several years, is continuing to gel," despite the election of Clinton. Identifying the *Atlantic* as the premier organ "of smug, elitist, knee-jerk liberalism," Bauer aptly reads Whitehead's vindication of Quayle as the most prominent of increasing "signs that the traditionalist revival among policy experts has not been snuffed out."[75]

Bauer understands the political implications of neo-family values discourse far better than do its propagators. Despite the collectivist aspirations of communitarian ideology, the political effects of identifying family breakdown as the crucible of all the social crises that have accompanied postindustrialization and the globalization of capitalism are privatistic and profoundly conservative. Clinton's own welfare reform proposals, which differed from those of the Republicans only in their lesser degree of severity rather than in their ideological presumptions about family breakdown and welfare dependency, should be persuasive on this score.

Particularly troubling, and ironic, have been the success of local appeals to homophobic family values among African American ministers and the electorate they influence. In November 1993, the religious right succeeded in winning support for repeal of a local gay rights protection ordinance from 56 percent of the voters in traditionally liberal black precincts in Cincinnati. Effectively portraying the gay and lesbian movement "as a group of well-off whites fighting for 'special rights,'" the right-wing family-values campaign convinced a majority of black voters that the interests and constituencies of the two movements were antagonistic.[76] Similar strategic alliances of right-wing family-values activists and African American clergy blocked the passage of the first referendum for domestic partners legislation in San Francisco in 1989.

Thus the rush to consensus on family values is not only premature; it is also undemocratic. The idea that we should all subscribe to a unitary ideal of family life is objectionable on social scientific, ethical, and political grounds. I had hoped, and Bauer and his associates had feared, that the 1992 electoral defeat of the right-wing family values campaign would signal an opportunity for democratic initiatives on family and social reforms, initiatives that would begin with a recognition of how diverse our families are and will continue to be. Instead, we have witnessed the startling resurrection of family-values ideology. Beneath its new, velvet gown is an old-fashioned, confining, one-size-fits-all corset. But our nation's families come in many shapes and sizes, and will continue to do so. A democratic family politics must address diverse bodily and spiritual desires in rhetoric people find at least as comfortable as the ever-popular combat uniform of family values.

TOWARD RECONFIGURING FAMILY VALUES

No sound-bite rebuttal can convey the complex, contradictory character of family and social turmoil. Still, it is important to disrupt the stampede to premature consensus on family values. To wage a viable countercultural campaign for *social* values, progressives need to confront the impoverishment of our national capacity to imagine human bonds beyond familial ones that can keep individuals safe from a "heartless" world. So atrophied is this cultural muscle that family impulses overcompensate.

Two media items illustrate the cultural ubiquity of this ideological translation. An op-ed by China scholar Franz Schurmann that lauded the cooperative, cultural traditions that have generated phenomenal economic growth in China concluded that "creating new *social power* is the key to reversing the United States' decline" (my emphasis). Not once did Schurmann use the ubiquitous "F" word, but the editorial page editor affixed the title "Families That Work are Helping China."[77]

More predictable was the photo caption, "The Post-Nuclear Family," which the *New York Times* ran over a picture of young Black "doughnut men" (joyride car thieves) in Newark, New Jersey. The photo accompanied a story identifying family decline as the source of delinquency as well as the impetus for parental appeals to "government, schools and whatever communal vestiges remain in a mobile and complex society" for help in rearing law-abiding youth.[78]

We cannot counter the flawed, reductionist logic of family-values ideology, however, unless we resist using knee-jerk, symmetrical responses, like a feminist bumper sticker Whitehead cites effectively to mock feminism: "Unspoken Traditional Family Values: Abuse, Alcoholism, Incest."[79] Portraying nuclear families primarily as sites of patriarchal violence, as some feminists have done, is inaccurate and impolitic.[80] It reinforces a stereotypical association of feminism with antifamilism, which does not even accurately represent feminist perspectives on the subject. Certainly, protecting women's rights to resist and exit unequal, hostile, dangerous marriages remains a crucial project, but one we cannot advance by denying that many women, many of them feminists, sustain desires for successful and legally protected relationships with men and children. We must steer a tenuous course between cultural warriors who blame public violence on (patriarchal) family decline, and those who blame family decline on (patriarchal) domestic violence.

A better strategy is to work to redefine family values democratically by extending full rights, obligations, resources, and legitimacy to a diversity of intimate bonds. We might take our lead here from the only partly parodic family-values campaign currently blossoming among gays and lesbians. Progressives could appeal to the rhetoric of the neo-family-values crusade in order to advocate full marital, reproductive, and custody rights for homosexuals. Such a strategy requires bridging the rift between gays and African Americans, first by disputing the erroneous notion that these are distinct communities, and second by addressing racism among white gays and black homophobia at the grassroots level. African American heterosexuals and all homosexuals, supported by a full-spectrum rainbow coalition, must come to recognize mutual interests in democraticizing family rhetoric, rights, and resources.

Another way to reconfigure family values is to up the ante in the revisionist bid to elevate the cultural status and responsibilities of fatherhood. Here I agree with Blankenhorn that the sort of family-values campaign we must urgently need is one to revise popular masculinities. Familyless fathers, be they married or single, do seem to be disproportionately harmful to women, children and civil society, as well as to themselves. Normative masculine behavior among the overpaid ranks of greedy, competitive, corporate, and professional absent fathers and also among more overtly macho, underpaid, underemployed, undereducated, volatile "Boyz in the 'hood" can lead women, as well as men, to idealize cinematic visions of Victorian patriarchy. We sorely need cultural efforts to deglamorize violence, predatory sexuality, and sexism, such as the one that was announced in 1994 by an organization of Black professional women. We need to challenge the destructive androcentric logic behind "the clockwork of male careers."[81] Unfortunately, currently the most prominent initiatives of this sort—the Christian men's movement, Promise Keepers, and the African-American Million Man March that was called by Farrakhan—seem to share with Blankenhorn nostalgic affection for a world of *Father Knows Best*. The democratic challenge is to find ways to affirm the laudable sentiments these movements tap while enticing them to follow a more egalitarian drummer.

Rethinking family values requires dodging ideological corners into which revisionists deftly paint feminists and other progressives. First, we must concede that the best familial interests of women (or men) and children do not always coincide. While research demonstrates that high-conflict marriages are at least as destructive to children as is parental divorce, clearly there *are* some unhappy marriages whose adult dissatisfactions harm children much less than do their post-divorce circumstances. Certainly, some divorces *are* better for the adults who initiate them than for the children who must adjust to them.

Likewise, just as there are His and Her marriages, so too divorce is often better for one spouse (not always the male) than the other, as are many remarriages and the stepfamilies they create. When the best interests of the genders collide, it is not easy to say whose should prevail. However, it is also not easy to say whether the genders actually do have incompatible interests in making all marriages harder to leave. The vast majority of women, men, and their children derive clear benefits from living in loving, harmonious, secure relationships, but men and women in marriages like these rarely choose to divorce. What is really at issue in the great divorce controversy is the extent to which easy access to divorce encourages individuals to indulgently throw in the towel on marriages that are not too wet to be saved. In other words, how many marriages that now end in divorce could have been saved, and would have been better off for all parties if they had been?

Research does not, and probably cannot, shed much useful light on this question. No doubt "divorce culture," as critics call it, does foster some undesirable instances of capricious divorce. But how large is that incidence, and at what cost do we deter it? Contrary to the claims of the antidivorce campaigners, there is little evidence that most parents regard divorce as a casual, impulsive, or easy decision. Nor is there evidence that divorce restrictions are likely to achieve their intended effect of buttressing marital commitment. They are at least as likely to deter people from marrying in the first place, and more likely to encourage unhappily married individuals to resort to extralegal forms of desertion and separation. These practices have become so widespread in Roman Catholic countries that even Ireland has taken measures to legalize divorce. For better and worse, governmental attempts to socially engineer the quality, as opposed to the legal form, of intimate relationships have an abysmal historical track record.

The campaign against single mothers calls for an analogous response. We do not need to defend single mothers from the open season of cultural bounty hunters by denying that two compatible, responsible, committed, loving parents generally *can* offer greater economic, emotional, physical, intellectual, and social resources to their children than can one from a comparable cultural milieu. Of course, if two parents are generally better than one, three or four might prove better yet. A version of Barbara Ehrenreich's Swiftian proposal—that to lift their families out of poverty, Black women should wed, "Two, Three, Many Husbands,"[82] is unlikely to win popular affection. Still, we might draw upon communitarian sentiments to foster much more collective responsibility for children. Spontaneously, many childless and childfree adults are choosing to become unofficial para-parents by forming nurturant, long-term relationships with the children of overburdened parents (a category from which few parents would exclude themselves). Children's advocates might actively promote and seek social protection for these voluntary extended kin relationships, which, as the *New York Times* put it, treat "children as a collective commitment that is more than biological in its impulse."[83] No doubt such proposals would prove more appealing and constructive than polyandry.

Similarly, we should not feel obliged to reject the claim that in industrial societies, teenage motherhood often does not augur well for the offspring. The rising age of marriage since the 1950s is a positive, rather than a negative trend, but one which leads to more nonmarital sexuality and pregnancies. Yet countries like Sweden, which do not stigmatize unwed births but make sex education, contraception, and abortion services widely and cheaply available to all, witness few unwanted births and few births to teen mothers. The misguided drive to restigmatize "illegitimacy" demands renewed struggle to destigmatize abortion among both the populace and health providers and to vastly increase its accessibility. A reinvigorated campaign for comprehensive reproductive rights, perhaps reviving that old Planned Parenthood slogan, "Every child, a wanted child," should promote a full panoply of contraceptive options. like RU-486. It might include a take-back-our-bodies drive to wrest exclusive control over abortion provision from doctors, particularly when so few of these in the U.S. have proven willing to subject their professional status, personal safety, perhaps even their lives, to the formidable risks that the antiabortion movement imposes on abortion providers.[84] At the same time, we should resist the misrepresentation of feminism as hostile to motherhood or "life" by continuing the struggle for genuine, humane, workplace and welfare reforms (rather than repeals) that make it possible for women to choose to mother or to reject maternity.

Feminists are particularly well placed to promote this humane brand of progressive family values. Unlike revisionists, we understand that it is not "the family" but one, historically specific, system of family life (the "modern nuclear family") that has broken down. We understand, too, that this has had diverse effects on people of different genders, races, economic resources, sexual identities, and generations. Some have benefited greatly; others have lost enormously; most have won a few new rights and opportunities and lost several former protections and privileges. The collapse of our former national consensus on family values, like the collapse of our prosperous economy to which it was intricately tied, has not been an equal opportunity employer. Indeed, women, especially poor and minority women, have been some of the biggest winners, and most of the biggest losers. Those who do not want to count feminism, liberalism, or human compassion casualties of the emergent new consensus on neo-family values had better disrupt the mesmerizing, but misguided, campaign.

NOTES

This essay is excerpted from the author's *In the Name of the Family* (Beacon, 1997).

1. Whitehead, "Dan Quayle Was Right," 47–84.
2. Whitehead, "Was Dan Quayle Right?" 13. For sample retreads, see, Charen, "Hey, Murphy, Quayle was Right," and Fields, "Murphy's Chorus of Enlightened Celebrities," B9.
3. Popenoe, "The Controversial Truth: Two-Parent Families Are Better"; Popenoe, "Scholars Should Worry about the Disintegration of the American Family"; Beck, "What's Good for Babies: Both Parents."
4. Moynihan, "Defining Deviancy Down," 17–30; Wilson, "The Family-Values Debate," 24–31.
5. Stacey, *Brave New Families.*
6. Fields, "Murphy's Chorus," B9.
7. Popenoe, "Scholars Should Worry," A48. For the statement and list of council members, see "Family and Child Well-Being: Eight Propositions," 11.
8. Personal interview conducted April 6, 1994, Oakland, California.
9. Quoted in Karen Winkler, "Communitarians Move Their Ideas Outside Academic Arena," A7.
10. Kamarck and Galston, "Putting Children First."
11. Blankenhorn, Elshtain, and Bayme, eds., *Rebuilding the Nest;* National Commission on Children, *Beyond Rhetoric.*
12. Personal interview, April 6, 1994.

13. Whitehead, "A New Familism?" 5.
14. Wilson, "The Family-Values Debate," 31.
15. Klein, "The Out-of-Wedlock Question," 37.
16. Quoted in Kranish, "In Bully Pulpit, Preaching Values," 17.
17. Wilson, "The Family-Values Debate," 24.
18. The debate took place on an ABC radio call-in program, *The Gil Gross Show,* broadcast on Jan. 18, 1993.
19. Whitehead, "Dan Quayle Was Right," 47.
20. Ibid, 80.
21. Wilson, "The Family-Values Debate," 31. Syndicated columnist Suzanne Fields, abridged Whitehead's *Atlantic* story, charging that Dan Quayle was punished like a messenger in a Greek tragedy when he attacked Murphy Brown, "knocked about for delivering bad news that contradicted the biases of the media, the morality chic of the beautiful people, and the scholarship of ideological feminists, among others." After ridiculing media stars who spoke up for Murphy Brown, Fields remarked, "We can't expect wisdom from celebrities, but feminist academics at good universities peddle similar claptrap. Sociologist Judith Stacey of UC, Davis describes a postmodern future for women in which none of us are oppressed by the nuclear family." Fields, "Murphy's Chorus," 89.
22. Gillis suggested the term during a discussion of an early draft of this paper with the "family values" seminar at the Center for Advanced Studies in the Social and Behavioral Sciences, November 29, 1993.
23. Popenoe, "The Controversial Truth."
24. Whitehead, "Dan Quayle Was Right," 48.
25. Whitehead, "The Expert's Story of Marriage," quoted in Moynihan, "Defining Deviancy Down," 24.
26. *Beyond Rhetoric* essays by Blankenhorn, Elshtain, Popenoe, Sylvia Hewlett, and other contributors to Blankenhorn, Elshtain and Bayme, eds., *Rebuilding the Nest*.
27. Popenoe, "Scholars Should Worry."
28. Council on Families in America, "Family and Child Well-Being: Eight Propositions," p. 11.
29. Popenoe, "Controversial Truth."
30. To sample the diversity of scholarly views, see a careful evaluation of the inconclusive findings of research on the impact of divorce on children Furstenberg and Cherlin, *Divided Families*. For a review of the research on gay and lesbian parenting, see Patterson, "Children of Lesbian and Gay Parents," 1,025–42. Indeed, even Sara McLanahan, who Whitehead's *Atlantic* essay portrayed as recanting her earlier views on the benign effects of single parenting, provides a more nuanced analysis of the sources of whatever disadvantages the children of single parents experience than Whitehead leads readers to believe. She acknowledges that research does not demonstrate that children of "mother only" households would have been better off if their two biological parents had married or never divorced. See McLanahan and Booth, "Mother-Only Families: Problems, Prospects, and Politics," 557–80.
31. Demo, "Parent-Child Relations: Assessing Recent Changes," 104.
32. Ibid., 110.
33. Wallerstein and Kelly, *Surviving the Breakup*; Wallerstein and Blakeslee, *Second Chances*.
34. Demo, "Parent-Child Relations," 110. For an even more comprehensive and equally balanced survey of research on the impact of divorce on children, see Furstenberg and Cherlin, *Divided Families*.
35. See Furstenberg and Cherlin for a summary of this research.
36. Murray, "The Time Has Come to Put a Stigma Back on Illegitimacy."
37. Murray appeared on *This Week with David Brinkley*, November 29, 1993. The op-ed by Hoover Institute scholar, John Bunzel, aired on "Perspective," KQED-FM, San Francisco, December 21, 1993.
38. Blankenhorn, Elshtain, and Bayme, *Rebuilding the Nest*, 21.
39. Quoting from an essay he wrote in 1965, Moynihan, "Defining Deviancy Down," 26.
40. Klein, "The Out-of-Wedlock Question," 37.
41. The quotes from Shalala and the unidentified liberal appear in Klein, "Out-of-Wedlock Question."
42. See Kamarck and Galston, "Putting Children First: A Progressive Family Policy for the 1990s," 9.

43. Many feminists fear that even employing the concept "postfeminism" cedes important political ground to the backlash. I disagree and use the term to indicate a culture that has both assimilated and tamed many of the basic ideas of second-wave feminism. For a fuller discussion of this use of this term, see Rosenfelt and Stacey, "Second Thoughts on the Second Wave."

44. Popenoe, "Scholars Should Worry."

45. Blankenhorn, Elshtain, and Bayme, *Rebuilding the Nest*, 19.

46. Wilson, 31.

47. Lefkowitz, "Where Dad Belongs," A12.

48. Chira, "Push to Revamp Ideal for American Fathers," 10. Blankenhorn presents an extended, polemical exposition of his neotraditional fatherhood ideology in his *Fatherless America*. Blankenhorn's ideology has become too conservative even for some of his colleagues at the Institute for American Values. Originally Popenoe and Blankenhorn contracted to coauthor *Fatherless America*, but due to ideological differences, Popenoe wrote his own book on this subject, *Life Without Father*, which was released in April 1996.

49. For my earlier critiques of Elshtain, Friedan, and Hewlitt, see Stacey, "The New Conservative Feminism"; and Rosenfelt and Stacey, "Second Thoughts on the Second Wave."

50. Blankenhorn, for example, is interpreted approvingly by a *Wall Street Journal* columnist as providing intellectual justification for "laws that mandate spousal notification prior to all abortions. Today laws in most states consider fetuses the property of pregnant women. Unfortunately, this posture leads to the view that children are the sole responsibility of mothers." Lefkowitz, "Where Dad Belongs."

51. Whitehead, "A New Familism?" 2.

52. Popenoe, "Modern Marriage: Revising the Cultural Script," 2.

53. Glenn, "A Plea for Objective Assessment of the Notion of Family Decline," 543; Wilson, "Family-Values Debate," 25.

54. Johnson, "No-Fault Divorce is Under Attack," A 8.

55. Ibid.

56. Weitzman, *The Divorce Revolution*, is the most significant albeit controversial treatment of no-fault divorce.

57. Ahrons, *The Good Divorce*, p. 35.

58. Popenoe applies this term to me and other critics of "family-values" ideology in "Scholars Should Worry."

59. Glenn, "Plea for an Objective View," 544.

60. Wilson, "Family-Values Debate," 29.

61. Popenoe, "American Family Decline, 1960–1990," 529.

62. Moynihan, "Defining Deviancy Down," 26; Whitehead, "Dan Quayle was Right," 70.

63. Blankenhorn, Elshtain, and Bayme, *Fatherless America*, 233.

64. Elshtain, "Family and Civil Life," 130. In Blankenhorn, Elshtain, and Bayme, *Rebuilding the Nest*.

65. Stacey, chapter 5, *In the Name of the Family* (in press).

66. Moynihan quoted in Winkler, "Communitarians Move Their Ideas," A13.

67. Batteiger, "Bigotry for Bucks," 19. For primary evidence of the prominence of homophobic appeals in right-wing organizing, see, for example, James C. Dobson, "1993 in Review," *Focus on the Family Newsletter*, January 1994.

68. White, "Christian Right Tries to Capitalize on antiGay Views," A6.

69. Toner, "Republican Factions Gather Under One Tent, Then Argue."

70. Traube, "Family Matters," 63.

71. Moynihan, *The Negro Family*.

72. Murray, "The emerging white underclass and how to save it," A15.

73. Wilson defines this index as the ratio of employed Black males per 100 Black females in the same age group. He charts a decline in this ratio from 70 in 1960 to 40 in 1986, and the disparity is reflected in the decline of Black marriage rates. William J. Wilson, *The Truly Disadvantaged*.

74. Married voters ages 18–34 with children voted 48 percent for Bush, 39 percent for Clinton, and 22

percent for Perot; singles (with and without children) in that age group voted 58 percent for Clinton, 20 percent for Bush, and 19 percent for Perot. Poll data were reported in a *Washington Post* story by Vobejda, reprinted as "'Family Gap' Found in Post-Election Poll," A4.

75. Bauer, "Family Values Matter!" 16.
76. Suggs and Carter, "Cincinnati's Odd Couple," A11.
77. *San Francisco Chronicle*, December 23, 1993.
78. Smothers, "Tell It to Mom, Dad and the Authorities," 2. For an astute analysis of media treatment of the Newark car theft panic, see Gregory, "Time to Make the Doughnuts: On the Politics of Subjugation in the 'Inner City,'" paper presented at American Anthropological Association Meetings, Washington, D.C., November 1993.
79. Whitehead, "Dan Quayle Was Right," 55.
80. Academic feminists indulge this impulse as well. For an example, see Probyn's otherwise incisive critique of postfeminist TV family fare, "Television's *Unheimlich* Home."
81. Hochschild, "Inside the Clockwork of Male Careers," 47–81.
82. Ehrenreich, "Two, Three, Many Husbands," 183–87.
83. Schwartz, "Children's New Bonds: Para-Dads, Para-Moms," B1, B4.
84. For an astute and moving account of the experiences of some of the heroic doctors who have paid these costs, see Joffe, *Doctors of Conscience.*

BIBLIOGRAPHY

Ahrons, Constance. 1994. *The Good Divorce.* New York: HarperCollins.

Batteiger, John. 1993. Bigotry for Bucks. *San Francisco Bay Guardian.* 7 Apr., 19.

Bauer, Gary L. 1993. Family Values Matter! *Focus on the Family Citizen* 7, n. 5, May, 16.

Beck, Joan. 1993. What's Good for Babies: Both Parents. *The Press Democrat* 7 Mar., G1, G6.

Blankenhorn, David. 1995. *Fatherless America: Confronting Our Most Urgent Social Problem.* New York: Basic Books.

Blankenhorn, David, Jean Bethke Elshtain, and Steven Bayme, eds. 1990. *Rebuilding the Nest: A New Commitment to the American Family.* Milwaukee: Family Service America.

Charen, Mona. 1993. Hey, Murphy, Quayle was Right. *Orange County Register* 29 Mar., B9.

Chira, Susan. 1994. Push to Revamp Ideal for American Fathers. *New York Times,* 19 June, 10.

Council on Families in America. 1994. Family and Child Well-Being: Eight Propositions. *Family Affairs* 6, no. 1–2, Winter, 11.

Demo, David H. 1992. Parent-Child Relations: Assessing Recent Changes. *Journal of Marriage and the Family* 54 Feb., 104.

Ehrenreich, Barbara. 1990. Two, Three, Many Husbands. In *The Worst Years of Our Lives: Irreverent Notes from a Decade of Greed.* New York: Pantheon, 183–87.

Fields, Suzanne. 1993. Murphy's Chorus of Enlightened Celebrities. *Orange County Register* 29 Mar., B9.

Furstenberg Jr., Frank, and Andrew J. Cherlin. 1991. *Divided Families: What Happens to Children When Parents Part.* Cambridge: Harvard University Press.

Glenn, Norval D. 1994. A Plea for Objective Assessment of the Notion of Family Decline. *Journal of Marriage and the Family* 55, no. 3. Aug. 543.

Gregory, Steven. 1993. Time to Make the Doughnuts: On the Politics of Subjugation in the 'Inner City.' Paper presented at American Anthropological Association Meetings, Washington, D.C. Nov.

Hochschild, Arlie. Inside the Clockwork of Male Careers.

Joffe, Carole. 1996. *Doctors of Conscience.* Boston: Beacon Press.

Johnson, Dirk. 1991. No-Fault Divorce is Under Attack. *New York Times.* Feb. 12, A8.

Kamarck, Elaine Ciulla, and William A. Galston, 1990. Putting Children First: A Progressive Family Policy for the 1990s" Progressive Policy Institute pamphlet, Sept. 27.

Klein, Joe. 1993. The Out-of-Wedlock Question. *Newsweek.* 13 Dec.

Kranish, Michael. 1993. In Bully Pulpit, Preaching Values. *Boston Globe,* 10 Dec., 17.

Lefkowitz, Jay. 1993. Where Dad Belongs. *Wall Street Journal,* 18 June, A12.

McLanahan, Sara, and Karen Booth. 1989. Mother-Only Families: Problems, Prospects, and Politics. *Journal of Marriage and the Family,* 51, Aug., 557–80.

Moynihan, Daniel Patrick. 1993. Defining Deviancy Down. *American Scholar,* Winter, 17–30.

Murray, Charles. 1993. The Time has Come to Put a Stigma Back on Illegitimacy. *Wall Street Journal,* 2 Oct. Forum.

———. 1993. The Emerging White Underclass and How to Save It. *Philadelphia Inquirer.* 15 Nov. A15.

National Commission on Children. 191. *Beyond Rhetoric: A New American Agenda for Children and Families.* Washington, D.C.: Library of Congress.

Patterson, Charlotte J. 1992. Children of Lesbian and Gay Parents. *Child Development* 63, 1,025–42.

Popenoe, David. 1992. The Controversial Truth: The Two-Parent Family Is Better. *New York Times,* 26 Dec. 13.

———. 1993a. American Family Decline, 1960–1990: A Review and Appraisal. *Journal of Marriage and the Family* 55, n. 3, 527–44.

———. 1993b. Scholars Should Worry About the Disintegration of the American Family. *Chronicle of Higher Education,* 14 April, A48.

———. 1992. Modern Marriage: Revising the Cultural Script. Council on Families in American Working Paper, no. WP17. New York: Institute for American Values. Aug. 2.

———. *Life Without Father.* New York: Free Press.

Probyn, Elsbeth. 1994. "Television's Unheimlich Home." In *The Politics of Everyday Fear.* Brian Massumi. Minneapolis: University of Minnesota Press.

Rosenfelt, Deborah and Judith Stacey. 1987. Second Thoughts on the Second Wave. *Feminist Studies* 13, n. 2, 341–61.

Schwartz, Pepper. 1995. Children's New Bonds: Para-Dads, Para-Moms. *New York Times,* 9 Nov., B1, B4.

Smothers, Ronald. 1993. Tell It to Mom, Dad and the Authorities. *New York Times,* Week in Review, 14 Nov., 2.

Stacey, Judith. 1983. The New Conservative Feminism. *Feminist Studies* 9, n. 3, 559–83.

———. 1986. Are Feminists Afraid to Leave Home? The Challenge of Profamily Feminism. In *What is Feminism?* Ed. Juliet Mitchell and Ann Oakley, 219–48. London: Basil Blackwell.

———. 1990. *Brave New Families: Stories of Domestic Upheaval in Late Twentieth Century America.* New York: Basic Books.

———. 1996. *In the Name of the Family: Rethinking Family Values in the Postmodern Age.* Boston: Beacon Press.

Toner, Robin. 1993. Republican Factions Gather Under One Tent, Then Argue. *New York Times,* 11 May.

Traube, Elizabeth. Family Matters. *Visual Anthropology.*

Vobejda, Barbara. 1992. Family Gap Found in Post-Election Poll. *San Francisco Chronicle,* 27 Nov., A4.

Wallerstein, Judith, and Joan B. Kelly. 1980. *Surviving the Breakup: How Children and Parents Cope with a Divorce.* New York: Basic Book.

Wallerstein, Judith, and Sandra Blakeslee. 1989. *Second Chances: Men, Women, and Children a Decade After Divorce.* New York: Basic Books.

Weitzman, Lenore J. 1985. The Diverse Revolution: The Unexpected Social and Economic Consequences for Women and Children. New York: Free Press.

White, Evelyn C. 1994. Christian Right Tries to Capitalize on antiGay Views. *San Francisco Chronicle,* 12 Jan., A6.

Whitehead, Barbara Dafoe. 1993. Dan Quayle Was Right. *The Atlantic* 271, n. 4., April, 47–84.

———. 1992. A New Familism? *Family Affairs* 5, no. 1–2, Summer, 5.

———. 1994. Was Dan Quayle Right? Family Affairs 6, no. 1–2. Winter, 13.

Wilson, James Q. 1993. The Family-Values Debate. *Commentary* 95, n. 4, 24–31.

Wilson, William J. 1987. *The Truly Disadvantaged: The Inner City, The Underclass, and Public Policy.* Chicago: University of Chicago Press.

Winkler, Karen. 1993. Communitarians Move Their Ideas Outside Academic Arena. *Chronicle of Higher Education,* 21 April, A7.

Part Eight

TRAVELING THEORY

Transnational
and Postcolonial
Interlocutions

31 The Consumption
of Color and the Politics
of White Skin in Post-Mao China

Louisa Schein

MOBILE IMAGES/COLOR POLITICS

It is dusk in the Miao mountains of Guizhou, China, September 1993—a quintessential site for Western ethnological and Chinese nativist imaginings alike. A wedding is underway. The couple being wed are educated local youth with good jobs—she an elementary school teacher, he the manager of the subcontracted state dry goods outlet in the Miao market town of Xijiang. Amidst firecrackers, the guests are arriving bearing shoulder poles of gifts—pork, sticky rice, home-brewed liquor, quilts, fabric. The bride stays in the nuptial chamber while guests are received at a long table in the central room of the groom's house, offered a welcoming meal and some shots of home-brew. Languorously the bride makes up her face with powder, blush, lipstick, eyeliner, then dresses in Miao finery—a full length pleated skirt layered with a circle of embroidered bands, a jacket laden with brocade, necklaces of delicately handwrought silver. Her hair is thickened with extra strands and combed upward into a topknot dense enough to support the weighty silver ornaments that will complete the ensemble.

Just then a group of city friends arrive, classmates from the days when the couple attended high school in the prefecture seat. The firecrackers they set off are so noisy as to put the local village guests to shame. Then, the *pièce de resistance*—the gift borne on shoulder poles. It is an ostentatious yard-long wall hanging behind glass—a photographic decoration slated for the walls of the nuptial chamber. The picture, in a bizarre juxtaposition with or even upstaging of the bride, is of a blonde model in a hot pink g-string bikini lying atop a snazzy racing car. Lovingly, the hanging is given front center placement among the other gifts—heaps of quilts and household goods—on display in the nuptial chamber for guests to review. Upon completion of her ethnic adornment, the bride poses with the thing.

As representations of white women continue to deluge the globe, an initial task of this essay will be to explore *how* (more so than *what*) such renderings mean within particular Chinese contexts. The account above suggests that the erotic codes through which most Westerners read the expo-

Louisa Schein teaches Anthropology at Rutgers University, New Brunswick. She specializes in ethnicity and gender in China and in transnational processes. She is presently writing a book on cultural politics in China's post-Mao era and conducting multi-site research on the forging of transnationality between Hmong refugees in the U.S. and the Miao in China.

sure of female-gendered flesh may be idiomatic. That a young woman of China's Miao minority would, in the midst of her own beautification as bride, welcome the inclusion of a g-stringed other woman as one of the accoutrements of her future home indicates that the heterosexual gaze common to Western consumption of such images[1] is not necessarily dominant in other contexts. In the popular culture of a China that is currently in the thick of an encounter with global capitalism, the surface of the white female body virtually prickles with polysmy. Meanings have multiplied in keeping with the velocity with which the images have traveled transnationally. In this process, as will be seen below, both the sexual and the political have become complexly entangled with the commodity.

Assuming the white woman represents a figure of alterity in China, this essay will ask: For what or whom does she constitute the other? Through an investigation of this problematic, I hope to show the ways in which self other binarisms may be unraveling in the 1990s reform climate. Specifically, an earlier nationalist vision that organized identity chiefly in terms of Chinese versus non-Chinese identities appears to be giving way to more locally based alliances on the one hand, and to supranational identifications on the other. It might be argued that structural reforms such as differential development policies, marketization of the economy, decentralization of state social services and the lifting of the ban on internal migration have precipitated such realignments. These processes, however, yield only a partial picture, one that remains incomplete without a consideration of the wild circulation of signs and of their varied localizations.[2] These signs saturate Chinese popular culture in the form of television, film, video, the print media, school curricula, advertising, packaging, shop display, etc. They are both domestically produced and imported; they are not unitary in form or content, but disjunctive in the sense by which Appadurai (1990) characterized global cultural flows; and they play obsessively with figures of the (raced) feminine. But the issue remains: How is this feminine read? Or, how is this feminine localized?

To address this question I will turn, in the latter part of the essay, to another alterity, one that is taking on a particular cast in 1990s China and one that entails the analytical counterposition of color and whiteness. "Color" is used here to connote a medium of contrast that has the potential to evade the straitjacketing of bipolar categories such as black/white and by extension Chinese/non-Chinese or self/other. "Color" is strategic precisely because, in a cognitive lexicon of race-marked categories, whiteness can become not the absence of color but instead one of many colors, one to which myriad desires attach. But the notion of "color" is also brought in here because it evokes the other key alterity to be discussed below. This is the alterity of the feminized folk, an internal site of difference that is constructed as anchoring China in authenticity and providing an antidote to the modernizing that is oft experienced as careering beyond control.

The Chinese term *duocai* (colorful, polychromatic) is regularly used by Chinese urbanites to describe the folk and minority cultures (not skin tones) of the countryside.[3] This color, then is what the increasingly impoverished interior has to offer in the eyes of coastal elites whose newfound prosperity cannot completely assuage an accompanying sense of the dull grayness of industrialized metropolitan life. It circulates not only through popular imagings but also through the actual movement out of the rural interior of folk and minority women who become both productive hands and consumption objects for privileged urbanites. My argument, then, is that both color and whiteness constitute significant alterities in the ongoing Chinese project of what Jing Wang has called "self-positioning" (Wang 1993).

The reflections in this work arise out of the imponderabilia of ethnographic encounters together with readings of current intellectual and popular discourses. The timespan of my field experiences in China (1982–1993) was effectively coterminous with the "post-Mao" period of liberalization and economic reform that began in 1979 and continues to the present.[4] The extra-textual ways of knowing that inform my accounts have included not only long-term residence in a Miao minority village but also deep immersion in the consumption practices of peasants and urbanites as the commodity landscape shifted over those years, as well as innumerable instances of politically charged interchanges that were thickly inflected by my own white femaleness.[5]

COMPLICATING "WHITENESS" IN THE CHINESE IMAGINARY

At first glance, China's voracious consumption of "the" Western woman might appear uncomplicated. "She" signifies modernity in a neat voluptuous embodiment, often bedecked in finery to stress her material stature and to remind the doubtful that modernity means prosperity. "She" is femininity, an essentialized and potent difference much cherished after the gender flattenings of the Cultural Revolution. "She" is liberation, a sign of cultural self-expression conveyed through the metaphorical unmasking encoded in her relentless undress. Desire for the Western woman may seem so predictable as to be trite—possessing her means, most crassly; possessing the wealth, power, and civility of whiteness. Frantz Fanon's unforgettable words still resonate:[6]

> I marry white beauty, white culture, white whiteness. When my restless hands caress those white breasts, they grasp white civilization and dignity and make them mine. (Fanon 1967 [1952]: 63)

In China too, such desire has fused the sexual and the political. As will be seen below, any eroticism of the white woman's body has been written over by a palimpsest of other meanings—including freedom, individualism, democracy, progress, and also abandon, critique of morality, nonconformism, subversion.

Neither is the representation of "the" white woman unitary. White women, in their multifarious costumings, groomings, and poses, can be wholesome figures of self-possessed independence (as I was often read), or fashionable models of bourgeois consumer expertise, or sultry practitioners of erotic extremity. They appear in sites with different social valences—foreign students' dormitories, tourist hotels, advertisements, pornographic videos. They possess varying degrees of corporeality depending on whether they are actual women or those consumed in multiple mediated formats. Despite the discontinuities, however, these variations together form a complex that is densely interreferential. The picture becomes ever more complicated. Reflexive Chinese subjects, both within the Chinese mainland and overseas—as well as Westerners like myself who write about them—are deliberating: Is Chinese enthrallment with the Western woman a nauseating capitulation? Is her consumption incompatible with a self-respecting nationalism? Is her ubiquity in Chinese pop culture a vehicle for furthering Chinese and Western cultural entanglement or merely a reflection of a *fait accompli*?

These dilemmas were underscored when art students during the 1989 demonstrations at Tiananmen square erected the statue of the "Goddess of Democracy." The figure's referentiality to the Statue of Liberty has been debated and highly troubling for those concerned with the integrity of Chinese nationalism.[7] Five years after Tiananmen, however, even with the waning of political activism, the white woman's presence has endured, albeit in other venues. Zha Jianying recounts how, in 1994, China's Ministry of Culture transformed its official publication:

> For years the [China Culture Gazette] had been an infamous stronghold of the hard-line apparatchiks, choking with dull, harsh propaganda. With a new issue of its *Cultural Weekend* edition, the paper changed color overnight: from red to yellow. The pictures did the trick. On that day, the four-page *Cultural Weekend* displayed many nude and half-nude photographs (mostly of busty Western women in languidly seductive poses); instantly it became known as "the coolest paper in Beijing." (Zha 1994: 373)

THE MODERN AS GENDERED COMMODITY

The white woman's unwavering presence in Chinese popular culture prompts a number of questions beyond that of "what does she signify?" I wonder: *Is* she intransigent? And *is* she polluting?

But in some moments these questions seem tired and wrong-headed, superseded by another process that seems these days to be displacing all others: *the white woman sells*. On a 1993 research trip, I wandered through the print and photographic media on sale in streetfront shops in cities of China's southwest provinces. Predictably, there was a shop for all calendars in which perhaps one-third of the offerings were pin-up style images of Western women in various degrees of dress and undress. Not so predictably, however, there was also a magazine stand in which not only love and fashion magazines but also journals such as *Democracy and the Legal System (Minzhu yu Fazhi)* were adorned with similarly provocative women on their front covers. When I asked Chinese consumers why the image of the white woman was so ubiquitous as a commodity *and* in the packaging of other commodities, I was sometimes told that she represented "modernity" or "beauty." But other times I was told that there was simply no meaning intended, that commodity producers slapped on the image because *the white woman sells*.

As the heady days of Tiananmen activism fade and the marketizing transformation proceeds apace, one begins to muse: Is the fetish of the white woman with all her multivalent significations being supplanted by that old fetish—of the commodity form itself? A comment from the proprietor of the calendar shop was telling in this regard: People are less and less interested in stripped-down images of seminude women, he explained. Instead they want her to be at least partially dressed, bedecked and bejewelled—a textbook on fashion. Or they want background—buildings, foreign cities, or a panoply of desirable objects as indexed, for instance, in the twelve months of the *1994 Modern Lifestyles (Xiandai Shenghuo)* calendar, which showed furniture, ornaments, luxury foods, pets, and the like on each of its polychrome pages.

These days, then, Chinese consumers-in-training are looking to the body of the white woman as a catalogue of consumption style. With a subtlety that Judith Williamson (1986) identified for Western capitalist advertising, this woman is both the object of consumption and its agent. What better instructor in the magic of the commodity than the Western woman who has had it bound to her as the limit of her domain? In China, then, could it be that the white woman not only signifies in the semiotic economy of political struggle, but that she is now guiding Chinese consumers-to-be into the privatized world of fetishized things?

IMAGINED COSMOPOLITANISM

Shifting meanings notwithstanding, the white woman still recurs with regularity. But, I would venture, of late she recurs with a little more caprice. As her meaning has destabilized, as her pointedly oppositional charge has corroded in places, it is less clearly scripted where she will appear. I noted with some surprise in 1993 that in what used to be her unequivocal place—pin-up calendars, condom wrappers, pantyhose packages, department store mannequins—there were a growing number of Asian women similarly underdressed, similarly (?) enticing.

In the 1980s, the oppositional force of the Western woman in large part derived from her occupation of an "other" category, one that Chinese women would never be seen in. She was simultaneously an object of longing and a symbol of lack. Those Chinese persons who wanted to change themselves were consigned to a specular positioning, watching her flit across movie screens and book covers, or into their workunit for a brief stay—always somehow inaccessible. She was mobile while they were held in stasis by censors, by visa officials, by planned economics. By the 1990s, however, the open door policy of *kaifang* had brought MTV into urban Chinese living rooms, had flooded the shops with imported or imitation-Western goods, had curtailed many of the former restrictions on travel. Now politics barely intervened anymore in accessing the West; it seemed that all you needed was money and you too could have it all.

For those with sufficient resources, the Western look was to be had in the most intimate way—not simply by dangling a beeper from one's belt or donning fishnet stockings and spike heels, but by cosmetic surgery to amend the Asian body, deracializing it in some small measure to shorten the distance between "us" and "them." Orville Schell's account of a visit to a private Beijing "clinic" for eye and nose jobs evidences the transformation its patrons were seeking. Schell interviewed the doctor who singlehandedly ran the operation:

> When I asked him what services his small, and seemingly primitive, clinic provided, he explained that he could remove acne scars, . . . create epicanthic folds, and widen eyes, . . . or raise noses . . . right there in his clinic. "But for patients who wish to have their breasts enlarged, their thighs or fanny reduced, or their legs lengthened, we must go to the hospital," he said matter-of-factly. (Schell 1989: 82)

Were it not for compelling postcolonial critiques of derivative discourse, I would be tempted to view this process as a kind of internalization or indigenization (cf. Appardurai 1988: 5) of that which had once been intractably alien.[8] In the 1980s, more than ten thousand people altered themselves at a single Shanghai hospital (Schell 1989: 84). The Westerner was resituated, with fleshly reality, within the Chinese body. But what was created in this process were *hybrid* physical forms. While they could be seen as capitulations to white aesthetics of physical beauty, these forms could also be taken as evidence of the kind of creolizing artifice that Mercer (1990) described for the relaxing and dyeing of black hair—a set of practices that refused the impermeability of race categories.

What I am arguing for the 1990s is that the effect of the saturation of Chinese cultural space with Western presence was the beginning dissolution of a self/other binarism between China and the West. In the process the Western woman was desexualized (when she signified political transgression) and sometimes resexualized (when she recurred in the marketing of commodities and porn through erotic titillation). Likewise, she was politicized and depoliticized. Increasingly, she vaporized, disappearing into the commodities she sold or into the bodies she transformed.

It would be simplistic, then, to say that Chinese had become more Westernized than they used to be. These agents were fashioning themselves more and more as participants in a global culture of late capitalist consumption. This process of identity redistribution could be described as "imagined cosmopolitanism."[9] Cosmetic surgery might supply one of its most potent tactics.[10] The election of cosmetic surgery, or any number of other practices in which the West is fused with Chineseness, mocks the hardness of national boundaries.

UNMAPPING NATIONALISM

Whither nationalism? It has by no means gone away. Nor is it the sole province either of elite intellectuals or of government hardliners who, for instance, have banned Chinese students' celebrations of Christmas, Easter, and Valentine's Day in order to "preserve stable cultural traditions at universities and uphold the national life of China" (*China News Digest*, March 6, 1994). Nationalism is also vibrant among the entrepreneurs of "greater China" (including other Pacific Rim countries and overseas Chinese) as well as their academic scribes who, as Aihwa Ong has recently documented (n.d.), are busy articulating an alternative version of modernity that will not be dictated by the form of modernity exemplified by the West (Ong n.d.: 34). What I am going to suggest, though, is that while a certain nationalist discourse re-asserts Chinese difference, there are two trends that continually undermine the original East-West distinction that produced the fetish of the white woman and of things Western. The first is the "imagined cosmopolitanism" that I described above. The second is the mobility of the other, which I will describe forthwith.

The disruption and recuperation of the East-West binary as the overarching structure of identity in reform China cannot be separated from a context in which there has been a tremendous proliferation of alterities. In the productive process that casts and recasts selfhood, the potency of that particular East-West dyad does not preclude the presence of additional, and perhaps equally potent, dyadic relations inside China.[11] Although the notion of "the Other" implies two poles, I want to stress that a given subject position can include relations to *more than one* other. These relations tend not to be parallel, but to be ranked in the minds of cultural agents on a vertical axis. The "significant other," so to speak, varies with the different moments in which the self is envisioned, but these multiple alterities also converge in cultural struggles over hierarchized positionings. Over the twentieth century, then, China's internal others have been variously imaged but routinely portrayed as subjugated, inferior, and in need of being liberated from feudal oppression. Emancipation narratives—whether for women, for peasants, or for peasant women—have relied on the naturalization of those in the "other" category as requiring help; in the process their stigma has been reproduced.

Turning to the "folk"—particularly the non-Han folk[12]—the conflation of "inferior" categories is further intensified. As exemplified in 1980s "Fifth Wave" films[13] an idealized folk that was both feminized and peasantized pulsed with native culture, serving as a counterweight to Westernization, but at the same time legitimating a thinly veiled civilizing mission—the charge of urban elites.[14] I have called this representational logic "internal orientalism" (Schein 1990). Not independent from the West, it was nonetheless a turning away from the West in a fervent attempt to cast off the inferior positioning assigned to China in the dyadic relation with the West. I call this latter practice "displacing subalternity." My reading of the cultural production that suffused China in the post-1979 reform period (and much earlier) revealed an ongoing effort on the part of a nationalist state *and* of nonstate cultural agents[15] to place both tradition and lack of civilization squarely on the shoulders of an internal and contrastive other.

The folk, then, were at once constitutive of the self and yet a flawed and backward version of it. While the West may have bequeathed a relational scale structured by the notion of unitary "modernity" toward which "China" was ambivalently proceeding, the question of whom *within* China occupied the inferior pole and spoke the native voice was still contested. This is how discursive maneuverings brought about the mobility of the other: At least in the post-Mao period and, I would suggest, since May Fourth (1919), not just intellectuals but also an array of cultural producers, from urban academies to hinterland villages, energetically shifted "native-ness" onto a rural, ethnically distinct other. This other's voice could be appropriated for the nationalist consolidation of difference from the West, but its reviled backwardness did not have to be incurred in the process.

WHO CONSUMES THE FOLK

In the 1980s, with the advent of reform, I found the attraction-repulsion toward the internal other to saturate Chinese popular culture. Troubled both by the grayness of metropolitan life that was the legacy of the Cultural Revolution and, simultaneously, by the specter of "total Westernization" (*quanpan xifanghua*) that was the feared consequence of the Open Door policy, elites and cultural producers fetishized the feminized folk with a passion that rivaled that directed toward the Western woman. The folk woman, emblem of pastoral rawness, yielded color and essence. Her extravagantly costumed image proliferated in films, in amateur art, in magazines, in ethnic performances, even on the new state currency issued after 1980 that pictured headdressed minorities on each of the small denominations. She was consumed through burgeoning domestic tourism, folk fashion and, varieties of urban spectatorship. Accordingly, folk culture was packaged and streamlined in the service of either national politics or the commodity.

In the 1990s, by contrast, contemporaneous with the imagining of cosmopolitanism, I found a strikingly decreased fascination with the exotic domains of the internal folk other. It seemed as if the embrace of the West was less problematized, was even naturalized, to the point that, for most Chinese, demarcating the self and the other was simply less of a concern, and, concomitantly, the folk woman as resource was less routinely called upon. The following trends seem to have been intimately interdependent: (1) Western culture was no longer a distant object of tabooed longing, (2) the place of the erotic/modern Western woman was no longer so circumscribed, but could be occupied by Chinese women as well, and (3) the function of the folk woman as resistant to an engulfing West was no longer so salient.

There was, however, a domain in which a newer form of nationalist nostalgia was emerging. This was among the affluent urbanites of the mainland who had made their fortunes and had had their fill in dealing with the West. The colorful cultures of the interior have been rediscovered by these coastal[16] entrepreneurs, who have made the folk one of their consumption habits alongside video *karaoke* and big-band dancing. These consumers look to Hong Kong as their model for style, and Hong Kongers, less unsure of their privileged modernity, have long known the pleasures of consuming the mainland other as ethnic trinket and of plundering it for new and improved commodity styles. In 1993 William Tang, a major Hong Kong clothes designer, traveled to western Hunan where the media reported that he was "charmed and amazed" by the local Miao people. He was "powerfully tempted to tear off all his clothes and swim naked in a river with the natives from a Miao village and he . . . spent a lot of time gazing at women's skirts" after which he "immersed himself in a study of Miao embroidery, weaving, fabric-dyes and pleating methods" and pledged to incorporate them in his work.[17] In the eyes of coastal mainlanders who would emulate Tang's commercial success, this kind of model renders obsolete the distaste that they had harbored for the "less-than-modern" character of their inland compatriots, replacing it instead with a more straightforwardly celebratory raiding impulse.

FOLK COLOR AS PRODUCT

As a consequence of these new consumption patterns, cultural producers among the "folk" are learning hard lessons about marketing. Performers in the Song and Dance Troupes of Guizhou province told me of their economic woes in the 1990s now that their mission is less scripted and subsidized by the state. They are no longer given assignments to travel to urban and rural sites to disseminate their cultural products to the masses. Instead they have to rely on their own resourcefulness to make ends meet. Some have been more "successful" than others. Those most versatile at trafficking in the recent demand for authenticity have gotten busy repackaging themselves for a new set of consumption desires. One enterprising troupe, hailing from southeast Guizhou, has had engagements in clubs in Shanghai, Shenzhen, Beijing, and other sites where nostalgia has created acute demand for them. Much of their acclaim has been based on their unprocessed demeanor—they collect costumes from the countryside, they replay rituals onstage, they dance in unrecognizable ways that appear primitive. The romance with wildness even extends to the literally animal. One of the most successful ventures of this troupe was when they loaded water buffaloes onto the train to Beijing and staged a rural festival in an outdoor auditorium complete with bullfights. Beijingers paid dearly (by Guizhou standards—five *yuan* a seat) to witness this bestial display. When demand continued unabated, the troupe enhanced their profits further by selling the animals, leaving them in the capital for a lifetime of clashing horns for the titillation of metropolitan audiences.

The taste for this raw cultural style might be understood as a Western import, but its localization among the affluent, entrepreneurial elite of China bespeaks consumption meanings concerned not only with China's difference but also with the anxious marking of difference or displacing of subalternity within China, a practice that is inseparable from the growing gulf that divides such producers and consumers in terms of wealth. To have "made it" in the crazy world of China's mixed economy may mean that one not only can carry a cellular phone or drink European wine, but that one also can consume the interior with abandon and unambiguous pleasure.[18]

THE POLITICS AND ECONOMICS OF OTHER WOMEN

It is a muggy October day in Shenzhen, China, October 1993—that site of putative economic miracles on which the desires of transnational capital and impoverished interior wage-seekers alike have become transfixed. I am doing a few days of fieldwork with the Miao young people who work in the China Folk Culture Villages (*Zhongguo Minsu Wenhua Cun*), a theme park that showcases through live re-enactments the customs and lifestyles of China's ethnic groups. I sit for hours with my friend, a twenty-two-year-old whom I have known since I stayed in her village home in 1985. Sweltering in a pleated skirt and heavy brocade jacket that she brought from the cool mountains of her Guizhou home, she smilingly serves tourists sugared tea and a nonalcoholic replica of sweet rice wine for 1 *yuan* a cup, assuring them that they are imbibing a traditional Miao beverage. Here in Shenzhen her body and her soul have become a site of conquest. By day, I find her accosted by a white missionary who comes in from his base in Hong Kong to proselytize among the unwitting employees of the theme park—young kids like herself from the countryside whose job requires them to be pleasant to foreigners. By night—she confides with a hint of fear—she has taken up with a Cantonese man, twenty years her senior, who buys her everything but has threatened to beat her if she even hints at having casual friendships with other males.

I take a walk around the life-sized recreation of a Miao village. In one of the replica houses, a fiftyish Chinese man speaks to me in accented English. "This bedroom is traditional style; this one is modernized," he explains with an air of authority. I discern his Cantonese accent and query, "How do you know?" Proudly, he gestures to his companion. "She is a Miao," he boasts. The girl acts bashful. She is taller that he and dressed in the unisex sightseeing garb of Hong Kong: jeans, athletic shoes, a baseball cap, a white button-down shirt. Her hair is pulled back in a ponytail. Her style is undistinguishable from his, except for the expensive jewelry that ornaments her ear lobes and her soft forearms—she doesn't look as if she's done physical labor for some time. Seeing that she doesn't speak English I shift into Chinese. In Mandarin, I ask how old she is, where she's from. Her eyes barely meet mine and she turns to the Hong Kong man as if he could translate. Gradually I realize that she doesn't even speak much Mandarin and I wonder how she communicates with him since I am sure she doesn't speak Cantonese and even surer that he doesn't speak Miao or the regional Chinese dialect of her hometown. But I don't wonder long: the ways they brush against each other make it probable that they have been more intimate. It is also clear that she doesn't speak for herself in his presence. This is what he tells me: She is nineteen, from the Xiangxi Miao area of Hunan. She is in Shenzhen visiting her brother with whom he does business when he comes in from Hong Kong. Because her brother wasn't available that day she accompanied him for sightseeing instead. That's all.

These two accounts, taken together, suggest the cultural/economic logic that compels folk women of the interior to travel to the coast and become the ethnic playthings of wealthier nostalgic men. The desire for them is premised both on identity and on difference. In one sense they are Chinese, putatively more authentically so than the Cantonese men whom they fascinate. But at the same time, their allure is caught up with their constituting an other, one who appears as less privileged, more traditional, more feminine, more exotic, etc. This is especially in contradistinction to contemporary Chinese urban women, whose ardent adoption of the styles and trappings of Western femininity has come to be read as "liberated"—in some cases undesirably so because of its potential to threaten time-honored masculine positionings. Folk women, it would seem, are caught in a bizarre and rarefied backlash. Reform-era gender shifts have been either critiqued or lauded as a post–Cultural Revolution recuperation of the gender difference and sexual objectification characteristic both of the "modern" West and of earlier Chinese days, and therefore as indicative, for some, of a postsocialist trajectory (back) toward women's increasingly unequal positioning.[19] But the men who seek folk women, on the contrary, regret these same shifts as corrupting of a putatively indigenous and purer femininity. To the extent that they reflect Western influence, these men fear contemporary changes as marks of a capitulation to what *they* see as more independent, emancipated forms of womanhood. Ironically, what their desire has fixed upon is the mirage of an uncontaminated woman, while their actual objects have long since been made over by the Maoist revolution if not by the current cultural sea-change.

For the purposes of this discussion, folk women have figured thus far as pawns or objects. They exemplify with a vengeance what Lata Mani described as the process by which women become sites for debates over tradition and modernity (Mani 1987). Some of these women, however, also emerge as agentive in these encounters, if only because of their having consented to situate themselves in these relationships for whatever economic advantages they expect to gain. Undoubtedly, there are those who are taken by force and held captive—either physically or economically—in the appropriation of folk women by coastal men, but this is not the only story. The tactics deployed by interior women in their negotiation of the exchanges precipitated by coastal-interior difference complicate the purported effacement of Chinese women's subjectivity that we saw with the fetish of the white woman. The white woman inspires in these young women, as aspiring consumers themselves, another kind of desire, one that has to do with a vicarious experience of affluence accessed precisely through the ways in which cosmopolitan images act upon Chinese men.

CONCLUSION

The project of this paper has been twofold: to chart a shift that has taken place in the politics of difference over China's reform period (the 1980s and early 1990s) and to point to some related spatial realignments that may still be underway. The shift that has taken place over time is fragmented, but can be analyzed in context as cohering around commoditization and enmeshment in the global economy. I have highlighted several facets of this process. First, the white woman, still an object of desire, has shed some of her political charge as her otherness has been eroded. She has become less and less a sign of the inaccessible or the forbidden; at the same time, the eroticized domain that she once monopolized is increasingly populated by Asian women. The imaging of both Western and Asian women is more intimately linked to the marketing of commodities and thus delinked from the asexual political symbolism of such images as the "Goddess of Democracy." Second, with the tantalizing dance of foreign goods and cultural products across television screens and on store shelves, even those who can't afford them are imagining themselves as participants in a cosmopolitan world of consumption. This "imagined cosmopolitanism" coincides with a diminishing enunciation of a unitary and oppositional Chinese identity. In its place are discrete pockets of anxious nationalism, about which I will say more below. Third, the figure of the folk woman, once an unequivocal symbolic reservoir for the cultural material on which an oppositional Chinese nationalism could be produced, has become more an object of localized consumption practices. Largely forgotten in the mainstream media, she is now craved mostly by those on the coast who would slake their nostalgia by possessing her. In keeping with the commoditization process, possessing her can be quite literal, as in the case of the numerous stolen daughters of the interior who are sold into marriage, mistresshood, or prostitution to sate the desires of more affluent men in China's boom regions.[20]

This latter point leads to my other project: a rethinking of the Chinese landscape in terms of internal difference and in terms of the weakening of the boundary with the outside. In my discussion above I talked about the woman/peasant/folk as an internal other. But to even speak of another that is "internal" implies a national unit that is analytically intact. This intactness seemed profoundly difficult to retain in the 1993 China that I visited. Policies of decentralization along with the chaotic arrival of transnational capital all over the Chinese map have made China as a unit seem more and more elusive. Goods and cultural products are flowing across borders and via satellite with tremendous velocity. At the same time, more localized alliances are being forged with global forces—including interest groups as disparate as diaspora communities or conservationists, as well as capital—illustrating yet another potential case of what Appadurai (1993) characterized as a reorganization of the global order through *postnational* linkages that supplant or rival territorial nation-states. At the same time, the pockets of nativism that have sprung up effectively fracture Chinese space despite their aspirations to the celebration of some kind of generalized Chineseness. Women move physically and symbolically in the remaking of difference that is underway. Constructed upon the ground of uneven development and asymmetrical exchange between regions, the cultural practices we might call nationalist can be seen to deepen cleavages and to reaffirm a unilineal hierarchy through the displacing of subalternity onto the interior folk. This kind of practice, and this kind of hierarchy, is unconcerned with the political borders that mark the nation. The consumption of color, then, may ultimately be inseparable from the politics of white skin.

NOTES

I am especially grateful to the following persons for their encouragement and incisive commentary: Vincanne Adams, Connie Clark, Nina Cornyetz, Micaela di Leonardo, Jillana Enteen, Rebecca Etz, Dorothy Hodgson, Cora Kaplan, Laurel Kendall, Roger Lancaster, Ralph Litzinger, Laura Liu, Michael Moffatt, and Rujie Wang.

This work is dedicated to my dear friend and colleague, the late Mark Saroyan, whose untimely loss to the theorizing of ethnic politics will be long felt, and whose inspiration cannot be extinguished.

1. The heterosexual character of this gaze, as that of a male viewing subject upon an (eroticized) female object, may not be universal but has nearly monopolized codings of maleness and femaleness, at least in commodified representations. Among the challenges to this scopic structure see Kaplan (1983); see also Clark (1991) on commodity lesbianism for another move that dislocates the heterosexual consuming gaze within the West.

2. See Barlow (1991) for a theorization of the contestation that occurs around the localization of *imported* signs in the Chinese context. My treatment considers localizations of signs *within* China in terms of the ways in which this process enables the production of internal differences—gender, class, ethnic, regional, etc.—through the fecund medium of malleable alterity.

3. Although dark or black *(hei)* skin tone is popularly associated with peasants because of their excessive exposure to the sun during agricultural labor and thereby comes to constitute a significant class (as opposed to race) marker, my emphasis here is on the figurative sense of color as denoting exotic indigenous customs and lifeways. The overlap with physical looks is only to the extent that such lifeways include extravagant costume, grooming, and ornament—objects of abiding fascination for urbanites.

4. For research support during these years, I would like to thank the Committee on Scholarly Communications with the People's Republic of China, the Fulbright-Hays Doctoral Dissertation Research Abroad Program, the Samuel T. Arnold Fellowship Program of Brown University, the University of California, Berkeley, and the Rutgers University Research Council, as well as numerous institutions and individuals in China who sponsored or otherwise facilitated my work.

5. I have in mind here a range of experiences involving both state and nonstate agents, experiences such as: surveillance and scrutiny of my body, grooming me and dressing me up, "covering" me in the media, nurturing me as quintessentially fragile, protecting me from danger and rape, questioning me as to sexual mores, approaching me as an unindividuated object of desire, and segregating me from undesirable categories of people.

6. I stress *resonance* here, and do not mean to imply an uncritical transposition of colonial/postcolonial frames to the Chinese context—an intellectual maneuver that is currently under active consideration in the field of Chinese studies. See, for just two examples of counterposed voices in this debate, Hershatter (1993) and Wang (1993).

7. See Chow (1991) and Zhang L. (1992) for divergent perspectives on the "Goddess" from U.S.-based Chinese intellectuals.

8. See Chatterjee (1986) for the original discussion of "derivative discourse" in terms of the modes by which nationalist discourse reproduced colonial/capitalist formulations. Barlow (1991) gives a compelling treatment of such processes among intellectuals in contemporary China. Unlike more neutral formulations such as indigenization or traveling theory, both authors retain a sense of

asymmetrical power/prestige that impacts the global movement of theories and cultural forms. "Derivative" or "colonial" discourse, then, is characterized by a more unidirectional and powered flow, not simply an endless recombination of meanings/practices to suit local contexts.

9. My formulation of "cosmopolitanism" owes much to the possibilities opened up by Robbins (1992)—building on Clifford (1992)—for attending to "discrepant" cosmopolitanisms may be not only the practices of metropolitan elites but also the province and the project of particular, local, and less privileged sectors. But while Robbins's vision incorporates variants of actual global mobility (such as diasporas or labor migrations), I want to add here an *imagining* of mobility through the consumption of foreign objects and media and through the potential for global access implied by the "opening" policy.

10. As Anne Balsamo's (1992: 226) work suggests, cosmetic surgery looses difference from its mooring in a "naturalized body," thus making space for people to mean with their bodies beyond what is circumscribed by race and sex categories. See Kaw (1993) for an opposing view based on analysis of Asian-American women's use of cosmetic surgery, which holds that this practice serves to entrench hierarchical racial ideology through its naturalization of white features as beautiful.

11. On the contours of internal difference within China, see Crossley (1990) for a recuperation of the importance of ethnic difference in early modern China; Honig (1992), Lipman (1984), and Siu (1993) for the ways in which regional difference has been inflected ethnically; and Leeming (1993: 170–80), Wang and Hague (1993), and Goodman (1989) (especially Cannon's "National Minorities and the Internal Frontier" in the latter) for the political economy of regional difference. Dikotter's (1992) treatment of the discourse of race in China gives some historical depth concerning formulations of racial difference that apply to "barbarians" both within and beyond the Chinese purview. Diamond (1988), Schein (1993), and Litzinger (1994) theorize the social effects of dominant representations of the non-Han; and Harrell (1990) and Gladney (1990) give perspectives on the relationship between state policy in the socialist period and the formation of ethnic identities.

12. The vast majority (approximately 92 percent) of the mainland Chinese population is reckoned in government statistics in terms of the unitary ethnic category "Han." The remaining 8 percent of the population comprise 55 officially recognized "minority nationalities" (*shaoshu minzu*). Totalling over 91 million people, these groups include Tibetans, Mongolians, Manchu, Islamic groups such as Uighurs, highland and lowland groups across the South and Southwest (including the Miao, on whom this essay is focused), and smaller groups with transnational identifications such as Russians and the "*Jing*," cousins of the Vietnamese.

13. A "romantic folk" genre was a subset of what was called the Fifth Wave of Chinese filmmaking. Emerging after the end of the Cultural Revolution in 1976, the Fifth Wave was characterized by a delinking of artistic production from the Party politics that had directed content since Mao's "Talks at the Yanan Forum on Art and Literature" in 1942.

14. For a reading of the role of minorities in mainland film see Clark (1987), and of minority women in films since 1949 see Yau (1989). Gladney (1993) discusses Fifth Wave film and several of the 1980s films that deal with minorities. See Litzinger (1994: 314–38) for a compelling alternative to the above approaches, one that positions members of the Yao minority as subjects, not merely objects, in the production of cultural difference. See also Schein 1997.

15. By "cultural agents" I mean writers, journalists, artists, filmmakers, designers, advertisers, musicians, academics, researchers, etc., including both those whose work was sponsored by the state and those who worked independently.

16. The "coast" or "coastal" (*yanhai*) has become an everyday vocabulary term in mainland parlance, connoting internationalized cities and Special Economic Zones not only on the literal coast but also elsewhere on the economic-cultural frontier with foreign capital. This figurative space includes Beijing and several other inland cities, but is cognitively centered on the Shanghai-Fujian-Guangdong corridor in the Southeast.

17. *South China Morning Post*, June 2, 1993.

18. Antecedents to what I have described in the foregoing two sections are suggested in Levenson's (1967, 1971) analysis, written in the mid-1960s, of cosmopolitanism and provincialism. Levenson argued that, for Chinese, Confucianism had once been cosmopolitan, worldly, absolute; and that it was only with "modern" nationalism—when China sought to take its place among parallel nations—that Confucianism was rendered provincial (see Duara 1993 for a critique of this periodization as overly disjunctive). Chinese Communists, then, in Levenson's view, were confronted with a further dilemma: charged both with enacting an internationalist script and with consolidating the nation, they provincialized the provinces. Tradition—once that same "universalized" Confucianism—became quaint, museumified, staged. What we are seeing in the current period may be the latest incarnation of this process. But my move, analytically, is to deprovincialize the provinces as well by showing how saturated they too are, if only through imagining, with cosmopolitanism.

19. Feminist scholars, both Chinese and Western, are divided on the effects of reform for women's status. While the Maoist period (1949–1979) fell far short of utopia, many point to negative, retrogressive trends in the current years such as intensification of the gendered division of labor, discrimination in the workplace and in education, a rise in arranged marriage and female infanticide practices, the kidnapping and sale of women, the erotic depersonalization of women's bodies in pornography and prostitution, etc. But many also stress that the current period is conditioned by several decades of at least partially successful attempts to overhaul Chinese gender norms as well as by the possibilities for women's economic autonomy eventuated by the increase in waged work opportunities under reform. For just a few representative pieces in these deliberations, see Croll (1983), Gao (1994), Honig and Hershatter (1988), Rai (1992), Woo (1994), Young (1989), and Zhang (1992). For comparative works on gender and postsocialism see Einhorn (1993), Rai et al (1992), and Funk and Mueller (1993).

20. One report stated that "police processed more than 15,000 cases of gangs that kidnapped and sold women into marriage" (*China News Digest*, February 24, 1994). Another reported that "rural women in Guangxi Province, lured to cities with promises of jobs, have been raped and then sold for prostitution . . . more than 50,000 abductions of women and children were reported in 1991–92" (*China News Digest*, May 24, 1994.)

REFERENCES

Appadurai, Arjun. 1988. "Why Public Culture?" *Public Culture* 1(1): 5–9.
———. 1990. "Disjuncture and Difference in the Global Cultural Economy." *Public Culture* 2(2): 1–24.
———. 1993. Patriotism and Its Futures. *Public Culture* 5(3): 411–29.
Balsamo, Anne. 1992. "On the Cutting Edge: Cosmetic Surgery and the Technological Production of the Gendered Body." *Camera Obscura* 28: 207–37.
Barlow, Tani E. 1991. "*Zhishifenzi* (Chinese Intellectuals) and Power." *Dialectical Anthropology* 16(3–4):209–32.
Cannon, Terry. 1989. "National Minorities and the Internal Frontier." In *China's Regional Development.* Ed. David S.G. Goodman, pp. 164–79. London: Routledge.
Chatterjee, Partha. 1986. *Nationalist Thought and the Colonial World: A Derivative Discourse.* Minneapolis: University of Minnesota Press.
Chow, Rey. 1991. "Violence in the Other Country: China as Crisis, Spectacle, and Woman." In *Third World Women and the Politics of Feminism.* Ed. Chandra Talpade Mohanty et al., pp. 80–100. Bloomington and Indianapolis: University of Indiana Press.
Clark, Danae. 1991. "Commodity Lesbianism." *Camera Obscura* 25–26: 180–201.
Clark, Paul. 1987. "Ethnic Minorities in Chinese Films: Cinema and the Exotic." *East-West Film Journal* 1(2): 15–31.
Clifford, James. 1992. "Traveling Cultures." In *Cultural Studies.* Ed. Lawrence Grossberg et al., pp. 96–116. New York: Routledge.

Croll, Elisabeth. 1983. *Chinese Women Since Mao*. London: Zed Books.

Crossley, Pamela. 1990. "Thinking About Ethnicity in Early Modern China." *Late Imperial China* 11(1): 1–34.

Diamond, Norma. 1988. "The Miao and Poison: Interactions on China's Southwest Frontier." *Ethnology* 27(1) :1–25.

Dikotter, Frank. 1992. *The Discourse of Race in Modern China*. Stanford, CA: Stanford University Press.

Duara, Prasenjit. 1993. "De-Constructing the Chinese Nation." *Australian Journal of Chinese Affairs* 30(July): 1–26.

Einhorn, Barbara. 1993. *Cinderella Goes to Market: Citizenship, Gender and Women's Movements in East Central Europe*. London: Verso.

Fanon, Frantz. 1967 (1952). *Black Skin, White Masks*. New York: Grove Weidenfeld.

Funk, Nanette, and Magda Mueller. 1993. *Gender Politics and Post-Communism: Reflections from Eastern Europe and the Former Soviet Union*. New York: Routledge.

Gao Xiaoxian. 1994. "China's Modernization and Changes in the Social Status of Rural Women." In *Engendering China: Women, Culture and the State*. Ed. Christina Gilmartin et al., pp. 80–97. Cambridge: Harvard University Press Contemporary China Series 10.

Gladney, Dru C. 1990. *Muslim Chinese: Ethnic Nationalism in the People's Republic of China*. Cambridge, MA: Council on East Asian Studies, Harvard University.

———. 1994. "Representing Nationality in China: Refiguring Majority/Minority Identities." *Journal of Asian Studies* 53(1) :92–123.

Goodman, David S. G. 1989. *China's Regional Development*. London: Routledge.

Harrell, Stevan. 1990. "Ethnicity, Local Interests and the State: Yi Communities in Southwest China." *Comparative Studies in Society and History* 32(3):515–48.

Hershatter, Gail. 1993. "The Subaltern Talks Back: Reflections on Subaltern Theory and Chinese History." *Positions* 1(1): 103–30.

Honig, Emily. 1992. *Creating Chinese Ethnicity: Subei People in Shanghai 1850–1980*. New Haven: Yale University Press.

Honig, Emily and Gail Hershatter. 1988. *Personal Voices: Chinese Women in the 1980s*. Stanford, CA: Stanford University Press.

Kaplan, E. Ann. 1983. "Is the Gaze Male?" In *Powers of Desire: The Politics of Sexuality*. Ed. Ann Snitow et al., pp. 309–27. New York: Monthly Review Press.

Kaw, Eugenia. 1993. "Medicalization of Racial Features: Asian American Women and Cosmetic Surgery." *Medical Anthropology Quarterly* 7(1): 74–89.

Leeming, Frank. 1993. *The Changing Geography of China*. Oxford: Blackwell.

Levenson, Joseph R. 1967. "The Province, the Nation and the World: The Problem of Chinese Identity." In *Approaches to Modern Chinese History*. Ed. Albert Feuerwerker, pp. 268–88. Berkeley: University of California Press.

———. 1971. *Revolution and Cosmopolitanism: The Western Stage and the Chinese Stages*. Berkeley: University of California Press.

Lipman, Jonathan N. 1984. "Ethnicity and Politics in Republican China." *Modern China* 10(3): 285–316.

Litzinger, Ralph A. 1994. "Crafting the Modern Ethnic: Yao Representation and Identity in Post-Mao China." Ph.D. dissertation, Department of Anthropology, University of Washington.

Mani, Lata. 1987. "Contentious Traditions: The Debate on SATI in Colonial India." *Cultural Critique* 7: 119–56.

Mercer, Kobena. 1990. "Black Hair/Style Politics." In *Out There: Marginalization and Contemporary Culture*. Ed. Russell Ferguson et al., pp. 247–64. New York: New Museum of Contemporary Art; and Cambridge, MA: MIT Press.

Ong, Aihwa. 1996. "Anthropology, China, and Modernities: The Geopolitics of Cultural Knowledge." In *The Future of Anthropological Knowledge*. Ed. Henrietta Moore. pp. 60–92. London: Routledge.

Rai, Shirin. 1992. "'Watering Another Man's Garden': Gender, Employment and Educational Reforms in China." In *Women in the Face of Change: The Soviet Union, Eastern Europe and China.* Ed. Shirin Rai et al., pp. 20–40. London: Routledge.

Robbins, Bruce. 1992. "Comparative Cosmopolitanism." *Social Text* 31/32: 169–86.

Schein, Louisa. 1990. "Barbarians Beautified: The Ambivalences of Chinese Nationalism." Unpublished ms.

———. 1993. "Popular Culture and the Production of Difference: The Miao and China." Ph.D. dissertation, Department of Anthropology, University of California, Berkeley.

———. 1997. "Gender and Internal Orientalism in China." *Modern China* 23(1): 69–98.

Schell, Orville. 1989. *Discos and Democracy: China in the Throes of Reform.* New York: Anchor Books.

Siu, Helen F. 1993. "Cultural Identity and the Politics of Difference in South China." *Daedalus* 122(2): 19–43.

Wang Jing. 1993. "The Mirage of 'Chinese Postmodernism': Ge Fei, Self-Positioning, and the Avant-Garde Showcase." *Positions* 1(2): 349–88.

Wang Ya Ping and Cliff Hague. 1993. "Territory Planning in China: A New Regional Approach." *Regional Studies* 27(6): 561–73.

Williamson, Judith. 1986. "Woman Is an Island: Femininity and Colonization." In *Studies in Entertainment.* Ed. Tania Modleski, pp. 99–118. Bloomington and Indianapolis: University of Indiana Press.

Woo, Margaret Y. K. 1994. "Chinese Women Workers: The Delicate Balance between Protection and Equality." In *Engendering China: Women, Culture and the State.* Christina Gilmartin et al., eds. pp. 279–95. Cambridge: Harvard University Press Contemporary China Series 10.

Yau, Esther. 1989. "Is China the End of Hermeneutics? Or, Political and Cultural Usage of Non-Han Women in Mainland Chinese Films." *Discourse* 11(2): 115–36.

Young, Marilyn. 1989. "Chicken Little in China: Some Reflections on Women." In *Marxism and the Chinese Experience.* Ed. Arif Dirlik and Maurice Meisner, pp. 253–68. Armonk, NY: M.E. Sharpe, Inc.

Zha Jianying. 1994. "Communism Lite in Beijing: China Goes Pop; Mao Meets Muzak." *The Nation* 258(11): 373–76.

Zhang Junzuo. 1992. "Gender and Political Participation in Rural China." In *Women in the Face of Change: The Soviet Union, Eastern Europe and China.* Ed. Shirin Rai et al., pp. 41–56. London: Routledge.

Zhang Longxi. 1992. "Western Theory and Chinese Reality." *Critical Inquiry* 19(1): 15–30.

32   The Enterprise of Empire

Race, Class, Gender, and Japanese National Identity

Jacalyn D. Harden

My officemates and I were off to Osaka for our section trip. We had saved money for one year in order to be able to afford these 36 hours of hectic "rest." As we boarded the Shinkansen, Kanada-sensei gave me a sympathetic smile, handed me my ticket, and told me that I would be sitting next to Endo-sensei for the two-hour trip. I knew that he had a reputation for being sukebe *(lecherous), especially when he drank, but I also knew that he had spent a summer in California with a black high-school principal and had plenty of interesting stories about his trip to the states. I was only mildly wary. Yet as soon as the train pulled out of Hamamatsu station and the sake bottles appeared, Endo-sensei begged my forgiveness for the sensitive question he was about to ask me: "Why do American teenagers become sexually active so early in life? . . . And by the way when did you have your first lover?" Endo-sensei must have sensed by my rapid flipping through my dictionary that I was upset. Not being able to find the word that I was looking for, I asked him if he would talk about sex with a Japanese woman like this. He quickly apologized and said, "Japanese girls are not like black girls or Filipinas . . . they are just different."*

My experiences in Japan like the one above suggest that images of Western "others" are used to make claims about authentic Japanese national identity as well as about Japan's position in the world. They also confirm that many Japanese citizens use images of blacks in an "attempt to deal with their own ambiguous racio-cultural status in a Eurocentric world" (Russell 1991a: 6). I suggest that images of women's sexual nature, such as those hinted at by Endo-sensei, reflect efforts to build a Japanese national collective identity. In what follows, I construct an interpretation of Japanese national identity that centers on the trope Micaela di Leonardo names "exotics at home" (forthcoming). As Japanese politics, economics, and Japan's position in the world have changed over the past century, "other" women's sexual behavior has been deployed in creating an image of genuine Japanese culture that has served to define out those women who could not or would

---

Jacalyn D. Harden has an M.A. in justice studies from Arizona State University (1988), and is currently a Ph.D. candidate in anthropology at Northwestern University. From 1988 to 1991 she worked for Monbusho, the Ministry of Education, in Shizuoka prefecture, Japan. Her dissertation is an historical ethnography of Japanese nationals and Japanese Americans in post–World War II Chicago.

not fit into their "proper place." I argue here that Japanese constructions of race and national pride are deeply intertwined with images of women's sexuality, past and present.

In the last five to ten years, critics have called Japan every "-ist" label imaginable—racist, sexist, nationalist, infantile capitalist, protectionist—and Japan currently occupies an ambiguous position in Western representations. Global public culture allows many in the West, the United States in particular, to claim an imagined superiority and sophistication over Japan by suggesting that the West is not as racist nor as sexist as the Japanese.[1] Statements by a Japanese prime minister about racial minorities or lazy U.S. workers and their role in the decline of America coexist with increases in "Japan-bashing"—revamped World War II "Yellow Perilism"—that suggest a Japanese predilection for racial and sexual discrimination. For black Americans in particular, Japan symbolizes blatant discriminatory attitudes. At the same time, the myth persists across international boundaries that Japan and Japanese people have little experience in dealing with other "others."

Thus this article is in part a response to the "Westerners" of varied backgrounds who, when they hear of my previous job, routinely ask, "How did you, a black woman, make it over there? Those people are so racist and sexist." It is about the two years that I worked for the Japanese Ministry of Education in a city of 500,000 people in Shizuoka prefecture. During those twenty-six months the same questions and comments (Why do you sing so well? I bet you can run fast. By the way, I really love the blues!) that I also received at home in the United States were part of my personal experience and were represented in Japanese mass media and popular culture. For most of my colleagues, neighbors, and friends I was one of a few Western women and probably the first and the last black woman from any nation they would ever see in the flesh. Yet they were often able to identify the differences between the "real" shy and naive Japanese woman and the "real" loose and promiscuous American (read, Western) woman. I sensed a strong tendency on the part of many Japanese people among whom I lived and worked to suggest that "color" as diversity was a threat to the economic strength of the West. However, I argue that current Japanese notions of sexuality and race that I experienced were due neither to some overpowering Western influence nor to qualities intrinsic to Japan. Things were no better, but certainly no worse than in America, for me as a black woman in Japan. Endo-sensei is Japanese, but his questions and assumptions could have been made anywhere by anyone. Ideas about race, gender, and nationality are both lucrative and commonplace throughout the world today.

Much has been written by Western scholars about the Japanese incorporation of Western ideologies in the creation of the "modern Japan," yet little work deals with state policies and gender construction (see Nolte and Hastings 1991). Moreover, what is also lacking is the manner in which women's sexuality, race, and "proper place" have been used in the creation of "modern Japan." In other words, how did representations of "traditional" sexuality and moral strength become tied to Japanese economic growth and national image (Tamanoi 1991)? Here I take issue with much of the research concerned with Japanese cultural constructions. Consistently, it has left out the concept of race, even when dealing with sexuality and class (see Bernstein 1991; Tobin 1992; Gordon 1993). Thus the illusion has persisted that the Japanese are unaware of an outside world of others in which racism against them as Asians exists; unaware of what Kelly (1986) calls Japan's "double image" in the Western world.

I begin by an examination of how recent research on other areas of the world has dealt with nationalism, race, sexuality, and the politics of empire. Following O'Brien and Roseberry's suggestion (1991) that the construction of women's sexuality is situated within social, economic, and political processes, I then analyze the ways in which global capital and nationalist agendas combine with race and class to create a national image of Japan's cultural superiority embraced both domestically and internationally. Bernstein (1991) states that Japanese women's experience of womanhood historically had more to do with social class and age than with race, religion, or ethnicity, but I suggest that more than two tools must be used to understand Japan's "other" meanings.

THE ENTERPRISE OF EMPIRE

The Boundaries of Opportunity and Allegiance

Empire building over the past century has almost always required some level of economic gain, political opportunity, and imperial allegiance. In order to hoist flags over new acquisitions, those engaged in colonial projects simultaneously had to support and muster troops to keep the banners of the empire waving. Colonial officials could define and defend the importance of national culture abroad, but the colonial enterprise also necessitated sufficient economic returns to concerned investors back home. However, I want to stress the importance of the everyday mechanics of empire construction along with the symbolic contexts that give them structure and meaning. For example, policies that served the interests of the privileged few had to be sold to the masses, who would be called on repeatedly to sacrifice their lives or life styles in the name of the empire. Going beyond simple functionalism or utilitarianism, then, colonial life, its various boundaries, and the hierarchies that it necessitated must be viewed in light of *cui bono* (for whose gain). The important question thus becomes: Who gained from the enterprise of empire and from hierarchies of opportunity and allegiance to the colonial project, which handicapped many or defined others as good colonial subjects, leaders, and resistors?[2]

The dynamics inherent in the enterprise of empire—with regard to economics, culture, and political sovereignty—are part of both the colonial past and the global political economy of the present. The notion of domestic empire building suggests that there is a need to create a nationalized collective identity that can go beyond geographical boundaries. The construction of national identity can only take place if individuals in government, business, and the various "publics" become familiar and comfortable with the relevant signs and symbols of national success, be they defined as a strong military presence, kiwi fruit, computer software, or "strong family values." Thus even if not in faraway places, the building of national empires and notions of what active participants will "look like" and how their lives will benefit the nation is both continuous and complex. Symbolic goals and material realities in the context of the enterprise of empire are not just about Japan over the past one hundred years but also about current aggregations of power in the world today. Thus, if being a good member of an empire mandates referencing oneself with respect to "others" at home and abroad, then of course "Japanese girls are not like black girls or Filipinas." But we need to know why and how "they are just different."

Actions committed by colonial powers that are motivated by profit but justified under the guise of moral uplift, cultural betterment, and indubitable destiny have been well documented. Likewise, it has been noted that formerly colonized political elites and intellectuals often become nation builders who use the tools of their former colonial masters to build up their new national homes (Chatterjee 1989). Others have examined the ways in which colonial powers in general have profited from gendered inequalities. There has also been discussion about the proper balance of race, class, and gender within analyses of national identity (see Gilroy 1991). Linking these literatures together raises questions that are central to the notion of the Japanese construction of domestic empire: How was it that colonial discourse used the colonized woman as a means of constructing proper place and racial superiority? Who benefited from these constructions? What needs were met by them? How did they affect the lives of those men and women who were actors—willing and unwilling—within colonial projects? Why is it that current notions of race are entangled with a history of past imperial projects and present global political economies?

These queries buttress a belief that race, class, and gender are more than just a holy trinity to be invoked in our research. I am thus attempting the crowd-pleasing yet difficult feat of juggling multiple balls at once. It does involve more work to give consideration to all of the "categories"; however, holding something constant while dealing with the more obvious does not do the trick. Likewise, conflating gender with sexuality or using class as shorthand for race is relatively easy and seductive. No matter how gallant the effort, single- or double-ball theories only suppress an understanding of world history, politics, and identities. Absent culture, economy, and politics on a global level, a train ride in which a middle-aged Japanese male school teacher tells a young black woman from the United States about "Japanese womanhood" is only another ambiguous expatriate tale.

In 1868, the Meiji oligarchs, just having overthrown the Tokugawa shogunate, took the first steps toward what was perceived in Japan as becoming more Western. Part of the new government's plan was to increase contact with the West and to modernize Japan in the hopes of avoiding the colonization by Europe that was taking place throughout Asia. Partly because the Meiji oligarchs had come to power through loosely defined promises to deal with the West, the Meiji period entailed limited increases in the number of Westerners entering Japan, either as missionaries or as consular officials. Yet at the same time, perhaps more importantly, many Japanese officials were being sent abroad to bring back firsthand knowledge of the West and how it functioned. These government trips were to aid the transformation of a primarily agricultural economy into an industrial one. With this scrutinization of the West, there came to be a core of upper-class Japanese—for the most part sons of the former samurai armed with primary source readings, translations of major Western theorists, and friendships with Western thinkers such as Herbert Spencer—who became concerned with the notion that a society's place on the social evolutionary scale could be determined by the character of its women (Sievers 1983).

In 1872 the central government instituted a nationwide family registry system (*honseki*). What was perhaps the most significant part of this new system was that the Meiji government validated and generalized the model of the *ie* (house) system that had been before limited strictly to the upper classes. With the acceptance of the family registry as national exigency, the unification of Japan became linked to a chain of authority and accountability: "Individuals were made legally accountable to their househeads who were in turn, accountable to government officials" (Bryant 1991: 116). Yet with the establishment of a family unit recognized and mandated by the central government in Tokyo, the "woman's question" was well on its way to being structured in terms of national goals, allegiance to empire, and externally marked hierarchies.

There was tremendous debate in *Meiroku Zashii* (Meiji Six Magazine) and in public forums on how to preserve the "natural Japanese state" while moving ahead with modernization. Much of what was written in the magazine in its one year of publication (1874–1875) dealt with Western thought and how it would affect Japan's new place in the world. Sakatani Shiroshi, a contributor to the magazine wrote: "The wise men of Japan, China, and the West are agreed in holding that marriage is the foundation from which the fine qualities of nations emerge since it is the basis of morality and the source of propriety as well as the institution upon which the conduct of the people rests" (Sakatani 1875: 392–93). Sakatani felt that it was the duty of the more privileged class to set the standard for the lower classes. The lower classes in Japan would be influenced by the upper class just as grass blew with the wind. But in looking at class in Japan, Europe, and the United States, Sakatani concluded that middle- and lower-class Westerners were "barbaric" because of their tacit acceptance of sexual immorality.

Mori Asano, the magazine's editor-in-chief, likewise saw that the more privileged classes must set the standard for all of Japan (Braisted 1976). He suggested that men who didn't realize the need for wives to be treated as equals were not qualified to legislate needed changes in the newly formed legislative assembly. Ultimately, the responsibility for morality was supposed to be shared by all. There was great concern expressed in the magazine, however, that equal rights for men and women (*danjo doken*) would cause the Japanese household to resemble a Western one in which women dictated to men.

It was in keeping with this same nation-building project that Tsuda, another contributor, took on the subject of prostitution. He argued that because "ignorant" commoners destroyed their homes by squandering their family fortunes on prostitutes, which in turn posed a serious threat to "the splendid Japanese Empire," the immediate eradication of prostitution was the means by which every Japanese citizen would prosper (Tsuda 1875: 517). Statements such as these helped structure public sentiment for new plans to keep Japan an empire untouched by foreign powers. They also suggest that public calls to escape poverty and colonization were often put in terms of class and gender roles within the newly "modernized" Japan. There was a thin line between equal rights for women and oppression of men; upper-class women would adopt a new role and lead the way toward modernization and Japan's proper place in the world, and lower-class women would follow.

Many of the views expressed in *Meiroku Zashii* took it for granted that female virtue in Japan had long been in decay well before any attempts to modernize. However, the debates and concerns of Meiji officials about the importance of women to a "new" Japan and about which women would lead the changes are especially important because much of the Western criticism of Japan centered on the Japanese woman's "traditional" position in society. Not only because of the debates on the proper place of women in creating a domestic empire, but also because of the increase in numbers of those Westerners who felt qualified to give advice to Meiji policymakers, there were numerous calls from both home and abroad to look at the women question. The government set up educational programs and supported prescriptive public campaigns to create a *ryosai kenbo* (good wife and wise mother) nation (Nolte and Hastings 1991). The concept was influenced at least on the surface by early twentieth-century Western notions of moral motherhood.

Debate about the *fujin mondai* (women question) was not limited to Japan's early industrial period. Throughout Japan's twentieth-century history, the state utilized various sexual images projected by expert "public men" journalists, intellectuals, and public figures. It was able to "capitalize on an immense capacity to amass knowledge and exercise power" (Tamanoi 1991: 795). However, during the Meiji period, more "public women"—mainly upper class—also used an archetype of nationalized Japanese womanhood to suggest that women being in control of their lives and their sexual behavior was key to women's equal position in Japanese society (Sievers 1983). Early women's groups like the *seito* (bluestockings) argued in their own magazines for cultural and later economic change for the Japanese woman. Yet the Japanese woman in question was usually of the upper class.[3]

It was also the Meiji government's goal of industrialization coupled with cultural learning that led to an increase in the number of women who began to work in factories (Hane 1986).[4] But as the words in the Meiroku magazine would suggest, the women who were to lead the way for all Japanese were again those of the upper classes. The textile industry was chosen as a primary site for this new female responsibility because it was already established and well recognized in world markets. Textile exports to the West could provide quick capital for industrial growth and government policies, including imperial expansion. So in clear illustration of the power of symbolism in conjunction with material realities, those first women who were called to help the Japanese textile industry in its early stages were daughters of the ex-samurai class. However, this soon changed as factory workers became mostly the "good daughters" of the poor.

Labor for wages had a tremendous influence on both men and women of Japan's lower classes (Ueno 1987; Uno 1991). But it is the construction of factory girls and their position within Japan's efforts to become economically strong that should be noted. Factory girls were seen as workers who, if controlled by their families, government, and business, were crucial to Japanese economic vitality. The factory girl was both an exemplar to the women of Japan and testimony to the Western world about the use of women in the creation of an industrialized power. It was soon clear that rural and lower-class women would do the bulk of industrial labor. Government and business leaders, as well as early Japanese feminists, could speak of young women working in factories in terms of their allegiance to both Western (virginal) and Japanese (filial piety) values. Responsible for upholding notions fabricated out of the nationalist thoughts of ex-samurai government elites, young powerless women provided the needed labor for Japan's grand entrance as both a colonial and economic power. Yet as the need for female factory workers continued to increase, ideas about female virtue and working women soon came to represent a "new view of womanhood presented in the guise of tradition" (Uno 1991: 38).[5]

SHADOWED PICTURES

Part of my self-imposed regime of language study was to watch the evening news (the one not dubbed in English) every day and ask my coworkers the next morning about anything that had happened that I didn't understand. I remember watching the story about Miyazaki-san during August of 1989. I heard the news anchor say that Miyazaki had lived with his mother and had been obsessed with pornographic videos, including those of his own mutilation murders of four young girls. The next morning in the teacher's room, I didn't have to ask anyone about the story; my coworkers were all talking about the horrible crime and how unbelievable it was. Yamaguchi-sensei, both a mathematics teacher and a Buddhist priest, asked me what I thought about Miyazaki. I said that I had seen the story the night before but could not understand the role of the videos in his crime. He then proceeded to explain to me that it was the 6,000 videos that Miyazaki owned that had caused him to abduct, sexually abuse, and kill his victims. He added that this was not normal Japanese behavior, it was in part the result of the increase in gaijin *(foreigners) in Japan.*

What are traditional Japanese values? Almost a century after factory girls were called upon by their government in the name of Japanese tradition to work in factories modeled after those in Europe and the United States, ideas of what it means to be Japanese are often juxtaposed to a single Western culture. Why was it important to him that an increase in foreigners could be linked to a heinous sex crime? How would he have answered if I had asked him to which foreigners was he referring? Did he mean the legions of blond native speakers/teachers of English escaping bad job prospects in their own countries? Or did he mean the increasing numbers of Brazilian laborers who lived in our town who were also part of the global shifts of capital and labor? Did he mean me, an employee of the prefectural government? Constructs of memory, history, and "tradition" are invented and reinvented constantly (see Hobsbawm and Ranger 1983; O'Brien and Roseberry 1991). In Japan, an analysis of constructions of both past and present representations suggests that what constitutes "Japan" has varied across different time periods (Kelly 1991; Tobin 1992).[6] Once again, looking at gender helps to illuminate the links between nation, allegiance, and collective memories.

As a result of influence from China before the Meiji era, Japanese women had been expected to adhere to Confucian constructions of womanly virtues, which included obedience, purity, good will, frugality, modesty, and diligence (Walthall 1991). However, with the economic shifts and government policies noted above, what had been reserved for the elite became central to popular notions of the proper place for Japanese women of all classes within the reconstituted definition of Japanese economic and cultural success. As in the enterprise of empire elsewhere, according to their particular defined place, many Japanese women were being asked by their government to prove their allegiance in economic terms. However, the notion that Japanese women should be judged on a personal level was growing in popularity. The two icons discussed below suggest how ideas of work, sexuality, gender, and the utility of references to "Western culture" and un-Japanese behavior served to create hierarchies within which individual women could be judged and ranked. Those women who couldn't or wouldn't be part of the enterprise of empire were linked to accepted constructions of Western sexual behavior and attitudes.

Komori

Tamanoi's (1991) study of the *komori* (nursemaids) provides evidence of the creation of hierarchies in conjunction with national goals during the beginning of this century. These preteen girls from poor rural families were sold and used as indentured servants, serving as nursemaids and often as apprentices to those "masters," who often were tradespeople. Shifts in what the *komori* symbolized changed as the needs of government and business changed also. As would be expected from the discussion above, at the beginning of the Meiji period reforms, the *komori* were hailed in the press as model citizens and as evidence of the benefits of increased labor productivity for the good of Japanese military projects. Glowing accounts of the *komori* soon were replaced, however, with reports that their behavior was considered a threat to Japanese tradition. Why? Quite possibly because of shifting ideas of what the *komori*, as lower-class women, could provide the domestic project. As proper allegiance to the empire came to mean that upper- and middle-class women's principal duties to their country's economic success were to raise their children and keep their husbands' homes satisfactorily—in accordance with *ryosai kenbo* policies—*komori* technically were not needed in their employers' homes. The *komori* could, however, prove their allegiance to Japan by providing needed factory labor. But, the public explanation in the newspapers of the day was that the *komori* were a bad influence on their charges, Japan's future citizens. This allegation referred in part to the *komori*'s improper references to body parts and sexual intercourse in their daily language.[7]

The "traditional" circumspection according to which the *komori* were being judged was neither fully accepted nor venerable. The state campaigns and debates of the early twentieth century, which sought to define and redefine Japanese women's sexuality, tended to disregard or ignore the existence before the turn of the century of *Yoshiwara* (pleasure quarters) or the trade in young girls from southern Japan as prostitutes to various parts of Asia (Hane 1982). Young Japanese women from poor, oftentimes rural, homes were "sold" for sex work and would serve out contracts in cities like Tokyo, Osaka, Singapore, and Shanghai; their families would receive a small sum of money. Their customers were often the same men who were developing appeals to Japanese "traditional" values. Yet the "tradition" that was being invented was less about women's sexual chastity and more about the desire to commodify labor rather than sex. Also, the illusions of virginal and chaste "traditions" collapse when compared to accounts of village *yobai* (night wandering) documented by at least one Meiji era ethnographer, Yanagita Kunio (Walthall 1991). The disapproval of the *komori* expressed in newspapers ignored the type of nightly premarital sexual behavior between young men and women that was tolerated and in many cases even encouraged by their communities (Smith and Wissell 1982).

THE MODERN GIRL

Despite a down cycle in the world economy, by the Taisho era (1912–1926) Japan had gained economic strength and was increasing the scope of its imperial empire in Asia. On the basis of the changes in the Japanese economy during the Meiji era, one might assume that the ideal Japanese woman at this time would either be in the home practicing typical Japanese activities, in a factory working for the good of the economy, or farming in a traditional Japanese manner. Although this picture may be part of a collective Japanese memory today, during the 1920s what a woman was doing was more varied, and ideas about what a woman should be doing with her life were still subject to debate.

The Taisho period in Japan—as in most of the world at the time—was a time of recession. Regardless of economic difficulties, early Japanese feminists were asking for equal rights while female factory workers were participating in labor strikes. Meanwhile Japan's emerging middle class was in trouble. Young single and married women—future and present good wives and wise mothers—were working in order to help their families survive, although for some middle-class women working was a way in which to experience independence and self-reliance. Regardless of their motives, middle-class women who worked in newly formed pink- and white-collar jobs were discriminated against in the work force. Many women across class lines were openly showing disregard for their expected places of loyalty. As an image of unpatriotic behavior, the modern girl became a means for a variety of Japanese to address the proper place of working women through their sexual behavior. The Westernized actions of the modern girl ultimately permitted decadence and economic failure to be linked to the West.

The modern girl as an image of the late 1920s in Japan was part symbol and part reality. Even though first appearing in a woman's magazine, the concept of a free and easy "new working woman" of the department stores and offices of urban centers soon became a recognized image in the 1920s. By their consumption patterns, middle-class working women (*chūryū shokugyō fujin*), who as a group admired and sometimes aspired to the modern-girl image, were a source of patronage for department stores and a booming *biyoin* (beauty salon) industry. These outlets for working women's wages were encouraged by businesses and the government. In purely economic terms, middle-class working women could spend their wages on goods and services, which in turn helped the Japanese economy.

Yet at the same time the image of the "modern girl" became synonymous with "unnatural," "inauthentic" behavior, with selfishness, and with a disruption of Japan's progress. As an example of Western frivolity, it became the object of nationalist criticism. In political terms, the modern girl in part symbolized working women, who by the 1930s were clearly demanding equal rights from the government and their employers. In an increasingly nationalistic atmosphere, the image of a "natural" or "authentic" patriotic woman was becoming indispensible in defining what was Japanese and what was not.

The "modern girl" took on different meanings for different groups of Japanese. Feminists of privilege who had been influenced by Marxist theory through education or trips abroad could use the construct of the modern girl as evidence of a "ruling class in decline" without fully recognizing the way the imagery played upon negative depictions of working-class women (Silverberg 1991). The women who were at the forefront of Japan's first feminist movement in the Taisho era in various organizations rarely incorporated working class or rural women into their efforts. Women's organizations at this time were varied and by no means shared a common agenda. Yet whether in the Reform Society or the appropriately named Women's Patriotic Association, Japan's early feminists rarely made connections with working-class women (Sievers 1983). Their own class positions provided access to Western political thought and feminist theory, yet shielded them from working women's daily experiences.

For those who would most openly criticize the modern girl—the government and the right-wing magazines—she was a threat to both traditional Japan and the emergent economic system. Because part of the image of the modern girl was that of a spoiled selfish woman who had multiple sex partners, to be called a modern girl in public insinuated that a woman had allegiance to no one, something that was not Japanese. Working women who had no loyalty were out of control and were in direct opposition to state policies and moral education, which centered on the family. Disregard for tradition also involved appearance. Modern girls were depicted as discarding the kimono for Western dress and wearing bobbed hairstyles instead of long hair. The modern girl was thus seen as an example of increasing Japanese consumption of Western commodities and "over-Westernization." She wanted too many things from the West and not enough from Japan.

The *komori*'s shifting value to the Japanese industrial project, and the modern girl's negative image during a period of slow economic growth, were images that were tied to both government and popular conceptions of nationalized womanhood. Both illustrate how, as Japanese women began to occupy more prominent public space as consumers, laborers, legal subjects, and political activists, images were manipulated by Japanese government and businesses for economic and political consumption during a mercurial period in Japan's history. They were images—occasionally used to illustrate the fundamental inadequacies in Western culture—that served as referents, whether accepted or not, for the lives of individual Japanese women and their families.

From this sketch of images found in Western research on pre–World War II Japan, nationalized womanhood and allegiance aided both government and women's rights activists in supporting different assumptions about women's role in Japan. Increasingly, sexual behavior was portrayed in newspapers and magazines as a national trait through which hierarchies could be drawn between women and across class and nation. In either case, constructed images served to hide material realities and soon became part of collective Japanese memories.

RACE, CLASS, GENDER—JAPANESE STYLE

Another part of my self-imposed "better yourself in Japan" regime was to exercise at a gym after work at least three times a week. Usually I would shower afterward and put back on the same clothing that I had worn to my office. On this day, for some reason, I didn't put my pantyhose back on. Instead I went barelegged and wore my tennis shoes. When I got to the train station, I realized that I needed to buy a new train card. While I was digging through my bag looking for my money purse, I saw two policemen watching me. I paid them no mind and bought my vending card and then with it bought my ticket. I began to walk to the ticket wicket, but remembered I had left my umbrella back at the ticket machine. As I turned to go get my umbrella, I heard one of the policemen ask me in English, "May I see your passport please." Flustered, shocked, and a little frightened, I asked back in Japanese, "Naze? Watashi wa muzai desu. Dorobo dewa arimasen" (Why? I'm innocent. I'm not a thief). I then told them I didn't have a passport with me, but I did have my gaijin card.[8] When they saw where I worked and for whom, things changed. My ID showed that I had the highest status visa given out by the Japanese government—the same as that of a foreign diplomat in Japan. As the policemen apologized and begged my pardon, one of them began to explain that because I was not wearing pantyhose, I had been mistaken for a Filipina (read, prostitute/bar hostess).

To the policemen who interrogated me that evening, I was "unreadable" or perhaps maybe even too easily read. I was someone who didn't seem to fit into a set framework of proper behavior for a woman in the train station late at night, but at the same time I could be put into a convenient if inappropriate category of unsavory foreign woman. I must have caused them great distress. Yet what would my own stress level have been if I had forgotten my identification that evening? What if I truly had been a Filipina? Was I unfair to read a misreading of my national identity as an accusation of prostitution? I couldn't help wondering as I was riding home that night why the policeman had used my lack of pantyhose as an excuse for mistaken identity. If my lack of proper dress was not the real reason, then why did he choose that as the way to apologize for a misreading of my status in Japan? Of which aspects of raced, classed, and gendered images and the hierarchies they create in Japan was I unaware?

DIALOGUE IN ABSENTIA

Suzuki-sensei called one day and asked if I would like to meet a friend of hers who had recently returned from a summer in the United States and wanted to meet me. Invitations like this were very common, considering my relative "celebrity" status; however, I did not always accept. This time I did, because I knew Suzuki-sensei was very involved with the Japanese teachers' union. I believe to this day that it was this membership that, in the politically conservative Shizuoka prefecture, put her at risk in her job. I sensed that meeting her friend would not end up as a "guest gaijin" experience.[9] We met at a coffee shop and I was surprised to learn that Ishida-san had married into a ready-made family—her husband had two teenage children from a previous marriage—and she had gone alone over the recent summer vacation to do a homestay in Atlanta. Listening to the two women talk, I realized that they were both very conscious of many current political and social issues and were willing to talk to me about them, which was quite refreshing. As we began to discuss discrimination in Japan and the United States, Ishida-san confessed that she had felt "closer" to the black people in Atlanta than the white people. She continued in English, "While I was in Atlanta, I felt what it was like to be a minority for the first time. I knew when I went to the shops that some of the workers did not approve of me and I received unfamiliar stares sometimes. I had the opportunity to go to a black church one Sunday. I had known before that blacks could sing well and had a very natural sense of music, but there I could experience it for the first time. The women wore such beautiful hats and the children were so well behaved. I was deeply moved. I found in my stay that the blacks were much more natural than whites. They had more soul."[10]

In 1921 Uesugi Sumio, a self-professed Christian minister, concluded after visiting numerous United States cities that whites were insincere and that he preferred the friendliness of negroes such as the Garveyites (Hill 1984). Uesugi planned to send Garvey pamphlets back to Japan in order to make his government aware of the strength of the Garvey movement. Uesugi's experience with the Universal Improvement Association was a sign of the times. Ishida-san's report to me almost seventy years later is also indicative of the time in which it took place. As a middle-class housewife in a ready-made family who visited the United States alone, Ishida-san's experience says something about the realities of "women's" position in Japan today. As a woman who was interested in social issues, her preconceived images and observations are both ironic and predictable in a world in which ideas about behavior and identity are up for global consumption. Why did she feel closer to blacks in Atlanta? What does Ishida-san's tale suggest about the racial experiences of Japanese in the United States as well as the stereotypes about blacks in Japan and elsewhere?

An increased number of Japanese middle-class businessmen and their families are returning to Japan—reminiscent of the Meiji period—with firsthand knowledge of what it is like "over there." As their numbers have increased, so have the calls for returnees from abroad to play a central part in preparing Japan for its latest global role. History cannot really repeat itself—or can it? Looking at the historical record illustrates that eerie similarities and ironic contradictions are part of both the historical past and present.

Arnold Rubin (1974) and John Russell (1991a, 1991b) suggest that, beginning with Japan's contact with Portuguese black slave crews in the 1500s and Commodore Perry's Black Ship's minstrel shows in the late 1800s, the Japanese have continuously either sympathized with blacks or tried to outdo the West when it comes to racist attitudes. It is surely part of the complexity of Japanese attitudes toward race that the Japanese noted in their version of war propaganda that racism lay at the root of American atrocities against the Japanese. Images of the mistreatment of blacks were used by the Japanese government in both Japan and abroad as justification of World War II.[11] Americans were simply unable to think of colored people as humans (Dower 1986). In its war propaganda, the United States portrayed the Japanese as monkeys, a slur used historically in the West to refer to blacks.

Even though Uesugi's Garvey pamphlets might fall on deaf ears in Japan today, Japanese notions of race have been and continue to be contingent upon domestic thoughts about global issues. There has never been one single Japanese stand on the "black question" in Japan. However, the efforts of dominant classes in Japan to find a place in the "new world order" cannot be separated from the dissemination in Japanese popular culture of images of the unemployed welfare mother of color with six children and of the notion that the decline of America is the result of the loss of "traditional American values."

PROSCRIPTIONS FOR SUCCESS

Was there a colonial collective "language of domination" that over the years has become a collective language of discrimination? If so, did those who stood to gain the most in Japan—in the form of government allegiance and business profits—use these forms of discourse to place Japan within a global system, which at its core advanced racial differences and hierarchies? Japan's social structure has never been the kind of unified, homogeneous society it is portrayed to be by the Japanese or believed to have been by many Western scholars. In their defense, Japanese officials often have responded to the idea of "Japan the colonizer of Asia" by insisting that the same discussion must examine notions of "Japan the occupied little brother of the West" (Aoki 1990). Japan's politicians have often said that they have no experience in dealing with a minority perspective and thus must be forgiven for any transgressions they commit. Individual citizens also do the same; Endo-sensei and the police officer in the train station apologized to me in much of the same way. The long history in Japan of "dealing" with minority groups such as the Ainu, native-born Koreans, and *burakumin* (a stigmatized caste group) just doesn't seem to count.

Any refined notion of national identity—even in Japan—mandates a historical contextualization of race, class, and gender in relationship to the global political economy. The present narrative of the reasons for "the Japanese Miracle," as it is told and inscribed into public discourse both inside and outside of Japan, is the result of a long period of defining and redefining the acceptable behavior of the productive citizenry of successful industrial powers.

Cecilia and I couldn't be more physically different from each other. She is quite fair with white/blond hair and blue eyes, while I am dark and tall with very curly hair and brown eyes. We became quite good friends after we met in our first weeks in Japan, despite the fact that we were different in other ways too. I was the "big city American" and she was from an economically depressed rural area in the north of England. Cecilia and I would sometimes compare mental "notes," jokingly trying to outdo each other in degrees of "standing out" in different situations. In Tokyo, as a kokujin (black person), I was often able to claim greater standout status, while at festivals it was Cecilia who received the fuss and comments. Our jobs often required an appearance at government functions, where we, along with other employees, would act as representatives of the kokusai (international) efforts of our prefectural government. We were often called upon to give speeches about how internationalism worked in our home countries. At one of these functions Cecilia—who still lives in Japan and is married to a Japanese man—and I found ourselves constantly being asked to have our pictures taken together, despite the fact that there were six other Westerners there also. That day numerous people asked if the two of us would come to their homes as a pair, while others stood at a distance, in what appeared to be a mixture of awe and fright. Later that evening, we both agreed that together we had probably been something of a sensory overload that day. Cecilia commented, "I guess that we provide a chance to see what is only seen in the movies, but together we would be a novelty anywhere."

Who benefited from Cecilia and me living and working in Japan—our students, neighbors, the Japanese government, us? The official reason for our presence was the "internationalization" of Japan. Yet it was rumored that some Japanese government officials also thought of us as trade balancers between Japan and the West, like oranges from California or tins of biscuits from Harrods. The fact that we symbolized various things in Japan not only speaks to Cecilia's adopted homeland, but also hints at other configurations of globalized privilege and stratification.

Without ever having been in Japan in large numbers, Western women have been in an "interlocution" of sorts with Japanese women for approximately a century. Encouraged by the government and business expectations and constructions of proper behavior for a model Japanese woman, a dialogue in absentia with the West has also been a means through which some Japanese women—usually those who could "afford" it—have questioned the position of women in Japan during the twentieth century. This dialogue has recently become more and more face to face, as Cecilia's and my presence in Japan illustrates. As more foreigners enter Japan, the cultural hierarchies that helped build an empire in gendered terms will become increasingly more useful for those Japanese who wish to distinguish among various groups of Japanese and foreigners. The Japanese men and women whose voices are heard throughout this text are real-life Japanese citizens. Their words suggest that even if individuals dispute the way things "are" in Japan, their belief in fundamental principles of being Japanese structures their individual understandings of national identities (Field 1993). For some, especially the men whose views appear here, hierarchies based on popularized stereotypes help to form a notion of collective respectability and a Japanese sense of cultural pride. The linkage between continued Japanese economic and cultural success and the assemblage of a Japanese national identity has continually been made through the popularization and interconnection of assumptions about sexual preferences, class obligations, duties to family and nation, and the proper calibration of Japanese tradition and Western morality.

Images of Japanese women's sexuality, work, and proper place must be placed within the various domestic and international contexts in which they were generated. Examining these images and the shifts within the global political economy to which they are connected suggests that the longer the twentieth-century's domestic empire building has been going on, the more important sexual behavior has become in categorizing both the material and the symbolic aspects of the enterprise. Ironically, the Western colonialism that the Meiji era leaders were desperately struggling to avoid has become a source for an image of women's sexuality and in particular of the image of "colored" women as behaving differently from women who show allegiance to the empire. I believe that images of traditional Japanese women's sexuality are currently being contrasted with those of women who are, for whatever reason, "colored" not Japanese.

The last century of colonial passion plays on a world stage has allowed Japan, the national actor, often to play a cameo—but always well choreographed—part. Current thoughts in the world about what it means to be a successful nation in cultural, political, and economic terms resemble in many ways the hierarchies of the past that allowed colonial empires to survive and prosper. Official and unofficial power hierarchies—as well as the creation of a popular domestic image of what it means to be "Japanese"—are part of continuing global relationships of dominance and power and thus underscore the notion that national identity as an image nurtures the same kind of environment as colonial enterprises. In such realities, the struggle for acceptance or efforts to resist are often made in terms that cross varied material existences. Feminists from the Meiji era, striking female workers, and Ishida-san, as resistors to the enterprise of empire, nevertheless fight with "accepted" ideas of Japan and the rest of the world. The creation of a specific national identity in gendered terms, like colonial projects abroad, benefits those who hold economic and cultural capital. Regardless of how lines are drawn between individuals, both inside and outside nations, the enterprise of building a collective national identity is deeply embedded in a world of power differentials, cultural imagery, and complex histories.

NOTES

This paper owes much thanks to the many Japanese people in Japan who made my first experience in Japan "the toughest job I ever loved." Special credit goes to Hasegawa Akiko who taught me how grass can blow in the wind and survive. I also wish to thank Norma Field and Ogawa Setsuko for understanding why I sometimes do not follow the advice they always generously give to me. I am especially grateful to Micaela di Leonardo and Michele Mitchell for their constructive comments, suggestions, and encouragement which are always beyond the call of duty.

1. Many of the remarks such as those made by Prime Minister Nakasone in 1986, which trace the decline of the United States to increasing numbers of blacks and Latinos, are used by Americans of all identities to criticize the Japanese. U.S. newspapers in particular often report Japanese corporations' disregard for Western ideas concerning sexual and racial discrimination (see Reich 1992).

2. European colonial projects provided a kind of universal whiteness that privilege lower- and middle-class expatriates over colonial subjects. Thus colonial officials and the like were able to become honorary members of the upper class.

3. Most certainly these groups were influenced by socialist debate going on throughout the world during the early part of this century. Besides arguing for a change in women's role in the family, for example, Japan's women socialists also offered critiques of the Japanese colonial empire. Interestingly enough, they voiced concern that Japanese military and economic campaigns in Asia were "emulating the worst traditions of Western imperialism" (Sievers 1983).

4. A strong connection between the government and private business was in part an acknowledgment by the Japanese government that industrial growth and a build-up of Japan's military were the primary means through which colonization by the West was to be avoided (Tsurumi 1990).

5. Until the Meiji period, lack of virtue was linked not to sexual promiscuity but more to disregard for Confucian principles of filial piety (Nolte and Hastings 1991).

6. Many aspects of Japan's writing, religion, agriculture, and food production have been adopted from imports and contact with the greater Asian continent, dating back to the Yayoi period (around 300 B.C.–300 A.D.). Much of what was then and still is today considered by the Japanese to be "unique culture" has its roots elsewhere.

7. Tamanoi concludes that in this environment, language soon became a viable form of resistance for the *komori*. See Abu-Lughod (1990) and Gal (1991) for a discussion of young women's use of language and resistance to notions of tradition.

8. All resident aliens must register at their local city hall, be fingerprinted, and carry what is called among English speakers a "gaijin card." This identification card that I showed the policeman included where I lived, whom I worked for, and my nationality.

9. I use the term here as it was often used by expatriates in Japan while I was there. Guest Gaijin experiences implied being treated like a recent arrival to Japan, regardless of how long one had lived there, and often revolved around being "shown off" to neighbors or relatives. Quite often these invitations resulted in a request to be the "living English" expert and rate the English ability of the children of the household.

10. This Japanese fascination/romanticism concerning blacks can be seen in Japanese mass media (CM's or television commercials), the popularity of *nama* (real-life) jazz tours of New York City, Japanese dreadlocked "rastafarians," novels by Japanese women revealing the unknown secrets of sex with black mens as well as in the 1989 New Year's Eve Red and White Show, which included a performance by a Japanese rap group complete with crotch-grabbing musicians and references in English to "fly girls."

11. Dower (1986) mentions that during World War II, the Japanese government sent an operative to the American Nation of Islam, which led to members of the Nation undergoing investigation by the federal government for sedition. The reason behind "stirring up the Negroes" by the Japanese has been forgotten for the most part. Japan's involvement in the Nation of Islam is not presented here to suggest that the Japanese government's involvement was purely altruistic, especially in light of the research on the history of Japanese negative attitudes toward blacks in literature and science (see Wagamatsu 1967). Instead, I point out here that the Japanese have had a history of dealing with Western racism and have not always been totally "ignorant" of western attitudes toward blacks. Rubin traces these shifts back even further by suggesting that during the fifteenth and sixteenth centuries, "Japanese attitudes towards slavery were generally antipathetic" (1974: 9). Perhaps some Japanese attitudes about slavery were even stronger considering that some Japanese were enslaved by Portuguese sailors while they were in Japan during this 200-year period. Rubin also notes that Japanese also served as slaves for the African and Indian slaves of the Portuguese, which Jesuit missionaries in Japan at the time considered to be an obstacle to their efforts to convert Japan to Christianity.

REFERENCES

Aoki, Tamotsu.
   1990. *Nihonbunkaron no henyo: sengonihon no bunka to aidentitii*. Tokyo: Chūōkōronsha.
Abu-Lughod, Lila.
   1990. The romance of resistance tracing transformations of power through Bedouin women. *American Ethnologist* 17(1): 41–55.
Bernstein, Gail Lee, ed.
   1991. Recreating Japanese women, 1600–1945. Berkeley: University of California Press.
Braisted, William R.
   1976. *Meiroku Zasshi: Journal of the Japanese Enlightenment*. Cambridge: Harvard University Press.

Bryant, Tamie.
    1991. For the sake of the country, for the sake of the family: The oppresssive impact of family registra-
        tion on women and minority in Japan. *UCLA Law Review*. 39: 109–68.
Chatterjee, Partha.
    1989. Colonialism, nationalism, and colonized women: The contest in India. *American Ethnologist* 16
        (4): 622–33.
Cooper, Frederick, and Ann L. Stoler.
    1989. Tensions of empire: Colonial control and visions of rule. *American Ethnologist* 16 (4): 609–21.
di Leonardo, Micaela.
    Forthcoming. *Exotics at Home*. Chicago: University of Chicago Press.
Dower, John W.
    1986. *War Without Mercy: Race and Power in the Pacific War*. New York: Pantheon.
Field, Norma.
    1993. *In the Realm of a Dying Emperor: A Portrait of Japan at Century's End*. New York: Vintage Books.
Gilroy, Paul.
    1991. *"There Ain't No Black in the Union Jack": The Cultural Politics of Race and Nation*. Chicago: Univer-
        sity of Chicago Press.
Gordon, Andrew, ed.
    1993. *Postwar Japan as History*. Berkeley: University of California Press.
Hane, Mikiso.
    1982. *Peasants, Rebels, and Outcastes: The Underside of Modern Japan*. New York: Pantheon Books.
    1986. *Modern Japan: A Historical Survey*. Boulder, CO: Westview.
Hill, Robert A., ed.
    1984. *The Marcus Garvey and Universal Negro Improvement Association Papers*. Los Angeles: University of
        California Press.
Hobsbawm, Eric, and Terence Ranger, eds.
    1983. *The Invention of Tradition*. Cambridge: Cambridge University Press.
Kelly, William W.
    1986. Rationalization and nostalgia: Cultural dynamics of new middle class Japan. *American Ethnologist*
        13 (4): 603–18.
    1991. Directions in the anthropology of contemporary Japan. *Annual Review of Anthropology*. 20:
        395–431.
Nolte, Sharon H., and Sally Ann Hastings.
    1991. The Meiji state's policy towards women, 1890–1910. In *Recreating Japanese women, 1600–1945*,
        ed. Gail Lee Bernstein, 151–74. Berkeley: University of California Press.
O'Brien, Jay, and William Roseberry, eds.
    1991. *Golden Ages, Dark Ages: Imagining the Past in Anthropology and History*. Berkeley: University of
        California Press.
Reich, Robert B.
    1992. Is Japan really out to get us? *New York Times*, 9 February, pp. 1, 24, 25.
Rubin, Arnold.
    1974. *Black Nanban: Africans in Japan During the Sixteenth Century*. Bloomington: Indiana University,
        African Studies Program.
Russell, John.
    1991a. Race and reflexivity: The black other in contemporary Japanese mass culture. *Cultural Anthro-
        pology* 6 (1): 3–25.
    1991b. Narratives of denial: Racial chauvinism and the black other in Japan. *Japan Quarterly* 38 (4): 416–28.
Sakatani, Shiroshi.
    1875 [1976]. On concubines. In *Meiroku Zashii*, ed. William Reynolds Braisted, 392–99. Tokyo: Uni-
        versity of Tokyo Press.

Sievers, Sharon L.

    1983. *Flowers in Salt: The Beginnings of Feminist Consciousness in Modern Japan.* Stanford, CA: Stanford University Press.

Silverbury, Miriam.

    1991. The modern girl as militant. In *Recreating Japanese Women, 1600–1945,* ed. Gail Lee Bernstein, pp. 239–66. Berkeley: University of California Press.

Smith, Robert J., and Elle Wiswell.

    1982. *The Women of Suye Mura.* Chicago: University of Chicago Press.

Tamanoi, Mariko Asano.

    1991. The culture and history of *komori* (nursemaids) in modern Japan. *Journal of Asian Studies* 50 (4): 793–817.

Tobin, Joseph J., ed.

    1992. *Re-made in Japan: Everyday Life and Consumer Taste in a Changing Society.* New Haven: Yale University Press.

Tsuda, Mamichi.

    1875 [1976]. On destroying prostitution. In *Meiroku Zashii,* ed. William Reynolds Braisted, 517–18. Tokyo: University of Tokyo Press.

Tsorumi, E. Patricia.

    1980. *Factory Girls: Women in the Thread Mills of Meiji Japan.* Princeton: Princeton University Press.

Ueno, Chizuko.

    1987. The position of Japanese women reconsidered. *Current Anthropology Supplement* 28 (4): 75–84.

Uno, Kathleen S.

    1991. Women and changes in the household division of labor. In *Recreating Japanese Women, 1600–1945,* ed. Gail Lee Bernstein, 17–41. Berkeley: University of California Press.

Wagamatsu, Hiroshi.

    1967. The social perception of skin color in Japan. *Daedulus* 96: 407–43.

Walthall, Anne.

    1992. The life cycle of farm women in Tokugawa Japan. In *Recreating Japanese Women, 1600–1945,* ed. Gail Lee Bernstein, 42–70. Berkeley: University of California Press.

33 Movie Stars and Islamic Moralism in Egypt

Lila Abu-Lughod

In Egypt, local westernized elites are singled out as sources of corruption and moral decadence by Islamic groups deploying a populist rhetoric. An absence of faith is portrayed as the cause of this elite's immorality and greed, while the embracing of Islam is offered as the solution to the country's considerable social and economic problems. Despite the efforts such groups have made to provide social services, and especially medical clinics, for the poor who are not well served by overtaxed state institutions now under IMF and USAID pressure to privatize, they seem to have no serious programs for wealth distribution, while at the same time they support capitalism and private property.[1] An important question that no one seems to have explored is why a political discourse in which morality displaces class as the central social problem is so appealing.

Instead of focusing on the social programs or philosophies of such groups, I want to explore this question by way of a close analysis of a sensationalized phenomenon: the decision by some female film and stage stars to give up their careers and take on the *higab*, the new kind of head-covering that is the most visible symbol of the growing popularity of a self-consciously Muslim identity in Egypt and elsewhere in the Muslim world. The complex reactions of rural and poor women toward these stars, I will argue, illuminate the dynamics of the Islamist appeal. Leila Ahmed has suggested, with some justification, that the dominance of the new veiling and the affiliation with Islamism it represents mark "a broad demographic change—a change that has democratized mainstream culture and mores," whereby the emergent middle classes, rather than the formerly culturally dominant upper and middle classes, define the norms.[2] I will argue, however, that the case of the media stars shows how the discourse of morality associated with the new veil works to produce a false sense of egalitarianism that distracts from the significant and ongoing problems of class inequality in Egypt.

Lila Abu-Lughod teaches anthropology at New York University. Her books include two ethnographies: *Veiled Sentiments* (California, 1986), a study of how Bedouin women in Egypt use oral poetry to express sentiments that violate the moral code; and *Writing Women's Worlds: Bedouin Stories* (California, 1993), a critical ethnography that uses the everyday stories of these women to challenge a variety of stereotypes about gender relations in Arab societies. She also edited *Remaking Women: Feminism and Modernity in the Middle East* (Princeton, forthcoming), a book that examines the legacy of turn-of-the-century feminism in contemporary politics, including Islamism.

BORN AGAIN STARS

On display during the first months of 1993 in the bookstores and street stalls of Cairo was a small but controversial book marking (and marketing) what it claimed was a major social phenomenon. On the front cover was a bold announcement that the book, published in 1991, was in its eighth printing; on the back cover, a quote from the widely popular conservative religious figure Sheikh Al-Sharawi, himself a media star because of his weekly television program: "After more than 20 actresses and radio personalities had adopted the veil [*higab*] . . . war was declared on them . . . those carrying the banner of this war are the 'sex stars' and 'merchants of lust.'"[3]

Entitled *Repentant Artists and the Sex Stars*, the book was coauthored by a man and a woman, 'Imad Nasif and Amal Khodayr. Yet only a photo of the man can be found on the title page: he is youthful, wearing a loud patterned shirt and sitting thoughtfully at a desk. One presumes that the coauthor is veiled and does not want to appear. Below the photo is a quotation, unattributed, suggesting the authors' admiration for what they represent as the courage of these embattled "born again" stars: "The most honorable eagle is the one that flies against the wind and the powerful fish is the one who swims against the current . . . and truth is worth dying to achieve." On the following pages are the assertion of copyright protection (the book has no publisher and only lists the post office box and fax number of the authors) and a quote from the Koran about how God loves those who repent.

Intended to promote the so-called repentant actresses, this little book includes lengthy interviews with many of these famous actresses, belly dancers, and singers, stars of film and stage, who have given up their careers and have taken on the veil. The women tell their stories and present "confessions." The book also contains some interviews with their supportive husbands, an approving interview with Sheikh Al-Sharawi, and a brief section at the end in which prominent actresses still in the business tersely give their opinions on what their "repentant artist" sisters have done (usually stressing individuals' freedom of choice) and defend the value and religious correctness of acting and of "true art" (often in distinction from the commercial productions of the last fifteen years).

As the pitiful confession of Hala Al-Safy, a famous belly dancer, illustrates, the discourse of these repentant stars demonizes the world of performing and portrays their renunciation of it as a way of becoming closer to God. The authors state that she wrote, in her own hand, the following words for the book:

> I confess and acknowledge that I, Suhayr Hasan Abdeen and famous as the dancer Hala Al-Safy . . . left my life in the hands of the Devil to play with and to do what he wanted without my feeling the sins of what I did, until God willed and desired to remove me from this swamp . . . and I acknowledge and confess that the life that they call the life of art . . . is empty of art and I acknowledge that I lived this life. . . . Just as I acknowledge and confess that I regret . . . regret . . . regret every moment that I lived far from God in the world of night and art and parties. . . . I entrust God to accept my remorse and my repentance. (33)

The dramatic story told by Shams Al-Barudy, a movie star whose name, according to the authors, "was associated with seduction roles" (49) repeats these themes. Some lengthy quotes give the full flavor of the "born again" narratives. Al-Barudy recounts two experiences as transformative: reading a modern poem about veiling, and going to Mecca to perform the lesser pilgrimage *('umra)*:

> I was at home preparing sweets when my little daughter Nariman came in. She was happy carrying her schoolbag. She kissed me and I hugged her lovingly to my breast. She said, "Mom, Mom look at the present my teacher gave me for getting good grades." She was talking about a book of poetry. I kissed her and took the book from her. I skimmed through it and my eyes stopped at one poem that began this way: "Let them talk about my veil, I swear to God I don't care. / My religion has protected me with the veil and deemed me lawful. / Shyness will always be my makeup and modesty my capital."

And another verse in which the poet says:

"They cheated her by saying she was beautiful, the beautiful are duped by praise." When I read these verses I had a strange feeling. I sat down wearily and found tears falling from my eyes. I repeated what I'd just read. I said to myself, modesty and bashfulness don't describe me so I don't have any capital. At this moment I realized the secret behind the continuous anxiety that had spoiled the happy moments of my life. Those who told me that I was an actress of great beauty had cheated me. Those who had put my picture on the covers of magazines and in their pages had duped me. It struck me in the heart and after that my life changed completely. I started hating acting and art. My pictures on the billboards disgusted me. I started thinking about everything . . . myself, my husband, my children, death. (50–51)

She then recounts that her father suggested they go to Mecca to perform the lesser pilgrimage. She was overwhelmed by the holy places and remorseful about her life. Her discourse here turns on the Devil, prefaced by the lament, "Oh, this damn Devil who steals the best years of our lives and we only recognize him after it is too late" (51). Then comes the description of the epiphany while in Mecca:

At night I felt a constricting of my chest as if all the mountains in the world were on top of me. My father asked me why I couldn't sleep. I told him I wanted to go the Grand Mosque [Haram]. He was surprised but pleased that I had requested this. When we got to the sanctuary and I greeted it and began to circumambulate, my body began to tremble. I started sweating. My heart seemed to be jumping out of my chest and I felt at that moment as if there was a person inside trying to strangle me. Then he went out. Yes, the Devil went out and the pressure that was like all the mountains of the world weighing on my breast lifted. The worries were gone. And I found my tongue burst forth with prayers for my children and my husband and I began crying so hard that it was as if a volcano had burst and no one could stop it.

As I reached the shrine of the Prophet Ibrahim, I stood up to pray and recited the opening verse of the Koran as if for the first time. I started recognizing its beauty and meaning as if God had graced me. I felt there was a new world around me. Yes I was reborn. I felt I was a bride and that the angels were walking in my wedding march. Everything around me brought me happiness. I felt I was a pure white bird who wanted to fly in the sky, singing and warbling, setting down on flowers and green branches. I felt the world around me had been created for me. I would no longer feel fatigue, anxiety, or misery. (52–53)

She then describes how her father had come for her; when he took her by the hand, she felt like a small child, totally innocent. She prayed the dawn prayer among her Muslim sisters and from then on began wearing the veil (higab). She concludes her interview with the following words, again invoking the Devil:

I'll never go back to acting. I won't go back to the Devil who stole everything from me. I've tasted the sweetness of faith and closeness to God . . . just as I tasted the Devil's life. (58)

IMMORAL LIVES

The first time I had heard about this new phenomenon was in the summer of 1987. Two adolescent girls in the Bedouin community in Egypt's Western Desert where I was doing research were entertaining themselves by flipping through a clandestine movie magazine. One was literate, the other had never been to school. The latter, who stared carefully at the grainy black-and-white photographs, stopped when she got to one. This actress, she pointed out approvingly, had given it all up and taken on the higab. By way of explanation she added, somewhat harshly, "She got cancer and they had to chop off her breasts." After a pause, to make sure I had understood, she said, "God had punished her for exposing them."

In this girl's reaction is a key to the complex attitudes ordinary women in Egypt have toward the world of media stars. She had conflated immoral life styles with an absence of religion, as if only religion guided women to live proper, respectable lives. God had punished the actress for her sins and, as a result, she had come to recognize the importance of religious faith. The girl could feel self-righteous and yet, there she was, poring over a magazine filled with news of the others who were still part of that fascinating world.

Although film and radio stars are among the most widely known and popular public figures in Egypt, the "repentant artists'" demonization and religious renunciation of the world they represent is not so surprising. Nor is the widespread approval of these women's choices. But I think the roots of this acceptance are complex, confounded by ordinary people's continuing and simultaneous infatuation with media stars.

The born-again discourse of performance as the work of the Devil carries weight, first, because it resonates with long standing traditional views in the Muslim world that performers are disreputable. Women performers mixed with strange men and appeared in public when no other women did; they were also linked, justifiably or not, to "the oldest profession." More important, in the contemporary period, media stars are criticized for their immoral lifestyles and, in the lingo of the religious critics, for their involvement in the world of animal instinct, sexual desire, and temptation. My young Bedouin friend's interpretation of the film star's breast cancer as due to the wrath of God is indicative of a widespread recognition that media stars are the victims and perpetrators of what we call "sexploitation."

Women stars today are perceived as problematic for a host of related reasons, however. First, they are the most public of women and the most visibly independent of family control, violating some basic assumptions about gender in rural and many segments of urban Egypt. Many stars, especially dancers, use stage names, as the confession of Hala Al-Safy above illustrates, frequently with only a first name—Lucy, Shirihan, Yusra, or Sabrin, for example. This is a striking sign of their difference, and particularly their independence from family ties and genealogical definitions in a country where the father's name is always one's second name, and the grandfather's is often the surname.

Their denial of family responsibility, widely assumed to be part of a woman's self-definition, is also problematic. A recurring theme in the narratives of the reformed actresses, bolstered by the interviews with their husbands that accompany their stories, is how their careers had caused them to neglect their husbands and children. As Shams Al-Barudy notes, "I now live a happy life in the midst of my family, with my noble husband who stood by me and encouraged me and congratulated me on each step . . . and my three children" (56). Her husband, a former actor and movie director, explains, "I had long wished that Shams would retire from acting and live for her household" (60).

This husband is echoing a sentiment being widely disseminated in the press and other media, especially in the last two decades of increasing unemployment, that women's proper place is in the home with their families. Actresses and other show business personalities epitomize the challenge to that domestic model and are targeted in part because they are the most extreme and visible cases of a widespread phenomenon: working women.

That the problem is also class related—the working women being criticized are privileged—is apparent in a short article by Anis Mansour, an establishment journalist, in the official government newspaper *Al-Ahram* in 1989. In alarmist language it lays out the links between careerist mothers and unhappy children, stressing actresses' special culpability as women who are wealthy enough to send their children to boarding schools. It was translated in *The Egyptian Gazette* as follows:

Obsessed with her career and the cut-throat competition with others to ascend the ladder of success, today's mother has not got enough time to look after her children and get to grips with their problems. Thus in her scramble for business success, the mother leaves behind her poor children for nannies and servants to bring up. Many film stars are characteristically interested in sending their children away to be brought up and receive their education. There is no doubt that this lifestyle takes its toll on the mental and psychological growth of these children who develop a devastating sense of powerlessness and even feel unwanted and isolated. . . . The whole issue boils down to the fact that unless the child gets enough parental care and protection he is bound to fall into the abyss of brothels, drug dens and deviation.[4]

Ultimately, the problem with stars is that they represent a nouveau-riche westernized elite. Their sexual immorality is often associated with Western life styles, but there is also a general impression that they are different from ordinary Egyptians. The women wear expensive, fashionable clothes, plenty of makeup, and dramatic hairdos, perceived by Egyptians to be "Western." Moreover, many of the most famous actors and actresses are known to travel to Europe for film festivals and holidays.

The statements of a Cairene domestic who was especially immersed in and knowledgeable about the media world affirm this association of actors with the immorality, and even illegality, of the wealthy. Commenting on an actor in a rerun of a television serial, she said he had just died a few months previously. He was at a seaside resort, having a good time. He had an asthma attack but he probably died because he was snorting drugs and had a fatal overdose. She added that all the "artists" do drugs; they have lots of money and that is what they do with it. When I asked her how she knew this, she said it was reported in the newspapers, on radio, and on television. This particular actor had been arrested a few years earlier, his apartment raided, and drugs seized. But he was acquitted. When I expressed surprise that she said he had also been a prosecuting attorney, she tried to convince me that "all these people" are rich and run the country. By contrast, she concluded, it was only people like her (ordinary poor people) who were suffering these days, barely managing to cope with rising prices.

ENTITLEMENT AND DISTANCE

From these attitudes toward stars and the repentant stars' own denunciations of their former lives, one might expect that most women in Egypt are wholly disapproving of actresses and other media stars. And yet, my recent fieldwork in a village in Upper Egypt suggests that this is certainly not the case. The Bedouin girl who so self-righteously condemned the actress with cancer spoke with the confidence of someone who was part of a community that had maintained enough independence from the urban centers and from state institutions to retain a sense of pride about their different social and moral standards. She was part of a wealthy family that did not need to feel shame.[5]

In the Upper Egyptian village in which I have been working, however, most people were relatively poor. Many men were forced to migrate to the city or abroad to find work, and people generally were aware of the disdain with which they were regarded by urban and wealthier Egyptians. They knew this from migrants but also because they were more involved in state institutions and more connected to mass media than the Awlad 'Ali Bedouin families I had known.[6] The younger generation especially could not manage the same pride, although most saw more dignity in their customs and community than other Egyptians granted.

The villagers spoke about media stars with a mix of entitlement and distance. They seemed to feel as if the stars were "theirs," somehow belonging to them as viewers as much as they belonged to anyone else in Egypt. All except the old men and women knew the names of stars who appeared on their television screens, volunteering their previous roles and often some tidbits about their off-screen lives in answer to my questions about television drama plots. Many offered opinions about the popularity and success of various careers.

Yet no one would have considered the stars as like themselves. In this, stars resembled the films and television serials in which they acted, which villagers appreciated as having been broadcast for their pleasure but, as I describe in more detail elsewhere, perceived as depicting the lives of others who had different problems, followed different rules, and did not belong to the local moral community.[7]

The black-and-white televisions on which most villagers watch these stars sit in rooms of mud-brick houses whose walls are decorated with odd bits of gift wrap and newspaper, small posters of Egyptian soccer teams, and abstract hangings fashioned from the foil wrappers of a popular candy bar advertised on television. These are different from the rooms they see in the serials, where even village homes are depicted with decent furniture and identified by primitivist wall hangings showing village scenes, the kind of weavings popular only with tourists and affluent westernized Egyptians.

The village might be considered atypical. School teachers from the nearby town believed it was unusually liberal, the people kinder, more hospitable, and less attached to their traditions and customs (implied negative) than in other communities in Upper Egypt. It was certainly extraordinary in its enmeshment in the tourist industry. A Pharaonic temple was set in its midst, and many men made some kind of living through work with the Antiquities Organization and foreign archaeological missions. One heard octogenarians reminiscing about the Met, others praising New York University, and yet others mentioning the work they had done for the Germans, the Poles, the Canadians, and the French. Even village women had seen foreigners close up; several middle-aged tourists had married young men in the village, buying them hotels or taxis. One American expatriate had built himself a house in the village and a number of folklorists had set up shop there, collecting funeral laments or simply using the village as a base while studying epic poets further south. When I arrived, a friend of these folklorists, I was asked their news and asked if I didn't know other foreigners and urban Egyptians people knew—a miscellany of filmmakers, journalists, architects, and others.

Despite their savvy about other worlds, some of it derived, as in other villages across Egypt, from watching television, these villagers were typical of other rural Egyptians in the problems they confronted. Trying to make ends meet with low wages and unemployment, many children, and insufficient land to be farmed, were not the problems dramatized in television serials or faced by movie stars. As in other agricultural areas, land was distributed unevenly; the largest landowner worked hundreds of *feddans* (approximately acres), while most of the families fortunate enough to own land counted it in *qirats* (1/24 of a *feddan*). Some families were embarrassed to admit, when I found them picking through the stubble of a recently harvested wheat field, that they were grateful when kind landowners permitted them to glean the grains of wheat left behind.

Women lived in a different world from the film stars. They worked hard at household chores like baking bread and with the tasks associated with raising animals as large as water buffalo and sheep and as small as pigeons. When rented or owned fields were close by, the women cut the *barseem* (clover) for the animals and carried it home in large bundles on their heads or on donkeys their sons brought out to the fields. They worried about sons failing in school or about getting daughters married. Some were fortunate in their husbands; others put up with husbands who were unhappy and cruel or who had migrated to Cairo only to take second wives. Some had good in-laws, some did not. Some had brothers who were generous with them; others found themselves in disputes over inheritance.

And they certainly did not perceive the stars as part of their moral community. For village women, matters of reputation were crucial. Although relations between men and women seemed more relaxed than in the Bedouin community I had known, with men and women greeting each other more readily and people who had known each other for a long time sitting and talking together, the men still sat perched on the benches while the women sat on the floor. In large extended households where everyone did watch television together, the women tended to be circumspect. All but the young generation of school-age women still wore heavy black dresses and head coverings when they went on formal visits or to the nearby town. Even around the village they were careful to wrap shawls around their heads and straighten out their black overdresses. Young women were delighted when they got water piped into their houses because they could avoid the public exposure of fetching water, since people were so ready to judge each other and talk about how women and girls behaved.

In contrast, the villagers displayed a kind of tolerance and suspension of moral judgment toward the media stars. This was striking in its difference from their critical evaluations of neighbors and kin. The story I heard from a mother of a married daughter shows the way discourses of morality are crucial in discrediting others. As in many patrilineal societies, in which brothers are expected to share a household even after marriage, in-marrying wives are prone to conflict, their interests being at odds, especially regarding the division of the patrimony at the death of their father-in-law. To explain why a high wall had been built between the house of her daughter and her husband and his brother's family, this old woman, the wife of a wealthy landowner in another hamlet of the village, constructed it as a matter of moral difference between her daughter and the sister-in-law. *That* woman, she began, was from a village in which all the people are worthless. But the real difference could be seen in these women's teenaged daughters. Her grandchild, she explained proudly, was like a cat. No one ever saw her. She would come out to say hello to you and then disappear. She never went out and wouldn't let even the best known and most harmless male family friends into the house if her mother was not home. The other woman's daughter, she went on, had gone across the river in a car to Luxor (the large town) alone with an old European man who had bought her things. He had fallen in love with the girl and moved into the house. She claimed that the young girl would go up to his room.

I happened to know this family she was disparaging and had been told by her daughter's vibrant and friendly rival about the old Norwegian man who had, she claimed, not been comfortable at his hotel and so they had given him a room in their house. He had been generous with them, she implied, because he pitied their circumstances. They ran a small restaurant in their front room that catered to budget tourists, the business they had started after her lame husband had been fired from his job as the cook for the German Archaeological Mission—because he drank, others told me. She had showed me the Norwegian's room, still kept for him, but the old man had never returned after the Gulf War.

Other women in the village, ones less directly involved, told the story somewhat differently. One woman told me that an old European had befriended the family and helped them out financially. She didn't know why he had done this but thought he must have had no family of his own. She explained that he had taken a liking to one of the girls, but she made it seem more innocent. She did disapprove strongly of the fact that he took the girl to Luxor to buy her things.

Whether they assumed the worst and loudly condemned the behavior, in order to side with a daughter against her sister-in-law in a dispute over their husbands' share of an inheritance as well as the disparities in standing (the other brother having taken over the disgraced brother's position with the German archaeologists), or whether they withheld final judgment, the moral standards were clear and the scrutiny of neighbors and kin considered absolutely appropriate.

Knowing the standards by which the villagers judged one another, I was always shocked by what people took for granted on television. For instance, no one blanched at the fact that the highly anticipated annual "quiz shows" *(fawazir)* of Ramadan, the holy month of fasting, involved sexy women wearing extravagant, skin-tight costumes, dancing western-style and Arab numbers. In 1990, people were excited at the return of Nelly to the small screen. She was blonde, petite, and quite agile; she was reputed to be sixty years old. In 1993, her replacement Shirihan was watched with more ambivalence, everyone impressed with her total recovery from a serious back injury (treated abroad, they all stressed) suffered in a car accident under scandalous circumstances. Despite the whispers and the rumors about these circumstances, women and children in the village watched every evening. They had no idea what the riddles meant, and even the references of her costumes (sometimes 1920s flappers, sometimes Caribbean, sometimes Arab) must have passed them by. Yet that was one of the things Ramadan was about.

A favorite Ramadan program in 1993 was *Without Talk,* a kind of celebrity charades that pitted teams of stars against each other: men on one side, women on the other. When they are being themselves, out of costume and without lines, one can sense how fundamentally urban, sophisticated, and westernized the media stars are. Again, though, what I found surprising was how easily village children related to the program. Those with whom I watched it were so excited that they eventually started reproducing it in the field in front of their house, down to the competition between girls and boys. And when I remarked on the stars' clothing—many of the women were in slacks or sporty culottes that were far from anything one would see on local women—some adolescent girls explained knowledgeably that this was the fashion. They knew, they said, because they'd seen city women who came as tourists.

It was touching to see young adolescents even seeking ways to sympathize with the plights of these stars. Some girls were anxious to tell me that Yusra, one of the most westernized and sophisticated film stars, had never married.[8] There was pathos in what they added: "She says she loves children and has photos of children on her walls."

The television and film industries, of course, have a strong interest in fostering viewers' attachment to the stars. They do so through television programs in which actors and actresses are interviewed about productions currently being filmed, compete in often silly games like relay races at the Pyramids, and invite viewers into their homes. There are programs showing highlights of new works, and magazines devoted to the world of cinema and stage. Most recently, a new biweekly newspaper called *Stars* began publication. Only the adolescent and young men in the villages had access to the latter since they were literate and, for school or work, went into a town where such reading matter was sold. But everyone was exposed to the television promotions of these stars.

The pleasures village women and girls took in their access to the world of the stars was undeniable. They could not only tolerate the differences in these women's life-styles, so far removed from their own, but they also were fascinated by them. I never sensed any envy of the stars, or fantasies about joining them, although one evening when left on their own with no interesting shows to watch, the children in one family had what they described to me as a party. The eldest daughter played the role of a broadcaster and each of her siblings took the name of a movie star. She interviewed them about such things as how many films they had made and about their marital lives. It was great fun but make-believe. What one sensed was that viewers enjoyed being entertained by the stars, in their roles on- and off-screen, and in having a very different and glamorous world to know about, to discuss, and to include in their gossip.

What happens when these stars change, taking on the veil and renouncing that world is that they are suddenly brought closer. They seem to step out of their screen worlds and enter into the same world these village women live in, a world where religion and morality are taken for granted as the foundation of social existence. This, I believe, provokes a certain satisfaction while lending moral weight to the women's ambivalence about the world of stars. For women who know they are peripheral and disadvantaged compared to the urban and the wealthy, the confirmation provided by these actresses enables them to more freely express, as did my young Bedouin friend, their self-righteous disapproval of the immorality of that world and to feel good about their own.

FALSE VINDICATION

The "repentant" actresses have done what an increasing number of urban Egyptian women have done: adopted the new modest dress as part of what they conceive of as their religious awakening.[9] Because they are such well-known figures, their actions have been publicized and capitalized on by the Islamists to further legitimize the trend toward women's veiling and to support their call for women's return to the home.

Secularists and progressives, many of whom see feminist ideals as integral to their projects, are opposed to veiling as a sign of "backwardness." Whether they are westernized liberals of the cultural elite for whom women's emancipation has been of longstanding interest, advocated first by turn-of-the-century reformists and "modernizers"—like the well-known figure, Qasim Amin, and upper-class women whose work we are only now discovering—or leftists carrying the banner of Nasser's policies of state feminism in the 1960s (stressing general employment and education), they see in veiling the loss of women's rights.[10]

Some feminist intellectuals and political activists, like television writer Fathiyya al-'Assal, who is also a leading member of the Egyptian leftist party *(hizb al-tagammu')*, suspiciously accuse these actresses of taking fat salaries from the Islamic groups for hosting study groups at which conservative religious authorities or unqualified women proselytize. Others concerned with women's issues, like the liberal writer Wafiyya Kheiry, express resentment when censors interfere with their productions. Noting that most of the censors for television are veiled women, Kheiry asks, "How can I accept a veiled woman dictating to me what can and cannot be said? If I am veiled, won't my thinking be veiled too?"

But such study groups have cropped up everywhere, and the decision to adopt the *higab*—while initially, in the late 1970s, mostly a form of political action by intelligent university women, usually the first in their families to be educated—has now spread down to working women of the lower middle classes and up to a few rebellious upper-class adolescents and movie stars. In rural areas, educated girls declare their difference from their uneducated kinswomen, without jeopardizing their respectability, by means of this form of dress.[11] Adopting the *higab* now has an extraordinary number of meanings and co-implications that need to be distinguished.

And yet, just as the Western press treats the phenomenon monolithically, as a simple sign of fundamentalism, so most women in Egypt (except the urban middle-class secularists described above and Coptic Christians, most of whom share the Western view) read the new veiling simply as a sign of piety and morality. When such women see prominent women known to have operated under very different rules from themselves—performing, traveling abroad, wearing Western fashions, living independent of family constraints, seemingly unconcerned with reputation and respectability—take on the veil, they interpret this as a renunciation of such foreign values and an embracing of the same morality and religious identity that they see as guiding their own lives.

The stars' choice to veil is taken as a vindication of the life patterns of these other women, who live in communities or come from classes that do not offer the other choices to women—the choices of wearing makeup or high heels on an everyday basis, of having careers, or of going to glamorous parties. The women delude themselves into thinking that these stars are now women like themselves, sharing their moral values and thus other aspects of their situation. This is especially true for the younger women who, if they attend school, begin to take on the same *higab* they see their teachers wearing in communities that have become less lax about religious matters in the past decade.

When asked about how his wife had changed, the actress Shams Al-Barudy's husband was quoted in *Repentant Artists and the Sex Stars* as saying, "Shams has now become a wife who cares for her husband . . . and a mother who tends her children *and lives her life like any other wife* . . . she is a mother with a calling [to raise her children in a Muslim way]" (61, my emphasis).

Yet she is not like "any other wife"—especially a wife in rural Egypt. The home she gives up her career for is comfortable, with fancy furniture, shiny bathrooms, and plenty of servants. It is not mud-brick, with insufficient room for expansion when her sons marry, or requiring constant battle with flies because of the sheep and water buffalo housed within. Her closets are stocked with clothes, the old fashionable ones now replaced with "modest dress" that nevertheless is of high quality fabric and color coordinated. She does not have to wait for the religious feasts to get a piece of fabric to make a new dress. She probably has savings and a husband with a decent income, not a migrant laborer who has left her with five children to feed and fields to be worked, or an asthmatic husband who makes $35 per month working for the Antiquities Organization. She never walks back from the market carrying her purchases on her head, or is forced to squeeze into a crowded bus or climb into the back of a pickup truck fitted with narrow benches; she drives or, more likely, is driven around in an imported car. It is this which allows her the leisure to tend to her husband and to oversee the raising of her children, helping them with their homework, taking them for lessons or to the club for swimming, or delivering them to their friends' birthday parties.

Veiling and retiring from acting do not change her class position and its privilege. Nor do they affect the bourgeois ideas about domesticity informing her (not to mention her husband's) vision of herself as wife and mother, ideas very different from the ones guiding women in this village in Upper Egypt and elsewhere.[12]

To take on the *higab* is a very different thing from having always worn some sort of head covering, having always thought of yourself as religious and moral, or having never left the bounds of family control. Yet, in the new Islamic consciousness in Egypt, a discourse of morality serves to erase the distinctions between these experiences and to mask the persistent divisions of class and lifestyle. This gives poor and rural women the comforting illusion of equality with their Muslim sisters everywhere, something no other political discourse can offer.

NOTES

This paper was written as the 1995 Sabbagh Lecture at the University of Arizona. Research in Egypt was supported by fellowships from New York University, the Near and Middle East Committee of the Social Science Research Council, and the American Research Center of Egypt. I am grateful for the research assistance of Hala Abu-Khatwa, to Boutros Wadi' for first alerting me to the phenomenon of the repentant artists, and to my friends in the Upper Egyptian village for their hospitality.

1. The literature on the Islamic groups in Egypt is considerable. Some important sources are Ali E. Hillal Dessouki, ed., *Islamic Resurgence in the Arab World* (New York: Praeger, 1982); Saad Eddin Ibrahim, "Anatomy of Egypt's Militant Islamic Groups," *International Journal of Middle East Studies* 12 (1980): 423–53; Gilles Kepel, *The Prophet and Pharaoh: Muslim Extremism in Egypt* (London: El Saqi Books, 1985); Gudrun Kramer, "The Change of Paradigm: Political Pluralism in Contemporary Egypt," *Peuples méditerranéens* 41–2 (1987–88): 283–302; Barbara Stowasser, ed., *The Islamic Impulse* (Washington, D.C.: Center for Contemporary Arab Studies, Georgetown University, 1987). Two more recent special issues on political Islam make *Middle East Report* 179 (November–December 1992) and 183 (July–August 1993) especially useful.

2. Leila Ahmed, *Women and Gender in Islam* (New Haven, Conn.: Yale University Press, 1992), 225.

3. Barbara Stowasser's "Religious Ideology, Women and the Family: The Islamic Paradigm," in her *The Islamic Impulse*, 262–96, gives a good sense of the views of Sheikh Al-Sharawi.

4. Anis Mansour, "Victims," *The Egyptian Gazette*, 6 November 1989, 3.

5. I have written extensively about the pride of this community and its sense of difference from the rest of Egypt. See, for example, Lila Abu-Lughod, *Veiled Sentiments: Honor and Poetry in a Bedouin Society* (Berkeley: University of California Press, 1986) and *Writing Women's Worlds: Bedouin Stories* (Berkeley: University of California Press, 1993).

6. For a rich analysis of the place of Sáidis (Upper Egyptians) in the imaginaries of urban Egyptians, see Martina Reicker, "The Sa'id and the City." Unpublished dissertation, Temple University, 1996.

7. See my "The Objects of Soap Opera," in *Worlds Apart: Modernity Through the Prism of the Local*, ed.

Daniel Miller (London: Routledge, 1995), 190–210.

8. The news of her marriage in 1993 was the cover story on numerous Arabic magazines.

9. The phenomenon of "the new veiling" is extremely complex and interesting. Among those who have written insightfully on it, showing clearly how the religious motivation for it needs to be balanced by an understanding of how veiling contributes to greater freedom of movement in public, easier work relations in mixed sex settings, respectability in the eyes of neighbors and husbands, greater economy, and social conformity, are Leila Ahmed, *Women and Gender in Islam* (New Haven, Conn.: Yale University Press, 1992); Fadwa El Guindi, "Veiling Infitah with Muslim Ethic," *Social Problems* 28 (1981): 465–85; Mervat Hatem, "Economic and Political Libera(liza)tion in Egypt and the Demise of State Feminism," *International Journal of Middle East Studies* 24 (1992): 231–51; Valerie Hoffman-Ladd, "Polemics on the Modesty and Segregation of Women in Contemporary Egypt," *International Journal of Middle East Studies* 19 (1987): 23–50; and Arlene MacLeod, *Accommodating Protest* (New York: Columbia University Press, 1990). Elizabeth Fernea's documentary film, *A Veiled Revolution*, is especially good at revealing many meanings of the new modest dress.

10. I discuss these progressives and the issue of feminism in my unpublished paper, "The Marriage of Feminism and Islamism in Egypt. Good sources on feminism in Egypt include Leila Ahmed, op. cit.; Beth Baron, *The Women's Awakening in Egypt* (New Haven, Conn.: Yale University Press, 1994); and Margot Badran, *Feminists, Islam, and Nation* (Princeton, N.J.: Princeton University Press, 1995). For a discussion of Nasser's state feminism, see Mervat Hatem, "Economic and Political Liberalization."

11. See Abu-Lughod, *Writing Women's Worlds*, op. cit., chap. 5.

12. For a discussion of the difference between urban and Islamist notions about the roles of wives and mothers and those with which some rural women work, see my "The Marriage of Feminism and Islamism in Egypt."

34 Sex Acts and Sovereignty

Race and Sexuality in the Construction of the Australian Nation

Elizabeth A. Povinelli

INTRODUCTION

In 1788 on the shores of Botany Bay Australia, Watkins Tench, captain of the British Marine Corps, had "scarcely landed five minutes" when his party was met "by a dozen Indians, naked as at the moment of their birth."[1] Eager to aid in bringing "about an intercourse between [the] old and new masters" of the continent and "to take possession of [the] new territory,"[2] Tench entices the Aboriginal group forward by "baring" the bottom of a five-year-old convict boy and "showing the whiteness of [his] skin."[3] This enticing display of a small boy's bottom was not the only way in which the British used the body to take possession of the Land Down Under. During this same meeting, in order to make his own sex clear and to construct a distinction between old and new masters, Tench describes how he reached into his—or perhaps a convict's—breeches and pulled out his penis only to be met with "the most immoderate fits of laughter" by the Aboriginal men. Or so I interpret the manner by which Tench made the sex of his party "understood"—the text itself remaining ambiguous on this point by skating between reference to a direct, shameless display of anatomies and a performance of European reticence and modesty.

In Tench's *A Narrative of the Expedition to Botany Bay with an Account of New South Wales* and in other colonial officials' memoirs, this juxtaposition of bodily action and reaction will occur again and again; Europeans attempt to use bodies to effect a "rational intercourse" across cultures, only to be thwarted by Aborigines' apparently immoderate and unproportional sexual and emotional responses. While Tench first offers the hope of peaceful and productive relations between Europeans and Aborigines, the reader soon learns that indigenous Australians' sexual and emotional irregularity "signify" *terra Australis* is *terra nullius*—an empty land lawfully available for the expression of British land desire. Thus in a colonial memoir offered as "amusement and information" to its readers, a military leader in the British penal colony in Australia imbricates racial,

---

Elizabeth A. Povinelli is Associate Professor of Anthropology at the University of Chicago, and is the author of *Labor's Lot: The Power, History, and Culture of Aboriginal Action* (Chicago, 1993). Her research centers on sexual, racial, and cultural discrimination as technologies of power in colonial and postcolonial Australia and the United States. She is also politically active in indigenous land rights struggles in Australia, and in Gay, Lesbian, and Queer human rights issues in the U.S.

sexual, and national discourses that simultaneously construct British sovereignty and the Aboriginal and European bodies and passions on which that sovereignty will rest.

Almost 210 years later, the textual accounts of race, sexuality, and nationalism that in the eighteenth century produced a legal context for British sovereignty claims not only no longer produced sovereignty also but were now hurting the Australian state's standing in the international community, especially in east and southeast Asia. Not surprisingly, then, on 3 June 1992 the Australian High Court, in the decision *Eddie Mabo v. the State of Queensland*, overturned the doctrine that Australia was *terra nullius* (a land belonging to no-one) at the point of settlement. It further found that the *terra nullius* claim had rested on a "discriminatory denigration of indigenous inhabitants, their social organization and customs"[5] and that for Commonwealth, State, or Territory governments to extinguish native title now, they must meet the nondiscriminatory standards laid out in the Commonwealth *Racial Discrimination Act 1975* that, in effect, bars the taking of Aboriginal land without just compensation. The broad scope of this decision potentially subjected all unalienated Crown lands in Australia to a traditional Aboriginal land claim.

This essay juxtaposes a set of colonial memoirs[6] covering the period 1788–1802 to the contemporary *Mabo* debate. It compares how colonial writers represented the "emptiness" of Aboriginal social life in order to establish sovereignty over *terra Australis* to how contemporary courts and politicians represent the "traditions" of indigenous people in order to adjudicate land claims. I argue that although the Traditional Aboriginal Man, steward of family, clan, and land, has replaced the naked satyricon as the nation's reference point for sovereignty claims, each has allowed the nation-state to consolidate and legitimate its power through reference to imaginary Aboriginal sex acts.

Reading across these two historical periods and sets of texts necessitates crossing traditional boundaries in social criticism and cultural and historical studies. My purpose here is, therefore, not primarily ethnographic, although I do provide a counter-reading of colonial and postcolonial constructions of Aboriginal social life based on my twelve-year relationship with the Belyuen community, an indigenous community in northern Australia. These counter-readings—some imaginary, some ethnographic—are intended to shake the narrative and cultural coherences, thus "grip," of current accounts of Aboriginal sexuality and social practice. They should not be taken as *the* Aboriginal counter-discourse, but rather an attempt to "synthesize an understanding of local movements and class culture, on the one hand, and large-scale state dynamics, on the other" (Dirks, Eley, and Ortner 1994, 5).

1. Sexual Irregularity and Sovereign Desires, 1788–1802

The military and civil administrations who, in 1788, arrived on the shores of the land down under brought with them more than a cargo store of convicts, foods, and materials. They also brought with them emerging but interlocking understandings of sexual regularity, civil progress, and international rules for establishing sovereignty that provided them with grounds for intervening in local social practices.[6] It was within these social, economic, and legal frameworks that the Australian colonial administrations "discovered" Aboriginal sex and temperament and put it to colonial use.

Two points are I think critical to understanding this process of "discovery." The first is that colonial administrators were not simply manipulating preconstituted representations of "savages" in order to gain their lands. Instead, administrators were reacting to and adjusting symbolic frameworks in a way that allowed them to see themselves as gaining local lands and resources without taking them from anyone and as creating humane governance on barbaric shores. In other words, their representations of indigenous people were motivated by economic and psychic desires that created complex, often incoherent, portraits of local people, culled from rapid and confusing encounters with them. Second, the "emptiness" of (Ab)Original society was saturated with British meaning. *Terra nullius* was one of three ways a nation could legally establish sovereignty over a stretch of land (the other two being cession and conquest). But *terra nullius* did not refer to any specific state of "emptiness"; rather it simply signified that "some form" of social vacuity existed. Without any necessary social form to discover, administrators flooded their memoirs, their governance policies, and their disputes with their own views, incoherences, and ambivalences about what a *terra nullius* society might signify (or what it might be ethnologically).

Good Natives, Bad Natives

The civil government led by Arthur Philip the first governor of the colony and the Lieutenant-Colonel and Judge-Advocate John Collins advocated—in the beginning—gaining mastery over the indigenous population through a new form of colonial humanism. In doing so they were participating in the British attempt to distinguish the "humanity" of the Protestant Ascendancy from the atrocities of the Spanish Catholic "black conquest."[7] A key method Philip advocated for introducing a rational and humane order between settler and colonized group was through linguistic "intercourse"[8] and through noninterference in local practices and especially the prevention of "transport crews from having [sexual] intercourse with the Native."[9]

In the first parts of their memoirs, the civil officers are exuberant over how well their plan is going. Phillip and his faction, especially Collins and Tench, continually note the "moderating" effect that officers have on "native" behavior. The bodies of officers seemed to have an almost magical power to sway the actions of local people, and Philip is not shy in saying so: "When I first landed in Botany Bay the natives appeared on the beach and were easily persuaded to receive what was offered to them, and, tho' they came armed, very readily returned the confidence I placed in them, laying down their spears when desired."[10] The response of local people to Phillip's gestures seemed "another proof how tractable these people are, when no insult or injury is offered, and when proper means are used to influence the simplicity of their minds" (Phillip 1789, 51). Extreme tractability would indeed be needed if local men and women were to respond placidly to the British offer—if you give us your land we'll take it, if you don't we'll shoot you.

These wondrous meetings came to a rapid halt when Philip was nearly fatally speared after attempting, one too many times, to cool a supposedly savage scene. As officials were implicated in the provocation of violence and they themselves became targets of it, a significant narrative shift occurred. The content of (Ab)Original "emptiness" shifted away from describing local men, although simple and primitive, as manly, brave, and affable. Instead, on the one hand, discussions focused more exclusively on local familiar and gender relations and, especially white men's protection of black women from black men.[11] And, on the other hand, discussions of Aborigines shifted from the early positive descriptions of aboriginal temperament to negative ones—of unpredictable, unprincipled, and sanguinary people.

Sex and Temperament

Given the gender discourse in Britain at the time,[12] it is not surprising that the civil government focused its attention on a battered group of Aboriginal women, whose own moral instincts were constantly put into question.[13] Intervening in gender relations allowed the civil government to produce simultaneously its own rationality and Aboriginal men and women's irrationality. For example, Governor Arthur Phillip is constantly portrayed as attempting to moderate the temper of two Aboriginal men, Coalby and Banalang, in relations to their "wives" and various other unnamed women. Although Philip always suffers setbacks, at one point is near-fatally speared, and ultimately laments the unrecuperable nature of the men, by these textual moves, he and other colonial administrators are constantly being portrayed as (at least) attempting to rationalize the sexual (and economic) relations of male and female Aborigines. Moreover, Aboriginal men and women's resistance to British sociosexual intervention is folded back into the account as further evidence of the irrationality of the indigenous group (note, not "person"), a point writers linger over, as did John Hunter, Post Captain in the Royal Navy, who noted that Banalang "laughed when he was told that it was wrong to beat a woman" (Hunter 1793, 475). In the process of producing moral and immoral colonial subjects, these representations of gender and sexuality performed the colonial prerequisites of sovereignty: making contact with the natives and establishing a just and orderly regime.

But along with performing sovereignty, the colonial government's official policy regarding sexual relations between European men and Aboriginal women helped transform European economic appropriations into fair economic transactions. By representing themselves as morally restrained and restraining the immorality of the criminal class "locked up" at Port Jackson (forbidding convicts any "contact" with native women)[14] writers established a substitutional relationship between European sexual restraint and imperial desire. Always addressing Aboriginal men (the putative "owners" of the women and the land—although this could never be said directly since it contradicted *terra nullius* claims), writers established a narrative relationship between woman-as-property and land-as-property which made their land appropriation appear to be a fair economic deal: we won't take your women, we *will* take your land; we won't take your women, *if* you give us your land; *if* you don't give us your land, we'll take your women; or perhaps even, we didn't *also* take their women like real sexual savages do (i.e., the Spanish).[15]

One way that colonial writers made this "deal" seem fair, just, and humane was by contrasting their willingness to "order" (withhold) their passions for local women to local men's inability to control their sexual and emotional temperaments. For example, "beatings" were described as the foreplay of Aboriginal "lovemaking."[16] Men "lent out" their wives even though they seemed to show, at those times they weren't beating them, a great tenderness and jealousy for them.[17] Relatedly, while many administrators who wrote of their recollections of the first years of the New South Wales colony professed a real admiration for the various mainly Aboriginal men they "befriended" (often by kidnapping), the male Aboriginal "temper"—Aboriginal men's sexual and emotional practices—were represented as irrational and inscrutable. Aboriginal men were portrayed as explicitly irrational in the way they lashed out against those Europeans and aborigines alike who tried to help them in their "frequent" brawls;[18] i.e., they were portrayed as unable to differentiate friend from foe. Likewise, Aboriginal men showed a passive face in the context of the harshest initiation rites,[19] but they also showed the same face in the presence of their best friends and close family;[20] i.e., they were portrayed as unable to differentiate torture and familial solace. Because of these mixed-up and unbridled emotions, writers claimed that Aboriginal socio-sexual organization defied classification. Perhaps the surest sign that all was not right in the realm of Aboriginal sexuality was, however, the observation that the civil markers of natural sex difference failed to signify in this land down under.[21]

Aboriginal sexual and emotional interactions were irregular, writers claimed, because the passions, not social convention or reason, were the agent of all Aboriginal action. The passions (an emotion category inflected by class and race) snatched the Aboriginal body and were the motivating forces of Aboriginal temperament, sexuality, and other interpersonal affairs. John Hunter, for instance, described how Banalang reacted to British intervention in his relationship with a young Aboriginal woman: "Reasoning with him was now out of the question; the savage fury which took possession of him when he found himself kept from the girl, who was lying senseless, is not to be described" (1793, 482). It is not to be described, in part, because describing it would only restrict the Western readers' imaginary relationship to "savage fury" inflected by class, cultural difference, and the spatio-temporal vertigo that Hunter's text evokes. For, where are we-the-reader? At home in England "now," where moral panics over the informal sexual practices of the lower and climbing classes are threatening the foundations of civil society? Or are we in the colony "then," where savage fury and criminal licentiousness threatened the best efforts of colonial leaders to create "order and useful arrangement" from "tumult and confusion" (Philip 1789, 121)? Moreover, by positing a disordered social and emotional realm, authors and readers of these colonial texts could extend from the social to the economic and demographic: no wonder, the

British mused, the Australian continent had such a low population and its people such a "primitive" economy; contradictory sexual and emotional practices impeded the establishment of advanced civil forms.[22]

Representations of local men and women's sex and temperament were not simply cover for colonial acquisition (although they were *also* cover for colonial acquisition); they also produced emotional reactions in English settlers that had devastating results for local men and women. In short, these racisms, articulated through discourses on gender and sexuality,[23] caused settlers to react to imaginary specters, even as they gave settlers a way of understanding their reactions as rational responses. In order to suggest the functions of race and sexuality in colonial narrative strategies, I look here at an extended passage wherein a colonial military writer maintains, in a clearly confused scene, the distinction between the rational and rationalizing European and the irrational and violent Aborigine. The account comes from the journal of John Murray and describes what happened to his first mate, Mr. Bowen, when he came suddenly upon a group of Aboriginal men in the year 1801.[24]

According to Murray, Bowen—"knowing I [Murray] was extremely anxious to have, if possible, a friendly intercourse with them" immediately set off to meet them. Each of the local men had "a bundle of spears in their hands," but "did not seem at all alarmed" when the white men "hollowed to them" or when the boat came nearer. Because of the vast tidal mud flats ("a bank of mud") that characterize the Australian coast, Bowen could only maneuver his boat "about 200 yards" away from the group. He therefore, "singly got out and began to walk towards them, which when they perceived they jumped up on their feet, and it now was perceived that one of them was a very old man with a large bushy beard, and the rest of his face besmeared with red oaker; the others were young men"—the "old man seemed to have command over the others." As Mr. Bowen got closer to this group of men a series of exchanges occurred. First the local men "pulled off their dress ('Apposums [skins] as far as the middle') and made signs to the officer, that before he came any nearer he must do the same." Bowen "immediately complied," adding a Christian signature to this first exchange by "plucking a root of fern . . . [and] holding it up." Although "they seemed to understand it as it was meant," when Bowen got within a few yards of the group "the old man seemed rather uneasy and began to handle his spears." Bowen then initiates a second series of exchanges; tomahawks, handshakes, bread, and ducks are offered to the local men, Murray commenting on what the men take (what they seem to desire and thus what might be useful in winning them over), what they leave. He is especially careful to note their seeming lack of knowledge about firearms: "On getting some ducks they took no other notice of them than to examine in what manner they were killed. What their ideas on that head we know not, as they did not take the least notice of our firearms even when, towards the latter end of the parley, it was found necessary to point one at the breast of the old man, who all along was very suspicious of our designs."

After noting these exchanges the narrative returns to a series of bodily "intercourses." Murray notes that a young Aboriginal man commented on Mr. Bowen's body ("All this time they expressed a good deal of wonder at the colour of Mr. Bowen's skin, and one of the young men made very significant signs to him that he must have washed himself very hard"), that women who joined the party "shook their hands" and little boys "laughed and whooped" as the naked Bowen tried to warm himself by their fire; and finally, that the old man insisted that all Bowen's party get "out of the boat stark naked . . . and [walk] somewhat near the natives, on which the old man sent the boys away to the women, and he, after having in a great passion made signs for us to go to the boat, began to retire with his face to us, and brandishing his spear, so that every one thought he would heave." Murray continues, "When our people turned their backs the young men seemed more quiet." But realizing that "all hope of further intercourse for the present was at an end," Mr. Bowen ordered one of his men "to fire his piece over their heads in order to make good his retreat to the boat. This had the desired effect, as they one and all were out of sight in an instant."

What then of this "singular" and "strange" first contact event? Let me pursue two lines of inquiry. First, is this account exposing the "rawness" of all bodies in this social scene? If not, how does the narrative allow the British body to remain wrapped in its self-evident and productive virtue? Second, how is the use or meaning of the body being used to produce cultural difference, and how could a rereading show the pragmatic work the text is performing in the realm of sovereignty?

There are several ways the narrative wraps the European body even while relying on nakedness to act as a sign of the unraveling of social relations. First, while Murray describes some of the actions that occur around the European body, he does not say what Bowen or he makes of these events. Murray focuses, instead, on how Mr. Bowen productively initiates and handles a series of semiotic, "gestural," economic, and weaponry exchanges. British action remains transitive, producing semiotic and economic exchanges and inciting, supposedly, a jealous fit in the senior Aboriginal man. Second, by avoiding the experiential effect of being "looked over," Murray is able to abstain from providing the reader with an inversion of the colonial gaze. The irreverent gaze and parodic commentary of the young Aboriginal men—let alone the women—on the stark naked body of the British male and the susceptibility of this body to damage in the harsh climate all potentially displace the European body from the defining center of the narrative—in the logic of colonial narrative, the British inspect, record, and graphically represent the colonized body. Irrespective of the actual events happening in the field, the perspective of the Aboriginal group, especially a senior male, is not allowed to assume this definitive ground in the text. How then does the narrative resist, even forbid, such a displacement?

The narrative resists such racial and social decenterings, in part, by selecting what elements of the bodily gesture, on either side, are understood as meaningful. On the European side we "see" the European skin, in particular, its scrubbed whiteness. Moreover, the defining purity of the European body is remarked on *by the Aborigines* who, along with ridiculing, are described as commenting on the excessive cleanliness of it. How better to show the natural hierarchies of bodies than to have "the blacks" announce the symbolic connection between bodily types and purity? No matter that the explorers' bodies could hardly have been that clean or healthy looking given the environmental conditions that they had just navigated: the mud, the sun, the sandflies, the rotten food. We do not, and it is significant that we do not, hear of the potential disfigurements of these European bodies. Did Bowen carry scars? Was he circumcised? What of his ex-convict sailors? Did they appear to Aborigines with their backs flayed and laced with scars inflicted by what Robert Hughes has called the sadistic excesses of the convict system: skin and flesh lashed away and shoulder bones protruding? And what of their foreskins? There or not? Obviously the "full" truth of the European bodies appearing on this scene must remain partial to colonial readers in order to maintain the position of the colonial subject; but they did not appear in this partiality to the senior Aboriginal man who initially sought to read these colonial objects. Let us turn to him for a moment.

What might have been his motivations for inspecting the European bodies, and why did they so offend him? Why did the young men quiet down when the British turned their backs to them? Was the European penis so perverse, or were the scars on their backs more interesting reading? Although left unsaid, but well-known to colonists by 1801,[25] we can be fairly confident that the senior man was asking Bowen and his crew to present the meaning of their social selves by undressing—an action that for the senior man (perhaps interrupted in ceremonial instruction, note the mention of the red ochre) would convey more than all the waving of ferns (Bowen's reenactment of Eden?), handkerchiefs, and passing of tomahawks. For the Aboriginal group, status was, in part, written on the body and stored in the knowledge individuals had of the countryside and its rituals (Muecke 1988). Whereas ritual and everyday action unveiled a man's and woman's comparative level of knowledge, a more preliminary social assessment could be had in reading the body's physical inscriptions—or; in this case, its lack thereof. "Natural" sex difference was never the sufficient social determinant, rather the social body necessitated a physically inscribed supplement. Thus when the lily-white, potentially uncircumcised and unscarred Mr. Bowen approaches—a body *tabula rasa*—"the old man seemed rather uneasy and began to handle his spears" as he might do with any novice male intruding upon his land. In the end, a gun blast rationalizes and productively orders a scene that narratively is, for no apparent reason, rapidly unraveling.

While both the civil and military groups present Aboriginal sexual and emotional irregularity as the cause of the British's violent and nonviolent social and physical interventions, the narrative representation of Aboriginal sexuality and passion as irrational actually allowed these violent social interventions and through them the legal fictions that supported British land appropriation. Drawing on eighteenth-century notions of savage sexuality and passion and of social progressivity and sovereignty, the emerging Australian government could present itself not as appropriating an ordered land but as ordering an as-yet-unordered, unappropriated land, a social *terra nullius*. Sexual, emotional, and social disorder were the necessary, and thus narrativized, form Aboriginal life had to take for colonial military and civil writers.

2. Sexual Regularity and Sovereignty Discussions, 1966–1994

Some 210 years have passed since the "first contact" texts were composed and the first penal colony was begun in a corner of Aboriginal country. Since then, social theory and international law have significantly changed in relation to non-Western indigenous societies. Traditional Aborigines, and other traditional indigenous societies, are no longer portrayed as sexually unregulated and irrational. Instead, and with particular regard to Australian Aborigines, critical studies in Marxism (*Origin of the Family*), Freudian psychoanalytics (*Totem and Taboo*), Durkhiemian functionalism and Levi-Straussian structuralism (*Primitive Classification, Totemism*), have all turned to the dominating constraining logic of Aboriginal totemism, kinship, and marriage (or descent and alliance systems) to solve much broader puzzles in human psychology, political economy, and society.

Not only has social theory supposedly come around to recognizing the inherent order in Aboriginal sexual and gender practices, so supposedly have international and national High Courts and parliaments. In Australia, no surer sign of this is there, we are told, than the series of legislative acts and juridical decisions that have occurred since the mid-1960s, culminating in the very recent decision *Eddie Mabo v. the State of Queensland*, in which the court rejected the doctrine that Australia was *terra nullius* at the point of European colonization.[26] This narrative of recognition and reconciliation obscures, however, the *similarities* between the past and present courts, government and media. It also pulls our attention away from seeing how this "new recognition" of Aboriginal land rights is restructuring contemporary Aboriginal sociosexual practices even as the courts claim to be acknowledging them.

Protecting the Integrity of "Our" Economy and Law

Most Aboriginal leaders and activists have applauded the High Court's recognition that Australia was already peopled and possessed when the first boatload of Europeans stepped onto its shores. But this High Court decision did not come without heated response from the Aboriginal and non-Aboriginal communities. Popular media personalities, international business corporations, and the chief ministers of Australian State and Territory governments predicted that the *Mabo* decision would result in everything from the last breath of Australian racism, to the last gasp of the Australian economy, to the last stage of Aboriginal dispossession. Conservative (Liberal and National Party) state leaders foreground forcefully what they saw as the catastrophic economic implications of *Mabo*. For instance, the *Sydney Morning Herald* (3 December 1993) reported that "the Chief Minister of the Northern Territory, Mr. Marshall Perron, warned that the Federal bill 'set the scene for the greatest battle between Aboriginal and non-Aboriginal interests Australia has ever seen.'" Such a response by the Northern Territory's Chief Minister is not surprising given that many in the northern government and business communities lament racist attitudes toward indigenous people primarily because they scare away Asian investment.

While conservative state governments have foregrounded economic reasons for overturning *Mabo*, the Australian Labor (although hardly leftist) Prime Minister, Mr. Paul Keating, vacillated between social justice and constitutional pragmatism as the motivation for his proposed "land-mark . . . reconciliation"[27] between Aborigines and non-Aboriginal Australians. In the face of advice from some in his own party, Keating set for himself the daunting task of using these dis-cursive frames to navigate stridently divided political, economic, and social communities and coming up with a legislative package that would, in some way, acknowledge the Court's decision. On 19 October 1993, seemingly "against all odds,"[28] Mr. Keating persuaded his cabinet to approve a compromise package that recognized native title and provided "social justice" for Abo-rigines, while at the same time safeguarded, as an editorial in the *Australian* put it, the "integrity of *our* land management system as one of the foundations of *our* economy"[29] (my emphases). On 22 December, the Australian Parliament passed the *Native Title Act*.

While "social justice" may be a better "guiding principle" for the left than other minor- and meta-narratives (Morris 1988; Hebdige 1991), it also provides political groups from the left, center, and right with a discursive framework that masks other motivations for and implications of social legislation. By framing his stance in terms of social justice, for instance, Keating need not acknowledge any inevitable right of Aboriginal people to determine land interests in Australia. Thus it is not "social justice" or Aboriginal rights to self-determination *per se* that centers the public articulation of Keating's vision—neither would be sufficient or persuasive—but rather it is the court's legitimate right to rule and the economic legacy of that ruling that Keating claims has forced the Australian government's hand in "finally" solving the indigenous legacy of the colonial period.

Whereas in the first contact period the state gained international support by showing it could produce order from cross-cultural and social disorder, and justified its sovereignty claims by posit-ing that no (and not dickering over what degree of) social order preceded European settlement, now the state gains international legitimacy by showing it can reconcile itself to a multiplicity of cross-cultural social orders and can discriminate among degrees of cultural authenticity.[30] The state and its juridical apparata are what is "on the line" in this debate, not the lives of indigenous people. The recognition of "native title" rights and the discourse of social justice is as bent on representing Aboriginal sexual and social systems in a way that would make them compatible with governing needs as was the previous colonial strategy. The state's recognition of "traditions" is, on the one hand, creating a narrow chute that restricts Aboriginal access to land and, on the other hand, acting as a discursive virus that expresses state needs through Aboriginal social forms—in other words, the discussion of "traditions" allows the state to restrict Aboriginal claims, legitimate the actions of European governance, and transform Aboriginal practices.

ABORIGINAL TRADITIONS, THE RESTRICTION OF RECOGNITION

At heart, the High Court overturned *terra nullius* as a legal basis for non-Aboriginal Australian sovereignty because "the theory that the indigenous inhabitants of a 'settled' colony had no pro-prietary interest in the land . . . depended upon a discriminatory denigration of indigenous inhabitants, their social organization and customs" (Brennan 1992, 27). The High Court announced in *Mabo* that it *now* recognizes that "traditional" Aboriginal people have a highly structured social system for regulating sexuality, marriage, and property that is the very opposite of irrational. It is rather the dominating institution in their lives.

The chute through which Aboriginal groups can gain access to land has narrowed rather than expanded based on the preliminary legislative fallout of the *Mabo* decision. In perhaps the most drastic example of this narrowing, the *Native Title Act* overrides the Commonwealth *Racial Dis-*

crimination Act 1975 (RDA), which was passed to reflect the United Nations *Convention on the Elimination of All Forms of Racial Discrimination* (CERD) and to which the High Court referred as restricting the ability of the Commonwealth, State, and Territory governments to take Aboriginal land. By overriding the RDA the Commonwealth government is now able to extinguish native title without paying "just compensation." Less startling but equally as threatening to an indigenous group's ability to determine how human-land and human-human relations will be legally conceived is the proposed establishment of tribunals to hear Aboriginal claims. These tribunals, whose constitution is still not settled, would among other things determine whether the "general nature of the connection between the indigenous people and the land remains" and thus whether a land claim is viable (Brennan 1992, 59).

While the RDA applies Australian-wide, only in the Northern Territory has there been a Commonwealth Act pertaining to Aboriginal land rights: *Aboriginal Land Rights (Northern Territory) Act of 1976* (hereafter ALR). Examining how "the connection between the indigenous people and land" was operationized in it allows us to imagine how Aboriginal claims might be assessed in the climate of a *Native Title Act*. In the ALR, Aboriginal groups have to pass through a series of social and cultural tests and performances before being granted traditional title to their country (Gumbert 1981; Weaver 1984). Specifically, an Aboriginal group must prove that they are the "traditional Aboriginal owners" of the land under claim. In the ALR, "traditional Aboriginal owners" are: "a local descent group of Aborigines who—(a) have common spiritual affiliation to a site on the land, being an affiliation that place the group under a primary spiritual responsibility for that site and for the land, and (b) are entitled by Aboriginal tradition to forage as of right over the land."[31]

In other words, the law constructs the local descent group as a heterosexually defined genealogical family group reckoned through the mother or father's line (or, in some recent decisions, both) that has as its apical ancestor a Dreaming (or totem, say a long yam Dreaming) whose spiritual center is on the land under claim (say a rock or banyan tree). The ALR leans on a definition of the Dreaming as the Aboriginal belief that the extant world was formed by the actions and travels of Dreamtime men and women (say, the Blue Crab Man and the Stringbag Woman) who, at certain places in the countryside, left a mark (e.g., stone, banyan tree, waterhole) and remain there today. In the best of all *legal worlds*, land commissioners, anthropologists, and local indigenous groups construct a genealogical map, draw a circle around the descent group, locate that group's Dreaming (totem) on a map, and the case is settled. That group owns that land. No where else; no one else.

This legal portrait of Aboriginal culture drew on dominant anthroplogical models of Aboriginal society. Ian Keen has described the relationship between the definition of "traditional Aboriginal owners" and "the 'orthodox model' of Aboriginal tenure" (1984, 25; see also Gumbert 1981; Maddock 1983). In particular Keen draws out the connections between the Act's use of the phrases "local descent group," "common spiritual affiliation," "primary spiritual responsibility," and "to forage as of right over the land," and structural-functionalist discussions of the differences between aboriginal land-holders and land-users (especially, Berndt and Berndt 1964; Radcliffe-Brown 1930–31; Stanner 1965). Land-holders were posited to be an exogamous patrilineal descent group (or "clan"). In contrast, land-users (bands or "hordes") were thought to be a looser confederation of families and friends actually living on and using the clan territory. Land-holders were a heterosexually and genealogically defined group with spiritual ties to a stretch of the countryside, while land-users were defined by their affective relations to one another and their economic interests in the land.

Human sexual reproduction and the heterosexual form of the family within a totemic framework (often portrayed as "mystifying" or ideological, but never granted a real nature) are, therefore, the underpinnings of European legal recognition of Aboriginal traditions. But while the law specifies a type of sexuality and a form of cultural belief as defining Aboriginal legal rights to land, it does not in any way inspect sexuality as a cultural category.[32] The courts would confront severe problems in delimiting the realm of sexuality in Aboriginal (and non-Aboriginal) communities, but not examining the contours of sexuality and the body has a severely distorting effect on Aboriginal and European understandings of land rights and land relations. While a full articulation is beyond the scope of this essay, here I simply want to suggest that in many Aboriginal communities humans are not seen as the only subjects involved in reproduction and eroticism and that rights do not only accrue through Western-defined heterosexual families.

Many Aboriginal men and women at Belyuen describe human-human sexuality and erotics as determined by a set of kinship and Dreaming (totemic) relationships. Persons come into the world with some of these kinship and Dreaming relationships already determined. Others of these relationships are negotiated in speech acts or practices. For example, erotic relationships between "parallel cousins" are considered reprehensible by members of the community. But who is a parallel cousin rather than, say, a "cross-cousin" (an ideal sexual and erotic partner) can be negotiated in speech or practice. A person can argue that if one "tracks" kinship and Dreaming relationships between people in a certain way, then those who first appeared to be parallel cousins are revealed to be cross-cousins. Thus erotic partners are "produced" not only by a system of kinship and Dreaming relationships but also by men and women innovatively negotiating relationships within these systems. Of additional importance to this discussion is the fact that these kinship and Dreaming relationships are often used to establish erotic relationships between persons of the same sex.

Thus human-human desire, eroticism, and sexuality do not simply work to produce "marriages," even granting an expansion of one's marriageable choices from cross-sex to cross- and same-sex partners. Desire and eroticism are also tools Belyuen men and women use to build mobile and diffuse affective relations between groups vis-à-vis individuals. For instance, after periods of intense emotional stress, people often demand that the community come together for "play." At these times, corroborees are sung and danced and people urged to tease each other sexually and otherwise. Women dance erotically toward each other or men, perhaps mocking the dance style of a male suitor or a female "rival." Adult same-sex cousins will urge each other's sons and daughters to dance together erotically, teasing them and each other mercilessly, often in explicitly sexual terms—both teasings a form of emotional and bodily pleasure, recognition, and alliance. Old people will pursue young people and everyone will be urged to "be serious" as they throw dog, cow, or horse manure at each other and are uproariously mocked and laughed at. These mandatory pleasures are just formalized examples of the constant erotic teasings and bodily interactions that occur on northern Aboriginal communities and that create the dense same-sex and cross-sex, generational and cross-generational emotional networks that can be relied upon to secure economic and social assets. This pleasure, this sexual excess—which is seen in everyday conversation and joust and is composed of sexual discourses from putatively Aboriginal and non-Aboriginal sources—is not simply the topsy-turvy world of Bakhtinian carnival, because it does not simply invert the normal order. Instead, it performs the available "tracks," not all of which are utilizable for adult reproduction, that cement alliances, make contacts, connect persons and through them places. In short, it is a large part of what generates the "normal order." Human-human relations are, in large part, discussed as a question of how to get people and places to desire one another, sexually or affectively, and thus form a flexible, but dense, community of resources—an abundance of affectivity rather than the thin line of descent courts and parliaments now recognized. These dense networks of affectivity/sexuality/eroticism are part of the reason that certain people are found in certain places and subsequently form the human-land attachments described below.

While Aboriginal understandings of human-human sexuality and erotics provide some problems for current legislative attempts to delimit the realm of property, Aboriginal understandings of human-land relations provide somewhat different problems. Human-land relations (reproduction, desire, bodily pleasures), or The Dreaming, are implicated in but escape current legislative definitions of sexuality in three main ways. First, northern Aboriginal groups do have what are usually called descent Dreamings (totems). The reproduction of human life (having kids) is the occasion for these descent Dreamings to maintain their here-and-now being in the world with their there-and-then origination at a site. An example helps. The long yam is, through my father, brought to life in me. Through my mother's family Dreaming, I am the red kangaroo. I, the temporary human manifestation of the Dreaming yam and kangaroo, may travel anywhere, but my origination site, where I-the-Dreaming yam and kangaroo emerged from, traveled to, and submerged in the Dreamtime, is marked with one or a series of geological features, such as one or a series of waterholes; i.e., descent Dreamings are both a place and a being.

But while the courts essentialize Aboriginal human-land relations to this form of reproductive heterosexuality—conversant with its own notions of the genealogy of emotional obligations and legal property—indigenous men and women have many forms of human-land, or Dreaming, relations none of which are essential in the sense of being reducible to the other. For instance, northern persons also recognize Dreaming relationships between persons and places based on conception,[33] on ceremonial ties, and on naming practices.

Thus, as others have long noted, indigenous land-rights legislation quantitatively restricts the type of group and the number of people who can make proprietary claims to an unalienated piece of land.[34] The Australian parliament's and the courts' recognition of "the local totemic descent group" (patrilineal or matrilineal) as the only legitimate basis for land-ownership under the *ALR* allows the state to restrict indigenous understandings of human-human and human-land relations in a way that best fits emerging nineteenth- and twentieth-century Western notions and institutions for the descent of rights and goods.[35] By only recognizing the "local totemic descent group," the state is provided with historically predictable and delineable, relatively immobile sets of heterosexually defined families through which and only through which property is passed. When these narrowly defined groups die or change their beliefs "significantly," land reverts to the state. Thus when the state says it recognizes the local totemic descent group, it is in fact recognizing its own needs, compatibilities, and wants within it—it recognizes the distribution of property rights through human reproduction anchored in the cultural topography of the Dreaming.

Equally important to the quantitative restriction (from many totems to the one totem) that the Courts impose is the qualitative perversion of the meaning of the Dreaming in relation to Aboriginal notions of bodies, desire, and land. It is a narrowing of the senses in which land-human affectivity and desire is understood as a contextually based, emergent, and ongoing relationship between people and places: something that cannot be known *a priori* or fixed by genealogical referent. Northern Aboriginal people discuss human-land relations, like they discuss human-human relations, as a problem of how to get people and places to desire one another and thus form flexible but dense bonds of attractions.

ASSESSING DIFFERENCE

Irrespective of these cultural conceptions of human-land relations, in the context of a post-*Mabo* tribunal system, future land commissioners or tribunal members would, arguably, turn to the wording of the High Court and Parliamentary debate to determine the scope and meaning of "traditions" (how "traditions" were conceived as a cultural litmus for land rights). Tribunal members would be looking for some way of deciding what constitutes "traditions": what would be the essential component of cultural continuity or the diacritic of cultural loss? At first glance the High Court seems to provide some mobility for cultural expression. For instance, Brennan's discussion of cultural change seems quite broad; for traditions to maintain their legal veracity, Aboriginal groups must simply continue "to acknowledge the laws" and "to observe the customs *so far as practicable.*" Likewise, in their decisions in the *Mabo* case, Deane and Gaudron bow to the dynamism of culture. In their view an Aboriginal society can change and still retain traditional rights to their land "*pro-*

vided any changes do not diminish or extinguish the relationship between a particular tribe or other group and particular land." But there is a limit to change. For instance, Brennan argues that where "the tide of history has washed away any real acknowledgement of traditional law and any real observance of traditional customs, the foundation of native title has disappeared" (Brennan 1992, 49).

But whether recognizing frozen culture or more fluid fields, government rights are re-entrenched as they are represented as liberal accommodations by establishing a testable, factual basis for a claim that looks at degrees of change rather than static states. Arguing that there are degrees past which the grounds for "special rights" pass into the grounds for "equal rights"—"our traditions are different but equal thus laws relating to us differ" to "our traditions are the same thus laws relating to us must be the same"—courts and parliament gain the backing of the "reasonable person"[36] who does not want to turn a cold eye to the atrocities of colonial history but who also wants some contemporary basis for the differential treatment of Aboriginal people. By framing Aboriginal land rights as "special rights" that can be extinguished either by previous acts of land alienation or by the ongoing process of cultural change, the state gains the benefit of recognizing the rights of authentic Aboriginal culture subjects (acting on principle for "social justice" in classic cultural relativistic terms: culture should be seen to be legitimate *in its own right*) as it maintains the right to evaluate that subjectivity and to distribute the rights the authentic cultural subject retains. In the process the court has reestablished the dynamics, if not the explicit discourse, of a theory of cultural stagism and social progressivity ("our law which is more advanced can incorporate your law"). For the state also *only* recognizes Aboriginal cultural subjectivity as legitimate if it is *in its own right* (viz., as "special" and "other") and if *it is seen to be* by official institutions (in this case the state or Commonwealth tribunals).

This "multicultural" turn in Australian law can thus be seen to mask a malignant institutionalization of European discrimination of Aboriginal social organization in the imperative sense of "distinguish as distinct," if not "denigrate as degenerate."[37] Why denigrate the indigenous cultural subject if it is always and already undermined by the question of cultural corruption and cultural tainting? Like sexual misconduct, cultural corruption need not be proven or even pressed for the possibility of taint to undermine the unity of an authentic voice. The "ideal" image of the Traditional Aboriginal Man hovering in the background—a man who does not exist, who never existed—is enough. His specter continually undermines real men and women's practices as legitimate bases for material claims.

In short, while political leaders and the High Court have discussed native title legislation as a move beyond the "discriminatory denigration of indigenous inhabitants, their social organization and customs," they rely on socioeconomic and cultural change to limit, and eventually halt, the ability of Aboriginal men and women to make claims. Moreover, government discourse needs to be read against national and international business communities who continue to mobilize a discourse of social progressivity. Thus, for example, the business community framed its responses to *Mabo* within a model of socioeconomic progressivity. Mr. Rob Davies of the investing banking house Lehman Brothers told the AAP in London that the *Mabo* decision threatened Australia's ability to maintain a "modern economy"—"If this decision stands, Australia could *go back* to being a Stone Age culture of 200,000 people living on witchetty grubs" (*The Australian*, 14 June 1993, my emphasis). And, we can be sure that, as they did in virtually every land claim case in the Northern Territory, local governments and businesses will, in the post-*Mabo* world, challenge every Aboriginal claim on the basis of its social referent's social, cultural, and historical authenticity.

While political and jural activities catch most people's attention as those which threaten or supports Aboriginal practices, cultural hegemonic understandings of sexuality threaten to undermine Aboriginal practices in court and in practice. "Fringe" increasingly becomes an interior position: what is within the group that cannot be shown outside, and what itself has or seems to have been changed by dominant cultural views? For example, if an Aboriginal community attempts to create dense affective networks of relations predicated on a kinship system that weighs

degree-of-relation more heavily than sex, but also knows from the public realm that sexual identity is a form of subjectivity that exists "outside" kinship ("I am a homo-poof" versus "that is my
same-sex marriage partner"), into which system will it place the name of same-sex desire and
eroticism? And how will this name differ within the community, the courtroom, the media?
Whereas in Western society "at large" homosexuality is a counter-discourse to the hegemony of
heterosexism and hetero-presumptions, in an Aboriginal context this oppositional framework
undermines and transforms local systems of desire, sexuality, and economy and thus land
use/ownership. And how much more stigmatized is same-sex eroticism and desire than single-
motherhood and miscegenation, which the non-Aboriginal public sees as evidence of the breakdown of "traditional Aboriginal values"? On television shows, in public welfare pamphlets, and in
scholarly essays, the single Aboriginal mother of multiple children is described as a "social condition" produced by unemployment, the loosening of belief in the Dreaming, and the devastating
effects of drug addictions. It is not proclaimed, as it is in some Aboriginal communities, as a new
form of polygamy. Likewise, light skin is metaphorically linked to the draining of culture: miscegenation is a bodily sign of cultural loss, not a new form of cultural inclusion. For the single
mother herself or the two same-sex cousins or the child of Aboriginal, Anglo-Celtic or Asian
parents, the cultural condition of "single motherhood," "homosexuality," and "half-caste"
becomes that which distinguishes between authentic and "buggered-up" Aboriginal subjects;
thus, that which can be told, known, accepted, embraced. "Homosexuality," "miscegenation,"
and "single motherhood" not only function within Aboriginal communities to refashion bodily
practices and desires, but also, from a Western legal perspective at least, function as a sign of cultural decay, the loss of "specialness" in the realm of culture, and thus the loss of any basis to claim
land rights in Australia.

A closing caution. While Western constructions of sexuality bear on Aboriginal understandings of human-human and human-land relations, Aborigines' rearticulated, dialogical conceptions and practices of eros and affectivity will never be Western but will always slip outside it
because it will always be speaking with and against something that is itself always moving.[38]

WHAT GUILT ALLOWS: A CONCLUSION

In many ways, this essay is simply an elaborate discussion of how a discourse of guilt allows the
contemporary state to keep while giving away and the historical role that sexuality has played in
this game of fort-da. Rather than position itself as opposing Aboriginal land rights, easily rede-
ployed by Aboriginal activists as oppressing Aboriginal people and thus easily entangled in a
human rights controversy, the Australian government positions itself as, on the one hand, expressing sorrow for the effects on Aboriginal people of past European misunderstandings (although
those Aboriginal groups who suffered most gain least) and, on the other hand, supporting multiculturalism as it relates to state definitions of Aboriginal traditions. But in the midst of elaborate
displays of remorse and appeals for reconciliation, the state has managed to maintain its control
over both the type of Aboriginal sexuality that will be legally productive and the manner by
which sovereignty (ultimate authority over people and places) and sexuality will be articulated.

A comparison of colonial and postcolonial representations of Aboriginal sexuality, hopefully,
makes it clear that *this* sexuality has no real social referent. State representation and implementation of legally recognized "traditions" serve to articulate it to state needs even as it purports to be
recognizing Aboriginal traditional institutions and legalizing a multicultural approach to land
tenure. Loosely articulated, mobile but dense, same- and cross-sex, human-human and human-
land desires and affectivities have no place in an ordered society or the law that seeks to uphold
it—even though, in the postmodern context of current national and international business communities, mobile worker populations and facile commodity desire figure strongly (Harvey 1989).
In short, the sexuality that government officials overtly and covertly invoke is but a marker and
site of non-Aboriginal uses of culture as a means to and maintenance power.

NOTES

I would like to thank the editors Roger Lancaster and Micaela di Leonardo for their insightful comments on the form and content of this essay.

1. Tench (1789, 24).
2. Tench (1789, 24).
3. Tench (1789, 25). See also White (1986, 171).
4. Brennan (1992, 27).
5. The texts I refer to are: Phillips (1789; Collins (1802); Barrington (1800); Tench (1789); Hunter (1793); Grant (1803); and Murray in Labilliere (1878).
6. For a history of colonial Australia see Hughes (1986). For discussions of the British social elite's discussions of class and sexuality see MacFarlane (1986), Mitchison and Leneman (1989), and Parker (1992). For a discussion of the relationship between sexual and civil order see Amussen (1988), Mosse (1985), and Hyam (1990).
7. Phillip (1789, 44–45); see also Grant (1803, 170).
8. See also the convict Barrington's description of the same (1800, 75–76). See also Fabian (1986) for a discussion of a language and colonialism.
9. Tipping (1988, p. 20).
10. *Historical Records of Australia*, series 1, volume 1, p. 24.
11. Gayatri Spivak has noted the broader context of this "protection": "Imperialism's image as the establisher of the good society is marked by the espousal of the woman as *object* of protection from her own kind" (1988, 299). See also Stoler (1992).
12. See Amussen (1988) and Hyam (1990).
13. See Phillip (1789, 81–82).
14. See Collins (1802, 473).
15. For example, see Tench (1789, 26, 28, 40).
16. "Making love in this country is always prefaced by a beating" (Hunter 1793, 510–11).
17. See for example Phillip (1789, 78, 82); Hunter (1793, 475).
18. See Hunter (1793, 474).
19. See Hunter (1793, 503–7).
20. See Grant (1803, 106, 151).
21. "These people seemed at a loss to know (probably from our want of beards) of what sex we were, which having understood, they burst into the most immoderate fits of laughter, talking to each other at the same time with such rapidity and vociferation as I had never heard before."
22. See Grant (1803, 131). Foucault long ago noted that sex emerged in the eighteenth century not in the form of a "general theory of sexuality" but in the form of "analysis, stocktaking, classification, and specification, of quantitative or causal studies" (Foucault 1978, 23–25).
23. In a series of critical readings inspired by the work of Frantz Fanon, Homi K. Bhabha (1994) argues that race and sexuality are the two key forms of difference articulated in the production of the colonial subject. See also Robert Young (1995) and Toni Morrison (1992).
24. In Labilliere (1878, 68–69).
25. See Barrington (1800, 112), Tench (1789, 35), and Hunter (1793, 505).
26. For a history of Aboriginal land rights see Williams (1986) and McRae, Nettheim, and Beacroft (1991, 151–2).
27. *Sydney Morning Herald* (1 December 1993).
28. *Manchester Guardian Weekly*, 31 October 1993, "Justice at last for an invisible people."
29. *Australian*, 3 September 1993, "Editorial."
30. Tellingly, during the initial political sallies over the Keating government's policy paper—framed by some in explicitly racist and Eurocentric terms—supporters of Sydney's quest against Beijing's for the 2000 Summer Olympics compared the two cities in terms of their respective nation-state's record on multiculturalism and human rights.
31. *Aboriginal Land Rights (Northern Territory) Act 1976*, section 3, pp. 3–4. (Sydney: Government Printer).

32. See especially essays collected in *Positions, East Asia Cultures Critique* 2(1) Spring 1994.

33. See Merlan (1986) for a discussion of conception dreamings.

34. For a similar argument see Keen (1984, 27); Gumbert (1981); Hiatt (1984). See Hamilton (1982) and Myers (1986) for a discussion of noncognatic methods of affiliation to sites.

35. See Myers (1989) for an insightful account of Aboriginal notions of "property."

36. See Abrams (1992) and P. Williams (1991).

37. See also Hamilton's (1984) and Gunew's (1990).

38. See also Sahlins (1993, 864).

BIBLIOGRAPHY

Abrams, Kathryn. 1992. "Social construction, roving biologism, and reasonable women: A response to Professor Epstein." *DePaul Law Review* 41: 1021–40.

Amussen, Susan Sawyer. 1988. *An Ordered Society: Gender and Class in Early Modern England.* New York: Basil Blackwell.

Australian, 14 June 1993.

Australian, "Editorial," 3 September 1993.

Australian, 3 December 1993.

Barrington, George. 1800. *A Voyage to New South Wales with a Description of the Country, the Manners, Customs, Religion Etc. of the Natives in the Vicinity of Botany Bay.* Philadelphia: Stewart.

Berndt, R. M., and C. H. Berndt 1964. *The World of the First Australians.* Sydney: Ure Smith.

Bhabha, Homi K. 1994. "The other question: Stereotype, discrimination and the discourse of colonialism." In *The Location of Culture,* pp. 66–84. London and New York: Routledge.

Brennan, J. 1992. In *Eddie Mabo v. The State of Queensland.* 3 June 1992, F.C. 92/014.

Collins, John. 1802. *An Account of the English Colony in New South Wales.* London: Strahan.

Deane, J., and J. Gaudron. 1992. *Decision regarding Eddie Mabo v. The State of Queensland.* 3 June 1992, F.C. 92/014.

Dirks, Nichols, Geoff Eley, and Sherry Ortner. 1994 *Culture/Power/History.* Princeton, NJ: Princeton University Press.

Fabian, Johannes. 1986. *Language and Colonial Power.* Cambridge: Cambridge University Press.

Foucault, Michel. 1978. *The History of Sexuality.* Volume 1. New York: Vintage.

Grant, James. 1803. *The Narrative of a Voyage of Discovery Performed in His Majesty's Vessel The Lady Nelson, of Sixty Tons Burthen with Sliding Keels in the Years 1800, 1801, and 1802 to New South Wales.* London: Roworth.

Gumbert, Marc. 1981. "Paradigm Lost: Anthropological models and their effect on Aboriginal land rights." *Oceania* 52: 103–123.

Gunew, Sneja. 1990. "Denaturalizing cultural nationalisms: Multicultural readings of 'Australia.'" In *Nation and Narration,* ed. Homi K. Bhabha, pp. 99–120. New York: Routledge.

Hamilton, Annette. 1982. "Descended from father, belonging to country: rights to land in the Australian Western Desert." In *Politics and History in Band Societies.* Eds. Eleanor Leacock and Richard Lee, pp. 85–108. Cambridge: Cambridge University Press.

———. 1984. "Spoonfeeding the Lizards, Culture and Conflict in Central Australia." *Meanjin* 43(3): 341–62.

Harvey, David. 1989. *The Condition of Postmodernity: An Enquiry into the Origins of Cultural Change.* Cambridge, MA: Blackwell.

Hebdige, Dick. 1991. "After the Masses." In *New Times: The Changing Face of Politics in the 1990s,* ed. S. Hall and M. Jacques. London: Verso.

Hiatt, L.R. 1984. "Traditional land tenure and contemporary land claims." In *Aboriginal Landowners, Contemporary Issues in the determination of Traditional Aboriginal Land Ownership.* ed. L. R. Hiatt, pp. 11–23. Sydney: University of Sydney.

Hughes, Robert. 1986. *The Fatal Shore.* New York: Knopf.

Hunter, John. 1793. *An Historical Journal of the Transactions at Port Jackson and Norfolk Island.* London: John Stockdale.

Hyam, Ronald. 1990. *Empire and Sexuality: The British Experience*. New York: St. Martin's Press.

Keen, Ian. 1984. "A question of interpretation: the definition of 'traditional Aboriginal owners' in the Aboriginal Land Rights (N.T.) Act." In *Aboriginal Landowners, Contemporary Issues in the determination of Traditional Aboriginal Land Ownership*, ed. L. R. Hiatt, pp. 24–45. Sydney: University of Sydney.

Labilliere, Francis Peter. 1878. *Early History of the Colony of Victoria, From Its Discovery to Its Establishment as a Self-Governing Province of the British Empire*. London: Sampson Low, Marston, Searle, and Rivington.

Mabo, The High Court Decision on Native Title. 1992, 3 June. Canberra: Commonwealth Government Printer.

MacFarlane, Alan. 1986. *Marriage and Love in England: Modes of Reproduction, 1300–1840*. New York: Basil Blackwell.

Maddock, Kenneth. 1983. *Your Land is Our Land, Aboriginal Land Rights*. Ringwood: Penguin. *Manchester Guardian Weekly*. "Justice at last for an invisible people." 149(18), 31 October 1993.

McRae, H., G. Nettheim, and L. Beacroft. 1991. *Aboriginal Legal Issues*. Butterworth.

Merlan, Francesca. 1986. "Australian Aboriginal conception beliefs revisited." *Man* 12: 474–93.

Mitchison, Rosalind and Leah Leneman. 1989. *Sexuality and Social Control: Scotland 1660–1780*. New York: Basil Blackwell.

Morris, Meagan. 1988. *The Pirate's Fiancee: Feminism Reading Postmodernism*. London: Verso.

Morrison, Toni. 1992. *Playing in the Dark, Whiteness and the Literary Imagination*. New York: Vintage.

Mosse, George. 1985. *Nationalism and Sexuality: Respectability and Abnormal Sexuality in Modern Europe*. New York: H. Fertige.

Muecke, S. 1988. "Body, Inscription, Epistemology: Knowing Aboriginal Texts." In *Connections, Essays in Black Literatures*. ed. E. Nelson, pp. 41–52. Canberra: Aboriginal Studies Press.

Myers, Fred. 1986. *Pintupi Country, Pintupi Self: Sentiment, Place and Person among the Western Desert Aborigines*. Washington, DC: Smithsonian Institute Press.

Parker, Stephen. 1990. *Informal Marriage, Cohabitation and the Law, 1750–1989*. New York: St. Martin's Press.

Phillip, Arthur. 1789. *The Voyage of Governor Phillip to Botany Bay with an Account of the Establishment of Port Jackson and Norfolk Island*. London: John Stockdale.

Povinelli, Elizabeth. 1993. *Labor's Lot: The Culture, History and Power of Aboriginal Action*. Chicago: University of Chicago Press.

Radcliffe-Brown, A. 1930–31. "The Social Organization of Aboriginal Tribes." *Oceania* 1: 34–63.

Sahlins, Marshall. 1993. "Cery cery fuckabede." *American Ethnologist* 20(4): 848–67.

Spivak, Gayatri C. 1988. "Can the Subaltern Speak?" In *Marxism and the Interpretation of Culture*, Cary Nelson and Lawrence Grossberg, pp. 271–313. Chicago and Urbana: University of Illinois Press.

Stanner, W. E. H. 1965. "Aboriginal territorial organization: Estate, range, domain, and regime." *Oceania* 36: 1–26.

Stoler, Ann. 1992. "Sexual affronts and racial frontiers: European identities and the cultural politics of exclusion in colonial Southeast Asia." *Comparative Studies in Society and History* 34: 514–51.

Sydney Morning Herald, 1 December 1993.

Sydney Morning Herald, 3 December 1993.

Tench, Watkin. 1789. *Narrative of the Expedition to Botany Bay with an Account of New South Wales*. London: Swords.

Tipping, Garry R. *The Official Account Through Governor Phillip's Letters to Lord Sydney*. Sydney, Mitchell Library, photocopy, 1988, p. 20 [n.d. on letter, before leaving].

Weaver, Sally. 1984. "Struggles of the nation-state to define Aboriginal ethnicity: Canada and Australia." In *Minorities and Mother Country Imagery*, ed. Gerald L. Gold, pp. 182–210. Social and Economic Papers No. 13, Institute of Social and economic Research. Newfoundland: Memorial University of Newfoundland.

White, Allon. 1986. "Bourgeoisie hysteria and the Carnivalesque." In *Politics and Poetic of Transgression*, ed. Peter Stallybrass and Allon White. Ithaca, NY: Cornell University Press.

Williams, Patricia. 1991. *The Alchemy of Race and Rights*. Cambridge, MA: Harvard University Press.

Young, Robert. 195. *Colonial Desire: Hybridity in Theory, Culture and Race*. London and New York: Routledge.

Part Nine

RE-IMAGINING

BODIES

35 Excerpt from "Introduction" to *Bodies That Matter*

Judith Butler

INTRODUCTION

> Why should our bodies end at the skin, or include at best other beings encapsulated by skin?
> —Donna Haraway, *A Manifesto for Cyborgs*

> If one really thinks about the body as such, there is no possible outline of the body as such. There are thinkings of the systematicity of the body, there are value codings of the body. The body, as such, cannot be thought, and I certainly cannot approach it.
> —Gayatri Chakravorty Spivak, "In a Word," interview with Ellen Rooney

> There is no nature, only the effects of nature: denaturalization or naturalization.
> —Jacques Derrida, *Donner le Temps*

Is there a way to link the question of the materiality of the body to the performativity of gender? And how does the category of "sex" figure within such a relationship? Consider first that sexual difference is often invoked as an issue of material differences. Sexual difference, however, is never simply a function of material differences that are not in some way both marked and formed by discursive practices. Further, to claim that sexual differences are indissociable from discursive demarcations is not the same as claiming that discourse causes sexual difference. The category of "sex" is, from the start, normative; it is what Foucault has called a "regulatory ideal." In this sense, then, "sex" not only functions as a norm but also is part of a regulatory practice that produces the bodies it governs, that is, whose regulatory force is made clear as a kind of productive power, the power to produce—demarcate, circulate, differentiate—the bodies it controls. Thus,

Judith Butler is Chancellor Professor in the Departments of Rhetoric and Comparative Literature at the University of California at Berkeley. She is the author of *Subjects of Desire: Hegelian Reflections in Twentieth Century France* (Columbia, 1987); *Gender Trouble: Feminism and the Subversion of Identity* (Routledge, 1990); and *Bodies that Matter: On the Discursive Limits of "Sex"* (Routledge, 1993). She has recently completed two books: *The Psychic Life of Power: Theories in Subjection* (Stanford, 1997), which concerns the double meaning of "subjection" (to be subordinated by another, and to become a subject), and *Excitable Speech: A Politics of the Performative* (Routledge, 1997), which treats the performative power of language as it has emerged in contemporary political debates and in recent reflections on speech acts.

"sex" is a regulatory ideal whose materialization is compelled, and this materialization takes place (or fails to take place) through certain highly regulated practices. In other words, "sex" is an ideal construct that is forcibly materialized through time. It is not a simple fact or static condition of a body, but a process whereby regulatory norms materialize "sex" and achieve this materialization through a forcible reiteration of those norms. That this reiteration is necessary is a sign that materialization is never quite complete, that bodies never quite comply with the norms by which their materialization is impelled. Indeed, it is the instabilities, the possibilities for rematerialization, opened up by this process that mark one domain in which the force of the regulatory law can be turned against itself to spawn rearticulations that call into question the hegemonic force of that very regulatory law.

But how, then, does the notion of gender performativity relate to this conception of materialization? In the first instance, performativity must be understood not as a singular or deliberate "act" but, rather, as the reiterative and citational practice by which discourse produces the effects that it names. What will, I hope, become clear in what follows is that the regulatory norms of "sex" work in a performative fashion to constitute the materiality of bodies and, more specifically, to materialize the body's sex, to materialize sexual difference in the service of the consolidation of the heterosexual imperative.

In this sense, what constitutes the fixity of the body, its contours, its movements, will be fully material, but materiality will be rethought as the effect of power, as power's most productive effect. And there will be no way to understand "gender" as a cultural construct which is imposed upon the surface of matter, understood either as "the body" or its given sex. Rather, once "sex" itself is understood in its normativity, the materiality of the body will not be thinkable apart from the materialization of that regulatory norm. "Sex" is, thus, not simply what one has, or a static description of what one is: it will be one of the norms by which the "one" becomes viable at all, that which qualifies a body for life within the domain of cultural intelligibility.[1]

At stake in such a reformulation of the materiality of bodies will be the following: (1) the recasting of the matter of bodies as the effect of a dynamic of power, such that the matter of bodies will be indissociable from the regulatory norms that govern their materialization and the signification of those material effects; (2) the understanding of performativity not as the act by which a subject brings into being what she/he names, but, rather, as that reiterative power of discourse to produce the phenomena that it regulates and constrains; (3) the construal of "sex" no longer as a bodily given on which the construct of gender is artificially imposed, but as a cultural norm which governs the materialization of bodies; (4) a rethinking of the process by which a bodily norm is assumed, appropriated, taken on as not, strictly speaking, undergone *by a subject*, but rather that the subject, the speaking "I," is formed by virtue of having gone through such a process of assuming a sex; and (5) a linking of this process of "assuming" a sex with the question of *identification*, and with the discursive means by which the heterosexual imperative enables certain sexed identifications and forecloses and/or disavows other identifications. This exclusionary matrix by which subjects are formed thus requires the simultaneous production of a domain of abject beings, those who are not yet "subjects" but who form the constitutive outside to the domain of the subject. The abject[2] designates here precisely those "unlivable" and "uninhabitable" zones of social life, which are nevertheless densely populated by those who do not enjoy the status of the subject, but whose living under the sign of the "unlivable" is required to circumscribe the domain of the subject. This zone of uninhabitability will constitute the defining limit of the subject's domain; it will constitute that site of dreadful identification against which—and by virtue of which—the domain of the subject will circumscribe its own claim to autonomy and to life. In this sense, then, the subject is constituted through the force of exclusion and abjection, one which produces a constitutive outside to the subject, an abjected outside, which is, after all, "inside" the subject as its own founding repudiation.

The forming of a subject requires an identification with the normative phantasm of "sex," and this identification takes place through a repudiation that produces a domain of abjection, a repudiation without which the subject cannot emerge. This is a repudiation that creates the valence of "abjection" and its status for the subject as a threatening spectre. Further, the materialization of a given sex will centrally concern *the regulation of identificatory practices* such that the identification with the abjection of sex will be persistently disavowed. And yet, this disavowed abjection will threaten to expose the self-grounding presumptions of the sexed subject, grounded as that subject is in repudiation whose consequences it cannot fully control. The task will be to consider this threat and disruption not as a permanent contestation of social norms condemned to the pathos of perpetual failure, but rather as a critical resource in the struggle to rearticulate the very terms of symbolic legitimacy and intelligibility.

Lastly, the mobilization of the categories of sex within political discourse will be haunted in some ways by the very instabilities that the categories effectively produce and foreclose. Although the political discourses that mobilize identity categories tend to cultivate identifications in the service of a political goal, it may be that the persistence of *dis*identification is equally crucial to the rearticulation of democratic contestation. Indeed, it may be precisely through practices which underscore disidentification with those regulatory norms by which sexual difference is materialized that both feminists and queer politics are mobilized. Such collective disidentifications can facilitate a reconceptualization of which bodies matter, and which bodies are yet to emerge as critical matters of concern.

FROM CONSTRUCTION TO MATERIALIZATION

The relation between culture and nature presupposed by some models of gender "construction" implies a culture or an agency of the social which acts upon a nature, which is itself presupposed as a passive surface, outside the social and yet its necessary counterpart. One question that feminists have raised, then, is whether the discourse which figures the action of construction as a kind of imprinting or imposition is not tacitly masculinist, whereas the figure of the passive surface, awaiting that penetrating act whereby meaning is endowed, is not tacitly or—perhaps—quite obviously feminine. Is sex to gender as feminine is to masculine?[3]

Other feminist scholars have argued that the very concept of nature needs to be rethought, for the concept of nature has a history, and the figuring of nature as the blank and lifeless page, as that which is, as it were, always already dead, is decidedly modern, linked perhaps to the emergence of technological means of domination. Indeed, some have argued that a rethinking of "nature" as a set of dynamic interrelations suits both feminist and ecological aims (and has for some produced an otherwise unlikely alliance with the work of Gilles Deleuze). This rethinking also calls into question the model of construction whereby the social unilaterally acts on the natural and invests it with its parameters and its meanings. Indeed, as much as the radical distinction between sex and gender has been crucial to the de Beauvoirian version of feminism, it has come under criticism in more recent years for degrading the natural as that which is "before" intelligibility, in need of the mark, if not the mark, of the social to signify, to be known, to acquire value. This misses the point that nature has a history, and not merely a social one, but, also, that sex is positioned ambiguously in relation to that concept and its history. The concept of "sex" is itself troubled terrain, formed through a series of contestations over what ought to be decisive criterion for distinguishing between the two sexes; the concept of sex has a history that is covered over by the figure of the site or surface of inscription. Figured as such a site or surface, however, the natural is construed as that which is also without value; moreover, it assumes its value at the same time that it assumes its social character, that is, at the same time that nature relinquishes itself as the natural. According to this view, then, the social construction of the natural presupposes the cancellation of the natural by the social. Insofar as it relies on this construal, the sex/gender distinction founders along parallel lines; if gender is the social significance that sex assumes within a given culture—and for the sake of argument we will let "social" and "cultural" stand in an uneasy interchangeability—then what, if anything, is left of "sex" once it has assumed its social character as gender? At issue is the meaning of "assumption," where to be "assumed" is to be taken up into a more elevated sphere, as in "the Assumption of the Virgin." If gender consists of the social meanings that sex assumes, then sex does not *accrue* social meanings as additive properties but, rather, *is replaced by* the social meanings it takes on; sex is relinquished in the course of that assumption, and gender emerges, not as a term in a continued relationship of opposition to sex, but as the term which absorbs and displaces "sex," the mark of its full substantiation into gender or what, from a materialist point of view, might constitute a full *de*substantiation.

When the sex/gender distinction is joined with a notion of radical linguistic constructivism, the problem becomes even worse, for the "sex" which is referred to as prior to gender will itself be a postulation, a construction, offered within language, as that which is prior to language, prior to construction. But this sex posited as prior to construction will, by virtue of being posited, become the effect of that very positing, the construction of construction. If gender is the social construction of sex, and if there is no access to this "sex" except by means of its construction, then it appears not only that sex is absorbed by gender, but also that "sex" becomes something like a fiction, perhaps a fantasy, retroactively installed at a prelinguistic site to which there is no direct access.

But is it right to claim that "sex" vanishes altogether, that it is a fiction over and against what is true, that it is a fantasy over and against what is reality? Or do these very oppositions need to be rethought such that, if "sex" is a fiction, it is one within whose necessities we live, without which life itself would be unthinkable? And if "sex" is a fantasy, is it perhaps a fantasmatic field that constitutes the very terrain of cultural intelligibility? Would such a rethinking of such conventional oppositions entail a rethinking of "constructivism" in its usual sense?

The radical constructivist position has tended to produce the premise that both refutes and confirms its own enterprise. If such a theory cannot take account of sex as the site or surface on which it acts, then it ends up presuming sex as the unconstructed and so concedes the limits of linguistic constructivism, inadvertently circumscribing that which remains unaccountable within the terms of construction. If, on the other hand, sex is a contrived premise, a fiction, then gender does not presume a sex that it acts upon, but rather gender produces the misnomer of a prediscursive "sex," and the meaning of construction becomes that of linguistic monism, whereby everything is only and always language. Then, what ensues is exasperated debate that many of us have tired of hearing: Either (1) constructivism is reduced to a position of linguistic monism, whereby linguistic construction is understood to be generative and deterministic—critics making that presumption can be heard to say, "If everything is discourse, what about the body?"; or (2) when construction is figuratively reduced to a verbal action which appears to presuppose a subject, critics working within such a presumption can be heard to say, "If gender is constructed, then who is doing the constructing?"; though, of course, (3) the most pertinent formulation of this question is the following: "If the subject is constructed, then who is constructing the subject?" In the first case, construction has taken the place of a godlike agency that not only causes but also composes everything which is its object; it is the divine performative, bringing into being and exhaustively constituting that which it names, or, rather, it is that kind of transitive referring that names and inaugurates at once. For something to be constructed, according to this view of construction, is for it to be created and determined through that process.

In the second and third cases, the seductions of grammar appear to hold sway; the critic asks, Must there not be a human agent, a subject, if you will, who guides the course of construction? If the first version of constructivism presumes that construction operates deterministically, making a mockery of human agency, the second understands constructivism as presupposing a voluntarist subject who makes its gender through an instrumental action. A construction is understood in this latter case to be a kind of manipulable artifice, a conception that not only presupposes a subject but also rehabilitates precisely the voluntarist subject of humanism that constructivism has, on occasion, sought to put into question.

If gender is a construction, must there be an "I" or a "we" who enacts or performs that construction? How can there be an activity, a constructing, without presupposing an agent who precedes and performs that activity? How would we account for the motivation and direction of construction without such a subject? As a rejoinder, I would suggest that it takes a certain suspicion toward grammar to reconceive the matter in a different light. For if gender is constructed, it is not necessarily constructed by an "I" or a "we" who stands before that construction in any spatial or temporal sense of "before." Indeed, it is unclear that there can be an "I" or a "we" who has not been submitted, subjected to gender, where gendering is, among other things, the differentiating relations by which speaking subjects come into being. Subjected to gender, but subjectivated by gender, the "I" neither precedes nor follows the process of this gendering, but emerges only within and as the matrix of gender relations themselves.

This then returns us to the second objection, the one which claims that constructivism forecloses agency, preempts the agency of the subject, and finds itself presupposing the subject that it calls into question. To claim that the subject is itself produced in and as a gendered matrix of relations is not to do away with the subject, but only to ask after the conditions of its emergence and operation. The "activity" of this gendering cannot, strictly speaking, be a human act or expression, a willful appropriation, and it is certainly *not* a question of taking on a mask; it is the matrix through which all willing first becomes possible, its enabling cultural condition. In this sense, the matrix of gender relations is prior to the emergence of the "human." Consider the medical interpellation that (the recent emergence of the sonogram notwithstanding) shifts an infant from an "it" to a "she" or a "he," and in that naming, the girl is "girled," brought into the domain of language and kinship through the interpellation of gender. But that "girled" of the girl does not end there; on the contrary, that founding interpellation is reiterated by various authorities and throughout various intervals of time to reenforce or contest this naturalized effect. The naming is at once the setting of a boundary and also the repeated inculcation of a norm.

Such attributions or interpellations contribute to that field of discourse and power that orchestrates, delimits, and sustains that which qualifies as "the human." We see this most clearly in the examples of those abjected beings who do not appear properly gendered; it is their very humanness that comes into question. Indeed, the construction of gender operates through *exclusionary* means, such that the human is not only produced over and against the inhuman but also through a set of foreclosures, radical erasures, that are, strictly speaking, refused the possibility of cultural articulation. Hence, it is not enough to claim that human subjects are constructed, for the construction of the human is a differential operation that produces the more and the less "human," the inhuman, the humanly unthinkable. These excluded sites come to bound the "human" as its constitutive outside, and to haunt those boundaries as the persistent possibility of their disruption and rearticulation.[4]

Paradoxically, the inquiry into the kinds of erasures and exclusions by which the construction of the subject operates is no longer constructivism, but neither is it essentialism. For there is an "outside" to what is constructed by discourse, but this is not an absolute "outside," an ontological thereness that exceeds or counters the boundaries of discourse;[5] as a constitutive "outside," it is that which can only be thought—when it can—in relation to that discourse, at and as its most tenuous borders. The debate between constructivism and essentialism thus misses the point of deconstruction altogether, for the point has never been that "everything is discursively constructed"; that point, when and where it is made, belongs to a kind of discursive monism or linguisticism that refuses the constitutive force of exclusion, erasure, violent foreclosure, abjection, and its disruptive return within the very terms of discursive legitimacy.

And to say that there is a matrix of gender relations that institutes and sustains the subject is not to claim that there is a singular matrix that acts in a singular and deterministic way to produce a subject as its effect. That is to install the "matrix" in the subject-position within a grammatical formulation which itself needs to be rethought. Indeed, the propositional form "Discourse constructs the subject" retains the subject-position of the grammatical formulation even as it reverses the place of subject and discourse. Construction must mean more than such a simple reversal of terms.

There are defenders and critics of construction, who construe that position along structuralist lines. They often claim that there are structures that construct the subject, impersonal forces, such as Culture or Discourse or Power, where these terms occupy the grammatical site of the subject after the "human" has been dislodged from its place. In such a view, the grammatical and metaphysical place of the subject is retained even as the candidate that occupies that place appears to rotate. As a result, construction is still understood as a unilateral process initiated by a prior subject, fortifying that presumption of the metaphysics of the subject that where there is activity, there lurks behind it an initiating and willful subject. On such a view, discourse or language or the social becomes personified, and in the personification the metaphysics of the subject is reconsolidated.

In this second view, construction is not an activity, but an act, one that happens once and whose effects are firmly fixed. Thus, constructivism is reduced to determinism and implies the evacuation or displacement of human agency.

This view informs the misreading by which Foucault is criticized for "personifying" power: if power is misconstrued as a grammatical and metaphysical subject, and if that metaphysical site within humanist discourse has been the privileged site of the human, then power appears to have displaced the human as the origin of activity. But if Foucault's view of power is understood as the disruption and subversion of this grammar and metaphysics of the subject, if power orchestrates the formation and sustenance of subjects, then it cannot be accounted for in terms of the "subject" which is its effect. And here it would be no more right to claim that the term "construction" belongs at the grammatical site of subject, for construction is neither a subject nor its act, but a process of reiteration by which both "subjects" and "acts" come to appear at all. There is no power that acts, but only a reiterated acting that is power in its persistence and instability.

What I would propose in place of these conceptions of construction is a return to the notion of matter, not as site or surface, but as *a process of materialization that stabilizes over time to produce the effect of boundary, fixity, and surface we call matter.* That matter is always materialized has, I think, to be thought in relation to the productive and, indeed, materializing effects of regulatory power in the Foucaultian sense.[6] Thus, the question is no longer, How is gender constituted as and through a certain interpretation of sex? (a question that leaves the "matter" of sex untheorized), but rather, Through what regulatory norms is sex itself materialized? And how is it that treating the materiality of sex as a given presupposes and consolidates the normative conditions of its own emergence?

Crucially, then, construction is neither a single act nor a causal process initiated by a subject and culminating in a set of fixed effects. Construction not only takes place *in* time, but also is itself a temporal process which operates through the reiteration of norms; sex is both produced and destabilized in the course of this reiteration.[7] As a sedimented effect of a reiterative or ritual practice, sex acquires its naturalized effect, and, yet, it is also by virtue of this reiteration that gaps and fissures are opened up as the constitutive instabilities in such constructions, as that which escapes or exceeds the norm, as that which cannot be wholly defined or fixed by the repetitive labor of that norm. This instability is the *de*constituting possibility in the very process of repetition, the power that undoes the very effects by which "sex" is stabilized, the possibility to put the consolidation of the norms of "sex" into a potentially productive crisis.[8]

Certain formulations of the radical constructivist position appear almost compulsively to produce a moment of recurrent exasperation, for it seems that when the constructivist is construed as a linguistic idealist, the constructivist refutes the reality of bodies, the relevance of science, the alleged facts of birth, aging, illness, and death. The critic might also suspect the constructivist of a certain somatophobia and seek assurances that this abstracted theorist will admit that there are, minimally, sexually differentiated parts, activities, capacities, hormonal and chromosomal differences that can be conceded without reference to "construction." Although at this moment I want to offer an absolute reassurance to my interlocutor, some anxiety prevails. To "concede" the undeniability of "sex" or its "materiality" is always to concede some version of "sex," some formation of "materiality." Is the discourse in and through which that concession occurs—and, yes, that concession invariably does occur—not itself formative of the very phenomenon that it concedes? To claim that discourse is formative is not to claim that it originates, causes, or exhaustively composes that which it concedes; rather, it is to claim that there is no reference to a pure body which is not at the same time a further formation of that body. In this sense, the linguistic capacity to refer to sexed bodies is not denied, but the very meaning of "referentiality" is altered. In philosophical terms, the constative claim is always to some degree performative.

In relation to sex, then, if one concedes the materiality of sex or of the body, does that very conceding operate—performatively—to materialize that sex? And further, how is it that the reiterated concession of that sex—one which need not take place in speech or writing but might be "signaled" in a much more inchoate way—constitutes the sedimentation and production of that material effect?

The moderate critic might concede that *some part* of "sex" is constructed but some other is certainly not, and then, of course, find him or herself not only under some obligation to draw the line between what is and is not constructed but also to explain how it is that "sex" comes in parts whose differentiation is not a matter of construction. But as that line of demarcation between such ostensible parts gets drawn, the "unconstructed" becomes bounded once again through a signifying practice, and the very boundary which is meant to protect some part of sex from the taint of constructivism is now defined by the anticonstructivist's own construction. Is construction something which happens to a ready-made object, a pregiven thing, and does it happen *in degrees?* Or are we perhaps referring on both sides of the debate to an inevitable practice of signification, of demarcating and delimiting that to which we then "refer," such that our "references" always presuppose—and often conceal—this prior delimitation? Indeed, to "refer" naively or directly to such an extradiscursive object will always require the prior delimitation of the extradiscursive. And insofar as the extradiscursive is delimited, it is formed by the very discourse from which it seeks to free itself. This delimitation, which often is enacted as an untheorized presupposition in any act of description, marks a boundary that includes and excludes, that decides, as it were, what will and will not be the stuff of the object to which we then refer. This marking off will have some normative force and, indeed, some violence, for it can construct only through erasing; it can bound a thing only through enforcing a certain criterion, a principle of selectivity.

What will and will not be included within the boundaries of "sex" will be set by a more or less tacit operation of exclusion. If we call into question the fixity of the structuralist law that divides and bounds the "sexes" by virtue of their dyadic differentiation within the heterosexual matrix, it will be from the exterior regions of that boundary (not from a "position," but from the discursive possibilities opened up by the constitutive outside of hegemonic positions), and it will constitute the disruptive return of the excluded from within the very logic of the heterosexual symbolic.

The trajectory of this text, then, will pursue the possibility of such disruption, but proceed indirectly by responding to two interrelated questions that have been posed to constructivist accounts of gender, not to defend constructivism per se, but to interrogate the erasures and exclusions that constitute its limits. These criticisms presuppose a set of metaphysical oppositions between materialism and idealism embedded in received grammar which, I will argue, are critically redefined by a poststructuralist rewriting of discursive performativity as it operates in the materialization of sex.

PERFORMATIVITY AS CITATIONALITY

When, in Lacanian parlance, one is said to assume a "sex," the grammar of the phrase creates the expectation that there is a "one" who, upon waking, looks up and deliberates on which "sex" it will assume today, a grammar in which "assumption" is quickly assimilated to the notion of a highly reflective choice. But if this "assumption" is *compelled* by a regulatory apparatus of hetero-sexuality, one that reiterates itself through the forcible production of "sex," then the "assumption" of sex is constrained from the start. And if there is *agency*, it is to be found, paradoxically, in the possibilities opened up in and by that constrained appropriation of the regulatory law, by the materialization of that law, the compulsory appropriation and identification with those normative demands. The forming, crafting, bearing, circulation, signification of that sexed body will not be a set of actions performed in compliance with the law; on the contrary, they will be a set of actions mobilized by the law, the citational accumulation and dissimulation of the law that pro-duces material effects, the lived necessity of those effects as well as the lived contestation of that necessity.

Performativity is thus not a singular "act," for it is always a reiteration of a norm or set of norms, and to the extent that it acquires an act-like status in the present, it conceals or dissimu-lates the conventions of which it is a repetition. Moreover, this act is not primarily theatrical; indeed, its apparently theatricality is produced to the extent that its historicity remains dissimu-lated (and, conversely, its theatricality gains a certain inevitability given the impossibility of a full disclosure of its historicity). Within speech act theory, a performative is that discursive practice that enacts or produces that which it names.[9] According to the biblical rendition of the perfor-mative—i.e., "Let there be light!"—it appears that it is by virtue of *the power of a subject or its will* that a phenomenon is named into being. In a critical reformulation of the performative, Derrida makes clear that this power is not the function of an originating will, but is always derivative:

> Could a performative utterance succeed if its formulation did not repeat a "coded" or iterable utter-ance, or in other words, if the formula I pronounce in order to open a meeting, launch a ship or a marriage were not identifiable as conforming with an iterable model, if it were not then identifiable in some way as a "citation"? . . . in such a typology, the category of intention will not disappear; it will have its place, but from that place it will no longer be able to govern the entire scene and system of utterance [*l'énonciation*].[10]

To what extent does discourse gain the authority to bring about what it names through citing the conventions of authority? And does a subject appear as the author of its discursive effects to the extent that the citational practice by which he/she is conditioned and mobilized remains unmarked? Indeed, could it be that the production of the subject as originator of his/her effects is precisely a consequence of this dissimulated citationality? Further, if a subject comes to be through a subjection to the norms of sex, can we read that "assumption" as precisely a modality of this kind of citationality? In other words, the norm of sex takes hold to the extent that it is "cited" as such a norm, but it also derives its power through the citations that it compels. And how it is that we might read the "citing" of the norms of sex as the process of approximating or "identifying with" such norms?

Further, to what extent within psychoanalysis is the sexed body secured through identificatory practices governed by regulatory schemas? Identification is used here not as an imitative activity by which a conscious being models itself after another; on the contrary, identification is the assimilating passion by which an ego first emerges.[11] Freud argues that "the ego is first and fore-most a bodily ego," that this ego is, further, "a projection of a surface,"[12] what we might redescribe as an imaginary morphology. Moreover, I would argue, this imaginary morphology is not a presocial or presymbolic operation, but is itself orchestrated through regulatory schemas that produce intelligible morphological possibilities. These regulatory schemas are not timeless structures, but historically revisable criteria of intelligibility that produce and vanquish bodies that matter.

If the formulation of a bodily ego, a sense of stable contour, and the fixing of spatial boundary is achieved through identificatory practices, and if psychoanalysis documents the hegemonic workings of those identifications, can we then read psychoanalysis for the inculcation of the heterosexual matrix at the level of bodily morphogenesis? What Lacan calls the "assumption" or "accession" to the symbolic law can be read as a kind of *citing* of the law, and so offers an opportunity to link the question of the materialization of "sex" with the reworking of performativity as citationality. Although Lacan claims that the symbolic law has a semi-autonomous status prior to the assumption of sexed positions by a subject, these normative positions, i.e., the "sexes," are only known through the approximations that they occasion. The force and necessity of these norms ("sex" as a symbolic function is to be understood as a kind of commandment or injunction) is thus functionally *dependent on* the approximation and citation of the law; the law without its approximation is no law or, rather, it remains a governing law only for those who would affirm it on the basis of religious faith. If "sex" is assumed in the same way that a law is cited, then "the law of sex" is repeatedly fortified and idealized as the law only to the extent that it is reiterated as the law, produced as the law, the anterior and inapproximable ideal, by the very citations it is said to command. Reading the meaning of "assumption" in Lacan as citation, the law is no longer given in a fixed form *prior* to its citation, but is produced through citation as that which precedes and exceeds the mortal approximations enacted by the subject.

In this way, the symbolic law in Lacan can be subject to the same kind of critique that Nietzsche formulated of the notion of God: the power attributed to this prior and ideal power is derived and deflected from the attribution itself.[13] It is this insight into the illegitimacy of the symbolic law of sex that is dramatized to a certain degree in the contemporary film *Paris is Burning*: the ideal that is mirrored depends on that very mirroring to be sustained as an ideal. And though the symbolic appears to be a force that cannot be contravened without psychosis, the symbolic ought to be rethought as a series of normativizing injunctions that secure the borders of sex through the threat of psychosis, abjection, psychic unlivability. And further, that this "law" can only remain a law to the extent that it compels the differentiated citations and approximations called "feminine" and "masculine." The presumption that the symbolic law of sex enjoys a separable ontology prior and autonomous to its assumption is contravened by the notion that the citation of the law is the very mechanism of its production and articulation. What is "forced" by the symbolic, then, is a citation of its law that reiterates and consolidates the ruse of its own force. What would it mean to "cite" the law to produce it differently, to "cite" the law in order to reiterate and coopt its power, to expose the heterosexual matrix and to displace the effect of its necessity?

The process of that sedimentation or what we might call *materialization* will be a kind of citationality, the acquisition of being through the citing of power, a citing that establishes an originary complicity with power in the formation of the "I."

In this sense, the agency denoted by the performativity of "sex" will be directly counter to any notion of a voluntarist subject who exists quite apart from the regulatory norms which she/he opposes. The paradox of subjectivation (*assujetissement*) is precisely that the subject who would resist such norms is itself enabled, if not produced, by such norms. Although this constitutive constraint does not foreclose the possibility of agency, it does locate agency as a reiterative or rearticulatory practice, immanent to power, and not a relation of external opposition to power.

As a result of this reformulation of performativity, (a) gender performativity cannot be theorized apart from the forcible and reiterative practice of regulatory sexual regimes; (b) the account of agency conditioned by those very regimes of discourse/power cannot be conflated with voluntarism or individualism, much less with consumerism, and in no way presupposes a choosing subject; (c) the regime of heterosexuality operates to circumscribe and contour the "materiality" of sex, and that "materiality" is formed and sustained through and as a materialization of regulatory norms that are in part those of heterosexual hegemony; (d) the materialization of norms requires those identificatory processes by which norms are assumed or appropriated, and these identifications precede and enable the formation of a subject, but are not, strictly speaking, performed by a subject; and (e) the limits of constructivism are exposed at those boundaries of bodily life where abjected or delegitimated bodies fail to count as "bodies." If the materiality of sex is demarcated in discourse, then this demarcation will produce a domain of excluded and delegitimated "sex." Hence, it will be as important to think about how and to what end bodies are constructed as is it will be to think about how and to what end bodies are *not* constructed and, further, to ask after how bodies which fail to materialize provide the necessary "outside," if not the necessary support, for the bodies which, in materializing the norm, qualify as bodies that matter.

How, then, can one think through the matter of bodies as a kind of materialization governed by regulatory norms in order to ascertain the workings of heterosexual hegemony in the formation of what qualifies as a viable body? How does that materialization of the norm in bodily formation produce a domain of abjected bodies, a field of deformation, which, in failing to qualify as the fully human, fortifies those regulatory norms? What challenge does that excluded and abjected realm produce to a symbolic hegemony that might force a radical rearticulation of what qualifies as bodies that matter, ways of living that count as "life," lives worth protecting, lives worth saving, lives worth grieving?

NOTES

1. Clearly, sex is not the only such norm by which bodies become materialized, and it is unclear whether "sex" can operate as a norm apart from other normative requirements on bodies. This will become clear in later sections of this text.

2. Abjection (in Latin, *ab-jicere*) literally means to cast off, away, or out and, hence, presupposes and produces a domain of agency from which it is differentiated. Here the casting away resonates with the psychoanalytic notion of *Verwerfung*, implying a foreclosure which founds the subject and which, accordingly, establishes that foundation as tenuous. Whereas the psychoanalytic notion of *Verwerfung*, translated as "foreclosure," produces sociality through a repudiation of a primary signifier which produces an unconscious or, in Lacan's theory—the register of the real, the notion of *abjection* designates a degraded or cast-out status within the terms of sociality. Indeed, what is foreclosed or repudiated *within* psychoanalytic terms is precisely what may not reenter the field of the social without threatening psychosis, that is, the dissolution of the subject itself. I want to propose that certain abject zones within sociality also deliver this threat, constituting zones of uninhabitability which a subject fantasizes as threatening in its own integrity with the prospect of a psychotic dissolution ("I would rather die than do or be that!"). See the entry under "Forclusion" in Jean Laplanche and J.-B. Pontalis, *Vocabulaire de la psychanalyse* (Paris: Presses Universitaires de France, 1967), pp. 163–67.

3. See Sherry Ortner, "Is Female to Male as Nature Is to Culture?" in *Woman, Culture, and Society*, ed. Michele Rosaldo and Louise Lamphere (Stanford: Stanford University Press, 1974), pp. 67–88.

4. For different but related approaches to this problematic of exclusion, abjection, and the creation of "the human," see Julia Kristeva, *Powers of Horror: An Essay on Abjection*, tr. Leon Roudiez (New York: Columbia University Press, 1982); John Fletcher and Andrew Benjamin, eds., *Abjection, Melancholia and Love: The Work of Julia Kristeva* (New York and London: Routledge, 1990); Jean-François Lyotard, *The Inhuman: Reflections on Time*, tr. Geoffrey Bennington and Rachel Bowlby (Stanford: Stanford University Press, 1991).

5. For a very provocative reading that shows how the problem of linguistic referentiality is linked with the specific problem of referring to bodies, and what might be meant by "reference" in such a case, see Cathy Caruth, "The Claims of Reference," *Yale Journal of Criticism*, vol. 4, no. 1 (Fall 1990): pp. 193–206.

6. Although Foucault distinguishes between juridical and productive models of power in *The History of Sexualtiy, Volume One*, tr. Robert Hurley (New York: Vintage, 1978), I have argued that the two

models presuppose each other. The production of a subject—its subjection (*assujetissement*)—is one means of its regulation. See my "Sexual Inversions," in *Discourses of Sexualtiy* ed. Domna Stanton (Ann Arbor: University of Michigan Press, 1992), pp. 344–61.

7. It is not simply a matter of construing performativity as a repetition of acts, as if "acts" remain intact and self-identical as they are repeated in time, and where "Time" is understood as external to the "acts" themselves. On the contrary, an act is itself a repetition, a sedimentation, and congealment of the past which is precisely foreclosed in its act-like status. In this sense an "act" is always a provisional failure of memory. In what follows, I make use of the Lacanian notion that every act is to be construed as a repetition, the repetition of what cannot be recollected, of the irrecoverable, and is thus the haunting specter of the subject's deconstitution. The Derridean notion of iterability, formulated in response to the theorization of speech acts by John Searle and J. L. Austin, also implies that every act is itself a recitation, the citing of a prior chain of acts which are implied in a present act and which perpetually drain any "present" act of its presentness. See note 9 below for the difference between a repetition in the service of the fantasy of mastery (i.e., a repetition of acts which build the subject, and which are said to be the constructive or constituting acts of a subject) and a notion of repetition-compulsion, taken from Freud, which breaks apart that fantasy of mastery and sets its limits.

8. The notion of temporality ought not to be construed as a simple succession of distinct "moments," all of which are equally distant from one another. Such a spatialized mapping of time substitutes a certain mathematical model for the kind of duration that resists such spatializing metaphors. Efforts to describe or name this temporal span tend to engage spatial mapping, as philosophers from Bergson through Heidegger have argued. Hence, it is important to underscore the effect of *sedimentation* that the temporality of construction implies. Here, what are called "moments" are not distinct and equivalent units of time, for the "past" will be the accumulation and congealing of such "moments" to the point of their indistinguishability. But it will also consist of that which is refused from construction, the domains of the repressed, forgotten, and the irrecoverably foreclosed. That which is not included—exteriorized by boundary—as a phenomenal constituent of the sedimented effect called "construction" will be as crucial to its definition as that which is included; this exteriority is not distinguishable as a "moment." Indeed, the notion of the "moment" may well be nothing other than a retrospective fantasy of mathematical mastery imposed upon the interrupted durations of the past.

To argue that construction is fundamentally a matter of iteration is to make the temporal modality of "construction" into a priority. To the extent that such a theory requires a spatialization of time through the postulation of discrete and bounded moments, this temporal account of construction presupposes a spatialization of temporality itself, what one might, following Heidegger, understand as the reduction of temporality to time.

The Foucaultian emphasis on *convergent* relations of power (which might in a tentative way be contrasted with the Derridean emphasis on iterability) implies a mapping of power relations that in the course of a genealogical process from a constructed effect. The notion of convergence presupposes both motion and space; as a result, it appears to elude the paradox noted above in which the very account of temporality requires the spatialization of the "moment." On the other hand, Foucault's account of convergence does not fully theorize what is at work in the "movement" by which power and discourse are said to converge. In a sense, the "mapping" of power does not fully theorize temporality.

Significantly, the Derridean analysis of iterability is to be distinguished from simple repetition in which the distances between temporal "moments" are treated as uniform in their spatial extension. The "betweenness" that differentiates "moments" of time is not one that can, within Derridean terms, be spatialized or bounded as an identifiable object. It is the nonthematizable différance which erodes and contests any and all claims to discrete identity, including the discrete identity of the "moment." What differentiates moments is not a spatially extended duration, for, if it were, it would also count as a "moment," and so fail to account for what falls between moments. This "entre," that which is at once "between" and "outside," is something like nonthematizable space and nonthematizable time as they converge.

Foucault's language of construction includes terms like "augmentation," "proliferation," and "convergence," all of which presume a temporal domain not explicitly theorized. Part of the problem here is that whereas Foucault appears to want his account of genealogical effects to be historically specific, he would favor an account of genealogy over a philosophical account of temporality. In "The Subject and Power" (Hubert Dreyfus and Paul Rabinow, eds., *Michel Foucault: Beyond Structuralism and Hermeneutics* [Chicago: Northwestern University Press, 1983]), Foucault refers to "the diversity of . . . logical sequence" that characterizes power relations. He would doubtless reject the apparent linearity implied by models of iterability which link them with the linearity of older models of historical sequence. And yet, we do not receive a specification of "sequence": Is it the very notion of "sequence" that varies historically, or are there configurations of sequence that vary, with sequence itself remaining invariant? The specific social formation and figuration of temporality is in some ways unattended by both positions. Here one might consult the work of Pierre Bourdieu to understand the temporality of social construction.

9. See J. L. Austin, *How to Do Things With Words*, eds. J. O. Urmson and Marina Sbisà (Cambridge, Mass.: Harvard University Press, 1955), and *Philosophical Papers* (Oxford: Oxford University Press, 1961), especially pp. 233–252; Shoshana Felman, *The Literary Speech-Act: Don Juan with J. L. Austin, or Seduction in Two Languages*, tr. Catherine Porter (Ithaca: Cornell University Press, 1983); Barbara Johnson, "Poetry and Performative Language: Mallarmé and Austin," in *The Critical Difference: Essays in the Contemporary Rhetoric of Reading* (Baltimore: Johns Hopkins University Press, 1980), pp. 52–66; Mary Louis Pratt, *A Speech Act Theory of Literary Discourse* (Bloomington: Indiana University Press, 1977); and Ludwig Wittgenstein, *Philosophical Investigations*, tr. G. E. M. Anscombe (New York: Macmillan, 1958), part 1.

10. Jacques Derrida, "Signature, Event, Context," in *Limited, Inc.*, ed. Gerald Graff, tr. Samuel Weber and Jeffrey Mehlman (Evanston, IL: Northwestern University Press, 1988), p. 18.

11. See Michel Borch-Jacobsen, *The Freudian Subject*, tr. Catherine Porter (Stanford: Stanford University Press, 1988). Whereas Borch-Jacobsen offers an interesting theory of how identification precedes and forms the ego, he tends to assert the priority of identification to any libidinal experience, where I would insist that identification is itself a passionate or libidinal assimilation. See also the useful distinction between an imitative model and a mimetic model of identification in Ruth Leys, "The Real Miss Beauchamp: Gender and the Subject of Imitation" in *Feminists Theorize the Political*, ed. Judith Butler and Joan Scott (New York :Routledge, 1992), pp. 167–214; Kaja Silverman, *Male Subjectivity at the Margins* (New York: Routledge, 1992), pp. 262–70; Mary Ann Doane, "Misrecognition and Identity," in *Explorations in Film Theory: Selected Essays from Ciné-Tracts*, ed. Ron Burnett (Bloomington: Indiana University Press, 1991), pp. 15–25; and Diana Fuss, "Freud's Fallen Women: Identification, Desire, and 'A Case of Homosexuality in a Woman,'" *Yale Journal of Criticism*, vol. 6, no. 1 (1993), pp. 1–23.

12. Sigmund Freud, *The Ego and the Id*, ed. James Strachey; tr. Joan Riviere (New York: Norton, 1960), p. 16.

13. Nietzsche argues that the ideal of God was produced "in the same measure" as a human sense of failure and wretchedness, and that the production of God was, indeed, the idealization which instituted and reenforced that wretchedness; see Friedrich Nietzsche, *On the Genealogy of Morals*, tr. Walter Kaufmann (New York: Vintage, 1969), section 20. That the symbolic law in Lacan produces "failure" to approximate the sexed ideals embodied and enforced by the law is usually understood as a promising sign that the law is not fully efficacious, that it does not exhaustively constitute the psyche of any given subject. And yet, to what extent does this conception of the law produce the very failure that it seeks to order, and maintain an ontological distance between the laws and its failed approximations such that the deviant approximations have no power to alter the workings of the law itself?

36   The End of the Body?

Emily Martin

Why is the body such an intense focus of attention in the academy today? Perhaps all this attention has come about simply because the body is now a central feature of contemporary Western social forms. Certainly, numerous historical forces could be said to have played a role in producing the current salience of the body: European state formation, creating and protecting individual rights, produced citizens who, one per body, voted, fought, paid taxes, and sowed their seed (Corrigan and Sayer 1985). Industrialization, which incorporated workers into factory structures separated from family and community, controlled and harnessed individual bodies in new ways. Modern forms of power, deployed in the normalizing discourses of sciences such as psychiatry and biology, led us to spill the contents of our inner lives into the waiting arms of new disciplines of knowledge. This power "seeps into the very grain of individuals, reaches right into their bodies, permeates their gestures, their posture, what they say, how they learn to live and work with other people" (Foucault, quoted in Sheridan 1980: 217).

Given all this, it is no wonder that the body is so often a focus of social and cultural analysis. However, I would argue that there is another way of explaining why the body is such an intense focus of academic attention today. In *Tristes Tropiques* (1967), Lévi-Strauss described how phenomena become the focus of attention in the academy precisely when they are ending; he was speaking of the "primitive," which was in the process of disappearing for the last time. Is one reason so many of us are energetically studying the body precisely that we are undergoing fundamental changes in how our bodies are organized and experienced? Some have claimed that the body as a bounded entity is in fact ending under the impact of commodification, fragmentation, and the proliferation of images of body parts (Kroker and Kroker 1987: 20). Without discounting these claims, I would argue they need to be seen in a particular context. In the following I

Emily Martin is Professor of Anthropology at Princeton University. Her work on ideology and power in Chinese society was published in *The Cult of the Dead in a Chinese Village* (Stanford) and *Chinese Ritual and Politics* (Cambridge). Beginning with *The Woman in the Body: A Cultural Analysis of Reproduction* (Beacon, 1987), she has been working on the anthropology of science and reproduction in the U.S. Her latest research is described in *Flexible Bodies: Tracking Immunity in America from the Days of Polio to the Age of AIDS* (Beacon, 1994).

will suggest that people in the United States (and perhaps elsewhere) are now experiencing a dramatic transition in body perception and practice, from bodies suited for and conceived in the terms of the era of Fordist mass production to bodies suited for and conceived in the terms of the era of flexible accumulation. We are seeing not the end of the body, but rather the end of one kind of body and the beginning of another kind of body.

THE FORDIST BODY

Imagery in reproductive biology exemplifies what I mean by the Fordist body. In reproductive biology, bodies are organized around principles of centralized control and factory-based production. Men continuously produce wonderfully astonishing quantities of highly valued sperm, women produce eggs and babies (though neither efficiently) and, when they are not doing this, either produce scrap (menstruation) or undergo a complete breakdown of central control (menopause). The models that confer order are hierarchical pyramids, with the brain firmly located at the top and the other organs ranged below. The body's products all flow out over the edge of the body, through one orifice or another, into the outside world. Steady, regular output is prized above all, preferably over the entire life span, as exemplified by the production of sperm (Martin 1987; 1991).

In contemporary cell biology, similar motifs are present. Inside the cell, the nucleus with its genetic material is seen as the privileged head of the cell "family":

> The master-molecule has become, in DNA, the unmoved mover of the changing cytoplasm. In this cellular version of the Aristotelian cosmos, the nucleus is the efficient cause (as Aristotle posited the sperm to be) while the cytoplasm (like Aristotle's conception of the female substrate) is merely the *material* cause. The nuclear DNA is the essence of domination and control. Macromolecule as machomolecule. [Beldecos et al. 1988: 70]

These models of the body seem related in form and function to early twentieth-century Fordist mass-production systems. Such systems sought efficiency by means of economies of scale in production; they were geared to producing large quantities of standardized products put together from standardized components.

During the establishment of Fordist forms of organization in the United States, Antonio Gramsci wrote that Fordism implied "the biggest collective effort to date to create, with unprecedented speed, and with a consciousness of purpose unmatched in history, a new type of worker and a new type of man" (quoted in Harvey 1989a: 126). The success of Fordist production would rely on new constructions of sexuality, reproduction, family life, moral ideals, masculinity, and femininity. New habits would preserve, "outside of work, a certain psycho-physical equilibrium which [would] prevent the physiological collapse of the worker, exhausted by the new method of production." This equilibrium could become internalized "if it [were] proposed by a new form of society, with appropriate and original methods" (Gramsci 1971: 303). Some means by which a new form of society was "proposed" involved coercion. Henry Ford sent investigators into workers' homes to intervene in their private lives. One hundred fifty investigators admonished workers to practice thrifty and hygienic habits and to avoid smoking, gambling, and drinking. These early social workers decided which workers "because of unsatisfactory personal habits or home conditions" were not eligible to receive the full five-dollar wage Ford offered (Gelderman 1981: 56–57). Other means, we might speculate, could operate at a less obvious level. Perhaps scientific body imagery, capturing the essential features of Fordist production, was one "appropriate and original method" that could lead people to internalize a new form of society. Perhaps the two sets of interrelated imageries in the body and in society were used to think thoughts and organize practice about time, space, substance, productivity, efficiency, and so on.

FLEXIBILITY: THE BODY IN LATE CAPITALISM

In the course of my fieldwork on contemporary concepts of the immune system, I began to wonder whether the Fordist body was being transformed.[1] Far from being reminiscent of Fordist production, talk about the immune system seems to share its logic with a different social formation, one that began to coalesce sometime in the 1970s. Are new modes of "living and thinking and feeling life" (Gramsci, quoted in Harvey 1989a: 126) coming into being alongside wrenching new forms of social organization? Could the writing of these new modes into the body, via what we think of as scientific "truth," be a particularly powerful way in which certain principles are literally being internalized, making an important contribution to creating a "new type of worker and a new type of man [and woman]," a new "shape of life" (Flax 1990: 39)?

Called variously late capitalism (Ernst Mandel) or the regime of flexible accumulation (David Harvey), the new formation has as its hallmarks technological innovation, specificity, and rapid, flexible change. It entails "flexible system production with [an] emphasis upon problem solving, rapid and often highly specialized responses, and adaptability of skills to special purposes"; "an increasing capacity to manufacture a variety of goods cheaply in small batches" (Harvey 1989a: 155); "an acceleration in the pace of product innovation together with the exploration of highly specialized and small-scale market niches"; and "new organizational forms (such as the 'just-in-time' inventory-flows delivery system, which cuts down radically on stocks required to keep production flow going)" (Harvey 1989a: 156).

Laborers experience a speed-up in the processes of labor and an intensification in the deskilling and reskilling that are constantly required. New technologies in production reduce turnover time dramatically, entailing similar accelerations in exchange and consumption. "Improved systems of communication and information flow, coupled with rationalizations in techniques of distribution (packaging, inventory control, containerization, market feedback, etc.), make it possible to circulate commodities through the market system with greater speed" (Harvey 1989a: 285). Time and space are compressed, as the time horizons of decision making shrink and instantaneous communications and cheaper transport costs allow decisions to be effected over a global space (Harvey 1989a: 147). Multinational capital operates in a globally integrated environment: ideally, capital flows unimpeded across all borders, all points are connected by instantaneous communications, and products are made as needed for the momentary and continuously changing market.

The imagery used to describe the immune system in the body strongly evokes these descriptions of the operation of global capital. In the scientific discipline of immunology, the body is depicted as a whole, interconnected system complete unto itself. The body is seen as "an engineered communications system, ordered by a fluid and dispersed command-control-intelligence network" (Haraway 1989: 12). One example of this is a line drawing from a college textbook showing the complex communications among three types of immune system cells: macrophages, T cells, and B cells. The macrophage has taken the foreign bacterium, the antigen, inside itself, processed it, and put it back on the surface along with a protein called MHC, which marks cells in this particular body as "self." This allows a T cell to "recognize" the foreign antigen as something to be dealt with, and it sends the first activation "signal" to a B cell. At the same time the B cell recognizes the foreign material directly. Meanwhile the macrophage is sending signals to both T and B cells. Then other T cells send further signals to the B cell, leading it to differentiate and start producing antibodies, which will eliminate the foreign matter that the macrophage ingested in the first place. This is only a tiny portion of the total system of communication and control involved. One further element is crucial: at a later stage, another kind of T cell is activated; called the T suppressor cell, it is a "controlling mechanism that turn[s] off the proliferation of reactive cells and limit[s] the extent of the response" (Sell 1987: 224).

The classroom version of this tends to be elaborate chalkboard sketches with countless arrows showing signals from one cell to another in the system, accompanied by frequent statements that all functions are interrelated. This is a homeostatic, self-regulating system, complete unto itself. This way of seeing the immune system is far from limited to an esoteric scientific community. As part of a three-year research project, several graduate students and I have done over 100 extensive interviews on health concepts and practices with residents of several urban neighborhoods. We have found that people convey the systemic character of the immune system in various ways:

> Bill Walters (service worker in his twenties): I don't even think about the heart anymore; I think about the immune system as being the major thing that's keeping the heart going in the first place, and now that I think about it I would have to say yeah, the immune system is really . . . important . . . and the immune system isn't even a vital organ, it's just an act, you know?
>
> Peter Herman (corporate employee in his twenties): It's like a complete . . . If one thing fails, I mean if—
>
> Bill Walters: If something goes wrong, the immune system fixes it; it's like a back-up system. It's a perfect balance.

Next, consider what kind of production is associated with the immune system. The essence of contemporary scientific descriptions of the immune system is careful regulation of production in orientation to specific needs, not efficient production on a mass scale as in the Fordist model. When I was taking my first course in immunology, I was struck by the repeated emphasis on the "specificity" of immune system cells, both T cells and B cells. For example, as a B cell matures, it develops surface receptors that will be "committed to a single specificity . . . a specificity to a single antigen." One of the first lectures in the course, on immunoglobulins (also called antibodies), started out with "immunoglobulin facts to amaze you":

> There are 6×10^{16} immunoglobulin molecules per ml of blood, 5 liters of blood in the body, or 3×10^{20} molecules of immunoglobulin in the body. A visiting lecturer will say there are 10^6 or 10^8 different specificities possible. In theory it is possible to have 6×10^{10} molecules of different specificity in each ml of serum. Potentially there are a lot of preformed specificities for an organism to encounter. There are a lot of these little suckers running around.

The visiting lecturer called them "tailor-made specificities."

But this specificity is not a mechanical sort of specificity. Referring to a diagram of the immunoglobulin molecule, depicted as a Y-shaped molecule whose forked end can lock into antigens (foreign material), the lecturer went on: "Exquisite specificity was a term used earlier, but it is not clear now how exquisite the specificity is because of the flexibility at the hinge region. . . . They can move and lock in." What is emphasized is specificity *and* flexibility, so that any possible foreign molecule or protein can be matched from the body's store of specific/flexible antibodies.

In flexible accumulation, the stress is on constant innovation, which is the basis for flexible response to new markets. In the immune system the basis for all the "tailor-made specificities" in the body is genetic mutation, which produces a constant flow of new specificities in certain immune system cells, B cells. These new specificities wait in the body like bits of potentially useful information until (if it ever happens) a match is made with a foreign antigen. Then antibodies are produced, in just the right amount needed.

Finally, consider how time and space are depicted in descriptions of the immune system. With the transition from Fordism to flexible accumulation, we experience

> an intense phase of time-space compression that has had a disorienting and disruptive impact upon political-economic practices. . . . Spaces of very different worlds seem to collapse upon each other, much as the world's commodities are assembled in the supermarket and all manner of sub-cultures get juxtaposed in the contemporary city. [Harvey 1989a: 284, 301–1]

In Harvey's view, time/space compression is a phenomenon that "so revolutionize[s] the objective qualities of space and time that we are forced to alter, sometimes in quite radical ways, how we represent the world to ourselves" (Harvey 1989a: 240).

When, in our interviews about the immune system, people are asked to move in imagination to the world inside the body, they often find the experience spatially dislocating. After people have talked at length about their conceptions of the immune system, immunity, health, and illness, we then show them micrographs of greatly magnified immune system cells, such as macrophages or T cells. Many people have seen these before in popular magazines or educational movies. Here is a typical response:

> Dave Potter (accountant in his twenties, looking at a micrograph of cells): That's, see to me, that's what's incredible. . . . I mean that one cell is unto its own. It doesn't have a brain, your brain isn't connected to it, and it's got its own. . . . God! It's so incredible, I mean it's phenomenal! . . . It's like being in two different worlds.
>
> Interviewer: Really?
>
> Dave Potter: Yeah, I mean, even though I've seen all these kinds of things before and I realize that these are the exact same kinds of things that are in my body, it's still distanced somehow. I mean *these cells act on their own, you know, there's no connection between being a human and having, there's no connection between me being a conscious human being and this cell that's inside me.*

The self has retreated inside the body, is a witness to itself, a tiny figure in a cosmic landscape, which is the body. This scene is one that is both greatly exciting and greatly bewildering.

Dramatic forms of spatial disorientation are particularly apparent in the large numbers of people who interpret scientific images as visions of something colossal and distant inside us: these images look, as Nancy Harris puts it, "like star wars," "like space sharks," "like the sun and the moon." Consider the remarks of John Marcellino, a community organizer in his forties:

> It's funny, . . . when you think about the inside of your body, I think about outer space. It's like those are the only things that look like this, you know, they're that far away from you. It's weird because outer space is like, way out there, and your body is just right here, but it's about the same, it's the same thing.

No wonder it is disconcerting: the unimaginably small and the unimaginably large coalesced in the same image, agency residing in cells, the person becoming an observer of the agency of others inside him or herself. The "I" who used to wear the body like a closely fitting set of clothes is now miniaturized, and is dwarfed by its body. The "I" is made a passive and powerless witness to the doings of the components of the body. Somewhere in the system lies agency; the "I" can only watch.

It is much less clear to me what is happening with representations of time. In popular texts about the immune system, it is striking how many different historical periods are "plundered" to depict the workings of this postmodern instantaneous information deployment system. Here are some typical images: an ancient city (Jewler 1989), an ancient walled castle (Kobren 1989), ancient Japanese warriors (Schindler 1988), conventional contemporary arms (Brownlee 1990; Lertola 1984). Perhaps these images convey a sense of being unmoored in time, unable to unify past, present, and future, a disorientation in time to match a disorientation in space.

I am suggesting that the science of immunology is helping to render a kind of aesthetic or architecture for our bodies that captures some of the essential features of flexible accumulation. Presumably these images in science developed in complex interaction with many changing social forms and practices. Here I have space only to point out that the era of flexible accumulation is usually said to have begun in the early 1970s (with some seeds present in the 1960s) (Harvey

1989a: 141–172). The ideas in immunology that I have discussed emerged at roughly the same time. It was not until the late 1960s that the concept of an immune *system* as such existed (Moulin 1989), and it was not until the early 1970s that departments of immunology existed in American or other universities. Knowledge of how specificity in antibodies works came at this time too: Edelman and Porter shared the Nobel prize for studies of the structural basis of immunological specificity in 1972 (Silverstein 1989: 134–35).

SELF / NONSELF: THE WAR SCENE

To see further complexities of the late twentieth-century body, we must turn to a different picture, one that exists alongside the flexible response system I have outlined. This is a portrait of the body as a nation-state, organized around a hidden discourse of gender, race, and class, the "hierarchical, localized organic body" (Haraway 1989: 14). In this picture, which is taught in biology classes and conveyed in the popular media, the boundary between the body ("self") and the external world ("nonself") is rigid and absolute: "At the heart of the immune system is the ability to distinguish between self and nonself. Virtually every body cell carries distinctive molecules that identify it as self" (Schindler 1988: 1). These molecules are class 1 MHC proteins, present on every nucleated cell in an individual's body and different from every other individual's. One popular book calls these our "trademarks" (Dwyer 1988: 37). The maintenance of the purity of self within the borders of the body is seen as tantamount to the maintenance of the self: a chapter called "The Body Under Siege," in the popular book on the immune system *In Self Defense*, begins with the epigraph, "'To be or not to be, that is the question' (William Shakespeare)" (Mizel and Jaret 1985: 1).

As one of the interviews I quoted hints, talk about the immune system's maintenance of a clear boundary between self and nonself is often accompanied by a conception of the nonself world as foreign and hostile. Our bodies are faced with masses of cells bent on our destruction: "To fend off the threatening horde, the body has devised astonishingly intricate defenses" (Schindler 1988: 13). As a measure of the extent of this threat, contemporary popular publications depict the body as the scene of all-out war between ruthless invaders and determined defenders: "Besieged by a vast array of invisible enemies, the human body enlists a remarkably complex corps of internal bodyguards to battle the invaders" (Jaret 1986: 702). A site of injury is "transformed into a battle field on which the body's armed forces, hurling themselves repeatedly at the encroaching microorganisms, crush and annihilate them" (Nilsson 1985: 20).

Small white blood cells called granulocytes are "kept permanently at the ready for a blitzkrieg against microorganisms" and constitute the "infantry" of the immune system: "Multitudes fall in battle, and together with their vanquished foes, they form the pus which collects in wounds" (Nilsson 1985: 24). Larger macrophages are another type of white blood cell, the "armored unit" of the defense system: "These roll forth through the tissues, . . . devouring everything that has no useful role to play there" (Nilsson 1985: 25). Another part of the immune system, the complement system, can "perforate hostile organisms so that their lives trickle to a halt" (Nilsson 1985: 24). The components of the complement system function as "'magnetic mines.' They are sucked toward the bacterium and perforate it, causing it to explode" (Nilsson 1985: 72). When the system "comes together in the right sequence, it detonates like a bomb, blasting through the invader's cell membrane" (Jaret 1986: 720). Certain T lymphocytes, whose technical scientific name is the "killer cells," are the "immune system's special combat units in the war against cancer"; killer cells "strike," "attack," and "assault" (Nilsson 1985: 96, 98, 100). "The killer T cells are relentless. Docking with infected cells, they shoot lethal proteins at the cell membrane. Holes form where the protein molecules hit, and the cell, dying, leaks out its insides" (Jaroff 1988: 59).

Not surprisingly, identities involving gender, race, and class are present in this war scene. Compare two categories of immune system cells, macrophages, which surround and digest foreign organisms, and T cells, which kill by transferring toxin to them. The macrophages are a lower form of cell, evolutionarily, and are even found in such primitive organisms as worms (Roitt, Brostoff, and Male 1985: 2.1); they are called a "primeval tank corps" (Michaud, Feinstein, and Editors 1989: 3). T cells are more evolutionarily advanced and have higher functions such as memory (Jaroff 1988: 60; Roitt, Brostoff, and Male 1985: 2.5). It is only these advanced cells which "attend the technical colleges of the immune system" (Nilsson 1985: 26).

There is clearly a hierarchical division of labor here, one that is to some extent overlaid with our gender categories. Specifically, there are obvious female associations with the engulfing and surrounding that macrophages do and obvious male associations with the penetrating or injecting that killer T cells do. In addition, many scholars have pointed out the frequent symbolic association of the female with lower functions, and especially with a lack of or lesser degree of mental functions.

Beyond this, macrophages are the cells that are the "housekeepers" (Jaret 1986) of the body, cleaning up the dirt and debris, including the "dead bodies" of both self and foreign cells (one immunologist called them "little drudges"):

> The first defenders to arrive would be the phagocytes [a category of "eating" cells that includes macrophages]—the scavengers of the system. Phagocytes constantly scour the territories of our bodies, alert to anything that seems out of place. What they find, they engulf and consume. Phagocytes are not choosy. They will eat anything suspicious that they find in the bloodstream, tissues, or lymphatic system. [Jaret 1986: 715]

Given their uncultivated origins, it should not be surprising that after eating, macrophages "burp": "After [a macrophage] finishes its meal, it burps out pieces of the enemy and puts them out on its surface" (Michaud, Feinstein, and Editors 1989: 6). As macrophages feed, they may be described as "angry" or in a "feeding fury," an image combining uncontrolled emotions with an obliterating, engulfing presence, both common cultural ascriptions of females. In addition, as is often the case with the lower orders of human females, the macrophage harbors disease. It is the macrophage that is the reservoir of HIV. "Unlike T 4 cells, the macrophage is not killed by HIV. It may serve as a reservoir for the virus" (Gallo and Montagnier 1989).

Gender might not be the only overlay on this division of labor. Racial overtones could be there as well, although I have less convincing evidence for them. Macrophages are the cells that actually eat other cells belonging to the category "self," and so engage in a form of "cannibalism." Cannibalism is often associated with the attribution of a lower animal nature to those who engage in it (Arens 1979). In immunology, macrophages are seen as feminized in some ways but as simply "uncivilized" in other ways. These "cannibals" are indiscriminate eaters, barbaric and savage in their willingness to eat any manner of thing at all. Sometimes macrophages are feminized "housekeepers," and sometimes they seem to be racially marked, as when they are described as "roving garbage collectors" (Brownlee 1990: 50).

A more certain reason for the lowliness of macrophages is that they lack the highly valued characteristic (given a regime of flexible accumulation) of specificity. In a class lecture, I heard that macrophages are "the dumb cells of the immune system. They don't have any specificity, while T cells do have specificity."

To explore the hierarchy of cells further, we need to look at another immune system cell, the B cell. B cells are clearly ranked far above the lowly macrophage. They are not educated in the college of the thymus, but they are "educated" in the bone marrow (Dwyer 1988: 47) and they have enormous specificity. However, they rank below the T cell, which is consistently termed the "orchestrator" of the immune response and which activates B cells. In one popular book, the T cell is said to give the B cell "permission" to attack invading organisms (Dwyer 1988: 47). (This assertion is frequently made in spite of the interlocking nature of all the elements of the system.) B cells exist in two stages, virgin or immature B cells and, when stimulated by an antigen of the right specificity, mature B cells. Mature B cells are the cells that, with T cell "permission," rapidly produce antibodies against invading antigen. A B cell starts out a virgin, is stimulated by the right nonself antigen and the T cell, and thereupon starts to produce antibodies like mad.

In one lecture I heard, T cells were said to "sidle up" to B cells as a part of their orchestration of B cell responses to antigen. I think that in most American courtship behavior, It would be the man who sidled up to the woman. So this suggests that B cells are sometimes feminized but rank much higher in the hierarchy than the lowly macrophage. In the B cell, then, we may have a kind of upper-class female, a suitable partner for the top-ranked T cell. Far below her in terms of class and race is the macrophage, angry, scavenging, engulfing, housekeeping, and harboring disease.

The cartoon on a recent cover of the technical journal *Immunology Today* provides clear evidence for the picture I am drawing. This cartoon depicts a B cell with long eyelashes and high heels, silently taking orders from a T cell called a gamma/delta cell, drawn as a doctor with a stethoscope and a hypodermic needle. The gamma/delta T cell is kicking the B cell. In the next frame the gamma/delta T cell kicks another kind of T cell, one unmarked by any adornments, but this T cell registers a verbal protest, "Ouch!" In the final frame, two gamma/delta T cells are shown standing on top of a macrophage, while one of them shouts into a megaphone, "Come on—the action's here!!" (Born et al. 1990).

So we have T cells, masculine and high ranking; B cells, feminine and high-ranking; and macrophages, feminine, perhaps racially marked, and low ranking on all counts. What is missing? Low-ranking males, revealing by their invisibility in this system (even as they seem to be "invisible" in the U.S. social structure) how salient a system of race and class is to the understanding of relationships among these cells.

In this system, gendered distinctions are not limited to male and female, they also encompass the distinction heterosexual and homosexual. T cells convey aspects of male potency, cast as heterosexual potency. There is evidence that T cells are for many researchers the virile heroes of the immune system, highly trained commandos who have been selected for and then educated in the technical college of the thymus gland. T cells are referred to as the "master regulators of the immune system" (Sell 1987: 26). Some T cells, killer cells, are masculine in the old-fashioned mold of a brawny, brutal he-man: in a mail advertisement for a book on the immune system, we are told, "You owe your life to this little guy, the Rambo of your body's immune system." Other T cells, T 4 cells, have a different kind of masculinity, one focused on abilities required in the contemporary world of global corporations, especially strategic planning and corporate team participation. The T 4 cell is often called the quarterback of the immune system, because he orchestrates everything else and because he is the brains and memory of the team. As it is put in one popular source, "Besides killer t-cells . . . there are also helper [T 4] and suppressor T-cells. *Somebody* has to make strategic decisions" (Michaud, Feinstein, and Editors 1989: 10). A popular manual on the immune system, *Fighting Disease*, clinches the heterosexuality of the T cell:

> In order to slip inside a cell, a virus has to remove its protein coat, which it leaves outside on the cell membrane. The viral coat hanging outside signals the passing T cell that viral hanky panky is going on inside. Like the jealous husband who spots a strange jacket in the hall closet and *knows* what's going on in the upstairs bedroom, the T cell takes swift action. It bumps against the body cell with the virus inside and perforates it. [Michaud, Feinstein, and Editors 1989: 8]

CONTRADICTORY FORMATIONS

So far I have described two coexisting "bodies": a body organized as a global system with no internal boundaries and characterized by rapid flexible response, and a body organized around nationhood, warfare, gender, race, and class. In logical terms, these two bodies are contradictory: if the system were really self-regulatory, there would be no "waste" for the macrophage to clean up; "waste" could be described as nourishment instead. If the system were really a complex interlocking series of feedback loops, then no one would be more in charge than anyone else; T 4 cells could be seen as playing their part in the system but as being no more or less important that macrophages. In the world outside the body, there are concrete reasons why two contradictory formations like these would coexist. David Harvey writes of the geopolitical dangers attached to the rapidity of time-space compression:

> The serious diminution of the power of individual nation states over fiscal and monetary policies, for example, has not been matched by any parallel shift towards an internationalization of politics. Indeed there are abundant signs that localism and nationalism have become stronger precisely because of the quest for the security that place always offers in the midst of all the shifting that flexible accumulation implies. [1989: 306]

Another reason relates more directly to the particular form flexible accumulation has taken in the United States. In the United States, the establishment of global capital has been accompanied by dramatic restructuring. Harrison and Bluestone describe how heightened international economic competition after the mid-1960s led to a profit squeeze. They argue that although some sectors of U.S. industry undertook experiments in new forms, changing the scale and manner of work, the prevalent response was industrial restructuring. Among other things, companies

> abandoned core businesses, invested offshore, shifted capital into overtly speculative ventures, subcontracted work to low-wage contractors here and abroad, demanded wage concessions from their employees, and substituted part-time and other forms of contingent labor for full-time workers. [1988: viii]

In tandem, many policies of the federal government added to constraints on and containment of wages.

The result is what Therborn (1986) has called "Brazilianization": mass unemployment as a permanent feature; at the bottom the permanently unemployed and the marginals, on welfare (or, in the United States, destitute); in the middle the regularly employed (but often underemployed), increasingly divided by enterprise, sector, gender, and race; and at the top the few of increasing wealth and income (Hall 1988). Even among middle managers, restructuring and mergers have produced massive dislocations (Harrison and Bluestone 1988: 13, 38). As the international flow of capital and communication systems link the United States to global systems, borders and cleavages inside this nation-state have become deeper and wider (Davis 1984).

How would such a context shed light on the two organizational forms I have argued coexist in the body? The key lies in the hallmark of the late twentieth-century U.S. body, flexibility: the ability to respond to constant change in the environment and the nature and kind of work one does in a context of widespread fear of mortal loss of employment, status, housing, and health. I came upon one example of this in a quintessential postmodern architectural spectacle, Baltimore's famous Harborplace, the waterfront tourist and financial attraction developed by the Rouse Company. A local publication brought to light that some of the retailers (Baltimore residents) were being forced to give up their leases if they refused to change product lines frequently. One retailer, Cathy Crymes, explained how she had built her hobby of collecting stuffed bears into a successful Harborplace shop. After seven years she was told by the Rouse company, in July, "We are tired of bears. We want to get rid of all your bears by October 1. . . . [W]e think bears are passé and your sales are down. We would like you to stay but we'd like you to come up with a new idea, like a store selling sweatshirts or sweaters." She said, "I know nothing about selling sweatshirts. People look at me and they know I'm the Bear Lady" (Macsherry 1990: 8–10). The flexibility required of Cathy Crymes is entailed by the increasing specificity of marketing. In an article explaining how Harborplace was "fine-tuning" itself, a spokesman for the International Council of Shopping

Centers was quoted: "There's no such thing as a mass market anymore. . . . Developers are tailoring their retail mixes to attract increasingly specific groups of people" (Tyner 1990a).

In the nineteenth century, fatigue "provided the key to the efficient utilization of the body's energies by determining its internal limit" (Rabinbach 1986; see also 1982); in our day, flexibility may play a similar role. A Harborplace merchant said: "In this business, change is what it's about. . . . If you don't upgrade your concept and your merchandising *and* your presentation every three to five years, you're going to be behind the 8-ball and not abreast of the marketplace" (Macsherry 1990: 10). Lacking flexibility of that kind, people face ominous boundaries close at hand. Even for middle-class people, business failure is all too common; the Bear Lady lost her lease.

From the point of view of almost any worker in such an environment, the menacing vision of falling over fearful internal borders into unemployment, underemployment, or destitution would give "flexibility" a compelling character. There may be productive relationships between, on the one hand, concepts of the body with its immune system poised for flexible response to fearful biological threats at any moment and, on the other, a world that now requires "flexibility" as the price of earning a wage. The "flexible specificity" in the scientific descriptions of antibodies exemplify the bodily dimension of how we experience the world, and they give evidence of a new bodily percept emerging in the present.

SEXUALITY, FAMILY, AND DISPOSABLE PEOPLE

When Fordism was becoming established in the United States, deliberate efforts were made to transform workers' concepts of sexuality and domestic life. Are similar processes occurring today? Earlier I described both the virile, heterosexualized T cell and the dominance hierarchy among immune system cells. These descriptions take on a stark significance in light of the fact that HIV is killing off precisely the high-ranking cells, the masculinized T cells, in gay men and minority drug users (the demographic groups now most affected by HIV in Baltimore). HIV especially depletes the T 4 cell, the particular cell that is compared to that most masculine of figures, the quarterback in football, because it directs and orchestrates the other T cells (Redfield and Burke 1989: 64). After all, "We are not all born equal when it comes to the T cell system" (Dwyer 1988: 46).

The way HIV is seen as destroying the virile T cell made me wonder whether the men at the hospice where I volunteer as an AIDS "buddy" experienced the weakening of the body as a defeat on several fronts. My buddy training manual explains, "Think of lots of rebels and a government dictatorship protected by the army. As soon as your immune system gets impaired (your army dies) all the diseases which you have been carrying for years can run amok (the rebels seize power)" (*Washington HIV News 1988,* quoted in Health Education Resource Organization 1989). It seemed possible that the weakening of the body these men experienced was being linked in scientific language to a loss of heterosexual potency. It was not simply that you were no longer a "man" but that your body as a centralized nation-state had lost its virility.

I had these thoughts in mind before my buddy, Mark Scott, was presented at grand rounds. Grand rounds are elaborate, formal presentations of cases, held in a large lecture hall. Although Mark was extremely ill, recovering from a serious toxoplasmosis infection, he was elated at the prospect of being presented at grand rounds. He told me the week before that he was the one and only patient his doctor, John Aubrey, wanted to present. He said that he was going to try to get across the patient's need to be responsible for his own illness, no matter how sick. He wanted to convey the importance of not taking a doctor's word for it and of learning as much as possible by asking questions. When he told me this, he was in the hospital, unable to walk or even sit up. Three days later—by dint of incredible determination—he was shaved, with a fresh haircut, dressed in a dark double-breasted suit, leaning on the arm of Aubrey as they walked across the stage at grand rounds.

Mark was asked a series of detailed questions in which the various stages of his disease were constructed entirely in terms of the progressive elimination of T 4 cells:

Dr. Aubrey: Mr. Scott has an identical twin, and he underwent a series of leukocyte infusions from the identical twin, followed by bone marrow transplantation. Before the bone marrow transplantation, do you know what the status of your immune system was?

Mark Scott: Yes I do.

Dr. Aubrey: What was it?

Mark Scott: My T 4 count was 60.

Dr. Aubrey: 60. OK. The normal value at that laboratory was 600, 800? So you had less than 10 percent of the normal number of helper T cells. Had you had that test done before?

[Mark Scott looks puzzled.]

Dr. Aubrey: The T cell count, before you went to NIH.

Mark Scott: In 1984 it was normal.

Dr. Aubrey: So over a period of three or four years, the helper T cells, the primary target of HIV, had fallen from near normal, a near normal range, down to a very low range of a T 4 count of 60. What happened with bone marrow transplantation?

Mark Scott: I believe to this day that I got a boost. I was very strong for a while after the bone marrow. I went back to college and studied word processing, and was making a 4 point while working a full-time job. Only in the last six months was I ill.

Dr. Aubrey: And in terms of the laboratory, evaluations that they did . . . clearly functionally you did extremely well. You were working full-time, functioning entirely normally. The laboratory tests that they did to monitor you, what did that show?

[Mark Scott shakes his head uncomprehendingly.]

Dr. Aubrey: The T cells, did they change?

Mark Scott: My T cells went up after the bone marrow to about 180 and stayed there for about three months before coming back down to 60.

Dr. Aubrey: So there was a *transient* increase in your helper T cells, but functionally you felt fine.

Mark's condition was relentlessly defined by his T 4 cell count, and in the process, given the significance of T 4 cells in the armamentarium of the body, Mark was defined as impotent and feeble. The force of this drama could not have struck deeper when later many doctors came down onto the stage to congratulate Mark and his doctor: they said that Mark's presence had "given AIDS a human face."

Could this scientific imaging of the body be seen as an aspect of secular opposition to homosexuality? There are broad social currents in the United States today, especially in the New Right, that seek to "restore heterosexual patriarchy, the control of men over their wives and children":

> Homosexuality is characterized by "pro-family" representatives as "unnatural," "evil," and psychologically "perverse"; but male homosexuality is even more dangerous than female, in the "pro-family" view, because it signals a breakdown of "masculinity" itself—or what one right-wing ideologue calls the "male spirit," or the "male principle." [Petchesky 1981: 231]

Or this diminishment of the homosexual body might be related to ideas brought to life with the weakening of the liberal state and of the state's responsibility to provide for social welfare needs. Withdrawal of government support from social services of all kinds makes the nuclear family seem to be the only source of these glues to the social fabric, and conservative efforts to buttress the heterosexual family ideologically may reflect this perception. The depiction of body cells that privileges some as heterosexually potent has a part to play here and operates at a particularly subtle, invisible, and therefore insidious level.

It may be that while flexibility in adjusting to retraining, deskilling, part-time work, home-based work, periodic unemployment, relocation, changing product lines, downward mobility, and all the other ways restructuring bears on wage earners is desirable, flexibility in domestic arrangements is threatening to this very restructuring. Part-time work, home-based work, service sector work without health benefits or retirement benefits, and unemployment themselves seem to entail dependence on the family to fill in the gaps in order to enable the work force to reproduce itself. Contemporary conservative publications are filled with exactly this logic:

> Teachers at urban schools speak of chaotic, scattered families, of gross parental irresponsibility, of small schoolchildren who witness open sexual activity at home. The cycle perpetuates itself across generations: a teenage mother, abused as a child, cannot read, write, add or subtract. She is pregnant with her third child and living on welfare. She has zero skills, zero work habits, zero future. Work at a fast food restaurant seems beyond her capacity. She is neglecting her 3-year-old, who is often sick and ill-fed. She shunts the child off to relatives as often as she can.
>
> These poor neighborhoods and families are radically different from their counterparts of two decades ago. People talk now of an inability to cope with life's most rudimentary demands, such simple things as getting up in the morning to go to work. Idleness and irresponsibility pave the tragic road to self-destruction: teenage pregnancy, long-term welfare dependence, drugs, crime, prison and death. [Lochhead 1989: 10, 11]

If restructuring makes the heterosexual family seem to some a necessary prop to the social fabric, restructuring also makes some people seem superfluous. Flexible accumulation goes along with high levels of "structural unemployment" and an increase in a labor market periphery that lacks job security (Harvey 1989a: 149–50. These conditions affect disadvantaged groups disproportionately: not all groups seem equally superfluous. A growing sense that some groups of people are superfluous must surely be related to the recent increase in intolerance in the United States, a willingness to openly express racist, classist, homophobic, or misogynistic sentiments and act on them. The poor are said to have become "American untouchables" (Kozol 1990). Young black males are said to have become an "endangered species" (Corey 1990). We read in the paper of a student "hospitalized speechless after racial threats": "A [black] freshman at Emory University was found in her dormitory room curled in the fetal position and unable to speak . . . following the latest episode in a reported campaign of racial terror against her" (Smith 1990). Here is how this climate feels to John Marcellino, a community leader in a chronically poor, mostly white neighborhood in Baltimore:

> [The person in charge of commercial redevelopment in this area] says the area, the problems in this area, will not improve until this community changes, until the people who live here are no longer here. And so you won't get rid of the drug abuse or the prostitution or the crime or stuff until the people who live here are no longer here. And that to me is the same as the underclass thing, disposable people. . . . As soon as they can't figure out a need for us, they'll get rid of us.
> Interviewer: What's the need for you right now?
> John Marcellino: We still make money for somebody or another. They still need us some, like they needed people to come up out of the south to work in the mills, so they attract them all up. Now there's not as much need for the people to work in the mills; they need some people in the service economy, they try to retrain . . . but if not they're no use, they'll put you in jail, . . . they'll choke you off so that you can't make a living doing anything else, so they get rid of you, or you know, hopefully you'll go back to Virginia or somewhere else, right? You know, you'll crawl in a crack or you won't have children or something.

As with secular opposition to homosexuality, scientific imagery has a role to play here too. We know that nineteenth-century anthropology had a view of the natural order of the world which could be used to justify denying women the privileges of citizenship in the Enlightenment project and to justify the colonization, enslavement, and exploitation of people of color. If women and people of color were simply lower on the evolutionary scale, doing them harm became less bothersome (Stocking 1987: 230–37). In present-day circumstances—with poor whites as "disposable people," poor blacks as an "endangered species," the Secretary of Health and Human services comparing the calamitous situation of blacks in the United States today to slavery (Corey 1990)—the popularization of the notion of a world within the body with cells ranked by gender, race, and class is not trivial. Learning that our bodies are made up of hierarchically ranked kinds of cells, with dumb, uncouth, barbaric "females" at the bottom and smart, educated, civilized, executive "males" at the top, has its part to play in showing us why it is all right to think some kinds of people are not as worthy of life in human society as others.

In describing a "collective effort" that is pushing us toward new modes of living, thinking, and feeling, I have only hinted at how these modes actually get instantiated in our lives. Part of the full story would obviously involve the "media" in Raymond Williams's social sense (1977). Many of the images I have discussed are from newspapers, magazines, or mass-market books, and it would be easy to add images from films such as *The Miracle of Life* and *The Fighting Edge*, innumerable television specials or talk shows, and amusements such as the "Wonder of Life" ride at Epcot Center near Disney World.

Another part of the story would involve individuals or groups who are explicit advocates of links between biological knowledge of the body and social control. For example, James D. Watkins, who was the head of Ronald Reagan's AIDS commission, said in an interview:

> We have an opportunity to restructure what a healthy lifestyle is all about. . . . [T]oo often we assume a child in our society will be healthy. . . . [This] may have been true years ago, but society is changing. One third of youngsters today are born into poverty. Now we are hardening an underclass and there is a strong overlay between that underclass and AIDS. It is mainly Hispanic and Black Americans. AIDS brings into focus a variety of flaws in our system. . . . [T]he job of educators then is to help people learn in a fundamental way about human biology and their own bodies so they can possess lifelong strategies for healthy wholesome lifestyles.

The interviewer broke in: "You are talking about trying to get at health care problems by getting students to understand the nature of human biology!?" And Watkins answered, "Absolutely" (Newman 1988). Watkins put it all together: the social control entailed in disseminating biological knowledge of the body; the fear and threat of AIDS, linked to "flaws in our system," among them homosexuals, people of color, and people living in poverty.

I have emphasized the wrenching effects of a new mode of being. Hence my focus has been on how people stretch and are stretched to adjust, rather than on the other side of this process, always potentially present: how people revise and bend ideas and events to fit their circumstances. Mark Scott used grand rounds to flatter and please a doctor whose experimental protocol he wanted to join; AIDS activists have produced films and publications, among them *Ecstatic Antibodies: Resisting the AIDS Mythology* (Boffin and Gupta 1990), which create more enabling body imagery. John Marcellino has organized the "disposable people" in his community into alliances with people from poor black neighborhoods and Native American groups in the city and elsewhere; Cathy Crymes has relocated her stuffed bear shop outside Harborplace. These actions might well turn out to be examples of the kinds of political resistance, based on reimaging, relocation, and rearrangement of alliances, that are possible and efficacious in a regime of flexible accumulation (Harvey 1989b: 274).

I have sketched a transformation in embodiment, from Fordist bodies held by disciplined order in time and space and organized for efficient mass production, to late capitalist bodies learning flexible response in rapidly collapsing time and space, bodies that nonetheless contain (contradictorily) increasingly sharp and terrible internal divisions. I am suggesting that there are changes afoot in our embodied dispositions, changes that will surely take importantly different forms among different people and groups. We are experiencing not so much the end of the body as the ending of one organizational scheme for bodies and persons and the beginning of another. The depth of the transformations that are entailed accounts for at least some of the academy's justifiable fascination with the subject of the body, even as the body's borders waver, its internal parts become invested with agency, and its responses become ever more flexibly specific.

NOTE

Jonathan Parry (1989) was the inspiration for my title. This article is a revision of the Distinguished Lecture I gave at the 1990 meeting of the American Ethnological Society, which was organized around the theme "The Body in Society and Culture." For criticism and editorial advice, I thank Don Brenneis, Ashraf Ghani, Erica Schoenberger, and Sharon Stephens.

This essay was the 1990 Distinguished Lecture at the meetings of the American Ethnological Society. For a complete and fully-annotated version of this essay, see *American Ethnologist* vol. 19, no. 1 (1992): 121–40.

1. The fieldwork I refer to involves participant observation in a university department of immunology, an immunology research lab, several urban neighborhoods, several community organizations dedicated to the AIDS crisis, an AIDS hospice, and the AIDS ward of an inner-city nursing home. The argument below draws on a limited segment of the ongoing research. Other work in progress will describe the impact of the AIDS crisis on immunology and the impact of grassroots political organizations dealing with HIV infection on scientific research.

REFERENCES

Arens, W. 1979. The Man-Eating Myth: *Anthropology and Anthropophagy.* Oxford: Oxford University Press.
Beldecos, Athena, et al. 1988. The Importance of Feminist Critique for Contemporary Cell Biology. *Hypatia* 3(1): 61–76.
Boffin, Texxa, and Sunil Gupta, eds. 1990. *Ecstatic Antibodies: Resisting the AIDS Mythology.* London: Unwin Hyman.
Born, Willi, et al. 1990. Recognition of Heat Shock Proteins and Gamma Delta Cell Function. *Immunology Today* 11(2): 40–43.
Brownlee, Sharon. 1990. The Body at War. *U.S. News and World Report,* 2 July: 48–54.
Business Week. 1984. The "Blunders" Making Millions for 3M. *Business Week* 2851 (16 July): 118.
Corey, Mary. 1990. Endangered Species: Officials Look for Ways to Reduce Risks in Being Young, Black and Male. The Sun (Baltimore), 4 April: 1E.
Corrigan, Philip, and Derek Sayer. 1985. *The Great Arch: English State Formation as Cultural Revolution.* Oxford: Blackwell.
Crimp, Douglas, ed. 1988. *AIDS: Cultural Analysis, Cultural Activism.* Cambridge, MA: MIT Press.
Crimp, Douglas and Adam Ralston, eds. 1990. AIDS Demo Graphics. Seattle: Bay Press.
Davis, Mike. 1984. *The Political Economy of Late-Imperial America.* New Left Review 143: 6–38.
Durning, Alan B. 1990. Ending Poverty. In *State of the World 1990.* Lester R. Brown et al., eds., pp. 135–53. New York: Norton.
Dwyer, John M. 1988. *The Body at War: The Miracle of the Immune System.* New York: New American Library.
Ferrell, J. E. 1990. Surgeons Removed and Sold His Spleen Cells: Should He Get a Cut? *The Sun* (Baltimore), 21 January: 5E.
Flax, Jane. 1990. Postmodernism and Gender Relations in Feminist Theory. In *Feminism/Postmodernism.* Linda J. Nicholson, ed., pp. 39–62. New York: Routledge.
Gallo, Robert C., and Luc Montagnier. 1989. The AIDS Epidemic. In *The Science of AIDS: Readings from Scientific American Magazine,* pp. 1–11. New York: W. H. Freeman.
Gelderman, Carol. 1981. *Henry Ford: The Wayward Capitalist.* New York: St. Martin's Press.
Gibbs, Jewelle. 1988. Young Black Males in America: Endangered, Embittered, and Embattled. In *Young, Black, and Male in America: An Endangered Species.* Jewelle Gibbs et al., eds. pp. 1–36. Dover, MA: Auburn House.

Glassner, Barry. 1988. Bodies: *Why We Look the Way We Do and How We Feel about It*. New York: G.P. Putnam's Sons.

Gramsci, Antonio. 1971. *Selections from the Prison Notebooks of Antonio Gramsci*. Q. Hoare and G.N. Smith, eds. New York: International Publishers.

Hall, Stuart. 1988. *The Hard Road to Renewal: Thatcherism and the Crisis of the Left*. London: Verso.

Haraway, Donna. 1985. A Manifesto for Cyborgs: Science, Technology, and Socialist Feminism in the 1980s. *Socialist Review* 80: 65–108.

———. 1989. The Biopolitics of Postmodern Bodies: Determinations of Self in Immune System Discourse. *Differences* 1(1): 3–43.

Hardison, O. B. 1989. *Disappearing through the Skylight*. New York: Viking.

Harrison, Bennett, and Barry Bluestone. 1988. *The Great U-Turn: Corporate Restructuring and the Polarizing of America*. New York: Basic Books.

Harvey, David. 1989a. *The Condition of Postmodernity: An Enquiry into the Origins of Cultural Change*. Oxford: Basil Blackwell.

———. 1989b. *The Urban Experience*. Baltimore, MD: Johns Hopkins University Press.

Health Education Resource Organization. 1989. *Health Education Resource Organization Buddy Training Manual*. Baltimore, MD: Health Education Resource Organization.

Jaggar, Alison M., and Susan R. Bordo. 1989. *Gender/Body/Knowledge: Feminist Reconstructions of Being and Knowing*. New Brunswick, NJ: Rutgers University Press.

Jameson, Fredric. 1984. Postmodernism, or the Cultural Logic of Late Capitalism. *New Left Review* 146: 53–92.

Jaret, Peter. 1986. Our Immune System: The Wars Within. *National Geographic* 169(6): 702–35.

Jaroff, Leon. 1988. Stop That Germ! *Time* 131(21): 56–64.

Jewler, Donald. 1989. Diabetes and the Immune System. *Diabetes Forecast*, August: 32–40.

Johnson, Mark. 1987. *The Body in the Mind: The Bodily Basis of Meaning, Imagination, and Reason*. Chicago: University of Chicago Press.

Jordanova, J. J. 1989. *Sexual Visions: Images of Gender in Science and Medicine between the Eighteenth and Twentieth Centuries*. Madison: University of Wisconsin Press.

Kash, Don E. 1989. *Perpetual Innovation: The New World of Competition*. New York: Basic Books.

Kobren, Gerri. 1989. A Body on the Fritz. To Your Health. *The Sun* (Baltimore), 3 October: 4–6.

Kozol, Jonathan. 1990. The New Untouchables. *Newsweek* (Winter/Spring special issue) 114(27): 48–53.

Kroker, Arthur, and Marilouise Kroker. 1987. *Body Invaders: Panic Sex in America*. New York: St. Martin's Press.

Law, Sylvia. 1988. Homosexuality and the Social Meaning of Gender. *Wisconsin Law Review* 2: 187–235.

Lertola, Joe. 1984. The Virus Invasion. *Time* 123(18): 67.

Lévi-Strauss, Claude. 1967. *Tristes Tropiques: An Anthropological Study of Primitive Societies in Brazil*. John Russell, trans. New York: Atheneum.

Lipuma, Edward, and Sarah Keene Meltzoff. 1989. Toward a Theory of Culture and Class: An Iberian Example. *American Ethnologist* 16: 313–34.

Lochhead, Carolyn. 1989. Poor Neighborhoods Fall to a Widening Decay. *Insight* 5(14): 10–12.

Macsherry, Clinton. 1990. Harbor Sights: As Harborplace Turns 10, Some Merchants Grouse about Rouse. *City Paper* 14(10): 8–10.

Martin, Emily. 1987. *The Woman in the Body: A Cultural Analysis of Reproduction*. Boston: Beacon Press.

———. 1991. The Egg and the Sperm: How Science Has Constructed a Romance Based on Stereotypical Male-Female Roles. *Signs* 16(3): 1–18.

Michaud, Ellen, Alice Feinstein, and the Editors of Prevention Magazine. 1989. *Fighting Disease: The Complete Guide to Natural Immune Power*. Emmaus, PA: Rodale Press.

Mizel, Steven B., and Peter Jaret. 1985. *In Self Defense*. San Diego, CA: Harcourt Brace Jovanovich.

Moulin, Anne Marie. 1989. The Immune System: A Key Concept for the History of Immunology. *History and Philosophy of the Life Sciences* 11: 221–36.

Newman, Frank. 1988. AIDS, Youth and the University: An Interview with Admiral Watkins. *Change* 20(5): 39–44.

Nilsson, Lennart. 1985. *The Body Victorious.* New York: Delacorte Press.

Outram, Dorinda. 1989. *The Body and the French Revolution: Sex, Class, and Political Culture.* New Haven, CT: Yale University Press.

Parry, Jonathan. 1989. The End of the Body. In *Fragments for a History of the Human Body.* Part 2. Zone, no. 4. Michael Feher, ed. pp. 491–517. New York: Zone (distributed by MIT Press).

Petchesky, Rosalind Pollack. 1981. Antiabortion, Antifeminism and the Rise of the New Right. *Feminist Studies* 7(2): 206–246.

Piore, Michael J., and Charles F. Sabel. 1984. *The Second Industrial Divide: Possibilities for Prosperity.* New York: Basic Books.

Rabinbach, Anson. 1982. The Body Without Fatigue: A Nineteenth-Century Utopia. In *Political Symbolism in Modern Europe: Essays in Honor of George L. Mosse.* Seymour Drescher, David Sabean, and Allan Sharlin, eds. pp. 42–62. New Brunswick, NJ: Transaction Books.

———. 1986. The European Science of Work: The Economy of the Body at the End of the Nineteenth Century. In *Work in France: Representations, Meaning, Organization, and Practice.* Steven Laurence Kaplan and Cynthia J. Koepp, eds. pp. 475–513. Ithaca, NY: Cornell University Press.

Redfield, Robert, and Donald S. Burke. 1989. HIV Infection: The Clinical Picture, In *The Science of AIDS: Readings from Scientific American Magazine.* pp. 64–73. New York: W. H. Freeman.

Roitt, Ivan, Jonathan Brostoff, and David Male. 1985. *Immunology.* St. Louis, MO: C. V. Mosby.

Schindler, Lydia Woods. 1988. *Understanding the Immune System.* Washington, DC: U.S. Department of Health and Human Services.

Schoenberger, Erica. 1987. Technological and Organizational Change in Automobile Production: Spatial Implications. *Regional Studies* 21(3): 199–214.

Sell, Stewart. 1987. *Basic Immunology: Immune Mechanisms in Health and Disease.* New York: Elsevier.

Sheridan, Alan. 1980. *Michel Foucault: The Will to Truth.* London: Tavistock.

Silver, Edward A., and Rein Peterson. 1985. *Decision Systems for Inventory Management and Production Planning.* New York: Wiley.

Silverstein, Arthur M. 1989. *A History of Immunology.* San Diego, CA: Academic Press.

Smith, Ben. 1990. Ga. Student Hospitalized Speechless after Racial Threats. *The Sun* (Baltimore), 14 April: 1A, 3A.

Stocking, George. 1987. *Victorian Anthropology.* New York: Free Press.

Stromberg, Peter G. 1990. Ideological Language in the Transformation of Identity. *American Anthropologist* 92: 42–56.

Therborn, Goran. 1986. *Why Some Peoples Are More Unemployed Than Others.* London: Verso.

Treichler, Paula. 1987. Aids, Homophobia, and Biomedical Discourse: An Epidemic of Signification. *Cultural Studies* 1(3): 263–305.

Tyner, Joan. 1990a Overhaul Will Bring New Retailers to Harborplace. *The Sun* (Baltimore), 18 April: 1E, 5E.

———. 1990b. Making the Grade. Maryland Business Weekly. *The Sun* (Baltimore), 2 April: 10–13.

USAir Magazine. 1990. A Decade of Post-its. *USAir Magazine* 12(4): 10.

Washington HIV News. 1988. *A Layman's Guide to HIV.*
Washington HIV News 1(1): 5.

Williams, Raymond. 1977. *Marxism and Literature.* Oxford: Oxford University Press.

37 Guto's Performance

Notes on the Transvestism of Everyday Life

Roger N. Lancaster

THE BLOUSE

It was early evening at the end of a typically sweltering day in Managua.[1] Aida, my *comadre*, had returned home from work with an exquisite rarity in Nicaragua's devastated economy: a new blouse, a distinctly feminine blouse, soft to the touch, with good threadwork and careful attention to detail. It had been sent from the United States—not to Aida, but to one of her coworkers by a relative living abroad.

In Nicaragua, if commodities could speak they'd recount peripatetic tales of endless digressions. How Aida had obtained the blouse is its own circuitous story. She had netted this enviable catch through a complex series of trades and transactions involving the blouse's designated recipient and two other coworkers: four transactions in all. Such were the convolutions of everyday economic life at the end of the revolutionary dispensation.[2]

When Aida arrived home, she beckoned everyone to come see her new raiment. Her teenage brother, Guto, arose from where he had been lounging shirtless in the living room, watching the standard TV fare. The drama that ensued took me completely by surprise. With a broad yet pointed gesture, Guto wrapped himself in the white, frilly blouse, and began a coquettish routine that lasted for fifteen or twenty minutes. Sashaying about the three cramped rooms of his mother's house, the seventeen year old added a purse and necklace to his ensemble. Brothers, sisters, even his mother, egged on this performance, shouting festive remarks: *¡Qué fina, bonita, muñe quita!*—these cries punctuated by whistles, kissing noises . . . Someone handed Guto a pair of clip-on earrings. With cheerful abandon, he applied a bit of blush and touch of make-up. His performance intensified, to the pleasure of the audience. After disappearing for a moment into the bedroom, he returned wearing a blue denim skirt. "*Hombrote*" (Big Guy), he shot in my direction, nuancing his usually raspy voice as though to flirt with me.

Roger N. Lancaster teaches anthropology and cultural studies at George Mason University. He is the author of two books on revolutionary Nicaragua, including the critical ethnography *Life is Hard: Machismo, Danger, and the Intimacy of Power in Nicaragua* (California, 1992), which won both the C. Wright Mills Award (Society for the Study of Social Problems) and the Ruth Benedict Prize (Society of Lesbian and Gay Anthropologists). He is currently completing *The Queer Body* (California, in progress), a book of revisionist gay theory about carnal desire, sensuous practice, and everyday culture.

I was astonished, and no doubt my visible surprise was part of the clowning of the evening. "See, Róger," Aida kept remarking. "Look, Guto's a *cochón*," a queer. At first, I had imagined that such banter might dissuade Guto from his increasingly extravagant performance—that the sting of the term, "cochón," might somehow discipline his unruly antics. Not so. If anything, the challenge prodded him to new heights of dramaturgic excess. The young man luxuriated in *femininity*. His sisters played the role of macho cat-callers, hooting their remarks. Laughing, teasing, everyone seemed to enjoy the ritual. Guto beamed.

THEORY AND LAUGHTER

> Both body and meaning can do a cartwheel.
> — Mikhail Bakhtin[3]

When later, in solemn seriousness, I tried to "interview" participants on what had transpired, no one would give me a *straight* answer. Reviving the spirit of the evening, jest, mockery, and levity colored the responses: "Maybe Guto's queer," his sister Clara laughed. No one had ever seriously suggested such an opinion before. Quite the contrary, it was typically Guto who taunted his younger brother, Miguel, calling him a "cochón."[4] "Of course, he's a little queen," his mother said, tossing off a laugh. "I was flirting with you, stupid," Guto told me, winking.

How to adequately describe such antics?

Or better yet, what exactly had happened here?

The demands of classical ethnographic description would seem to set before us a series of mutually exclusive options: either this was a serious performance, or it was play acting. Either the onlookers were approving, or they were disapproving. Obviously, these are not the terms of a purely "descriptive" approach—whatever that might be. They are in fact already full-fledged analyses of events: claims about perception, staged in terms of an event, its references, and its broader context.

Theorizing these capers proves no less problematic, for theory, too, would put before us a set of dreary options: either Guto was making fun of women, or he was celebrating femininity. Either this was a screen for homosexual flirtation, or it was a way of getting rid of those very desires. Either the audience was making fun of cochones, or it was suspending the usual prejudices to celebrate them. Either Guto was transgressing gender forms, or he was intensifying them. Such acts either constitute a radical challenge to the system of gender norms, or they merely effect a periodic blowing-off of steam that enables the system to reproduce itself despite its many tensions.[5] With such options, we are invited to choose sides, to pick a team, and to play a game whose outcome is already decided.

An interpretive apparatus, an analytical technology, hums its familiar noise: parody or praise, subversion or intensification, deviation or norm, resistant or enabling, play or serious . . . A series of claims, a chain of diagrams. All the parts are already in place; a syntax is prepared; categories are allotted. One need do no more than mark off the performance, catalogue its parts, and fill in the details. Such tedious work! Guto's delirious gestures and swirls would thus be packaged into neat little boxes—theoretical closures, as final as the denouement of a familiar play.

In a famous passage, Geertz argued that "thick description" is telling the difference between a wink and a twitch.[6] Surely, nuance is everything in the phenomenology of a transvestic performance. But what if a dramatic moment *en cours* is overwhelmed by nuance and ambiguity? And how does one think through a continuous play of winks and gestures, looks and movements, to read what lies behind it all: from the twinkle in Guto's eye to the tone of women's laughter?

It is indeed a slippery task to think about the slipperiness of copy-cat gestures. The whole point of such fun and games is that a final meaning evades us.

What I want to offer here is a set of closely woven arguments about performances of the sort just described and about those rituals of masquerade cast on the wider stages of Carnival. Guto was indeed play acting—and play is fun or it is nothing at all. But play is not a trivial thing, and the simultaneously destructive and creative power of laughter should never be underestimated. An essay, then, in praise of folly, and some questions about the utility of extravagance.

THE CLOSET OF EPISTEMOLOGY: INTENTIONAL AMBIGUITIES7

Now, I can scarcely frame my own presence out of the events I've recounted. I was part of the audience, and such performances are always intended, if not exactly *for* an audience, then always *with* an audience in mind. My flat-footedness when everyone else knew the steps, my not getting it when others were in on a joke, were clearly part of the evening's merriment. In the argot of show biz, I played the "straight man."

Or did I? Is it possible that my reactions were being probed here? That Guto and his family were attempting to clarify, by reading my reactions, what I was determined to keep ambiguous if not secret? Certainly, events are more or less consistent with this logic. Although the subject of my own sexual preferences almost never came up as a direct topic of query, I am relatively certain that suspicions circulated.

However, I am not willing to simply settle on this reading of the situation, for one's social identity is scarcely a unidimensional or straightforward matter. If implicitly conducted as something of an experiment in which I was the subject, my hosts might have been trying to get some insight into my reactions as a person of unknown sexuality. Or they might have been probing my reactions as a representative North American, as a white person, as a college-educated man, as a somewhat awkward person . . . The possible bases of inquiry, the kinds of questions that might be posed, are perhaps too numerous to count.

To make matters yet more complicated, cultural differences occlude the medium of communication, problematizing any notion of a straightfoward inquiry into stable identities. As I was constantly reminded, my own conceptions of homosexuality did not exactly match up with those of my informants.8 It is not even quite clear to me what would have constituted a "queer" response on my part—to play along, as the cochón's *macho* companion? Or to join in the transvestic frolic? To stand agape?

These are questions that one cannot settle definitively or unequivocally, for what would count as evidence? The word of one's informants counts for something, but in this case those words were double-edged (and necessarily so, as *playful* speech). And even assuming a serious response, how would one weigh divided or shifting subject matters? More vexing still, the acts of not just one but of plural *others* almost never offer themselves up as a transparent window on intention. And when plural others are *playing*, ambiguities multiply geometrically. In such situations, by their very nature, the one intention conceals the other, takes refuge in the other, leads to another.

I dwell on this point to put aside the obvious temptation toward ready finality and easy closure.

In both cultural feminism and in a section of gay/lesbian studies, it has become commonplace to offer one's *own self* up: as subject, evidence, argument, and analysis.9 Like Descartes's philosophical introspections, this approach begins with what is most proximate and can—presumably—be best known: one's own self, one's own body, one's own experiences. From a fortified interior, one can then venture generalizations about an exterior—about others, about the social world.

Only a naive and vulgar model could delude us into thinking that the self enjoys some special access to its self. In the first place, the presence of the self and its effects on others are necessarily occulted. We can never quite see our own eye seeing, hear our own ear hearing, or touch our own finger touching.10 A self, then, cannot directly observe itself. Precisely *because* all knowledge filters through a situated self, that self, the nature and scope of its effects, constitute something of a blind spot—and necessarily so. It is a problem no mirrors or interlocutions can ultimately solve (for they can only provide additional refractions, each with its own blind-spots).

In the second place, a self is ever only partially revealed, even to the self, for consciousness is always "consciousness of something." A self exists because it projects into the world. If a self tries to trap itself,

> if consciousness tries to recover itself, to coincide with itself, all warm inside with the shutters closed, it becomes nothing. This need of consciousness to exist as consciousness of something other than itself is what Husserl calls "intentionality."[11]

As a swarm of intentions, interlacing with the world, the self is always beyond itself. Its effects are infinitely refracted in the world and through other selves.

To narrow the practice of interpretation to one or two singular dimensions, as recollected from the position of an authoritative self, is to short-circuit everything that goes into the complexity of a moment, the richness of a situation, the contingencies of self-understanding, and the very *sociability* of the social. For much of what happens in the give and take of social life is tentative, unarticulated, inarticulate. Meanings are negotiated: we don't quite know what we meant until a response comes from someone else. Our best thinking is serendipitous: we're not quite sure what we suspected until some evidence appears. We're not quite sure what we're looking for until we find it. A gaze roves until it catches something unexpected . . . as we might have expected. What is self, no less than what is other, is out there, in the world, between us, and in play.

Unless it is to decompose into a virtual parody of its nemesis, positivism, reflexivity, too, must practice a sort of reflexivity—and be modest in its pretensions. In the end, I cannot say whether Guto's performance was a test *for me*, and if so, how it was conceived or even how the evidence would have been read; whether it was an *a priori* event, and my reactions were probed *ex post facto*; whether it would have happened in my absence; whether it was staged for my benefit or for others' amusement. It happened, and I was there, a part of it. That is all.

Existential Fuzz: A Dramatization

So I can only begin to fathom the complexities of intention that lay behind Guto's performance. This is not just a problem of audience reception but also of performative conception. Transvestism lends itself to performances of gender and sexuality, race and class, desire and repulsion, ego and alter—not to mention the physical body, its carnal practices, and its ideal representations. Such practices are multiply nuanced—and without doubt, complexly intended.

I hope I am being clear about the nature of this enigma. It is really an extension of the blind spots of self-knowledge just described—as seen from the other side. If one's own identity is always and necessarily complex, compound, and multifaceted; if one's own intentions are therefore somewhat ambiguous, even to one's own self; and if one's own self, and its effects, are therefore multiply refracted in the world of others, then one can hardly expect less from others.

If *ambiguity* rules a wide continent of the self, its intentions, its refractions through others, then *ambivalence* is the degree zero of such performances that dramatize and intensify everyday existential fuzz. In such moments, identity, identification, and intention are simultaneously revealed, concealed, performed, manipulated, and denied . . .

To leave matters in their properly productive ambiguity: Guto was acting the part of a woman, no doubt. He was also imitating queers, as the audience's cries suggest. But he was also playing the role of a man in drag—that is, he was performing a performance. And that is something too, and not at all the same thing as simply *practicing* a gender or sexuality. For in reality, what woman, what queer, what cochón, really acts that way—unless they, too, are deliberately underscoring their action with a broadly performative gesture? No matter who acts them out, such performative performances can never simply *imitate* or *mimic* some original practice, person, or type—for they are always *in excess* of their target. That is what distinguishes them as "performances." This "excess" invariably slides around: Guto is now a woman, now a cochón, now a low-class prostitute, now a refined and affected matron, now *negra*, now *blanca*, now just Guto, his own self, in a dress, now something else entirely . . .

In this manner, transvestic performance is multiply transversal. It effects a rapid shuttle between shifting subject matters: between male and female, between femininity and effeminacy, between the real and the imaginary, between the given and the improvised. It is thus not quite correct to say that transvestism defines a space of parody or transgression.[12] Nor is it correct to say that it represents a ritual of intensification. Rather, it represents a profound equivocation. It takes up a space in between. Contrary, even antagonistic intentions are held in suspension, but nothing is canceled out. Not only are multiple intentions refracted through a given gesture, but moreover many possible selves—and others—are always *in play*. The performative performance is a rich, nuanced, and *crowded* practice.

PHENOMENOLOGY OF TRANSVESTISM

> A movement is learned when the body has understood it.
> —Merleau-Ponty[13]

Such is the everyday world of transvestic performance, a mode of physical simulation far wider than literally cross-dressing—and far broader than any genre of gay camp:

A man quotes a woman. He pitches his voice high to mimic a woman's speech; he thereby takes her part in some reported conversation. Neither in Nicaragua nor in the United States is this an unusual occurrence. Men do this all the time. Or, to seal an argument or establish the reality of a claim, a man extends his gestures a little further than usual to affect either a feminine or homosexual role—a roll of the eyes, a flick of the wrist, a toss of the head . . . In recounting events or developing an argument, he thus slides into a genre of "transvestic" performance: that is, he strikes a pose, intended to act out the part of some other person, some other role, some other being . . . He thus models his body's demeanor and disposition in the style of another. In these everyday miniature theaters, a sort of momentary stage arises: the performer necessarily monitors his audience, his interlocutors, to see whether a performance is working or misfiring, to gauge whether his act is appreciated or resented, to know whether it is amusing or annoying, and to decide how far he can take the conceit.

A woman does the same when she enacts the presumed radical alterity of cochones—a gesture in the air, a swirl of the hands, a facial expression, a mincing gait, an inflection understood as "effeminate" . . . a glance at the audience, out of the corner of her eye. And in a less parodical context, women are always appropriating what are otherwise marked as "male" words, male speech patterns, male roles.

> "I am the head of the family now," I told my children, "the mother and the father, and what I say goes."

Thus Doña Jazmina recounts herself speaking to her children in a new paternal voice after the death of her husband, just before taking a job in a factory to do "men's work."[14] Her statement itself is a kind of doubly transversal act: she is quoting herself at some past moment affecting a man's role: a performance of self performing another gender. My own citations keep the circuitry going—triply, quadruply.

Like ventriloquism, these practices "throw" one's voice, one's gestures, one's demeanor—one's self—into the position of another. This happens more often than we might at first acknowledge.

Conversation would likely be impossible without such give and take, for transvestic figuration is almost implicit in "reported speech," which is itself a necessary component of dialogue.[15] If we thus marked as "transvestic" every iteration, quotation, and pantomime that crossed the lines of gender or sexuality, we would understand such performances in all their startling density: as routine, habit, convention, and second nature.

These transvestics, whether linguistically or theatrically performative—whether affected through words, tone of voice, or physical comportment—all involve what Judith Butler describes as a kind of "citationality."[16] In other words, they trade against some representational convention or shared image: a standard gender, a normal body, a scripted role, the usual way some being is thought to act. But as long as the analysis remains fixed at this preliminary level, the analyst can only chose between two equally improbable options: either the performance *enacts* or it *violates* an ideal script.[17] Performativity becomes a variant of Normativity, and we fall into the familiar trap of seeing every practice as the blossoming forth of an Idea. Since everything happens on the plane of an abstract and disembodied concept, we fail to understand, and cannot even really pose, the question of performance in its carnal materiality. At the same time, we forget what physical fun it is to play. A more impractical understanding of practice, and more disembodied approach to the body, would be hard to imagine. For the moment we reduce carnal perception to symbolic language, the body becomes non-sense. In making the body one representation, one meaning, among others, we necessarily withdraw analysis to a contemplative retreat far removed from all those carnal ways of knowing and making the world that ought to properly focus the constructionist interrogative from the start: viz., how human subjects are crafted through the practical engagements of living flesh with the fabric of the world.

Before treating performance as a question of citation, then, it might be more productive to think through how a being moves, perceives, and practices. For what occurs in any transvestic performance is an extension and dramatization of rather more mundane movements, themselves implicit in the work of perception and in the logic of the senses.

Telescoping arguments from Merleau-Ponty: "to perceive" something is "to figure" it: to foreground it while backgrounding everything else.[18] Perceptual attention thus draws us both "toward" and "into" the thing attended. Necessarily, we do not attend to the eye when seeing, but *from* the eye *to* what is seen.[19] In reaching, we do not know the body but rather what is touched or grasped. In the absorption of observation, subject/viewer and object/viewed are momentarily fused. We thus lose ourselves in finding the object, only to recover ourselves among objects—which become extensions of our own limbs, "encrustations in our own flesh."[20] The "operational intentionality"—or better yet, the carnal "ecstasis"[21]—of sense perception means that we are always entangled with others, with objects, with the world; that by its very nature, the body locates itself only by going beyond its place of standing; that we find ourselves and lose ourselves in the same gesture, the same glance.

Now if this work of the senses is interactive and creative; if in the primacy of perception we are always losing and finding ourselves; if our bodies are open to the experiences of other bodies; then the senses themselves are given to carnal cross-overs, to physical empathies, and—if you will—to assorted transvestics and polymorphics.

Every act of attention, every physical appropriation, every empathic power of the flesh, involves a kind of crossing-over, a loss and recovery of the self. These quotidian practices are continuous with a host of other cross-over desires, and would seem implicit in the social structure of perception. It could not be otherwise. Because we are social creatures, "self" is always found in an "other." And because our sociability is carnal in its very nature, the desire for another, the desire to be another, is part of the fundamental magnetism the world exerts on us.

Perhaps the full impact of these arguments ought to be stated carefully. First, *all* reported conversation, even self-reportage, and *all* instances of acting-out—even the acting out of one's own self—entail a kind of cross-over. Therein lies the power—and the risk—of the practice. Second, *all* practice, insofar as it engages the senses, lays the body open to the world and to others in the fashion dramatized—starkly but not uniquely—by transvestic performance. Finally, no one learns (or unlearns) anything—a gender or a sexuality or an identity or even a meaning—except through some process of physical modeling, sensuous experimentation, and bodily play. In the least perception, we are perpetually crossing over and becoming entangled, finding and losing the self, making and dissolving the world.

HOSTILE MIMICRY AND PLAY ACTING

When gays perform drag, when straights pantomime gays, when men mimic women, when children act out adult roles, what often happens is a mockery or a burlesque. We need not imagine that these acts are complimentary.

Yet even in the worst-case scenario—even in, say, a homophobic performance of homosexuality, a misogynist enactment of femininity, in clear cases of hostile mimicry—a certain *other* lesson is also, undeniably, drawn, or at any rate made available for those who might draw it. For to act out the part of the Other plays off the contingencies of identity: it implies that one's body is malleable; that these gestures are, after all, just extensions of the gestures one already makes—indeed, that everyone is capable of making. As a problem of movement, the transversal performance is an exploration of a space not appropriate but proximate to the space already known. One attempts to abandon one's own horizon so as to see another's horizon, a different landscape. In inhabiting that space, the Other is a possible Self given to extravagance and excess.

Performances can, of course, "misfire." As Austin shows in his catalogue of performative types—a typology organized precisely around how performances might fall short of or exceed their intended mark—the definition of a misfire depends on nonperformative constraints: on context.[22] In gay camp, one mimics the gesture or words or another (even if that other is sometimes the self) not quite literally, but *ironically*. The audience must both see the irony and find it amusing. In this case, a performance misfires when its irony is lost or when its intention is judged too mean or too obvious. (Of course, all these judgments are relative to the taste, sophistication, and demands of the audience.)[23]

In certain Drag Balls, however, a "good" performance is a *convincing* one. As deBarge intimates, and as every commentator on "Paris Is Burning" has noted, effective drag produces "the effects of the real." In this case a misfiring is one that fails to achieve the illusion of "reality."

For a parodically intended straight male performance of either women or gay men, however, a "misfired" performance is one in which the style of being of the other all too readily sticks to the self of the performer. The act is all too convincing, for not enough space lies between the actor and the acted. The parody thus lacks its intended irony—or, that irony is deliberately denied as a countermove in the game of negotiated meanings. A hostile critic of the transvestic performance in this case might note: "It is altogether quite conceivable that this is the way you act, that you are at home in this style, that these gestures become you, that this is the way you *are*. Your gestures, your own body, give you away." This implies, further, a category of "nonvoluntary performances"—by definition, misfirings of attempts to affect one or another effect.

To return to the performance that stimulated these arguments: It would be altogether too easy to understand Guto's drag act as hostile mimicry. There was that, no doubt, but there was also an affectionate, almost sentimental staging of the stock-figure queen, *la loca*. There was, certainly, the sense that the transvestic cochón is exotic, but attractively, copiably so, with a force that draws imitation. There was indeed the indication that such antics are extreme, but in pleasurable senses: in physical abandon, visceral mirth, creative frivolity . . .

Performances of this type suggest a variant of transvestics, partly taking in several other genres, and making them all possible. It involves trying things on, trying things out. Playful, exploratory, and ambiguous, this mode belongs to the genre of children's games, to free play, to friendly banter, and to Carnival. I shall call this variant by its familiar name, *play acting*. As infectious as laughter itself, it necessarily invites us to play along. Guto's performance was almost certainly an example of this genre.

CARNIVAL DREAMS: BENT-OVER ACTS AND CROSS-OVER DESIRES

"Let's go to *Carnaval* to see the cochones," people often say upon the approach of Masaya's harvest festival.[24] Someone will invariably note, without apparent irony or guile: "The cochones at Carnival are very, very beautiful." And then someone else will launch into a generous enumeration of the characteristics and qualities of transvestic beauty, perhaps illustrating his argument with a mincing gait, or by clutching an imaginary skirt . . .

The pleasures we partook in Guto's performance were very much in the spirit of Carnival, "the festival of disguises." Indeed, his antics put people to talking for several days about the visual and visceral joys of that much anticipated ritual. At Carnival, audience reaction to cochones is much what it was with Guto's Carnivalesque performance: solicitous festivity, teasing banter, and good-spirited encouragement.

Many of the "cochones" performing on the stage of Carnival are indeed "queers" in real life. But some are men who are not. The difference is not always apparent. Some affect their role with regal demeanor and glamorous adornment. Others are just men in rather plain dresses. No matter. Although onlookers clearly savor flamboyance over simplicity, all are graced with the familiar sobriquet "queer." The best performers receive this mockery in the good spirit of Carnival humor, giving as well as they get. A stately queen approached me at one Carnival procession— coquettishly, flirtatiously—but upon closer approach, reacted sharply, as though a bad odor were emanating from me. Theatrically, she took leave . . . to gales of laughter from onlookers. Such is Carnival's humor, with its turning of tables and inversion of expectations.

One could make selective sense of Carnivalesque festivities through the idioms of gender and sexuality, which are visibly salient features of the experience. Carnival is, in part, the Revolt of the Queers. Much of its whimsy plays off slippages, contradictions, and ambiguities in the propositions of the prevailing sexual culture. Much of its "gay ambivalence" reverses the usual valences associated with queers, homosexuality, effeminacy, and desire.[25] Things hidden somersault into the open; passivity and activity exchange places; bad sport becomes good humor . . . In the ensuing vertigo, everyone becomes a little bit queer. The whole world is flaming.

But Carnival also—wildly—exceeds questions of gender and sexuality. One might say: the theory and practice of the flesh renewed each year at Carnivaltime *subtends* questions of gender and sexuality. If Carnival lends itself to ritual reversals in the performance of *gender and sexuality*, it no less takes up questions of *race, class, and ethnicity*. The famous peach-complexioned masks of Monimbó, with their rosy cheeks and pencil mustaches, recall the Spanish gentry and reveal the colonial dimension of Carnival's history: Indians take on the color, wear the face, mimic the dances—and thereby mime the powers—of white Spaniard rulers.[26] More modern Carnival images likewise traffic in depictions of class, administrative, or neocolonial power. Images include a transvestic whiteface jazzercise class, white-coated physicians with vaudevillian implements, bankers, politicians, *internacionalistas* . . .

Carnival, then, is the occasion for remembering, interrogating, and *playing with* the history of systems of domination. This reading locates Carnival in its proper historical and political-economic context. But such an approach still remains limited. The danger of leaving matters here is the danger of a false reduction, where everything is settled even before a question can be posed. Like transvestic performance, Carnival becomes either a contestation or a ratification of the forms of power it so clearly dissects, yet we have short-circuited the whole inquiry. We never understand *how* it could, in and of itself, perform either function, or *why* the other should be so fascinating to start with.

An alternative reading: When Carnival comes to Masaya, when the Fiesta de Santo Domingo is celebrated in Managua, or when any of a dozen such festivities comes to towns and barrios across Nicaragua, what happens is a profusion of masks, a merry confounding of intentions, and a proliferation of cross-over desires. In Carnival time, "gay ambiguity" embraces not just the imagery of the social, political, and economic world but also the physical world, the natural world. Carnival's working materials are sights, colors, smells, and tastes. Its repertoire is the entire sensorium, an ever-shifting kaleidoscope.

Consider, then, a host of other images. Humans take on animal forms, and people become fantastic creatures: cows, bulls, birds, insects, Diablos, Diablitos . . . Saints walk among savages, alongside an occasional beast comprised of sparklers and fireworks. Images pile up: not as a composed and singular picture, but as a work in progress; as an unfinished process of experimentation, excess, and play . . . These images play at sacrilege: a travestied crucifixion scene, with a Transvestic Jesus and two Drag Thieves, all bearing crosses . . . They also risk a rupture with coherence altogether: animated objects gambol perplexingly among funny monsters, fused bodies, and creatures that are half-human and half-animal—like the stirrings of a psychedelic dream. Transvestics become panvestics, as social discriminations oscillate, natural distinctions blur, and the contours of the body are stretched and tested.[27]

Bakhtin's discussion of the sensibility of the mask is instructive:

> The mask is connected with the joy of change and reincarnation, with gay relativity and with the merry negation of uniformity and similarity; it rejects conformity to oneself. The mask is related to transition, metamorphoses, the violation of natural boundaries, to mockery and familiar nicknames. It contains the playful element in life; it is based on a peculiar interrelation of reality and image, characteristic of the most ancient rituals and spectacles.[28]

Beside Bakhtin's celebration of Carnival metamorphosis, we might set Merleau-Ponty's understanding of the body in its very existence. For it is precisely in metamorphosis, fusion, and confusion—in that space in between perceiver and perceived—that body and self take shape.

> A human body is present when, between the see-er and the visible, between touching and touched, between one eye and the other, between hand and hand a kind of crossover occurs, when the spark of the sensing/sensible is lit.[29]

Like the "mirror's phantom" contemplated by Merleau-Ponty, the mask

> draws my flesh into the outer world, and at the same time . . . my body can invest its psychic energy in the other bodies I see. Hence my body can include elements drawn from the body of another, just as my substance passes into them.[30]

Reflections of beings, infinitely refracted, Carnival whimsy plays off those powers of perception that extend the body beyond its contours, to consolidate the body in and through the world—in the very act of dispersing it.

Masks—crossovers, transvestics—no less than mirrors, "are instruments of a universal magic that converts things into spectacles, spectacles into things, myself into another, and another into myself."[31]

The horizons of Carnival are as wide as perception itself, and as sensuous as practice itself. Intentionality and identity are caught up in playful equivocations that are simultaneously productive, destructive, and instructive. Abandoning the self-conformity of our own contours, our own horizons, we try out other bodies, other horizons, all possible worlds. Hand with eye and body to world, the Carnival celebrant grapples with the problem of aesthetics in its original and broadest sense: the perception of reality.[32] Through non-sense, we unmake a sense of self, while making a new sense of reality—in open air, as play.

Seen in the context of Carnivalesque festivity, impersonations like Guto's are most richly understood not as discrete representations, nor even as enactments of gender or sexuality alone, but as practices continuous with the expression of other crossover desires. Such performances turn on physical excess, carnal ambivalence, and gay ambiguity. They model a body exposed to the gravitational pull of other bodies; an open, ambiguous body, given to all kinds of crossovers and reversals; a body malleable and in flux, because perception opens it to the world; a self thus lost, and recovered, but only in others and in the world.

THE SOCIABILITY OF THE SOCIAL: GAY LAUGHTER

A helicopter passes overhead. A bad omen, the helicopter, in war-torn Nicaragua. On its first pass, it drops loads and loads of dirt on us. It turns, preparing for a second pass. With grit in our mouths and shaking dirt from our hair, we Carnival celebrants scramble to take refuge under the awnings of the buildings that line Masaya's narrow, cobbled streets. But on its second pass, the helicopter drops gently scented flower petals, which slowly rain on the panicked people left stranded in the street. And now we are laughing, all laughing—at life, at ourselves, at our bodies, at our fears no less than our pleasures. Carnival is like that: it assaults you and it pleasures you; it plays bait-and-switch with your sensibilities; it plays tricks on you, and it makes you laugh. I always leave these festivities more than a little giddy: intoxicated from so much laughter, and largely unable to explain later just what was so funny.

Laughter—deep, visceral laughter—resonates throughout the Carnival experience. An intimate breath reverberates from the belly, acquires a voice, gushes through the air, and flows from body to body. Like that very "respiration of Being" Merleau-Ponty writes about,[33] this inspired laughter erases the distinction between seer and seen, performer and audience, laugher and laughed at. Such laughter is the very medium of Carnival connectivity, its carnal form of sociability. This laughter is *felt*, intimately and viscerally, but it is also shared and universal. In the dialectical play of opposites described by Bakhtin, laughter lifts us up even as it debases; it "dooms the existing world to the regenerating flames of Carnival."[34] All the popular genius of Carnival, all its mastery of visual tricks and physical games, come to so much funny playing, so many ways of trying things out.

THEORY POST-FESTUM: PLAYING AND KNOWING

Guto, of course, was just playing around. At first I dismissed his eruption as an unusual and marginal occurrence—until I considered just how densely such ludic interludes punctuate daily life. Guto's performance suggests that Carnivalesque leaps of body and meaning are implicit in a wide range of figurings. And just what happens when these everyday suspensions of the normal break out? What happens when people play act? What might it imply to get "carried away" by an act, a mask, a dramatic moment? Are we transported, as it were, bodily, to another space? Do we *live*, if only for a moment, that which we *do*?

Taken as a total situation and seen in the wider context of Carnival, Guto's performance and his audience's interactions suggest the special affinities between play and exploration, knowledge and jest. There was a practical knowledge, a kind of familiarity, to it all, and everyone—save me—seemed to know their parts. Once Guto initiated the evening's gag, my hosts all played along, with a physical understanding, much as one might follow the steps of a dance. There was a joke—it was all so much tomfoolery—but it is precisely the "gestic" or gestural element of jest that, in catching the *gist* of what it mimes, allows it to conceal so many obscure truths, so much manifold sobriety, such a detailed and carnal knowledge of the world.[35]

Huizinga's classic, *Homo Ludens*, provides a set of useful insights for thinking about the relationship between play and other forms of practice, and for theorizing play as both a human universal and as a base condition of culture. In a narrow sense, play is easily distinguished from routine activity and work. Play is "fun." It is some surplus exertion beyond utility and in excess of reason: unproductive, impractical, even irrational. As superfluous activity, voluntarily chosen, play is "free," and this "quality of action" distingishes it from the practices of ordinary life. Thus, play is bounded against nonplay: as a playtime, on a playground.[36]

But in a broader sense, play has consequences far beyond its own space and time, and any distinction between play and nonplay begins to waver. As a functional matter, play and rules imply each other. Through repetition, variation, and memory, "play creates order, is order"; at the same time, an action becomes playful only through the gridwork of certain expectations, certain regularities. If "play" and "rules" thus come into being simultaneously, the forces they set in motion are anything but trivial.[37]

Huizinga's generalist anthropology traces the play-spirit through a variety of serious practices. Play's affinities with ritual are especially compelling: both are time-bounded activities, restricted to a special place, simultaneously rule governed and rule generating. As suspensions of the ordinary, both involve a "loss of self" in the action of the event. Despite its "imaginary" or "make-believe" character, play is efficacious: it creates a community of players, a community that lingers after the play is over—just as ritual leaves in its wake a community of believers.[38]

Finally, as an open-ended alternation of give-and-take, move-and-countermove, play is *tense*.[39] It solicits us. Poised to move in response, we want to see what happens next. This dynamic of tension and solution both gives play its fascination and fosters the cultivation of certain habits, the development of certain skills. The conduct of play brings together physical attention, mental alertness, bodily exertion, carnal learning, and tests of performative competence. As a result, the player's body and dispositions are, to varying degrees, reshaped by his engagement with sport.

From Huizinga's perspective, play embraces culture: it comes before it; it lies beneath it; and it is spread out before it. If the play-spirit lies at the origin of aesthetics, art, myth, ritual, and religion, then it is difficult to think of any "higher order" activity that is not infused with the spirit of play. *Play is the very quality of action that both encompasses structure and makes it possible.*

Is it such a far step to ask whether what social constructionism attempts to describe is also a kind of play? Would it really be so outlandish to suggest that play is "the matrix of identity,"[40] that very surplus of activity whose consequences entail "subjects," "selves," and "groups?"

It no doubt goes too far to suggest that we literally become what we play at being, that we make the make-believe become the real. Only a charlatan or a madman claims that. Play, *by itself*, has no power to make anything happen. "Play is tense" means, in part, that sinew and fiber resist certain activities. The freedom of play is meaningful, and faculties are reshaped by its exertions, precisely because both body and world are encountered as obstacles, resistances, counterforces. Play is exhilarating because it is experienced counter to work, to routine, to other practices. Huizinga's heuristic origins stories aside, we are never in the position of the first to play. We thus play our games freely, but we are not free to play them just any way we choose.

And yet, play does come to something. Put another way: Play is a special genre of practice—that form most perfectly aligned with what Marx calls "sensuous practice," or "practice as sensuous activity."[41] It embodies practice at its freest and most creative. In this engagement of body and world, we test the plasticity of the world against the dexterity of the body—not "to do" something else (as in work), but for no good reason at all. Play can either follow or violate a script, but that is not the major point. If play has some part in making the world, as Huizinga argues, it also has a part in unmaking the world, as Bakhtin shows. Either alternative is possible because play engages sense, body, and world in a particularly *impractical* way—and thereby liberates practice from its seriousness, its commitment to a given end, its inertia. In the form of play, practice displays its most potent possibilities (but not its most direct results).

In the model suggested here, play is to identity as sense is to body: it locates and orients us, but it also goes beyond and exceeds us. In this making of identity, the body is neither "given" nor "made-up." A body is a self

> not by transparency, like thought, which never thinks anything except by assimilating it, constituting
> it, transforming it into a thought—but a self by confusion, narcissism, inherence of the see-er in the
> seen, the toucher in the touched, the feeler in the felt—a self, then, that is caught up in things.[42]

All of existence is caught up together as an unbroken circuit of perception and practice, but to play is to leap and throw oneself, consciously (if not always voluntarily)—an especially instructive way of being "caught up in things." It is a way of knowing. We learn something when we play. The body remembers it. But against all temptation to see the body as a kind of clay, passively stamped by other forces, and permanently shaped into a closed subject, play also reminds us that plasticity is reciprocal; that body and world come into being together.

IDENTITY, POLITICS, PRACTICE

In ordinary life, ambiguities and crossovers—the promiscuity of the senses—are held in check. Routine practices constellate narrow and habitual relations between self, others, world. When the world is thus held constant, the polymorphous potential of the flesh is still at work, but its surplus capacities are bracketed off and—as it were—backgrounded. "Being" thus brokers a compromise with the forces of its own composition: we attend *to* certain regularities, and thus *from* a body, a self, held constant. Understood this way, "identity" means nothing more than a temporary cessation of the overflow of the senses. (It is to this side of perception that Bourdieu's theory of practice restricts itself: that is, with what memory *forgets*, with what perception *omits*.[43])

And yet, in the give-and-take of social life, carnivalized subjects and dispersed intentionalities are perpetually breaking through all that is stable, structural, and singular. In the metamorphic figurations of everyday practice; in the implicitly transvestic conceits of reported speech; in speculation on the compound identities and mixed motives of other people; in deconstructive double-talk, pun, and verbal play; in every way of longing for a new identity, another body, a fresh perspective—by myriad such devices, what is alter is also ego, what is "beyond" is also "within," and ambiguity lives at the core of identity. Implicit in the nature of our bond with the world, even the most habituated habitus can be the source of new experiences. Through the magic of perception, even the most objectified object can be dislodged from its inertia to reveal new facets. Even the most consolidated self retains in the senses a perpetually-available resource for going beyond its self. "All flesh, even that of the world, radiates beyond itself."[44]

The kind of playfulness I have been sketching—aesthetic, plastic, and creative—is often understood as a variety of leisure, as an index of education, or as a function of privilege. Bourdieu thus separates critical thought from ordinary perception, and reflection from activity.[45] But perceptual intelligence is not necessarily on the side of the higher orders, with inertia on the side of the lower. No one is ever so impoverished or exploited as to be without capacity for empathy, mimicry, laughter, and double-talk. Even at the height of war, social dislocation, and economic scarcity—especially then—people make time for funny games and Carnival laughter.

Not all cultures publicly elaborate these powers: some celebrate Carnival; others do not. Yet like the existentialist idea of freedom, these capacities are always there, always here, always available for some engagement. Play is always available for some work. Everyday transvestics, assorted plays off ambiguity, and temporary transpositions of identity are simultaneously so germane and so mundane that the work they do often goes unnoticed.

Here, in a nutshell, is my argument about that work: identity, like hermeneutic knowledge, is a matter of locating and stabilizing a *self* by way of the detour of the *other*.[46] Identity, then, is not self-identical. Experience is not a receptacle. Like learning to see, or learning to walk, learning a gender or a sexuality—or any other kind of self/identity—relies on physical explorations, carnal transpositions, corporeal learning, and practice. Transvestics and other kinds of body-play are absolutely necessary to secure stable genders—but they also carry the danger that play always implies: a game can, at any moment, run away with the players. In engaging the world and each other, subjects make themselves, but they also—through intentionalities without intention—lay themselves open to risks without which they could not "exist" at all.

This volatile and creative capacity is not simply "given," a force outside of history, society, and meaning. Like language, it is a universal human capacity that must nonetheless be learned and developed in all its specifics, in all its variable forms. Although it is "volitional," it represents the will of no given subject; rather, it is that very plurality of wills through which subjects are realized. It takes distinctive forms but is not just a terminal form of social practice; it is also both a medium and a *font* of sociability. Surely, it is meaningful, but not in the purely "conceptual" sense of Saussurean semiotics; it is, rather, that creative and slippery way of grounding meaning, through perception, at the interface between flesh and world. This "ecstatic" power, then, is historical but it does not belong to history the way an object fits in a box. We should say, rather, that this capacity—what we do when we play no less than when we labor—is both constitutive in and constituted by history. It is the flesh and blood of history.[47]

Since playful practice is a social power, its effects are differentially distributed. The politics of play is thus anything but a straightforward matter. Fascist Right no less than anti-authoritarian Left embodies a kind of play-spirit. No one wants to be on the receiving end of certain kinds of play—to be "toyed with," as a "play-thing." Doña Jazmina is being inventive, but she is not being funny, when she appropriates a partly masculine identification. Cross-dressing has different social implications, depending on who crosses to what, for whom, and in what context. Men and women, rich and poor, "straight" and "queer," all *play*, but they do not and cannot all play the same way, with the same intentions, to the same effects.

Understood in this sense, such fun and games become difficult to distinguish rigorously from ritual at its most solemn—or from the seriocomic practices of gender in everyday life. In this wider sense, Guto's performance was neither the exception nor the rule. Rather, it embodied the kind of practice capable of making or breaking rules. These practices locate us at the heart of practice and in the matrix of identity—not where identity is "produced" or directly made as the consequence of some activity, but where unmotivated intentionalities are caught up with unintended consequences; not where signifier joins signified, nor where a code is either cited or parodied, but rather where sense both precedes and exceeds meaning; where hand and eye connect to the world; where, between eye and hand, body and world, ego and alter, a kind of combustion occurs; where the creative powers of perception bear witness to the birth of the world, and where the world is made new again at every moment.

These practices happen, unnoticed, all the time. Hand to substance, we give something shape; we know it by its touch and feel. We then indicate that something with a gesture, when the word escapes us. Hand with eye and touch to matter, we learn a technique of labor or a style of expression. We know something because we have explored it from all its angles; we have passed into it, and it into us. There is no cultural activity that is without some element of physical play and corporeal learning. Applying hand to object, we learn the materiality of things. Applying sense memory to body image, we practice at being someone.

This is not to say that transvestism lies at the origin of culture, which is Marjorie Garber's provocative claim in *Vested Interests*.[48] People have argued that stranger things lie at the origin of culture, but it seems to me that this staging of the claim puts the terms backwards. Undoubtedly, transvestism is implicit in any gender system—and is likely necessary for gender to exist at all. But it might be better to say that the kind of manipulation, learning, and play that goes into a transvestic ritual goes into every other cultural practice as well; that where there is gender, there must also be transvestism.

Sometimes this playful practice or sensuous epistemology is understood as "mimesis."[49] But as Huizinga notes, play is less "mimetic" (imitative representation) than "*methectic*": "a helping out of the action." Its efficacy implies less a distinctive "play instinct" or "mimetic faculty" than the general powers of perception and practice.

It would also be too straightforward simply to assert that all identity is playfully performative—that, for a moment there, Guto really *was* a cochón, or a woman, or a transgendered person; that play *directly* makes things happen; that play *is* construction; that gender *is* transvestism. Rather, it might be better to say that playful practices put us at the fulcrum of a phenomenological vector, into a position from which we might spring in any number of different directions. To play act, to play at Carnival, to play at transvestism, is to explore those possibilities.

Guto's "Breasts": The Transvestism of the Body

> There are several ways for a body to be body . . .
> —Merleau-Ponty[50]

I do not want to close out this essay with a sense of finality—a notion opposed, at any rate, to Carnival play. I do not even know whether it is germane—how does one ever claim to know such things?—to mention this:

After adolescence, Guto, like some other boys in his extended family, had begun to grow small breasts. His older brother Charlie claimed that his own nipples sometimes produced *leche*, milk, as I discovered one day when I encountered him, concentratedly squeezing his nipples and asked him what he was doing. Now, other than Guto's small "breasts" and Charlie's occasional "lactation," the young men's physiques were scarcely "feminine." If anything, their solidly muscular frames could only be seen as "masculine." I surmise that, as Doña Flora's family had come from a rural province, where they lived until moving to Managua, her children may have been exposed to pesticides, including DDT. Some pesticides, when they decompose, mimic the effects of estrogen, giving rise to such phenomena as "breasts" in young men.

When Guto acted out his transvestic part, he had recently undergone a minor operation to remove the breasts. A pair of small, crescent-shaped scars cupped his nipples. Guto made no effort to conceal them and did not seem self-conscious about these odd-looking marks, which resembled nothing so much as happy-face smiles inscribed on his chest.

Notes

Thanks to Florence Babb, Daniel Balderston, John Beverley, Samuel Colón, Micaela di Leonardo, Jean Franco, Donna Guy, Lois Horton, Ann Palkovich, Ileana Rodríguez, and Paul Smith for critical readings of early drafts. Additional thanks to those who were collegial during trying times at Columbia, and who gave my work supportive criticism and helpful feedback: Caroline Bynum, Elaine Combs-Schilling, Linda Green, Jean Howard, Katherine Newman, and Gayatri Spivak. Students rarely get the credit they deserve for stimulating a professor's thinking; special thanks are in order for Andy Bickford, Alex Costley, Marcial Godoy. And of course, thanks to all the cultural studies students at George Mason University. Finally, these arguments are deeply indebted to Judith Butler's sharp and disciplined formulations—when departing from them no less than when applying them.

1. Some readers may recognize these characters, the subjects of my book, *Life Is Hard: Machismo, Danger, and the Intimacy of Power in Nicaragua* (Berkeley: University of California Press, 1992).

2. Ibid., 52–68.

3. Mikhail Bakhtin, *Rabelais and His World* (Bloomington: Indiana University Press), 415.

4. Lancaster, *Life Is Hard*, 245.

5. Transvestism, transsexuality, and related forms of transgression have lent themselves to various interpretations. See, for instance, Judith Butler, "Critically Queer," *GLQ* 1 (1) (1993): 17–32, esp.
21–24; Judith Butler, *Bodies that Matter: On the Discursive Limits of "Sex"* (New York: Routledge,
1993), esp. 121–40; Majorie Garber, *Vested Interests: Cross-Dressing and Cultural Anxiety* (New York:
Routledge, 1992); Esther Newton, *Mother Camp: Female Impersonators in America* (Chicago: University of Chicago Press, 1972, 1979); Janice Raymond, *The Transsexual Empire: The Making of the She-
Male* (Boston: Beacon, 1979); Nancy Scheper-Hughes, *Death Without Weeping: The Violence of
Everyday Life in Brazil* (Berkeley: University of California Press, 1992): 490–97; Judith Shapiro,
"Transsexualism: Reflections on the Persistence of Gender and the Mutability of Sex," in Julia Epstein and Straub, eds., *Body Guards* (New York: Routledge, 1991), 248–79; of course, Richard
Parker, *Bodies, Pleasures, and Passions: Sexual Culture in Contemporary Brazil* (Boston: Beacon 1991)
and this volume.
6. Clifford Geertz, "Thick Description," in *The Interpretation of Cultures* (New York: Basic Books,
1973, 3–30); 12, 16.
7. With apologies to Eve Kosofsky Sedgwick, whose *Epistemology of the Closet* (Berkeley: University of
California, 1990) continues to inspire thinking about the closed and the open, the hidden and the
revealed.
8. Lancaster, *Life is Hard*, 235–78.
9. See Roger Lancaster, "The Use and Abuse of Reflexivity," *American Ethnologist* 23 (1) (February
1996): 130–31.
10. See Maurice Merleau-Ponty, *Phenomenology of Perception* (London: Routledge and Kegal Paul,
1962), 90–91; see also Drew Leder, *The Absent Body* (Chicago: University of Chicago Press, 1990),
an extended investigation into how the body "disappears" as a function of sensuous engagements.
11. Jean-Paul Sartre, "Intentionality" [1939]. Reprinted in Jonathan Crary and Sanford Kwinter, eds.,
Incorporations (New York: Zone, 1992), 387–91, 389.
12. See Judith Butler, *Gender Trouble: Feminism and the Subversion of Identity* (New York: Routledge,
1990), 128–49; Butler, *Bodies that Matter*, 121–40. See also Eve Kosofsky Sedgwick, "Queer Performativity: Henry James's *The Art of the Novel*," *GLQ* 1 (1) (1993): 1–16; and Judith Butler,
"Critically Queer."
13. Maurice Merleau-Ponty, *Phenomenology of Perception*, 139.
14. Lancaster, *Life Is Hard*, 179–80.
15. I am extending Vološinov's ideas, from the end of *Marxism and the Philosophy of Language*
(Cambridge: Harvard University Press, [1929] 1986).
16. See especially Butler, *Bodies that Matter*, 12–16.
17. See Sedgwick's arguments in "Queer Performativity."
18. I am drawing freely on various texts by Merleau-Ponty: *Phenomenology of Perception*; *The Primacy of
Perception* (Evanston, IL: Northwestern University Press, 1964): *Sense and Non-Sense* (Evanston, IL:
Northwestern University Press, 1964), and *The Visible and the Invisible* (Evanston: Northwestern
University Press, 1968).
19. See Leder's precise discussion of "the From and the To" in *The Absent Body*, 15–17.
20. Merleau-Ponty, "Eye and Mind" [1960], in Galen A. Johnson, ed., *The Merleau-Ponty Aesthetics
Reader* (Evanston, IL: Northwestern University Press, 1993), 121–49), 125.
21. If the term "intentionality" carries the Cartesian baggage of an implicitly "mental" (not "physical")
act, the word *ecstasis* "describes the operation of the lived body. The body always has a determinate
stance — it is that whereby we are located and defined. But the very nature of the body is to project outward from its place of standing" (Leder, *The Absent Body*, 21–22). Readers may note that
throughout this essay, I have gradually unfolded these concepts, beginning with Sartre's description
of Husserl's "intentionality," working toward the "operative intentionality" of Merleau-Ponty's early
work, and ending with the "ecstasis" that occupied Merleau-Ponty's later writings.
22. J. L. Austin, *How to Do Things with Words*, 2d ed. (Cambridge: Harvard University Press, 1962,
1975).

23. For wide-ranging analyses of gay camp, see David Bergman, ed. *Camp Grounds: Style and Homosexuality* (Amherst: University of Massachusetts, 1993).

24. On Nicaraguan popular festivities, see Roger Lancaster, *Thanks to God and the Revolution: Popular Religion and Class Consciousness in the New Nicaragua* (New York: Columbia University Press, 1988), and *Life is Hard*; 233, 251–52. And of course, for the definitive study of Carnival, in a different setting, see Richard Parker, *Bodies Pleasures and Passions*, and his essay in this volume.

25. Felicitously and throughout the text, the English translator of Bakhtin's *Rabelais and His World* gives such terms as "gay ambiguity," "gay ambivalence," "gay laughter," and especially "gay matter." These terms — with their emphasis on change, flux, and carnal engagement — are fully resonant with the perspective of this essay.

26. See Roger N. Lancaster, "The Festival of Disguises," *The Progressive* (November 1986): 50.

27. See Georges Bataille, *Theory of Religion* (New York: Zone), 54.

28. Bakhtin, *Rabelais and His World*, 39–40.

29. Merleau-Ponty, "Eye and Mind," 125.

30. Ibid., 130.

31. Ibid.

32. See arguments by Susan Buck-Morss, "Aesthetics and Anaesthetics: Walter Benjamin's Artwork Essay Reconsidered," *October* 62 (Fall 1992): 3–41.

33. Merleau-Ponty, "Eye and Mind," 129.

34. Bakhtin, *Rabelais and His World*, 394.

35. On "gest," see Bertolt Brecht, *Brecht on Theatre: The Development of an Aesthetic*, Ed. John Willet (New York: Hill and Wang, 1964). On "gesture," see Merleau-Ponty, especially *The Primacy of Perception*, 7.

36. Johan Huizinga, *Homo Ludens: A Study of the Play Element in Culture* (Boston: Beacon, [1944] 1955): 2–3, 8, 9–10.

37. Ibid., 10ff.

38. Ibid., 12, 18–27.

39. Ibid., 11.

40. To invoke a much-used concept. See, for instance, Butler's formulations in *Bodies That Matter*, esp. 7–8, 31.

41. See especially the "Theses on Feuerbach" in *Karl Marx: Selected Writings*, ed. David McLellan (Oxford: Oxford University Press, 1977), 156–58; see also Marx's arguments about sense, sensuousness, human sense, corporeality, and practice in *The Economic and Philosophical Manuscripts of 1844* (Buffalo, NY: Prometheus, 1988).

42. Merleau-Ponty, "Eye and Mind," 124.

43. Pierre Bourdieu, *The Logic of Practice* (Stanford, CA: Stanford University Press, 1980), esp. 52–97.

44. Merleau-Ponty, "Eye and Mind," 143.

45. Bourdieu, *The Logic of Practice*.

46. See Diana Fuss's fine discussion of perspectives from Freud and Lacan, through Sedgwick, Butler, and others on "identity" and "identification" in *Identification Papers* (New York: Routledge, 1995): 1–19.

47. See Merleau-Ponty's discussion of praxis theory, "Marxism and Philosophy," in *Sense and Non-Sense*, 125–36.

48. Marjorie Garber, *Vested Interests: Cross-Dressing and Cultural Anxiety* (New York: Routledge, 1992), 34.

49. See especially Micael Taussig, *Mimesis and Alterity: A Particular History of the Senses* (New York: Routledge, 1993).

50. Merleau-Ponty, *Phenomenology of Perception*, 124.